Fodor's 2014

ENGLAND

WELCOME TO ENGLAND

From medieval cathedrals to postmodern towers, from prehistoric stones to one-pub villages, England is a spectacular tribute to the strength—and flexibility—of tradition. In the capital city of London and beyond, you can explore grand manors and royal castles steeped in history, and also discover cutting-edge art, innovative cultural scenes, and trendy shops. Quintessentially English treasures like the Georgian town of Bath, academic Oxford, and eccentric Brighton remain vibrant, and silvery lakes and green hills provide enduring grace notes.

TOP REASONS TO GO

★ **London:** Landmarks, top theater, museums, village-like neighborhoods—it's all here.

★ **Idyllic Towns:** The Cotswolds' stone cottages, Cornwall's seaside charmers, and more.

★ **Pubs:** For a pint or a chat, a visit to one of "England's living rooms" is essential.

★ **History:** Sights from Stonehenge to Windsor Castle bring the country's past to life.

★ **Great Walks:** Classic trails await in the Lake District and Yorkshire's dales and moors.

★ **Gardens:** Roses, flower borders, and sculpted landscapes flaunt a national talent.

Fodor's ENGLAND 2014

Publisher: Amanda D'Acierno, *Senior Vice President*

Editorial: Arabella Bowen, *Executive Editorial Director*; Linda Cabasin, *Editorial Director*

Design: Fabrizio La Rocca, *Vice President, Creative Director*; Tina Malaney, *Associate Art Director*; Chie Ushio, *Senior Designer*; Ann McBride, *Production Designer*

Photography: Melanie Marin, *Associate Director of Photography*; Jessica Parkhill and Jennifer Romains, *Researchers*

Maps: Rebecca Baer, *Senior Map Editor*; David Lindroth, Inc., Mark Stroud (Moon Street Cartography), *Cartographers*

Production: Linda Schmidt, *Managing Editor*; Evangelos Vasilakis, *Associate Managing Editor*; Angela L. McLean, *Senior Production Manager*

Sales: Jacqueline Lebow, *Sales Director*

Marketing & Publicity: Heather Dalton, *Marketing Director*; Katherine Fleming, *Senior Publicist*

Business & Operations: Susan Livingston, *Vice President, Strategic Business Planning*; Sue Daulton, *Vice President, Operations*

Fodors.com: Megan Bell, *Executive Director, Revenue & Business Development*; Yasmin Marinaro, *Senior Director, Marketing & Partnerships*

Copyright © 2014 by Fodor's Travel, a division of Random House LLC.

Writers: Robert Andrews, Julius Honnor, Kate Hughes, Jack Jewers, James O'Neill, Ellin Stein, Alex Wijeratna

Editors: Linda Cabasin, lead project editor; Bethany Beckerlegge, Mark Sullivan

Production Editor: Carrie Parker

ISBN 978-0-7704-3269-0

ISSN 1558-870X

SPECIAL SALES

This book is available at special discounts for bulk purchases for sales promotions or premiums. For more information, e-mail specialmarkets@randomhouse.com

PRINTED IN COLOMBIA

10 9 8 7 6 5 4 3 2 1

CONTENTS

Fodor's Features

CONTENTS

CONTENTS

CONTENTS

ABOUT THIS GUIDE

Fodor's Recommendations

Everything in this guide is worth doing—we don't cover what isn't—but exceptional sights, hotels, and restaurants are recognized with additional accolades. Fodor'sChoice★ indicates our top recommendations; and **Best Bets** call attention to notable hotels and restaurants in various categories. Care to nominate a new place? Visit Fodors.com/contact-us.

Trip Costs

We list prices wherever possible to help you budget well. Hotel and restaurant price categories from $ to $$$$ are noted alongside each recommendation. For hotels, we include the lowest cost of a standard double room in high season. For restaurants, we cite the average price of a main course at dinner or, if dinner isn't served, at lunch. For attractions, we always list adult admission fees; discounts are usually available for children, students, and senior citizens.

Hotels

Our local writers vet every hotel to recommend the best overnights in each price category, from budget to expensive. Unless otherwise specified, you can expect private bath, phone, and TV in your room. For expanded hotel reviews, facilities, and deals visit Fodors.com.

Restaurants

Unless we state otherwise, restaurants are open for lunch and dinner daily. We mention dress code only when there's a specific requirement and reservations only when they're essential or not accepted. To make restaurant reservations, visit Fodors.com.

Credit Cards

The hotels and restaurants in this guide typically accept credit cards. If not, we'll say so.

Top Picks
★ Fodor'sChoice

Listings
✉ Address
✉ Branch address
☎ Telephone
🖷 Fax
⊕ Website
✍ E-mail
🎫 Admission fee
☉ Open/closed times
Ⓜ Subway
⊕ Directions or Map coordinates

Hotels & Restaurants
🛏 Hotel
🛏 Number of rooms
🍴 Meal plans
✕ Restaurant
🍴 Reservations
🏛 Dress code
⊟ No credit cards
$ Price

Other
⇨ See also
☞ Take note
🏌 Golf facilities

EXPERIENCE
ENGLAND

ENGLAND TODAY

England is the biggest region of the United Kingdom (or U.K.), the nation that also includes Scotland, Wales, Northern Ireland, and the Channel Islands (Guernsey and Jersey). Some but not all of these are also part of Great Britain (or just Britain), which is made up of the contiguous regions of England, Scotland, and Wales on the main British isle. It's worth noting that, while England, Scotland, and Wales are all part of Britain and the U.K., Wales and Scotland aren't part of England, and vice versa. Get that one wrong at your peril—you haven't seen angry until you've seen a Welshman referred to as English.

Although it's about the size of Louisiana, England has a population 12 times as large: 51 million people find space to live on its green rolling hills and in its shallow valleys and crowded cities.

Coalition Country

The current government in the United Kingdom is a coalition government. In the last election in 2010, no single party won more than 50% of the vote, so the leading vote-winner, the Conservative Party, joined together with a small moderate party, the Liberal Democrats, to form a government led by Prime Minister David Cameron, a Conservative, and Deputy Prime Minister Nick Clegg, a Liberal Democrat. This uncomfortable alliance between two parties that had long been political enemies is controversial with some voters because both parties are forced to compromise on complex issues: nobody gets everything they want. Matters were exacerbated in the 2013 local elections by the gain of seats by the relatively new UKIP (UK Independence Party), led by Nigel Farage. This party favors tighter control on immigration and an "amicable divorce" from the European Union.

Caught up as the United Kingdom is in the ongoing global economic crisis, you could say that London was put in an unfair test, having been chosen in 2005 as the venue for the 2012 Olympic Games. Costs ran at least five times the original £2.4 billion budget, and whether this overspending outweighed all other benefits—in terms of sports, urban regeneration, and architecture—will never be less than controversial.

Despite the economic crisis, the money invested in the Olympic and Paralympic Games of 2012, which were universally regarded as an outstanding success, was regarded as money well spent. The games also contributed to a rekindling of the British sense of pride. The site of the games, renamed the Queen Elizabeth Olympic Park, has not kept its stunning wildflower meadow but is undergoing transformation into the capital's largest urban park.

Analyzing how the different political parties respond to everything from a politician lying over personal speeding offenses to discussion of holding a referendum over the European Union is a national hobby. And there's much to consider: provoking continuing discussion are changes affecting welfare and social care, reorganization of the National Health Service, and the problems caused by the fact that people are now living longer. The issues of unemployment and the lack of opportunity among England's youth on one hand, and corporate greed and crony capitalism on the other, are a constant. Social networking sites have aided and abetted the debates.

The Royals Reinvented

How things have changed for the Windsor family. Essentially a figurehead monarchy but with a symbolic political role, the Royal Family has teetered on the brink of obsolescence. After the death of Princess Diana in 1997 and the royal scandals and divorces that littered the late 20th century, the idea of ending the monarchy's political role—and its government subsidy—was widely discussed publicly. Maintaining the Royal Family costs the country £42 million (more than $65 million) each year, and that amount was increasingly difficult to justify as the popularity of the family—aside from the beloved Queen—plummeted.

It's not surprising, then, that some in the media maintain that when Prince William married the appealing Catherine Middleton he saved the monarchy. The young couple's popularity is enormous, particularly after the birth of their son, George, Prince of Cambridge, in July 2013 The Queen capped her successful Diamond Jubilee year in 2012 by playing a starring role as a Bond girl in the much-lauded Olympic Opening Ceremony. Now in her late eighties and with no thought of retiring, she is scaling down her public engagements, gradually transferring them to her son, Prince Charles, and other members of the Royal Family.

Fashionable Britannia

Known for their quirky, creative, and bold style, British fashion designers have been influential on the global stage for decades. Whether it's from top-of-the-line companies like Burberry and Mulberry or from individual designers such as Paul Smith, Stella McCartney, Victoria Beckham, and the late Alexander McQueen, clothes made by British designers are sought after.

According to the British Fashion Council, the British fashion industry is worth £21 billion and is still growing.

Catherine, the Duchess of Cambridge, still holds sway as chief ambassador for British fashion. The "Kate effect," first fired by her wedding dress, has not diminished; constant analysis of her attire and that of her offspring continues. Choosing to mix high fashion with moderately priced high-street clothing, she's caused such chains as Reiss, LK Bennett, Hobbs, and Whistles to sell out the moment she dons their garments, and the cachet of such designers such as Jenny Packham and Jimmy Choo to rocket.

Last Call for Alcohol

According to published studies, Britain is only the 11th-heaviest drinking nation in Europe, but on a Friday night in any town center that rating can be hard to believe. The British refer to some busy towns as "no-go areas" after 11 pm, because they're packed with raucous, drunken young people stumbling out of pubs. Even normally staid towns, such as Harrogate in Yorkshire and Rochester in Kent, can take on a spring break atmosphere after the pubs close on a Friday night. Seaside towns tend to have the most problems, including Bristol, Newquay, and Hastings.

The main cause, experts say, is a binge-drinking culture, particularly among the young. While, overall, Britain may rank quite low in drinking studies, for people under 25 the results are quite different. A recent study ranked British youth as the third-heaviest drinkers in their age group in Europe. Now government programs, including price increases, are underway to try and change the nation's gulp-it-down approach to alcohol.

WHAT'S WHERE

The following numbers refer to chapters.

2 London. Not only Britain's financial and governmental center but also one of the world's great cities, London has mammoth museums, posh palaces, double-decker buses, and iconic sights such as Big Ben. Intriguing village-like neighborhoods from Notting Hill to Bloomsbury call out to be explored. When you need a break, pop into a pub or relax in one of the city's sprawling parks.

3 The Southeast. This compact green and pleasant region within day-trip distance of London takes in Canterbury and its cathedral, funky seaside Brighton, the appealing towns of Rye and Lewes, Dover's white cliffs, and castles such as Bodiam, Leeds, and Hever. Noted gardens as different as smaller, romantic Sissinghurst and large-scale Wisley add to the mix.

4 The South. Hampshire, Dorset, and Wiltshire have quintessential English countryside, with gentle hills and green pastures. Explore the stone circles at Stonehenge and Avebury, take in Winchester (Jane Austen country) and Salisbury, and discover Highclere Castle and Lyme Regis.

5 The West Country. Somerset, Devon, and Cornwall are sunnier and warmer than the rest of the country, with sandy beaches. Cornwall has lush gardens and a stunning coast. Of the cities, Bristol is the largest and most vibrant, while Wells and Exeter are attractive and compact. Take in the brooding heaths and moors of Exmoor and Dartmoor, too.

6 The Thames Valley. London's commuter belt takes in Windsor, where the Queen spends time, and Eton. Then there are the spires of Oxford and peaceful river towns such as Henley and Marlow; in all of these you have the opportunity for some relaxing river excursions. Among the stately homes not to be missed are over-the-top Blenheim Palace and Waddesdon Manor.

7 Bath and the Cotswolds. The grand Georgian town of Bath is one of England's highlights, with the Roman Baths and golden-stone 18th- and 19th-century architecture. Nearby, pretty as a picture, the Cotswolds region is justly famous for tranquil, stone-built villages, such as Chipping Campden, Stow-on-the-Wold, and Tetbury. Notable gardens include those at Hidcote Manor and Sudeley Castle.

WHAT'S WHERE

8 Stratford-upon-Avon and the Heart of England. One hundred miles northwest of London, Stratford-upon-Avon is the place to see Shakespeare's birthplace and watch his plays, and Warwickshire has Warwick and Kenilworth castles, too. Nearby Birmingham offers a modern urban experience. You can explore the Industrial Revolution museums of Ironbridge Gorge, Ludlow's half-timber buildings, medieval Shrewsbury, and popular Chester with its centuries-old walls.

9 Lancashire and the Peaks. Liverpool rides the Beatles' coattails but, like Manchester, has transformed its warehouses and docks into sleek hotels, restaurants, and shops. Buzzing nightlife and excellent museums are highlights in both cities. The Peak District has great opportunities for walking and stately homes such as Chatsworth and Haddon Hall.

10 The Lake District. A popular national park, this is a startlingly beautiful area of craggy hills, wild moorland, stone cottages, and glittering silvery lakes. Nature lovers and hikers crowd the area in summer. Among the literary high points are the homes of Wordsworth and Beatrix Potter.

11 East Anglia. The biggest lure in this green, flat, low-key region is Cambridge, with its medieval halls of learning. The countryside is dominated by the cathedrals of Ely and Norwich, and by time-warp towns such as Lavenham. Coastal spots such as Aldeburgh add a salty flavor.

12 Yorkshire. This wilder part of England has great appeal for lovers of the outdoors, but ancient walled York is also a center of attention. To York's west are the moors and dales that inspired the Brontës, and in east Yorkshire the moors collide with the sea at towns such as Whitby. Leeds is a vibrant urban center.

13 The Northeast. Here travelers can walk in the footsteps of Roman soldiers along Hadrian's Wall. Bamburgh and Dunstanburgh castles guard the coast; Alnwick Castle has stunning gardens. The small city of Durham is a medieval gem, a contrast to modern Newcastle.

14 Wales. Clinging to the western edge of England, Wales is green and ruggedly beautiful, with mountains and magnificent coastline. Except for Cardiff and Swansea, this is a rural country, with three national parks. Wales is also known for its castles.

ENGLAND PLANNER

When to Go

The English tourist season peaks from mid-April to mid-October, and during July and August accommodations in popular resorts and areas are in high demand. Many historic houses close from October to Easter. The winter cultural season in London is lively, however, and hotel rates are lower then, too. Spring and fall can be good alternatives to summer, as prices are still below high-season rates, and crowds are thinner. Generally, the climate in England and Wales is mild. Summer temperatures can reach the mid-80s, but it's more likely to be cooler and cloudier than you expect. In winter there can be heavy frost, thin snow, thick fog, and rain, rain, rain. Here are average daily maximum and minimum temperatures for two cities.

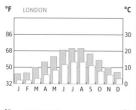

Getting Here

You can arrive in England by plane, train, or boat, and there are many places to disembark. Most international flights arrive at either London's Heathrow Airport (LHR) or at Gatwick Airport (LGW). A third, much smaller airport, Stansted (STN), handles mainly European and domestic traffic, as does Luton Airport (LLA). These airports have good train and bus options for getting into London.

Manchester (MAN) in northwest England handles some flights from the United States, as does Birmingham (BHX) in the Midlands. Most people fly into London, but other airports can be useful. *For more details, see Getting Here and Around in Travel Smart England.*

Getting Around

England isn't a large country: the entire United Kingdom (including England, Scotland, Wales, and Northern Ireland) is about the size of Oregon, so you're less likely to fly within the country. The country's train and bus systems are extensive and relatively well maintained; in major towns and cities there's generally no need to rent a car. To see castles and historic houses—which can be far from towns—you may have to rent a car or join a tour. Driving is on the left, and gas (petrol) is expensive at $5.10 a gallon. Train tickets tend to be two to three times more expensive than bus fares, but trains are usually at least twice as fast as buses. *For more details, see Getting Here and Around in Travel Smart England.*

FROM LONDON TO	BY CAR	BY TRAIN
Newquay, Cornwall	6½ hours	5 hours
The Lake District	5½ hours	4 hours
York	3½ hours	2 hours
Liverpool	4 hours	2 ½ hours
Bath	2 hours	1½ hours
The Cotswolds	1½ hours	2 hours
Oxford	1½ hours	1 hour

Restaurants: The Basics

What you should eat in England depends on where you are, as food is surprisingly regional. Fresh seafood dominates the coastal areas, but lamb and beef lead the way in the inland regions. The ethnic communities in each region also influence local cuisine. England is increasingly a foodie country with a good restaurant scene and a strong food culture in cities, especially London, and increasingly in the countryside. The Thames Valley in particular is well stocked with award-winning restaurants.

In the rural north—Cumbria, Yorkshire, and Northumberland—you'll get hearty meals in family-friendly pubs and inns. York and Harrogate have better options, and Leeds, Manchester, and Liverpool have good food scenes. Look for local lamb and beef in this area. Birmingham, in the Midlands, is famous for its Indian restaurants serving spicy curries. In Cornwall, Devon, and Dorset it's all about great fresh seafood. However, don't overlook Cornish pasties (hand-size meat-and-potato pies), sold everywhere. *For details, see Eating Out in Travel Smart England.*

Lodging: The Basics

London is in part about sleek, modern hotels, where enormous amounts of money get you relatively small amounts of space. One way to get a good deal in the capital is to book a chain—such as Millennium/Copthorne or Premier—online well in advance. Check for off-season deals, too. Budget hotels in London can be unattractive; it can be better to look for a special offer at a better chain.

In major towns you have more options than in rural areas. Hotels are harder to come by in the countryside, and you may stay in a small bed-and-breakfast attached to a pub. Prices may be half of or less than what you'll pay in London. Some B&Bs are gorgeous, and many are in handy locations; others are neither, so be careful. B&Bs are popular with British travelers and can be a great way to meet locals. You might also stay in an old coaching inn from the stagecoach era. There are modern twists on the theme, with chains operating cheap modern hotels with bland pub-restaurants. Some older hotels can be old-fashioned but also less pricey.

House and apartment rentals, in cities or in the countryside, can be a good, sometimes cheaper alternative to hotels. *For details, see the Lodging Primer in this chapter and Accommodations in Travel Smart England.*

Saving Money

Here are ways to start pinching your pennies.

■ Take advantage of free breakfasts if your hotel or B&B offers them. Or grab a croissant at a coffee shop.

■ Many pubs serve lunches for less than £10; most restaurants offer cheap lunch deals.

■ Make one meal a prepared sandwich from a grocery store or sandwich shop.

■ In London, consider staying in a house or apartment. Outside London, stay in a B&B or small guesthouse.

■ Check the websites of major chains for deals, especially in the off-season.

■ Buy a prepaid Oyster Card in London to save on the Tube and buses.

■ Ask about family tickets at major sights.

■ Get your culture kicks in free national museums.

■ Check out a sightseeing pass such as the National Trust Touring Pass.

■ Purchase a BritRail train pass or regional passes.

Visitor Information

These sites have information useful for planning.

Contacts VisitBritain ⊕ *www. visitbritain.com.* **VisitEngland** ⊕ *www.enjoyengland.com.*

ENGLAND
TOP ATTRACTIONS

London

(A) Packed with treasures and pleasures, London entices with superb museums, royal pageantry, and exciting theater, shopping, and nightlife. Its iconic sights include the Houses of Parliament, Westminster Abbey, the Tower of London, and the British Museum, but parks and pubs offer memorable diversions as well. *(⇨ See Chapter 2.)*

Yorkshire Dales

(B) Shaped by ice and sliced by rivers, the dales (valleys) are bounded either by wild, rocky formations and crags or soft-rounded hills. Cascades of waterfalls, drystone walls, and enchanting cottage gardens invite hikes, which can be as easy or challenging as you please. *(⇨ See Chapter 12.)*

Stonehenge and Avebury

(C) Prehistoric monuments dot England's landscape, silent but tantalizing reminders of the distant past. Of these, the great circle of stones at Stonehenge is one of the country's icons. Nearby, the Avebury Stone Circles surround part of a village and are also deeply intriguing. *(⇨ See Chapter 4.)*

Brighton and Its Seafront

(D) England is more than stately homes and pretty towns. This longtime seaside resort lives it up with classic seaside fun as well as the eccentric Royal Pavilion. Good shopping and restaurants, plus energetic nightlife, keep the action going nonstop. *(⇨ See Chapter 3.)*

Bath

(E) Exquisitely preserved but entertaining, this Georgian town still centers on the hot mineral springs that made it a fashionable spa for the wealthy in the 18th and early 19th centuries. Streets lined with Palladian buildings made of golden limestone, an ancient abbey, boutiques, and the ruined Roman baths give Bath real character. *(⇨ See Chapter 7.)*

Hadrian's Wall

(F) Begun in AD 122, the thick stone wall built by the Emperor Hadrian across the rugged far north of the country is a remarkable survivor from Roman Britain, where it protected Roman soldiers from invading tribes. Biking, hiking, and horseback riding are wonderful ways to explore. (⇨ *See Chapter 13.*)

Oxford and Cambridge

(G) It's hard to choose a favorite between these two ancient university towns. Oxford is larger and more cosmopolitan, but lovely with its fairytale cityscape of steeples and towers. In Cambridge you can stroll through the colleges, visit the university's museums, and relax in the city's pubs. (⇨ *See Chapters 6 and 11.*)

Coastal Cornwall

(H) The coasts of Cornwall, in the far southwest, are beloved by many (too many, in summer) for different reasons. The rugged northern coast has cliffs that drop to tiny coves and beaches; ruined, cliff-top Tintagel Castle and Padstow with its lively harbor are here. The south coast has resort towns such as Penzance and arty St. Ives. (⇨ *See Chapter 5.*)

Cotswold Villages

(I) Marked by rolling uplands, green fields, and mellow limestone cottages with prim flower beds, the Cotswolds, 100 miles west of London, make a peaceful getaway. There's little to do in idyllic villages, but that's exactly the point. Exquisite gardens and stately homes add further charm. (⇨ *See Chapter 7.*)

Lake District

(J) Sprawling across northwest England, this area of 16 major lakes and jagged mountains inspired Romantic poets. You can hike the trails or view the mountains from a boat, or visit the retreats of Wordsworth and Beatrix Potter. (⇨ *See Chapter 10.*)

QUINTESSENTIAL ENGLAND

Pints and Pubs

Pop in for a pint at a pub to encounter what has been the center—literally the "public house"—of English social life for centuries. The basic pub recipe calls for a variety of beers on draft—dark creamy stouts like Guinness; bitter, including brews such as Tetley's and Bass; and lager, the blondest and blandest of the trio—a dartboard, oak paneling, and paisley carpets. Throw in a bunch of young suits in London, a generous dash of undergrads in places such as Oxford or Cambridge, and, in rural areas, a healthy helping of blokes around the television and ladies in the corner sipping their *halves* (half pints) and having a *natter* (gossip). In smaller pubs, listen in and enjoy the banter among the regulars—you may even be privy to the occasional *barney* (harmless argument). Make your visit soon: the encroachment of gastro-pubs is just one of the forces challenging traditional pub culture.

Daily Rags

To blend in with the English, stash your smart phone and slide a newspaper under your arm. If you're on the move, pick up free copies of the *Evening Standard* (in London) and *Metro* (in London and on local trains and buses in various other cities), or head for a park bench or café and lose yourself in one of the national dailies for insight into Britain's worldview. The ramifications of the Leveson Inquiry into the role and relationships of the media in 2012 rumble on in the press from the tabloid *Sun*, the biggest-selling daily (though there is discussion that the topless model on Page 3 might be dropped), to the *i*, the cheapest and shortest of the dailies, and the Sunday papers, such as the *Observer* and the more conservative *Sunday Telegraph*. For a more satirical view, the fortnightly *Private Eye*, with its hallmark cartoons and parodies, offers British wit at its best.

If you want to get a sense of contemporary English culture, and indulge in some of its pleasures, start by familiarizing yourself with the rituals of daily life. Here are a few highlights—things you can take part in with relative ease.

A Lovely Cuppa

For almost four centuries the English and tea have been immersed in a love affair passionate enough to survive revolutions, rations, tariffs, and lattes, but also soothing, as "putting the kettle on" heralds moments of quiet comfort in public places and in homes and offices across the nation. The ritual known as "afternoon tea" had its beginnings in the early 19th century, in the private chambers of the duchess of Bedford, where she and her "ladies of leisure" indulged in afternoons of pastries and fragrant blends. Department stores, hotels, and tearooms offer everything from simple tea and biscuits to shockingly overpriced spreads with sandwiches and cakes that would impress even the duchess herself. Some restaurants are now even offering a different tea with each course of the meal. But, if tea isn't your cup of tea, coffee is fine too.

Sports Fever

Whoever says England isn't an overtly religious country hasn't considered the sports mania that's descended here, and not merely because of the effects of the 2012 Olympic Games in London or Andy Murray winning Wimbledon in 2013. Whether water events (such as Henley, Cowes, and the Head of the River Race) or a land competition (the Grand National steeplechase, the Virgin Money London Marathon, a good football match), most bring people to the edge of their seats— or more often the living room couch. To partake in the rite, you'll need Pimm's (the drink for swank spectators of the Henley Royal Regatta) or beer (the drink for most everything else). You may experience the exhilaration yourself—which, you'll probably sense, is not for the love of *a* sport, but for the love of *sport* itself.

IF YOU LIKE

Castles and Stately Homes

Exploring the diversity and magnificence of England's castles and stately homes can occupy most of a blissful vacation. You'll find clusters in the southeast, west of Salisbury, in the Cotswolds, and on the remote northeastern coast. Note that most stately homes are open only from spring through fall. If your itinerary extends to Wales, look for Edward I's "iron ring" of castles, including Caernarfon and Conwy.

Blenheim Palace, Thames Valley. This baroque extravaganza is touted as England's only rival to Versailles.

Buckingham Palace, London. Glimpse royal life in the magnificent state rooms, open in August and September.

Hever Castle, Southeast. The childhood home of Anne Boleyn is the archetypal castle with battlements, turrets, and moat.

Holkham Hall, East Anglia. The splendid 60-foot-tall Marble Hall and salons filled with old masters distinguish this Palladian house.

Knole, Southeast. Within the seven courtyards of this 16th-century family home are silver furniture and a golden bed.

Petworth House, the Southeast. One of the National Trust's glories, it's known for art by J.M.W. Turner.

Stourhead, the South. A visit here brings you what is considered by many the most beautiful house and landscape garden in Europe.

Wilton House, the South. The Double Cube room designed by Inigo Jones is one of the country's best interior designs.

Windsor Castle, Thames Valley. The Queen's favorite residence has a fabulous art collection.

Idyllic Towns and Villages

Year after year, armies of tourists with images of green meadows, thatched roofs, and colorful flower beds flock to England's countryside. Most will find their way to famously adorable towns along the Thames, timeless seaside resorts in the West Country, and a smattering of fairy-tale hamlets in the Cotswolds. But don't dismiss the pastoral flatlands and historic villages of East Anglia beyond Cambridge, the Norfolk coast, or the mountainside hamlets and sleepy seaside resorts of Wales.

Clovelly, Southwest. A steep cobbled street threads between flower-bedecked cottages down to the tiny harbor on the south Devon coast.

Henley-on-Thames, Thames Valley. Famous for its Regatta, the affluent town has a lovely position on the Thames and is ideal for strolling.

Lavenham, East Anglia. This village is full of Tudor buildings, the former houses of wool merchants and weavers.

Ludlow, Stratford-upon-Avon and the Heart of England. Medieval and Georgian buildings cluster below a castle in this town, whose restaurants have made it a foodie favorite.

Rye, Southeast. Writers and artists have always been drawn to the cobbled streets and timber houses of this historic little town.

Whitby, Yorkshire. A ruined abbey and a cliff-lined harbor combine with a rich fishing and whaling legacy to enhance this coastal gem.

Winchcombe, Bath and the Cotswolds. Cottages of honey-color stone line the streets of this quintessential Cotswold town.

Glorious Gardens

Despite being cursed with impertinent weather and short summers, English gardeners need no encouragement to grab their gardening tools. A pilgrimage to a garden is an essential part of any spring or summer trip. Green havens thrive all over England, but perhaps the most fertile hunting grounds are in Oxfordshire, Gloucestershire (including the Cotswolds), and Kent (the "Garden of England").

Eden Project, Southwest. Much ingenious thought and inspiration has gone into presenting the world's plants from three climate zones in huge geodesic domes in Cornwall.

Hidcote Manor, Bath and the Cotswolds. A masterful example of the Arts and Crafts garden, it is divided into garden rooms and contains the stunning Red Border.

Kew Gardens, London. A tree-top walk, huge 19th-century greenhouses, and a pagoda, as well as swaths of colorful flower beds, adorn this center of academic research.

Sissinghurst Castle Garden, Southeast. Vita Sackville-West's masterpiece, set within the remains of a Tudor castle, is busy in summer and spectacular in autumn.

Stourhead, South. One of the country's most impressive house-and-garden combinations is an artful 18th-century sanctuary with a tranquil lake, colorful shrubs, and grottoes.

Wisley, Southeast. The Royal Horticultural Society's garden splendidly blends the pretty and the practical in its inspirational displays and glasshouses.

Urban Excitement

London has everything a world capital should have—rich culture and history, thrilling art and theater scenes, world-class restaurants and sensational shopping—along with crowds, traffic, and high prices. It's not to be missed, but if you appreciate modern cities, spend time in some of England's reviving urban centers, including those in its former industrial heartland. Here blossoming multiculturalism has paved the way for a unique vibe.

Birmingham, Heart of England. Interlaced with canals, the country's second-largest city is a vibrant center for culture and cuisine and has a unique Jewellery Quarter.

Brighton, Southeast. Bold, bright, and boisterous are the words to describe a seaside charmer that has everything from the dazzling Royal Pavilion to the trendy shops of the Lanes.

Bristol, West Country. With its lively waterfront and music and food culture, this youthful city has vibrant nightlife as well as a long history.

Leeds, Yorkshire. A former industrial city now polishing its Victorian buildings, Leeds is known for its shopping arcades and a spirited music scene.

Liverpool, Lancashire and the Peaks. Dramatic regeneration, a historic waterfront, Beatles sites, and the stellar museums of the Albert Dock are stars of this city.

Manchester, Lancashire and the Peaks. Much more than football, the city offers chic urban shopping, bars and clubs, and fabulous museums, reflective of its industrial heritage.

Ancient Mysteries

Stone circles as well as ancient stone and earthen forts and mounds offer intriguing hints about Britain's mysterious prehistoric inhabitants. The country's southwestern landscape, particularly the Salisbury Plain, Dorset, and the eastern side of Cornwall, has a notably rich concentration of these sites, perplexing mysteries that human nature compels us to try to solve.

Avebury Stone Circles, South. Large and marvelously evocative, these circles surround part of the village of Avebury. You can walk right up to these stones.

Castlerigg Stone Circle, Lake District. The setting of this Neolithic creation, surrounded by brooding peaks, is as awesome as the surviving remains.

Maiden Castle, South. The largest Iron Age hill fort in England has impressive rings of ramparts and ditches that fire your sense of history.

Stanton Drew Circles, West Country. Use your imagination to visualize the vast size of the two avenues of standing stones, three rings, and burial chamber that now lie in a field.

Stonehenge, South. The stone circle begun 5,000 years ago stands on the wide Salisbury Plain. Hypotheses about its purpose range from the scientific (ancient calendar) to the fantastic (a gift from extinct giants).

Vale of the White Horse, Thames Valley. The gigantic horse here was actually carved into the chalky hillside around 1750 BC.

Wonderful Walks

England seems to be designed with walking in mind—footpaths wind through the contours of the landscape, and popular routes are well endowed with cozy bed-and-breakfasts and pubs. You can walk the whole or small chunks of the many long-distance trails or ramble through one of England's national parks. Famous walking spots are in the Lake District (congested in summer) and Yorkshire's dales and moors. Wherever you hike, always be prepared for storms or fogs. Check out www.nationaltrail.co.uk for inspiration and advice.

Borrowdale, Lake District. Have a color-pencil kit handy to capture the beauty of the dramatically verdant valleys and jagged peaks.

Brecon Beacons, Wales. The windswept uplands here are crossed with easy paths and are uncrowded.

Cotswolds Way, Bath and the Cotswolds. Hike the Cotswold Way and combine open grassland, pretty villages and sweeping views to the Malvern Hills and Severn Valley.

Peak District, Lancashire and the Peaks. Its rocky outcrops and vaulting meadows make some people say this is the country's most beautiful national park.

Snowdonia, Wales. Ferocious peaks in the national park promise challenging hikes.

South West Coast Path, West Country. Spectacular is the word for the 630-mile trail that winds from Minehead in Somerset to Poole Harbour in Dorset.

Thames Path, Thames Valley. Follow the Thames from its source through water meadows and riverside villages to the heart of London.

Thrilling Theater

There's no better antidote to an overdose of stately homes and well-groomed gardens than a face-to-face encounter with another British specialty, the theater. London is the heart and soul of the action: here companies consistently churn out superb productions. Still, be sure to sample theater outside London. Stratford-upon-Avon may be the Bard's hometown, but festivals all over the country celebrate Shakespeare's work—among the best is London's Shakespeare Under the Stars at Regent's Park. Or try a university production.

Chichester Festival Theatre, Southeast. This modernist building is known for its innovative performances.

Harrogate International Festival, Yorkshire. See street theater at the north of England's best arts festival.

Minack Theatre, West Country. The open-air theater in coastal Cornwall, near Land's End, nuzzles the slope of a sandy cliff.

Royal Shakespeare Company, Stratford-upon-Avon and the Heart of England. Seeing any Shakespeare play is a treat in the home of the Bard.

Stephen Joseph Theater, Scarborough, Yorkshire. Alan Ayckbourn's plays are performed here.

Theatre Royal, Bath, Bath and the Cotswolds. Pre- or post-London tours often visit this Regency-era theater.

Theatre Royal, York, Yorkshire. Traditional pantomime—with dames (men dressed as ladies), slapstick, and music takes place in December and January.

Yvonne Arnaud Theatre, Guildford, the Southeast. The productions at this theater on an island often travel to London.

Country-House Hotels

In all their luxurious glory, country-house hotels are an essential part of the English landscape, particularly in the southern part of the country. Some hotels are traditional, but there's a newer modern breed as well, and many will have spas, pools, and sports available. If you can't spend a night, consider dinner or afternoon tea. The Cotswolds and the Thames Valley are prime ground for these retreats. One tip: Ask if a wedding party will be using the hotel during your stay; these can take over a smaller establishment.

Calcot Manor, Bath and the Cotswolds. Luxury and opulence join with family-friendly amenities here where traditional and modern mix.

Cliveden House, Thames Valley. This very grand stately pile, once the Astors' home, offers champagne boat trips on the River Thames.

Coworth Park, Thames Valley. It's 18th century on the outside but very 21st century within: this retreat combines playful luxury with spacious grounds.

Gidleigh Park, West Country. Beautiful grounds in a wooded valley on edge of Dartmoor are the backdrop for superb food and antiques-filled rooms.

Lime Wood, South. This woodland hideaway in a Regency house has the added treat of a fabulous spa.

Miller Howe, Lake District. Stunning views of Windermere, Arts and Crafts touches, and superior service are the appeal here.

Thornbury Castle, West Country. A stay in this 16th-century castle with a royal pedigree connects you to history but also includes plenty of modern pampering.

FLAVORS OF ENGLAND

The New Food Scene

England has never lacked a treasure store of nature's bounty: lush green pastures, fruitful orchards, and the encompassing sea. Over the past few decades, dowdy images of English cooking have been sloughed off. A new focus on the land and a new culinary confidence and expertise are exemplified by the popularity and influence of celebrity chefs such as Rick Stein, Heston Blumenthal, Gordon Ramsay, Jamie Oliver, and Mary Berry. The chefs are only one indicator of change: all over the country, artisanal food producers and talented cooks are indulging their passion for high-quality, locally sourced ingredients. And television programs on home baking have proved phenomenally popular.

Food festivals, farmers' markets (some organic), and farm shops have sprung up in more cities and towns. Alongside the infiltration of supermarkets, much opposed by some people, comes a more discriminating attitude to food supplies. Outdoors-reared cows, sheep, and pigs; freshly caught fish; and seasonal fruits and vegetables provide a bedrock upon which traditional recipes are tempered with cosmopolitan influences. The contemporary English menu takes the best of Mediterranean and Asian cuisines and reinterprets them with new enthusiasm.

Natural Bounty

Cask ales. The interest in the provenance of food extends to beer, encouraging microbreweries to develop real or cask ales: beer that's unfiltered and unpasteurized, and that contains live brewer's yeast. The ales can be from kegs, bottles, or casks, and they range from pale amber to full-bodied. The Casque Mark outside pubs signals their availability.

Dairy produce. The stalwart Cheddar, Cheshire, Double Gloucester, and Stilton cheeses are complemented by traditional and experimental cheeses from small, local makers. Some cheeses come wrapped in nettles or vine leaves, others stuffed with apricots, cranberries, or herbs. Dairies are producing more sheep and goat cheeses, yogurts, and ice creams.

Game. In the fall and winter, pheasant, grouse, partridge, and venison are prominent on restaurant menus, served either roasted, in rich casseroles, or in pies. Duck (particularly the Gressingham and Aylesbury breeds), rabbit, and hare are available all year-round.

Meat. Peacefully grazing cattle, including Aberdeen Angus, Herefordshire, and Welsh Black varieties, are an iconic symbol of the countryside. When hung and dry-aged for up to 28 days, English beef is at its most flavorsome. Spring lamb is succulent, and salt-marsh lamb from Wales and the Lake District, fed on wild grasses and herbs, makes for a unique taste. Outdoors-reared and rare breeds of pig, such as Gloucester Old Spot, often provide the breakfast bacon.

Preserved foods. Marmalade is a fixed item on the breakfast menu, and a wide variety of jams, including the less usual quince, find their place on the tea-shop table. Chutneys made from apples or tomatoes mixed with onions and spices are served with cheese at the end of a meal or as part of a pub lunch.

Seafood. The traditional trio of cod, haddock, and plaice is still in evidence, but declining fishing stocks have brought other varieties to prominence. Hake, bream, freshwater trout, wild salmon, sardines, pilchards, and mackerel are on the restaurant table, along with crab, mussels, and oysters. The east and Cornish coasts are favored fishing grounds.

Traditional Dishes

Good international fare is available, and you shouldn't miss the Indian food in England. But do try some classics.

Black pudding. In this dish, associated with Lancashire, Yorkshire, and the Midlands, onions, pork fat, oatmeal, herbs, and spices are blended with the blood from a pig. At its best this dish has a delicate, crumbly texture and can be served at breakfast or as a starter to a meal.

Fish-and-chips. This number-one seaside favorite not only turns up in every seaside resort, but in fish-and-chip shops and restaurants throughout the land. Fish, usually cod, haddock, or plaice, is deep-fried in a crispy batter and served with thick french fries (chips) and, if eaten out, wrapped up in paper. The liberal sprinkling of salt and vinegar, and "mushy" (processed) peas are optional.

Meat pies and pasties. Pies and pasties make a filling lunch. Perhaps the most popular is steak-and-kidney pie, combining chunks of lean beef and kidneys mixed with braised onions and mushrooms in a thick gravy, topped with a light puff- or short-pastry crust. Other combinations are chicken with mushrooms or leek and beef slow-cooked in ale (often Guinness). Cornish pasties are filled with beef, potato, rutabaga, and onions, all enveloped in a circle of pastry folded in half.

Sausages. "Bangers and mash" are sausages, most commonly made with pork but sometimes beef or lamb, served with mashed potatoes and onion gravy. Lincolnshire sausage consists of pork flavored with sage. Cumberland sausage comes in a long coil and has a peppery taste.

Shepherd's and cottage pie. These classic pub dishes have a lightly browned mashed-potato topping over stewed minced meat and onions in a rich gravy. Shepherd's pie uses lamb, cottage pie beef.

Meals Not to Be Missed

Full English breakfast. The "full English" is a three-course affair. Starting with orange juice, cereals, porridge, yogurt, or stewed fruit, it's followed by any combination of sausages, eggs, bacon, tomatoes, mushrooms, black pudding, baked beans, and fried bread. The feast finishes with toast and marmalade and tea or coffee. Alternatives to the fry-up are kippers, smoked haddock, or boiled eggs. Some cafés serve an all-day breakfast.

Ploughman's lunch. Crusty bread, English cheese (perhaps farmhouse Cheddar, blue Stilton, crumbly Cheshire, or waxy red Leicester), and tangy pickles with a side-salad garnish make up a delicious light lunch, found in almost every pub.

Roast dinners. On Sunday, the traditional roast dinner is still popular. The meat, either beef, pork, lamb, or chicken, is served with roast potatoes, carrots, seasonal green vegetables, and Yorkshire pudding, a savory batter baked in the oven until crisp, and then topped with a rich, dark, meaty gravy. Horseradish sauce and English mustard are on hand for beef; a mint sauce accompanies lamb; and an apple sauce enhances pork.

Tea in the afternoon. Tea, ideally served in a country garden on a summer afternoon, ranks high on the list of England's must-have experiences. You may simply have a scone with your tea, or you can opt for a more ample feast: dainty sandwiches with the crusts cut off; scones with jam and clotted cream; and an array of homemade cakes.

ENGLAND LODGING PRIMER

If your England dreams involve staying in a cozy cottage with a lovely garden, here's some good news: you won't have to break the bank. Throughout the country you'll find stylish lodging options—from good-value hotels and intimate bed-and-breakfasts to chic apartments and unique historic houses—in all price ranges.

For resources and contacts, and information on hotel grading and booking, see Travel Smart England.

Apartments and House Rentals

For a home base with cooking facilities that's roomy enough for a family, consider renting furnished "flats" (the word for apartments in England). These are popular in cities and towns throughout the country and can save you money. They also provide more privacy than a hotel or B&B.

Cottages and other houses are available for weekly rental in all areas. These vary from quaint older homes to brand-new buildings in scenic surroundings. For families and large groups they offer the best value-for-money accommodations, but because they're often in isolated locations, a car is vital. Living Architecture offers stays in one-of-a-kind architect-designed country houses. Lists of rental properties are available free of charge from VisitBritain. You may find discounts of up to 50% on rentals during the off-season (October through March).

Bed-and-Breakfasts

A special English tradition, and the backbone of budget travel, B&Bs are usually in a family home. Typical prices (outside London) range from £45 to £100 a night. They vary in style and grace, but these days most have private bathrooms. B&Bs range from the ordinary to the truly elegant. The line between B&Bs

and guesthouses is growing increasingly blurred, but the latter are often larger.

Some Tourist Information Centres in cities and towns can help you find and book a B&B even on the day you show up in town. Many private services also deal with B&Bs. *For reservation services in London, see the Where to Stay section in Chapter 2.*

Farmhouses

Over the years farmhouses have become popular; their special appeal is the rural experience, whether in Cornwall or Yorkshire. Consider this option only if you are touring by car, because farmhouses may be in remote locations. Prices are generally reasonable. Ask VisitBritain for the booklet "Stay on a Farm" or contact Farm Stay UK. Regional tourist boards may have information as well.

Historic Buildings

Looking for a unique experience and want to spend your vacation in a Gothic banqueting house, an old lighthouse, or maybe in an apartment at Hampton Court Palace? Several organizations, such as the Landmark Trust, National Trust, English Heritage, and Vivat Trust, have specially adapted historic buildings to rent. Many of these have kitchens, and some may require minimum stays.

Hotels

England is a popular vacation destination, so be sure to reserve hotel rooms weeks (months for London) in advance. The country has everything from budget chain hotels to luxurious retreats in converted country houses. In many towns and cities you'll find old inns that are former coaching inns; these served travelers as they journeyed around the country in horse-drawn carriages and stagecoaches.

GREAT
ITINERARIES

HIGHLIGHTS
OF ENGLAND:
UNFORGETTABLE IMAGES

12 days
London

Day 1. The capital is just the jumping-off point for this trip, so choose a few highlights that grab your interest. If it's the Changing of the Guard at Buckingham Palace, check the time to be sure you catch the pageantry. If Westminster Abbey appeals to your sense of history, arrive as early as you can. Pick a museum (many are free, so you needn't linger if you don't want to), whether it's the National Gallery in Trafalgar Square, the British Museum in Bloomsbury, or a smaller gem like the Queen's Gallery. Stroll Hyde Park or take a boat ride on the Thames before you find a pub or Indian restaurant for dinner. End with a play; the experience of theatergoing may be as interesting as whatever work you see.

Windsor

Day 2. Resplendent with centuries of treasures, Windsor Castle is favored by the Queen, and has been by rulers for centuries. Tour it to appreciate the history and wealth of the monarchy. The State Apartments are open if the Queen isn't in residence, and 10 kings and queens are

buried in magnificent St. George's Chapel. Time permitting, take a walk in the adjacent Great Park. If you can splurge for a luxurious stay (versus making Windsor a day trip from London), head up the valley to Cliveden, the Thames Valley's most spectacular hotel.

Logistics: Trains from Paddington and Waterloo stations leave about twice hourly and take less than one hour. Green Line buses depart from the Colonnades opposite London's Victoria Coach Station.

Salisbury and Stourhead

Day 3. Visible for miles around, Salisbury Cathedral's soaring spire is an unforgettable image of rural England. See the Magna Carta in the cathedral's Chapter House as you explore this marvel of medieval engineering, and walk the town path to get the view John Constable painted. Pay an afternoon visit to Stourhead to experience the finest example of the naturalistic 18th-century landscaping for which England is famous; the grand Palladian mansion here is a bonus.

Logistics: For trains to Salisbury from Windsor Riverside, head back to London's Clapham Junction to catch a train on the West of England line.

Bath and Stonehenge

Day 4. Bath's immaculately preserved, golden-stone Georgian architecture helps you recapture the late 18th century. Take time to stroll; don't miss the Royal Crescent (you can explore the period interior of No. 1), and sip the Pump Room's vile-tasting water as Jane Austen's characters might have. The Roman Baths are an amazing remnant of the ancient empire, complete with curses left by soldiers. Today you can do as the Romans did as you relax in the warm mineral waters at the Thermae Bath Spa. There's plenty to do in Bath (museums, shopping, theater), but you might make an excursion to Stonehenge (by car or tour bus). Go early or late to avoid the worst crowds at Stonehenge, and use your imagination—and the good audio guide—to appreciate this enigma.

Logistics: Trains and buses leave hourly from Salisbury to Bath.

The Cotswolds

Day 5. Antiques-shop in fairy-tale Stow-on-the-Wold and feed the ducks at the brook in Lower Slaughter for a taste of the mellow stone villages and dreamy green landscapes for which the area is beloved. Choose a rainy or off-season day to visit Broadway or risk jams of tourist traffic. Another great experience is a walk on the Cotswold Way or any local path.

Logistics: Drive to make the best of the beautiful scenery. Alternatively, opt for a guided tour bus.

Oxford and Blenheim Palace

Day 6. Join a guided tour of Oxford's glorious quadrangles, chapels, and gardens to get the best access to these centuries-old academic treasures. This leaves time for a jaunt to Blenheim, a unique combination of baroque opulence (inside and out) and naturalistic parkland, the work of the great 18th-century landscape designer Capability Brown. For classic Oxford experiences, rent a punt or join students and go pub-crawling around town.

Logistics: Hourly trains depart from Bath for Oxford. Buses frequently depart from Oxford's Gloucester Green for Blenheim Palace.

Stratford-upon-Avon

Day 7. Skip this stop if you don't care about you-know-who. Fans of Shakespeare can see his birthplace and Anne Hathaway's Cottage (walking there is a delight), and then finish with a memorable performance at the Royal Shakespeare Company's magnificently renovated main stage. Start the day early and be prepared for crowds.

Logistics: From Oxford there are direct trains and a less frequent Stagecoach bus service.

Shrewsbury to Chester

Day 8. Head north to see the half-timber buildings of Shrewsbury, one of the best preserved of England's Tudor towns. Strolling is the best way to experience it. In Chester the architecture is more or less the same (though not always authentic), but the Rows, a series of two-story shops with medieval crypts beneath, and the fine city walls are sights you can't pass by. You can walk part or all of the city walls for views of the town and surrounding area.

Logistics: For Shrewsbury, change trains at Birmingham. The train ride to Chester is 55 minutes.

The Lake District

Days 9 and 10. In the area extending north beyond Kendal and Windermere, explore the English lakes and beautiful surrounding mountains on foot in the Lake District National Park. This area is jam-packed with hikers in summer and on weekends, so rent a car to seek out the more isolated routes. Take a cruise on Windermere or Coniston Water, or rent a boat, for another classic Lakeland experience. If you have time for one Wordsworth-linked site, head to Dove Cottage; you can even have afternoon tea there.

Logistics: Train to Oxenholme with a change at Warrington Bank Quay. At Oxenholme you can switch to Windermere.

York

Day 11. This historic cathedral city is crammed with 15th- and 16th-century buildings, but don't miss York Minster, with its stunning stained glass, and the medieval streets of the Shambles. Take your pick of the city's museums or go shopping; have tea at Betty's or unwind at a pub. A walk along the top of the city walls is fun too.

Logistics: By train from Oxenholme, switch in Preston, or from Carlisle change at Newcastle.

Cambridge

Day 12. Spend the afternoon touring King's College Chapel and the Backs—gardens and sprawling meadows—and refining your punting skills on the River Cam. The excellent Fitzwilliam Museum, full of art and antiquities, is another option, as is the Polar Museum. To relax, join the students for a pint at a pub.

Logistics: For train service, switch at Peterborough or Stevenage. Trains leave Cambridge for London frequently.

TIPS

■ Train travelers should keep in mind that regional "Rovers" and "Rangers" offer unlimited train travel in one-day, three-day, or weeklong increments. See ⊕ www.nationalrail.co.uk/promotions for details. Also check out BritRail passes, which must be purchased before your trip.

■ Buses are time-consuming, but more scenic and cheaper than train travel. National Express offers discounts including fun fares—fares to and from London to various cities (including Cambridge) for £7.50 and under if booked more than 24 hours in advance. Or check out low-cost Megabus.

■ To cut the tour short, consider skipping Chester and Shrewsbury and proceed to the Lake District from Stratford-upon-Avon on day eight. Likewise, you can consider passing up a visit to Cambridge if you opt for Oxford. You can add the time to your London stay or another place you want to linger.

■ It's easy to visit Stonehenge from Salisbury, as well as from Bath, whether you have a car or want a guided excursion.

■ Buy theater tickets well in advance for Stratford-upon-Avon.

GREAT
ITINERARIES

STATELY HOMES AND LANDSCAPES TOUR

11 days

Hampton Court Palace

Day 1. Start your trip royally at this palace a half hour from London by train. It's two treasures in one: a Tudor palace with magnificent baroque additions by Christopher Wren. As you walk through cobbled courtyards, Henry VIII's State Apartments, and the enormous kitchens, you may feel as if you've been whisked back to the days of the Tudors and William and Mary. A quiet stroll through the 60 acres of immaculate gardens—the sculpted yews look like huge green gumdrops—is recommended. Be sure to get lost in the 18th-century maze—if it's open (diligent maintenance leads to occasional closures). It's easy to spend a whole day here, so start early.

Logistics: Tube to Richmond, then Bus R68; or catch the train from Waterloo to Hampton Court Station.

Knole and Ightham Mote

Days 2 and 3. Clustered around Royal Tunbridge Wells south of London is the highest concentration of stately homes in England, and, as if that weren't enough, the surrounding fields and colorful orchards are often wrapped in clouds of mist, creating a picture-perfect scene. We've picked two very different homes to visit, leaving you plenty of time to tour at a leisurely pace. Knole, Vita Sackville-West's sprawling childhood home, has dark, baroque rooms and a famous set of silver furniture. Ightham Mote, a smaller, moated house, is a vision from the Middle Ages. Its rooms are an ideal guide to style changes from the Tudor to Victorian eras. Spend the evening at one of the many good restaurants in Royal Tunbridge Wells.

Logistics: Take the train from London's Charing Cross to Sevenoaks, from which it's a 20-minute walk to Knole. There's no public transportation to Ightham Mote.

Petworth House

Day 4. Priceless paintings by Gainsborough, Reynolds, and Turner (19 by Turner alone) embellish the august rooms of Petworth House, present-day home to Lord and Lady Egremont and one of the National Trust's treasures. Check out Capability Brown's 700-acre deer park or the Victorian kitchens, and for the perfect lunch peruse the offerings in the winding lanes of Petworth town. Head to Chichester for the evening, along a route passing through the rolling grasslands and deep valleys of the South Downs.

Logistics: Train to Chichester, switching in Redhill, then bus to Petworth.

Wilton House

Day 5. Base yourself in Salisbury for two days, taking time to see the famous cathedral with its impressively tall spire and to walk the town path from the Long Bridge for the best view of it. Visit neoclassical Wilton House (in nearby Wilton) first, where the exquisite Double Cube Room contains a spectacular family portrait by Van Dyck and gilded furniture that accommodated Eisenhower when he contemplated the Normandy invasion here. On your way back make a detour to Stonehenge to view the wide-open Salisbury Plain and ponder the enigmatic stones.

Logistics: Take a train from Chichester to Salisbury, with a switch in Cosham or Southampton; then bus it to Wilton House.

Stourhead to Longleat House

Day 6. Day-trip west from Salisbury to Stourhead to experience perhaps the most stunning house-garden combination in the country, and either spend the day here (climb Alfred's Tower for a grand view of the house) or leave some time for nearby Longleat House—a vast, treasure-stuffed Italian Renaissance palace complete with safari park and a devilish maze. If you want to see the safari park, you'll need plenty of time here. Once back in Salisbury, relax in one of New Street's many cafés.

Logistics: Bus to Warminster and then a taxi for the 5-mile journey to Longleat; for Stourhead, take the train to Gillingham from Salisbury, followed by a short cab ride.

Blenheim Palace

Day 7. Home of the dukes of Marlborough and birthplace of Winston Churchill, Blenheim Palace uniquely combines exquisitely designed parklands (save time to walk) and one of the most ornate baroque structures in the world. After your visit, have afternoon tea at Blenheim Tea Rooms in the adorable village of Woodstock. Overnight in Oxford; do your own pub crawl.

Logistics: From Salisbury by train, change at Basingstoke for Oxford, then catch a bus to Blenheim.

Snowshill Manor and Sudeley Castle

Days 8 and 9. Here you can take in the idyllic Cotswold landscape, a magical mix of greenery and mellow stone cottages and ancient churches (built with wool-trade money), along with some famous buildings. Spend the first night in Broadway to explore nearby Snowshill Manor—with its delightfully eccentric collection of Tibetan scrolls, Persian lamps, and samurai armor—in the unspoiled village of Snowshill. If you have a car, don't linger in busy Broadway. Instead, head to Chipping Campden, one of the best-preserved Cotswolds villages, which nestles in a secluded valley. Move to another charming town, Winchcombe, on the second day. Take a stroll past honey-color stone cottages and impeccably well-kept gardens. Visit Sudeley Castle, once home to Catherine Parr (Henry VIII's last wife), a Tudor-era palace with romantic gardens (only a few rooms are now open to the public). Another option near Winchcombe is Stanway House, a Jacobean manor owned by Lord Neidpath; hours are limited, but this timeworn home and its gabled gatehouse are typically English.

Logistics: Take a train from Oxford to Moreton-in-Marsh for the bus to Broadway; from Broadway, walk the 2½ miles to Snowshill Manor; for Sudeley Castle, take a bus from Broadway to Winchcombe, then walk.

Chatsworth House, Haddon Hall, and Hardwick Hall

Days 10 and 11. For the final stops, head north, east of Manchester, to a more dramatic landscape. In or near the craggy Peak District, where the gentle slopes of the Pennine Hills begin their ascent to Scotland, are three of England's most renowned historic homes. Base yourself in Bakewell, and spend your first day taking in the art treasures amassed by the dukes of Devonshire at Chatsworth House. The gardens, grounds, shops, and farmyard exhibits make it easy to spend a day here. If you have any time left over, get out of Bakewell and take a walk in the hills of the Peak District National Park (maps are available at the town's tourist information center).

On the second day, devote the morning to the crenellations and boxy roofs of medieval Haddon Hall, a quintessentially English house. Give your afternoon to Hardwick Hall, an Elizabethan stone mansion with a facade that's "more glass than wall"—a truly innovative idea in the 16th century. Its collections of period tapestries and embroideries are remarkable reminders of the splendor of the age.

Logistics: Take a train back to Oxford and then up to Manchester for the connection to Buxton; then catch a bus to Bakewell.

TIPS

■ All stately homes in this itinerary, with the exception of Hampton Court Palace and Longleat House, are closed for winter, though gardens may remain open. Even homes open April through October may not be open every day. It's best to confirm all hours before visiting.

■ A car is best for this itinerary, as some houses are remote. Use a GPS or get good maps.

■ Country roads around the Peak District are hard to negotiate; be especially careful when driving to Chatsworth House, Haddon Hall, and Hardwick Hall. Drives will take longer than you expect.

■ Look into discount passes, such as those from the National Trust or English Heritage (⇨ *See Sightseeing Passes in Essentials in Travel Smart England*), which provide significant savings on visits to multiple sites. Memberships are also available.

LONDON

WELCOME TO LONDON

TOP REASONS TO GO

★ **The abbey and the cathedral:** The pillars of Westminster Abbey stand around the final resting place of the people who built Britain. To the east, St. Paul's Cathedral takes the breath away.

★ **Buckingham Palace:** Not the prettiest royal residence, but a must-see for the glimpse it affords of modern royal life. The Queen's Gallery is next door.

★ **Tower of London:** The Tower is London at its majestic, idiosyncratic best. This is the heart of the kingdom, with foundations dating back nine centuries.

★ **Museum marvels:** The National Gallery has old masters, the Tate Modern the latest thing. Treasures from around the globe fill the British Museum. These are just a few top museums.

★ **A city of villages:** London has dozens of neighborhoods bursting with life. Parks, shops, pubs: walk around and make the city your own.

1 Westminster, St. James's, and Royal London. This is the place to embrace the "tourist" label. Snap pictures of the mounted Horse Guards, play with the pigeons in Trafalgar Square, and visit stacks of art in the national galleries. It's well worth braving the crowds to wander ancient Westminster Abbey and its historic bounty.

2 Soho and Covent Garden. More sophisticated than seedy these days, the heart of London puts Theaterland, strip joints, Chinatown, and the trendiest of film studios side by side. Nearby Charing Cross Road is a bibliophile's dream; hectic hordes fill Leicester Square, London's answer to Times Square.

GETTING ORIENTED

London grew from a wooden bridge built over the Thames in the year AD 43 to its current 600 square miles and 7 million souls in haphazard fashion, meandering from its two official centers: Westminster, seat of government and royalty, to the west, and the City, site of finance and commerce, to the east. In this city of urban villages, the neighborhoods continue to evolve. If the city's great parks such as Hyde Park are, in Lord Chatham's phrase, "the lungs of London," then the River Thames remains its backbone.

3 Bloomsbury and Holborn. Once London's intellectual center, elegant Bloomsbury is now mostly a business district. Stop for a good while in the incomparable British Museum; the University of London is worth a passing glance.

4 The City. London's Wall Street might be the oldest part of the capital, but thanks to futuristic skyscrapers and a sleek Millennium Bridge, it looks like the newest. Fans of ages gone by won't be disappointed, however: head for St. Paul's Cathedral, Tower Bridge, and the Tower of London.

5 The South Bank. The Royal National Theatre and Royal Festival Hall, the National Film Theatre, Shakespeare's Globe, and the Tate Modern make this area a creative hub. Take it all in from the Shard.

6 Kensington, Knightsbridge, and Mayfair. The museums are awe-inspiring; the Science Museum and the Natural History Museum are the most fun for children. Flash your cash at Harrods and Harvey Nichols.

7 Regent's Park and Hampstead. London becomes noticeably calmer and greener as you head north from Oxford Street. This area will provide a taste of how laid-back (moneyed) Londoners can be.

8 Up and Down the Thames. The quaint Thames-side streets of Greenwich have some brilliant sights. Other excursions include Kew Gardens and Hampton Court Palace.

Updated by
Julius Honnor,
Jack Jewers,
James O'Neill,
Ellin Stein,
and Alex
Wijeratna

London is an ancient city whose history greets you at every turn; it's also one of the coolest cities in the world. If the city contained only its famous landmarks—the Tower of London, Big Ben, Westminster Abbey, Buckingham Palace—it would still rank as one of the world's top cities. But London is so much more.

To gain a sense of its continuity, stand on Waterloo Bridge at sunset. To the east, the great globe of St. Paul's Cathedral glows golden in the fading sunlight as it has since the 17th century, still majestic amid the modern glass towers. To the west stand the mock-medieval ramparts of Westminster, home to the "Mother of Parliaments," which has met here or hereabouts since the 1250s. Past them both snakes the swift, dark Thames, which flowed past the Roman settlement of Londinium nearly 2,000 years ago.

The city beckons with great museums, royal pageantry, and history-steeped houses. There's no other place like it in its medley of styles, in its mixture of the green loveliness of parks and the modern gleam of neon. Modern-day London largely reflects its tangled medieval layout. Even Londoners, most of whom own a dog-eared copy of an indispensable *London A–Z* street finder, get lost in their own city.

You should not only visit St. Paul's Cathedral and the Tower of London, but also set aside some time for random wandering; the city repays every moment spent exploring on foot. Walk in the city's backstreets and mews, around Park Lane and Kensington. Pass up Buckingham Palace for Kensington Palace. Take in the National Gallery, but don't forget London's "time machine" museums, such as the 19th-century home of Sir John Soane. Abandon the city's chain stores for its wonderful markets.

Today the city's art, style, fashion, and dining scenes, not to mention its financial muscle, make headlines around the world. London's chefs have become superstars. Its fashion designers have conquered Paris, avant-garde artists have caused waves at the Royal Academy of Arts, the raging after-hours scene is packed with music mavens ready to catch the Next Big Thing, and the theater continues its tradition of radical, shocking productions.

Then there's that greatest living link with the past—the Royal Family. Don't let the tag of "typical tourist destination" stop you from enjoying the pageantry of the Changing of the Guard at Buckingham Palace, one of the greatest free shows in the world.

Be prepared to be taken by surprise. The great 18th-century author Samuel Johnson said that a man who is tired of London is tired of life. Armed with energy and curiosity, you can find, to quote Dr. Johnson again, "in London all that life can afford."

LONDON PLANNER

WHEN TO GO

The heaviest tourist season runs mid-April through mid-October, with another peak around Christmas—though the tide never really ebbs. Spring is the time to see the royal London parks and gardens at their freshest; fall to enjoy near-ideal exploring conditions. In late summer, be warned: air-conditioning is rarely found in places other than department stores, modern restaurants, hotels, and cinemas in London, although it's really needed for only a few days. Winter can be rather dismal, but all the theaters, concerts, and exhibitions go full speed ahead.

Avoid the February and October "half-terms" when schools in the capital take a break for a week and nearly all attractions are flooded by children. The start of August can be a very busy time, and the weather makes Tube travel a nightmare. Shopping in central London the week before Christmas is an idea best left only to desperate Londoners who have forgotten to buy presents.

GETTING HERE AND AROUND

ADDRESSES

Central London and its surrounding districts are divided into 32 boroughs—33, counting the City of London. More useful for finding your way around, however, are the subdivisions of London into postal districts. The first one or two letters give the location: N means north, NW means northwest, etc.

AIR TRAVEL

For information about airports and airport transfers, see Getting Here and Around in Travel Smart England.

BUS TRAVEL

In central London Transport for London (TfL) buses are traditionally bright red double- and single-deckers. Not all buses run the full length of their route at all times, so check with the driver. In central London you must purchase tickets from machines at bus stops along the routes before you board. The main bus stops have a red TfL symbol on a white background. When the word "Request" is written across the sign, you must flag the bus down. Buses are a good way to see the town, but don't take one if you're in a hurry.

All journeys cost £2.40, and there are no transfers. If you plan to make a number of journeys in one day, consider buying a Travelcard, good for both Tube and bus travel. Also consider getting a prepaid Oyster card, as single journeys are just over a pound using a prepaid card. Travelcards are also available in one-, three-, or seven-day combinations. Visitor Oyster cards cost £5 and can be topped up. They are available from ticket desks at Gatwick and Stansted airports or at any Tube station. Traveling without a valid ticket makes you liable for a fine (£20).

Night buses, denoted by an "N" before their route numbers, run from midnight to 5 am on a more restricted route than day buses. However, some night bus routes should be approached with caution and the top deck avoided. All night buses run by request stop, so flag them down if you're waiting or push the button if you want to alight.

Buses, or "coaches," as privately operated bus services are known here, operate mainly from London's Victoria Coach Station to more than 1,200 major towns and cities. *For information, see Getting Here and Around in Travel Smart England.*

Contact Transport for London ☎ *0843/222–1234* ⊕ *www.tfl.gov.uk.*

CAR TRAVEL

The major approach roads to London are six-lane motorways. Motorways (from Heathrow, M4; from Gatwick, M23 to M25, then M3; Stansted, M11) are usually the faster option for getting in and out of town, although rush-hour traffic is horrendous. Stay tuned to local radio stations for updates.

The simple advice about driving in London is: don't. The city never had a central street plan, and the result is a chaotic winding mass, made no easier by the one-way street systems. If you must drive, remember to drive on the left and stick to the speed limit (30 mph on most city streets, 20 mph near schools and in some residential areas).

Designed to reduce traffic through central London, a congestion charge has been instituted. Vehicles (with some exemptions) entering central London on weekdays from 7 am to 6 pm (excluding public holidays) have to pay a £10 daily fee. One day's payment is good for all access into the charging zone on that day. Traffic signs designate the entrance to congestion areas, and cameras read car license plates and send the information to a database. Drivers who don't pay the congestion charge by midnight of the next charging day following the day of driving are penalized £120, which is reduced to £60 if paid within 14 days.

TAXI TRAVEL

Taxis are expensive, but if you're with several people they can be practical. Hotels and main tourist areas have taxi ranks; you can also hail taxis on the street. If the yellow "For Hire" sign is lighted on top, the taxi is available. Drivers often cruise at night with their signs unlighted, so if you see an unlighted cab, keep your hand up. Fares start at £2.40 and charge by the minute—a journey of a mile (which might take between 5 and 12 minutes) will cost anything from £4.90 to £8.60 (the fare goes up between 10 pm and 6 am—a system designed to persuade more taxi drivers to work at night). A surcharge of £2 is applied to a telephone booking. You can, but do not have to, tip taxi drivers 10% of the tab. Usually passengers round up to the nearest pound.

2

TRAIN TRAVEL

London has eight major train stations, each serving a different area of the country, all accessible by Underground or bus. Trains are operated by a number of private companies, but National Rail Enquiries acts as a central rail information number. *For further information on train travel, see Getting Here and Around in Travel Smart England.*

Contact **National Rail Enquiries** ☎ 0845/748–4950, 020/7278–5240 outside U.K. ⊕ www.nationalrail.co.uk.

UNDERGROUND (TUBE) TRAVEL

London's extensive Underground (Tube) system has color-coded routes, clear signs, and extensive connections. Trains run out into the suburbs, and all stations are marked with the London Underground circular symbol. (In Britain, the word "subway" means "pedestrian underpass.") Some lines have branches (Central, District, Northern, Metropolitan, and Piccadilly), so be sure to note which branch is needed for your destination. Electronic platform signs tell you the final stop and route of the next train and how many minutes until it arrives.

London is divided into six concentric zones (ask at Underground ticket booths for a map and booklet, which give details of the ticket options). For one-way fares paid in cash, a flat £4.50 price per journey now applies across all six zones, whether you're traveling one stop or 12 stops. If you're planning several trips in one day, it's much cheaper to buy a tourist Oyster card or even a Travelcard, which is good for unrestricted travel on the Tube, buses, and some Above-ground trains for the day. The off-peak Oyster-card fare for Zones 1–2, for example, is £2.10. A one-day Travelcard for Zones 1–2 costs £8.80 if purchased before 9:30 am, and £7.30 if bought after 9:30 am. The more zones included in your travel, the more the Travelcard will cost.

Trains begin running just after 5 am Monday to Saturday; the last services leave central London between midnight and 12:30 am. On Sunday trains start two hours later and finish about an hour earlier. The frequency of trains depends on the route and the time of day, but normally you should not have to wait more than 10 minutes in central areas.

DISCOUNTS AND DEALS

All national collections (such as the Natural History Museum, Science Museum, Victoria & Albert Museum) are free, a real bargain for museumgoers. *For other discounts, see Sightseeing Passes in Essentials in Travel Smart England.*

TOUR OPTIONS

BIKE TOURS

A 24-hour cycle-for-hire scheme, the Barclays Cycle Hire, introduced in 2010 to enable Londoners to pick up a bicycle at one of more than 570 docking stations and return it at another, has proved very popular. The first 30 minutes are free. After that, charges rise incrementally from £1 for one hour up to £50 for the entire 24 hours. There is also a £1 per-day access charge. Fees are payable online, by phone, or at docking stations, by credit or debit cards only—cash is not accepted. But whether you join the scheme or just rent a bike from a shop, remember that London is still a busy metropolis: the best way to see it on two wheels is probably to contact one of the excellent cycle tour companies.

Tour Operators **Barclays Cycle Hire** ☎ *0845/026–3630 within U.K., 208/216–6666 from outside U.K.* ⊕ *www.tfl.gov.uk/roadusers.* **Cycle Tours of London** ☎ *0778/899-4430* ⊕ *www.biketoursoflondon.com.* **Fat Tire Bike Tours** ☎ *0788/233-8779* ⊕ *www.fattirebiketours.com.* **London Bicycle Tour Company** ☎ *020/3318-3088* ⊕ *www.londonbicycle.com.*

BOAT TOURS

Year-round, but more frequently from April to October, boats cruise the Thames, offering a different view of the London skyline. Most leave from Westminster Pier, Charing Cross Pier, and Tower Pier. Downstream routes go to the Tower of London, Greenwich, and the Thames Barrier via Canary Wharf. Upstream destinations include Kew, Richmond, and Hampton Court (mainly in summer). Most of the launches seat between 100 and 250 passengers, have a public-address system, and provide a running commentary on passing points of interest. Some include musical entertainment. Depending upon the destination, river trips may last from one to four hours.

The tranquil side of London can be found on narrow boats that cruise the city's two canals, the Grand Union and Regent's Canal; most vessels operate on the latter, which runs between Little Venice in the west (nearest Tube: Warwick Avenue on the Bakerloo Line) and Camden Lock (about 200 yards north of Camden Town Tube station). Fares start at £9 for 1½-hour round-trip cruises.

Contacts **Bateaux London** ☎ *020/7695-1800* ⊕ *www.bateauxlondon.com.* **Canal Cruises** ☎ *020/8440-8962* ⊕ *www.londoncanalcruises.com.* **Jason's Trip** ☎ *020/7286-3428* ⊕ *www.jasons.co.uk.* **London Duck Tours** ☎ *020/7928-3132* ⊕ *www.londonducktours.co.uk.* **Thames Cruises** ☎ *020/7928-9009* ⊕ *www.thamescruises.com.* **Thames River Boats** ☎ *020/7930-2062* ⊕ *www.wpsa.co.uk.* **Thames River Services** ☎ *020/7930-4097* ⊕ *www.thamesriverservices.co.uk.*

BUS TOURS

Guided sightseeing tours from the top of double-decker buses, which are open-top in summer, are a good introduction to the city, as they cover all the main central sights. A number of companies run daily bus tours that depart (usually between 8:30 and 9 am) from central points. In hop-on, hop-off fashion, you may board or alight at any of the numerous stops to view the sights, and reboard on the next bus. Most companies offer this hop-on, hop-off feature, but others, such as Best Value, remain guided tours in traditional coach buses. Tickets can be bought from the driver and are good all day. Prices vary according to the type of tour, although £25 is the benchmark.

For that more personal touch, try out a tour in a guided taxi. Other guided bus tours, like those offered by Golden, are not open-top or hop-on, hop-off, but enclosed (and more expensive) coach bus versions.

Contacts **Best Value Tours** ☎ *0870/803–1316* ⊕ *www.bestvaluetours.co.uk.* **Big Bus Tours** ☎ *020/7233-9533* ⊕ *www.bigbustours.com.* **Black Taxi Tour**

2

of London ☎ *020/7935-9363* ⊕ *www.blacktaxitours.co.uk.* **Golden Tours** ☎ *0844/880-5050 in U.K., 800/509-2507 in U.S.* ⊕ *www.goldentours.co.uk.* **Original London Sightseeing Tour** ☎ *020/8877-1722* ⊕ *www.theoriginaltour. com.* **Premium Tours** ☎ *020/7713-1311, 888/990-1209 from the US* ⊕ *www.premiumtours.co.uk.*

WALKING TOURS

One of the best ways to get to know London is on foot, and there are many guided and themed walking tours from which to choose. Richard Jones's London Walking Tours includes the Jack the Ripper Walk, following in the footsteps of the titular killer, as does the Blood and Tears Walk. Other tours include Secret London, the West End with Dickens, and Hampstead—A Country Village. Context London's expert docents lead small groups on walks with art, architecture, and similar themes. The London Walks Company hosts more than 100 walks every week.

Contacts Blood and Tears Walk ☎ *07905/746-733* ⊕ *www.shockinglondon. com.* **Blue Badge** ☎ *020/7403-1115* ⊕ *www.blue-badge-guides.com.* **Context London** ☎ *020/3514-1780, 800/691-6036 in U.S.* ⊕ *www.contexttravel.com/ london.* **London Walks** ☎ *020/7624-3978* ⊕ *www.walks.com.* **Richard Jones's London Walking Tours** ☎ *020/8530-8443* ⊕ *www.walksoflondon.co.uk.* **Shakespeare City Walk** ☎ *07905/746-733* ⊕ *www.shakespeareguide.com.*

VISITOR INFORMATION

You can get good information at the Travel Information Centres at Victoria Station and St. Pancras International train station. These are helpful if you're looking for brochures for London sights, or if something's gone wrong with your hotel reservation—as they have a useful reservations service. There are also Travel Information Centres at Euston and Liverpool Street train stations, Heathrow Airport, and Piccadilly Circus. There are also London Tourist Information Centres in Greenwich and some other Outer London locations.

Information ⊕ *www.visitlondon.com.*

EXPLORING LONDON

Westminster and the City contain many of the grand buildings that have played a central role in British history: the Tower of London and St. Paul's Cathedral, Westminster Abbey and the Houses of Parliament, Buckingham Palace, and the older royal palace of St. James's.

Within a few minutes' walk of Buckingham Palace lie St. James's and Mayfair, neighboring quarters of elegant town houses built for the nobility during the 17th and early 18th centuries and now notable for shopping opportunities. Westminster Abbey's original vegetable patch (or convent garden), which became the site of London's first square, Covent Garden, is now a popular stop.

Hyde Park and Kensington Gardens, preserved by past kings and queens for their own hunting and relaxation, create a swath of parkland across the city center. A walk across Hyde Park brings you to the museum district of South Kensington, with the Natural History Museum, the

Science Museum, and the Victoria & Albert Museum. The South Bank has many cultural highlights: the theaters of the South Bank Centre, the Tate Modern, and the reconstruction of Shakespeare's Globe theater. The London Eye observation wheel here gives stunning city views, or you can walk across the Millennium or Hungerford Bridge. Farther downstream is the gorgeous 17th- and 18th-century symmetry of Greenwich, and its maritime attractions.

WESTMINSTER, ST. JAMES'S, AND ROYAL LONDON

If you have time to visit only one part of London, this is it. Westminster, St. James's, and Royal London might be called "London for Beginners." If you went no farther than these few acres, you would have seen many of the famous sights, from the Houses of Parliament, Big Ben, Westminster Abbey, and Buckingham Palace, to two of the world's greatest art collections, in the National and Tate Britain galleries. You can truly call this area Royal London, since it is bounded by the triangle of streets that make up the route that the Queen usually takes when journeying from Buckingham Palace to Westminster Abbey or to the Houses of Parliament on state occasions. The three points on this royal triangle are Trafalgar Square, Westminster, and Buckingham Palace. Naturally, in an area that regularly sees the pomp and pageantry of royal occasions, the streets are wide and the vistas long. This is concentrated sightseeing, so pace yourself. For a large part of the year much of Royal London is floodlighted at night, adding to the theatricality of the experience.

GETTING HERE Trafalgar Square—easy to access and smack-dab in the center of the action—is a good place to start. Take the Tube to Embankment (District and Circle lines) and walk north until you cross the Strand, or alight at Charing Cross (Bakerloo, Jubilee, and Northern lines), where the Northumberland Avenue exit deposits you on the southeast corner of the Square.

PLANNING A lifetime of exploring may still be insufficient to cover this histori-
YOUR TIME cally rich part of London. But don't fret: two to three days can take in the highlights. For royal pageantry begin with Buckingham Palace, Westminster Abbey, and the Guards Museum. For more constitutional sightseeing, there's the Houses of Parliament. For art, the National Gallery and the Tate Britain head anyone's list.

TOP ATTRACTIONS

Fodor's Choice **Buckingham Palace.** It's rare to get a chance to see how the other half—
★ well, other minute fraction—lives and works. But when the Queen heads off to Scotland on her annual summer holiday (you can tell because the Union Jack flies above the palace instead of the Royal Standard), the palace's 19 State Rooms open up to visitors, although the north wing's private apartments remain behind closed doors. With fabulous gilt moldings and walls adorned with masterpieces by Rembrandt, Rubens, and other old masters, the State Rooms are the grandest of the palace's 775 rooms.

A classic photo op: don't miss the cavalry from the Queen's Life Guard at Buckingham Palace.

The **Grand Hall,** followed by the **Grand Staircase** and **Guard Room,** give a taste of the marble, gold leaf galore, and massive, twinkling chandeliers that embellish the palace. Don't miss the theatrical **Throne Room,** with the original 1953 coronation throne, or the sword in **the Ballroom,** used by the Queen to bestow knighthoods and other honors. Royal portraits line the **State Dining Room,** and the **Blue Drawing Room** is splendor in overdrive. The bow-shape **Music Room** features lapis lazuli columns between arched floor-to-ceiling windows, and the alabaster-and-gold plasterwork of the **White Drawing Room** is a dramatic crescendo. Spend some time ambling around the splendid gardens, a gorgeous epilogue to the visit.

The **Changing the Guard,** also known as **Guard Mounting,** remains one of London's best free shows and culminates in front of the palace. Marching to live bands, the old guard proceeds up the Mall from St. James's Palace to Buckingham Palace. Shortly afterward, the new guard approaches from Wellington Barracks. Then within the forecourt, the captains of the old and new guards symbolically transfer the keys to the palace. Get there by 10:30 to grab a spot in the best viewing section for the Changing the Guard (www.changing-the-guard. com), daily at 11:30 from May until the end of July (varies according to troop deployment requirements) and on alternate days for the rest of the year, weather permitting. ✉ *Buckingham Palace Rd., St. James's* ☎ *020/7766–7300* ⊕ *www.royalcollection.org.uk/visit* ✒ *£19 (includes audio tour)* ☉ *Open Aug. daily 9:30–7 (last admission 4:45); Sept. daily 9:30–6:30 (last admission 3:45). Times subject to change; check website* Ⓜ *Victoria, St. James's Park, Green Park.*

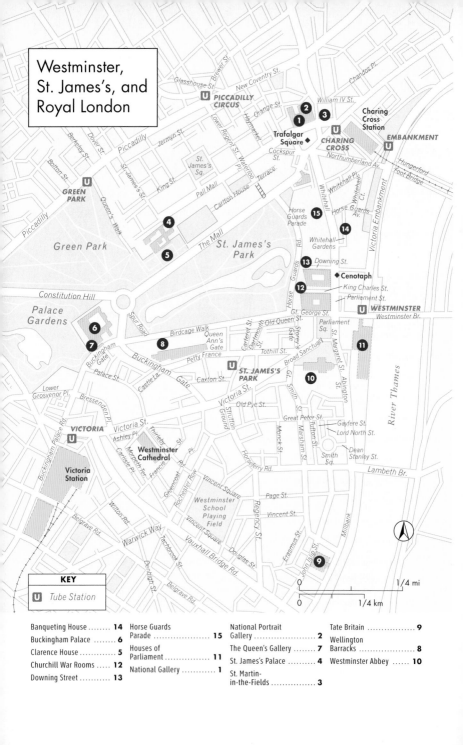

Westminster, St. James's, and Royal London

PICCADILLY CIRCUS

New Coventry St.
Glasshouse St.   Brewer St.
William IV St.
Chandos Pl.
Orange St.

Charing Cross Station

EMBANKMENT

Trafalgar Square ◆
Cockspur St.

CHARING CROSS

Dover St.
Berkeley St.
Piccadilly
Jermyn St.
St. James's Sq.
Haymarket
Lower Regent St.
Waterloo Pl.
Northumberland Av.
Hungerford Foot Bridge

Bolton St.

GREEN PARK

St. James's St.
King St.
Pall Mall
Carlton House Terrace

Queen's Walk

Whitehall
Horse Guards Av.
Whitehall Pl.
Whitehall Ct.

Green Park

The Mall
St. James's Park

Horse Guards Parade ⑮

⑭

Piccadilly

④
⑤

Victoria Embankment

Constitution Hill

Horse Guards Rd.

Downing St.
◆ Cenotaph
⑬
King Charles St.
Parliament St.

⑫

River Thames

Palace Gardens

Spur Road
Birdcage Walk
Queen Ann's Gate
Old Queen St.
Gt. George St.
Parliament Sq.
Storey's Gate
St. Margaret St.

WESTMINSTER
Westminster Br.

⑥
⑦
⑧

Buckingham Gate
Buckingham Gate
Petty France
Carteret St.
Dartmouth St.
Tothill St.
Broad Sanctuary
⑪

Palace St.
Castle La.
Caxton St.
ST. JAMES'S PARK

Lower Grosvenor Pl.
Bressenden Pl.
Victoria St.
Old Pye St.
Strutton Ground
Smith St.
⑩
Abingdon St.

VICTORIA
Ashley Pl.
Thirleby Pl.
Meredith Ter.
Carlisle Pl.
Frances St.
Great Peter St.
Monck St.
Marsham St.
Tufton St.
Gayfere St.
Lord North St.
Dean Stanley St.
Lambeth Br.

Westminster Cathedral

Smith Sq.

Buckingham Palace Rd.

Victoria Station

Greencoat Pl.
Rochester Row
Vincent Square
Page St.
Erasmus St.
Millbank

Belgrave Rd.
Wilton Rd.
Warwick Way
Tachbrook St.
Vauxhall Bridge Rd.
Denbigh St.
Westminster School Playing Field
Vincent Square
Douglas St.
Regency St.
Vincent St.
John Islip St.
⑨

KEY

U Tube Station

0   1/4 mi
0   1/4 km

Banqueting House **14**	Horse Guards Parade **15**
Buckingham Palace **6**	Houses of Parliament **11**
Clarence House **5**	National Gallery **1**
Churchill War Rooms **12**	National Portrait Gallery **2**
Downing Street **13**	The Queen's Gallery **7**
	St. James's Palace **4**
	St. Martin-in-the-Fields **3**
Tate Britain **9**	
Wellington Barracks **8**	
Westminster Abbey **10**	

FAMILY **Churchill War Rooms.** It was from this small warren of underground rooms—beneath the vast government buildings of the Treasury—that Winston Churchill and his team directed troops in World War II. Designed to be bombproof, the whole complex has been preserved almost exactly as it was when the last light was turned off at the end of the war. Every clock shows almost 5 pm, and the furniture, fittings, and paraphernalia of a busy, round-the-clock war office are in situ, down to the colored map pins.

A great addition to the War Rooms is the Churchill Museum, a tribute to the stirring politician and defiant wartime icon himself. Different zones explore his life and achievements—and failures, too—through objects and documents, many of which, such as his personal papers, had never previously been made public. ⊠ *Clive Steps, King Charles St., Westminster* ☎ *020/7930–6961* ⊕ *www.iwm.org.uk* ⊠ *£17 (includes audio guide)* ⊗ *Daily 9:30–6; last admission 5; disabled access* Ⓜ *Westminster.*

FAMILY **Horse Guards Parade.** Following its brief transformation into the beach volleyball arena for the 2012 Olympics, the Horse Guards Parade is most known for the annual Trooping the Colour ceremony, in which the Queen takes the salute, her official birthday tribute, on the second Saturday in June. (Like Paddington Bear, the Queen has two birthdays; her real one is on April 21.) In what was once the tiltyard for jousting tournaments, there is still pageantry galore, with marching bands and throngs of onlookers, and the ceremony is televised. Throughout the rest of the year the changing of two mounted sentries known as the **Queen's Life Guard** at the Whitehall facade of Horse Guards provides what may be London's most popular photo opportunity. The ceremony last about half an hour. ⊠ *Whitehall* ☎ *020/7930–4832* ⊗ *Changing of the Queen's Life Guard at 11 am Mon.–Sat. and 10 am Sun.; inspection of the Queen's Life Guard daily at 4 pm* Ⓜ *Westminster.*

Houses of Parliament. If you want to understand some of the centuries-old traditions and arcane idiosyncrasies that make up constitutionless British parliamentary democracy, the Palace of Westminster, as the complex is still properly called, is the place to come. The architecture in this 1,100-room labyrinth impresses, but the real excitement lies in stalking the corridors of power. A palace was first established on this site by Edward the Confessor in the 11th century. William II started building a new palace in 1087, and this gradually became the seat of English administrative power. However, fire destroyed most of the palace in 1834, and the current complex dates largely from the middle of the 19th century.

Visitors aren't allowed to snoop too much, but the **Visitors' Galleries** of the House of Commons do afford a view of democracy in process when the banks of green-leather benches are filled by opposing MPs (members of Parliament). When they speak, it's not directly to each other but through the Speaker, who also decides who will get time on the floor. **Westminster Hall,** with its remarkable hammer-beam roof, was the work of William the Conqueror's son William Rufus. It's one of the largest remaining Norman halls in Europe, and its dramatic interior was the scene of the trial of Charles I. After the 1834 fire, the Clock Tower—renamed the **Elizabeth Tower** in 2012, in honor of the

Queen's Diamond Jubilee—was completed in 1858, and contains the 13-ton bell known as **Big Ben.** At the southwest end of the main Parliament building is the 323-foot-high Victoria Tower. The only guided tour nonresidents can go on is the paid-for (£15) tour offered on Saturday, or Monday to Saturday during August and September (book through *www.ticketmaster.co.uk*).

The most romantic view of the Houses is from the opposite (south) bank, across Lambeth Bridge. It is especially dramatic at night when floodlighted green and gold. ⊠ *St. Stephen's Entrance, St. Margaret St., Westminster* ☎ *020/7219–4272 Information, 0844/847–1672 Public Tours* ⊕ *www.parliament.uk/visiting* ☑ *Free; tours £15 (must book ahead)* ⊙ *Tours: Aug., Mon., Tues., Fri., and Sat. 9:15–4:30, Wed. and Thurs. 1:15–4:30; Sept., Mon., Fri., and Sat. 9:15–4:30, Tues., Wed., and Thurs. 1:15–4:30. Call to confirm hrs for Visitors Galleries.* Ⓜ *Westminster.*

FAMILY
Fodor's Choice
★

National Gallery. Standing proudly on the north side of Trafalgar Square, this is truly one of the world's supreme art collections, with more than 2,300 masterpieces on show. Picasso, van Gogh, Michelangelo, Leonardo, Monet, Turner, and more—all for free. Watch out for special temporary exhibitions too.

This brief selection is your jumping-off point, but there are hundreds of other paintings to see, enough to fill a full day. In chronological order: (1) **Van Eyck** (circa 1395–1441), *The Arnolfini Portrait*—a solemn couple holds hands, the fish-eye mirror behind them mysteriously illuminating what can't be seen from the front view. (2) **Holbein** (1497–1543), *The Ambassadors*—two wealthy visitors from France stand surrounded by what were considered luxury goods at the time. Note the elongated skull at the bottom of the painting, which takes shape when viewed from an angle. (3) **Leonardo da Vinci** (1452–1519), *The Virgin and Child*—this exquisite black-chalk "Burlington Cartoon" depicts the master's most haunting Mary. (4) **Velazquez** (1599–1660), *Christ in the House of Martha and Mary*—in this enigmatic masterpiece the Spaniard plays with perspective and the role of the viewer. (5) **Turner** (1775–1851), *Rain, Steam and Speed: The Great Western Railway*, the whirl of rain, mist, steam, and locomotion is nothing short of astonishing (spot the hare). (6) **Caravaggio** (1573–1610), *The Supper at Emmaus*—a freshly resurrected Christ blesses bread in an astonishingly domestic vision from the master of chiaroscuro. (7) **Van Gogh** (1853–1890), *Sunflowers*—painted during his sojourn with Gauguin in Arles, this is quintessential Van Gogh. (8) **Seurat** (1859–91), *Bathers at Asnières*—this summer day's idyll is one of the pointillist extraordinaire's best-known works. One-hour free, guided tours start at the Sainsbury Wing daily at 11:30 and 2:30 (also Friday at 7pm). ⊠ *Trafalgar Sq., Westminster* ☎ *020/7747–2885* ⊕ *www.nationalgallery.org.uk* ☑ *Free; charge for special exhibitions; audio guide £3.50* ⊙ *Sun.–Thurs. 10–6, Fri. 10–9* Ⓜ *Charing Cross, Embankment, Leicester Sq.*

FAMILY

Fodor's Choice

★

National Portrait Gallery. Tucked around the corner from the National Gallery, the National Portrait Gallery was founded in 1856 with a single aim: to gather together portraits of famous (and infamous) British men and women. More than 150 years and 160,000 portraits later, it is an essential stop for all history and literature buffs. The spacious galleries make it a pleasant place to visit, and you can choose to take in a little or a lot. Need to rest those legs? Then use the Portrait Explorer in the Digital Space on the ground-floor mezzanine for interactive, computer-aided exploration of the gallery's extensive collection. If you visit with little ones, ask at the desk about the excellent Family Trails, which make exploring the galleries with children much more fun. On the top floor, the Portrait Restaurant (check website for details) will delight skyline aficionados. ▇ TIP➔ **The restaurant vista will reveal stately London at its finest: a panoramic view of Nelson's Column and the backdrop along Whitehall to the Houses of Parliament.**

Galleries are arranged clearly and chronologically, from Tudor times to contemporary Britain. In the Tudor Gallery—a modern update on a Tudor long hall—is a Holbein cartoon of Henry VIII. Joshua Reynolds's self-portrait hangs in the refurbished 17th-century rooms. Portraits of notables, including Shakespeare, the Brontë sisters, Jane Austen, and the Queen are always on display. ⊠ *St. Martin's Pl., Westminster* ☎ *020/7312–2463, 020/730–0555 recorded switchboard information* ⊕ *www.npg.org.uk* ✉ *Free; charge for special exhibitions; audiovisual guide £3* ☉ *Mon.–Wed. and weekends 10–6, Thurs. and Fri. 10–9; last admission 1 hr before closing* Ⓜ *Charing Cross, Leicester Sq.*

The Queen's Gallery. Twenty years after it was destroyed in an air raid in 1940, this former chapel at the south side of Buckingham Palace was redeveloped, at the say-so of the Queen, into a gallery fit to house the Royal Collection—and what a collection it is! Technically speaking, the sovereign doesn't "own" these rare and exquisite works of art, she merely holds them in trust for the nation. Only a selection from the Royal Collection is on view at any one time, presented in themed exhibitions. Let the excellent audio guide take you through the elegant galleries filled with some of the world's greatest art works. ▇ TIP➔ **The E-gallery provides an interactive electronic version of the collection, allowing the user to open lockets, remove a sword from its scabbard, or take apart the tulip vases. It's probably the closest you could get to eyeing practically every diamond in the sovereign's glittering diadem.** ⊠ *Buckingham Palace, Buckingham Palace Rd., St. James's* ☎ *020/7766–7301* ⊕ *www.royalcollection.org.uk* ✉ *£9.50 with free audio guide; joint ticket with Royal Mews £15.75* ☉ *Daily 10–5:30; last admission 4:30* Ⓜ *Victoria, St. James's Park, Green Park.*

FAMILY

Fodor's Choice

★

St. James's Park. In a city of royal parks, this one—bordered by three palaces (the Palace of Westminster, the Tudor **St. James's Palace,** and Buckingham Palace)—is the most regal of them all. It's not only London's oldest park, but also its smallest and most ornate. Once marshy meadows, the land was acquired by Henry VIII in 1532 as royal deer-hunting grounds (with dueling and sword fights strictly forbidden). In the early 19th century, John Nash redesigned the landscape in a more naturalistic, romantic style, and if you gaze down the lake toward Buckingham

Where to See the Royals

The Queen and the Royal Family attend hundreds of functions a year, and if you want to know what they are doing on any given date, turn to the Court Circular, printed in the major London dailies, or check out the Royal Family website, ⊕ *www.royal.gov. uk*, for the latest events on the Royal Diary. Trooping the Colour is usually held on the second Saturday in June, to celebrate the Queen's official birthday. This spectacular parade begins when she leaves Buckingham Palace in her carriage and rides down the Mall to arrive at Horse Guards Parade at 11 exactly. To watch, just line up along the Mall with your binoculars!

Another time you can catch the Queen in all her regalia is when she and the Duke of Edinburgh ride in

state to open the Houses of Parliament. The famous black and gilt-trimmed Irish State Coach travels from Buckingham Palace—on a clear day, it's to be hoped, for this ceremony takes place in late October or early November. The Gold State Coach, an icon of fairy-tale glamour, is used for coronations and jubilees only.

But perhaps the most relaxed, least formal time to see the Queen is during Royal Ascot, held at the racetrack near Windsor Castle—a short train ride out of London—usually during the third week of June (Tuesday–Friday). After several races, the Queen invariably walks down to the paddock on a special path, greeting race goers as she proceeds. If you meet her, remember to address her as "Your Majesty."

Palace, you could believe yourself to be on a country estate. From April to September the deck chairs (charge levied) come out, crammed with office workers at midday, lunching while being serenaded by music from the bandstands. The popular Inn the Park restaurant is a wood-and-glass pavilion with a turf roof that blends in beautifully with the surrounding landscape; it's an excellent stopping place for a meal or a snack on a nice day. ⊠ *The Mall or Horse Guards approach or Birdcage Walk, St. James's* ⊕ *www.royalparks.gov.uk* ☉ *Daily 5 am–midnight* Ⓜ *St. James's Park, Westminster.*

FAMILY

Fodor's Choice ★

Tate Britain. The stately neoclassical institution may not be as ambitious as its sibling Tate Modern on the South Bank, but Tate Britain's bright galleries lure only a fraction of the Modern's crowds and are a great place to explore British art from 1500 to the present. First opened in 1897, funded by the sugar magnate Sir Henry Tate, the museum includes the Linbury Galleries on the lower floors, which stage temporary exhibitions, whereas the upper floors show the permanent collection. From early 2014, much more of the Tate's collection will be on permanent display as part of a major redevelopment of the galleries. So you'll have no excuse not to pop in and view classic works by John Constable, Thomas Gainsborough, David Wilkie, Francis Bacon, Duncan Grant, Barbara Hepworth, and Ben Nicholson and an outstanding display from J.M.W. Turner in the Clore Gallery, including many later vaporous and light-infused works such as *Sunrise with Sea Monsters*. Sumptuous Pre-Raphaelite pieces are a major drawcard while the Contemporary British Art galleries bring you face to face with Damien

Hirst's *Away from the Flock* and other recent conceptions. The Tate Britain also hosts the annual Turner Prize exhibition, with its accompanying furor over the state of contemporary art, from about October to January each year. Details of activities for families are on the website.

■ TIP➔ **Craving more art? Head down the river on the Tate to Tate (£5.50 one way) to the Tate Modern, running between the two museums every 40 minutes. A River Roamer ticket (£13.60) permits a day's travel, with stops including the London Eye and the Tower of London.** ⊠ *Millbank, Westminster* ☎ *020/7887–8888* ⊕ *www.tate.org.uk/britain* ▣ *Free, special exhibitions £9–£15* ⊙ *Sat.–Thurs. 10–6 (last entry at 5:15), Fri. 10–10 (last entry at 9:15)* Ⓜ *Pimlico.*

Fodor'sChoice
★

Westminster Abbey. A monument to the nation's rich—and often bloody— history, the abbey is one of London's most iconic sites. The atmospheric gloom of the lofty medieval interior is home to more than 600 statues, tombs, and commemorative tablets. About 3,300 people, from kings to composers to wordsmiths, are buried in the abbey. It has hosted 38 coronations—beginning in 1066 with William the Conqueror—and no fewer than 16 royal weddings, the latest being that of Prince William and Kate Middleton in 2011.

But be warned: there's only one way around the abbey, and as a million visitors flock through its doors each year, you'll need to be alert to catch the highlights. Enter by the north door then turn around and look up to see the **painted-glass rose window**, the largest of its kind. As you walk east toward the apse you'll see the **Coronation Chair**, at the foot of the Henry VII Chapel, which has been briefly graced by nearly every regal posterior since Edward I ordered it in 1301. Elizabeth I is buried above arch enemy Mary Tudor in the tomb just to the north, while Mary Queen of Scots rests in the tomb to the south. In front of the **High Altar**, which was used for the funerals of Princess Diana and the Queen Mother, is a black-and-white marble pavement laid in 1268. The intricate Italian Cosmati work contains three Latin inscriptions, one of which states that the world will last for 19,683 years.

Continue through the South Ambulatory to the **Chapel of St. Edward the Confessor**, which contains the shrine to the pre-Norman king. Because of its great age, you must join the vergers' tours to be admitted to the chapel (details available at the admission desk; there is a £3 charge), or attend Holy Communion within the shrine on Tuesdays at 8 am. To the left, you'll find **Poets' Corner**. Geoffrey Chaucer was the first poet to be buried here in 1400, and other statues and memorials include those to William Shakespeare, D.H. Lawrence, T.S. Eliot, and Oscar Wilde as well as non-poets, Laurence Olivier and George Frederick Handel among them; look out for the 700-year old frescoes.

The medieval Chapter House is adorned with 14th-century frescoes and a magnificent 13th-century tiled floor, one of the finest in the country. The King's Council met here between 1257 and 1547. Near the entrance is Britain's oldest door, dating from the 1050s. Continue back to the nave of the abbey. In the choir screen, north of the entrance to the choir, is a marble **monument to Sir Isaac Newton**. If you walk toward the West Entrance, you'll see **a plaque to Franklin D. Roosevelt**—one

Historic Westminster Abbey is a beautiful setting for any choral performance.

of the Abbey's very few tributes to a foreigner. The poppy-wreathed **Grave of the Unknown Warrior** commemorates soldiers who lost their lives in both world wars; nearby is a portrait of Richard II.

Arrive early if possible, but be prepared to wait in line to tour the abbey. Photography is not permitted. ⊠ *Broad Sanctuary, Westminster* ☎ *020/7222–5152* ⊕ *www.westminster-abbey.org* ✎ *Abbey and museum £16; audio tour free* ☉ *Abbey, Mon., Tues., Thurs., Fri. 9:30–4:30; Wed. 9:30–7; Sat. 9:30–2.30; last admission is one hour before closing time; Sun. open for worship only. Museum, Mon.– Sat. 10:30–4. Cloisters daily 8–6. College Garden, Apr.–Sept., Tues.– Thurs. 10–6; Oct.–Mar., Tues.–Thurs. 10–4. Chapter House, daily 10:30–4. Services may cause changes to hrs, so call ahead* Ⓜ *Westminster, St James's Park.*

WORTH NOTING

Banqueting House. James I commissioned Inigo Jones, one of England's great architects, to undertake a grand building on the site of the original Tudor Palace of Whitehall, which was (according to one foreign visitor) "ill-built, and nothing but a heap of houses." Jones' Banqueting House, finished in 1622 and the first building in England to be completed in the neoclassical style, bears all the hallmarks of the Palladian sophistication and purity which so influenced Jones during his sojourn in Italy. ⊠ *Whitehall, Westminster* ☎ *020/3166–6154, 020/3166–6155, 020/3166–6153 concert information* ⊕ *www.hrp.org.uk* ✎ *£5, includes audio guide* ☉ *Mon.–Sat. 10–5, last admission 4:15. Closed Christmas wk. Liable to close at short notice for events, so calling first is advisable* Ⓜ *Charing Cross, Embankment, Westminster.*

Clarence House. The London home of Queen Elizabeth the Queen Mother for nearly 50 years, Clarence House is now the residence of the Prince of Wales, Camilla, Duchess of Cornwall, and Prince Harry. The Regency mansion was built by John Nash for the Duke of Clarence (later to become William IV) who considered next-door St. James's Palace to be too cramped for his liking, although postwar renovation work means that little remains of Nash's original. Since then it has remained a royal home for princesses, dukes, and duchesses, including the present monarch, Queen Elizabeth, as a newlywed before her coronation. Clarence House is usually open only for the month of August and tickets must be booked in advance. ⊠ *St. James's Palace, The Mall, St. James's* ☏ *020/7766–7303* ⊕ *www.royalcollection.org.uk* 💷 *£9* ⊘ *Aug. 1–Sept. 1: Mon.–Fri. 10–4 (last admission 3); Sat.–Sun. 10–5:30 (last admission 4:30)* Ⓜ *Green Park*.

Downing Street. Looking like an unassuming alley but for the iron gates at both its Whitehall and Horse Guards Road approaches, this is the location of the famous **No. 10,** London's modest equivalent of the White House. The Georgian entrance is deceptive, though, since the old house now leads to a large mansion behind it, overlooking the Horse Guards Parade. ⊠ *Whitehall* Ⓜ *Westminster*.

St. James's Palace. Commissioned by Henry VIII, this Tudor brick palace was the residence of kings and queens for more than 300 years; indeed, it remains the official residence of the Sovereign even though since Queen Victoria's day all monarchs have lived up the road in the more expansive Buckingham Palace. Today it contains various royal apartments and offices, including the working office of Charles, Prince of Wales. It's not open to the public. ⊠ *Friary Ct., St. James's* ⊕ *www. royal.gov.uk* Ⓜ *Green Park*.

FAMILY **St. Martin-in-the-Fields.** One of London's best-loved and most welcoming of churches is more than just a place of worship. The church is also a haven for music lovers; the internationally known Academy of St. Martin-in-the-Fields was founded here, and a popular program of concerts continues today. (Although the interior is a wonderful setting for a recital, beware the hard wooden benches!) The crypt is a hive of activity, with a popular café and shop, plus the **London Brass-Rubbing Centre,** where you can make your own life-size souvenir knight, lady, or monarch from replica tomb brasses, with metallic waxes, paper, and instructions from about £5. Also watch out for a new alfresco café set to open in summer 2013. ⊠ *Trafalgar Sq., Westminster* ☏ *020/7766–1100, 020/7839–8362 brass rubbings, 020/7766–1122 evening-concert credit-card bookings* ⊕ *www.smitf.org* 💷 *Free; concerts £7–£30* ⊘ *Open all day for worship; sightseeing: Mon., Tue., and Fri. 8:30–1 and 2–6; Wed. 8:30–1:15 and 2–5; Thurs. 8:30–1.15 and 2–6; Sat. 9:30–6; Sun. 9:30–5* Ⓜ *Charing Cross, Leicester Sq.*

FAMILY **Wellington Barracks.** These are the headquarters of the Guards Division, the Queen's five regiments of elite foot guards (Grenadier, Coldstream, Scots, Irish, and Welsh) who protect the sovereign and, dressed in tunics of gold-purled scarlet and tall bearskin caps, patrol her palaces. If you want to learn more about the guards, visit the **Guards**

Museum, which has displays on all aspects of a guardsman's life in conflicts dating back to 1642; the entrance is next to the Guards Chapel. Next door is the **Guards Toy Soldier Centre,** a great place for a souvenir. ⊠ *Birdcage Walk, Westminster* ☎ *020/7414–3428* ⊕ *www. theguardsmuseum.com* ⌑ *£5* ⊙ *Daily 10–4; last admission 3:30* Ⓜ *St. James's Park, Green Park.*

SOHO AND COVENT GARDEN

Soho, which, along with Covent Garden is loosely known as "the West End," has long been known as the entertainment and arts quarter of London's center. Bordered to the north by Oxford Street, Regent Street to the west, and Chinatown and Leicester Square to the south, the narrow, winding streets of Soho are unabashedly devoted to pleasure. Wardour Street bisects the neighborhood, with lots of interesting boutiques and some of London's best-value restaurants to the west (especially around Foubert's Place and on Brewer and Lexington streets). Nightlife central lies to the east—including London's gay mecca, Old Compton Street—and beyond that is the city's densest collection of theaters, on Shaftesbury Avenue. London's compact Chinatown is wedged between Soho and Leicester Square. A bit of erudition surfaces to the east of the square on Charing Cross Road, famous for its secondhand bookshops, and on tiny Cecil Court, a pedestrianized passage lined with small antiquarian booksellers.

To the east of Charing Cross Road lies Covent Garden, the famous marketplace turned shopping mall. Although boutiques and haute fashion shops line the surrounding streets, many Londoners come to Covent Garden for its two outposts of culture: the Royal Opera House and the Donmar Warehouse, one of London's best and most innovative theaters. The Strand leads to the huge, stately piazza of Somerset House, a vibrant center of contemporary arts and home to the many masterpieces on view at the Courtauld Institute Gallery.

GETTING HERE   Almost all Tube lines cross the Covent Garden and Soho areas, so it's easy to hop off for a dinner or show in the hippest area of London. For Soho, take any train to Piccadilly Circus, or Leicester Square, Oxford Circus, or Tottenham Court Road. For Covent Garden, get off at the Covent Garden station on the Piccadilly line. It might be easier to exit the Tube at Leicester Square or Holborn and walk. Thirty buses connect to the Covent Garden area from all over London.

PLANNING   You can comfortably tour all the sights in Covent Garden in a day. Visit
YOUR TIME   the small but perfect Courtauld Institute Gallery on Monday before 2 pm when it's free. That leaves plenty of time to visit the marketplace, watch the street entertainment, and do a bit of shopping, with energy left over for a night on the town (or "on the tiles," as the British say) in Soho.

TOP ATTRACTIONS

Courtauld Institute Gallery. One of London's most beloved art collections, the Courtauld is to your right as you pass through the archway into the grounds of the beautifully restored, grand 18th-century neoclassical **Somerset House.** Founded in 1931 by the textile magnate Samuel Courtauld to house his remarkable private collection, this is one of

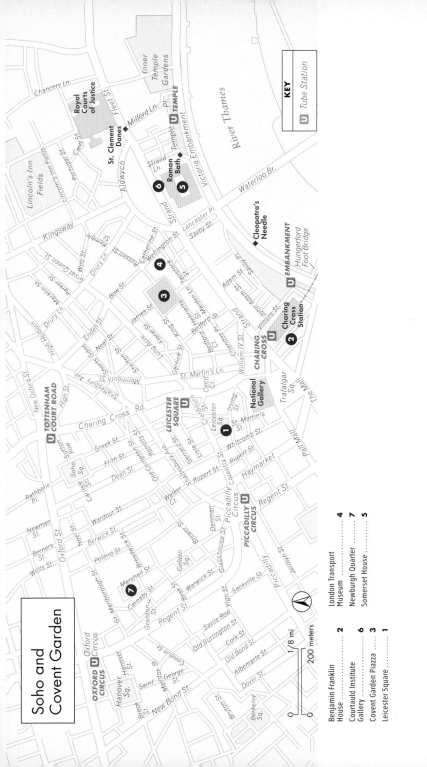

Soho and Covent Garden

KEY

U Tube Station

0 ___ 1/8 mi
0 ___ 200 meters

Benjamin Franklin
House **2**
Courtauld Institute
Gallery **6**
Covent Garden Piazza **3**
Leicester Square **1**
London Transport
Museum **4**
Newburgh Quarter **7**
Somerset House **5**

Pure street theater: you can't miss the buskers performing in the streets of Soho and Covent Garden.

the world's finest Impressionist and post-Impressionist galleries, with artists ranging from Bonnard to van Gogh. ⊠ *Somerset House, Strand, Covent Garden* ☎ *020/7848–2526* ⊕ *www.courtauld.ac.uk* ☎ *£6, free Mon. 10–2, except bank holidays* ☉ *Daily 10–6; last admission 5:30* Ⓜ *Temple, Covent Garden.*

Covent Garden Piazza. Once home to London's main flower market, where *My Fair Lady*'s Eliza Doolittle peddled her blooms, the square around which Covent Garden pivots is known as the Piazza. In the center, the fine old market building now houses stalls and shops selling higher-class clothing, plus several restaurants and cafés and knick-knack stores that are good for gifts. One particular gem is Benjamin Pollock's Toyshop at No. 44 in the market. Established in the 1880s, it sells delightful toy theaters. The superior **Apple Market** has good crafts stalls on most days, too. On the south side of the Piazza, the indoor **Jubilee Market,** with its stalls of clothing, army-surplus gear, and more crafts and knickknacks, has a distinct flea-market feel. In summer it may seem that everyone you see around the Piazza (and the crowds are legion) is a fellow tourist, but there's still plenty of office life in the area. Londoners who shop here tend to head for Neal Street and the area to the north of Covent Garden tube station rather than the market itself. In the Piazza, street performers—from global musicians to jugglers and mimes—play to the crowds, as they have done since the first English Punch and Judy Show, staged here in the 17th century. ⊠ *Covent Garden* ⊕ *www.coventgardenlondonuk.com* Ⓜ *Covent Garden.*

2

FAMILY **London Transport Museum.** Housed in the old flower market at the southeast corner of Covent Garden, this stimulating museum is filled with impressive vehicle, poster, and photograph collections. As you watch the crowds drive a Tube-train simulation and gawk at the horse-drawn trams (and the piles of detritus that remained behind) and steam locomotives, it's unclear who's enjoying it more, children or adults. ▥TIP→ **Tickets are valid for unlimited entry for 12 months.** ⊠ *Covent Garden Piazza, Covent Garden* ☎ *020/7565–7298* ⊕ *www.ltmuseum. co.uk* ⊠ *£13.50* ☉ *Sat.–Thurs. 10–6 (last admission 5:15), Fri. 11–6 (last admission 5:15)* Ⓜ *Covent Garden, Leicester Sq.*

Fodor'sChoice **Newburgh Quarter.** Want to see the hip style of today's London? Find
★ it just one block east of Carnaby Street—where the look of the '60s "Swinging London" was born—in an adorable warren of cobblestone streets now lined with specialty boutiques, edgy stores, and young indy upstarts. Here, not far from roaring Regent Street, the future of England's fashion is being incubated in stores like Lucy in Disguise and Sweaty Betty. A check of the ingredients reveals one part 60's London, one part Futuristic Fetishism, one part Dickensian charm, and one part British street swagger. The Nouveau Boho look best flourishes in shops like Peckham Rye, a tiny boutique crowded with rockers and fashion plates who adore its grunge-meets-*Brideshead Revisted* vibe. Or continue down Newburgh Street to Beyond the Valley, an art-school showcase whose designers have successfully paired graphic art-prints with kitschy outfits. ⊠ *Newburgh St., Foubert's Pl., Ganton St., and Carnaby St., Soho* ⊕ *carnaby.co.uk.*

FAMILY **Somerset House.** In recent years this huge complex—the work of Sir
Fodor'sChoice William Chambers (1726–96), and built during the reign of George III
★ to house offices of the Navy—has completed its transformation from dusty government offices to one of the capital's most buzzing centers of culture and the arts, hosting several interesting exhibitions at any one time. The **Courtauld Institute Gallery** (⇨ *see above*) occupies most of the north building, facing the busy Strand. Across the courtyard are the Embankment Galleries, with a vibrant calendar of design, fashion, architecture, and photography exhibitions. Creative activities for children are a regular feature (the website has details). The East Wing has another fine exhibition space and events are sometimes also held in the atmospherically gloomy cellars below the Fountain Court. ⊠ *Strand, Covent Garden* ☎ *020/7845–4600* ⊕ *www.somersethouse. org.uk* ⊠ *Embankment Galleries price varies, Courtauld Gallery £6, other areas free* ☉ *Daily 10–6; last admission 5:30* Ⓜ *Charing Cross, Waterloo, Blackfriars.*

WORTH NOTING

Benjamin Franklin House. This architecturally significant 1730 house is the only surviving residence of American statesman, scientist, writer, and inventor Benjamin Franklin, who lived and worked here for 16 years preceding the American Revolution. The restored Georgian town house has been left unfurnished, the better to show off the original features—18th-century paneling, stoves, beams, bricks, and windows. Visitors are led around the house by the costumed character of Polly Hewson, the daughter of Franklin's landlady. ⊠ *36 Craven St., Covent*

Garden ☎ *020/7839–2006, 020/7925–1405 booking line* ⊕ *www. benjaminfranklinhouse.org* ✉ *Historical experience £7; architectural tour £3.50* ⊙ *Historical Experience Wed.–Sun. noon, 1, 2, 3:15 and 4:15; Architectural tour Mon. noon, 1, 2, 3:15 and 4:15.*

Leicester Square. Looking at the neon of the major movie houses, the fast-food outlets, and the disco entrances, you'd never guess that this square (pronounced *Lester*) was a model of formality and refinement when it was first laid out around 1630. By the 19th century the square was already bustling and disreputable, and although it's not a threatening place, you should still be on your guard, especially at night—any space so full of people is bound to attract pickpockets, and Leicester Square certainly does. Although there's a bit of residual glamour (red-carpet film premieres), Londoners generally tend to avoid the place, though it's worth a visit for its hustle and bustle, its mime artists, and a pleasant green area in its centre. ✉ *Covent Garden* Ⓜ *Leicester Sq.*

BLOOMSBURY AND HOLBORN

Bloomsbury is anchored by the British Museum and the University of London, which houses—among other institutions—the internationally ranked London School of Economics and the School of Oriental and African Studies. As a result, the streets and cafés around Bloomsbury's Russell Square are often crawling with students and professors engaged in heated conversation, while literary agents and academics surf the shelves of the antiquarian bookstores nearby.

The character of an area of London can change visibly from one street to the next. Nowhere is this so clear as in the contrast between fun-loving Soho and intellectual Bloomsbury, a mere 100 yards to the north-east, or between arty, trendy Covent Garden and—on the other side of Kingsway—sober Holborn (pronounced *hoe*-bun). Bloomsbury is known for its famous flowering of literary-arty bohemia, personified during the first three decades of the 20th century by the clique known as the Bloomsbury Group, including Virginia Woolf, E. M. Forster, Vanessa Bell, and Lytton Strachey.

Bloomsbury also happens to be where London's legal profession was born. In fact, the buildings associated with Holborn were some of the few structures spared during the Great Fire of 1666, and so the serpentine alleys, cobbled courts, and historic halls ooze centuries of history. The Gothic-style Royal Courts of Justice ramble all the way to the Strand, and the Inns of Court are where most British trial lawyers have offices to this day.

GETTING HERE   You can easily get to where you need to be on foot in Bloomsbury, and the Russell Square Tube stop on the Piccadilly Line leaves you right at the corner of Russell Square. The best Tube stops for the Inns of Court are Holborn on the Central and Piccadilly lines or Chancery Lane on the Central Line. Tottenham Court Road on the Northern and Central lines or Russell Square (Piccadilly Line) are best for the British Museum.

The massive, glass-roofed Great Court in the British Museum has a couple of cafés.

PLANNING YOUR TIME Bloomsbury can be seen in a day, or in half a day, depending on your interests. If you plan to visit the Inns of Court as well as the British Museum, and you'd also like to get a feel for the neighborhood, then you may devote an entire day to this literary and legal enclave, or come back on another day to visit the vast British Museum. It's a pleasure to wander through the quiet, leafy squares at your leisure.

TOP ATTRACTIONS

FAMILY **British Library.** This collection of around 18 million volumes, formerly in the British Museum, now has a home in state-of-the-art surroundings. The library's greatest treasures are on view to the general public: the Magna Carta, a Gutenberg Bible, Jane Austen's writings, Shakespeare's First Folio, and musical manuscripts by G.F. Handel as well as Sir Paul McCartney are on display in the Sir John Ritblat Gallery. ⊠ *96 Euston Rd., Bloomsbury* ☎ *0843/208–1144* ⊕ *www.bl.uk* ✉ *Free, donations appreciated; charge for special exhibitions* ☉ *Mon. and Wed.–Fri. 9:30–6, Tues. 9:30–8, Sat. 9:30–5, Sun. and public holidays 11–5* Ⓜ *Euston, Euston Sq., King's Cross/St Pancras.*

Fodor's Choice **British Museum.** With a facade like a great temple, this celebrated treasure house, filled with plunder of incalculable value and beauty from around the globe, occupies an immense, imposing, neoclassical building in the heart of Bloomsbury. Inside are some of the greatest relics of humankind: the Parthenon Sculptures (Elgin Marbles), the Rosetta Stone, the Sutton Hoo Treasure—almost everything, it seems, but the Ark of the Covenant. The three rooms that comprise the **Sainsbury African Galleries** are a must-see in the Lower Gallery—together they present 200,000 objects, highlighting such ancient kingdoms as Benin

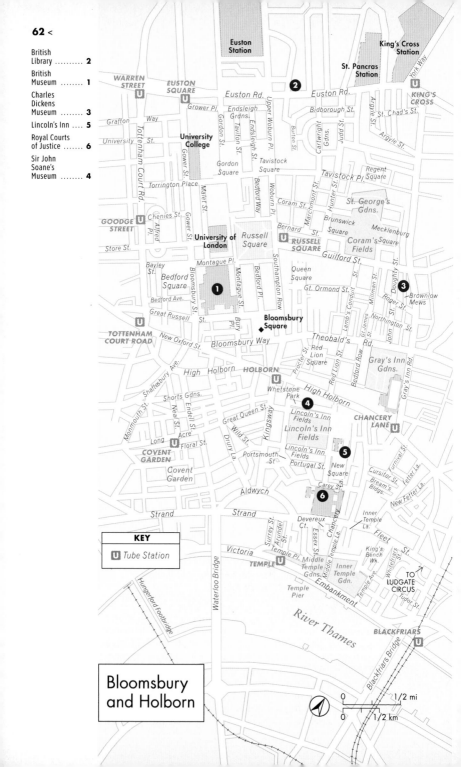

Bloomsbury and Holborn

KEY

Ⓤ Tube Station

and Asante. The museum's focal point is the **Great Court**, a brilliant modern design with a vast glass roof that reveals the museum's covered courtyard. The revered **Reading Room** has a blue-and-gold dome and hosts temporary exhibitions. If you want to navigate the highlights of the almost 100 galleries, join the free **eyeOpener** 30- to 40-minute tours by museum guides (details at the information desk). Or alternatively, hire a multimedia guide for £5.

The collection began when Sir Hans Sloane, physician to Queen Anne and George II, bequeathed his personal collection of antiquities to the nation. It grew quickly, thanks to enthusiastic kleptomaniacs after the Napoleonic Wars—most notoriously the seventh Earl of Elgin, who acquired the marbles from the Parthenon and Erechtheion in Athens during his term as British ambassador in Constantinople. Here follows a highly edited résumé (in order of encounter) of the British Museum's greatest hits: close to the entrance hall, in Room 4, is the **Rosetta Stone,** found by French soldiers in 1799, and carved in 196 BC by decree of Ptolemy V in Egyptian hieroglyphics, demotic (a cursive script developed in Egypt), and Greek. This inscription provided the French Egyptologist Jean-François Champollion with the key to deciphering hieroglyphics. Also in Room 4 is the colossal statue of Ramesses II, a 7-ton likeness of this member of the 19th dynasty's (ca. 1270 BC) upper half. Maybe the **Parthenon Sculptures** should be back in Greece, but while the debate rages on, you can steal your own moment with the Elgin Marbles in Room 18. Carved in about 400 BC, these graceful decorations are displayed along with a high-tech exhibit of the Acropolis. Upstairs are some of the most popular galleries, especially beloved by children: Rooms 62–63, where the **Egyptian mummies** live. Nearby are the glittering 4th-century **Mildenhall Treasure** and the equally splendid 8th-century Anglo-Saxon **Sutton Hoo Treasure** (with magnificent helmets and jewelry). A more prosaic exhibit is that of Pete Marsh, sentimentally named by the archaeologists who unearthed the **Lindow Man** from a Cheshire peat marsh; poor Pete was ritually slain in the 1st century, and lay perfectly pickled in his bog until 1984. ⊠ *Great Russell St., Bloomsbury* ☎ *020/7323–8299* ⊕ *www.britishmuseum.org* 🖃 *Free; donations encouraged* ⊙ *Galleries Sat.–Thurs. 10–5:30, Fri. 10–8:30. Great Court Sat.–Thurs. 9–6, Fri. 9–8:30* Ⓜ *Russell Sq., Holborn, Tottenham Court Rd.*

Charles Dickens Museum. This is one of the few London houses Charles Dickens (1812–70) inhabited that is still standing—and is the place where the master wrote *Oliver Twist* and *Nicholas Nickleby* and finished *Pickwick Papers*. The house looks exactly as it would have in Dickens's day, complete with first editions, letters, and a tall clerk's desk (where the master wrote standing up, often while chatting with visiting friends and relatives). ⊠ *48 Doughty St., Bloomsbury* ☎ *020/7405– 2127* ⊕ *www.dickensmuseum.com* 🖃 *£8* ⊙ *Daily 10–5 (last admission 4:30)* Ⓜ *Chancery La., Russell Sq.*

Fodor's Choice
★
Sir John Soane's Museum. A wonderful, eccentric jewel of a place, Sir John (1753–1837), architect of the Bank of England, bequeathed his house to the nation on one condition: that nothing be changed. It's a house full of surprises. In the Picture Room, for instance, two of Hogarth's *Rake's Progress* series are among the paintings on panels that swing away to

reveal secret gallery pockets with even more paintings. Everywhere, mirrors and colors play tricks with light and space, and split-level floors worthy of a fairground fun house disorient you. ⊠ *13 Lincoln's Inn Fields, Bloomsbury* ☎ *020/7405–2107* ⊕ *www.soane.org* ✉ *Free; tours £10* ⊙ *Tues.–Sat. 10–5; also 6–9 on 1st Tues. of month* Ⓜ *Holborn.*

WORTH NOTING

Lincoln's Inn. There's plenty to see at one of the oldest, best preserved, and most attractive of the Inns of Court—from the Chancery Lane Tudor brick gatehouse to the wide-open, tree-lined, atmospheric Lincoln's Inn Fields and the 15th-century chapel remodeled by Inigo Jones in 1620. Visitors are welcome to attend Sunday services in the chapel; otherwise, you must pre-book a place on of the official tours. But be warned: they tend to prefer group bookings of 15 or more, so it's best to check the website or call for details. ⊠ *Chancery La., Bloomsbury* ☎ *020/7405–1393* ⊕ *www. lincolnsinn.org.uk* ✉ *Free* ⊙ *Gardens and chapel, weekdays noon–2:30; services Sun. at 11:30 during legal term* Ⓜ *Chancery La.*

Royal Courts of Justice. Here is the vast Victorian Gothic pile of 35 million bricks containing the nation's principal law courts, with 1,000-odd rooms running off 3½ miles of corridors. This is where the most important civil law cases—that's everything from divorce to fraud, with libel in between—are heard. You can sit in the viewing gallery to watch any trial you like, for a live version of Court TV. ⊠ *The Strand, Bloomsbury* ☎ *020/7947–6000, 020/7947–7684 tour reservations* ⊕ *www.hmcourts-service.gov.uk (search for 'Royal Courts of Justice' in A–Z option)* ✉ *Free; tours £12* ⊙ *Weekdays 9–4:30* Ⓜ *Temple, Holborn, Chancery La.*

THE CITY

The City, as opposed to the city, is the capital's fast-beating financial heart. Behind a host of imposing neoclassical facades lie the banks and exchanges whose frantic trade determines the fortunes that underpin London—and the country. But the "Square Mile" is much more than London's Wall Street—the capital's economic engine room also has currency as a religious and political center. St. Paul's Cathedral has looked after Londoners' souls since the 7th century, and the Tower of London—that moat-surrounded royal fortress, prison, and jewel house—has taken care of beheading them. The City's maze of backstreets is also home to a host of old churches, marketplaces, and cozy pubs.

Twice the City has been nearly wiped off the face of the earth. The Great Fire of 1666 necessitated a total reconstruction, in which Sir Christopher Wren had a big hand, contributing not only his masterpiece, St. Paul's Cathedral, but 49 additional parish churches. The second wave of destruction was dealt by the German bombers of World War II. The ruins were rebuilt, but slowly, and with no overall plan, leaving the City a patchwork of the old, the new, the interesting, and the flagrantly awful. Since a mere 8,000 or so people call it home, the nation's financial center can feel deserted on weekends, with restaurants shuttered.

Crossing the Millennium Bridge from the Tate Modern to St. Paul's is one of the finest walks in London for views of the river and the cathedral that towers over it.

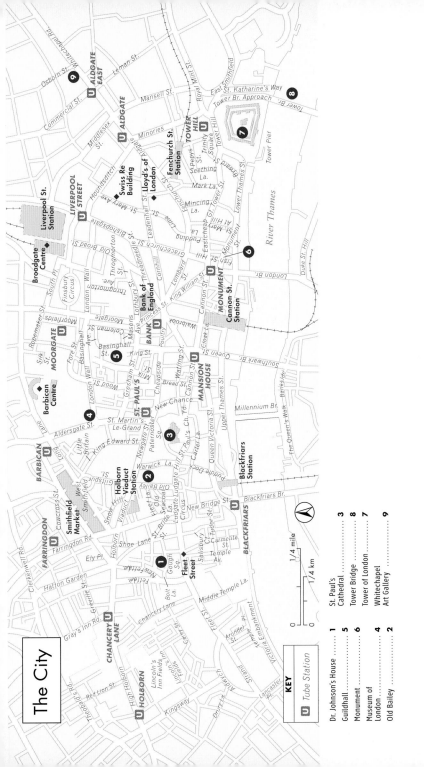

The City

GETTING HERE The City is well served by a concentrated selection of underground stops. St Paul's and Bank, on the Central Line, and Mansion House, Cannon Street, and Monument, on the District and Circle lines, deliver visitors to the heart of the City. Liverpool Street and Aldgate border the City's eastern edge, while Chancery Lane and Farringdon lie to the west. Barbican and Moorgate provide easy access to the theaters and galleries of the Barbican, while Blackfriars, to the south, leads to Ludgate Circus and Fleet Street.

PLANNING YOUR TIME   The "Square Mile" is compact, making it easy to dip into the City for an afternoon stroll. For full immersion in the Tower of London, set aside half a day, especially if seeing the Crown Jewels is a priority. Allow an hour minimum each for the Museum of London, St. Paul's Cathedral, and the Tower Bridge. On weekends the City is nearly deserted, making it hard to find lunch—and yet this is when the major attractions are at their busiest. So if you can manage to come on a weekday, do so.

TOP ATTRACTIONS

FAMILY   **Monument.** Commemorating the "dreadful visitation" of the Great Fire of London, in 1666, this is the world's tallest isolated stone column. It is the work of Sir Christopher Wren and Dr. Robert Hooke, who were asked to erect it "on or as neere unto the place where the said Fire soe unhappily began as conveniently may be." And so here it is—at 202 feet, exactly as tall as the distance it stands from Farriner's baking house in Pudding Lane, where the fire started (note the gilded urn of fire at the column's pinnacle). If climbing the 311 steps is enough to put you off your lunch, cheat a little and watch the live views that are relayed from the top. ⊠ *Monument St., The City* ☎ *020/7626–2717* ⊕ *www. themonument.info* ⊠ *£3; combined ticket with Tower Bridge exhibition £9* ⊙ *Daily 9:30–5:30, last admission 5* Ⓜ *Monument.*

FAMILY   **Museum of London.** If there's one place to absorb the history of London, from 450,000 BC to the present day, it's here: Oliver Cromwell's death mask, Queen Victoria's crinoline gowns, Selfridges' art deco elevators, the London's Burning exhibition, fans, guns and jewelry, an original Newgate Prison door, and the incredible late-18th-century Blackett Dolls House—7,000 objects to wonder at in all. The museum appropriately shelters a section of the 2nd- to 4th-century London wall, which you can view through a window, and permanent displays highlight Pre-Roman, Roman, Medieval, and Tudor London. The Galleries of Modern London are equally enthralling: experience the "Expanding City," "People's City," and "World City," each gallery dealing with a section of London's history from 1666 until the 21st century. Innovative interactive displays abound, and you can even wander around a 19th-century London street with impressively detailed shopfronts and interiors, including a pawnbroker's, a pub, a barber's, and a bank manager's office, in case you're running short on holiday money. There's also a fine schedule of temporary exhibitions. ⊠ *London Wall, The City* ☎ *020/7001–9844* ⊕ *www.museumoflondon.org.uk* ⊠ *Free* ⊙ *Mon.– Sun. 10–6; last admission 5:30* Ⓜ *Barbican, St. Paul's.*

Continued on page 74

THE TOWER OF LONDON

The Tower is a microcosm of the city itself—a sprawling, organic hodgepodge of buildings that inspires reverence and terror in equal measure. See the block on which Anne Boleyn was beheaded, marvel at the Crown Jewels, and pay homage to the ravens who keep the monarchy safe.

An architectural patchwork of time, the oldest building of the complex is the fairytale White Tower, conceived by William the Conqueror in 1078 as both a royal residence and a show of power to the troublesome Anglo-Saxons he had subdued at the Battle of Hastings. Today's Tower has seen everything, as a palace, barracks, a mint for producing coins, an armoury, and the Royal menagerie (home of the country's first elephant). The big draw is the stunning opulence of the Crown Jewels, kept on-site in the heavily fortified Jewel House. Most of all, though, the Tower is known for death: it's been a place of imprisonment, torture, and execution for the realm's most notorious traitors as well as its martyrs. These days, unless you count the killer admission fees, there are far less morbid activities taking place in the Tower, but it still breathes London's history and pageantry from its every brick and offers hours of exploration.

TOURING THE TOWER

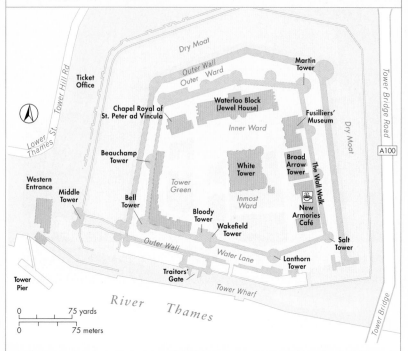

Dry Moat

Martin Tower

Outer Wall
Outer Ward

Ticket Office

Tower Hill Rd

Chapel Royal of St. Peter ad Vincula

Waterloo Block (Jewel House)

Fusilliers' Museum

Inner Ward

Lower Thames St.

Beauchamp Tower

Broad Arrow Tower

White Tower

The Wall Walk

Western Entrance

Middle Tower

Bell Tower

Tower Green

Inmost Ward

New Armouries Café

Bloody Tower

Wakefield Tower

Salt Tower

Outer Wall

Water Lane

Lanthorn Tower

Tower Pier

Traitors' Gate

Tower Wharf

Tower Bridge Road

A100

Dry Moat

River Thames

Tower Bridge

0 — 75 yards
0 — 75 meters

Entry to the Tower is via the **Western Entrance** and the **Middle Tower,** which feed into the outermost ring of the Tower's defenses.

Water Lane leads past the dread-inducing **Traitors' Gate,** the final point of entry for many Tower prisoners.

Toward the end of Water Lane, the **Lanthorn Tower** houses by night the ravens rumored to keep the kingdom safe, and by day a timely high-tech reconstruction of the Catholic Guy Fawkes's plot to blow up the Houses of Parliament in 1605.

The **Bloody Tower** earned its name as the apocryphal site

of the murder of two young princes, Edward and Richard, who disappeared from the Tower after being put there in 1483 by their uncle, Richard III. Two little skeletons (now in Westminster Abbey) were found buried close to the White Tower in 1674 and are thought to be theirs.

The **Beauchamp Tower** housed upper-class miscreants: Latin graffiti about Lady Jane Grey can be glimpsed today on its walls.

Like a prize gem set at the head of a royal crown, the **White Tower** is the center-piece of the complex. Its four towers dominate the Inner

GOLD DIGGER?

Keep your eyes peeled as you tour the Tower: according to one story, Sir John Barkstead, goldsmith and Lieutenant of the Tower under Cromwell, hid £20,000 in gold coins here before his arrest and execution at the Restoration of Charles II.

Ward, a fitting and forbidding reminder of Norman strength at the time of the conquest of England.

Once inside the White Tower, head upstairs for the **Armouries,** where the biggest attraction, quite literally,

Jewel House, Waterloo Barracks

TIME KILLERS

Some prisoners managed to keep themselves plenty amused: Sir Walter Raleigh grew tobacco on Tower Green, and in 1561 suspected sorcerer Hugh Draper carved an intricate astronomical clock on the walls of his Salt Tower cell.

is the suit of armor worn by a well-endowed Henry VIII. There is a matching outfit for his horse.

Other fascinating exhibits include the set of Samurai armor presented to James I in 1613 by the emperor of Japan, and the tiny set of armor worn by Henry VIII's young son Edward.

The **Jewel House** in Waterloo Block is the Tower's biggest draw, perfect for playing pick-your-favorite-crown from the wrong side of bul-

letproof glass. Not only are these crowns, staffs, and orbs encrusted with heavy-duty gems, they are invested with the authority of monarchical power in England, dating back to the 1300s.

Outside, pause at **Tower Green,** permanent departure point for those of noble birth. The hoi polloi were dispatched at nearby Tower Hill. The Tower's most famous female victims—Anne Boleyn, Margaret Countess of Salisbury, Catherine Howard, and Lady Jane Grey—all went this "priviledged" way.

Behind a well-kept square of grass stands the **Chapel Royal of St. Peter ad Vincula,** a delightful Tudor church and final resting place of six beheaded Tudor bodies. ▇ TIP→ **Visitors are welcome for services and can also enter after 4:30 pm daily.**

The **Salt Tower,** reputedly the most haunted corner of the complex, marks the start of the **Wall Walk,** a bracing promenade along the stone spiral steps and battlements of the Tower that looks down on the trucks, taxis, and shimmering high-rises of modern London.

The Wall Walk ends at the **Martin Tower,** former home of the Crown Jewels and now host to the crowns and diamonds exhibition that explains the art of fashioning royal headwear and tells the story of some of the most famous stones.

On leaving the Tower, browse the **gift shop,** and wander the wharf that overlooks the Thames, leading to a picture-postcard view of Tower Bridge.

WHO ARE THE BEEFEATERS?

First of all, they're Yeoman Warders, but probably got the nickname "beefeater" from their position as Royal Bodyguards which entitled them to eat as much beef as they liked. Part of the "Yeoman of the Guard," started in the reign of Edmund IV, the warders have formed the Royal Bodyguard as far back as 1509 when Henry VIII left a dozen of the Yeoman of the Guard at the Tower to protect it.

Originally, the Yeoman Warders also served as jailers of the Tower, doubling as torturers when necessary. (So it would have been a Beefeater tightening the thumb screws, or ratchetting the rack another notch on some unfortunate prisoner. Smile nicely.) Today 36 Yeoman Warders (men and women since 2007), along with the Chief Yeoman Warder and the Yeoman Gaoler, live within the walls of the Tower with their families, in accommodations in the Outer Ward. They stand guard over the Tower, conduct tours, and lock up at 9:53 pm every night with the Ceremony of the Keys.

■ TIP➜ **Free tickets to the Ceremony of the Keys are available by writing several months in advance; check the Tower Web site for details.**

HARK THE RAVENS!

Legend has it that should the hulking black ravens ever leave, the White Tower will crumble and the kingdom fall. Charles II, no doubt jumpy after his father's execution and the monarchy's short-term fall from grace, made a royal decree in 1662 that there should be at least six of the carrion-eating nasties present at all times. There have been some close calls. During World War II, numbers dropped to one, echoing the precarious fate of the war-wracked country. In 2005, two (of eight) died over Christmas when Thor—the most intelligent but also the largest bully of the bunch—killed new recruit Gundolf, named after the Tower's 1070 designer. Pneumonia put an end to Bran, leaving lifelong partner Branwen without her mate.

■ DID YOU KNOW? **In 1981 a raven named Grog, perhaps seduced by his alcoholic moniker, escaped after 21 years at the Tower. Others have been banished for "conduct unbecoming."**

The six that remain, each one identified by a colored band around a claw, are much loved for their fidelity (they mate for life) and their cheek (capable of 440 noises, they are witty and scolding mimics). It's not only the diet

of blood-soaked biscuits, rabbit, and scraps from the mess kitchen that keeps them coming back. Their lifting feathers on one wing are trimmed, meaning they can manage the equivalent of a lop-sided air-bound hobble but not much more. For the first half of 2006 the ravens were moved indoors full-time as a preventive measure against avian flu but have since been allowed out and about again. In situ they are a territorial lot, sticking to Tower Green and the White Tower, and lodging nightly by Wakefield Tower. They've had free front-row seats at all the most grisly moments in Tower history— Anne Boleyn's execution included.

■ TIP➜ **Don't get too close to the ravens: they are prone to pecking and not particularly fond of humans, unless you are the Tower's Raven Master.**

And *WHAT* are they wearing?

A **pike** (or halberd), also known as a partisan, is the Yeoman Warder's weapon of choice. The Chief Warder carries a staff topped with a miniature silver model of the White Tower.

Anyone who refers to this as a costume will be lucky to leave the Tower with head still attached to body: this is the ceremonial uniform of the Yeoman Warders, and it comes at a cool £13,000 a throw.

The black Tudor **bonnet** is made of velvet; the blue undress consists of a felt top hat, with a single Tudor rose in the middle.

This **Tudor-style ruff** helps date the ceremonial uniform, which was first worn in 1552.

Insignia on a Yeoman Warder's upper right arm denote the rank he carried in the military.

The **medals** on a Yeoman Warder's chest are more than mere show: all of the men and women have served for at least 22 years in the armed forces.

This version of the **royal livery** bears the insignia of the current Queen ("E" for Elizabeth) but originally dates from Tudor times. The first letter changes according to the reigning monarch's Christian name; the second letter is always an "R" for *rex* (king) or *regina* (queen).

Slits in the **tunic** date from the times when Beefeaters were expected to ride a horse.

Red socks and **black patent shoes** are worn on special occasions. Visitors are more likely to see the regular blue undress, introduced in 1858 as the regular working dress of the Yeoman Warders.

The **red lines down the trousers** are a sign of the blood from the swords of the Yeoman Warders in their defense of the realm.

(IN)FAMOUS PRISONERS OF THE TOWER

Anne Boleyn   Lady Jane Grey   Sir Walter Raleigh

Sir Thomas More. A Catholic and Henry VIII's friend and chancellor, Sir Thomas refused to attend the coronation of Anne Boleyn (Henry VIII's second wife) or to recognize the multi-marrying king as head of the Church. Sent to the Tower for treason, in 1535 More was beheaded.

Anne Boleyn. The first of Henry VIII's wives to be beheaded, Anne, who failed to provide the king with a son, was accused of sleeping with five men, including her own brother. All six got the chop in 1536. Her severed head was held up to the crowd, and her lips were said to be mouthing prayer.

Margaret, Countess of Salisbury. Not the best-known prisoner in her lifetime, she has a reputation today for haunting the Tower. And no wonder: the elderly 70-year-old was condemned by Henry VIII in 1541 for a potentially treacherous bloodline (she was the last Plantagenet princess) and hacked to death by the executioner after she refused to put her head on the block like a common traitor and attempted to run away.

Queen Catherine Howard. Henry VIII's fifth wife was locked up for high treason and infidelity and beheaded in 1542 at age 20. Ever eager to please, she spent her final night practicing how to lay her head on the block.

Lady Jane Grey. The nine-days-queen lost her head in 1554 at age 16. Her death was the result of sibling rivalry gone seriously wrong, when Protestant Edward VI slighted his Catholic sister Mary in favor of Lady Jane as heir, and Mary decided to have none of it.

Guy Fawkes. The Roman Catholic soldier who tried to blow up the Houses of Parliament and kill the king in the 1605 Gunpowder plot was first incarcerated in the chambers of the Tower, where King James I requested he be tortured in ever-worsening ways. Perhaps unsurprisingly, he confessed. He met his seriously grisly end in the Old Palace Yard at Westminster, where he was hung, drawn, and quartered in 1607.

Sir Walter Raleigh. Once a favorite of Elizabeth I, he offended her by secretly marrying her Maid of Honor and was chucked in the Tower. Later, as a conspirator against James I, he paid with his life. A frequent visitor to the Tower (he spent 13 years there in three stints), he managed to get the Bloody Tower enlarged on account of his wife and growing family. He was finally executed in 1618 in Old Palace Yard, Westminster.

Josef Jakobs. The last man to be executed in the Tower was caught as a spy when parachuting in from Germany and executed by firing squad in 1941. The chair he sat in when he was shot is preserved in the Royal Armouries' artifacts store.

FOR FURTHER EVIDENCE . . .

A trio of buildings in the Inner Ward, the **Bloody Tower, Beauchamp Tower,** and **Queen's House,** all with excellent views of the execution scaffold in Tower Green, are the heart of the Tower's prison accommodations and home to a permanent exhibition about notable inmates.

TACKLING THE TOWER (without losing your head)

✉ H.M. Tower of London, Tower Hill
☎ 0844/482-7777/7799 ⊕ www.hrp.org.uk
🎟 Adult: £19.50, children under 16: £9.75, Family tickets (2 adults, 2 children): £52, children under 5, free. ⊙ Mar.–Oct., Tues.–Sat. 9–5:30, Sun. and Mon. 10–5:30; last admission at 5. Nov.–Feb., Tues.–Sat. 9–4:30, Sun. and Mon. 10–4:30; last admission at 4 Ⓤ Tower Hill

▥ TIP➔ **You can buy tickets from automatic kiosks on arrival, or up to seven days in advance at any Tube station. Avoid lines completely by booking by telephone (0844 482 7777/7799 weekdays 9–5), or online.**

MAKING THE MOST OF YOUR TIME:
Without doubt, the Tower is worth two to three hours. A full hour of that would be well spent by joining one of the Yeoman Warders' tours (included in admission). It's hard to better their insight, vitality, and humor—they are knights of the realm living their very own fairytale castle existence.

The Crown Jewels are worth the wait, the White Tower is essential, and the Medieval Palace and Bloody Tower should at least be breezed through.

▥ TIP➔ **It's best to visit on weekdays, when the crowds are smaller.**

WITH KIDS: The Tower's centuries-old cobblestones are not exactly stroller-friendly, but strollers are permitted inside most of the buildings. If you do bring one, be prepared to leave it temporarily unsupervised (the stroller, that is—not your child) outside the White Tower, which has no access. There are baby-changing facilities in the Brick Tower restrooms behind the Jewel House. Look for regular free children's events such as the Knight's school where children can have a go at jousting, sword-fighting, and archery.

▥ TIP➔ **Tell your child to find one of the Yeoman Warders if he or she should get lost; they will in turn lead him or her to the Byward Tower, which is where you should meet.**

IN A HURRY? If you have less than an hour, head down Wall Walk, through a succession of towers, which eventually spit you out at the Martin Tower. The view over modern London is quite a contrast.

TOURS: Tours given by a Yeoman Warder leave from the main entrance near Middle Tower every half-hour from 10–4, and last about an hour. Beefeaters give occasional 30-minute talks in the Lanthorn Tower about their daily lives. Both tours are free. Check website for talks and workshops

Fodor'sChoice   **St. Paul's Cathedral.** St. Paul's is simply breathtaking, especially now that
★   the scaffolding has been removed after 15 years of major restoration work.
The structure is Sir Christopher Wren's masterpiece, completed in 1710
after 35 years of building, and, much later, miraculously spared (mostly)
by World War II bombs. St. Paul's simply would not be St. Paul's as we
know it without the dome, the third largest in the world. Even so, from
inside the vast cathedral the dome may seem smaller than you'd expect—
the inner dome is 60 feet lower than the lead-covered outer dome. Beneath
the lantern is Wren's famous and succinct epitaph, which his son composed and had set into the pavement: "Lector, si monumentum requiris,
circumspice"—"Reader, if you seek his monument, look around you."
The epitaph also appears on Wren's memorial in the Crypt.

Up 163 spiral steps is the **Whispering Gallery,** an acoustic phenomenon;
you whisper something to the wall on one side, and a second later it
transmits clearly to the other side, 107 feet away. Ascend to the **Stone
Gallery,** which encircles the base of the dome. Farther up (280 feet from
ground level) is the small **Golden Gallery,** the dome's highest point.
From both these galleries (if you have a head for heights) you can walk
outside for a spectacular panorama of London.

The remains of the poet John Donne, who was Dean of St. Paul's for
his final 10 years (he died in 1631), are in the south choir aisle. The
vivacious choir-stall carvings nearby are the work of Grinling Gibbons,
as are those on the **great organ,** which Wren designed. Behind the high
altar is the **American Memorial Chapel,** dedicated to the 28,000 GIs
stationed in the United Kingdom who lost their lives in World War II.
Among the famous figures whose remains lie in the **Crypt** are the Duke
of Wellington and Admiral Lord Nelson. The Crypt also has a gift
shop and a café. ⊠ *St. Paul's Churchyard, The City* ☎ *020/7236–4128*
⊕ *www.stpauls.co.uk* ⊠ *£15 (includes multimedia guides and guided
tours)* ⊗ *Mon.–Sat. 8:30–4; Shop Mon.–Sat. 9–5, Sun. 10–4.30; Crypt
Café Mon.–Sat. 9–5, Sun. 12–4* Ⓜ *St. Paul's.*

FAMILY   **Tower Bridge.** Despite its medieval, fairy-tale appearance, this is a Victo-
Fodor'sChoice   rian youngster. Constructed of steel, then clothed in Portland stone, the
★   Horace Jones masterpiece was deliberately styled in the Gothic persuasion to complement the Tower next door. The **Tower Bridge Exhibition** is
a child-friendly tour where you can discover how one of the world's most
famous bridges actually works before heading out onto the walkways for
the wonderful city views. ⊠ *Tower Bridge Rd., The City* ☎ *020/7403–
3761* ⊕ *www.towerbridge.org.uk* ⊠ *£8* ⊗ *Apr.–Sept., daily 10–6; Oct.–
Mar., daily 9:30–5.30; last admission 30 min before closing* Ⓜ *Tower Hill.*

FAMILY   **Tower of London.**
Fodor'sChoice   *See the highlighted feature in this section.*
★

WORTH NOTING

Dr. Johnson's House. This is where Samuel Johnson lived between 1748
and 1759. Built in 1700, the elegant Georgian residence, with its paneled rooms and period furniture, is where the Great Bear (as he was
known) compiled his *Dictionary of the English Language* in the attic
as his health deteriorated. Two early editions are on view, among other

mementos of Johnson and his friend, diarist, and later, his biographer, James Boswell. After soaking up the atmosphere, repair around the corner in Wine Office Court to the famed **Ye Olde Cheshire Cheese** pub (⇨ *See Feeling Peckish?*), once Johnson and Boswell's favorite watering hole. ✉ *17 Gough Sq., The City* ☎ *020/7353–3745* ⊕ *www. drjohnsonshouse.org* ✉ *£4.50* ☉ *May–Sept., Mon.–Sat. 11–5:30; Oct.– Apr., Mon.–Sat. 11–5* Ⓜ *Holborn, Chancery Lane, Temple.*

Guildhall. The Corporation of London, which oversees The City, has ceremonially elected and installed its Lord Mayor here for the last 800 years. The Guildhall was built in 1411, and though it failed to avoid either the 1666 or 1940 flames, its core survived. To the right of Guildhall Yard is the **Guildhall Art Gallery,** which includes portraits of the great and the good, cityscapes, famous battles, and a slightly cloying pre-Raphaelite section. The construction of the gallery in the 1980s led to the exciting discovery of London's only **Roman amphitheater,** which had lain underneath Guildhall Yard undisturbed for more than 1,800 years. It was excavated, and now visitors can walk among the remains, although most of the relics can be seen at the Museum of London. ✉ *Aldermanbury, The City* ☎ *020/7606–3030, 020/7332–3700 gallery* ⊕ *www.cityoflondon.gov.uk* ✉ *Free (fee for some gallery exhibitions)* ☉ *Mon.–Sat. 9:30–5; gallery Mon.–Sat. 10–5, Sun. noon–4, last admission 4:30 or 3:30* Ⓜ *St. Paul's, Moorgate, Bank, Mansion House.*

Old Bailey. This is the place to watch the real-life drama of justice in action in one of the 16 courtrooms that are open to the public. Previous trials have included those of Crippen and Christie, two of England's most notorious wife murderers, as well as the controversial trials of Oscar Wilde and the notorious East End gangsters, the Kray twins. The day's hearings are posted on the sign outside, but your best bet is to consult the previous day's tabloid newspapers for an idea of the trials that are making waves. There are security restrictions, and children under 14 are not allowed in; call the information line first. ✉ *Newgate St., The City* ☎ *020/7248–3277 information* ⊕ *www.cityoflondon.gov.uk* ☉ *Public Gallery weekdays 9.45–12.45 and 1.45–4 (approx.); line forms at Newgate St. entrance or in Warwick St. Passage; closed bank holidays and day after* Ⓜ *St. Paul's.*

Whitechapel Art Gallery. Established in 1897 and recently expanded, this large, independent East End gallery is one of London's most innovative and consistently interesting. Jeff Wall, Bill Viola, Gary Hume, and Mark Rothko have exhibited here and there is an interesting program of events as well as an excellent restaurant. ✉ *80–82 Whitechapel High St., Shoreditch* ☎ *020/7522–7888* ⊕ *www.whitechapel.org* ✉ *Free* ☉ *Tues., Wed., Fri.–Sun. 11–6, Thurs. 11–9* Ⓜ *Aldgate East.*

THE SOUTH BANK

Culture, history, sights: the South Bank has it all. High-caliber art, music, film, and theater venues sit alongside the likes of an aquarium, historic warships, and Borough Market, a foodie favorite. Pedestrians cross between the north and south banks using the futuristic Hungerford Bridge and the curvaceous Millennium Bridge, as they take in the compelling views of the Thames.

The Tate Modern is the star attraction, installed in a 1930s power station, with the eye-catching Millennium Bridge linking its main door across the river to the City. Near the theaters of the South Bank Centre, the London Eye observation wheel gives you a flight over the city. The South Bank of the Thames isn't beautiful, but this area of theaters and museums has Culture with a capital C.

It's fitting that so much of London's artistic life should once again be centered on the South Bank—in the past, Southwark was the location of theaters, taverns, and cockfighting arenas. The Globe Theatre, in which Shakespeare acted and held shares, was one of several here. In truth the Globe was as likely to stage bear baiting as Shakespeare, but today, at the reconstructed "Wooden O," you can see only the latter. Be sure to take a walk along Bankside, the embankment along the Thames from Southwark to Blackfriars Bridge.

GETTING HERE For the South Bank, use the Embankment on the District, Circle, Northern, and Bakerloo lines and walk across the Golden Jubilee Bridges; or Waterloo on the Northern, Jubilee, and Bakerloo lines, from where it's a 10-minute walk. London Bridge on the Northern and Jubilee lines is five minutes from Borough Market and Southwark Cathedral.

PLANNING YOUR TIME Don't attempt to explore the area south of the Thames all in one go. Not only will you exhaust yourself, but you will miss out on the varied delights that it has to offer. The Tate Modern alone deserves a whole morning or afternoon, especially if you want to do justice to both the temporary exhibitions and the permanent collection. The Globe requires about two hours for the exhibition theater tour and two to three hours for a performance.

TOP ATTRACTIONS

Fashion and Textile Museum. The bright yellow and pink museum (it's hard to miss) designed by Mexican architect Ricardo Legorreta features changing exhibitions devoted to developments in fashion design, textiles, and jewelry from the end of World War II in 1945 to the present. Founded by designer Zandra Rhodes, an icon of Swinging London, and now owned by Newham College, the FTM is a favorite with fashionistas and offers weekday lectures on aspects of fashion history and fashion-based workshops. The excellent gift shop sells books on fashion and one-of-a-kind pieces by local designers. After your visit, check out the many trendy restaurants, cafés, and boutiques that have bloomed on Bermondsey Street. ⊠ *83 Bermondsey St., Bermondsey* ☎ *020/7407–8664* ⊕ *www.ftmlondon. org* 🎟 *£7* ⊗ *Tues.–Sat. 11–6; last admission 5:15* Ⓜ *London Bridge.*

FAMILY **Golden Hinde.** Famed Elizabethan explorer Sir Francis Drake circumnavigated the globe in a little galleon just like this one. Launched in 1973, this exact replica made two round-the-world voyages and called in at ports—many along the Pacific and Atlantic coasts of the United States—to do duty as a maritime museum. ⊠ *St. Mary Overie Dock, Cathedral St., Bankside* ☎ *020/7403–0123* ⊕ *www.goldenhinde.com* 🎟 *£6* ⊗ *Daily 10–5:30* Ⓜ *London Bridge.*

FAMILY
Fodor'sChoice
★ **London Dungeon.** Here's the goriest, grisliest, most gruesome attraction in town, where unfortunate prisoners (or at least realistic waxworks) are subjected in graphic detail to all the historical horrors that the Tower

of London merely describes. Perhaps most shocking are the crowds of children roaring to get in—kids absolutely adore this place, although those with more a sensitive disposition may find it too frightening (that goes for adults as well). Since moving to new quarters next to the London Aquarium in March 2013, this attraction has eschewed its former penny-dreadful aesthetic in favor of a more "theatrical, history-based" approach. ■■ TIP➔ Expect long lines on weekends and during school holidays. Savings are available for online booking. ☒ *County Hall, Westminster Bridge Rd., South Bank* ☎ *020/7403–7221* ⊕ *www. thedungeons.com* ☒ *From £16* ⊙ *Mar.–July, Fri.–Wed. 10–6, Thurs. 11–6; Aug., Fri.–Wed. 10–7, Thurs. 11–7; Sept.–Feb., Fri.–Wed. 10–5, Thurs. 11–5; phone or check website to confirm times* Ⓜ *Waterloo.*

FAMILY **London Eye.** To mark the start of the new millennium, architects David Marks and Julia Barfield conceived a beautiful and celebratory structure that would allow people to see this great city from a completely new perspective. They came up with a giant Ferris wheel, which, as well as representing the turn of the century, would also be a symbol of regeneration. The London Eye is the largest cantilevered observation wheel ever built and among the tallest structures in London. The 25-minute slow-motion ride inside one of the enclosed passenger capsules is so smooth you'd hardly know you were suspended over the Thames. ■■ TIP➔ Buy your ticket online to avoid the long lines and get a 10% discount. ☒ *Westminster Bridge Rd., Riverside Bldg., County Hall, South Bank* ☎ *0870/990–8883* ⊕ *www.londoneye.com* ☒ *£18.90; cruise £12.50* ⊙ *June and Sept., daily 10–9; July and Aug., daily 10–9:30; Oct.–Mar., daily 10–8:30* Ⓜ *Waterloo.*

FAMILY **Shakespeare's Globe Theatre.** This spectacular theater is a replica of
Fodor's Choice Shakespeare's open-roof, wood-and-thatch Globe Playhouse (built
★ in 1599 and burned down in 1613), where most of the Bard's greatest works premiered. American actor and director Sam Wanamaker worked ceaselessly for several decades to raise funds for the theater's reconstruction 200 yards from its original site, using authentic materials and techniques, a dream realized in 1997. "Groundlings"—patrons with £5 standing-only tickets—are not allowed to sit during the performance. Fortunately, you can reserve an actual seat on any one of the theater's three levels, but you will want to rent a cushion for £1 (or bring your own) to soften the backless wooden benches. The show must go on, rain or shine, warm or chilly—so come prepared for anything. Umbrellas are banned, but you can bring a raincoat or buy a cheap Globe rain poncho, which doubles as a great souvenir.

Shakespeare's Globe Exhibition, a museum under the theater (the entry is adjacent), provides background material on the Elizabethan theater and the construction of the modern-day Globe. Admission to the museum also includes a tour of the theater. On matinee days the tour visits the archaeological site of the nearby (and older) Rose Theatre. ☒ *21 New Globe Walk, Bankside* ☎ *020/7902–1400 box office, 020/7401–9919 Exhibition* ⊕ *www.shakespearesglobe.com* ☒ *Exhibition and Globe Theatre tour £13.50 (£2 reduction with valid performance ticket); ticket prices for plays vary, £5–£39* ⊙ *Exhibition: May–early Oct., daily 10–5; mid-Oct.–Apr., daily 9–12:30 and 1–5; plays: April 23–Oct., call for performance schedule* Ⓜ *London Bridge; Mansion House, then cross Southwark Bridge.*

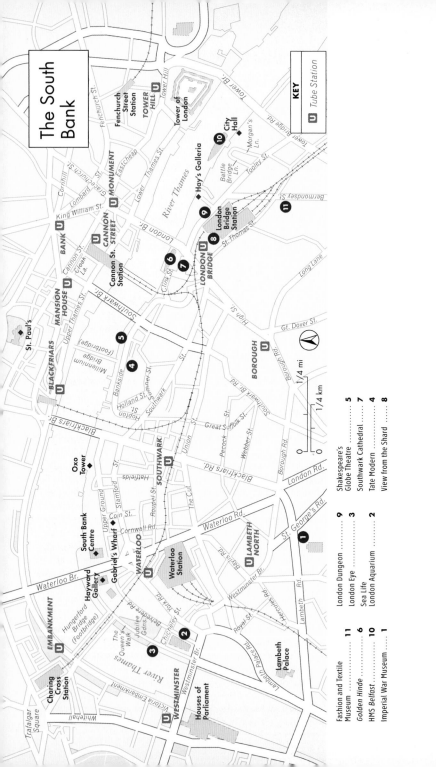

The South Bank

KEY

U Tube Station

Fashion and Textile
Museum **11**

Golden Hinde **6**

HMS Belfast **10**

Imperial War Museum **1**

London Dungeon **9**

London Eye **3**

Sea Life
London Aquarium **2**

Shakespeare's
Globe Theatre **5**

Southwark Cathedral **7**

Tate Modern **4**

View from the Shard **8**

FAMILY

Fodor'sChoice

★

Tate Modern. This spectacular renovation of a mid-20th-century power station is one of the most-visited museums of modern art in the world. Its great permanent collection, which starts in 1900 and ranges from modern masters like Matisse to the most cutting-edge contemporary artists, is arranged thematically—Landscape, Still Life, and the Nude. Its blockbuster temporary exhibitions showcase the work of individual artists like Gauguin, Roy Lichtenstein, and Gerhard Richter. The vast **Turbine Hall** is a dramatic entrance point used to showcase big, audacious installations that tend to generate a lot of publicity. The **Material Gestures** galleries on Level 3 feature an impressive offering of post–World War II painting and sculpture. Room 7 contains a breathtaking collection of Rothkos and Monets; there are also paintings by Matisse, Pollock, and Picasso, and newer works from the likes of the sculptor Anish Kapoor. Head to the Restaurant on Level 7 or the Espresso Bar on Level 3 for stunning vistas of the Thames. The view of St. Paul's from the Espresso Bar's balcony is one of the best in London. An extension to the front of the building is not only ambitious but also controversial— you won't be alone if you don't care for it. ⊠ *Bankside* ☎ *020/7887– 8888* ⊕ *www.tate.org.uk/modern* 🖼 *Free, charge for special exhibitions* ⊙ *Sun.–Thurs. 10–6, Fri. and Sat. 10–10 (last admission to exhibitions 45 min before close)* Ⓜ *Southwark, Mansion House, St. Paul's.*

WORTH NOTING

FAMILY

HMS *Belfast*. At 613.5 feet, this is one of the last remaining big-gun armored warships from World War II, in which it played an important role in protecting the Arctic convoys and supporting the D-Day landings in Normandy; the ship later saw action during the Korean War. The *Belfast* has been moored in the Thames as a maritime branch of the **Imperial War Museum** since 1971. ⊠ *Morgan's La., Tooley St., Borough* ☎ *020/7940–6300* ⊕ *www.iwm.org.uk* 🖼 *£14.50* ⊙ *Mar.–Oct., daily 10–6; Nov.–Feb., daily 10–5; last admission 1 hr before closing* Ⓜ *London Bridge.*

Imperial War Museum. Despite its title, this museum of 20th-century warfare does not glorify bloodshed but emphasizes understanding through evoking what life was like for citizens and soldiers alike through the two world wars and beyond. After reopening its doors in summer 2013 after an enormous renovation, this museum is even more spectacular than before. A redesigned atrium will tower over six storeys, and this dramatic space will hold some of the collection's top items. The renovation's heart, however, will be the new First World War Galleries, noted for using sights, sounds, and smells to re-create the very uncomfortable Trench Experience of this most carnage-filled war. ⊠ *Lambeth Rd., South Bank* ☎ *020/7416–5000* ⊕ *www.iwm.org.uk* 🖼 *Free (charge for special exhibitions)* ⊙ *Daily 10–6* Ⓜ *Lambeth North.*

FAMILY

Sea Life London Aquarium. The curved, colonnaded, neoclassical former County Hall that once housed London's local government administration is now home to a superb three-level aquarium full of sharks and stingrays, along with many other acquatic species, both common and rare. There are also feeding and hands-on displays, including a tank full of shellfish that you can touch. It's not the biggest aquarium you've ever seen, but the educational exhibits are particularly well arranged, with areas for different oceans, water environments, and climate zones ranging from a stunning coral reef to a rain forest. Regular feeding times and free talks are offered throughout the day. ✉ *County Hall, Westminster Bridge Rd., South Bank* ☎ *0871/663–1678* ⊕ *www.sealife. co.uk* ⎙ *£20.50* ⊘ *Mon.–Thurs. 10–6, Fri.–Sun. 10–7, last admission 1 hr before closing* Ⓜ *Westminster, Waterloo.*

Southwark Cathedral. Pronounced "Suth-uck," this is the oldest Gothic church in London, with parts dating back to the 12th century. It remains off the beaten track, despite being the site of some remarkable memorials and a concert program that offers recitals of works for the organ at lunchtime on Mondays (except in August and December) and classical music at 3:15 on Tuesdays (except in December). Originally the priory church of St. Mary Overie (as in "over the water"—on the South Bank), it became a palace church under Henry VIII and was only promoted to cathedral status in 1905. Look for the gaudily renovated 1408 tomb of the poet John Gower, friend of Chaucer, and for the Harvard Chapel. Another notable buried here is Edmund Shakespeare, brother of William. ▮**TIP**➜ **The Refectory serves full English breakfasts, light lunches, and tea 8:30–6 Monday–Friday, 10–6 weekends.** ✉ *London Bridge, Bankside* ☎ *020/7367–6700* ⊕ *www.southwark.anglican.org* ⎙ *Free, suggested donation £4* ⊘ *Daily 8–6* Ⓜ *London Bridge.*

The View from the Shard. At 1,016 feet, this 2012 addition to the London skyline is currently the tallest building in Western Europe and, as a design of noted architect Renzo Piano, has attracted both admiration and opprobrium. While the building itself is generally highly regarded—although there are those who wonder how such a tall building can appear so squat and graceless—many feel it would be better sited in Canary Wharf (or, indeed, Dubai) as it spoils views of St. Paul's Cathedral from traditional vantage points such as Hampstead's Parliament Hill. No matter how you feel about the building, there's no denying that it offers a spectacular 360-degree view *over* London (extending to 40 miles on a clear day) from viewing platforms on floors 68, 69, and 72—almost twice as high as any other vantage point in the city. ✉ *32 London Bridge St., Borough* ☎ *0844/499–7111* ⊕ *www. theviewfromtheshard.com* ⎙ *£24.95* ⊘ *Daily 9 am–10 pm, last admission 8:30* Ⓜ *London Bridge.*

KENSINGTON, KNIGHTSBRIDGE, AND MAYFAIR

Splendid houses with pillared porches, as well as fascinating museums, stylish squares, and glittering antiques shops, line the streets of this elegant area of the Royal Borough of Kensington. Also here is Kensington Palace (the former home of both Diana, Princess of Wales, and Queen Victoria), which put the district literally on the map back in the 17th century. To Kensington's east is one of the highest concentrations of important artifacts in London, the "museum mile" of South Kensington. Kensington first became the *Royal* Borough of Kensington (and Chelsea) when William III, who suffered from the Thames mists over Whitehall, decided in 1689 to buy Nottingham House in the rural village of Kensington.

Hyde Park and Kensington Gardens together form by far the biggest of central London's royal parks. It's probably been centuries since any major royal had a casual stroll here, but the parks remain the property of the Crown, and it was the Crown that saved them from being devoured by the city's late-18th-century growth spurt.

Wealthy Knightsbridge is shop-'til-you-drop territory of the highest order. Two world-famous department stores, Harrods and Harvey Nichols, are a few hundred yards apart, and every bit of space around is taken up with designer boutiques, chain stores, and jewelers.

Around the borders of Hyde Park are several of London's most beautiful and posh neighborhoods. To the south of the park and a short carriage ride from Buckingham Palace is the splendidly aristocratic enclave of Belgravia. Its white-stucco buildings and grand squares—particularly Belgrave Square—are Regency-era jewels. On the eastern border of Hyde Park is Mayfair, which gives Belgravia a run for its money as London's wealthiest district.

GETTING HERE There's good Tube service to these areas. On the Central Line, Marble Arch and Bond Street (also Jubilee Line) take you to the heart of Mayfair; the Hyde Park Corner stop on the Piccadilly line is at the southeast corner of the park, near Apsley House. South Kensington and Gloucester Road on the District, Circle, and Piccadilly lines are convenient stops for the South Kensington museums; Knightsbridge on the Piccadilly line leaves you close to Harrods and many retail temptations.

PLANNING YOUR TIME The best way to approach these neighborhoods is to treat Knightsbridge shopping and the South Kensington museums as separate days out, although the three vast museums may be too much to take in at once. The parks are best in the growing seasons and during fall, when the foliage is turning; the summer roses in Regent's Park are stunning. On Sunday the Hyde Park and Kensington Gardens railings all along the Bayswater Road are hung with mediocre art, which may slow your progress; this is prime perambulation day for locals.

TOP ATTRACTIONS

Fodor'sChoice ★ **Apsley House (Wellington Museum).** The mansion built by Robert Adam and presented to the Duke of Wellington in thanks for his victory over Napoléon at the Battle of Waterloo in 1815 was long celebrated as the best address in town. The mansion was the residence of the Duke of Wellington from 1817 until his death in 1852. The duke's former residence shows off his uniforms, weapons, a fine collection of paintings (partially looted from his war campaigns), and his porcelain and plate collections acquired as a result of his military success, such as a Sèvres dessert service commissioned by Napoléon for his empress, Josephine. Wellington's extensive art collection, much of it presented to him by admirers, includes works by Brueghel, Van Dyck, and Rubens, as well as the famous Veláquez portrait of Pope Innocent X and a portrait of the duke on horseback by Goya. ⊠ *149 Piccadilly, Hyde Park Corner, Mayfair* ☎ *020/7499–5676* ⊕ *www.english-heritage.org.uk* ⚏ *£6.50 (includes audio tour); joint ticket with Wellington Arch £8.20* ☉ *Mar.– Oct., Wed.–Sun. and bank holiday Mon. 11–5; Nov.–Feb., Sat.–Sun. 10–4* Ⓜ *Hyde Park Corner.*

FAMILY
Fodor's Choice
★

Hyde Park. Along with the smaller St. James's and Green parks to the east, Hyde Park started as Henry VIII's hunting grounds. Along its south side runs Rotten Row, once Henry's royal path to the hunt—the name is a corruption of *Route du Roi* (route of the king). It's still used by the Household Cavalry, who live at the Hyde Park Barracks—a high-rise and a low, ugly, red block—to the left. This is where the brigade that mounts the guard at Buckingham Palace resides, and you can see them leave to perform their duty, in full regalia, at about 10:30, or await the return of the guard around noon. Hyde Park is wonderful for strolling, watching the locals, or just relaxing by the Serpentine, the long body of water near its southern border. On the south side, by the 1930s **Serpentine Lido**, is the site of the **Diana Princess of Wales Memorial Fountain**, which opened in 2003 and is a good spot to refuel at one of the cafés. On Sunday, Speakers' Corner, in the park near Marble Arch, is an unmissable spectacle of vehement, sometimes comical, and always entertaining orators. ⊠ *Hyde Park* ☎ *030/0061–2000* ⊕ *www.royalparks.gov.uk* ☉ *Daily 5 am–midnight* Ⓜ *Hyde Park Corner, Knightsbridge, Lancaster Gate, Marble Arch.*

FAMILY
Fodor's Choice
★

Kensington Gardens. Laid out in 1689 by William III, who commissioned Christopher Wren to build Kensington Palace, the gardens are a formal counterpart to neighbouring Hyde Park. Just to the north of the palace itself is the Dutch-style **Sunken Garden**. Nearby, the 1912 bronze statue of *Peter Pan* commemorates the boy in J.M. Barrie's story who lived on an island in the Serpentine and never grew up. The lovely **Diana Princess of Wales Memorial Playground** has sections inspired by Peter's other imaginary home, *Neverland*. Nearby, the **Serpentine Gallery** holds often controversial exhibitions of contemporary works. ⊠ *Kensington* ☎ *030/0061–2000* ⊕ *www.royalparks.gov.uk* ☉ *Daily 6–dusk* Ⓜ *High Street Kensington, Lancaster Gate, Queensway, South Kensington.*

Kensington Palace. Neither as imposing as Buckingham Palace nor as charming as Hampton Court, Kensington Palace is something of a Royal Family commune, with various close relatives of the Queen occupying large apartments in the private part of the palace. Bought in 1689 by Queen Mary and King William III, it was converted into a palace by Sir Christopher Wren and Nicholas Hawksmoor, and Royals have been in residence ever since. Its most famous resident, Princess Diana, lived here with her sons after her divorce, and this is where Prince William now lives with his wife, Catherine, Duchess of Cambridge. The State Apartments, however, are open to the public, and galleries showcase three permanent exhibitions that delve into palace history: Queen Victoria (with the theme "love, duty, and loss"); William and Mary and Queen Anne ("the private life of the Queen"); and George II ("the curious world of the court"). There is also a changing temporary exhibition during the summer months. ⊠ *The Broad Walk, Kensington Gardens, Kensington* ☎ *0844/482–7799 advance booking, 0844/482–7777 information, 0203/166–6000 from outside U.K.* ⊕ *www.hrp.org.uk* ☎ *£14.50 (subject to change)* ☉ *Mar.–Sept., daily 10–6; Oct.–Feb., daily 10–5; last admission 1 hr before closing* Ⓜ *Queensway, High Street Kensington.*

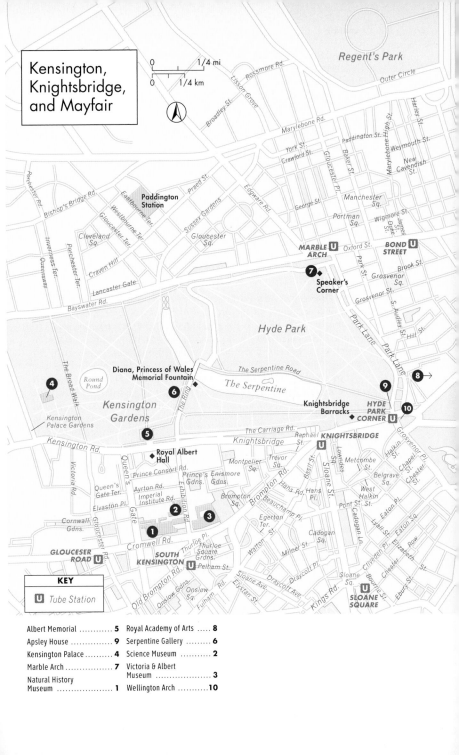

Kensington, Knightsbridge, and Mayfair

0 1/4 mi
0 1/4 km

Regent's Park
Outer Circle

Rossmore Rd.
Lisson Grove
Broadley St.
Marylebone Rd.
York St.
Crawford St.
Gloucester St.
Baker St.
Paddington St.
Marylebone High St.
Harley St.
Weymouth St.
New Cavendish St.
Manchester Sq.
George St.
Portman Sq.
Wigmore St.
James St.
Duke St.
Orchard St.

Porchester Rd.
Bishop's Bridge Rd.
Eastbourne Ter.
Paddington Station
Praed St.
Westbourne Ter.
Gloucester Ter.
Sussex Gardens
Edgware Rd.
Gloucester Sq.

MARBLE [U] Oxford St. **BOND** [U]
ARCH **STREET**

Cleveland Sq.
Craven Hill
Lancaster Gate
Inverness Ter.
Porchester Ter.
Queensway
Bayswater Rd.

Grosvenor St.
Brook St.
Grosvenor Sq.
S. Audley St.
Park St.
Park Lane

7 ♦
Speaker's Corner

Hyde Park

Hill St.
Park Lane

The Serpentine Road
Diana, Princess of Wales Memorial Fountain
6 ♦
The Serpentine

4
Round Pond
The Broad Walk
The Ring

Kensington Gardens

Kensington Palace Gardens

9
8 →

Knightsbridge Barracks **HYDE PARK CORNER** [U]
5

The Carriage Rd.
KNIGHTSBRIDGE
Kensington Rd.
Victoria Rd.
Queen's Gate
Knightsbridge
Raphael St.
[U]
10
Grosvenor Pl.

Royal Albert Hall ♦
Prince Consort Rd.
Prince's Gdns.
Ennismore Gdns.
Montpelier Sq.
Trevor Sq.
Basil St.
Metcombe St.
Halkin St.
Chapel Pl.
Chester St.

Queen's Gate Ter.
Ayrton Rd.
Imperial Institute Rd.
2
3
Brompton Sq.
Brompton Rd.
Hans Rd.
Hans Pl.
Sloane St.
Lowndes Square
Belgrave Sq.
West Halkin St.
Pont St.
Cadogan Ln.

Cornwall Gdns.
Elvaston Pl.
Cromwell Rd.
1
Thurloe Pl.
Thurloe Square Gdns.
Egerton Ter.
Beauchamp Pl.
Walton St.
Cadogan Sq.
Lyall St.
Eaton Pl.
Eaton Sq.

GLOUCESER ROAD [U]
SOUTH KENSINGTON [U]
Pelham St.
Milner St.
Cadogan Pl.
Cliveden Pl.
Elizabeth St.

Old Brompton Rd.
Onslow Gdns.
Onslow Sq.
Fulham Rd.
Elystan St.
Draycott Pl.
Draycott Ave.
Sloane Ave.
Sloane Sq.
Kings Rd.
SLOANE SQUARE [U]
Bourne St.
Chester Row
Ebury St.
Gloucester Rd.
Queen's Gate

KEY
[U] *Tube Station*

FAMILY
Fodor's Choice
★

Natural History Museum. The ornate terracotta facade of this enormous Victorian museum is strewn with relief panels depicting living creatures to the left of the entrance and extinct ones to the right (although some species have subsequently changed categories). It's an appropriate design, for within these walls lie more than 70 million different specimens. Only a small percentage is on public display, but you could still spend a day here and not come close to seeing everything. The museum is full of cutting-edge exhibits, with all the wow-power and interactives necessary to secure interest from younger visitors. You'll also come face to face with a giant animatronic Tyrannosaurus rex—who is programmed to sense when human prey is near and "respond" in character. When he does, you can hear the shrieks of fear and delight all the way across the room. A dizzyingly tall escalator takes you into a giant globe in the **Earth Galleries,** where there's a choice of levels—and Earth surfaces—to explore. Don't leave without checking out the earthquake simulation in Gallery 61. ⊠ *Cromwell Rd., South Kensington* ☎ *0207/942–5000* ⊕ *www.nhm.ac.uk* ✉ *Free (some fees for special exhibitions)* ⊙ *Daily 10–5:50, last admission at 5:30* Ⓜ *South Kensington.*

Fodor's Choice
★

Royal Academy of Arts. Burlington House was built in 1664, with later Palladian additions for the 3rd Earl of Burlington in 1720. The house itself is home to the draw-card tenant, the Royal Academy of Arts. The statue of the academy's first president, Sir Joshua Reynolds, palette in hand, is prominent in the piazza of light stone with fountains by Sir Phillip King. Within the house and up the stairs are statues of creative giants J.W.M. Turner and Thomas Gainsborough. Free tours show off part of the RA collection, some of it housed in the John Madejski Fine Rooms, and the RA hosts excellent temporary exhibitions. ⊠ *Burlington House, Piccadilly, Mayfair* ☎ *020/7300–8000, 0207/300–5839 lectures, 0207/300–5995 family programs* ⊕ *www.royalacademy.org.uk* ✉ *Prices vary with exhibition from £7–£15* ⊙ *Sat.–Thurs. 10–6, Fri. 10–10; tours Tues. 1, Wed.–Fri. 1 and 3, Sat. 11:30* Ⓜ *Piccadilly Circus, Green Park.*

FAMILY
Fodor's Choice
★

Victoria & Albert Museum. Known to all as the V&A, this huge museum is devoted to the applied arts of all disciplines, all periods, and all nationalities. Full of innovation, it's a wonderful, generous place in which to to get lost. First opened as the South Kensington Museum in 1857, it was renamed in 1899 in honor of Queen Victoria's late husband and has since grown to become one of the country's best-loved cultural institutions. Many collections at the V&A are presented not by period but by category—textiles, sculpture, jewelry, and so on. Nowhere is the benefit of this more apparent than in the **Fashion Gallery** (Room 40), where formal 18th-century court dresses are displayed alongside the haute couture styles of contemporary designers, creating an arresting sense of visual continuity. The **British Galleries** (rooms 52–58 and 118–125), devoted to British art and design from 1500 to 1900, are full of beautiful diversions—among them the Great Bed of Ware (immortalized in Shakespeare's *Twelfth Night*). The V&A is a tricky building to navigate, so be sure to use the free map. ⊠ *Cromwell Rd., South Kensington* ☎ *020/7942–2000* ⊕ *www.vam.ac.uk* ✉ *Free; charge for some special exhibitions (from £5)* ⊙ *Sat.–Thurs. 10–5:45, Fri. 10–10* Ⓜ *South Kensington.*

These ice-skaters outside the Natural History Museum in South Kensington are making the best of London's winter.

WORTH NOTING

Albert Memorial. This gleaming, neo-Gothic shrine to Prince Albert created by Sir Gilbert Scott epitomizes the Victorian era. After Albert's early death from typhoid in 1861, his grieving widow, Queen Victoria, had this elaborate confection erected to the west of where the Great Exhibition had been held a decade before. ⊠ *Kensington Gardens, Hyde Park, Kensington* Ⓜ *South Kensington, High Street Kensington.*

Marble Arch. John Nash's 1827 arch, moved here from Buckingham Palace in 1851, stands amid the traffic whirlpool where Bayswater Road segues into Oxford Street, at the top of Park Lane. The arch actually contains three small chambers, which served as a police station until the mid-20th century. Cross over (or under) to the northeastern corner of Hyde Park for Speakers' Corner, a parcel of land long-dedicated to the principle of free speech, and where every Sunday people of all views—or none at all—come to pontificate, listen, and debate about anything and everything under the sun. ⊠ *Park La., Mayfair* Ⓜ *Marble Arch.*

Science Museum. This, one of the three great South Kensington museums, stands next to the Natural History Museum in a far plainer building. It has lots of hands-on, painlessly educational exhibits, with entire schools of children apparently decanted inside to interact with them, but don't dismiss the Science Museum as just for kids. Highlights include the Launch Pad gallery, which demonstrates basic laws of physics; *Puffing Billy,* the oldest steam locomotive in the world; and the actual *Apollo 10* capsule. ⊠ *Exhibition Rd., South Kensington* ☎ 0870/870–4868 ⊕ *www.sciencemuseum.org.uk* ✉ *Free; charge for special exhibitions,* *cinema shows and simulator rides* ⊙ *Daily 10–6, 10–7 during school holidays (check website)* Ⓜ *South Kensington.*

Serpentine Gallery. Built in 1934 as a tea pavilion in Kensington Gardens, the Serpentine has an international reputation for exhibitions of modern and contemporary art. Man Ray, Henry Moore, Andy Warhol, Bridget Riley, Damien Hirst, and Rachel Whiteread are a few of the artists who have had exhibits here. An extension to the gallery is scheduled to open in the fall of 2013. The annual Summer Pavilion, a striking temporary structure designed by a different leading architect every year, is always worth catching. ⊠ *Kensington Gardens, Kensington* ☎ *020/7402–6075* ⊕ *www.serpentinegallery.org* 🎟 *Free* ⊙ *Daily 10–6* Ⓜ *Lancaster Gate, Knightsbridge, South Kensington.*

Wellington Arch. Opposite the Duke of Wellington's mansion, Apsley House, this majestic stone arch surveys the traffic rushing around Hyde Park Corner. Designed by Decimus Burton and built in 1828, it was created as a grand entrance to the west side of London and echoes the design of that other landmark gate, Marble Arch ⇨ *See above.* ⊠ *Hyde Park Corner, Mayfair* ☎ *020/7930–2726* ⊕ *www.english-heritage.org. uk* 🎟 *£4* ⊙ *Sun.–Wed. 10–5, but platform sometimes closed for exhibition installations; check website* Ⓜ *Hyde Park Corner.*

REGENT'S PARK AND HAMPSTEAD

Besides lovely Regent's Park and its attractions, this area is the showcase for some of the most aristocratic architecture in the world, thanks to the town houses of John Nash, 19th-century design whiz. They provide the setting for some splendid sights, from Keats House to—Strawberry Beatles Forever!—Abbey Road, the favorite studio of the Fab Four. Northward lies Hampstead, which continues its historic tradition of providing a haven for literati and some of the most stunning town-house architecture in England (think any Merchant Ivory film) while Primrose Hill is home to models and movie stars. Excellent bookshops, contemporary boutiques, and cozy cafés line tree-shaded blocks.

GETTING HERE
To get to Regent's Park, take the Bakerloo Line to Regent's Park Tube station or, for Primrose Hill, the Chalk Farm stop on the Northern Line. Reaching Hampstead by Tube is as easy as it looks: Simply take the Edgware branch of the Northern Line to the Hampstead station, or the aboveground North London line to Hampstead Heath. The south side of Hampstead Heath can also be reached by the Gospel Oak station on the North London line.

PLANNING YOUR TIME
Depending on your pace and inclination, Regent's Park and Hampstead can realistically be covered in a day. It might be best to spend the morning in Hampstead, then head south toward Regent's Park in the afternoon so that you're closer to central London come nightfall, if that is where your hotel is located.

TOP ATTRACTIONS

FAMILY
Fodor's Choice
★
Hampstead Heath. For an escape from the ordered prettiness of Hampstead, head to the Heath—a unique remnant of London's pre-industrial countryside, with habitats ranging from wide grasslands

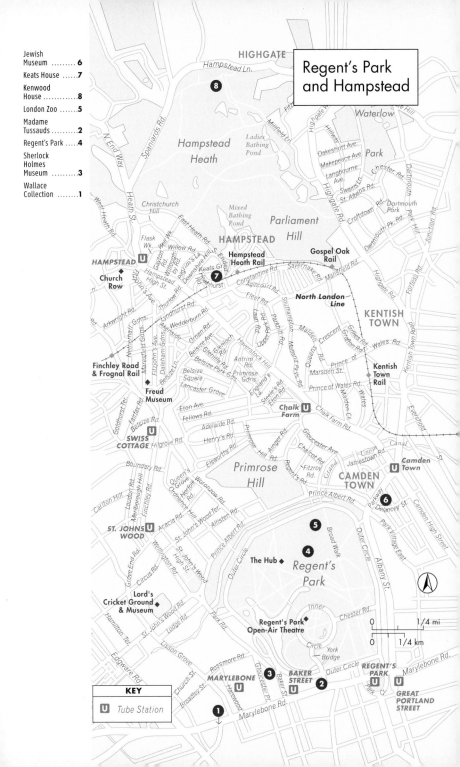

Regent's Park
and Hampstead

HIGHGATE

Hampstead Ln.

8

Waterlow

Hampstead
Heath

Ladies'
Bathing
Pond

Park

Oakeshott Ave.

Makepeace Ave.

Langbourne
Ave.

Swains Ln.

St. Albans Rd.

Croftdown

Rd.

Dartmouth
Park

Christchurch
Hill

Mixed
Bathing
Pond

Parliament
Hill

HAMPSTEAD

Dartmouth Pk. Rd.

Dartmouth Pk. Hill

Junction Rd.

Flask
Wk.

Willow Rd.

Keats Grove

Gospel Oak
Rail

HAMPSTEAD **U**

Church
Row

Hampstead
High St.

7

Downshire Hill

Hempstead
Heath Rail

Constantine Rd.

Savernake Rd.

Mansfield Rd.

Highgate Rd.

North London
Line

**KENTISH
TOWN**

Arkwright Rd.

Lyndhurst Rd.

Fleet Rd.

Agincourt Rd.

Southampton

Parkhill Rd.

Malden Rd.

Queen's Crescent

Grafton Rd.

Gilles Rd.

Wales Rd.

Finchley Road
& Frognal Rail

Mansfield Gdns.

Nethehall Gdns.

Fitzjohn's Ave.

Belsize Ave.

Glenloch Rd.

Glenilla Rd.

Antrim
Rd.

Belsize Park Gdns.

Primrose
Gdns.

Haverstock Hill

Prince of
Wales Rd.

Marsden St.

**Kentish
Town
Rail**

Wales

Evershot

**Freud
Museum**

Belsize
Square

Lancaster Grove

England's
La.

Steele's Rd.

Eton Rd.

Prince of Wales Rd.

Malden Rd.

Goldhurst Ter.

Fairfax Rd.

Belsize Rd.

Eton Ave.

Fellows Rd.

**Chalk
Farm** **U**

Chalk Farm Rd.

Canal

**SWISS
COTTAGE** **U**

Hilgrove Rd.

Adelaide Rd.

Henry's Rd.

Primrose
Hill Rd.

Gloucester Ave.

Union

Jamestown Rd.

Grand

**Camden
Town**

St.

Boundary Rd.

Elsworthy Rd.

Fitzroy
Rd.

Chalcot Rd.

**CAMDEN
TOWN** **U**

Camden High Street

Carlton Hill

Loudon Rd.

Marlborough Hill

Finchley Rd.

Queen's
Grove

Ordnance Hill

Norfolk
Rd.

Woronzow Rd.

**Primrose
Hill**

Regent's Rd.

Prince Albert Rd.

Parkway

Delancey St.

6

Park Village East

Albany St.

**ST. JOHNS
WOOD** **U**

Acacia Rd.

Grove End Rd.

Wellington Rd.

St. John's Wood Ter.

St. John's
Wood
High St.

Allitsen Rd.

Prince Albert Rd.

Outer Circle

5

Broad Walk

Outer Circle

**REGENT'S
PARK** **U**

Circus Rd.

The Hub ◆

4

**Regent's
Park**

**GREAT
PORTLAND
STREET** **U**

**Lord's
Cricket Ground
& Museum** ◆

St. John's Wood Rd.

Lodge Rd.

Park Rd.

Inner

Chester Rd.

Outer Circle

0 ___ 1/4 mi

Hamilton Ter.

Lisson Grove

Regent's Park
Open-Air Theatre ◆

Circle

York
Bridge

0 ___ 1/4 km

Edgware Rd.

Church St.

Bradley St.

Rossmore Rd.

MARYLEBONE **U**

3

Gloucester Pl.

Harewood

**BAKER
STREET** **U**

Baker St.

2

Outer Circle

Marylebone Rd.

1

Marylebone Rd.

to ancient woodlands spread over some 791 acres. **Parliament Hill,** one of the highest points in London, offers a stunning panorama over the city. ✉ *Hampstead* ☎ *020/7482–7073 Heath Education Centre* ⊕ *www.cityoflondon.gov.uk/hampstead* ✏ *Free* Ⓜ *Gospel Oak, Hampstead Heath for south of Heath; Hampstead for east of Heath; Golders Green, then Bus 210, 268 to Whitestone Pond for north and west of Heath.*

Keats House. It was in February 1820 that John Keats (1795–1821) coughed blood up into his handkerchief and exclaimed, "That drop of blood is my death warrant. I must die." Here you can see the plum tree under which the young Romantic poet composed *Ode to a Nightingale;* many of his original manuscripts; his library; and other possessions he managed to acquire in his short life. ▥TIP➜ Picnics can be taken into the grounds during the summer. ✉ *Wentworth Pl., Keats Grove, Hampstead* ☎ *020/7332–3868* ⊕ *www.keatshouse.cityoflondon.gov.uk* ✏ *£5* ⊙ *Apr.–Oct., Tues.–Sun. 1–5; Nov.–Mar., Fri.–Sun. 1–5; closed Good Friday and Christmas wk* Ⓜ *Hampstead; North London Line overground: Hampstead Heath from Highbury & Islington.*

FAMILY **Kenwood House.** This gracious Georgian villa was first built in 1616 and remodeled by Robert Adam between 1764 and 1779. Adam refaced most of the exterior and added the splendid library, which, with its curved painted ceiling and gilded detail, is the highlight of the house for lovers of the decorative arts and interior design. Kenwood is also home to the **Iveagh Bequest,** an extraordinary collection of paintings that the Earl of Iveagh gave the nation in 1927, including a wonderful self-portrait by Rembrandt and works by Reynolds, Van Dyck, Hals, Gainsborough, and Turner. Most iconic amongst them is Vermeer's *Guitar Player,* considered by many to be among the most beautiful paintings in the world. ✉ *Hampstead La., Hampstead* ☎ *020/8348–1286* ⊕ *www.english-heritage.org.uk* ✏ *Free* ⊙ *House daily 11:30–4. Gardens daily dawn–dusk* Ⓜ *Golders Green, then Bus 210.*

FAMILY
Fodor's Choice
★
London Zoo. Owned by the Zoological Society of London (a charity), the zoo opened in 1828. A recent modernization program has seen the introduction of several big attractions, with a focus on wildlife conservation, education, and the breeding of endangered species. The huge **BUGS** pavilion (Biodiversity Underpinning Global Survival) is a self-sustaining, contained ecosystem with 140 species of exotic plants, animals, and creepy-crawlies. At **Gorilla Kingdom** you can watch the four residents— Effie, Kesho, Jookie, and Zaire—at close range. **Rainforest Life** is a recreated nighttime rain-forest environment, home to tiny marmosets and other rain-forest-dwelling creatures, including bats. The new **Children's Zoo** allows kids to see a host of unusual creatures up close, including aardvarks and mongooses. It also contains play areas and a petting zoo. ▥TIP➜ Check the website or the information board out front for free events, including creature close encounters and "ask the keeper" sessions. ✉ *Outer Circle, Regent's Park* ☎ *020/7722–3333* ⊕ *www.zsl.org* ✏ *£20* ⊙ *Mid-Nov.–Feb., daily 10–4; Mar.–early Sept., daily 10–6; early-Sept.–Oct., daily 10–5:30; early–mid-Nov., daily 10–4:30; last admission 1 hr before closing* Ⓜ *Camden Town, then Bus 274.*

A TRIP TO ABBEY ROAD

For countless Beatlemaniacs and baby boomers, No. 3 Abbey Road is one of the most beloved spots in London. Here, outside the legendary Abbey Road Studios, is the most famous zebra crossing in the world, immortalized on the Beatles' 1969 *Abbey Road* album. This footpath became a mod monument when, on August 8 of that year, John, Paul, George, and Ringo posed for photographer Iain Macmillan's famous cover shot. The recording facility's Studio 2 is where the Beatles recorded their entire output, from "Love Me Do" onward, including *Sgt. Pepper's Lonely Hearts Club Band* (early 1967).

Meanwhile, there's never any shortage of tourists re-creating "the photo" outside. One of the best—and safer—ways Beatle lovers can enjoy

the history of the group is to take one of the excellent walking tours offered by **Original London Walks** (☎ *020/7624–3978* ⊕ *www.walks. com*), including **The Beatles In-My-Life Walk** (11:20 am outside Marylebone Underground on Saturday and Tuesday) and **The Beatles Magical Mystery Tour** (Wednesday at 2 pm, February to November, and Thursday and Sunday at 11 am, year-round, at Underground Exit 3, Tottenham Court Road), which cover nostalgic landmark Beatles spots in the city.

Abbey Road is in the elegant neighborhood of St. John's Wood, a 10-minute ride on the Tube from central London. Take the Jubilee line to the St. John's Wood Tube stop, head southwest three blocks down Grove End Road, and be prepared for a view right out of Memory Lane.

FAMILY **Regent's Park.** Cultivated and formal, compared with the relative wildness of Hampstead Heath, Regent's Park was laid out in 1812 by John Nash in honor of the Prince Regent, who was later crowned George IV. The idea was to re-create the feel of a grand country residence close to the center of town. Your nostrils should lead you to **Queen Mary's Gardens,** a fragrant 17-acre circle that riots with 400 different varieties of roses in summer. ⊠ *Marylebone Rd., Regent's Park* ☎ *0300/061–2000* ⊕ *www.royalparks. gov.uk* ⌑ *Free* ☉ *5 am–dusk* Ⓜ *Baker St., Regent's Park, Great Portland St.*

Sherlock Holmes Museum. Outside Baker Street station, by the Marylebone Road exit, is a 9-foot-high bronze statue of the celebrated detective. Nearby is number 221B Baker Street—the address of Arthur Conan Doyle's fictional detective. Inside, Mrs. Hudson, "Holmes's housekeeper," conducts you into a series of Victorian rooms full of Sherlock-abilia. There's more than enough photo ops, and it's all carried off with such genuine enthusiasm that you almost believe that the fictional detective really lived here. ⊠ *221B Baker St., Regent's Park* ☎ *020/7224–3688* ⊕ *www.sherlock-holmes.co.uk* ⌑ *£6* ☉ *Daily 9:30–6* Ⓜ *Baker St.*

FAMILY
Fodor'sChoice
★
Wallace Collection. This exquisite labyrinth of an art gallery is housed in Hertford House, an 18th-century mansion that was bequeathed to the nation, along with its contents, by the widow of Sir Richard Wallace (1818–1890). The full list of painters in the collection reads like a roll call of classical European masters, from Rubens, Rembrandt, and Van Dyck to Canaletto, Titian, and Velázquez. English works include paintings by Gainsborough and Turner, plus a dozen by Joshua Reynolds.

⊠ *Hertford House, Manchester Sq., Marylebone* ☎ *020/7563–9500*
⊕ *www.wallacecollection.org* 🗐 *Free* ☉ *Daily 10–5* Ⓜ *Bond St.*

WORTH NOTING

Jewish Museum. This fascinating museum on the history of the Jewish people in Britain contains precious little from before the 17th century–and with good reason. Judaism was outlawed in England for almost four centuries, until the Jews were finally allowed to settle once more in 1656. "History: A British Story" provides a general overview of this and other facets of the Jewish story in Britain over the centuries, through a mix of rare artifacts and interactive displays. ⊠ *Raymond Burton House, 129–131 Albert St., Camden Town* ☎ *020/7284–7384* ⊕ *www.jewishmuseum. org.uk* 🗐 *£7.50* ☉ *Sun.–Thurs. 10–5, Fri. 10–2; last admission 30 min before closing. Closed on major Jewish festivals* Ⓜ *Camden Town.*

FAMILY **Madame Tussauds.** One of London's busiest tourist attractions, this is nothing less—but also nothing more—than the world's most famous exhibition of lifelike waxwork models of celebrities. Madame T. learned her craft while making death masks of French Revolution victims, and in 1835 she set up her first show of the famous ones near this spot. Top billing still goes to the murderers in the Chamber of Horrors, who stare glassy-eyed at visitors—one from an electric chair, one sitting next to the tin bath where he dissolved several wives in quicklime. ∎ TIP➔ **Beat the crowds by booking timed entry tickets in advance. You can also buy non-dated, "priority access" tickets via the website (at a premium).** ⊠ *Marylebone Rd., Regent's Park* ☎ *0870/400–3000 for timed entry tickets* ⊕ *www.madame-tussauds.com* 🗐 *£15–£35 according to time; call or check website. Combination ticket with London Eye, London Dungeons, and London Aquarium from £35–£57.* ☉ *Early Apr. and mid-Jul.–Aug., daily 9–7; Sept.–Mar. and mid-Apr.–mid-Jul., weekdays 9–5:30 (last admission); weekends 9:30–6 (last admission).* Ⓜ *Baker St.*

UP AND DOWN THE THAMES

Downstream—meaning seaward, or east—from central London, Greenwich has enough riches, especially if the maritime theme is your thing, that you should allow a very full day to see them. Upstream, the royal palaces and grand houses that dot the area were built not as town houses but as country residences with easy access to London by river; Hampton Court Palace is the best and biggest of all.

GREENWICH

8 miles east of central London.

Greenwich makes an ideal day out from central London, thanks to its historic and maritime attractions. Sir Christopher Wren's Royal Naval College and Inigo Jones's Queen's House reach architectural heights; the Old Royal Observatory measured time for the entire planet; and the Greenwich Meridian divides the world in two. You can stand astride it with one foot in either hemisphere. The National Maritime Museum will appeal to seafaring types, and landlubbers can stroll the parkland that surrounds the buildings, the pretty 19th-century houses, and the weekend crafts and antiques markets.

Docklands Light Railway (DLR) is a zippy way to get to Cutty Sark station, from Canary Wharf and Bank Tube stations in the City. Or take the DLR to Island Gardens and walk the old Victorian Foot Tunnel under the river. The best way to arrive, however—time and weather permitting—is like a sea captain of old: by water.

Fodor's Choice
★

Cutty Sark. This sleek, romantic clipper was built in 1869, one among fleets and fleets of tall-masted wooden ships that plied the oceanic highways of the 19th century, trading in exotic commodities—in this case, tea. *Cutty Sark* (named after an old Scottish term for women's undergarments) was the fastest, sailing the London–China route in 1871 in only 107 days. The ship re-opened in 2012, with hugely improved visitor facilities; not only can you tour the painstakingly restored ship in its entirety, but the glittering new visitor center (above which the ship now rests, in an enormous gold mount) allows you to view the hull from below. ⊠ *King William Walk, Greenwich* ☎ *020/8858-4422* ⊕ *www.rmg.co.uk* ☒ *£12* ☉ *Daily, 10-5; last admission 4* Ⓜ *DLR: Cutty Sark.*

Fodor's Choice
★

National Maritime Museum. From the time of Henry VIII until the 1940s Britain was the world's preeminent naval power, and the collections here trace half a millennium of that seafaring history. The story is as much about trade as it is warfare; the "Atlantic Worlds" gallery explores how trade in goods—and people—helped shape the New World, while "Voyagers: Britons and the Sea" focuses on stories of the ordinary people who took to the waves over the centuries. One gallery is devoted to Admiral Lord Nelson, Britain's most famous naval commander, and among the exhibits is the uniform he was wearing, complete with bloodstains, when he died at the Battle of Trafalgar in 1805. The adjacent **Queen's House** is home to the museum's art collection, the largest collection of maritime art in the world, including works by William Hogarth, Canaletto, and Joshua Reynolds. ⊠ *Romney Rd., Greenwich* ☎ *020/8858-4422* ⊕ *www.rmg.co.uk* ☒ *Free* ☉ *Daily 10-5; last admission 30 min before closing* Ⓜ *DLR: Greenwich.*

QUICK BITES

Trafalgar Tavern. With its excellent vista of the Thames, there is no more handsomely situated pub in Greenwich than the Trafalgar Tavern. Featured in Charles Dickens's *Our Mutual Friend,* it's still as grand a place to have a pint and some (upscale) pub grub as it ever was. ⊠ *Park Row, Greenwich* ☎ *020/8858-2909* ⊕ *www.trafalgartavern.co.uk.*

Old Royal Naval College. Begun by Christopher Wren in 1694 as a rest home for ancient mariners, the college became instead a school for young ones in 1873. Today the University of Greenwich and Trinity College of Music have classes here. Architecturally, you'll notice how the structures part to reveal the **Queen's House** across the central lawns. Behind the college are two more buildings you can visit: the **Painted Hall,** the college's dining hall, derives its name from the baroque murals of William and Mary (reigned 1689–95; William alone 1695–1702) and assorted allegorical figures. ⊠ *Old Royal Naval College, King William Walk, Greenwich* ☎ *020/8269-4747* ⊕ *www.ornc.org* ☒ *Free, guided tours £6* ☉ *Painted Hall and chapel daily 10–5 (Sun. chapel from 12:30); grounds 8–6* Ⓜ *DLR: Greenwich.*

Among the botanical splendors of Kew Gardens is the Waterlily House.

FAMILY **Royal Observatory.** Greenwich is on the prime meridian at 0° longitude, and the ultimate standard for time around the world has been set here since 1884, when Britain was the world's largest and most important maritime power. The observatory is actually split into two sites, a short walk apart—one devoted to astronomy, the other to the study of time. The enchanting **Peter Harrison Planetarium** is London's only planetarium, its bronze-clad turret poking out of the ground like a crashed UFO. Shows on black holes and how to interpret the night sky are enthralling and enlightening. Even better for kids are the high-technology rooms of the **Astronomy Galleries,** where cutting-edge touch screens and interactive programs give young explorers the chance to run their own space missions to Ganymede, one of Jupiter's moons. Across the way is **Flamsteed House,** designed by Christopher Wren in 1675 for John Flamsteed, the first Royal Astronomer. In the **Time Galleries,** linger over the superb workmanship of John Harrison (1693–1776), whose famous **Maritime Clocks** won him the Longitude Prize for solving the problem of accurate timekeeping at sea and greatly improved navigation.

A brass line laid among the cobblestones here marks the meridian, one side being the Eastern, one the Western hemisphere. As darkness falls, a funky green laser shoots out across London for several miles, following exactly the path of the meridian line. ⊠ *Romney Rd., Greenwich* ☎ *020/8858–4422* ⊕ *www.rog.nmm.ac.uk* ✉ *Astronomy Galleries free; Flamstead house and Meridian Line courtyard £7; planetarium shows £6.50; combined ticket £11.50.* ☯ *Daily 10–5 (May–Aug., Meridian courtyard until 6); last entry 30 min before closing; last planetarium show 4* Ⓜ *DLR: Greenwich.*

HAMPTON COURT PALACE
20 miles southwest of central London.

FAMILY

Fodor'sChoice

★

Hampton Court Palace. The beloved seat of Henry VIII's court, sprawled elegantly beside the languid waters of the Thames, this beautiful palace really gives you two for the price of one: the magnificent Tudor red-brick mansion, begun in 1514 by Cardinal Wolsey to curry favor with the young Henry, and the larger 17th-century baroque building, which was partly designed by Christopher Wren (of St. Paul's fame). The earliest buildings on this site belonged to a religious order founded in the 11th century and were expanded over the years by its many subsequent residents, until George II moved the royal household closer to London in the early 18th century.

Wander through the **State Apartments,** decorated in the Tudor style, complete with priceless paintings, and on to the wood-beamed magnificence of **Henry's Great Hall,** before taking in the strikingly azure ceiling of the **Chapel Royal.** Well-handled reconstructions of Tudor life take place all year, from live appearances by "Henry VIII" and his elaborately-costumed court, to a small retinue of cook-historians preparing authentic Tudor feasts in the 15th-century **Henry's Kitchens.** Latter-day masters of the palace, the joint rulers William and Mary (reigned 1689–1702), were responsible for the beautiful **King's and Queen's Apartments** and the elaborate baroque of the **Georgian Rooms.** Don't miss the famous **maze** (the oldest hedge maze in the world), its half mile of pathways among clipped hedgerows still fiendish to negotiate. There's a trick, but we won't give it away here: It's much more fun just to go and lose yourself. ⊠ *Hampton Court Rd., East Molesley, Surrey* ☎ *0844/482–7799 tickets, 0844/482–7777 information (24 hr.)* ⊕ *www.hrp.org.uk/hamptoncourtpalace* ⊠ *Palace, maze, and gardens £17; maze only £3.85; gardens only £5.50 (free Oct.–Mar.)* ☉ *Late Mar.–Oct., daily 10–6; Nov.–late Mar., daily 10–4:30; last admission one hr before closing; last entry to maze 45 mins before closing); check website before visiting* Ⓜ *Richmond, then bus R68; National Rail: Hampton Court Station, 35 min from Waterloo (most trains require change at Surbiton).*

KEW GARDENS
6 miles southwest of central London.

FAMILY

Kew Gardens. Enter the Royal Botanic Gardens, as Kew Gardens are also known, and you are enveloped by blazes of color, extraordinary blooms, hidden trails, and lovely old follies. Beautiful though it all is, Kew's charms are secondary to its true purpose as a major center for serious research. First opened to the public in 1840, Kew has been supported by royalty and nurtured by landscapers, botanists, and architects since the 1720s. Today the gardens, now a Unesco World Heritage site, hold more than 30,000 species of plants, from every corner of the globe. Although the plant houses make Kew worth visiting even in the depths of winter, the flower beds are, of course, best enjoyed in the fullness of spring and summer. Architect Sir William Chambers built a series of temples and follies, of which the crazy 10-story **Pagoda,** visible for miles around, is the star turn. Two great 19th-century greenhouses—the **Palm House** and the **Temperate House**—are filled with exotic blooms, and many of the plants have been there since the final glass panel was fixed into place. The Princess of Wales Conservatory houses 10 climate zones, and the Rhizotron and Xstrata Treetop Walkway takes you 59 feet up into the air. ☒ *Kew Rd. at Lichfield Rd., for Victoria Gate entrance, Kew* ☎ *020/8332–5655* ⊕ *www.kew.org* ☛ *£16* ☾ *Mid-Feb.–mid Mar., daily 9:30–5:30; mid-Mar.–Aug., weekdays 9:30–6:30, weekends 9:30–7:30; Sept. and Oct., daily 9:30–6; Nov.–mid-Feb. daily 9:30–4:15. Glasshouses and galleries close 5:30 (3:45 Nov.–mid-Feb., 5 mid-Feb.–late Mar.); Palm House closes 2 on Tues.* Ⓜ *Kew Gardens. National Rail: Kew Gardens, Kew Bridge.*

Fodor'sChoice
★

Kew Palace and Queen Charlotte's Cottage. The elegant red-brick exterior of the smallest of Britain's royal palaces seems almost humble when compared with the grandeur of, say, Buckingham or Kensington palaces. Yet inside is a fascinating glimpse into life at the uppermost end of society from the 17th to 19th centuries. This is actually the third of several palaces that stood here; once known as Dutch House, it was one of the havens to which George III retired when insanity forced him to withdraw from public life. ☒ *Kew Gardens, Kew Rd. at Lichfield Rd., Kew* ☎ *0844/482 7777 (only in U.K.), 020/3166–6000* ⊕ *www.hrp. org.uk* ☛ *£6, in addition to ticket for Kew Gardens* ☾ *Apr.–Sept., daily 10–5:15; Oct., Thurs.–Sun 11–4; also daily during school holidays, late Oct. and late Feb. (call to confirm times)* Ⓜ *Kew Gardens.*

QUICK BITES	**The Original Maids of Honour.** This most traditional of Old English tearooms, is named for a type of jam tart invented here and still baked by hand on the premises. Tea is served daily 2:30–6, lunch in two sittings at 12:30 and 1:30. Or opt for take-out to picnic at Kew Gardens or on Kew Green. ☒ *288 Kew Rd., Kew* ☎ *020/8940–2752* ⊕ *www. theoriginalmaidsofhonour.co.uk.*

WHERE TO EAT

Use the coordinate (✛ B2) at the end of each listing to locate a site on the corresponding map.

As anyone knows who reads the papers, London's had a restaurant boom, or rather, a restaurant atomic-bomb explosion. More than ever, Londoners love their restaurants—all 6,700 of them—from its be-here-right-now, wow-factor West End gastro-emporiums to its tiny neighborhood joints. You, too, will be smitten, because you'll be spending, on average, 25% of your travel budget on eating out.

Today nearly everything on the culinary front has dramatically changed from the days of steamed suet puddings and over-boiled Brussels sprouts. Everyone's mad about food, while a wall of City and hot global money has souped up standards remarkably. Celebrity chefs abound. One week it's Wolfgang Puck at CUT at 45 Park Lane that's the flavor of the month, the next it's Jason Atherton at the Pollen Street Social in Mayfair. Thankfully, pride in the best of authentic British food—local, seasonal, regional, wild, and foraged—has made a resurgence and appears on more menus by the day. The new wave of waste-not, want-not "nose-to-tail" eating—where every scrap of meat is deemed fair game for the plate—made its first spectacular comeback at St. John in Clerkenwell, and chimes perfectly with the new age of austerity.

These days, standards are higher and poor-quality shepherd's pie has been largely replaced by the city's unofficial dish, the ubiquitous spiced Indian curry. London's food quake is built on its incredible ethnic diversity, and you'll find the quality of other international cuisines has also grown immeasurably in recent years, with London becoming known for its Chinese, Japanese, Indian, Thai, Spanish, Italian, French, Persian, and North African restaurants. With all the choices, traditional British food, when you track it down, appears as just one more exotic cuisine in the pantheon.

PRICES AND SAVING MONEY

London is a very pricey city by global standards. A modest meal for two can easily cost £40, and the £110-a-head meal is not unknown. Damage-control strategies include making lunch your main meal—the top places have bargain midday menus—going for early- or late-evening deals, or sharing an à la carte entrée and ordering a second appetizer instead. Seek out fixed-price menus, and watch for hidden extras on the check, that is, bread or vegetables charged separately.

TIPPING AND TAXES

Do not tip bar staff in pubs and bars—though you can always offer to buy them a drink. In restaurants, tip 12.5% of the check for full meals if service is not already included; tip a small token if you're just having coffee or tea. If paying by credit card, double-check that a tip has not already been included in the bill.

WESTMINSTER, ST. JAMES'S, AND ROYAL LONDON

ST. JAMES'S

$$$

MODERN
EUROPEAN

Fodor'sChoice

★

✕ **Le Caprice.** Celeb-*ville* grande dame Le Caprice commands the deepest loyalty of any restaurant in London. *Why?* Because of the *memories* . . . and because it gets practically everything right—*every* time. It's the 30-year celebrity history—think Liz Taylor, Joan Collins and Lady Di—the haunting David Bailey black-and-white portraits, designer Martin Brudnizki's updated décor, charming Bolivian-born Jesus Adorno the veteran maître'd, the perfect service, and the long-standing menu that sits somewhere between Euro peasant and trendy fashion plate. Sit at the raised counter or at a corner table and enjoy calves' liver with crispy bacon, roast pheasant with caramalized quince—all served with an ample dollop of *"SHHush! Don't-Look-Now-Dear!"* star spotting. $ *Average main: £23* ⊠ *Arlington House, Arlington St., St. James's* ☎ *020/7629–2239* ⊕ *www.caprice-holdings.co.uk* ⬥ *Reservations essential* Ⓜ *Green Park* ✛ *D4.*

$$$$

BRITISH

✕ **Wiltons.** Aristos, blue bloods, and the *extremely* well-to-do blow the family bank at this old-fashioned bastion of English fine dining on pedigreed Jermyn St. (the place first opened on the Haymarket as a shellfish stall in 1742). Invariably fresh from a little snooze in their nearby St. James's gentlemen's clubs, male diners are required to wear jackets at all times at this clubby time capsule and *frightfully* snooty ode to all things

BEST BETS FOR LONDON DINING

Where can I find the best food London has to offer? Fodor's writers and editors have selected their favorite restaurants by price, cuisine, and experience in the lists below. In the first column, the Fodor's Choice properties represent the "best of the best" across price categories. You can also search by neighborhood for excellent eating experiences—just peruse our complete reviews on the following pages.

Fodor's Choice ★

10 Greek Street, $$, p. 97

Brasserie Zédel, $, p. 100

Bubbledogs, $, p. 105

CUT at 45 Park Lane, $$$$, p. 116

Dabbous, $$, p. 106

The Delaunay, $$, p. 102

Dinner by Heston Blumenthal, $$$$, p. 113

The Giaconda Dining Rooms, $$, p. 101

Great Queen Street, $$, p. 103

Harwood Arms, $$, p. 113

The Ledbury, $$$, p. 120

Le Caprice, $$, p. 95

Mari Vanna, $$$, p. 115

Petrus, $$, p. 115

Pollen Street Social, $$$, p. 118

Rules, $$$, p. 104

Spuntino, $, p. 102

St. John, $$, p. 108

Tom Aikens, $$$$, p. 112

Viajante, $$$, p. 109

Zucca, $, p. 112

Best by Price

$

Brasserie Zédel, p. 100

Busaba Eathai, p. 100

Côte, p. 102

Golden Hind, p. 119

$$

10 Greek Street, p. 97

Dabbous, p. 106

The Delaunay, p. 102

Giaconda Dining Rooms, p. 101

Great Queen Street, p. 103

Harwood Arms, p. 113

Lima, p. 101

The Riding House Café, p. 118

St. John, p. 108

Zucca, p. 112

$$$

The Ledbury, p. 120

Mari Vanna, p. 115

Petrus, p. 115

Viajante, p. 109

$$$$

Scott's, p. 119

Tom Aikens, p. 112

Best by Cuisine

BRITISH

Great Queen Street, $$, p. 103

Harwood Arms, $$, p. 113

Hereford Road, $$, p. 120

The Orange, $$, p. 113

St. John, $$, p. 108

FRENCH

The Delaunay, $$, p. 102

La Petite Maison, $$$, p. 117

The Ledbury, $$$, p. 120

Petrus, $$$, p. 115

The Riding House Café, $$, p. 118

ITALIAN

Bocca di Lupo, $$, p. 100

Cecconi's, $$$, p. 116

L'Anima, $$$, p. 107

Best by Experience

HOT SPOTS

CUT at 45 Park Lane, $$$$, p. 116

Pollen Street Social, $$$$, p. 118

The Ledbury, $$$, p. 120

Scott's, $$$$, p. 119

Spuntino, $, p. 102

GASTRO-PUBS

Great Queen Street, $$, p. 103

Harwood Arms, $$, p. 113

The Orange, $$, p. 102

HISTORIC

Rules, $$$, p. 104

Sweetings, $$, p. 107

Wiltons, $$$$, p. 95

2

English. Signet ring–wearing posh patrons like to take half-a-dozen finest Colchester oysters, followed by grilled Dover sole on the bone, or fabulous native game in season, such as grouse, woodcock, partridge, or teal. There are long-forgotten savories like anchovies or mushrooms on toast, plus nursery desserts like sherry trifle and bread and butter pudding. Service, naturally, would put Jeeves to shame. $ *Average main: £32* ✉ *55 Jermyn St., St. James's* ☎ *020/7629–9955* ⊕ *www.wiltons. co.uk* ⌕ *Reservations essential* 🏛 *Jacket required* ☉ *Closed weekends* Ⓜ *Green Park* ✛ *D3.*

$$
AUSTRIAN
FAMILY
Fodor's Choice
★

✕ **The Wolseley.** The whole of beau London comes for the always-on-show spectacle and soaring elegance at this Viennese-style *Mitteleuropa* grand café on Piccadilly. Framed with black laquerware and silver service, and a few doors down from the Ritz, this all-day brasserie begins its long decadent days with breakfast at 7 am and serves until midnight. Don't be shy to pop in on spec (they hold seats back for walk-ins) to enjoy such highlights as Hungarian goulash, Austrian pork belly, chicken soup with salt beef sandwich, eggs Benedict, kedgeree, or the breaded *Wiener Schnitzel.* Book a return table to savor the Viennoise pastries at one of their classy £9.75 to £32.50 afternoon teas. $ *Average main: £18* ✉ *160 Piccadilly, St. James's* ☎ *020/7499–6996* ⊕ *www. thewolseley.com* ⌕ *Reservations essential* Ⓜ *Green Park* ✛ *D4.*

SOHO AND COVENT GARDEN

SOHO

$$
MODERN
EUROPEAN
Fodor's Choice
★

✕ **10 Greek Street.** There may only be 28 seats and 9 counter stools overlooking the open kitchen at this stripped-back, Formica-topped, indy-spirited, and upstart Modern European humdinger, but talented Aussie chef Cameron Emirali and former wine merchant Luke Wilson dish up the gourmet goods and have seriously got their schtick together. Great food? *Tick.* Cheap wine? *Tick.* Cute service? *Tick.* Decent prices? *Tick.* Buzz? *Tick.* The only negative is the no reservations policy in the evenings, but most happily saunter off for a quick shifty in the pub, three doors down, and wait to be called back on their cell phones. Once seated, expect simple interchangeable starter/mains like grilled sardines with salsify and salsa verde, or octopus carpaccio with caperberries, chili, and lemon. Gutsy meats like Welsh Black ribeye with horseradish, hare and polenta, or venison with parsnips and cranberry are big and bold, and swing with the seaons, as are the top-value £4–£6 puds, like lemon delicious, rum pannacotta, or quince and apple pie. $ *Average main: £16* ✉ *10 Greek Street, Soho* ☎ *020/7734 4677* ⊕ *www.10greekstreet.com* ☉ *Closed Sun.* ✛ *E3.*

$$
MEDITERRANEAN

✕ **Andrew Edmunds.** Well-worn, candlelit, and with an overwhelming Dickensian vibe to it, Andrew Edmunds is a permanently packed, deeply romantic olde-world Soho institution—though it could be larger, less creaky underfoot, and the reclaimed church-pew wooden bench seats more forgiving. Tucked away behind Carnaby St., it's a cozy favorite with the insider Soho media mafia that come for daily changing, hand-written, fixed-price lunch menus and the overall quirky/historic vibe. Satisfyingly rustic and keenly priced starters and mains draw on the tastes of Ireland, the Med, and the Middle East. Harissa-spiced

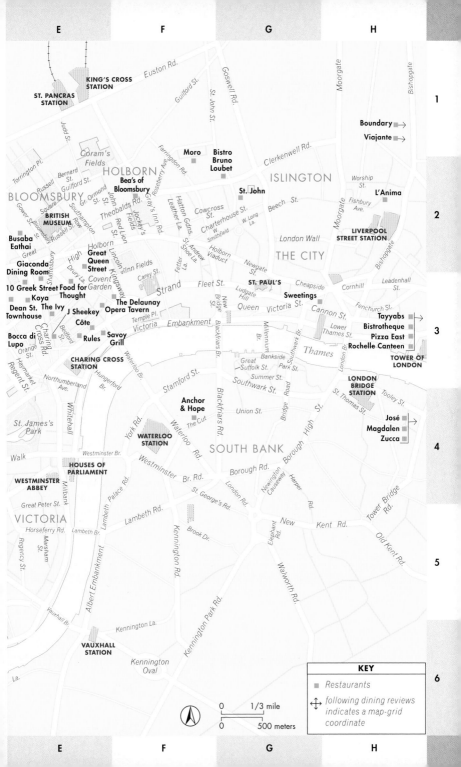

mackerel, woodcock on toast, goose rillettes, seafood paella, and pork belly with apple purée are all hale and hearty. $ *Average main: £16* ✉ *46 Lexington St., Soho* ☎ *020/7437 5708* ⚠ *Reservations essential* Ⓜ *Oxford Circus, Piccadilly Circus* ⊹ *D3.*

$$
ITALIAN
✕ **Bocca di Lupo.** The place is always packed, the tables are too close together, and the acoustics suck, but everyone tips up for the buzz and chef Jacob Kenedy's punchy and unusual regional Italian rustic fare. Red-brick fronted and set in an unlikely street off Soho's red-light district, this popular family-run place offers a procession of small plates and peasant-based dishes from Piedmont to Emilia, Lombardy to Campania. Try drop-dead offerings like buffalo mozzarella, suckling pig, teal, polenta with anchovies, Sicilian lobster spaghetti, or *baccala* home-salted pollack. Limber up with a colorful Aperol spritz before plunging into the regional Italian-focused wine list, which weaves from Gavi di Gavi to rare Barolo's. $ *Average main: £16* ✉ *12 Archer St., Soho* ☎ *020/7734–2223* ⊕ *www. boccadilupo.com* ⚠ *Reservations essential* Ⓜ *Piccadilly Circus* ⊹ *D3.*

$
BRASSERIE
FAMILY
Fodor's Choice
★
✕ **Brasserie Zédel.** Vichyssoise *soupe du jour* with sliced baguette, butter, and a jug of water for £2.25? A prix-fixe with steak haché and frites in a silver cup for £8.75? Or a 3-course daily set meal with salade Mâche, confit duck, a glass of red, water, and coffee for £19.75? *And* just off Piccadilly, in a glam and gilded art deco/Beaux Arts gastro and jazz-bar basement emporium? *Surely* some mistake? But no, these are a few indecently priced steals on offer at restaurateurs Corbin and King's *magnifique* take on an all-day Parisian-style brasserie ("Chartier by way of La Coupole," says King), just north of Piccadilly Circus. Save centimes on a classic *céleri rémoulade* for £2.95 or *soupe de poisson* for £4.95 in a soaring salon of leather banquettes, marbled columns, mirrors, and stained birch tops. Afterward, imbibe at the swank Bar Américain, or enjoy live jazz or cabaret at the in-house The Crazy Coqs. $ *Average main: £8* ✉ *20 Sherwood St., Soho* ☎ *020/7734 4888* ⊕ *www.brasseriezedel.com* Ⓜ *Piccadilly Circus* ⊹ *D3.*

$
THAI
FAMILY
✕ **Busaba Eathai.** It's top Thai nosh for little *moolah* at this sleek and sultry modern Thai canteen in the heart of Soho. Fitted with dark-wood bench seats and hardwood tables, this flagship restaurant has communal dining, rapid service, low lighting, and often fast-moving queues out front. Pour yourself a lemongrass tea, then try ginger beef with Thai pepper, classic crunchy green papaya salad, chicken with shiitake mushrooms, jungle curry, vermicelli with prawns, squid, and scallops, or other tasty winners. You'll escape for about £15 a head, and all in all, this makes for a top-value tummy-filler and a fine pit-stop during a West End shopping safari. $ *Average main: £11* ✉ *106–110 Wardour St., Soho* ☎ *020/7255–8686* ⊕ *www.busaba.com* ⚠ *Reservations not accepted* Ⓜ *Tottenham Court Rd.* ⊹ *E2.*

$$
BRITISH
✕ **Dean Street Townhouse.** Everyone feels ten times more glamorous once they step into this buzzy Soho mustering point, attached to the stylish 39-room Georgian hotel of the same name. Soft lighting, dark-wood floors, red leather banquettes, raised bar seats, and walls crammed with Brit-pack drawings and daubings create a hip hang-out for London's good-looking media elite. No-frills, no-fuss retro-British favorites include pea and ham soup, plain mince and potatoes, twice-baked smoked haddock

soufflé, chicken, bacon and mushroom pie, or toad-in-the-hole, plus yum-milicous sherry trifle, Trinity burnt cream, or sticky toffee pudding. You'll find fruit scones and buttered crumpets for afternoon tea, Welsh rarebit for "high tea," and a decent smattering of vaguely-familiar looking celebs fiddling around on their iPhones. $ *Average main: £19* ⊠ *69–71 Dean St., Soho* ☎ *020/7434–1775* ⊕ *www.deanstreettownhouse.com* ⌒ *Reservations essential* Ⓜ *Tottenham Court Rd.* ✛ *E3.*

$$

MODERN
EUROPEAN
Fodor's Choice
★

✕ **The Giaconda Dining Rooms.** A gastro-landmark with an indie spirit on Denmark Street's Tin Pan Alley—think Bowie, Marley, and The Clash—off Tottenham Court Road, this super friendly Australian-run dining room has an eclectic menu that is both distinctive and inspired. Chef Paul Merrony describes his food as "French-ish, with a couple of day trips to Italy thrown in," and this relaxed approach is reflected as he nonchalantly sends out mighty starters—creamed shallots with horserad-ish, crispy pig's trotters, or baked eggs with cream and tomatoes—and a full range of luscious entrées at decent prices. Try the ox tongue, rack of lamb with gnocchi "alla Romana," guinea fowl with prunes, or heartier dishes like veal kidneys, black pudding with potatoes, or ham hock hash with a fried egg on top. $ *Average main: £16* ⊠ *9 Denmark St., Soho* ☎ *020/7240–3334* ⊕ *www.giacondadining.com* ⌒ *Reservations essential* ◐ *Closed Sun. No lunch Sat.* Ⓜ *Tottenham Court Rd.* ✛ *E3.*

$

JAPANESE

✕ **Koya.** Is it the hours of foot kneading—albeit under canvas, to allay hygene concerns—that makes the hand-pulled Sanuki udon wheat-flour noodles here so springy, spongy, slurpy, and *so* addictive? Lines of Japa-nese diners and hip and heritage-clad Soho-ites are a testament to the allure of the tasty dishes served at this tiny Zen-like cult *udon-ya*, or noodle house, on Frith Street. Once inside, start with cold udon on a bamboo basket with pungent miso and pickled pork, and then—*if* you're up for it—slurp hot udon with smoked mackerel and Japanese green leaves, or fried tofu and green onions. There's also pickled plums, prawn tempura, duck-and-rice-in-a-bowl all-in-ones, seaweed salad, slow-cooked *onsen tamago* poached eggs, and braised pork belly dishes, but it's the mighty udon noodle that prevails. $ *Average main: £12* ⊠ *49 Frith St., Soho* ☎ *020/7434–4463* ⊕ *www.koya.co.uk* ⌒ *Reservations not accepted* Ⓜ *Tottenham Court Rd.* ✛ *E3.*

$$

PERUVIAN

✕ **Lima.** Wicked pisco sours and out-of-this-world biodiversity-driven modern Peruvian cuisine by chef Virgilio Martinez have blasted Lima to the top rank of London's new-wave Peruvians. Kick back in an informal sky-lit dining room scattered with cushions and Inca-style stitched banquettes, and put yourselves in the hands of the famously bubbly staff, who'll guide you first to frisky pisco sours, made with clear grape brandy, sugar syrup, bitters, and foamy egg white. Next *has* to be a killer raw-fish sea bream ceviche, doused in lime-y white tiger's milk ("leche de tigre"), with a tangle of sweet onion and inka corn. Charred chunks of braised octopus on white quinoa with purple botija olive blobs is as vibrant a dish as any, and mains like suckling pig with Amazonian cashews and lentils, or crab with purple corn, 4000m native *huayro* potato, and red *kiwich* (an Andean super-grain) will blow you sky high. $ *Average main: £18* ⊠ *31 Rathbone Pl., Soho* ⊕ *www.limalondon.com* Ⓜ *Tottenham Court Rd.* ✛ *D2.*

$

BARBECUE

Fodor'sChoice

★

× **Pitt Cue Co.** Everyone's gone bonkers for the super-smokey and cheap-as-chips Midwest American BBQ-ed ribs and pulled pork-in-a-bun meal combos here. A tiny, no-reservations hipster hangout, Pitt Cue has only 18 basement seats, plus a few pavement berths and eight counter stools in the ground-level bourbon-and-rye crush bar—little wonder queues often snake down the street. Many order the £9.50 to £12.50 finger-lickin' spreads, which come replete with authentic slaw and house pickles (and are even served up in regulation-white enamel and blue-rimmed *Shawshank Redemption* baker-wear dishes). Charred rib-tips, sausages, baked beans, and bone marrow mash sides are other temptation, but the devout devour the sliders and sticky ribs (with their mucky paws). Ⓢ *Average main: £12* ✉ *1 Newburgh St., Soho* ⊕ *www.pittcue.co.uk* ⌒ *Reservations not accepted* ☾ *Closed Sun.* Ⓜ *Oxford Circus* ✛ *D3.*

$

DINER

Fodor'sChoice

★

× **Spuntino.** Moody tin-tile ceilings, dangly low-wattage filament light bulbs, tattooed waitstaff, bluegrass tunes, and only 26 raised counter stools at this pewter-topped rectangular bar and Lower East Side/Italian-inspired Soho diner makes this the absolute, undisputed, most unimaginably cool gig in town. Naturally, there's no phone, no reservations, and minimal signage, but that only adds to the speakeasy vibe. Once seated after a wait, try truffled egg toast, grits, softshell crab, or Yankee sliders—like ground beef and bone marrow, or spiced mackerel—but don't forget there's mac and cheese or steak and eggs. How could you leave without trying the famed peanut butter and jelly sandwich or the Nutella pizzetta? And wash it all down with a shot or two of Elijah Craig or Knob Creek bourbon. Ⓢ *Average main: £12* ✉ *61 Rupert St., Soho* ⊕ *www.spuntino.co.uk* ⌒ *Reservations not accepted* Ⓜ *Piccadilly Circus* ✛ *D3.*

COVENT GARDEN

$

BISTRO

FAMILY

× **Côte.** Where else can you get a great two-course French meal in Covent Garden for £9.95? The Côte brasserie chain—softly lit and smoothly decked out with natty gray-and-white striped awnings, banquettes, and Parisian-style round café tables—does just the trick, and offers these meal deals weekdays from noon until 7 pm, weekends from noon until 6 pm. With four choices per course, you'll find all your French brasserie favorites: tuna Niçoise salad, bœuf Bourguignon, chargrilled Breton chicken, *Moules marinières* (mussels with white wine), steak haché, and crème caramel for afters. If you're so lucky to be attending the nearby Royal Opera House, this is perfect for pre-theater . . . *or* post-theater, come to that. Ⓢ *Average main: £10* ✉ *17-21 Tavistock St., Covent Garden* ☎ *020/7379–9991* ⊕ *www.cote-restaurants.co.uk* ⌒ *Reservations essential* Ⓜ *Covent Garden* ✛ *E3.*

$$

AUSTRIAN

Fodor'sChoice

★

× **The Delaunay.** It's all *fin de siècle* Vienna and the "Radetsky March" at this magnificent low-lit and elegant art deco–style take on an all-day grand Central European café and Viennese coffeehouse located on the Aldwych. Want to feel Emperor Franz Joseph I fabulous? Here's a majestic 60-item menu that would do the dual-monarchy and Austro-Hungarian Empire proud. Dishes are von Trapp delicious: impressive Weiner schnitzels, goulash, and Viennese hot dogs, served with sauerkraut and onions. Desserts delight too, including *Apfelstrudel*

2

and an evocative three-peaked Salzburg soufflé. Classy breakfasts, brunch, Viennese pastries, and afternoon teas are served, and be sure to sniff out the hidden café within the café to while away a long lost afternoon. $ *Average main: £21* ⊠ *55 Aldwych, Covent Garden* ☎ *020/7499 8558* ⊕ *www.thedelaunay.com* Ⓜ *Covent Garden, Charring Cross, Aldwych* ✢ *F3.*

$$
MODERN BRITISH
Fodor's Choice
★

✕ **Great Queen Street.** Expect a wraparound din and a noisy British foodie-loving crowd at Covent Garden's top gastropub, one that showcases the kind of retro-British classics that Londoners now devour with gusto. Not far from the Royal Opera House, the stripped-back eaterie is done up in burgundy-walls-bare-oak-floor-and-table setting. Overexcited pear-and-prosecco and wine-fueled diners dive into old-fashioned offerings like pressed tongue, pickled herrings, chicken pie, partridge, or smoked mackerel with rhubarb. You'll find dishes from a bygone era, like brown crab on toast, or faggots with apple mash, plus roasts for the whole table—think 7-hour shoulder of lamb with dauphinoise potatoes (£64 for 4)—although green veggies are few and far between. $ *Average main: £18* ⊠ *32 Great Queen St., Covent Garden* ☎ *020/7242–0622* ⌂ *Reservations essential* ◷ *No dinner Sun.* Ⓜ *Covent Garden, Holborn* ✢ *E2.*

$$
BRITISH

✕ **The Ivy.** The triple-A list spurn The Ivy for its upstairs private members' club (and other luxe spots like Scott's and J Sheekey) but, nonetheless, this luvvies landmark still receives a thousand calls a day! A bewitching mix of daytime-and-satellite TV stars, gawkers, and out-of-towners dine on salt beef hash, squash risotto, Thai-baked sea bass, salmon fish cakes, pork meatballs, eggs Benedict, and English classics like shepherd's pie or kedgeree (curried rice with smoked haddock, egg and parsley) in a handsome mullioned stained-glass and oak-paneled dining salon. Service is flawless, and for low-to-mid wattage West End star-spotting this is a prime spot. ▮▮**TIP→ Tip: If you can't snag a table by phone, try walking in on spec—it's been known to work.** $ *Average main: £21* ⊠ *1–5 West St., Covent Garden* ☎ *020/7836–4751* ⊕ *www. the-ivy.co.uk* ⌂ *Reservations essential* Ⓜ *Covent Garden* ✢ *E3.*

$$$
SEAFOOD
Fodor's Choice
★

✕ **J Sheekey.** West End and Hollywood superdooper stars slide into this classy 1896 alley-walk seafood haven, a top alternative to Scott's, Nobu, or 34. Umbilically linked with the surrounding Theaterland district, J Sheekey is one of Londoners' all-time favorite West End haunts. Magnificently orchestrated by incorrigibly amusing maître'd John Andrews, the place charms with warm wood paneling, vintage showbiz black-and-white portraits, a warren of alcove tables, and lava-rock bar tops. Opt for snappingly fresh Atlantic prawns, pickled Arctic herrings, crab bisque, slip soles, scallop, shrimp and salmon burgers, or famous Sheekey fish pie. Better still, sip Gaston Chiquet Champagne and polish off half a dozen Lindisfarne rock oysters at the old mirrored raised-counter oyster bar for the ultimate in true romance, or alternatively take advantage of the £26.50 weekend 3-course set lunch deals. $ *Average main: £24* ⊠ *28–32 St. Martin's Ct., Covent Garden* ☎ *020/7240–2565* ⊕ *www.j-sheekey.co.uk* ⌂ *Reservations essential* Ⓜ *Leicester Sq.* ✢ *E3.*

Fried calamari is typically delicious fare at Busaba Eathai, a good-value Thai favorite.

$
TAPAS
✕ **Opera Tavern.** Mouthwatering acorn-rich Ibérico pig's-head terrine? Chargrilled salt-marsh lamb with broad beans? Mini Ibérico pork and foie gras burgers? These are three of the outstanding Spanish and Italian tapas dishes presented at the handily situated Opera Tavern, opposite the historic Drury Lane theater, and not far from Covent Garden piazza and the Royal Opera House. Clamber in at the overcrowded ground-floor tapas bar (avoiding the accoustically challenged second-floor dining salon if you can) and, after enjoying an amuse-bouche of crispy pig's ears, opt for the empanadas of venison, braised cuttlefish, or Venetian-style sardines. Authentic? The menu warns that all game here may have "shot" in it. ■ TIP➜ Watch out too for the £40 to £45 set tapas meals for groups of 7 up. $ *Average main: £15* ⊠ *23 Catherine St., Covent Garden* ☎ *020/7836–3680* ⊕ *www.operatavern.co.uk* ⌂ *Reservations essential* Ⓜ *Covent Garden, Holborn* ✛ *E3.*

$$$
BRITISH
Fodor's Choice
★
✕ **Rules.** Come, escape the 21st century. Opened by Thomas Rule in 1798, London's oldest restaurant is, according to some, still London's most *beautiful.* The main dining salons are, indeed, an all-round olde-world wonderland, what Maxim's is to Paris. The décor begins with the plush red banquettes, lacquered yellow walls, and spectacular etched-glass skylights. Then, in High Victorian fashion, every nook and cranny is covered with vintage needlepoints, Regency oil paintings, antique clocks, stuffed pheasants, antlers, bronze figurines, and hundreds of framed prints. Little wonder Rules has been a stage across which everyone from Charles Dickens to Laurence Olivier has pranced. For your shining day—be sure to ask for a table in one of the "glass house" sky-light rooms, the bar area, or the cute Maggie Thatcher corner—dig into the menu's pricey and historic British dishes, such as steak-and-kidney

pie, jugged hare, or roast beef and Yorkshire pudding. For a real taste of the 18th century, you can choose, in season, daily specials of fabulous game from the restaurant's High Pennines estate, including grouse, partridge, snipe, and woodcock. $ *Average main: £29* ⊠ *35 Maiden Lane, Covent Garden* ☎ *020/7836–5314* ⊕ *www.rules.co.uk* ⚑ *Reservations essential* 🎩 *Jacket required* Ⓜ *Covent Garden* ✛ *E3.*

$$$ ✕ **The Savoy Grill.** You can *feel* the history in the room at this glamor-
BRITISH ous 1889 art deco power dining salon, which has hosted all the greats
FAMILY from Oscar Wilde and Frank Sinatra to Elizabeth Taylor and Marilyn Monroe. Nowadays—buffed up with Swarovski chandeliers, velvet coverings, gold leaf-backed tortoiseshell walls, and period photos and mirrors—it caters to business barons and dreamy top-end tourists who come for the Grill's famous table-side trolley, which might trundle up with roasts like saddle of lamb, crown of pork, or traditional beef Wellington. Savoy dishes like omelette Arnold Bennett (with smoked haddock, Parmesan, and cream) or old-favorite egg cocotte with smoked bacon, wild mushrooms, and red wine sauce are to the fore, and there's impressive classics like T-bone, Chateaubriand, and Porterhouse steaks, plus oysters, Dover sole, and lobster Thermidor. $ *Average main: £30* ⊠ *The Savoy, 100 Strand, Covent Garden* ☎ *020/7592–1600* ⊕ *www. gordonramsay.com/thesavoygrill* ⚑ *Reservations essential* Ⓜ *Charing Cross, Covent Garden* ✛ *E3.*

BLOOMSBURY AND HOLBORN

BLOOMSBURY

$ ✕ **Bea's of Bloomsbury.** We don't know how it happened, but London's
AMERICAN turned into cupcake central, and Bea's of Bloomsbury is one of the best American cupcake and tea shops in town. With its on-site bakery, Bea's churns out freshly baked sugary delights like blackberry cupcake with vanilla sponge and butter cream and a fresh blackberry on top, or heavenly chocolate fudge cupcake with fudge icing. Don't miss the brightly colored peanut butter, praline, or carrot cake cupcakes, and try not to drool over the cornucopia of three-layered chocolate truffle cakes, New York cheesecakes, lemon drizzle Bundts, fruit cakes, and pecan pies. Afternoon tea (2 pm to 7 pm weekdays, noon to 7 pm on weekends) with cupcakes, scones, mini-meringues, flavored marshmallows, and Valrhona brownies is £19. $ *Average main: £6* ⊠ *44 Theobald's Rd., Bloomsbury* ☎ *020/7242–8330* ⊕ *wwww.beasofbloomsbury.com* ✛ *F2.*

FITZROVIA

$ ✕ **Bubbledogs.** Hot dogs and *Champagne?* Why didn't *we* think of that!
AMERICAN Bubbledogs has come up with one of the most unlikely food combina-
FAMILY tions this side of milk shakes and fries—and has miraculously hit the
Fodor's Choice jackpot. Husband-and-wife team Sandia Chang and chef James Knap-
★ pett have combined their respective loves of New York hot dogs and small-production-house Champagne, and gone back to basics with a bar menu that pays due homage to both. Classic 7-by-1 inch, all-British pork, beef, or vegetarian hot dogs cost a mere £6–£7.50, while the handcrafted Champagnes are some of the cheapest in town—including £6.50 for a glass of Gaston Chiquet or £7.50 for Christophe Mignon.

Sit at raised counters with dog cartoons, brick walls, and cozy log-cabin paneling, and choose scrumbilicious hot dogs in baskets ranging from a superior BLT, to a Sloppy Joe (with chili and cheese), or a K-DAWG (with kimchi and red bean paste). They only take reservations for groups of six or more. $ *Average main: £7* ⊠ *70 Charlotte St., Fitzrovia* ☎ *020/7637–7770* ⊕ *www.bubbledogs.co.uk* ⌁ *Reservations not accepted* ⊘ *Closed Sun. and Mon.* Ⓜ *Goodge St.* ✣ *D2.*

$$
MODERN
EUROPEAN
Fodor's Choice
★
✕**Dabbous.** It's a triumph of taste over technology at wunderkind Ollie Dabbous's extraordinary game-changer off Charlotte Street. Startlingly stripped-back, pure, inventive, and seasonally based new-wave dishes elicit *Oohs!, Aahhs!, Wows!* and *Oh-my-goshes!!* in a flummery-free NYC–industrial chic setting of exposed concrete, overhead ducting, and heavy metal screens and cages. Phenomenal flavors abound. Dishes like peas and mint ping your taste buds with frozen mint tea, edible violets, and broad-bean flowers, and a coddled hen's egg with woodland mushrooms and smoked butter sits handsomely in a cute bowl of hay. Palette-popping barbecued Ibèrico pork with acorn praline, turnip tops, and apple vinegar; halibut with coastal herbs (sea aster and oyster leaf); and brittle and crumbly chocolate ganache with green basil moss are *instant* classics, and set Dabbous apart as one of London's most dazzling young talents. Sorry: you have to book months ahead. $ *Average main: £18* ⊠ *39 Whitfield St., Fitzrovia* ☎ *020/7323–7323* ⊕ *www.dabbous.co.uk* ⌁ *Reservations essential* ⊘ *Closed Sun. and Mon.* Ⓜ *Goodge St.* ✣ *D2.*

$
MODERN INDIAN
Fodor's Choice
★
✕**Roti Chai.** Incredible Indian street food hits the spot at this bright, yellow-ceilinged, superior curry canteen found behind Selfridges. The kitchen specializes in grub inspired by Indian street-cart vendors, roadside "dhaba" cafés, and bustling Victorian railway stations found across the subcontinent. You'll find a good sprinkling of smart Indians tucking in—often heartily with their fingers—into glass bowls of spicy street snacks like nibbly *bhel puri* (puffed rice with onion, cumin, and tamarind), fiery white cubes of "Hakka" chili paneer cheese, or flayed Keralan chicken "lollipops," which come with an irresistible coriander dip. There's Punjabi aloo (potato) *bun tikki* mini-burgers, and a tender tomato-based "Railway" lamb curry with chapatis (straight out of Bombay's Victoria Terminus station). You can imagine you're on the road with the authentic hot curried chickpea spreads, pea samosas, or Indian mango ice cream on a stick. This is a trip to India for which you need no passport. $ *Average main: £12* ⊠ *3 Portman Mews S, Fitzrovia* ☎ *020/7408–0101* ⊕ *www.rotichai.com* Ⓜ *Marble Arch* ✣ *C3.*

THE CITY AND ENVIRONS

THE CITY

$$
BRASSERIE
Fodor's Choice
★
✕**Boundary.** Restaurateur and design-guru Sir Terence Conran scores a bull's-eye at Boundary at this eponymous boutique hotel and foodie complex in über-trendy Hoxton/Shoreditch. A theatrically glass-fronted open kitchen, sparkly lighting, smart acoustics, and plush red-and-blue upholstered throne-like seats make this swanky, chic, and gayly carpeted modern French basement brasserie the glamorati's East End dining destination of choice. The menu's a wish list of crowd-pleasers designed to impress: classics like twice-baked soufflé Suisse, lobster Thermidor, cod

2

cassoulet, pigeon *pot-au-feu*, and red wine-heavy bœuf Bordelaise are all big and brassy, and are well served by timeless sides like Dauphinois potatoes or cauliflower gratin. Look out, too, for the £19.50 or £24.50 prix fixe deals. $ *Average main: £20* ⊠ *2–4 Boundary St.(entrance at 9 Redchurch St.), The City* ☎ *020/7729–1051* ⊕ *www.theboundary.co.uk* ⊜ *Reservations essential* ☉ *No lunch Mon.* Ⓜ *Liverpool St.* ✛ *H1.*

$$$　✕ **L'Anima.** Top-notch southern Italian cuisine in a love-it-or-loathe-it
ITALIAN　modern glass-sided shoe-box of a restaurant characterizes the breezy business-based scene here near Liverpool Street in the City. Italian chef Francesco Mazzei draws inspiration from Sicily, Puglia, Sardinia, and Calabria, and prowls the high-ceilinged bar, floor, and clear-fronted kitchen like the proud owner he is. Simple, fresh, modern, and restrained dishes like wild mushroom and black truffle *tagliolini* and Sardinian fish stew are near perfection, as is the wood-roasted turbot with artichoke and Calabrian sausage—as succulent as you could wish. Desserts, like liquorice zabayon wine custard, are *bellissimo*, and the winning wine list, naturally, is practically all Italian. $ *Average main: £26* ⊠ *1 Snowden St., The City* ☎ *020/7422–7000* ⊕ *www.lanima.co.uk* ☉ *Closed Sun.* Ⓜ *Liverpool St.* ✛ *H2.*

$$　✕ **Moro.** Up from the City, near Clerkenwell and Sadler's Wells dance
MEDITERRANEAN　theater, is Exmouth Market, a cluster of cute indie shops, artisan bakeries, bookstores, an Italian church, and more fine restaurants like Moro. Lovingly led for more tha a decade by husband-and-wife chefs Sam and Sam Clark, the menu includes a mélange of Spanish and Moorish North African flavors. Rustic tapas—like *baba ganoush* and Syrian lentils, baby squid with harissa, or grilled chorizo—compete with spiced meats, Serrano ham, salt cod, and char-grilled offerings. Wood-fired seabass with hispi cabbage or grilled sea bream with chickpea salad are among the stand-out mains. Sidle up to the zinc bar, or squeeze into a tiny table and lean in—it's *really* noisy here, but fun. $ *Average main: £19* ⊠ *34–36 Exmouth Market, The City* ☎ *020/7833–8336* ⊕ *www.moro.co.uk* ⊜ *Reservations essential* ☉ *Closed Sun.* Ⓜ *Farringdon, Angel* ✛ *F1.*

$$　✕ **Sweetings.** A time-warp City seafood institution, Sweetings was estab-
SEAFOOD　lished in 1889 and it powers serenely on as if the sun never set on the British Empire. There are some things Sweetings really *doesn't* do: dinner, reservations, coffee, or weekends. It does, mercifully, do seafood—and rather well. Not far from St. Paul's Cathedral, it's patronized by self-assured old school City gents who down pewter tankards of Black Velvet (Guinness and Champagne) and like to eat lobster salad, roe on toast, Dover sole, Cornish brill, and succulent skate wings with black butter sauce, all this at linen-covered raised counters or tables. The snooty long-serving wait staff wear whites, the oysters are plump and fresh, and desserts, like fruit crumble and baked jam roll, are old boarding school favorites. $ *Average main: £19* ⊠ *39 Queen Victoria St., The City* ☎ *020/7248–3062* ⊜ *Reservations not accepted* ☉ *Closed weekends. No dinner* Ⓜ *Mansion House* ✛ *H3.*

$　✕ **Tayyabs.** Unloved City bankers and doctors from the nearby Royal
PAKISTANI　London Hospital swamp this neon-lit, high-turnover Pakistani curry specialist (set in the eastern part of the Whitechapel part of The City). Expect queues after dark, and bear in mind it's BYO, jam-packed, noisy,

and often maddeningly chaotic. Nonetheless, prices are keen and you can OD and gorge handsomely for under £20 on a mixed char-grill extravaganza, which might include fiery Tandoori chicken and fish tikka. Other best bets include Karachi okra, slow-cooked "dry meat," minced meat *seekh* kebabs, Karachi prawns, hot steaming naan breads, and Tayyab's famous spicy char-grilled Karachi lamb chops (cooked to a secret receipe). [$] *Average main: £12* ✉ *83 Fieldgate St., The City* ☎ *020/7247–9543* 🌐 *www.tayyabs.co.uk* ✍ *Reservations not accepted* [M] *Aldgate East* ✥ *H3.*

CLERKENWELL

$$ FRENCH

🍴 **Bistrot Bruno Loubet.** Seasoned French chef Bruno Loubet rules the roost at this ever-buzzy hotel dining room and bistrot at the Zetter hotel in historic-yet-cutting-edge Clerkenwell. Loubet tinkers away and creates so many must-try dishes it's genuinely hard to pick: deliciously pink quail comes with prune, Roquefort, and sautéed wild mushrooms, while guinea fowl *boudin blanc* sausages sit perfectly with leeks and chervil sauce, just to name two winners. You'll find wonderful sea bream with Pernod *beurre blanc*, yummy Mauricette snails and meatballs, and rabbit *royale*, followed by tarragon poached pear, or *crêpe* Suzettes (served with a touch of cardamom in a shiny copper pan). The ground-floor bistro is kitted out with appealing retro lamps and artifacts and overlooks St. John's Square. [$] *Average main: £19* ✉ *The Zetter, 86–88 Clerkenwell Rd.Clerkenwell* ☎ *020/7324–4455* 🌐 *www.bistrotbrunoloubet.com* ✍ *Reservations essential* [M] *Farringdon St., Barbican* ✥ *G2.*

$$ MODERN BRITISH Fodor's Choice ★

🍴 **St. John.** Foodies travel the globe for pioneering chef Fergus Henderson's ultra-British nose-to-tail cooking at this no-frills, stark-white converted ham-and-bacon smokehouse near famed Smithfield Market in Clerkenwell. Henderson famously uses *all* parts of a carcass, and his waste-not, want-not chutzpah is laudable and chimes perfectly with the new age of austerity: one appetizer is pig's skin, and others, like ox heart or pig's ear and calves' brain and chichory, are marginally less extreme. St. John signatures like bone marrow and parsley salad, chitterlings with dandelion, or pheasant and pig's trotter pie appear stark on the plate, but arrive with aplomb. Expect a cracking all-French wine list and finish with apple pie with custard, Eccles cakes and Lancashire cheese, or half a dozen golden Madeleines. [$] *Average main: £23* ✉ *26 St. John St., Clerkenwell* ☎ *020/3301–8069* 🌐 *www.stjohnrestaurant.com* ✍ *Reservations essential* 🕒 *No dinner Sun.* [M] *Farringdon, Barbican* ✥ *G2.*

THE EAST END

$ MODERN EUROPEAN Fodor's Choice ★

🍴 **Bistroteque.** You'll need a GPS or Google Maps to find this East London fashionista G-spot, and all-round cool-hunters HQ, down a side alley in jam-hot Bethnal Green. Once inside, the striking first-floor loft dining space and Manchichi bar is a bubbly post-industrial chic setting of all-white tiled walls and white concrete floor, factory pipes and beams, Crittal windows, dangly lights, marble-top tables, and black bentwood chairs. All the men seem to wear caps, spats, 'tashes, Trilbys, skinny Acne jeans, or '30s tweed three-piece deer-stalker suits, while the Alexa Chung lookalike women are in capes, *Emmanuelle 2* organza get-ups, and oversized Scooby-Doo specs. French- and English-based dishes range from steak tartar, Croque Madame, and towering cheese-burgers, to cod and clams, or lamb rump with chestnuts and sage. Be sure to catch Xavior, the resident pianist, at weekend brunch, camping up everything from Girls Aloud to Katy Perry on the baby grand. $ *Average main: £15* ✉ *23-27 Wadeson St., East End* ☎ *020/8983 7900* ⊕ *www.bistroteque.com* Ⓜ *Bethnal Green* ✚ *H3*.

$ ✕**Pizza East.** The whole *Wham!*-glam East End demimonde seems to
PIZZA have taken up residence at this knockabout gourmet pizza parlor, which
FAMILY serves up chewy, 10-inch, wood-fired, thin-crust, crispy pizzas in a former tea warehouse—actually, an achingly au courant setting of exposed concrete walls, raw brickwork, pillars, pipes, and industrial ducting. Amid a soundscape of Stone Roses, Baby Shambles, and vintage Bowie, mix things up at the long refractory-style shared tables with a starter of sea bass carpaccio with fennel and chili, or broad beans with pecorino, before tearing into the one of the eleven £8–£14, semolina-crust, rich pizzas, which might be topped with San Daniele ham, ricotta and pesto, or pancetta, eggplant, and scamorza (an Italian cow's-milk cheese). There's wine by the tap, cocktails by the jug (if you ask *nicely*), plus karaoke, slam poetry, hip-hop, or old-school tune sessions in the downstairs Concrete basement bar. $ *Average main: £12* ✉ *56 Shoreditch High St., East End* ☎ *020/729–1888* ⊕ *www.pizzaeast.com* Ⓜ *Rail: Shoreditch High Street* ✚ *H3*.

$ ✕**Rochelle Canteen.** You feel quite the foodie insider once you've finally
BRITISH found the quirky Rochelle Canteen—it is set in the renovated bicycle shed of the old restored Victorian-era Rochelle School (off Arnold Circus in Shoreditch, not far from the boutiques of Redchurch Street and Liverpool Street station). Ring a buzzer next to a pale blue door, go in through the "Boys" entrance (passing a former playground) and enter chef Margot Henderson's long white, austere "canteen," which has an open kitchen and two long Formica tables, Ercol school chairs, and Shaker pegs on the wall. Gloriously understated British fare arrives at a convivial pace, from simple deviled kidneys on toast to a retro plate of Yorkshire ham, carrots, and parsley sauce. Bump along with the art/architecture/designer crowd, and enjoy seasonal guinea fowl with bacon, or skate and capers, and finish with quince jelly or lemon posset. Note it is no-liquor-license BYO (£5 corkage), and only open Monday to Friday, for breakfast, elevenses, lunch, and tea. $ *Average main: £16* ✉ *Rochelle School, Arnold Circus, Shoreditch* ☎ *020/7729 5677* ⊕ *www.arnoldandhenderson.com* ☾ *Closed weekends* Ⓜ *Liverpool St.* ✚ *H3*.

$$$ ✕**Viajante.** It's quite a *schlep* from the West End to Viajante in Beth-
MODERN nal Green, but Portuguese chef/patron/cultural leader Nuno Mendes's
EUROPEAN ultra-contemporary, avant-garde cuisine is some of the hottest, most
Fodor's Choice exciting in town. Armed with tweezers in a fascinating open-kitchen, El
★ Bulli-trained Mendes doubles down with 3 to-12-course tasting extravaganzas (£35–£95) in the à la modishly converted former Bethnal Green Town Hall. Unusual tastes, textures, and flavors abound—like skate with roasted yeast, set crab milk with beach herbs, or Thai basil panna cotta—but every dish tastes incredible, and *looks* like high art. Expect rare micro-herbs and Hackney's finest local urban foraged goodies, such as wood sorrel, sweet violets, and honeysuckle, and don't be surprised

to be served at your table by the great man Mendes himself. Our advice is simple: *Go.* $ *Average main: £25* ✉ *Town Hall Hotel, Patriot Sq., Bethnal Green, East End* ☎ *020/7871–0461* ⊕ *www.viajante.co.uk* ⟁ *Reservations essential* ⊘ *No lunch Sun.* Ⓜ *Bethnal Green Tube/rail, Cambridge Heath rail* ✛ *H1.*

THE SOUTH BANK

$$
MODERN BRITISH

✕ **Anchor & Hope.** Hearty meaty dishes at wallet-friendly prices emerge from the open kitchen at this permanently packed, no-reservations leading gastropub on The Cut (between Waterloo and Southwark Tube), a few doors down from the excellent Young Vic contemporary theater. Pot roast duck, Herefordshire beef, deep-fried pig's head, pumpkin gratin, and cuttlefish with bacon stand out. Bear in mind that it's noisy, cramped, informal, and always overflowing. That said, the kitchen is highly original, and there are great dishes for groups—like the famous slow-roasted shoulder of lamb. Eager diners wait for a table over a drink in the pub's convivial saloon bar, and be prepared to share a wooden dining table with others once seated, too. $ *Average main: £17* ✉ *36 The Cut, South Bank* ☎ *020/7928–9898* ⟁ *Reservations not accepted* ⊘ *No dinner Sun. No lunch Mon.* Ⓜ *Waterloo, Southwark* ✛ *F4.*

$$$
MODERN FRENCH
Fodor'sChoice
★

✕ **Chez Bruce.** Deeply flavorsome French and Mediterrean cuisine, faultless service, a winning wine list, and a glossy neighborhood vibe make for one of London's all-time favorite destination restaurants. Take a train or cab south of the Thames to lauded chef Bruce Poole's cozy, gimmick-free haunt overlooking Wandsworth Common and then get ready for an endless procession of wonders, ranging from delicious home-made charcuterie or offal to lighter, simply grilled fish dishes. Pot roast pig's cheek with polenta, pollack with wild mushrooms, and roast monkfish with scallops, ham hock, and Jerusalem artichokes are all immaculately conceived. The wine and desserts are stunning, the sommelier's superb and, pound-for-pound, Chez Bruce is nigh impossible to beat. Weekday lunches are £27.50; three-course dinners are £45. $ *Average main: £26* ✉ *2 Bellevue Rd., Wandsworth* ☎ *020/8672–0114* ⊕ *www.chezbruce.co.uk* ⟁ *Reservations essential* Ⓜ *Tube: Wandsworth Common rail* ✛ *B6.*

$
TAPAS

✕ **José.** Rising Spanish chef José Pizarro packs 'em in like so many slices of *jamón* at this tapas-and-sherry treasure trove on happening Bermondsey Street, south of the river near Guy's Hospital and London Bridge. With only 30 seats and no reservations, you'll be hard-pressed to find a spot at the tapas bar or a perch at an upturned barrel after 6 pm, but stick with it, *hombre*—the tapas is astounding. Quaff a glass of Amontillado or Orloroso sherry, and keep those expertly-crafted small white plates a comin': patatas bravas . . . croquetas . . . pisto and crispy duck eggs . . . hake and aioli . . . razor clams with chorizo . . . paprika-specked Ibérico pork fillets. You'll either love or hate the crush. $ *Average main: £7* ✉ *104 Bermondsey St., South Bank* ☎ *020/7403–4902* ⊕ *josepizzaro.com* ⟁ *Reservations not accepted* Ⓜ *London Bridge* ✛ *H4.*

2

BRITISH TO A "T": TOP TEAS IN TOWN

It was a peckish Anna, 7th Duchess of Bedford, who began the tradition of British afternoon tea in the 1840s, and taking tea is now once more the height of fashion. Here are the best around, plus some places that are gently priced.

Tea at the Palm Court at the **Ritz** (✉ The Ritz, 150 Piccadilly ☎ 020/7300–2345 ⊕ www. theritzlondon.com) would moisten the eye of Marie Antoinette and is still an ultimate afternoon tea experience, with a rococo starburst of gilt work, crystal chandeliers, and floral displays. Expect egg and cress-and-cucumber sandwiches on three-tiered silver cake stands, plus fruit scones, cakes, and dainty British pastries (£45–£64).

In the northern reaches of Mayfair, a Hungarian quartet plays at hallowed **Claridge's** (✉ Brook St. ⊕ www. claridges.co.uk ☎ 020/7107–8872), where the green-and-white-striped porcelain tea service is straight out of the Mad Hatter's Tea Party. You'll find 40 loose-leaf teas to choose from, including rare Darjeeling First Flush tea (prices from £39, or £63 for a rosé Champagne tea). Nearby, off Mount Street in Mayfair, fashionistas splurge on flourless caramel sponge cake at the soigné **Connaught** (✉ Carlos Pl. ⊕ www. the-connaught.co.uk ☎ 020/7107–8861). Loyalists enjoy the open fires, Laurent-Perrier bubbles,

smoked-salmon finger sandwiches, Christine Ferber jams, and looseleaf Ceylon tea.

If you can't afford to stay at London's best hotel, why not take tea for an hour or two and indulge in the fantasy of Noël Coward's favorite city spot for a fraction of the cost? Just a few blocks over from Mayfair on the Strand, the **Savoy** (✉ Strand ⊕ www.fairmont.com/ savoy-london ☎ 020/7420–2111) offers the prettiest settings in London. In the heavenly glass-cupolacovered Upper Thames Foyer—all pink orchids and a black-and-white chinoiserie fabric—you can savor the Savoy's Afternoon, Champagne, and High Teas (£40–£60).

For cheaper tea options, there's a £10.50 Cream Tea, or an exquisite £34 Afternoon Tea with quail-eggand-caviar sandwiches, in a quirky *Alice in Wonderland* meets *The Enchanted Wood* setting at the Glade at **Sketch** (✉ 9 Conduit St. ☎ 020/7659–4500 ⊕ www.sketch. uk.com). Similarly, the Soho crowd sinks into comfy velvet chairs with frilly cushions for Afternoon Tea at the Parlour anteroom at **Dean Street Townhouse** (✉ 69–71 Dean St. ⊕ www.deanstreettownhouse. com ☎ 020/7434–1775) restaurant for eminently affordable £16.75 teas, with buttered crumpets, Battenberg cake, or cheesy buck rarebit with an egg on top.

$$ ✕ **Magdalen.** South of the river between London and Tower bridges,
MODERN BRITISH Magdalen is a self-assured beacon of class in a markedly up-and-coming part of town. It specializes in inventive but unpretentious modern British cuisine at keen prices; poached hake with fennel (£9), calves' sweetbreads with salsify (£18), wild turbot and clams (£19), and treacle tart for £7 will hardly break the bank. With dark-wood and bentwood chairs, chandeliers, tea candles, the pleasing ox-blood-colored surrounds invite you to sit back with the clever wine list and ponder

whether to have a feast of whole hare or the stuffed suckling pig instead. $ *Average main: £17* ⊠ *152 Tooley St., South Bank* ☎ *020/7403–1342* ⊕ *www.magdalenrestaurant.co.uk* ⌕ *Reservations essential* ⊗ *No lunch Sat. Closed Sun.* Ⓜ *London Bridge* ✛ *H4.*

$$
Fodor's Choice
★

✕ **Zucca.** River Café alumnus Sam Harris has nailed the elusive winning formula for London's *ultimate*—and commendably inexpensive—modern Italian on buzz-hot Bermondsey Street, doors down from the fab White Cube gallery (and other happening eateries like tapas joints José and Pizzaro). Anywhere that notes on its menu that "The use of mobile phones is both unsociable and unnecessary" has got its head screwed on right, and this sure touch is in evidence throughout, from the white melamine tables and open kitchen to the passionately prepared, all-homemade Italian breads, pasta, and ice cream. Start off sharing a punchy £5.50 antipasto like salt cod with chickpeas, then swoon over the Piedmontese egg-yoke-colored pappardelle pasta with veal ragu, or the incredible Le Marche white truffle *vincisgrassi* pasta bake. You'll only find three fish or meat mains to chose from, but anything like the ink-black squid with white polenta, or a perfect blush-pink veal chop with spinach and lemon will be *molto bellissimo.* The desserts and all-Italian wine list rock, too. $ *Average main: £16* ⊠ *184 Bermondsey St., South Bank* ☎ *020/7378–6809* ⊕ *www.zuccalondon.com* ⊗ *Closed Mon. No dinner Sun.* Ⓜ *London Bridge* ✛ *H4.*

KENSINGTON, KNIGHTSBRIDGE, AND MAYFAIR

KENSINGTON

$$$$
FRENCH
Fodor's Choice
★

✕ **Tom Aikens.** Is so-called wonderchef Tom Aikens the real thing? Indeed. The flame-haired, former kitchen bad boy was always popping up in the gossip columns for having bust-ups with his staff, winning awards, hobnobbing with the gentry, or flirting with bankrupcy. Nonetheless, he's stripped all the *ancien régime* flummery away and it's now all freed up, colorful, joyous technique-*and*-ingredient-driven fireworks on the plate at his starkly revamped Nordic-style gastro-lair in tony Chelsea, and everyone's impressed. You'll bliss out over his marinated hand-dived scallops with apple vinegar, his new-found vegetable numbers—like baked celeriac, a jumbled-up raw turnip salad, or braised leeks with whey and marjoram—and his mains are even better: try the braised beef short rib with bone marrow and melting tendons, or herb-coated sea bass with clams and brown shrimps to encounter a grandmaster at work. $ *Average main: £32* ⊠ *43 Elystan St., Kensington* ☎ *020/7584–2003* ⊕ *www.tomaikens.co.uk* ⌕ *Reservations essential* ⊗ *Closed Sun. No lunch Sat.* Ⓜ *South Kensington* ✛ *B5.*

$$
JAPANESE

✕ **Yashin.** *Without Soy Sauce . . . but if you want to* proclaims the neon sign on the glazed green-tiled wall behind the open chefs' counter at London's *best* sushi bar (right off Ken High Street). Take their advice, bag a ringside counter seat, and watch head chef and co-founder Yashuhiro Mineo and Co. tease, slice, tweak, and blowtorch their way through dish after dish of the most awesome/fresh/funky/spunky/colorful and exquisite "omakase" sushi, sashimi, salads, and carpaccios that you're likely to find this side of the East China Sea. Tofu-topped miso cappucino comes in a Victoriana cup-and-saucer, and softshell blue crab salad is a tangle of zingy mizuna leaves. Delectable 8, 11, or 15-piece omakase sushi spreads (£30–£60) might mesmerize with ponzu-spiked salmon, Japanese sea bream with rice cracker dust, salted wagyu, or Japanese botan prawns with foie gras. Alternatively, the bargain £12.50 5-piece salmon nigiri set-lunch, with hot miso and bracing salad, is a smashing way to sample Yashin's below-the-radar brilliance. $ *Average main: £22 ⊠ 1A Argyll Road, Kensington ☎ 020/7938 1536 ⊕ www. yashinsushi.com Ⓜ High Street Kensington ⊹ A4.*

CHELSEA

$$ ✕ **The Harwood Arms.** Modern British game doesn't get any better—or more inventive—than at this exceptional gastropub and game-lovers' paradise off Fulham Broadway. Enthusiast and co-owner Mike Robinson shoots and bags all the wild venison on the menu here in season (the 2-star Aussie chef Brett Graham is another co-owner), and you'll find a catalogue of awesome game-based dishes like haunch of Berkshire roe deer with tarragon mustard or North Yorkshire grouse with Earl Grey–soaked prunes. Tuck into game pie with Somerset cider jelly or Herdwick lamb with rosemary curd in a relaxed comfy-sofas-and-newspapers Sloaney-pub type setting. A number of fine dishes are served on a slab of wood, and there are popular carve-your-own whole-roast beef, lamb, or pork joints for the table—and, *yes,* you can ask for doggy bags on the way out! $ *Average main: £19 ⊠ 27 Walham Grove, Chelsea ☎ 020/7386– 1847 ⊕ www.harwoodarms.com* ⊜ *Reservations essential ⊗ No lunch Mon. Last dinners served 9 to 9:30pm* Ⓜ *Fulham Broadway ⊹ A6.*

MODERN BRITISH

Fodor's Choice

★

$$ ✕ **The Orange.** Four-square and handsome, this debs-delight Pimlico gastropub (with upstairs guest rooms) seems to get everything right, which is why it's packed with braying locals most nights and seemingly all weekend. The stage is set—light and airy, with stripped wood, a tony ocher color-scheme, and mini-potted orange trees—for service that is noticeably smiley, polite, and (dare we say it?) well-mannered. You can't go wrong with the chicken liver parfait, Treacly Farm cured meat platters, and the wood-fired spelt-based pizzas, or alternatively enjoy a leisurely Sunday roast like 28-day Castle of Mey beef rib, Kilravock pork rack, or Suffolk chicken with sage and bacon stuffing, all served with crispy duck-fat roast potatoes, seasonal vegetables, and traditional Yorkshire puddings. $ *Average main: £16 ⊠ 37 Pimlico Rd., Chelsea ☎ 020/7881–9844 ⊕ www.theorange.co.uk* ⊜ *Reservations essential* Ⓜ *Sloane Sq. ⊹ C5.*

MODERN BRITISH

FAMILY

KNIGHTSBRIDGE

$$$$ ✕ **Dinner by Heston Blumenthal.** Exceptional olde English-inspired dishes executed with ultra-modern precision in an open kitchen is the *schtick* at Ashley Palmer-Watts' acclaimed award-winner at the Mandarin Oriental in Knightsbrige (Palmer-Watts is the protégée of superstar chef Heston Blumenthal, who is still closely involved in the restaurant). As you take in the view of Hyde Park, you simply must slice into a Meat Fruit starter (c.1500), deceptively shaped like a mandarin, but encasing the smoothest, most creamy chicken liver parfait on the *planet.* A plate of Rice and Flesh (c.1390) is a picture of yellow saffron rice with calf's tails and red wine, and fans will recognise the snail-and-girolle Savoury

BRITISH

Fodor's Choice

★

LOCAL CHAINS WORTH A TASTE

When you're on the go or don't have time for a leisurely meal, you might want to try a local chain restaurant or sandwich bar. *The ones listed below are well priced and are the best in their category.*

Byron: Bright and child-friendly, this 19-strong line of superior hamburger joints storms the burger market with its delicious Scotch beef hamburgers, onion rings, Cobb salads, and french fries. ⊕ www.byronhamburgers.com.

Busaba Eathai: It's always jam-packed at these eight Thai canteen supremos where you'll find Thai noodles, rice dishes, and spicy all-in-one meals in a bowl in sultry dark-wood surrounds. ⊕ www.busaba.com.

Café Rouge: A classic 35-strong French bistro chain that's been around for eons and churns out great £9.95–£14.50 *plats rapides* and prix-fixe deals—so enduringly uncool that it's now almost fashionable. ⊕ www.caferouge.co.uk.

Carluccio's Caffè: The Carluccio's chain of 14 all-day Italian café–bar–food shops are freshly sourced, family-friendly, and make for brilliant pasta and salad stops on a shopping spree. ⊕ www.carluccios.com.

Côte: High quality and very reliable £11.70–£13.65 classic French brasserie meal deals are order of the day at this upmarket and smartly decked out 21-strong chain. ⊕ www.cote-restaurants.co.uk.

Ed's Easy Diner: Overdose on milk shakes, ice-cream floats, chili dogs, blues burgers, and other made-to-order hamburgers at this five-strong chain of shiny, retro-'50s-theme, American-style diners. ⊕ www.edseasydiner.com.

Gail's Artisan Bakery: Chunky artisanal-bread sandwiches, fine breakfasts, and lunches like chorizo, butternut squash, and quinoa salad are found at this spanking-clean chain of 12 brilliant bakeries. ⊕ www.gailsbread.co.uk.

Le Pain Quotidien: Try Belgian tartine open sandwiches, soups, salads, and cakes at the communal wooden tables. There are 15 branches, including ones at the soaring St. Pancras station and Eurostar terminus. ⊕ www.lepainquotidien.co.uk.

Pret a Manger: London's high street take-out supremo isn't just for wholesome store-made sandwiches: there are great-tasting wraps, toasties, noodles, sushi, salads, fruit, porridge, and tea cakes, too. ⊕ www.pret.com.

Wagamama: Londoners love to drain endless bowls of Asian ramen and noodle soups at this high-tech, child-friendly chain of canteens. ⊕ www.wagamama.com.

Porridge (c.1660) from Blumenthal's Berkshire flagship, The Fat Duck. There's juicy Beef Royale (c.1720) cooked *sous vide* at 56°C for 72 hours, plus tender cod in cider with mussels and chard (c. 1940). Head off with the marvelous spit roasted pineapple Tipsy cake (c.1810)—a triumphant homage to traditional English spit-roasting from centuries past. For conversation-piece dishes, you can do no better. [$] *Average main: £32* ⊠ *Mandarin Oriental Hyde Park, 66 Knightsbridge, Knightsbridge* ☎ *020/7201–3833* ⊕ *www.dinnerbyheston.com* ⚄ *Reservations essential* [M] *Knightsbridge* ✛ *C4.*

$$$ RUSSIAN Fodor's Choice ★ 🍴 **Mari Vanna.** All of London's Russian molls, dolls, and porcelain-skinned *babushkas* squeeze into this kitsch White Russian fantasy dining salon in Knightsbridge, which overflows with a fay-gray and maximalist décor of antique chandeliers, Tiffany lamps, knick-knacks, pickles, tchotchkes, vintage books, pics, mirrors, Cheburashkas, and a Russian *pechka* stove. Note the crochet and linen-covered tables tended by chirpy Russian staff (some in dirndls) and dishes proffered with what feels like great aunt Vanna's old family silver and jumbled crockery. Then snap into character with a horseradish vodka shot or two, then carb-up on Pirogi sea bass savories, clear Siberian Pelmeni dumpling soup, classic Russian "Olivier" ox-tongue salad, or feather-light smoked salmon blinis. There's highly pleasing borsch, dill and potaotes, and creamy beef Stroganoff with mash and wild mushrooms, and let's not forget the sweet crêpes with condensed milk. But it's the nostalgic dacha-like antebellum home-from-home setting that makes you feel like you're in some kind of *Anna Karenina*-esque episode. [$] *Average main: £26* ✉ *116 Knightsbridge, Knightsbridge* ☎ *020/7225 3122* 🌐 *www.marivanna.co.uk* [M] *Knightsbridge* ⊕ *C4.*

$$$ MODERN FRENCH Fodor's Choice ★ 🍴 **Petrus.** Gordon Ramsay protégé Sean Burbidge presides over an absolutely flawless, world-class, modern French *experience* at Tripadvisor's top-ranked London restaurant in very posh Belgravia. The softly carpeted dining salon may be a bit beige and circa G. Ramsay-late-'90s, and a central circular glass wine cellar a touch *passé,* but add in the warm welcome, bonhomie, impeccable nibbles, *bonnes bouches*, petit fours, assured sommelier, stonking cheese board, and charming, fleet-footed service, and you've got an unparalleled all-around gastro-embrace. Burbidge's go-forward cuisine is all *technique, technique, technique*, and it's impossible not to swoon at starters like exemplary Les Landes duck foie gras with grape jelly, or perfect lobster ravioli swimming in creamed leaks and Champagne velouté. Bliss out on pink 25-day Casterbridge beef fillet with braised shin and sticky Barolo sauce, and watch out for surprises towards the end, like the honeycomb-and-dark-chocolate sphere that theatrically melts in front of your eyes, cute cones with syllabub, or white choc-ices on sticks that emerge from a bowl of dry ice. [$] *Average main: £28* ✉ *1 Kinnerton St., Belgravia, Knightsbridge* ☎ *020/7592–1609* 🌐 *www.gordonramsay.com/petrus* [M] *Knightsbridge* ⊕ *C4.*

$$$$ INDIAN 🍴 **Rasoi.** Star Indian chef Vineet Bhatia showcases the best new-wave Indian cuisine in London at this tony Victorian town house off the King's Road. Ring the front door bell on arrival at this romantic celebration venue, which is decked out with colorful Indian prints, silks, masks, bells, and ornaments. Bhatia pushes the boundaries with creative signatures like popcorn prawns, crab lollies with lime and coconut soup, wild mushroom rice with tomato ice cream, Bordeaux rogan-josh lamb shanks, or Darjeeling tea grilled chicken. Naturally the prices are pretty fiery for such inventive cuisine, but be sure not to leave without sampling Madras coffee cheesecake or the famous warm chocolate samosas, dubbed "Chocamosas." Two-course lunches are £22, while dinners range from £49 to £89. [$] *Average main: £32* ✉ *10 Lincoln St., Knightsbridge* ☎ *020/7225–1881* 🌐 *www.rasoirestaurant.co.uk* ✍ *Reservations essential* ⏲ *No lunch Sat.* [M] *Sloane Sq.* ⊕ *C5.*

Harwood Arms has a modern take on Scotch eggs, a classic British dish.

MAYFAIR

$$ ITALIAN

🍴 **Cecconi's.** Spot the odd A-list celeb and revel in all-day buzz at this ever-fashionable upscale Italian brasserie wedged handsomely between Old Bond Street, Cork Street, and Savile Row, and across from the Royal Academy of Arts. The *vaguely* familiar and important-looking Miu Miu, offshore tax exile, and private jet set spill out onto the street for breakfast, brunch, and *cicchetti* (Italian tapas), and return later in the day for something more substantial. À la mode designer Ilse Crawford's luxe green-and-brown interior is a stylish backdrop for classics like stuffed baby squid, Umbrian sausages, lobster spaghetti, and a flavorful pick-me-up tiramisu. It's just the spot for a high-end pit stop during an ill-advised kamakazi West End shopping spree. [$] *Average main: £23* ✉ *5A Burlington Gardens, Mayfair* ☎ *020/7434–1500* 🌐 *www.cecconis.co.uk* ✍ *Reservations essential* [M] *Green Park, Piccadilly Circus* ✥ *D3.*

$$$$ STEAKHOUSE Fodor's Choice ★

🍴 **CUT at 45 Park Lane.** 87 quid for an 8 oz steak?! NOW we're talkin'! US-based Austrian übernoober star-chef Wolfgang Puck amps up the steak stakes at this counter-intuitive and strangely *smokin'* high-end steak extravaganza on Park Lane. Against a neo-'90s hotel-lobby luxe backdrop of polished marble, Damien Hirsts, and glitzy globe lights, and an '80s soundtrack of Elton John and Lynryd Skynyrd, an army of private equity, petro-dollar, and hedge fund knuckleheads go gangbusters for perfectly-seared prime cuts from the U.S., Chile, England, and Australia. Grilled over charcoal and hardwood, and finished under a 650°C broiler, there's awesome Arkansas Creekstone filet mignon for £34, incredible 35-day USDA Black Angus New York sirloins for £38 or £50, or outstandingly tender-is-the-night rib-eye of Wagyu beef from Araucanía in Chile for a top ranked £87! Add bone marrow, French fries, Béarnaise, and creamed spinach with a fried egg on top for the whole nine yards. $ *Average main: £35* ✉ *45 Park Lane, Mayfair* ☎ *020/7493–4545* ⊕ *www.45parklane.com* ⌂ *Reservations essential* Ⓜ *Marble Arch, Green Park* ✛ *C3.*

$$$$ ✕ **Hélène Darroze at the Connaught.** London's *crème de la crème* flock to
FRENCH French virtuoso Hélène Darroze at the exclusive Connaught hotel for her dazzling regional French haute cuisine, all served up in an impressive Edwardian wood-paneled dining salon sumptuously kitted out by Parisian *It*-designer India Mahdavi. Taking inspiration from Les Landes in southwest France, Darroze sallies forth with a procession of magical dishes. Caviar d'Acquitaine wows with oyster tartare in a sleek Martini glass, topped with black caviar jelly and white haricot bean velouté. Spit-roasted and flambéed pigeon is served gloriously pink, with duck foie gras and mini–Brussels sprouts. To finish, choose pear jelly or apple compote with black Sawarak pepper cream. Darroze may be perfect for celebrations but beware the high prices: £35 for lunch, £55 for Saturday brunch, and £80 to £115 for dinner. $ *Average main: £35* ✉ *The Connaught, Carlos Place, Mayfair* ☎ *020/7107-8880* ⊕ *www.the-connaught.co.uk* ⌂ *Reservations essential* 🛆 *Jacket required* ⊙ *Closed Sun. and Mon.* Ⓜ *Green Park* ✛ *C3.*

$$$$ ✕ **Hibiscus.** Is chunky chef Claude Bosi the *new* Heston Blumenthal?
MODERN FRENCH Such is the acclaim showered on this burly French chef that—*whisper it!*—Bosi's now talked about in the same breath as Blumenthal, Britain's supernova TV chef. Bosi, unsurprisingly, bosses the scene at this disarmingly neutral Mayfair spot with peerless, take-no-prisoners nouvelle dishes like carpaccio of hand-dived Isle of Skye scallops with blobs of truffle and pickled radish, or Cornish John Dory with specs of Morteau sausage and *girolle* mushrooms. The desserts are as *original* as his mains, with an unlikely but flavorsome cep tart standing out. Celebrations, CEOs, and global gastro-tourists are well served by a copious wine list, which features a hefty selection of top-rank "orange" biodynamic, organic, and unadulterated fine wines. $ *Average main: £35* ✉ *29 Maddox St., Mayfair* ☎ *020/7629–2999* ⊕ *www.hibiscusrestaurant.co.uk* ⌂ *Reservations essential* ⊙ *Closed Sun. and Mon.* Ⓜ *Oxford Circus, Piccadilly* ✛ *D3.*

$$$ ✕ **La Petite Maison.** Movie star and blogger Gwyneth Paltrow rates see-
FRENCH and-be-seen La Petite Maison, off New Bond St., as one of her favorite
FAMILY London restaurants, and no wonder—there's nothing on the impressively well-sourced carbo-lite French Mediterranean, Côte d'Azur, and Provençale menu that fails to entice. Try figure-friendly broad bean and Pecorino salad, the soft white Burrata cheese with Datterini tomato and basil spread, or the wonderfully aromatic baked turbot with artichokes, chorizo, five spices, and white wine sauce. Based on the style of the original La Petite Maison in Nice in France, dishes come to the table as and when they're ready, and the chirpy, *jolie,* and informal wait staff make for a convivial Gucci Gucci Gangnam-style party-*ish* vibe. Rosé, anyone? $ *Average main: £26* ✉ *53–54 Brook's Mews, Mayfair* ☎ *020/7495–4774* ⊕ *www.lpmlondon.co.uk* ⌂ *Reservations essential* Ⓜ *Bond St.* ✛ *C3.*

$$$$ FRENCH

🍴 **Le Gavroche.** Enthusiastic "MasterChef" judge Michel Roux Jr. thrives and works the floor at this clubby basement national institution in Mayfair—established by his uncle and father in 1967—and which many still rate to this day as the best *formal* dining in London. With silver domes and old-fashioned unpriced ladies' menus, Roux's mastery of technically precise and classical French cuisine hypnotizes all comers with signature dishes like foie gras with cinnamon-scented crispy duck pancake, langoustine with snails and Hollandaise, pig's trotters, or saddle of rabbit with Parmesan cheese. Desserts like Roux's famous chocolate omelette soufflé or upside-down apple tart are searingly accomplished. Weekday 3-course set lunches (£52) are the best and sanest way to experience such unashamed overwrought flummery—with a half bottle of wine, water, coffee, and petit fours thrown in. The decor is 80s-traditional-luxe: some might find it dated, but the V.I.P.s here must adore it. [$] *Average main: £40* ✉ *43 Upper Brook St., Mayfair* ☎ *020/7408–0881* 🌐 *www.le-gavroche.co.uk* ✍ *Reservations essential* 👔 *Jacket required* 🕒 *Closed Sun. and 10 days at Christmas* [M] *Marble Arch, Bond St.* ✣ *C3.*

$$$ MODERN EUROPEAN Fodor's Choice ★

🍴 **Pollen Street Social.** El Bulli–trained and stratospheric star chef Jason Atherton knocks the London dining scene for a loop at this smash-hit set in a quaint side alleyway off Regent Street. Gobsmacked fans mix-and-max on edgy, witty, and refined small-or-larger dishes ranging from a "full English" starter—a cute deconstructed minature of poached egg, bacon, morels, tomato purée, and croutons—to sublime Dingley Dell pork belly, or tender Atlantic hake with cod cheeks and seaweed. Glamorous diners often move from their tables to perch at counter seats at London's first dessert bar, and watch the dessert staff chop, slice, fiddle about, and prepare immaculate creamy goat-milk rice pudding with hay ice cream or sensational sashimi-like pressed watermelon with an unlikely basil sorbet. Look out for Atherton, who's often around, and note the £27.50 3-course lunches. [$] *Average main: £26* ✉ *8–10 Pollen St., Mayfair* ☎ *020/7290–7600* 🌐 *www.pollenstreetsocial.com* ✍ *Reservations essential* [M] *Oxford Circus, Piccadilly Circus* ✣ *D3.*

$ BURGER FAMILY

🍴 **The Riding House Café.** Stuffed squirrel lamp holders peer down on trendy London diners at this groovy New York–style small-plates-and-luxe-burgers all-day brasserie just north of Oxford Circus. Everything's appropriately salvaged or bespoke here, so you'll find stuffed birds and other taxidermy dotted around, reclaimed theater seats at the long counter bar, bright orange leather banquettes, or old snooker table legs holding up your dining table. Opt for the £5 small plates of sea bass ceviche with lime and chili or veal and pork meatballs with pomarola sauce, and then head for the poached egg chorizo hash browns, pearl-barley salt marsh lamb broth, a decadent cheeseburger, with gherkin and chips—a bargain at £12.50—or their famed tummy-filling lobster lasagna (£18.80). Service is NYC-standard friendly, and you'll find all-day breakfasts, hard shakes, and cocktails, plus sundaes on the kids menu. [$] *Average main: £14* ✉ *43-51 Great Titchfield St., Noho* ☎ *020/7927* 🌐 *www.ridinghousecafe.co.uk* ✍ *Reservations essential* [M] *Oxford Circus* ✣ *D2.*

$$$$ SEAFOOD Fodor's Choice ★ 🍴 **Scott's.** Liveried doormen greet the A-list with a discreet nod at this glamorlicious seafood haven and crustacea bar on fashion-central Mount Street, the new heart of Mayfair. Orginally founded in 1851, and a former haunt of James Bond author Ian Fleming (he adored the potted shrimps), these days you're more likely to see Bill Clinton in one corner, Kate Winslet in another, and former hell-raiser Brit-pack artists, Damien Hirst or Tracy Emin, playing up on a banquette nearby. Scott's draws London's *real* movers and shakers and the attendant beautiful ones, who enjoy day-boat fresh Lindisfarne oysters, baked crab, cod cheeks, shrimp burgers, and lobster Americaine. Magnificent standouts like sautéed razor clams with wild boar sausages or sole Colbert with maître'd hôtel butter are to die for. Prices would make a Saudi shiekh blanch, but fear not: this really is the *hottest* joint in town. [$] *Average main: £32* ✉ *20 Mount St., Mayfair* ☎ *020/7495–7309* 🌐 *www.scotts-restaurant.com* ✍ *Reservations essential* [M] *Bond St., Green Park* ✥ *C3.*

MARYLEBONE

$$ BRASSERIE 🍴 **Galvin Bistrot de Luxe.** The accomplished Chris and Jeff Galvin brothers blaze a trail for the French *bistrot de luxe* approach on a fast-moving stretch of Baker Street. Seasoned fans and a more discerning crowd go for the impeccable food and service in a handsome slate-floor, bentwood chair, and mahogany-paneled Parisian-style salon. There's no finer Dorset crab lasagna in town, and mains consistently punch above their weight: Cornish brill, calves liver with Alsace bacon, stuffed pig's trotter, and sumptious daube of venison with quince and chestnuts are all devilishly tasty, each one a superbly executed gastro triumph. The £19.50 3-course set lunches or £21.50 early evening dinners (6–7 pm) are top value, and look out for occasional live Sunday afternoon jazz. [$] *Average main: £19* ✉ *66 Baker St., Marylebone* ☎ *020/7935–4007* 🌐 *www.galvinrestaurants.com* ✍ *Reservations essential* [M] *Baker St.* ✥ *C2.*

$ SEAFOOD 🍴 **The Golden Hind.** You'll catch some of the best fish-and-chips in London at this great British "chippy" (or traditional fish-and-chip shop), run by a long-standing Greek family in a retro 1914 art deco café. Gaggles of tourists and hungry Marylebone village locals alike hunker down for the homemade cod fishcakes, skate wings, feta fritters, and breaded scampi tails, but it's the neatly prepared and non-greasy deep-fried or steamed battered cod, plaice, and haddock from Grimsby (£4-£6.50), the classic hand-cut Maris Piper chips, and the traditional mushy peas that are the big draws. It's BYO and take away, but note it's only open noon–3 pm weekdays, and 6–10 pm Mon–Sat. [$] *Average main: £6* ✉ *73 Marylebone La., Marylebone* ☎ *020/7486–3644* ✍ *Reservations not accepted* ⏲ *No lunch Sat. Closed Sun.* [M] *Bond St.* ✥ *C2.*

NOTTING HILL AND BAYSWATER

NOTTING HILL

$ MODERN ASIAN 🍴 **E&O.** Gywneth, Madonna, Stella, and a gazillion *flashionistas* and the Learjet set, give a well-manicured thumbs up to this long-standing Asian tapas supremo off Portobello Road market. E&O's figure-friendly medley of Japanese, Chinese, Vietnamese, and Thai all-star favorite dishes includes dim sum, sushi, tempura, and sashimi, with a slew of low-carb options. Don't skip lychee Martinis in the see-and-be-scene bar, before moseying over to the moody monochrome dining room for miso black cod, snow crab maki, papaya salad, Thai rare beef, or lamb rendang; the sea bass sashimi is achingly fresh. There are pavement tables and curb-side bench seats to people-watch on Blenheim Crescent, and it's good for a girly girls' night get-together. $ *Average main: £15* ⊠ *14 Blenheim Crescent, Notting Hill* ☎ *020/7229–5454* ⊕ *www.rickerrestaurants. com/e-and-o* ⊜ *Reservations essential* Ⓜ *Ladbroke Grove* ✠ *A3.*

$$$

MODERN FRENCH

Fodor's Choice

★

✕ **The Ledbury.** Sensational Aussie chef Brett Graham wins hearts, minds— and global accolades—at this high-ceilinged destination dining landmark on the crumbier edges of Notting Hill. In a handsome four-square room full of drapes, mirrored walls, and plush seats, you won't find a more inventive vegetable dish than Graham's ash-baked celeriac with hazelnut and wood sorrel, and it's impossible to best his roast quail with walnut cream, roe deer with bone marrow, or Cornish turbot with fennel and elderflower. Besides an *obsessive* interest in game, Graham's also famous for incredible desserts, so why not finish with thinly sliced figs with ewes milk yogurt and fig-leaf ice cream? Pro service and a top sommelier round out this winning proposition, now considered one of London's very best eateries by many foodies. $ *Average main: £31* ⊠ *127 Ledbury Rd., Notting Hill* ☎ *0207/7792–9090* ⊕ *www.theledbury.com* ⊜ *Reservations essential* ☉ *No lunch Mon.* Ⓜ *Westbourne Park, Ladbroke Grove* ✠ *A2.*

$

MODERN BRITISH

✕ **The Mall Tavern.** It's all things unapologetically British at this embrac-ing 1856 Notting Hill gastropub, which overflows with relaxed but discerning locals. Check out the Coronation mugs, royal wedding, and Prince Charles and Lady Diana crockery and memorabilia after sam-pling some great British bar snacks, like pork scratchings, brawn (head cheese), or lop-eared sausage rolls. Move through to dine on chef Jess Dunford Wood's hearty cow pie with bone marrow poking through the crust, or wallow in '70s nostalgia with chicken Kiev, macaroni cheese, or high-quality fish fingers, mushy peas, and tartare sauce. There's old-school Artic Roll ice cream, "Hello to the Queen!" glacé bananas with hot chocolate sauce, and some strong farmhouse cheeses, like Mrs Kirkham's Lancashire, and Shorrock's Bomb. ▮TIP➔ Note the bargain £10 lunches from Tuesday to Friday. $ *Average main: £13* ⊠ *71 Palace Gardens Terr., Notting Hill* ☎ *020/7229–3374* ⊕ *www.themalltavern. com* ⊜ *Reservations essential* Ⓜ *Notting Hill Gate* ✠ *A3.*

BAYSWATER

$$

MODERN BRITISH

✕ **Hereford Road.** Bespeckled chef and co-owner Tom Pemberton mans the front-of-house grill station at this must-visit Bayswater favorite, renowed for its pomp-free, pared-down, and ingredient-driven seasonal British fare. With an accent on well-sourced honest-to-goodness regional and seasonal British produce, many dishes are as unfussy as you'll find. Work your way though uncluttered combinations like steamed mussels with cider and thyme, lemon sole with sea dulse, duck breast with pickled wal-nuts, and English rice pudding and jam. Expect to brush past the entire well-heeled Tory party senior leadership and Notting Hill set on the way out, and ▮TIP➔ NB: the express £9.50, or set £13 or £15.50 lunches are arguably the best high-quality lunch deals in town. $ *Average main: £16* ⊠ *3 Hereford Rd., Bayswater* ☎ *020/7727–1144* ⊕ *www.herefordroad. org* ⊜ *Reservations essential* Ⓜ *Bayswater, Queensway* ✠ *A3.*

REGENT'S PARK AND HAMPSTEAD

$ 🍴 **Lemonia.** Hollywood-*ville* Primrose Hill's favorite Greek Cypriot restaurant, vine-decked and '80s taverna-style Lemonia is large and light, and always packed with hordes of hungry locals. Besides an endless supply of small-dish *mezédes* dips and starters, there are rustic mains like slow-baked *kleftiko* lamb in lemon, aubergine and potato *moussaka,* and beef stewed in red wine. Expect generous Greek hospitality, tons of noise, and the odd fly-by from the ritzy boho-chic Primrose Hill/super-megastar set. Top-value weekday luncheons are a bargain £12.50. [$] *Average main: £14* ✉ *89 Regent's Park Rd., Regent's Park* ☎ *020/7586–7454* ✍ *Reservations essential* 🕐 *No lunch Sat. No dinner Sun.* [M] *Chalk Farm* ✥ *B1.*

GREEK

PUBS

The city's pubs, public houses, or "locals" dispense beer, good cheer, and casual grub in settings that range from ancient wood-beam rooms to ornate Victorian interiors to utilitarian modern rooms. Pubs in the capital are changing: 90-year-old licensing laws have finally been modernized, gastropub fever has swept London, and smoking in all pubs has been illegal since 2007. At many places char-grills are being installed in the kitchen out back, and up front the faded wallpapers are being replaced by abstract paintings. Some showcase nouveau pub grub, but whether you have Moroccan chicken or the usually dismal ploughman's special, do order a pint. Note that American-style beer is called "lager" in Britain, whereas the real British brew is "bitter" (usually served cellar temperature, which is cooler than room temperature but not actually chilled). Order up your choice in two sizes—pints or half pints. Some London pubs also sell "real ale," which is less gassy than bitters and, many would argue, has a better flavor.

The list below offers a few pubs selected for central location, historical interest, a pleasant garden, music, or good food, but you might just as happily adopt your own temporary local.

SOHO AND COVENT GARDEN

Lamb & Flag. This refreshingly un-gentrified 17th-century pub was once known as the Bucket of Blood because the upstairs room was used as a ring for bare-knuckle boxing. Now it's a friendly—and bloodless—place, serving food (lunch only) and real ale. It's on the edge of Covent Garden, up a hidden alley off Garrick Street. ✉ *33 Rose St., Covent Garden* ☎ *020/7497–9504* 🌐 *www.lambandflagcoventgarden.co.uk* [M] *Covent Garden.*

White Hart. Claiming to be the oldest licensed pub in London, this elegant, family-owned place on Drury Lane had already been here for more than 500 years when it served highwayman Dick Turpin in 1739, just before he was hanged. Nowadays it is one of the best places to mix with cast and crew of the stage. A female-friendly environment, a cheery skylight above the lounge area, and above-average pub fare make the White Hart a particularly sociable spot for a drink. ✉ *191 Drury La., Covent Garden* ☎ *020/7242–2317* [M] *Holborn, Covent Garden, Tottenham Court Rd.*

2

BLOOMSBURY AND HOLBURN

The Lamb. Charles Dickens and his contemporaries drank here, but today's enthusiastic clientele make sure this intimate and eternally popular pub avoids the pitfalls of feeling too old-fashioned. For private chats at the bar, you can close a delicate etched-glass "snob screen" to the bar staff, opening it only when you fancy another pint. ⌧ *94 Lamb's Conduit St., Bloomsbury* ☎ *020/7405–0713* ⊕ *www.youngs. co.uk* Ⓜ *Russell Sq.*

Museum Tavern. Across the street from the British Museum, this friendly and classy Victorian pub makes an ideal resting place after the rigors of the culture trail. Karl Marx unwound here after a hard day in the Library. He could have spent his *Kapital* on any of seven well-kept beers available on tap. ⌧ *49 Great Russell St., Bloomsbury* ☎ *020/7242–8987* Ⓜ *Tottenham Court Rd.*

THE CITY

Fodor's Choice
★
Black Friar. A step from Blackfriars Tube station, this spectacular pub has an Arts and Crafts interior that is entertainingly, satirically ecclesiastical, with inlaid mother-of-pearl, wood carvings, stained glass, and marble pillars all over the place. In spite of the finely lettered temperance tracts on view just below the reliefs of monks, fairies, and friars, there is a nice group of ales on tap from independent brewers. The 20th-century poet Sir John Betjeman once led a successful campaign to save the pub from demolition. ⌧ *174 Queen Victoria St., The City* ☎ *020/7236–5474* ⊕ *www. nicholsonspubs.co.uk/theblackfriarblackfriarslondon* Ⓜ *Blackfriars.*

Fodor's Choice
★
Craft Beer Company. With 37 beers on tap and 300 more in bottles (some brewed exclusively for the Craft Beer Company), the main problem here is knowing where to start. Luckily, friendly and knowledgeable staff are happy to advise or give tasters—or why not sign up for a guided tasting session? A huge chandelier and a mirrored ceiling lend antique charm to the interior, and a smattering of tourists and beer pilgrims break up the crowds of Leather Lane workers and locals. ⌧ *82 Leather La., Clerkenwell* ⊕ *thecraftbeerco.com* Ⓜ *Chancery Lane.*

Fodor's Choice
★
Jerusalem Tavern. Owned by the well-respected St. Peter's Brewery from Suffolk, the Jerusalem Tavern is one-of-a-kind: small, and endearingly eccentric. Ancient Delft-style tiles meld with wood and concrete in a converted watchmaker and jeweler's shop dating back to the 18th century. The beer, both bottled and on tap, is some of the best available anywhere in London. It's loved by Londoners and often busy, especially after work. ⌧ *55 Britton St., Clerkenwell* ☎ *020/7490–4281* ⊕ *www. stpetersbrewery.co.uk/london-pub* Ⓜ *Farringdon.*

Ye Olde Cheshire Cheese. Yes, this extremely historic pub (it dates from 1667, the year after the Great Fire of London) is full of tourists, but it deserves a visit for its sawdust-covered floors, low wood-beam ceilings, and the 14th-century crypt of Whitefriars' monastery under the cellar bar. This was the most regular of Dr. Johnson's and Dickens's many locals. Food is served, except on Sunday (when it's only open from noon to 3). ⌧ *145 Fleet St., The City* ☎ *020/7353–6170* Ⓜ *Blackfriars.*

SOUTH BANK

Fodor's Choice
★
Anchor & Hope. One of London's most popular gastropubs, the Anchor & Hope doesn't take reservations (except for Sunday lunch). Would-be diners snake around the red-walled, wooden-floored pub, kept happy by some good real ales and a fine wine list as they wait for hours for a table. The excellent, meaty English food is old-fashioned English—think salt cod, tripe, and chips (fries)—with a few modern twists. ⊠ *36 The Cut, South Bank* ☎ *020/7928–9898* Ⓜ *Southwark.*

Market Porter. Opposite the foodie treasures of Borough Market, this atmospheric pub opens at 6 am for the stallholders, and always seems busy. Remarkably, the place manages to remain relaxed, with helpful staff and happy customers spilling out onto the road right through the year. The wide selection of real ales is lovingly tended. The pub was used as a set for one of the Harry Potter movies. ⊠ *9 Stoney St., Borough* ☎ *020/7407–2495* ⊕ *www.markettaverns.co.uk* Ⓜ *London Bridge.*

KENSINGTON, KNIGHTSBRIDGE, AND MAYFAIR

The Nag's Head. The landlord of this idiosyncratic little mews pub in Belgravia runs a tight ship, and no cell phones are allowed. If that sounds like misery, the lovingly collected artifacts (including antique penny arcade games) that decorate every inch of the place, high-quality beer, and old-fashioned pub grub should make up for it. ⊠ *53 Kinnerton St., Belgravia* ☎ *020/7235–1135* Ⓜ *Knightsbridge, Hyde Park Corner.*

Fodor's Choice
★
Punch Bowl. In a quiet corner of Mayfair, the cozy little Punch Bowl has a worn wood floor and well-spoken staff dressed in pale checked shirts. The pub dates from 1750 and the interior remains steadfastly old-fashioned, with a painting of Churchill, candles, polished dark wood, and engraved windows. Try the place's eponymous ale, made specially in Scotland by Caledonian. A special dining area at the rear buzzes at lunchtime with locals who come for the upscale English pub grub. ⊠ *41 Farm St., Mayfair* ☎ *020/7493–6841* ⊕ *www.punchbowllondon.com* Ⓜ *Green Park, Bond St.*

WHERE TO STAY

Use the coordinate (✛ B2) at the end of each listing to locate a site on the corresponding map.

Queen Elizabeth hasn't invited you this time? No matter. Staying at one of London's grande-dame hotels is the next-best thing to being a guest at the palace—and some say it's even better. Happily, however, there is no dearth of options where friendliness outdistances luxe—London, thank goodness, has plenty of atmospheric places that won't cost a king's ransom.

That noted, until fairly recently it was extremely difficult to find a decent hotel in the center for less than £150 per night. Things have improved, thanks in part to the global recession, but also to a flurry of new midprice hotels that have sprung up in the last few years.

WHERE SHOULD I STAY?

	NEIGHBORHOOD VIBE	PROS	CONS
Westminster, St. James's, and Royal London	This historic section, aka "Royal London," is home to major tourist attractions like Buckingham Palace.	Central area near tourist sites; easy Tube access; considered a safe area to stay.	Mostly expensive lodging options; few restaurants and entertainment venues nearby.
Soho and Covent Garden	A tourist hub with endless entertainment on the streets and in theaters and clubs—it's party central for young adults.	Buzzing area with plenty to see and do; late-night entertainment abounds; wonderful shopping district.	The area tends to be noisy at night; few budget hotels; keep your wits about you at night, and watch out for pickpockets.
Bloomsbury, Holborn, Hampstead, and Islington	Diverse area that is part bustling business center and part tranquil respite with tree-lined streets and meadows.	Easy access to Tube, and 15 minutes to city center; major sights, like British Museum are here; buzzing nightlife in Islington.	Busy streets filled with honking trucks and roving students; the area around King's Cross can be sketchy—particularly at night.
The City and South Bank	London's financial district, where most of the city's banks and businesses are headquartered.	Central location with easy transportation access; great hotel deals in South Bank; many major sights nearby.	It can be as quiet as a tomb after 8 pm; many nearby restaurants and shops close over the weekend.
East End	Increasingly trendy area east of the town center with a great arts scene.	Great for art lovers, shoppers, and business execs with meetings in Canary Wharf.	Still a transitional area, parts of Hoxton can be a bit dodgy at night; 20-minute Tube ride from central London.
Kensington, Knightsbridge, and Mayfair	This is one of London's most upscale neighborhoods and a center of London's tourist universe. A glittering galaxy of posh department stores, boutiques, and fabulous hotels.	Diverse hotel selection; great area for meandering walks; superb shopping district; London's capital of high-end shopping.	Depending on where you are, the nearest Tube might be a hike; residential area might be too quiet for some. Few budget hotel or restaurant options; beware of pickpockets.
Notting Hill and Bayswater	This is an upscale, trendy area favored by locals, with plenty of good hotels.	Hotel deals abound if you know where to look; gorgeous greenery in Hyde Park; great shopping districts.	Choose the wrong place and you may end up in a flea pit; residential areas may be too quiet at night for some.
Regent's Park and Hampstead	A mix of arty, fashionable districts with a villagelike feel in other places.	Good access to central London; easy to fall in love with this part of town.	Some distance from center; lack of hotel/dining options.

It's all so different if money is no object. London has some of the very best and most luxurious hotels in the world. On the other hand, freshly minted billionaires favor the rash of new hot spots, like the Corinthia, while fashion plates always book Kit Kemp's super-stylish hotels (such as the Covent Garden). But even these places have sales, and you can sometimes snag a bargain within the reach of ordinary mortals—particularly in the off-season—or just be a spectator to all the glamour by visiting for that most traditional of high-society treats, afternoon tea. The top end has also seen a spectacular new arrival, with the rebirth of the gorgeous Victorian-meets-modern St. Pancras Hotel, which lay closed and virtually untouched for nearly 80 years.

Meanwhile, several midrange hotels have dropped their average prices in response to the choppy waters of the global economy, which has pulled some fantastic places, such as Hazlitt's and Town Hall, back into the affordable category. And there's a clutch of new, stylish, and super-cheap hotels that are a real step forward for the city. The downside is that these places tend to be a little out of the way, but that's often a price worth paying. Another attractive alternative includes hotels in the Premier and Millennium chains, which offer sleek, modern rooms, lots of up-to-date conveniences, and sales that frequently bring room prices well below £100 a night.

You should confirm *exactly* what your room costs before checking in. In January and February you can often find reduced rates, and large hotels with a business clientele have frequent weekend packages. The usual practice these days in all but the cheaper hotels is for quoted prices to cover room alone; breakfast, whether Continental or "full English," costs extra. V.A.T. (value-added tax—sales tax) follows the same rule, with the most expensive hotels excluding a hefty 20%; middle-of-the-range and budget places include it in the initial quote. *Prices in the reviews are the lowest cost of a standard double room in high season. For additional choices, visit Fodors.com.*

WESTMINSTER, ST. JAMES'S, AND ROYAL LONDON

For expanded hotel reviews, visit Fodors.com.

WESTMINSTER

$$ B&B/INN **B&B Belgravia.** At this modern guesthouse near Victoria Station, a clean, chic white color scheme, simple modern furniture, and a lounge where a fire crackles away in the winter are all geared to stylish comfort. **Pros:** nice extras like free use of a laptop in the hotel lounge; coffee and tea always available. **Cons:** rooms and bathrooms are small; unimaginative breakfasts; can be noisy, especially on lower floors. [$] *Rooms from: £135* ✉ *64–66 Ebury St., Victoria* ☎ *020/7259–8570* 🌐 *www.bb-belgravia.com* *17 rooms* 🍴 *Breakfast* [M] *Sloane Square, Victoria* ✣ *E5.*

$$$$ HOTEL Fodor's Choice ★ **The Corinthia.** A star in the firmament of new hotels that have opened in London in this decade, the Corinthia is design heaven-on-earth, with levels of service that make anyone feel like a VIP. **Pros:** so much luxury and elegance you'll feel like royalty. **Cons:** prices jump to the stratosphere once the cheapest rooms sell out. [$] *Rooms from: £420*

⊠ *Whitehall Pl., Westminster* ☎ *020/7930–8181* ⊕ *www.corinthia.com*
🛏 *294 rooms* ⧠⊘⧠ *Breakfast* Ⓜ *Embankment* ✛ *F4.*

$$$
HOTEL
FAMILY

🏨 **DoubleTree by Hilton Hotel London Westminster.** Spectacular views of the river, Big Ben, and the London Eye fill the floor-to-ceiling windows in this rather stark, steel-and-glass building steps from the Tate Britain, and a plethora of techy perks await inside. **Pros:** amazing views; flat screens and other high-tech gadgetry. **Cons:** small bedrooms; tiny bathrooms; TV has to be operated through a computer (confusing if you're not used to it). Ⓢ *Rooms from: £230* ⊠ *30 John Islip St., Westminster* ☎ *020/7630–1000* ⊕ *doubletree3.hilton.com* 🛏 *444 rooms, 16 suites* ⧠⊘⧠ *Some meals* Ⓜ *Westminster, Pimlico* ✛ *F5.*

$$$$
HOTEL
Fodor's Choice
★

🏨 **Hotel 41.** Designer credentials and high-tech gadgets are everywhere in the impeccably coordinated black-and-white rooms, some split-level and all gorgeously furnished with extraordinary pieces drawn from every corner of the globe. **Pros:** unique place opposite Buckingham Palace; great service; unlimited free Wi-Fi. **Cons:** unusual design is not for everyone. Ⓢ *Rooms from: £323* ⊠ *41 Buckingham Palace Rd., Victoria* ☎ *020/7300–0041* ⊕ *www.41hotel.com* 🛏 *26 rooms, 4 suites, 2 apartments* ⧠⊘⧠ *Breakfast* Ⓜ *Victoria* ✛ *E5.*

$$
HOTEL

🏨 **The Luna Simone Hotel.** This delightful and friendly little family-run hotel, a short stroll from Buckingham Palace, is a real find for the price in central London. **Pros:** friendly and well run; family rooms are outstanding value; superb location. **Cons:** dated style; tiny bathrooms; no elevator or air-conditioning. Ⓢ *Rooms from: £120* ⊠ *47–49 Belgrave Rd., Pimlico* ☎ *020/7834–5897* ⊕ *www.lunasimonehotel.com* 🛏 *36 rooms* ⧠⊘⧠ *Breakfast* Ⓜ *Pimlico, Victoria* ✛ *E6.*

$
RENTAL

🏨 **Studios @ 82.** A great little side operation from B&B Belgravia, these self-catering apartments represent fantastic value for money; they're pleasant, contemporary spaces that have everything you need, plus a few useful extras such as free Wi-Fi. **Pros:** great price; lovely location; all the independence of self-catering. **Cons:** lots of stairs and no elevator. Ⓢ *Rooms from: £99* ⊠ *64–66 Ebury St., Victoria* ☎ *020/7259–8570* ⊕ *www.bb-belgravia. com* 🛏 *9 apartments* ⧠⊘⧠ *Breakfast* Ⓜ *Knightsbridge* ✛ *E5.*

ST. JAMES'S

$$$$
HOTEL
FAMILY
Fodor's Choice
★

🏨 **Claridge's.** The original art deco public spaces of this super-glamorous London institution are gloriously unspoiled (down to the grand staircase and elevator, complete with upholstered sofa). **Pros:** serious luxury everywhere—this is an old-money hotel; comics, books, and DVDs to help keep kids amused. **Cons:** better pack your designer wardrobe—guests in the hotel bar can be almost cartoonishly snobbish. Ⓢ *Rooms from: £390* ⊠ *Brook St., St. James's* ☎ *020/7629–8860, 866/599–6991 in U.S.* ⊕ *www.claridges.co.uk* 🛏 *203 rooms* ⧠⊘⧠ *Breakfast* Ⓜ *Bond St.* ✛ *E3.*

$$$
HOTEL
Fodor's Choice
★

🏨 **The Stafford London by Kempinski.** This is a rare find: a posh hotel that's equal parts elegance and friendliness, and it's in one of the few peaceful spots in the area, down a small lane behind Piccadilly. **Pros:** great staff; big, luxurious rooms; quiet location. **Cons:** traditional style is not to all tastes; men must wear jackets in the bar. Ⓢ *Rooms from: £260* ⊠ *St. James's Pl., St. James's* ☎ *020/7493–0111* ⊕ *www.kempinski.com/ london* 🛏 *81 rooms* ⧠⊘⧠ *Breakfast* Ⓜ *Green Park* ✛ *E4.*

BEST BETS: LONDON LODGING

SOHO AND COVENT GARDEN

For expanded hotel reviews, visit Fodors.com.

SOHO

$$
HOTEL
Fodor's Choice
★

Dean Street Townhouse. Discreet and unpretentious, but oh-so-stylish—
and right in the heart of Soho—this place has a bohemian vibe and
an excellent modern British restaurant, hung with art by, among
others, Peter Blake and Tracy Emin. **Pros:** über-cool; resembles an
upper-class pied à terre. **Cons:** full rate reflects location rather than
what you get; some rooms are small; rooms at the front can be noisy,
especially on weekends; occasional 2-night minimum stay. $ *Rooms
from: £188* ⊠ *69–71 Dean St., Soho* ☎ *020/7434–1775* ⊕ *www.
deanstreettownhouse.com* ↘ *39 rooms* ⚭ *Breakfast* Ⓜ *Leicester Sq.,
Tottenham Court Rd.* ✛ *F3.*

$$$
HOTEL

Hazlitt's. This disarmingly friendly place, full of personality, robust
antiques, and claw-foot tubs, occupies three connected early-18th-
century houses, one of which was the last home of essayist William
Hazlitt (1778–1830). **Pros:** great for lovers of art and antiques; historic
atmosphere with lots of small sitting rooms and wooden staircases;
truly beautiful and relaxed. **Cons:** no in-house restaurant; breakfast
is £12 extra; no elevators. $ *Rooms from: £216* ⊠ *6 Frith St., Soho*

☎ 020/7434–1771 🌐 *www.hazlittshotel.com* 🛏 *20 rooms, 3 suites* 🍴 *No meals* [M] *Tottenham Court Rd.* ✥ *F3.*

COVENT GARDEN

$$$$ HOTEL Fodor's Choice ★ 🏨 **Covent Garden Hotel.** It's little wonder this is now the London home-away-from-home for off-duty celebrities, actors, and style mavens, with its Covent Garden location and guest rooms that are *World of Interiors*-stylish. **Pros:** great for star-spotting, super-trendy. **Cons:** you can feel you don't matter if you're not famous; setting in Covent Garden can be a bit boisterous. [$] *Rooms from: £315* ✉ *10 Monmouth St., Covent Garden* ☎ *020/7806–1000, 800/553–6674 in U.S.* 🌐 *www.firmdale.com* 🛏 *55 rooms, 3 suites* 🍴 *Some meals* [M] *Covent Garden* ✥ *F3.*

$$$$ HOTEL Fodor's Choice ★ 🏨 **ME London.** One can only imagine the endless concept meetings that went into this shiny luxury hotel at the end of the Strand, but the result—a happy mix of high fashion and futuristic hipster—is almost achingly on-trend. **Pros:** very fashionable; full of high-tech comforts; excellent service. **Cons:** design can sometimes verge on form over function; very small closets and in-room storage areas. [$] *Rooms from: £340* ✉ *336 The Strand, Covent Garden* ☎ *0845/601–8980* 🌐 *www.melia.com* 🛏 *141 rooms, 16 suites* 🍴 *Breakfast* ✥ *G3.*

$$$$ HOTEL Fodor's Choice ★ 🏨 **The Savoy.** One of London's most famous hotels has emerged from a £220 million renovation, and the old girl is looking like a superstar again. **Pros:** the best hotel in London, period; Thames-side location; less snooty than many others of its pedigree. **Cons:** everything comes with a price tag; bedrooms can be surprisingly noisy, particularly on lower floors; right off the super-busy Strand. [$] *Rooms from: £375* ✉ *Strand, Covent Garden* ☎ *020/7836–4343, 800/257–7544 in U.S.* 🌐 *www.fairmont.com/savoy-london* 🛏 *268* 🍴 *Breakfast* [M] *Covent Garden, Charing Cross* ✥ *G3.*

BLOOMSBURY AND HOLBORN

For expanded hotel reviews, visit Fodors.com.

BLOOMSBURY

$ B&B/INN 🏨 **Alhambra Hotel.** One of the best bargains in Bloomsbury is a stone's throw from King's Cross and the Eurostar terminal, and though rooms are very small and the neighborhood is still "edgy," few places are this cheery and clean for the price. **Pros:** low price, with breakfast included; friendly service; central location. **Cons:** zero frills; stairs to climb; some rooms have shared bathrooms. [$] *Rooms from: £75* ✉ *17–19 Argyle St., Bloomsbury* ☎ *020/7837–9575* 🌐 *www.alhambrahotel.com* 🛏 *52 rooms* 🍴 *Breakfast* [M] *King's Cross* ✥ *G1.*

$$ B&B/INN 🏨 **Arosfa Hotel.** Simple, friendly, and pleasantly quirky, this little B&B, once the home of pre-Raphaelite painter Sir John Everett Millais, is on an elegant Georgian street within walking distance of the West End and the British Museum. **Pros:** friendly staff; check-in from 7 am; good location for museums and theaters; free Wi-Fi. **Cons:** some rooms are very small; bathrooms have showers only; few services. [$] *Rooms from: £110* ✉ *83 Gower St., Bloomsbury* ☎ *020/7636–2115* 🌐 *www.arosfalondon.com* 🛏 *15 rooms* 🍴 *Breakfast* [M] *Goodge St., Euston Sq.* ✥ *F2.*

The Corinthia

The Connaught

The Dorchester

Covent Garden Hotel

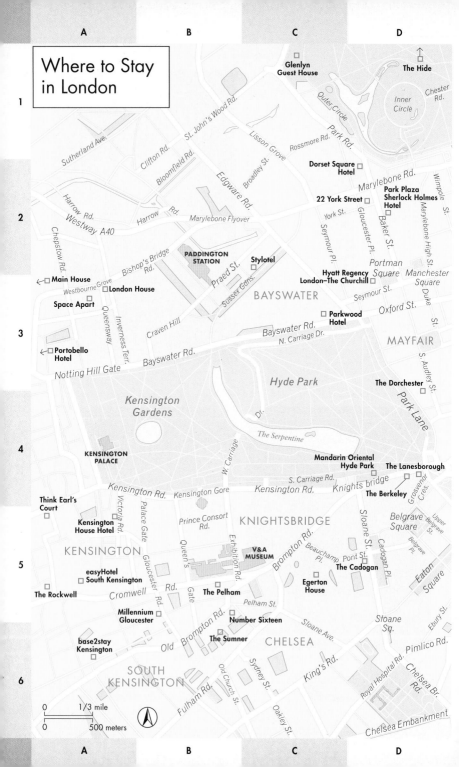

Where to Stay in London

A **B** **C** **D**

1

Glenlyn Guest House

The Hide

Inner Circle

Chester Rd.

Outer Circle

St. John's Wood Rd.

Sutherland Ave.

Clifton Rd.

Bloomfield Rd.

Lisson Grove

Rossmore Rd.

Park Rd.

Dorset Square Hotel

Marylebone Rd.

Edgware Rd.

Broadley St.

22 York Street

Park Plaza Sherlock Holmes Hotel

Wimpole St.

Marylebone High St.

2

Harrow Rd.

Westway A40

Harrow Rd.

Marylebone Flyover

York St.

Seymour Pl.

Gloucester Pl.

Baker St.

Chepstow Rd.

Bishop's Bridge Rd.

PADDINGTON STATION

Praed St.

Stylotel

Portman Square

Manchester Square

Duke St.

Main House

Westbourne Grove

London House

Sussex Gdns.

BAYSWATER

Hyatt Regency London–The Churchill

Seymour St.

Oxford St.

Space Apart

Queensway

Inverness Terr.

Craven Hill

Bayswater Rd.

N. Carriage Dr.

Parkwood Hotel

MAYFAIR

3

Portobello Hotel

Bayswater Rd.

Notting Hill Gate

Hyde Park

S. Audley St.

The Dorchester

Park Lane

Kensington Gardens

W. Carriage Dr.

The Serpentine

KENSINGTON PALACE

Kensington Rd.

Kensington Gore

Kensington Rd.

S. Carriage Rd.

Mandarin Oriental Hyde Park

Knightsbridge

The Lanesborough

Grosvenor Cres.

The Berkeley

4

Think Earl's Court

Victoria Rd.

Palace Gate

Prince Consort Rd.

KNIGHTSBRIDGE

Belgrave Square

Upper Belgrave St.

belgrave Pl.

Kensington House Hotel

KENSINGTON

Gloucester Rd.

Queen's Gate

Exhibition Rd.

V&A MUSEUM

Brompton Rd.

Beauchamp Pl.

Sloane St.

Cadogan Pl.

Pont St.

The Cadogan

Eaton Square

5

easyHotel South Kensington

The Rockwell

Cromwell Rd.

The Pelham

Pelham St.

Egerton House

Sloane Sq.

Ebury St.

Millennium Gloucester

Old Brompton Rd.

Number Sixteen

Sloane Ave.

Pimlico Rd.

Chelsea Br. Rd.

base2stay Kensington

The Sumner

CHELSEA

King's Rd.

Royal Hospital Rd.

SOUTH KENSINGTON

Fulham Rd.

Old Church St.

Sydney St.

Oakley St.

Chelsea Embankment

6

0 1/3 mile

0 500 meters

A **B** **C** **D**

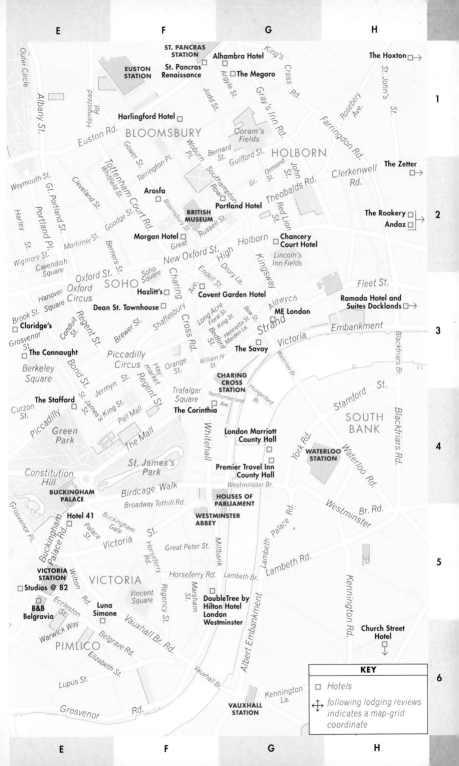

Claridge's

The Stafford London by Kempinski

$$ 🛏 **Harlingford Hotel.** The most contemporary of the Cartwright Gar-
HOTEL dens hotels offers sleek, quiet, and comfortable bedrooms and per-
fectly appointed public rooms. **Pros:** good location; friendly staff; use
of private garden; wider breakfast choice than at many small London
hotels. **Cons:** rooms are quite small; no elevator. $ *Rooms from: £120*
⊠ *61–63 Cartwright Gardens, Bloomsbury* ☎ *020/7387–1551* ⊕ *www.
harlingfordhotel.com* ⤳ *43 rooms* ⫤ *Breakfast* Ⓜ *Russell Sq.* ✛ *F1.*

$$ 🛏 **The Megaro.** Directly across the street from St. Pancras International
HOTEL station (for Eurostar), the snazzy, well-designed, modern bedrooms
here surround guests with startlingly contemporary style and amenities that include powerful showers and espresso machines. **Pros:** comfortable beds; great location for Eurostar; short hop on Tube to city
center. **Cons:** neighborhood isn't great; standard rooms are small; interiors may be a bit stark for some. $ *Rooms from: £160* ⊠ *Belgrove
St., King's Cross* ☎ *020/7843–2222* ⊕ *www.hotelmegaro.co.uk* ⤳ *49
rooms* ⫤ *Breakfast* ✛ *G1.*

$$ 🛏 **Morgan Hotel.** Don't expect many bells or whistles in this former
B&B/INN Georgian house, but the rooms are sunny and attractive and it overlooks
the British Museum and is close to West End theaters. **Pros:** friendly
staff; double and triple rooms are large by London standards; good
location. **Cons:** mattresses are quite thin, as are walls; no elevator.
$ *Rooms from: £135* ⊠ *24 Bloomsbury St., Bloomsbury* ☎ *020/7636–
3735* ⊕ *www.morganhotel.co.uk* ⤳ *15 rooms, 5 apartments* ⫤ *Break-
fast* Ⓜ *Tottenham Court Rd., Russell Sq.* ✛ *F2.*

$ 🛏 **The Portland Hotel.** Around the corner from leafy Russell Square and
HOTEL an easy walk to the British Museum and Covent Garden, the Portland
offers spacious and comfortable bedrooms, with large bathrooms, seat-
ing areas, and kitchenettes. **Pros:** great location; large rooms; kitchen-
ettes offer alternative to restaurants; staff is friendly. **Cons:** restaurant
is in neighboring hotel, requiring a walk down the street to breakfast;
prices rise hugely after cheap rooms are sold. $ *Rooms from: £91* ⊠ *31–
32 Bedford Pl., Bloomsbury* ☎ *020/7580–7088* ⊕ *www.grangehotels.
com* ⤳ *18 rooms* ⫤ *Breakfast* Ⓜ *Holborn Rd.* ✛ *G2.*

$$$ 🛏 **St. Pancras Renaissance.** Reopened in 2011 after nearly a century of
HOTEL dereliction, this stunningly restored Victorian landmark—replete with
Fodor's Choice gingerbread turrets and castle-like ornaments—started as a love letter
★ to the golden age of railways; now it's one of London's most sophisticated places to stay (bait-and-switch department: note that the guest
rooms are modern and sleek). **Pros:** Victorian heaven (in parts); unique
and beautiful; faultless service; just an elevator ride to the Eurostar.
Cons: very popular bar and restaurant; streets outside are always busy.
$ *Rooms from: £230* ⊠ *Euston Rd., King's Cross* ☎ *020/7841–3540*
⊕ *www.marriott.com* ⤳ *207 rooms, 38 suites* ⫤ *Breakfast* Ⓜ *Kings
Cross St. Pancras. National Rail: Kings Cross St. Pancras* ✛ *F1.*

HOLBORN

$$$ 🛏 **Chancery Court Hotel.** So striking it was featured in the movie *How-
HOTEL ards End,* this landmark structure (built by the Pearl Assurance Com-
pany in 1914) now houses a beautiful hotel with a clubby feel and
extra-spacious guest rooms. **Pros:** gorgeous space; great spa; your
every need catered to. **Cons:** area is deserted at night and on weekends.

Mandarin Oriental Hyde Park

Church Street Hotel

The Hoxton

Number Sixteen

The Zetter

The Rookery

2

$ *Rooms from: £212 ⊠ 252 High Holborn, Holborn ☎ 020/7829–9888 ⊕ www.chancerycourthotel.com ⤳ 342 rooms, 14 suites ⦿ Some meals Ⓜ Holborn ✛ G2.*

$$$
HOTEL
Fodor's Choice
★

🏨 **The Zetter.** The dizzying five-story atrium, art deco staircase, and slick European restaurant hint at the delights to come in this converted warehouse—a breath of fresh air with its playful color schemes, elegant wallpapers, and wonderful views of The City from the higher floors. **Pros:** huge amounts of character; big rooms; free Wi-Fi; gorgeous "Rainforest" showers. **Cons:** rooms with good views cost more. $ *Rooms from: £234 ⊠ 86–88 Clerkenwell Rd., Holborn ☎ 020/7324–4444 ⊕ www.thezetter.com ⤳ 59 rooms ⦿ Breakfast Ⓜ Farringdon ✛ H2.*

THE CITY

For expanded hotel reviews, visit Fodors.com.

$$
HOTEL
Fodor's Choice
★

🏨 **The Rookery.** An absolutely unique and beautiful 1725 town house, the Rookery is the kind of place where you want to allow quality time to enjoy and soak up the atmosphere. **Pros:** helpful staff; free Wi-Fi; good deals in the off-season. **Cons:** breakfast costs extra; short Tube ride to tourist sites. $ *Rooms from: £144 ⊠ 12 Peter's La., at Cowcross St., The City ☎ 020/7336–0931 ⊕ www.rookeryhotel.com ⤳ 30 rooms, 3 suites ⦿ No meals Ⓜ Farringdon ✛ H2.*

THE EAST END

For expanded hotel reviews, visit Fodors.com.

$$
HOTEL

🏨 **Andaz.** Swanky and upscale, this hotel boasts a modern, masculine design, and novel check-in procedure—instead of standing at a desk, guests sit in a lounge while a staff member with a handheld computer takes their information. **Pros:** nice attention to detail; guests can borrow an iPod from the front desk; no standing in line to check in; "healthy minibars" are stocked with nuts, fruit, and yogurt. **Cons:** sparse interior design is not for all; rates rise significantly for midweek stays. $ *Rooms from: £154 ⊠ 40 Liverpool St., East End ☎ 020/7961–1234, 800/492–8804 in U.S. ⊕ www.andaz.hyatt.com ⤳ 267 rooms ⦿ Breakfast Ⓜ Liverpool St. ✛ H2.*

$
HOTEL
Fodor's Choice
★

🏨 **The Hoxton Hotel.** The design throughout this trendy East London lodging is contemporary—but not so modern as to be absurd—and in keeping with a claim to combine a country-lodge lifestyle with true urban living, a fire crackles in the lobby. **Pros:** cool vibe; neighborhood known for funky galleries and boutiques; huge weekend discounts; way-cool restaurant; one hour of free international calls. **Cons:** price rockets during the week; away from tourist sights; £1 rooms sell out months ahead. $ *Rooms from: £90 ⊠ 81 Great Eastern St., East End ☎ 020/7550–1000 ⊕ www.hoxtonhotels.com ⤳ 205 ⦿ Breakfast ✛ H1.*

$$
HOTEL

🏨 **Ramada Hotel and Suites Docklands.** Many of the sleek and modern rooms at this hotel, dramatically set at the edge of the river in the rejuvenated Docklands area of East London, have water views, while others have views of the city. **Pros:** waterfront views. **Cons:** lacks character; area is tumbleweed quiet on weekends; about a 20-minute Tube ride to central London. $ *Rooms from: £129* ✉ *ExCel, 2 Festoon Way, Royal Victoria Dock, East End* ☎ *020/7540–4820* ⊕ *www.ramadadocklands. co.uk* ⇆ *224 rooms* ⟡ *Breakfast* Ⓜ *Old St.* ✛ *H3.*

THE SOUTH BANK

For expanded hotel reviews, visit Fodors.com.

$ 🏛 **Church Street Hotel.** Like rays of sunshine in gritty South London, these rooms above a popular tapas restaurant are individually decorated in rich, bold tones and authentic Central American touches—elaborately painted crucifixes; tiles handmade in Guadalajara; homemade iron bed frames. **Pros:** unique and arty; great breakfasts; lovely staff; closer to central London than it might appear. **Cons:** a trendy but not great part of town (stay out of neighboring Elephant and Castle); would suit adventurous young things more than families; a mile from a Tube station (though bus connections are handier); some rooms have shared bathrooms. $ *Rooms from: £90* ✉ *29–33 Camberwell Church St., Camberwell, South East* ☎ *020/7703–5984* ⊕ *www.churchstreethotel. com* ⇆ *28 rooms* ⟡ *Breakfast* Ⓜ *Oval St.* ✛ *H6.*

HOTEL
Fodors Choice
★

$$$ 🏛 **London Marriott Hotel County Hall.** This grand hotel on the Thames enjoys perhaps the most iconic view in the city—right next door is the London Eye, and directly across the River Thames are the Houses of Parliament and Big Ben. **Pros:** handy for South Bank arts scene, London Eye, and Westminster; great gym; good weekend discounts. **Cons:** interior design is overdone; breakfasts are pricey; rooms facing the river inevitably cost extra. $ *Rooms from: £266* ✉ *County Hall, Westminster Bridge Rd., South Bank* ☎ *020/7928–5200, 888/236–2427 in U.S.* ⊕ *www.marriott.com* ⇆ *200 rooms* ⟡ *Breakfast* Ⓜ *Westminster, Waterloo. National Rail: Waterloo* ✛ *G4.*

HOTEL

$$ 🏛 **Premier Travel Inn County Hall.** The small but nicely decorated rooms at this budget choice share the County Hall complex with the grander London Marriott Hotel County Hall, and though they have none of the spectacular river views they share the convenient location—at a decidedly lower price. **Pros:** good location for the South Bank; bargains to be had if you book in advance, including very cheap breakfast and dinner rates; kids stay free. **Cons:** no river views; limited services. $ *Rooms from: £132* ✉ *Belvedere Rd., South Bank* ☎ *0871/527–8648* ⊕ *www.premiertravelinn.com* ⇆ *313 rooms* ⟡ *Breakfast* Ⓜ *Westminster, Waterloo. National Rail: Waterloo* ✛ *G4.*

HOTEL
FAMILY

KENSINGTON, KNIGHTSBRIDGE, AND MAYFAIR

For expanded hotel reviews, visit Fodors.com.

KENSINGTON

$$ 🏛 **base2stay Kensington.** This near-budget option in a creamy white Georgian town house offers comfortable double rooms that have a stylish, modern look and tiny kitchenettes—and some even have bunk beds for traveling friends or children. **Pros:** great value alternative to hotel; attractive rooms; handy mini-kitchens; free WiFi. **Cons:** bathrooms are small but well designed; 15-minute Tube ride to central

RENTAL

2

London. $ *Rooms from: £135* ⊠ *25 Courtfield Gardens, South Kensington* ☎ *020/7244–2255, 800/511–9821 in U.S.* ⊕ *www.base2stay. com* ⤳ *67 rooms* ⦿⦿ *No meals* Ⓜ *Earls Court* ⊹ *A6.*

$
HOTEL
☷ **easyHotel South Kensington.** London's first "pod hotel" has tiny rooms with a double bed, private shower room, and little else, each brightly decorated in the easyGroup's trademark orange and white (to match their budget airline easyJet). **Pros:** amazing price; safe and pleasant space. **Cons:** not for the claustrophobic; most rooms have no windows; six floors and no elevator. $ *Rooms from: £44* ⊠ *14 Lexham Gardens, Kensington* ☎ *020/7216–1717* ⊕ *www.easyhotel.com* ⤳ *34 rooms* ⦿⦿ *No meals* Ⓜ *Gloucester Rd.* ⊹ *A5.*

$$
HOTEL
☷ **Kensington House Hotel.** A short stroll from High Street Kensington and Kensington Gardens, this refurbished 19th-century town house has streamlined, contemporary rooms with large windows letting in plenty of light, comfortable beds with luxurious fabrics and soft comforters. **Pros:** attractive design; relaxing setting; free Wi-Fi. **Cons:** rooms are small; bathrooms are minuscule; the elevator is Lilliputian. $ *Rooms from: £144* ⊠ *15–16 Prince of Wales Terr., Kensington* ☎ *020/7937–2345* ⊕ *www.kenhouse.com* ⤳ *39 rooms, 2 suites* ⦿⦿ *Breakfast* Ⓜ *High Street Kensington* ⊹ *A5.*

$$
HOTEL
☷ **Millennium Gloucester.** With a Tube station opposite and Kensington's many attractions nearby, this hotel is both convenient and alluring, its sleek and opulent lobby, with polished wood columns, a warming fireplace, and glittering chandeliers giving way to guest rooms with a traditionally masculine look. **Pros:** good deals available if you book in advance. **Cons:** lighting in some bedrooms is a bit too subtle; bathrooms are relatively small but have all you need; public areas and restaurant can get crowded. $ *Rooms from: £150* ⊠ *4–18 Harrington Gardens, Kensington* ☎ *020/7373–6030* ⊕ *www.millenniumhotels.co.uk/millenniumgloucester* ⤳ *143 rooms* ⦿⦿ *Breakfast* Ⓜ *Gloucester Rd.* ⊹ *B5.*

$$$
HOTEL
Fodor's Choice
★
☷ **Number Sixteen.** Guest rooms at this lovely luxury guesthouse, just around the corner from the Victoria & Albert Museum, look like they come from the pages of *Architectural Digest*, and the delightful garden is an added bonus. **Pros:** just the right level of helpful service; interiors are gorgeous. **Cons:** no restaurant; small elevator. $ *Rooms from: £285* ⊠ *16 Sumner Pl., South Kensington* ☎ *020/7589–5232, 888/559–5508 in U.S.* ⊕ *www.firmdale.com* ⤳ *42 rooms* ⦿⦿ *Breakfast* Ⓜ *South Kensington* ⊹ *B5.*

$$$
HOTEL
Fodor's Choice
★
☷ **The Pelham Hotel.** One of the first and most stylish of London's famed "boutique" hotels, this still-chic choice is but a short stroll away from the Natural History, Science, and V&A museums. **Pros:** great location for museum-hopping; gorgeous marble bathrooms; soigné interior design; lovely staff; good package deals for online booking. **Cons:** taller guests will find themselves cursing the top-floor rooms with sloping ceilings. $ *Rooms from: £252* ⊠ *15 Cromwell Pl., South Kensington* ☎ *020/7589–8288, 888/757–5587 in U.S.* ⊕ *www.pelhamhotel.co.uk* ⤳ *47 rooms, 4 suites* ⦿⦿ *Breakfast* Ⓜ *South Kensington* ⊹ *B5.*

$$
HOTEL
☷ **The Rockwell.** Despite being on the notoriously traffic-clogged Cromwell Road, this excellent little place is one of the best boutique hotels in this part of London—and windows have good soundproofing. **Pros:**

large bedooms; stylish surroundings; helpful staff. **Cons:** on a busy, unattractive road; 20-minute Tube ride to central London. $ *Rooms from: £180* ⊠ *181 Cromwell Rd., South Kensington* ☎ *020/7244–2000* ⊕ *www.therockwell.com* ⤳ *38 rooms, 2 suites* ⦿❘ *Breakfast* ✛ *A5.*

$$ ⛫ **The Sumner.** You can feel yourself relaxing the minute you enter this

HOTEL elegant Georgian town house. **Pros:** excellent location for shopping; small enough that the staff knows your name; attractive conservatory and garden. **Cons:** services are limited but prices high. $ *Rooms from: £180* ⊠ *54 Upper Berkley St., Marble Arch, Marylebone* ☎ *020/7723–2244* ⊕ *www.thesumner.com* ⤳ *20 rooms* ⦿❘ *Breakfast* Ⓜ *Marble Arch* ✛ *B6.*

$$ ⛫ **Think Earl's Court.** These serviced apartments are a stone's throw from

RENTAL Kensington High Street and a short walk from both Earl's Court and Olympia. **Pros:** brand-new building; self-catering offers greater independence. **Cons:** payment is made when you book; bland, officelike exterior. $ *Rooms from: £168* ⊠ *26A Adam and Eve Mews, Kensington* ☎ *020/3465–9100* ⊕ *www.think-apartments.com* ⤳ *133 rooms* ⦿❘ *No meals* Ⓜ *High Street Kensington* ✛ *A5.*

CHELSEA

$$$ ⛫ **The Cadogan Hotel.** This elegant and luxurious hotel is one of Lon-

HOTEL don's most historically naughty hotels—once the home of scandalous actress Lillie Langtry (King Edward's mistress in the 1890s), and where Oscar Wilde was staying (in Room 118) when he was arrested for "indecency" with a young man on April 6, 1895. **Pros:** luxurious but not stuffy; friendly staff; great location for shopping; good advance discounts online. **Cons:** rooms are quite small. $ *Rooms from: £234* ⊠ *75 Sloane St., Chelsea* ☎ *020/7235–7141* ⊕ *www.cadogan.com* ⤳ *65 rooms* ⦿❘ *Breakfast* Ⓜ *Sloane Sq.* ✛ *D5.*

KNIGHTSBRIDGE

$$$$ ⛫ **The Berkeley.** Convenient for Knightsbridge shopping, the very ele-

HOTEL gant Berkeley is known for its renowned restaurants and luxuries that culminate—literally—in a splendid penthouse swimming pool. **Pros:** lavish and elegant; attentive service; prices aren't quite as stratospheric as some high-end places. **Cons:** You'll need your best designer clothes to fit in. $ *Rooms from: £390* ⊠ *Wilton Pl., Knightsbridge* ☎ *020/7235–6000, 800/637–2869 in U.S.* ⊕ *www.the-berkeley.co.uk* ⤳ *103 rooms, 55 suites* ⦿❘ *Breakfast* Ⓜ *Knightsbridge* ✛ *D4.*

$$$ ⛫ **Egerton House.** Sensationally soigné, chicly decorated, and feeling like

HOTEL your own private London home, this option has some gorgeous pluses, including guest rooms lavishly decorated with luxurious fabrics in rich colors, a knockout white-on-gold dining room. **Pros:** lovely staff; great location; magnificent interiors; striking art. **Cons:** some style touches a little too frou-frou—but Toulouse-Lautrec would have approved. $ *Rooms from: £281* ⊠ *17–19 Egerton Terr., Knightsbridge* ☎ *020/7589–2412, 877/955–1515 in U.S.* ⊕ *www.egertonhousehotel.co.uk* ⤳ *23 rooms, 6 suites* ⦿❘ *Breakfast* Ⓜ *Knightsbridge, South Kensington* ✛ *C5.*

$$$$ ⛫ **The Lanesborough.** A gilded cocoon for the seriously wealthy, this

HOTEL hotel exudes a spectacular richness and, when built by a Texan heiress, was the talk of the town, thanks to the magnificent 19th-century antiques, the personal butler service, and that 1770 cognac on the

2

menu. **Pros:** lap of luxury; your wish is their command. **Cons:** prices are extraordinary; not everybody likes the constantly hovering service. $ *Rooms from: £495* ✉ *Hyde Park Corner, Belgravia* ☎ *020/7259–5599, 800/999–1828 in U.S.* ⊕ *www.lanesborough.com* ⤳ *52 rooms, 43 suites* ⦿ *Breakfast* Ⓜ *Hyde Park Corner* ✛ *D4.*

$$$$ 🔲 **Mandarin Oriental Hyde Park.** Built in 1880, the Mandarin Oriental
HOTEL welcomes you with one of the most exuberantly Victorian facades in
Fodor's Choice town, then fast-forwards you to high-trend modern London, thanks to
★ striking and luxurious guest rooms filled with high-tech gadgets. **Pros:** Great shopping at your doorstep; amazing views of Hyde Park; excellent service. **Cons:** nothing comes cheap; you must dress for dinner (and lunch and breakfast) $ *Rooms from: £570* ✉ *66 Knightsbridge, Knightsbridge* ☎ *020/7235–2000* ⊕ *www.mandarinoriental.com/london* ⤳ *177 rooms, 23 suites* ⦿ *Breakfast* Ⓜ *Knightsbridge* ✛ *D4.*

MAYFAIR

$$ 🔲 **22 York Street.** This Georgian town house has a cozy, family feel,
B&B/INN with polished pine floors and plenty of quilts and French antiques in the homey, individually furnished bedrooms. **Pros:** outstanding location for shoppers; friendly hosts; very flexible check-in times; entirely no-smoking. **Cons:** if you take away the great location, you're paying a lot for a B&B; not everyone enjoys socializing with strangers over breakfast. $ *Rooms from: £130* ✉ *22 York St., Mayfair* ☎ *020/7224–2990* ⊕ *www.22yorkstreet.co.uk* ⤳ *10 rooms* ⦿ *Breakfast* Ⓜ *Baker St.* ✛ *D2.*

$$$$ 🔲 **The Connaught.** A huge favorite of the "we wouldn't dream of staying
HOTEL anywhere else" monied set since its opening in 1917, the Connaught has
Fodor's Choice many dazzlingly modern complements to its famously historic delights.
★ **Pros:** legendary hotel; great for star-spotting. **Cons:** history comes at a price; bathrooms are small. $ *Rooms from: £400* ✉ *Carlos Pl., Mayfair* ☎ *020/7499–7070, 866/599–6991 in U.S.* ⊕ *www.the-connaught.co.uk* ⤳ *92 rooms* ⦿ *Breakfast* Ⓜ *Bond St.* ✛ *E3.*

$$$$ 🔲 **The Dorchester.** The glamour level is off the scale here, with gold leaf
HOTEL and marble public rooms and guest quarters awash in English country-
Fodor's Choice house-style furnishings, with more than a hint of art deco—yet few
★ hotels this opulent manage to be as personable as the Dorchester. **Pros:** historic luxury in 1930s building; lovely views of Hyde Park; top-notch star-spotting; lots of modern technology, including web TVs. **Cons:** traditional look is not to all tastes; prices are high; some rooms are rather small. $ *Rooms from: £365* ✉ *Park Lane, Mayfair* ☎ *020/7629–8888* ⊕ *www.thedorchester.com* ⤳ *195 rooms, 55 suites* ⦿ *Breakfast* Ⓜ *Marble Arch, Hyde Park Corner* ✛ *D4.*

MARYLEBONE

$$$ 🔲 **Dorset Square Hotel.** Reopened in June 2012 after extensive updates
HOTEL and refurbishment, this boutique hotel, in one of London's most fash-
Fodor's Choice ionable neighborhoods, occupies a charming town house. **Pros:** ideal
★ location; lovely design; welcoming vibe. **Cons:** some rooms are small; no bathtub in some rooms; fee for WiFi. $ *Rooms from: £260* ✉ *39 Dorset Sq., Marylebone* ☎ *020/7723–7874* ⊕ *www.firmdalehotels.com* ⤳ *35 rooms, 3 suites* ⦿ *Breakfast* Ⓜ *Baker St.* ✛ *D2.*

$$$ HOTEL Fodor's Choice ★ 🏨 **Hyatt Regency London – The Churchill.** Even though it's one of London's largest hotels, the Churchill is always abuzz with guests smiling at the purring perfection they find here, including warmly personalized service and calmly alluring guest rooms. **Pros:** Comfortable and stylish; efficient service; up to three can stay in one room **Cons:** Feels more geared to business than leisure travelers. [$] *Rooms from: £260* ✉ *30 Portman Sq., Marylebone* ☎ *020/7486–5800* 🌐 *www.london.churchill.hyatt.com* 🛏 *389 rooms, 45 suites* 🍴 *Breakfast* [M] *Marble Arch* ✣ *D3.*

$$ HOTEL 🏨 **Park Plaza Sherlock Holmes Hotel.** In honor of the fictional detective who had his home on Baker Street, rooms here have a masculine edge with lots of earth tones and pinstripe sheets (along with hyper-modern bathrooms stocked with fluffy bathrobes). **Pros:** nicely decorated; near Marylebone High Street; international electrical outlets, including those that work with American equipment. **Cons:** have to walk through the bar to get to reception; not well soundproofed from the noisy street. [$] *Rooms from: £180* ✉ *108 Baker St., Marylebone* ☎ *020/7486–6161* 🌐 *www.sherlockholmeshotel.com* 🛏 *99 rooms, 20 suites* 🍴 *Breakfast* [M] *Baker St.* ✣ *D2.*

NOTTING HILL AND BAYSWATER

For expanded hotel reviews, visit Fodors.com.

NOTTING HILL

$$ B&B/INN Fodor's Choice ★ 🏨 **The Main House.** A stay in this delightfully welcoming B&B feels more like sleeping over at a friend's house than in a hotel—albeit a particularly wealthy and well-connected friend. **Pros:** unique and unusual place; charming and helpful owners. **Cons:** few services; two-night minimum stay. [$] *Rooms from: £110* ✉ *6 Colvile Rd., Notting Hill* ☎ *020/7221–9691* 🌐 *www.themainhouse.com* 🛏 *4 rooms* 🍴 *Breakfast* [M] *Notting Hill Gate* ✣ *A3.*

$$ HOTEL 🏨 **The Portobello Hotel.** One of London's quirkiest hotels, the little Portobello (formed from two adjoining Victorian houses) is seriously hip, attracting scores of celebrities to its small but stylish rooms that are decorated with joyous abandon. **Pros:** stylish; celebrity vibe; guests have use of nearby gym and pool. **Cons:** most rooms are quite small; may be too eccentric for some. [$] *Rooms from: £174* ✉ *22 Stanley Gardens, Notting Hill* ☎ *020/7727–2777* 🌐 *www.portobello-hotel.co.uk* 🛏 *24 rooms* 🕒 *Closed 10 days at Christmas* 🍴 *Breakfast* [M] *Notting Hill Gate* ✣ *A3.*

BAYSWATER

$$ HOTEL 🏨 **London House Hotel.** Set in a row of white Georgian town houses, this excellent new budget option in hit-or-miss Bayswater is friendly, well run, and spotlessly clean. **Pros:** friendly and efficient; emphasis on value for money; good location. **Cons:** some public areas feel a bit too clinical; smallest rooms are tiny. [$] *Rooms from: £105* ✉ *81 Kensington Garden Sq., Bayswater* ☎ *020/7243–1810* 🌐 *www.londonhousehotels.com* 🛏 *100 rooms* 🍴 *Breakfast* [M] *Queensway, Bayswater* ✣ *A3.*

$ B&B/INN 🏨 **Parkwood Hotel.** Just seconds from Hyde Park in one of London's swankiest enclaves (the Blairs live a few doors away), this sweet little guesthouse is an oasis of value-for-money, with warm and helpful

APARTMENT RENTALS & HOME EXCHANGES

APARTMENT RENTALS

For a home base that's roomy enough for a family and that comes with cooking facilities, consider renting furnished "flats" (the British word for apartments). These can save you money, especially if you're traveling as a family or with a group.

INTERNATIONAL AGENTS

Interhome. Dozens of flats (apartments) all over London, starting at about £750 per week per person, are on Interhome's books. Properties range from suburban *pied-à-terres* to luxurious city-center apartments. $ *Rooms from: £110* ☎ *800/882–6864* ⊕ *www.interhome. us* ⊙*| No meals.*

Villas International. Exclusively priced flats all over London are available through Villas International, starting at around £1,800 per week—although as some sleep up to 10 people it can work out as a viable option for large groups. $ *Rooms from: £250* ✉ *17 Fox La., San Anselmo, California, USA* ☎ *415/499–9490, 800/221–2260* ⊕ *www.villasintl.com.*

LOCAL AGENTS

The Apartment Service. This agency specializes in executive apartments for business travelers, so prices are high, but so is the quality. $ *Rooms from: £75* ✉ *5 Francis Grove, Wimbledon* ☎ *020/8944–1444* ⊕ *www.apartmentservice.com.*

The Bed and Breakfast Club. Contact this company for delightful little London apartments, in Kensington, Chelsea, and Knightsbridge, costing from around £50–£125 per night with full English breakfasts. $ *Rooms from: £50* ✉ *405 Kings Rd., Suite 192,* *Chelsea* ☎ *01243/370-692* ⊕ *www. thebedandbreakfastclub.co.uk*

Coach House London Vacation Rentals. This company arranges stays in the properties of Londoners who are temporarily away. $ *Rooms from: £120* ✉ *2 Tunley Rd., Balham* ☎ *020/8133–8332* ⊕ *www.rentals. chslondon.com* ☞ *Payment by credit card only; 10% deposit required.*

Landmark Trust. Specializing in unusual and historic buildings, this agency has London apartments starting at around £100 a night, but many properties require a minimum stay of seven days. $ *Rooms from: £100* ✉ *Shottesbrooke, Maidenhead, Berkshire* ☎ *01628/825–925* ⊕ *www.landmarktrust.org.uk.*

One Fine Stay. What sets this agency apart is the quality of the properties on offer and the outstanding support you get during your stay—fresh linen, toiletries, a kitchen full of basic supplies, iPhones helpfully loaded with maps, and, in a lovely touch, a package of tips about the area from the owners themselves. $ *Rooms from: £90* ☎ *020/7097–8948* ☏ *N/A* ⊙*| No meals.*

HOME EXCHANGES

If you would like to exchange your home for someone else's, join a home-exchange organization, which will send you its updated listings of available exchanges for a year and will include your own listing in at least one of them. It's up to you to make specific arrangements.

Exchange Clubs Intervac U.S. It costs from $8.50 per month for a listing and online access with this company. ☎ *800/756–4663* ⊕ *www.intervacus.com.*

hosts and bright bedrooms. **Pros:** lovely hosts; free Wi-Fi; hotel guarantees to match or beat price of any other hotel of its class in the area. **Cons:** often booked up in advance; no elevator; front-facing rooms can be noisy. [$] *Rooms from: £85* ✉ *4 Stanhope Pl., Bayswater* ☎ *020/7402–2241* 🌐 *www.parkwoodhotel.com* 🛏 *18 rooms* 🍴 *Breakfast* [M] *Marble Arch* ✣ *C3.*

$$ RENTAL 🏨 **Space Apart Hotel.** These studio apartments near Hyde Park are done in soothing tones of white and gray, with polished wood floors and attractive modern kitchenettes equipped with all you need to make small meals. **Pros:** especially good value for the money; the larger suites have space for four people; handy location. **Cons:** no in-house restaurant or bar; minimum two-night stay required. [$] *Rooms from: £140* ✉ *32–37 Kensington Gardens Sq., Bayswater* ☎ *020/7908–1340* 🌐 *www.aparthotel-london.co.uk* 🛏 *30 rooms* 🍴 *No meals* [M] *Bayswater* ✣ *A3.*

$ HOTEL 🏨 **Stylotel.** Just around the corner from Paddington station, this funky-looking little place has small, functional rooms—done to death in contemporary style—and even tinier bathrooms, but it's clean, cheerful, and perfectly comfortable. **Pros:** bargain price; helpful staff; unique style. **Cons:** style will be *too* unique for some; small bedrooms and bathrooms. [$] *Rooms from: £95* ✉ *160–162 Sussex Gardens Sq., Bayswater* ☎ *0207/223–1026* 🌐 *www.stylotel.com* 🛏 *40 rooms* 🍴 *Breakfast* [M] *Paddington, Edgware Rd. National Rail: Paddington* ✣ *C2.*

REGENT'S PARK AND HAMPSTEAD

For expanded hotel reviews, visit Fodors.com.

$ B&B/INN 🏨 **Glenlyn Guest House.** An excellent option for travellers who don't mind being a long Tube ride away from the action, this converted Victorian town house offers a high standard of accomodation a few miles north of Hampstead. **Pros:** comfortable and friendly; you get more for your money than you would in central London; adjoining rooms can be converted to family suites; 5-minute walk to Tube station. **Cons:** you have to factor in the cost and inconvenience of a half-hour Tube ride to central London; no restaurant. [$] *Rooms from: £85* ✉ *6 Woodside Park Rd., North Finchley* ☎ *020/8445–0440* 🌐 *www.glenlynhotel.com* 🛏 *27* 🍴 *Breakfast* [M] *Woodside Park* ✣ *C1.*

$ HOTEL Fodor's Choice ★ 🏨 **The Hide.** This cozy, chic, little bolt-hole is exceptional value for money and exceeds virtually anything you could hope to find in central London for the price; the great downside is that the half-hour Tube ride into town can start to feel like penance at the end of a long day's sightseeing. **Pros:** excellent value for money; great service; free Wi-Fi; close to Tube station. **Cons:** far from the center; dull neighborhood. [$] *Rooms from: £100* ✉ *230 Hendon Way, Hendon, Hampstead* ☎ *020/8203–1670* 🌐 *www.thehidelondon.com* 🛏 *22 rooms* 🍴 *Breakfast* [M] *Hendon Central* ✣ *D1.*

NIGHTLIFE AND THE ARTS

London is a veritable utopia for excitement junkies, culture fiends, and those who like to party. Most who visit London will be mesmerized by the city's energy, which reveals itself in layers. Whether you prefer a romantic evening at the opera, rhythm and blues with fine French food, the gritty guitar riffs of east London, a pint and gourmet pizza at a local gastro-pub, or swanky cocktails and sushi at London's sexiest lair, the U.K. capital is sure to feed your fancy. Admission prices are not always bargain-basement, but when you consider how much a London hotel room costs, the city's arts and nightlife diversions are a bargain.

NIGHTLIFE

There isn't *a* London nightlife scene—there are lots of them. As long as there are crowds for obscure teenage rock bands, Dickensian-style pubs, comedy cabarets, and "bodysonic" dance nights, someone will create clubs and venues for them in London. The result? London has become a veritable utopia for excitement junkies, culture fiends, and those who—simply put—like to party.

WESTMINSTER, ST. JAMES'S, AND ROYAL LONDON

BARS

American Bar. Festooned with a chin-dropping array of club ties, signed celebrity photographs, sporting mementos, and baseball caps, this sensational hotel cocktail bar has superb martinis. The name dates from the 1930s, when hotel bars in London started to cater to growing numbers of Americans crossing the Atlantic in ocean liners, but it wasn't until the 1970s, when a customer left a small carved wooden eagle, that the collection of parephenalia was started. ⊠ *Stafford Hotel, 16–18 St. James's Pl., St. James's* ☎ *020/7493–0111* ⊕ *www.thestaffordhotel. co.uk* ⊘ *Daily 11:30 am–1 am* Ⓜ *Green Park.*

Bedford and Strand. The wine bar enjoyed something of a renaissance in the first decade of the 21st century in London, and this is one of the best of a new generation. It's sunk atmospherically down below the streets of Covent Garden, with dark wood and hanging shades; the wine list is short but well chosen, the service is faultless, and the bistro food is created with plenty of care. ⊠ *1A Bedford St., Charing Cross* ☎ *020/7836–3033* ⊕ *www.bedford-strand.com* ⊘ *Mon.–Fri. noon–midnight; Sat. 5 pm–midnight* Ⓜ *Charing Cross.*

SOHO AND COVENT GARDEN

BARS

Le Salon Bar. Renowned chef Joël Robuchon's intimate, relaxed, and elegant bar with red undertones is in the same premises as his L'Atelier and La Cuisine restaurants. New cocktails await you, as the drink menu changes every six months, with new flavors and textures sure to entice your taste buds. ⊠ *13–15 West St., Soho* ☎ *020/7010–8600* ⊕ *www.joel-robuchon.com* ⊘ *Mon.–Sat. noon–2 am, Sun. noon–10:30 pm* Ⓜ *Leicester Sq.*

Nordic. With shooters called "Husky Poo" and "Danish Bacon Surprise" and crayfish tails and meatballs on the smorgasbord menu, Nordic takes its Scandinavian feel the whole way. This secluded, shabby-chic bar serves many couples cozied up among travel brochures promoting the Viking lands. If you can't decide what to drink, the cocktail roulette wheel on the wall may help. ✉ *25 Newman St., Soho* ☎ *020/7631–3174* ⊕ *www.nordicbar.com* ⊙ *Mon.–Wed. 5 pm–midnight, Thurs. noon–midnight, Fri. noon–2am, Sat. 5 pm–midnight* Ⓜ *Tottenham Court Rd.*

Sketch. One seat never looks like the next at this collection of esoteric living-room bars. The exclusive Parlour, a patisserie during the day, exudes plenty of rarefied charm; the intimate East Bar at the back is reminiscent of a sci-fi film set; and in the Glade it's permanently sunset in a forest. ✉ *9 Conduit St., Soho* ☎ *020/7659–4500* ⊕ *www.sketch. uk.com* ⊙ *Parlour Mon.–Fri. 8 am–2 am, Sat. 10 am–2 am; The Glade 6:30 pm–2 am* Ⓜ *Oxford Circus.*

COMEDY AND CABARET

Comedy Store. Known as the birthplace of alternative comedy, this is where the United Kingdom's funniest stand-ups have cut their teeth before being launched onto prime-time TV. Comedy Store Players, a team with six comedians doing improvisation with audience suggestions, entertain on Wednesday and Sunday; the Cutting Edge steps in every Tuesday. Thursday, Friday, and Saturday have the best stand-up acts. There's also a bar with food. Note that children under 18 are not admitted to this venue. ✉ *1A Oxendon St., Soho* ☎ *0844/847–1728* ⊕ *www. thecomedystore.co.uk* 🎫 *£14–£28* ⊙ *Shows daily 7:30 or 8 pm, with extra shows Fri. and Sat. at 11 pm* Ⓜ *Piccadilly Circus, Leicester Sq.*

Fodor's Choice
★

Soho Theatre. This innovative theater's programs include comedy shows by established acts and up-and-coming comedians and new writers. The relaxed Soho Theatre Bar has food, free Wi-Fi, simple tables, and a late license until 1 am for members and ticket holders. Check local listings or the website for what's on, and book tickets in advance. ✉ *21 Dean St., Soho* ☎ *020/7478–0100* ⊕ *www.sohotheatre.com* 🎫 *£10–£30* ⊙ *Mon.–Sat. usually 7–11 although show times vary* Ⓜ *Tottenham Court Rd.*

JAZZ AND BLUES

Fodor's Choice
★

Pizza Express Jazz Club Soho. One of the capital's most ubiquitous pizza chains also runs a great Soho jazz venue. The dimly lighted restaurant hosts top-quality international jazz acts every night. The Italian-style thin-crust pizzas are good, too, though on the small side. ✉ *10 Dean St., Soho* ☎ *0845/602–7017* ⊕ *www.pizzaexpresslive.com* 🎫 *£10–£25* ⊙ *Daily 11:30 am–midnight for food; music after 7:30 pm (timings vary)* Ⓜ *Tottenham Court Rd.*

THE GAY SCENE

Candy Bar. London's top girls' bar is intimate, chilled, and cruisey, with DJs mixing the latest sounds. Live music, DJs, speed dating, and comedy are also featured on some nights. Men are welcome only as guests of female patrons. ✉ *4 Carlisle St., Soho* ☎ *020/7287–5041* ⊕ *www.candybarsoho.com* 🎫 *Free–£5* ⊙ *Mon.–Sat. 1 pm–3 am, Sun. 1 pm–12:30 am* Ⓜ *Tottenham Court Rd.*

London's dance clubs present all kinds of live music in venues both large and small.

Fodor's Choice
★
Friendly Society. This haute moderne hot spot hops with activity almost any night of the week; the basement feels a bit like something out of *Star Trek* with its white-leather pod seats. The place is known for being gay yet female-friendly. ☒ *79 Wardour St., Soho* ☎ *020/7434–3805* ⊙ *Weekdays 4–11, Sat. 2–11, Sun. 2–10:30* Ⓜ *Leicester Sq.*

Fodor's Choice
★
Heaven. With the best light show on any London dance floor, Heaven is unpretentious, loud, and huge, with a labyrinth of rooms, bars, and live-music parlors. Friday and Saturday nights there's a gay comedy night (£10 in advance, 7–10 pm). Tuesday, Wednesday, and Thursday often have live performances. If you go to just one gay club in London, Heaven should be it. ☒ *The Arches, Villiers St., Covent Garden* ☎ *020/7930–2020* ⊕ *www.heavennightclub-london.com* ☒ *£4–£12* ⊙ *Mon. 11 pm–5:30 am, Tues.–Fri. 11 pm–5 am, Sat. 10:30 pm–5 am* Ⓜ *Charing Cross, Embankment.*

The Shadow Lounge. This fabulous little lounge and dance club glitters with faux jewels and twinkling fiber-optic lights over its sunken dance floor, which comes complete with pole for those inclined to do their thing around it. It has a serious A-list celebrity factor, with the glamorous London glitterati camping out in the VIP booth. Members are given entrance priority when the place gets full, especially on weekends, so show up early, book onto the guestlist online, or prepare to wait in line. ☒ *5–7 Brewer St., Soho* ☎ *020/7317-9270* ⊕ *www.theshadowlounge. co.uk* ☒ *Mon. free, Tues.–Thurs. £5, Fri.–Sat. £10* ⊙ *Mon.–Sat. 10 pm–3 am* Ⓜ *Leicester Sq.*

BLOOMSBURY AND HOLBURN

BARS

All Star Lanes. One of London's most chic bars is an unlikely combination—it's in a sleek, underground, retro bowling alley in the heart of literary Bloomsbury. Here, surrounded by 1950s Americana, you can sit on the red leather seats and choose from the largest selection of bourbons in London. DJs play on Friday and Saturday nights; there are also locations in Bayswater, Brick Lane, and Stratford. ⊠ *Victoria House, Bloomsbury Pl., Bloomsbury* ☎ *020/7025–2676* ⊕ *www.allstarlanes.co.uk* ☉ *Mon.–Wed. 4–11:30, Thurs. 4–midnight, Fri. noon–2 am, Sat. 11 am–2 am, Sun. 11–11* Ⓜ *Holborn.*

THE EAST END

DANCE CLUBS

Cargo. Housed under a series of old railroad arches, this vast brick-wall bar, restaurant, dance floor, and live-music venue pulls a young, international crowd with its hip vibe and diverse selection of music. Long tables bring people together, as does the food, which draws on global influences and is served tapas-style. Drinks, though, are expensive. ⊠ *83 Rivington St., Shoreditch* ☎ *020/7739–3440* ⊕ *www.cargo-london.com* ⌐ *Free–£20* ☉ *Mon.–Thurs. 6 pm–1 am, Fri. 6 pm–3 am, Sat. 6 pm–3 am, Sun. 6 pm–midnight (restaurant opens at noon)* Ⓜ *Old St.*

Fabric. This sprawling subterranean club opposite Smithfield Meat Market is now a firm fixture on the London scene and is regularly voted as one of the top clubs in the world. "FabricLive" hosts drum 'n' bass, dubstep, and hip-hop crews and live acts on Friday; international big-name DJs play slow, sexy bass lines and cutting-edge music on Saturday. The devastating sound system and vibrating "bodysonic" dance floor ensure that bass riffs vibrate through your entire body. ▓ TIP→ **Get there early to avoid a lengthy queue, and don't wear a suit.** ⊠ *77A Charterhouse St., The City* ☎ *020/7336–8898* ⊕ *www.fabriclondon.com* ⌐ *£15–£20; discounts after 3 or 4 am* ☉ *Fri. 10 pm–6 am, Sat. 11 pm–8 am, Sun. 11 pm–6 am* Ⓜ *Farringdon.*

THE SOUTH BANK

BARS

The Dogstar. This popular South London hangout is frequented by local hipsters and counterculture types. It was the first DJ bar in the world and has since enjoyed a fabulous reputation. The vibe at this "surrealist boudoir" is unpretentious, with top-name DJs playing cutting-edge sounds every night (free Tuesday–Thursday) and pizza available until midnight. ⊠ *389 Coldharbour La., Brixton* ☎ *020/7733–7515* ⊕ *www.antic-ltd.com/dogstar* ⌐ *Free–£8* ☉ *Tues.–Wed. 4 pm–11 pm, Thurs. 4 pm–2 am, Fri. 4 pm–4 am, Sat. noon–4 am, Sun. noon–10:30 pm* Ⓜ *Brixton.*

DANCE CLUBS

Ministry of Sound. It's more of an industry than a club, with its own record label, online radio station, and international DJs. Though it's too much a part of the establishment these days to be at the forefront of cool, the stripped-down warehouse-style club has a super sound system and still pulls in the world's most legendary names in dance. There are chill-out rooms, two bars, and three dance floors. ☒ *103 Gaunt St., Borough* ☎ *020/740–8600* ⊕ *www.ministryofsound.com* 💷 *£15–£23* 🕙 *Fri. 10 pm–5 am, Sat. 11 pm–7 am* Ⓜ *Elephant & Castle.*

ECLECTIC MUSIC

Fodor's Choice ★ **O2 Academy Brixton.** This legendary Brixton venue has seen it all—mods and rockers, hippies and punks—and it remains one of the city's top indie and rock venues. Despite a capacity for almost 5,000, this refurbished Victorian hall with original art deco fixtures retains a clublike charm; it has plenty of bars and upstairs seating. ☒ *211 Stockwell Rd., Brixton* ☎ *020/7771–3000* ⊕ *www.o2academybrixton.co.uk* 💷 *£10–£50* 🕙 *Opening hrs vary* Ⓜ *Brixton.*

KENSINGTON, KNIGHTSBRIDGE, AND MAYFAIR

BARS

Fodor's Choice ★ **The Blue Bar at the Berkeley Hotel.** With low-slung dusty-blue walls, this hotel bar is ever so slightly sexy. Immaculate service, an excellent cocktail list—try the Sex in the City—and a trendy David Collins design make this an ideal spot for a romantic tête-à-tête, complete with jazzy music in the background. ☒ *Wilton Pl., Knightsbridge* ☎ *020/7235–6000* ⊕ *the-berkeley.co.uk* 🕙 *Mon.–Sat. 9 am–1 am, Sun. 9 am–11 pm* Ⓜ *Knightsbridge.*

Fodor's Choice ★ **Claridge's Bar.** This elegant Mayfair meeting place remains unpretentious even when it brims with beautiful people. The bar has an art deco heritage made hip by the sophisticated touch of designer David Collins. A library of rare champagnes and brandies as well as a delicious choice of traditional and exotic cocktails—try the Flapper or the Black Pearl—will occupy your taste buds. Request a glass of vintage Cristal in the darkly moody Fumoir. ☒ *55 Brook St., Mayfair* ☎ *020/7629–8860* ⊕ *www.claridges.co.uk* 🕙 *Mon.–Sat. noon–1 am, Sun. noon–midnight* Ⓜ *Bond St.*

JAZZ AND BLUES

Dover Street Restaurant & Jazz Bar. Dance the night away after you've feasted from the French Mediterranean menu. Fun for dates as well as groups, Dover Street Restaurant has three bars, a DJ, and a stage with the latest live bands performing everything from jazz to soul to R&B, all this encircling linen-covered tables with a friendly staff catering to your every whim. ☒ *8–10 Dover St., Mayfair* ☎ *020/7491–7509* ⊕ *www.doverst.co.uk* 💷 *£7–£15* 🕙 *Mon.–Thurs. 5:30 pm–3 am, Fri.–Sat. 7 pm–3 am* Ⓜ *Green Park.*

NOTTING HILL

BARS

Beach Blanket Babylon. In a Georgian house in Notting Hill, close to Portobello Market, this always-packed bar is distinguishable by its eclectic indoor-outdoor spaces with Gaudí-esque curves and snuggly corners—like a fairy-tale grotto or a medieval dungeon. A sister restaurant-bar-gallery offers a slightly more modern take on similar themes in an ex-warehouse in Shoreditch (19–23 Bethnal Green Rd.; 020/7749–3540). ☒ *45 Ledbury Rd., Notting Hill* ☎ *020/7229–2907* ⊕ *www.beachblanket.co.uk* 🕙 *Daily noon–midnight* Ⓜ *Notting Hill Gate.*

DANCE CLUBS

Notting Hill Arts Club. Rock stars like Liam Gallagher and Courtney Love have been seen at this small basement club-bar. What the place lacks in looks it makes up for in mood, and an alternative crowd swills beer to eclectic music that spans Asian underground, hip-hop, Latin-inspired funk, deep house, and jazzy grooves. ⊠ *21 Notting Hill Gate, Notting Hill* ☎ *020/7460–4459* ⊕ *www.nottinghillartsclub.com* 🖃 *Free–£8* ⊙ *Tues. noon–2 am, Wed.–Thurs. 7 pm–2 am, Fri.–Sat. 7 pm–midnight* Ⓜ *Notting Hill Gate.*

REGENT'S PARK AND HAMPSTEAD

DANCE CLUBS

KOKO. This Victorian theater, formerly known as Camden Palace, has seen acts from Charlie Chaplin to Madonna, and genres from punk to rave. Updated with lush reds not unlike a cockney Moulin Rouge, this is still one of London's most stunning venues. Sounds of live indie rock, cabaret, funky house, and club classics keep the big dance floor moving, even when it's not heaving. ⊠ *1A Camden High St., Camden Town* ☎ *0870/432–5527* ⊕ *www.koko.uk.com* 🖃 *£6–£25* ⊙ *Opening hrs vary, depending on shows* Ⓜ *Mornington Crescent.*

ECLECTIC

Union Chapel. The beauty of this sublime old chapel and its impressive multicultural programming make this spot one of London's best musical venues, especially for acoustic shows. Performers have included Björk, Beck, and Goldfrapp, though now you're more likely to hear lower-key alternative country, world music, and jazz, alongside poetry and literary events. ⊠ *Compton Terr., Islington* ☎ *020/7226–1686 Venue (no box office; ticket sales numbers vary with each event)* ⊕ *www.unionchapel. org.uk* 🖃 *Free–£25* ⊙ *Opening hrs vary* Ⓜ *Highbury & Islington.*

JAZZ AND BLUES

Jazz Café. A palace of high-tech cool in bohemian Camden, this remains an essential hangout for fans of both the mainstream end of the jazz repertoire and hip-hop, funk, world music, and Latin fusion. It's also the unlikely venue for Saturday "I Love the 80s" nights. Book ahead if you want a prime table in the balcony restaurant overlooking the stage. ⊠ *5 Parkway, Camden Town* ☎ *020/7688–8899 restaurant reservations, 020/7485–6834 venue info, 0844/847–2514 Tickets (Ticketmaster)* ⊕ *venues.meanfiddler.com/jazz-cafe/home* 🖃 *£6–£35* ⊙ *Daily 7 pm–2 am* Ⓜ *Camden Town.*

ROCK

Barfly Club. At one of the finest small clubs in the capital, punk, indie guitar bands, and new metal rock attract a nonmainstream crowd. Weekend club nights upstairs host DJs (and live bands) who rock the decks. ⊠ *49 Chalk Farm Rd., Camden Town* ☎ *020/7424-0800 Venue, 0870/9070-999 Tickets* ⊕ *www.barflyclub.com* 🖃 *£5–£11* ⊙ *Mon. and Tues. 7–midnight, Wed. and Thurs. 7 pm–2 am, Fri. and Sat. 7 pm–3 am* Ⓜ *Camden Town, Chalk Farm.*

THE ARTS

"All the world's a stage," said Shakespeare, and whether you prefer your art classical or modern, or as a contemporary twist on a time-honored classic, you'll find that London's vibrant cultural scene holds its own on the world stage. Divas sing original-language librettos at the Royal Opera House, Shakespeare's plays are brought to life at the reconstructed Globe Theatre, and challenging new writing is produced at the Royal Court.

To find out what's showing now, the free weekly magazine *Time Out* (issued every Tuesday in print and online at ⊕ *www.timeout.com*) is invaluable. The free *Evening Standard* carries listings, many of which are also available online at ⊕ *www.thisislondon.co.uk*. *Metro*, London's other widely available free newspaper, is also worth checking out. You can pick up the free fortnightly *London Theatre Guide* from hotels and tourist-information centers.

MAIN PERFORMING ARTS CENTERS

FAMILY **Barbican Centre.** Opened in 1982, the Brutalist-style Barbican is the largest performing arts center in Europe. The main concrete theater is most famous as the home of the London Symphony Orchestra. As well as the LSO (⊕ *www.lso.co.uk*), the Barbican is also the frequent host of the English Chamber Orchestra and the BBC Symphony Orchestra, and has an excellent concert season of big-name virtuosos. Performances by British and international theater companies make up part of its year-round **BITE** (Barbican International Theatre Events), which also features groundbreaking performance, dance, drama, and musical theater. Innovative exhibitions of 20th-century and current art and design are shown in the Barbican Gallery and the Curve (usually free). In addition to Hollywood films, obscure classics and film festivals with Screen Talks are programmed in the three movie theaters here. Saturday Family Film Club has adventure and animation to please all ages. You could listen to Elgar or watch some Russian theater, see some 1960's photography or an exhibition on art and science, and catch some German animation with live musical accompaniment, possibly all in one evening. ⊠ *Silk St., The City* ☎ *020/7638–8891 box office* ⊕ *www.barbican.org.uk* ⊗ *Mon.–Sat. 9 am–11 pm, Sun noon–11 pm* Ⓜ *Barbican.*

Southbank Centre. The Royal Festival Hall is one of London's best spaces for large-scale choral and orchestral works and is home to the Philharmonia and London Philharmonic orchestras. Other venues in the Southbank Centre host smaller-scale music performances: The Queen Elizabeth Hall is a popular venue for chamber orchestras and top-tier soloists, and the intimate Purcell Room is known for chamber music and solo recitals. Southbank also hosts everything from the London International Mime festival to large-scale dance performances, including a diverse and exciting season of international and British-based contemporary dance companies. Also part of the complex is the **Hayward Gallery** (10–6 daily), a landmark Brutalist-style 1960s building and one of London's major venues for contemporary art exhibitions. ⊠ *Belvedere Rd., South Bank* ☎ *020/7960–4200, 0844/875–0073 box office* ⊕ *www.southbankcentre.co.uk* Ⓜ *Waterloo, Embankment.*

CLASSICAL MUSIC

Whether it's a concert by cellist Yo-Yo Ma or Mozart's Requiem by candlelight, it's possible to hear first-rate musicians in world-class venues almost every day of the year. If you can't book in advance, arrive at the hall an hour before the performance for a chance at returns.

■TIP→ Lunchtime concerts take place all over the city in smaller concert halls, the big arts-center foyers, and churches; they usually cost less than £5 or are free, and feature string quartets, singers, jazz ensembles, or gospel choirs. St. John's, Smith Square, and St. Martin-in-the-Fields are popular locations. Performances usually begin about 1 pm and last one hour.

A great British tradition since 1895, the **Henry Wood Promenade Concerts** (more commonly known as the "Proms" ⊕ *www.bbc.co.uk/proms*) run eight weeks, from July to September, at the Royal Albert Hall. Despite an extraordinary quantity of high-quality concerts, it's renowned for its (atypical) last night: a madly jingoistic display of singing "Land of Hope and Glory," Union Jack–waving, and general madness. For regular Proms, tickets run £5–£90, with hundreds of standing tickets for £5 available at the hall on the night of the concert. ■TIP→ The last night is broadcast in Hyde Park on a jumbo screen, but even here a seat on the grass requires a paid ticket that can set you back around £25.

Royal Albert Hall. Built in 1871, this splendid iron-and-glass–dome auditorium hosts music programs in a wide range of genres. Its terra-cotta exterior surmounted by a mosaic frieze depicting figures engaged in artistic, scientific, and cultural pursuits, this domed, circular 5,223-seat auditorium was made possible by the Victorian public, who donated the money to build it. The RAH hosts everything from pop and classical headliners to Cirque du Soleil, ballet on ice, awards ceremonies, and Sumo wrestling championships, but is best-known as the venue for the annual July–September BBC Promenade Concerts—the "Proms". ⊠ *Kensington Gore, Kensington* ☎ *020/7589–8212, 0845/401–5034 box office* ⊕ *www.royalalberthall.com* Ⓜ *South Kensington.*

St. Martin-in-the-Fields. Popular lunchtime concerts (free but £3.50 donation suggested) are held in this lovely 1726 church, as are regular evening concerts. ■TIP→ Stop for a snack at the Café in the Crypt. ⊠ *Trafalgar Sq., Westminster* ☎ *020/7766–1100* ⊕ *www.stmartin-in-the-fields.org* Ⓜ *Charing Cross.*

Fodor'sChoice ★ **Wigmore Hall.** Hear chamber music and song recitals in this charming hall with near-perfect acoustics. Don't miss the Sunday morning concerts (11:30 am). ⊠ *36 Wigmore St., Marylebone* ☎ *020/7935–2141* ⊕ *www.wigmore-hall.org.uk* Ⓜ *Bond St.*

DANCE

Dance fans in London can enjoy the classicism of the world-renowned Royal Ballet, as well as innovative works by several contemporary dance companies—including Rambert Dance Company, Matthew Bourne's New Adventures, and the Wheeldon Company—and scores of independent choreographers. The English National Ballet and visiting international companies perform at the Coliseum and at Sadler's Wells, which also hosts various other ballet companies and dance troupes.

Encompassing the refurbished Royal Festival Hall, the Southbank Centre has a seriously good contemporary dance program that hosts top international companies and important U.K. choreographers, as well as multicultural offerings ranging from Japanese Butoh and Indian Kathak to hip-hop. The Place and the Lilian Bayliss Theatre at Sadler's Wells are where you'll find the most daring, cutting-edge performances. Also check ⊕ *www.londondance.com* for performances and fringe venues.

Dance Umbrella. The biggest annual event is Dance Umbrella, ten days in October that host international and British-based artists at various venues across the city. ☎ *020/7407–1200* ⊕ *www.danceumbrella.co.uk.*

The Place. The Robin Howard Dance Theatre at The Place is London's only theater dedicated to contemporary dance, and with tickets often under £15 it's good value, too. "Resolution!" is the United Kingdom's biggest platform event for new choreographers. ✉ *17 Duke's Rd., Bloomsbury* ☎ *020/7121–1100* ⊕ *www.theplace.org.uk* Ⓜ *Euston.*

Fodor's Choice
★
Sadler's Wells. This gleaming building opened in 1998, the seventh on the site in its 300-year history, and is devoted to presenting leading classical and contemporary dance companies. The Random Dance Company is in residence, and the little Lilian Bayliss Theatre hosts avant-garde work. ✉ *Rosebery Ave., Islington* ☎ *0844/412–4300 tickets, 020/7863-8198 general enquiries* ⊕ *www.sadlerswells.com* Ⓜ *Angel.*

FILM

There are many lovely movie theaters in London and several that are committed to nonmainstream cinema, notably the National Film Theatre. Most of the major houses, such as the Odeon Leicester Square and the Empire, are in the Leicester Square–Piccadilly Circus area, where tickets average £15. Monday and matinees are often cheaper, at around £6–£10, and there are also fewer crowds.

FAMILY
BFI Southbank. With the best repertory programming in London, the three movie theaters and studio at what was previously known as the National Film Theatre are effectively a national film center run by the British Film Institute. They show more than 1,000 titles each year, favoring art-house, foreign, silent, overlooked, classic, noir, and short films over Hollywood blockbusters. The center also has a gallery, bookshop, and "mediatheque," where visitors can watch film and television from the National Archive for free (closed Mon). ✉ *Belvedere Rd., South Bank* ☎ *020/7928–3535 information, 020/7928–3232 box office* ⊕ *www.bfi.org.uk* Ⓜ *Waterloo.*

Curzon Soho. This popular, comfortable movie theater runs a vibrant and artsy program of mixed repertoire and mainstream films, with a good calendar of director talks and other events, too. There are branches in Mayfair, Bloomsbury, Chelsea, and Richmond. ✉ *99 Shaftesbury Ave., Soho* ☎ *0330/500–1331* ⊕ *www.curzoncinemas.com* Ⓜ *Piccadilly Circus, Leicester Sq.* ✉ *38 Curzon St., Mayfair* ☎ *0330/500–1331* Ⓜ *Green Park.*

FAMILY
The Electric Cinema. This refurbished Portobello Road art house screens mainstream and international movies. The emphasis is on comfort, with leather sofas for two, armchairs, footstools, and mini–coffee tables for your tapas-style food and wine. Saturday matinees for kids are popular. Edible Cinema combines experimental food and cocktails with the

The Proms at Royal Albert Hall have standing tickets for £5 on the night of the concerts.

cinema experience. The Electric also has another sumptuous movie theater in east London—the Aubin, on Redchurch Street, with sofas and wine-coolers. ⊠ *191 Portobello Rd., Notting Hill* ☎ *020/7908–9696* ⊕ *www.electriccinema.co.uk* ✉ *£12.50–£22.50* Ⓜ *Ladbroke Grove, Notting Hill Gate.*

OPERA

The two key players in London's opera scene are the Royal Opera House (which ranks with the Metropolitan Opera House in New York) and the more innovative English National Opera (ENO), which presents English-language productions at the London Coliseum. Only the Theatre Royal, Drury Lane, has a longer theatrical history than the Royal Opera House—the third theater to be built on the site since 1858.

Despite occasional performances by the likes of Björk, the Royal Opera House struggles to shrug off its reputation for elitism and ticket prices that can rise to £800. It is, however, more accessible than it used to be—the cheapest tickets are less than £10. Conditions of purchase vary; call for information. Prices for the ENO are generally lower, ranging from around £20 to £95.

In summer, the increasingly adventurous Opera Holland Park presents the usual chestnuts alongside some obscure works under a canopy in leafy Holland Park. International touring companies often perform at Sadler's Wells, the Barbican, the Southbank Centre, and Wigmore Hall, so check the weekly listings for details.

The London Coliseum. A vertiable architectural extravaganza of Edwardian exoticism, the restored baroque-style theater (1904) has a magnificent auditorium and a rooftop glass dome with a bar and great views.

As one of the city's largest and most venerable theaters, the Coliseum functions mainly as the home of the English National Opera. Seemingly in better financial shape than it has been for some time, ENO continues to produce innovative opera, sung in English, for lower prices than the Royal Opera House. During opera's off-season, the house hosts a number of dance troupes, including the English National Ballet (⊕ *www.ballet.org.uk*). Guided tours (every Saturday at 11:30 am) cost £10. ⊠ *St. Martin's La., Covent Garden* ☎ *0871/911–0200 box office, 020/7836–0111 enquiries* ⊕ *www.eno.org* Ⓜ *Leicester Sq.*

Opera Holland Park. In summer, well-loved operas and imaginative productions of relatively unknown works are presented under a spectacular new canopy against the remains of Holland House, one of the first great houses built in Kensington. Ticket prices range from £12 to £67.50, with 1,100 tickets offered free to young people ages 9–18 every season. Tickets go on sale in April. ⊠ *Holland Park, Kensington High St., Kensington* ☎ *0300/999–1000 box office (opens late Apr.), 020/7361–3570 enquiries* ⊕ *www.operahollandpark.com* Ⓜ *High Street Kensington, Holland Park.*

Fodor'sChoice **Royal Opera House.** Along with Milan's La Scala, New York's Metropoli-
★ tan, and the Palais Garnier in Paris, this is one of the world's greatest opera houses. The resident troupe has mounted famously spectacular productions in the past, though recent productions have tended toward starker, more contemporary operas. Tickets range in price from £8 to £800. The box office opens at 10 am, but lines for popular productions can start as early as 7 am; unsold tickets are offered at half price four hours before a performance. There are free lunchtime recitals most Mondays in the Crush Room (arrive early to get a ticket—between 11 am and noon; some tickets are available online from nine days before the event). ROH2, the Opera House's contemporary arm, stages more experimental dance and voice performances in locations including the Linbury Studio Theatre, a 400-seater space below the Opera House. ⊠ *Bow St., Covent Garden* ☎ *020/7304–4000* ⊕ *www.roh.org. uk* ☉ *Public areas generally 10–3:30; Auditorium tours daily at 4; Backstage tours Mon.–Fri. 10:30, 12:30, and 2:30, Sat. 10:30, 11:30, 12:30, and 1:30* Ⓜ *Covent Garden.*

THEATER

In London the play really *is* the thing, ranging from a long-running popular musical like *Mamma Mia!*, a groundbreaking reworking of Pinter, imaginative physical theater from an experimental company like *Complicite*, a lavish Disney spectacle, or a small fringe production above a pub. West End glitz and glamour continue to pull in the audiences, and so do the more innovative productions. Only in London will a Tuesday matinee of the Royal Shakespeare Company's *Henry IV* sell out a 1,200-seat theater.

In London the words "radical" and "quality," or "classical" and "experimental" are not mutually exclusive. The Royal Shakespeare Company (⊕ *www.rsc.org.uk*) and the National Theatre (⊕ *www. nationaltheatre.org.uk*) often stage contemporary versions of the classics. The Almeida, Battersea Arts Centre (BAC), Donmar Warehouse,

Royal Court Theatre, Soho Theatre, and Old Vic attract famous actors and have excellent reputations for new writing and innovative theatrical approaches. These are the venues where you'll see an original production before it becomes a hit in the West End or on Broadway (and for a fraction of the cost). The London theater scene remains vibrant throughout the summer months. Open-air productions of Shakespeare are particularly well served, whether in the faithful reconstruction of the Elizabethan Globe Theatre or under the stars in Regent's Park's Open Air Theatre.

Theatergoing isn't cheap. Tickets less than £10 are a rarity, although designated productions at the National Theatre have seats at this price. At the commercial theaters you should expect to pay from £15 for a seat in the upper balcony to at least £25 for a good one in the stalls (orchestra) or dress circle (mezzanine). However, last-minute returns available on the night may provide some good deals. Tickets may be booked through ticket agents, at individual theater box offices, or over the phone by credit card. Be sure to inquire about any extra fees—prices can vary enormously, but agents are legally obliged to reveal the face value of the ticket if you ask. All the larger hotels offer theater bookings, but they tack on a hefty service charge. ■ TIP→ Be very wary of ticket touts (scalpers) and unscrupulous ticket agents outside theaters.

Ticketmaster (☎ 0844/277–4321 ⊕ www.ticketmaster.co.uk) sells tickets to a number of different theaters, although it charges a booking fee. For discount tickets, **Society of London Theatre** (☎ 020/7557–6700 ⊕ www.tkts.co.uk) operates "tkts," a half-price ticket booth on the southwest corner of Leicester Square, and sells the best available seats to performances at about 25 theaters. It's open Monday–Saturday 9–7, Sunday 10:30–4:30; there's a £3 service charge (included in the price). Major credit cards are accepted.

THEATERS

Almeida Theatre. This Off–West End venue premieres excellent new plays and exciting twists on the classics, often featuring high-profile actors. There's a good cafe and a licensed bar that serves "sharing dishes" as well as tasty main courses. ⊠ Almeida St., Islington ☎ 020/7359–4404 ⊕ www.almeida.co.uk Ⓜ Angel, Highbury & Islington.

BAC. Battersea Arts Centre has a reputation for producing innovative new work. Check out Scratch events, low-tech cabaret theater by emerging artists where the audience provides feedback on works-in-progress. Tuesday shows often have pay-what-you-can entry. ⊠ 176 Lavender Hill, Battersea ☎ 020/7223–2223 ⊕ www.bac.org.uk Ⓜ National Rail: Clapham Junction.

Fodor's Choice
★ **Donmar Warehouse.** Hollywood stars often perform in this not-for-profit theatre in diverse and daring new works, bold interpretations of the classics, and small-scale musicals. Nicole Kidman, Gwyneth Paltrow, and Ewan McGregor have all been featured. ⊠ 41 Earlham St., Seven Dials, Covent Garden ☎ 0844/871–7624 ⊕ www.donmarwarehouse.com Ⓜ Covent Garden.

National Theatre. When this theater, designed by Sir Denys Lasdun, opened in 1976 Londoners weren't all so keen on the low-slung, multi-layered Brutalist block. Interspersed with the three theaters—the 1,120-seat Olivier, the 890-seat Lyttelton, and the 300-seat Cottesloe—is a multilayered foyer with exhibitions, bars, and restaurants, and free entertainment. Musicals, classics, and new plays are all performed by top-flight professionals. Some shows offer £12 ticket deals. ⊠ *Belvedere Rd., South Bank* ☎ *020/7452–3000 box office, 020/7452–3400 information* ⊕ *www.nationaltheatre.org.uk* ☎ *Tour £8.50* ☉ *Foyer Mon.–Sat. 9:30 am–11 pm; 75-min tour backstage up to 6 times daily weekdays, twice on Sat., often on Sun.* Ⓜ *Waterloo.*

The Old Vic. This grand old theater, former haunting grounds of such stage legends as John Gielgud, Vivien Leigh, Peter O'Toole, Richard Burton, and Judi Dench, is now masterminded by American actor Kevin Spacey. The theater had suffered decades of financial duress before being brought under the ownership of a dedicated trust headed by Spacey. His production record has had a few hiccups but his tenure is these days regarded by most as a success. As well as being artistic director, Spacey often appears on stage. ⊠ *The Cut, Southwark* ☎ *0844/871–7628 box office, 020/7928–2651* ⊕ *www.oldvictheatre.com* Ⓜ *Waterloo, Southwark.*

Fodor's Choice ★ **Open Air Theatre.** On a warm summer evening, open-air classical theater in the pastoral and royal Regent's Park is hard to beat for a magical adventure. Enjoy a supper before the performance, a bite during the intermission on the picnic lawn, or drinks in the spacious bar. The only downside is that warm summer nights in London are not always entirely reliable. ⊠ *Inner Circle, Regent's Park* ☎ *0844/826–4242* ⊕ *www.openairtheatre.com* Ⓜ *Baker St., Regent's Park.*

Royal Court Theatre. Britain's undisputed epicenter of new theatrical works, the RCT is now 50 years old and continues to produce gritty British and international drama. ▉**TIP**➔ Don't miss the best deal in town—four 10-pence standing tickets go on sale one hour before each performance, and £10 tickets are available on Monday. ⊠ *Sloane Sq., Chelsea* ☎ *020/7565–5000* ⊕ *www.royalcourttheatre.com* Ⓜ *Sloane Sq.*

Soho Theatre. This sleek theater in the heart of Soho is devoted to fostering new work and is a prolific presenter of plays by emerging writers, comedy performances, cabaret shows, and other entertainment. ⊠ *21 Dean St., Soho* ☎ *020/7478–0100* ⊕ *www.sohotheatre.com* Ⓜ *Tottenham Court Rd.*

Tricycle Theatre. Committed to representing the cultural diversity of its community, the Tricycle shows the best in black, Irish, Jewish, Asian, and South African drama, and also promotes new work. ⊠ *269 Kilburn High Rd., Kilburn* ☎ *020/7372 6611 information, 020/7328–1000 box office* ⊕ *www.tricycle.co.uk* Ⓜ *Kilburn.*

Young Vic. In a home near Waterloo, big names perform alongside young talent, often in daring, innovative productions of classic plays that appeal to a more diverse audience than is traditionally found in London theaters. ⊠ *66 The Cut, Waterloo, South Bank* ☎ *020/7922–2800, 020/7922–2922 box office* ⊕ *www.youngvic.org* Ⓜ *Southwark, Waterloo.*

SHOPPING

As befits one of the great trading capitals of the world, London's shops have been known to boast, "You name it, we sell it." Finding and buying "it" can be a delight (the private fitting rooms at couturier Vivienne Westwood) or a trial (mobbed Oxford Street on a Saturday morning). No matter where you head in this city, you'll find you can melt as much plastic as your wallet can stand. You can shop like royalty at Her Majesty's glove maker, run down a leather-bound copy of *Wuthering Heights* at a Charing Cross bookseller, or find flea-market goodies on Portobello Road. Whether out for fun—there's nothing like those amazing street markets to stimulate the acquisitive juices—or for fashion, London can be the most rewarding of hunting grounds.

Although it's impossible to pin down one particular look that defines the city, London style tends to fall into two camps: one is the quirky, individualistic, somewhat romantic look exemplified by homegrown designers like Matthew Williamson, Westwood, and Lulu Guinness. The other reflects Britain's celebrated tradition of classic knitwear and suiting, with labels like Jaeger, Pringle, and Brora, while Oswald Boateng, Paul Smith, and Richard James take tradition and give it a very modern twist. Traditional bespoke men's tailoring can be found in the menswear stores of Jermyn Street and Savile Row—there's no better place in the city to buy custom-made shirts and suits, while the handbags at Mulberry, Asprey, and Anya Hindmarch are pure classic quality. If your budget can't stretch this far, no problem; the city's chain stores like Topshop, Zara, and H&M, aimed at the younger end of the market, are excellent places to pick up designs copied straight from the catwalk at a fraction of the price, while mid-market chains like Reiss, Jigsaw, and L.K. Bennett offer smart design and better quality for the more sophisticated shopper.

If there's anything that unites London's designers, it's a commitment to creativity and originality, underpinned by a strong sense of heritage. This combination of posh and rock-n-roll sensibilities turns up in everyone from Terence Conran, who revolutionized product and housewares design in the '60s (and is still going strong), to Alexander McQueen, who combined the Punk aesthetic with the rigor of couture. You'll see it in fanciful millinery creations by Philip Treacy and Stephen Jones, and in the work of imaginative shoemakers Nicholas Kirkwood, United Nude, and Terry de Havilland; and it keeps going, right through to current hot designers Erdem, Christopher Kane, and Christopher Bailey, the latter responsible for making traditional label Burberry relevant again.

Apart from bankrupting yourself, the only problem you may encounter is exhaustion. London's shopping districts are spread out all over the city, so do as the locals do. Plan your excursion with military precision, taking in only one or two areas in a day, and stop for a hearty English lunch with a glass of wine or a pint at a pub.

LONDON'S SPECTATOR SPORTS

Sport in the capital comes into its own when it's watched, rather than participated in. You'll most easily witness London's fervent sporting passions in front of a screen in a pub with a pint in hand. And those passions run deep.

FOOTBALL

London's top teams—Chelsea, Arsenal, Tottenham Hotspur—are world-class (especially the first two) and often progress in the European Champions League. It's unlikely you'll be able to get tickets for anything except the least popular Premier League games during the August–May season, despite absurdly high ticket prices—as much as £41 for a standard, walk-up, match-day seat at Chelsea, and a whopping £126 for the dearest match-day tickets at Arsenal!

Arsenal. Arsenal (aka the Gunners) is historically London's most successful club. Under the managerial reign of Arsene Wenger they have shed their boring image to become proponents of tippy-tappy, attractive, free-flowing football—while hardly ever employing any English players. ⊠ *Emirates Stadium, 75 Drayton Park* ☎ *020/7619–5000* ⊕ *www.arsenal. com* Ⓜ *Arsenal.*

Chelsea. Chief rivals of Manchester United in the Premier League, Champions League winners in 2012, and Premier League title and FA Cup winners in 2009 and 2010, Chelsea (aka the Blues) is owned by one of Russia's richest oligarchs, Roman Abramovich. In recent years the team has been forged into a formidable and ruthless footballing machine. ⊠ *Stamford Bridge, Fulham Rd., Fulham* ☎ *0871/9841–905* ⊕ *www. chelseafc.com* Ⓜ *Fulham Broadway.*

Tottenham Hotspur. Tottenham Hotspur (aka Spurs)—bitter North London rivals of Arsenal—has under-performed for decades but there are strong hints of a revival with a bevy of England national team regulars. ⊠ *White Hart Lane, 748 High Rd.* ☎ *0844/499–5000* ⊕ *www. tottenhamhotspur.com* Ⓜ *National Rail: White Hart Lane.*

West Ham. Known as "The Hammers," West Ham, despite the name, is the team of the East End. The Hammers have created a more consistent team, but one unlikely to claim many trophies. ⊠ *Boleyn Ground, Green St., Upton Park* ☎ *0871/222–2700* ⊕ *www.whufc. com* Ⓜ *Upton Park.*

TENNIS

Wimbledon Lawn Tennis Championships. The Wimbledon Lawn Tennis Championships are famous for the green grass of Centre Court, Andy Murray never quite winning the Men's Final, and an old-school insistence on players wearing white. Whether you can get Centre Court tickets is literally down to the luck of the draw, because there's a ballot system (lottery) for advance purchase. For more information, see their website. You can also buy entry to roam matches on the outside courts, where even the top-seeded players compete early on. Five hundred show court tickets are also sold daily, but these usually go to those prepared to stand in line all night. ⊠ *The All England Lawn Tennis Club, Church Rd.* ☎ *020/8944–1066* ⊕ *www.wimbledon.com.*

WESTMINSTER, ST. JAMES'S, AND ROYAL LONDON

BEAUTY

Fodor's Choice ★ **Floris.** What do Queen Victoria and Marilyn Monroe have in common? They both used fragrances from Floris, one of the most beautiful shops in London, with gleaming glass-and-Spanish-mahogany showcases salvaged from the Great Exhibition of 1851. In addition to scents for both men and women, Floris makes its own shaving products, reflecting its origins as a barbershop. Other gift possibilities include goose-down powder puffs, a famous rose-scented mouthwash, and beautifully-packaged soaps and bath essences. There's another branch in Belgravia. ✉ 89 Jermyn St., St. James's ☎ 020/7930–2885 ⊕ www.florislondon. com ☾ Closed Sun. Ⓜ Piccadilly Circus, Green Park.

BOOKS AND STATIONERY

Fodor's Choice ★ **Hatchards.** This is London's oldest bookshop, open since 1797 and beloved by writers themselves (customers have included Oscar Wilde, Rudyard Kipling, and Lord Byron). Despite its wood-panelled, "gentleman's library" atmosphere, and eclectic selection of books, Hatchards is owned by the large Waterstone's chain. Nevertheless, the shop still retains its period charm, aided by the staff's old-fashioned helpfulness and expertise. Look for the substantial number of books signed by notable contemporary authors on the well-stocked shelves. ✉ 187 Piccadilly, St. James's ☎ 020/7439–9921 ⊕ www.hatchards. co.uk Ⓜ Piccadilly Circus.

CLOTHING: MENSWEAR

Fodor's Choice ★ **Turnbull & Asser.** This is *the* custom shirtmaker, dripping exclusivity from every fiber—after all, Prince Charles is a client and every filmic James Bond has worn shirts from here. At least 15 separate measurements are taken, and the cloth, woven to the company's specifications, comes in 1,000 different patterns—the cottons feel as good as silk. The first order must be for a minimum of six shirts, which start from £195 each. As well as jackets, cashmeres, suits, ties, pajamas, and accessories perfect for the billionaire who has everything, the store also carries less expensive, though still exquisite, ready-to-wear shirts. There's another branch in the City ✉ 71–72 Jermyn St., St. James's ☎ 020/7808–3000 ⊕ www. turnbullandasser.com ☾ Closed Sun. Ⓜ Green Park.

FOOD

Fodor's Choice ★ **Berry Bros. & Rudd.** Nothing matches Berry Bros. & Rudd for rare offerings and a unique shopping experience. A family-run wine business since 1698, "BBR" stores its vintage bottles and casks in vaulted cellars that are more than 300 years old. The shop has a quirky charm and the staff is extremely knowledgeable—and not snooty if you're on a budget. ✉ 3 St. James's St., St. James's ☎ 020/396–9600 ⊕ www. bbr.com ☾ Closed Sun. Ⓜ Green Park.

Fodor's Choice ★ **Fortnum & Mason.** Although F&M is popularly known as the Queen's grocer and the impeccably mannered staff wear traditional tailcoats, its celebrated food hall stocks gifts for all budgets, such as loads of irresistibly packaged luxury foods stamped with the gold "By Appointment" crest for less than £5. Try the teas, preserves (unusual products include rose-petal jelly), condiments, or Gentleman's Relish (anchovy

CAMDEN TOWN
cheap second-hand and club gear

CLERKENWELL
a historical hotspot for crafts and design

HOXTON & SHOREDITCH
edgy young designers

MARYLEBONE
small shops in village-like setting

NOTTING HILL
antiques, vintage clothing, and boho boutiques

OXFORD CIRCUS
global flagships, department stores, and street style on Carnaby

SOHO
books abound on Charing Cross Road

COVENT GARDEN
an urban-wear mecca around Seven Dials

MAYFAIR
catwalk names on Bond St., trad tailors on Savile Row

ST JAMES'S
old-fashioned specialists, from hatters to shirtmakers

KNIGHTSBRIDGE
luxe labels and, of course, Harrods

CHELSEA
the King's Rd. spans fashion to furniture

REGENT'S PARK

BLOOMSBURY

BAYSWATER

HYDE PARK

Green Park

St. James's Park

WESTMINSTER

BELGRAVIA

VICTORIA

LAMBETH

River Thames

0   1/2 mile
0   1/2 km

Choices, choices: there are plenty of prints—and much else—at the Portobello Road Market.

paste). If you start to flag, break for afternoon tea at one of the four other restaurants (one's an indulgent ice-cream parlor)—or a treatment in the Beauty Rooms. ⊠ *181 Piccadilly, St. James's* ☎ *020/7734–8040* ⊕ *www.fortnumandmason.com* Ⓜ *Green Park.*

TOYS

The Armoury of St. James's. The fine toy soldiers and military models in stock here are collectors' items. Painted and mounted knights only 6 inches high can cost up to £1,200 (though figures start at a mere £7.50 for a toy soldier). Besides lead and tin soldiers, the shop has regimental brooches, porcelain figures, military memorabilia, and military antiques. ⊠ *17 Piccadilly Arcade, St. James's* ☎ *020/7493–5082* ⊕ *www.armoury.co.uk* ☉ *Closed Sun.* Ⓜ *Piccadilly Circus.*

SOHO AND COVENT GARDEN

ACCESSORIES

Fodor's Choice
★

Peckham Rye. The epicenter of "Swinging London" in the mid-'60s has recently undergone a renaissance, particularly in the "Newburgh Quarter," the small cobblestone streets leading off Carnaby Street. Here's where you'll find small specialist boutiques such as Peckham Rye, a tiny bolt-hole showcasing heritage-style men's accessories—handmade silk and twill ties (the name is Cockney rhyming slang for same), bow ties, and scarves, all using traditional patterns from the archives of this family-run business that go back to 1799. More Ralph Lauren than Ralph Lauren, the socks, striped shirts, and handkerchiefs attract modern-day Beau Brummels such as Mark Ronson and David Beckham. ⊠ *11 Newburgh St., Soho* ☎ *0207/734–5181* ⊕ *www.peckhamrye.com* Ⓜ *Oxford Street.*

BOOKS AND PRINTS

Fodor's Choice
★
Foyles. Founded in 1903 by the Foyle brothers after they failed the Civil Service exam, this family-owned store, recently relocated into this historic 1930s art deco building, carries almost every title imaginable. One of London's best sources for textbooks, Foyles also stocks everything from popular fiction to military history, sheet music, medical tomes, graphic novels, and handsome illustrated fine arts books. It also offers the store-within-a-store Ray's Jazz (one of London's better outlets for music) and a cool café. Foyles has branches in the Southbank Centre, St. Pancras International train station (the Eurostar's U.K. terminus), and the Westfield shopping centers in Shepherd's Bush and Stratford. In 2014 they are planning a move right next door. ⊠ *107–109 Charing Cross Rd., Soho* ☎ *020/7437–5660* ⊕ *www. foyles.co.uk* Ⓜ *Tottenham Court Rd.*

Fodor's Choice
★
Grosvenor Prints. London's largest collection of 17th- to-early 20th-century prints emphasizes views of the city and architecture as well as sporting and decorative motifs. The selection is eclectic, with prices ranging from £5 into the thousands. ⊠ *19 Shelton St., Covent Garden* ☎ *020/7836–1979* ⊕ *www.grosvenorprints.com* ☾ *Closed Sun.* Ⓜ *Covent Garden, Leicester Sq.*

CLOTHING

Other. Aimed at men and women in search of stylish cool, this independent boutique stocks its own brand of entirely made-in-England clothing, as well as accessories, housewares, books, and clothing from other carefully selected brands such as b store, Opening Ceremony, Sophie Hulme, and Peter Jensen. The look is understated, slightly geeky, and totally contemporary. ⊠ *21 Kingly St., Soho* ☎ *020/7734–6846* ⊕ *www. other-shop.com* Ⓜ *Oxford Circus.*

Fodor's Choice
★
Paul Smith. British classics with an irreverent twist define Paul Smith's collections for women, men, and children. Beautifully tailored suits for men and women take hallmarks of traditional British style and turn them on their heads with humor and color, combining exceptional fabrics with flamboyant linings or unusual detailing. There are several branches throughout London, in Notting Hill, South Kensington, Chelsea, and Borough Market, plus a vintage furniture shop at 9 Albemarle Street in Mayfair and a shoes and accessories shop on Marylebone High Street. ⊠ *40–44 Floral St., Covent Garden* ☎ *020/7379–7133* ⊕ *www. paulsmith.co.uk* Ⓜ *Covent Garden.*

CLOTHING: WOMEN'S WEAR

Poste Mistress. The Office chain's more glamourous sibling, this boudoir-styled boutique features fashion-forward but wearable styles from some 40 brands including Stella McCartney, Acne, and Miu Miu. Casual alternatives such as Vivienne Westwood rubber booties and Converse sneakers are also available, and prices are not eye-watering. There's a branch devoted to men's designer shoes at 10 South Moulton Street in Mayfair. ⊠ *61–63 Monmouth St., Covent Garden* ☎ *020/7379–4040* ⊕ *www.office.co.uk* Ⓜ *Covent Garden.*

Reiss. With an in-house design team whose experience includes stints at Gucci and Calvin Klein and customers like Beyoncé and the Duchess of Cambridge (formerly Kate Middleton), who wore a Reiss dress for her official engagement picture, this hot chain brings luxury standards of tailoring and details to mass-market women's and menswear. The sleek and contemporary style is not cheap, but does offer value for money. There are branches in Knightsbridge, The City, Covent Garden, Chelsea, Hampstead, Notting Hill, Soho, and basically all over London. ⊠ *10 Barrett St., Fitzrovia* ☎ *020/7486–6557* ⊕ *www.reiss. com* Ⓜ *Oxford Street.*

Fodor's Choice ★ **Topshop.** A hotspot for straight-from-the-runway affordable fashion, Topshop is destination shopping for teenagers and fashion editors alike. Clothes and accessories are geared to the youthful end of the market, although women who are young at heart and girlish of figure can find plenty of wearable items here. However, you will need a high tolerance for loud music and busy dressing rooms. The store also features collections designed by a rotating roster of high-end designers as well as offering its own premium designer line called Topshop Unique. Topman brings the same fast-fashion approach to clothing for men. ▮▮▮ TIP→ If the crowds become too much, head to one of the smaller Topshops in Kensington High Street, Knightsbridge, Victoria, Marble Arch, or Holborn. ⊠ *36–38 Great Castle Street, Fitzrovia* ☎ *0844/848–7487* ⊕ *www.topshop.com* Ⓜ *Oxford Circus.*

Fodor's Choice ★ **United Nude.** Co-created by noted architect Rem D Koolhaas (who also designed this Covent Garden flagship store) and Galahad Clark (of the Clark's shoes dynasty), these distinctive, futuristic designs that use up-to-the-minute techniques such as carbon fiber heels and injection-molded soles are flattering and surprisingly comfortable. There's another branch in Knightsbridge. ⊠ *13 Floral St., Covent Garden* ☎ *0207/240-7106* ⊕ *www.unitednude.com* Ⓜ *Covent Garden.*

DEPARTMENT STORES

Fodor's Choice ★ **Liberty.** The wonderful black-and-white mock-Tudor facade, created from the timbers of two Royal Navy ships, reflects this store's origins in the late-19th-century's Arts and Crafts movement. Leading designers were recruited from this and the Aesthetic movement to create the classic art nouveau Liberty prints that are still a centerpiece of the brand, gracing everything from cushions and silk kimonos to embossed leather bags and photo albums. Inside, Liberty's is a labyrinth of nooks and crannies stuffed with thoughfully chosen merchandise. ⊠ *Regent St., Soho* ☎ *020/7734–1234* ⊕ *www.liberty. co.uk* Ⓜ *Oxford Circus.*

TOYS

FAMILY Fodor's Choice ★ **Benjamin Pollock's Toyshop.** This landmark shop still carries on the tradition of its eponymous founder, who sold minature theater stages made from richly-detailed paper from the late-19th century until his death in 1937. Today the antique model theaters tend to be expensive, but there are plenty of magical reproductions for under 10 pounds. There's also an extensive selection of new but nostalgic puppets, marionettes, teddy bears, spinning tops, jack-in-the-boxes, and similar traditional children's toys from the days before batteries were required. ✉ *44 Clare Market, The Piazza, Covent Garden* ☎ *020/7379–7866* ⊕ *www. pollocks-coventgarden.co.uk* Ⓜ *Covent Garden.*

FAMILY **Hamleys.** Besieged by pester power? Don't worry, help is at hand—this London institution has six floors of the latest dolls, soft toys, video games, and technological devices (plus such old-fashioned pleasures as train sets, drum kits, and magic tricks), with every must-have on the preteen shopping list. It's a madhouse at Christmastime, but Santa's grotto is one of the best in town. There's a smaller branch in St. Pancras International train station. ✉ *188–196 Regent St., Soho* ☎ *0800/280–2444* ⊕ *www.hamleys.com* Ⓜ *Oxford Circus, Piccadilly Circus.*

BLOOMSBURY AND HOLBORN

ACCESSORIES

James Smith & Sons Ltd. This has to be the world's ultimate umbrella shop, and a must for anyone interested in real Victorian London. The family-owned shop has been in this location on a corner of New Oxford Street since 1857, and sells every kind of umbrella, cane, and walking stick imaginable. The interior is unchanged since the 19th century; you will feel as if you have stepped back in time. If the umbrellas are out of your price range, James Smith also sells smaller accessories and handmade wooden bowls. ✉ *Hazelwood House, 53 New Oxford St., Bloomsbury* ☎ *020/7836–4731* ⊕ *www.james-smith.co.uk* ☺ *Closed Sun.* Ⓜ *Tottenham Court Rd., Holborn.*

ANTIQUES

Fodor's Choice **London Silver Vaults.** Housed in a basement vault, this extraordinary
★ space holds stalls from more than 30 silver dealers. Products range from the spectacularly over-the-top costing thousands to smaller items—like teaspoons, candlesticks, or a set of Victorian cake forks—starting at £25. ◼ TIP➜ **Most of the silver merchants actually trade out of room-size, underground vaults, which were originally rented out to London's upper crust to store their valuables.** ✉ *53–64 Chancery La., Holborn* ☎ *020/7242–3844* ⊕ *www.thesilvervaults.com* ☺ *Closed Sat. after 1 and Sun.* Ⓜ *Chancery La.*

THE CITY

JEWELRY

Fodor's Choice **Lesley Craze Gallery.** This serene gallery displays unique pieces by some
★ 100 innovative designers from around the world (with a strong British bias). A textiles room showcases colorful handmade scarves. Prices start at £45. ✉ *33–35A Clerkenwell Green, Clerkenwell* ☎ *020/7608–0393* ⊕ *www.lesleycrazegallery.co.uk* ☺ *Closed Sun.; open Mon. in Nov. and Dec. only* Ⓜ *Farringdon.*

THE EAST END

CLOTHING

Fodor's Choice
★
Junky Styling. This brand was launched by designers Annika Sanders and Kerry Seager, who used to "deconstruct" old clothing when they wanted something unique to wear clubbing. They recycled traditional suits and shirts into wild outfits, and the business grew from there. ✉ *21 Hackney Road, Shoreditch* ☎ *020/7247–1883* ⊕ *www.junkystyling.co.uk* Ⓜ *Old St. London Overground: Hoxton, Shoreditch High St.*

Fodor's Choice
★
The Laden Showroom. Sienna Miller and Victoria Beckham are among the celebs who regularly check out emerging talent at this East End showroom for young designers. The store retails the work of more than 50 new designers, some selling one-off items—so the look you find is likely to be original. ✉ *103 Brick La., Spitalfields* ☎ *020/7247–2431* ⊕ *www. laden.co.uk* Ⓜ *London Overground: Shoreditch High St.*

HATS

Fodor's Choice
★
Bernstock Speirs. Here since 1982, Paul Bernstock and Thelma Speirs turn traditional hats on their head with street-smart trilbies and knitted hats that feature unusual colors and quirky details. ✉ *234 Brick La., Spitalfields* ☎ *020/7739–7385* ⊕ *www.bernstockspiers.com* ☉ *Closed Mon.* Ⓜ *London Overground: Shoreditch High Street.*

HOUSEHOLD

Fodor's Choice
★
Labour & Wait. Although such household items as colanders and clothespins may not sound like ideal souvenirs, this shop may make you reconsider. The owners are on a mission to revive functional, old-fashioned British goods, such as enamel kitchenware, "Brown Betty" glazed teapots, Guernsey sweaters, and vintage Welsh blankets. ✉ *85 Redchurch St., Shoreditch* ☎ *020/7729–6253* ⊕ *www.labourandwait.co.uk* Ⓜ *London Overground: Shoreditch High St.*

MUSIC

Fodor's Choice
★
Rough Trade East. While many London record stores are struggling, this veteran indie-music specialist seems to have gotten the formula right. The spacious surroundings are as much a hangout as a shop, complete with a stage for live gigs, a café, and Internet access. There's another branch on Portobello Road in Notting Hill. ✉ *Dray Walk, Old Truman Brewery, 91 Brick La., Spitalfields* ☎ *020/7392–7788* Ⓜ *Liverpool St. London Overground: Shoreditch High St.*

STREET MARKETS

Old Spitalfields Market. This fine example of a Victorian market hall (once the East End's wholesale fruit and vegetable market), now restored to its original splendor, is at the center of the area's gentrified revival. The original building is now largely occupied by shops with traders' stalls in the courtyard, and a modern shopping precinct under a Norman Foster–designed glass canopy adjoins the old building, home to a large number of independent traders' stalls. Thursday is particularly good for antiques. And, from Spanish tapas to Thai satays, the food outlets (mostly small, upscale chains but some independent stallholders as well) offer cuisines from around the world. ✉ *16 Horner Sq., Brushfield St., Spitalfields* ☎ *020/7247–8556* ⊕ *www.spitalfields.co.uk* ☉ *Stalls Tues.–Fri. 10–5, Sun. 9–5; restaurants weekdays 11–11, Sun. 9–11; retail shops daily 10–7* Ⓜ *Liverpool St. London Overground: Shoreditch High Street.*

THE SOUTH BANK

STREET MARKETS

Fodor'sChoice
★
Borough Market. There's been a market in Borough since Roman times. This one, spread under the arches and railroad tracks leading to London Bridge Station, is the successor to a medieval market once held on London Bridge. Postmillennium, it has been transformed from a noisy collection of local produce stalls to a trendy foodie center that attracts some of London's best merchants of comestibles. Fresh coffees, gorgeous cheeses, olives, and baked goods complement the organically farmed meats, fresh fish, fruit, and veggies. Seven of the original Borough Market traders, including the celebrated Kappacasein Swiss raclette stand that serves heaping plates of melted Ogleshield cheese over new potatoes, baby pickles, and onion, have established a breakaway market on nearby Maltby Street, which operates on Saturday morning from 9 am. ⊠ *Southwark St., Borough* ☎ *020/7402–1002* ⊕ *www.boroughmarket.org.uk* ☾ *Mon.–Wed. 10–3 (lunch stalls only), Thurs. 11–5, Fri. noon–6, Sat. 8–5* Ⓜ *London Bridge.*

KENSINGTON, KNIGHTSBRIDGE, AND MAYFAIR

ANTIQUES

Fodor'sChoice
★
Alfie's Antique Market. This four-story, bohemian-chic labyrinth is London's largest indoor antiques market, housing dealers specializing in art, lighting, glassware, textiles, jewelry, furniture, and collectibles, with a particular strength in vintage clothing and 20th-century design. Come here to pick up Victorian and Edwardian clothes and textiles at Melinda Colthurst, 19th- and 20th-century furniture and decorative objects from Christopher, or a spectacular mid-20th-century Italian lighting fixture at Vincenzo Caffarrella. There's also a rooftop restaurant if you need a coffee break. In addition to the market, this end of Church Street is lined with excellent antiques shops. ⊠ *13–25 Church St., Marylebone* ☎ *020/7723–6066* ⊕ *www.alfiesantiques.com* ☾ *Closed Sun. and Mon.* Ⓜ *Marylebone.*

Fodor'sChoice
★
Rupert Cavendish. This most elevated of Chelsea dealers had the Biedermeier market cornered so has now expanded to Empire and art deco antiques. The shop is a museum experience. ⊠ *610 King's Rd., Fulham* ☎ *020/7731–7041* ⊕ *www.rupertcavendish.co.uk* Ⓜ *Fulham Broadway.*

ACCESSORIES

Fodor'sChoice
★
Anya Hindmarch. Exquisite leather bags and personalized, printed canvas totes are what made Hindmarch famous, along with her "I'm Not A Plastic Bag" eco-creation. Her designs are sold at Harrods, Liberty, and Harvey Nichols, but in her stores you can see her complete collection of bags and shoes, or order a bespoke piece such as the "Be A Bag," a tote bag imprinted with your chosen photo. There are also branches around the corner on Pont Street, in Mayfair, and in Notting Hill. ⊠ *157–158 Sloane St., Knightsbridge* ☎ *020/7730–0961* ⊕ *www.anyahindmarch. com* Ⓜ *Sloane Sq., Knightsbridge.*

Fodor'sChoice
★
Lulu Guinness. Famous for her flamboyantly themed bags (think the satin "bucket" topped with roses or the elaborately beaded red snakeskin "lips" clutch), Guinness also showcases vintage-inspired luggage and beauty accessories in this frilly little shop, which is just as whimsical as her designs. There are other branches in Mayfair and the City. ⊠ *3 Ellis St., Belgravia* ☎ *020/7823–4828* ⊕ *www.luluguinness.com* ⊙ *Closed Sun.* Ⓜ *Sloane Sq.*

Mulberry. Staying true to its roots in rural Somerset, this luxury goods company epitomizes *le style Anglais*, a sophisticated take on the earthtones and practicality of English country style. Best-known for highly desireable luxury handbags such as the Alexa and the Bayswater, the company also produces gorgeous leather accessories, from wallets to luggage, as well as shoes and clothing. ⊠ *50 New Bond St., Mayfair* ☎ *020/7491–3900* ⊕ *www.mulberry.com* Ⓜ *Bond St.*

Fodor'sChoice
★
Philip Treacy. Magnificent hats by Treacy are annual showstoppers on Ladies Day at the Royal Ascot races and regularly grace the glossy magazines' society pages. In addition to the extravagant, haute couture hats handmade in the atelier, ready-to-wear hats and bags are also for sale. ⊠ *69 Elizabeth St., Belgravia* ☎ *020/7730–3992* ⊕ *www.philiptreacy.co.uk* ⊙ *Closed Sun.* Ⓜ *Sloane Sq.*

Fodor'sChoice
★
Swaine Adeney Brigg. Providing practical supplies for country pursuits since 1750, Swaine Adeney Brigg, now in new Mayfair premises, carries beautifully crafted umbrellas, walking sticks, and hip flasks, or ingenious combinations of same, such as the umbrella with a slim tippleholding flask secreted inside the stem. The same level of quality and craftsmanship applies to the store's leather goods, which include attaché cases and wallets. You'll find scarves, caps, and the Herbert Johnson "Poet Hat," the iconic headgear (stocked since 1890) worn by Harrison Ford in every Indiana Jones film. Satellite branches are in the Piccadilly Arcade and the City. ⊠ *41 S. Audley St., Mayfair* ☎ *020/7409–7277* ⊕ *www.swaineadeney.co.uk* ⊙ *Closed Sun.* Ⓜ *Green Park.*

BOOKS AND STATIONERY

Smythson of Bond Street. Hands down, this is the most elegant stationer in Britain. No hostess of any standing would consider having a leatherbound guest book made by anyone else, and the shop's distinctive pale-blue–page diaries and social stationery are thoroughly British. Diaries, stationery, and small leather goods can be personalized. Smythson also produces a small range of leather handbags and purses. You'll find other branches in Chelsea, Notting Hill, and the City. ⊠ *40 New Bond St., Mayfair* ☎ *020/7629–8558* ⊕ *www.smythson.com* Ⓜ *Bond St., Oxford Circus.*

Waterstone's. At this mega-bookshop (Europe's largest) located in a former art deco department store near Piccadilly Circus, browse through your latest purchase or admire the view while sipping a glass of bubbly or getting a bite to eat at the sixth-floor Champagne and Seafood Bar, which is open until 9. Waterstone's is the country's leading book chain, and they've pulled out all the stops to make their flagship as comfortable and welcoming as a bookstore can be. There are several smaller branches located throughout the city. ⊠ *203–206 Piccadilly, Mayfair* ☎ *0843/290–8549* ⊕ *www.waterstones.com* Ⓜ *Piccadilly Circus.*

Bring your appetite to Borough Market on the South Bank; it's a foodie favorite.

CERAMICS

Emma Bridgewater. Here's where you'll find fun and funky casual plates, mugs, jugs, and breakfast tableware embellished with polka dots, hens, hearts and flowers, amusing mottoes, or matter-of-fact labels (sugar or coffee). There's another branch in Fulham. ✉ *81a Marylebone High St., Marylebone* ☎ *020/7486–6897* ⊕ *www.emmabridgewater.co.uk* Ⓜ *Regent's Park.*

CLOTHING

Fodor's Choice ★ **Dover Street Market.** Visiting this six-floor emporium isn't just about buying; with its creative displays and eclectic, well-chosen mix of merchandise, it's as much art installation as store. The creation of Comme des Garçons' Rei Kawakubo, it showcases all of the label's collections for men and women alongside a changing roster of other designers including Erdem, Alaia, and YSL—all of whom have their own customized mini-boutiques—plus avant-garde art books, vintage couture, and curiosities such as antique plaster anatomy models. With merchandise and configuration changing every six months, you never know what you will find, which is half the fun. ▇ **TIP**➔ **An outpost of the Rose Bakery on the top floor makes for a yummy break.** ✉ *17–18 Dover St., Mayfair* ☎ *020/7518–0680* ⊕ *www.doverstreetmarket.com* ☽ *Closed Sun.* Ⓜ *Green Park.*

Jack Wills. The British preppie's answer to Abercrombie & Fitch, Jack Wills specializes in heritage and country sports-inspired styles for men and women but gives them a youthful, sexy edge. Branches are in Notting Hill, Covent Garden, Islington, and Soho. ✉ *72 Kings Rd., Chelsea* ☎ *020/7581–0347* ⊕ *www.jackwills.com* Ⓜ *Sloane Sq.*

CLOTHING: MENSWEAR

Fodor's Choice ★ **Ozwald Boateng.** The dapper menswear by Ozwald Boateng (pronounced Bwa-teng) combines contemporary funky style with traditional Savile Row quality. His made-to-measure suits have been worn by trend-setters such as Jamie Foxx, Mick Jagger, and Laurence Fishburne, who appreciate the sharp cuts, luxurious fabrics, and occasionally vibrant colors (even the more conservative choices sport jacket linings in bright silk). ⊠ *30 Savile Row, Mayfair* ☎ *020/7437–2030* ⊕ *www. ozwaldboateng.co.uk* ⊗ *Closed Sun.* Ⓜ *Piccadilly Circus.*

CLOTHING: WOMEN'S WEAR

Fodor's Choice ★ **Alexander McQueen.** Since McQueen's untimely death in 2010, his right-hand woman Sarah Burton has been at the helm, receiving raves for continuing his tradition of theatrical, darkly romantic, and beautifully cut clothes incorporating corsetry, lace, embroidery, and hourglass sil-houettes, all of which were exemplified in Burton's celebrated wedding dress for Kate Middleton. Can't afford a gala gown? Go home with a skull-printed scarf. ⊠ *4–5 Old Bond St., Mayfair* ☎ *020/7355–0088* ⊕ *www.alexandermcqueen.com* Ⓜ *Bond St.*

Fodor's Choice ★ **Browns.** This shop—actually a collection of small shops—was a pio-neer designer boutique in the 1970s and continues to talent-spot the newest and best around. You may find the windows showcasing the work of top graduates from this year's student shows or displaying well-established designers such as Marni, Chloé, Dries Van Noten, or Temperley. The men's store at No. 23 has a similar designer selec-tion, while Browns Focus, across the street at Nos. 38–39, showcases youthful, hip designs and denim. There is a bargain outlet in Maryle-bone and a smaller boutique on Sloane Street. ⊠ *24–27 South Molton St., Mayfair* ☎ *020/7514–0000* ⊕ *www.brownsfashion.com* ⊗ *Closed Sun.* Ⓜ *Bond St.*

Fodor's Choice ★ **Jigsaw.** Jigsaw specializes in clothes that are classic yet trendy, ladylike without being dull. The style is epitomized by the former Kate Middle-ton, who was a buyer for the company before her marriage. The quality of fabrics and detailing belie the reasonable prices, and cuts are kind to the womanly figure. Although there are numerous branches across London, no two stores are the same. The pre-teen set have their own line, Jigsaw Junior. ⊠ *The Chapel, Duke of York Sq., King's Rd., Chel-sea* ☎ *020/730–4404* ⊕ *www.jigsawonline.com* Ⓜ *Sloane Sq.*

Rigby & Peller. Lovers of luxury lingerie shop here for brands like Prima Donna and Aubade, as well as R&P's own line. If the right fit eludes you and you fancy being fitted by the Queen's *corsetiére*, the made-to-measure service starts at around £300. Many of London's most affluent women shop here, not only because of the royal appointment but also because the quality is excellent and the service impeccably knowledgeable while being much friendlier than you might expect. There are also branches in Mayfair, Chelsea, and the City. ⊠ *2 Hans Rd., Knightsbridge* ☎ *020/7225–4760* ⊕ *www.rigbyandpeller.com* Ⓜ *Knightsbridge.*

Fodor'sChoice **Stella McCartney.** It's not easy emerging from the shadow of a Beatle
★ father, but Stella McCartney has become a major force in fashion in her
own right. Her signature jumpsuits and tuxedo pantsuits embody her
design philosophy, combining minimalist tailoring with femininity and
sophistication with ease of wear. ⊠ *30 Bruton St., Mayfair* ☎ *020/7518–*
3100 ⊕ *www.stellamccartney.com.uk* Ⓜ *Bond St.*

Vivienne Westwood. From beginnings as the most shocking and outré
designer around, Westwood has become a standard bearer for high-
style British couture. The Chelsea boutique is where it all started: the
lavish corseted ball gowns, the dandyfied nipped-waist jackets, and
the tartan with a punk edge that formed the core of her signature
look. Here you can still buy ready-to-wear, mainly the more casual
Anglomania diffusion line and the exclusive Worlds End label based
on the archives. The small Davies Street boutique sells only the more
exclusive, expensive Gold Label and Couture collections (plus bridal),
while the flagship Conduit Street store carries all of the above. ⊠ *44*
Conduit St., Mayfair ☎ *020/7439–1109* ⊕ *www.viviennewestwood.*
co.uk ☉ *Closed Sun.* Ⓜ *Oxford Circus* ⊠ *World's End Shop, 430*
King's Rd., Chelsea ☎ *020/7352–6551* ⊕ *www.worldsendshop.co.uk*
☉ *Closed Sun.* Ⓜ *West Brompton.*

DEPARTMENT STORES

Harrods. With an encyclopedic assortment of luxury brands, this
Knightsbridge institution has more than 300 departments and 20 restaurants, all spread over 1 million square feet on a 5-acre site. If you
approach Harrods as a tourist attraction rather than as a fashion hunting ground, you won't be disappointed. Focus on the spectacular food
halls, the huge ground-floor perfumery, the revamped toy and technology departments, the excellent Urban Retreat spa, and the Vegas-
like Egyptian Room. ■TIP➔ Be prepared to brave the crowds (avoid
visiting on a Saturday if you can), and be prepared to pay if you want to
use the bathroom on some floors(!). ⊠ *87–135 Brompton Rd., Knights-*
bridge ☎ *020/7730–1234* ⊕ *www.harrods.com* Ⓜ *Knightsbridge.*

Harvey Nichols. While visiting tourists flock to Harrods, true London
fashionistas shop at Harvey Nichols, aka "Harvey Nicks." The wom-
enswear and accessories departments are outstanding, featuring of-the-
moment designers like Roland Mouret, Peter Pilotto, and 3.1 Phillip
Lim. The furniture and housewares are equally gorgeous (and pricey),
though they become somewhat more affordable during the twice-annual
sales in January and July. The Fifth Floor restaurant is the place to
see and be seen, but if you're just after a quick bite, there's also a
more informal café on the same floor or sushi-to-go from Yo! Sushi.
⊠ *109–125 Knightsbridge, Knightsbridge* ☎ *020/7235–5000* ⊕ *www.*
harveynichols.com Ⓜ *Knightsbridge.*

Marks & Spencer. You'd be hard-pressed to find a Brit who doesn't
have something in the closet from Marks & Spencer (or "M&S," as
it's affectionately known). This major chain is known for its classic,
dependable clothing for men, women, and children—affordable cash-
mere and lambswool sweaters are particularly good buys—and occasionally scores a fashion hit with its Per Una and Autograph lines. The

food department at M&S is consistently superb, especially for frozen food, and a great place to pick up a sandwich or premade salad on the go (look for M&S Simply Food stores all over town). The flagship branch at Marble Arch and the Pantheon location at 173 Oxford Street have extensive fashion departments. ⊠ *458 Oxford St., Marylebone* ☎ *020/7935–7954* ⊕ *www.marksandspencer.com* Ⓜ *Marble Arch.*

Fodor'sChoice **Selfridges.** This giant, bustling store (the second-largest in the U.K. after
★ Harrods) gives Harvey Nichols a run for its money as London's most fashionable department store. Packed to the rafters with clothes ranging from midprice lines to the latest catwalk names, the store continues to break ground with its innovative retail schemes, especially the high-fashion Superbrands section, the ground-floor Wonder Room showcasing extravagant jewelry and luxury gifts, and the Concept Store, which features a rotating series of themed displays. ■ TIP→ Take a break with a glass of wine from the Wonder Bar, or pick up some rare tea in the Food Hall as a gift. ⊠ *400 Oxford St., Marylebone* ☎ *0800/123–400* ⊕ *www.selfridges.com* Ⓜ *Bond St.*

HOUSEHOLD

Fodor'sChoice **The Conran Shop.** This is the brainchild of Sir Terence Conran, who has
★ been informing British taste since he opened Habitat in the 1960s. Although he is no longer associated with Habitat, his eponymous stores are still bastions of similarly clean, unfussy modernist design. Both the flagship store and the branch on Marylebone High Street are bursting with great gift ideas. ⊠ *Michelin House, 81 Fulham Rd., South Kensington* ☎ *020/7589–7401* ⊕ *www.conranshop.co.uk* Ⓜ *South Kensington.*

Fodor'sChoice **Mint.** Owner Lina Kanafani has scoured the globe to curate an eclectic
★ mix of conceptual statement furniture, art, ceramics, and home accessories. Mint also showcases works by up-and-coming designers and sells plenty of limited edition and one-off pieces. If you don't want to ship a couch home, consider a miniature flower vase or a handmade ceramic pitcher. ⊠ *2 North Terr., South Kensington* ☎ *020/7225–2228* ⊕ *www.mintshop.co.uk* Ⓜ *South Kensington.*

JEWELRY

Asprey. Created by architect Norman Foster and interior designer David Mlinaric, this "global flagship" store displays exquisite jewelry—as well as silver and leather goods, watches, china, and crystal—in a discreet, very British setting that oozes quality, expensive good taste, and hushed comfort And, for the really well-heeled, there's a custom-made jewelry service available as well. ⊠ *167 New Bond St., Mayfair* ☎ *020/7493–6767* ⊕ *www.asprey.com* Ⓜ *Green Park.*

Fodor'sChoice **Butler & Wilson.** Long before anybody ever heard the word "bling,"
★ this shop was marketing the look—in diamanté, colored rhinestones, and crystal—to movie stars and secretaries alike. There's also another shop at 20 South Molton Street. ⊠ *189 Fulham Rd., South Kensington* ☎ *020/7352–3045* ⊕ *www.butlerandwilson.co.uk* Ⓜ *South Kensington.*

Fodor'sChoice **Kabiri.** A dazzling array of exciting contemporary jewelry by emerg-
★ ing and established designers from around the world is packed into this small shop. There is something to suit most budgets and tastes,

from flamboyant statement pieces to subtle, delicate adornment. Look out for British talent Johanne Mills, among many others. There's another branch in Chelsea. ✉ *37 Marylebone High St., Marylebone* ☎ *020/7317–2150* ⊕ *www.kabiri.co.uk* Ⓜ *Baker St.*

SHOES

Fodor's Choice ★ **Rupert Sanderson.** Designed in London and made in Italy, Sanderson's elegant shoes have been a huge hit in fashion circles. Ladylike styles, bright colors, smart details, and a penchant for peep toes are signature elements. Prices reflect the impeccable craftsmanship. There's now a tiny outpost next to Harrods at 2A Hans Road. ✉ *19 Bruton Pl., Mayfair* ☎ *0207/491–2260* ⊕ *www.rupertsanderson.com* ☾ *Closed Sun.* Ⓜ *Bond St., Green Park.*

NOTTING HILL

BOOKS

Books for Cooks. It may seem odd to describe a bookshop as delicious-smelling, but the aromas wafting out of Books for Cooks' test kitchen will whet your appetite even before you've opened one of the 8,000 cookbooks. Just about every world cuisine is represented along with a complete lineup of books by celebrity chefs. A tiny cafe at the back offers lunch dishes drawn from recipes on the shelves, as well as desserts and coffee. Menus change daily. ▉TIP➜ Before you come to London, visit the shop's website to sign up for a cooking class. ✉ *4 Blenheim Crescent, Notting Hill* ☎ *020/7221–1992* ⊕ *www.booksforcooks.com* ☾ *Closed Sun. and Mon.* Ⓜ *Notting Hill Gate, Ladbroke Grove.*

CLOTHING

Aimé. French-Cambodian sisters Val and Vanda Heng-Vong launched this shop to showcase the best of French clothing and designer housewares. Expect to find fashion by Isabel Marant, Forte Forte, and A.P.C. You can also pick up A.P.C. candles, Rice homewares, and a well-edited collection of ceramics. Just next door, Petit Aimé sells children's clothing. ✉ *32 Ledbury Rd., Notting Hill* ☎ *020/7221–7070* ⊕ *www.aimelondon.com* Ⓜ *Notting Hill Gate.*

MUSIC

Music & Video Exchange. This store is a music collector's treasure trove, with a constantly changing stock refreshed by customers selling and exchanging as well as buying. The main store focuses on rock pop, soul, and dance, both mainstream and obscure, in a variety of formats ranging from vinyl to CD, cassette, and even mini-disk. Don't miss the discounts in the basement and the rarities upstairs. Classical music is at No. 40 and there are branches in Soho and Greenwich. ✉ *38 Notting Hill Gate, Notting Hill* ☎ *020/7243–8574* ⊕ *www.mgeshops.com* Ⓜ *Notting Hill Gate.*

STREET MARKETS

Fodor's Choice ★ **Portobello Market.** London's most famous market still wins the prize (according to some) for the all-round best, stretching almost two miles from fashionable Notting Hill to the lively cultural melting pot of North Kensington, changing character as it goes. The southern end, starting at Chepstow Villas, is lined with shops, stalls, and arcades selling antiques, silver, and bric-a-brac on Saturday; the middle, above Westbourne Grove, is devoted on weekdays to fruit and veg, interspersed with excellent hot food stalls; On Friday and Saturday, the area between Talbot Road and the elevated highway (called the Westway) becomes more of a flea market specializing in household and mass-produced goods sold at a discount, while north of the Westway are more stalls selling even cheaper household goods. Some say Portobello Road has become a tourist trap, but if you acknowledge that it's a circus and get into the spirit, it's a lot of fun. Saturday is when the market in full swing. Serious shoppers avoid the crowds and go on Friday morning. ■ TIP➔ Bring cash (several vendors don't take credit cards) but keep an eye on it. ⊠ *Portobello Rd., Notting Hill* ⊕ *www. portobellomarket.org* ⊗ *Mon.–Wed., Fri.–Sat. 8–6:30, Thurs. 8–1 pm* Ⓜ *Notting Hill Gate.*

THE SOUTHEAST

WELCOME TO THE SOUTHEAST

TOP REASONS TO GO

★ **Amazing gardens:**
Gardens of all kinds are
an English specialty,
and at Sissinghurst and
Wisley, as well as in the
gardens of Hever Castle
and Chartwell, you can
easily spend an entire afternoon wandering through
acres of floral exotica.

★ **Bodiam, Dover, Hever,
and Herstmonceux castles:**
Take your pick: the most
evocative castles in a
region filled with them
dazzle you with their
fortitude and fascinate
you with their histories.

★ **Brighton:** With its nightclubs, sunbathing, and
funky atmosphere, this is
the quintessential modern
English seaside city.

★ **Canterbury Cathedral:**
This massive building,
a textbook of medieval
architecture, inspires awe
with its soaring towers
and flagstone corridors.

★ **Treasure houses:** Here
is one of England's richest
concentrations of historic
homes: among the superla-
tives are Petworth House;
sprawling Knole; Ightham
Mote; and Chartwell.

1 Canterbury, Dover,
and Environs. Dover's
distinctive chalk-white cliffs
plunging hundreds of feet
into the sea are just a part
of this region's dramatic
coastal scenery. Don't miss
Canterbury's medieval town
center, dominated by its
massive cathedral.

2 Rye, Lewes, and Environs. Medieval villages dot
the hills along this stretch
of Sussex coastline. The
centerpiece is Rye, a pretty
hill town of cobbled streets
lined with timbered homes.
Lewes, with its crumbling
castle, is another gem.

GETTING ORIENTED

For sightseeing purposes, the Southeast can be divided into four sections. The eastern part of the region takes in the cathedral town of Canterbury, as well as the port city of Dover. The next section stretches along the southern coast from the medieval hill town of Rye to picturesque Lewes. A third area reaches from the coastal city of Brighton inward to Chichester and to sprawling Guildford. The fourth section takes in the spa town of Royal Tunbridge Wells and western Kent, where stately homes and castles dot the farmland. Larger towns in the area can be easily reached by train or bus from London for a day trip. To visit most castles, grand country homes, or quiet villages, though, you need to rent a car or join a tour.

3 **Brighton, the Sussex Coast, and Surrey.** Funky, lively Brighton perfectly melds Victorian architecture with a modern vibe that includes the best shopping and dining on the coast. Outside town are beautiful old homes such as Petworth House and even a Roman villa.

4 **Tunbridge Wells and Environs.** From Anne Boleyn's regal childhood abode at Hever Castle to the medieval manor at Ightham Mote, this area is rich with grand houses. Spend a couple of days exploring them; Tunbridge Wells is a comfortable base.

TEA TIME IN ENGLAND

Tea is often called the national drink, and for good reason. Most people start their day with "a cuppa," have tea breaks in the afternoon, and a cup after dinner. Join in by lifting a cup, or try a cream tea with a scone or a fancier formal afternoon tea.

(*above*) Relaxing with tea and a scone with clotted cream and jam is a civilized pastime; (*top right*) Cucumber sandwiches at afternoon tea; (*right, bottom*) Tea store

It's hard to imagine a time when tea wasn't part of English culture. But there was no tea in Europe until the 1600s, when it was first brought by Portuguese and Dutch traders. Charles II and his wife, Catherine of Braganza, were tea drinkers. When coffeehouses in London began serving the drink in the mid-17th century, it was seen as an expensive curiosity. By the early 18th century tea was sold in coffeehouses all over the country, and consumed by all classes. The duchess of Bedford is credited with popularizing formal afternoon tea in the early 1800s. Dinner in those days was often not served until after 8 pm, so a light meal in late afternoon was welcome. The tradition faded when more people began working in offices in the 20th century—though the love of tea remains.

WHICH TEA?

England's most popular tea is English Breakfast tea, a full-bodied blend of black teas. Second in line is Earl Grey: oil of bergamot orange creates an elegant perfume, but it's an acquired taste. Assam is one of the major teas blended into English Breakfast, and it tastes similar, if a bit more brisk. By contrast, Darjeeling is light and delicate; it's perfect for afternoons.

3

CREAM TEA

In popular tourist areas in Britain, signs everywhere advertise "cream tea." This is the national shorthand for "tea and scones." The "cream" part is delectable clotted cream—a cream so thick it has a texture like whipped butter. Some scones are fruity and have raisins or dried fruit; others are more like a cross between American biscuits and shortbread. Along with the cream, you'll usually be offered jam. It's customary to put both jam and cream on the scone, treating the cream like butter.

Cream teas are widely offered in areas favored by travelers, such as Stratford-upon-Avon, the Cotswolds, Devon, and Canterbury. In those regions you'll see it advertised in pubs, restaurants, and dedicated tea shops. Cream tea is a casual afternoon affair: think of it as a coffee break, with tea. Your tea will likely be a teabag rather than loose tea. The cost is usually from £3 to £7.

AFTERNOON TEA

A pricey treat reserved for vacations and special occasions, afternoon tea (called "high tea" in America, but not in England, where that term referred to a meal between 5 and 7 pm) is served in upscale hotels in London, but also in Oxford, Cambridge, and Brighton, or anywhere popular with travelers. Along with tea—and you can choose from a variety of teas—you'll be served finger sandwiches (usually cucumber, egg, ham, and smoked salmon) and scones, as well as tiny cakes and pastries. These will usually be brought on tiered plate stands, with sweet options higher up and savory on the lower level. Tea will be brewed in a china pot and served with china cups and saucers; milk and lemon are accompaniments.

Afternoon tea is generally offered between 3 and 5:30 pm and can last for hours. It's generally quite formal, and most people dress up for the occasion. Expect to spend from £17 to £50.

TEA IN THE SOUTHEAST

Grand Brighton. Afternoon tea at the elegant Grand Brighton is a local tradition. Dress up to fit in. ✉ *97–99 Kings Rd., Brighton* ☎ *0871/222–4684* ⊕ *www.devere-hotels.co.uk.*

Michael Caines. In Canterbury, afternoon tea at Michael Caines at the Abode Hotel has all the requisite teas, sandwiches, cakes, and scones. ✉ *Abode Canterbury, 30–33 High St., Canterbury* ☎ *01227/766266* ⊕ *www.michaelcaines.com.*

Very good cream teas are served in the tearooms at all National Trust–run houses and gardens, as well as at most other historic estates open to the public. In the Southeast, the cafés at **Chartwell, Dover Castle, Knole, Wisley, Sissinghurst Castle Gardens,** and **Bodiam Castle** all offer excellent, affordable cream teas.

Updated by
Jack Jewers

Surrey, Kent, and Sussex form the breadbasket of England, where bucolic farmland stretches as far as the eye can see. Once a favorite destination of English nobility, this region is rich with history, visible in the great castles and stately homes that dot the countryside. Its cities are similarly historic, especially ancient Canterbury, with its spectacular cathedral and medieval streets. Along the coast, funky seaside towns have a more relaxed attitude, especially artsy Brighton, where artists and musicians use the sea as inspiration for their work.

Although it's close to London (both Surrey and Kent reach all the way to London's suburbs) and is one of the most densely populated areas of Britain, the Southeast feels far away from the big city. In Kent, acres of orchards burst into a mass of pink-and-white blossoms in spring, while Dover's white cliffs and brooding castle have become symbols of Britain. Historic mansions, such as Petworth House and Knole, are major draws for travelers, and lush gardens such as Vita Sackville-West's Sissinghurst and the Royal Horticultural Society's Wisley attract thousands to their vivid floral displays.

Because the English Channel is at its narrowest here, a great deal of British history has been forged in the Southeast. The Romans landed in this area and stayed to rule Britain for four centuries. So did the Saxons—*Sussex* means "the land of the South Saxons." The biggest invasion of them all took place here when William ("the Conqueror") of Normandy defeated the Saxons at a battle near Hastings in 1066, changing the island forever.

SOUTHEAST PLANNER

WHEN TO GO

It's best to visit in spring, summer, or early fall. Many privately owned castles and mansions are open only between April and September or October. Failing that, the parks surrounding the stately houses are often open all year. If crowds tend to spoil your fun, avoid August, Sunday, and national holidays, particularly in Canterbury and the seaside towns.

PLANNING YOUR TIME

With the exception of Brighton, you can easily see the highlights of each of the towns in less than a day. Brighton has more to offer, and you should allot at least two days to take it all in. Consider basing yourself in one town while exploring a region. For example, you could stay in Brighton and take in Lewes on a day trip. Base yourself in Rye for a couple of days while exploring Winchelsea, Battle, Hastings, and Herstmonceux Castle. Tunbridge Wells is a great place to overnight if you plan on exploring the many stately homes and castles nearby.

GETTING HERE AND AROUND

AIR TRAVEL

Heathrow is convenient for Surrey, but Gatwick Airport is a more convenient gateway for Kent. The rail station inside Gatwick has trains to Brighton and other major towns, and you can take a taxi from Heathrow to Guildford for around £50.

BUS TRAVEL

National Express buses serve the region from London's Victoria Coach Station. Trips to Brighton and Canterbury take two hours; to Chichester, three hours. Megabus runs buses at budget prices from Victoria Coach Station to many of the same destinations as National Express and can be cheaper, although luggage limits are strict.

Bus service between towns can be useful but is often intermittent. Out in the country, don't expect buses more often than once every half hour or hour. Sometimes trains are a better option; sometimes they're much worse. Traveline is the best central place to call for bus information, and local tourist information centers can be a big help.

Contacts Megabus ☎ 0900/160–0900 ⊕ www.megabus.co.uk.
National Express ☎ 0871/781–8178 ⊕ www.nationalexpress.com.
Traveline ☎ 0871/200–2233 ⊕ www.traveline.org.uk.

CAR TRAVEL

Traveling by car is the best way to get to the stately homes and castles in the region. Having a car in Canterbury or Brighton, however, is a nuisance; you'll need to park and walk. Major routes radiating outward from London to the Southeast are, from west to east, M23/A23 to Brighton (52 miles); A21, passing by Royal Tunbridge Wells to Hastings (65 miles); A20/M20 to Folkestone (58 miles); and A2/M2 via Canterbury (56 miles) to Dover (71 miles).

TRAIN TRAVEL

Trains are the fastest and most efficient way to travel to major cities in the region, but they don't stop in many small towns. From London, Southeastern trains serve Sussex and Kent from Victoria and Charing Cross stations, and South West trains travel to Surrey from Waterloo Station. Getting to Brighton takes about 1 hour, to Canterbury about 1½ hours, and to Dover between 1½ and 2 hours. A Network Railcard costing £28, valid throughout the southern and southeastern regions for a year, entitles you and three companions to one-third off many off-peak fares.

Contacts National Rail Enquiries ☎ *0845/748–4950* ⊕ *www.nationalrail. co.uk/railcard.* **Network Railcard** ☎ *0844/871-4036* ⊕ *www.railcard.co.uk.*

RESTAURANTS

If you're in a seaside town, look for that great British staple, fish-and-chips. Perhaps "look" isn't the word—just follow your nose. On the coast, seafood, much of it locally caught, is a specialty. Try local smoked fish (haddock and mackerel), or the succulent local oysters. Inland, sample fresh local lamb and beef. In cities such as Brighton and Tunbridge Wells there are numerous restaurants and cafés, but out in the countryside the best options are often pubs. *Prices in the reviews are the average cost of a main course at dinner or, if dinner isn't served, at lunch.*

HOTELS

All around the coast, resort towns stretch along beaches, their hotels standing cheek by jowl. Of the smaller hotels and guesthouses not all remain open year-round; many do business only from mid-April to September or October. Some hotels have all-inclusive rates for a week's stay. Prices rise in July and August, when the seaside resorts can get solidly booked, especially Brighton. (On the other hand, hotels may drop rates by up to 40% off season.) Places in Brighton may not take a booking for a single night in summer or on weekends. *Prices in the reviews are the lowest cost of a standard double room in high season, including 20% V.A.T.*

VISITOR INFORMATION

Tourist boards in the main towns can help with information, and many will also book local accommodations.

Contacts Southeast England Tourist Board ⊕ *www.visitsoutheastengland.com.*

CANTERBURY, DOVER, AND ENVIRONS

The cathedral city of Canterbury is an ancient place that has attracted travelers since the 12th century. Its magnificent cathedral, the Mother Church of England, remains a powerful draw. Even in prehistoric times, this part of England was relatively well settled. Saxon settlers, Norman conquerors, and the folk who lived here in late-medieval times all left their mark. From Canterbury there's rewarding wandering to be done in the gentle Kentish countryside between the city and the busy port of Dover. Here the landscape ravishes the eye in spring with apple blossoms, and in autumn with lush fields ready for harvest. It's a county of orchards, market gardens, and round oasthouses with their tilted, pointed roofs; they were once used for drying hops, but now many are expensive homes.

CANTERBURY

56 miles southeast of London.

Just mention Canterbury, and most people are taken back to memories of high-school English classes and Geoffrey Chaucer's *Canterbury Tales,* about medieval pilgrims making their way to Canterbury Cathedral. Judging from the tales, however, in those days Canterbury was as much a party town as it was a spiritual center.

The city has been the seat of the Primate of All England, the archbishop of Canterbury, since Pope Gregory the Great dispatched St. Augustine to convert the pagan hordes of Britain in 597. The height of Canterbury's popularity came in the 12th century, when thousands of pilgrims flocked here to see the shrine of the murdered archbishop St. Thomas à Becket. This southeastern town became one of the most visited in England, if not Europe. Buildings that served as pilgrims' inns (and that survived World War II bombing of the city) still dominate the streets of Canterbury's center, though it's tourists who flock to this city of about 40,000 people today.

Prices at city museums are higher than average, so if you plan to see more than one, ask at the tourist office if a combination ticket might be cheaper.

GETTING HERE AND AROUND

The fastest way to reach Canterbury from London is by train. Southeastern trains to Canterbury run every half hour in peak times from London's Charing Cross Station. The journey takes around 1½ hours. Canterbury has two centrally located train stations, Canterbury East Station (a 5-minute walk from the cathedral square) and Canterbury West Station (a 10-minute walk from the cathedral).

National Express and Megabus buses bound for Canterbury depart several times a day from London's Victoria Coach Station. Trips to Canterbury take around two hours, and drop passengers near the train stations. If you're driving, take the A2/M2 to Canterbury from London (56 miles). Park in one of the signposted parking lots at the edge of the town center.

Canterbury has a small, walkable town center. Although the town has good local bus service, you're unlikely to need it. Most major tourist sites are on one street that changes name three times—beginning as St. George's Street and then becoming High Street and St. Peter's Street.

Canterbury Guild of Guides provides walking tours with expert guides. Tours (£6.50) are at 11 am every, with an additional tour at 2 pm from April to October. VisitBritain offers an MP3 tour of Canterbury ($8.50) that you can download from its website.

TIMING

The town tends to get crowded around religious holidays—particularly Easter weekend—and on other national holiday weekends. If you'd rather avoid the tour buses, try visiting midweek.

ESSENTIALS

Visitor and Tour Information **Canterbury Guild of Guides** ✉ *Arnett House, Hawks La.* ☎ *01227/459779* ⊕ *www.canterbury-walks.co.uk.* **Canterbury Visitor Centre** ✉ *18 High St.* ☎ *01227/378100* ⊕ *www.canterbury.co.uk.* **VisitBritain** ⊕ *www.visitbritain.com.*

EXPLORING

TOP ATTRACTIONS

Fodor's Choice **Canterbury Cathedral.** The focal point of the city was the first of England's great Norman cathedrals. Nucleus of worldwide Anglicanism, the Cathedral Church of Christ Canterbury (its formal name) is a living textbook of medieval architecture. The building was begun in 1070, demolished, begun anew in 1096, and then systematically expanded over the next three centuries. When the original choir section burned to the ground in 1174, another replaced it, designed in the new Gothic style, with tall, pointed arches. The cathedral is popular, so arrive early or late in the day to avoid the crowds.

The cathedral was only a century old, and still relatively small, when Thomas Becket, the archbishop of Canterbury, was murdered here in 1170. Becket, as head of the church, had been engaged in a political struggle with his old friend Henry II. Four knights supposedly overheard Henry scream "will no one will rid me of this troublesome priest?" although there is no evidence that those were his actual words—the only contemporary record has his saying "what miserable drones and traitors have I nourished and brought up in my household, who let their lord be treated with such shameful contempt by a low-born cleric?"

Thinking they were carrying out the king's wishes, the knights went immediately to Canterbury and hacked Becket to pieces in one of the side chapels. Henry, racked with guilt, went into deep mourning. Becket was canonized and Canterbury's position as the center of English Christianity was assured.

For almost 400 years Becket's tomb was one of the most extravagent shrines in Christendom, until it was destroyed by Henry VIII's troops during the Reformation. In **Trinity Chapel,** which held the shrine, you can still see a series of 13th-century stained-glass windows illustrating Becket's miracles. (The actual site of Becket's murder is down a flight of steps just to the left of the nave.) Nearby is the tomb of Edward, the Black Prince (1330–76), warrior son of Edward III and a national hero. In the corner of Trinity Chapel, a second flight of steps leads down to the enormous Norman **undercroft,** or vaulted cellar, built in the early 12th century. A row of squat pillars engraved with dancing beasts (mythical and otherwise) supports the roof.

To the north of the Cathedral are the **cloisters** and a small compound of monastic buildings. The 12th-century octagonal water tower is still part of the cathedral's water supply. The Norman staircase in the northwest corner of the Green Court dates from 1167 and is a unique example of the architecture of the times. ✉ *Cathedral Precincts* ☎ *01227/762862* ⊕ *www.canterbury-cathedral.org* ⌂ *£9.50, free for services and ½ hr before closing; £5 tour; £3.50 for audio guide* ☉ *Cathedral: Mon.–Sat. 9–5:30 (9–5, Oct.–Easter), Sun.*

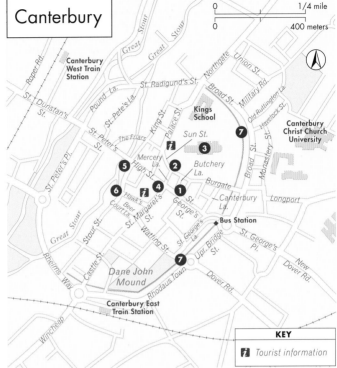

3

12:30–2:30. *Last entry ½ hr before closing. Restricted access during services. Tours: Apr.–Oct., weekdays 10:30, noon, and 2, Sat. 10:30, noon, and 1; Nov.–Mar., weekdays 10:30 (not Jan.), noon and 2, Sat. 10:30, noon, and 1.*

QUICK
BITES

The Custard Tart. A short walk from the cathedral, the Custard Tart serves freshly made sandwiches, pies, tarts, and cakes, along with steaming cups of tea and coffee. You can take your selection upstairs to the seating area. Arrive early, as it's not open for dinner. ⊠ *35A St. Margaret's St.* ☎ *01227/785178.*

Canterbury Roman Museum. Below ground, at the level of the remnants of Roman Canterbury, this museum features colorful mosaic Roman pavement and a hypocaust—the Roman version of central heating. Displays of excavated objects (some of which you can hold in the **Touch the Past** area) and computer-generated reconstructions of Roman buildings and the marketplace help re-create the past. ■ TIP→ Up to four kids get in free with an adult. ⊠ *Butchery La.* ☎ *01227/785575* ⊕ *www.canterbury.co.uk* ⊠ *£6; combined ticket with Canterbury Heritage Museum £10* ☉ *Daily 10–5; last admission 4:15. Closed last wk in Dec.*

Medieval city walls. For an essential Canterbury experience, follow the circuit of the 13th- and 14th-century walls, built on the line of the Roman walls. Roughly half survive; those to the east are intact, towering some 20 feet high and offering a sweeping view of the town. You can access these from a number of places, including Castle Street and Broad Street.

WORTH NOTING

FAMILY **Canterbury Heritage Museum.** The medieval Poor Priests' Hospital is the site of this quirky local museum, where exhibits provide an overview of the city's history and architecture from Roman times to World War II. It covers everything and everyone associated with the town, including the Blitz, the mysterious death of the 16th-century writer Christopher Marlowe, and the British children's book and TV characters Rupert the Bear and Bagpuss. Kids get in free with their parents. ✉ *20 Stour St.* ☎ *01227/475202* 🌐 *www.canterbury-museums.co.uk* 🎫 *£8; combined ticket with Canterbury Roman Museum £10* 🕑 *Daily 10–5.*

FAMILY **The Canterbury Tales.** Take an audiovisual tour of the sights, sounds (and smells) of 14th-century England at this cheesy but popular attraction. You'll "meet" Chaucer's pilgrims and view tableaus illustrating five of his tales. In summer, costumed actors perform scenes from the town's history. ✉ *St. Margaret's St.* ☎ *01227/479227* 🌐 *www.canterburytales.org.uk* 🎫 *£8.50* 🕑 *Nov.–Feb., daily 10–4:30; Mar.–June, Sept., and Oct., daily 10–5; July and Aug., daily 9:30–5.*

Christchurch Gate. This immense gate, built in 1517, leads into the cathedral close. As you pass through, look up at the sculpted heads of two young figures: Prince Arthur, elder brother of Henry VIII, and the young Catherine of Aragon, to whom Arthur was betrothed. After Arthur's death, Catherine married Henry. Her failure to produce a male heir after 25 years of marriage led to Henry's decision to divorce her, creating an irrevocable breach with the Roman Catholic Church and altering the course of English history.

Eastbridge Hospital of St. Thomas. The 12th-century building (which would now be called a hostel) lodged pilgrims who came to pray at the tomb of Thomas Becket. It's a tiny place, fascinating in its simplicity. The refectory, the chapel, and the crypt are open to the public. ✉ *25 High St.* ☎ *01227/471668* 🌐 *www.eastbridgehospital.org.uk* 🎫 *£2* 🕑 *Mon.–Sat. 10–5; last admission at 4:30.*

WHERE TO EAT

$ BRITISH 🍴 **City Fish Bar.** Long lines and lots of satisfied finger-licking attest to the deserved popularity of this excellent fish-and-chip shop in the center of town. Everything is freshly fried, the batter crisp and the fish tasty; the fried mushrooms are also surprisingly good. There's no seating, so your fish is wrapped up in paper and you eat it where you want, perhaps in the park. This place closes at 7. [$] *Average main: £7* ✉ *30 St. Margaret's St.* ☎ *01227/760873* 💳 *No credit cards.*

$ BRITISH 🍴 **The Goods Shed.** Next to Canterbury West Station, this vaulted wooden space with stone-and-brick walls was a storage shed in Victorian times. Now it's a farmers' market with a restaurant that has wooden tables and huge arched windows overlooking the market and

Impressive both inside and out, ancient Canterbury Cathedral dominates the town.

a butchers' stall. It's well known for offering fresh Kentish food—think locally caught fish and smoked meats, local cider, and freshly baked bread. Whatever is freshest that day appears on the menu, whether it's John Dory with garlic, or steak with blue cheese butter. $ *Average main: £15* ✉ *Station Rd. W.* ☎ *01227/459153* ⊕ *www.thegoodsshed.co.uk* ⊗ *Closed Mon. No dinner Sun.*

$$$

MODERN FRENCH

Fodors Choice

★

✕ **Michael Caines at ABode.** Canterbury's most sought-after tables are at Michael Caines (not the actor–the eminent British chef with a similar name). Occupying a light-filled corner of the trendy ABode Canterbury, with its pine tables, white walls, and sophisticated country style, this place is hugely popular with local foodies. The modern French cuisine is excellent; dishes change weekly but could include slow poached then roasted pheasant with pumpkin and cumin puree, or monkfish and braised oxtail with porcini mushroom fricassèe. Leave room for a dessert of pistachio soufflé, or perhaps chestnut mousse with chocolate cremeux, meringue, and chestnut ice cream. The seven-course tasting menu (£72, or £110 with matching wine) is great for special occasions. ■TIP➜ True aficionados will want to reserve the chef's table in the kitchen to watch the staff in action. $ *Average main: £24* ✉ *ABode Canterbury, 30–33 High St.* ☎ *01227/766266* ⊕ *www.michaelcaines.com* ➩ *Reservations essential.*

$

BRITISH

✕ **Old Brewery Tavern.** Although it's part of a hotel, this pub has a separate entrance leading to a room with polished floors, wooden tables, and whitewashed stone. The menu and kitchen are overseen by top chef Michael Caines, so it's a good place to try his food at a more reasonable price (a two-course lunch is £10). The atmosphere is relaxed and casual, except on weekend nights when the music gets turned up for the party crowd. Expect reliably good comfort food—juicy burgers, crispy fish-and-chips, or sirloin steak grilled to order. The courtyard is perfect for alfresco dining. $ *Average main: £13* ✉ *ABode Canterbury, 30–33 High St.* ☎ *01227/826682* ⊕ *www.michaelcaines.com.*

$ ✕ **Old Buttermarket.** A colorful, friendly old pub near the cathedral, the
BRITISH Buttermarket is a great place to grab a hearty lunch and sample some traditional English fare with a modern inflection. You can indulge in a fresh English ale from the changing selection while sampling a beef rib puff pastry pie with creamy mashed potato, or perhaps a wild boar and chorizo burger if you're feeling more adventurous. There's been a pub on this site for more than 500 years, so although the current building is a few hundred years younger than that, it's carrying on a fine tradition. $ *Average main: £11* ✉ *39 Burgate* ☎ *01227/462170* ⊕ *www. nicholsonspubs.co.uk.*

WHERE TO STAY

For expanded hotel reviews, visit Fodors.com.

$$ ⬚ **ABode Canterbury.** This glossy boutique hotel inside the old city walls
HOTEL offers an up-to-date style in traditional Canterbury. **Pros:** central location; luxurious handmade beds; great restaurants and bars. **Cons:** one of the priciest hotels in town; bar gets quite crowded; breakfast is extra. $ *Rooms from: £135* ✉ *30–33 High St.* ☎ *01227/766266* ⊕ *www. abodehotels.co.uk* ⤴ *73 rooms* ⦿ *No meals.*

$$ ⬚ **Canterbury Cathedral Lodge.** Small and modern, this hotel tucked
HOTEL away within the grounds of the cathedral has quiet, soothingly decorated rooms with creamy white walls and exposed oak trim. **Pros:** outstanding location; incredible views; free access to the cathedral. **Cons:** no restaurant; few services. $ *Rooms from: £120* ✉ *The Precincts* ☎ *01227/865350* ⊕ *www.canterburycathedrallodge.org* ⤴ *35 rooms* ⦿ *Breakfast.*

$$ ⬚ **Ebury Hotel.** Family-run, this hotel earns raves for its laid-back atti-
HOTEL tude and comfortable accommodations inside two big Victorian buildings. **Pros:** cozy lounge; comfortable rooms; free Wi-Fi. **Cons:** a bit of a walk to the town center; no elevator. $ *Rooms from: £140* ✉ *65–67 New Dover Rd.* ☎ *01227/768433* ⊕ *www.ebury-hotel.co.uk* ⤴ *15 rooms* ⦿ *Breakfast.*

$ ⬚ **Magnolia House.** A converted Georgian house with a walled garden,
B&B/INN this lovely B&B has a traditional air. **Pros:** adorable house; friendly atmosphere. **Cons:** a bit of a walk to the town center; some rooms are small; no elevator. $ *Rooms from: £95* ✉ *36 St. Dunstan's Terr.* ☎ *01227/765121* ⊕ *www.magnoliahousecanterbury.co.uk* ⤴ *7 rooms* ⦿ *Breakfast.*

$ ⬚ **The White House.** Reputed to have been the place in which Queen
B&B/INN Victoria's head coachman came to live upon retirement, this handsome Regency building sits on a quiet road off St. Peter's Street. **Pros:** historic house; spacious rooms; family-friendly atmosphere. **Cons:** a bit outside the center; no restaurant; no elevator. $ *Rooms from: £90* ✉ *6 St. Peter's La.* ☎ *01227/761836* ⊕ *www.whitehousecanterbury.co.uk* ⤴ *7 rooms* ▭ *No credit cards* ⦿ *Breakfast.*

NIGHTLIFE AND THE ARTS

NIGHTLIFE

Canterbury is home to a popular university, and the town's many pubs and bars are busy, often crowded with college-age folks.

Alberry's Wine Bar. With late-night jazz and hip-hop and a trendy crowd, Alberry's Wine Bar is one of Canterbury's coolest nightspots. ✉ *St. Margaret's St.* ☎ *01227/452378* ⊕ *www.alberrys.co.uk.*

Parrot. Built in 1370, the Parrot is an atmospheric old pub known for its real ale. They also do good food; Sunday lunch here is popular. ✉ *3–9 Church La.* ☎ *01227/762355* ⊕ *www.theparrotcanterbury.com.*

Thomas Becket. A traditional English pub, Thomas Becket has a fire crackling in winter, copper pots hanging from the ceiling, and a friendly crowd. They also serve decent pub grub. ✉ *21 Best La.* ☎ *01227/464384.*

THE ARTS

Canterbury Festival. The two-week-long Canterbury Festival fills the town with music, dance, theater, and other colorful events every October. ☎ *01227/787787* ⊕ *www.canterburyfestival.co.uk.*

Gulbenkian Theatre. Outside the town center, the Gulbenkian Theatre mounts all kinds of plays, particularly experimental works, and is a venue for dance performances, concerts, comedy shows, and films. ✉ *University of Kent, Giles La.* ☎ *01227/769075* ⊕ *www.kent.ac.uk/gulbenkian.*

New Marlowe. Check out this excellent performance space for theater, music, dance, and comedy. It is also a venue for popular touring shows. ✉ *The Friars, off King St.* ☎ *01227/787787* ⊕ *www.newmarlowetheatre.org.uk.*

SHOPPING

Canterbury's medieval streets are lined with shops, perfect for an afternoon of rummaging. The best are in the district just around the cathedral. The King's Mile, which stretches past the cathedral and down Palace Street and Northgate, is a good place to start.

925. This shop has a great selection of handmade silver jewelry. ✉ *57 Palace St.* ☎ *01227/785699* ⊕ *www.925-silver.co.uk.*

Burgate Antiques. This rambling shop is full of fine British and French antiques, mostly Georgian and Victorian, with both high-end and less expensive selections. It's a great place to nose around on a rainy day. ✉ *23a Palace St.* ☎ *01227/456500.*

Crowthers of Canterbury. For music lovers, Crowthers of Canterbury carries an extensive selection of musical instruments, gifts, and sheet music. ✉ *1 The Borough* ☎ *01227/763965* ⊕ *www.crowthersofcanterbury.co.uk.*

BROADSTAIRS

17 miles east of Canterbury.

Like other Victorian seaside towns such as Margate and Ramsgate, Broadstairs was once the playground of vacationing Londoners, and grand 19th-century houses line the waterfront. In the off-season Broadstairs is peaceful, but day-trippers pack the town in July and August.

Park your car in one of the town lots, and strike out for the crescent beach or wander down the residential Victorian streets. Make your way down to the amusement pier and try your hand in one of the game arcades. You can grab fish-and-chips to go and dine on the beach.

Charles Dickens spent many summers in Broadstairs between 1837 and 1851 and wrote glowingly of its bracing freshness.

GETTING HERE AND AROUND

By car, Broadstairs is about a two-hour drive (78 miles) from London, off A256 on the southeast tip of England. Trains run from London's St. Pancras and Victoria stations to Broadstairs once or twice an hour; it's a two-hour trip and sometimes involves a change in Rochester. Broadstairs Station is off the Broadway in the town center. National Express buses travel to Broadstairs from London several times a day; the journey takes about three hours.

EXPLORING

Dickens House Museum. This house was originally the home of Mary Pearson Strong, on whom Dickens based the character of Betsey Trotwood, David Copperfield's aunt. Dickens lived here from 1837 to 1839 while writing *The Pickwick Papers* and *Oliver Twist*. Some rooms have been decorated to look as they would have in Dickens' day, and there's a reconstruction of Miss Trotwood's room as described by Dickens. The house is in Broadstairs, 18 miles northeast of Canterbury. ⊠ *2 Victoria Parade* ☎ *01843/861232* ⊕ *www.dickensfellowship.org* ☜ *£3.50* ☉ *Apr. and May, daily 2–5; June–Oct., daily 10–5.*

NIGHTLIFE AND THE ARTS

Dickens Festival. For a week every June, Broadstairs is taken over by a sea of people in Victorian costume, as the town hosts its annual Dickens Festival—a tradition going back to 1937. The fun includes readings, a Dickensian cricket match, a Victorian bathing party, and vaudeville acts. ☎ *01843/861827* ⊕ *www.broadstairsdickensfestival.co.uk*.

DEAL

18 miles south of Broadstairs.

The large seaside town of Deal, known for its castle, is famous in history books as the place where Caesar's legions landed in 55 BC, and it was from here that William Penn set sail in 1682 on his first journey to the American colony he founded, Pennsylvania.

GETTING HERE AND AROUND

Southeastern trains travel to Deal twice an hour from London's St. Pancras Station, and once an hour from London's Charing Cross. The journey takes about two hours. You can also get a National Express bus

Canterbury, Dover, and Environs

from London's Victoria Coach Station, but there are only two buses a day (both late afternoon) and the trip takes 2½ to 3½ hours.

ESSENTIALS

Visitor Information Deal Tourist Information Centre ✉ *Landmark Centre, High St.* ☎ *01304/369576* ⊕ *www.deal.gov.uk.*

EXPLORING

Deal Castle. Erected in 1540 and intricately built to the shape of a Tudor rose, Deal Castle is the largest of the coastal defenses constructed by Henry VIII. A moat surrounds its gloomy passages and austere walls. The castle museum has exhibits about prehistoric, Roman, and Saxon Britain. ✉ *Victoria Rd.* ☎ *01304/372762* ⊕ *www.english-heritage.org. uk* 💷 *£5* ⊘ *Apr.–Sept., daily 10–6; Oct.–Mar., weekends 10–4.*

Walmer Castle and Gardens. Another of Henry VIII's coastal fortifications, this castle was converted in 1708 into a residence for the Lord Warden of the Cinque Ports, a ceremonial honor dating back to the early Middle Ages. Made up of four round towers around a circular keep, the castle has sprawling lavender gardens with gorgeous ocean views. Among its famous lord wardens were William Pitt the Younger; the duke of Wellington, hero of the Battle of Waterloo, who lived here from 1829 until his death here in 1852 (a small museum contains memorabilia); and Sir Winston Churchill. The drawing and dining rooms are open to the

The majestic White Cliffs of Dover are a national icon.

public except when the lord warden is in residence. The castle is about a mile south of Deal. ⊠ *A258* ☎ *01304/364288* ⊕ *www.english-heritage. org.uk* ✉ *£7.50* ⊘ *Mar., weekends 10–6; Apr.–Sept., daily 10–6; Oct.– early Nov., Wed.–Sun. 10–4.*

DOVER

8 miles south of Deal, 78 miles east of London.

The busy passenger port of Dover has for centuries been Britain's gateway to Europe and is known for the famous white cliffs. You may find the town itself disappointing; the savage bombardments of World War II and the shortsightedness of postwar developers left the city center an unattractive place. Roman legacies include a lighthouse adjoining a stout Anglo-Saxon church.

GETTING HERE AND AROUND

National Express buses depart from London's Victoria Coach Station for Dover about every 1½ hours. The journey takes about three hours. Drivers from London take the M20, which makes a straight line south to Dover. The 76-mile journey should take around two hours. Southeastern trains leave London's Charing Cross, Victoria, and St. Pancras stations about every 30 minutes for Dover Priory Station in Dover. The trip is between one and two hours; some services require changes in Ashford.

For the best views of the cliffs, you need a car or taxi; it's a long way to walk from town.

ESSENTIALS

Visitor Information **Dover Visitor Information Centre** ✉ *Dover Museum, Market Sq.* ☎ *01304/201066* 🌐 *www.whitecliffscountry.org.uk.*

HENRY VIII'S CASTLES

Why did Henry VIII rapidly (1539–42) build sturdy forts along the southern coast? After enraging the pope and Europe's Catholic monarchs with his marriages and by seizing control of the wealthy monasteries, he prepared for an impending French invasion. (It never came.) Today you can bike or walk along the beachfront between Deal and Walmer castles.

EXPLORING

FAMILY Fodor's Choice ★ **Dover Castle.** Spectacular and with plenty to explore, Dover Castle, towering high above the ramparts of the white cliffs, is a mighty medieval castle that has served as an important strategic center over the centuries. Most of the castle, including the keep, dates to Norman times. It was begun by Henry II in 1181 but incorporates additions from almost every succeeding century. There's a lot to see besides the castle rooms themselves, most notably the recently opened **secret wartime tunnels**. Dover Castle played a surprisingly dramatic role in World War II, and these well-thought-out interactive galleries tell the complete story. The tunnels themselves, originally built during the Napoleonic Wars, were used as a top-secret nerve center in the fight against Hitler. ✉ *Castle Rd.* ☎ *01304/211067* 🌐 *www.english-heritage.org.uk* 🎟 *£16.50* ⏲ *Apr.–July and Sept., daily 10–6; Aug., daily 9:30–6; Oct.–early Nov., daily 10–5; mid-Nov.–Mar., weekends 10–4.*

Roman Painted House. Believed to have been a hotel, the remains of this nearly 2,000-year-old structure were excavated in the 1970s. It includes some Roman wall paintings (mostly dedicated to Bacchus, the god of revelry), along with the remnants of an ingenious heating system. ✉ *New St.* ☎ *01304/203279* 🌐 *www.theromanpaintedhouse.co.uk* 🎟 *£3* ⏲ *Early–mid-Apr., Tues.–Sun. 10–5; late Apr.–May, Tues. and Sat. 10–5; June–late Sept, Tues.–Sun. 10–5; last admission 30 mins before closing.*

Fodor's Choice ★ **White Cliffs.** Plunging hundreds of feet into the sea, Dover's chalk-white cliffs are an inspirational site and a symbol of England. They stay white because of the natural process of erosion. Because of this, you must be cautious when walking along the cliffs—experts recommend staying at least 20 feet from the edge. The best places to see the cliffs are at Samphire Hoe, St. Margaret's Bay, or East Cliff and Warren Country Park. Signs will direct you from the roads to scenic spots. **TIP→ The visitor center at Langdon Cliffs has 5 miles of walking trails with some spectacular views.**

WHERE TO STAY

For expanded hotel reviews, visit Fodors.com.

$ HOTEL 🏨 **Premier Inn Dover.** By the waterfront, this modern hotel has spacious, quiet rooms, and a handy restaurant and bar. **Pros:** affordable rates; great location. **Cons:** busy neighborhood; no character; hotel restaurant is only so-so. [$] *Rooms from: £72* ✉ *Marine Court, Marine Parade* ☎ *0871/527–8306* 🌐 *www.premierinn.com* 🛏 *100 rooms* 🍴 *Breakfast.*

$$ **White Cliffs Hotel.** Literally in the shadow of the famous White Cliffs
B&B/INN   of Dover, this colorful little hotel is attached to a high-end homeware
store and a good restaurant. **Pros:** bags of character; beautiful location;
guests can use the spa at another local hotel. **Cons:** far from central
Dover; difficult to get here without a car. $ *Rooms from: £119* ⊠ *High
St., St. Margaret's-at-Cliffe* ☎ *01304/852229* ⊕ *www.thewhitecliffs.com*
⌐ *15 rooms* ⦿ *Breakfast.*

RYE, LEWES, AND ENVIRONS

From Dover the coast road winds west through Folkestone (a genteel
resort, small port, and Channel Tunnel terminal), across Romney Marsh
(famous for its sheep and, at one time, its ruthless smugglers), and on
to the delightful medieval town of Rye. The region along the coast is
noted for Winchelsea, the history-rich sites of Hastings, Herstmonceux,
and Bodiam, and the Glyndebourne Opera House festival, based outside
Lewes, a town celebrated for its architectural heritage. One of the three
steam railroads in the Southeast services part of the area: the Romney,
Hythe, and Dymchurch Railway.

RYE

68 miles southeast of London, 34 miles southwest of Dover.

Fodor's Choice   With cobbled streets and ancient timbered dwellings, Rye is an artist's
★   dream. It was an important port town until the harbor silted up and
the waters retreated more than 150 years ago; now the nearest harbor
is 2 miles away. Virtually every building in the little town center is
intriguingly historic. Rye is known for its many antiques stores and
also for its sheer pleasantness. This place can be easily walked without
a map, but the local tourist office has an interesting audio tour of the
town as well as maps.

GETTING HERE AND AROUND

If you're driving to Rye, take the M20 to A2070. Trains from Lon-
don's St. Pancras leave once an hour and take an hour, with a change
in Ashford.

ESSENTIALS

Visitor Information Rye Tourist Information Centre ⊠ *4 Lion St.*
☎ *01797/229049* ⊕ *www.ryesussex.co.uk.*

EXPLORING

TOP ATTRACTIONS

FAMILY   **Bodiam Castle.** Immortalized in paintings, photographs, and films,
Bodiam Castle rises out of the distance like a piece of medieval legend.
From the outside it's one of Britain's most impressive castles, with tur-
rets, battlements, a glassy moat and 2-foot-thick walls. Once you cross
the drawbridge to the interior there's little to see but ruins, albeit on an
impressive scale. Built in 1385 to withstand a threatened French inva-
sion, it was partly demolished during the English Civil War of 1642–46
and has been uninhabited ever since. Still, you can climb the towers to
take in sweeping countryside views, and kids love running around the

keep. The castle, 12 miles west of Rye, schedules organized activities for kids during school holidays. ✉ *Off B2244, Bodiam* ☎ *01580/830196* ⊕ *www.nationaltrust.org.uk* ⌸ *£7* ☉ *Mid-Feb.–Oct., daily 10:30–5; Nov. and Dec., Wed.–Sun. 11–4 or dusk; Jan.–mid-Feb., weekends 11–4; last admission 1 hr before closing.*

Church of St. Mary the Virgin. At the top of the hill at the center of Rye, this classic English village church is more than 900 years old and encompasses a number of architectural styles. The turret clock dates to 1561 and still keeps excellent time. Its huge pendulum swings inside the church nave. ■ TIP→ **Climb the tower for amazing views of the surrounding area.** ✉ *Church Sq.* ☎ *01797/224935* ⊕ *www.ryeparishchurch.org.uk* ⌸ *Free* ☉ *Daily 10–4.*

Fodor's Choice ★ **Great Dixter House and Gardens.** Combining a large timber-frame hall with a cottage garden on a grand scale, this place will get your green thumbs twitching. The house dates to 1464 (you can tour a few rooms) and was restored in 1910 by architect Edwin Lutyens, who also designed the garden. From these beginnings, the late horticulturist and writer Christopher Lloyd, whose home this was, developed a series of creative, colorful "garden rooms" and a dazzling herbaceous Long Border. The house is 9 miles northwest of Rye. ✉ *Off A28, Northiam* ☎ *01797/252878* ⊕ *www.greatdixter.co.uk* ⌸ *£10.50; gardens only £8.50* ☉ *Apr.–Oct., Tues.–Sun. and bank holidays 11–5 (house 2–5).*

Mermaid Street. One of the town's original cobbled streets (and perhaps its most quintissential view) heads steeply from the top of the hill to the former harbor. Its name supposedly came from the night a drunken sailor swore he heard a mermaid call him down to the sea. The houses here date from between the medieval and Georgian periods; a much-photographed pair have the delightfully fanciful names "The House With Two Front Doors" and "The House Opposite." Be careful on your feet—the cobbles are very uneven.

Ypres Tower. Down the hill past Church Square, Ypres Tower was originally built as part of the town's fortifications (now all but disappeared) in 1249; it later served as a prison. The stone chambers hold a rather random collection of local items, such as smuggling bric-a-brac and shipbuilding mementos. A row of defensive cannons are fixed to the rampart, which used to overlook the sea. ✉ *Gungarden* ☎ *01797/226728* ⊕ *www.ryemuseum.co.uk* ⌸ *£3; £4 combined ticket with Rye Castle Museum* ☉ *Apr.–Oct., daily 10:30–5; Nov.–Mar., daily 10:30–3:30; last admission 30 mins before closing.*

WORTH NOTING

Bodiam Boating Station. By far the prettiest way to approach Bodiam Castle is on a 45-minute river cruise through Sussex countryside. Boats leave from the riverbank by the old stone road bridge on the outskirts of Newenden (it's easy to find—the village is tiny). ✉ *Riverside Cottage, Rye Rd., Newenden* ☎ *01797/253838* ⊕ *www.bodiamboatingstation. co.uk* ⌸ *£6.50* ☉ *Apr.–Oct., Wed., weekends 10:30, 12:45, and 3 (return boats 1 hr later).*

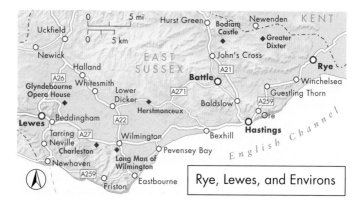

Rye, Lewes, and Environs

Chapel Down Winery. After decades as little more than the butt of jokes, the English wine industry is beginning to be taken seriously—and one of Britain's leading wine producers is a few miles north of Rye. You can visit the wine shop and explore the herb gardens for free. Book in advance and you can also take an hour-long guided tour of the rest of the grounds. ⊠ *Off B2082, Small Hythe, Tenterton* ☎ *01580/766111* ⊕ *www.chapeldown.com* ⊠ *£10 tour* ⊙ *Daily 10–5.*

Lamb House. Something about Lamb House, an early-18th-century dwelling, attracts writers. The novelist Henry James lived here from 1898 to 1916. E. F. Benson, onetime mayor of Rye and author of the witty *Lucia* novels (written in the 1920s and 1930s), was a later resident. The ground-floor rooms contain some of James's furniture and personal belongings. ⊠ *West St.* ☎ *01580/762334* ⊕ *www.nationaltrust.org.uk* ⊠ *£4.80* ⊙ *Apr.–Oct., Tues. and Sat. 2–6; last admission at 5:30.*

Rye Castle Museum. The diminutive Rye Castle Museum, below the remains of the castle wall, displays watercolors and examples of Rye pottery, for which the town was famous. ⊠ *3 East St.* ☎ *01797/226728* ⊕ *www.ryemuseum.co.uk* ⊠ *£1.50; £4 combined ticket with Ypres Tower* ⊙ *Weekends and bank holidays 10:30–5; last admission 30 mins before closing.*

Winchelsea. Like Rye, Winchelsea perches prettily atop its own small hill amid rolling farmland. Look for the splendid (though damaged) church built in the 14th century with stone from Normandy. Winchelsea was built on a grid system devised in 1283. This was once a walled town, and some original town gates still stand. Beneath the narrow streets are at least 56 medieval cellars; a few are accessible by guided tour (£5) on various dates from April to October. The tour, which is run by somewhat overenthusiastic volunteers, is interesting but long. See the town website or call 01797/224446 for recorded information. The town is 2 miles southwest of Rye. ⊠ *Winchelsea* ⊕ *www.winchelsea.net.*

WHERE TO EAT

$

ITALIAN

✕ **Simply Italian.** In a prime location near the marina, this popular Italian eatery packs in the crowds on weekend nights with its inexpensive classic pasta-and-pizza dishes. The atmosphere is cheerful and bright, and the food is straightforward and unfussy. Try tagliatelle with salmon in a creamy sauce, or grilled lemon sole with white wine sauce. Good pizza picks are the *quarto stagioni,* with mushrooms, salami, and peppers on a crisp crust, and pizza *reale* with red peppers, spinach, goat cheese, and red onion. [$] *Average main: £8* ✉ *The Strand* ☎ *01797/226024* 🌐 *www.simplyitalian.co.uk.*

$$ SEAFOOD Fodor's Choice ★ 🍴 **Webbes at the Fish Café.** One of Rye's most popular restaurants occupies a brick building that dates to 1907, but the interior has been redone in a sleek, modern style. The ground-floor café has a relaxed atmosphere, and upstairs is a more formal dining room. Most of the seafood here is caught nearby, so it's very fresh. Sample the shellfish platter with oysters, whelks, winkles, shrimp, and crab claws, or try the grilled squid with bok choi. Reservations are recommended for dinner. [$] *Average main: £15* ✉ *17 Tower St.* ☎ *01797/222226* 🌐 *www.webbesrestaurants.co.uk* 🕓 *Closed Mon. Oct.–Apr. No dinner Sun.*

WHERE TO STAY

For expanded hotel reviews, visit Fodors.com.

$$ HOTEL 🏨 **The George.** This attractive hotel on Rye's main road takes a boutique approach, cleverly mixing modern pieces with antiques in a sprawling Georgian building. **Pros:** elegant room design; very central. **Cons:** weddings are popular here—they can happen weekly in summer, take over public areas, and stay noisy until late. [$] *Rooms from: £135* ✉ *98 High St.* ☎ *01797/222114* 🌐 *www.thegeorgeinrye.com* 🛏 *24 rooms* 🍽 *Breakfast.*

$ B&B/INN 🏨 **Jeake's House.** Antiques fill the cozy bedrooms of this rambling 1689 house, where the snug, painted-and-paneled parlor has a wood-burning stove for cold days. **Pros:** pleasant atmosphere; delicious breakfasts; winter discounts. **Cons:** Mermaid Street is steep and cobbled; cheapest room has bathroom across the hall. [$] *Rooms from: £90* ✉ *Mermaid St.* ☎ *01797/222828* 🌐 *www.jeakeshouse.com* 🛏 *11 rooms, 10 with bath* 🍽 *Breakfast.*

$$ HOTEL Fodor's Choice ★ 🏨 **The Mermaid.** Steeped in a history of smuggling, the Mermaid is Rye's most historic inn, and one of the oldest in the country—it's been in business for 600 years. **Pros:** dripping in atmosphere; good restaurant; 24-hour room service. **Cons:** price is high for what's on offer; allegedly haunted. [$] *Rooms from: £150* ✉ *Mermaid St.* ☎ *01797/223065* 🌐 *www.mermaidinn.com* 🛏 *31 rooms* 🍽 *Multiple meal plans.*

$$ B&B/INN 🏨 **White Vine House Hotel.** Occupying a building from the late 1500s, this small hotel embraces tradition with features such as wood-paneled lounges with warming fireplaces. **Pros:** beautiful building; one of the area's best restaurants. **Cons:** main street location can be a bit noisy; few services. [$] *Rooms from: £130* ✉ *24 High St.* ☎ *01797/224748* 🌐 *www.whitevinehouse.co.uk* 🛏 *7 rooms* 🍽 *Breakfast.*

SHOPPING

Rye has great antiques shops, perfect for an afternoon of rummaging, with the biggest cluster at the foot of the hill near the tourist information center.

Britcher & Rivers. This traditional candy store is like something out of a bygone age. Choose from row upon row of tall jars packed with every imaginable type of candy, measured out into little paper bags. ✉ *89 High St.* ☎ *01797/227152.*

David Sharp Pottery. Like the distinctive ceramic name plaques that are a feature of the town? They are on offer at this sweet little shop. ✉ *55 The Mint* ☎ *01797/222620* ⊕ *www.studiopottery.com/.*

Glass Etc. A glorious collection of quality antique glass can be found in this colorful, friendly shop by the train station. ✉ *18-22 Rope Walk* ☎ *01797/226600* ⊕ *www.decanterman.com.*

The Paper Place. This little stationery boutique sells beautiful handmade paper and cards with intricate, Asian-influenced designs. ✉ *12 Market Rd.* ☎ *01797/222688* ⊕ *www.thepaperplaceonline.co.uk.*

HASTINGS

12 miles southwest of Rye, 68 miles southeast of London.

In the 19th century Hastings became one of England's most popular spa resorts. Tall Victorian row houses painted in lemony hues still cover the cliffs around the deep blue sea, and the views from the hilltops are extraordinary. The pretty Old Town, on the east side of the city, offers a glimpse into the city's 16th-century past. Hastings has been through difficult times in recent decades, and the town developed a reputation as a rough place. It's currently trying hard to reinvent itself—a clutch of trendy new boutique B&Bs has opened, also an important new art gallery—but the town center can still be quite rowdy after dark. Expect a handsome but tattered town, with a mix of traditional English seaside amusements: miniature golf, shops selling junk, fish-and-chip stands, and a rocky beach that stretches for miles.

GETTING HERE AND AROUND

If you're driving to Hastings from London (70 miles), take A21. Trains travel to Hastings every 30 minutes or so from London's Charing Cross and St. Pancras stations; the journey takes about 1½ hours. The station, Hastings Warrior Square, is in the town center, within easy walking distance of most sights. National Express buses travel from London to Hastings about twice a day in about 3½ hours.

ESSENTIALS

Visitor Information Hastings Tourist Information Centre ✉ *Queens Sq.* ☎ *01424/451111* ⊕ *www.visit1066country.com.*

EXPLORING

FAMILY **Hastings Castle.** Take a thrilling ride up the West Hill Cliff Railway from George Street precinct to the atmospheric ruins of the Norman fortress now known as Hastings Castle, built by William the Conqueror in 1069. All that remains are fragments of the fortifications, some ancient walls, and a number of gloomy dungeons. Nevertheless, you get an excellent view of the chalky cliffs, the rocky coast, and the town below. ✉ *West Hill* ☎ *01424/201609* 💷 *£4.50* ⊗ *Mid.-late Feb. and Apr.–Sept., daily 10–5; Mar., weeknds 10–5; last admission 30 mins before closing; closed Oct.–Jan.*

Fodor's Choice **The Jerwood Gallery.** A symbol of Hastings' slow but growing regeneration after decades of neglect, this new exhibition space in the Old Town ★ became one of the most talked about new galleries outside London when it opened in 2012. The permanent collection includes works by Augustus

John, Walter Sickert, and Stephen Lowry, and temporary exhibitions change every couple of months. The glazed tile building on the seafront was designed to reflect the row of distinctive old, blackened fishing sheds it sits alongside. ⊠ *Rock-a-Nore Rd.* ☎ *01424/728377* ⊕ *www.jerwoodgallery.org* ⊠ *£7* ☉ *Tues.– Fri., 11–5, weekends 11–6.*

FAMILY **Smuggler's Adventure.** The history of smuggling on the south coast is told through waxworks and other exhibits, inside this labyrinth of caves underneath the West Hill, a 15-minute walk from the Hastings Castle. ⊠ *St. Clement Caves* ☎ *01424/422964* ⊕ *www.smugglersadventure.co.uk* ⊠ *£7.50* ☉ *Apr.–Sept., daily 10–5:30; Oct.– Mar., daily 10–4; last admission 30 mins before closing.*

THE BATTLE OF HASTINGS

When William of Normandy attacked King Harold's army in 1066, a vicious battle ensued. Harold's troops had just successfully fended off the Vikings near York and marched across the country to take on the Normans. Utterly exhausted, Harold was no match, and William became known as William the Conqueror. It's worth noting that, though it was called the Battle of Hastings, the skirmish actually took place 6 miles away at a town now called, well, Battle.

WHERE TO EAT AND STAY

For expanded hotel reviews, visit Fodors.com.

$ ✕ **Blue Dolphin.** The crowds line up all day to make their way into this
SEAFOOD small fish-and-chips shop just off the seafront, down near the fish shacks. Although the decor is humble, reviewers consistently rank the battered fish and huge plates of double-cooked chips (chunky fries) as among the best in the country. Everything is steaming fresh, and it's all cheaper if you get it to take out. $ *Average main: £6* ⊠ *61 High St.* ☎ *01424/425778* ▭ *No credit cards* ☉ *No dinner.*

WHERE TO STAY

$ ⌂ **The Cloudesley.** No TVs and a general Zen vibe at this boutique B&B in
B&B/INN the quieter St. Leonard's district of Hastings make it a thoroughly relaxing place to stay. **Pros:** oasis of calm; great spa treatments; impeccable eco credentials. **Cons:** super-chilled vibe won't be for everyone; two-night minimum at certain times. $ *Rooms from: £75* ⊠ *7 Cloudesley Rd., St. Leonards-on-Sea* ☎ *07507/000148* ⊕ *www.thecloudesley.co.uk* ⇌ *5 rooms.*

$ ⌂ **Hastings House.** In Warrior Square at the edge of Hastings near St.
HOTEL Leonards-on-Sea, this renovated boutique guesthouse in a Victorian house takes a funky, modern approach. **Pros:** spacious rooms; near the sea. **Cons:** no restaurant; few services. $ *Rooms from: £95* ⊠ *9 Warrior Sq., St. Leonards-on-Sea* ☎ *01424/422709* ⊕ *www.hastingshouse. co.uk* ⇌ *8 rooms* ⦿ *Breakfast.*

$$ ⌂ **Swan House.** Originally a bakery, this extraordinary 15th-century
B&B/INN building has been beautifully converted into a welcoming, stylish B&B.
Fodor's Choice **Pros:** beautiful, historic building; welcoming hosts; delicious break-
★ fasts. **Cons:** some bathrooms have shower only. $ *Rooms from: £120* ⊠ *1 Hill St.* ☎ *01424/430014* ⊕ *www.swanhousehastings.co.uk* ⇌ *27 rooms* ⦿ *Breakfast.*

$$ 🛏 **Zanzibar International Hotel.** This spacious, light-filled hotel overlook-
HOTEL ing the sea has guest rooms designed as a playful, yet restrained hom-
age to exotic destinations. **Pros:** great facilities for a small hotel; sea
views; champagne is served with breakfast. **Cons:** a bit over the top
for some tastes; pricey for Hastings; nonrefundable deposit. $ *Rooms
from: £125* ⊠ *9 Everfield Pl., St. Leonards-on-Sea* ☎ *01424/460109*
⊕ *www.zanzibarhotel.co.uk* ↪ *9 rooms* ⚬| *Breakfast.*

BATTLE

7 miles northwest of Hastings, 61 miles southeast of London.

Battle is the actual site of the crucial Battle of Hastings, at which,
on October 14, 1066, William of Normandy and his army trounced
King Harold's Anglo-Saxon army. Today it's a sweet, quiet town, and
a favorite of history buffs.

GETTING HERE AND AROUND

Southeastern trains arrive from London's Charing Cross and Canon
Street stations every half hour. The journey takes 90 minutes. National
Express buses travel once daily in the early evening from London's
Victoria Coach Station. The trip takes around 2½ hours.

ESSENTIALS

Visitor Information Battle Information Point ⊠ *Yesterdays World, 89-90 High
Street* ☎ *01797/229049* ⊕ *www.visit1066country.com.*

EXPLORING

Battle Abbey. This great Benedictine abbey was erected by William the
Conqueror on the site of the Battle of Hastings—one of the most deci-
sive turning points in English history and the last time the country was
successfully invaded. A memorial stone marks the high altar, which in
turn was supposedly laid on the spot where Harold II, the last Saxon
king, was killed. All of this meant little to Henry VIII, who didn't spare
the building from his violent dissolution of the monasteries. Today
the abbey is just a ruin, but films and interactive exhibits help bring
it all to life. You can also take the mile-long walk around the edge of
the battlefield and see the remains of the abbey's former outbuildings.
⊠ *High St.* ☎ *01424/775705* ⊕ *www.english-heritage.org.uk* ✉ *£7.60*
⊙ *Apr.–Sept., daily 10–6; Oct.–early Nov., daily 10–4; early Nov.–Mar.,
weekends 10–4.*

FAMILY   **Herstmonceux.** A banner waving from one tower and a glassy moat crossed
Fodor'sChoice   by what was once a drawbridge—this fairy-tale castle has everything
★   except knights in shining armor. The redbrick structure was originally
built by Sir Roger Fiennes (ancestor of actor Ralph Fiennes) in 1444,
although it was altered in the Elizabethan age and again early in the 20th
century, after it had largely fallen to ruin. Canada's Queen's University
owns the castle, so only part of it is open for guided tours once or twice
a day (except Saturday). Highlights include the magnificent ballroom,
a medieval room, and the stunning Elizabethan-era staircase. Explore
the formal walled garden, lily-covered lakes, and miles of woodland—
the perfect place for a picnic on a sunny afternoon. There's a hands-on
science center for kids. When school isn't in session, the castle rents

out its small, plain guest rooms from £40 per night. The castle is 8 miles southwest of Battle. ✉ *Off A271, Hailsham* ☎ *01323/833816* 🌐 *www.herstmonceux-castle.com* 🎟 *Castle and grounds £6; castle, grounds, and science center £12.50; castle tours £2.50* ⏲ *Mid-Apr.–Sept., daily 10–6; Oct., daily 10–5; last admission 1 hr before closing.*

BEACH HUTS

As English as clotted cream, rows of tiny, cheerfully painted, one-room wooden beach huts brighten the shoreline in Sussex (look for them at the edges of Hastings and Brighton) and elsewhere. The huts originated in the Victorian wheeled bathing machines that were rolled into the water so that women could swim modestly behind them. Eventually the wheels came off, and they and similar structures became favored for storage and as a windbreak. Most huts lack electricity or plumbing but are beloved for their adorableness. Some are rented; others are owned, and prices can be surprisingly steep.

WHERE TO EAT AND STAY

For expanded hotel reviews, visit Fodors.com.

$$$ MODERN FRENCH

🍴 **The Sundial.** This 17th-century brick farmhouse with views of the South Downs is home to a popular Modern French restaurant. Wood-beamed rooms and white tablecloths provide a backdrop for the imaginative menu, which may include rack of lamb with rosemary cream sauce, or steak fillet with shallot tatin and Madeira sauce. Dessert may be pineapple carpaccio marinated in Malibu and star anise, or perhaps marscapone mousse with plum compote. The Sundial is near the castle in Herstmonceux, 8 miles southwest of Battle. [$] *Average main: £21* ✉ *Gardner St., Herstmonceux* ☎ *01323/832217* 🌐 *www.sundialrestaurant.co.uk* ⏲ *Closed Mon. No dinner Sun.*

EN ROUTE

Long Man of Wilmington. Wilmington, 9 miles southwest of Herstmonceux Castle on A27, has a famous landmark that people drive for miles to see. High on the downs to the south of the village (signposted off A27), a 226-foot-tall white figure with a staff in each hand, known as the Long Man of Wilmington, is carved into the chalk. His age is a subject of great debate, but some researchers think he might have originated in Roman times.

LEWES

24 miles east of Battle, 8 miles northeast of Brighton, 54 miles south of London.

Fodor's Choice ★

The town nearest to the celebrated Glyndebourne Opera House, Lewes is so rich in architectural history that the Council for British Archaeology has named it one of the 50 most important English towns. A walk is the best way to appreciate its steep streets and appealing jumble of building styles and materials—flint, stone, brick, tile—and the secret lanes (called "twittens") behind the castle, with their huge beeches. Here and there are smart antiques shops, good eateries, and secondhand-book dealers. Most of the buildings in the center date to the 18th and 19th centuries.

Something about this town has always attracted rebels. It was once the home of Thomas Paine (1737–1809), whose pamphlet *Common Sense* advocated that the American colonies break with Britain. It was also favored by Virginia Woolf and the Bloomsbury Group, early-20th-century countercultural artistic innovators.

Today Lewes's beauty and proximity to London mean that the counter-culture crew can't really afford to live here anymore, but its rebel soul still peeks through, particularly on Guy Fawkes Night (November 5), the anniversary of Fawkes's foiled attempt to blow up the Houses of Parliament in 1605. Flaming tar barrels are rolled down High Street and into the River Ouse; costumed processions fill the streets.

GETTING HERE AND AROUND

If you're driving to Lewes from London, take the M23 south. The 57-mile journey takes around an hour and 45 minutes. Southern trains run direct to Lewes from Victoria Station every 30 minutes or so on the Brighton line. It may be faster to take a train to Brighton and change to the regional service for Lewes. There's no easy way to get to Lewes by bus; you need to take a National Express or Megabus to Brighton and change to a regional bus line.

ESSENTIALS

Visitor Information Lewes Tourist Information Centre ⊠ *187 High St.* ☎ *01273/483448* ⊕ *www.lewes.gov.uk.*

EXPLORING

FAMILY **Anne of Cleves House.** This 16th-century structure, a fragile-looking, timber-frame building, holds a small collection of Sussex ironwork and other items of local interest, such as Sussex pottery. The house was part of Anne of Cleves's divorce settlement from Henry VIII, although she never lived in it. There are medieval dress-up clothes for kids. To get to the house, walk down steep, cobbled Keere Street, past lovely Grange Gardens, to Southover High Street. ⊠ *52 Southover High St.* ☎ *01273/474610* ⊕ *www.sussexpast.co.uk* ☎ *£4.90* ☉ *Feb.–Nov., Tues.–Sat. 10–5, Sun. and Mon. 11–5.*

Charleston. Art and life mixed at Charleston, the farmhouse Vanessa Bell—sister of Virginia Woolf—bought in 1916 and fancifully decorated, along with Duncan Grant (who lived here until 1978). The house became a refuge for the writers and artists of the Bloomsbury Group. On display are colorful ceramics and textiles of the Omega Workshop—in which Bell and Grant participated—and paintings by Picasso and Renoir, as well as by Bell and Grant themselves. You view the house on a guided tour except on Sunday. On Friday there's a special 90-minute tour that focuses on a different aspect of Charleston's history, such as the great influence French culture had on the Bloomsbury Group. ⊠ *Off A27, 7 miles east of Lewes, Firle* ☎ *01323/811626* ⊕ *www.charleston. org.uk* ☎ *£10; gardens only £4* ☉ *Late Mar.–June and Sept.–late Oct., Wed.–Sat. 1–6, Sun. and bank holidays 1–5:30; July and Aug., Wed.–Sat. noon–6, Sun. 1–5:30.*

Lewes Castle. High above the valley of the River Ouse stand the majestic ruins of Lewes Castle, begun in 1100 by one of the country's Norman conquerors, and completed 300 years later. The castle's barbican holds a

BONFIRE NIGHT IN LEWES

In 1605 a group of Catholic rebels attempted to blow up Parliament in the most famous failed coup in English history. Known as the Gunpowder Plot, it's still commemorated with fireworks every year on the Saturday closest to the anniversary on November 5. As befitting a 400-year-old custom, it's a night rich with tradition—nowhere more than in Lewes. Thousands parade through the town with flaming torches; many wear elaborate costumes and play instruments. Huge pyres are lit ("bonfires"), effigies of the plotters and other, more modern bogeymen are burned (recent examples include Osama bin Laden) and the fireworks carry on well into the night. Admittedly it may be too much for some visitors—anti-Catholic chants and the burning of a Papal effigy are genuinely in the spirit of tradition and bone-dry humor, rather than actual anti-Catholic sentiment—but it's a unique event with a carnival atmosphere. Similar, smaller parades happen in Rye and Hastings, usually on different weeks. For more details see 🌐 *www.lewesbonfirecelebrations.com* or check the town websites.

3

small museum with archaeology collections, a changing temporary exhibition gallery, and a bookshop. There are panoramic views of the town and countryside. ✉ *169 High St.* ☎ *01273/486290* 🌐 *www.sussexpast.co.uk* 🎫 *£6.80* 🕒 *Tues.–Sat. 10–5:30, Sun. and Mon.11–5:30.*

Monk's House. Of interest to Bloomsbury Group fans, this was the home of novelist Virginia Woolf and her husband, Leonard Woolf, who bought it in 1919. Leonard lived here until his death in 1969. Rooms in the small cottage include Virginia's study and her bedroom. Artists Vanessa Bell (Virginia's sister) and Duncan Grant helped decorate the house. The house is in Rodmell, 3 miles south of Lewes. ✉ *Off A27, Rodmell* ☎ *01273/474760* 🌐 *www.nationaltrust.org.uk* 🎫 *£4.90* 🕒 *Apr.–Oct., Wed.–Sun. and bank holidays 1–5:30.*

WHERE TO EAT

$ CAFÉ 🍴 **The Real Eating Company.** This light-filled restaurant has big windows overlooking the bustling shopping street outside. The heavy wood tables are perfect for lingering over the home-style cooking. Come at breakfast for the waffles with bacon and maple syrup, or perhaps some raspberry granola. For lunch you may opt for beer-battered cod and chips, or perhaps a grilled chicken Caesar. Great cakes and strong tea help to make this an ideal afternoon pitstop. [$] *Average main: £11* ✉ *18 Cliff High St.* ☎ *01273/402650* 🌐 *www.real-eating.co.uk* 🕒 *No dinner Sun.*

$ CAFÉ 🍴 **Robson's of Lewes.** Good coffee, fresh produce, and delicious pastries have made this coffee shop very popular with locals. A light-filled space with wood floors and simple tables creates a pleasant, casual spot to enjoy a cup of coffee with breakfast, a scone, or a light sandwich or salad lunch. You can also order to go. [$] *Average main: £5* ✉ *22A High St.* ☎ *01273/480654* 🌐 *www.robsonsoflewes.co.uk* 🕒 *No dinner.*

A mixture of architectural styles and good shops make Lewes a wonderful town for a stroll.

WHERE TO STAY

For expanded hotel reviews, visit Fodors.com.

$$
HOTEL
Crossways Hotel. Near the Long Man of Wilmington, this small "restaurant with rooms" in a whitewashed house with 2 acres of gardens is decorated in warm, upbeat colors that contrast with the lovely antique furniture. **Pros:** lovely location near Glyndebourne; spacious bedrooms. **Cons:** few frills. $ *Rooms from: £145* ⊠ *Lewes Rd., Polegate* ☎ *01323/482455* ⊕ *www.crosswayshotel.co.uk* ⌁ *7 rooms, 1 cottage* ⊠ *Breakfast.*

$$$
B&B/INN
Horsted Place. On 1,100 acres, this luxurious Victorian manor house was built as a private home in 1850; it was owned by a friend of Queen Elizabeth until the 1980s, and she was a regular visitor. **Pros:** historic building; amazing architecture; lovely gardens. **Cons:** too formal for some; creaky floors bother light sleepers. $ *Rooms from: £180* ⊠ *Off A26, Little Horsted* ☎ *01825/750581* ⊕ *www.horstedplace.co.uk* ⌁ *15 rooms, 5 suites* ⊠ *Breakfast.*

$
B&B/INN
The Ram Inn. Roaring fires, cozy rooms, and friendly locals give this 500-year-old inn its wonderful feeling of old-world authenticity. **Pros:** proper village pub atmosphere; good food; cozy, well-designed rooms. **Cons:** you need a car to get here from Lewes. $ *Rooms from: £90* ⊠ *The Street, West Firle* ☎ *01273/858222* ⊕ *www.raminn.co.uk* ⌁ *4 rooms.*

$$
B&B/INN
The Shelleys. The lounge and dining room in this 17th-century building are on the grand scale, furnished with antiques that set the tone for the rest of the lovely building. **Pros:** historic atmosphere; good, French-influenced cuisine. **Cons:** service a bit spotty; securing a table at the restaurant can be tough. $ *Rooms from: £130* ⊠ *High St.* ☎ *01273/472361* ⊕ *www.the-shelleys.co.uk* ⌁ *19 rooms* ⊠ *Breakfast.*

NIGHTLIFE AND THE ARTS

NIGHTLIFE

Lewes has a relatively young population and a nightlife scene to match; there are also many lovely old pubs.

Brewers' Arms. On High Street, this is a good pub with a friendly crowd. The half-timbered building dates from 1906, but a pub has stood on this spot since the 16th century. ⊠ *91 High St.* ☎ *01273/475524* ⊕ *www. brewersarmslewes.co.uk.*

King's Head. A traditional pub, the King's Head has a good menu with locally-sourced fish and meat dishes. ⊠ *9 Southover High St.* ☎ *01273/474628* ⊕ *www.thekingsheadlewes.co.uk.*

THE ARTS

Glyndebourne Opera House. Nestled beneath the Downs, this world-famous opera house combines first-class productions, a state-of-the-art auditorium, and a beautiful setting. Seats are *very* expensive (the cheapest are around £50) and you have to book months in advance, but it's worth every penny to aficionados, who traditionally wear evening dress and bring a hamper to picnic in the gardens. The main season runs from mid-May to the end of August. ■ TIP➔ **If you can't afford a seat, standing room costs about £10.** The Glyndebourne Touring Company performs here in October, when seats are cheaper. ⊠ *New Rd., off A26, Ringmer* ✥ *Near Lewes* ☎ *01273/813813* ⊕ *www.glyndebourne.com.*

SHOPPING

Antiques shops offer temptation along the busy High Street. Lewes also has plenty of tiny boutiques and independent clothing stores vying for your pounds.

Cliffe Antiques Centre. Cliffe Antiques Centre carries a fine mix of vintage English prints, estate jewelry, and art at reasonable prices. ⊠ *47 Cliffe High St.* ☎ *01273/473266.*

The Fifteenth Century Bookshop. A wide collection of rare and vintage books can be found at this ancient, timber-framed building in the center of Lewes. Antique children's books are a specialty. ⊠ *99–100 High St.* ☎ *01273/474160* ⊕ *www.oldenyoungbooks.co.uk.*

Louis Potts & Co. From frivolous knickkacks to full-on formal dining sets, Louis Potts specializes in stylish bone china and glassware. ⊠ *43 Cliffe High St.* ☎ *01273/472240* ⊕ *www.louispotts.com.*

BRIGHTON, THE SUSSEX COAST, AND SURREY

The self-proclaimed belle of the coast, Brighton is upbeat, funky, and endlessly entertaining. Outside town the soft green downs of Sussex and Surrey hold stately homes you can visit, including Arundel Castle and Petworth House. Along the way, you'll discover the largest Roman villa in Britain, the bustling city of Guildford, and Chichester, whose cathedral is a poem in stone.

BRIGHTON

9 miles southwest of Lewes, 54 miles south of London.

Fodor's Choice
★
For more than 200 years, Brighton has been England's most interesting seaside city, and today it's more vibrant, eccentric, and cosmopolitan than ever. A rich cultural mix—Regency architecture, specialty shops, sidewalk cafés, lively arts, and a flourishing gay scene—makes it unique and unpredictable.

In 1750 physician Richard Russell published a book recommending sea-water treatment for glandular diseases. The fashionable world flocked to Brighton to take Dr. Russell's "cure," and sea bathing became a popular pastime. Few places in the south of England were better for it, since Brighton's broad beach of smooth pebbles stretches as far as the eye can see. It's been popular with sunbathers ever since.

The next windfall for the town was the arrival of the Prince of Wales (later George IV). "Prinny," as he was called, created the Royal Pavilion, a mock-Asian pleasure palace that attracted London society. This triggered a wave of villa building, and today the elegant terraces of Regency houses are among the town's greatest attractions. The coming of the railway set the seal on Brighton's popularity: the *Brighton Belle* brought Londoners to the coast in an hour.

Londoners still flock to Brighton. Add them to the many local university students, and you have a trendy, young, laid-back city that does, occasionally, burst at its own seams. Property values have skyrocketed, but all visitors may notice is the good shopping and restaurants, attractive (if pebbly) beach, and wild nightlife. Brighton is also the place to go if you're looking for hotels with offbeat design and party nights.

GETTING HERE AND AROUND

Brighton-bound National Express and Megabus buses depart from London's Victoria Coach Station. The trip takes about two hours. South-eastern trains leave from London's Victoria and Charing Cross stations four or five times an hour. The journey takes 75 minutes, and the trains stop at Gatwick Airport. By car from London, head to Brighton on the M23/A23. The journey should take about 1½ hours.

Brighton (and the adjacent Hove) sprawls in all directions, but the part of interest to travelers is fairly compact. None of the sights is more than a 10-minute walk from the train station. You can pick up a town map at the station. City Sightseeing has a hop-on, hop-off tour bus that leaves Brighton Pier every 20 to 30 minutes. It operates May through mid-September (plus weekends, March and April) and costs £11.

TIMING

On summer weekends the town is packed with Londoners looking for a day by the sea. Oceanfront bars can be rowdy, especially on national holidays when concerts and events bring in crowds. But summer is also when Brighton looks its best, and revelers pack the shops, restaurants, and bars. At other times, it's much quieter. The Brighton Festival in May fills the town with music and other performances.

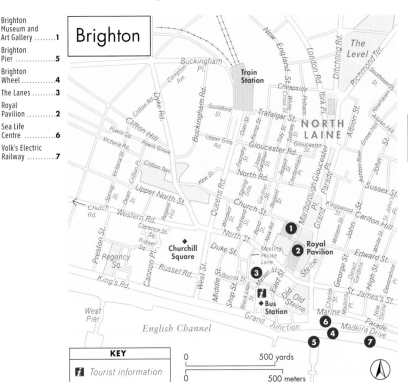

ESSENTIALS

Visitor and Tour Information **Brighton Visitor Information Centre**
✉ *Royal Pavilion Shop, Royal Pavilion* ☎ *01273/290337* ⊕ *www.visitbrighton.com.* **City Sightseeing** ☎ *01273/886200* ⊕ *www.city-sightseeing.com.*

EXPLORING

TOP ATTRACTIONS

Brighton Beach. Brighton's most iconic landmark is its famous beach, which sweeps smoothly from one end of town to the other. In summer sunbathers, swimmers, and hawkers selling ice cream and toys pack the shore; in winter people stroll at the water's stormy edge, walking their dogs and searching for seashells. The water is bracingly cold, and the beach is covered in a thick blanket of large, smooth pebbles (615 billion of them, according to the tourism office). ■TIP➔ Bring a pair of rubber swimming shoes if you're taking a dip-the stones are hard on bare feet.

Brighton Museum and Art Gallery. The grounds of the Royal Pavilion contain this museum, in a former stable block designed for the Prince Regent (1762–1830), son of George III. The museum has particularly interesting art nouveau and art deco collections. Look out for Salvador Dalí's famous sofa in the shape of Mae West's lips. The Fashion & Style Gallery has clothes from the Regency period to the present day, and

George IV loved the sea at Brighton and built the flamboyant Royal Pavilion as a seaside escape.

the Performance gallery has a collection of masks, puppets, and other theatrical curiosities. ⊠ *Royal Pavilion, Church St.* ☎ *0300/029–0900* ⊕ *www.brighton-hove-rpml.org.uk* ✉ *Free* ⊙ *Tues.–Sun. and bank holiday Mon., 10–5.*

FAMILY **Brighton Pier.** Opened in 1899, the pier is an amusement park set above the sea. In the early 20th century it had a music hall and entertainment; today it has roller coasters and other carnival rides, as well as game arcades, clairvoyants, candy stores, and greasy-food stalls. In summer it's packed with children by day and teenagers by night. The skeletal shadow of a pier you can see off in the water is all that's left of the old West Pier. ⊠ *Madeira Dr.* ☎ *01273/609361* ⊕ *www.brightonpier.co.uk* ⊙ *Daily 10–10.*

The Lanes. This maze of tiny alleys and passageways was once the home of fishermen and their families. Closed to vehicular traffic, the area's narrow cobbled streets are filled with interesting restaurants, boutiques, and antiques shops. Fish and seafood restaurants line the heart of the Lanes, at Market Street and Market Square. ⊠ *Bordered by West, North, East, and Prince Albert Sts..*

Fodor's Choice **Royal Pavilion.** The city's most remarkable building is this delightfully
★ over-the-top domed and pinnacled fantasy. Built as a simple seaside villa in the fashionable classical style of 1787 by architect Henry Holland, the Pavilion was rebuilt between 1815 and 1822 by John Nash for the Prince Regent (later George IV). The result was an exotic, foppish Eastern design with opulent Chinese interiors. The two great set pieces are the **Music Room**, styled in the form of a Chinese pavilion, and the **Banqueting Room**, with its enormous flying-dragon "gasolier," or gaslight chandelier, a revolutionary invention in the early 19th

century. The gardens, too, have been restored to Regency splendor, following John Nash's naturalistic design of 1826. ▦ TIP➜ For an elegant time-out, a tearoom serves snacks and light meals. ✉ *Old Steine* ☎ *03000/290900* ⊕ *www.royalpavilion.org.uk* 🎫 *£10* 🕐 *Oct.–Mar., daily 9:30–5:15; Apr.–Sept., daily 9:30–5:45; last admission 45 mins before closing.*

QUICK BITES

Mock Turtle. Less than a five-minute walk from the Royal Pavilion, the Mock Turtle is a great old-fashioned, homey café. Alongside a decent selection of teas and coffees are four types of rarebit, soups, and scones, as well as cakes and enormous doughnuts. It's closed Monday. ✉ *4 Pool Valley* ☎ *01273/327380.*

WORTH NOTING

FAMILY **Brighton Wheel.** Brighton's answer to the London Eye, this 50-metre (164-foot) Ferris wheel gives you a spectacular panorama of the town and the sea, from air-conditioned capsules. VIP tickets, including rides where wine or champagne is served, cost from £25 to £60 per person. ▦ TIP➜ There's a discount on all tickets if you book online. ✉ *Daltons Bastion, Madeira Dr.* ☎ *01273/722822* ⊕ *www.brightonwheel.com* 🎫 *£8* 🕐 *Sun.–Thurs. 10–9, Fri. and Sat. 10–11.*

FAMILY **Sea Life Centre.** Near Brighton Pier, this aquarium has many sea-dwelling creatures—from sharks to sea horses—in more than 30 marine habitats. A recent renovation added an octopus garden and a jellyfish disco (yes, really). ✉ *Marine Parade* ☎ *0871/423–2110* ⊕ *www.visitsealife.com/Brighton* 🎫 *£17.40* 🕐 *Apr.–Oct., daily 10–5; last admission 1 hr before closing.*

FAMILY **Volk's Electric Railway.** Built by inventor Magnus Volk in 1883, this was the first public electric railroad in Britain. In summer you can take the 1¼-mi trip along Marine Parade. ✉ *Marine Parade* ☎ *01273/292718* ⊕ *www.volkselectricrailway.co.uk* 🎫 *£3.50 round-trip* 🕐 *Easter–Sept., Mon. and Fri., 11:15–5; Tues.–Thurs., 10:15–5; weekends and bank holidays, 10:15–6.*

WHERE TO EAT

$$ SEAFOOD ✕ **Arch 139.** This casually chic restaurant looks out over the English Channel. Fresh local seafood is what the place is all about, so much so that the menu is divided not just by starters and mains, but also "crustacea" and "fruits de mer." Expect Asian-influenced flavors in such dishes as battered tiger prawns with sweet chili sauce, wok-fried crab or sea bass in a saffron and pernod sauce. More traditional dishes let the ingredients speak for themselves, as with the Sussex fish pie. Caviar, lobster, and three varieties of oyster add a touch of cut-glass sophistication. 🅢 *Average main: £16* ✉ *139 Kings Rd. Arches* ☎ *01273/821218* ⊕ *www.arch139.com* ⟲ *Reservations not accepted.*

Brighton and the Regent

The term "Regency" comes from the last 10 years of the reign of George III (1811–20), who was deemed unfit to rule because of his mental problems. Real power was officially given to the Prince of Wales, also known as the Prince Regent, who became King George IV and ruled until his death in 1830.

Throughout his regency, George spent grand sums indulging his flamboyant tastes in architecture and interior decorating—while failing in affairs of state.

The distinctive architecture of the Royal Pavilion is a prime, if extreme, example of the Regency style, popularized by architect John Nash (1752–1835) in the early part of the 19th century. The style is characterized by a diversity of influences—French, Greek, Italian, Persian, Japanese, Chinese, Roman, Indian—you name it. Nash was George IV's favorite architect, beloved for his interest in Indian and Asian art and for his neoclassical designs, as evidenced in his other most famous work—Regent's Park and its terraces in London.

$
CAFÉ

× **Bill's Produce.** Even groceries seem attractive at this casual, pleasant coffee shop–restaurant–deli. On tall shelves all around the light-filled dining room, bottles of olive oil and vinegars glisten alongside stacks of fresh fruit, vegetables, baskets, and flowers. Blackboards near the counter list the day's specials: these usually include a variety of salads, sandwiches (your choice of fresh breads), and a few hot dishes. Comfort food mains include burgers, fish pie, and mac and cheese. Breakfast is popular here, too. $ *Average main: £10* ⊠ *The Depot, 100 North Rd.* ☎ *01273/692894* ⊕ *www.bills-website.co.uk.*

$
MIDDLE EASTERN

× **Pomegranate.** A contemporary Kurdish restaurant, Pomegranate takes a lighthearted, fun approach to Middle Eastern cuisine. Its small dining area spreads over two floors and has large windows and exposed brick walls. The sprawling menu includes lamb with rosemary and lemon juice, or grilled chicken in a grape and honey sauce. For dessert, try the figs stuffed with walnuts and pomegranate. The lunch menu (£12.50 for three courses) is particularly good value. $ *Average main: £13* ⊠ *10 Manchester St.* ☎ *01273/628386* ⊕ *www.eatpomegranates.com.*

$$
SEAFOOD
Fodor's Choice
★

× **Riddle and Finns.** White tiles, bare metal tables, and sparkling chandeliers set the tone as soon as you walk through the door of this casually elegant restaurant—the more laid-back sister to ⇨ *Arch 139.* The house specialty is oysters, fresh and sustainably sourced, served with or without a tankard of black velvet (champagne and Guinness) on the side. Other options include sea bass with bubble and squeak (a traditional dish of fried vegetables and potatoes) or lobster, served with garlic and herb butter or thermidor. They don't take bookings, so come early or be prepared to wait. It's also open weekends for breakfast (and, yes, they serve oysters and champagne). $ *Average main: £16* ⊠ *12B Meeting House La.* ☎ *01273/323008* ⊕ *www.riddleandfinns.co.uk* ⌂ *Reservations not accepted.*

$$ MODERN BRITISH 🍴 **Seven Dials.** A former bank houses a restaurant that's undeniably striking and surprisingly laid-back, given the elegance of the cooking. Sophisticated Modern British cuisine rules the menu, with main dishes including rib eye with rosemary dauphine and purple sprouting broccoli, or black bream fillet with pearl barley. For dessert try the sticky toffee pudding (a sweet, steamed cake with toffee sauce) or red wine–poached pear with vanilla ice cream and pistachio praline. [$] *Average main: £15* ✉ *1 Buckingham Pl.* ☎ *01273/885555* 🌐 *www.sevendialsrestaurant.co.uk* ✍ *Reservations essential.*

$$ VEGETARIAN 🍴 **Terre à Terre.** This inspiring vegetarian restaurant is incredibly popular, so come early for a light lunch or later for a more sophisticated evening meal. Dishes have a pan-Asian influence, so you may start with Indian tandoori-spiced halloumi, before moving on to aubergine with tahini, sesame, and white miso. There's also an excellent collection of wines from around the globe. [$] *Average main: £15* ✉ *71 East St.* ☎ *01273/729051* 🌐 *www.terreaterre.co.uk* ⏲ *No lunch Tues. and Wed. in winter.*

WHERE TO STAY

For expanded hotel reviews, visit Fodors.com.

$ B&B/INN 🏨 **Brightonwave.** Chic and sleek, this hotel off the seafront but near Brighton Pier is all about relaxation. **Pros:** big, comfy beds; soothing decor. **Cons:** rooms on the small side; few extras. [$] *Rooms from: £95* ✉ *10 Madeira Pl.* ☎ *01273/676794* 🌐 *www.brightonwave.com* 🛏 *8 rooms* 🍽 *Breakfast.*

$$ HOTEL 🏨 **Drakes.** It's easy to miss the low-key sign for this elegant, modern hotel tucked away amid the frilly houses on Marine Parade; it's worth the trouble, because everything is cool, calm, and sleekly designed. **Pros:** attention to detail; well-designed bathrooms; excellent restaurant. **Cons:** 2-night minimum on weekends. [$] *Rooms from: £115* ✉ *43–44 Marine Parade* ☎ *01273/696934* 🌐 *www.drakesofbrighton.com* 🛏 *20 rooms* 🍽 *No meals.*

$$ HOTEL 🏨 **Grand Brighton.** The city's most famous hotel, this seafront landmark is a huge, creamy Victorian wedding cake of a building dating from 1864. **Pros:** as grand as its name; lovely sea views. **Cons:** a bit impersonal; prices can rise sharply at weekends. [$] *Rooms from: £160* ✉ *97–99 Kings Rd.* ☎ *01273/224300* 🌐 *www.devere-hotels.co.uk* 🛏 *200 rooms, 3 suites* 🍽 *Breakfast.*

$ HOTEL 🏨 **Granville Hotel.** Three grand Victorian buildings facing the sea make up this hotel where the themed guest quarters include the pink-and-white Brighton Rock Room and the art deco Noël Coward Room. **Pros:** creative design; friendly staff; rambunctious atmosphere. **Cons:** rooms are a bit too quirky; can get noisy. [$] *Rooms from: £89* ✉ *124 King's Rd.* ☎ *01273/326302* 🌐 *www.granvillehotel.co.uk* 🛏 *24 rooms* 🍽 *Breakfast.*

$$ HOTEL 🏨 **Hotel du Vin.** In the Lanes area, this outpost of a snazzy boutique chain has chic modern rooms. **Pros:** gorgeous rooms; comfortable beds; excellent restaurant. **Cons:** bar can get crowded; big price fluctuations in summer. [$] *Rooms from: £140* ✉ *Ship St.* ☎ *01273/718588* 🌐 *www.hotelduvin.com* 🛏 *40 rooms, 3 suites* 🍽 *No meals.*

3

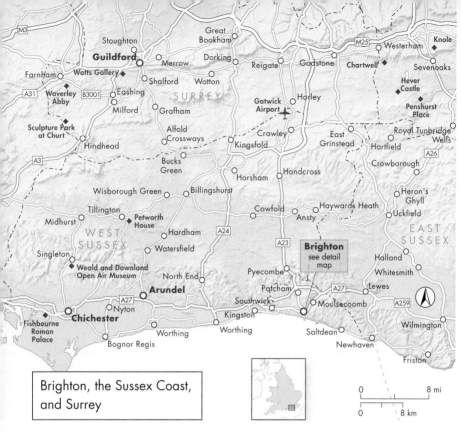

Brighton, the Sussex Coast, and Surrey

0 — 8 mi

0 — 8 km

$$
B&B/INN **Nineteen.** A calm oasis of white, this guesthouse is filled with contemporary art and designer accessories. **Pros:** relaxing rooms; innovative design; three nights for the price of two. **Cons:** not on the nicest street; two-night minimum on weekends. $ *Rooms from: £100* ✉ *19 Broad St.* ☏ *01273/675529* ⊕ *www.hotelnineteen.co.uk* ⤳ *8 rooms* ❑ *Breakfast.*

$
HOTEL **Oriental Brighton.** With a casual elegance that typifies Brighton, this Regency-era hotel sits close to the seafront. **Pros:** close to the beach; beautiful rooms. **Cons:** No restaurant; busy bar; minimum stay on weekends. $ *Rooms from: £85* ✉ *9 Oriental Pl.* ☏ *01273/205050* ⊕ *www.orientalbrighton.co.uk* ⤳ *9 rooms* ❑ *Breakfast.*

$
HOTEL **Pelirocco.** Here the imaginations of designers have been given free rein, and the result is a vicarious romp through pop culture and rock and roll. **Pros:** quirky design; laid-back atmosphere; near the beach. **Cons:** too form-over-function; no restaurant. $ *Rooms from: £99* ✉ *10 Regency Sq.* ☏ *01273/327055* ⊕ *www.hotelpelirocco.co.uk* ⤳ *18 rooms, 1 suite* ❑ *Breakfast.*

NIGHTLIFE AND THE ARTS
NIGHTLIFE

Brighton is a techno hub, largely because so many DJs have moved here from London. Clubs and bars present live music most nights, and on weekends the entire place can be a bit too raucous for some tastes. There's a large and enthusiastic gay scene.

Above Audio. The popular Above Audio, in an art deco building east of Brighton Pier, serves up a mix of house and underground music. ⊠ *10 Marine Parade* ☎ *01273/606906* ⊕ *www.audiobrighton.com.*

The Jazz Lounge at the Bohemia Grand Café. Every Thursday the best local jazz acts take over this upscale cafe-bar. It's arranged like a traditional jazz club, with table service and an old school vibe. ⊠ *54 Meeting House La.* ☎ *01273/777770* ⊕ *www.bohemiabrighton.co.uk.*

Proud Cabaret. A mixture of vintage and avant-garde cabaret and burlesque is on offer at this stylish nightclub, which also serves a 1920s-style three-course dinner from Thursday to Saturday. Booking is advisable. ⊠ *83 St. Georges Rd.* ☎ *01273/605789* ⊕ *www.brightoncabaret.com.*

The Tube. Underneath the Victorian arches on the seafront is one of Brighton's hottest nightclubs, with an eclectic range of dance, hip-hop, funk, soul, and indie playing until 6 am Wednesday to Saturday. ⊠ *169 King's Rd. Arches* ☎ *01273/725541.*

THE ARTS

Brighton Dome. West of the Royal Pavilion, the Brighton Dome was converted from the prince regent's stables in the 1930s. It includes a theater and a concert hall that stage pantomime (a traditional British children's play with songs and dance, usually featuring low-rent TV stars), and classical and pop concerts. ⊠ *Church St.* ☎ *01273/709709* ⊕ *www.brightondome.org.*

Brighton Festival. The three-week-long Brighton Festival, one of England's biggest and liveliest arts festivals, takes place every May in venues around town. The more than 600 events include drama, music, dance, and visual arts. ☎ *01273/709709* ⊕ *www.brightonfestival.org.*

Duke of York's Picture House. The elegant 1910 Duke of York's Picture House, a 10-minute walk north of the main train station, shows art-house movies. ⊠ *Preston Circus* ☎ *0871/902–5728* ⊕ *www.picturehouses.co.uk.*

Theatre Royal. Close to the Royal Pavilion, the Theatre Royal has a gem of an auditorium that's a favorite venue for shows on their way to or fresh from London's West End. ⊠ *35 Bond St.* ☎ *01273/328488.*

SHOPPING

Brighton Lanes Antique Centre. Although this shop specializes in gold and jewelry, it also has a good selection of furniture and ornaments. ⊠ *12 Meeting House La.* ☎ *01273/823121* ⊕ *www.brightonlanesantiques.co.uk.*

Colin Page. At the western edge of the Lanes, Colin Page stocks a wealth of antiquarian and secondhand books at all prices. ⊠ *36 Duke St.* ☎ *01273/325954.*

Cologne & Cotton. This lovely little bed-and-bath emporium sells vintage bed linens, blankets, bath products, and tableware. ⊠ *13 Pavilion Bldgs.* ☎ *01273/729666* ⊕ *www.cologneandcotton.com.*

Curiouser & Curiouser. This shop is filled with unique handmade jewelry, mostly sterling silver pieces with semiprecious stones. ⊠ *2 Sydney St.* ☎ *01273/673120* ⊕ *www.curiousersilverjewellery.co.uk.*

The Lanes. The main shopping area is the Lanes, especially for antiques or jewelry. It also has clothing boutiques, coffee shops, and pubs.

Lavender Room. This relaxing boutique tempts with scented calendars, glittery handmade jewelry, and little things you just can't live without. ⊠ *16 Bond St.* ☎ *01273/220380* ⊕ *www.lavender-room.co.uk.*

North Laine. Across North Street from the Lanes lies the North Laine, a network of narrow streets full of little stores. They're less glossy than those in the Lanes, but are fun, funky, and exotic.

Pavilion Shop. Next door to the Royal Pavilion, the Pavilion Shop carries well-designed toys, trinkets, books, and cards, all with a loose Regency theme. There are also high-quality fabrics, wallpapers, and ceramics based on material in the Pavilion itself. ⊠ *4–5 Pavilion Bldgs.* ☎ *03000/290900.*

Pecksniff's Bespoke Perfumery. The old-fashioned Pecksniff's Bespoke Perfumery mixes and matches ingredients to suit your wishes. ⊠ *45–46 Meeting House La.* ☎ *01273/723292.*

ARUNDEL

23 miles west of Brighton, 60 miles south of London.

The little hilltop town of Arundel is dominated by its great castle, the much-restored home of the dukes of Norfolk for more than 700 years, and an imposing neo-Gothic Roman Catholic cathedral (the duke is Britain's leading Catholic peer). The town itself is full of interesting old buildings and well worth a stroll.

GETTING HERE AND AROUND

Arundel is on the A27, about a two-hour drive south of central London. Trains from London's Victoria Station leave every half hour and take 90 minutes. No direct buses run from London, but you can take a National Express bus to Worthing or Chichester and change to a local bus to Arundel, though that journey could easily take five hours.

ESSENTIALS

Visitor Information Arundel Museum and Visitor Information Point ⊠ *1–3 Crown Yard Mews, off River Rd.* ☎ *01903/882419* ⊕ *www.sussexbythesea.com.*

EXPLORING

FAMILY

Fodor'sChoice

★

Arundel Castle. You've probably already seen Arundel Castle without knowing it—the striking resemblence to Windsor means that it's frequently used as a stand-in for its more famous cousin in movies and television. Begun in the 11th century, this vast castle remains rich with the history of the Fitzalan and Howard families and with paintings by Van Dyck, Gainsborough, and Reynolds. During the 18th century and in the Victorian era it was reconstructed in the fashionable Gothic style—although the keep, rising from its conical mound, is as old as the original castle (climb its 130 steps for great views of the River Arun), and the barbican and the Barons' Hall date from the 13th century. Among the treasures are the rosary beads and prayer book used by Mary, Queen of Scots, in preparing for her execution. The newly redesigned formal garden is a triumph of order and beauty. Although the castle's ceremonial entrance is at the top of High Street, you enter at the bottom, close to the parking lot. ⊠ *Mill Rd.* ☎ *01903/882173* ⊕ *www.arundelcastle. org* ⊠ *£17; grounds only £8* ☉ *Easter–early Nov., Tues.–Sun. and bank holidays 10–5 (keep closes 4:30); last admission 4.*

WHERE TO EAT AND STAY

For expanded hotel reviews, visit Fodors.com.

$$$
EUROPEAN
✕ **The Town House.** This small but elegant restaurant in a beautifully converted Regency town house (look up—the dining room ceiling is quite something) serves top-notch British and European cuisine. The fixed-price lunch and dinner menus change regularly, but could include roast partridge with spinach and wild mushrooms, or local sea bass with caramelized shallots and potato rosti. If you want to see more of the place, they also do bed and breakfast accommodation from £95 per night. $ *Average main: £24* ⊠ *65 High St.* ☎ *01903/883847* ⊕ *www. thetownhouse.co.uk.*

$$$$
HOTEL
Fodor's Choice
★
🏰 **Amberley Castle.** The lowering of the portcullis every night at midnight is a sure sign that you're in a genuine medieval castle. **Pros:** sleep in a real castle; lovely gardens and grounds. **Cons:** you have to dress for dinner. $ *Rooms from: £315* ⊠ *Off B2139, Amberley* ☎ *01798/831992* ⊕ *www.amberleycastle.co.uk* ⤶ *19 rooms* ⦿ *Breakfast.*

$
HOTEL
🏰 **Norfolk Arms Hotel.** Like the cathedral and the castle in Arundel, this 18th-century coaching inn on the main street was built by one of the dukes of Norfolk. **Pros:** charming building; historic setting. **Cons:** older rooms on the small side; a little old-fashioned. $ *Rooms from: £94* ⊠ *22 High St.* ☎ *01903/882101* ⊕ *www.norfolkarmshotel.com* ⤶ *34 rooms* ⦿ *Breakfast.*

NIGHTLIFE AND THE ARTS

Arundel Festival. The popular Arundel Festival presents dramatic productions and classical and pop concerts in and around the castle grounds for 10 days in late August or early September. ☎ *01903/883690* ⊕ *www. arundelfestival.co.uk.*

CHICHESTER

10 miles west of Arundel, 66 miles southwest of London.

The Romans founded Chichester, the capital city of West Sussex, on the low-lying plains between the wooded South Downs and the sea. The city walls and major streets follow the original Roman plan. This cathedral town, a good base for exploring the area, is a well-respected theatrical hub, with a reputation for attracting good acting talent during its summer repertory season. North of town is Petworth House, one of the region's finest stately homes.

GETTING HERE AND AROUND

From London, take A3 south and follow exit signs for Chichester. The 67-mile journey takes slightly more than two hours; much of it is on smaller highways. Southern trains run to Chichester several times an hour from Victoria Station, with a travel time of about 90 minutes. Buses leave from London's Victoria Coach Station every two hours and take just over three hours.

ESSENTIALS

Visitor Information **Chichester Tourist Information Centre** ⊠ *29A South St.* ☎ *01243/775888* ⊕ *www.visitchichester.org.*

EXPLORING

TOP ATTRACTIONS

Chichester Cathedral. Standing on Roman foundations, 900-year-old Chichester Cathedral has a glass panel that reveals Roman mosaics uncovered during restorations. Other treasures include the wonderful Saxon limestone reliefs of the raising of Lazarus and Christ arriving in Bethany, both in the choir area. Among the outstanding contemporary artworks are a stained-glass window by Marc Chagall and a colorful tapestry by John Piper. Free guided tours begin every day except Sunday at 11:15 and 2:30. You can also prebook tours that concentrate on subjects including the English Civil War and the cathedral's art collection; call or go online for details. ⊠ *West St.* ☎ *01243/782595* ⊕ *www. chichestercathedral.org.uk* ☞ *Free; £3 suggested donation* ☉ *Easter–Sept., daily 7:15–7; Oct.–Easter, daily 7:15–6.*

Fodor's Choice ★ **Fishbourne Roman Palace.** In 1960, workers digging a water-main ditch uncovered a Roman wall; so began nine years of archaeological excavation of this site, the remains of the largest, grandest Roman villa in Britain. Intricate mosaics (including Cupid riding a dolphin) and painted walls lavishly decorate what is left of many of the 100 rooms of the palace, built in the 1st century AD, possibly for local chieftain Tiberius Claudius Togidubnus. You can explore the sophisticated bathing and heating systems, along with the only example of a Roman garden in northern Europe. An expansion has added many modern attributes, including a video reconstruction of how the palace might have looked. The site is ½ mile west of Chichester. ⊠ *Salthill Rd., Fishbourne* ☎ *01243/785859* ⊕ *www.sussexpast.co.uk* ☞ *£8.50* ☉ *Feb. and Nov.–mid-Dec., daily 10–4; Mar.–Oct., daily 10–5; mid-Dec.–Jan., weekends 10–4.*

Fodor's Choice ★ **Pallant House Gallery.** This small but important collection of mostly modern British art includes work by Henry Moore and Graham Sutherland. It's in a modern extension to Pallant House, a mansion built for a wealthy wine merchant in 1712, and considered one of the finest surviving examples of Chichcester's Georgian past. At that time its state-of-the-art design showed the latest in complicated brickwork and superb wood carving. Appropriate antiques and porcelains furnish the faithfully restored rooms. Admission includes entry to the **Hans Fiebusch Studio,** nearby in St. Martin's Square, with an exact re-creation of the London studio of this exiled German artist (1898–1998) who was the last member of the so-called degenerate art group. ⊠ *9 N. Pallant* ☎ *01243/774557* ⊕ *www.pallant.org.uk* ☞ *£9* ☉ *Tues., Wed., Fri., and Sat. 10–5, Thurs. 10–8, Sun. and bank holidays 11–5.*

Fodor's Choice ★ **Petworth House.** One of the National Trust's greatest treasures, Petworth is the imposing 17th-century home of Lord and Lady Egremont and holds an outstanding collection of English paintings by Gainsborough,

Reynolds, and Van Dyck, as well as 19 oil paintings by J. M. W. Turner, the great proponent of romanticism who often visited Petworth and immortalized it in luminous drawings. A 13th-century chapel is all that remains of the original manor house. The celebrated landscape architect Capability Brown (1716–83) added a 700-acre deer park. Other highlights include Greek and Roman sculpture and Grinling Gibbons wood carvings, such as those in the spectacular Carved Room. Six rooms in the servants' quarters, among them the old kitchen, are also open to the public. A restaurant serves light lunches. You can reach the house off A283; Petworth House is 13 miles northeast of Chichester and 54 miles south of London. ⊠ *A283, Petworth* ☎ *01798/342207* ⊕ *www.nationaltrust.org.uk* 🎫 *£12.10; gardens only £4.70* ⊙ *House mid-Mar.–early Nov., Sat.–Wed. 11–5. Gardens Mar.–late Oct., Sat.–Wed. 11–6; Nov.–mid-Dec., Wed.–Sat. 10:30–6. Park daily 8–dusk.*

> ## A TEMPTING TOWN
>
> After you visit Petworth House, take time to explore the small town of Petworth, with its narrow old streets and timbered houses. Temptation awaits, too: this is a center for fine antiques and collectibles, with many excellent shops.

WORTH NOTING

FAMILY **Weald and Downland Open Air Museum.** On the outskirts of Singleton, a secluded village 5 miles north of Chichester, is this excellent museum, a sanctuary for historical buildings dating from the 13th to 19th centuries. Among the 45 structures moved to 50 acres of wooded meadows are a cluster of medieval houses, a water mill, a Tudor market hall, and an ancient blacksmith's shop. ⊠ *Town La., off A286, Singleton* ☎ *01243/811363* ⊕ *www.wealddown.co.uk* 🎫 *£11.50* ⊙ *Mar.–Dec., daily 10:30–6; Jan. and Feb., weekends and Wed. 10:30–4:30; last admission 1 hr before closing.*

WHERE TO EAT AND STAY

For expanded hotel reviews, visit Fodors.com.

$$$$ ✕ **Comme Ça.** The location, about a five-minute walk across the park
FRENCH from the Chichester Festival Theatre, makes this a popular spot for pre- and post-theater dinners. The dining room is relaxed and homey, with big windows and ceiling fans. The owner, Michel Navet, is French, and his chef produces sophisticated, authentic French dishes using fresh local produce. The prix-fixe menu changes regularly, but includes dishes like halibut wrapped in smoked salmon served with a horseradish and white wine velouté; or saddle of lamb in a brioche crust with thyme jus. The fixed-price lunch menu offers two courses for £22. $ *Average main: £30* ⊠ *67 Broyle Rd.* ☎ *01243/788724* ⊕ *www.commeca.co.uk* ⊙ *Closed Mon. No dinner Sun. No lunch Tues.*

$$ 🛏 **Ship Hotel.** Originally the home of Admiral George Murray, one of
HOTEL Admiral Nelson's right-hand men, this architecturally interesting hotel is known for its flying (partially freestanding) staircase and colonnade. **Pros:** well-restored building; good location. **Cons:** rooms are small; not many amenities. $ *Rooms from: £120* ⊠ *North St.* ☎ *01243/778000* ⊕ *www.theshiphotel.net* 🛏 *36 rooms* ⦿ *Multiple meal plans.*

NIGHTLIFE AND THE ARTS

Chichester Festival Theatre. The modernist Chichester Festival Theatre presents classics and modern plays from May through September and is a venue for touring companies the rest of the year. Built in 1962, it has an international reputation for innovative performances and attracts theatergoers from across the country. ⊠ *Oaklands Park, Broyle Rd.* ☎ *01243/781312* ⊕ *www.cft.org.uk.*

GUILDFORD

22 miles north of Petworth House, 35 miles north of Chichester, 28 miles southwest of London.

Guildford, the largest town in Surrey and the county's capital, has a lovely historic center with charming original storefronts. Gabled merchants' houses line the steep, pleasantly provincial High Street, where the remains of a Norman castle are tucked away in a peaceful garden, and the iconic clock on the old guildhall dates from 1683. The area around the train station is rather seedy and crowded, but once you make your way to the center it's a much more peaceful, pleasant town. Guildford is a good place to base yourself if you're planning to visit nearby attractions such as the Royal Horticulutral Society gardens in Wisley, or the ruins of Waverley Abbey.

GETTING HERE AND AROUND

From London, take A3 south and then exit onto the A31, following signs for Guildford. The 28-mile journey takes about an hour in traffic. Southwest trains run to Guildford every half hour from London's Waterloo Station; the trip takes between 30 minutes and an hour. Guildford Station is extremely busy and surrounded by traffic, but fortunately the center is a five-minute walk; just follow the signs for High Street. National Express buses travel from London to Guildford every couple of hours; the trip takes an hour.

ESSENTIALS

Visitor Information **Guildford Tourist Information Centre** ⊠ *155 High St.* ☎ *01483/444333* ⊕ *www.guildford.gov.uk.*

EXPLORING

TOP ATTRACTIONS

Fodor'sChoice ★ **Watts Gallery.** An extraordinary small museum that's often overlooked, Watts Gallery was built in tiny Compton in 1904 by the late-19th-century artist George Frederic Watts (1817–1904) to display his work. After a major renovation to the gallery, Watts' romantic, mystical paintings are beautifully displayed. His sculptures are astonishing both for their size and the near-obsessive attention to detail. Mary, his wife and a devotee of the art nouveau style, designed a stunning mortuary chapel nearby, covering the walls (inside and out) in elaborate paintings. It's about 50 yards from the museum in the village cemetery. The museum is 3 miles south of Guildford. ⊠ *Down La., Compton* ☎ *01483/810235* ⊕ *www.wattsgallery.org.uk* ⊠ *£7.50* ☉ *Tues.–Sat. and bank holiday Mon. 11–5, Sun. 1–5.*

Waverley Abbey. One of the oldest Cistercian abbeys in England, this was an important center of monastic power from 1128 until Henry VIII's dissolution of the monastries. What remains is a strikingly picturesque ruin surrounded by open countryside. Roofed sections of the undercroft and monks' dormitory survive, as does the refrectory tunnel and a magnificent yew tree in the former churchyard, thought to be around 700 years old. A more unexpected historical footnote sits on the banks of the abbey stream: moss-covered tank traps, overlooked from across a field by a pillbox (sniper station). They were placed here during World War II after British generals role-played a Nazi invasion and decided this was the route they'd choose to attack London. Unused plans later found in Berlin showed they were precisely right. The abbey is off the B3001, 9 miles southwest of Guildford. ⊠ *Waverley La., Farnham* ⊕ *www. english-heritage.org.uk* ⛭ *Free* ☉ *Daily dawn–dusk.*

Fodor'sChoice **Wisley.** In a nation of gardeners and garden goers, Wisley is the Royal
★ Horticultural Society's innovative and inspirational 240-acre showpiece. Both an ornamental and scientific center, it claims to have greater horticultural diversity than any other garden in the world. The flower borders and displays in the central area, the rock garden and alpine meadow in spring, and the large, modern conservatories are just a few highlights, along with an impressive bookstore and a garden center that sells more than 10,000 types of plants. The garden is 10 miles northeast of Guildford. ⊠ *A3, Woking* ☎ *0845/260–9000* ⊕ *www.rhs.org.uk/gardens/ wisley* ⛭ *£12* ☉ *Mar.–Oct., weekdays 10–6, weekends 9–6; Nov.–Feb., weekdays 10–4:30, weekends 9–4:30; last admission 1 hr before closing.*

WORTH NOTING

Guildford Museum. In the old castle building, this museum has exhibits on local history and archaeology, as well as memorabilia of Charles Dodgson, better known as Lewis Carroll, author of *Alice in Wonderland.* Dodgson spent his last years in a house on nearby Castle Hill and is buried in the Mount Cemetery, up the hill on High Street. Castle Arch, all that remains of the entrance of the old castle, displays a slot for a portcullis. ⊠ *Quarry St.* ☎ *01483/444751* ⊕ *www.guildfordmuseum. co.uk* ⛭ *Free* ☉ *Mon.–Sat. 11–5.*

Polesden Lacey. This gorgeous, creamy-yellow Regency mansion, built in 1824, contains impressive collections of furniture, paintings, porcelain, and silver gathered in the early part of the 20th century. Edwardian society hostess Mrs. Ronald Greville was responsible for the lavish interiors; the future King George VI stayed here for part of his honeymoon in 1923. On summer days you can wander its vast landscaped gardens or rent croquet equipment from the house and take advantage of its smooth lawns. The house is in Great Bookham, 8 miles from Guildford. ⊠ *Off A246, Great Bookham* ☎ *01372/458203* ⊕ *www.nationaltrust. org.uk* ⛭ *£11; gardens only £7* ☉ *House Mar.–Oct., weekdays 12:30–5, weekends 11–5; grounds daily 10–5 or dusk.*

FAMILY **Sculpture Park at Churt.** Set in a forested park 8 miles outside Guildford, this is a wild, fanciful place where giant metal spiders climb trees, bronze horses charge up hillsides, and metal girls and boys dance on lakes. You follow signposted paths across the parkland, spotting tiny sculptures up

HIKING IN THE SOUTHEAST

A walk on the South Downs provides some panoramic views.

For those who prefer to travel on their own two feet, the Southeast offers long sweeps of open terrain that makes walking a pleasure. Ardent walkers can explore all or part of the **North Downs Way** (153 miles) and the **South Downs Way** (106 miles), following ancient paths along the tops of the downs—the undulating treeless uplands typical of the area. Both trails are now part of the **South Downs National Park** (⊕ www.southdowns.gov.uk), but each maintains its separate identity.

TRAILS ON THE DOWNS

The North Downs Way starts outside Guildford, in the town of Farnham, alongside the A31. (You can park at the train station.) It passes along the White Cliffs of Dover and ends in the Dover town square. It follows part of the old Pilgrim's Way to Canterbury that so fascinated Chaucer.

The South Downs Way starts in Winchester, at Water Lane. It ends on the promenade in the seaside town of Eastbourne. Along the way it crosses the chalk landscape of Sussex Downs, with parts of the route going through deep woodland. Charming little villages serve the walkers cool ale in inns that have been doing precisely that for centuries.

The 30-mile **Downs Link** joins the two routes. Along the Kent coast, the Saxon Shore Way, stretching 143 miles from Gravesend to Rye, passes four Roman forts.

RESOURCES

Guides to these walks are available from the excellent website for **National Trails** (⊕ www. nationaltrail.co.uk). Tourist information offices throughout the region also have good information.

in trees, and walking through the legs of other more gigantic creations. You can also follow the footpath beside the little car park outside up to the **Devil's Jumps,** a rugged local beauty spot with views over the South Downs. The name derives from a piece of folklore: one night the devil stole a cauldron from a local witch, who gave chase on her broomstick. With each leap the devil kicked up huge clods of earth, which in turn became hills—hence "jumps." The park is off the A287 between Guildford and Farnham. ✉ *Jumps Rd., Churt* ☎ *01428/605453* 🌐 *www.thesculpturepark.com* 🎫 *£6* 🕓 *Weekdays 10–5, weekends 8:30–5.*

3

WHERE TO EAT

$ FRENCH 🍴 **Café Rouge.** Part of a chain of French-style cafés, this a great place to stop for a coffee, or to have a full lunch or dinner. The menu consists of bistro classics such as caesar salad, moules marinières, French onion soup, and steak frites. The wine list is decently priced, and the coffee is excellent. [$] *Average main: £12* ✉ *8–9 Chapel St.* ☎ *01483/451221* 🌐 *www.caferouge.co.uk.*

$ AMERICAN 🍴 **Gourmet Burger Kitchen.** This very popular place does what it says on the label—good burgers and not a lot else. You wait for a table, then order at the counter. All the burgers are excellent: try the Pesterella, with pesto and mozzarella; the Habernero, with spicy salsa; or the Wellington, with mushrooms and horseradish sauce. The enormous milk shakes are tasty diet-busters. One order of fries will be enough for two. [$] *Average main: £9* ✉ *10 Friary St.* ☎ *01483/572464* 🌐 *www.gbk.co.uk.*

$ BRITISH 🍴 **The Mill.** A short hop down the road from Waverley Abbey, this unusually handsome pub is in an old watermill (which is still working—you can see it in the lobby). The food is traditional British with a modern twist pub grub; beer-battered fish-and-chips is a specialty, or you might find tagliatelle, in a pumpkin, sage, and blue cheese sauce. The huge beer garden, overlooking the mill stream and usually patrolled by a flock of ducks, is an extremely popular spot in summer. The pub is on the B3001, 9 miles southwest of Guildford. [$] *Average main: £12* ✉ *Farnham Rd.* ☎ *01252/703333* 🌐 *www.millelstead.co.uk.*

$ THAI 🍴 **Rumwong.** With an incredibly long menu, Rumwong has dozens of choices from all over Thailand. Tasty dishes include the fisherman's soup, a spicy mass of delicious saltwater fish in a clear broth, or *yam pla muek,* a hot salad with squid. The owners also run an Asian supermarket next door. [$] *Average main: £9* ✉ *18–20 London Rd.* ☎ *01483/536092* 🌐 *www.rumwong.co.uk.*

WHERE TO STAY

For expanded hotel reviews, visit Fodors.com.

$ B&B/INN 🏨 **Old Great Halfpenny.** Surrounded by well-maintained grounds, this 16th-century half-timbered house looks like something out of a picture book. **Pros:** beautiful gardens; lovely old building; peace and quiet. **Cons:** a 15-minute drive out of town. [$] *Rooms from: £90* ✉ *Halfpenny La., St. Martha* ✥ *5 miles north of Guildford* ☎ *01483/567835* 🛏 *2 rooms* 💳 *No credit cards* 🍽 *Breakfast.*

Yvonne Arnaud Theatre. This horseshoe-shape theater on an island in the River Wey frequently previews West End productions. The smaller Mill Studio showcases more intimate productions. ⊠ *Off Millbrook* ☏ *01483/440000* ⊕ *www.yvonne-arnaud.co.uk*.

TUNBRIDGE WELLS AND ENVIRONS

England is famous for its magnificent stately homes and castles, but many of them are scattered across the country, presenting a challenge for travelers. Within a 15-mile radius of Tunbridge Wells, however, in that area of hills and hidden dells known as the Weald, lies a wealth of architectural wonder in historic homes, castles, and gardens: Penshurst Place, Hever Castle, Chartwell, Knole, Ightham Mote, Leeds Castle, and lovely Sissinghurst Castle Garden.

ROYAL TUNBRIDGE WELLS

39 miles southeast of London.

Nobody much bothers with the "Royal" anymore, but Tunbridge Wells is no less regal because of it. Because of its wealth and political conservatism, this historic bedroom community has been the subject of (somewhat envious) British humor for years. Its restaurants and lodgings make it a convenient base for exploring the many homes and gardens nearby.

The city owes its prosperity to the 17th- and 18th-century passion for spas and mineral baths. In 1606 a mineral-water spring was discovered here, drawing legions of royal visitors looking for eternal health. Tunbridge Wells reached its zenith in the mid-18th century, when Richard "Beau" Nash presided over its social life. The buildings at the lower end of High Street are mostly 18th century, but as the street climbs the hill north, changing its name to Mount Pleasant Road, structures become more modern.

GETTING HERE AND AROUND

Southeastern trains leave from London's Charing Cross Station every 15 minutes. The journey to Tunbridge Wells takes just under an hour. If you're traveling by car from London, head here on the A21; travel time is about an hour.

Tunbridge Wells sprawls in all directions, but the historic center is compact. None of the sights is more than a 10-minute walk from the main train station. You can pick up a town map at the station.

ESSENTIALS

Visitor Information **Royal Tunbridge Wells Tourist Information Centre** ⊠ *The Old Fish Market, The Pantiles* ☏ *01892/515675* ⊕ *www.visittunbridgewells.com.*

EXPLORING

All Saints Church. This modest 13th-century church holds one of the glories of 20th-century church art. The building is awash with the luminous yellows and blues of 12 windows by Marc Chagall (1887–1985),

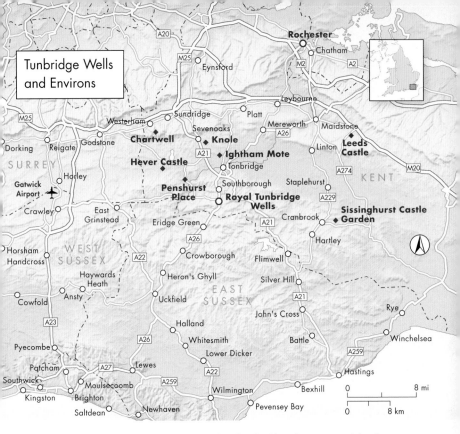

Rochester
Chatham
A20
M25
Eynsford
Leybourne
M2
A2
M25
Sundridge
Platt
Mereworth
Maidstone
Westerham
Sevenoaks
A26
Chartwell **Knole** Linton
Leeds
Godstone
A21 **Ightham Mote**
Castle
Dorking
Reigate
Hever Castle
Tonbridge
SURREY
A274
M20
Horley
Southborough
Staplehurst
KENT
Gatwick
Airport
Penshurst
Place
Royal Tunbridge
A229
East
Wells
Sissinghurst Castle
Crawley
Grinstead
Eridge Green
Cranbrook
Garden
A21
Horsham
WEST
A26
Hartley
Handcross
SUSSEX
A22
Crowborough
Flimwell
Haywards
Heron's Ghyll
Silver Hill
Heath
EAST
A21
Cowfold
Ansty
Uckfield
SUSSEX
Rye
A23
John's Cross
Halland
Winchelsea
Pyecombe
A26
Whitesmith
Battle
Patcham
Lower Dicker
A259
Southwick
A27
Lewes
Hastings
Kingston
Moulsecoomb
A259
Wilmington
Bexhill
Brighton
A22
0   8 mi
Saltdean
Newhaven
Pevensey Bay
0   8 km

commissioned as a tribute by the family of a young girl who was drowned in a sailing accident in 1963. The church is 4 miles north of Tunbridge Wells; turn off A26 before Tonbridge and continue a mile or so east along B2017. ⊠ *B2017, Tudeley* 🕾 *01732/808277* ⊠ *Free; £2.50 donation requested* ⊗ *Late Mar.–late Oct., daily 9–6; late Oct.– late Mar., daily 9–4.*

Church of King Charles the Martyr. Across the road from the Pantiles, this church dates from 1678, when it was dedicated to Charles I, who had been executed by Parliament in 1649. Its plain exterior belies its splendid interior, with a particularly beautiful plastered baroque ceiling. ⊠ *Chapel Pl.* 🕾 *01892/511745* ⊕ *www.kcmtw.org* ⊠ *Free* ⊗ *Mon.– Sat., 11–3.*

Pantiles. A good place to begin a visit is at the Pantiles, a famous promenade with colonnaded shops near the spring on one side of town. Its odd name derives from the Dutch "pan tiles" that originally paved the area. Now sandwiched between two busy main roads, the Pantiles remains an elegant, tranquil oasis, and the site of the actual well. ▌▌TIP➜ **You can still drink the waters when a "dipper" (the traditional water dispenser) is in attendance, from Easter through September.**

WHERE TO EAT

$
ASIAN
✕ **Himalayan Gurkha.** It's not what you might expect to find in the cozy confines of Tunbridge Wells, but the Nepalese cuisine at this friendly spot is popular with locals. Spicy mountain dishes are cooked with care in traditional clay ovens or barbecued on flaming charcoal. The vegetarian options are appealing, too. $ *Average main: £8* ⊠ *31 Church Rd.* ☎ *01892/527834* ⊕ *www.himalayangurkha.com.*

$
JAPANESE
Fodor's Choice
★
✕ **Kitsu.** Good Japanese food is often difficult to come by in England, so this tiny, unassuming restaurant seems an unlikely venue for the best sushi you're likely to find for miles. Everything is fresh and delicious, from the fragrant miso soup to the light tempura to the sushi platters that are big enough to share. For something heartier, try a bowl of steaming fried noodles or a katsu curry. There are only two drawbacks: the place doesn't take credit cards and doesn't serve alcohol, although you're welcome to bring your own. $ *Average main: £6* ⊠ *82a Victoria Rd.* ☎ *01892/515510* ⊕ *www.kitsu.co.uk* ⊟ *No credit cards.*

$$$$
FRENCH
✕ **Thackeray's House.** Once the home of Victorian novelist William Makepeace Thackeray, this mid-17th-century tile-hung house is now an elegant restaurant known for creative French cuisine. The menu changes daily, but often lists such dishes as roast beef with black truffle creamed potato, or poached lemon sole with pistachio crust and caremelized Belgium endive. $ *Average main: £25* ⊠ *85 London Rd.* ☎ *01892/511921* ⊕ *www.thackerays-restaurant.co.uk* ☯ *Closed Mon. and last wk in Dec. No dinner Sun.*

WHERE TO STAY

For expanded hotel reviews, visit Fodors.com.

$$
HOTEL
⌂ **Hotel du Vin.** An elegant sandstone house dating from 1762 has been transformed into a chic boutique hotel with polished wood floors and luxurious furnishings. **Pros:** historic building; luxurious linens. **Cons:** restaurant can get booked up; bar can be crowded. $ *Rooms from: £130* ⊠ *Crescent Rd., near Mount Pleasant Rd.* ☎ *01892/526455* ⊕ *www.hotelduvin.com* ⇌ *34 rooms* ⍩ *Breakfast.*

$
HOTEL
⌂ **Smart & Simple Hotel.** This small place near the train station takes a contemporary approach with rooms that are small but nicely decorated. **Pros:** handy location; free Wi-Fi. **Cons:** few services; no frills at all. $ *Rooms from: £75* ⊠ *54–57 London Rd.* ☎ *01892/552700* ⊕ *www. smartandsimple.co.uk* ⇌ *40 rooms* ⍩ *Some meals.*

$$
HOTEL
⌂ **Spa Hotel.** Carefully chosen furnishings and period-perfect details help maintain the country-house flavor of this 1766 Georgian mansion. **Pros:** lap-of-luxury feel; gorgeous views. **Cons:** breakfast is extra; very formal atmosphere; can be a bit stuffy. $ *Rooms from: £160* ⊠ *Mount Ephraim* ☎ *01892/520331* ⊕ *www.spahotel.co.uk* ⇌ *70 rooms* ⍩ *No meals.*

PENSHURST PLACE

7 miles northwest of Royal Tunbridge Wells, 33 miles southeast of London.

One of the best preserved of the great medieval houses in Britain, and surrounded by stunning landscaped gardens, Penshurst Place is like an Elizabethan time machine

GETTING HERE AND AROUND

To get to Penshurst, take the A26 north to Penshurst Road. The drive from Tunbridge Wells takes about 12 minutes. Buses 231 and 233 run from Tunbridge Wells to Penshurst; also 235 weekdays and 237 Saturdays only.

EXPLORING

Fodor's Choice ★ **Penshurst Place.** At the center of the adorable hamlet of Penshurst stands this fine medieval manor house, hidden behind tall trees and walls. Although it has a 14th-century hall, Penshurst is mainly Elizabethan and has been the family home of the Sidneys since 1552. The most famous Sidney is the Elizabethan poet Sir Philip, author of *Arcadia*. The **Baron's Hall,** topped with a chestnut roof, is the oldest and one of the grandest halls to survive from the early Middle Ages. Family portraits, furniture, tapestries, and armor help tell the story of this house that was first inhabited in 1341 by Sir John de Pulteney, the very wealthy four-time London mayor. On the grounds are a toy museum, a gift shop, and the enchanting 11-acre walled Italian Garden, which displays tulips and daffodils in spring, roses in summer. Take time to study the village's late-15th-century half-timber structures adorned with soaring brick chimneys. To get here from Tunbridge Wells, take the A26 and B2176. ⊠ *Rogues Hill, off Leicester Square* ☎ *01892/870307* ⊕ *www. penshurstplace.com* 🔳 *£10; grounds only, £8* ☉ *Mid-Feb.–late Mar., weekends 10:30–6; late Mar.–early Nov., daily 10:30–6. Last entry 1 hr before closing.*

WHERE TO EAT

For expanded hotel reviews, visit Fodors.com.

$ BRITISH ✕ **Spotted Dog.** This pub first opened its doors in 1520 and hardly appears to have changed. Its big inglenook fireplace and heavy beams give it character, the views from the hilltop are lovely, and the good food and friendly crowd make it a pleasure. Many ingredients are locally sourced, as is the ale. There's seating in the sunny garden in the summertime. The pub, which sells locally made ales, is a mile from Penshurst via the narrow B2188. 🜄 *Average main: £10* ⊠ *Smarts Hill* ☎ *01892/870253* ⊕ *www.spotteddogpub.co.uk.*

HEVER CASTLE

3 miles west of Penshurst, 10 miles northwest of Royal Tunbridge Wells, 30 miles southeast of London.

A fairy-tale medieval castle on the outside, and a Tudor mansion within, Hever contains layer on layer of history. It's one of the most unusual and romantic of the great English castles.

GETTING HERE AND AROUND

Hever Castle is best reached via the narrow, often one-lane B2026. From Tunbridge Wells, take A264 east then follow signs directing you north toward Hever.

EXPLORING

Fodor's Choice

★

Hever Castle. For some, 13th-century Hever Castle fits the stereotype of what a castle should look like: all turrets and battlements, the whole encircled by a water lily–bound moat. Here, at her childhood home, the unfortunate Anne Boleyn, second wife of Henry VIII and mother of Elizabeth I, was courted and won by Henry. He loved her dearly for a time but had her beheaded in 1536 after she failed to give birth to a son. He then gave Boleyn's home to his fourth wife, Anne of Cleves, as a present. Famous though it was, the castle fell into disrepair in the 19th century. When American millionaire William Waldorf Astor acquired it in 1903, he built a Tudor village to house his staff (it's now used for private functions) and created the stunning gardens, which today include an excellent yew maze, ponds, playgrounds, tea shops, gift shops, plant shops—you get the picture. There's a notable collection of Tudor portraits, and in summer activities are nonstop here, with jousting, falconry exhibitions, and country fairs, making this one of southern England's most rewarding castles to visit. In one of the Victorian wings, B&B rooms go for about £100 per night. ⊠ *Off B2026* ☎ *01732/865224* ⊕ *www.hevercastle.co.uk* ✉ *£15; grounds only £12.50* ⊙ *Castle Mar., Wed.–Sun., noon–5; Apr.–Oct., daily noon–6; Nov. and Dec., Wed.–Sun. 11–5. Grounds Mar., Wed.–Sun. 10:30–4; Apr.–Oct., daily 10:30–6; Nov. and Dec., Thurs.–Sun. 10:30–4; last admission 1 hr before closing.*

CHARTWELL

9 miles north of Hever Castle, 12 miles northwest of Royal Tunbridge Wells, 28 miles southeast of London.

Beloved of Winston Churchill, Chartwell retains a homely warmth despite its size and grandeur. Almost as lovely are the grounds, with a rose garden and magnificent views across rolling Kentish hills.

GETTING HERE AND AROUND

From Tunbridge Wells, take A21 north toward Sevenoaks, then turn east onto A25 and follow signs from there. You can travel to Chartwell by bus from the town of Sevenoaks. Take Go Coach 401, but check with the driver to make sure the bus passes near the mansion.

EXPLORING

Chartwell. A grand Victorian mansion with views over the Weald, Chartwell was the home of Sir Winston Churchill from 1924 until his death in 1965. Virtually everything has been kept as it was when he lived here, with his pictures, books, photos, and maps. There's even a half-smoked cigar that the World War II prime minister never finished. Churchill was an amateur artist, and his paintings show a softer side of the stiff-upper-lipped statesman. Admission to the house is by timed ticket available only the day of your visit. ■TIP→ Be sure to explore the rose gardens and take one of the walks in the nearby countryside. ⊠ *Off B2026*

☎ *01732/866368* ⊕ *www.nationaltrust.org.uk* ✉ *£12; garden only £6*
☻ *House Mar.–Oct., daily 11–5. Gardens Mar.–Oct., daily 10–5; Nov.–*
Feb., daily 11–4; last admission 45 mins before closing.

KNOLE

8 miles east of Chartwell, 11 miles north of Royal Tunbridge Wells, 27
miles southeast of London.

Perhaps the quintessential Tudor mansion, Knole is as famous for its
literary connections and impressive collection of furniture and tapestries
as it is for its elegant 15th and 16th century architecture.

GETTING HERE AND AROUND

To get to the town of Sevenoaks from Chartwell, drive north to Westerham, then pick up A25 and head east for 8 miles to A225. The route
is well signposted. Southeastern trains travel from London's Charing
Cross Station to Sevenoaks every few minutes and take about half an
hour. Knole is a 20-minute walk from the train station.

EXPLORING

Fodor's Choice **Knole.** The town of Sevenoaks lies in London's commuter belt, a world
★   away from the baronial air of its premier attraction, the grand, beloved
home of the Sackville family since the 16th century. Begun in the 15th
century and enlarged in 1603 by Thomas Sackville, Knole, with its
complex of courtyards and buildings, resembles a small town. You'll
need most of an afternoon to explore it thoroughly. The house is noted
for its tapestries, embroidered furnishings, and an extraordinary set of
17th-century silver furniture. Most of the salons are in the pre-baroque
mode, rather dark and armorial. The magnificently florid staircase was a
novelty in its Elizabethan heyday. Vita Sackville-West grew up here and
used it as the setting for her novel *The Edwardians*, a witty account of
life among the gilded set. Encircled by a 1,000-acre park where herds
of deer roam free, the house lies in the center of Sevenoaks, opposite
St. Nicholas Church. ✉ *Knole La., off A225* ☎ *01732/462100* ⊕ *www.*
nationaltrust.org.uk ✉ *House £10.40, gardens £5; parking £4* ☻ *House*
Mar., weekends noon–4; Apr.–Oct., Tues.–Sun., noon–4. Gardens Apr.–
Sept., Tues. 11–4. Last admission 30 mins before closing.

IGHTHAM MOTE

7 miles southeast of Knole, 10 miles north of Royal Tunbridge Wells,
31 miles southeast of London.

Almost unique among medieval manor houses in that it still has a moat
(although that has nothing to do with the name) Ightham is a captivating,
unreal-looking place reached down a warren of winding country lanes.

GETTING HERE AND AROUND

The house sits 6 miles south of Sevenoaks. From Sevenoaks, follow A25
east to A227 and then follow the signs. At the village of Ivy Hatch follow signs to tiny Mote Road, which winds its way to the house. The 404
bus from Sevenoaks stops here on Thursday and Friday only; otherwise
you'll have to get off in Ivy Hatch and walk just under a mile from there.

THE SOUTHEAST'S BEST HISTORIC HOUSES

Touring the Southeast's historic houses isn't just a procession of beautiful photo ops; it's a living history lesson. From modest manor houses to the sprawling stately homes of the aristocracy, each building has something to tell about private life or the history of the nation, and often the story is presented in an entertaining way.

(above) Penshurst Place gracefully evokes the Elizabethan era; (*right, top*) Bodiam Castle has a moat; (*right, bottom*) Hever Castle claims Tudor connections.

Historic houses reveal the evolution of the country, from medieval fortresses planned for defense to architectural wonders that displayed the owner's power. In time, gardens and grounds became another way to display status. Times, however, changed. And the aristocratic rewards of owning tracts of countryside, art, and family treasures encountered reality in the 20th century, as cash flow and death taxes presented huge challenges. Private owners opened homes to the public for a fee, some with marketing flair. Hundreds of other homes and castles are now owned by the National Trust or English Heritage, organizations that raise part of the money needed to maintain them through entrance fees.

BEYOND THE HOUSE

The idea of exploring historic houses may inspire joy—or, frankly, boredom. If the latter, please don't give up: many houses have gardens and extensive grounds that make a great day out for garden lovers or walkers. You may be able to purchase a ticket that includes only the grounds. Some houses have so many activities aimed at kids that the whole family will find something to do.

CHOOSING A HOUSE

We admit it: there are almost too many houses to visit in the Southeast, but they're conveniently close to each other. Here are the prime characteristics of some top spots to help you decide.

Arundel Castle: Still a family home for the duke of Norfolk, Arundel has its Norman-era keep and Barons' Hall, as well as magnificent examples of Gothic-style domestic remodeling by the Victorians.

Bodiam Castle: This place is what most of us picture when we think of a medieval castle, complete with turrets and an exquisite moat. However, the inside is mostly a ruin.

Chartwell: The National Trust owns this Victorian mansion, the former home of Winston Churchill. There's plenty of memorabilia, plus good woodland walks. Tours are by timed ticket.

Herstmonceux Castle: This romantic, moated 15th-century brick castle was saved by a 20th-century rehab. Only a few rooms are open (it's now a school), but they and the extensive gardens and grounds are evocative.

Hever Castle: Turrets, battlements, and a moat set the mood: Hever dates to the 13th century but has a Tudor link as the childhood home of Anne Boleyn, Henry VIII's second wife. The American Astors restored it after 1903. Gardens and activities—jousting, fairs—keep things entertaining.

Ightham Mote: Ideal for lovers of romantic antiquity, this 14th-century manor house also has a moat. The Great Hall is ancient, but there are Tudor and Victorian sections, too.

Knole: Home of the Sackvilles and now a National Trust property, this sprawling Tudor house resembles a village. Furnishings are dark and florid, and include a set of 17th-century silver furniture. Writer Vita Sackville-West grew up here.

Leeds Castle: The setting of this castle on two islands on a lake is amazing. The inside reflects a 20th-century refurbishing by the last owner, and family activities are plentiful. You can eat and spend the night here, too, at themed events.

Penshurst Place: For more than 500 years this medieval manor house has been the family home of the Sidneys. The medieval hall is famous, and the interior is Elizabethan. An 11-acre Italian garden and a toy museum are other interests.

Petworth House: Art lovers, take note: This sprawling 17th-century mansion has the National Trust's richest collection of paintings, including treasures by J. M. W. Turner, who visited here. Capability Brown's park is also a big draw.

Polesden Lacey: This National Trust property dates to the early 19th century but is famous for its lavish early 20th-century interiors.

TIPS FOR VISITING

Keep in mind that houses and castles are unique. You may be free to wander at will, or you may be organized into groups like prisoners behind enemy lines. Sometimes the exterior of a building may be spectacular, but the interior dull. And the gardens and grounds may be just as interesting as (or more so than) the house. Our individual reviews alert you to these instances, but you should study websites. You can often pay separately for the house and grounds.

Consider the kids. Some houses have activities or special events aimed at kids, especially in summer; some even have playgrounds.

Look into money-saving passes. If you plan to see lots of historic houses and castles, it might be cheaper to buy a pass, such as the ones from the National Trust or English Heritage, or to join an organization such as the National Trust (⇨ *Sightseeing Passes in Essentials in Travel Smart England*) and thus get free entry. Check entrance fees against your itinerary to be sure what you'll save.

Check seasonal opening hours. Hours can change abruptly, so call the day before or check online. Many houses are open only from April to October, and they may have unpredictable hours. In other cases the houses have celebrated parks and gardens that are open much of the year. Consider a trip in shoulder seasons if you can't take the crowds that pack the most popular houses. Some places are open during December.

Plan your transportation. Some places are very hard to reach without a car. Plan your transportation in advance—and remember that rural bus and train services can finish early!

Consider a stay at a property. You can rent a cottage from the **National Trust** (⊕ *www.nationaltrustcottages.co.uk*) or **English Heritage** (⊕ *www.english-heritage.org.uk/holidaycottages*).

Options include the servants' quarters, a lodge, or even a lighthouse. Some privately owned houses have cottages for rent on their estates; their websites generally have this information. The **Landmark Trust** (⊕ *www.landmarktrust.org.uk*) and **Vivat Trust** (⊕ *www.vivat-trust.org*) also have properties for rent.

EXPLORING

Ightham Mote. Finding Ightham (pronounced "Item") Mote requires careful navigation, but it's worth the effort to see a vision right out of the Middle Ages. To enter this outstanding example of a small manor house, you cross a stone bridge over a dry moat. This moat, however, doesn't relate to the "mote" in the name, which refers to the role of the house as a meeting place, or "moot." Built nearly 700 years ago, Ightham's magical exterior has changed little since the 14th century, but within you'll find that it encompasses styles of several periods, Tudor to Victorian. The Great Hall, Tudor chapel, and drawing room are all highlights. ✉ *Mote Rd., off A227, Sevenoaks* ☎ *01732/810378* ⊕ *www.nationaltrust.org.uk* 🎫 *£11.50; £5.75 in winter.* ⊘ *Mid-Mar.–Oct., Wed.–Mon. 11–5; Dec. (to 23rd), daily 11–3. Closed Nov., Jan., and Feb.*

> ### WORD OF MOUTH
>
> "Knole and Sissinghurst are two totally different animals. Into gardens and gardening? Definitely visit Sissinghurst. It is really amazing—but it does get VERY crowded, especially on weekends. Into major medieval stately homes? Knole fills the bill. (Very nice gardens there too, but they are only open once a week.) If it was me, I'd spend an overnight and see both plus Hever and Chartwell."
>
> –janisj

ROCHESTER

15 miles north of Ightham Mote, 28 miles southeast of London.

Positioned near the confluence of the Thames and the River Medway, this posh town has a history of Roman, Saxon, and Norman occupation, all of which have left architectural remains, including the vast castle at the town center. Novelist Charles Dickens called Rochester home for more than a decade, until his death in 1870, and would sometimes walk here all the way from London. You can take things at a much easier pace by strolling through the gardens of the Swiss-style chalet where he wrote. Every December the city hosts the Dickensian Christmas Festival.

Across the river from Rochester is Chatham, with a noted maritime museum and the Dickens World theme park.

GETTING HERE AND AROUND

To drive to Rochester, take the M2, turning off on the A2. The journey from London should take about 45 minutes. Southeastern trains run from several London stations, including St. Pancras, Victoria, and Charing Cross. The journey takes around 40 minutes.

ESSENTIALS

Visitor Information Rochester Visitor Information Centre ✉ *95 High St.* ☎ *01634/338141* ⊕ *www.visitmedway.org.*

EXPLORING

FAMILY **Dickens World.** Filling an aluminum-clad hangar in a giant shopping center, Dickens World is a literary theme park. Inside is a small but beautifully designed Victorian London scene where you can walk down an alley and climb the stairs in period houses. There's a schoolroom with a fierce

One of England's most notable stately homes, sprawling Knole displayed the power of the Sackvilles.

headmaster; a haunted house; a shop where you can buy Victorian-style trinkets; and a (silly but fun) boat ride down a narrow canal that's loosely based on the story of Pip and Magwitch in *Great Expectations*. The 3-D film about Dickens is actually pretty good. This place is very popular with school groups and families with young kids. ⊠ *Leviathan Way, Chatham* ☎ *01634/890421* ⊕ *www.dickensworld.co.uk* ⊠ *£13* ⊙ *Weekdays 10–4:30 (last admission 3), weekends 10–5:30 (last admission 4).*

Historic Dockyard. The buildings and 47 retired ships at the 80-acre dockyard across the River Medway from Rochester constitute the country's most complete Georgian-to-early-Victorian dockyard. Fans of maritime history could easily spend a day at the exhibits and structures. The dockyard's origins go back to the time of Henry VIII; some 400 ships were built here over the centuries. There's a guided tour of the submarine HMS *Ocelot*, the last warship to be built for the Royal Navy at Chatham. ■TIP→ Save your ticket, as it's good for a year. ⊠ *Chatham* ☎ *01634/823800* ⊕ *www.thedockyard.co.uk* ⊠ *£17.50* ⊙ *Mid-Feb.– Mar. and late Oct.–Dec., daily 10–4; Apr.–late Oct., 10–6; last admission 45 min before closing.*

Rochester Castle. The impressive ruins of Rochester Castle are a superb example of Norman military architecture. The keep, built in the 1100s using the old Roman city wall as a foundation, is the tallest in England. It's been shored up but left without floors, so that from the bottom you can see to the open roof and study the complex structure. At the shop you can pick up well-researched guides to the building. ⊠ *Boley Hill* ☎ *01634/402276* ⊕ *www.english-heritage.org.uk* ⊠ *£5.65* ⊙ *Apr.–Sept., daily 10–6; Oct.–Mar., daily 10–4; last admission 30 mins before closing.*

Rochester Cathedral. Augustine of Canterbury ordained the first English bishop in a small cathedral that stood on this site in the year 604. The current cathedral, England's second oldest, is a jumble of architectural styles. Much of the original Norman building from 1077 remains, including the striking west front, the highly carved portal, and the tympanum above the doorway. Some medieval art survives, including a 13th-century Wheel of Fortune on the choir walls; it's a reminder of how difficult medieval life was. ✉ *Boley Hill* ☎ *01634/843366* 🌐 *www.rochestercathedral.org* 🎟 *Free; £1 audio tour* 🕒 *Sun.–Fri. 7:30–6, Sat. 7:30–5. Tours Sun.–Fri. 10–4:30, Sat. 10–2.*

WHERE TO EAT AND STAY

For expanded hotel reviews, visit Fodors.com.

$ ITALIAN 🍴 **Don Vincenzo.** This lively Italian trattoria in the center of Rochester specializes in delicious pizza. One of the best is the simple *capriana*, topped with mozarella, goat cheese, tomato, and arugula. If that's just not enough to satisfy your appetite, try a hearty calzone stuffed with two types of Italian cheeses, tomatoes, and salami. There's also a good range of pasta, fish, and meat dishes. Best of all, the prices are reasonable. [$] *Average main: £10* ✉ *108 High St.* ☎ *01634/408373* 🌐 *www.donvincenzo.co.uk.*

$ B&B/INN 🏨 **Orchard Cottage.** Longtime Rochester locals Kevin and Sue Farrelly run this sweet little B&B overlooking the Kent countryside. **Pros:** friendly and helpful owners; you feel more like a houseguest than a customer. **Cons:** few frills; building isn't very interesting. [$] *Rooms from: £70* ✉ *11 View Rd.* ☎ *01634/222780* 🌐 *www.orchardcottagekent.co.uk* 🛏 *5 rooms* 🍽 *Breakfast.*

NIGHTLIFE AND THE ARTS

Fodor's Choice ★ **Dickensian Christmas Festival.** Rochester sponsors a Dickensian Christmas Festival on the first weekend in December. Thousands of people in period dress participate in reenactments of scenes from *A Christmas Carol*. A candlelight procession, mulled wine and roasted chestnuts, and Christmas carols at the cathedral add to the celebration. There's also a summer festival that takes place in early June. Two other important Dickens festivals take place in Broadstairs, 40 miles east, every June and December. ☎ *01634/306000* 🌐 *www.rochesterdickensfestival.org.uk.*

LEEDS CASTLE

12 miles south of Rochester, 19 miles northwest of Royal Tunbridge Wells, 40 miles southeast of London.

Every inch the grand medieval castle, Leeds is a like a storybook illustration of what an English castle should look like—from the fortresslike exterior to the breathtaking rooms within.

GETTING HERE AND AROUND

Just off the M20 motorway, signs direct you to Leeds Castle from every road in the area, so it's hard to miss.

EXPLORING

Fodor's Choice ★ **Leeds Castle.** The bubbling River Medway runs through Maidstone, Kent's county seat, with its backdrop of chalky downs. Nearby, the fairy-tale stronghold of Leeds Castle commands two small islands on a peaceful lake. Dating to the 9th century and rebuilt by the Normans in 1119, Leeds (not to be confused with the city in the north of England) became a favorite home of many medieval English queens. Henry VIII liked it so much he had it converted from a fortress into a grand palace. The interior doesn't match the glories of the much-photographed exterior, although there are fine paintings and furniture, including many pieces from the 20th-century refurbishment by the castle's last private owner, Lady Baillie. The outside attractions are more impressive and include a maze, a grotto, an aviary of native and exotic birds, and woodland gardens. The castle is 5 miles east of Maidstone. ✉ A20 ☎ 01622/765400 ⊕ www.leedscastle.org.uk ⛶ £20 ⊙ Apr.–Sept., daily 10:30–6 (last admission 4:30); Oct.–Mar., daily 10:30–4 (last admission 3).

SISSINGHURST CASTLE GARDEN

10 miles south of Leeds Castle, 53 miles southeast of London.

Impeccable literary credentials go hand in hand with enchanting grounds, magnificent countryside views, and even a working kitchen garden at this beautiful home in the Sussex countryside.

GETTING HERE AND AROUND

For those without a car, take a train from London's Charing Cross Station and transfer to a bus in Staplehurst. Direct buses operate on Tuesday, Friday, and Sunday between May and August; at other times, take the bus to Sissinghurst village and walk the remaining 1¼ mile. From Leeds Castle, make your way south on B2163 and A274 through Headcorn, and then follow signs.

EXPLORING

Fodor's Choice ★ **Sissinghurst Castle Garden.** One of the most famous gardens in the world, unpretentiously beautiful and quintessentially English, Sissinghurst rests deep in the Kentish countryside. The gardens, with 10 themed "rooms," were laid out in the 1930s around the remains of part of a moated Tudor castle by writer Vita Sackville-West (one of the Sackvilles of Knole, her childhood home) and her husband, diplomat Harold Nicolson. ■ TIP→ **Climb the tower to see Sackville-West's study and to get wonderful views of the garden and surrounding fields. The view is best in June and July, when the roses are in bloom.** The beautiful White Garden is filled with snow-color flowers and silver-gray foliage, while the herb and cottage gardens reveal Sackville-West's encyclopedic knowledge of plants. There are woodland and lake walks, too, making it easy to spend a half day or more here. Stop by the big tea shop for lunch made with the farm's fruits and vegetables. If you'd like to linger, the National Trust rents the Priest's House on the property for a minimum stay of three nights. ✉ A262 ☎ 01580/710700 ⊕ www.nationaltrust. org.uk ⛶ Jan.–Nov., £10.80; Dec., £5.40 ⊙ Garden: Mar.–early Nov., daily 11–5:30; Dec., 11–3:30; last admission at 4:30. Closed early–late Nov. Estate: daily dawn–dusk.

WHERE TO STAY

For expanded hotel reviews, visit Fodors.com.

$

B&B/INN

Bishopsdale Oast. This converted 18th-century double-kiln oasthouse (used for drying hops) makes an atmospheric place to stay in tiny Biddenden, near Sissinghurst. **Pros:** quiet and restful setting; owner is a chef, so breakfasts are great; nice garden. **Cons:** some rooms are small; car needed to get around. $ *Rooms from: £90 ⊠ Off Tenterden Rd., Biddenden* ☎ *01580/291027* ⊕ *www.bishopsdaleoast.co.uk* ⤶ *5 rooms* ⊺◯⊦ *Breakfast.*

$$$

B&B/INN

Fodor's Choice

★

Sissinghurst Castle Farmhouse. On the grounds of Sissinghurst Castle, this beautiful 1885 farmhouse was lovingly restored by the National Trust in 2009; bedrooms are simple but quite spacious, decorated in historical color schemes, and boast sumptuous views across the estate. **Pros:** beautiful location on the grounds of a historic home; lovely hosts; elevator makes building more accessible than most older B&Bs; discounts for two or more nights. **Cons:** few amenities; need a car to get here. $ *Rooms from: £165 ⊠ The Street, Sissinghurst* ☎ *01580/720992* ⊕ *www.sissinghurstcastlefarmhouse.com* ⤶ *7 rooms* ⊺◯⊦ *Breakfast.*

4

THE SOUTH

WELCOME TO THE SOUTH

TOP REASONS TO GO

★ **Salisbury Cathedral:** At one of England's most spectacular cathedrals, try a tour around the roof and spire for a fascinating angle on this must-see monument.

★ **Stonehenge:** At the right time of day (early or late is best), this mystical ring of stones can cast a memorable spell against the backdrop of Salisbury Plain.

★ **House and garden at Stourhead:** It's the perfect English combination. An 18th-century Palladian mansion plus acres of landscaped parkland, induce feelings of bliss.

★ **The New Forest:** Get away from it all in the South's most extensive woodland, crisscrossed by myriad trails that are ideal for horseback riding, hiking, and biking.

★ **Literary trails:** Jane Austen, Thomas Hardy, John Fowles, and Ian McEwan have made this area essential for book buffs, with a concentration of sights in Chawton, Dorchester, Chesil Beach, and Lyme Regis.

1 **Winchester, Portsmouth, and Southampton.** One of the region's most compelling and historically rich towns, Winchester lies a short distance from the well-heeled villages of New Alresford and Chawton and the great south-coast ports of Portsmouth and Southampton.

2 **Isle of Wight.** Osborne House, near Cowes, and Carisbrooke Castle, outside Newport, have much historic interest. The picturesque east-coast resorts of Ryde and Ventnor contrast with the dramatic Needles, the island's most iconic landmark, on the western tip.

GETTING ORIENTED

In the south of England, the inland county of Wiltshire's wide-open Salisbury Plain offers a sharp contrast to the sheltered villages of coastal Hampshire and Dorset and the bustle of the port cities of Southampton and Portsmouth. Spend your nights in the more culturally compelling towns of Salisbury and Winchester instead of these cities. One draw outside Salisbury is Stonehenge; you're also near the stone circles at Avebury. From there you can swing south to the New Forest. The southern coast of Dorset has a couple of popular vacation resorts, Bournemouth and Weymouth, and some historic sites: Corfe Castle, Maiden Castle, and Cerne Abbas. Lyme Regis, at the center of the wide arc of Lyme Bay, is a vacation favorite. It provides a gateway to the Jurassic Coast, a World Heritage Site that stretches between Swanage in the east and Exmouth in Devon.

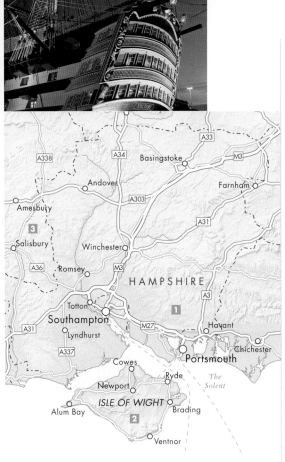

4 New Forest, Dorset, and the South Coast. The sparsely populated New Forest stretches between Southampton and Bournemouth. The route west passes Wimborne Minster, dominated by its church, and ruined Corfe Castle. Also worth a stop are the market towns of Shaftesbury and Sherborne, as well as Dorchester and coastal Weymouth and Lyme Regis.

3 Salisbury, Stonehenge, and Salisbury Plain. A tour of Wiltshire kicks off in the cathedral city of Salisbury, close to Wilton, Stonehenge, and Avebury. Farther afield are the great estates of Stourhead and Longleat.

FOSSIL HUNTING ON THE JURASSIC COAST

Besides the dramatic beauty of its jagged cliffs and hidden coves, the lure of the Jurassic Coast for visitors is fossils and fossil hunting. The varied and dramatic coastline is a World Heritage Site encompassing 200 million years of geological history, and constant erosion makes finding fossils a distinct possibility.

A geological journey through time, the Jurassic Coast stretches for 95 miles between the younger, Cretaceous chalk stacks at Studland Bay in Dorset in the east to the older, striking red Triassic cliffs at Exmouth (Devon) in the west. The earliest Jurassic cliffs of West Dorset formed in a tropical sea that flooded a vast desert. After the sea level dropped 140 million years ago, forest, swampland, and dinosaurs thrived, before the rising sea flooded the area once again. Fossils are continuously being uncovered, and both amateurs and professionals have made many important finds here. Coastal towns and villages act as gateways to the site, offering tourist information, boat trips, and guided fossil walks.

(above) Scenery can distract you from fossil hunting on the beautiful Jurassic Coast; (right, top) Intriguing fossil finds; (right, bottom) The coast near Charmouth

MARY ANNING

In 1811 a local child named Mary Anning (1799–1847) dug out an ichthyosaur skeleton near Lyme Regis; it's now on display in London's Natural History Museum. Anning's obsession with Jurassic remains left her labeled locally as the "fossil woman." Throughout her life she made many valuable discoveries that were sought after by museums and collectors in Britain, Europe, and beyond.

WHEN TO GO

If you're intent on collecting fossils, consider visiting in winter, when storms and rough seas encourage cliff erosion that sweeps fossils onto the beaches below. Search at low tide if you want the very best chance of making discoveries. Winter is less crowded, too. In summer the seas are calmer and the weather is more reliable. Although summer is busier with visitors, the days are longer and buses more frequent—a plus if you're exploring the coastal path.

WHAT TO LOOK FOR

Fossil hunters should stick to the area around Charmouth (the beach below Stonebarrow Hill, east of Charmouth, is especially fruitful) and Lyme Regis. The rock here is rich in fossils of the creatures that lived in the Jurassic oceans, and is especially prone to rapid erosion. You're free to pick and chip at the rocks; no permit is needed.

Keep your eyes peeled on the shore at low tide and you may well find ammonites. These chambered cephalopods from the Jurassic era, related to today's nautilus, are usually preserved in either calcite or iron pyrite ("fool's gold"); shinier, more fragile specimens may be found in aragonite. Visit the museums in Lyme Regis and Dorchester to remind you what to look for: the lustrous spirals are similar in heft and size to a brass coin, most smaller than a 10p

4

piece. Other common fossils include sea urchins, white oyster shells, and coiled worm tubes. Look out for belemnites, an extinct cephalopod.

SEEING THE COAST

The South West Coast Path National Trail, more than 600 miles long, passes through the area and is a great way to get closer to the Jurassic Coast. The First X53 bus travels along the Jurassic Coast from Poole to Weymouth and Exeter, and allows you to walk a section of the path and return by bus.

You can join a pro: information on guided walks is available from local tourist offices and the Lyme Regis Museum. Operators offer boat trips from gateway towns, an easy way to appreciate the coastline. See the boards at harbors, or ask at information centers. Fossil collector **Brandon Lennon** (☎ *07944/664757* ⊕ *www.lymeregisfossilsforsale.co.uk* ✉ *£7*) runs fossil-hunting expeditions with geologist Ian Lennon. A mile east of Lyme Regis, the **Charmouth Heritage Coast Centre** (☎ *01297/560772* ⊕ *www. charmouth.org* ✉ *£7.50 walks*) offers walks, kids' events, and a permanent exhibit. Late March through November, **Harry May** (☎ *07974/753287* ⊕ *www. mackerelfishinglymeregis.com* ✉ *£9*) operates mackerel fishing and sightseeing boat trips on the *Marie F* and the *Sunbeam* from the Cobb in Lyme Regis.

Updated by
Ellin Stein

Cathedrals, stately homes, stone circles—the South, made up of Hampshire, Dorset, and Wiltshire counties, holds all kinds of attractions, and not a few quiet pleasures. Two important cathedrals, Winchester and Salisbury (pronounced *sawls-bree*), are here, as are stately homes—Longleat, Stourhead, and Wilton House, among them—intriguing market towns, and hundreds of evocative prehistoric remains, two of which, Avebury and Stonehenge, shouldn't be missed.

These are just the tourist-brochure superlatives. Anyone spending time in these parts should rent a bike or a car and set out to discover the back-road villages. Close to London, the green fields of Hampshire divide the cliffs and coves of the West Country from the hustle and bustle of the big city. Even if you have a coastal destination in mind, hit the brakes—there's plenty to see. One of the many historical highlights was when Alfred the Great, a pioneer in establishing the rule of law and considered to be the first king of a united England, made Winchester his capital in the 9th century. Winchester is dominated by its imposing cathedral, the final resting place of notables ranging from Saxon kings to the son of William the Conqueror to Jane Austen. This town is a good base for visiting quiet villages where many of England's literary greats lived or died. The road to Austen's home at Chawton is a much-trodden path.

North of Hampshire and the New Forest lies the somewhat harsher terrain of Salisbury Plain, part of it owned by the British army and used for training and weapons testing. Two monuments, millennia apart, stand sentinel over the plain. One is the 404-foot-tall stone spire of Salisbury Cathedral, immortalized in oil by John Constable. Not far away is the most imposing and dramatic prehistoric structure in Europe: Stonehenge. The many theories about its construction and purpose only add to its mystical attraction.

Other districts have their own pleasures, and many have literary or historical associations. Turn your sights to the Dorset heathland, the countryside explored in the novels of Thomas Hardy. This district is spanned by grass-covered chalk hills—the downs—wooded valleys, meandering rivers, and meadows. Busy beach resorts sit next to hidden coves, interspersed with unspoiled market towns and villages. Dorset's Lyme Regis sits on the fossil-rich Jurassic Coast, while just of Hampshire is the Isle of Wight—Queen Victoria's favorite getaway—where colorful flags flutter from the many sailboats at Cowes, home of the famous regatta. The South has been quietly central to England's history for well over 4,000 years, occupied successively by prehistoric man, the Celts, the Romans, the Saxons, the Normans, and the modern British. History continues to be made here. On D-Day, Allied forces sailed for Normandy from this coast; nearly 40 years later, British forces set out to recover the Falklands.

SOUTH PLANNER

WHEN TO GO

In summer the coastal resorts of Bournemouth and Weymouth are crowded; it may be difficult to find the accommodations you want. The Isle of Wight gets its fair share of summer visitors, too, especially during the weeklong Cowes Regatta in late July or early August. Because ferries fill up to capacity, you may have to wait for the next one. The New Forest is most alluring in spring and early summer (for the foaling season) and fall (for the colorful foliage), whereas summer can be busy with walkers and campers. In all seasons, take waterproof boots for the mud and puddles. Major attractions such as Stonehenge and Longleat House attract plenty of people at all times; bypass such sights on weekends, public holidays, or school vacations. Don't plan to visit the cathedrals of Salisbury and Winchester on a Sunday, when your visit will be restricted, or during services, when it won't be appreciated by worshippers.

PLANNING YOUR TIME

The South has no obvious hub, though many people base themselves in one or both of the cathedral cities of Winchester and Salisbury and make excursions to nearby destinations. The coastal cities of Portsmouth and Southampton have their charms, but neither of these large urban centers is particularly attractive as an overnight stop. Busy Bournemouth, whose major sight is a Victorian-era museum, has quieter areas that are more conducive to relaxation. To escape the bustle, the New Forest, southwest of Southampton, offers space and semi wilderness. It's easy to take a morning or afternoon break to enjoy the activities it offers, whether on foot, by bike, or on horseback. The Isle of Wight needs more time, and is worth exploring at leisure over at least a couple of days.

GETTING HERE AND AROUND
BUS TRAVEL

National Express buses at London's Victoria Coach Station on Buckingham Palace Road depart every one to two hours for Bournemouth (2½ hours), Southampton (2¼), and Portsmouth (1¾ hours), and every two to three hours for Winchester (1¾). There are five buses daily to Salisbury (about three hours). Bluestar operates a comprehensive service in the Southampton and Winchester area, and Stagecoach South has service in Portsmouth and around Hampshire. Salisbury Red serves

Salisbury, More travels to Bournemouth and Poole, and First serves Portsmouth, Southampton, and Dorchester, and Southern Vectis covers the Isle of Wight. More and Salisbury Reds both offer one-day Dayrider or Explorer passes as well as weekly and monthly Period passes valid on all routes. Ask about the Megarider tickets offered by Stagecoach, Rover and Freedom tickets offered by Southern Vectis. Contact Traveline for all information on routes and tickets.

Bus Contacts Bluestar ☎ 023/8023–1950 ⊕ www.bluestarbus.co.uk. **First** ☎ 0871/200–2233 ⊕ www.firstgroup.com. **More** ☎ 0845/072–7093 ⊕ www.morebus.co.uk. **National Express** ☎ 0871/781–8178 ⊕ www. nationalexpress.com. **Salisbury Reds** ☎ 0845/072–093 ⊕ www.salisburyreds. co.uk. **Southern Vectis** ☎ 0871/200–2233 ⊕ www.islandbuses.info. **Stagecoach South** ☎ 0845/121–0190 ⊕ www.stagecoachbus.com. **Traveline** ☎ 0871/200–2233 ⊕ www.traveline.org.uk.

CAR TRAVEL

On the whole, the region is easily negotiable using public transportation. But for rural spots, especially the grand country estates, a car is useful. The well-developed road network includes M3 to Winchester (70 miles from London) and Southampton (77 miles); A3 to Portsmouth (77 miles); and M27 along the coast, from the New Forest and Southampton to Portsmouth. For Salisbury, take M3 to A303, then A30. A35 connects Bournemouth to Dorchester and Lyme Regis, and A350 runs north to Dorset's inland destinations.

TRAIN TRAVEL

South West Trains serves the South from London's Waterloo Station. Travel times average 1 hour to Winchester, 1½ hours to Southampton, 1¾ hours to Bournemouth, and 2¾ hours to Weymouth. The trip to Salisbury takes 1½ hours, and Portsmouth about 1¾ hours. A yearlong Network Railcard, valid throughout the South and Southeast, entitles you and up to three accompanying adults to one-third off most train fares, and up to four accompanying children ages 5–15 to a 60% discount off each child fare. It costs £28.

Train Contacts National Rail Enquiries ☎ 0845/748–4950 ⊕ www.nationalrail.co.uk. **South West Trains** ☎ 0845/600–0650 ⊕ www.southwesttrains.co.uk.

TOURS

The Guild of Registered Tourist Guides maintains a directory of qualified Blue Badge guides who can meet you anywhere in the region for private tours. Local organizations such as Wessexplore can also arrange Blue Badge tours. On the Isle of Wight, Southern Vectis operates open-top bus tours.

Tour Information Guild of Registered Tourist Guides ☎ 0207/403–1115 ⊕ www.britainsbestguides.org. **Wessexplore** ☎ 01722/326304 ⊕ www.dmac. co.uk/wessexplore.

RESTAURANTS

In summer, and especially on summer weekends, visitors can overrun the restaurants in small villages, so either book a table in advance or be prepared to wait. The more popular or upscale the restaurant, the more critical a reservation is. For local specialties, try fresh-grilled river trout or sea bass poached in brine, or dine like a king on New Forest's renowned venison. Hampshire is noted for its pig and sheep farming, and you might zero in on pork and lamb dishes on local restaurant menus. The region places a strong emphasis on seasonal produce, so venison, for example, is best sampled between September and February. *Prices in the reviews are the average cost of a main course at dinner or, if dinner isn't served, at lunch.*

HOTELS

Modern hotel chains are well represented, and in rural areas you can choose between elegant country-house hotels, traditional coaching inns (updated to different degrees), and modest guesthouses. Some seaside hotels don't accept one-night bookings in summer. If you plan to visit Cowes on the Isle of Wight during Cowes Week, the annual yachting jamboree in late July or early August, book well in advance. *Prices in the reviews are the lowest cost of a standard double room in high season, including 20% V.A.T.*

VISITOR INFORMATION

Visitor Information Tourism South East ☎ *023/8062–5400* ⊕ *www. visitsoutheastengland.com.* **Southwest Tourism Alliance** ☎ *0117/230–262* ⊕ *www.visitsouthwest.co.uk.*

WINCHESTER, PORTSMOUTH, AND SOUTHAMPTON

From the cathedral city of Winchester, 70 miles southwest of London, you can meander southward to the coast, stopping at the bustling ports of Southampton and Portsmouth to explore their maritime heritage. From either port you can strike out for the restful shores of the Isle of Wight, vacation destination of Queen Victoria and thousands of modern-day Britons.

WINCHESTER

66 miles southwest of London, 12 miles northeast of Southampton.

Winchester is among the most historic of English cities, and as you walk the graceful streets and wander the many public gardens, a sense of the past envelops you. Although it's now merely the county seat of Hampshire, for more than four centuries Winchester served first as the capital of the ancient kingdom of Wessex and then of England. Here, in AD 827, Egbert was crowned first king of England, and his successor, Alfred the Great, held court until his death in 899. After the Norman Conquest in 1066, William I ("the Conqueror") had himself crowned in London, but took the precaution of repeating the ceremony in Winchester. William also commissioned the local monastery to produce the Domesday Book, a land survey begun in 1085. The city remained the center of ecclesiastical, commercial, and political power until the 13th century, when that power shifted to London. Despite its deep roots in the past, Winchester is also a thriving market town living firmly in the present, with numerous shops and restaurants on High Street.

GETTING HERE AND AROUND

On a main train line and on the M3 motorway, Winchester is easily accessible from London. The train station is a short walk from the sights; the bus station is in the center, opposite the tourist office. The one-way streets are notoriously confusing, so find a parking lot as soon as possible. The city center is very walkable, and most of the High Street is closed to vehicular traffic. A walk down High Street and Broadway will bring you to St. Giles Hill, which has a panoramic view of the city.

TIMING

The city is busier than usual during the farmers' market, the largest in the country, held on the second and last Sunday of each month.

ESSENTIALS

Visitor and Tour Information Winchester Tourist Guides
⊕ www.winchestertouristguides.com. **Winchester Tourist Information Centre**
⊠ *The Guildhall, Broadway* ☎ *01962/840500* ⊕ *www.visitwinchester.co.uk.*

EXPLORING

TOP ATTRACTIONS

City Museum. This museum tells Winchester's past through displays of Celtic pottery, Saxon jewelry and coins, and reconstructed Victorian shops. It's an imaginative, well-presented collection that will appeal to children and adults alike—check out the history detective quiz and costumes of every period starting with the Romans for kids to try on, local ceramics, and domestic and agricultural bits and pieces from the Middle Ages, and, on the top floor, some well-restored Roman mosaics. Pick up an audio guide at the entrance (£2) to get the most out of the museum. ⊠ *The Square, next to cathedral* ☎ *01962/863064* ⊕ *www. winchester.gov.uk* ⊠ *Free* ⊙ *Nov.–Mar., Tues.–Sat. 10–4, Sun. noon–4; Apr.–Oct., Mon.–Sat. 10–5, Sun. noon–5.*

Great Hall. A short walk west of the cathedral, this hall is all that remains of the city's Norman castle, and it's still used today for events and ceremonies. It's thought the English Parliament had one of its first meetings here in 1246; Sir Walter Raleigh was tried for conspiracy against King James I in 1603; and Dame Alice Lisle was sentenced to death by the brutal Judge Jeffreys for sheltering fugitives, after Monmouth's Rebellion in 1685. The hall's greatest artifact hangs on its west wall: King Arthur's Round Table has places for 24 knights and a portrait of Arthur bearing a remarkable resemblance to King Henry VIII. In fact, the oak table dates back only to the 13th century and was painted by order of Henry in 1522 on the occasion of a visit by the Holy Roman Emperor Charles V; one theory is that the real Arthur was a Celtic chieftain who held off the invading Saxons after the fall of the Roman Empire in the 5th or 6th century. The Tudors were among several British monarchs who periodically revived the Arthurian legend for political purposes. Take time to wander through the garden named for two Queens, Eleanor of Provence and Eleanor of Castille—a re-creation of a medieval shady retreat. ⊠ *Castle Hill* ☎ *01962/846476* ⊕ *www.hants. gov.uk/greathall* ⊠ *Free* ⊙ *Daily 10–5.*

4

Fodor's Choice ★ **Highclere Castle.** Set in 1,000 acres of parkland designed by Capability Brown, the historic home of the actual Earls of Carnarvon—as opposed to the imaginary Earls of Grantham of period television drama *Downton Abbey*, which is shot here—owes its appearance to Sir Charles Barry, architect of the Houses of Parliament. Commissioned by the third Earl to transform a simpler Georgian mansion, Barry used golden Bath stone to create this fantasy castle bristling with "Gothic" turrets. Like its fictional counterpart, it served as a hospital during World War I. Highlights of the State Rooms include Van Dyke's equestrian portrait of Charles I in the Dining Room and the imposing library (Lord Grantham's retreat). There's also an exhibit of Egyptian antiquities collected by the 5th Earl, known for his pivotal role in the 1920s excavation of ancient Egyptian tombs, notably Tutankhamen's. Get good views of the house and countryside by walking the gardens and grounds. The house is 25 miles north of Winchester and 5 miles south of Newbury; there's train service from London and Winchester to Newbury, and taxis can take you the 5 miles to Highclere. ⊠ *Off A34, Highclere Park, Newbury* ☎ *01635/253204* ⊕ *www.highclerecastle.co.uk* ☎ *£16 castle, exhibition, and gardens; £9.50 castle and gardens or exhibition; £5 gardens only* ☉ *July–mid-Sept., Sun.–Thurs. 10:30–6; last admission at 4. Also selected days Apr.–June.*

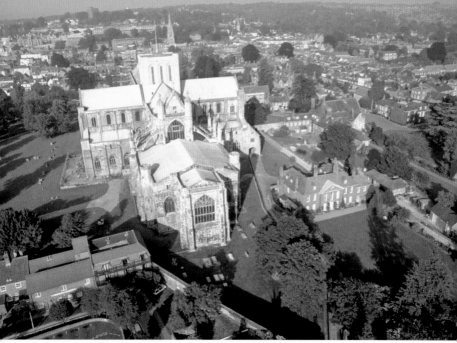

The historic city of Winchester, with its graceful cathedral, is well worth exploring.

King's Gate. One of two surviving gateways in the city's original ancient walls, this structure to the south of the Close is thought to date back to 1300. The tiny medieval **St. Swithun's Church** is on the upper floor. ⊠ *South of the Close.*

Fodor's Choice
★

Winchester Cathedral. The city's greatest monument, begun in 1079 and consecrated in 1093, presents a sturdy, chunky appearance in keeping with its Norman construction, so that the Gothic lightness within is even more breathtaking. Its tower, transepts, and crypt, and the inside core of the great Perpendicular nave, reveal some of the world's best surviving examples of Norman architecture. Other features, such as the arcades, the presbytery (behind the choir, holding the high altar), and the windows, are Gothic alterations carried out between the 12th and 14th centuries. Little of the original stained glass has survived, except in the large window over the entrance. When Cromwell's troops ransacked the cathedral in the 17th century, locals hid away bits of stained glass they found on the ground so that it could later be replaced. The Library and Triforium Gallery contains the Winchester Bible, one of the finest remaining 12th-century illuminated manuscripts.

Among the many well-known people buried in the cathedral are William the Conqueror's son, William II ("Rufus"), mysteriously murdered in the New Forest in 1100; Izaak Walton (1593–1683), author of *The Compleat Angler,* whose memorial window in Silkestede's Chapel was paid for by "the fishermen of England and America"; and Jane Austen, whose grave lies in the north aisle of the nave. The tombstone makes no mention of Austen's literary status, though a brass plaque in the wall, dating from 80 years after her death, celebrates her achievements, and modern panels provide an overview of her life and work. Firmly in the 20th century, Antony Gormley's evocative statue *Sound II* (1986) looms in the crypt, as often as not standing in water (as it was designed to do), because of seasonal flooding. You can also explore the bell tower—with far-reaching views in fair weather—and other recesses of the building on a tour. Special services or ceremonies may mean the cathedral is closed to visits, so call ahead. Outside the cathedral, explore the Close, the area to the south of the cathedral that boasts neat lawns and the Deanery, Dome Alley, and Cheyney Court. ⊠ *The Close, Cathedral Precincts* ☎ *01962/857200* ⊕ *www.winchester-cathedral.org.uk* ⊠ *Cathedral £7.50; bell tower £6; cathedral and bell tower £9.50* ⊙ *Cathedral Mon.–Sat. 10–4 (last admission 3), Sun. 12:30–2:30. Library and Triforium Gallery Apr.–Oct., Mon. 2–4, Tues.–Sat. and national holidays 10:30–4; Nov.–Mar., Sat. 10:30–3:30. Free tours on the hr Mon.–Sat. 10–3, bell tower tours May–Sept., Mon. and Fri. 2:15, Sat. 11:30 and 2:15; Oct.–mid-Nov., Jan.–Apr., Wed. 2:15, Sat. 11:30 and 2:15; late Nov.–Dec., "twilight tower tour," see website for details.*

ST. SWITHUN WEATHER

St. Swithun (died AD 862) is interred in Winchester Cathedral, although he requested outdoor burial. Legend says that when his body was transferred inside from the cathedral's churchyard, it rained for 40 days. Since then, folk wisdom says that rain on St. Swithun's Day (July 15) means 40 more days of wet weather. (Elsewhere in England the name is usually spelled "Swithin.") Near St. Swithun's Church at King's Gate, 8 College Street, is the house where Jane Austen died on July 18, 1817, three days after writing a comic poem about the legend of St. Swithun's Day (copies are usually available in the cathedral).

WORTH NOTING

City Mill. Set over the River Itchen, this working 18th-century water mill, complete with small island garden, is at the east end of High Street. The medieval mill on the site was rebuilt in 1743, remaining in use until the early 20th century. Restored by the National Trust, it still operates as a working mill on weekends, and you can purchase flour produced here in the gift shop. ⊠ *Bridge St.* ☎ *01962/870057* ⊕ *www.nationaltrust.org.uk* ⊠ *£3.90* ⊙ *Jan.–mid-Feb., Mon. and Fri.–Sun. 11–4; mid-Feb.–Nov., daily 10–5; early Dec.–Christmas, daily 10:30–4.*

FAMILY **Watercress Line.** New Alresford, 8 miles northeast of Winchester by A31 and B3046, is the starting point of the Watercress Line, a 10-mile-long railroad reserved for steam locomotives that runs to Alton. The line (named for the area's watercress beds) takes you on a nostalgic tour through reminders of 19th-century England. New Alresford, crossed by the River Alre, has some antiques shops and Georgian houses. ⊠ *New Alresford Railway Station, Station Rd., New Alresford* ☎ *01962/733810* ⊕ *www.watercressline.co.uk* ⊠ *£14* ⊙ *May–Sept., departures Tues.–Thurs. and weekends; Oct. and Dec.–Apr., weekends and national holidays; times vary.*

FAMILY **Westgate.** This atmospheric fortified medieval gateway with its stunning Tudor ceiling was a debtor's prison for 150 years, and now holds a motley assortment of artifacts relating to Tudor and Stuart times, displayed among the 16th-century graffiti by former prisoners. Child-size replicas of authentic 16th-century armor that can be tried on, as well as the opportunity to make brass rubbings, make it popular with kids. You can take in a view of Winchester from the roof. ✉ *Upper High St.* ☎ *01962/869864* 🎫 *Free* 🕓 *Apr.–Oct., Sat. 10–5, Sun. noon–5; early Nov.–Mar., Sat. 10–4, Sun. noon–4.*

Winchester College. One of England's oldest "public" (meaning private) schools was founded in 1382 by Bishop William of Wykeham, whose alabaster tomb sits in a chapel dedicated to him in Winchester Cathedral. The school's own chapel is notable for its delicately vaulted ceiling. Among the buildings still in use is Chamber Court, center of college life for six centuries. Notice the "scholars"—students holding academic scholarships—clad in their traditional gowns. Call about tours, sometimes canceled due to college events. ✉ *College St.* ☎ *01962/621209* 🌐 *www.winchestercollege.org* 🎫 *£6* 🕓 *1-hr tours Mon., Wed., Fri., and Sat. 10:45, noon, 2:15, and 3:30, Tues. and Thurs. 10:45 and noon, Sun. 2:15 and 3:30.*

WHERE TO EAT

$$ MODERN BRITISH 🍴 **The Bistro at Hotel du Vin.** Classic French and British fare is served with modern touches in this stylish bistro paneled in light wood, converted from a redbrick Georgian town house. Such dishes as sea bass en papillote are complemented by the many eclectic wine selections. In summer, meals are served on a terrace and in a walled garden. The hotel's luxurious rooms are richly furnished in crisp modern style. [$] *Average main: £18* ✉ *14 Southgate St.* ☎ *01962/841414* 🌐 *www.hotelduvin.com.*

$$ MODERN BRITISH 🍴 **Chesil Rectory.** The timbered and gabled building may be Old English—it dates back to the mid-15th century—but the cuisine is modern British, using locally sourced ingredients. Dishes might include venison carpaccio for a starter, followed by slow-cooked pork rib eye or oven-roasted halibut. Good-value fixed-price lunches and early-evening dinners are available. Service and the heritage charm of the surroundings enhance the quality of the food. [$] *Average main: £17* ✉ *1 Chesil St.* ☎ *01962/851555* 🌐 *www.chesilrectory.co.uk.*

$ CAFÉ 🍴 **Ginger Two for Tea.** This bright and airy corner café is the place to come for a relaxed afternoon tea. White walls and wooden furniture lend it a modern, rustic feel. The kitchen serves simple lunches, locally baked cakes and pastries, and a variety of teas and coffees. The cakes and coffees are acclaimed, the sandwiches and service less so. Try such seasonal dishes as butternut squash soup or crepes with salmon. You'll find this place on a quiet road off High Street. [$] *Average main: £6* ✉ *29 St. Thomas St.* ☎ *01962/877733* 🕓 *No dinner.*

$ BRITISH 🍴 **Green's Wine Bar.** Everything is served cafeteria style at this local favorite, which offers delicious comfort food like chicken and leek pie, lamb stew with dumplings, and panini at reasonable prices. The space is small, but sidewalk seating means there's plenty of space in good weather. In the evening, the place transforms into a busy bar, and there's a DJ and dancing on weekends. Despite the name, the atmosphere and beverage selection makes the place more like a lively pub than a sophisticated wine bar. $ *Average main: £8* ✉ *4 Jewry St.* 📞 *01962/869630.*

WHERE TO STAY

For expanded hotel reviews, visit Fodors.com.

$$$
HOTEL
Fodor's Choice
★

🏨 **Lainston House.** The 63 acres surrounding this elegant 17th-century country house retain many original features, including the walls of the kitchen garden (still in use), the apple trees in the former orchard, and a mile-long avenue of Linden trees, the longest in Europe. **Pros:** beautiful setting; atmospheric guest rooms. **Cons:** lower-priced modern rooms small; country house "shabby chic" not to everyone's taste. $ *Rooms from: £165* ✉ *Woodman La., off B3049, Sparsholt* 📞 *01962/776088* ⊕ *www.lainstonhouse.com* ⤴ *25 rooms, 25 suites or Jr. suites* 🍴 *Some meals.*

$$
B&B/INN

🏨 **Old Vine.** Blessed with an ideal location opposite the cathedral, this 18th-century inn, now a gastropub with rooms, has received a smart, modern makeover without losing any of its character. **Pros:** elegant rooms; delicious food; attentive service. **Cons:** rooms over the bar may be noisy on weekends. $ *Rooms from: £105* ✉ *8 Great Minster St.* 📞 *01962/854616* ⊕ *www.oldvinewinchester.com* ⤴ *6 rooms* 🍴 *Breakfast.*

$$
B&B/INN

🏨 **Wykeham Arms.** A watering hole since 1755, this pub with rooms near the cathedral and the college wears its Britishness proudly, with decor that features photos of such national heroes as Nelson and Churchill, military artifacts, and an assortment of pewter mugs hanging from the ceiling. **Pros:** quirky charm; lively bar; good food. **Cons:** rooms above the bar can be noisy; no kids under 14; small portions at restaurant. $ *Rooms from: £129* ✉ *75 Kingsgate St.* 📞 *01962/853834* ⊕ *www.fullershotels.com* ⤴ *13 rooms, 1 suite* 🍴 *Breakfast.*

SHOPPING

Kingsgate Books and Prints. This is a good stop for a selection of secondhand books, maps, and prints. ✉ *Kingsgate Arch, College St.* 📞 *01962/864710.*

King's Walk. Off Friarsgate, King's Walk has a number of stalls selling antiques, crafts, and bric-a-brac.

P&G Wells. The oldest bookshop in the country, P&G Wells has numerous books by and about Jane Austen, who had an account here and died almost next door in 1817. It also has the region's largest selection of children's books. ✉ *11 College St.* 📞 *01962/852016.*

CHAWTON

16 miles northeast of Winchester.

In Chawton you can visit the home of Jane Austen (1775–1817), who lived the last eight years of her life in the village; she moved to Winchester only during her final illness. The site has always drawn literary pilgrims, but with the ongoing release of successful films based on her novels, the town's popularity among visitors has grown enormously.

GETTING HERE AND AROUND

Hourly Stagecoach bus X64 service connects Winchester and New Alresford with Chawton. It's a 10-minute walk from the bus stop to Jane Austen's House. By car, take A31. Alternatively, take a 40-minute stroll along the footpath from Alton.

OPEN-AIR MARKETS

Among the best markets is the Winchester Farmers' Market held in Winchester's Middle Brook Street on the second and the last Sunday of each month. It specializes in local produce and goods. Also worth a look are Salisbury's traditional Charter Market (Tuesday and Saturday); Southampton's Bargate Market for artisanal foods, local produce, and leather goods (Friday), and arts and crafts and local produce (Saturday); and Dorchester's large market (Wednesday) and Farmers' Market (fourth Saturday). The largest of all is outside Wimborne Minster (Friday and Sunday).

EXPLORING

Fodor's Choice ★ **Jane Austen's House.** Here, in an unassuming redbrick house, Jane Austen wrote *Emma, Persuasion,* and *Mansfield Park,* and revised *Sense and Sensibility, Northanger Abbey,* and *Pride and Prejudice.* Now a museum, the house retains the modest but genteel atmosphere suitable to the unmarried daughter of a clergyman. In the drawing room there's a piano similar to the one Jane would play every morning before repairing to a small writing table in the family dining parlor—leaving her sister, Cassandra, to do the household chores ("I find composition impossible with my head full of joints of mutton and doses of rhubarb," Jane wrote). In the early 19th century the road near the house was a bustling thoroughfare, and one traveler reported that a window view proved that the Misses Austen were "looking very comfortable at breakfast." Jane was famous for working through interruptions, but one protection against the outside world was the famous door that creaked. She asked that its hinges remain unattended to because they gave her warning that someone was coming. It's often closed for special events, so call ahead. ✉ *Winchester Rd., signed off A31/A32 roundabout* ☎ *01420/83262* 🌐 *www.jane-austens-house-museum.org.uk* 🎟 *£7.50* 🕒 *Jan.–mid-Feb., weekends 10:30–4:30; mid-Feb.–May and Sept.–Dec., daily 10:30–4:30; June–Aug., daily 10–5; last admission 30 mins before closing.*

WHERE TO STAY

For expanded hotel reviews, visit Fodors.com.

$$$$ HOTEL 🏨 **Four Seasons Hotel Hampshire.** Although deep in the peaceful British countryside, this country-house hotel on a 500-acre estate is only a half hour from Heathrow. **Pros:** peaceful location; great spa; plenty of activities. **Cons:** dogs are welcome (a pro or a con); not in the center of any action. [$] *Rooms from: £225* ✉ *Dogmersfield Park, Chalky La., Hook* ☎ *01252/853000* 🌐 *www.fourseasons.com/hampshire* 🛏 *111 rooms, 22 suites* 🍴 *No meals.*

IN SEARCH OF JANE AUSTEN

Jane Austen used this tiny writing table at her home in Chawton.

Jane Austen country—a verdant landscape filled with relatively unspoiled villages—is where you can get a glimpse of the decorous 18th- and early-19th-century society she described with wry wit in novels such as *Emma, Persuasion, Sense and Sensibility,* and *Pride and Prejudice.* You can almost hear the clink of teacups raised by the likes of Elinor Dashwood and Mr. Darcy. Serious Janeites will want to retrace her life in the towns of Bath (⇨ *see Chapter 7),* Chawton, Winchester, and Lyme Regis.

BATH

Bath is the elegant setting that served as a backdrop for the society Austen observed with such razor sharpness. She lived in Bath between 1801 and 1806, and although she wrote relatively little while she was here, she used it as a setting for *Northanger Abbey* and *Persuasion.* Bath's Jane Austen Centre explores her relationship to the city.

CHAWTON

About 83 miles southeast of Bath is this tiny Hampshire village, the heart of Jane Austen country. Here you'll find the elegant but understated house, a former bailiff's cottage on her brother's estate, where Austen worked on three of her novels. It's now a museum that effectively evokes her life there.

WINCHESTER

Driving southwest from Chawton, take the A31 for about 15 miles to Winchester, where you can visit Austen's austere grave within the cathedral and view an exhibit about her life; then see the commemorative plaque on No. 8 College Street, where her battle with Addison's disease ended with her death on July 18, 1817.

LYME REGIS

Heading 110 miles southwest of Winchester you can visit Lyme Regis, the 18th-century seaside resort on the Devon border where Austen spent the summers of 1804 and 1805. Here, at the Cobb, the stone jetty that juts into Lyme Bay, poor Louisa Musgrove jumps off the steps known as Granny's Teeth—a turning point in Chapter 12 of *Persuasion.*

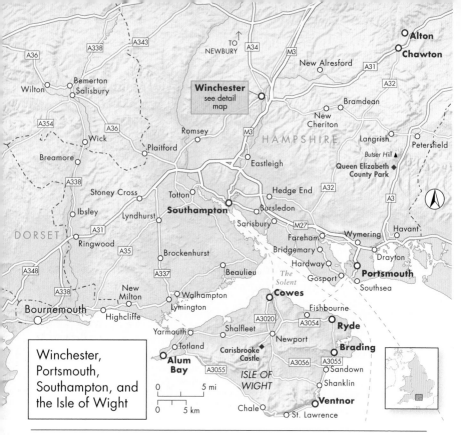

Winchester,
Portsmouth,
Southampton, and
the Isle of Wight

0   5 mi
0   5 km

PORTSMOUTH

24 miles south of Chawton, 77 miles southwest of London.

Portsmouth's historic harbor, revitalized waterfront, and working port make it an energetic place. At the newly developed Gunwharf Quays you'll find the soaring Spinnaker Tower, as well as shops, restaurants, bars, and a contemporary art gallery. The main attraction for many travelers is the extraordinary collection of maritime memorabilia, including well-preserved warships from the Napoleonic era, at the Portsmouth Historic Dockyard, and other museums. For others, Portsmouth is primarily of interest for the ferries that set off from here to the Isle of Wight and more distant destinations.

GETTING HERE AND AROUND

The M27 motorway from Southampton and the A3 from London take you to Portsmouth. There are also frequent buses and trains that drop you off at the Hard, the main transport terminus. It's only a few steps from the Historic Dockyard and Gunwharf Quays. Regular passenger ferries cross Portsmouth Harbour from the Hard for Gosport's Royal Navy Submarine Museum. Attractions in the nearby town of Southsea are best reached by car or by buses departing from the Hard.

ESSENTIALS

Visitor Information **Portsmouth Visitor Information Centre**
✉ *D-Day Museum, Clarence Esplanade, Southsea* ☎ *023/9282–6722*
⊕ *www.visitportsmouth.co.uk.*

EXPLORING

TOP ATTRACTIONS

FAMILY **D-Day Museum.** In the absorbing D-Day Museum in nearby Southsea, an eclectic range of exhibits illustrates the planning and logistics involved in the D-Day landings, as well as the actual invasion on June 6, 1944. The museum's centerpiece is the Overlord Embroidery ("Overlord" was the code name for the invasion), a 272-foot-long embroidered cloth with 34 panels illustrating the history of World War II, from the Battle of Britain in 1940 to D-Day and the first days of the liberation. ✉ *Clarence Esplanade, Southsea* ☎ *023/9282-7261* ⊕ *www. ddaymuseum.co.uk* ⬛ *£6.50* ☯ *Apr.–Sept., daily 10–5:30; Oct.–Mar., daily 10–5; last admission 30 mins before closing.*

FAMILY   **Portsmouth Historic Dockyard.** The city's most impressive attraction
Fodor'sChoice   includes an unrivaled collection of historic ships. The dockyard's
★   youngest ship, **HMS *Warrior*** (1860), was England's first ironclad battleship. British naval hero Admiral Lord Horatio Nelson's flagship, **HMS *Victory,*** is in the process of being painstakingly restored to appear as it did at the battle at Trafalgar (1805). You can inspect the cramped gun decks, visit the cabin where Nelson entertained his officers, and stand on the spot where he was mortally wounded by a French sniper. A museum opened in 2013 houses the ***Mary Rose,*** the former flagship of the Tudor navy. Built in this very dockyard more than 500 years ago, the boat sank in the harbor in 1545 before being raised in 1982. Described in the 16th century as "the flower of all the ships that ever sailed," it's berthed in a special enclosure where water continuously sprays the timbers to prevent them from drying out and breaking up.

The **National Museum of the Royal Navy** has extensive exhibits about Nelson and the battle of Trafalgar, a fine collection of painted figureheads, and galleries of paintings and mementos recalling naval history from King Alfred to the present. **Action Stations,** an interactive attraction, gives insight into life in the modern Royal Navy and tests your sea legs with tasks such as piloting boats through gales. **Dockyard Apprentice** showcases the skills of the shipbuilders and craftsmen who constructed and maintained the naval vessels, with illustrations of rope making, sail making, caulking, signals, and knots. You should allow one or two days to tour all the attractions in the Historic Dockyard. ■ **TIP→ The entrance fee includes a boat ride around the harbor.** ✉ *Historic Dockyard, Victory Gate* ☎ *023/9283–9766* ⊕ *www.historicdockyard.co.uk* ⬛ *£26 includes harbor tour* ☯ *Apr.–Oct., daily 10–5:30; Nov.–Mar., daily 10–5; last admission 1 hr before closing.*

Boathouse No. 7. In the heart of the Historic Dockyard, Boathouse No. 7 is a family-friendly eatery in a converted 18th-century boathouse a stone's throw from the HMS *Victory*. The kitchen dishes out traditional favorites like shepherd's pie and baked potatoes, as well as lighter options like freshly made sandwiches, salads, and soups. Kids can enjoy the "treasure trove" lunchbox filled with healthy snacks. You can eat here without purchasing a ticket to the museums. ⊠ *Historic Dockyard, Victory Gate* ☎ *023/9283–8060* ⊕ *www.historicdockyard.co.uk.*

Spinnaker Tower. On the lively Gunwharf Quays development of shops and bars, the Spinnaker Tower adds a striking visual focus to Portsmouth's skyline. The slender structure evokes a mast with a billowing sail, and rises to a height of 558 feet. An elevator whisks you to three viewing platforms 330 feet high, for thrilling all-around views over the harbor and up to 23 miles beyond. ⊠ *Gunwharf Quays* ☎ *023/9285–7520* ⊕ *www.spinnakertower.co.uk* ▭ *£8.55* ☉ *Sept.–July, daily 10–6; Aug., Sun.–Thurs. 10–7, Fri. and Sat. 10–6; last admission 30 mins before closing.*

WORTH NOTING

FAMILY   **Explosion!.** In a former arms depot near the Submarine Museum, the Museum of Naval Firepower gathers together munitions, mines, and missiles to relate the history of warfare at sea. The museum also tells the story of the local people who manufactured them. Interactive touch-screen exhibits explore all aspects of naval armaments, from guns to tactical nuclear weapons. ⊠ *Priddy's Hard, Gosport* ☎ *023/9250–5600* ⊕ *www.explosion.org.uk* ▭ *£10* ☉ *Apr.–Oct., daily 10–5; Nov.–Mar., weekends 10–4; last admission 1 hr before closing.*

Millennium Promenade. Starting at the Spinnaker Tower, the Millennium Promenade meanders through Old Portsmouth and along the seafront. The 4-mile self-guided walk, marked by a rope pattern on the sidewalk, passes though the original port, where fishing boats still dock, and where press gangs forcibly enlisted young men for the Royal Navy in the 18th century. Follow it to Clarence Pier in Southsea. ⊠ *Gunwharf Quays.*

Portchester Castle. Incorporating the walls of a Roman fort built more than 1,600 years ago, Portchester Castle claims to have the most complete set of Roman walls in northern Europe. In the 12th century a Norman castle (now in ruins) was built inside the impressive fortifications. From the keep's central tower you can take in a sweeping view of the harbor and coastline. ⊠ *Off A27, near Fareham* ☎ *023/9237–8291* ⊕ *www.english-heritage.org.uk* ▭ *£4.90* ☉ *Apr.–Sept., daily 10–6; Oct., daily 10–5; Nov.–Mar., weekends 10–4.*

FAMILY   **Royal Navy Submarine Museum.** The highlight here is a tour of the World War II submarine HMS *Alliance*, from the cramped quarters to the engine room. The museum fills you in on submarine history and lets you view Portsmouth Harbour through a periscope. There are plenty of submarine-related artifacts, as well as three actual subs spread around the large site. From Portsmouth Harbour, take the ferry to Gosport and walk along Millennium Promenade past the huge sundial clock. ✉ *Halsar Jetty Rd., Gosport* ☎ *023/9251–0354* 🌐 *www.submarine-museum.co.uk* 🎫 *£12.50* 🕒 *Apr.–Oct., daily 10–5:30; Nov.–Mar., Wed.–Sun.10–4:30; last tour 1 hr before closing.*

RULING THE WAVES

Great Britain invested heavily in its Royal Navy to defend its shores and, eventually, to access its far-flung empire. The first dry dock in Europe was built in 1495 in Portsmouth, by order of Henry VII. His son Henry VIII greatly built up the navy early in his reign, but it was still a smaller force than the Spanish Armada, whose attack the English beat back famously in 1588, during the reign of Elizabeth I. It would take another century for England to make its navy the largest, and the world's most powerful, a rank it held up to World War II.

WHERE TO EAT

$ MODERN BRITISH 🍴 **Abarbistro.** A relaxed, modern bistro midway between Old Portsmouth and Gunwharf Quays, this place is ideal for a snack, a full meal, or just a glass from the thoughtfully chosen wine list. The changing Modern British menu specializes in seafood dishes, mostly sourced from Portsmouth's fish market right opposite, and may include *moules marinière*, fish cakes, or salmon Wellington; alternatively, opt for the sirloin steak and fries, or mushroom risotto. You can sit indoors, in a garden at the back, or at Continental-style tables on the pavement. [$] *Average main: £12* ✉ *58 White Hart Rd.* ☎ *023/9281–1585* 🌐 *www.abarbistro.co.uk.*

$$$$ BRITISH 🍴 **Montparnasse.** Modern photographs on cinnamon walls add a contemporary touch to this relaxed restaurant. The fixed-price menus (£32.50 and £37.50) specialize in British classics with a twist, like pork belly with homemade sausage rolls or a mushroom-and-potato pavé with poached tomatoes. Desserts such as a macademia with praline parfait are to die for. The service is discreet but attentive and knowledgeable. [$] *Average main: £35* ✉ *103 Palmerston Rd., Southsea* ☎ *023/9281–6754* 🌐 *www.bistromontparnasse.co.uk* 🕒 *Closed Sun. and Mon.*

THE OUTDOORS

Queen Elizabeth Country Park. Designated an Area of Outstanding Natural Beauty, the park has 1,400 acres of chalk hills and shady beeches with 20 miles of scenic trails for hikers, cyclists, and horse riders. You can climb to the top of 888-foot-tall Butser Hill to take in a panoramic view of the coast. The park lies 15 miles north of Portsmouth, and 4 miles south of the Georgian market town of Petersfield, in a wide valley between wooded hills and open downs. A visitor center has a theater, café, and shop. ✉ *South Downs National Park, A3* ☎ *023/9259–5040* 🌐 *www.hants.gov.uk/qecp* 🎫 *Free* 🕒 *Park open 24 hrs; visitor center Mar.–Oct., daily 10–5:30; Nov.–late Dec. and mid–late Jan., daily 10–4:30; café open from 9 am.*

You can tour Admiral Nelson's famous flagship, the HMS *Victory*, at Portsmouth's Historic Dockyard.

SOUTHAMPTON

17 miles northwest of Portsmouth, 24 miles southeast of Salisbury, 77 miles southwest of London.

Southampton is England's leading passenger port, and as the home port of Henry V's fleet bound for Agincourt, the *Mayflower*, the *Queen Mary*, and the ill-fated *Titanic*, along with countless other great ocean liners of the 20th century, the city has one of the richest maritime traditions in England. Parts of the center can seem shoddy, having been hastily rebuilt after World War II bombing, but bits of the city's history peek out from between modern buildings. The Old Town retains its medieval feel, and considerable parts of Southampton's castellated town walls remain. Other attractions include a decent art gallery, extensive parks, and a couple of good museums. The Southampton Boat Show, a 10-day event in mid-September, draws huge crowds.

GETTING HERE AND AROUND

Located on the M3 motorway from London and Winchester, and on the M27 from Portsmouth, Southampton is also easily accessed by bus or train from these cities. The bus and train stations are a few minutes' walk from the tourist office, and the main sights can be reached by foot.

EXPLORING

Broadlands. This 60-room Palladian mansion located on 6,000 acres near the town of Romsey was the home of 19th-century British Prime Minister Lord Palmerston and later of Earl Mountbatten of Burma (1900–79), uncle of Prince Philip and mentor to Prince Charles, who, as the last Viceroy of India, was in charge of that country's transition to independence before being killed by the IRA. One of the the grandest houses in Hampshire, Broadstairs dates back to the 18th century and holds a large collection of antiques, Greek and Roman marbles, and old master paintings, including three Van Dycks. Landscape designer Capability Brown laid out the grounds, which include wide lawns sweeping down to the banks of the River Test. ✉ *A3090 Romsey Bypass, Romsey* ☎ *01794/505022* 🌐 *www.broadlandsestates.co.uk* 🎟 *£8* 🕒 *Late June–early Sept., weekdays 1–5:30; last admission at 4.*

Mayflower Park and the Pilgrim Fathers' Memorial. This memorial was built to commemorate the departure of 102 passengers on the North America–bound *Mayflower* from Southampton on August 15, 1620. A plaque also honors the 2 million U.S. troops who embarked from Southampton during World War II. ✉ *Western Esplanade.*

4

SeaCity Museum. Devoted to Southampton's storied maritime history, this museum brings together artifacts from Roman, Saxon, and medieval times with models, mementos, and pieces of furniture from the age of the great clippers and cruise ships. The Titanic gallery displays a wealth of memorabilia relating to one of the most famous of the cruise ships that sailed from the city—footage, photos, crew lists, and so on. Boat buffs will relish plenty of vital statistics dealing with the history of commercial shipping. ✉ *Havelock Rd.* ☎ *023/8083–3007* 🌐 *www.seacitymuseum.co.uk* 🎟 *£8.50* 🕒 *Daily 10–5.*

WHERE TO EAT AND STAY

For expanded hotel reviews, visit Fodors.com.

$$ BRASSERIE
🍴 **Oxford Brasserie.** Close to the docks, this informal place gets lively in the evening but it's calmer at lunchtime. Fresh fish is always available (the fixed-price menus are a particularly good value), along with Mediterranean fare. The restaurant has a tile floor and taupe walls that are enlivened by funky sections of brightly painted wood doors for a color-block effect . [$] *Average main: £16* ✉ *33–34 Oxford St.* ☎ *023/8063–5043* 🌐 *www.theoxfordbrasserie.co.uk.*

$$ B&B/INN
🏨 **The Pig In The Wall.** On a quiet street across from Mayflower Park, this snug hotel in two converted townhouses has guest rooms with a funky but chic aesthetic, with goose-down bedding and monsoon showers. **Pros:** stylish rooms; lovely common areas; limited but good menu. **Cons:** breakfast not included; top-floor room reachable via very steep stairs. [$] *Rooms from: £115* ✉ *8 Western Esplanade* ☎ *08450/779494* 🌐 *www.thepiginthewall.com* 🛏 *12 rooms* 🍽 *No meals.*

$$ HOTEL
Fodor's Choice ★
🏨 **TerraVina Hotel.** The public areas of this small and select boutique hotel outside the city invite lingering with their mix of contemporary and period furnishings, while the guest rooms—decorated in lively colors accentuating the contemporary lines—are spacious and have thoughtful touches like espresso machines. **Pros:** well-appointed rooms; fantastic food; good showers. **Cons:** some rooms small; a little remote from Southampton. [$] *Rooms from: £155* ✉ *174 Woodlands Rd., Woodlands, Netley Marsh* ☎ *023/8029–3784* 🌐 *www.hotelterravina.co.uk* 🛏 *11 rooms* 🍽 *No meals.*

NIGHTLIFE AND THE ARTS

Mayflower. This is one of the larger theaters outside London; the Royal Shakespeare Company and Barnum on Ice are among the productions that have attracted packed houses. ⊠ *Commercial Rd.* ☎ *023/8071–1811* ⊕ *www.mayflower.org.uk.*

Nuffield. At Southampton University, the Nuffield has a repertory company and also hosts national touring companies. ⊠ *University Rd.* ☎ *023/8067–1771* ⊕ *www.nuffieldtheatre.co.uk.*

ISLE OF WIGHT

A slightly tattered, slightly romantic place, this island sometimes gets so crowded it seems that it might sink beneath the weight of the throngs of summer visitors. Its appealingly dusty Victorian look comes courtesy of Queen Victoria, who made the Isle of Wight (pronounced white) fashionable by choosing it for the site of her favorite residence, Osborne House. She stayed as often as she could, and ultimately died here. The island attracted the cream of Victorian society, including Darwin, Thackeray, and Tennyson; the latter lived here until tourist harassment drove him away. Perhaps understandably, islanders have a love-hate relationship with the crowds of tourists that descend on this 23-mile-long island every summer thanks to the ferries and hydrofoils that connect the island with Southampton, Portsmouth, Southsea, and Lymington. The attractions include its vacation resorts—Ryde, Bembridge, Ventnor, and Freshwater (stay away from rather tacky Sandown and Shanklin)—and its rich vegetation, narrow lanes, thatched cottages, curving bays, sandy beaches, and walking paths. Although the fabulous ocean air is, to quote Tennyson, "worth six pence a pint," the island offers more than sailing and the sea. There's splendid driving to be done in the interior in such places as Brading Down, Ashley Down, Mersely Down, and along Military Road, and the occasional country house to visit, none more spectacular than former royal hideaway Osborne House.

GETTING HERE AND AROUND

Wightlink operates a car ferry between the mainland and the Isle of Wight. The crossing takes about 30 minutes from Lymington to Yarmouth, 45 minutes from Portsmouth to Fishbourne. The company also operates catamaran service between Portsmouth and Ryde (20 minutes). Red Funnel runs a car ferry (one hour) between Southampton and East Cowes and hydrofoil service (25 minutes) to West Cowes. Hovertravel runs a hovercraft shuttle between Southsea (Portsmouth) and Ryde (15 minutes). The island is covered by a good network of roads, and you can rely on a regular local bus service. Southern Vectis, the local bus company, operates open-top tours between March and early November. One goes to Dimbola Lodge, the Needles, and Alum Bay. You can board and disembark at different points for £10.

TIMING
Summer traffic slows things down considerably. Try to avoid Cowes Week in late July or early August, the Garlic Festival in mid-August, and the two major rock festivals that take place in mid-June and mid-September.

ESSENTIALS
Bus and Tour Information Southern Vectis ☎ *0871/200–2233*
⊕ *www.islandbuses.info.*

Ferry Information Hovertravel ☎ *08434/878887* ⊕ *www.hovertravel.co.uk.*
Red Funnel ☎ *0844/844–9988* ⊕ *www.redfunnel.co.uk.* **Wightlink**
☎ *0871/376–1000* ⊕ *www.wightlink.co.uk.*

COWES

7 miles northwest of Ryde.

If you embark from Southampton, your ferry will cross the Solent channel and dock at Cowes, near Queen Victoria's Osborne House. Cowes is a magic name in the sailing world because of the internationally known Cowes Week yachting festival (⊕ *www.cowesweek.co.uk*), held each July or August. At the north end of the high street, on the Parade, a tablet commemorates the 1633 sailing from Cowes of two ships carrying the first English settlers of the state of Maryland.

GETTING HERE AND AROUND
A car ferry and a hydrofoil shuttle passengers from Southampton. Southern Vectis runs numerous buses connecting Cowes with other destinations on the island.

ESSENTIALS
Visitor Information Isle of Wight Tourism ☎ *01983/813813*
⊕ *www.visitisleofwight.co.uk.*

EXPLORING
Carisbrooke Castle. Standing above the village of Carisbrooke, this castle was built by the Normans and enlarged in Elizabethan times. It had its moment of historical glory when King Charles I was imprisoned here during the English Civil War; note the small window in the north curtain wall through which he tried unsuccessfully to escape. You can walk along the battlements and visit the well house, which still uses donkeys to draw water, and also explore the Edwardian-style Princess Beatrice garden and a small museum devoted to Charles I and the English Civil War. The castle is about a mile southwest of the Isle of Wight's modern-day capital, Newport. From Cowes, take Bus 1 or 5 (1 from West Cowes, near Holmwood Hotel; 5 from East Cowes, near Osborne House) to Newport, from where you can walk (about 30 minutes) or pick up either Bus 6, 7, or 38—it's about a 10-minute walk from the bus stop in The Mall, Carisbrooke. ⊠ *Off B3401* ☎ *01983/522107* ⊕ *www.english-heritage.org.uk* 🎫£7.70 ⊙ *Apr.–Sept., daily 10–6; Oct.–Mar., weekends 10–4.*

Fodor's Choice ★ **Osborne House.** Queen Victoria's favorite residence, a massive pile designed by Prince Albert to replicate a grand Italian Renaissance palazzo, holds enormous interest for anyone drawn to the domestic side of history. The house reveals the engineer manqué in Prince Albert through his clever innovations, such as a kind of central heating, as well as evidence of Victoria's desperate attempts to give her children a normal but disciplined upbringing. A minibus will take you to the Swiss Cottage, a superior version of a playhouse built for the children. After Albert's death in 1861, the queen spent much of her time here mourning her loss in relative seclusion, and the antiques-filled rooms have scarcely been altered since her death here in 1901. The house and extensive grounds—which can be quite crowded during July and August—were used as a location for the 1998 movie *Mrs. Brown.* Since 2012, what used to be Victoria's private beach has been open to the public. In summer another minibus will take you there. **TIP→ Book ahead for guided tours of the house and gardens.** Buses 4 (from Ryde) and 5 (from Cowes and Newport) stop outside. ✉ *Off A3021, 1 mile southeast of Cowes* ☎ *01983/200022* 🌐 *www.english-heritage.org.uk* 🎟 *£13* 🕒 *House: Mar., weekends 10–4; Apr.–Sept., daily 10–5; Oct., daily 10–5; mid-Nov.–Feb., weekends by prebooked guided tour. Garden: Mar., weekends 10–4; Apr.–Sept., daily 10–6; Oct., daily 10–5; mid-Nov.–Feb., weekends 10–4.*

WHERE TO STAY

For expanded hotel reviews, visit Fodors.com.

$$ HOTEL 🏨 **Best Western New Holmwood Hotel.** The rooms may be unremarkable, but the views are special at this hotel occupying an unrivaled location above the western end of the Esplanade—ideal for watching yachters in the Solent. **Pros:** good sea views; friendly staff; within walking distance of passenger ferry. **Cons:** some dated bathrooms and public rooms. [$] *Rooms from: £112* ✉ *Queens Rd.* ☎ *01983/292508* 🌐 *www.newholmwoodhotel.co.uk* 🛏 *24 rooms, 2 suites* 🍴 *Breakfast.*

RYDE

7 miles southeast of Cowes.

The town of Ryde has long been one of the Isle of Wight's most popular summer resorts, with several family attractions. After the construction of Ryde Pier in 1814, elegant town houses sprang up along the seafront and on the slopes behind, commanding fine views of the harbor. In addition to its long, sandy beach, Ryde has a large lake (you can rent rowboats and pedal boats) and children's playgrounds.

GETTING HERE AND AROUND

From Portsmouth, catamaran service takes about 20 minutes; from Southsea a hovercraft gets you to Ryde in 10 minutes. If you're driving from Cowes, take the A3021 to the A3054.

WHERE TO EAT AND STAY

For expanded hotel reviews, visit Fodors.com.

$$ SEAFOOD ✕ **Seaview.** A strong maritime flavor defines this outstanding restaurant in the heart of a harbor village just outside Ryde. Choose between the two main dining areas, one a smaller Victorian room, the other

bright and modern with tables spilling out into a conservatory. The kitchen specializes in seafood and fresh island produce, much of it from the Seaview's own farm. You might start with the smoked salmon cannelloni with smoked mackerel mousse, then move on to panfried skate in a saffron and mussel sauce. A three-course fixed-price menu at £25 is a good deal. Simple fish dishes can be ordered in the two congenial bars, one modern, one traditional. Luxurious fabrics characterize the chic guest rooms in the adjoining hotel. $ *Average main: £17* ✉ *Seaview Hotel, High St., Seaview* ☎ *01983/612711* ⊕ *www. seaviewhotel.co.uk.*

$$
HOTEL

⛶ **Lakeside Park Hotel.** Halfway between Cowes and Ryde in the tiny town of Wootton Bridge, this waterfront hotel is perfectly located for exploring the northern part of the island. **Pros:** scenic location; pretty views; comfortable rooms. **Cons:** air-conditioning can be noisy; patchy service; somewhat characterless. $ *Rooms from: £120* ✉ *High St., Wootton Bridge* ☎ *01983/882266* ⊕ *www.lakesideparkhotel.com* ⇗ *44 bedrooms, 3 suites* ⍟ *Breakfast.*

$$
HOTEL
Fodor's Choice
★

⛶ **Priory Bay Hotel.** This country-house hotel has architectural flourishes that date back to Tudor times, 70 acres of grounds, and its own private sandy beach. **Pros:** quirky character; beautiful setting; restful atmosphere. **Cons:** sometimes shabby rather than shabby chic; not much to do in vicinity; minimum stay required. $ *Rooms from: £160* ✉ *Priory Dr., Seaview* ☎ *01983/613146* ⊕ *www.priorybay.com* ⇗ *18 rooms, 9 cottages* ⍟ *Breakfast.*

BRADING

3 miles south of Ryde on A3055.

In Brading, St. Mary's Church, dating from Norman times, contains monuments to the local Oglander family, whose ancestor from Normandy served William the Conqueror. You can still see the old lockup, dating from 1750, complete with stocks and whipping post at the Hall.

GETTING HERE AND AROUND
To get here from Ryde, take the Island Line trains or local bus services.

ESSENTIALS
Contacts **Island Line** ☎ *0845/600–0650* ⊕ www.southwesttrains.co.uk.

EXPLORING

FAMILY **Brading Roman Villa.** Housed within a striking wooden-walled, glass-roofed building, the remains of this substantial 3rd-century villa include walls, splendid mosaic floors, and a well-preserved heating system. The mosaics, depicting peacocks (symbolizing eternal life), gods, gladiators, sea beasts, and reclining nymphs, are a rare example of this type of floor preserved in situ in a domestic building. There's also a café at the site, 1 mile south of Brading. ✉ *Morton Old Rd., off A3055* ☎ *01983/406223* ⊕ *www.bradingromanvilla.org.uk* 🎫 *£6.50* ⊙ *Daily 9:30–5; last entry at 4.*

VENTNOR

11 miles south of Ryde.

The south-coast resorts are the sunniest and most sheltered on the Isle of Wight. Handsome Ventnor rises from such a steep slope that the ground floors of some of its houses are level with the roofs of those across the road.

GETTING HERE AND AROUND

Local bus service connects Ventnor with the rest of the island.

EXPLORING

Ventnor Botanic Garden. Laid out over 22 acres, these gardens contain more than 3,500 species of trees, plants, and shrubs. The impressive greenhouse includes banana trees and a waterfall; a visitor center puts the subtropical and display gardens into context. The admission price includes a guided tour. ✉ *Undercliff Dr.* ☎ *01983/855397* 🌐 *www.botanic.co.uk* 🎟 *£5* 🕒 *Oct.–Mar., daily 10–4; Apr.–Sept., daily 10–dusk.*

WHERE TO EAT

$$ MODERN BRITISH 🍴 **The Pond Café.** Overlooking a secluded, elongated pond in the hamlet of Bonchurch, a mile north of Ventnor, this quiet, understated restaurant is a good place to gently unwind. The simply furnished interior is compact and contemporary in style, and there are a few outdoor tables for eating alfresco when the weather permits. Come for a tea or coffee, or tuck into lunch or dinner. The lunch menu includes such dishes as local mushroom ravioli, roast venison with gnocchi and black cabbage, and sea bass with salsify and champagne sauce. There are fresh-baked breads and homemade ice creams, among other toothsome desserts, and a wide selection of cheeses. [$] *Average main: £15* ✉ *Bonchurch Village Rd., Bonchurch* ☎ *01983/855666* 🌐 *www.thehambrough.com.*

ALUM BAY AND THE NEEDLES

19 miles northwest of Ventnor, 18 miles southwest of Cowes.

At the western tip of the Isle of Wight is the island's most famous natural landmark, the **Needles,** a long line of jagged chalk stacks jutting out of the sea like monstrous teeth, with a lighthouse at the end. It's part of the Needles Pleasure Park, which has mostly child-oriented attractions. Adjacent is **Alum Bay,** accessed from the Needles by chairlift. Here you can catch a good view of the "colored sand" in the cliff strata or take a boat to view the lighthouse. **Yarmouth,** a quaint fishing village, is a 10-minute drive from Alum Bay.

GETTING HERE AND AROUND

Wightlink car and passenger ferries from Lymington dock at nearby Yarmouth. The spectacular A3055 runs along the southwest coast from Ventnor to Freshwater, the nearest town. From there you can follow the coast road to Alum Bay. Local bus services connect Freshwater with the rest of the island.

EXPLORING

Dimbola. This was the home of Julia Margaret Cameron (1815–79), the eminent Victorian portrait photographer and friend of Lord Tennyson. A gallery includes more than 60 examples of her work, including striking images of Carlyle, Tennyson, and Browning. There's also a room devoted to the various Isle of Wight rock festivals, most famously the five-day event in 1970 that featured the Who, the Doors, Joni Mitchell, and Jimi Hendrix. On the ground floor you'll find a shop and a good Alice in Wonderland-themed tearoom for snacks, hot lunches, and a traditional cream tea. ✉ *Terrace La., Freshwater Bay, Yarmouth* ☎ *01983/756814* ⊕ *www.dimbola.co.uk* ✆ *£4* ⊘ *Apr.–Oct., daily 10–5; Nov.–Mar., Tues.–Sun. and national holiday Mon. 10–4.*

SALISBURY, STONEHENGE, AND SALISBURY PLAIN

The roster of famous sights in this area takes in the attractive city of Salisbury, renowned for its glorious cathedral, and includes the renowned prehistoric sites at Stonehenge and Avebury. A trio of stately homes reveals the ambitions and wealth of their builders—Wilton House with its Inigo Jones–designed state rooms, Stourhead and its exquisite gardens, and the Elizabethan splendor of Longleat. Your own transportation is essential to see anything beyond Salisbury, other than Stonehenge or Avebury.

SALISBURY

24 miles northwest of Southampton, 44 miles southeast of Bristol, 79 miles southwest of London.

The silhouette of Salisbury Cathedral's majestic spire signals your approach to this historic city long before you arrive. Although the cathedral is the principal interest in the town, and the Cathedral Close one of the country's most atmospheric spots (best experienced on a foggy night), Salisbury has much more to see, not least its largely unspoiled— and relatively traffic-free—old center. Here are stone shops and houses that grew up in the shadow of the great church over the centuries. You're never far from any of the five rivers that meet here, or from the bucolic water meadows that stretch out to the west of the cathedral and provide the best views of it. Salisbury didn't become important until the early 13th century, when the seat of the diocese was transferred here from Old Sarum, the original settlement 2 miles to the north, of which only ruins remain. In the 19th century, novelist Anthony Trollope based his tales of ecclesiastical life, notably *Barchester Towers*, on life here, although his fictional city of Barchester is really an amalgam of Salisbury and Winchester. The local tourist office organizes walks—of differing lengths for varying stamina—to lead you to the treasures. And speaking of treasures, prehistoric Stonehenge is less than 10 miles away and easily visited from the city.

GETTING HERE AND AROUND

Salisbury is on main bus and train routes from London and South-ampton; regular buses also connect Salisbury with Winchester. The bus station is centrally located on Endless Street. Trains stop west of the center. After negotiating a ring-road system, drivers will want to park as soon as possible. The largest of the central parking lots is by Salisbury Playhouse. The city center is compact, so you won't need to use local buses for most sights. For Wilton House, take Bus Red 3 from New Canal, near Market Square.

TIMING

Market Square hosts general markets every Tuesday and Saturday and farmers' markets on the first and third Wednesday of the month. It's also the venue for other fairs and festivals, notably the one-day Food & Drink Festival in mid-September and the three-day Charter Fair in October. The city gets busy during the arts festival in May and June, when accommodation may be scarce.

TOURS

The Stonehenge Tour has hop-on, hop-off open-top buses leaving once or twice an hour all year from the train station and the bus station, and the route includes Old Sarum and Salisbury Cathedral as well as Stonehenge. Tickets cost £12; £20 includes a tour of Stonehenge and Old Sarum, £24 includes all three attractions. Salisbury City Guides offers 90-minute city tours by Blue Badge guides, departing from the tourist office at 11 every morning from April through October and on weekends the rest of the year. The cost is £5. Wessexplore has everything from walking tours to trips in luxury cars to a helicopter ride over Stonehenge.

ESSENTIALS

Visitor and Tour Information Salisbury City Guides ☎ 07873/212941 ⊕ *www.salisburycityguides.co.uk.* **Salisbury Information Centre** ✉ *Fish Row, off Market Sq.* ☎ 01722/342860 ⊕ *www.visitwiltshire.co.uk/salisbury.* **Stonehenge Tour** ☎ 0845/072–7093 ⊕ *www.thestonehengetour.co.uk.*

EXPLORING

TOP ATTRACTIONS

Cathedral Close. With its smooth lawns and splendid examples of archi-tecture from many periods creating a harmonious background, Salis-bury's Close forms probably the finest backdrop of any British cathedral. Some of the historic houses are open to the public. ✉ *Bounded by West Walk, North Walk, and Exeter St..*

Mompesson House. On the north side of Cathedral Close sits one of Brit-ain's most appealing Queen Anne houses, dating from 1701. As the display replicates a typical 18th-century family home, there are no trea-sures, but highlights include some fine original paneling and plaster-work, an exceptional carved oak staircase, and a fascinating collection of 18th-century drinking glasses. Tea and refreshments are served in a walled garden. ✉ *The Close* ☎ *01722/335659* ⊕ *www.nationaltrust.org. uk* 🖂 *£6.10* ⊙ *Mid-Mar.–Oct., Sat.–Wed. 11–5; last admission at 4:30.*

Old Sarum. Massive earthwork ramparts in a bare sweep of Wiltshire countryside are all that remain of this impressive Iron Age hill fort, which was successively taken over by Romans, Saxons, and Normans

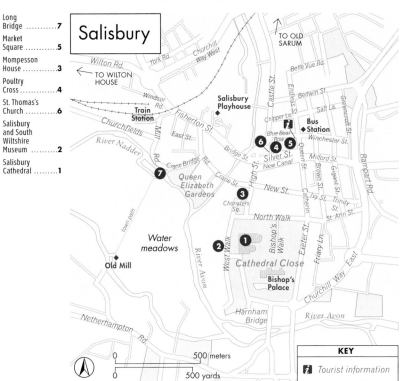

KEY

🚺 *Tourist information*

(who built a castle and cathedral within the earthworks). The site was still fortified in Tudor times, though the population had mostly decamped in the 13th century for the more amenable site of New Sarum, or Salisbury. You can clamber over the huge banks and ditches and take in the bracing views over the chalk downland to Salisbury Cathedral. ⊠ *Off A345, 2 miles north of Salisbury* ☎ *01722/335398* ⊕ *www.english-heritage.org.uk* ☜ *£3.90* ☉ *Apr.–June and Sept., daily 10–5; July and Aug., daily 9–6; Oct. and Mar., daily 10–4; Nov., Jan., and Feb., daily 11–4.*

Salisbury and South Wiltshire Museum. Opposite the cathedral's west front, this excellent museum is in the King's House, parts of which date back to the 15th century (James I stayed here in 1610 and 1613). Models and exhibits in the Stonehenge Gallery provide helpful background information for a visit to the famous stones. Also on view are skeletons, collections of costumes, lace, embroidery, Wedgwood pottery, and a collection of Turner watercolors, all dwarfed by the medieval pageant figure of St. Christopher, a 14-foot-tall giant, and his companion hobbyhorse, Hob Nob. A cozy café (closed Sunday) is in one of the oldest sections of the building. ⊠ *The King's House, 65 The Close* ☎ *01722/332151* ⊕ *www.salisburymuseum.org.uk* ☜ *£6* ☉ *July and Aug., Mon.–Sat. 10–5, Sun. noon–5; Sept.–June, Mon.–Sat. 10–5.*

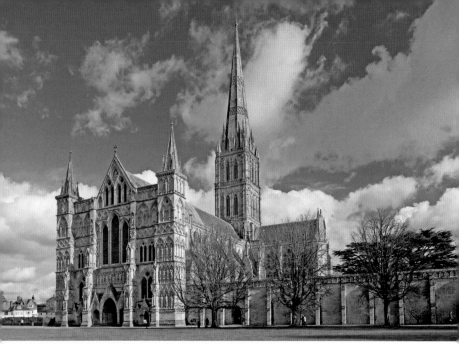
Salisbury Cathedral has a towering spire—the tallest in England—that you can tour.

★

Salisbury Cathedral. Salisbury is dominated by the towering cathedral, a soaring hymn in stone. It is unique among cathedrals in that it was conceived and built as a whole in the amazingly short span of 38 years (1220–58). The spire, added in 1320, is the tallest in England and a miraculous feat of medieval engineering—even though the point, 404 feet above the ground, is 2½ feet off vertical. For a fictional, keenly imaginative reconstruction of the drama underlying such an achievement, read William Golding's novel *The Spire*. The excellent model of the cathedral in the north nave aisle, directly in front of you as you enter, shows the building about 20 years into construction, and makes clear the ambition of Salisbury's medieval builders. For all their sophistication, the height and immense weight of the great spire have always posed structural problems. In the late 17th century Sir Christopher Wren was summoned from London to strengthen the spire, and in the mid-19th century Sir George Gilbert Scott, a leading Victorian Gothicist, undertook a major program of restoration. He also initiated a clearing out of the interior and removed some less-than-sympathetic 18th-century alterations, returning a more authentically Gothic feel. Despite this, the interior seems spartan and a little gloomy, but check out the remarkable lancet windows and sculpted tombs of crusaders and other medieval notables. Next to the cathedral model in the north aisle is a medieval clock—probably the oldest working mechanism in Europe, if not the world—made in 1386.

The **cloisters** are the largest in England, and the octagonal **Chapter House** contains a marvelous 13th-century frieze showing scenes from the Old Testament. Here you can also see one of the four original copies of the **Magna Carta,** the charter of rights the English barons forced King John to accept in 1215; it was sent here for safekeeping in the 13th century. ▦ TIP➔ **Join a free 45-minute tour of the church, leaving two or more times a day. There are also daily tours of the roof and spire (except on Sunday morning) that vary in frequency—check website.** For a peaceful break, the café in the cloister offers freshly baked cakes and pastries, plus hot lunches. ⊠ *Cathedral Close* ☏ *01722/555150* ⊕ *www.salisburycathedral.org.uk* ✉ *Cathedral and Chapter House free; suggested donation £6.50; tower tour £10* ⊙ *Cathedral Apr.–Sept., Mon.–Sat. 9–5, Sun. noon–4; Oct.–Mar., daily 10–4.30. Chapter House Mon.–Sat. 9:30–4:30, Sun. 12:45–3:45.*

Fodor'sChoice
★

Wilton House. This is considered to be one of the loveliest stately homes in England and, along with its grounds, a fine example of the English Palladian style. The seat of the earls of Pembroke since Tudor times, the south wing of the current building was rebuilt in the early 17th century by Isaac de Caus, with input from Inigo Jones, Ben Jonson's stage designer and the architect of London's Banqueting House. It was completed by James Webb, again with input from Jones, Webb's uncle-by-marriage, after the recently finished south wing was ravaged by fire in 1647. Most noteworthy are the seven state room in the south wing, among them the Single Cube Room (built as a perfect 30-foot cube) and one of the most extravagantly beautiful rooms in the history of interior decoration, the aptly named Double Cube Room. The name refers to its proportions (60 feet long by 30 feet wide and 30 feet high), evidence of Jones's classically inspired belief that beauty in architecture derives from harmony and balance. The room's headliner is the spectacular Van Dyck portrait of the Pembroke family. Elsewhere at Wilton House, the art collection includes several other old master paintings, including works by Rembrandt and members of the Brueghel family. Also of note are the lovely grounds, which have sweeping lawns dotted with towering oaks; the gardens; and the Palladian bridge crossing the small River Nadder, designed by the 9th Earl after the Rialto Bridge in Venice. ▦ TIP➔ **Be sure to explore the extensive gardens; children will appreciate the large playground.** The town of Wilton is 3 miles west of Salisbury. Buses 2, 13, 25, 26, 27, and Red 3 from Salisbury stop outside Wilton House. They depart every 10 to 15 minutes. ⊠ *Off A36, Wilton* ☏ *01722/746714* ⊕ *www.wiltonhouse.co.uk* ✉ *£14; grounds only £5.50* ⊙ *House Easter and May–Aug., Sun.–Thurs.11:30–5; grounds early Apr.–mid-Apr. and May–mid-Sept., daily 11–5:30.*

WORTH NOTING

Long Bridge. For a classic view of Salisbury, head to the Long Bridge and the Town Path. From the main street walk west to Mill Road, which leads you across Queen Elizabeth Gardens. Cross the bridge and continue on the Town Path through the water meadows from which you can see the vista John Constable painted to create that 19th-century icon, *Salisbury Cathedral,* now hung in the Constable Room of London's National Gallery.

Market Square. One of southern England's most popular markets fills this square on Tuesday and Saturday. Permission to hold an annual fair here was granted in 1221, and that right is still exercised for three days

With its art and gilded furniture, the Double Cube Room at Wilton House may well be one of England's most beautiful interiors.

every October, when the Charter Fair takes place. A narrow side street links Poultry Cross to Market Square. ⊠ *Market Sq.*

Poultry Cross. One of Salisbury's best-known landmarks, the hexagonal Poultry Cross is the last remaining of the four original medieval market crosses, and dealers still set up their stalls beside it. A cross on the site was first mentioned in 1307, and a poultry cross here was first named as such a century or so later. The canopy and flying buttresses were added in 1852. ⊠ *Silver St.*

St. Thomas's Church. This church contains a rare medieval Doom painting of Judgment Day, considered to be one of the best preserved and most complete of the few such works left in Britain. Created around 1470 and covering the chancel arch, the scenes of heaven and hell served to instill the fear of damnation into the congregation. ■ TIP→ It's best seen on a spring or summer evening when the light through the west window illuminates the details. ⊠ *St. Thomas's Sq.* ☎ *01722/322537* ⊕ *www. stthomassalisbury.co.uk* ☞ *Free* ☉ *Apr.–Oct., Mon.–Sat. 8:30–5, Sun. noon–6; Nov.–Mar., Mon.–Sat. 8:30–3, Sun. noon–6.*

QUICK
BITES

Fisherton Mill. A former grain mill, Fisherton Mill houses artist studios and exhibition spaces showcasing paintings, sculptures, textiles, and jewelry. Enjoy a light lunch or Wiltshire cream tea in the well-regarded café. It shuts down for the day at 5, except for Sunday when it's closed. ⊠ *108 Fisherton St.* ☎ *01722/415121* ⊕ *www.fishertonmill.co.uk.*

WHERE TO EAT

$ 🍴 **Anokaa.** For a refreshingly modern take on Indian cuisine, try this bustling restaurant a few minutes from the center. Classic recipes are taken as starting points for the artistically presented dishes, which include beef marinated in yogurt and rum, cinnamon-glazed duck breast stuffed with garlicky spinach, and black tiger prawns in a sauce of curry leaves and coconut oil. At lunchtime, choose from the buffet selection. The setting is contemporary and cosmopolitan, and service by staff in traditional dress is friendly and prompt. [$] *Average main: £12* ✉ *60 Fisherton St.* ☎ *01722/414142* 🌐 *www.anokaa.com.*
INDIAN

> **DOUBLE CUBE ROOM**
>
> Adorned with gilded furniture by William Kent, Wilton House's Double Cube was where Eisenhower and Churchill prepared plans for the D-Day landings during World War II. It has been used in many films, including *The Madness of King George*, *Mrs. Brown*, the 2005 version of *Pride and Prejudice*, Emma Thompson's adaptation of *Sense and Sensibility*, and *The Young Victoria*.

$ 🍴 **Boston Tea Party.** Specializing in quick, nourishing meals, this relaxed and child-friendly café serves hot and cold breakfasts, lunches, and afternoon snacks. Homemade meat and vegetarian burgers with interesting toppings like red-onion marmalade or chili sauce, come with potato wedges. The huge vegan Super Salad is enlivened with mango and grapefruit. Freshly roasted coffee and a wide selection of teas are a nice complement to the freshly baked cakes. You can eat upstairs in the spectacular Tudor great hall or the quieter side room. [$] *Average main: £7* ✉ *13 High St.* ☎ *01722/238116* 🌐 *www.bostonteaparty.co.uk* 🕒 *No dinner.*
CAFÉ

$ 🍴 **Charter 1227.** Casual and friendly but upscale, with red carpets and taupe leather seats, this second-floor restaurant enjoys a prime position overlooking Market Square. The menu blends traditional British and Mediterranean dishes, such as scallops wrapped in pancetta and slow-braised lamb shank. There are good-value fixed-price lunches. [$] *Average main: £14* ✉ *7 Ox Row, Market Sq.* ☎ *01722/333118* 🌐 *www.charter1227.co.uk* 🕒 *Closed Mon. No dinner Sun.*
BRITISH

$ 🍴 **Haunch of Venison.** This wood-paneled pub opposite the Poultry Cross has been going strong for more than six centuries. It brims with character, thanks to details such as the mummified hand of an 18th-century card player still clutching his cards and the last pewter-top bar in England. You can fortify yourself with one of the 80 or so malt whiskies or repair to the upstairs restaurant for dishes such as panfried sea bass or venison and bacon casserole. The pub can be crowded and the service (to nonlocals) brusque. [$] *Average main: £13* ✉ *1 Minster St.* ☎ *01722/411313* 🌐 *www.restaurant-salisbury.com.*
BRITISH

$$$$ 🍴 **Howard's House.** If you're after complete tranquillity, head for this early-17th-century house set on 2 acres of grounds in the Nadder Valley. The style is traditional and smart, and a terrace provides alfresco dining overlooking the tidy lawns in summer. Sophisticated contemporary fare makes up most of what's on the set-price menus, such as fillet of wild turbot with goat cheese gnocchi, and breast of guinea fowl
MODERN BRITISH

with seared foie gras. Nine luxuriously furnished guest rooms may tempt you into forgoing the 10-mile drive back to Salisbury. $ *Average main: £32* ⊠ *Off B3089, Teffont Evias* ☎ *01722/716392* ⊕ *www.howardshousehotel.co.uk.*

WHERE TO STAY

For expanded hotel reviews, visit Fodors.com.

$
B&B/INN
Cricket Field House. Located halfway between Wilton and Salisbury, this comfortable ex-gamekeeper's cottage overlooks a cricket ground and has a large, peaceful garden of its own. **Pros:** efficient, helpful management; well-maintained rooms; good breakfasts. **Cons:** dated decor; on a busy road; lacks charm. $ *Rooms from: £85* ⊠ *Wilton Rd.* ☎ *01722/322595* ⊕ *www.cricketfieldhouse.co.uk* ⟿ *18 rooms* ⦿| *Breakfast.*

$
B&B/INN
Rokeby Guest House. Easy to find on the east side of town, this four-story Edwardian B&B represents good value for your money with its spic-and-span, tastefully decorated interiors and a large, landscaped garden with a summerhouse. **Pros:** convenient location; helpful hosts; abundant and tasty breakfasts. **Cons:** not central. $ *Rooms from: £65* ⊠ *3 Wain-a-Long Rd.* ☎ *01722/329800* ⊕ *www.rokebyguesthouse.co.uk* ⟿ *10 rooms* ⦿| *Breakfast.*

$
B&B/INN
Wyndham Park Lodge. This simple Victorian house in a quiet part of town (off Castle Street) provides an excellent place to rest and a delicious breakfast, as well as a garden. **Pros:** efficient and hospitable owners; convenient location; good breakfast; handy parking. **Cons:** spotty Wi-Fi connection. $ *Rooms from: £55* ⊠ *51 Wyndham Rd.* ☎ *01722/416517* ⊕ *www.wyndhamparklodge.co.uk* ⟿ *3 rooms* ⦿| *Breakfast.*

NIGHTLIFE AND THE ARTS

Salisbury International Arts Festival. Held at the end of May and the beginning of June, the festival has outstanding classical concerts, recitals, plays, street theater, and outdoor events. ⊠ *87 Crane St.* ☎ *0845/241–9651* ⊕ *www.salisburyfestival.co.uk.*

Salisbury Playhouse. The playhouse presents high-caliber drama all year and is the main venue for the Salisbury Arts Festival. ⊠ *Malthouse La.* ☎ *01722/320333* ⊕ *www.salisburyplayhouse.com.*

SHOPPING

Most of the shops are gathered around Market Square, venue for twice-weekly markets and the annual Charter Fair, and along High Street, where chain stores predominate.

Dauwalders. This shop specializes in stamps, coins, medals, and models, including some quirky gift ideas. ⊠ *42 Fisherton St.* ☎ *01722/412100.*

FOOD AND DRINK FESTIVAL

Salisbury forces you to squeeze a lot in during its one-day **Food & Drink Festival** (☎ *01722/332241* ⊕ *www.salisburyfestival.co.uk*) in mid-September. There are wine and beer tents, a waiters' race, cooking demonstrations, barbecues, and festival menus in the restaurants. The main venue is Market Square.

Salisbury lives it up at the annual Salisbury International Arts Festival.

National Trust Shop. The range of traditional gifts here is large, from pottery to books, bags, soaps, jam, biscuits, honey, and garden-inspired accessories. ⊠ *House of Steps, 41 High St.* ☏ *01722/331884.*

SPORTS

Hayball Cyclesport. Bike rentals here cost about £15 per day or £70 per week, with a £25 cash deposit. ⊠ *26–30 Winchester St.* ☏ *01722/411378.*

STONEHENGE

8 miles north of Salisbury, 20 miles south of Avebury.

Fodor's Choice
★ **Stonehenge.** *For information about this site, see the feature Mysterious Stonehenge.*

AVEBURY

24 miles north of Stonehenge, 34 miles north of Salisbury, 25 miles northeast of Longleat, 27 miles east of Bath.

The village of Avebury was built much later than the stone circles that brought it fame; it has an informative museum with an outstanding collection of Bronze Age artifacts from the area around Stonehenge. You can also explore a cluster of other ancient sites nearby.

GETTING HERE AND AROUND

From Salisbury, follow A345 north to Upavon and take the A342 to Devizes; then continue 7 miles northeast on the A361. You can also take the hourly Stagecoach bus No. 49 from Swindon to Avebury (30 minutes).

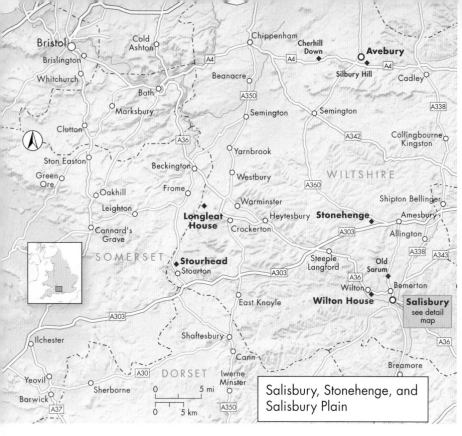

Salisbury, Stonehenge, and Salisbury Plain

EXPLORING

TOP ATTRACTIONS

FAMILY **Alexander Keiller Museum.** Archaeological finds from the Avebury area, and charts, photos, models, and home movies taken by archaeologist Alexander Keiller himself, put the Avebury Stone Circles and the site into context. Recent revelations suggest that Keiller, responsible for the excavation of Avebury in the 1930s, may have adapted the site's layout more in the interests of presentation than authenticity. The exhibits are divided between the **Stables Gallery,** showing excavated finds, and the more child-friendly, interactive **Barn Gallery.** You can also visit the Elizabethan manor house where Keiller lived, which has interactive exhibits on his work and the excavation. ⊠ *1 mi north of A4* ☎ *01672/539250* ⊕ *www.nationaltrust.org.uk* ☑ *£4.90* ☉ *Apr.–Oct., daily 10–6; Nov.– Mar., daily 10–4.*

Fodor's Choice **Avebury Stone Circles.** Surrounding part of Avebury village, the Ave-
★ bury Stone Circles are one of England's most evocative prehistoric monuments—not so famous as Stonehenge, but all the more powerful for their lack of commercial exploitation. The stones were erected around 2600 BC, about the same time the better-known monument. As with Stonehenge, the purpose of this stone circle has never been ascertained, although it most likely was used for similar ritual purposes.

Unlike Stonehenge, however, there are no certain astronomical alignments at Avebury, at least none that have survived. The main site consists of a wide, circular ditch and bank, about 1,400 feet across and more than half a mile around. Entrances break the perimeter at roughly the four points of the compass, and inside stand the remains of three stone circles. The largest one originally had 98 stones, although only 27 remain. Many stones on the site were destroyed centuries ago, especially in the 14th century when they were buried for unclear reasons, possibly religious fanaticism. Others were later pillaged in the 18th century to build the thatched cottages you see flanking the fields. You can walk around the circles at any time; early morning and early evening are recommended. ✉ *1 mile north of A4* ⊕ *www.nationaltrust.org.uk* 🖾 *Free* ☉ *Daily.*

> **WORD OF MOUTH**
>
> "I've been to Stonehenge three times and loved it each time but agree the fence there is not nice. The real gem is a few miles away at Avebury. Same stones, not as big but set in the middle of a little village. Just as surreal as to why they are there in the pattern they are in. You have complete freedom to roam the stones, visit the haunted pub, and marvel at the stones. I enjoyed it as much or more than Stonehenge."
>
> —smurcook

WORTH NOTING

Cherhill Down. Four miles west of Avebury, Cherhill Down is a prominent hill carved with a vivid white horse and topped with a towering obelisk. It's one of a number of hillside etchings in Wiltshire, all but two of which date back no farther than the late 18th century. This one was put there in 1780 to indicate the highest point of the downs between London and Bath. The views from the top are well worth the half-hour climb. The best view of the horse is from A4, on the approach from Calne. ✉ *A4.*

Kennet Stone Avenue. The Avebury monument lies at the end of the Kennet Stone Avenue, a sort of prehistoric processional way leading to the stone circles. The avenue's stones were spaced 80 feet apart, but only the half mile nearest the main monument survives intact. The lost stones are marked with concrete obelisks.

Silbury Hill. Rising 130 feet and comparable in height and volume to the roughly contemporary pyramids in Egypt, the largest man-made mound in Europe dates from about 2400 BC. Though there have been periodic excavations of the mound since the 17th century, its original purpose remains unknown The viewing area, less than 1 mile east of Avebury, is accessible only during daylight hours. ✉ *A4.*

West Kennet Long Barrow. One of the largest Neolithic chambered tombs in Britain, West Kennet Long Barrow was built around 3400 BC. You can explore all around the site and also enter the tomb, which was used for more than 1,000 years before the main passage was blocked and the entrance closed, around 2000 BC. More than 300 feet long, it has an elevated position with a great view of Silbury Hill and the surrounding countryside. It's about 1 mile east of Avebury. ✉ *A4.*

Continued on page 281

MYSTERIOUS
STONEHENGE

A circle of giant stones sitting on the wide sweep of Salisbury Plain, Stonehenge is one of the most famous prehistoric sites in England. It still has the capacity to fascinate and move those who view it, but Stonehenge can also be perplexing. The site seems to pose more questions than it answers about its 5,000-year-long history, and its meaning and purpose are continually reevaluated and debated. With some context, you can experience Stonehenge as it once was: deeply mystical and awe-inspiring.

The ineffable mystery of Stonehenge—the name derives from the Anglo-Saxon term for "hanging stones"—remains despite the presence of a busy road nearby and close to a million visitors a year. With an improved visitor center 1.5 miles away scheduled to be completed before 2014 and traffic re-routed as of mid-2014, the experience of seeing Stonehenge promises to be hugely improved. But timing your visit and taking advantage of what the site offers—including a good audio guide—are important.

It also helps to sort through the theories, and to look at the landscape. Stonehenge was created in, broadly speaking, three stages: the earliest stage around 3000 BC, the stone settings around 2500 BC, and the rearrangement of the stones around 2300 BC. It was built on Salisbury Plain, an area devoid of trees since the last ice age—but it does not stand in isolation. The Stonehenge part of the UNESCO World Heritage Site of Stonehenge and Avebury (a nearby stone circle) covers almost 6,500 acres containing more than 350 burial mounds and prehistoric monuments. Archaeologists continue to rewrite the site's history as they uncover more evidence about Stonehenge and the surrounding ancient structures.

—by Ellin Stein

Opposite: Theories about the sun and its alignment with Stonehenge continue to invite debate. Above: An aerial view provides perspective on the great stone circle.

VIEWING STONEHENGE TODAY

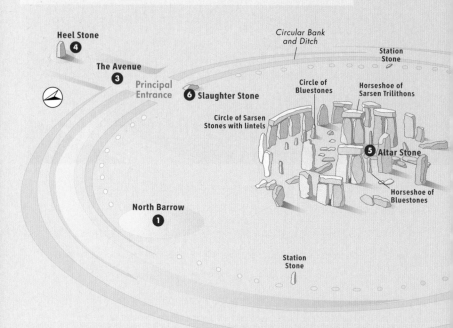

Heel Stone **4**

The Avenue **3**

Principal Entrance

6 Slaughter Stone

Circular Bank and Ditch

Station Stone

Circle of Bluestones

Horseshoe of Sarsen Trilithons

Circle of Sarsen Stones with lintels

5 Altar Stone

Horseshoe of Bluestones

North Barrow **1**

Station Stone

LAYOUT OF THE CIRCLE

Stonehenge today has an **outer circle of sarsen stones**, sandstone blocks from nearby Marlborough Downs. It is the only stone circle in the world with lintels. The huge stones are around 13 feet high, 7 feet wide, and weigh about 25 tons each. This sarsen circle surrounds a smaller **circle of bluestones**, a dolerite stone that appears blue when wet. Bluestones were possibly the first stones at the site, brought from the Preseli Hills in West Wales 150 miles away.

Sarsen stones form the **trilithons**, the tall (over 20 feet) pairs of upright stones with lintels across the top, in the center of the circle, part of an **inner horseshoe of sarsen stones and bluestones.** The sandstone **Altar Stone** is also in the center. The horseshoe's open end and central upright stones face midsummer sunrise and midwinter sunset.

The word "henge" refers to another feature of the site: a henge is a **circular earthwork bank with an internal ditch** surrounding flattened ground. Stonehenge is unusual in that the ditch is outside the earthwork bank.

OVER THE CENTURIES

Circular ditch with interior bank constructed

2850 BC Construction of nearby Avebury stone circles begins

2500 BC Large sarsen stones brought to Stonehenge; first bluestones brought from Wales

3000 BC   2800 BC   2500 BC   2400 B

Heel Stone

South Barrow

Secondary
Entrance

Aubrey Holes
2

HOW MANY STONES?
Many of the site's original stones have been lost over the years to builders of roads and houses and souvenir hunters, and some have fallen down. However, out of the original 30 large sarsen uprights, 17 remain, with 3 of the 5 trilithons still standing. Forty-three bluestones are left from the original 80 or so, and other major stones remain at the site.

❶ North Barrow. The outer ditch and bank intersect with the largely unexcavated North Barrow, thought to have been used for burials. The barrow may predate Stonehenge.

❷ Aubrey Holes. These 56 pits inside the outer bank, now with concrete markers, are named after John Aubrey, the antiquarian who identified them in 1666. Evidence suggests they may once have contained bluestone or timber uprights and were later used for cremated remains.

❸ The Avenue. The Avenue's parallel ditches and banks stretch over 2.8 km (1.7 miles) to the bank of the River Avon. It was discovered in 2009, but little remains. Periglacial stripes, a natural geographic feature, run parallel to the banks of the Avenue and align in place with the solstice axis.

❹ Heel Stone. This sarsen block stands at the entrance to the Avenue, on the edge of the current site. At midsummer solstice, the sun rises over the Heel Stone.

❺ Altar Stone. Now recumbent, the great sandstone Altar Stone stood nearly 6 feet tall at the center of Stonehenge. Unlike the sarsen stones, it probably came from Milford Haven in Wales. Despite the name, its purpose remains unknown. Today the

stone is the centerpiece for rituals around the summer and winter solstice.

❻ Slaughter Stone. This stone, originally upright, now lies within the northeast entrance, and may have formed part of a portal. It is stained a rusty red by rainwater acting on the iron in the stone, rather than by the blood of human sacrifice, as 18th-century legend says.

Trilithon standing stones

MOVING THE STONES
The first 80 bluestones were brought by sea and river over 150 miles from Wales around 2500 BC. People probably used rafts to transport the bluestones over water. The heavier sarsen stones were dragged about 25 miles over land from the Marlborough Downs, and tipped into pits dug in the chalk plain. It is possible that people used wooden rollers for transporting the stones.

4

IN FOCUS MYSTERIOUS STONEHENGE

2400 BC The Avenue constructed, leading to West Amesbury Henge at the River Avon

2300 BC Final rearrangement of bluestones into interior circle

1600 BC Concentric circles of Y and Z holes dug

LEGENDS, MYTHS, and CURRENT THEORIES

LEGENDARY STONEHENGE

Because of its prominence, Stonehenge has become steeped in myths assigning it any number of religious, mystical, and spiritual functions: it was built by the legendary Arthurian wizard Merlin, by the devil, giants, even aliens. The rebel queen Boudicca, who fought against the Romans, was said to have been buried at Stonehenge after the Romans fought the Druids, giving rise to the myth that the Druids built the stone circle to mark her tomb. One thing is certain: the Druids had nothing to do with the construction of Stonehenge, which had already stood for 2,000 years when they appeared.

WHO BUILT STONEHENGE?

The Neolithic and Bronze Age people who built Stonehenge, beginning around the time that the great pyramids in Egypt were built, had only hand tools for shaping the stones and their own manpower for moving them. No other stone circle contains such carefully shaped and meticulously placed stones. Some stones also show carvings of daggers and axes.

The first Neolithic people at what is now the World Heritage Site were semi-nomadic farmers who buried their dead in large, east-west facing barrows. Later, between 2500 and 2200 BC, the "Beaker People" started to use the site. Their name comes from their tradition of burying their dead with pottery (seen in displays at the Salisbury and South Wiltshire Museum), and they may have been sun worshipers. The final group was the Wessex people, around 1600 BC, who probably made the carvings in the stones and finalized Stonehenge's structure.

NEW THEORIES

Recent excavations have put forward two major new theories about its purpose. Evidence from the Stonehenge Riverside Project, a major ongoing archaeological study running since 2003, indicates that it was a domain of the dead: both a burial ground and a memorial. Numerous burials have been found all over the site and the surrounding area. Stonehenge is joined to Durrington Walls, the world's largest known henge and a nearby ancient

Above: Many stones have fallen, but Stonehenge is still a powerful sight.

settlement, by the River Avon and the Avenue. The journey along the river to Stonehenge may have been a ritual passage from life to death.

Another theory is that Stonehenge was a place of healing, accounting for the number of burials with physical injury and disease found in the tombs here as well as the unusual number of people who were not native to the area. That the bluestones were brought from so far away suggests that they were thought to harbor great powers.

STONEHENGE AND THE SUN

Stonehenge's design offers an intriguing clue as to its purpose, although there are no definitive answers. The horseshoe of trilithons and other stone settings align on the solstitial (midsummer sunrise and midwinter sunset) axis. This has led to much speculation and a variety of ideas. The centuries-old theory persists that Stonehenge was an astronomical observatory, a calendar, or a sun temple. It is fairly certain that it was a religious site, and worship here may have involved cycles of the sun.

On Summer Solstice (June 21), thousands gather to watch the sun rise over the Heel Stone. But the discovery of a neighboring stone to the Heel Stone questions even this, suggesting it may not itself have been a marker of sunrise, but part of a "solar corridor" that framed the sunrise.

Ongoing archaeological research, not to mention speculation, continues to revise the story of Stonehenge.

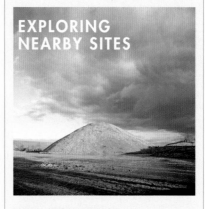

EXPLORING NEARBY SITES

NEAR STONEHENGE

Hundreds of Neolithic monuments and barrows dot the landscape around Stonehenge. Excavations at **Durrington Walls**, a couple of miles northeast of Stonehenge off A345, have unearthed a substantial settlement dating from around 2500 BC, probably occupied by Stonehenge's builders. Although there is little left of most Neolithic sites today, concrete posts mark nearby **Woodhenge** (also off A345), which dates from around 2300 BC. Its long axis is aligned to the midsummer sunrise and the midwinter sunset. Admission and parking are free at both these sites.

AVEBURY AND ENVIRONS

Twenty-four miles to the north lie Avebury and the **Avebury Stone Circles**, the largest stone circles in the world (dating to around 2850 BC). You can walk freely among the stones— a major attraction for those who prefer the site to Stonehenge.
Silbury Hill, the last of the great monuments, and **West Kennet Long Barrow**, a tomb, are close by.

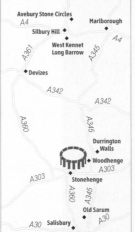

Above, Silbury Hill

MAKING THE MOST OF YOUR VISIT

WHEN TO VISIT

Come early before the crowds arrive, or in the evening when the light is low and skies darkening. Summer weekends and school holidays can be especially crowded. Stonehenge is packed at Summer Solstice, when visitors stay all night to watch the sun rise. If you want to visit at this time, use the dedicated bus service from Salisbury.

English Heritage, which manages the site, can arrange access to the inner circle (not a guided tour) outside of regular hours; each group is 26 people maximum. This requires application and payment of £16.30 well in advance, as Stone Circle Access visits are popular. Apply by mail or fax, call the booking office at ☎ 0870/333–0605, or email ✉ stonecircleaccess@englishheritage. org.uk. The booking form is available at ⊕ www.english-heritage.org.uk.

The site is in the midst of a major development program. Until 2014, facilities remain limited to a visitor center, shop, and refreshment stand. Check the English Heritage website for updates.

TIPS AND WHAT TO BRING

Since the stones are roped off, bring binoculars to see the prehistoric carvings on them. Spend a few hours: walk all around the site to get that perfect photo and to observe the changing light on the plain. The free audio guide is essential, and the shop sells plenty of books.

MAKING A DAY OF IT

The Salisbury and South Wiltshire Museum in Salisbury has finds from the site and burial reconstructions that help put Stonehenge into perspective. The smaller Alexander Keiller Museum in Avebury has finds from the area.

It's an easy drive between nearby prehistoric sites. Stonehenge is set in

Avebury, Wiltshire

1,500 acres of National Trust land with excellent walks. There is a proposal for a 45-mile, Great Stones Way, a walking path that will link Avebury with Stonehenge and will reach Old Sarum, near Salisbury.

GETTING HERE

By car, Stonehenge is 2 miles west of Amesbury off A344. The **Stonehenge Tour Bus** (⊕ www.thestonehengetour. info) departs from Salisbury rail and bus stations frequently; buses leave every half hour or hour. Tickets cost £12, or £20 with Stonehenge and Old Sarum admission. Other options are a taxi or an organized tour. **Salisbury and Stonehenge Guided Tours** (⊕ www.salis buryguidedtours.com ☎ 07775/674816 ✉ pat_shelley@btinternet.com) operates small-group tours from Salisbury and London.

VISITOR INFORMATION

✉ Junction of A303 and A360, near Amesbury ☎ 0870/333–1181, 0870/333–0605 for after-hours access ⊕ www.english-heritage.org.uk 🖻 £8 ⊙ Mid-Mar.–May and Sept.–mid-Oct., daily 9:30–6; June–Aug., daily 9–7; mid-Oct.–mid-Mar., daily 9:30–4. Last admission 30 mins before closing.

WHERE TO EAT AND STAY

For expanded hotel reviews, visit Fodors.com.

$ ✕**Waggon and Horses.** A 16th-century thatched building, this traditional
BRITISH inn and pub is a two-minute drive from the prehistoric circle. Dickens
mentioned the building in the *Pickwick Papers*. Excellent lunches and
dinners are served beside a fire. Homemade dishes include steak, kidney,
and ale pie, pork terrine, and goat's cheese and spinach rissoto. In high
season it's something of a tourist hub. $ *Average main: £10* ⊠ *A4, east
of A361, Beckhampton* ☎ *01672/539418.*

$$$ 🛏 **The Lodge.** The spacious rooms of this charming B&B are full of char-
B&B/INN acter, thanks to the eclectic decor, rare prints, and antique furnishings,
but its special appeal is its one-of-a-kind location within the Avebury
Stone Circles, which the two guest rooms look out on. **Pros:** great views;
comfortable rooms; friendly host **Cons:** can book up. $ *Rooms from:
£175* ⊠ *High St.* ☎ *01672/539023* ⊕ *www.aveburylodge.co.uk* 🛏 *2
rooms* ⦿ *Breakfast.*

LONGLEAT HOUSE

*31 miles southwest of Avebury, 6 miles north of Stourhead, 19 miles
south of Bath, 27 miles northwest of Salisbury.*

With its popular safari park and a richly decorated Italian Renaissance–
style house to explore. Longleat can provide a day of diversions.

GETTING HERE AND AROUND

Longleat House is off A36 between Bath and Salisbury. The nearest
train station is Warminster, about 5 miles away. Your best option is to
take a taxi from there.

ESSENTIALS

Visitor Information Warminster Information Centre ⊠ *Central car park, off
Station Rd.* ☎ 01985/218548 ⊕ www.visitwiltshire.co.uk.

EXPLORING

FAMILY **Longleat House.** Home of the Marquess of Bath, Longleat House is one of
southern England's most famous private estates, and possibly the most
ambitiously, even eccentrically, commercialized, as evidenced by the
presence of a drive-through safari park (open since 1966) with giraffes,
zebras, monkeys, rhinos, and lions. The Italian Renaissance-style build-
ing was largely completed in 1580 (for more than £8,000, an astro-
nomical sum at the time) and contains outstanding tapestries, paintings,
porcelain, and furniture, as well as notable period features such as the
Victorian kitchens, an Elizabethan minstrels' gallery, and the great hall
with its massive wooden beams. Giant antlers of the extinct Irish elk
decorate the walls, as do the present marquess's occasionally raunchy
murals—described as "keyhole glimpses into my psyche" that range
from philosophical subjects to depictions of the Kama Sutra. Besides
the safari park, Longleat has a butterfly garden, a miniature railway, an
extensive (and fairly fiendish) hedge maze, and an adventure castle, all
of which make it extremely popular, particularly in summer and during
school vacations. ■TIP➡ You can easily spend a whole day here. Visit
the house in the morning, when tours are more relaxed, and the safari

park in the afternoon. A safari bus service is available (£4) for those arriving without their own transport. ✉ *Off A362* ☎ *01985/844400* 🌐 *www.longleat.co.uk* 🎟 *£29.50; house and grounds only, £14.50* 🕒 *Mar., daily 10–5; Apr.–mid-July and mid-Sept.–late Oct., daily 10–6; late July–early Sept., daily 10–7:30; Nov. and Dec., call in advance.*

WHERE TO STAY

For expanded hotel reviews, visit Fodors.com.

$$ HOTEL **Bishopstrow House.** This ivy-covered Georgian manor house set in 27 acres has been converted into a relaxed country-house hotel that combines well-chosen antiques with modern amenities such as DVD players. **Pros:** country-house ambience; impressive suites; excellent leisure facilities. **Cons:** expensive extras; restaurant lacks charm; some standard rooms dark; unpredictable heating. [$] *Rooms from: £145* ✉ *Boreham Rd.* ☎ *01985/212312* 🌐 *www.bishopstrow.co.uk* 🛏 *29 rooms, 3 suites* 🍴 *Breakfast.*

STOURHEAD

9 miles southwest of Longleat, 15 miles northeast of Sherborne, 30 miles west of Salisbury.

England has many memorable gardens, but Stourhead holds a high place in this pantheon. Naturalistic landscaping and well-sited temples and other decorative features are spectacular; the Palladian house is a bonus but also worth a look.

GETTING HERE AND AROUND

By car, you can reach Stourhead via B3092. It's signposted off the main road. From London, board a train to Gillingham and take a five-minute cab ride to Stourton.

EXPLORING

Fodor's Choice ★ **Stourhead.** Close to the village of Stourton lies one of Wiltshire's most breathtaking sights—Stourhead, a country-house-and-garden combination that has few parallels for beauty anywhere in Europe. Most of Stourhead was built between 1721 and 1725 by Henry the Magnificent, the wealthy banker Henry Hoare. A fire gutted the center of the house in 1902, but it was reconstructed with only a few differences. Many rooms in the Palladian mansion contain Chinese and French porcelain, and some have furniture by Chippendale. The elegant Regency library and picture gallery were built for the cultural enrichment of this cultivated family. Still, the house takes second place to the adjacent gardens designed by Henry Hoare II, which are the most celebrated example of the English 18th-century taste for "natural" landscaping. Temples, grottoes, and bridges have been placed among shrubs, trees, and flowers to make the grounds look like a three-dimensional oil painting. A walk around the artificial lake (1½ miles) reveals changing vistas that conjure up the 17th-century landscapes of Claude Lorrain and Nicolas Poussin; walk counterclockwise for the best views. **TIP→ The best time to visit is early summer, when the massive banks of rhododendrons are in full bloom, or mid-October for autumn color, but the gardens are beautiful at any time of year.** You can get a fine view of the surrounding area from Alfred's Tower, a 1772 folly (a structure built for picturesque effect). A restaurant and plant shop are on the grounds. All in all, it's easy to spend half a day here. ✉ *Off B3092, northwest of Mere* ☎ *01747/841152* 🌐 *www.nationaltrust.org.uk* 🎟 *House £14.20 house; gardens £8.50; Alfred's Tower £3.50* 🕐 *House mid-Mar.–Oct., daily 11–4:30. Gardens Apr.–Sept., daily 9–7; Oct., daily 9–5. Alfred's Tower Mar.–Oct., weekends noon–4.*

WHERE TO STAY

For expanded hotel reviews, visit Fodors.com.

$$ 🏨 **The Spread Eagle.** You can't stay at Stourhead, but you can stay at
B&B/INN this popular inn built at the beginning of the 19th century just inside the main entrance. **Pros:** period character; lovely rooms; free access to Stourhead. **Cons:** needs some modernization; food can be disappointing and service brusque. [$] *Rooms from: £120* ✉ *Off B3092, northwest of Mere* ☎ *01747/840587* 🌐 *www.spreadeagleinn.com* 🛏 *5 rooms* 🍴 *Breakfast.*

4

NEW FOREST, DORSET, AND THE SOUTH COAST

Tucked southwest of Southampton, the New Forest was once the hunting preserve of William the Conqueror and his royal descendants. Thus protected from the deforestation that has befallen most of southern England's other forests, this relatively wild, scenic expanse offers great possibilities for walking, riding, and biking. West of here stretches the green, hilly, and largely unspoiled county of Dorset, the setting for most of the books of Thomas Hardy, author of *Far from the Madding Crowd* and other classic Victorian-era novels. "I am convinced that it is better for a writer to know a little bit of the world remarkably well than to know a great part of the world remarkably little," he wrote as he immortalized the towns, villages, and fields of this rural area, not least the county capital, Dorchester, an ancient agricultural center. North of here is the unspoiled market town of Sherborne. Other places of historic interest such as Maiden Castle and the chalk-cut giant of Cerne Abbas are close to the bustling seaside resorts of Bournemouth and Weymouth. You may find Lyme Regis (associated with another writer, John Fowles) and the villages along the route closer to your ideal of coastal England. The Jurassic Coast is the place to search for fossils.

LYNDHURST

26 miles southeast of Stonehenge, 18 miles southeast of Salisbury, 9 miles west of Southampton.

Lyndhurst is famous as the capital of the New Forest. Although some popular spots can get crowded in summer, there are ample parking lots, picnic areas, and campgrounds. Miles of trails crisscross the region.

GETTING HERE AND AROUND

From Salisbury, follow A36, B3079, and continue along A337 another 4 miles or so. To explore the depths of the New Forest, take A35 out of Lyndhurst (the road continues southwest to Bournemouth) or

New Forest, Dorset, and the South Coast

A337 south. The New Forest Tour, a hop-on, hop-off open-top bus, runs a circular route through the New Forest between mid-June and mid-September (adults £10 per day, tickets on board). There are eight departures daily, and the bus will stop anywhere. Regular bus services are operated by Bluestar and Wilts & Dorset.

Many parts of the New Forest are readily accessible by train from London via the centrally located Brockenhurst Station.

ESSENTIALS

Visitor and Tour Information Lyndhurst Visitor Information Centre
✉ *Main Car Park, High St.* ☎ *023/8028–2269* ⊕ *www.thenewforest.co.uk.*
New Forest Tour ⊕ *www.thenewforesttour.info.*

EXPLORING

Fodor'sChoice ★ **New Forest.** This area consists of 150 square miles of open countryside interspersed with dense woodland, a natural haven for herds of free-roaming deer, cattle, and, most famously, hardy New Forest ponies. The forest was "new" in 1079, when William the Conqueror cleared the area of farms and villages and turned it into his private hunting grounds. An extensive network of trails makes it a wonderful place for biking, walking, and horseback riding. ⊕ *www.thenewforest.co.uk.*

FAMILY **New Forest Centre.** This visitor complex contains fascinating and informative background on the region. The exhibits focus on the area's fauna, flora, and social traditions and are linked by quizzes, and there are other interactive elements that will keep children engaged. ⊠ *Main car park, High St.* ☎ *023/8028–3444* ⊕ *www.newforestcentre.org.uk* ⌹ *£4* ☉ *Daily 10–5; last entry at 4.*

St. Michael and All Angels. Lyndhurst's High Street is dominated by this redbrick, high Victorian church, which holds stained glass from William Morris's studio and a large fresco of the Parable of the Virgins by Frederick Leighton. Fans of Lewis Carroll's *Alice in Wonderland* should note that Alice Hargreaves (née Liddell), the inspiration for the fictional Alice, is buried in the churchyard. ⊠ *High St.* ☎ *023/8028–2154* ⊕ *www.newforestparishes.com.*

4

WHERE TO EAT AND STAY
For expanded hotel reviews, visit Fodors.com.

$$ ✕ **The Pig.** Funkier sister of glamorous Lime Wood, this New Forest
MODERN BRITISH "restaurant with rooms" puts the emphasis on localism and seasonality
Fodor'sChoice and is a local favorite. Lunch and dinner are served in a large conser-
★ vatory overlooking lawns, and 95% of the ingredients come from the kitchen garden or other sources within 15 miles. The frequently changing menu may include dishes like honey and smoked chili crispy pork belly salad or Lyme Bay scallops with bacon. As the name suggests, porcine dishes feature prominently. You can overnight in one of the 26 comfortable rooms in the main building (an 18th-century former royal hunting lodge) or the converted stable block. All combine a slightly retro, shabby-chic style with modern bathrooms. You may accompany the "staff forager" on expeditions to find edible fauna like wild garlic. $ *Average main: £16* ⊠ *Beaulieu Rd., Brockenhurst* ☎ *01590/622354* ⊕ *www.thepighotel.com.*

$$$$ ☖ **Chewton Glen Hotel and Spa.** This grand early-19th-century country-
HOTEL house hotel and spa on extensive manicured grounds ranks among Britain's most acclaimed—and most expensive—lodgings. **Pros:** classic English luxury; top-notch leisure facilities; high staff-to-guest ratio. **Cons:** expensive rates. $ *Rooms from: £325* ⊠ *., Christchurch Rd., New Milton* ☎ *01425/275341, 800/344–5087 in U.S.* ⊕ *www.chewtonglen. com* ⤳ *35 rooms, 35 suites* ❙❍❙ *No meals.*

$$$$ ☖ **Lime Wood.** If you're looking for a discreet, luxurious hideaway in a
HOTEL woodland setting with uninterrupted views and an excellent spa, this
Fodor'sChoice hugely relaxing country-house hotel is hard to beat. **Pros:** great location;
★ stylish decor; friendly staff. **Cons:** hard to reach without a car; breakfast not included $ *Rooms from: £295* ⊠ *Beaulieu Rd.* ☎ *02380/287177* ⊕ *www.limewoodhotel.co.uk* ⤳ *14 rooms, 15 suites* ❙❍❙ *No meals.*

$ ☖ **Rufus House.** Personal service and easy access to the New Forest are
B&B/INN the draws at this turreted Victorian house run by a Japanese-Italian couple. **Pros:** friendly owners; delicious breakfasts; great location. **Cons:** traffic noise in front rooms; some rooms and beds are small. $ *Rooms from: £80* ⊠ *Southampton Rd.* ☎ *023/8028–2930* ⊕ *www.rufushouse. co.uk* ⤳ *10 rooms* ❙❍❙ *Breakfast.*

SPORTS AND THE OUTDOORS

Largely unspoiled and undeveloped, yet accessible even to those not normally given to long walks or bike rides, the New Forest offers countless opportunities to explore the outdoors. Bike rental and horseback riding are widely available. Numerous trails lead through thickly wooded country, across open heaths, and through the occasional bog. With very few hills, it's fairly easy terrain, and rich with wildlife. You're almost guaranteed to see ponies and deer, and occasionally free-roaming cattle and pigs.

BIKING

Cycle Experience. The range of trails weaving through the New Forest makes this one of Britain's best terrains for off-road biking. For £16 per day you can rent bikes at Cycle Experience. ⊠ *2–4 Brookley Rd., Brockenhurst* ☎ *01590/624204.*

HORSEBACK RIDING

Burley Manor Riding Stables. There are rides for all levels at Burley Manor Riding Stables. Hour-long rides are £33. ⊠ *Burley Manor Hotel, Ringwood Rd., Burley* ☎ *01425/403489.*

Forest Park Riding Centre. You can arrange a ride at Forest Park Riding Centre for £33 per hour. ⊠ *Rhinefield Rd., Brockenhurst* ☎ *01590/623429.*

WALKING

New Forest walks. The area is crisscrossed with short, easy trails, as well as longer hikes. For an easy walk (about 4 mi), start from Lyndhurst and head directly south for Brockenhurst, a commuter village. The path goes through woods, pastureland, and heath—and you'll see plenty of New Forest ponies. ⊠ *Lyndhurst.*

BEAULIEU

7 miles southeast of Lyndhurst.

The unspoiled village of Beaulieu (pronounced *byoo*-lee) has three major attractions in one at Beaulieu Abbey and is near the museum village of Buckler's Hard.

GETTING HERE AND AROUND

Beaulieu is best reached by car on B3056 from Lyndhurst or B3054 from Lymington. It's signposted off A326 from Southampton. Bus 112 has a limited service (twice daily on Tuesday and Thursday, once on Saturday) between Beaulieu and Lymington and Hythe.

EXPLORING

FAMILY **Beaulieu.** With a ruined abbey, a stately home, and an automobile museum, Beaulieu can satisfy different interests. In 1204 King John established **Beaulieu Abbey** for the Cistercian monks, who gave their new home its name, which means "beautiful place" in French. It was badly damaged as part of the suppression of Catholicism during the reign of Henry VIII, leaving only the cloister, the doorway, the gatehouse, and two buildings. A well-planned exhibition in one building re-creates daily life in the monastery. **Palace House** incorporates the abbey's 14th-century gatehouse and has been the home of the Montagu family since they purchased it in 1538, after the dissolution of the monasteries. Inside you can see drawing rooms, dining halls, and fine family portraits. The present Lord Montagu is noted for his work in establishing the **National Motor Museum,** which traces the development of motor transport from 1895 to the present. You can see more than 250 classic cars and motorcycles. Museum attractions include a monorail, audiovisual presentations, and a trip in a 1912 London bus. ⊠ *Off B3056* ☎ *01590/612345* ⊕ *www.beaulieu.co.uk* 🎫 *Abbey, Palace House, and Motor Museum £20* ⊙ *Late May–late Sept., daily 10–6; late Sept.–late May, daily 10–5.*

Buckler's Hard. Among the area's more interesting attractions is this museum village 2 miles south of Beaulieu. This restored 18th-century hamlet is home to a fascinating **Maritime Museum** that tells the story of Lord Nelson's favorite ship, HMS *Agamemnon.* Exhibits and model ships trace the town's shipbuilding history. Also part of the museum are four building interiors in the hamlet that re-create 18th-century village life. Easter through October, you can take a cruise on the Beaulieu River. The **Master Builder's House Hotel** has a bar and restaurant. ⊠ *Off B3056* ☎ *01590/616203* ⊕ *www.bucklershard.co.uk* 🎫 *£6.20* ⊙ *Mar.–June, Sept., and Oct., daily 10–5; July and Aug., daily 10–5:30; Nov.–Feb., daily 10–4:30; last entry 30 mins before closing.*

EN ROUTE From Beaulieu, take any of the minor roads leading west through wide-open heathland to Lymington and pick up A337 for the popular seaside resort of Bournemouth, a journey of about 18 miles.

BOURNEMOUTH

26 miles southwest of Southampton, 26 miles south of Salisbury, 24 miles east of Dorchester.

Bournemouth has 7 miles of beaches, and the waters are said to be some of southern England's most pristine. The resort was founded in 1810 by Lewis Tregonwell, an ex-army officer. He settled near what is now the Square and planted the first pine trees in the distinctive steep little valleys—or chines—cutting through the cliffs to the Bournemouth sands. The scent of fir trees was said to be healing for consumption (tuberculosis) sufferers, and the town grew steadily.

Today the city has expanded to swallow up neighboring settlements, making it a somewhat amorphous sprawl on first view. Its stodgier, more traditional side is kept in check by the presence of a lively student population—partly made up of foreign-language students from abroad. Gardens laid out with trees and lawns link the Square and the beach. This is an excellent spot to relax and listen to music wafting from the Pine Walk bandstand. Regular musical programs take place at the Pavilion.

GETTING HERE AND AROUND
From the New Forest, take A35 or A31/A338 southwest to Bournemouth. The center of town is best explored on foot, but to reach East Cliff or Boscombe you'll need to drive or hop aboard the frequent local buses. Fast trains from London take about two hours.

ESSENTIALS
Visitor Information **Bournemouth Tourist Information Centre** ⊠ *Westover Rd., near bandstand* ☎ *0845/051–1701* ⊕ *www.bournemouth.co.uk.*

EXPLORING

Bournemouth Beach. With miles of beaches tucked beneath its cliffs, Bournemouth is said to enjoy some of the country's warmest sea temperatures. Taking the zigzag paths through the leafy public gardens, you can descend to the seafront, where Bournemouth Pier juts into the channel from the pristine sandy beach. If you're not tempted to swim, you can stroll the nearby promenade. Europe's first artificial **surf reef** was constructed here to attract surf fans as well as create an area of calm water that's perfect for children—surfers, however, have reported that the reef is more suitable for bodyboarding than standing up. Windsurfing, sailing, and other water sports are also big here.

Russell-Cotes Art Gallery and Museum. Perched on East Cliff, this unusual late-Victorian mansion overflows with vintage paintings and collectibles from around the world, such as cases of butterflies and treasures from Asia that include an exquisite suit of Japanese armor. Members of the Russell-Cotes family, wealthy hoteliers who traveled widely, assembled the items. Small landscaped gardens surround the house. ⊠ *East Cliff* ☎ *01202/451858* ⊕ *www.russell-cotes.bournemouth.gov.uk* ✆ *Oct.– Mar. free; Apr.–Sept. £5* ☉ *Tues.–Sun. 10–5.*

St. Peter's. This parish church is easily recognizable by its 200-foot-high tower and spire. Lewis Tregonwell, founder and developer of Bournemouth, is buried in the churchyard. Here, too, is the elaborate tombstone of Mary Shelley, author of *Frankenstein* and wife of the great Romantic poet Percy Bysshe Shelley, whose heart is buried with her. ⊠ *Hinton Rd.*

WHERE TO EAT AND STAY

For expanded hotel reviews, visit Fodors.com.

$$
SEAFOOD

✕ **WestBeach.** Superbly positioned right on the marine promenade, close to Bournemouth Pier, this place has views over sand and sea. It also serves the best seafood in town, whether grilled, baked, or in fish pies and stews. The menu usually lists halibut, sea bass, plaice, and shellfish (oysters, mussels, lobster). Nonfish dishes may include rib-eye steak and sesame mille-feuille with grilled sweet potato and eggplant. The simple wooden tables and large glass front lend a modern, minimalist feel, and there's a narrow deck and terrace for open-air dining. In summer you can pick up ice cream and snacks from the adjacent takeout. $ *Average main: £17* ⊠ *Pier Approach* ☎ *01202/587785* ⊕ *www.west-beach.co.uk.*

$$
HOTEL

▥ **The Urban Beach.** A short walk from the seafront, this funky boutique hotel provides the contemporary style and energy so needed by Bournemouth. **Pros:** designer decor; friendly staff; great food. **Cons:** not central; rooms over bar can be noisy. $ *Rooms from: £138* ⊠ *23 Argyll Rd., Boscombe* ☎ *01202/301509* ⊕ *www.urbanbeachhotel.co.uk* ⤴ *12 rooms* ⫶◯⫶ *Breakfast.*

$
B&B/INN

▥ **Wood Lodge Hotel.** Small and sedate, this family-run hotel in a Victorian building near the shore offers good value. **Pros:** welcoming staff; close to beach; reasonable rates. **Cons:** dated in places; some bathrooms need improving; upper-floor shower water pressure may be weak. $ *Rooms from: £88* ⊠ *10 Manor Rd., East Cliff* ☎ *01202/290891* ⊕ *www.woodlodgehotel.co.uk* ⤴ *15 rooms* ⫶◯⫶ *Breakfast.*

WIMBORNE MINSTER

7 miles northwest of Bournemouth via A341.

The impressive minster of this quiet market town makes it seem like a miniature cathedral city. The town is exceptionally quiet on Sunday.

GETTING HERE AND AROUND

To reach Wimborne Minster from central Bournemouth, take any main road heading west, following signs for A341 or A349, or take advantage of the regular bus service.

ESSENTIALS

Visitor Information Wimborne Minster Tourist Information Centre
✉ *29 High St.* ☎ *01202/886116* ⊕ *www.wimborneminster.net.*

EXPLORING

Kingston Lacy. Sir Charles Barry, co-architect of the Houses of Parliament in London, altered this grand 17th-century house in the 19th century. It has a notable picture collection including works by Titian, Rubens, Van Dyck, and Velásquez, as well as the fabulous Spanish Room, lined with gilded leather and topped by an ornate Venetian ceiling. There's also a fine collection of Egyptian artifacts. Parkland with walking paths surrounds the house. ✉ *B3082, 1½ mile northwest of Wimborne Minster* ☎ *01202/883402* ⊕ *www.nationaltrust.org.uk* 🎟 *£13; park and garden only, £7* ⊙ *House mid-Mar.–Oct., Wed.–Sun. 11–5, last admission at 4. Garden and park mid-Mar.–Oct., daily 10:30–6; Nov.–mid-Mar., daily 10:30–4.*

Priest's House Museum. On the main square in an Elizabethan town house with a garden, this museum features rooms furnished in period styles and a Victorian kitchen. It also has Roman and Iron Age exhibits, including a cryptic, three-faced Celtic stone head. In the garden are displays of agricultural and horticultural tools plus a tearoom. ✉ *23–27 High St.* ☎ *01202/882533* ⊕ *www.priest-house.co.uk* 🎟 *£4.50* ⊙ *Apr.–Oct., Mon.–Sat. 10–4:30; Nov.–Mar., call ahead.*

Wimborne Minster. The crenellated and pinnacled twin towers of Wimborne Minster present an attractive patchwork of gray stone. The church's Norman nave has zigzag molding interspersed with carved heads, and the Gothic chancel has tall lancet windows. ■TIP→ See the chained library, a survivor from the days when books were valuable enough to keep locked up. Look out for the 14th-century astronomical clock on the inside wall of the west tower. ✉ *High St.* ☎ *01202/884753* ⊕ *www.wimborneminster.org.uk* 🎟 *£2 for guided tour of church and library* ⊙ *Church Mar.–Dec., Mon.–Sat. 9:30–5:30, Sun. 2:30–5:30; Jan. and Feb., Mon.–Sat. 9:30–4, Sun. 2:30–5:30. Chained library Easter–Oct., weekdays 10:30–12:30 and 2–4, Sat. 10–12:30; Nov.–Easter, Sat. 10–12:30.*

WHERE TO STAY

For expanded hotel reviews, visit Fodors.com.

$$
B&B/INN
🏠 **Museum Inn.** It's worth making the detour 10 miles north of Wimborne Minster to find this characterful inn known for fine Modern British cooking; despite a stylish transformation, the building remains in

harmony with its 17th-century beginnings, retaining its flagstone floors and inglenook fireplace. **Pros:** pretty village location; great food. **Cons:** remote from Wimborne Minster. $ *Rooms from: £120* ⊠ *Off A354, near Blandford Forum, Farnham* ☎ *01725/516261* ⊕ *www.museuminn. co.uk* ⇱ *8 rooms* ¶⊙¶ *Breakfast.*

CORFE CASTLE

25 miles south of Wimborne Minster, 15 miles south of Poole, 5 miles southeast of Wareham.

The village of Corfe Castle is best known for the ancient, ruined castle that overlooks it.

ESSENTIALS

Visitor Information Discover Purbeck Information Centre ⊠ *Wareham Library, South St.* ☎ *01929/552740* ⊕ *www.visitswanageandpurbeck.co.uk.*

EXPLORING

Corfe Castle. One of the most impressive ruins in Britain, Corfe Castle overlooks the appealing gray limestone village of the same name. The castle site guards a gap in the surrounding Purbeck Hills. The present ruins are of the castle built between 1086, when the great central keep was erected by William the Conqueror, and the 1270s, when the outer walls and towers were built. Cromwell's soldiers blew up the castle in 1646 during the Civil War, after a long seige during which its Royalist chatelaine, Lady Bankes, led its defense. ⊠ *A351* ☎ *01929/477060* ⊕ *www.nationaltrust.org.uk* 🎫 *£8.50* ⊙ *Mar. and Oct., daily 10–5; Apr.–Sept., daily 10–6; Nov.–Feb., daily 10–4.*

OFF THE BEATEN PATH

Clouds Hill. This brick-and-tile cottage near the Tank Museum served as the retreat of T.E. Lawrence (Lawrence of Arabia) before he was killed in a motorcycle accident on the road from Bovington in 1935. The house remains very much as he left it, with photos and memorabilia from the Middle East. It's particularly atmospheric on a gloomy day, as there's no electric light. Clouds Hill is 8 miles northwest of Corfe. ⊠ *off B3390, Morton* ☎ *01929/405616* ⊕ *www.nationaltrust. org.uk* 🎫 *£5.50* ⊙ *Mid-Mar.–Oct., Wed.–Sun. and national holiday Mon. 11–5, last admission 4:30 or dusk.*

Swanage Railway. Largely volunteer-run, this railroad makes 25-minute scenic trips in vintage train carriages (steam and diesel engines) across the Isle of Purbeck—more a peninsula—from Norden in the center to the seaside town of Swanage via Corfe Castle. Small, pretty stations with details like flower baskets, painted signs, and water bowls for dogs add to the excursion's charm. Trains leave approximately every 80 minutes in low season, and every 40 minutes in high season. ⊠ *Station House, Springfield Rd., Swanage* ☎ *01929/425800* ⊕ *www. swanagerailway.co.uk* 🎫 *£1–£6.20* ⊙ *Apr.–Oct., daily 10–5:20; Nov.– Mar., weekends 10–5:20.*

The ruins of Corfe Castle, destroyed during the 17th-century English Civil War, are evocative after a snowfall.

WHERE TO EAT AND STAY

For expanded hotel reviews, visit Fodors.com.

$ ✕ **The Fox Inn.** A traditional pub that claims to have been in business
BRITISH since the 16th century, the Fox has a fine view of Corfe Castle from its
beer garden. There's an ancient well in the lounge bar and more timeworn stonework in an alcove, as well as a 13th-century fireplace. The
bar menu includes soups and sandwiches, as well as steaks and fish
dishes, though quality is variable. Even though it can sometimes have
a locals-only vibe, this place is popular, with congestion and resulting
slow service in summer. $ *Average main: £10* ✉ *West St., Corfe Castle*
☎ *01929/480449.*

$ ⊡ **Castle Inn.** This family-run inn has a thatched roof, flagstone bar, and
B&B/INN other 16th-century features. **Pros:** close to Lulworth Cove; historic vibe;
for dog lovers. **Cons:** shabby in places; some rooms are over the noisy
bar. $ *Rooms from: £95* ✉ *Main Rd., 10 miles west of Corfe Castle,*
West Lulworth ☎ *01929/400311* ⊕ *www.thecastleinn-lulworthcove.*
co.uk ⤲ *11 rooms* ⦿ *Breakfast.*

Hardy's Dorset

Among this region's proudest claims is its connection with Thomas Hardy (1840–1928), one of England's most celebrated novelists. If you read some of Hardy's novels before visiting Dorset—re-created by Hardy as his part-fact, part-fiction county of Wessex—you may well recognize some places immediately from his descriptions. The tranquil countryside surrounding Dorchester is lovingly described in *Far from the Madding Crowd,* and Casterbridge, in *The Mayor* *of Casterbridge,* stands for Dorchester itself. Any pilgrimage to Hardy's Wessex begins at the author's birthplace in Higher Bockhampton, 3 miles east of Dorchester. Salisbury makes an appearance as "Melchester" in *Jude the Obscure.* North of Dorchester, walk in the footsteps of Jude Fawley by visiting the village of Shaftesbury— "Shaston"—and its steep Gold Hill, a street lined with cottages. Today many of these sights seem frozen in time, and Hardy's spirit is ever present.

DORCHESTER

21 miles west of Corfe on A351 and A352, 30 miles west of Bournemouth, 43 miles southwest of Salisbury.

In many ways Dorchester, the Casterbridge of Thomas Hardy's novel *The Mayor of Casterbridge,* is a traditional southern country town. The town owes much of its fame to its connection with Hardy, whose bronze statue looks westward from a bank on Colliton Walk. He was born in a cottage in the hamlet of Higher Bockhampton, about 3 miles northeast of Dorchester. "Hardy country" includes a number of hidden-away villages in the rolling hills of Dorest. Two important historical sites, as well as his former residence, are a short drive from Dorchester.

Dorchester has many reminders of the Roman presence in the area. The Romans laid out the town about AD 70, and a stroll along Bowling Alley Walk, West Walk, and Colliton Walk follows the approximate line of the original Roman town walls. On the north side of Colliton Park lies an excavated Roman villa with a marvelously preserved mosaic floor. The high street was tranquil in Hardy's day, but today it's usually busy with vehicle traffic. The tourist office has walking itineraries that cover the main points of interest along quieter routes and help you appreciate the town's contemporary character.

GETTING HERE AND AROUND

Dorchester can be reached from Corfe Castle via A351 and A352. From Salisbury take A354. Park wherever you can (pay parking lots are scattered around the center) and explore the town on foot.

ESSENTIALS

Visitor Information Dorchester Tourist Information Centre ⊠ *11 Antelope Walk* ☎ *01305/267992* ⊕ *www.visit-dorset.com.*

EXPLORING

TOP ATTRACTIONS

Athelhampton House and Gardens. Fine 19th-century gardens enhance an outstanding example of 15th-century domestic Tudor architecture at Athelhampton House and Gardens. Thomas Hardy called this place Athelhall in some of his writings, referring to the legendary King Aethelstan, who had a palace on this site. The current house includes the Great Hall, with much of its original timber roof intact, the King's Room, and the Library, with oak paneling and more than 3,000 books. The 10 acres of landscaped gardens have a dozen giant yew pyramids. ⊠ *A35, 5 miles east of Dorchester* ☎ *01305/848363* ⊕ *www.athelhampton.co.uk* ☒ *£12.50* ⊙ *Mar.–Oct., Sun.–Thurs. 10:30–5; Nov.–Feb., Sun. 11–dusk.*

Dorset County Museum. This labyrinthine museum contains ancient Celtic remains from nearby Maiden Castle and Roman remains from town, a rural crafts gallery, and a local-history gallery. It's better known for its large collection of Hardy memorabilia, and there's a gallery focusing on the nearby Jurassic Coast. ⊠ *High West St.* ☎ *01305/262735* ⊕ *www.dorsetcountymuseum.org* ☒ *£6.50* ⊙ *Apr.–Oct., Mon.–Sat. 10–5; Nov.–Mar., Mon.–Sat. 10–4.*

QUICK BITES **Potters Café Bistro.** Drop into Potters Café, in a 17th-century cottage, for cream teas and delicious cakes and pastries, as well as homemade soups and pannini. The lunch specials, such as smoked haddock fishcakes or cassoulet, are excellent, and the pleasant courtyard garden provides outdoor seating, weather permitting. ⊠ *19 Durngate St.* ☎ *01305/260312.*

Maiden Castle. This castle is one of the most important pre-Roman archaeological sites in England. It's not an actual castle but an enormous Iron Age hill fort of stone and earth with ramparts that enclose about 45 acres. England's Neolithic inhabitants built the fort some 4,000 years ago, and many centuries later it was a Celtic stronghold. In AD 43 invading Romans, under the general (later emperor) Vespasian, stormed the fort. Finds from the site are on display in the Dorset County Museum in Dorchester. To experience an uncanny silence and sense of mystery, climb Maiden Castle early in the day. Leave your car in the lot at the end of Maiden Castle Way, a 1½-mile lane. ⊠ *A354, 2 miles southwest of Dorchester.*

WORTH NOTING

FAMILY **Dinosaur Museum.** The popular Dinosaur Museum has life-size models, interactive displays, and a hands-on Discovery Gallery. ⊠ *Icen Way, off High East St.* ☎ *01305/269880* ⊕ *www.thedinosaurmuseum. com* ☒ *£6.99* ⊙ *Apr.–Sept., daily 10–5; Oct.–Mar., daily 10–4. Closed mid–late Dec.*

Hardy's Cottage. The small thatch-and-cob cottage, where the writer was born in 1840, was built by his grandfather and is little altered since that time. From here Thomas Hardy would make his daily 6-mile walk to school in Dorchester. Among other things, you can see the desk at which the author completed *Far from the Madding Crowd*. Access is on foot only, via a woodland walk, or country lane from the parking lot. ✉ *Brockhampton Ln., ½ mile south of Blandford Rd., Higher Bockhampton* ☎ *01305/262366* 🌐 *www.nationaltrust.org.uk* 🎟 *£5* 🕒 *Mid-Mar.–Oct., Wed.–Sun. and holiday Mon. 11–5 or dusk.*

Maumbury Rings. These remains of a Roman amphitheater on the edge of town were built on a prehistoric site that later served as a place of execution. (Hardy's *Mayor of Casterbridge* contains a vivid evocation of the Rings.) As late as 1706 a girl was burned at the stake here. ✉ *Maumbury Rd., off Weymouth Ave.*

WORD OF MOUTH

"Another thought: at the end of the walk I stayed in Dorchester, just north of Weymouth. Three miles northeast of Dorchester is Thomas Hardy's cottage and beautiful country garden run by the National Trust. It's a nice change of pace from the Trust's many great piles."

—MmePerdu

Max Gate. Thomas Hardy lived in Max Gate from 1885 until his death in 1928. An architect by profession, Hardy designed the house himself, and visitors can now see the study where he wrote *Tess of the d'Urbevilles, The Mayor of Casterbridge,* and *Jude the Obscure.* The dining room, the drawing room, and the garden are open to the public. ✉ *Allington Ave., 1 mi east of Dorchester on A352* ☎ *01305/262538* 🌐 *www.nationaltrust.org.uk* 🎟 *£5.50* 🕒 *Mar.–Oct., Wed.–Sun. and holiday Mon. 11–5, last entry 4:30.*

OFF THE BEATEN PATH

Poundbury. Owned by the Duchy of Cornwall and under the aegis of the Prince of Wales, this development in a traditional vernacular style showcases Prince Charles's vision of urban planning and community living. The emphasis is on conservation and energy efficiency; private houses coexist with shops, offices, small-scale factories, and leisure facilities. Central Pummery Square is dominated by the colonnaded Brownsword Hall. Dorchester's Farmers' Market is held in the Queen Mother's Square the first Saturday of the month. Poundbury, a mile west of Dorchester on the B3150, has attracted the ire of modernist architects, but any properties for sale are quickly snapped up.

WHERE TO EAT AND STAY

For expanded hotel reviews, visit Fodors.com.

$$ BRASSERIE

🍴 **No. 6.** Just behind the County Museum, this pleasant neighborhood brasserie makes an ideal stop for a relaxed lunch or evening meal. The menu may list locally caught king scallops in a lime and ginger sauce for a starter, and fillet steak with cracked-peppercorn sauce and brandy or venison marinated in thyme and port for main courses. The atmosphere is intimate without being chichi, and the tiled floor and sidewalk tables lend a Continental air. [$] *Average main: £16* ✉ *6 North Sq.* ☎ *01305/267679* 🌐 *www.no6-restaurant.co.uk* 🕒 *Closed Sun. and Mon.*

$$$ MODERN BRITISH

🍴 **Yalbury Cottage.** Oak-beamed ceilings, exposed stone walls, and inglenook fireplaces add to the charm of this restaurant in a 300-year-old cottage. It specializes in superior Modern British cooking using locally sourced produce, such as Portland dressed crab, roast loin of lamb with a mustard and herb crust, and pan-fried Dorset Coast sea bass. A three-course fixed-price dinner menu (£36) offers good value. Eight comfortable bedrooms are available in an extension overlooking gardens or fields. Lower Bockhampton is signposted off the A35, 1½ miles east of Dorchester. [$] *Average main: £24* ✉ *Bockhampton La., Lower Bockhampton* ☎ *01305/262382* 🌐 *www.yalburycottage.com* 🕒 *No dinner Sun. or Mon.*

$$ B&B/INN 🏨 **The Casterbridge.** Small but full of character, this family-owned inn in a Georgian building dating from 1790 is elegantly decorated with period antiques. **Pros:** central location; period setting; good breakfasts. **Cons:** traffic noise in front rooms; annex rooms are small and lack character; limited parking. [$] *Rooms from: £110* ✉ *49 High East St.* ☎ *01305/264043* 🌐 *www.thecasterbridge.co.uk* 🛏 *14 rooms* 🍴 *Breakfast.*

SHOPPING

Wednesday Market. You can find Dorset delicacies such as Blue Vinney cheese (which some connoisseurs prefer to Blue Stilton) in the market. ✉ *Fairfield parking lot, off Weymouth Ave.*

THE OUTDOORS

Thomas Hardy Society. From April through October, the Thomas Hardy Society organizes guided walks that follow in the steps of Hardy's novels. Readings and discussions accompany the walks, which range from a couple of hours to most of a day. ☎ *01305/251501* 🌐 *www.hardysociety.org.*

CERNE ABBAS

6 miles north of Dorchester.

The village of Cerne Abbas, worth a short exploration on foot, has some Tudor houses on the road beside the church. Nearby you can also see the original village stocks.

GETTING HERE AND AROUND

Cerne Abbas is best reached by car from Dorchester to the south or Sherborne to the north via A352.

EXPLORING

Cerne Abbas Giant. This colossal and unblushingly priapic figure, 180 feet long, dominates a hillside overlooking the village of Cerne Abbas. The giant carries a huge club and may have originated as a pre-Roman tribal fertility symbol. Alternatively, historians have tended to believe he is a representation of Hercules dating back to the 2nd century AD, but more recent research suggests he may be a 17th-century gibe at Oliver Cromwell. The figure's outlines are formed by 1-foot-wide trenches cut into the ground to reveal the chalk beneath. The best place to view the figure is from the A352 itself, where you can park in one of the numerous nearby turnouts. ✉ *A352* 🌐 *www.nationaltrust.org.uk.*

Cerne Abbey. Little remains of this 10-century Benedictine abbey, but its South Gatehouse has been incorporated into the nearby Abbey House (a private residence). On the abbey grounds are the remains of the early 16th-century Abbot's Porch, adorned with carvings of small animals and a double oriel window, along with the15th-century hospice, one of the few surviving monastic guest houses. ✉ *A352* 🎟 *Suggested donation £1.*

SHERBORNE

12 miles north of Cerne Abbas, 20 miles north of Dorchester, 15 miles west of Shaftesbury, 40 miles west of Wilton, 43 miles west of Salisbury.

Once granted cathedral status, until deferring to Old Sarum in 1075, this unspoiled market town is awash with medieval buildings built with the honey-color local stone. The focal point of the winding streets is the abbey church. Also worth visiting here are the ruins of the 12th-century Old Castle and Sherborne Castle with its grounds.

GETTING HERE AND AROUND

Hourly trains from Salisbury take 45 minutes to reach Sherborne. The station is at the bottom of Digby Road, near the abbey. Drivers should take A30, passing through Shaftesbury.

ESSENTIALS

Visitor Information Sherborne Tourist Information Centre ⊠ *3 Tilton Ct., Digby Rd.* ☎ *01935/815341* ⊕ *www.visit-dorset.com.*

EXPLORING

Shaftesbury. The model for the town of Shaston in Thomas Hardy's *Jude the Obscure* is still a small market town. It sits on a ridge overlooking Blackmore Vale—you can catch a sweeping view of the surrounding countryside from the top of Gold Hill, a steep street lined with cottages, so picturesque it was used in an iconic TV commercial to evoke the quintessential British village of yore. Shaftesbury is 20 miles west of Salisbury and 15 miles east of Sherbourne.

Sherborne Abbey. The glory of Sherbourne Abbey, a warm, "old gold" stone church, is the delicate and graceful 15th-century fan vaulting that extends the length of the soaring nave and choir. ("I would pit Sherborne's roof against any contemporary work of the Italian Renaissance," enthused Simon Jenkins in his *England's Thousand Best Churches.*) If you're lucky, you might hear "Great Tom," one of the heaviest bells in the world, pealing out from the bell tower. Guided tours are offered from April through September on Tuesday (10:30) and Friday (2:30), or by prior arrangement. ⊠ *Abbey Close* ☎ *01935/812452* ⊕ *www.sherborneabbey.com* ⊡ *Free* ⊙ *Apr.–Sept., daily 8–6; Oct.–Mar., daily 8–4.*

Sherborne Castle. Built by Sir Walter Raleigh in 1594, this castle remained his home for 10 years before it passed to the custodianship of the Digby family. The castle has interiors from a variety of periods, including Tudor, Jacobean, and Georgian. The Victorian Gothic rooms are notable for their splendid plaster moldings on the ceiling. After admiring the extensive collections of Meissen and Asian porcelain, stroll around the lake and landscaped grounds, the work of Capability Brown. The house is less than a mile southeast of town. ⊠ *Off A352* ☎ *01935/812072* ⊕ *www.sherbornecastle.com* ⊡ *£10; gardens only, £5* ⊙ *Castle Apr.–Oct., Tues.–Thurs. and Sun. 11–5, Sat. 2–5. Gardens Apr.–Oct., Tues.–Thurs. and Sun. 11–5, Sat. 11–5.*

WHERE TO STAY

For expanded hotel reviews, visit Fodors.com.

$ 🛏 **The Alders.** In a secluded stone house, this homey B&B with a walled
B&B/INN garden opposite a 13th-century church is in a quiet, unspoiled village
3 miles north of Sherborne. **Pros:** peaceful setting; hospitable owners.
Cons: a bit remote; nothing to do in evening. $ *Rooms from: £60 ⊠ Off
B3145, Sandford Orcas ☎ 01963/220666 ⊕ www.thealdersbb.com ➵ 3
rooms* 🖃 *No credit cards* ⦿ *Breakfast.*

WEYMOUTH

4

8 miles south of Dorchester, 28 miles south of Sherbourne.

West Dorset's main coastal resort, Weymouth, is known for its sandy
and pebble beaches and its royal connections. King George III began
bathing here for his health in 1789, setting a trend among the wealthy
and fashionable people of the day. Popularity left Weymouth with many
fine buildings, including the Georgian row houses lining the Esplanade.
Striking historical details command attention: a wall on Maiden Street
holds a cannonball that was embedded in it during the English Civil
War. Not far away, a column commemorates the launching of U.S.
forces from Weymouth on D-Day.

Weymouth and its lively harbor offer the full bucket-and-spade seaside
experience: donkey rides, sand castles, and plenty of fish-and-chips.
Weymouth and Portland hosted the 2012 Olympic sailing events.

GETTING HERE AND AROUND

You can reach Weymouth on frequent local buses and trains from
Dorchester, or on less frequent services from Bournemouth. The bus
and train stations are close to each other near King's Statue, on the
Esplanade. If you're driving, take A354 from Dorchester and park
on or near the Esplanade—an easy walk from the center—or in a lot
near the harbor.

ESSENTIALS

EXPLORING

Chesil Beach. A 5-mile-long spit jutting south from Weymouth leads to
the Isle of Portland, well known for its limestone and as the setting for
Ian McEwan's novel of the same name. The spit is the eastern end of
the unique geological curiosity known as Chesil Beach—a 200-yard-
wide, 30-foot-high bank of pebbles that decrease in size from east to
west. The beach extends for 18 miles. A powerful undertow makes
swimming dangerous, and tombstones in local churchyards attest to
the many shipwrecks the beach has caused. There are walking and cycle
trails along the rugged coastline.

WHERE TO EAT

$ ✕ **Old Rooms Inn.** This popular pub has great views over the harbor. The
BRITISH extensive menu ranges from wraps and salads to grilled steaks, curries,
burgers, and comfort food. There are two separate dining areas and
tables outside, or you can mix with the locals at the bar. $ *Average
main: £8 ⊠ 2 Cove Row ☎ 01305/771130.*

Sunrise is lovely at the Cobb, the harbor wall built by Edward I in Lyme Regis.

$
BISTRO
✕ **Time for Tea.** Tucked away from the busy harbor, this French-owned haven serves classic Gallic dishes and superlative baked goods. The onion or fish soups, cassoulet, and *croque-monsieur* are favorites. If you're looking for an afternoon pit stop, try the substantial, and very English, cream tea selection with homemade cakes and scones. The place serves a fixed-price dinner (£20 for two courses, £25 for three) on the third Friday and Saturday of each month. ⓢ *Average main: £8* ✉ *8 Cove St.* ☎ *01305/777500* ⊗ *No dinner.*

ABBOTSBURY

10 miles northwest of Weymouth.

Pretty Abbotsbury is at the western end of Chesil Beach and has a swannery. In other parts of the village, you can also visit a children's farm, housed in an impressive medieval barn, and subtropical gardens.

GETTING HERE AND AROUND

By car, take B3157 from Weymouth, or the steep and very minor road passing through Martinstown off A35 from Dorchester; the latter route has marvelous views of the coast.

ESSENTIALS

Visitor Information Abbotsbury Tourist Information Centre ✉ *Bellenie's Bakehouse, 11 Market St.* ☎ *01305/871990* ⊕ *www.abbotsbury.co.uk.*

EXPLORING

Abbotsbury Swannery. A lagoon outside the village serves as a famous breeding place for swans. Originally tended by Benedictine monks as a source of meat in winter, the swans have remained for centuries, drawn by the lagoon's soft, moist eelgrass, a favorite food, and fresh water. They now build nests in reeds provided by the swannery. Cygnets hatch between mid-May and late June. Try to visit during feeding time, at noon and 4 pm. ✉ *New Barn Rd.* ☎ *01305/871858* ⊕ *www.abbotsburyswannery.co.uk* 🖾 *£11, £15 including gardens* ☉ *May–Aug., daily 10–6; mid-Mar.–Apr., Sept., and Oct., daily 10–5; last admission 1 hr before closing.*

LYME REGIS

19 miles west of Abbotsbury.

Fodor's Choice
★

"A very strange stranger it must be, who does not see the charms of the immediate environs of Lyme, to make him wish to know it better," wrote Jane Austen in *Persuasion*. Judging from the summer crowds, most people appear to be not at all strange. The ancient, scenic town of Lyme Regis and the so-called Jurassic Coast are highlights of southwest Dorset. The crumbling seaside cliffs in this area are especially fossil rich.

GETTING HERE AND AROUND

Lyme Regis is off the A35, extending west from Bournemouth and Dorchester. Drivers should park as soon as possible—there are lots at the top of town—and explore the town on foot. First buses run here from Dorchester and Axminster, 6 miles northwest; the latter town is on the main rail route from London Waterloo and Salisbury, as is Exeter, from which you can take the X53 bus.

ESSENTIALS

Visitor Information Lyme Regis Tourist Information Centre ✉ *Guildhall Cottage, Church St.* ☎ *01297/442138* ⊕ *www.lymeregis.org.*

EXPLORING

Cobb. Lyme Regis is famous for its curving stone harbor breakwater, the Cobb, built by King Edward I in the 13th century to improve the harbor. The duke of Monmouth landed here in 1685 during his ill-fated attempt to overthrow his uncle James II, and the Cobb figured prominently in the movie of John Fowles's novel *The French Lieutenant's Woman*, as well as in the film version of Jane Austen's *Persuasion*.

FAMILY **Dinosaurland Fossil Museum.** Located in a former church, this compact museum displays an excellent collection of local fossils and gives the background on regional geology and how fossils develop. It also provides information on guided fossil-hunting walks. The shop on the ground floor sells minerals and fascinating fossils. ✉ *Coombe St.* ☎ *01297/443541* ⊕ *www.dinosaurland.co.uk* 🖾 *£5* ☉ *Mid-Feb.–mid-Oct., daily 10–5; mid-Oct.–mid-Feb., hrs vary.*

Lyme Regis Philpot Museum. In a gabled and turreted Edwardian building, this lively museum contains engaging items that illustrate the town's maritime and domestic history, as well as a section on local writers and a good selection of local fossils. It also offers a series of fossil hunting and local history walks throughout the year. ✉ *Bridge St.* ☎ *01297/443370* ⊕ *www.lymeregismuseum.co.uk* 🖾 *£3.95* ☉ *Easter–Oct., Mon.–Sat. 10–5, Sun. 11–5; Nov.–Easter, Wed.–Sun. 11–4.*

FAMILY **Marine Aquarium.** This small but child-friendly aquarium offers the usual up-close look at maritime creatures, from spider crabs to fish found in nearby Lyme Bay. Children love feeding the gray mullets. ✉ *End of the Cobb* ☎ *01297/444230* 🌐 *www.lymeregismarineaquarium.co.uk* 🎟 *£5* ⏲ *Mar.–Oct., daily 10–5.*

WHERE TO EAT AND STAY

For expanded hotel reviews, visit Fodors.com.

$ BRITISH 🍴 **The Bell Cliff Restaurant and Tea Rooms.** This cozy, welcoming, child-friendly place in a 17th-century building at the bottom of Lyme Regis's main street makes a great spot for a light lunch or tea, although it can get noisy and cramped. Apart from teas and coffees, you can order seafood, including salmon, cod, and breaded plaice, or a gammon steak (a thick slice of cured ham) or vegetarian lasagna. [$] *Average main: £9* ✉ *5–6 Broad St.* ☎ *01297/442459* ⏲ *No dinner Nov.–Mar.*

$$ SEAFOOD 🍴 **Hix Oyster & Fish House.** This coastal outpost of one of London's trendiest restaurants combines stunning views from a height overlooking the Cobb with the celebrity chef's trademark high standards and originality. Simply cooked and beautifully presented seafood rules here, including Portland whole sea bass with creamed wild garlic. As the name suggests, the variety of local oysters is a particular specialty. Non-fish-eaters have limited choices, but the dessert menu is extensive, including cider-brandy chocolate truffles, and buttermilk pudding. A selection of three appetizers (like sardines cured in local cider) is good value at £12. Book well ahead to sit by the floor-to-ceiling windows or on the small terrace. [$] *Average main: £17* ✉ *Cobb Rd.* ☎ *01297/446910* 🌐 *www.hixoysterandfishhouse.co.uk* ✍ *Reservations essential* ⏲ *Closed Sun. and Mon. evenings in Jan. and Feb.*

$$$ HOTEL 🏨 **Alexandra.** Magnificently sited above the Cobb, the family-owned Alexandra combines contemporary decor with the genteel charm of yesteryear. **Pros:** great garden; deck overlooking the sea; central location. **Cons:** cheaper rooms have no sea views; small bathrooms; restricted parking. [$] *Rooms from: £177* ✉ *Pound St.* ☎ *01297/442010* 🌐 *www.hotelalexandra.co.uk* 🛏 *24 rooms* ⏲ *Closed late Dec.–late Jan.* 🍽 *Breakfast.*

$ B&B/INN 🏨 **Coombe House.** In a stone house tucked away on one of the oldest (14th century) lanes in Lyme, and one minute from the seafront, this uncluttered, stylish B&B has genial hosts and airy, modern guest rooms decorated in maritime blue and white. **Pros:** friendly owners; pleasant rooms; central location; Wi-Fi access. **Cons:** only two rooms; little parking. [$] *Rooms from: £70* ✉ *41 Coombe St.* ☎ *01297/443849* 🌐 *www.coombe-house.co.uk* 🛏 *2 rooms* 💳 *No credit cards* 🍽 *Breakfast.*

SPORTS AND THE OUTDOORS

Dorset Coast Path. The 72-mile Dorset Coast Path—a section of the 630-mile-long Southwest Coast Path—runs east from Lyme Regis to Poole, bypassing Weymouth and taking in the quiet bays, shingle beaches, and low chalk cliffs of the coast. Some highlights are Golden Cap, the highest point on the south coast; the Swannery at Abbotsbury; Chesil Beach; Durndle Door; and Lulworth Cove (between Weymouth and Corfe Castle). Villages and isolated pubs dot the route, as do many rural B&Bs. ☎ *01392/383560* 🌐 *www.southwestcoastpath.com.*

5

THE WEST COUNTRY

WELCOME TO THE WEST COUNTRY

TOP REASONS TO GO

★ **A coastal walk:**
For high, dramatic cliff scenery, choose the Exmoor coast around Lynmouth or the coast around Tintagel. The South West Coast Path is 630 miles long.

★ **Seafood in Padstow:**
Celebrity chef Rick Stein rules the roost in this small, pretty Cornish port, and any of his establishments will strongly satisfy.

★ **Tate St. Ives:** There's nowhere better to absorb the local arts scene than this offshoot of London's Tate in the pretty seaside town of St. Ives. A rooftop café claims views over Porthmeor Beach.

★ **A visit to Eden:** It's worth the journey west for Cornwall's Eden Project alone: a wonderland of plant life in a former clay pit. Two gigantic geodesic "biomes" are filled with flora.

★ **Wells Cathedral:**
A perfect example of medieval craftsmanship, the building is a stunning spectacle.

1 Bristol, Wells, and North Devon. Bristol is filled with remnants of its long history, but you need to explore small towns like Wells and Glastonbury to get the full flavor of the region. West of here, Exmoor National Park has an unfettered, romantic appeal, with some entrancing coastline.

2 Cornwall. You're never more than 20 miles from the sea in this western outpost of Britain, and the maritime flavor imbues such port towns as Padstow and Falmouth. A string of good beaches and resort towns such as St. Ives pull in the summer crowds.

GETTING ORIENTED

Going from east to west, the counties of Somerset, Devon, and Cornwall make up the West Country. A circular tour of the West Country peninsula covers stark contrasts, from the bustling city of Bristol in the east to the remote and rocky headlands of Devon and Cornwall to the west. On the whole, the northern coast is more rugged, the cliffs dropping dramatically to tiny coves and beaches, whereas the south coast shelters many more resorts and wider expanses of sand. The crowds gravitate to the southern shore, but there are many remote inlets and estuaries, and you don't need to go far to find a degree of seclusion. The national parks of Exmoor on the northern part of the pen-insula and Dartmoor, with their wilder landscapes, add even more variety.

5

3 Plymouth and Dart-moor. Though modern in appearance, Plymouth has some important historical sights. To the northeast, the open heath and wild moorland of Dartmoor National Park invite walking and horseback riding; towns such as Chagford make a good base for exploring.

4 Exeter, Torbay, Totnes, and Dartmouth. Exeter's sturdy cathedral dominates the historic city, from which you can make an easy foray to Topsham. South of Exeter, relaxed Totnes and bustling Dartmouth lie close to the English Riviera resorts of Torquay and Brixham.

WEST COUNTRY BEACHES

When the British travel to Cornwall and Devon, they're heading for the beach. This region has the best beaches in the country, whether on the Atlantic or the English Channel: crescents of ivory sand at the foot of plunging cliffs, all washed by clear, deep blue water. Bring your swimsuit and join the fun.

(above) Clear water adds appeal at some of Cornwall's beaches; (right, top) Granite cliffs at Porthcurno Beach; (right, bottom) Boats add coastal charm.

Carved out by ancient volcanic activity or by the creative erosion of wind and waves, the beaches here are often uniquely beautiful. North Cornwall beaches are rugged and often pounded by surf: those near Newquay and Padstow are beloved by the young surfer crowd. The more sheltered south coast tends to be popular with families due to the calmer waves. In the far west, the beaches can be a bit wilder and equally spectacular, although the best are often off the beaten track—and well worth the drive. Most beaches are free (but you may pay to park), and rare is the beach that doesn't have an ice-cream truck nearby. Expect to bring your own towels, chairs, and floats.

GOOD TO KNOW

The waters off the coasts of England are very cold: brace yourself. Undertows are common due to the nature of the shoreline; beware of fast-moving tides. At most beaches, red-and-yellow flags show the limits of safe swimming. A blue flag means that the beach is excellent. The Blue Flag plan grades cleanliness, water quality, access, and facilities; it's used in Europe and parts of North America.

These Devon and Cornwall beaches include top picks for families, surfers, and those who love stunning landscapes.

WOOLACOMBE BAY

One of the most famous beaches in the country, North Devon's Woolacombe is hugely popular with surfers for its waves and with families for its soft sand and tidal pools for the kids to explore. This beach has all you could need for a dreamy day: cafés, chairs and surfing equipment to rent, lifeguards, ice cream—you name it. But if you're not looking for crowds and kids, you may want to go elsewhere. The beach is 17 miles west of Lynton: to get here, take A361 and follow signs.

BLACKPOOL SANDS

Near Dartmouth on Start Bay in South Devon, this privately managed beach sits at the edge of an extraordinary natural setting of meadows and forest. It's favored for its clear water and long, wide stretch of sand. Great for swimming (not so great for surfing), the beach is big enough that you can always find a quiet stretch. Take A379 south of Dartmouth for about 3 miles and look for signs.

FISTRAL BAY

This favorite of serious surfers near Newquay in North Cornwall is a long stretch of flat, soft sand, renowned for its powerful tides and strong currents.

Surf shops rent equipment and offer lessons on the beach, or you can just check the scene. Lifeguards watch the water in summer, and there are cafés and shops selling beach supplies. The beach is off Headland Road at the western edge of Newquay.

PORTHCURNO

A protected, blue bay in South Cornwall, Porthcurno has a crescent moon of white sand (from crushed shells) at the foot of imposing dark, blocklike granite cliffs. The extraordinary Minack Theatre—carved from solid rock—is on one side, and there are pubs and cafés nearby. A steep slope can make swimming a challenge at times, but one area near a stream is good for families. The town and beach are signed off B3315, about 3 miles southeast of Land's End.

SENNEN COVE

Located in the aptly named Whitesand Bay, Sennen Cove is a gorgeous expanse of creamy soft sand on the western tip of Cornwall. When the tide is coming in, the waves attract legions of surfers. When the tide's out, kids paddle in the tidal pools and the sand stretches as far as you can see. Cafés are nearby, and surfing equipment is for rent on the beach. Sennen is off A30 less than 2 miles north of Land's End: follow signs.

—by Christi Daugherty

5

GREAT COASTAL DRIVES

The best way to explore the West Country is by car. The coast and countryside here are wondrously varied, but the area isn't well traversed by buses or trains. A drive can take you from spectacular ocean views to mysterious moors in an hour, and the routes are nearly endless.

(above) Exploring coastal towns such as Tintagel is a West Country pleasure; (right, top) Romantic sunset at Tintagel; (right, below) Coastal view in Cornwall

Choose your ideal coastal tour based on the scenery that appeals to you. For plunging cliffs and crashing seas, you'll want the north Devon and Cornwall coast. For sheltered white beaches carved out of rocky shores, southern Cornwall is the place for you. You can combine your driving route with breaks for sightseeing or for bike riding, walking on the South West Coast Path, or even surfing. If you prefer a more relaxed option, stop at a café for a cup of tea and a scone; treat yourself to the clotted cream. Stretch your coastal tour out over days, or pack it all into one busy afternoon: your route can fit your own plans. Either way, you're bound to see something beautiful along the way.

BE PREPARED

Gas stations (called petrol stations here) are fairly frequent on major roads but rare on rural lanes. Don't let your tank get low if you're spending your time on small country roads. Coastal roads will be more crowded on summer weekends than weekdays, as you might expect. Heavy traffic is generally limited to the most popular towns and beaches. Outside towns, there are few lights at night—it gets very dark.

THE ATLANTIC HIGHWAY

Length and driving time: 55 miles one-way; about 5 hours with stops, 2 hours without stops

Difficulty: Moderate, with some steep, narrow roads

Running from the top of Devon down to the tip of Cornwall, A39, known as the Atlantic Highway, takes a handy route along the peninsula's northern coast, and you can hop off and on it to see the sights. Starting at the charming hillside town of Clovelly, you can explore the steep streets and adorable cottages before driving south on A39 to Boscastle (30 miles; turn off on B3266 and follow signs), a stone-built village at the foot of a steep, forested ravine. Stop for tea and spend some time browsing Boscastle's pottery shops before driving 4 miles (on B3263) to Tintagel with its cliff-top castle ruins (linked to King Arthur). The ocean views are breathtaking. Back on A39, drive 20 miles to the beachfront town of Padstow, a perfect place to stop for the day, and perhaps indulge in a meal at one of Rick Stein's famous seafood restaurants.

ST. IVES TO CAPE CORNWALL, VIA PENZANCE

Length and driving time: 44 miles; about 4 hours with stops, 1½ hours without stops

Difficulty: Moderate, with narrow, winding roads

You can spend hours in St. Ives looking through its art galleries and relaxing on the beach, but when you're ready to explore, strike out for Penzance, 8 miles south on B3311. Park in the lots by the sea and take in the shops and cafés of Chapel Street before heading to Mousehole, 3 miles away along the seafront. In this tiny village, the Lilliputian cottages are scattered around the harbor.

From Mousehole, the winding B3315 road will take you the 10 miles to Land's End, the tip of Cornwall: you can either join in the tourist fest of the amusement park there, or strike out on foot along the coastal path for some stunning scenery.

It's less than 8 miles from Land's End to Cape Cornwall on B3306, but the road twists and turns. It can take time to get there, particularly if you're lured by awesome coastal views along the way. Cape Cornwall is a promontory where Atlantic currents split, heading south to the English Channel or north toward Bristol. The dramatic, rocky shoreline has spectacular views and makes a great picnic spot; there's plenty of well-marked parking.

From Cape Cornwall, you're only 14 miles from St. Ives on B3306, completing your coastal loop.

—by Christi Daugherty

Updated
by Robert
Andrews

England's West Country is a land of granite promontories, windswept moors, hideaway hamlets, and—above all— the sea. Leafy, narrow country roads lead through miles of buttercup meadows and cider-apple orchards to heathery heights and mellow villages. With their secluded beaches and dreamy backwaters, Somerset, Devon, and Cornwall can be some of England's most relaxing regions to visit.

The counties of the West Country each have their own distinct flavor, and each comes with a regionalism that borders on patriotism. Somerset is noted for its rolling green countryside; Devon's wild and dramatic moors—bare, boggy, upland heath dominated by heathers and gorse— contrast with the restfulness of its many sandy beaches and coves; and Cornwall has managed to retain a touch of its old insularity, despite the annual invasion of thousands of people lured by the Atlantic waves or the ripples of the English Channel.

The historic port of Bristol is where you come across the first unmistakable burrs of the western brogue. Its Georgian architecture and a dramatic gorge create a backdrop to what has become one of Britain's most dynamic cities. To the south lie the cathedral city of Wells and Glastonbury, with its ruined abbey and Arthurian associations. Abutting the north coast is heather-covered Exmoor National Park.

There's more wild moorland in Devon, where Dartmoor is famed for its ponies roaming amid an assortment of strange tors: rocky outcroppings eroded into weird shapes. Devon's coastal towns are as interesting for their cultural and historical appeal—many were smuggler havens—as for their scenic beauty. Parts of south Devon resemble some balmy Mediterranean shore—hence its soubriquet, the English Riviera.

Cornwall, England's westernmost county, has always regarded itself as separate from the rest of Britain, and the Arthurian legends really took root here, not least at Tintagel Castle, the legendary birthplace of Arthur. The south coast is filled with sandy beaches, delightful coves, and popular resorts.

WEST COUNTRY PLANNER

WHEN TO GO

In July and August, traffic chokes the roads leading into the West Country. Somehow the region squeezes in all the "grockles," or tourists, and the chances of finding a remote oasis of peace and quiet are severely curtailed. The beaches and resort towns are either bubbling with zest or unbearably tacky, depending on your point of view. In summer your best option is to find a secluded hotel and make brief excursions from there. Avoid traveling on Saturday, when weekly rentals start and finish and the roads are jammed. Most properties that don't accept business year-round open for Easter and close in late September or October. Those that remain open have reduced hours. Winter has its own appeal: the Atlantic waves crash dramatically against the coast, and the austere Cornish cliffs are at their most spectacular.

The most notable festivals are Padstow's Obby Oss, a traditional celebration of the arrival of summer that takes place around May 1; the Cornish-themed Golowan Festival in Penzance in late June; and the St. Ives September Festival of music and art in mid-September. In addition, many West Country maritime towns host regattas over summer weekends. The best times to visit Devon are late summer and early fall, during the end-of-summer festivals, especially popular in the coastal towns of east Devon.

PLANNING YOUR TIME

The elongated shape of Britain's southwestern peninsula means that you may well spend more time traveling than seeing the sights. The key is to base yourself in one or two places and make day trips to the surrounding region. The cities of Bristol, Exeter, and Plymouth make handy bases from which to explore the region, but they can also swallow up a lot of time, at the expense of smaller, less demanding places. The same is true of the resorts of Torquay, Newquay, and Falmouth, which can get very busy. Choose instead towns and villages such as Wells, Lynmouth, Port Isaac, St. Mawes, and Fowey to soak up local atmosphere. If you stick to just a few towns in Somerset and Devon (Bristol, Wells, and Exeter) you could get a taste of the area in four or five days. If you intend to cover Cornwall, at the end of the peninsula, you'll need at least a week. Allow time for aimless rambling—the best way to explore the moors and the coast—and leave enough free time for doing nothing at all.

GETTING HERE AND AROUND

AIR TRAVEL

Bristol International Airport, a few miles southwest of the city, has frequent flights from London, as well as from Dublin, Amsterdam, and other international cities. Exeter International Airport is 5 miles east of the city. Newquay Cornwall Airport, 5 miles northeast of town, has daily flights to London Gatwick.

Airport Information Bristol International Airport ✉ *A38, Lulsgate Bottom* ☎ *0871/334–4444* ⊕ *www.bristolairport.co.uk.* **Exeter International Airport** ✉ *A30, Clyst Honiton* ☎ *01392/367433* ⊕ *www.exeter-airport.co.uk.* **Newquay Cornwall Airport** ✉ *Off A3059, St. Mawgan, Newquay* ☎ *01637/860600* ⊕ *www.newquaycornwallairport.com.*

BUS TRAVEL

National Express buses leave London's Victoria Coach Station for Bristol (2¾ hours), Exeter (4–5 hours), Plymouth (5½ hours), and Penzance (8½–9½ hours). Megabus (book online to avoid premium-line costs) offers cheap service to Bristol, Exeter, Plymouth, Newquay, and Penzance. There's also a good network of regional bus services. First buses serve Somerset, Devon, and Cornwall, and Stagecoach South West covers mainly south Devon and the north Devon coast. Western Greyhound operates mostly in Cornwall. All three companies offer money-saving one- or seven-day passes good for unlimited bus travel. Traveline can help you plan your trip.

Bus Contacts First ☎ *0845/600–1420* ⊕ *www.firstgroup.com.* **Megabus** ☎ *0900/160–0900* ⊕ *www.megabus.com.* **National Express** ☎ *0871/781–8178* ⊕ *www.nationalexpress.com.* **Stagecoach South West** ☎ *01392/427711* ⊕ *www.stagecoachbus.com.* **Traveline** ☎ *0871/200–2233* ⊕ *www.travelinesw. com.* **Western Greyhound** ☎ *01637/871871* ⊕ *www.westerngreyhound.com.*

CAR TRAVEL

Unless you confine yourself to a few towns—for example, Exeter, Penzance, and Plymouth—you'll be at a huge disadvantage without your own transportation. The region has a few main arteries, but you should take minor roads whenever possible, if only to see the real West Country at a leisurely pace.

The fastest route from London to the West Country is via the M4 and M5 motorways. Allow at least two hours to drive to Bristol, three to Exeter. The main roads heading west are the A30 (burrowing through the center of Devon and Cornwall all the way to the tip of Cornwall), the A39 (near the northern shore), and the A38 (near the southern shore, south of Dartmoor and taking in Plymouth).

TRAIN TRAVEL

Rail travelers can make use of a fast service connecting Exeter, Plymouth, and Penzance. First Great Western and South West Trains serve the region from London's Paddington and Waterloo stations. Average travel time to Exeter is 2½ hours, to Plymouth 3½ hours, and to Penzance about 5½ hours. Once you've arrived, however, you'll find trains to be of limited use in the West Country, as only a few branch lines leave the main line between Exeter and Penzance.

Regional Rail Rover tickets provide three days of unlimited travel throughout the West Country in any seven-day period, or eight days in any 15-day period; localized Ranger passes cover Devon or Cornwall.

Train Contacts National Rail Enquiries ☎ *0845/748–4950* ⊕ *www.nationalrail.co.uk.*

RESTAURANTS

The last several years have seen a food renaissance in England's West Country. In the top restaurants the accent is firmly on local and seasonal products. Seafood is the number one choice along the coasts, from Atlantic pollock to Helford River oysters, and it's available in places from haute restaurants to harborside fish shacks. Celebrity chefs have marked their pitch all over the region, including Michael Caines in

Exeter and Dartmoor, the Tanner brothers in Plymouth, Rick Stein in Padstow and Falmouth, and Jamie Oliver in Newquay. Better-known establishments are often completely booked on Friday or Saturday, so reserve well in advance. *Prices in the reviews are the average cost of a main course at dinner or, if dinner isn't served, at lunch.*

HOTELS

Accommodations include national hotel chains, represented in all of the region's principal centers, as well as ancient inns and ubiquitous bed-and-breakfast places. Availability can be limited on the coasts during August and during the weekend everywhere, so book well ahead. Many farmhouses also rent out rooms—offering tranquil rural surroundings—but these lodgings are often difficult to reach without a car. If you have a car, though, renting a house or cottage with a kitchen may be ideal. It's worth finding out about weekend and winter deals that many hotels offer. *Prices in the reviews are the lowest cost of a standard double room in high season, including 20% V.A.T.*

Visitor Information Contacts South West Tourism ⊕ www.visitsouthwest. co.uk. **Visit Cornwall** ✉ Pydar House, Pydar St., Truro ☎ 01872/322900 ⊕ www.visitcornwall.com. **Visit Devon** ⊕ www.visitdevon.co.uk. **Visit Somerset** ☎ 01934/750833 ⊕ www.visitsomerset.co.uk.

5

BRISTOL, WELLS, AND NORTH DEVON

On the eastern side of this region is the vibrant city of Bristol. From here you might head south to the pretty cathedral city of Wells and continue on via Glastonbury, which just might be the Avalon of Arthurian legend. Proceed west along the Somerset coast into Devon, skirting the moorlands of Exmoor and tracing the northern shore via Clovelly.

BRISTOL

120 miles west of London, 46 miles south of Birmingham, 45 miles east of Cardiff, 13 miles northwest of Bath.

The West Country's biggest city (population 430,000), Bristol has in recent years become one of the country's most vibrant centers, with a thriving cultural scene encompassing some of the best contemporary art, theater, and music. Buzzing bars, cafés, and restaurants, and a largely youthful population make it an attractive place to spend time.

Now that the city's industries no longer rely on the docks, the historic harbor along the River Avon has been given over to recreation. Arts and entertainment complexes, museums, and galleries fill the quayside. The pubs and clubs here draw the under-25 set and make the area fairly boisterous (and best avoided) on Friday and Saturday night.

Bristol also trails a great deal of history in its wake. It can be called the "birthplace of America" with some confidence, for John Cabot and his son Sebastian sailed from the old city docks in 1497 to touch down on the North American mainland, which he claimed for the English crown. The city had been a major center since medieval times, but in the 17th and 18th centuries it became the foremost port for trade with North

America, and played a leading role in the Caribbean slave trade. Bristol was the home of William Penn, developer of Pennsylvania, and a haven for John Wesley, whose Methodist movement played an important role in colonial Georgia.

GETTING HERE AND AROUND

Bristol has good connections by bus and train to most cities in the country. From London, calculate about 2½ hours by bus or 1¾ hours by train. From Cardiff it's about 50 minutes by bus or train. By train, make sure you get tickets for Bristol Temple Meads Station (not Bristol Parkway), which is a short bus or taxi ride from the center. The bus station is more central, near the Broadmead shopping center. Most sights can be visited on foot, though a bus or a taxi is necessary to reach the Clifton neighborhood.

ESSENTIALS

Visitor Information **Bristol Tourist Information Centre** ⊠ *E Shed, Canon's Rd.* ☎ *0906/711–2191* ⊕ *www.visitbristol.co.uk.*

EXPLORING

TOP ATTRACTIONS

FAMILY

Fodor's Choice

★

At-Bristol. One of the country's top family-friendly science centers, this multimedia attraction provides a "hands-on, minds-on" exploration of science and technology in more than 300 interactive exhibits and displays. "All About Us" is dedicated to the inner workings of the human body. Another section allows you to create your own animations. A planetarium in a gleaming stainless-steel sphere takes you on a 25-minute voyage through the galaxy. There are up to 10 shows a day, bookable when you buy your ticket. A popular exhibit lets kids test their skills at creating animations. Allow at least three hours to see it all. ⊠ *Anchor Rd., Harbourside* ☎ *0845/345–1235* ⊕ *www.at-bristol.org.uk* ☜ *£11.70* ☉ *Weekdays 10–5; weekends, national holiday Mon., and school vacations 10–6.*

QUICK
BITES

Watershed. The excellent café-restaurant upstairs at Watershed overlooks part of the harbor side. Sandwiches and hot snacks are served during the day, along with coffees and cakes. ⊠ *1 Canon's Rd., Harbourside* ☎ *0117/927–6444* ⊕ *www.watershed.co.uk.*

OFF THE
BEATEN
PATH

Berkeley Castle. In the sleepy village of Berkeley (pronounced *bark*-ley) this castle is perfectly preserved, down to its medieval turrets, and full of family treasures. It witnessed the murder of King Edward II in 1327—the cell in which it occurred can still be seen. Edward was betrayed by his French consort, Queen Isabella, and her paramour, the earl of Mortimer. Roger De Berkeley, a Norman knight, began work on the castle in 1153, and it has remained in the family ever since. Magnificent furniture, tapestries, and pictures fill the state apartments, but even the ancient buttery and kitchen are interesting. The castle is 20 miles north of Bristol, accessed from M5. ⊠ *Off A38, Berkeley* ☎ *01453/810332* ⊕ *www.berkeley-castle.com* ☜ *£9.50* ☉ *Apr. and Oct., Sun. 11–5; May–Sept., Sun.–Wed. 11–5; last admission at 4.*

Church of St. Mary Redcliffe. Built by Bristol merchants who wanted a place in which to pray for the safe (and profitable) voyages of their ships, the rib-vaulted, 14th-century church was called "the fairest in England" by Queen Elizabeth I. High up on the nave wall hang the

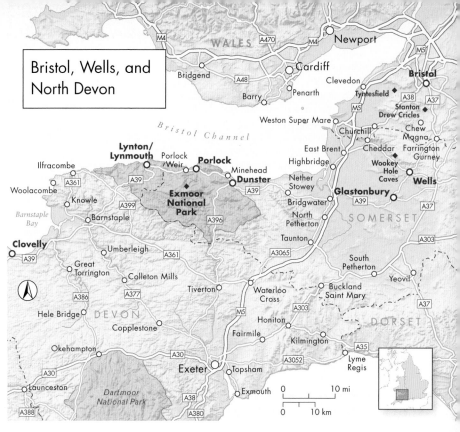

Bristol, Wells, and
North Devon

arms and armor of Sir William Penn, father of the founder of Pennsylvania. The church is a five-minute walk from Temple Meads train
station toward the docks. ⊠ *Redcliffe Way* ☎ *0117/929–1487* ⊕ *www.
stmaryredcliffe.co.uk* ✆ *Free* ☾ *Mon.–Sat. 8:30–5, Sun. 8–8.*

Clifton Suspension Bridge. A monument to Victorian engineering, this
702-foot-long bridge spans the Avon Gorge. Work began on Isambard
Kingdom Brunel's design in 1831, but the bridge wasn't completed
until 1864. Free hour-long guided tours usually take place at 3 on
weekends between April and October, departing from the tollbooth
at the Clifton end of the bridge. At the far end of the bridge, the **Clifton Suspension Bridge Interpretation Centre** has a small exhibition on
the bridge and its construction, including a 10-minute video. Near the
bridge lies **Clifton Village,** studded with boutiques, antiques shops, and
smart crafts shops in its lanes and squares. Bus number 8 from Bristol Temple Meads Station and the city center stops in Clifton Village.
⊠ *Bridge Rd., Leigh Woods* ☎ *0117/974–4664* ⊕ *www.cliftonbridge.
org.uk* ✆ *Free* ☾ *Daily 10–5.*

Fodor's Choice
★

M Shed. In a refurbished transit shed on the harbor side, this museum
is dedicated to the city's history. The collection comprises three main
galleries—Bristol People, Bristol Places, and Bristol Life—that focus
on everything from the slave trade to scientific inventions to recent

cultural innovations associated with the city. Check out the artifacts, photos, and sound and video recordings of and by Bristolians, all jazzed up with the latest interactive technology. ⊠ *Princes Wharf, Wapping Rd.* ☏ *0117/352–6600* ⊕ *www.mshed.org* ⊡ *Free* ☉ *Tues.–Fri. 10–5, weekends and bank holiday Mon. 10–6.*

SS *Great Britain*. On view in the harbor is the first iron ship to cross the Atlantic. Built by the great English engineer Isambard Kingdom Brunel in 1843, it remained in service until 1970, first as a transatlantic liner and ultimately as a coal storage hulk. Everything from the galley to the officers' quarters comes complete with sounds and smells of the time. You can descend into the ship's dry dock for a view of the hull and propeller. Your ticket admits you to an exhibit on the ship's history. A replica of the *Matthew,* the tiny craft that carried John Cabot to North America in 1497, may be moored alongside (when it's not sailing on the high seas). ⊠ *Great Western Dockyard, Gas Ferry Rd.* ☏ *0117/926–0680* ⊕ *www.ssgreatbritain.org* ⊡ *£12.95* ☉ *Apr.–Oct., daily 10–5:30; Nov.–Mar., daily 10–4:30; last entry 1 hr before closing.*

WORTH NOTING

FAMILY   **Bristol Zoo Gardens.** Alongside the leafy expanse of Clifton Down is one of the country's most famous zoos. More than 400 animal species live in 12 acres of gardens; the Seal and Penguin coasts, with underwater viewing, are rival attractions for Gorilla Island, Bug World, and Twilight World. Take Bus 8 or 9 from Temple Meads Station or the city center. ⊠ *Clifton Down* ☏ *0117/974–7399* ⊕ *www.bristolzoo.org.uk* ⊡ *£14* ☉ *Apr.–Oct., daily 9–5:30; Nov.–Mar., daily 9–5; last entry 1 hr before closing.*

New Room. John Wesley and Charles Wesley were among the Dissenters from the Church of England who found a home in Bristol, and in 1739 they built the New Room, a meeting place that became the first Methodist chapel. Its simplicity contrasts with the style of Anglican churches and with the modern shopping center hemming it in. Upstairs you can visit the Preachers' Rooms, now containing a small museum. ⊠ *36 The Horsefair* ☏ *0117/926–4740* ⊕ *www.newroombristol.org.uk* ⊡ *Free* ☉ *Mon.–Sat. 10–4.*

OFF THE
BEATEN
PATH

Stanton Drew Circles. Three rings, two avenues of standing stones, and a burial chamber make up the Stanton Drew Circles, one of the largest and most mysterious monuments in Britain, dating from 3000 to 2000 BC. It's far less well known than Stonehenge and other circles, however. The size of the circles suggests that the site was once as important as Stonehenge for its ceremonial functions, although little of great visual impact remains. English Heritage supervises the stones, which stand on private land. Access is given at any reasonable time, and a small admission fee or donation may be requested. ■ TIP→ You have to walk through a farmyard to reach the field where the site lies, so wear sturdy shoes. To get here from Bristol, head south on the A37 and turn right after about 5 miles onto the B3130, marked Stanton Drew. The circles are just east of the village, where more of the stones may be seen in the garden of the Druid's Arms pub. ⊠ *B3130, Stanton Drew* ☏ *0117/975–0700* ⊕ *www.english-heritage.org.uk.*

Fodor's Choice ★ **Tyntesfield.** The National Trust is gradually restoring this extravagant, 35-bedroom Victorian–Gothic Revival mansion. Every ornate detail of this decorative-arts showcase compels attention. Besides magnificent woodwork, stained glass, tiles, and original furniture and fabrics, the house contains the modern conveniences of the 1860s, such as a heated billiards table, and the servants' quarters are equally absorbing. There's a restaurant and family play area, too. You can see the house, garden, and chapel at your own pace. **TIP→ Arrive early in the day to avoid the crowds competing for timed tickets—Monday and Tuesday are the quietest days.** Tyntesfield is 7 miles southwest of Bristol; take Bus 354 or 361 from the city every day except Sunday. ✉ *B3128, Wraxall* ☎ *01275/461900* 🌐 *www.nationaltrust.org.uk* 🎫 *£13.20; gardens only £8.10* ⏲ *House early Feb.–early Mar., Sat.–Wed. 11–3; early Mar.–early July, Sat.–Wed. 11–5; early July–Oct., Fri.–Wed. 11–5; early Dec.–mid-Dec., Mon.–Wed. and Fri. 11–3. Gardens early Mar.–early Nov., daily 10–6, early Nov.–early Mar., 10–5 or dusk.*

5

WHERE TO EAT

$ MODERN BRITISH 🍴 **Bordeaux Quay.** This converted riverside warehouse is dedicated to food, incorporating a delicatessen, a wine bar, a brasserie, a formal restaurant, and a cookery school. The lively street-level brasserie (open daily) is recommended for breakfasts of buttermilk pancakes or eggs Florentine and dinners centered on locally sourced mussels, duck leg confit, or sirloin steak. With its large skylight and harbor views, the upstairs dining room (open weekends) offers more sophisticated dining, including such dishes as sea bass with clams, mussels, and saffron sauce, and desserts like rhubarb cheesecake with ginger ice cream. [$] *Average main: £12* ✉ *Canon's Way, Harbourside* ☎ *0117/943–1200* 🌐 *www.bordeaux-quay.co.uk* ⏲ *Restaurant closed weekdays. No lunch Sat. No dinner Sun.*

$ BRITISH 🍴 **Boston Tea Party.** Despite the name, this laid-back and vaguely eccentric place is quintessentially English, and ideal for a relaxed lunch away from the nearby rigors of the Park Street shopping scene. Tasty sandwiches can be taken out or eaten in the terraced backyard or the upstairs sofa salon, a comfy spot for a cup of tea with orange and almond cake. Generous salads and burgers are also available. Get here early, as the restaurant closes at 8 (7 on Sunday). [$] *Average main: £7* ✉ *75 Park St.* ☎ *0117/929–8601* 🌐 *www.bostonteaparty.co.uk.*

$$ MODERN BRITISH 🍴 **Riverstation.** Occupying a former police station, this modern, clean-lined restaurant affords serene views over the passing swans and boats. Book early for a window seat. Upstairs, the more formal restaurant serves such delicately cooked dishes as braised rabbit haunch and pan-fried brill, and some irresistible desserts, including pistachio crème brûlée with marinated figs. The bar has a more rough-and-ready menu that includes warm savory tarts and Thai-spiced mussels. With its terrace seating, this place also makes a great spot for breakfast, afternoon coffee, or evening drinks. [$] *Average main: £17* ✉ *The Grove, Harbourside, Bristol* ☎ *0117/914–4434* 🌐 *www.riverstation.co.uk* ⏲ *No dinner Sun.*

$$ MODERN BRITISH 🍴 **Source Food Hall.** In the heart of the old city, this trendy eatery benefits from its location in the St. Nicholas Market by offering a range of fresh seasonal produce, either to eat in or take out from the deli, meat, or fish counters. The wholesome lunch menu might feature asparagus

EATING WELL IN THE WEST COUNTRY

Sheer indulgence: a cream tea with scones, clotted cream, and jam is compulsory in the West Country.

From cider to cream teas, many specialties tempt your palate in the West Country. Lamb, venison, and, in Devon and Cornwall, seafood, are favored in restaurants, which have risen to heights of gastronomic excellence, notably through the influence of Rick Stein's seafood-based culinary empire in Padstow, in Cornwall. Seafood is celebrated at fishy frolics that include the Newlyn Fish Festival (late August) and Falmouth's Oyster Festival (early or mid-October).

WHAT TO EAT

Cheddar. Somerset is the home of Britain's most famous cheese—the ubiquitous cheddar, originally from the Mendip Hills village of the same name. Make certain that you sample a real farmhouse cheddar, made in the traditional barrel shape known as a truckle.

Cream teas. Devon's caloric cream teas consist of a pot of tea, homemade scones, and lots of strawberry jam and thickened clotted cream (a regional specialty, which is sometimes called Devonshire cream).

Pasties. Cornwall's specialty is the pasty, a pastry shell filled with chopped meat, onions, and potatoes. The pasty was devised as a handy way for miners to carry their dinner to work; today's versions are generally pale imitations of the original, though you can still find delicious home-cooked pasties if you're willing to search a little.

Seafood. In many towns in Devon and Cornwall, the day's catch is unloaded from the harbor and transported directly to eateries. The catch varies by season, but lobster is available year-round, as is crab, stuffed into sandwiches at quayside stalls and in pubs.

WHAT TO DRINK

Perry. This is similar to cider but made from pears.

Scrumpy. For liquid refreshment, try scrumpy, a homemade dry cider that's refreshing but carries a surprising kick.

Sheer indulgence: A cream tea with scones, clotted cream, and jam is compulsory in the West Country.

Wine and mead. English wine, similar to German wine, is made in all three counties (you may see it on local menus), and in Devon and Cornwall you can find a variant of age-old mead made from local honey.

soup with cream and chives or Hereford beef burgers, while the evening menu includes a range of steaks and seafood. The breakfasts and coffees are energizing, making this an ideal place to kick off a sightseeing excursion or take a pause en route. The attractive Bath-stone building has an airy, high-ceilinged interior. [$] *Average main: £15* ✉ *St. Nicholas Market, 1–3 Exchange Ave.* ☎ *0117/927–2998* 🌐 *www.source-food.co.uk* ⏲ *Closed Sun. No dinner Mon.–Wed.*

WHERE TO STAY

For expanded hotel reviews, visit Fodors.com.

$ HOTEL 🏨 **Hotel24seven.** Bristol's best budget option has furnishings and decor that are simple but modern. **Pros:** good value; clean rooms; self-catering. **Cons:** no reception; no breakfast; cheapest rooms have shared bathrooms. [$] *Rooms from: £60* ✉ *1 Dean La., Southville* ☎ *0844/770 9411* 🌐 *www.hotel24seven.com* 🛏 *30 rooms* 🍴 *No meals.*

$$ HOTEL 🏨 **Hotel du Vin.** This hip chain has brought high-tech flair to six former sugar-refining warehouses, built in 1728 when the River Frome ran outside the front door. **Pros:** tastefully restored old building; great bathrooms; excellent bar and bistro. **Cons:** traffic-dominated location; dim lighting in rooms; limited parking. [$] *Rooms from: £129* ✉ *Narrow Lewins Mead* ☎ *0844/736–4252* 🌐 *www.hotelduvin.com* 🛏 *36 rooms, 4 suites* 🍴 *No meals.*

$$$ HOTEL Fodor's Choice ★ 🏨 **Thornbury Castle.** An impressive lodging, Thornbury has everything a genuine 16th-century Tudor castle needs: huge fireplaces, moody paintings, mullioned windows, and a large garden. **Pros:** grand medieval surroundings; sumptuous rooms; doting service. **Cons:** many steps to climb; village is dull. [$] *Rooms from: £170* ✉ *Castle St., off A38, Thornbury* ☎ *01454/281182* 🌐 *www.thornburycastle.co.uk* 🛏 *22 rooms, 5 suites* 🍴 *Breakfast.*

$ HOTEL 🏨 **Victoria Square Hotel.** In two mellow Victorian buildings overlooking one of Clifton's leafiest squares, this hotel makes an excellent base for exploring Bristol. **Pros:** good advance-booking deals; pleasant location; pretty garden. **Cons:** numerous steps; some rooms need sprucing up. [$] *Rooms from: £77* ✉ *Victoria Sq., Clifton* ☎ *0117/973–9058* 🌐 *www.victoriasquarehotel.co.uk* 🛏 *41 rooms* 🍴 *Breakfast.*

NIGHTLIFE AND THE ARTS

Arnolfini. In a converted warehouse on the harbor, the Arnolfini is one of the country's most prestigious contemporary-art venues, known for uncovering innovative yet accessible art. There are galleries, a cinema, a bookshop, and a lively bar and bistro. ✉ *16 Narrow Quay* ☎ *0117/917–2300* 🌐 *www.arnolfini.org.uk.*

St. George's. A church built in the 18th century, St. George's now serves as one of the country's leading venues for classical, jazz, and world music. Stop by for lunchtime concerts. ✉ *Great George St., off Park St.* ☎ *0845/402–4001* 🌐 *www.stgeorgesbristol.co.uk.*

Watershed. A contemporary arts center by the harbor, the Watershed also has a movie theater that screens excellent international films. ✉ *1 Canon's Rd., Harbourside* ☎ *0117/927–5100* 🌐 *www.watershed.co.uk.*

WELLS

22 miles south of Bristol, 132 miles west of London.

England's smallest cathedral city, with a population of 10,000, lies at the foot of the Mendip Hills. Although set in what feels like a quiet country town, the great cathedral is a masterpiece of Gothic architecture—the first to be built in the Early English style. The city's name refers to the underground streams that bubble up into St. Andrew's Well within the grounds of the Bishop's Palace. Spring water has run through High Street since the 15th century. Seventeenth-century buildings surround the ancient marketplace, which hosts market days on Wednesday and Saturday.

GETTING HERE AND AROUND

Regular First buses from Bristol take 1¼ hours to reach Wells; the bus station is a few minutes south of the cathedral. Drivers should take A37, and park outside the compact and eminently walkable center.

ESSENTIALS

Visitor Information **Wells Visitor Information Service** ✉ *Wells Museum, 8 Cathedral Green* ☎ *01749/671770* ⊕ *www.wellssomerset.com.*

EXPLORING

Bishop's Palace. The Bishop's Eye gate leading from Market Place takes you to the magnificent, moat-ringed Bishop's Palace, which retains parts of the original 13th-century residence. Most rooms are closed to the public, but you can see the private chapel, the gatehouse, and the ruins of a late-13th-century great hall in the peaceful grounds. The hall lost its roof in the 16th century because Edward VI needed the lead it contained. ✉ *Market Pl.* ☎ *01749/988111* ⊕ *www.bishopspalacewells. co.uk* ⊠ *£6.35* ☉ *Early Feb.–Mar. and Nov.–late Dec., daily 10–4; Apr.–Oct., daily 10–6; last admission 1 hr before closing.*

Fodor'sChoice ★ **Cathedral Church of St. Andrew.** The great west towers of this medieval structure, the oldest surviving English Gothic church, can be seen for miles. Dating from the 12th century, the cathedral derives its beauty from the perfect harmony of all of its parts, the glowing colors of its original stained-glass windows, and its peaceful setting among stately trees and majestic lawns. To appreciate the elaborate west-front facade, approach the building from the cathedral green, accessible from Market Place through a great medieval gate called "penniless porch" (named after the beggars who once waited here to collect alms from worshippers). The cathedral's west front is twice as wide as it is high, and some 300 statues of kings and saints adorn it. Inside, vast inverted arches—known as scissor arches—were added in 1338 to stop the central tower from sinking to one side.

The cathedral has a rare and beautiful medieval clock, the second-oldest working clock in the world, consisting of the seated figure of a man called Jack Blandifer, who strikes a bell on the quarter hour while mounted knights circle in a joust. Near the clock is the entrance to the Chapter House—a small wooden door opening onto a great sweep of stairs worn down on one side by the tread of pilgrims over the centuries. Free guided tours lasting up to an hour begin at the back of the

Harmonious and stately, Wells Cathedral has a monumental west front decorated with medieval statues of kings and saints.

cathedral. A cloister restaurant serves snacks and teas. ⊠ *Cathedral Green* ☎ *01749/674483* ⊕ *www.wellscathedral.org.uk* ✉ *£6 suggested donation* ⊗ *Apr.–Sept., daily 7–7; Oct.–Mar., daily 7–6. Tours Apr.–Oct., Mon.–Sat. at 10, 11, 1, 2, and 3; Nov.–Mar., Mon.–Sat. at 11, noon, and 2.*

QUICK BITES

Sadler Street Café. This little café and patisserie near the cathedral serves exquisite cakes and pastries, chocolate concoctions, and excellent coffee. Soups, sandwiches, and light meals are also available, and French country dishes are served Wednesday to Saturday evening. ⊠ *5 Sadler St.* ☎ *01749/673866.*

Vicar's Close. To the north of the cathedral, the cobbled Vicar's Close, one of Europe's oldest streets, has terraces of handsome 14th-century houses with strange, tall chimneys. A tiny medieval chapel here is still in use.

OFF THE BEATEN PATH

Wookey Hole Caves. These limestone caves in the Mendip Hills, 2 miles northwest of Wells, may have been the home of Iron Age people. Here, according to ancient legend, the Witch of Wookey turned to stone. You can tour the caves, dip your fingers in an underground river (artful lighting keeps things lively), and visit a museum, a penny arcade full of Victorian amusement machines, and a working paper mill that once supplied banknotes for the Confederate States of America. There's plenty for kids. ⊠ *Off High St., Wookey Hole* ☎ *01749/672243* ⊕ *www. wookey.co.uk* ✉ *£18* ⊗ *Apr.–Oct., daily 10–6; Nov., Feb., and Mar., daily 10–5; Dec. and Jan., weekends 10–5; last tour 1 hr before closing.*

WHERE TO EAT AND STAY

For expanded hotel reviews, visit Fodors.com.

$$ MEDITERRANEAN 🍴 **The Old Spot.** For relaxed but top-notch dining in the heart of Wells, this sociable bistro with wood paneling and creamy white walls hits all the right notes. The Modern British and Mediterranean dinner menu varies seasonally, but might include a starter of smoked haddock fritters with tartar sauce, followed by a main course of tagine of lamb with hummus, eggplant, and North African spicy sausage. Set-price two-course lunches are £15.50. Arrive early for a table at the back, where there are views of the cathedral's west front. [$] *Average main: £17* ✉ *12 Sadler St.* ☎ *01749/689099* 🌐 *www.theoldspot.co.uk* 🕒 *Closed Mon. No lunch Tues. No dinner Sun.*

$$ B&B/INN 🏨 **Ancient Gate House.** This venerable hostelry makes a convenient base for exploring the area. **Pros:** historic character; cathedral views; handy base. **Cons:** steps to climb; cramped rooms; occasional restaurant odors at front. [$] *Rooms from: £115* ✉ *20 Sadler St.* ☎ *01749/672029* 🌐 *www.ancientgatehouse.com* 🛏 *9 rooms* 🍽 *Breakfast.*

$$ HOTEL 🏨 **Swan Hotel.** A former coaching inn built in the 15th century, the Swan has an ideal spot facing the cathedral. **Pros:** professional service; some great views; good restaurant. **Cons:** some rooms need updating; occasional noise issues; parking lot tricky to negotiate. [$] *Rooms from: £147* ✉ *11 Sadler St.* ☎ *01749/836300* 🌐 *www.swanhotelwells.co.uk* 🛏 *51 rooms, 1 suite* 🍽 *Breakfast.*

GLASTONBURY

5 miles southwest of Wells, 27 miles south of Bristol, 27 miles southwest of Bath.

Fodor's Choice ★ A town steeped in history, myth, and legend, Glastonbury lies in the lea of Glastonbury Tor, a grassy hill rising 520 feet above the drained marshes known as the Somerset Levels. The Tor is supposedly the site of crossing ley lines (hypothetical alignments of significant places), and, in legend, Glastonbury is identified with Avalon, the paradise into which King Arthur was reborn after his death.

Partly because of these associations but also because of its world-class rock-music festival, the town has acquired renown as a New Age center, mixing crystal gazers with druids, yogis, and hippies, variously in search of Arthur, Merlin, Jesus—and even Elvis. **TIP→ Between April and September, a shuttle bus runs every half hour between all of Glastonbury's major sights. Tickets are £3, and are valid all day.**

GETTING HERE AND AROUND

Frequent buses link Glastonbury to Wells and Bristol, pulling in close to the abbey. Drivers should take the A39. You can walk to all the sights or take the shuttle bus, though you'll need a stock of energy for ascending the tor.

ESSENTIALS

Visitor Information Glastonbury Tourist Information Centre ✉ *The Tribunal, 9 High St.* ☎ *01458/832954* 🌐 *www.glastonburytic.co.uk.*

EXPLORING

Glastonbury Abbey. The ruins of this great abbey, in the center of town, are on the site where, according to legend, Joseph of Arimathea built a church in the 1st century. A monastery had certainly been erected here by the 9th century, and the site drew many pilgrims. The ruins are those of the abbey completed in 1524 and destroyed in 1539, during Henry VIII's dissolution of the monasteries. A sign south of the Lady Chapel marks the sites where Arthur and Guinevere were supposedly buried. Between April and October, guides in period costumes are on hand to point out some of the abbey's most interesting features. The visitor center has a scale model of the abbey as well as carvings and decorations salvaged from the ruins. ⊠ *Magdalene St.* ☎ *01458/832267* ⊕ *www.glastonburyabbey.com* ☏ *£6* ☉ *Mar.–May, Sept. and Oct., daily 9–6; June–Aug., daily 9–8; Nov.–Feb., daily 9–4; last admission 30 mins before closing.*

> ### TALE OF THE GRAIL
>
> According to tradition, Glastonbury was where Joseph of Arimathea brought the Holy Grail, the chalice used by Jesus at the Last Supper. Centuries later, the Grail was said to be the objective of the quests of King Arthur and the Knights of the Round Table. When monks claimed to have found the bones of Arthur and Guinevere at Glastonbury in 1191, the popular association of the town with the mythical Avalon was sealed. Arthur and Guinevere's presumed remains were lost to history after Glastonbury Abbey was plundered for its riches in 1539.

Glastonbury Tor. At the foot of Glastonbury Tor is **Chalice Well,** the legendary burial place of the Grail. It's a stiff climb up the tor, but your reward is the fabulous view across the Vale of Avalon. At the top stands a ruined tower, all that remains of **St. Michael's Church,** which collapsed after a landslide in 1271. Take the Glastonbury Tor bus to the base of the hill.

FAMILY **Somerset Rural Life Museum.** Occupying a Victorian farmhouse and a 14th-century abbey tithe barn, this museum tells the story of life in Somerset. More than 90 feet in length, the barn once stored the one-tenth portion of the town's produce that was owed to the church. Exhibits illustrate 19th-century farming practices, and there's a cider-apple orchard nearby. Events designed for children take place most weekends during school holidays. ■ **TIP→ For a good walk, take the scenic footpath from the museum that leads up to the tor, a half mile east.** ⊠ *Chilkwell St.* ☎ *01458/831197* ⊕ *www.somerset.gov.uk* ☏ *Free* ☉ *Tues.–Sat. and national holiday Mon. 10–5.*

WHERE TO EAT AND STAY

For expanded hotel reviews, visit Fodors.com.

$ ✗ **Who'd a Thought It.** As an antidote to the natural-food cafés of
BRITISH   Glastonbury's High Street, try this traditional backstreet inn for some more down-to-earth fare that doesn't compromise on quality. Bar classics such as beef-and-ale pie with a suet pastry appear alongside sizzling steaks and the chef's special "curry of the day." The beers and ciders are local, and the pub's quirky decor—including ancient radios, a red

telephone box, and a bicycle on the ceiling—has a definite entertainment quotient. [$] *Average main: £12* ✉ *17 Northload St.* ☎ *01458/834460* 🌐 *www.whodathoughtit.co.uk.*

$ HOTEL 🏨 **George and Pilgrim Hotel.** Pilgrims en route to Glastonbury Abbey stayed here in the 15th century. **Pros:** historic surroundings; steps from the abbey. **Cons:** limited parking; some rooms need refreshing. [$] *Rooms from: £90* ✉ *1 High St.* ☎ *01458/831146* 🌐 *www.relaxinnz.co.uk* 🛏 *14 rooms* 🍴 *Breakfast.*

$ B&B/INN 🏨 **The Glastonbury White House.** You'll receive warm hospitality from the owner of this eco-friendly B&B a few minutes from High Street. **Pros:** friendly host; lots of period details; flexible breakfasts. **Cons:** not great for families. [$] *Rooms from: £65* ✉ *21 Manor House Rd.* ☎ *01458/830886* 🌐 *www.theglastonburywhitehouse.com* 🛏 *2 rooms* 💳 *No credit cards* 🍴 *No meals.*

NIGHTLIFE AND THE ARTS

Glastonbury Festival. Held a few miles away in Pilton, the Glastonbury Festival is England's biggest and perhaps best annual rock festival. For five days over the last weekend in June, it hosts hundreds of bands—established and up-and-coming—on three main stages and myriad smaller venues. Tickets are steeply priced—over £200—and sell out months in advance; they include entertainment, a camping area, and service facilities. ✉ *Pilton* 🌐 *www.glastonburyfestivals.co.uk.*

DUNSTER

35 miles west of Glastonbury, 43 miles north of Exeter.

Lying between the Somerset coast and the edge of Exmoor National Park, Dunster is a picture-book village with a broad main street. The eight-sided yarn-market building on High Street dates from 1589.

GETTING HERE AND AROUND

To reach Dunster by car, follow the A39. By bus, there are frequent departures from nearby Minehead and Taunton. Dunster Castle is a brief walk from the village center. In the village is the Exmoor National Park Visitor Centre, which can give you plenty of information about local activities.

ESSENTIALS

Visitor Information **Exmoor National Park Visitor Centre** ✉ *Dunster Steep* ☎ *01643/821835* 🌐 *www.exmoor-nationalpark.gov.uk.*

EXPLORING

Fodor's Choice ★ **Dunster Castle.** A 13th-century fortress remodeled in 1868, Dunster Castle dominates the village from its site on a hill. Parkland and unusual gardens with subtropical plants surround the building, which has fine plaster ceilings, stacks of family portraits (including one by Joshua Reynolds), 17th-century Dutch leather hangings, and a magnificent 17th-century oak staircase. The climb to the castle from the parking lot is steep. ✉ *Off A39* ☎ *01643/821314* 🌐 *www.nationaltrust.org.uk* 🎟 *£9; gardens only, £5.20* 🕒 *Castle early Mar.–early Nov., daily 11–5; early Dec.–late Dec., weekends 11–3. Gardens early Mar.–early Nov., daily 10–5; early Nov.–early Mar., daily 11–4.*

The hugely popular Glastonbury Festival attracts music lovers and free spirits from all over the world.

WHERE TO STAY

For expanded hotel reviews, visit Fodors.com.

$$
B&B/INN **Luttrell Arms.** In style and atmosphere, this classic inn harmonizes perfectly with Dunster village and castle; it was used as a guesthouse by the abbots of Cleeve in the 14th century. **Pros:** central location; historic trappings; good dining options. **Cons:** some standard rooms are small and viewless; no parking. *$ Rooms from: £130 ⊠ High St. ☎ 01643/821555 ⊕ www.luttrellarms.co.uk ➹ 28 rooms ⊓⊙⊦ Breakfast.*

EXMOOR NATIONAL PARK

16 miles southwest of Dunster.

When you're headed to Exmoor National Park, stop by the visitor information centers at Dulverton, Dunster, and Lynmouth for information and maps. Guided walks, many of which have themes (archaeology, for example), cost £3 to £5. If you're walking on your own, check the weather, take water and a map, and tell someone where you're going.

GETTING HERE AND AROUND

A car is usually necessary for getting around the inner reaches of Exmoor. Bus 300, a vintage open-top double-decker run by Quantock Motor Services, traces the coast between Minehead and Lynmouth. Bus 398, operated by Beacon Bus, runs from Minehead to Dunster and inland to Dulverton.

ESSENTIALS

Bus Contacts Beacon Bus ☎ *01805/804240* ⊕ *www.beaconbus.co.uk.* **Quantock Motor Services** ☎ *01823/430202* ⊕ *www.quantockmotorservices.co.uk.*

Visitor Information **Dulverton**
National Park Centre ✉ *7–9 Fore St.*
☎ *01398/323841* ⊕ *www.exmoor-
nationalpark.gov.uk/visiting/national-
park-centres/dulverton.* **Lynmouth
National Park Centre** ✉ *Lyndale
Car Park, Lynmouth* ☎ *01598/752509*
⊕ *www.exmoor-nationalpark.gov.uk/
visiting/national-park-centres/lynmouth.*

EXPLORING

Exmoor National Park. Less wild and forbidding than Dartmoor to its south, 267-square-mile Exmoor National Park is no less majestic for its bare heath and lofty views. The park extends right up to the coast and straddles the county border between Somerset and Devon. Some walks offer spectacular views over the Bristol Channel. Taking one of the more than 700 miles of paths and bridle ways through the bracken and heather (at its best in fall), you might glimpse the ponies and red deer for which the region is noted. ■TIP➔ Be careful: the proximity of the coast means that mists and squalls can descend with alarming suddenness. ✉ *Exmoor National Park Authority, Exmoor House* ☎ *01398/323665* ⊕ *www. exmoor-nationalpark.gov.uk*.

SOUTH WEST COAST PATH

Britain's longest national trail, the South West Coast Path, wraps around the coast of the peninsula for 630 miles from Minehead (near Dunster, Somerset) to South Haven Point, near Poole (Dorset). To complete the trail takes 50 to 60 days.

South West Coast Path Association. An annual guide to hiking in the region is published by the South West Coast Path Association. ⊕ *www.southwestcoastpath. org.uk.*

PORLOCK

6 miles west of Dunster, 45 miles north of Exeter.

Buried at the bottom of a valley, with the slopes of Exmoor all about, the small, unspoiled town of Porlock lies near "Doone Country," the setting for R. D. Blackmore's swashbuckling saga *Lorna Doone*. Porlock had already achieved a place in literary history by the late 1790s, when Samuel Taylor Coleridge declared it was a "man from Porlock" who interrupted his opium trance while the poet was composing "Kubla Khan."

GETTING HERE AND AROUND

Porlock is best reached via the A39 coastal route. Quantock Motor Services operates several buses between Porlock and Minehead. The village can be easily explored by foot.

ESSENTIALS

Visitor Information **Porlock Visitor Centre** ✉ *The Old School, High St.*
☎ *01643/863150* ⊕ *www.porlock.co.uk.*

EXPLORING

Coleridge Way. The 36-mile Coleridge Way passes through the northern fringes of the Quantock Hills, the isolated villages of the Brendon Hills, and parts of Exmoor National Park on the way from Nether Stowey (site of Coleridge's home) to Porlock. ⊕ *www.coleridgeway.co.uk.*

Porlock Hill. As you're heading west from Porlock to Lynton, the coast road A39 mounts Porlock Hill, an incline so steep that signs encourage drivers to "keep going." The views across Exmoor and north to the Bristol Channel and Wales are worth it. Less steep but quieter and equally scenic routes, up the hill on toll roads, can be accessed from Porlock and Porlock Weir.

Porlock Weir. Two miles west of Porlock, this tiny harbor is the starting point for an undemanding 2-mile walk along the coast through chestnut and walnut trees to **Culbone Church,** reputedly the smallest and most isolated church in England. Saxon in origin, it has a small Victorian spire and is lighted by candles. It would be hard to find a more enchanting spot.

WHERE TO EAT

$$
MODERN BRITISH
✕ **The Café.** Don't be put off by its unassuming name, because this self-styled "café-with-rooms" in a sea-facing Georgian building is pure, relaxed, English country house. Run by a husband-and-wife team, it offers top-quality food and accommodations. You can settle down in its spacious dining room for a cream tea with warm scones, or opt for a light lunch or more ambitious fare, including a seafood platter with oysters, lobster, crab, and scallops (ordering a day ahead). The five reasonably priced guest rooms are done in restful hues. $ *Average main: £16* ⊠ *Dunster Steep, Porlock Weir* ☎ *01643/863300* ⊕ *www. thecafeatporlockweir.co.uk* ☉ *Closed Mon. and Tues.*

LYNTON AND LYNMOUTH

13 miles west of Porlock, 60 miles northwest of Exeter.

A steep hill separates this pretty pair of Devonshire villages, which are linked by a Victorian cliff railway you can still ride. Lynmouth, a fishing village at the bottom of the hill, crouches below 1,000-foot-high cliffs at the mouths of the East and West Lyn rivers; Lynton is higher up. The poet Percy Bysshe Shelley visited Lynmouth in 1812, in the company of his 16-year-old bride, Harriet Westbrook. During their nine-week sojourn, the poet found time to write his polemical *Queen Mab.* The grand landscape of Exmoor lies all about, with walks to local beauty spots: Watersmeet, the Valley of Rocks, or Hollerday Hill, where rare feral goats graze.

GETTING HERE AND AROUND

These towns are best reached via the A39. Lynton is a stop on Quantock Motor Services Bus 300, which runs daily from Minehead between April and October. Lynton and Lynmouth are both walkable, but take the cliff railway to travel between them.

ESSENTIALS

Visitor Information **Lynton and Lynmouth Tourist Information Centre** ⊠ *Lee Rd., Lynton* ☎ *0845/458–3775* ⊕ *lynton-lynmouth-tourism.co.uk.*

EXPLORING

Exmoor Coast Boat Cruises. Cruise around the dramatic Devon coast on these boats that depart from Lynmouth Harbour. The round-trip journey to Lee Bay costs £10 and takes 45 minutes; the 75-minute excursion to Woody Bay and beyond, costing £15, lets you experience the clamorous birdlife on the cliffs. ⊠ *Lynmouth Harbour, Watersmeet Rd., Lynmouth* ☎ *01598/753207.*

Lynton and Lynmouth Cliff Railway. Water and a cable system power the 862-foot cliff railway that connects these two towns. As they ascend a rocky cliff, you are treated to fine views over the harbor. Inaugurated in 1890, it was the gift of publisher George Newnes, who also donated Lynton's imposing town hall, near the top station on Lee Road. ⊠ *The Esplanade, Lynmouth* ☎ *01598/753908* ⊕ *www.cliffrailwaylynton. co.uk* 🎫 *£3.20 round-trip* ⊗ *Mar. and Oct., daily 10–5; Apr.–late May and mid-Sept.–late Sept., daily 10–6; late May–late July and early Sept.– mid-Sept., daily 10–7; late July–early Aug., daily 10–8; early Aug.–early Sept., daily 10–9; early Nov., daily 10–4.*

WHERE TO EAT AND STAY

For expanded hotel reviews, visit Fodors.com.

$$ | MODERN BRITISH — ✕ **Rising Sun.** A 14th-century inn and a row of thatched cottages make up this restaurant with great views over the Bristol Channel. The kitchen specializes in local cuisine with European influences, so expect such dishes as a smoked haddock tartlet, or duck confit with tomato and olive ragout. There's a superb game menu December to February. In the attached hotel, corridors and creaking staircases lead to cozy guest rooms decorated in stylish print or solid fabrics. $ *Average main: £16* ⊠ *Riverside Rd., Lynmouth* ☎ *01598/753223* ⊕ *www. risingsunlynmouth.co.uk.*

$$ | B&B/INN — 🏨 **Shelley's Hotel.** Centrally located, this well-maintained hotel has bright and spacious rooms with generous windows and excellent views. **Pros:** harbor views from most rooms; great breakfasts; hospitable owners. **Cons:** some rooms overlook public car park; no restaurant; no kids under 12. $ *Rooms from: £100* ⊠ *8 Watersmeet Rd., Lynmouth* ☎ *01598/753219* ⊕ *www.shelleyshotel.co.uk* ⤴ *11 rooms* ⏐◯⏐ *Breakfast.*

SPORTS AND THE OUTDOORS

West of Lynton, the Atlantic-facing beaches of Saunton Sands, Croyde Bay, and Woolacombe Bay are much beloved of surfers, with plenty of outlets renting equipment and offering lessons. Croyde Bay and Woolacombe Bay are more family-friendly.

CLOVELLY

40 miles southwest of Lynton, 60 miles northwest of Exeter.

Fodor's Choice
★

Lovely Clovelly always seems to have the sun shining on its flower-lined cottages and stepped and cobbled streets. Alas, its beauty is well known, and day-trippers can overrun the village in summer. Perched precariously among cliffs, a steep, cobbled road—tumbling down at such an angle that it's closed to cars—leads to the toylike harbor with its 14th-century quay. Allow about two hours (more if you stop for a drink or a meal) to take in the village. Hobby Drive, a 3-mile cliff-top carriageway laid out in 1829 through thick woods, gives scintillating views over the village and coast.

Clovelly may have it all: cobbled streets, quaint houses, and the endless blue sea.

GETTING HERE AND AROUND

To get to Clovelly by bus, take Stagecoach service 319 from Barnstaple or Bideford. If you're driving, take the A39 and park at the Clovelly Visitor Centre for £6.50. The center of town is steep and cobbled. The climb from the harbor to the parking lot can be exhausting, but from Easter through October a reasonably priced shuttle service brings you back.

EXPLORING

Clovelly Visitor Centre. Here you'll see a 20-minute film that puts Clovelly into context. In the village you can visit a 1930s-style fisherman's cottage and an exhibition about Victorian writer Charles Kingsley, who lived here as a child. The admission fee includes parking. ■ TIP➔ To avoid the worst crowds, arrive early or late in the day. ⊠ Off A39 ☎ 01237/431781 ⊕ www.clovelly.co.uk ✆ £6.50 ⊙ June–Sept., daily 9–6; late Mar.–May and Oct., daily 9:30–5:30; Nov.–late Mar., daily 10–4.

WHERE TO STAY

For expanded hotel reviews, visit Fodors.com.

$$ 🛏 **Red Lion Hotel.** You can soak up the tranquillity of Clovelly after the
HOTEL day-trippers have gone at the 18th-century Red Lion, located right on the harbor in this coastal village. **Pros:** superb location; clean and comfortable; good service. **Cons:** some rooms are small; food is inconsistent. Ⓢ *Rooms from: £147* ⊠ *The Quay* ☎ 01237/431237 ⊕ www.clovelly. co.uk ⇨ 11 rooms ❧ Breakfast.*

CORNWALL

Cornwall stretches west into the sea, with plenty of magnificent coast-line to explore, along with tranquil towns and some bustling resorts. One way to discover it all is to travel southwest from Boscastle and the cliff-top ruins of Tintagel Castle, the legendary birthplace of Arthur, along the north Cornish coast to Land's End. This predominantly cliff-lined coast, interspersed with broad expanses of sand, has many tempting places to stop, including Padstow (for a seafood feast), Newquay (a surfing and tourist center), or St. Ives (a delightful artists' colony).

From Land's End, the westernmost tip of Britain, known for its savage land- and seascapes and panoramic views, return to the popular seaside resort of Penzance, the harbor town of Falmouth, and the river port of Fowey. The Channel coast is less rugged than the northern coast, with more sheltered beaches. Leave time to visit the excellent Eden Project, with its surrealistic-looking conservatories in an abandoned clay pit, and to explore the boggy, heath-covered expanse of Bodmin Moor.

BOSCASTLE

15 miles north of Bodmin, 30 miles south of Clovelly.

In tranquil Boscastle, some of the stone-and-slate cottages at the foot of the steep valley date from the 1300s. A good place to relax and walk, the town is centered on a little harbor and set snug within towering cliffs. Nearby, 2 miles up the Valency valley, is St. Juliot's, the "Endel-stow" referred to in Thomas Hardy's *A Pair of Blue Eyes*—the young author was involved with the restoration of this church while he was working as an architect.

GETTING HERE AND AROUND

Drivers can reach Boscastle along A39 and B3263. There are regular Western Greyhound buses from Bodmin Parkway, the nearest rail connection. The village is easily explored on foot.

ESSENTIALS

Visitor Information Boscastle Visitor Centre ⊠ *The Harbour* ☎ *01840/250010* ⊕ *www.visitboscastleandtintagel.com.*

WHERE TO STAY

For expanded hotel reviews, visit Fodors.com.

$

B&B/INN

Fodor'sChoice

★

The Old Rectory. While restoring St. Juliot's Church, Thomas Hardy stayed in the building that now holds this delightful B&B. **Pros:** secluded setting; romantic ambience; helpful hosts. **Cons:** a little hard to find; minimum stay might be required. $ *Rooms from: £90* ⊠ *Off B3263, St. Juliot* ☎ *01840/250225* ⊕ *www.stjuliot.com* 4 *rooms* ⊗ *Closed mid-Nov.–mid-Feb.* ⏽ *Breakfast.*

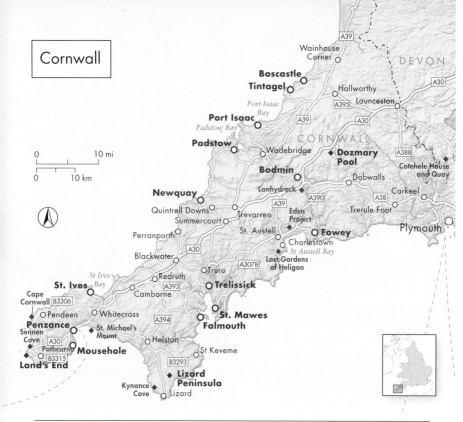

TINTAGEL

3 miles southwest of Boscastle.

The romance of Arthurian legend thrives around Tintagel's ruined castle on the coast. Ever since the somewhat unreliable 12th-century chronicler Geoffrey of Monmouth identified Tintagel as the home of Arthur, son of Uther Pendragon and Ygrayne, devotees of the legend cycle have revered the site. In the 19th century Alfred, Lord Tennyson described Tintagel's Arthurian connection in *The Idylls of the King*. Today the village has its share of tourist junk—including Excaliburgers. Never mind: the headland around Tintagel is splendidly scenic.

GETTING HERE AND AROUND

To drive to Tintagel, take the A39 to the B3263. Numerous parking lots are found in the village center. There's a bus stop near the tourist office for Western Greyhound buses from Bodmin Parkway, the nearest train station. Between April and October a shuttle service brings mobility-impaired passengers to the castle.

ESSENTIALS

Visitor Information **Tintagel Visitor Centre** ⊠ *Bossiney Rd.* ☎ *01840/779084.*

EXPLORING

Old Post Office. This gorgeous 14th-century stone manor house with yard-thick walls, smoke-blackened beams, and an undulating slate-tile roof has been furnished with items from the 17th and 18th centuries. The walls are hung with "samplers"—embroidered poems and prayers usually produced by young girls. One room originally served as a post office and has been restored to its Victorian appearance. ⊠ *Fore St.* ☎ *01840/770024* ⊕ *www.nationaltrust.org.uk* ☞ *£3.60* ☉ *Mid-Feb.–late Mar., and Oct.–early Nov., daily 11–4; late Mar.–Sept., daily 10:30–5:30.*

> **DONKEYS AT WORK**
>
> Donkey stables, donkey rides for kids, and abundant donkey souvenirs in Clovelly recall the days when these animals played an essential role in town life, carrying food, packages, and more up and down the village streets. Even in the 1990s, donkeys helped carry bags from the hotels. Today sleds do the work, but the animals' labor is remembered.

Fodor'sChoice **Tintagel Castle.** Although all that remains of the ruined cliff-top Tintagel ★ Castle, legendary birthplace of King Arthur, is the outline of its walls, moats, and towers, it requires only a bit of imagination to conjure up a picture of Sir Lancelot and Sir Galahad riding out in search of the Holy Grail over the narrow causeway above the seething breakers. Archaeological evidence, however, suggests that the castle dates from much later—about 1150, when it was the stronghold of the earls of Cornwall. Long before that, Romans may have occupied the site. The earliest identified remains here are of Celtic (AD 5th century) origin, and these may have some connection with the legendary Arthur. Legends aside, nothing can detract from the castle ruins, dramatically set off by the wild, windswept Cornish coast, on an island joined to the mainland by a narrow isthmus. Paths lead down to the pebble beach and a cavern known as **Merlin's Cave.** Exploring Tintagel Castle involves some arduous climbing on steep steps, but even on a summer's day, when people swarm over the battlements and a westerly Atlantic wind sweeps through Tintagel, you can feel the proximity of the distant past. ⊠ *Castle Rd., ½ mile west of the village* ☎ *01840/770328* ⊕ *www.english-heritage.org.uk* ☞ *£5.90* ☉ *Apr.–Sept., daily 10–6; Oct.–early Nov., daily 10–5; early Nov.– Mar., weekends 10–4.*

PORT ISAAC

6 miles southwest of Tintagel.

A mixture of granite, slate, and whitewashed cottages tumbles precipitously down the cliff to the tiny harbor at Port Isaac, still dedicated to the crab-and-lobster trade. Low tide reveals a pebbly beach and rock pools. Relatively unscathed by tourists, it makes for a peaceful and secluded stay. For an extra slice of authentic Cornwall life, you can hear the local choir sing shanties at the harborside on Friday nights in summer.

The coast near Tintagel Castle has lovely views.

GETTING HERE AND AROUND

If you're driving, Port Isaac is reached via the A39, then the B3314. Park at the lot at the top of the village rather than attempting to drive into the center. By bus, take Western Greyhound service 555 from the train station at Bodmin Parkway, changing to 584 at Wadebridge.

WHERE TO STAY

For expanded hotel reviews, visit Fodors.com.

$$ | 🛏 **Slipway Hotel.** This 16th-century inn on the harbor front has low ceilings, exposed timbers, and steep staircases that lead to rooms with simple but stylish modern furnishings. **Pros:** friendly staff; great location. **Cons:** some rooms are cramped and viewless; remote parking. ⑂ *Rooms from: £110* ✉ *Harbourfront* ☎ *01208/880264* ⊕ *www.portisaachotel. com* ⇄ *8 rooms, 2 suites* ⦿ *Breakfast.*

PADSTOW

10 miles southwest of Port Isaac.

A small fishing port at the mouth of the River Camel, Padstow attracts attention and visitors as a center of culinary excellence, largely because of the presence here since 1975 of pioneering seafood chef Rick Stein. Stein's empire includes two restaurants, a café, a fish-and-chips joint, a delicatessen, a patisserie, and a cooking school where classes fill up months in advance.

Even if seafood isn't your favorite fare, Padstow is worth visiting. The cries of seagulls fill its lively harbor, a string of fine beaches lies within a short ride—including some choice strands highly prized by surfers—and

All About King Arthur

Legends about King Arthur have resonated through the centuries, enthusiastically taken up by writers and poets, from 7th-century Welsh and Breton troubadours to Tennyson and Mark Twain in the 19th century and T. H. White in the 20th century.

WHO WAS ARTHUR?

The historical Arthur was probably a Christian Celtic chieftain battling against the heathen Saxons in the 6th century, although most of the tales surrounding him have a much later setting, thanks to the vivid but somewhat fanciful chronicles of his exploits by medieval scholars.

The virtuous warrior-hero of popular myth has always been treated with generous helpings of nostalgia for a golden age. For Sir Thomas Malory (circa 1408–71), author of *Le Morte d'Arthur,* the finest medieval prose collection of Arthurian romance, Arthur represented a lost era of chivalry and noble romance before the loosening of the traditional bonds of feudal society and the gradual collapse of the medieval social order.

FINDING KING ARTHUR

Places associated with Arthur and his consort, Guinevere, the wizard Merlin, the knights of the Round Table, and the related legends of Tristan and Isolde (or Iseult) can be found all over Europe, but the West Country claims the closest association. Arthur was said to have had his court of Camelot at Cadbury Castle (17 miles south of Wells) and to have been buried at Glastonbury.

Cornwall holds the greatest concentration of Arthurian links, notably his supposed birthplace, Tintagel, and the site of his last battle, on Bodmin Moor. However tenuous the links—and, barring the odd, somewhat ambiguous inscription, there's nothing in the way of hard evidence of Arthur's existence—the Cornish have taken the Once and Future King to their hearts, and his spirit is said to reside in the now-rare bird, the Cornish chough.

two scenic walking routes await: the Saints Way across the peninsula to Fowey, and the Camel Trail, a footpath and cycling path that follows the river as far as Bodmin Moor. If you can avoid peak visiting times—summer weekends—so much the better.

GETTING HERE AND AROUND

Regular buses connect Padstow with Bodmin, the main transportation hub hereabouts, and on the main Plymouth–Penzance train line. To get here from Port Isaac, change buses at Wadebridge. Alternatively, take the bus to Rock and the passenger ferry across the river. There are numerous direct buses on the Newquay–Padstow route. Drivers should take A39/A389 and park in the waterside parking lot before reaching the harbor.

ESSENTIALS

Visitor Information Padstow Tourist Information Centre ⊠ *North Quay* ☎ *01841/533449* ⊕ *www.padstowlive.com.*

Eating seafood is a must in Cornwall: celebrity chef Rick Stein's outposts in Padstow are excellent options.

WHERE TO EAT AND STAY

For expanded hotel reviews, visit Fodors.com.

$$$$ MODERN BRITISH 🍴 **Paul Ainsworth at Number 6.** There is more to Padstow's culinary scene than Rick Stein, as this intimate bistro persuasively demonstrates. Diners seated in a series of small, stylish rooms can feast on ingeniously concocted dishes that make the most of local and seasonal produce. Try the blow-torched mackerel with celeriac and Parma ham for starters, and baked hake with saffron *milanese* or Cornish saddleback pork for the main course, leaving space for some astounding desserts. Set-price lunches are a particularly good value. The atmosphere is warm and lively, with swift, amiable service. [$] *Average main: £26* ✉ *6 Middle St., Padstow* ☎ *01841/532093* 🌐 *www.number6inpadstow.co.uk* 🕒 *Closed Sun. and Mon.*

$$$$ SEAFOOD Fodor's Choice ★ 🍴 **The Seafood Restaurant.** Just across from where the lobster boats and trawlers unload their catches, Rick Stein's flagship restaurant has built its reputation on the freshest fish and the highest culinary artistry. The exclusively fish and shellfish menu includes everything from grilled Padstow lobster with herbs to monkfish in an Indonesian-style curry sauce. Choose between sitting formally at a table or grabbing a stool at the Seafood Bar in the center of the modern, airy restaurant (no reservations for bar). Don't want to move after your meal? Book one of the sunny, individually designed guest rooms overlooking the harbor. [$] *Average main: £30* ✉ *Riverside* ☎ *01841/532700* 🌐 *www.rickstein.com* ✍ *Reservations essential.*

$$$ FRENCH 🍴 **St. Petroc's Bistro.** Part of chef Rick Stein's empire, this bistro with contemporary art adorning its walls has a secluded feel. In fine weather you can dine in the sunny walled garden. The French-inspired menu

features such dishes as rib-eye steak with béarnaise sauce and *pommes frites* (french fries). If you want to stay, the spacious bedrooms are individually decorated with stylish modern pieces. [$] *Average main: £20* ⊠ *4 New St.* ☎ *01841/532700* ⊕ *www.rickstein.com.*

$$$$
B&B/INN
St. Edmund's House. The most luxurious Rick Stein venture has a sophisticated minimalist style. **Pros:** stylish bedrooms; select ambience; great on-site dining. **Cons:** no public rooms; short walk to breakfast; a bit of noise in ground-floor rooms. [$] *Rooms from: £285* ⊠ *St. Edmund's La.* ☎ *01841/532700* ⊕ *www.rickstein.com* ⇆ *6 rooms* ⫿ *Breakfast.*

SPORTS AND THE OUTDOORS

BIKING

Trail Bike Hire. Bikes of all shapes and sizes can be rented at Trail Bike Hire, at the start of the Camel Trail. ⊠ *South Quay* ☎ *01841/532594* ⊕ *www.trailbikehire.co.uk.*

SURFING

Harlyn Surf School. This school can arrange two-hour to four-day surfing courses at its base in Harlyn Bay, 3 miles west of Padstow. ⊠ *Harlyn Bay Beach* ☎ *01841/533076* ⊕ *www.harlynsurfschool.co.uk.*

WALKING

Saints Way. This 30-mile inland path takes you between Padstow and the Camel Estuary on Cornwall's north coast to Fowey on the south coast. It follows a Bronze Age trading route, later used by Celtic pilgrims to cross the peninsula. Several relics of such times can be seen along the way.

NEWQUAY

14 miles southwest of Padstow, 30 miles southwest of Tintagel.

The biggest, most developed resort on the north Cornwall coast is a fairly large town established in 1439. It was once the center of the trade in pilchards (a small herringlike fish), and on the headland you can still see a white hut where a lookout known as a "huer" watched for pilchard schools and directed the boats to the fishing grounds. Newquay has become Britain's surfing capital, and in summer young California-dreamin' devotees can pack the wide, cliff-backed beaches.

GETTING HERE AND AROUND

A branch line links Newquay with the main Plymouth–Penzance train line at Par, and there are regular buses from Padstow, Bodmin, and St. Austell. Train and bus stations are both in the center of town. Newquay has good road connections with the rest of the peninsula via the A30 and A39. The best beaches are a long walk or a short bus ride from the center.

ESSENTIALS

Visitor Information **Newquay Tourist Information Centre** ✉ *Marcus Hill* ☎ *01637/854020* 🌐 *www.visitnewquay.org.*

WHERE TO EAT

$$$$ ITALIAN Fodor's Choice ★ 🍴 **Fifteen Cornwall.** Bright and modern, this Italian restaurant has won plaudits both for its fabulous food and for its fine location overlooking magnificent Watergate Bay, a broad beach much beloved of water-sports enthusiasts. It's run by one of Britain's culinary heroes, Cockney chef Jamie Oliver, who trains local young people for careers in catering. To provide the staff with the widest possible repertoire, the £60 sampling menu changes frequently and lists five courses that might include a starter of gnocchi with oxtail and sage, followed by duck with polenta and *salsa verde* for a main course and *affogato al caffè* (ice cream soaked in black coffee) to finish. A fixed-price lunch is a cheaper option at £28. Watergate Bay lies 3 miles east of Newquay. [$] *Average main: £60* ✉ *Watergate Rd., Watergate Bay* ☎ *01637/861000* 🌐 *www.fifteencornwall.co.uk.*

SPORTS AND THE OUTDOORS

Surfing is Newquay's raison d'être for many of the enthusiasts who flock here throughout the year. Great Western and Tolcarne beaches are most suitable for beginners, while Fistral Beach is better for those with more experience. There are dozens of surf schools around town, many offering accommodation packages, and rental outlets are also ubiquitous.

Extreme Academy. One of the West Country's water-sports specialists, Extreme Academy offers courses in wave-skiing, kite-surfing, kite-buggying, paddle-surfing, and just plain old surfing, as well as equipment for hire. ✉ *The Hotel, Trevarrian Hill, Watergate Bay* ☎ *01637/860543* 🌐 *www.watergatebay.co.uk.*

ST. IVES

25 miles southwest of Newquay, 10 miles north of Penzance.

Fodor's Choice ★ James McNeill Whistler came here to paint his landscapes, Barbara Hepworth to fashion her modernist sculptures, and Virginia Woolf to write her novels. Today sand, sun, and superb art continue to attract thousands of vacationers to the fishing village of St. Ives, named after Saint Ia, a 5th-century female Irish missionary said to have arrived on a floating leaf. Many come to St. Ives for the sheltered beaches; the best are Porthmeor, on the northern side of town, and, facing east, Porthminster—the choice for those seeking more space to spread out.

GETTING HERE AND AROUND

St. Ives has good bus and train connections with Bristol, Exeter, and Penzance. Train journeys usually involve a change at St. Erth (the brief St. Erth–St. Ives stretch is one of the West Country's most scenic train routes). The adjacent bus and train stations are within a few minutes' walk of the center. Drivers should avoid the center—parking lots are well marked in the higher parts of town.

ESSENTIALS

Visitor Information **St. Ives Tourist Information Centre** ✉ *The Guildhall, Street-an-Pol* ☎ *0905/252–2250* 🌐 *www.stivestic.co.uk.*

EXPLORING

Barbara Hepworth Museum and Sculpture Garden. The studio and garden of Dame Barbara Hepworth (1903–75), who pioneered abstract sculpture in England, are now a museum and sculpture garden, managed by the Tate St. Ives. The artist lived here for 26 years. ⊠ *Trewyn Studio, Barnoon Hill* ☎ *01736/796226* ⊕ *www.tate.org.uk* ⛌ *£6, £10 combined ticket with Tate St. Ives* ☉ *Mar.–Oct., daily 10–5:20; Nov.–Feb., Tues.–Sun. 10–4:20.*

FAMILY **Geevor Tin Mine.** The winding B3306 coastal road southwest from St. Ives passes through some of Cornwall's starkest yet most beautiful countryside. Barren hills crisscrossed by low stone walls drop abruptly to granite cliffs and wide bays. Evidence of the ancient tin-mining industry is everywhere. Now a fascinating mining heritage center, the early-20th-century Geevor Tin Mine employed 400 men, but in 1985 the collapse of the world tin market wiped Cornwall from the mining map. Wear sturdy footwear for the surface and underground tours. A museum, shop, and café are on the site. ⊠ *B3306, Pendeen* ☎ *01736/788662* ⊕ *www.geevor.com* ⛌ *£10.50* ☉ *Apr.–Oct., Sun.–Fri. 9–5; Nov.–Mar., Sun.–Fri. 9–4; last admission 1 hr before closing.*

St. Ives Society of Artists Gallery. Local artists display selections of their current work for sale at this gallery in the former Mariners' Church. The Crypt Gallery in the basement is used for private exhibitions. ⊠ *Norway Sq.* ☎ *01736/795582* ⊕ *www.stisa.co.uk* ☉ *Mar.–Easter and mid-Oct.–early Jan., Mon.–Sat. 10:30–5:30; Easter–mid-Oct., Mon.–Sat. 10:30–5:30, Sun. 2:30–5:30.*

Tate St. Ives. The spectacular sister of the renowned London museum displays the work of artists who lived and worked in St. Ives, mostly from 1925 to 1975. There's also a selection of pieces from the museum's rich collection. It occupies a modernist building—a fantasia of seaside art deco–period architecture with a panoramic view of rippling ocean. The rooftop café is excellent for the food and views. ⊠ *Porthmeor Beach* ☎ *01736/796226* ⊕ *www.tate.org.uk* ⛌ *£7, £10 combined ticket with Barbara Hepworth Museum and Sculpture Garden* ☉ *Mar.–Oct., daily 10–5:20; Nov.–Feb., Tues.–Sun. 10–4:20.*

QUICK BITES

Sloop Inn. One of Cornwall's oldest pubs, the 1312 Sloop Inn serves simple lunches as well as evening meals in wood-beam rooms that display the work of local artists. If the weather's good, you can eat at the tables outside and watch the harbor. ⊠ *The Wharf* ☎ *01736/796584* ⊕ *www. sloop-inn.co.uk.*

WHERE TO EAT

$$$

MODERN BRITISH **✕ The Garrack.** This family-run restaurant is known for the panoramic sea views from its hilltop location and for relaxed and undemanding fine dining. The pretheater (£13.50 and £17.50), set-price (£23 and £26.50), and à la carte menus specialize in local fish and seafood, including seared scallops, as well as Cornish beef. Breads are made on the premises, and the wine list features some Cornish vineyards. Some rooms at the attached hotel are furnished in traditional style; others are more modern. $ *Average main: £21* ⊠ *Burthallan La.* ☎ *01736/796199* ⊕ *www.garrack.com* ☉ *No lunch Mon.–Sat.*

$$ **✕ Gurnard's Head.** This pub with bright, homey furnishings and a
MODERN BRITISH relaxed ambience looks past green fields to the ocean beyond. The frequently changing menu features fresh, inventively prepared meat and seafood dishes; look for braised beef with orange and parsnip puree, or fish stew with saffron potatoes, spinach, and sprouting broccoli. Seven smallish rooms provide guest accommodations. The inn sits near the curvy coast road 6 miles west of St. Ives. $ *Average main: £16* ✉ *B3306, near Zennor, Treen* ☎ *01736/796928* ⊕ *www.gurnardshead. co.uk* ⚴ *Reservations essential.*

$$ **✕ Porthminster Café.** Unbeatable for its location alone—on the broad,
SEAFOOD golden sands of Porthminster Beach—this sleek, modern eatery prepares imaginative lunches, teas, and evening meals that you can savor while you take in the marvelous vista across the bay. The accent is on Mediterranean and Asian flavors, and typical choices include seafood linguine, monkfish curry, and roast venison haunch. The sister Porthgwidden Beach Café, in the Downalong neighborhood, has a smaller and cheaper menu that's equally strong on fish. $ *Average main: £19* ✉ *Porthminster Beach* ☎ *01736/795352* ⊕ *www.porthminstercafe.co.uk* ☉ *Closed Mon. Nov.–Easter. No dinner Sun.–Wed. Nov.–Easter.*

WHERE TO STAY

For expanded hotel reviews, visit Fodors.com.

$ ⛱ **Cornerways.** Everything in St. Ives seems squeezed into the tiniest
B&B/INN of spaces, and this cottage B&B in the quiet Downalong quarter is no exception. **Pros:** friendly owners and staff; stylish decor; excellent cooked breakfast. **Cons:** rooms are mostly small; narrow stairways to climb; very limited parking. $ *Rooms from: £95* ✉ *1 Bethesda Pl.* ☎ *01736/796706* ⊕ *www.cornerwaysstives.com* ⛵ *6 rooms* ═ *No credit cards* ⱺ⫯ *Breakfast.*

$$ ⛱ **Primrose Valley Hotel.** Blending the elegance of an Edwardian villa
HOTEL with clean-lined modern style, this family-friendly hotel has the best of both worlds. **Pros:** close to beach and train and bus stations; friendly atmosphere; attention to detail. **Cons:** some rooms are small and lack views; tricky access to car park; steps to negotiate. $ *Rooms from: £125* ✉ *Porthminster Beach* ☎ *01736/794939* ⊕ *www.primroseonline.co.uk* ⛵ *8 rooms, 1 suite* ⱺ⫯ *Breakfast.*

LAND'S END

17 miles southwest of St. Ives, 9 miles southwest of Penzance.

The coastal road, B3306, ends at the western tip of Britain at what is, quite literally, Land's End.

GETTING HERE AND AROUND

Frequent buses serve Land's End from St. Ives (taking around one hour, 40 minutes) and Penzance (around 55 minutes). In summer an open-top double-decker tracks the coast between St. Ives and Penzance, taking in Land's End en route.

EXPLORING

Land's End. The sea crashes against the rocks at Land's End and lashes ships battling their way around the point. ■TIP➔ Approach from one of the coastal footpaths for the best panoramic view. Over the years, sightseers have caused some erosion of the paths, but new ones are constantly being built, and Cornish "hedges" (granite walls covered with turf) have been planted to prevent erosion. The scenic grandeur of Land's End remains undiminished. The Land's End Hotel here is undistinguished, though the restaurant has good views.

Porthcurno Beach. Porthcurno Beach, 3 miles east of Land's End, has a stunning strip of cliff-backed sand that's good for both walkers (the coastal path is nearby) and anyone ready to relax on a beach. ✉ *Off B3315, Porthcurno.*

Sennen Cove. Less than 2 miles north of Land's End, lovely Sennen Cove can be reached by car or by a walk on the South West Coast Path. You can enjoy the view or try the surfing. ✉ *Off A30, Sennen.*

MOUSEHOLE

7 miles east of Land's End, 3 miles south of Penzance.

Fodor's Choice
★

Between Land's End and Penzance, Mousehole (pronounced *mow*-zel, the first syllable rhyming with "cow") merits a stop—and plenty of people do stop—to see this archetypal Cornish fishing village of tiny stone cottages. It was the home of Dolly Pentreath, supposedly the last person to speak solely in Cornish, who died in 1777.

GETTING HERE AND AROUND

Frequent buses take 20 minutes to travel from Penzance to Mousehole. From Land's End, change buses at Newlyn. Drivers should take the B3315 coastal route and park in one of the lots before entering the village.

WHERE TO EAT AND STAY

For expanded hotel reviews, visit Fodors.com.

$$ ✕ **2 Fore Street.** Within view of Mousehole's tiny harbor, you can dine
MODERN BRITISH on the freshest seafood in this popular bistro. The seasonal, Mediterranean-inspired menu takes in everything from Newlyn crab with spiced brown shrimp butter to roasted monkfish with curried mussels, fennel, and bok choi. Meat eaters are also well catered to with dishes like pan-roasted chicken with lentils, spinach, and smoked bacon. The bright, white-walled dining room has a maritime flavor, and there are tables in the sheltered back garden. $ *Average main: £15* ✉ *2 Fore St.* ☎ *01736/731164* ⊕ *www.2forestreet.co.uk* ☉ *Closed Jan.*

$$ ⌂ **Old Coastguard.** The best views of Mousehole can be enjoyed from
HOTEL the bedrooms of this lodging; some rooms have balconies and four-poster beds, and all come with proper coffee with fresh milk and Cornish tea. **Pros:** panoramic views; walking paths; cheerful staff. **Cons:**

unprepossessing exterior; could do with a scrub-up in places. [$] *Rooms from: £110* ✉ *The Parade* ☎ *01736/731222* 🌐 *www.oldcoastguardhotel.co.uk* 🛏 *13 rooms, 1 suite* 🍴 *Breakfast.*

EN ROUTE

About 2 miles north of Mousehole on B3315, **Newlyn** has long been Cornwall's most important fishing port. The annual Fish Festival takes over the town at the end of August. Newlyn became the magnet for artists at the end of the 19th century, and a few of the fishermen's cottages that first attracted them remain. Today the village has a good gallery of contemporary art.

PENZANCE

3 miles north of Mousehole, 1½ miles north of Newlyn, 10 miles south of St. Ives.

Superb views over Mount's Bay are one lure of this popular, unpretentious seaside resort. Even though it does get very crowded in summer, Penzance makes a good base for exploring the area. The town's isolated position has always made it vulnerable to attack from the sea. During the 16th century, Spanish raiders destroyed most of the original town, and the majority of old buildings date from as late as the 18th century. The main street is Market Jew Street, a folk mistranslation of the Cornish expression Marghas Yow, which means "Thursday Market." Where Market Jew Street meets Causeway Head is Market House, an impressive, domed granite building constructed in 1837, with a statue of locally born chemist Humphry Davy in front.

In contrast to artsy St. Ives, Penzance is a no-nonsense working town. Though lacking the traffic-free lanes and quaint cottages of St. Ives, Penzance preserves pockets of handsome Georgian architecture.

GETTING HERE AND AROUND

The main train line from Plymouth terminates at Penzance, which is also served by National Express buses. Bus and train stations are next to each other at the east end of town. A car is an encumbrance here, so use one of the parking lots near the tourist office and the bus and train stations.

ESSENTIALS

Visitor Information **Penzance Tourist Information Centre** ✉ *Station Approach* ☎ *01736/335530.*

EXPLORING

Chapel Street. One of the prettiest thoroughfares in Penzance, Chapel Street winds down from Market House to the harbor. Its predominantly Georgian and Regency houses suddenly give way to the extraordinary **Egyptian House,** whose facade recalls the Middle East. Built around 1830 as a geological museum, today it houses vacation apartments. Across Chapel Street is the 17th-century **Union Hotel,** where in 1805 the death of Lord Nelson and the victory of Trafalgar were first announced. Near the Union Hotel on Chapel Street is the **Turk's Head,** an inn said to date from the 13th century.

The stunning ocean setting of the open-air Minack Theatre near Penzance may distract you from the on-stage drama.

Penlee House Gallery and Museum. A small collection in this gracious Victorian house in Penlee Park focuses on paintings by members of the so-called Newlyn School from about 1880 to 1930. These works evoke the life of the inhabitants of Newlyn, mostly fisherfolk. The museum also covers 5,000 years of West Cornwall history through archaeology, decorative arts, costume, and photography exhibits. ⊠ *Morrab Rd.* ☎ *01736/363625* ⊕ *www.penleehouse.org.uk* ✉ *£4.50, Sat. free* ☉ *Easter–Sept., Mon.–Sat. 10–5; Oct.–Easter, Mon.–Sat. 10:30–4:30; last admission 30 mins before closing.*

Fodor's Choice ★ **St. Michael's Mount.** Rising out of Mount's Bay just off the coast, this spectacular granite-and-slate island is one of Cornwall's greatest natural attractions. The 14th-century castle perched at the highest point—200 feet above the sea—was built on the site of a Benedictine chapel founded by Edward the Confessor. In its time, the island has served as a church (Brittany's island abbey of Mont St. Michel was an inspiration), a fortress, and a private residence. The castle rooms you can tour include the Chevy Chase Room—a name probably associated with the Cheviot Hills or the French word *chevaux* (horses), after the hunting frieze that decorates the walls of this former monks' refectory. Family portraits include works by Reynolds and Gainsborough. Don't miss the wonderful views from the castle battlements. Around the base of the rock are buildings from medieval to Victorian, but they appear harmonious. Fascinating gardens surround the Mount, and many kinds of plants flourish in its microclimate.

To get to the island, walk the cobbled causeway from the village of Marazion or, when the tide is in during summer, take the £2 ferry. There are pubs and restaurants in the village, but the island also has a café and restaurant. **TIP→ Wear stout shoes for your visit, which requires a steep climb.** Visits may be canceled in severe weather. ✉ *A394, 3 miles east of Penzance, Marazion* ☎ *01736/710507* 🌐 *www.stmichaelsmount.co.uk* 🎟 *£9.60, castle only £7.60, garden only £4* 🕒 *Castle mid-Mar.–June, Sept., and Oct., Sun.–Fri. 10:30–5; July and Aug., Sun.–Fri. 10:30–5:30; Nov.–mid-Mar., tours Tues. and Fri. 11 and 2. Garden mid-Apr.–June, weekdays 10:30–5; July and Aug., Thurs. and Fri. 10:30–5:30; Sept., Thurs., and Fri. 10:30–5; last admission 45 mins before closing.*

WHERE TO EAT

$ BRITISH 🍴 **Admiral Benbow.** One of the town's most famous inns, the 17th-century Admiral Benbow was once a smugglers' pub—look for the figure of a smuggler on the roof. Seafaring memorabilia, a brass cannon, model ships, and figureheads fill the place. In the family-friendly dining room, decorated to resemble a ship's galley, you can enjoy seafood or a steak-and-ale pie. [$] *Average main: £12* ✉ *46 Chapel St.* ☎ *01736/363448.*

$$$ SEAFOOD 🍴 **Harris's.** Seafood is the main event in the two small, boldly colored rooms of this restaurant off Market Jew Street. The menu showcases whatever the boats bring: crab Florentine, grilled on a bed of spinach with a cheese sauce, is usually available. Meat dishes might include noisettes of Cornish lamb with fennel puree and rosemary sauce in spring and summer, or breast of pheasant in winter. An inexpensive brasserie menu is also available for lunch or dinner. The semiformal style is intimate, elegant, and traditional. [$] *Average main: £20* ✉ *46 New St.* ☎ *01736/364408* 🌐 *www.harrissrestaurant.co.uk* 🕒 *Closed Sun. Closed Mon. Nov.–June and 4 wks Nov.–Mar.*

WHERE TO STAY

For expanded hotel reviews, visit Fodors.com.

$$ HOTEL Fodor's Choice ★ 🏨 **Abbey Hotel.** Co-owned by former 1960s model-icon Jean Shrimpton, this Wedgwood-blue-color hotel off Chapel Street is marvelously homey. **Pros:** full of character; inspiring views; solicitous staff. **Cons:** some rooms slightly cramped; limited parking. [$] *Rooms from: £130* ✉ *Abbey St.* ☎ *01736/366906* 🌐 *www.theabbeyonline.co.uk* 🛏 *6 rooms, 2 apartments* 🕒 *Closed late Dec.–mid-Feb.* 🍽 *Breakfast.*

$ B&B/INN 🏨 **Camilla House.** This flower-bedecked Georgian house close to the harbor has spacious, smartly decorated guest rooms, with sea views from those at the front. **Pros:** friendly and helpful management; quiet location near seafront. **Cons:** some rooms are small; a bit far from bus and train stations. [$] *Rooms from: £77* ✉ *12 Regent Terr.* ☎ *01736/363771* 🌐 *www.camillahouse.co.uk* 🛏 *8 rooms* 🍽 *Breakfast.*

$ HOTEL 🏨 **Union Hotel.** Strong on historical and nautical details, this central lodging housed the town's assembly rooms, where news of Admiral Nelson's victory at Trafalgar and of the death of Nelson himself were first announced from the minstrels' gallery in 1805. **Pros:** historic character; central location; good value. **Cons:** dowdy in places; sparse staff; no elevator. [$] *Rooms from: £73* ✉ *Chapel St.* ☎ *01736/362319* 🌐 *www.unionhotel.co.uk* 🛏 *28 rooms* 🍽 *Breakfast.*

NIGHTLIFE AND THE ARTS

Fodor's Choice
★

Minack Theatre. The open-air Minack Theatre perches high above a beach 3 miles southeast of Land's End and about 6 miles southwest of Penzance. The slope of the cliff forms a natural amphitheater, with bench seats on the terraces and the sea as a magnificent backdrop. Different companies present everything from classic dramas to modern comedies, as well as operas and concerts, on afternoons and evenings between Easter and late September. An exhibition center tells the story of the theater's creation. ⊠ *Off B3315, Porthcurno* ☎ *01736/810181* ⊕ *www.minack.com* 🖾 *Exhibition center £4, performances £8–£9.50* ☉ *Apr.–Sept., daily 9:30–5:30; Oct.–Mar., daily 10–4.*

SPORTS AND THE OUTDOORS

Many ships have foundered on Cornwall's rocky coastline, resulting in an estimated 3,600 shipwrecks. The area around Land's End has some of the best diving in Europe, in part because the convergence of the Atlantic and the Gulf Stream here results in impressive visibility and unusual subtropical marine life.

Cornwall Divers. This company offers year-round dive excursions in the waters around Falmouth. ⊠ *Marine Crescent, Bar Rd., Falmouth* ☎ *01326/311265* ⊕ *www.cornwalldivers.co.uk.*

LIZARD PENINSULA

23 miles southwest of Penzance.

Fodor's Choice
★

The southernmost point on mainland Britain, this peninsula is a government-designated Area of Outstanding Natural Beauty, named so for the rocky, dramatic coast rather than the flat and boring interior. The huge, eerily rotating dish antennae of the Goonhilly Satellite Earth Station are visible from the road as it crosses Goonhilly Downs, the backbone of the peninsula. There's no coast road, unlike Land's End, but the coastal path offers marvelous opportunities to explore on foot—and is often the only way to reach the best beaches. With no large town (Helston at the northern end is the biggest, and isn't a tourist center), it's far less busy than the Land's End peninsula.

GETTING HERE AND AROUND

If you're driving, take A394 to reach Helston, gateway town to the Lizard Peninsula. From Helston, A3083 heads straight down to Lizard Point. Helston is the main public transport hub, but bus service to the villages is infrequent.

EXPLORING

Kynance Cove. A path close to the tip of the peninsula plunges down 200-foot cliffs to this tiny cove dotted with a handful of pint-size islands. The sands here are reachable only during the 2½ hours before and after low tide. The peninsula's cliffs are made of greenish serpentine rock, interspersed with granite; souvenirs of the area are carved out of the stone.

5

FALMOUTH

8 miles northeast of Lizard Peninsula.

The bustle of this resort town's fishing harbor, yachting center, and commercial port only adds to its charm. In the 18th century Falmouth was the main mail-boat port for North America, and in Flushing, a village across the inlet, you can see the slate-covered houses built by prosperous mail-boat captains. A ferry service now links the two towns. On Custom House Quay, off Arwenack Street, is the King's Pipe, an oven in which seized contraband was burned.

GETTING HERE AND AROUND

Falmouth can be reached from Truro on a branch rail line or on frequent buses, and is also served by local and National Express buses from other towns. Running parallel to the seafront, the long, partly pedestrianized main drag links the town's main sights. Visitors to Pendennis Castle traveling by train should use Falmouth Docks Station, from which it's a short walk. Alternatively, drive or take a local bus to the castle to save legwork.

ESSENTIALS

Visitor Information **Falmouth Visitor Information Centre** ⊠ *Prince of Wales Pier, 11 Market Strand* ☎ *0905/325–4534* ⊕ *www.falmouth.co.uk.*

EXPLORING

FAMILY   **National Maritime Museum Cornwall.** The granite-and-oak-clad structure by the harbor is an excellent place to come to grips with Cornish maritime heritage, weather lore, and navigational science. You can view the collection of 140 or so boats, examine the tools associated with Cornish boatbuilders, and gaze down from the lighthouselike lookout, which is equipped with maps, telescopes, and binoculars. In the glass-fronted Tidal Zone below sea level, you come face-to-face with the sea itself. ⊠ *Discovery Quay* ☎ *01326/313388* ⊕ *www.nmmc.co.uk* ☜ *£11* ⊙ *Daily 10–5.*

FAMILY   **Pendennis Castle.** At the end of its own peninsula stands this formi-
Fodor's Choice   dable castle, built by Henry VIII in the 1540s and improved by his
★   daughter Elizabeth I. You can explore the defenses developed over the centuries. In the Royal Artillery Barracks, the Pendennis Unlocked exhibit explores the castle's history and its connection to Cornwall and England. The castle has sweeping views over the English Channel and across to St. Mawes Castle, designed as a companion fortress to guard the roads. There are also occasional performances, jousting, and shows for kids. ⊠ *Pendennis Head* ☎ *01326/316594* ⊕ *www.english-heritage.org.uk* ☜ *£6.70* ⊙ *Apr.–June, Sept. and Oct., Sun.–Fri. 10–5, Sat. 10–4; July and Aug., Sun.–Fri. 10–6, Sat. 10–4; Nov.–Mar., weekends 10–4.*

WHERE TO EAT AND STAY

For expanded hotel reviews, visit Fodors.com.

$$ ✕ **Gylly Beach Café.** For views and location, this beachside eatery with a
MODERN BRITISH   crisp, modern interior and deck seating can't be beat. By day, it's a breezy café offering burgers, salads, and sandwiches, while the evening menu presents a judicious balance of meat, seafood, and vegetarian dishes,

from "seafood taster" of freshly caught fish to slow-braised saddle of lamb with garlic and rosemary mash. There are barbecues in summer, and live music on Sunday evening. [$] *Average main: £15* ✉ *Gyllyngvase Beach, Cliff Rd.* ☎ *01326/312884* 🌐 *www.gyllybeach.com.*

$ BRITISH 🍴 **Pandora Inn.** This thatched pub on a creek 4 miles north of Falmouth is a great retreat, with both a patio and a moored pontoon for summer dining. Maritime memorabilia and fresh flowers provide decoration, and you can eat in the bar, in the oak-beamed room upstairs, or outside. The menu highlight is fresh seafood—try the fish pie in a shallot and Pernod cream sauce—though there's a good selection of game in winter. [$] *Average main: £12* ✉ *Restronguet Creek, Mylor Bridge* ☎ *01326/372678* 🌐 *www.pandorainn.com.*

$ SEAFOOD 🍴 **Rick Stein's Fish & Chips.** Celebrity chef Rick Stein has expanded his seafood empire to Falmouth, where this no-frills takeaway and restaurant opposite the National Maritime Museum makes a welcome addition to the local dining scene. The mackerel, plaice, and monkfish are grilled, fried to a golden hue, or charcoal-roasted and served with salad. Local scallops, oysters, and rump steak are also on the menu in the white-tiled dining room, and there are fixed-price deals for lunch and dinner. Across the square, Stein's Deli stocks all the fixings for a picnic. [$] *Average main: £12* ✉ *Discovery Quay* ☎ *01841/532700* 🌐 *www.rickstein.com.*

$$$$ HOTEL 🏨 **St. Michael's Hotel.** A cool, contemporary ambience pervades this seaside hotel overlooking Falmouth Bay and fronted by a lush, subtropical garden. **Pros:** excellent facilities; attentive and amiable staff. **Cons:** cheapest rooms are small and viewless; 20-minute walk to center. [$] *Rooms from: £230* ✉ *Gyllyngvase Beach* ☎ *01326/312707* 🌐 *www.stmichaelshotel.co.uk* 🛏 *58 rooms, 3 suites* 🍽 *Breakfast.*

TRELISSICK

6 miles northeast of Falmouth.

Trelissick is known for the colorful Trelissick Garden, owned by the National Trust.

GETTING HERE AND AROUND

Between May and October, the most rewarding way to arrive at Trelissick is by ferry from Falmouth or St. Mawes. There are also frequent year-round buses from these towns. By car, it's on B3289, between A39 and A3078.

EXPLORING

King Harry Ferry. A chain-drawn car ferry, the King Harry runs to the scenically splendid Roseland Peninsula each day three times an hour. From its decks you can see up and down the Fal, a deep, narrow river with steep, wooded banks. The river's great depth provides mooring for old ships waiting to be sold; these mammoth shapes lend a surreal touch to the riverscape. On very rare occasions, you may even spot deer swimming across. ✉ *B3289* ☎ *01872/862312* 🌐 *www.falriver.co.uk* 🎟 *£5* 🕑 *Apr.–Sept., Mon.–Sat. 7:20 am–9:20 pm, Sun. 9 am–9:20 pm; Oct.–Mar., Mon.–Sat. 7:20 am–7:20 pm, Sun. 9 am–7:20 pm.*

Trelissick Garden. Cornwall's mild climate has endowed it with some of the country's most spectacular gardens, among which is Trelissick Garden on the banks of the River Fal. Famous for its camellias, azaras, and photinias, the terraced garden is set within 375 acres of wooded parkland, offering wonderful panoramic views and making this a paradise for walkers. ✉ *B3289, Feock* ☎ *01872/862090* 🌐 *www.nationaltrust.org.uk* 🎟 *£7.20* 🕒 *Mid-Feb.–Oct., daily 10:30–5:30 or dusk; Nov.–mid-Feb., daily 11–4 or dusk; last admission 30 mins before closing.*

ST. MAWES

6 miles south of Trelissick, 16 miles east of Falmouth.

Fodor's Choice ★ At the tip of the Roseland Peninsula is the quiet, unspoiled village of St. Mawes, where subtropical plants thrive. The peninsula itself is a lovely backwater with old churches, a lighthouse, and good coast walking. One or two sailing and boating options are available in summer, but most companies operate from Falmouth.

GETTING HERE AND AROUND

By road, St. Mawes lies at the end of A3078. You could drive from Falmouth, but it's easier to hop on a ferry crossing the estuary. Shuttling passengers between the ports in Falmouth and St. Mawes, the St. Mawes Ferry passes by two atmospheric castles along the way. It runs all year from Falmouth's Prince of Wales Pier and, between June and September, the Custom House Quay.

ESSENTIALS

Ferry Contacts **St. Mawes Ferry** ☎ *01872/861910* 🌐 *www.falriver.co.uk/smf.*

EXPLORING

St. Just in Roseland. North of St. Mawes on the A3078 is St. Just in Roseland, one of the most beautiful spots in the West Country. The tiny hamlet has a 13th-century church set within a subtropical garden, often abloom with magnolias and rhododendrons, as well as a holy well and a graveyard on the banks of a secluded creek. ✉ *Roseland.*

St. Mawes Castle. Outside the village, the well-preserved Tudor-era St. Mawes Castle has a cloverleaf shape that makes it seemingly impregnable, yet during the Civil War its Royalist commander surrendered without firing a shot. (In contrast, Pendennis Castle in Falmouth held out at this time for 23 weeks before submitting to a siege.) ✉ *Castle Dr.* ☎ *01326/270526* 🌐 *www.english-heritage.org.uk* 🎟 *£4.50* 🕒 *Apr.–June and Sept., Sun.–Fri. 10–5; July and Aug., Sun.–Fri. 10–6; Oct., daily 10–5; Nov.–Mar., weekends 10–4.*

WHERE TO STAY

For expanded hotel reviews, visit Fodors.com.

$$ HOTEL 🏨 **Lugger Hotel.** It's worth the winding drive on some of Cornwall's narrowest roads to get to this waterfront hideaway in a tiny fishing village. **Pros:** unforgettable location; outstanding food; attentive staff. **Cons:** remote and isolated; some rooms are cramped with limited views; some noise intrusion. [$] *Rooms from: £130* ✉ *Portloe* ☎ *01872/501322* 🌐 *www.luggerhotel.co.uk* 🛏 *22 rooms* 🍴 *Breakfast.*

$$$$ HOTEL Fodor's Choice ★ 🏨 **Tresanton Hotel.** It's the Cornish Riviera, Italian style: this former yachtsman's club, owned by hotelier Olga Polizzi, makes for a luxuriously relaxed stay. **Pros:** relaxed but professional service; terrific views; stylishly luxurious setting. **Cons:** some steps to climb; some rooms are small; distant parking lot. [$] *Rooms from: £260* ✉ *Lower Castle Rd.* ☎ *01326/270055* 🌐 *www.tresanton.com* 🛏 *24 rooms, 6 suites* 🍴 *Breakfast.*

FOWEY

25 miles northeast of St. Mawes.

Fodor's Choice ★ Nestled in the mouth of a wooded estuary, Fowey (pronounced Foy) is still very much a working china-clay port as well as a focal point for the sailing fraternity. Increasingly, it's also a favored home of the rich and famous. Good and varied dining and lodging options abound; these are most in demand during Regatta Week in mid- to late August and the annual Daphne du Maurier Festival in mid-May. The Bodinnick and Polruan ferries take cars as well as foot passengers across the river for the coast road on to Looe.

5

A few miles west of Fowey are a pair of very different gardens: the Eden Project, a futuristic display of plants from around the world, and the Lost Gardens of Heligan, a revitalized reminder of the Victorian age.

GETTING HERE AND AROUND

Fowey isn't on any train line, but the town is served by frequent buses from St. Austell. Don't attempt to drive into the steep and narrow-lane town center, which is ideal for strolling around. Parking lots are signposted on the approach roads.

ESSENTIALS

Visitor Information Fowey Tourist Information Centre ✉ *Du Maurier Literary Centre, 5 South St.* ☎ *01726/833616* 🌐 *www.fowey.co.uk.*

EXPLORING

FAMILY Fodor's Choice ★ **Eden Project.** Spectacularly set in a former china-clay pit, this garden presents the world's major plant systems in microcosm. The crater contains more than 70,000 plants—many of them rare or endangered species—from three climate zones. Plants from the temperate zone are outdoors, and those from other zones are housed in hexagonally paneled geodesic domes. In the Mediterranean Biome, olive and citrus groves mix with cacti and other plants indigenous to warmer climates. The Rainforest Biome steams with heat, resounds to the gushing of a waterfall, and blooms with exotic flora. The emphasis is on conservation and ecology, but is free of any editorializing. A free shuttle helps the footsore, and well-informed guides provide information. An entertaining exhibition in the visitor center gives you the lowdown on the project, and the Core, an education center, provides amusement and instruction for children. There are open-air concerts in summer and an ice-skating rink in winter. The Eden Project is 3 miles northeast of Charleston and 5 miles northwest of Fowey. There's frequent bus service from Fowey to St. Austell. ✉ *Bodelva Rd., off A30, A390, and A391, St. Austell* ☎ *01726/811911* 🌐 *www.edenproject.com* 🎟 *£23.50, £19.50* *if arriving by bike, on foot, or on public transport* 🕒 *Apr.–Oct., daily 9:30–6; Nov.–Mar., daily 10–4; last admission 90 min before closing.*

Fodor's Choice ★ **Lost Gardens of Heligan.** These sprawling grounds have something for all garden lovers, as well as an intriguing history. Begun by the Tremayne family in the late 18th century, they were rediscovered and spruced up in the early 1990s by former rock music producer Tim Smit (the force behind the Eden Project). In Victorian times the gardens displayed plants from around the British Empire. The Jungle Zone contains surviving plants from this era, including a lone Monterey pine, as well as giant redwood and clumps of bamboo. The Italian Garden and walled Flower Gardens are delightful, but don't overlook the Fruit and Vegetable gardens or Flora's Green, bordered by a ravine. It's easy to spend half a day here. Guided tours costing £2 are available daily at 11:30. **TIP→ Travel via St. Austell to avoid confusing country lanes, then follow signs to Mevagissey.** ✉ *B3273, Pentewan* ☎ *01726/845100* 🌐 *www.heligan.com* 🎟 *£11* 🕒 *Apr.–Sept., daily 10–6; Oct.–Mar., daily 10–5; last entry 1½ hrs before closing.*

RENT A COTTAGE

You can experience rural peace in a rented cottage in the West Country, but book early for summer.

Classic Cottages
☎ *01326/555555*
🌐 *www.classic.co.uk.*

Cornish Cottage Holidays
☎ *01326/573808* 🌐 *www.cornishcottageholidays.co.uk.*

Cornish Traditional Cottages
☎ *01208/821666*
🌐 *www.corncott.com.*

Helpful Holidays
☎ *01647/433593*
🌐 *www.helpfulholidays.com.*

WHERE TO EAT AND STAY

For expanded hotel reviews, visit Fodors.com.

$ AMERICAN 🍴 **Sam's.** This small and buzzing bistro has a rock-and-roll flavor, thanks to the walls adorned with posters of music icons. Diners squeeze onto benches and into booths to savor dishes made with local seafood, including a majestic bouillabaisse, or just a simple "Samburger." You may have to wait for a table, but there's a slinky lounge-bar upstairs for a preprandial drink. [$] *Average main: £12* ✉ *20 Fore St.* ☎ *01726/832273* 🌐 *www.samsfowey.co.uk* ✍ *Reservations not accepted.*

$$$$ HOTEL FAMILY 🏨 **Fowey Hall.** A showy Victorian edifice, all turrets and elaborate plasterwork, this hotel with 5 acres of gardens, a spa, and a pool is a great place for families. **Pros:** grand manorial setting; family-friendly rates. **Cons:** some rooms distant from the main house; not ideal for anyone seeking an adult ambience. [$] *Rooms from: £230* ✉ *Hanson Dr.* ☎ *01726/833866* 🌐 *www.foweyhallhotel.co.uk* 🛏 *24 rooms, 12 suites* 🍽 *Breakfast.*

SPORTS AND THE OUTDOORS

Fowey River Expeditions. Between June and September, Fowey River Expeditions runs daily canoe trips up the tranquil River Fowey, the best way to observe the abundant wildlife. Kayaks are also available to rent. ✉ *17 Passage St.* ☎ *01726/833627* 🌐 *www.foweyriverexpeditions.co.uk.*

BODMIN

12 miles north of Fowey.

Bodmin was the only Cornish town recorded in the 11th-century Domesday Book, William the Conqueror's census. During World War I, the Domesday Book and the Crown Jewels were sent to Bodmin Prison for safekeeping. From the Gilbert Memorial on Beacon Hill you can see both of Cornwall's coasts. Lanhydrock, a stately home, is also near Bodmin.

GETTING HERE AND AROUND

At the junction of A38 and A30, Bodmin is a major transport hub for north Cornwall. Trains stop at Bodmin Parkway, 3 miles southeast of the center. A car is your best bet for touring Bodmin Moor and visiting Lanhydrock.

ESSENTIALS

Visitor Information Bodmin Tourist Information Centre ⊠ *The Shire Hall, Mount Folly* ☎ *01208/76616* ⊕ *www.bodminlive.com.*

EXPLORING

Dozmary Pool. For a taste of Arthurian legend, follow A30 northeast out of Bodmin across the boggy, heather-clad granite plateau of Bodmin Moor. After about 10 miles, turn right at Bolventor to get to Dozmary Pool. A lake rather than a pool, it was here that King Arthur's legendary magic sword, Excalibur, was supposedly returned to the Lady of the Lake after Arthur's final battle.

Fodor's Choice ★ **Lanhydrock.** One of Cornwall's greatest country piles, Lanhydrock gives a look into the lives of the upper classes in the 19th century. The former home of the powerful, wealthy Robartes family was originally constructed in the 17th century but was totally rebuilt after a fire in 1881. Its granite exterior remains true to the house's original form, however, and the long picture gallery in the north wing, with its barrel-vaulted plaster ceiling depicting 24 biblical scenes, survived the devastation. A small museum shows photographs and letters relating to the family. The house's endless pantries, sculleries, dairies, nurseries, and linen cupboards bear witness to the immense amount of work involved in maintaining this lifestyle. About 900 acres of wooded parkland border the River Fowey, and in spring the gardens present an exquisite ensemble of magnolias, azaleas, and rhododendrons. Allow two hours to see the house and more time to stroll the grounds. The house is 3 miles southeast of Bodmin. ⊠ *Off A30, A38, and B3268* ☎ *01208/265950* ⊕ *www.nationaltrust.org.uk* ✉ *£11; grounds only, £6.50* ☉ *House Apr.–Sept., Tues.–Sun. 11–5:30; Mar. and Oct., Tues.–Sun. 11–5; garden mid-Feb.–Oct., daily 10–6; park daily dawn–dusk; last admission 30 mins before closing.*

PLYMOUTH AND DARTMOOR

Just over the border from Cornwall is Plymouth, an unprepossessing city but one with a historic old core and splendid harbor that recall a rich maritime heritage. North of Plymouth, you can explore the vast, boggy reaches of hilly Dartmoor, the setting for the Sherlock Holmes classic *The Hound of the Baskervilles*. This national park is a great place to hike or go horseback riding away from the crowds.

PLYMOUTH

48 miles southwest of Exeter, 124 miles southwest of Bristol, 240 miles southwest of London.

Devon's largest city has long been linked with England's commercial and maritime history. The Pilgrims sailed from here to the New World in the *Mayflower* in 1620. Although much of the city center was destroyed by air raids in World War II and has been rebuilt in an uninspiring style, there are worthwhile sights. A harbor tour is also a good way to see the city.

GETTING HERE AND AROUND

Frequent trains arrive from Bodmin, Penzance, and Exeter. From London Paddington, trains take around four hours; Megabus and National Express buses from London's Victoria Coach Station take five–six hours. The train station is 1 mile north of the seafront, connected by frequent buses. Long-distance buses stop at the centrally located bus station off Royal Parade. Drivers can leave their cars in one of the numerous parking lots, including a couple right by the harbor. The seafront and central city areas are best explored on foot.

ESSENTIALS

Visitor Information **Plymouth Tourism Information Centre** ⊠ *Plymouth Mayflower, 3–5 The Barbican* ☎ *01752/306330* ⊕ *www.visitplymouth.co.uk.*

EXPLORING

TOP ATTRACTIONS

Barbican. East of the Royal Citadel is the Barbican, the oldest surviving section of Plymouth. Here Tudor houses and warehouses rise from a maze of narrow streets leading down to the fishing harbor and marina. Many of these buildings have become antiques shops, art shops, and cafés. It's well worth a stroll for the atmosphere.

Elizabethan House. In the heart of the Barbican section, this former sea captain's home offers a fascinating insight into how well-to-do Plymothians lived during the city's golden age. The three floors of the timber-frame house are filled with 16th- and 17th-century furnishings, and there's a reconstructed kitchen and a spiral staircase built around a ship's mast. ⊠ *32 New St.* ☎ *01752/304774* ⊕ *www.plymouth.gov.uk* 🎫 *£2.60* ◔ *Apr.–Sept., Tues.–Sat. and national holidays 10–noon and 1–5.*

Hoe. From the Hoe, a wide, grassy esplanade with crisscrossing walkways high above the city, you can take in a magnificent view of the inlets, bays, and harbors that make up Plymouth Sound.

Upstairs, downstairs: at Lanhydrock you can tour both the elegant picture gallery and the vast kitchens, pantries, and sculleries.

FAMILY **National Marine Aquarium.** This excellent aquarium on the harbor presents aqueous environments, from a freshwater stream to a seawater wave tank to a huge "shark theater." Not to be missed is the extensive collection of sea horses, part of an important breeding program, and the chance to walk under sharks in the Mediterranean tank. Feeding times are fun for the kids, and Waves café, with its harbor views, makes a good spot for a rest and refreshment. ⊠ *Rope Walk, Coxside* ☎ *0844/893–7938* ⊕ *www.national-aquarium.co.uk* ✑ *£12.75* ⏱ *Apr.–Sept., daily 10–6; Oct.–Mar., daily 10–5; last admission 1 hr before closing.*

FAMILY **Plymouth Mayflower Exhibition.** On three floors, this interactive exhibition narrates the story of Plymouth, from its beginnings as a fishing and trading port to the modern industrial city it is today. Along the way, you'll take in the stories of various expeditions that embarked from here to the New World, including the *Mayflower* itself. The city's tourist office is also in this building. ⊠ *3–5 The Barbican* ☎ *01752/306330* ⊕ *www. visitplymouth.co.uk* ✑ *£2* ⏱ *Apr.–Oct., Mon.–Sat. 9:30–5, Sun. 10:30–4; Nov.–Mar., weekdays 9:30–5, Sat. 10–4.*

Saltram. An exquisite 18th-century home with many of its original furnishings, Saltram was built around the remains of a late-Tudor mansion. Its jewel is one of Britain's grandest neoclassical rooms, a vast, double-cube salon designed by Robert Adam and hung with paintings by Sir Joshua Reynolds, first president of the Royal Academy of Arts, who was born nearby in 1723. Fine plasterwork adorns many rooms, and three have original Chinese wallpaper. The outstanding garden includes rare trees and shrubs, and there's a restaurant and a cafeteria. Saltram is 3½ miles east of Plymouth city center. ⊠ *South of A38, Plympton* ☎ *01752/333503*

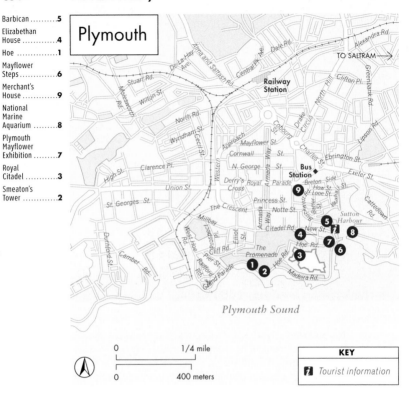

Plymouth Sound

KEY

🛈 *Tourist information*

⊕ *www.nationaltrust.org.uk* ✉ *£9.70; garden only £5* ⊘ *House early Mar.–early Nov., Sat.–Thurs. noon–4:30; last admission at 3:45. Garden early Mar.–early Nov., daily 11–5; early Nov.–early Mar., daily 11–4.*

WORTH NOTING

Mayflower Steps. By the harbor you can visit the Mayflower Steps, where the Pilgrims embarked in 1620; the **Mayflower Stone** marks the exact spot. They had sailed from Southampton but had to stop in Plymouth because of damage from a storm. ✉ *The Barbican.*

Merchant's House. Near the Barbican, just off the Royal Parade, this largely 17th-century house is a museum of local history. ✉ *33 St. Andrew's St.* ☎ *01752/304774* ✉ *£2.60* ⊘ *Apr.–Sept., Tues.–Sat. and national holidays 10–noon and 1–5.*

Plymouth Boat Trips. Harbor cruises and longer scenic trips on the rivers Tamar and Yealm leave from the Mayflower Steps and Cremyll Quay between April and November. ✉ *Mayflower Steps, 225 Commercial Wharf* ☎ *01752/253153* ⊕ *www.plymouthboattrips.co.uk.*

Royal Citadel. This huge citadel was built by Charles II in 1666 and still operates as a military center. Note that photography is not permitted. ✉ *End of the Hoe* ☎ *01752/306330* ⊕ *www.english-heritage. org.uk* ✉ *£5* ⊘ *Early May–late Sept., Tues. and Thurs. 1¼-hr guided tours at 2:30.*

Smeaton's Tower. This lighthouse, transferred here at the end of the 19th century from its original site 14 miles out to sea, provides a sweeping vista over Plymouth Sound and the city as far as Dartmoor. Gird yourself for the 93 steps to the top. ✉ *Hoe Rd.* ☎ *01752/304774* 🎟 *£2.60* ⏲ *Apr.–Sept., Tues.–Fri. 10–noon and 1–4:30, Sat. 10–noon and 1–4; Oct.–Mar., Tues.–Sat. 10–noon and 1–3.*

WHERE TO EAT AND STAY

For expanded hotel reviews, visit Fodors.com.

$ MODERN BRITISH 🍴 **River Cottage Canteen & Deli.** Renowned chef and food campaigner Hugh Fearnley-Whittingstall has set up an outpost of his culinary chain in the old naval depot in Plymouth's newly fashionable Stonehouse neighborhood. The menu is strong on seafood—including mackerel fishcakes and bouillabaisse—but also features braised beef-and-ale stew and beetroot spelt risotto with goat's cheese. Sit indoors in the large, open dining area or at tables outside, where you can take in views over a yacht marina and across to wooded slopes. From the deli counter you can choose from an enticing range of locally produced ham, bread, pasties, cheese, cider, and wine. [$] *Average main: £12* ✉ *Royal William Yard, Stonehouse, Plymouth* ☎ *01752/252702* 🌐 *www.rivercottage.net.*

$$$ MODERN BRITISH 🍴 **Tanners.** One of the city's oldest buildings, the 15th-century Prysten House, is the setting for the highly regarded, inventive cuisine of brothers Chris and James Tanner. The seasonal à la carte and fixed-price menus may include slow-cooked shoulder of lamb, or whole lemon sole with sea greens, mussels, and clams. One of the two lattice-windowed dining rooms has a well inside it, and the other is hung with tapestries. A canopied courtyard is ideal for alfresco dining. The brothers also operate the Barbican Kitchen, a more casual, less pricey offshoot at the Black Friars Distillery on Southside Street. [$] *Average main: £20* ✉ *Finewell St.* ☎ *01752/252001* 🌐 *www.tannersrestaurant.com* ✍ *Reservations essential* ⏲ *Closed Sun. and Mon.*

$ B&B/INN 🏨 **The Bowling Green.** Friendly and unpretentious, this Georgian house overlooks Sir Francis Drake's bowling green on Plymouth Hoe. **Pros:** convenient base for sightseeing; welcoming management. **Cons:** limited parking. [$] *Rooms from: £75* ✉ *9–10 Osborne Pl.* ☎ *01752/209090* 🌐 *www.thebowlinggreenplymouth.com* 🛏 *6 rooms* 🍽 *Breakfast.*

$ HOTEL 🏨 **Holiday Inn.** Grandly sited in a tall block overlooking Plymouth Hoe, this modern chain hotel has a businesslike tone but doesn't skimp on comforts. **Pros:** excellent location; large rooms; fantastic views. **Cons:** impersonal feel; dated decor; tight parking. [$] *Rooms from: £83* ✉ *Armada Way* ☎ *01752/639988* 🌐 *www.ihg.com* 🛏 *211 rooms* 🍽 *Breakfast.*

NIGHTLIFE AND THE ARTS

Theatre Royal. Plymouth's Theatre Royal presents ballet, musicals, and plays by some of Britain's best companies. ✉ *Royal Parade* ☎ *01752/267222* 🌐 *www.theatreroyal.com.*

SHOPPING

Black Friars Distillery. At the Black Friars Distillery, Plymouth's most famous export, gin, has been distilled since 1793. You can purchase bottles of sloe gin, damson liqueur, fruit cup, or the fiery "Navy Strength" gin that traditionally was issued to the Royal Navy. Learn the full story on walking tours around the distillery, ending with a sampling in the wood-paneled Refectory Bar. The building originally housed a friary, and was where the Pilgrims spent their last night on English soil in 1620. ⌧ *60 Southside St.* ☎ *01752/665292* ⊕ *www.plymouthdistillery.com.*

EN ROUTE From Plymouth you have a choice of routes northeast to Exeter. If rugged, desolate, moorland scenery appeals to you, take A386 and B3212 northeast across Dartmoor. There's plenty to stir the imagination.

DARTMOOR NATIONAL PARK

10 miles north of Plymouth, 13 miles west of Exeter.

GETTING HERE AND AROUND

Public transport services are extremely sparse on Dartmoor, making a car indispensable for anywhere off the beaten track. The peripheral towns of Okehampton and Tavistock are well served by bus from Exeter and Plymouth, and Chagford also has direct connections to Exeter, but central Princetown has only sporadic links with the outside world.

EXPLORING

Fodor's Choice ★ **Dartmoor National Park.** Even on a summer's day, the brooding hills of this sprawling wilderness appear a likely haunt for such monsters as the hound of the Baskervilles, and it seems entirely fitting that Sir Arthur Conan Doyle set his Sherlock Holmes thriller in this landscape. Sometimes the wet, peaty wasteland of Dartmoor National Park vanishes in rain and mist, although in clear weather you can see north to Exmoor, south over the English Channel, and west far into Cornwall. Much of Dartmoor consists of open heath and moorland, unspoiled by roads—wonderful walking and horseback-riding territory but an easy place to lose your bearings. Dartmoor's earliest inhabitants left behind stone monuments and burial mounds that help you envision prehistoric man roaming these pastures. Ponies, sheep, and birds are the main animals to be seen.

Several villages scattered along the borders of this 368-square-mile reserve—one-third of which is owned by Prince Charles—make useful bases for hiking excursions. Accommodations include simple inns and some elegant havens. **Okehampton** is a main gateway, and **Chagford** is a good base for exploring north Dartmoor. Other scenic spots include **Buckland-in-the-Moor,** a hamlet with thatch-roof cottages; **Widecombe-in-the-Moor,** whose church is known as the Cathedral of the Moor; and **Grimspound,** the Bronze Age site featured in Conan Doyle's most famous tale. Transmoor Link buses connect most of Dartmoor's towns and villages. The **High Moorland Visitor Centre** in Princetown is a good place to start your trip, as are centers in Postbridge and Haytor. You can also pick up information in Ivybridge, Okehampton, Moretonhampstead, Tavistock, and Buckfastleigh. ⌧ *High Moorland Visitor Centre, Tavistock Rd., Princetown* ☎ *01822/890414* ⊕ *www.dartmoor-npa.gov.uk.*

Pony trekking in Dartmoor National Park lets you get off the beaten path.

SPORTS AND THE OUTDOORS

Hiking is extremely popular in Dartmoor National Park. The areas around Widgery Cross, Becky Falls, and the Bovey Valley, as well as the short but dramatic walk along Lydford Gorge, have wide appeal, as do the many valleys around the southern edge of the moors. Guided hikes, typically costing £3 to £8, are available through the park's visitor information centers. Reservations are usually not necessary. Longer hikes in the bleak, less-populated regions—for example, the tors south of Okehampton—are appropriate only for most experienced walkers. Dartmoor is a great area for horseback riding; many towns have stables for guided rides.

TAVISTOCK AND ENVIRONS

13 miles north of Plymouth.

On the River Tavy, the ancient town of Tavistock historically owed its importance to its Benedictine abbey (dissolved by Henry VIII in the 16th century) and to its status as a stannary town, where tin was weighed, stamped, and assessed. Today the town of 11,000 preserves a prosperous, predominantly Victorian appearance, especially at the bustling indoor Pannier Market off central Bedford Square. Tavistock makes a useful base for exploring a scattering of nearby sights—Buckland Abbey, Cotehele House, and Morwellham Quay—and for touring Dartmoor's western reaches.

Plymouth, Exeter, and South Devon

GETTING HERE AND AROUND

Tavistock, on A386 and A390, is easily accessed via the frequent buses from Plymouth, which take about an hour. You'll need your own transportation to visit the attractions scattered around it, however.

ESSENTIALS

Visitor Information Tavistock Tourist Information Centre ⊠ *The Archway, Bedford Sq.* ☎ *01822/612938* ⊕ *www.dartmoor.co.uk.*

EXPLORING

Buckland Abbey. A 13th-century Cistercian monastery, Buckland Abbey became the home of Sir Francis Drake in 1581. Today it's filled with mementos of Drake and the Spanish Armada and has a restaurant. The house is 6 miles south of Tavistock; to get here, take A386 south to Crapstone and then head west. ⊠ *Off A386, Yelverton* ☎ *01822/853607* ⊕ *www.nationaltrust.org.uk* ⧉ *£8.55; grounds only £4.50* ☉ *House mid Feb.–early Mar. and early Dec.–late Dec., daily noon–4; early Mar.–early Nov., daily 11:30–4:30; early Nov.–early Dec., Fri.–Sun. noon–4. Grounds mid Feb.–early Nov. and early Dec.–late Dec., daily 10:30–5:30; early Nov.–early Dec., Fri.–Sun. 10:30–5:30. Last admission 45 mins before closing.*

Cotehele House and Quay. About 4 miles west of Buckland Abbey and 9 miles southwest of Tavistock, Cotehele House and Quay was formerly a busy port on the River Tamar, but it is now usually visited for the well-preserved, atmospheric late-medieval manor, home of the Edgcumbe family for centuries. The house has original furniture, tapestries, embroideries, and armor, and you can also visit the impressive gardens, a quay museum, and a restored mill (usually in operation on Tuesday and Thursday). A limited number of visitors are allowed per day, so arrive early and be prepared to wait during busy periods. Choose a bright day, because the rooms have no electric light. Shops, crafts studios, a gallery, and a restaurant provide other diversions. **TIP→ Take advantage of the shuttle bus that runs every half hour between the house, quay, and mill.** ✉ *Off A390, St. Dominick* ☎ *01579/351346* 🌐 *www.nationaltrust.org.uk* 🎟 *£9; gardens and mill only, £5.40* 🕒 *House mid-Mar.–early Nov., Sat.–Thurs. 11–4. Mill early Mar.–Sept., daily 11–5; Oct–early Nov., daily 11–4:30. Gardens daily dawn–dusk.*

STAY ON A FARM

One way to experience the authentic rural life in Somerset, Devon, and Cornwall is to stay on a farm. **Cartwheel Holidays** (🌐 *www.cartwheelholidays.co.uk*) has details about working farms that supply accommodations—including bed-and-breakfasts and house rentals—throughout the region. Other reference points are **Visit Devon** (🌐 *www.visitdevon.co.uk*), for farms in Devon, and **Cornish Farm Holidays** (🌐 *www.cornishfarmholidays.co.uk*), for Cornwall.

FAMILY **Morwellham Quay.** In the 19th century, Morwellham (pronounced More-*wel*-am) was England's main copper-exporting port, and it has been carefully restored as a working museum, with quay workers and coachmen in costume. Visitors can board a special train that goes along the River Tamar and into the Charlotte and George Copper Mine. You can hear live folk music played on Sunday afternoons. The site lies 2 miles east of Cotehele House and 5 miles southwest of Tavistock. ✉ *Off B3257, Morwellham* ☎ *01822/832766* 🌐 *www.morwellham-quay.co.uk* 🎟 *£7.95, mine train £3.50* 🕒 *Easter–late July and early Sept.–Oct., daily 10–5; late July–early Sept., daily 10–5:30; Nov.–Easter, daily 10–4.*

WHERE TO EAT AND STAY

For expanded hotel reviews, visit Fodors.com.

$$$$ | MODERN BRITISH | Fodor's Choice ★

🍴 **Horn of Plenty.** The restaurant within this Georgian house has magnificent views across the wooded, rhododendron-filled Tamar Valley. The sophisticated menu favors local and seasonal ingredients. Beef Rossini–a roast sirloin with seared foie gras, Jeruslaem artichoke puree, and truffle jus—is a typical main course. There are several fixed-price menus (lunch £19.50 and £24.50, dinner £49.50); the best value is Monday evening's potluck menu (£29). A converted coach house and the main house contain 10 sumptuously furnished guest rooms. It's 3 miles west of Tavistock. [$] *Average main: £49* ✉ *A390, Gulworthy* ☎ *01822/832528* 🌐 *www.thehornofplenty.co.uk.*

$$ Browns. With its mustard-and-brown color scheme, plush furnishings,
HOTEL   and fresh-feeling conservatory, this former coaching inn feels contempo-
rary, but its lattice windows and exposed stone walls suggest a longer
pedigree. **Pros:** friendly, professional staff; mixes modern and tradi-
tional; delicious food. **Cons:** some rooms and bathrooms are cramped;
tricky parking. *$ Rooms from: £129 ☒ 80 West St. ☎ 01822/618686
⊕ www.brownsdevon.com ↩ 20 rooms, 1 suite ¡○¡ Breakfast.*

LYDFORD GORGE

7 miles north of Tavistock, 24 miles north of Plymouth.

GETTING HERE AND AROUND

The gorge is easily accessed on Beacon buses from Tavistock (which has
frequent bus connections to Plymouth) and Okehampton (connected
to Exeter). By car, take A386 between Tavistock and Okehampton.

EXPLORING

Fodor'sChoice   **Lydford Gorge.** The River Lyd carved a spectacular 1½-mile-long chasm
★   through the rock at Lydford Gorge, outside the pretty village of Lyd-
ford, midway between Okehampton and Tavistock. Two paths follow the
gorge past gurgling whirlpools and waterfalls with evocative names such
as the Devil's Cauldron and the White Lady. ■ TIP→ **Sturdy footwear is
recommended.** Although the walk can be quite challenging, the paths can
still get congested during busy periods. In winter, access is restricted to the
main waterfall and the top of the gorge. ☒ *Off A386* ☎ *01822/820320
⊕ www.nationaltrust.org.uk ☜ £6 ۩ Early Mar.–early Oct., daily 10–5;
early Oct.–early Nov., daily 10–4; early Nov.–early Mar., call for times.*

WHERE TO EAT AND STAY

For expanded hotel reviews, visit Fodors.com.

$$ ✕ **Dartmoor Inn.** Locals and visitors alike make a beeline for this gastro-
MODERN BRITISH   pub in a 16th-century building with a number of small dining spaces done
in spare, contemporary country style. The elegantly presented dishes may
include pork belly, fish casserole with a ragout of leeks and saffron sauce,
or fillet of duck with vanilla-apple puree, prunes, and toasted almonds.
Set-price menus may be available, and there's a separate, reasonably
priced bar menu. Three spacious guest rooms make it possible to linger.
*$ Average main: £17 ☒ School Rd., off A386 ☎ 01822/820221 ⊕ www.
dartmoorinn.com ۩ No dinner Sun. Closed Mon.*

$ Castle Inn. In the heart of Lydford village, this 16th-century inn sits
B&B/INN   next to Lydford Castle. **Pros:** antique character; peaceful rural setting. **Cons:** shabby in places; some small rooms. *$ Rooms from: £70
☒ School Rd., off A386 ☎ 01822/820241 ⊕ www.castleinndartmoor.
co.uk ↩ 8 rooms ¡○¡ Breakfast.*

$$$ Lewtrenchard Manor. Paneled rooms, stone fireplaces, leaded-glass win-
HOTEL   dows, and handsome gardens outfit this spacious 1620 manor house on
Fodor'sChoice   the northwestern edge of Dartmoor. **Pros:** beautiful Jacobean setting; con-
★   scientious service; outstanding food. **Cons:** rooms in outbuildings have
less atmosphere; minimum stay on summer weekends; not very child-
friendly. *$ Rooms from: £175 ☒ Off A30, Lewdown ☎ 01566/783222
⊕ www.lewtrenchard.co.uk ↩ 10 rooms, 4 suites ¡○¡ Breakfast.*

A walk in Lydford Gorge takes you through lush forest.

SPORTS AND THE OUTDOORS

Cholwell Riding Stables. One- and two-hour horseback rides through some of Dartmoor's wilder tracts are available with Cholwell Riding Stables. Riders of all abilities are escorted, and equipment is provided. The stables are about 2 miles south of Lydford. ☒ *Off A386, Mary Tavy* ☎ *01822/810526* ⊕ *www.cholwellridingstables.co.uk.*

OKEHAMPTON

8 miles northeast of Lydford Gorge, 28 miles north of Plymouth, 23 miles west of Exeter.

This town at the confluence of the rivers East and West Okement is a good base for exploring north Dartmoor. It has a fascinating museum dedicated to the moor, as well as a helpful tourist office.

GETTING HERE AND AROUND

There's good bus service to Okehampton from Tavistock and Exeter, and on summer Sundays you can travel by train from Exeter. If you're driving, the town is on A30 and A386; parking is easy in the center of town.

ESSENTIALS

Visitor Information Okehampton Tourist Information Centre ☒ *Museum Courtyard, 3 West St.* ☎ *01837/53020* ⊕ *www.okehamptondevon.co.uk.*

EXPLORING

FAMILY **Museum of Dartmoor Life.** The three floors of this informative museum contain historical artifacts, domestic knickknacks, traditional agricultural and mining tools, and fascinating insights into the lives of ordinary folk living on the moor. ☒ *Museum Courtyard, 3 West St.* ☎ *01837/52295*

🌐 *www.museumofdartmoorlife.org.uk* 🎫 *£2.50* ⏲ *Late Mar.–late Nov., weekdays 10:15–4:15, Sat. 10:15–1.*

Okehampton Castle. On the riverbank a mile southwest of the town center, the jagged ruins of this Norman castle occupy a verdant site with a picnic area and woodland walks. ✉ *Castle Lodge, off B3260* ☎ *01837/52844* 🌐 *www.english-heritage.org.uk* 🎫 *£3.90* ⏲ *Apr.–June and Sept.–early Nov., daily 10–5; July and Aug., daily 10–6.*

WHERE TO STAY

For expanded hotel reviews, visit Fodors.com.

$ B&B/INN 🏨 **White Hart Hotel.** This venerable 17th-century coaching inn has counted the eminent statesman William Pitt the Elder among its guests, and little has changed since he visited in the 18th century: the rooms retain their low doors and sloping floors, for example. **Pros:** central location; historical character. **Cons:** breakfast costs extra; would benefit from a thorough updating; some street noise in front rooms. [$] *Rooms from: £80* ✉ *Fore St.* ☎ *01837/52730* 🌐 *www.thewhitehart-hotel.com* 🛏 *19 rooms* 🍴 *No meals.*

SPORTS AND THE OUTDOORS

Eastlake Riding Stables. A couple of miles outside Okehampton, Eastlake Riding Stables arranges horseback rides throughout the year. Trips last one or two hours or a full day. ✉ *Off A30, Belstone* ☎ *01837/52513* 🌐 *www.eastlakeridingstables.co.uk.*

CHAGFORD

9 miles southeast of Okehampton, 30 miles northeast of Plymouth.

Once a tin-weighing station, Chagford was an area of fierce fighting between the Roundheads and the Cavaliers during the English Civil War. Although officially a "town" since 1305, Chagford is more of a village, with taverns grouped around a seasoned old church and a curious "pepper-pot" market house on the site of the old Stannary Court. With a handful of cafés and shops to browse around, it makes a convenient base from which to explore north Dartmoor.

GETTING HERE AND AROUND

Infrequent local buses connect Chagford with Okehampton and Exeter (except on Sunday, when there's no service). The village is off A382; a car or bicycle is the best way to see its far-flung sights.

EXPLORING

Castle Drogo. Northeast of Chagford, this castle looks like a stout medieval fortress, complete with battlements, but construction actually took place between 1910 and 1930. Designed by noted architect Sir Edwin Lutyens for Julius Drewe, a wealthy grocer, the castle is only half finished (funds ran out). Inside, this magisterial pile combines medieval grandeur and early-20th-century comforts, and there are awesome views over Dartmoor's Teign Valley. Renovation work will be ongoing until 2018, which means that walls may be hidden behind scaffolding and some rooms will be closed to visitors. Turn off the A30 Exeter–Okehampton road at Whiddon Down to reach the castle. ✉ *Off A30* *and A382, Drewsteignton* ☎ *01647/433306* ⊕ *www.nationaltrust.org. uk* ☜ *£8.70; grounds only, £5.50* ⊘ *Castle early Mar.–early Nov., daily 11–5; early Nov.–late Dec., weekends 11–4. Grounds early Mar.–early Nov., daily 10–5:30 or dusk; early Nov.–early Mar., daily 11–4.*

Devon Guild of Craftsmen. The southwest's most important contemporary arts-and-crafts center, the Devon Guild is in a converted 19th-century coach house in the village of Bovey Tracey, 10 miles southeast of Chagford and 14 miles southwest of Exeter. The center has excellent exhibitions of local, national, and international crafts, as well as a shop and café. ✉ *Riverside Mill, Fore St., Bovey Tracey* ☎ *01626/832223* ⊕ *www. crafts.org.uk* ☜ *Free* ⊘ *Daily 10–5:30.*

QUICK
BITES

The Old Cottage Tea Shop. This is the real deal, perfect for a light lunch or, even better, a cream tea served on bone china. Warm scones come in baskets, with black currant and other homemade jams and plenty of clotted cream. It's closed Wednesday afternoon and all day Sunday. ✉ *20 Fore St., Bovey Tracey* ☎ *01626/833430.*

WHERE TO EAT AND STAY

For expanded hotel reviews, visit Fodors.com.

$$$$
MODERN BRITISH
Fodor'sChoice
★

✕ **Gidleigh Park.** One of England's foremost country-house hotels, Gidleigh Park occupies an enclave of landscaped gardens and streams. It's reached via a lengthy, winding country lane and private drive at the edge of Dartmoor. The extremely pricey contemporary restaurant, directed by chef Michael Caines, has been showered with culinary awards. You may see why when you dig into the turbot and scallops with leeks, wild mushrooms, and chive butter sauce, one of the choices often on the prix-fixé menus (£42 for two courses at lunch, £110 for three courses at dinner). The locally pumped spring water is like no other. Antiques fill the long, half-timber building, built in 1928 in Tudor style; there are 24 luxurious guest rooms. $ *Average main: £105* ✉ *Gidleigh Park* ☎ *01647/432367* ⊕ *www.gidleigh.com* ⚑ *Reservations essential.*

$$$$
HOTEL
FAMILY
Fodor'sChoice
★

🏯 **Bovey Castle.** With the grandeur of a country estate and the amenities of a modern hotel, Bovey Castle, built in 1906 for Viscount Hambledon, has it all. **Pros:** baronial splendor; range of activities. **Cons:** service can be slow; overpriced food and extras. $ *Rooms from: £249* ✉ *Off B3212, North Bovey* ☎ *0844/474–0077* ⊕ *www.boveycastle.com* ⚐ *64 rooms, 14 lodges* ⦿*Breakfast.*

$
B&B/INN

🏯 **Easton Court.** Discerning travelers such as C.P. Snow, Margaret Mead, John Steinbeck, and Evelyn Waugh—who completed *Brideshead Revisited* here—made this their Dartmoor home-away-from-home. **Pros:** helpful hosts; peaceful ambience. **Cons:** minimum stay required on weekends in high season; rooms upstairs accessed by exterior stairs; a drive from the village. $ *Rooms from: £75* ✉ *Easton Cross* ☎ *01647/433469* ⊕ *www.easton.co.uk* ⚐ *5 rooms* ⦿*Breakfast.*

EXETER AND SOUTH DEVON

The ancient city of Exeter, Devon's county seat, has preserved some of its historical character despite wartime bombing. From Exeter you can explore southeast to the estuary village of Topsham. Sheltered by the high mass of Dartmoor to the west, the coastal resort area of Torbay, known as the English Riviera, enjoys a mild, warm climate that allows for subtropical vegetation, including palm trees. To the east, on the banks of the River Dart, is the pretty market town of Totnes, while the well-to-do yachting center of Dartmouth lies south of Torbay at the river's estuary.

EXETER

18 miles east of Chagford, 48 miles northeast of Plymouth, 85 miles southwest of Bristol, 205 miles southwest of London.

Exeter has been the capital of the region since the Romans established a fortress here 2,000 years ago. Evidence of the Roman occupation remains in the city walls. Although it was heavily bombed in 1942, Exeter retains much of its medieval character, as well as examples of the gracious architecture of the 18th and 19th centuries. It's convenient to both Torquay and Dartmoor.

GETTING HERE AND AROUND

Hourly train service from London Paddington takes about two hours, 45 minutes; the cheaper Megatrain service takes 3 hours, 20 minutes and leaves London Waterloo four times daily. From London's Victoria Coach Station, National Express buses leave every two hours and Megabus has three daily departures, all taking around 4 hours, 30 minutes. Exeter is a major transportation hub for Devon. Trains from Bristol, Salisbury, and Plymouth stop at Exeter St. David's, and connect to the center by frequent buses. Some trains also stop at the more useful Exeter Central. The bus station is off Paris Street near the tourist office. Cars are unnecessary in town, so park yours as soon as possible—all the sights are within an easy walk.

TOURS Free 90-minute walking tours of Exeter by Red Coat Guided Tours take place daily all year, focusing on different aspects of the city. See ⊕ *www.exeter.gov.uk/guidedtours* for details, or contact the tourist office. You can also pick up a leaflet on self-guided walks from here.

ESSENTIALS

Visitor Information and Tours Exeter Visitor Information and Tickets ✉ *Dix's Field* ☎ *01392/665700* ⊕ *www.heartofdevon.com.* **Red Coat Guided Tours** ☎ *01392/265203* ⊕ *www.exeter.gov.uk/guidedtours.*

EXPLORING

TOP ATTRACTIONS

Fodor's Choice ★ **Cathedral of St. Peter.** At the heart of Exeter, the great Gothic cathedral was begun in 1275 and completed almost a century later. Its twin towers are even older survivors of an earlier Norman cathedral. Rising from a forest of ribbed columns, the nave's 300-foot stretch of unbroken Gothic vaulting is the longest in the world. Myriad statues, tombs, and memorial plaques adorn the interior. In the minstrels' gallery, high up on the left of the nave, stands a group of carved figures singing and playing musical instruments, including bagpipes. Outside in Cathedral Close, don't miss the 400-year-old door to No. 10, the bishop of Crediton's house, ornately carved with angels' and lions' heads. ⊠ *Cathedral Close* ☎ *01392/255573* ⊕ *www.exeter-cathedral.org.uk* ⊠ *£6* ⊗ *Mon.–Sat. 9–5, Sun. open for services only. Guided tours weekdays at 11, 12:30, and 2:30, Sat. at 11 and 12:30.*

OFF THE BEATEN PATH

Powderham Castle. Seat of the earls of Devon, this notable stately home 8 miles south of Exeter is famed for its staircase hall, a soaring fantasia of white stuccowork on a turquoise background, constructed in 1739–69. Other sumptuous rooms, adorned with family portraits by Sir Godfrey Kneller and Sir Joshua Reynolds, were used in the Merchant-Ivory film *Remains of the Day.* A tower built in 1400 by Sir Philip Courtenay, ancestor of the current owners, stands in the deer park. "Safari" rides (a tractor pulling a trailer) to see the 600-odd fallow deer depart daily at 1:45 (also at 2:45 and 4:15 in summer), and there are also falconry displays. The restaurant serves light lunches, and there's a children's play area, a farm shop, and a plant center. ⊠ *A379, Kenton* ☎ *01626/890243* ⊕ *www.powderham.co.uk* ⊠ *£11, deer park £2.50* ⊗ *Apr.–late July, Sept., and Oct., Sun.–Fri. 11–4:30; late July–Aug., daily 11–5:30.*

FAMILY

Fodor's Choice

★

Royal Albert Memorial Museum. This family-friendly museum is housed in a recently refurbished Victorian building. The centerpiece is the extensive Making History gallery, a giddy mix of objects imaginatively illustrating the city's history and covering everything from Roman pottery to memorabilia from World War II. The geology section is thrillingly enhanced by the latest video technology, and there are also excellent ethnography and archaeological collections, natural-history displays, and works by West Country artists. ⊠ *Queen St.* ☎ *01392/265858* ⊕ *www.rammuseum.org.uk* ⊠ *Free* ⊗ *Tues.–Sun. 10–5.*

WORTH NOTING

Custom House. Exeter's historic waterfront on the River Exe was the center of the city's medieval wool industry, and the Custom House, built in 1682, attests to the city's prosperity. Victorian warehouses flank the city's earliest surviving brick building. ⊠ *The Quay.*

Guildhall. On the city's main shopping street, this is said to be the oldest municipal building in the country still in use. The current hall, with its Renaissance portico, dates from 1330, although a guildhall has occupied this site since at least 1160. Its timber-braced roof, one of the earliest in England, dates from about 1460. ⊠ *High St.* ☎ *01392/665500* ⊠ *Free* ⊗ *Weekdays 10:30–1 and 2–4, Sat. 10–12:30.*

Quay House. This late-17th-century stone warehouse houses a visitor center where you can view documents on the city's maritime history and an audiovisual display. ⊠ *The Quay* ☎ *01392/271611* ⊠ *Free* ⊗ *Apr.–Oct., daily 10–5; Nov.–Mar., weekends 11–4.*

5

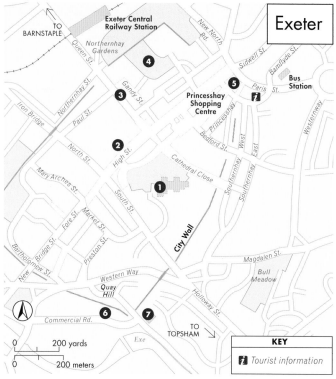

Exeter

KEY

Tourist information

0   200 yards

0   200 meters

QUICK BITES

The Prospect. At this pub you can contemplate the quayside comings and goings over a pint of real ale and a hot or cold meal. The nautical theme comes through in pictures and the ship's wheel hanging from the ceiling. ⊠ *The Quay* ☎ *01392/273152* ⊕ *www.heavitreebrewery.co.uk.*

Rougemont Gardens. These gardens behind the Royal Albert Memorial Museum were laid out at the end of the 18th century. The land was once part of the defensive ditch of Rougemont Castle, built in 1068 by decree of William the Conqueror. The gardens contain the original Norman gatehouse and the remains of the Roman city wall, the latter forming part of the ancient castle's outer wall. ⊠ *Off Queen St.*

FAMILY   **Underground Passages.** Exeter's Underground Passages, which once served as conduits for fresh water, are the only medieval vaulted passages open to the public in Britain. They date to the mid-14th century, although some were enlarged by the Victorians. An exhibition and video precede the 25-minute guided tour. Many of the passages are narrow and low: be prepared to stoop. The tours often sell out during school vacations, so come early. Children under five are not permitted in the tunnels. ⊠ *2 Paris St.* ☎ *01392/665887* ⊕ *www.exeter.gov.uk* ☎ *£5.60* ⊙ *June–Sept. and school vacations, Mon.–Sat. 9:30–5:30, Sun. 10:30–4; Oct.–May, Tues.–Fri. 11:30–5:30, Sat. 9:30–5:30, Sun. 11:30–4; last tours 1 hr before closing.*

WHERE TO EAT

$ ✕ **Ask.** This outpost of an Italian chain has secured an enviable site in

ITALIAN a part-medieval, part-Georgian building opposite the cathedral. The large windows in the three dining areas offer superb views across the Close, and the courtyard is perfect for warm days. Although the food is unadventurous and of varying quality, there are good antipasti and salads and a generous selection of pizzas and pastas. $ *Average main: £11* ✉ *5 Cathedral Close* ☎ *01392/427127* ⊕ *www.askitalian.co.uk.*

$ ✕ **Herbie's.** A mellow stop, this friendly vegetarian bistro with wood

VEGETARIAN floors and simple tables is ideal for unwinding over leisurely conversation. You can snack on pita bread with hummus and salad, or tackle the spicy vegetable satay or Greek vegetable pie. All the wines and the superb ice cream are organic. $ *Average main: £10* ✉ *15 North St.* ☎ *01392/258473* ⊙ *Closed Sun. No dinner Mon.*

$$$ ✕ **Michael Caines Restaurant.** Perfectly located within the Cathedral Close,

MODERN BRITISH this ultrachic restaurant is in the centuries-old building that is now the

Fodor'sChoice ABode Exeter. Master chef Michael Caines oversees the kitchen, which

★ serves eclectic contemporary fare like glazed Creedy Carver duck breast with a honey-rutabaga puree and orange confit, or Brixham sea bass with stir-fried shiitake mushrooms, bean sprouts, and lemongrass sauce. Fixed-price lunch and early evening menus are more affordable. Alternatively, a more relaxed (and more affordable) café-bar next door serves meals all day, including good fixed-price lunches, and hosts live jazz on alternate Friday evenings. $ *Average main: £24* ✉ *ABode Exeter, Cathedral Close* ☎ *01392/223638* ⊕ *www.michaelcaines.com* ⊙ *Closed Sun.*

$ ✕ **Ship Inn.** Here you can lift a tankard of stout in the very rooms where

BRITISH Sir Francis Drake and Sir Walter Raleigh enjoyed their ale. Drake, in fact, once wrote, "Next to mine own shippe, I do most love that old 'Shippe' in Exon." The pub dishes out casual bar fare, from curries to beef and ale pie, either in the bar or in the beamed and paneled upstairs restaurant. $ *Average main: £8* ✉ *St. Martin's La.* ☎ *01392/272040* ⊕ *www.gkpubs.co.uk.*

WHERE TO STAY

For expanded hotel reviews, visit Fodors.com.

$$ ⛉ **ABode Exeter.** Claimed to be the first inn in England to be described as

HOTEL a "hotel," the 1769 Royal Clarence (the old name still appears outside) has been transformed into a strikingly modern boutique hotel. **Pros:** superb central location; wonderful views from front; mixes old and new. **Cons:** some rooms are small and viewless; no parking. $ *Rooms from: £160* ✉ *Cathedral Close* ☎ *01392/319955* ⊕ *www.abodehotels. co.uk* ⌖ *53 rooms* ⫟⊙⫟ *No meals.*

$$$ ⛉ **Combe House.** Rolling parkland surrounds this luxurious Elizabethan

HOTEL manor house 16 miles east of Exeter. **Pros:** beautiful rural surroundings;

Fodor'sChoice romantic ambience; attentive but informal staff. **Cons:** rather remote;

★ decor a bit tired in places. $ *Rooms from: £215* ✉ *Off A30, Gittisham* ☎ *01404/540400* ⊕ *www.thishotel.com* ⌖ *13 rooms, 2 suites, 1 cottage* ⫟⊙⫟ *Breakfast.*

$$ ⛉ **The Magdalen Chapter.** This former hospital has been reimagined

HOTEL as a modish hotel with a zippy, happening vibe, and add-ons that include an indoor-outdoor pool, a fitness room, and spa treatments.

5

Pros: contemporary style; eager staff; health facilities. **Cons:** rooms on the small side; no parking. $ *Rooms from: £135* ✉ *Magdalen St., Exeter* ☎ *01392/281000* ⊕ *www.themagdalenchapter.com* ⤴ *59 rooms* ⦿ *Multiple meal plans.*

$

B&B/INN

🛏 **Raffles.** A 10-minute walk from the center, this quirky B&B in a quiet neighborhood makes an ideal base for a night or two in town. **Pros:** peaceful location; plenty of character; handy parking. **Cons:** not very central for sights; occasional noise from trains in front-facing rooms. $ *Rooms from: £78* ✉ *11 Blackall Rd.* ☎ *01392/270200* ⊕ *www. raffles-exeter.co.uk* ⤴ *6 rooms* ⦿ *Breakfast.*

$

HOTEL

🛏 **White Hart.** Guests have been welcomed to this inn since the 15th century, and it is said that Oliver Cromwell stabled his horses here. **Pros:** close to center; historic building; friendly service. **Cons:** can be noisy; tight parking. $ *Rooms from: £84* ✉ *66 South St.* ☎ *01392/279897* ⊕ *www.whitehartpubexeter.co.uk* ⤴ *55 rooms* ⦿ *Breakfast.*

NIGHTLIFE AND THE ARTS

Exeter Festival of South West Food and Drink. This festival, which showcases local producers, chefs, and their gastronomic specialties, takes place in Rougemont Gardens and Northernhay Gardens over three days in April or May. Live music is offered in the evenings. ⊕ *www. exeterfoodanddrinkfestival.co.uk.*

Northcott Theatre. Some of the country's most innovative companies stage plays at the Northcott Theatre. ✉ *Stocker Rd.* ☎ *01392/493493* ⊕ *www.exeternorthcott.co.uk.*

SHOPPING

Many of Exeter's most interesting shops are along Gandy Street, off the main High Street drag, with several good food and clothes outlets. Exeter was the silver-assay office for the West Country, and the earliest example of Exeter silver (now a museum piece) dates from 1218; Victorian pieces are still sold. The Exeter assay mark is three castles.

Bruford's of Exeter. This shop stocks antique jewelry and silver. ✉ *Guildhall Centre, Queen St.* ☎ *01392/254901* ⊕ *www.brufords.co.uk.*

SPORTS AND THE OUTDOORS

Saddles and Paddles. Renting bikes, kayaks, and canoes, this shop is handily placed for a 7-mile trip along the scenic Exeter Canal Trail, which follows the River Exe and the Exeter Ship Canal. ✉ *4 Kings Wharf* ☎ *01392/424241* ⊕ *www.sadpad.com.*

TOPSHAM

4 miles southeast of Exeter on B3182.

This small town, full of narrow streets and hidden courtyards, was once a bustling river port, and it remains rich in 18th-century houses and inns.

GETTING HERE AND AROUND

Frequent bus service connects Topsham with Exeter; the village is also a stop for twice-hourly trains running between Exmouth and Exeter. Topsham is best negotiated on foot.

EXPLORING

A la Ronde. The 16-sided, nearly circular A la Ronde was built in 1798 by two cousins inspired by the Church of San Vitale in Ravenna, Italy. Among the 18th- and 19th-century curiosities here is an elaborate display of feathers and shells. The house is 5 miles south of Topsham. ⊠ *Summer La.* ☎ *01395/265514* ⊕ *www.nationaltrust.org.uk* ⊡ *£7.50* ⊙ *Early Jan.–early Feb. and early Nov.–mid-Dec., weekends noon–4; mid-Feb.–early Nov., daily 11–5.*

Topsham Museum. Occupying a 17th-century Dutch-style merchant's house beside the river, this museum has period-furnished rooms and displays on local and maritime history. One room has memorabilia belonging to the late actress Vivien Leigh, who spent much time in the region. ⊠ *25 The Strand* ☎ *01392/873244* ⊡ *Free* ⊙ *Apr.–July, Sept., and Oct., Mon., Wed., Thurs., and weekends 2–5; Aug., Mon.–Thurs. and weekends 2–5.*

EN ROUTE The **Jurassic Coast** (⊕ *www.jurassiccoast.org*), from Exmouth to Studland Bay in Dorset, 95 miles to the east, has been designated a World Heritage Site because of the rich geological record of ancient rocks and fossils exposed here. The reddish, grass-topped cliffs of the region are punctuated by quiet seaside resorts such as Budleigh Salterton, Sidmouth, and Seaton. *For more information, see Chapter 4, The South.*

TORQUAY

26 miles south of Topsham, 23 miles south of Exeter.

The most important resort area in South Devon, Torquay envisions itself as the center of the "English Riviera." Since 1968 the towns of Paignton and Torquay (pronounced tor-*kee*) have been amalgamated under the common moniker of Torbay. Torquay is the supposed site of the hotel in the popular British television comedy *Fawlty Towers* and was the home of mystery writer Agatha Christie. Fans should check out the exhibit devoted to Christie at the town museum, and visit Greenway, her holiday home on the River Dart. Torquay's tourist office has leaflets outlining an Agatha Christie Trail that takes in all the Christie-related places in town.

The town has shed some of its old-fashioned image in recent years, with modern hotels, luxury villas, and apartments that climb the hillsides above the harbor. Still, Torquay is more like Brighton's maiden aunt in terms of energy and fizz, though a pubs-and-clubs culture makes an appearance on Friday and Saturday nights. Palm trees and other semitropical plants (a benefit of being near the warming Gulf Stream) flourish in the seafront gardens; the sea is a clear and intense blue.

GETTING HERE AND AROUND

Buses arrive near Torquay's harbor and the tourist office. The train station is close to Torre Abbey, but other points in town are best reached on local buses or by taxi. Drivers should take A38 and A380 from Exeter.

ESSENTIALS

Visitor Information Torquay Visitor Information Centre ⊠ *5 Vaughan Parade* ☎ *0844/474–2233* ⊕ *www.englishriviera.co.uk.*

EXPLORING

Cockington. Just a mile outside the heart of Torbay by bus or car lies this chocolate-box village with thatched cottages, a 14th-century forge, and the square-tower Church of St. George and St. Mary. Repair to the Old Mill for a café lunch or head to the Drum Inn, designed by Sir Edwin Lutyens to be an archetypal pub. On the village outskirts lies Cockington Court—a grand estate with crafts studios, shops, and an eatery. Cockington has, however, more than a touch of the faux: cottages that don't sell anything put up signs to this effect.

FAWLTY TOWERS

John Cleese was inspired to write the TV series *Fawlty Towers* after he and the Monty Python team stayed at a hotel in Torquay while filming the series *Monty Python's Flying Circus* in the early 1970s. The "wonderfully rude" owner became the model for Basil Fawlty, the exasperated, accident-prone manager in the series. The owner died in 1981, but his hotel, the Gleneagles, is still going strong—though happily nothing like the chaotic Fawlty Towers.

FAMILY Fodor's Choice ★ **Torre Abbey.** For lovers of fine things, Torquay's chief attraction is Torre Abbey, surrounded by parkland but close to the seafront. The abbey itself, founded in 1196, was razed in 1539, though you can still see traces of the old construction. The mansion that now occupies the site was the home of the Cary family for nearly 300 years, and it was later converted into a museum and art gallery. Artistic riches lie within the main building: marine paintings, Victorian sculptures, Pre-Raphaelite window designs, and drawings by William Blake. There are plenty of family-friendly activities, including brass-rubbing. ✉ *King's Dr.* ☎ *01803/293593* 🌐 *www.torre-abbey.org.uk* 🎟 *£7.50* 🕒 *Feb.–Nov., Wed.–Sun. 10–5; last admission at 4.*

WHERE TO EAT AND STAY

For expanded hotel reviews, visit Fodors.com.

$$ MODERN BRITISH 🍴 **The Elephant.** Set back from Torquay's harbor, this elegant eatery offers sophisticated but relaxed dining, either in the dining room upstairs with views over Torbay or in the less formal street-level brasserie. In the latter, you can tuck into such dishes as River Exe mussels, beef fillet with watercress salad and a brandy cream sauce, and treacle tart with vanilla ice cream. The upstairs dining room, with its high-back chairs, antique lighting fixtures, and polished floorboards, has more innovative concoctions, available on fixed-price menus, which may include scallops with pickled beets as a starter, and lamb and chicken roulade with smoked garlic, asparagus, and pea mousse for a main course. [$] *Average main: £18* ✉ *3–4 Beacon Terr.* ☎ *01803/200044* 🌐 *www.elephantrestaurant.co.uk* 🕒 *Closed Sun., Mon., and 2 wks early Jan.; upstairs restaurant closed Oct.–mid-Apr. No lunch in upstairs restaurant.*

$$ SEAFOOD Fodor's Choice ★ 🍴 **Number 7 Fish Bistro.** Seafood fans can indulge their passion at this unpretentious, convivial spot near the harbor; wood floors, white walls, and plenty of maritime knickknacks set the mood. Fresh, locally caught fish is brought to your table for inspection before being simply but imaginatively prepared. The extensive menu offers dishes ranging from humble—but abundant and beautifully cooked—fish-and-chips

to lobster and crab grilled with garlic and brandy. $ *Average main: £18* ⊠ *7 Beacon Terr.* ☎ *01803/295055* ⊕ *www.no7-fish.com* ⊜ *Reservations essential* ⊙ *Closed Sun. Oct.–June, Mon. Nov.–May. No lunch Sun.–Tues.*

$$
HOTEL

🏨 **The Imperial Hotel Torquay.** This enormous pile perched above the sea exudes slightly faded Victorian splendor. **Pros:** grand setting; great views; good online rates. **Cons:** renovation overdue; poor gym facilities; expensive parking. $ *Rooms from: £139* ⊠ *Park Hill Rd.* ☎ *01803/294301* ⊕ *www.pumahotels.co.uk* ⇌ *139 rooms, 13 suites* ⏐⊙⏐ *Breakfast.*

$$
B&B/INN

🏨 **Lanscombe House.** Located in the postcard-pretty village of Cockington, this family-run Victorian guesthouse offers spacious bedrooms with floral wallpaper and period furnishings, and a walled garden where you can try your hand at croquet. **Pros:** quiet atmosphere; traditional setting; pleasant garden. **Cons:** touristy environment; car necessary for local sights. $ *Rooms from: £120* ⊠ *Cockington La., Cockington* ☎ *01803/606938* ⊕ *www.lanscombehouse.co.uk* ⇌ *7 rooms* ⊙ *Closed mid-Oct.–Easter* ⏐⊙⏐ *Breakfast.*

SPORTS AND THE OUTDOORS

Torbay's beaches, a mixture of sand and coarse gravel, have won awards for their water quality and facilities, and can get crowded in summer. Apart from the central Torre Abbey Sands, they're mainly to the north of town, often separated by the crumbly red cliffs characteristic of the area. To sun and swim, head for Anstey's Cove, a favorite spot for scuba divers, with more beaches farther along at neighboring Babbacombe.

TOTNES

8 miles west of Torquay, 28 miles southwest of Exeter.

This busy market town on the banks of the River Dart preserves plenty of its medieval past, and on summer Tuesdays vendors dress in period costume for the Elizabethan Market. Market days are Friday and Saturday, when the town's status as a center of alternative medicine and culture becomes especially clear, and on the third Sunday of the month, when there's a local produce market on Civic Square. The historic buildings include a guildhall and St. Mary's Church.

GETTING HERE AND AROUND

Totnes is on a regular fast bus route between Plymouth and Torbay, and is a stop for main-line trains between Plymouth and Exeter. Buses pull into the center, and the train station is a few minutes' walk north of the center. Drivers should take A38 and A385 from Plymouth or A385 from Torbay.

ESSENTIALS

Visitor Information Totnes Tourist Information Centre ⊠ *The Town Mill, Coronation Rd.* ☎ *01803/863168* ⊕ *www.totnesinformation.co.uk.*

EXPLORING

Brixham. At the southern point of Tor Bay, Brixham has kept much of its original charm, partly because it still has an active fishing harbor. Much of the catch goes straight to restaurants as far away as London. Sample fish-and-chips on the quayside, where there's a (surprisingly petite) full-scale reproduction of the vessel on which Sir Francis Drake circumnavigated the world. The village is 10 miles southeast of Totnes by A385 and A3022. ✉ *Brixham.*

FAMILY **South Devon Railway.** Steam trains of this railway run through 7 miles of the wooded Dart Valley between Totnes and Buckfastleigh, on the edge of Dartmoor. Call about special trips around Christmas. ✉ *Dart Bridge Rd., Buckfastleigh* ☎ *0843/357–1420* 🌐 *www.southdevonrailway.co.uk* 🎫 *£12 round-trip* 🕒 *Mid-Mar.–Oct., daily; call for hours.*

Totnes Castle. You can climb up the hill in town to the ruins of this castle—a fine Norman motte and bailey design—for a wonderful view of Totnes and the River Dart. ✉ *Castle St.* ☎ *01803/864406* 🌐 *www.english-heritage.org.uk* 🎫 *£3.60* 🕒 *Apr.–Sept., daily 10–6; Oct., daily 10–5; Nov.–Mar., weekends 10–4.*

WHERE TO STAY

For expanded hotel reviews, visit Fodors.com.

$$ HOTEL 🏨 **Royal Seven Stars Hotel.** Conveniently located at the bottom of the main street, this centuries-old coaching inn has counted Daniel Defoe and Edward VII among its former guests. **Pros:** central location; friendly staff; spotless rooms. **Cons:** some accommodations are small; rooms over bars can be noisy; busy public areas. [$] *Rooms from: £119* ✉ *The Plains* ☎ *01803/862125* 🌐 *www.royalsevenstars.co.uk* 🛏 *16 rooms* 🍴 *Breakfast.*

NIGHTLIFE AND THE ARTS

Dartington Hall. One of the foremost arts centers of the West Country, Dartington Hall lies 2 miles northwest of Totnes. There are concerts, film screenings, and exhibitions. The gardens, free year-round, are the setting for outdoor performances of Shakespeare in summer. There's a café, and you can stay overnight in rooms in the hall. ✉ *Off A384 and A385, Dartington* ☎ *01803/847070* 🌐 *www.dartington.org/arts.*

SHOPPING

Shops at Dartington. Near Dartington Hall, 15 stores and two restaurants in and around an old cider press make up the Shops at Dartington. Open daily, it's a good place to find handmade Dartington crystal glassware, kitchenware, crafts, books, and toys. The farm shop sells fudge, ice cream, and cider, and Cranks is an excellent vegetarian restaurant. ✉ *Shinners Bridge, Dartington* ☎ *01803/847500* 🌐 *www.dartington.org/shops.*

DARTMOUTH

13 miles southeast of Totnes, 35 miles east of Plymouth, 35 miles south of Exeter, 5 miles southwest of Brixham.

An important port in the Middle Ages, Dartmouth is today a favorite haunt of yacht owners. Traces of its past include the old houses in Bayard's Cove at the bottom of Lower Street, where the Mayflower made a stop in 1620; the 16th-century covered Butterwalk, and the two castles guarding the entrance to the River Dart. The Royal Naval College, built in 1905, dominates the heights above the town. A few miles south of Dartmouth on Start Bay there are a number of pretty beaches including Blackpool Sands, popular with families.

GETTING HERE AND AROUND

Frequent buses connect Dartmouth with Plymouth and Totnes. Drivers coming from the west should follow A381 and A3122. Approaching from the Torbay area via A3022 and A379, you can save mileage by using the passenger and car ferries crossing the Dart. Travelers on foot can take advantage of a vintage steam train service operating between Paignton and Kingswear, where there are ferry connections with Dartmouth. River ferries also link Dartmouth with Totnes.

ESSENTIALS

Visitor Information Dartmouth Tourist Information Centre ⊠ *The Engine House, Mayors Ave.* ☎ *01803/834224* ⊕ *www.discoverdartmouth.com.*

EXPLORING

FAMILY **Dartmouth Steam Railway.** These lovingly restored trains chug along on tracks beside the River Dart between Paignton and Kingswear (across the river from Dartmouth). You can combine a train ride with a river excursion between Dartmouth and Totnes and a bus between Totnes and Paignton on a £23 Round Robin ticket. ⊠ *5 Lower St.* ☎ *01803/555872* ⊕ *www.dartmouthrailriver.co.uk* ⊠ *£11* ⊗ *Mid-Feb.–early Nov., call for departure times.*

Fodor's Choice **Greenway.** A rewarding way to experience the River Dart is to join
★ a cruise from Dartmouth's quay to visit Greenway, the 16th-century riverside home of the Gilbert family (Sir Humphrey Gilbert claimed Newfoundland on behalf of Elizabeth I), more famous today for its association with the crime writer Agatha Christie. Mrs. Mallowan (Christie's married name) made her holiday home beginning in 1938, and the house displays collections of archaeological finds, china, and silver. The gorgeous gardens are thickly planted with magnolias, camellias, and rare shrubs, and richly endowed with panoramic views. Beware, however, that the grounds are steeply laid out, and those arriving by boat face a daunting uphill climb. Allow three hours to see everything; timed tickets for the house are given on arrival. Parking spaces here are restricted and must be booked in advance. Alternatively, ask at the tourist office about walking and cycling routes to reach the house (non-car-users get discounted entry). ⊠ *Greenway Rd., Galmpton* ☎ *01803/842382* ⊕ *www.nationaltrust.org.uk* ⊠ *£9* ⊗ *Mid-Feb.–late July and mid-Sept.–early Nov., Wed.–Sun. 10:30–5; late July–mid-Sept., Tues.–Sun. 10:30–5.*

Greenway Cruises. A round-trip ticket between Dartmouth and Greenway costs £7.50 on Greenway Cruises. ☎ *01803/882811* ⊕ *www. greenwayferry.co.uk*

WHERE TO EAT AND STAY

For expanded hotel reviews, visit Fodors.com.

$$$ ✕ **The Seahorse.** In a prime riverside location, this seafood restaurant
SEAFOOD epitomizes the region's ongoing food revolution. The knowledgeable staff will guide you through the Italian-inspired menu, which primarily depends on the day's catch: look for scallops with garlic and

white port, grilled monkfish, and poached skate wing. The meat dishes are equally enticing, while the formidable desserts are well worth leaving space for. The owner, celebrity chef Mitch Tonks, also runs a much more relaxed fish-and-chips restaurant a few doors along called RockFish, open daily. [$] *Average main: £24* ✉ *5 S. Embankment* ☎ *01803/835147* 🌐 *www.seahorserestaurant.co.uk* 🕒 *Closed Mon. No dinner Sun., no lunch Tues.*

$$$ HOTEL 🏨 **Royal Castle Hotel.** This hotel has truly earned the name "Royal"—several monarchs have slept here. **Pros:** historical resonance; superb central location; superb breakfasts. **Cons:** some cheaper rooms are nondescript; no elevator. [$] *Rooms from: £170* ✉ *11 The Quay* ☎ *01803/833033* 🌐 *www.royalcastle.co.uk* 🛏 *25 rooms* 🍴 *Breakfast.*

THE THAMES
VALLEY

WELCOME TO
THE THAMES VALLEY

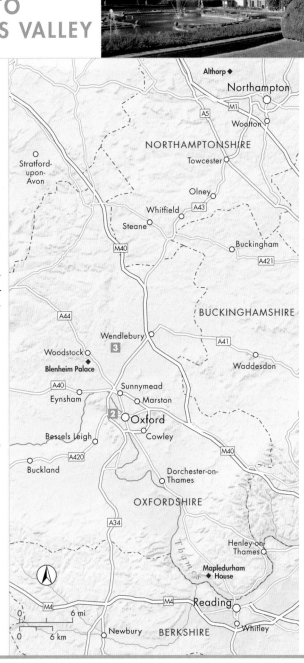

TOP REASONS
TO GO

★ **Blenheim Palace:**
The only British historic
home to be named a
World Heritage Site has
magnificent baroque
architecture, stunning parkland, and remembrances
of Winston Churchill.

★ **Boating on the Thames:**
Life is slower on the river,
and renting a boat or taking a cruise is an ideal way
to see verdant riverside pastures and villages. Windsor,
Marlow, Henley, and
Oxford are good options.

★ **Mapledurham
House:** This is the house
that inspired Toad Hall
from *The Wind in the
Willows;* you can picnic
here on the grounds and
drink in the views.

★ **Oxford:** While scholars'
noses are buried in their
books, you get to sightsee
among Oxford University's
ancient stone buildings
and memorable museums.

★ **Windsor Castle:**
The mystique of eight successive royal houses of the
British monarchy permeates
Windsor and its famous
castle, where a fraction
of the current Queen's
vast wealth is displayed.

1 **Windsor, Marlow, and Environs.** Gorgeous Windsor has its imposing and battlemented castle, stone cottages, and tea shops, and nearby Eton is also charming. The meadows and villages around Marlow and Henley are lovely in summer when the flowers are in bloom. Mapledurham House near Henley-on-Thames is an idyllic stop; you can take a boat here.

2 **Oxford.** Wonderfully walkable, this university town has one handsome, golden-stone building and museum after another to explore. Take a punt on the local waterways for a break. Oxford's good bars, pubs, and restaurants keep you going late at night as well.

3 **Oxfordshire and Environs.** So many grand manor houses, so little time: around the Thames Valley are many intriguing stops. Blenheim is a vast, ornate, extraordinary place that takes the better part of a day to see. Althorp, home of the late Princess Diana, seems almost small by comparison, although it's actually enormous.

GETTING ORIENTED

An ideal place to begin any exploration of the Thames Valley is the town of Windsor, about an hour's drive west of central London. From there you can follow the river to Marlow and to Henley-on-Thames, site of the famous regatta, and then make a counterclockwise sweep west to the area around Henley-on-Thames. To the north is Oxford, with its pubs, colleges, and museums; it can make a good base for exploring some of the area's charming towns and notable stately homes. If you're extending your itinerary, west of the region but nearby are both the Cotswolds and Stratford-upon-Avon.

6

BOATING ON THE THAMES

Whether you're drifting lazily along in your own boat or taking a sightseeing cruise past crucial points of English history, you'll see the River Thames from a new and delightful vantage point when you're out on the water.

(above) Views of tranquil countryside are one pleasure of boating on the Thames; (right, top) Riverside towns add interest; (right, bottom) Colorful boats in Henley

"There is nothing—absolutely nothing—half so much worth doing as simply messing about in boats." So says the Water Rat in Kenneth Grahame's timeless children's novel *The Wind in the Willows*. So take Ratty's advice: it's hard to beat gliding peacefully on the river, water meadows on either side of you, and then tying up for a picnic or lunch at a riverside pub. You can just putter about in a rowboat for an hour or so, or hire a boat and organize your own itinerary for a few days. If this doesn't appeal, go on a romantic lunch cruise or take one of the many organized trips. There are 125 miles of navigable water to explore, quieter nearer the source of the Thames in the Cotswolds, perhaps most picturesque between Pangbourne and Marlow, and busiest nearer London. Wherever you go, your pace of life will slow right down: boats aren't allowed to travel above 5 mph.

CHOOSE A BOAT

Most boats rented by the hour accommodate four people. Motorboats are noisy, but you can opt for electric canoes or launches that have the benefit of canopies. Punts (flat-bottom wooden boats) require a strong arm so you can maneuver the long wooden pole and push the boat along. Narrowboats carried freight on canals but are now well equipped for pleasure trips. For information, see ⊕ www.visitthames.co.uk.

MESS ABOUT ON THE RIVER

The main hubs for hiring self-drive boats on the Thames are at Windsor, Henley-on-Thames, Oxford, and Lechlade. The cost varies from £15 an hour for a rowboat, £25 for an electric boat, £60 for half a day with a punt, to £125 a day for a motor cruiser. A short trip for four on a narrowboat from Oxfordshire Narrowboats ranges from around £160 to £1,000.

Cotswold Boat Hire ⊠ *Faringdon Rd., Lechlade* ☎ *01793/727083* ⊕ *www.cotswoldboat.co.uk.*

Hobbs of Henley ⊠ *Station Rd., Henley-on-Thames* ☎ *01491/572035* ⊕ *www.hobbs-of-henley.com.*

John Logie Motorboats ⊠ *The Promenade, Barry Ave., Windsor* ☎ *07774/983809.*

Oxford River Cruises ⊠ *Folly Bridge, Oxford* ☎ *01865/269889* ⊕ *www.oxfordrivercruises.com.*

Oxfordshire Narrowboats ⊠ *Heyford Wharf, Station Rd., Lower Heyford* ☎ *01869/340348* ⊕ *www.oxfordshire-narrowboats.co.uk.*

PUSH THE BOAT OUT IN STYLE

Hire an Edwardian electric launch with your own skipper (£90 per hour) from the Compleat Angler in Marlow; take a vintage boat (from £140 per hour) or Champagne cruise (£47) from Cliveden; climb aboard the gleaming Victorian steam launch *Nuneham* for

summertime afternoon tea (£38) or lunch (£32.50) cruises from Windsor with the French Brothers.

Cliveden ⊠ *Off 404, near Maidenhaed, Taplow* ☎ *01628/668561* ⊕ *www.clivedenhouse.co.uk.*

Compleat Angler ⊠ *Marlow Bridge, Bisham Rd., Marlow* ☎ *0844/879–9128* ⊕ *www.macdonaldhotels.co.uk/compleatangler.*

French Brothers ⊠ *The Promenade, Barry Ave., Windsor* ☎ *01753/851900* ⊕ *www.boat-trips.co.uk.*

PICK AN ORGANIZED CRUISE

Windsor Castle, Runnymede, and Henley, where you can stop for the River and Rowing Museum, and Mapledurham all lie on the banks of the Thames. Thames River Cruise has outings to Mapledurham from Caversham on weekends. Salter's Steamers runs short round-trips out of Windsor, Henley, Oxford, and Marlow, and French Brothers *(see above)* offers round-trips from Windsor. Oxford River Cruises *(see above)* offers a one-hour cruise from Folly Bridge in Oxford and a longer trip (2½ hours) up to Godstow.

Salter's Steamers ⊠ *Folly Bridge, Oxford* ☎ *01865/243421* ⊕ *www.salterssteamers.co.uk.*

Thames River Cruise ⊠ *Bridge St., Reading* ☎ *0118/948–1088* ⊕ *www.thamesrivercruise.co.uk.*

Updated by
Kate Hughes

Easy proximity to London made the Thames Valley enormously popular with the rich and powerful throughout the country's history. They built the lavish country estates and castles, including Windsor, that form the area's most popular tourist attractions today. Some of these, as well as Oxford and its university, are easy day trips from London. Consider exploring this stretch of the River Thames by boat, either jumping aboard a cruiser or getting behind the oars. Windsor, Henley, and Marlow all make good starting points.

Once an aquatic highway connecting London to the rest of England and the world, the Thames was critical to the power of the city when the sun never set on the British Empire. By the 18th century the Thames was one of the world's busiest water systems, declining in commercial importance only when the 20th century brought other means of transportation to the forefront. Traditionally, the area west of London is known as the Thames Valley, and the area to the east is called the Thames Gateway.

Anyone who wants to understand the mystique of the British monarchy should visit Windsor, home to the medieval and massive Windsor Castle. Farther upstream, the green quadrangles and graceful spires of Oxford are the hallmarks of one of the world's most famous universities. Within 10 miles of Oxford the storybook village of Woodstock and gracious Blenheim Palace, one of the grandest houses in England, are both well worth your time.

The railroads and motorways carrying traffic to and from London have turned much of this area into commuter territory, but you can still find timeless villages and miles of relaxing countryside. The stretches of the Thames near Marlow, Henley, and Henley-on-Thames are lovely, with rowing clubs, piers, and sturdy waterside cottages and villas. It all conspires to make the Thames Valley a wonderful find, even for experienced travelers.

THAMES VALLEY PLANNER

WHEN TO GO

High summer is lovely, but droves of visitors have the same effect on some travelers as bad weather. Consider visiting in late spring or early fall, when the weather isn't too bad and the crowds have headed home. Book tickets and accommodations well in advance for Henley's Royal Regatta at the cusp of June and July and Ascot's Royal Meeting in mid-June. Visiting at Eton and the Oxford colleges is much more restricted during term time (generally September to late March and late April to mid-July). Most stately homes are open March through September or October only—call in advance if you're planning an itinerary. Avoid any driving in the London area during morning and afternoon rush hours.

PLANNING YOUR TIME

The major towns of the Thames Valley are easy to visit on a day trip from London. A train to Windsor, for example, takes about an hour, and you can fully explore Windsor and its environs in a day. Base yourself in Oxford for a couple of days, though, if you want to make a thorough exploration of the town and the surrounding countryside. To visit the great houses and the rural castles you'll need to either rent a car or join an organized tour. Blenheim Palace and Waddesdon Manor require at least half a day to do them justice, as do Stowe Landscape Gardens and Woburn Abbey.

GETTING HERE AND AROUND

BUS TRAVEL

Oxford and the area's main towns are convenient by bus from London, as is Windsor (although trains are faster), but St. Albans is best reached by train.

You can travel between the major towns by local bus, but it's complicated and can require changing more than once. For information, contact Traveline. If you want to see more than one town in this area in a day, it would be best to rent a car or join a tour.

Contacts Arriva ☎ *0871/200–2233* ⊕ *www.arrivabus.co.uk.* **First** ☎ *01344/782222* ⊕ *www.firstgroup.com.* **Megabus** ☎ *0871/266–3333 Inquiries, 0900/160–0900 booking line, calls cost 60p per minute* ⊕ *www.megabus.co.uk.* **Oxford Bus Company** ☎ *01865/785400* ⊕ *www.oxfordbus.co.uk.* **Reading Buses** ☎ *0118/959–4000* ⊕ *www.reading-buses.co.uk.* **Stagecoach Oxford Tube** ☎ *01865/772250* ⊕ *www.oxfordtube.com.* **Traveline** ☎ *0871/200–2233* ⊕ *www.traveline.org.uk.*

CAR TRAVEL

Most towns in this area are within a one- or two-hour drive of central London—except during rush hour, of course. Although the roads are good, this wealthy section of the commuter belt has heavy traffic, even on the secondary roads. Parking in towns can be a problem, so take advantage of public parking lots near the outskirts of town centers.

TRAIN TRAVEL

Trains to Oxford (one hour) and the region depart from London's Paddington Station. Trains bound for Ascot (50 minutes) leave from Waterloo every 30 minutes. Trains to St. Albans (20 minutes) leave from St. Pancras Station. A number of lines, including Chiltern and First Great Western, serve the area; National Rail Enquiries has information.

Contacts **National Rail Enquiries** ☎ *0845/748–4950* ⊕ *www.nationalrail.co.uk.*

RESTAURANTS

Londoners weekend here, and where they go, stellar restaurants follow. Bray (near Windsor), Marlow, and Great Milton (near Oxford) claim some excellent tables; you will need to book months ahead for these. Simple pub food, as well as classic French cuisine, can be enjoyed in waterside settings at many restaurants beside the Thames. Even in towns away from the river, well-heeled commuters and Oxford professors support top-flight establishments. Reservations are often not required but are strongly recommended, especially on weekends. *Prices in the reviews are the average cost of a main course at dinner or, if dinner isn't served, at lunch.*

HOTELS

From converted country houses to refurbished Elizabethan inns, the region's accommodations are rich in history and distinctive in appeal. Many hotels cultivate traditional gardens and retain a sense of the past with impressive collections of antiques. Book ahead, particularly in summer; you're competing for rooms with many Londoners in search of a getaway. *Prices in the reviews are the lowest cost of a standard double room in high season, including 20% V.A.T.*

VISITOR INFORMATION

Contacts **River Thames Alliance** ⊕ *www.visitthames.co.uk.*
Tourism Southeast ⊕ *www.visitsoutheastengland.com.*

WINDSOR, MARLOW, AND ENVIRONS

Windsor Castle is one of the jewels of the area known as Royal Windsor, but a journey around this section of the Thames has other classic pleasures. The town of Eton holds the eponymous private school, Ascot has its famous racecourse, and Cliveden is a stately home turned into a grand hotel.

The stretch of the Thames Valley from Marlow to Henley-on-Thames is enchanting. Walking through its fields and along its waterways, it's easy to see how it inspired Kenneth Grahame's classic 1908 children's book *The Wind in the Willows.* Whether by boat or on foot, you can discover some of the region's most delightful scenery. On each bank are fine wooded hills, with spacious homes, greenhouses, flower gardens, and neat lawns that stretch to the water's edge. Grahame wrote his book in Pangbourne, and his illustrator, E. H. Shepard, used the great house at Mapledurham as the model for Toad Hall. It all still has the power to inspire.

WINDSOR

21 miles west of London.

Only a small part of old Windsor—the settlement that grew up around the town's famous castle in the Middle Ages—has survived. The town isn't what it was in the time of Sir John Falstaff and the *Merry Wives of Windsor,* when it was famous for its convivial inns—in 1650, it had about 70 of them. Only a handful remain, with the others replaced, it seems, by endless cafés. Windsor can feel overrun by tourists in summer, but even so, romantics will appreciate cobbled Church Lane and noble Queen Charlotte Street, opposite the castle entrance.

GETTING HERE AND AROUND

Fast Green Line buses leave from the Colonnades opposite London's Victoria Coach Station every half hour for the 70-minute trip to Windsor. National Express and First Group have frequent services from Heathrow Airport's Terminal 5; the journey takes less than an hour. First Group also offers regional bus services to small towns and villages near Windsor.

Trains travel from London Waterloo every 30 minutes, or you can catch a more frequent train from Paddington and change at Slough. The trip takes less than an hour from Waterloo and around 30 minutes from Paddington. If you're driving, the M4 from London takes around an hour. Park in one of the public lots near the edge of the town center.

TOURS In summer, Orchard Poyle Carriage Rides offers 30-minute (£40) and one-hour (£80) horse-drawn carriage rides around the historic district. Tours leave from the Harte & Garter Hotel in central Windsor and tour the town and Windsor Great Park. City Sightseeing has hop-on, hop-off tours of Windsor and Eton, though it's easy to explore compact Windsor on foot; the price is £10.50.

TIMING

Windsor is at its best in winter and fall when it's not as crowded with tour groups. In summer it can be uncomfortably packed. Queen Elizabeth is in residence when her banner flies above the palace—everybody perks up a bit when that happens.

ESSENTIALS

Bus Contacts First Group ☎ 0175/352–4144 ⊕ www.firstgroup.com. **Green Line** ☎ 0844/801–7261 ⊕ www.greenline.co.uk. **National Express** ☎ 0871/781–8181 ⊕ www.nationalexpress.com.

Tour Information City Sightseeing ☎ 0780/871–3938 ⊕ www.city-sightseeing.com. **Orchard Poyle Carriage Rides** ☎ 0783/676–6027 ⊕ www.orchardpoyle.co.uk.

Visitor Information Royal Windsor Information Centre ✉ Old Booking Hall, Windsor Royal Station, Thames St. ☎ 01753/743900, 01753/743907 for accommodations ⊕ www.windsor.gov.uk.

EXPLORING

Fodor's Choice **Windsor Castle.** From William the Conqueror to Queen Victoria, the ★ kings and queens of England added towers and wings to this brooding, imposing castle, visible for miles and now the largest inhabited castle in the world. Despite the multiplicity of hands involved in its design,

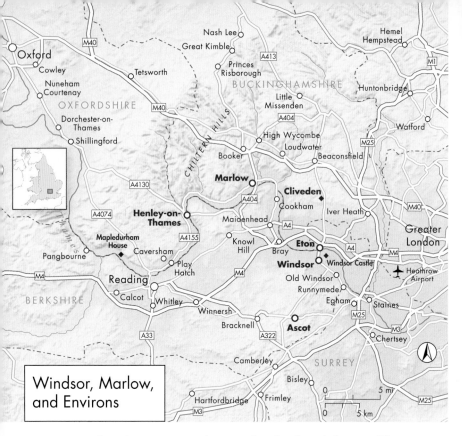

Windsor, Marlow,
and Environs

the palace manages to have a unity of style and character. The most
impressive view of Windsor Castle is from the A332 road, coming into
town from the south. Admission includes an audio guide and, if you
wish, a guided tour of the castle precincts. Entrance lines can be long in
season and you're likely to spend at least half a day here, so come early.

William the Conqueror began work on the castle in the 11th century,
and Edward III modified and extended it in the mid-1300s. One of
Edward's largest contributions was the enormous and distinctive **Round
Tower.** Later, between 1824 and 1837, George IV transformed the still
essentially medieval castle into the fortified royal palace you see today.
Most of England's kings and queens have demonstrated their undying
attachment to the castle, the only royal residence in continuous use by
the Royal Family since the Middle Ages.

As you enter the castle, **Henry VIII's gateway** leads uphill into the wide
castle precincts, where you're free to wander. Across from the entrance
is the exquisite **St. George's Chapel** (closed Sunday). Here lie 10 of the
kings of England, including Henry VI, Charles I, and Henry VIII (Jane
Seymour is the only one of his six wives buried here). One of the noblest
buildings in England, the chapel was built in the Perpendicular style
popular in the 15th and 16th centuries, with elegant stained-glass windows; a high, vaulted ceiling; and intricately carved choir stalls. The

colorful heraldic banners of the Knights of the Garter—the oldest British Order of Chivalry, founded by Edward III in 1348—hang in the choir. The ceremony in which the knights are installed as members of the order has been held here with much pageantry for more than five centuries.

The **North Terrace** provides especially good views across the Thames to Eton College, perhaps the most famous of Britain's exclusive "public" boys' schools. From the terrace, you enter the **State Apartments,** which are open to the public most days. On display to the left of the entrance to the State Apartments in Windsor Castle, **Queen Mary's Dolls' House** is a perfect miniature Georgian palace-within-a-palace, created in 1923. Electric lights glow, the doors all have tiny keys, and a miniature library holds Lilliputian-size books written especially for the young queen by famous authors of the 1920s. Five cars, including a Daimler and Rolls-Royce, stand at the ready.

Although a fire in 1992 gutted some of the State Apartments, hardly any works of art were lost. Phenomenal repair work brought to new life the **Grand Reception Room,** the **Green and Crimson Drawing Rooms,** and the **State and Octagonal Dining Rooms.** A green oak hammer-beam (a short horizontal roof beam that projects from the tops of walls for support) roof looms magnificently over the 600-year-old **St. George's Hall,** where the Queen gives state banquets. The State Apartments contain priceless furniture, including a magnificent Louis XVI bed and Gobelin tapestries; and paintings by Canaletto, Rubens, Van Dyck, Holbein, Dürer, and Brueghel. The tour's high points are the **Throne Room** and the **Waterloo Chamber,** where Sir Thomas Lawrence's portraits of Napoléon's victorious foes line the walls. You can also see arms and armor—look out for Henry VIII's ample suit. A visit between October and March also includes the Semi-State rooms, the private apartments of George IV, resplendent with gilded ceilings.

■ TIP➜ To see the castle come magnificently alive, check out the Changing of the Guard, which takes place daily at 11 am from April through July and on alternate days at 11 am from August through March. Confirm the exact schedule before traveling to Windsor. When the Queen is in town, the guard and a regimental band parade through town to the castle gate; when she's away, a drum-and-fife band takes over. ⊠ *Castle Hill* ☎ *020/7766–7304 tickets, 01753/831118 recorded information* ⊕ *www. royalcollection.org.uk* ⊒ *£17.75 for Precincts, State Apartments, Gallery, St. George's Chapel, and Queen Mary's Dolls' House; £9.70 when State Apartments are closed* ⊙ *Mar.–Oct., daily 9:45–5:15, last admission at 4; Nov.–Feb., daily 9:45–4:15, last admission at 3.*

QUICK BITES

Crooked House of Windsor. With two tiny rooms in a 300-year-old house, the Crooked House of Windsor is a traditional favorite for tea and plates of cakes and scones for £8.50. It's open daily until 5:30. ⊠ *51 High St.* ☎ *01753/857534* ⊕ *www.crooked-house.com.*

Windsor Great Park. The remains of an ancient royal hunting forest, this park stretches for some 5,000 acres south of Windsor Castle. Much of it is open to the public and can be seen by car or on foot, including its geographical focal points, the romantic **Long Walk,** a 3-mile-long path designed by Charles II to join castle and park, and **Virginia Water,** a 2-mile-long lake. **Valley Gardens** is particularly vibrant in April and May, when the dazzling multicolored azaleas are in full bloom. The park also contains one of Queen Victoria's most treasured residences, the sprawling white mansion called **Frogmore House.** It's only open for a few days in May and August. A spectacular visitor center offers a good introduction to the surrounding landscape. ✉ *Entrances on A329, A332, B383, and Wick La.* ☎ *01784/435544* 🌐 *www.theroyallandscape.co.uk* 🎟 *Free* 🕒 *Daily dawn–dusk.*

TIME FOR A CUPPA

This is a tea-and-scones town, so having some in one of Windsor's many charming tearooms simply feels right. After taking in the castle and wandering the town's winding medieval lanes, a nice "cuppa," as the locals call it, is just perfect.

Savill Garden. The main horticultural delight of Windsor Great Park, the exquisite Savill Garden is about 4 miles from Windsor Castle. The 35 acres of ornamental gardens contain an impressive display of 2,500 rose bushes and a tremendous diversity of trees and shrubs. The Savill Building, easily recognizable by its undulating roof in the shape of a leaf, holds a visitor center, restaurant, and terrace where you can dine overlooking the garden, as well as a large shopping area where there are plenty of gifts, cards, and original art work. ✉ *Wick Rd., Egham* ☎ *01784/435544* 🌐 *www.theroyallandscape.co.uk* 🎟 *£9 Mar.–Oct., £6.50 Nov.–Feb.* 🕒 *Mar.–Oct., daily 10–6; Nov.–Feb., daily 10–4:30; parking charge.*

Windsor and Royal Borough Museum. Local history is on display in this small museum—Bronze Age artifacts, Roman coins, and paintings of British monarchs, as well as dioramas of royal occasions. If you head upstairs to the Council Chamber you can see where the wedding of Prince Charles and the Duchess of Cornwall, and the civil partnership of Elton John and David Furnish took place. The museum was opened by Queen Elizabeth in 2011. ✉ *Guildhall, High St.* ☎ *01628/685686* 🌐 *www.rbwm.gov.uk/web/museum.htm* 🎟 *£2* 🕒 *Tues.–Sat. 10–4; Sun. noon–4.*

WHERE TO EAT

Bray, a tiny village 6 miles outside Windsor, is known for its restaurants more than anything else.

$$ MODERN BRITISH

🍴 **Bel and the Dragon.** Sit streetside and watch as village life streams by, or cozy up in the oak-beamed bar of this historic inn dating from the 11th century. Old meets new as inglenook fireplaces and stone walls are juxtaposed with colorfully painted chairs and paneling. The menu shows the same judicious mixture; served by a young and friendly staff, the creative dishes might include wild garlic and white onion soup, pink peppercorn squid with chili jam, roasted suckling pig or slow-cooked shoulder of lamb. Don't miss out on the delicious thyme and duck-fat roasted potatoes from the rotisserie. [$] *Average main: £17* ✉ *Thames St.* ☎ *01753/866056* 🌐 *www.belandthedragon-windsor.co.uk.*

$$$$
MODERN BRITISH
Fodor's Choice
★

✕ **Fat Duck.** One of the top restaurants in the country, and ranked by some reviewers among the best in the world, this extraordinary Bray establishment packs in fans of hypercreative, hyperexpensive cuisine. "Culinary alchemist" Heston Blumenthal is famed for bizarre taste combinations—scrambled-egg-and-bacon ice cream, for example—and the laboratory-like kitchen in which this advocate of molecular gastronomy creates his dishes. The 12 items on the tasting menu (£195) include such dishes as snail porridge, mock turtle soup, and salmon poached in a licorice gel. Like the food, the interior blends traditional and contemporary elements—modern art, exposed-brick walls, and ancient wooden beams. The place is discreet and so is the sign; look for the duck-inspired implements hanging outside. Reserve a table two months in advance. $ *Average main: £180* ✉ *High St., Bray-on-Thames* ☎ *01628/580333* ⊕ *www.fatduck.co.uk* ✍ *Reservations essential* ☽ *Closed Mon. and Sun.*

$$$
MODERN BRITISH

✕ **Hinds Head.** Fat Duck's esteemed chef Heston Blumenthal owns this traditional pub across the road, where he sells less extreme dishes at more reasonable prices. The atmosphere and dress code are relaxed, and the look of the place is historic, with exposed beams, polished wood-panel walls, and brick fireplaces. A brilliant modern take on traditional English cuisine, the menu includes tea-smoked salmon with soda bread as a starter, followed by lemon sole with samphire and pickled cucumber, or Hereford rib-eye steak with bone-marrow sauce and triple-cooked fries. There's also a menu for kids. $ *Average main: £23* ✉ *High St., Bray-on-Thames* ☎ *01628/626151* ⊕ *www.hindsheadbray. com* ☽ *No dinner Sun.*

$$
BRITISH

✕ **Two Brewers.** Locals congregate in a pair of low-ceiling rooms at this 17th-century establishment by the gates of Windsor Great Park. Those under 18 aren't allowed inside the pub (though they can be served at a few outdoor tables), but adults will find a suitable collection of wine, espresso, and local beer, plus an excellent menu with such dishes as sausages with mash and pea gravy, fish cakes, and a good selection of sandwiches. On Sundays the pub serves a traditional, hearty lunchtime roast. $ *Average main: £15* ✉ *34 Park St.* ☎ *01753/855426* ⊕ *www.twobrewerswindsor.co.uk* ✍ *Reservations essential* ☽ *No dinner Fri.–Sun.*

WHERE TO STAY

For expanded hotel reviews, visit Fodors.com.

$
B&B/INN

🛏 **Alma Lodge.** This friendly little bed-and-breakfast in an early-Victorian house retains some of the original features, including ornate ceilings and ornamental fireplaces. **Pros:** very welcoming; beautiful fireplaces. **Cons:** few frills; can be too quiet for some. $ *Rooms from: £95* ✉ *58 Alma Rd.* ☎ *01753/855620* ⊕ *www.almalodge.co.uk* ⇆ *4 rooms* ⦿ *Breakfast.*

$$
B&B/INN
FAMILY

🛏 **Langton House.** A former residence for representatives of the crown, this Victorian mansion on a quiet, leafy road is a 10-minute walk from Windsor Castle. **Pros:** soothing decor; family-friendly environment. **Cons:** not for those who prefer their privacy; a little out of town. $ *Rooms from: £110* ✉ *46 Alma Rd.* ☎ *01753/858299* ⊕ *www. langtonhouse.co.uk* ⇆ *5 rooms* ⦿ *Breakfast.*

6

No T-shirts here: at Eton College, students wear the school's traditional shirts, coats, and pinstripe pants.

$$ HOTEL **Mercure Windsor Castle Hotel.** You're treated to an exceptional view of Windsor Castle's changing of the guard ceremony from this former coaching inn, parts of which date back to the 16th century. **Pros:** excellent location; wonderful afternoon tea. **Cons:** older rooms are small; furniture is faux antique. *Rooms from: £140 ✉ 18 High St. ☎ 01753/252800 ⊕ www.mercure.com ⇒ 108 rooms, 4 suites ¶ Breakfast.*

$$ HOTEL **Oakley Court.** A romantic getaway on the Thames, this Victorian-era mansion stands on landscaped grounds 3 miles west of Windsor. **Pros:** stunning mansion; lots of pampering; friendly staff. **Cons:** most rooms in modern wings; river views cost more. *Rooms from: £150 ✉ Windsor Rd., Water Oakley ☎ 01753/609988 ⊕ www.oakleycourt.co.uk ⇒ 106 rooms, 12 suites ¶ Breakfast.*

$ B&B/INN **Rainworth House.** Ducks come knocking at the door of this country house with an expansive green lawn 2 miles from Windsor. **Pros:** peaceful setting; tennis court. **Cons:** out of town. *Rooms from: £98 ✉ Oakley Green Rd. ☎ 01753/856749 ⊕ www.rainworthhouse.com ⇒ 7 rooms ¶ Breakfast.*

$$$$ HOTEL Fodor's Choice ★ **Stoke Park.** On a 350-acre estate, Stoke Park's neoclassical grandeur can make Windsor Castle, visible in the distance, seem almost humble in comparison. **Pros:** luxurious rooms; sweeping grounds; wonderful for antiques lovers. **Cons:** not for those lukewarm about golf. *Rooms from: £265 ✉ Park Rd., Stoke Poges ☎ 01753/717171 ⊕ www.stokeparkclub.com ⇒ 77 rooms ¶ Breakfast.*

NIGHTLIFE AND THE ARTS

FAMILY **Firestation Arts Centre.** Windsor's former fire station has a whole new lease of life as a contemporary arts venue, offering films, theater, music, dance, and comedy, with plenty of events for kids. ⊠ *The Old Court, St. Leonard's Rd.* ☎ *01753/866865* ⊕ *www.firestationartscentre.com.*

Theatre Royal. Windsor's Theatre Royal, where productions have been staged since 1910, is one of Britain's leading provincial theaters. It puts on plays and musicals year-round, including a pantomime for five weeks around Christmas. ⊠ *Thames St.* ☎ *01753/853888* ⊕ *www. theatreroyalwindsor.co.uk.*

Windsor Festival. Concerts, poetry readings, and children's events highlight the two-week Windsor Festival, held over the last two weeks in September, with events occasionally taking place in the castle. A similar festival is held over a weekend in March. ☎ *01753/743585* ⊕ *www. windsorfestival.com.*

SHOPPING

Check out Peascod Street, opposite the castle, for a good selection of independent stores selling gifts, jewelry, toiletries, chocolates, and more.

Windsor Royal Station. In a Victorian-era train station, Windsor Royal Station is where you'll find Jaeger, Viyella, Hobbs and Whistles. ⊠ *5 Goswell Hill* ☎ *01753/797070.*

SPORTS AND THE OUTDOORS

John Logie Motorboats. From Easter to September, John Logie Motorboats rents motorboats and rowboats by the half hour and hour. ⊠ *Barry Ave.* ☎ *07774/983809.*

ETON

23 miles west of London.

Some observers may find it symbolic that almost opposite Windsor Castle—which embodies the continuity of the royal tradition—stands Eton, a school that for centuries has educated many leaders of the country. With High Street, its single main street, leading from the river to the famous school, the old-fashioned town of Eton is much quieter than Windsor.

GETTING HERE AND AROUND

Eton is linked to Windsor by a footbridge across the Thames. Most visitors barely notice passing from one to the other.

EXPLORING

Fodor's Choice **Eton College.** Signs warn drivers of "Boys Crossing" as you approach
★ the splendid Tudor-style buildings of Eton College, the distinguished boarding school for boys ages 13 through 18 that was founded in 1440 by King Henry VI. It's all terrifically photogenic, because during the college semester students still dress in pin-striped trousers, swallow-tailed coats, and stiff collars. Rivaling St. George's at Windsor in terms of size, the Gothic **Chapel** contains superb fifteenth-century grisaille wall paintings juxtaposed against modern stained glass by John Piper. Beyond the cloisters are the school's playing fields where, according to

the duke of Wellington, the Battle of Waterloo was really won, since so many of his officers had learned discipline and strategy during their school days. Among the country's prime ministers to be educated here is David Cameron. The **Museum of Eton Life** has displays on the school's history and vignettes of school life. ✉ *Brewhouse Yard, Eton, Berkshire* ☎ *01753/671177* 🌐 *www.etoncollege.com* 🎟 *£7.50* ⏲ *Guided tours at 2 and 3:15: mid-Mar.–mid-Apr. and July–early Sept., daily; mid-Apr.–June and mid-Sept.–early Oct., Wed. and Fri.–Sun.*

WHERE TO EAT AND STAY

For expanded hotel reviews, visit Fodors.com.

$$ MODERN BRITISH 🍴 **Gilbey's Eton.** Just over the bridge from Windsor, this restaurant at the center of Eton's Antiques Row serves a changing menu of imaginative fare, from quail, mushroom, and pistachio rillettes with pickled rhubarb to mustard crust lamb with black-eyed beans and shallots. The £19.50 lunch and early-dinner menu is a good deal. Well-priced wines, both French and from their own English vineyard are a specialty, as are the savories—think meat, fish, and vegetarian pâtés—and scrumptious cakes served with afternoon tea on weekends. The conservatory, with its colorful scattering of cushions, is a pleasant place to sit, as is the courtyard garden. [$] *Average main: £17* ✉ *82–83 High St., Eton, Berkshire* ☎ *01753/854921* 🌐 *www.gilbeygroup.com.*

$$ HOTEL 🏨 **Christopher Hotel.** This former coaching inn on the village's main shopping street has spacious rooms in the handsome main building as well as in the courtyard mews. **Pros:** a nice mix of modern and historic; good restaurant. **Cons:** steep stairs; courtyard rooms can be noisy. [$] *Rooms from: £150* ✉ *110 High St., Eton, Berkshire* ☎ *01753/852359* 🌐 *www.thechristopher.co.uk* 🛏 *34 rooms* 🍽 *Breakfast.*

SHOPPING

JaM. This shop has a lovely selection of ceramic and jewelry pieces by contemporary artists. ✉ *81 High St., Eton, Berkshire* ☎ *01753/622333* 🌐 *www.jam-eton.co.uk.*

ASCOT

8 miles southwest of Windsor, 28 miles southwest of London.

The posh town of Ascot (pronounced *as*-cut) has for centuries been famous for horse racing and for style. Queen Anne chose to have a racecourse here, and the first race meeting took place in 1711. The impressive show of millinery for which the Royal Meeting, or Royal Ascot, as it is also known, was immortalized in *My Fair Lady,* in which a hat with osprey feathers and black-and-white silk roses transformed Eliza Doolittle into a grand lady. Betting on the races at England's most prestigious course is as important as dressing up; it's all part of the fun.

GETTING HERE AND AROUND

If you're driving, leave M4 at Junction 6 and take A332. Trains from London leave Waterloo Station every half hour, and the journey takes 50 minutes. The racecourse is a seven-minute walk from the train station.

The horses at Royal Ascot are beautiful, and so is the formal attire of the memorably dressed spectators.

EXPLORING

Ascot Racecourse. The races run regularly throughout the year, and Royal Ascot takes place annually in mid-June. **TIP→ Tickets for Royal Ascot generally go on sale in November, so buy them well in advance.** Prices range from £12 for standing room on the heath to £73 for seats in the stands. Car parking costs £20. ✉ *A329* ☎ *0844/346–3000* 🌐 *www.ascot.co.uk*.

WHERE TO STAY

For expanded hotel reviews, visit Fodors.com.

$$$$ HOTEL Fodor's Choice ★ **Coworth Park.** Much imagination and thoughtful renovation has transformed this 18th-century mansion, set in 240 acres of parkland, into a playful and contemporary lodging. **Pros:** country-house atmosphere; attentive and friendly service; free activities for kids. **Cons:** bathrobes weigh you down. [$] *Rooms from: £305* ✉ *Blacknest Rd.* ☎ *01344/876600* 🌐 *www.coworthpark.com* 🛏 *55 rooms, 15 suites* 🍴 *Breakfast.*

CLIVEDEN

8 miles northwest of Windsor, 16 miles north of Ascot, 26 miles west of London.

This grand stately home, designed by Charles Barry, the architect of the Houses of Parliament, and the setting of the notorious Profumo affair in the 1960s, has spectacular gardens and sweeping views to the Thames.

GETTING HERE AND AROUND

If you're driving, take the M4 to the A4, where brown signs lead you to the entrance off the A4094.

EXPLORING

Cliveden. Described by Queen Victoria as a "bijou of taste," Cliveden is a magnificent country mansion that has for more than 300 years lived up to its Georgian heritage as a bastion of aesthetic delights. The house, set in 376 acres of gardens and parkland above the River Thames, was rebuilt for the duke of Sutherland by Sir Charles Barry in 1851; the Astors, who purchased it in 1893, made it famous. In the 1920s and 1930s the Cliveden Set met here at the strongly conservative (not to say fascist) salon presided over by Nancy Astor, an American who nevertheless was the first woman to sit in Parliament. The public can visit the spectacular gardens and woodland that run down to bluffs overlooking the Thames, as well as the Octagon Temple and ground-floor rooms in the house. Book your timed ticket for the house beforehand or early on the day. Boat hire and trips are available daily in July and August. ⊠ *Cliveden Rd.* ⊹ *Near Maidenhead* 🕾 *01628/605069, 01494/755562 recorded information* ⊕ *www.nationaltrust.org.uk* 🖃 *Garden and woodland £8.60, house £1.50* ☉ *Grounds mid-Feb.–Oct., daily 10–5.30; Nov. and Dec., daily 10–4. House Apr.–Oct., Thurs. and Sun. 3–5:30. Last admission 30 mins before closing.*

WHERE TO STAY

For expanded hotel reviews, visit Fodors.com.

$$$$
HOTEL
Fodor's Choice
★

Cliveden. If you've ever wondered what it would feel like to be an Edwardian grandee, then sweep up the drive to this stately home, one of Britain's grandest hotels. **Pros:** like stepping back in time; outstanding sense of luxury; beautiful grounds. **Cons:** airplanes fly overhead; no tea- or coffee-making facilities in rooms. 🖫 *Rooms from: £265* ⊠ *Cliveden Rd.* 🕾 *01628/668561* ⊕ *www.clivedenhouse.co.uk* ⟿ *22 rooms, 16 suites, 1 cottage* |❂| *Breakfast.*

OUTDOORS

Cliveden Boathouse. Here you can rent two vintage boats and a vintage electric canoe that ply the Thames. The 45-minute champagne sunset cruise (most days April through September at 5 and 6) is the most affordable at £47 per person. ⊠ *Cliveden, Cliveden Rd.* 🕾 *01628/668561.*

MARLOW

7 miles west of Cliveden, 15 miles northwest of Windsor.

Just inside the Buckinghamshire border, Marlow and the surrounding area overflow with Thames-side prettiness. The unusual suspension bridge was built in the 1830s by William Tierney Clark, architect of the bridge in Hungary linking Buda and Pest. Marlow has a number of striking old buildings, particularly the privately owned Georgian houses along Peter and West streets. In 1817 the Romantic poet Percy Bysshe Shelley stayed with friends at 67 West Street and then bought **Albion House** on the same street. His second wife, Mary, completed her Gothic novel *Frankenstein* here. Ornate **Marlow Place,** on Station Road, dating from 1721, is reputedly the finest building.

Marlow hosts its own one-day regatta in mid-June. The town is a good base from which to join the **Thames Path** to Henley-on-Thames. On summer weekends tourism can often overwhelm the town.

GETTING HERE AND AROUND

Trains leave London from Paddington every half hour and involve a change at Maidenhead; the journey takes an hour. By car, leave M4 at Junction 8/9, following A404 and then A4155. From M40, join A404 at Junction 4.

ESSENTIALS

Visitor Information **Marlow Tourist Information Centre** ✉ *55a High St.* ☎ *01628/483597* 🌐 *www.visitbuckingamshire.org.*

6

EXPLORING

Swan-Upping. This traditional event, which dates back 800 years, takes place in Marlow during the third week of July. By bizarre ancient laws, the Queen owns the country's swans, so each year swan-markers in skiffs start from Sunbury-on-Thames, catching the new cygnets and marking their beaks to establish ownership. The Queen's Swan Marker, dressed in scarlet livery, presides over this colorful ceremony. ☎ *01628/523030.*

WHERE TO EAT AND STAY

For expanded hotel reviews, visit Fodors.com.

$$$$ FRENCH 🍴 **Vanilla Pod.** Discreet and intimate, this restaurant is a showcase for the French-inspired cuisine of chef Michael Macdonald, who, as the name implies, holds vanilla in high esteem. The fixed-price menu includes smoked salmon in Bourbon vanilla, and you can sample Tahitian vanilla both in the desserts of rice pudding with spiced plums and bitter chocolate soup with spiced bread. The three-course lunch menu is a fantastic bargain at £19.50, and the seven-course *menu gourmand* for £55 is a tour de force. Vegetarians have a separate menu. [$] *Average main: £45* ✉ *31 West St.* ☎ *01628/898101* 🌐 *www.thevanillapod.co.uk* ✍ *Reservations essential* 🕒 *Closed Sun. and Mon.*

$$$ HOTEL 🏨 **Macdonald Compleat Angler.** Although fishing aficionados consider this luxurious 17th-century Thames-side inn the ideal place to stay, the place is stylish enough to attract those with no interest in casting a line. **Pros:** gorgeous rooms; great views of the Thames. **Cons:** river views cost more except Rooms 9 and 10; need a car to get around. [$] *Rooms from: £170* ✉ *Marlow Bridge, Bisham Rd.* ☎ *0844/879–9128* 🌐 *www.macdonaldhotels.co.uk/compleatangler* 🛏 *61 rooms, 3 suites* 🍽 *Breakfast.*

HENLEY-ON-THAMES

7 miles southwest of Marlow, 8 miles north of Reading, 36 miles west of central London.

Fodor's Choice
★

Henley's fame is based on one thing: rowing. The Henley Royal Regatta, held at the cusp of June and July on a long, straight stretch of the River Thames, has made the little riverside town famous throughout the world. Townspeople launched the Henley Regatta in 1839, initiating the Grand Challenge Cup, the most famous of its many trophies. The best amateur oarsmen from around the globe compete in crews of eight, four, or two, or as single scullers. For many spectators, the event is on par with Royal Ascot and Wimbledon.

The town is set in a broad valley between gentle hillsides. Henley's historic buildings, including half-timber Georgian cottages and inns (as well as one of Britain's oldest theaters, the Kenton), are all within a few minutes' walk. The river near Henley is alive with boats of every shape and size, from luxury cabin cruisers to tiny rowboats.

GETTING HERE AND AROUND

Frequent First Great Western trains depart for Henley from London Paddington; journey time is around an hour. If you're driving from London or from the west, leave M4 at Junction 8/9 and follow A404(M) and then A4130 to Henley Bridge. From Marlow, Henley is a 7-mile drive southwest on A4155.

ESSENTIALS

Visitor Information Henley Visitor Information Centre ✉ *Henley Town Hall, Market Pl.* ☎ *01491/578034* ⊕ *www.henley-on-thames.org.*

EXPLORING

Mapledurham House. This section of the Thames inspired Kenneth Grahame's 1908 *The Wind in the Willows*, which began as a bedtime story for Grahame's son Alastair while the family lived at Pangbourne. Some of E.F. Shepard's illustrations are of specific sites along the river—none more fabled than this redbrick Elizabethan mansion, bristling with tall chimneys, mullioned windows, and battlements. It became the inspiration for Shepard's vision of Toad Hall. Family portraits, magnificent oak staircases, wood paneling, and plasterwork ceilings abound. Look out for the lifesize deer guarding the fireplace in the entrance hall. There's also a 15th-century working grain mill on the river. The house is 10 miles southwest of Henley-on-Thames. ✉ *Off A074, Mapledurham* ☎ *0118/972–3350* ⊕ *www.mapledurham.co.uk* 🎫 *House and mill £8.50; grounds £1* ☉ *Easter–Sept., weekends and national holidays Mon. 2–5:30; Oct., Sun. 2–5:30; last admission 30 mins before closing.*

Thames River Cruise. On summer weekends you can reach Mapledurham House by boat from Caversham Promenade in Reading. Departures are at 2 pm, and travel time is 45 minutes. ☎ *0118/948–1088* ⊕ *www.thamesrivercruise.co.uk*

FAMILY **River & Rowing Museum.** Focusing on the history and sport of rowing, this absorbing museum includes exhibits devoted to actual vessels, from a Saxon log boat to an elegant Victorian steam launch. One gallery tells the story of the Thames as it flows from its source to the ocean, while

The rowing competitions at the Henley Royal Regatta draw spectators all along the river.

another explores the history of the town and its famed regatta. A *Wind in the Willows* exhibit evokes the settings of the famous children's book. ✉ *Mill Meadows* ☎ *01491/415600* ⊕ *www.rrm.co.uk* 🎫 *£8* ⊗ *May–Aug., daily 10–5:30; Sept.–Apr., daily 10–5.*

St. Mary's Church. With a 16th-century "checkerboard" tower, St. Mary's is a stone's throw from the bridge over the Thames. The adjacent, yellow-washed **Chantry House,** built in 1420, is one of England's few remaining merchant houses from the period. It's an unspoiled example of the rare timber-frame design, with upper floors jutting out. You can enjoy tea here on Sunday afternoons in summer. ✉ *Hart St.* ☎ *01491/577340* ⊕ *www.stmaryshenley.org.uk* 🎫 *Free* ⊗ *Church daily 9–5.*

WHERE TO EAT AND STAY

For expanded hotel reviews, visit Fodors.com.

$$
MODERN BRITISH
✕ **Crooked Billet.** It's worth negotiating the maze of lanes leading to this cozy 17th-century country pub 6 miles west of Henley-on-Thames. You could choose English rose veal chop with rosemary cream and manchego croquette, or saddle of rabbit baked in pancetta with young carrots. British cheeses and filling desserts round off the meal. There's a garden for open-air dining and live music on many evenings. Fixed-price lunches are a good deal. The restaurant is popular, so book ahead. 💲 *Average main: £18* ✉ *Newlands La., Stoke Row* ☎ *01491/681048* ⊕ *www.thecrookedbillet.co.uk.*

$
B&B/INN
🏠 **Falaise House.** The rooms in this B&B, a Georgian town house in the center of Henley, are individually furnished in a soft and warm contemporary style that mixes traditional and modern pieces. **Pros:** family-run; great breakfasts; fluffy towels. **Cons:** on the main road;

two-night minimum on summer weekends. [$] *Rooms from: £95* ✉ *37 Market Pl.* ☎ *01491/573388* ⊕ *www.falaisehouse.com* ⟿ *6 rooms* ⏐⊙⏐ *Breakfast.*

$$ ⌂ **Hotel du Vin.** A sprawling brick
HOTEL brewery near the river has been transformed into a distinctively modern architectural showplace. **Pros:** striking decor; lovely river views from upper floors; good for oenophiles. **Cons:** won't thrill traditionalists; a charge for parking. [$] *Rooms from: £120* ✉ *New St.* ☎ *01491/848400* ⟿ *41 rooms, 2 suites* ⏐⊙⏐ *Breakfast.*

NIGHTLIFE AND THE ARTS

Henley Festival. A floating stage and spectacular musical events from classical to folk draw a dress-code-abiding crowd to the upscale Henley Festival during the week after the regatta in July. Book ahead. ☎ *01491/843404* ⊕ *www.henley-festival.co.uk.*

SPORTS AND THE OUTDOORS

Henley Royal Regatta. A series of rowing competitions attracting participants from many countries, the annual Henley Royal Regatta takes place over five days in late June and early July. Large tents are erected along both sides of a straight stretch of the river known as Henley Reach, and every surrounding field becomes a parking lot. There's plenty of space on the public towpath from which to watch the early stages of the races. ▮ TIP➔ **If you want to attend, book a room months in advance.** After all, 500,000 people turn out for the event. ☎ *01491/571900* ⊕ *www.hrr.co.uk.*

OXFORD

FodorsChoice With arguably the most famous university in the world, Oxford has
★ been a center of learning since 1167, with only the Sorbonne preceding it. It doesn't take more than a day or two to explore its winding medieval streets, photograph its ivy-covered stone buildings and ancient churches and libraries, and even take a punt down one of its placid waterways. The town center is compact and walkable, and at its heart is Oxford University. Alumni of this prestigious institution include 48 Nobel Prize winners, 26 British prime ministers (including David Cameron), and 28 foreign presidents (including Bill Clinton), along with poets, authors, and artists such as Percy Bysshe Shelley, Oscar Wilde, and W. H. Auden.

> ### WALK THE CHILTERNS
>
> Part of the Chiltern Hills is an **Area of Outstanding Beauty** (⊕ *www.chilternsaonb.org*), a nature reserve that stretches over 320 square miles, taking in chalk hills, valleys, forests, lakes, and pretty towns. Its springtime bluebell woods are famed, and its autumn colors are glorious. The distinctive chestnut-color birds soaring above you will be red kites. You'll likely drive in and out of the Chilterns as you explore, or you could walk part of the circular 134-mile Chiltern Way. An easy 5-mile circular walk starts from Henley and takes in the picturesque Hambleden Valley.

Oxford is 55 miles northwest of London, at the junction of the rivers Thames and Cherwell. The city is more interesting and more cosmopolitan than Cambridge, and although it's also bigger, its suburbs aren't remotely interesting to visitors. The interest is all at the center, where the old town curls around the grand stone buildings, good restaurants, and historic pubs. Victorian writer Matthew Arnold described Oxford's "dreaming spires," a phrase that has become famous. Students rush past you on the sidewalks on the way to their exams, clad with marvelous antiquarian style in their requisite mortar caps, flowing dark gowns, stiff collars, and crisp white bow ties. ■ TIP➔ **Watch your back when crossing roads, as bikes are everywhere.**

GETTING HERE AND AROUND

Megabus, Oxford Bus Company, and Stagecoach Oxford Tube all have buses traveling from London 24 hours a day; the trip takes between 1 hour 40 minutes and 2 hours. In London, Megabus and Oxford Bus Company depart from Victoria Coach Station, and Stagecoach Oxford Tube has pickup points opposite Victoria Coach Station and the Marble Arch underground station. Oxford Bus Company also offers round-trip shuttle service from Gatwick (£32) every hour and Heathrow (£29) every half hour. Most of the companies have multiple stops in Oxford, with Gloucester Green, the final stop, being the most convenient for most travelers. You can easily traverse the town center on foot, but the Oxford Bus Company offers a one-day ticket (£4) for unlimited travel in and around Oxford.

Trains to Oxford depart from London's Paddington Station for the one-hour trip. Oxford Station is just at the western edge of the historic town center on Botley Road.

To drive, take the M40 northwest from London. It's an hour's drive, except during rush hour, when it can take twice as long. In-town parking is notoriously difficult, so use one of the five free park-and-ride lots and pay for the bus to the city. The Thornhill Park and Ride and the St. Clement's parking lot before the roundabout that leads to Magdalen Bridge are convenient for the M40.

TOURS The Oxford Tourist Information Centre has information on the many guided walking tours of the city. The best way of gaining access to the collegiate buildings is to take the two-hour university and city tour, which leaves the Tourist Information Centre daily at 11 and 2. City Sightseeing offers hop-on, hop-off bus tours (£13.50) with 19 stops around Oxford; your ticket, purchased from the driver, is good for 24 hours.

TIMING

You can explore major sights in town in a day or so, but it takes more than a day to spend an hour in each of the key museums and absorb the scene at the colleges. Some colleges are open only in the afternoons during university terms. When the undergraduates are in residence, access is often restricted to the chapels, dining rooms, and libraries, too, and you're requested to refrain from picnicking in the quadrangles. All are closed certain days during exams, usually from mid-April to late June.

6

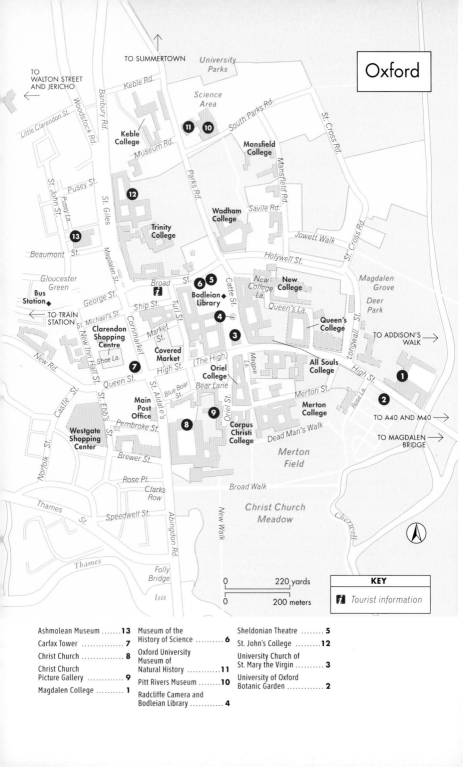

Oxford

TO SUMMERTOWN
University Parks
TO WALTON STREET AND JERICHO
Little Clarendon St.
Woodstock Rd.
Banbury Rd.
Keble Rd.
Science Area
South Parks Rd.
St. Cross Rd.
Keble College
Museum Rd.
11 **10**
Mansfield College
Mansfield Rd.
St. Giles
Pusey St.
St. John St.
Pusey La.
Parks Rd.
Wadham College
Savile Rd.
Jowett Walk
St. Cross Rd.
12
Trinity College
13
Beaumont St.
Magdalen St.
Holywell St.
Magdalen Grove
Gloucester Green
Broad St.
New College La.
New College
Deer Park
Bus Station
George St.
Ship St.
Turl St.
Catte St.
Queen's La.
TO TRAIN STATION
St. Michael's St.
Cornmarket
Broad St.
Bodleian Library
6 **5**
4
Queen's College
TO ADDISON'S WALK
Clarendon Shopping Centre
Market St.
3
All Souls College
Longwall St.
High St.
Rose La.
New Rd.
New Inn Hall St.
Shoe La.
Covered Market
High St.
(The High)
Oriel College
Magpie La.
Bear Lane
Merton St.
1
7
Queen St.
St. Aldate's
Blue Boar St.
Oriel St.
9
Merton College
2
TO A40 AND M40
Castle St.
St. Ebb's St.
Main Post Office
8
Corpus Christi College
Dead Man's Walk
TO MAGDALEN BRIDGE
Westgate Shopping Center
Pembroke St.
Brewer St.
Merton Field
Norfolk St.
Rose Pl.
Clarks Row
Broad Walk
Cherwell
Thames St.
Speedwell St.
Abingdon Rd.
New Walk
Christ Church Meadow
Thames
Folly Bridge
Isis

0 — 220 yards
0 — 200 meters

KEY
ℹ Tourist information

ESSENTIALS

Bus Contacts **Megabus** ☎ 0871/266–3333 Inquiry line, 0960/160–900 booking line, calls cost 60p per minute ⊕ www.megabus.com. **Oxford Bus Company** ☎ 01865/785400 ⊕ www.oxfordbus.co.uk. **Stagecoach Oxford Tube** ☎ 01865/772250 ⊕ www.oxfordtube.com.

Visitor and Tour Information City Sightseeing ☎ 01865/790522 ⊕ www.citysightseeingoxford.com. **Oxford Tourist Information Centre** ✉ 15/16 Broad St. ☎ 01865/252200 ⊕ www.visitoxfordandoxfordshire.com.

EXPLORING

Oxford University isn't one easily identifiable campus, but a sprawling mixture of 38 colleges scattered around the city center, each with its own distinctive identity and focus. Oxford students live and study at their own college, and also use the centralized resources of the overarching university. The individual colleges are deeply competitive. Most of the grounds and magnificent dining halls and chapels are open to visitors, though the opening times (displayed at the entrance gates) vary greatly.

The **city center** of Oxford is bordered by High Street, St. Giles, and Longwall Street. Most of Oxford University's most famous buildings are within this area. **Jericho,** the neighborhood where many students live, is west of St. Giles, just outside the city center. Its narrow streets are lined with lovely cottages. The area north of the center around Banbury and Marston Ferry Roads is called **Summertown,** and the area east of the center, along St. Clement's Street, is known as **St. Clement's.**

TOP ATTRACTIONS

Fodor's Choice ★ **Ashmolean Museum.** Britain's oldest public museum displays its rich and varied collections from the Neolithic to the present day over five floors. Innovative and spacious galleries on the theme of "Crossing Cultures, Crossing Time" explore connections between the priceless Egyptian, Greek, Roman, Chinese, and Indian artifacts, and also display a superb art collection. Among the highlights are drawings by Raphael, the shell-encrusted mantle of Powhatan (father of Pocahontas), the lantern belonging to Guy Fawkes, and the Alfred Jewel. This ancient piece features a large semiprecious stone set in gold carved with the words "*Aelfred mec heht gewyrcan*," which translates from old English as "Alfred ordered me to be made." The piece dates from the reign of King Alfred the Great (ruled 871–899). ■ TIP→ There's too much to see in one visit, but the free admission makes return trips easy. The Ashmolean Dining Room, Oxford's first rooftop restaurant, is a good spot for refreshments. ✉ *Beaumont St.* ☎ *01865/278002* ⊕ *www.ashmolean. org* ✏ *Free* ☉ *Tues.–Sun. and national holidays 10–6.*

Christ Church. Built in 1546, the college of Christ Church is referred to by its members as "The House." This is the site of Oxford's largest quadrangle, Tom Quad, named after the huge bell (6¼ tons) that hangs in the Christopher Wren–designed gate tower and rings 101 times at five past nine every evening in honor of the original number of Christ Church scholars. The vaulted, 800-year-old chapel in one corner has been Oxford's cathedral since the time of Henry VIII. The college's medieval dining hall, re-created for the Harry Potter films, contains portraits of many famous alumni, including 13 of Britain's prime ministers. ■ TIP→ Plan carefully, as the dining hall is only open weekdays 10:30–11:40 and 2:30–4:30 and weekends 2:30–4:30. Lewis Carroll, author of *Alice in Wonderland,* was a teacher of mathematics here for many years; a shop opposite the meadows on St. Aldate's sells Alice paraphernalia. ✉ *St. Aldate's* 🕾 *01865/276492* ⊕ *www.chch.ox.ac.uk* 🎫 *£8; £8.50 in July and Aug.* ⊙ *Mon.–Sat. 10–5, Sun. 2–5; last admission 30 mins before closing.*

Christ Church Picture Gallery. This connoisseur's delight in Canterbury Quadrangle exhibits works by the Italian masters as well as Hals, Rubens, and Van Dyck. Drawings in the 2,000-strong collection are shown on a changing basis. ✉ *Oriel Sq.* 🕾 *01865/276172* ⊕ *www.chch. ox.ac.uk* 🎫 *£3* ⊙ *June, Mon. and Wed.–Sat. 10:30–5, Sun. 2–5; July– Sept., Mon.–Sat. 10:30–5, Sun. 2–5; Oct.–May, Mon. and Wed.–Sat. 10:30–1 and 2–4:30, Sun. 2–4:30.*

Fodor'sChoice
★
Magdalen College. Founded in 1458, with a handsome main quadrangle and a supremely monastic air, Magdalen (pronounced *maud*-lin) is one of the most impressive of Oxford's colleges and attracts its most artistic students. Alumni include such diverse people as P.G. Wodehouse, Oscar Wilde, and John Betjeman. The school's large, square tower is a famous local landmark. ■ TIP→ To enhance your visit, take a stroll around the Deer Park and along Addison's Walk; then have tea in the Old Kitchen, which overlooks the river. ✉ *High St.* 🕾 *01865/276000* ⊕ *www.magd. ox.ac.uk* 🎫 *£5* ⊙ *July–Sept., daily noon–7 or dusk; Oct.–June, daily 1–6 or dusk.*

FAMILY
Oxford University Museum of Natural History. This highly decorative Victorian Gothic creation of cast iron and glass, more a cathedral than a museum, is worth a visit for its architecture alone. Among the eclectic collections of entomology, geology, mineralogy, and zoology are the towering skeleton of a *Tyrannosaurus rex* and casts of a dodo's foot and head. There's plenty for children to explore and touch. ✉ *Parks Rd.* 🕾 *01865/272950* ⊕ *www.oum.ox.ac.uk* 🎫 *Free* ⊙ *Daily 10–5.*

FAMILY
Fodor'sChoice
★
Pitt Rivers Museum. More than half a million intriguing archaeological and anthropological items from around the globe, based on the collection bequeathed by Lieutenant-General Augustus Henry Lane Fox Pitt Rivers in 1884, are crammed into a multitude of glass cases and drawers. Items are organized thematically rather than geographically, an eccentric approach that's surprisingly thought-provoking. Labels are handwritten, and children are given flashlights to explore the farthest corners and spot the world's smallest dolly. Give yourself plenty of time to wander through the displays of shrunken heads, Hawaiian

feather cloaks, and fearsome masks. Children will have a field day. ✉ *S. Parks Rd.* ☎ *01865/270927* ⊕ *www.prm.ox.ac.uk* ✍ *Free, suggested donation £3* ⊘ *Mon. 10–4:30, Tues.–Sun. and national holidays noon–4:30.*

Radcliffe Camera and Bodleian Library. A vast library, the domed Radcliffe Camera is Oxford's most spectacular building, built in 1737–49 by James Gibbs in Italian baroque style. It's usually surrounded by tourists with cameras trained at its golden-stone walls. The Camera contains part of the Bodleian Library's enormous collection, begun in 1602. Much like the Library of Congress in the United States, the Bodleian contains a copy of every book printed in Great Britain and grows by 5,000 items a week. Tours reveal the magnificent Duke Humfrey's Library, which was the original chained library and completed in 1488. (The ancient tomes are dusted once a decade.) Guides will show you the spots used for Hogwarts School in the Harry Potter films. ■ TIP→ **Arrive early to secure tickets for the three to six daily tours. These are sold on a first-come, first-served basis (except for the extended tour on Wednesday and Saturday, which can be prebooked).** Audio tours, the only tours open to kids under 11, don't require reservations. Call ahead to confirm tour times. ✉ *Broad St.* ☎ *01865/277216* ⊕ *www.bodleian.ox.ac.uk* ✍ *Audio tour £2.50, minitour £5, standard tour £7, extended tour £13* ⊘ *Bodleian and Divinity School weekdays 9–5, Sat. 9–4:30, Sun. 11–5.*

Sheldonian Theatre. This fabulously ornate theater is where Oxford's impressive graduation ceremonies are held, conducted almost entirely in Latin. Dating to 1663, it was the first building designed by Sir Christopher Wren when he served as professor of astronomy. The D-shape auditorium has pillars, balconies, and an elaborately painted ceiling. The stone pillars outside are topped by 18 massive stone heads. Climb the stairs to the cupola for the best view of the city's "dreaming spires." ✉ *Broad St.* ☎ *01865/277299* ⊕ *www.sheldon.ox.ac.uk* ✍ *£2.50* ⊘ *Mon.–Sat. 10–1 and 2–4:30. Closed for 10 days at Christmas and Easter.*

St. John's College. One of Oxford's most attractive campuses, St. John's has seven quiet quadrangles surrounded by elaborately carved buildings. You enter the first through a low wooden door. This college dates to 1555, when Sir Thomas White, a merchant, founded it. His heart is buried in the chapel (by tradition, students curse as they walk over it). The Canterbury Quad represented the first example of Italian Renaissance architecture in Oxford, and the Front Quad includes the buildings of the old St. Bernard's Monastery. ✉ *St. Giles* ☎ *01865/277300* ⊕ *www.sjc.ox.ac.uk* ✍ *Free* ⊘ *Daily 1–5.*

QUICK
BITES

Eagle and Child. Close to St. John's College, this pub is a favorite not only for its good ales (try the local Old Hooky) and sense of history, but also for its literary associations. From the 1930s to the 1960s this was the meeting place of C.S. Lewis, J.R.R. Tolkien, and their circle of literary friends who called themselves the "Inklings." ✉ *49 St. Giles* ☎ *01865/302925.*

6

WORTH NOTING

Carfax Tower. Passing through Carfax, the center of Oxford and where four roads meet, you can spot this tower. It's all that remains of **St. Martin's Church,** where Shakespeare stood as godfather for William Davenant, who himself became a playwright. Every 15 minutes, little mechanical "quarter boys" mark the passage of time on the tower front. ■TIP→ Climb up the 99 steps of the dark stairwell for a good view of the town center. ⊠ *Queen St. and Cornmarket* ☏ *01865/792653* ☏ *£2.30* ⊙ *Apr.–Sept., daily 10–5:30; Oct.–Mar., daily 10–dusk.*

Museum of the History of Science. The Ashmolean, the world's oldest public museum, was originally housed in this 1683 building, which now holds scientific and mathematical instruments, from astrolabes to quadrants. Here you'll find Lewis Carroll's camera box and the chalkboard Einstein used in a lecture on the theory of relativity. There are guided tours on Thursday (2:15 and 3) and Saturday (11:15 and noon). ⊠ *Broad St.* ☏ *01865/277280* ⊕ *www.mhs.ox.ac.uk* ☏ *Free; suggested donation £2* ⊙ *Tues.–Fri. noon–5, Sat. 10–5, Sun. 2–5.*

Rousham Park House and Garden. About 15 miles north of Oxford and wonderfully uncommercialized, Rousham has an expansive 18th-century English landscape park as well as the austere, gray Dormer family mansion, built in 1635. The design of gardener William Kent (1685–1748) is preserved almost unaltered in the groves, ponds, cascades and monuments, and the walled garden. Longhorn cattle, with fearsome bull, add an exotic touch to the English landscape. The house is only open to groups that book in advance, but the remarkable gardens are open all year. ■TIP→ There's no food, so bring a picnic and plenty of water. Children under 15 are not allowed, nor are dogs. ⊠ *Off B4030, Rousham* ✛ *Near Steeple Aston* ☏ *01869/347110* ⊕ *www.rousham.org* ☏ *£5* ⊙ *Gardens daily 10–4:30.*

University Church of St. Mary the Virgin. Seven hundred years' worth of funeral monuments crowd this galleried and spacious church, including the tombstone, on the altar steps, of Amy Robsart, the wife of Robert Dudley, Elizabeth I's favorite. One pillar marks the site of Thomas Cranmer's trial under Queen Mary for his marital machinations on behalf of Henry VIII. ■TIP→ The top of the 14th-century tower has a panoramic view of the city's skyline. It's worth the 127 steps. The Vaults and Garden Café, a part of the church accessible from Radcliffe Square, serves breakfasts and cream teas as well as good lunches. ⊠ *High St.* ☏ *01865/279111* ⊕ *www.university-church.ox.ac.uk* ☏ *Church free, tower £3* ⊙ *Mon.–Sat. 9–5, Sun. noon–5; last admission 30 mins before closing.*

University of Oxford Botanic Garden. Founded in 1621 as a healing garden, this is the oldest of its kind in the British Isles. Set on the river, the diverse garden displays 6,000 species ranging from lilies to citrus trees. There is a spacious walled garden, six luxuriant glass houses, including an insectiverous and a lily house, and interesting medicinal, rock and bog gardens to explore. ⊠ *Rose La.* ☏ *01865/286690* ⊕ *www.botanic-garden.ox.ac.uk* ☏ *£4.50* ⊙ *Mar., Apr., Sept., and Oct., daily 9–5; May–Aug., daily 9–6; Nov.–Feb., daily 9–4; last admission 45 mins before closing.*

OFF THE BEATEN PATH

Vale of the White Horse. Stretching up into the foothills of the Berkshire Downs between Swindon and Oxford is a wide fertile plain known as the Vale of the White Horse. Here, off B4507, cut into the turf of the hillside to expose the underlying chalk, is the 374-foot-long, 110-foot-high **figure of a white horse,** an important prehistoric site. Some historians believed that the figure might have been carved to commemorate King Alfred's victory over the Danes in 871, whereas others date it to the Iron Age, around 750 BC. More current research suggests that it's at least 1,000 years older, created at the beginning of the second millennium BC. **Uffington Castle,** above the horse, is a prehistoric fort. English Heritage maintains these sites. To reach the Vale of the White Horse from Oxford (about 20 miles), follow A420, then B4508 to the village of Uffington.

WHERE TO EAT

The city's pubs offer more options for a quick bite.

$$ FRENCH 🍴 **Brasserie Blanc.** Raymond Blanc's sophisticated brasserie in the Jericho neighborhood, a hipper cousin of Le Manoir aux Quat' Saisons in Great Milton, is one of the best places to eat in Oxford. Wood floors, pale walls, and large windows keep the restaurant open and airy. The changing menu always lists innovative, visually stunning adaptations of bourgeois French fare, sometimes with Mediterranean or Asian influences. Try the pasta with Jervaulx blue cheese, chestnut, and apple or the chicken stuffed with Armagnac-soaked prunes. There's a good selection of steaks as well. The £11.50 fixed-price lunch is a good value, and kids have their own menu. [$] *Average main: £15* ✉ *71–72 Walton St.* ☎ *01865/510999* 🌐 *www.brasserieblanc.com.*

$$ SEAFOOD 🍴 **Fishers.** Everything is remarkably fresh at what is widely viewed as the city's best fish restaurant. Seafood is prepared with a European touch and frequently comes with butter, cream, and other sauces: bream is served with fennel and black olive butter, for instance. Hot and cold shellfish platters are popular, as are the mussels on white wine and oysters in shallot vinegar. The interior has a casual nautical theme with wooden floors and tables, porthole windows, and red sails overhead. Lunches are a very good value. [$] *Average main: £16* ✉ *36–37 St. Clement's St.* ☎ *01865/243003* 🌐 *www.fishers-restaurant.com.*

$$ MODERN BRITISH 🍴 **Gee's.** With its glass-and-steel framework, this former florist's shop just north of the town center makes a charming plant-filled conservatory dining room. The menu concentrates on the best of Oxfordshire produce. You could start with small bites of cured wild boar and salt cod fritters and continue with such dishes as prosciutto and wild garlic pizzetta, bream with fennel and tapenade from the wood-fired oven, or pork, venison, and lamb chops from the charcoal grill. Chocolate and espresso tart and blood orange sorbet make fine desserts. [$] *Average main: £16* ✉ *61 Banbury Rd.* ☎ *01865/553540* 🌐 *www.gees-restaurant.co.uk.*

$ CAFÉ 🍴 **Grand Café.** Golden-hue tiles, towering columns, and antique marble tables make this café both architecturally impressive and an excellent spot for sandwiches, salads, or other light fare. It's packed with tourists and the service can be slow, but this is still a pretty spot for afternoon

6

tea. From Thursday through Saturday night, it transforms into a popular cocktail bar. $ *Average main: £8* ⊠ *84 High St.* ☎ *01865/204463* ⊕ *www.thegrandcafe.co.uk.*

$$
ITALIAN
⤬ **Jamie's Italian.** Freshly made pasta, multicolor gourds, and abundant hams hanging from the ceiling set the tone of this buzzing eatery. Chef Jamie Oliver's mission is to re-create the best rustic Italian fare, as shown in a diverting range of antipasti and mains such as tuna fusilli slow-cooked with tomatoes and cinnamon, and steak tagliata with crunchy fennel and garlic. The various dishes servied on a wood plank are a steal, desserts are light and refreshing—tutti frutti lemon meringue pie and fruit sorbets, for example—and the lively crowd appreciates it all. $ *Average main: £15* ⊠ *24–26 George St.* ☎ *01865/838383* ⊕ *www.jamieoliver.com.*

$$$$
FRENCH
Fodor's Choice
★
⤬ **Le Manoir aux Quat' Saisons.** Standards are high at this 15th-century stone manor house, a hotel with a cooking school and one of the country's finest kitchens. Chef Raymond Blanc's epicurean touch shows at every turn. Decide from among such innovative French creations as terrine of baby beetroot with horseradish sorbet or roasted duck breast with caramelized chicory, clementines, and jasmin tea sauce. You can dine à la carte, but if money is no object you might like to try one of the fixed-price menus ranging from £134 to £154; the five-course set-price lunch at £79 is easier on the wallet. There is a separate vegetarian menu, too. You need to book up to three months ahead in summer. A stroll through the hotel's herb and Japanese tea gardens is de rigueur. The pretty town of Great Milton is 7 miles southeast of Oxford. $ *Average main: £50* ⊠ *Church Rd., Great Milton* ☎ *01844/278881* ⊕ *www. manoir.com* ⌁ *Reservations essential.*

$
BRITISH
⤬ **Trout Inn.** More than a century ago, Lewis Carroll took three children on a Thames picnic. "We rowed up to Godstow, and had tea beside a haystack," he told a friend at Christ Church; "I told them the fairy tale of Alice's adventures in Wonderland." The haystacks are gone, but you can stop at the creeper-covered pub 2 miles north of the city center. Expect stone-baked pizzas, fresh pastas, steaks and salads, and a range of daily specials. This place is at the heart of the tourist trail and can get crowded; service may falter. $ *Average main: £14* ⊠ *195 Godstow Rd., Wolvercote* ☎ *01865/510930* ⊕ *www.thetroutoxford.co.uk.*

WHERE TO STAY

Oxford is pricey; for the cheapest lodging, contact the tourist information center for bed-and-breakfasts in locals' homes.

For expanded hotel reviews, visit Fodors.com.

$
B&B/INN
Brown's Guest House. At the southern edge of central Oxford, this redbrick Victorian house is a good bet in a town that has precious few affordable guesthouses. **Pros:** comfortable rooms; friendly owners. **Cons:** a long walk to the center; single rooms lack private bathroom. $ *Rooms from: £85* ⊠ *281 Iffley Rd.* ☎ *01865/246822* ⊕ *www. brownsguesthouse.co.uk* ⤙ *11 rooms, 7 with bath* ⊚ *Breakfast.*

$
B&B/INN
Burlington House. This Victorian guesthouse in Summertown, on the outskirts of Oxford, shows flair in its decoration, creativity in its breakfasts, and attentive, helpful service. **Pros:** friendly staff; superior

breakfasts; double-glazed windows throughout. **Cons:** 10-minute bus ride to the center; main road location. $ *Rooms from: £94* ⊠ *374 Banbury Rd.* ☎ *01865/513513* ⊕ *www.burlington-hotel-oxford.co.uk* ⟳ *12 rooms* ⦿ *Breakfast.*

$$$$
HOTEL
Fodor's Choice
★
🏨 **Le Manoir aux Quat'Saisons.** One of the original gastronomy-focused hotels, Le Manoir was opened in 1984 by chef Raymond Blanc, whose culinary talents have earned the hotel's restaurant two Michelin stars—which it has held for an incredible 29 years and running. **Pros:** one of the top Michelin-starred restaurants in Britain; attentive service; decor is plush, but not stuffy; perfect for romance, but also accommodates kids; famous on-site cooking school. **Cons:** every room is different, so if you have specific requirements, let them know when booking; tough on the wallet and waistline. $ *Rooms from: £545* ⊠ *Church Road, Great Milton, Oxford, England* ☎ *44/(01844) 278 881* ⊕ *www.manoir.com* ⟳ *32 rooms* ⦿ *Breakfast.*

$$$
HOTEL
🏨 **Macdonald Randolph.** A 19th-century neo-Gothic landmark, this hotel is ideally situated near the Ashmolean Museum. **Pros:** handy location; grand building. **Cons:** on a busy street; some small bathrooms; formality can be a bit daunting. $ *Rooms from: £200* ⊠ *Beaumont St.* ☎ *0844/879–9132* ⊕ *www.macdonaldhotels.co.uk/randolph* ⟳ *151 rooms* ⦿ *Breakfast.*

$$$
HOTEL
🏨 **Malmaison Oxford Castle.** Housed in what was a 19th-century prison, this high-concept boutique hotel remains true to its unusual history by showing off the original metal doors and exposed-brick walls. **Pros:** modern luxury; historic building; great bar and restaurant. **Cons:** prison life isn't for everyone; expensive parking. $ *Rooms from: £210* ⊠ *3 Oxford Castle* ☎ *01865/268400* ⊕ *www.malmaison.com* ⟳ *86 rooms, 8 suites* ⦿ *Breakfast.*

$
B&B/INN
🏨 **Newton House.** This handsome Victorian mansion, a five-minute walk from all of Oxford's action, is a sprawling, friendly place on three floors. **Pros:** great breakfasts; handy parking lot. **Cons:** on a main road; no elevator. $ *Rooms from: £90* ⊠ *82 Abingdon Rd.* ☎ *01865/240561* ⊕ *www.oxfordcity.co.uk/accom/newton* ⟳ *14 rooms, 13 with bath* ⦿ *Breakfast.*

$$$
HOTEL
🏨 **Old Bank Hotel.** From the impressive collection of modern artwork throughout the hotel to the sleek furnishings in the guest rooms, this stately converted bank building offers contemporary style in a city that favors the traditional. **Pros:** excellent location; interesting artwork at every turn. **Cons:** standard rooms can be small; breakfast costs extra. $ *Rooms from: £220* ⊠ *91–94 High St.* ☎ *01865/799599* ⊕ *www.oldbank-hotel.co.uk* ⟳ *42 rooms* ⦿ *Breakfast.*

$$$
HOTEL
🏨 **Old Parsonage.** A 17th-century gabled stone house in a small garden next to St. Giles Church. **Pros:** interesting building; complimentary walking tours. **Cons:** pricey given what's on offer; some guest rooms on small side. $ *Rooms from: £220* ⊠ *1 Banbury Rd.* ☎ *01865/310210* ⊕ *www.oldparsonage-hotel.co.uk* ⟳ *26 rooms, 4 suites* ⦿ *Breakfast.*

$$
HOTEL
🏨 **Royal Oxford Hotel.** This efficiently run hotel, a few steps from the train station, has bright, light, and modern rooms with simple contemporary furniture. **Pros:** comfortable rooms; good for travelers. **Cons:** not many amenities. $ *Rooms from: £150* ⊠ *17 Park End St.* ☎ *01865/248432* ⊕ *www.royaloxfordhotel.co.uk* ⟳ *26 rooms* ⦿ *Breakfast.*

$ B&B/INN 🏨 **Tilbury Lodge.** What this modern house on the city's western outskirts lacks in history it makes up for in hospitality; the homemade tea and scones that greet you on arrival set just the right tone. **Pros:** quiet location; free Wi-Fi; well-appointed bathrooms. **Cons:** away from the attractions; not good for families with young kids. [$] *Rooms from: £98* ✉ *5 Tilbury La., Botley* ☎ *01865/862138* 🌐 *www.tilburylodge.com* 🛏 *9 rooms* 🍴 *Breakfast.*

A LITTLE NIGHT MUSIC

Choral music. Choral music at the city's churches is a calming way to spend the early evening. Drop by weekdays during term time at 6 pm at Magdalen (except Monday), New College (except Wednesday), or Christ Church to hear evensong.

NIGHTLIFE AND THE ARTS

NIGHTLIFE AND PUBS

Nightlife in Oxford centers around student life, which in turn focuses on the local pubs, though you may find a few surprises, too. The popular Jericho area, around Walton Street north of the old city walls and within walking distance of the center of town, has good restaurants and pubs.

Head of the River. Near Folly Bridge, the terrace at the Head of the River is the perfect place to watch life on the water. You can also enjoy a pint in the clubby interior. ✉ *St. Aldate's* ☎ *01865/721600.*

Kings Arms. The capacious Kings Arms, popular with students and fairly quiet during the day, carries excellent local brews as well as inexpensive pub grub. ✉ *40 Holywell St.* ☎ *01865/242369.*

Raoul's. This trendy cocktail bar is located in the equally trendy Jericho neighborhood. ✉ *32 Walton St.* ☎ *01865/553732.*

Turf Tavern. Off Holywell Street, the Turf Tavern has a higgledy-piggledy collection of little rooms and outdoor spaces where you can enjoy a quiet drink and inexpensive pub food. ✉ *Bath Pl.* ☎ *01865/243235.*

White Horse. The cozy White Horse, one of the city's oldest pubs, serves real ales and traditional food all day. ✉ *52 Broad St.* ☎ *01865/728318.*

THE ARTS

CONCERTS **Music at Oxford.** This acclaimed series of weekend classical concerts takes place October through June in such esteemed venues as Christ Church Cathedral and the Sheldonian Theatre. ☎ *01865/244806 Box Office* 🌐 *www.musicatoxford.com.*

Oxford Coffee Concerts. This program of Sunday-morning chamber concerts, string quartets, piano trios, and soloists presents baroque and classical pieces in a 1748 hall. ✉ *Holywell Music Room, Holywell Rd.* ☎ *0751/847–9062* 🌐 *www.coffeeconcerts.co.uk.*

FESTIVALS Fodor's Choice ★ **Oxford Literary Festival.** The festival takes place during the last week of March at Christ Church College and other university venues. Leading authors come to give lectures and interviews. ✉ *Christ Church College, St. Aldate's* ☎ *0870/343–1001* 🌐 *oxfordliteraryfestival.org.*

Continued on page 412

SEE YOU AT THE PUB

Pubs have been called "England's living rooms": more than just a bar or a place to drink, they are gathering places, conversation zones. A trip to a pub ranks high on most visitors' list of things to do, and that's not surprising: in many ways, pubs *are* England. You simply haven't experienced the country properly until you've been to one.

Pubs started appearing in the late 15th century, when whole communities would gather at the pub to meet and swap news. The very name—pub is short for "public house"—sums up their role. As towns grew into cities, the humble pub came to be seen as an antidote to the anonymity of modern life. "The local," as Brits call it, is a place to relax and socialize. It's not all about drinking. Pubs can be good places for lunch as well, and during the day they're often family environments, before giving way to a lively, adults-only crowd at night.

Despite all this, the pub industry faces changing times and tastes, and competition from modern entertainment. In 2013 pubs were closing at the rate of around 14 per week. Although the adage about English town centers having a pub on every corner still just about rings true, times are tough—but still, the pub endures.

—by Jack Jewers

(Top) People gather outside the Market Porter pub at Borough Market in London, (bottom) Discovery Blonde Beer, Fuller's

CHOOSING A PUB

Pubs vary enormously, and that's a wonderful thing: in cities you may find splendid Victorian survivors; in the country there are Tudor pubs with atmospheric wood beams and warm fires. Or perhaps a simple pub with a sincere welcome is all you need.

To find a pub, ask the locals: everyone knows the good ones. Otherwise, if a pub looks attractive and well kept, check it out. Telltale signs that it's probably not the best include banners advertising lagers and "2-for-1" deals, or TV sports channels. Some basic definitions are useful:

A **freehouse** is a pub that is not tied to a single brewery, which means it can sell as many varieties of beer and wine as it likes. **Chain pubs** affiliated with particular breweries are middle-of-the-road, inexpensive franchises that serve decent food and drink. Bass, Wetherspoons, Courage, Whitbread, and Young's are chains; you will see their names on the pub's sign. The **gastropub** serves very high-quality food, but a pub with good food isn't necessarily a gastropub: the name implies culinary aspirations, and some expense. Another useful term is **"the local,"** shorthand for a favorite pub in your town. Everybody has a "local"— but the term is also used generally to refer to any pub that's good for cozy, convivial conversation.

CAN I TAKE MY KIDS TO THE PUB?

As pubs emphasize what's coming out of the kitchen rather than what's flowing out of the tap, whether to bring the kids has become a question. By law, patrons must be 18 in order to drink alcohol in a pub. Children 14 to 17 may enter a pub, but, children under 14 are not permitted in the bar area of a pub unless it has a "children's certficate" and they are accompanied by an adult. In general, however, some pubs have a section set aside for families—especially during the day. Check with the bartender. Some pubs actively encourage families and have play areas and a kid-friendly menu.

(Left) The Flask, Hampstead, London, (Right) Lamb and Flag pub, Covent Garden, London

PUB ETIQUETTE AND BASICS

Ordering: You order drinks from the bartender, known in England as the "barman" or "barmaid"—and pay up front. Don't be put off by a crowd at the bar. Never be impatient; wait as close to the bar as possible and they'll get to you. At most pubs you also order food from the bar and it is brought to you. Credit cards are common but likely require a minimum of £10.

Tipping: If you're only buying drinks, don't tip.

The round: If you're with friends, generally everyone takes turns buying drinks for the group. This is called a "round."

Smoking: Sorry, no: smoking has been banned since 2007.

Hours: In small towns, most pubs stick to the traditional hours of 11 am–11 pm (10:30 pm on Sunday), with the exception of Friday and Saturday nights. In large towns and cities, a few stay open past midnight, sometimes as late as 2 am. A handful are open 24 hours, but they are invariably dives.

Music: Some pubs have live music, usually local bands that vary in quality; but even big stars started out like this. You're not usually expected to pay.

Conversation: People don't generally get involved in a stranger's discussions, but for the best chance to chat with locals, hang out at the bar.

"Last orders please!": This is the traditional call of a landlord 20 minutes before closing, usually accompanied by a bell and a rush to buy drinks. When 20 minutes is up, they'll yell "Time please!" Then you have a few minutes to finish up.

DO I HAVE TO DRINK?

It's fine to go to a pub and not drink alcohol. They're social places first, watering holes second. All pubs serve soft drinks and most have tea and coffee. Other popular alternatives include lime and soda water; orange juice and lemonade; and a St. Clement's, a mixture of orange and bitter lemon (like lemonade, only more sour).

WHEN TO GO?

The English take their drink seriously, and pubs are where people go to hang out and, sometimes, drink heavily. Unless you're checking a place out on recommendation (a good idea), you may want to pick a midweek night for your first pub experience. On Friday and Saturday nights, rowdy young drinkers can take over some pubs.

KNOW YOUR BEER

Whether you're ordering a pint (the usual quantity), or a "half" (for half-pint), you have plenty of options, including imported beers. You can discuss your choice with the barman and then turn to your neighbor, raise your glass, and utter that amiable toast, "Cheers!"

ALE. The most quintessentially English type of beer is brewed from barley and hops and usually served at cellar (cooler than room, but not chilled) temperature. The term *real ale* distinguishes the traditionally made product, containing only authentic ingredients and no carbonation, from mass-produced alternatives; real ales have a devoted following. The flavor of ales varies greatly, from nutty and bitter to light and sweet. *Common varieties include Adnams Broadside; Greene King I.P.A.; Newcastle Brown Ale; Well's Waggle Dance.*

Adnams Broadside

BITTER. This is the generic name given to bitter types of ale. They vary greatly in strength; bitters with the word "best" after their name are medium; "premium," "strong," or "special" are the strongest. *Bitters to try include London Pride and Courage Directors.*

LAGER. Often imported, these carbonated, light, pale beers are usually mass produced, and they're extremely popular. Lager is always served chilled. What Americans call beer, the British call lager, including beers from continental Europe.

London Pride

STOUT. Something of an acquired taste, stouts are dark beers made with roasted barley or malt. A stronger variant, known as porter, was popular in the 18th and 19th centuries, and a handful of bottled kinds are sold in pubs today. *Try Guinness (the Irish favorite) or Fuller's London Porter.*

WHEAT BEER. These beers brewed from wheat are mostly imported from Europe. They are often white in color and have a malty taste. *Try Hoegaarden or Erdinger.*

Fuller's London Porter

MORE CHOICES

CIDER. Made with apples, cider is like its American namesake—but alcoholic. Ciders can be sweet or dry. Try Magners or Strongbow.

LAGER TOPS. A pint of lager with a splash of lemonade on top is a lager top. A 50/50 version of the same thing is called a shandy; this traditional summer afternoon drink is worth a try.

SNAKEBITE. Half lager and half cider, snakebite is usually served with a splash of blackcurrant cordial as a "snakebite and black."

(top) Magners cider, (bottom) Newcastle Brown Ale

EATING AT THE PUB

(left) Traditional ploughman's lunch, (right) Steak and kidney pie

In the 1980s, the best you might hope for in a pub was a sandwich or a plate of cold meats and cheese. The gastropub revolution of the 1990s forced everybody to raise their game. Popular chain pubs, such as Wetherspoons and The Slug and Lettuce, offer decent meals, especially at lunchtime. Don't want a full meal? Most pubs will fix you a bowl of chips (thick-cut French fries) or other hot nibbles. If pubs have specials boards or a menu prominently displayed outside, they're probably worth a shot for a meal. Pub fare includes anything from lasagna to burgers, but look for these traditional favorites:

■ Savory pies, such as steak and ale or chicken and bacon. Just make sure they're homemade.

■ Bangers and mash (sausage links and mashed potato), especially if the sausages are "butchers" or "local."

■ Ploughman's lunch, with cheese, pickles, and crackers.

■ Fish and chips may seem like a good pick, but avoid it in city pubs because proper fish and chips shops are usually better. Near the coast, though, pubs that advertise local seafood may be the best place for fish and chips.

■ Sunday roasts, another culinary tradition, are hearty feasts—and pubs are usually the best places to sample them. Even pubs not noted for their food can pull out excellent roasts at Sunday lunchtime, and the best places get packed; you may need a reservation. The centerpiece is roast beef, chicken, pork, or lamb, served with roast potatoes and vegetables, covered in thin, rich, dark gravy. Each meat has its traditional accompaniment; Yorkshire pudding (light, fluffy batter, resembling a soufflé) and horseradish sauce with beef; mint jelly with lamb. It's a treat to savor.

PUB QUIZZES AND GAMES

Many pubs hold general knowledge quizzes on a weekday evening, and anybody can enter. It's usually a pound each, which goes into a pot as prize money. Quizzes are a fun and relaxed way to socialize with locals, although it helps to know some British sports and pop culture.

Video gaming machines are a common, if jarringly modern feature, in many pubs. They're the latest additions to a longtime custom, though. Traditional pub games include darts, dominoes, and chess—plus more arcane pastimes now found only rarely in the countryside. These include bar billiards, a miniature version of pool crossed with skittles; and Nine Men's Morris, similar to backgammon.

THEATER   **New Theatre.** Oxford's main performance space, the New Theatre stages popular shows, comedy acts, and musicals. ✉ *George St.* ☎ *0844/871–3020* ⊕ *www.newtheatreoxford.org.uk.*

Oxford Playhouse. This theater presents classic and modern dramas as well as dance and music performances. ✉ *Beaumont St.* ☎ *01865/305305* ⊕ *www.oxfordplayhouse.com.*

SHOPPING

Small shops line High Street, Cornmarket, and Queen Street; the Clarendon and Westgate shopping centers, leading off them, have branches of several nationally known stores.

Alice's Shop. This store sells all manner of *Alice in Wonderland* paraphernalia. ✉ *83 St. Aldate's* ☎ *01865/723793.*

Blackwell's. Family-owned and family-run since 1879, Blackwell's stocks an excellent selection of books. Inquire about the literary and music walking tours that run from April through September. ✉ *48–51 Broad St.* ☎ *01865/792792.*

Fodor's Choice   **Covered Market.** This is a fine place for a cheap sandwich and a leisurely
★   browse; the smell of pastries and coffee follows you from cake shop to jeweler to cheesemonger. ✉ *High St.* ⊕ *www.oxford-covered-market.co.uk.*

Scriptum Fine Stationery. Cards, stationery, handmade paper, and leatherbound journals can be found at Scriptum Fine Stationery, as well as quills, sealing wax, and Venetian masks. ✉ *3 Turl St.* ☎ *01865/200042.*

Shepherd & Woodward. This traditional tailor specializes in university gowns, ties, and scarves. ✉ *109–113 High St.* ☎ *01865/249491.*

Taylors Deli. If you're planning a picnic, Taylors Deli has everything you need. There are cakes and pastries, as well as first-rate teas and coffees. There's a shop on the High Street as well. ✉ *31 St. Giles* ☎ *01865/558853.*

University of Oxford Shop. Run by the university, the University of Oxford Shop sells authorized clothing, ceramics, and tea towels, all emblazoned with university crests. ✉ *106 High St.* ☎ *01865/247414* ⊕ *www.oushop.com.*

SPORTS AND THE OUTDOORS

BIKING

Bainton Bikes. Bicycles can be rented from Bainton Bikes, a family-owned company that's happy deliver to your hotel. You can also hire a two-wheeler outside the train station in the summer. ✉ *78 Walton St.* ☎ *01865/311610* ⊕ *www.baintonbikes.com.*

PUNTING

Fodor's Choice   You may choose, like many an Oxford student, to spend a summer
★   afternoon **punting,** while dangling your Champagne bottle in the water to keep it cool. Punts—shallow-bottom boats that are poled slowly up the river—can be rented in several places, including at the foot of the Magdalen Bridge.

Cherwell Boathouse. From mid-March through mid-October, Cherwell Boathouse will rent you a boat and, if you wish, someone (usually an Oxford student) to punt it. Rentals are £14 (£17 on weekends) per hour or £70 (£85 on weekends) per day, and should be booked ahead. The facility, a mile north of the heart of Oxford, also includes a stylish restaurant. ⊠ *Bardwell Rd.* ☎ *01865/515978* ⊕ *www. cherwellboathouse.co.uk.*

Salter's Steamers. At the St. Aldates Road end of Folly Bridge, Salter's Steamers rents out punts and skiffs (rowboats) for £20 per hour, £60 per half day, and £100 per day. Its chauffeured punts are £60 per hour, booked in advance. ⊠ *Folly Bridge* ☎ *01865/243421* ⊕ *www. salterssteamers.co.uk.*

SPECTATOR SPORTS

Eights Week. At the end of May, during Oxford's Eights Week, men and women from the university's colleges compete to be "Head of the River." Because the river is too narrow for the eight-member teams to race side by side, the boats set off one behind another. Each boat tries to catch and bump the one in front.

Oxford University Cricket Club. The highly regarded Oxford University Cricket Club competes against leading county teams in late spring and summer, as well as major foreign teams visiting Britain each summer. In the middle of the sprawling University Parks—itself worthy of a walk— the club's playing field is truly lovely. ⊕ *www.cricketintheparks.org.uk.*

OXFORDSHIRE AND ENVIRONS

The River Thames takes on a new graciousness as it flows along the borders of Oxfordshire for 71 miles; each league it increases in size and importance. Three tributaries swell the river as it passes through the landscape: the Windrush, the Evenlode, and the Cherwell. Tucked among the hills and dales are one of England's impressive stately homes, an Edenic little town, and a former Rothschild estate. Closer to London in Hertfordshire is St. Albans, with its cathedral and Roman remains.

WOODSTOCK AND BLENHEIM PALACE

8 miles northwest of Oxford on A44.

Handsome 17th- and 18th-century houses line the trim streets of Woodstock, at the eastern edge of the Cotswolds. It's best known for nearby Blenheim Palace, and in summer tour buses clog the village's ancient streets. On a quiet fall or spring afternoon, however, Woodstock is a sublime experience: a mellowed 18th-century church and town hall mark the central square, and along its backstreets you can find flower-bedecked houses and quiet lanes right out of a 19th-century etching.

GETTING HERE AND AROUND

The public bus service S3 runs (usually every half hour) between Oxford and Woodstock and costs £3.40 one way. It can drop you at the gates at Blenheim Palace.

EXPLORING

Fodor'sChoice **Blenheim Palace.** This grandiose palace was named a World Heritage
★ Site, the only historic house in Britain to receive the honor. Designed
by Sir John Vanbrugh in the early 1700s in collaboration with Nicholas Hawksmoor, Blenheim was given by Queen Anne and the nation
to General John Churchill, first duke of Marlborough, in gratitude
for his military victories (including the Battle of Blenheim) against the
French in 1704. The exterior is mind-boggling, with its huge columns,
enormous pediments, and obelisks, all exemplars of English baroque.
Inside, lavishness continues in monumental extremes: you can join a free
guided tour or simply walk through on your own. In most of the opulent
rooms family portraits look down at sumptuous furniture, elaborate
carpets, fine Chinese porcelain, and immense pieces of silver. Exquisite
tapestries in the three state rooms illustrate the first duke's victories.
■ TIP→ Book a tour of the current duke's private apartments for a more
intimate view of ducal life. For some visitors, the most memorable room
is the small, low-ceiling chamber where Winston Churchill (his father
was the younger brother of the then-duke) was born in 1874; he's buried in nearby Bladon.

Sir Winston wrote that the unique beauty of Blenheim lay in its perfect
adaptation of English parkland to an Italian palace. Its 2,000 acres of
grounds, the work of Capability Brown, 18th-century England's best-
known landscape gardener, are arguably the best example of the "cun-
ningly natural" park in the country. Blenheim's formal gardens include
notable water terraces and an Italian garden with a mermaid fountain,
all built in the 1920s.

The Pleasure Gardens, reached by a miniature train that stops outside the palace's main entrance, contain some child-pleasers, including
a butterfly house, a hedge maze, and giant chess set. The herb-and-
lavender garden is also delightful. Blenheim Palace stages a concert of
Beethoven's *Battle Symphony* in mid-July, combined with a marvelous
fireworks display. There are many other outdoor events throughout the
summer, including jousting tournaments. ⊠ *Off A4095* ☎ *0800/849–
6500 information line* ⊕ *www.blenheimpalace.com* ✉ *Palace, park,
and gardens £21; park and gardens £12* ☉ *Palace mid-Feb.–Oct., daily
10:30–4:45; Nov.–mid-Dec., Wed.–Sun. 10:30–4:45; park mid-Feb.–
mid-Dec., daily 9–6 or dusk.*

WHERE TO EAT AND STAY

For expanded hotel reviews, visit Fodors.com.

$ ✕ **Falkland Arms.** It's worth detouring a bit for this supremely appeal-
BRITISH   ing pub on the village green at Great Tew, about 8 miles northwest of
Fodor'sChoice   Woodstock. The bar stocks fruit wines and snuff as well as local ales,
★   and there's a fine selction of mugs and jugs hanging from the beams.
The small restaurant chalks up a traditional but creative menu, which
includes such items as smoked fish pie with cheese sauce, pies of the
day and sharing platters. Book ahead on weekends. If you can't bear
to leave, a spiral stone staircase leads to five guest rooms. $ *Average
main: £10* ⊠ *19–21 The Green, Great Tew* ☎ *01608/683653* ⊕ *www.
falklandarms.co.uk* ⚑ *Reservations essential.*

Fountains and formal Italian gardens set off the monumental baroque pile that is Blenheim Palace.

$ B&B/INN **Blenheim Guest House & Tea Rooms.** Small and unassuming, this modestly furnished three-story guesthouse stands in the quiet village cul-de-sac that leads to the back gates of Blenheim Palace. **Pros:** handy tearoom downstairs; good location. **Cons:** no frills; floors are a bit creaky. [$] *Rooms from: £75* ✉ *17 Park St.* ☎ *01993/813814* 🌐 *www.theblenheim.co.uk* 🛏 *6 rooms* 🍴 *Breakfast.*

$$$ HOTEL **The Feathers.** Antiques-bedecked guest rooms fill this stylish inn, which was cobbled together from five 17th-century houses in the heart of town. **Pros:** beautiful modern decor; great food. **Cons:** pricey; two-night minimum stay on weekends in summer. [$] *Rooms from: £200* ✉ *Market St.* ☎ *01993/812291* 🌐 *www.feathers.co.uk* 🛏 *16 rooms, 5 suites* 🍴 *Breakfast.*

$$ HOTEL **Macdonald Bear.** Tudoresque wood paneling, beamed ceilings, wattle-and-daub walls, and blazing fireplaces help define this as an archetypal English coaching inn. **Pros:** plenty of character; historic house. **Cons:** creaky floors; you can knock yourself silly on those old beams. [$] *Rooms from: £160* ✉ *Park St.* ☎ *0844/879–9143* 🌐 *www.macdonaldhotels.co.uk/bear* 🛏 *46 rooms, 8 suites* 🍴 *Breakfast.*

EN ROUTE

After taking in Blenheim Palace, stop by **Bladon,** 2 miles southeast of Woodstock on A4095 and 6 miles northwest of Oxford, to see the small, tree-lined churchyard that's the burial place of Sir Winston Churchill. His grave is all the more impressive for its simplicity.

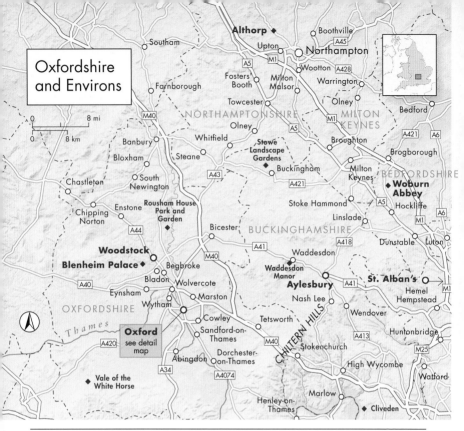

AYLESBURY

22 miles east of Oxford, 46 miles northwest of London.

Aylesbury makes a good base for exploring the surrounding country-side, including stately homes and gardens. It's a pretty, historic place with a 13th-century church surrounded by small Tudor lanes and cottages. This market town has been associated with the Aylesbury duck since the 18th century, when flocks were walked 40 miles to the London markets. Kids will appreciate a visit to the Roald Dahl's Children's Gallery, which is open all year.

GETTING HERE AND AROUND

From London, Chiltern Railways runs frequent trains from Marylebone Station (one hour). The town is easily accessible from Oxford by Arriva Bus 280, which runs every 30 minutes; travel time is 80 minutes. If you're driving from Oxford, take A40 and A418. From London, follow M1 and A41 and allow 90 minutes.

ESSENTIALS

Visitor Information Aylesbury Tourist Information Centre ⊠ *King's Head Passage, off Market Sq.* ☎ *01296/330559* ⊕ *www.visitbuckinghamshire.org.*

EXPLORING

Fodor's Choice ★ **Stowe Landscape Gardens.** This superb example of a Georgian garden was created for the Temple family by the most famous gardeners of the 18th century. Capability Brown, Charles Bridgeman, and William Kent all worked on the land to create 980 acres of pleasing greenery in the valleys and meadows. More than 40 striking monuments, follies, and temples dot the landscape of lakes, rivers, and pleasant vistas; this is a historically important place, but it's not for those who want primarily a flower garden. Allow at least half a day if you want to explore the grounds. Stowe House, at its center, is now a fancy school with some magnificently restored rooms; it's open for tours most afternoons from Sunday through Thursday, but call ahead. The gardens are about 3 miles northwest of Buckingham, which is 14 miles northwest of Aylesbury. You enter the gardens through the New Inn visitor center, where there are period parlor rooms to explore. ✉ *New Inn Farm, off A422, Stowe, Buckingham* ☎ *01280/817156, 01280/818166 house information line, 01289/818002 house tours* 🌐 *www.nationaltrust.org.uk* 🎟 *Gardens £8.20; house £5.50; house and gardens £13.25* 🕒 *Mar.–late Oct., daily 10–6; late Oct.–Feb., daily 10–4; last admission 90 mins before closing.*

Fodor's Choice ★ **Waddesdon Manor.** Many of the regal residences created by the Rothschild family throughout Europe are gone now, but this one is still a vision of the 19th century at its most sumptuous. G.H. Destailleur built the house in the 1880s for Baron Ferdinand de Rothschild in the style of a 16th-century French château, with perfectly balanced turrets and towers and walls of creamy stone. Although intended only for summer weekend house parties, it was lovingly furnished over the course of 35 years with Savonnerie carpets, Sèvres porcelain, furniture made by Riesener for Marie Antoinette, and paintings by Guardi, Gainsborough, and Reynolds. An exquisite 21st-century broken porcelain chandelier by Ingo Maurer in the Blue Dining Room brings the collection up-to-date. The gardens are equally extraordinary, with an aviary, colorful plantings, and winding trails that provide panoramic views. In the restaurant you can dine on English or French fare and order excellent Rothschild wines if your pocketbook can take the hit. **TIP→ Admission is by timed ticket; arrive early or book in advance.** ✉ *Silk St., Waddesdon* ✥ *On A41 west of Aylesbury* ☎ *01296/653226* 🌐 *www.waddesdon.org.uk* 🎟 *House and gardens £16.20; gardens only £7.20* 🕒 *House Apr.–Oct. and mid-Nov.–Dec., Wed.–Fri. noon–4, weekends and national holidays Mon. 11–4; gardens Jan.–Mar., weekends 10–5; Apr.–Oct., Wed.–Sun. and national holidays Mon. 10–5; last admission 45 mins before closing.*

WHERE TO STAY

For expanded hotel reviews, visit Fodors.com.

$$ B&B/INN 🏨 **Five Arrows.** Fancifully patterned brick chimneys and purple gables decorate this elegant building next to the main entrance of Waddesdon Manor. **Pros:** historic building; lovely grounds. **Cons:** some rooms are small; on a busy main road. [$] *Rooms from: £105* ✉ *High St., Waddesdon* ☎ *01296/651727* 🌐 *www.thefivearrows.co.uk* 🛏 *9 rooms, 2 suites* 🍴 *Breakfast.*

THAMES VALLEY HIKING AND BIKING

The Thames Valley is a great area to explore on foot or by bike. It's not too hilly, and pubs and easily accessible lodgings dot the riverside and small towns. The Thames is almost completely free of car traffic along the Thames Path, a 184-mile national trail that traces the river from the London flood barrier to the river's source near Kemble, in the Cotswolds. The path follows towpaths from the outskirts of London, through Windsor, Oxford, and Lechlade.

Good public transportation in the region makes it possible to start and stop easily anywhere along this route. In summer the walking is fine and no special gear is necessary, but in winter the path often floods—check before you head out.

For the best information on the Thames paths, contact the National Trails Office or the Ramblers' Association, both good sources of information, advice, and maps. The Chiltern Conservation Board promotes walking in the Chilterns peaks.

Biking is perhaps the best way to see the Chilterns. Routes include the 99-mile Thames Valley Cycle Route from London to Oxford, and the 87-mile Ridgeway Path from Uffington that follows the Chilterns; the National Trails Office has information. The Thames Path also has plenty of biking opportunities.

CONTACTS AND RESOURCES

Chiltern Conservation Board ☎ *01844/355500* 🌐 *www.chilternsaonb.org.*

Chiltern Way ☎ *01494/771250* 🌐 *www.chilternsociety.org.uk.*

National Trails Office 🌐 *www.nationaltrail.co.uk.*

Ramblers' Association ☎ *020/7339–8500* 🌐 *www.ramblers.org.uk.*

$$$$ HOTEL Fodor's Choice ★ 🏨 **Hartwell House.** Part Jacobean, part Georgian, this magnificent stately home offers formal luxury in an opulent country setting. **Pros:** truly elegant; soothing views of the gardens. **Cons:** may feel too formal; spa is open to the public. [$] *Rooms from: £290* ✉ *Oxford Rd.* ☎ *01296/747444* 🌐 *www.hartwell-house.com* 🛏 *33 rooms, 13 suites* 🍴 *Breakfast.*

ST. ALBANS

25 miles east of Aylesbury, 20 miles northwest of London.

A lively town on the outskirts of London, St. Albans is known for its historic cathedral, and it also holds reminders of a long history. From AD 50 to 440, the town then known as Verulamium was one of the largest communities in Roman Britain. You can explore this past in the Verulamium Museum and splendid Roman sites around the area. For activities more focused on the present, every Wednesday and Saturday the Market Place on St. Peter's Street bustles with traders from all over England, selling everything from fish and farm produce to clothing and CDs. A 20-minute drive away from St. Albans is Warner Bros. Harry Potter Studio Tour, which has sets and props from the successful films.

GETTING HERE AND AROUND

About 20 miles northwest of London, St. Albans is off the M1 and M25 highways, about an hour's drive from the center of the capital. First Capital Connect has frequent trains from London's St. Pancras Station, arriving in St. Albans in 30 minutes. The main train station is on Victoria Street, in the town center. A second station on the south side of town, St. Albans Abbey Station, serves smaller towns in the surrounding area. Bus service is slow and not direct. Central St. Albans is small and walkable. There's a local bus service, but you're unlikely to need it. Taxis usually line up outside the train stations.

ESSENTIALS

Train Contacts First Capital Connect ☎ *0845/026–4700* ⊕ *www.firstcapitalconnect.co.uk.*

Visitor Information St. Albans Tourist and Information Centre ⊠ *Town Hall, Market Pl.* ☎ *01727/864511* ⊕ *www.stalbans.gov.uk.*

EXPLORING

TOP ATTRACTIONS

Fodor'sChoice
★

Hatfield House. Six miles east of St. Albans, this outstanding brick mansion surrounded by lovely formal gardens stands as a testament to the magnificence of Jacobean architecture. Robert Cecil, earl of Salisbury, built Hatfield near an earlier palace where the first Queen Elizabeth spent much of her youth in 1611, and his descendants still live here. The interior, with its dark-wood paneling, lush tapestries, and Tudor and Jacobean portraits, reveals much about the era. Perhaps its finest feature is the ornate Grand Staircase, with carved wooden figures on the banisters. The knot garden is a highlight of the West Garden. Wednesday is the only day on which the East Garden, with topiaries, parterres, and rare plants, is open to the public. The Park has lovely woodland paths and masses of bluebells. There are open-air concerts and shows throughout the season. ⊠ *Great North Rd., Hatfield* ☎ *01707/287010* ⊕ *www.hatfield-house.co.uk* ◫ *House, West Garden, and Park £15.50; East Garden £4; park £4.50* ☉ *House Easter–Sept., Wed.–Sun. and national holiday Mon. noon–5; West Garden Tues.–Sun. and national holiday Mon. 10–5; East Garden Wed. 11–5; Park Tues.–Sun. and national holiday Mon. 11–5:30.*

St. Albans Cathedral. Medieval pilgrims came from far and wide to hilltop St. Albans Cathedral to honor its patron saint, a Roman soldier turned Christian martyr. His red-canopied shrine beyond the choir has a rare loft from where guards kept watch over gifts that were left. Construction of the mainly Norman cathedral began in the early 11th century, but the nearly 300-foot-long nave dates from 1235; the pillars are decorated with 13th- and 14th-century paintings. The tower is even more historic, and contains bricks from ancient Roman buildings. ⊠ *Holywell Hill* ☎ *01727/860780* ⊕ *www.stalbanscathedral.org* ◫ *Donations welcome* ☉ *Daily 8:30–5:45; guided tours weekdays 11:30, Sat. 11:30 and 2, Sun. 2:30.*

FAMILY **Verulamium Museum.** With exhibits on everything from food to burial practices, the Verulamium Museum, on the site of the ancient Roman city, explores life 2,000 years ago. The re-created Roman rooms contain colorful mosaics that are some of the finest in Britain. Every second weekend of the month, "Roman soldiers" invade the museum and demonstrate the skills of the Imperial Army. ⊠ *St. Michael's St.* ☎ *01727/751810* ⊕ *www.stalbansmuseums.org.uk* ⊡ *£3.80* ☉ *Mon.– Sat. 10–5:30, Sun. 2–5:30.*

FAMILY
Fodor'sChoice
★

Warner Bros. Harry Potter Studio Tour. Muggles, take note: this spectacular attraction opened for wizarding business just outside Watford in 2012. From the Great Hall of Hogwarts to magical props, each section of this attraction showcases the real sets, props, and special effects used in the eight movies. Visitors enter the Great Hall, a fitting stage for costumes from each Hogwarts house. The spooky charm of the Defense Against the Dark Arts Classroom will tempt some to start experimenting, but others will hurry on to the comforting confines of Dumbledore's office. Tickets, pegged to a 30-minute arrival time slot, must be prebooked online. The studio tour is a 20-minute drive from St. Albans. You can also get here by taking a 20-minute train ride from London's Euston Station (then a 15-minute shuttle bus ride). Via car from London, use M1 and M25 and enjoy the free parking. ⊠ *Studio Tour Dr., Leavesden* ☎ *0845/084–0900* ⊕ *www.wbstudiotour.co.uk* ⊡ *£29* ☉ *Daily 10–4 (until 6:30 at some times of year).*

WORTH NOTING

Roman Theater. Your imagination can take you back to AD 130 as you walk around the ruins of this 2,000-seat Roman Theater, one of the few in the country. Next to the theater are the ruins of a Roman town house, shops, and a shrine. ⊠ *Bluehouse Hill* ☎ *01727/835035* ⊕ *www.romantheatre. co.uk* ⊡ *£2.50* ☉ *Easter–Nov., daily 10–5; Dec.–Easter, daily 10–4.*

Shaw's Corner. From 1906 to his death in 1950, the famed Irish playwright George Bernard Shaw lived in the small village of Ayot St. Lawrence, 9 miles northeast of St. Albans. Today his small Edwardian home, Shaw's Corner, remains much as he left it. The most delightful curiosity is his little writing hut in the garden, which can be turned to face the sun. ⊠ *Off Hill Farm La., Ayot St. Lawrence* ☎ *01438/820307* ⊕ *www. nationaltrust.org.uk* ⊡ *£6.30* ☉ *House mid-Mar.–Oct., Wed.–Sun. 1–5; gardens mid-Mar.–Oct., Wed.–Sun. noon–5:30. Last entry at 4.30.*

FAMILY
Verulamium Park. Adjacent to the Verulamium Museum, this park contains the usual—playground, wading pool, lake—and the unusual— Roman ruins that include part of the town hall and a hypocaust, or central-heating system. The hypocaust dates to AD 200 and included one of the first heated floors in Britain. Brick columns supported the floor, and hot air from a nearby fire was drawn underneath the floor to keep bathers warm. ⊠ *St. Michael's St.* ☎ *01727/751810* ⊕ *www. stalbansmuseums.org.uk* ⊡ *Free* ☉ *Hypocaust Apr.–Sept., Mon.–Sat. 10–4:30, Sun. 2–4:30; Oct.–Mar., Mon.–Sat. 10–3:45, Sun. 2–3:45.*

WHERE TO EAT AND STAY
For expanded hotel reviews, visit Fodors.com.

$
BELGIAN

✕ **Waffle House.** Indoors or outside, you can enjoy a great budget meal at the 16th-century Kingsbury Watermill, near the Verulamium Museum. The organic flour for the sweet-and-savory Belgian waffles comes from Redbournbury Watermill, just north of the city. In the main dining room you can see the wheel churn the water of the River Ver. $ *Average main: £7* ✉ *Kingsbury Watermill, St. Michael's St.* ☎ *01727/853502* ⊕ *www. wafflehouse.co.uk* ☾ *No dinner.*

$
BRITISH
✕ **Ye Olde Fighting Cocks.** Some claim this is England's oldest pub, although that's a contentious category. Still, this octagonal building certainly looks suitably aged. The building was moved to this location in the 16th century, but the foundations date back to the 8th century. The small rooms with low ceilings make a cozy stop for a pint and good home-cooked food. Be prepared for crowds. $ *Average main: £11* ✉ *16 Abbey Mill La.* ☎ *01727/869152* ⊕ *www.yeoldefightingcocks.co.uk.*

$$$
HOTEL
🏨 **St. Michael's Manor.** In the same family for three generations, this luxurious 16th-century manor house close to the center of St. Albans is set in 5 acres of sweeping grounds. **Pros:** spacious rooms; excellent food; beautiful grounds. **Cons:** a little too grand for some. $ *Rooms from: £175* ✉ *Fishpool St.* ☎ *01727/864444* ⊕ *www.stmichaelsmanor. com* ⤳ *30 rooms* ⦿ *Breakfast.*

WOBURN ABBEY

6

30 miles west of St. Albans, 10 miles northeast of Aylesbury.

A stunning drive through the deer park at Woburn Abbey leads to a superb art collection within the Georgian mansion and roaming wildlife in the Safari Park.

GETTING HERE AND AROUND

Woburn Abbey is easily accessible for drivers from M1 at Junction 12 or 13; a car is needed to tour the safari park. The nearest train station, Flitwick, is a 15-minute taxi ride away. Frequent trains connect with St. Albans and London's St. Pancras Station in 50 minutes.

ESSENTIALS

Train Contacts First Capital Connect ☎ 0845/026–4700 ⊕ www.firstcapitalconnect.co.uk.

EXPLORING

FAMILY
Woburn Abbey. Still the ancestral residence of the duke of Bedford, Woburn Abbey houses countless Grand Tour treasures and old master paintings, including 20 stunning Canalettos that practically wallpaper the crimson dining salon, and excellent works by Gainsborough and Reynolds. The Palladian mansion contains a number of etchings by Queen Victoria, who left them behind after she stayed here. Outside, 10 species of deer roam grounds that include an antiques center and small restaurant. The adjacent **Woburn Safari Park** is a popular drive-through wildlife experience, home to big game from around the world. Be prepared for fearless monkeys who like to go for a ride on your car. There are plenty of play areas, a boating lake with swan boats, and walkabouts with small animals such as wallabies. ■ TIP→ Allow at least half a day for the safari park. If you buy a joint ticket with the house, you can use it on another day. ✉ *A4012, off A5* ☎ *01525/290333 abbey, 01525/290407 safari park* ⊕ *www.woburn.co.uk* 🎟 *House, gardens, and deer park £14; safari park £19.99; combination ticket £25.99* ☾ *House Apr.–Sept., daily 11–4. Safari park mid-Feb.–early Nov., daily 10–5. Gardens daily 10–5 or dusk.*

WHERE TO STAY

For expanded hotel reviews, visit Fodors.com.

$$ ⛺ **The Inn at Woburn.** In the center of this small Georgian town, this for-
HOTEL mer coaching inn has uncluttered and comfortable bedrooms. **Pros:** close
to Woburn Abbey; light-filled spaces. **Cons:** standard rooms are small;
small bathrooms. $ *Rooms from: £147* ✉ *George St.* ☎ *01525/290441*
⊕ *www.woburn.co.uk/inn* ↰ *48 rooms, 7 suites.*

ALTHORP

5 miles west of Northampton, 27 miles northwest of Woburn Abbey.

Althorp is known as the childhood home and burial place of Princess
Diana. There is an exhibition devoted to her life, as well as fine archi-
tecture and paintings, both old masters and new.

GETTING HERE AND AROUND

Signposted at Junction 16 of M1, Althorp is most easily reached by car.
However, if you ask the driver, Stagecoach Bus 96 from Northampton's
train station will drop you here (Monday through Saturday). Buses run
every hour.

ESSENTIALS

Train Contacts **Stagecoach** ☎ *0871/200–2233 Traveline*
⊕ *www.stagecoachbus.com.*

EXPLORING

Althorp. Deep in the heart of Northamptonshire sits the ancestral home
of the Spencers, the family of Diana, Princess of Wales. Here, on a
tiny island in a lake known as the Round Oval, is Diana's final resting
place. Diana and her siblings found the house too melancholy, calling it
"Deadlock Hall." What the house does have are rooms filled with Van
Dycks, Reynoldses, and Rubenses—all portraits of the Spencers going
back 500 years—and an entry hall that architectural historian Niko-
laus Pevsner called "the noblest Georgian room in the country." Two
paintings by contemporary artist Mitch Griffiths stand out in complete
contrast. To these attractions, Diana's brother, Earl Spencer, has added
a visitor center devoted to her, which includes her wedding dress, child-
hood memorabilia, and an exhibition on her charitable work. A literary
festival is held here in mid-June. On the west side of the estate park is
Great Brington, the neighboring village where the church of St. Mary
the Virgin holds the Spencer family crypt; it's best reached by the des-
ignated path from Althorp. ✉ *Rugby Rd., off A428* ☎ *01604/770107*
⊕ *www.spencerofalthorp.com* 🎫 *£15.50* ⊗ *July and Aug., grounds and
exhibition daily noon–5, house daily 1–5; last entry at 4.*

BATH AND THE COTSWOLDS

WELCOME TO BATH AND THE COTSWOLDS

TOP REASONS TO GO

★ **Architecture of Bath:**
Bath is perhaps the most perfectly preserved and harmonious English city. Close up, the elegance and finesse of the Georgian buildings is a perpetual delight.

★ **Cotswold pubs:**
The classic pubs here press all the right buttons— low wooden beams, horse brasses, and inglenook fireplaces.

★ **Hidcote Manor Gardens:** In a region rich with imaginative garden displays, Hidcote lays good claim to eminence. Exotic shrubs from around the world and the famous "garden rooms" are the highlights of this Arts and Crafts masterpiece.

★ **Perfect villages:**
With their stone cottages, Cotswold villages tend to be improbably picturesque; the hamlets of Upper and Lower Slaughter are among the most seductive.

★ **Roman Baths, Bath:**
Take a break from the town's Georgian elegance and return to its Roman days on a tour around this ancient bath complex.

1 Bath and Environs.
With the Roman Baths— renovated and embellished in the 18th century—and the late-medieval Bath Abbey at its heart, Bath is one of the country's comeliest towns. You can also soak up its thriving cultural scene and many shops.

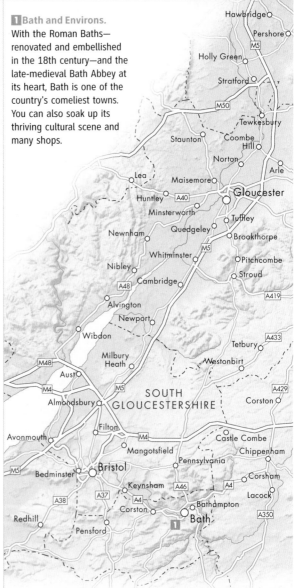

GETTING ORIENTED

The major points of interest in this part of west-central England—Bath, the Cotswolds, and Cheltenham—are one way to organize your explorations. Bath, in the southwestern corner of this area, is a good place to start; it can also be visited on a day trip out from London. The Cotswolds, about two hours northwest of London by car, cover some of southern England's most beautiful terrain. The area's small roads make for wonderful exploring, but public transportation is limited. To the west of the Cotswolds lies the city of Cheltenham, an elegant former spa town.

7

Map labels

Alderminster
A429
Halford
Hidcote Manor Gardens
Evesham
A46
A44
Broadway
Chipping Campden
A429
Teddington
Moreton-in-Marsh
A44
Chastleton
Winchcombe
Upper Slaughter
Chipping Norton
Lower Slaughter
Stow-on-the-Wold
Cheltenham
Bourton-on-the-Water
A40
A424
Andoversford
GLOUCESTERSHIRE
A40
Burford
A417
Fossebridge
A429
Bibury
Cirencester
A417
Lechlade
Kemble
A419
Latton
2 The Cotswolds.
Crudwell

With a scattering of picture-postcard towns and villages separated by sequestered valleys and woods, the Cotswolds are rural England at its best. Nearby Cheltenham, a larger town, with busy cafés and shops, provides a lively counterpoint.

M4
Swindon
WILTSHIRE

0 ——— 5 mi
0 ——— 5 km

GREAT WALKS IN THE COTSWOLDS

The gentle Cotswolds countryside, designated an Area of Outstanding Natural Beauty, is threaded with more than 3,000 miles of pleasant walking routes that enable you to appreciate these upland tracts at their best. It's easy to plan an afternoon walk or a multiday exploration.

(above) The Cotswold Way traverses some of England's loveliest countryside; (right, top) Stone bridge at Lower Slaughter; (right, below) Helpful sign on the Cotswold Way

The Cotswolds are a delight: wherever you turn, green areas are dotted with church steeples and stone roofs, restful on the eye and nourishing for the soul. To enjoy them to the fullest, do as the locals do—hoist on some walking shoes, don a sun (or rain) hat, and set forth on foot. Waymarked routes crisscross the area, and none of them is too challenging. No specialized equipment is required; it's healthy and it's free. Walks come in all lengths, but unless you decide to tackle one of the more ambitious regional trails, it may be easiest to pick a circular route. Just look for the "Public Footpath" and "Public Bridleway" signs, which indicate a right of way even when this passes through private property. Before you know it, you'll be opening gates and crossing stiles on the trails along with everyone else.

BRING WITH YOU

Light walking shoes or boots are essential, as are rain gear (even if it's sunny out), water, and a map. The walks may not be strenuous, but wear pants you won't mind getting dirty as you pass through fields. A fleece will keep the wind at bay, though in cold weather bundle up as needed. Carry a day pack for anything you don't want to hold or wear; you'll need your hands free to open gates along the trails.

CHOOSE YOUR WALKING ROUTE

The most celebrated route traversing the area is the **Cotswold Way** (⊕ *www.nationaltrail.co.uk*), a 102-mile national trail that traces the escarpment marking the western edge of the Cotswolds, stretching north to south between Chipping Campden and Bath, and taking in Broadway, Winchcombe, and Painswick, among many other villages. The trail has incomparable views across the Severn Vale to the Malvern Hills and takes you through varied scenery: limestone grasslands crossed by dry-stone walls, beech woodlands, and stone-built villages with ancient churches. You can select a route rather than walk the entire trail, which might take 7–10 days.

The **Heart of England Way** (⊕ *www.heartofenglandway.org*) runs a linear route from Bourton-on-the-Water north to Lower Slaughter, Bourton-on-the-Hill, and Chipping Campden, and continues north into the West Midlands. It's 100 miles in all, and the Cotswold section takes in hills and deep wooded valleys.

The **Warden's Way** and the **Windrush Way** both run between Winchcombe and Bourton-on-the-Water, 14-mile rambles that link the Cotswold Way (at Winchcombe) with the Oxfordshire Way (at Bourton-on-the-Water). The Warden's Way takes you through Upper and Lower Slaughter; the Windrush Way follows the meandering River Windrush and touches on Sudeley Castle, but without entering any village en route. You could make a circular walk of this, one day per leg.

Part of the Cotswold Way can be incorporated into an easy circular route between **Chipping Campden and Broadway,** along mostly level ground but including the elevated viewpoints of Dover's Hill and Broadway Tower. The circular route adds up to around 12 miles.

One of the most scenic Cotswolds walks explores the **Coln Valley,** a 6-mile (10-km) circular route beginning and ending at Bibury. The path follows the banks of the lovely River Coln for part of the way, through meadows and woodland.

RESOURCES

Tourist information centers carry local walking maps and publications describing longer trails. The most useful map for walkers in the area is Ordnance Survey Explorer OL45 (1:25,000). The **National Trail** website (⊕ *www.nationaltrail.co.uk*) outlines circular walks of 2–6 miles from the Cotswold Way.

Cotswold Voluntary Wardens conduct free guided walks of 2–10 miles (no booking needed). The free *Cotswold Lion* newspaper at tourist offices lists these. The website of the Cotswolds Area of Outstanding National Beauty (⊕ *www. cotswoldsaonb.org.uk*) is another resource.

Walk the Landscape (⊕ *www.walkthelandscape. co.uk*) organizes guided and self-guided hikes with luggage transfer and accommodation.

Compass Holidays (⊕ *www.compass-holidays. com*) arranges short walking trips in the Cotswolds, and **Sherpa Van** (⊕ *www. sherpavan.com*) offers a luggage transfer and accommodation booking service.

7

Updated by
Kate Hughes

The rolling uplands of the Cotswolds represent the quintessence of rural England, as immortalized in countless books, paintings, and films. In eloquently named settlements from Bourton-on-the-Water to Stow-on-the-Wold, you can taste the glories of the old English village—its stone slate roofs, low-ceiling rooms, and gardens; the atmosphere is as thick as honey, and equally as sweet. On the edge of the Cotswolds is Bath, among the most alluring small cities in Europe.

The blissfully unspoiled Cotswolds, deservedly popular with visitors and convenient to London, occupy much of the county of Gloucestershire, in west-central England. They also take in slices of neighboring Oxfordshire, Worcestershire, and Somerset. Together these make up a sweep of land stretching from close to Stratford-upon-Avon and Shakespeare Country in the north almost as far as the Bristol Channel in the south. On the edge of the area, two historic towns have absorbed, rather than compromised, the flavor of the Cotswolds: Bath, offering up "18th-century England in all its urban glory," to use a phrase by writer Nigel Nicolson, and Regency-era Cheltenham, like Bath, a spa town with elegant architecture.

Bath rightly boasts of being the best-planned town in England. Although the Romans founded the city when they discovered here the only true hot springs in England, its popularity during the 17th and 18th centuries luckily coincided with one of Britain's most creative architectural eras. Today people come to walk in the footsteps of Jane Austen, visit Bath Abbey and the excavated Roman baths, shop in an elegant setting, or have a modern spa experience at the stunning Thermae spa.

North of Bath are the Cotswolds—a region that more than one writer has called the very soul of England. This idyllic region, which from medieval times grew prosperous on the wool trade, remains a vision of rural England. Here are time-defying churches, sleepy hamlets, sequestered ancient farmsteads, and such fabled abodes as Sudeley Castle. The Cotswolds can hardly claim to be undiscovered, but the area's poetic appeal has survived the tour buses and antiques shops.

BATH AND THE COTSWOLDS PLANNER

WHEN TO GO

This area contains some of England's most popular destinations, and it's best to avoid weekends in the busier areas of the Cotswolds. During the week, even in summer, you may hardly see a soul in the more remote spots. Bath is particularly congested in summer, when students flock to its language schools. On the other hand, Cheltenham is a relatively workaday place that can absorb many tour buses comfortably.

Book your room well ahead if you visit during the two weeks in May and June when the Bath International Music Festival hits town, or if you visit Cheltenham during the National Hunt Festival (horse racing) in mid-March. Note that the private properties of Hidcote Manor, Snowshill Manor, and Sudeley Castle close in winter; Hidcote Manor Garden is at its best in spring and fall.

PLANNING YOUR TIME

Bath and Cheltenham are the most compelling larger towns in the region, and the obvious centers for an exploration of the Cotswolds. Cheltenham is closer to the heart of the Cotswolds and is far less touristy, but it has less immediate appeal. Bath is 29 miles from Cirencester in the southern Cotswolds, and 45 miles from Stow-on-the-Wold in the north. It's also worth finding accommodation in the smaller Cotswold settlements, though overnight stops in this well-heeled area can be costly. Good choices include Cirencester, Stow-on-the-Wold, and Broadway.

You can get a taste of Bath and the Cotswolds in three hurried days; a weeklong visit gives you plenty of time for the slow wandering this small region deserves. Near Bath, it's an easy drive to Lacock and Castle Combe, two stately villages on the southern edge of the Cotswolds, and Winchcombe makes a good entry into the area from Cheltenham. At the heart of the Cotswolds, Stow-on-the-Wold, Bourton-on-the-Water, and Broadway should on no account be missed. Within a short distance of these, Chipping Campden and Moreton-in-Marsh are less showy, with a more relaxed feel. Northleach is fairly low-key but boasts a fine example of a Cotswold wool church, while Bibury and Upper and Lower Slaughter are tiny settlements that can easily be appreciated on a brief passage. On the southern fringes of the area, Burford, Tetbury, and Cirencester have antiques and tea shops galore while avoiding the worst of the crowds.

GETTING HERE AND AROUND

AIR TRAVEL

This area is about two hours from London; Bristol and Birmingham have the closest regional airports.

BUS TRAVEL

National Express buses head to the region from London's Victoria Coach Station. Megabus, a budget bus company best booked online, also serves Cheltenham and Bath from London. It takes about three hours to get to both Cheltenham and to Bath. Bus service between some towns can be extremely limited. The First company covers the area around Bath. Stagecoach, Castleways, Johnson's Coaches, Cotswold

Green, Swanbrook, Pulham's Coaches, and Wessex Connect operate in the Cotswolds region. Traveline has comprehensive information about all public transportation.

Contacts **Castleways** ☏ *01242/602949* ⊕ *www.castleways.co.uk.* **Cotswold Green** ☏ *01453/835153.* **First** ☏ *0871/200–2233* ⊕ *www.firstgroup. com.* **Johnson's Coaches** ☏ *01564/797070* ⊕ *www.johnsonscoaches. co.uk.* **Megabus** ☏ *0871/266–3333 for general inquiries, 0900/160–0900 for bookings; calls cost 60p per minute* ⊕ *www.megabus.com.* **National Express** ☏ *0871/781–8178* ⊕ *www.nationalexpress.com.* **Pulham's Coaches** ☏ *01451/820369* ⊕ *www.pulhamscoaches.com.* **Stagecoach** ☏ *0871/200–2233* ⊕ *www.stagecoachbus.com.* **Swanbrook** ☏ *01452/712386* ⊕ *www.swanbrook.co.uk.* **Traveline** ☏ *0871/200–2233* ⊕ *www.traveline.info.* **Wessex** ☏ *0117/321–3190* ⊕ *www.wessexbus.com.*

CAR TRAVEL

A car is the best way to make a thorough tour of the area, given the limitations of public transportation. M4 is the main route west from London to Bath and southern Gloucestershire; expect about a two-hour drive. From Exit 18, take A46 south to Bath. From Exit 20, take M5 north to Cheltenham; from Exit 15, take A419 to A429 north to the Cotswolds. From London you can also take M40 and A40 to the Cotswolds, where a network of minor roads link the villages.

TRAIN TRAVEL

First Great Western trains serve the region from London's Paddington Station; First Great Western and CrossCountry trains connect Cheltenham and Birmingham. Travel time from Paddington to Bath is about 90 minutes. Most trains to Cheltenham (two hours and 20 minutes) involve a change at Swindon or Bristol. Train service within the Cotswold area is extremely limited, with Kemble (near Cirencester) and Moreton-in-Marsh being the most useful stops, both serviced by regular trains from London Paddington. A three-day or seven-day Heart of England Rover pass is valid for unlimited travel within the region. National Rail Enquiries can help with schedules and other information.

Contacts **National Rail Enquiries** ☏ *0845/748–4950* ⊕ *www.nationalrail.co.uk.*

RESTAURANTS

Good restaurants dot the region, thanks to a steady flow of fine chefs seeking to cater to wealthy locals and waves of demanding visitors. The country's food revolution is in full evidence here. Restaurants have never had a problem with a fresh food supply: excellent regional produce, salmon from the rivers Severn and Wye, local lamb and pork, venison from the Forest of Dean, and pheasant, partridge, quail, and grouse in season. Also look for Gloucestershire Old Spot pork, bacon (try a delicious Old Spot bacon sandwich), and sausage on area menus. *Prices in the reviews are the average cost of a main course at dinner or, if dinner isn't served, at lunch.*

HOTELS

The hotels of this region are among Britain's most highly rated—from bed-and-breakfasts in village homes and farmhouses to luxurious country-house hotels. Many hotels present themselves as deeply traditional rural retreats, but some have opted for a sleeker, fresher style, with boldly contemporary or minimalist furnishings. Spas are becoming increasingly popular at these hotels. Book ahead whenever possible and brace yourself for some high prices. B&Bs are a cheaper alternative to the fancier hotels, and most places offer two- and three-day packages. Note that the majority of lodgings in Bath and many in the Cotswolds require a two-night minimum stay on weekends and holidays; rates are often higher on weekends. Accommodation in Cheltenham and the Cotswolds is especially hard to find during the week of Cheltenham's National Hunt Festival in March.

There are numerous possibilities for renting a cottage in and around Bath and the Cotswolds, usually available by the week. Check out Manor Cottages or Jigsaw Holidays for a range of self-catering options.

Prices in the reviews are the lowest cost of a standard double room in high season, including 20% V.A.T.

Contacts **Jigsaw Holidays** ☎ *01993/849484* ⊕ *www.jigsawholidays.co.uk.* **Manor Cottages** ☎ *01993/824252* ⊕ *www.manorcottages.co.uk.*

VISITOR INFORMATION

The South West Tourism website has information about the entire region; the Cotswolds site is a government one that has a useful section on tourism. The major towns have Tourist Information Centres that provide advice and help with accommodations.

Contacts **The Cotswolds** ☎ *01452/328321* ⊕ *www.cotswolds.com.* **South West Tourism** ⊕ *www.visitsouthwest.co.uk.*

BATH AND ENVIRONS

On the eastern edge of the county of Somerset, the city of Bath has strong links with the Cotswolds stretching north, the source of the wool that for centuries underpinned its economy. The stone mansions and cottages of that region are recalled in Bath's Georgian architecture and in the mellow stone that it shares with two of the villages across the Wiltshire border, Lacock and Castle Combe.

BATH

13 miles southeast of Bristol, 115 miles west of London.

Fodor's Choice
★

"I really believe I shall always be talking of Bath. Oh! Who can ever be tired of Bath," enthuses Catherine Morland in Jane Austen's *Northanger Abbey,* and today plenty of people agree with these sentiments. In Bath, a UNESCO World Heritage Site, you're surrounded by magnificent 18th-century architecture, a lasting reminder of the vanished world described by Austen. In the 19th century the city lost its fashionable luster and slid into a refined gentility that still remains. Bath is no museum, though: it's lively, with good dining and shopping, excellent art galleries and museums, the remarkable excavated Roman baths, and theater, music, and other performances all year. Many people rush through Bath in a day, but there's enough to do to merit an overnight stay—or more. In summer, the sheer volume of sightseers may hamper your progress.

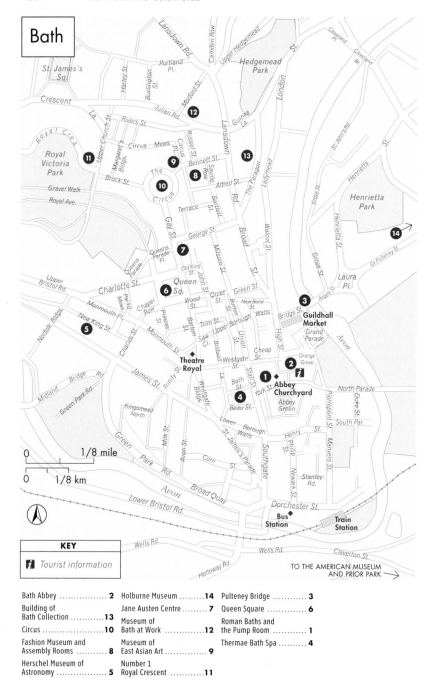

Bath

St. James's Sq.

Crescent

Royal Cres.

Royal Victoria Park

Gravel Walk

Royal Ave.

Lansdown Rd.

Camden Row

Upper Hedgemead

Hedgemead Park

Cleveland Pl.

Cleveland Br.

Portland Pl.

Harley St.

Burlington St.

Julian Rd.

Morford St.

London St.

St. John's Rd.

Rivers St.

Guinea La.

Lansdown

The Paragon

Grove St.

Henrietta St.

Henrietta Park

Circus Mews

Margaret Bldgs.

Upper Church St.

Circus Pl.

Russel St.

Bennett St.

Saville Row

Alfred St.

Laura Pl.

Gt. Pulteney St.

Brock St.

The Circus

Terrace

Bartlett St.

Walcot St.

Broad St.

Henrietta St.

Gay St.

George St.

Milsom St.

Queens Parade Pl.

Old King St.

John St.

Green St.

New Bond St.

Bridge St.

Argyle St.

Queen Sq.

Quiet St.

Barton St.

Watts

Guildhall Market

Upper Bristol Rd.

Charlotte St.

Chapel Row

Perla Mews

Princes St.

Wood St.

High St.

Grand Parade

Avon

Monmouth Pl.

Monmouth St.

Trim St.

Upper Borough

Union St.

Cheap St.

Orange Grove

New King St.

Charles St.

Saw Cl.

Bilbury

Westgate St.

Stall St.

Bath St.

Abbey Churchyard

North Parade

Norfolk Bldgs.

James St.

Trinity St.

Theatre Royal

Westgate Bldgs.

York St.

Beau St.

Abbey Green

Pierrepont St.

Duke St.

Manvers St.

Midland Bridge Rd.

Green Park Rd.

Kingsmead North

Milk St.

Avon St.

Lower Borough Walls

St. James's Parade

Henry St.

Philip St.

South Par.

0   1/8 mile

0   1/8 km

Green Park Rd.

Corn St.

Southgate

Newark St.

Stanley Rd.

Avon

Broad Quay

Lower Bristol Rd.

Dorchester St.

Bus Station

Train Station

KEY

🛈 *Tourist information*

Wells Rd.

Wells Rd.

Holloway Rd.

Claverton St.

TO THE AMERICAN MUSEUM
AND PRIOR PARK →

The Romans put Bath on the map in the 1st century when they built a temple here, in honor of the goddess Minerva, and a sophisticated network of baths to make full use of the mineral springs that gush from the earth at a constant temperature of 116°F (46.5°C). ■ TIP→ Don't miss the remains of the baths, one of the city's glories. Visits by Queen Anne in 1702 and 1703 brought attention to the town, and soon 18th-century "people of quality" took it to heart. Assembly rooms, theaters, and pleasure gardens were built to entertain the rich and titled when they weren't busy attending the parties of Beau Nash (the city's master of ceremonies and chief social organizer, who helped increase Bath's popularity) and having their portraits painted by Gainsborough.

GETTING HERE AND AROUND

Frequent trains from Paddington and National Express buses from Victoria connect Bath with London. The bus and train stations are close to each other south of the center. By car from London, take M4 to Exit 18, from which A46 leads 10 miles south to Bath.

Drivers should note that parking is extremely limited within the city, and any car illegally parked will be ticketed. Fees for towed cars can be hundreds of pounds. Public parking lots in the historic area fill up early, but the park-and-ride lots on the outskirts provide inexpensive shuttle service into the center, which is pleasant to stroll around.

TOURS Free two-hour walking tours of Bath are offered year-round by the Mayor of Bath's Honorary Guides. Individuals can just show up outside the main entrance to the Pump Room. Tours are Sunday through Friday at 10:30 and 2, Saturday at 10:30, and there's an additional tour at 7 pm Tuesday and Thursday from May to September. The Jane Austen Centre arranges Jane-themed walking tours on weekends. City Sightseeing runs 50-minute guided tours of Bath on open-top buses year-round, leaving two to four times an hour from High Street, near the abbey. Tickets, valid for 24 hours, give discounts on entry to some of Bath's top attractions. Mad Max Tours runs full-day tours from Bath through the Cotswolds on Tuesday, Thursday, and Sunday, stopping at Tetbury, Upper Slaughter and Lower Slaughter, and either Bourton-on-the-Water or Stow-on-the-Wold. The departure point is the Best Western Hotel, North Parade, near Bath Abbey, at 8:45 am. The company also has tours to Castle Combe, Lacock, Avebury, and Stonehenge.

TIMING

Schedule a visit to Bath during the week, as weekends see an influx of visitors. The city gets similarly crowded during its various festivals, though the added conviviality and cultural activity during these events are big draws in themselves.

ESSENTIALS

Visitor and Tour Information **Bath Tourist Information Centre**
⊠ Abbey Chambers, Abbey Churchyard ☎ 0844/847–5257, 0844/847–5256 booking accommodation service ⊕ www.visitbath.co.uk. **City Sightseeing** ☎ 01225/444102 ⊕ www.city-sightseeing.com. **Mad Max Tours** ☎ 0799/050–5970 ⊕ www.madmaxtours.co.uk. **Mayor of Bath's Honorary Guides** ☎ 01225/477411 ⊕ www.bathguides.org.uk.

The remains of the Roman Baths evoke the days when the Romans gathered here to socialize and bathe.

EXPLORING

TOP ATTRACTIONS

Bath Abbey. Dominating Bath's center, this 15th-century edifice of golden, glowing stone has a splendid west front, with carved figures of angels ascending ladders on either side. Notice, too, the miter, olive tree, and crown motif, a play on the name of the building's founder, Bishop Oliver King. More than 50 stained-glass windows fill about 80% of the building's wall space, giving the interior an impression of lightness. The abbey was built in the Perpendicular (English late-Gothic) style on the site of a Saxon abbey, and the nave and side aisles contain superb fan-vaulted ceilings. Look for the expressively carved angels on the choir screens. There are five services on Sunday, including choral even-song at 3:30. Forty-five-minute **tower tours**, allowing close-up views of the massive bells and panoramic cityscapes from the roof, take place daily except Sundays; the 212 dizzying steps demand a level of fitness. ⊠ *Abbey Churchyard* ☎ *01225/422462* ⊕ *www.bathabbey.org* ✉ *Abbey £2.50 suggested donation, tower tours £6* ⊗ *Abbey Mon. 9:30–6, Tues.–Sat. 9–6, Sun. 1–2:30 and 4:30–5:30. Tower tours Apr., May, Sept., and Oct., Mon.–Sat. 10–4 hourly; June–Aug., Mon.–Sat. 10–5 hourly; Nov.–Mar., Mon.–Sat. 11, noon, and 2.*

Circus. John Wood designed the masterful Circus, a circle of curving, perfectly proportioned Georgian houses interrupted just three times for intersecting streets. Wood died shortly after work began; his son, the younger John Wood, completed the project. Notice the carved acorns atop the houses: Wood nurtured the myth that Prince Bladud founded Bath, ostensibly with the help of an errant pig rooting for acorns (this is one of a number of variations of Bladud's story). A garden fills the center of the Circus. The painter Thomas Gainsborough (1727–88) lived at No. 17 from 1760 to 1774. ⊠ *Intersection of Bennett, Brock, and Gay sts.*

QUICK BITES

Bea's Vintage Tea Rooms. After surveying the Royal Crescent and the Circus, fast forward into the 1940s with a visit to these charming tearooms. Breakfasts, light lunches, and afternoon teas are all served on vintage china and hand-embroidered tablecloths. Teapots come with egg timers for the correct length of brew. ⊠ *6–8 Saville Row, Bath* 🕾 *01225/464552* ⊕ *www.beasvintagetearooms.com* ☉ *No dinner.*

Fodor'sChoice
★

Fashion Museum and Assembly Rooms. In its role as the **Assembly Rooms,** this neoclassical building was one of the leading centers for social life in 18th-century Bath. Jane Austen came here often, and it's in the Ballroom that Catherine Morland has her first, disappointing encounter with Bath's beau monde in *Northanger Abbey*; the Octagon Room is the setting for an important encounter between Anne Elliot and Captain Wentworth in *Persuasion*. Built by John Wood the Younger in 1771, the building was badly damaged by wartime bombing in 1942 but was faithfully restored. Its stunning chandeliers are the 18th-century originals. Throughout the year, classical concerts are given here, just as they were in bygone days. The Assembly Rooms are also known today for the entertaining **Fashion Museum,** displaying apparel from Jacobean times up to the present. You can see examples of what would have been worn in the heydays here, as well as glamorous frocks from the 20th century—a dress of the year is an annual addition. Besides admiring the changing exhibits, you can have fun trying on corsets and crinolines. An audio guide is included in the admission. ⊠ *Bennett St.* 🕾 *01225/477789* ⊕ *www.museumofcostume.co.uk* 🗪 *£2 for Assembly Rooms; £7.75 for Assembly Rooms and Fashion Museum; £16.25 combined ticket includes Roman Baths* ☉ *Mar.–Oct., daily 10:30–6; Nov.–Feb., daily 10:30–5; last admission 1 hr before closing.*

Fodor'sChoice
★

Holburne Museum. One of Bath's gems, this elegant 18th-century building and its modern extension house a superb collection of 17th- and 18th-century decorative arts, ceramics, and silverware. Highlights include paintings by Gainsborough (*The Byam Family*, on indefinite loan) and George Stubbs (*Reverend Carter Thelwall and Family*), and a hilarious collection of caricatures of the Georgian city's fashionable elite. In its original incarnation as the Sydney Hotel, the house was one of the pivots of Bath's high society, which came to perambulate in the pleasure gardens (Sydney Gardens) that still lie behind it. One visitor was Jane Austen, whose main Bath residence was No. 4 Sydney Place, a brief stroll from the museum. There's an excellent café and tea garden. ⊠ *Great Pulteney St.* 🕾 *01225/388569* ⊕ *www.holburne.org* 🗪 *Free* ☉ *Mon.–Sat. 10–5, Sun. and national holidays 11–5.*

Jane Austen Centre. The one place in Bath that gives Austen any space provides a briefly diverting exhibition about the influence of Bath on her writings; *Northanger Abbey* and *Persuasion* are both set primarily in the city. There's a 15-minute introductory talk, and displays give a pictorial overview of life in Bath around 1800. The cozy Georgian

7

house, a few doors up from where the writer lived in 1805 (one of several addresses she had in Bath), also includes the Austen-themed Regency Tea Rooms, open to the public. ■TIP→ Buy tickets here for Jane Austen walking tours, which leave from the Abbey Churchyard at 11 on weekends and holidays (also at 4 on Friday and Saturday in July and August). A tour ticket entitles you to a 10% reduction for entry to the exhibition. ⊠ *40 Gay St.* ☎ *01225/443000* ⊕ *www. janeausten.co.uk* ☑ *£8, tours £6* ☉ *Late Mar.–June, Sept., and Oct, daily 9:45–5:30; July and Aug., Sun.–Wed. 9:45–5:30, Thurs.–Sat. 9:45–7; Nov.–late Mar., Sun.–Fri. 11–4:30, Sat. 9:45–5:30.*

> ### JANE AUSTEN IN BATH
>
> Though born and brought up in Hampshire, Jane Austen had close connections with Bath and lived here from 1801 to 1806. She wasn't overly fond of the place, peppering her letters with caustic comments about it (interspersed with gossip and effusions on bonnets and trimmings). Austen wrote her sister, Cassandra, that she left "with what happy feelings of escape." However, she is thought to have fallen in love here, and she received her only known offer of marriage while in Bath. Bath's eight-day Jane Austen Festival celebrates the writer in late September.

Fodor's Choice ★ **Number 1 Royal Crescent.** The majestic arc of the Royal Crescent, much used as a film location, is the crowning glory of Palladian architecture in Bath. The work of John Wood the Younger, these 30 houses fronted by 114 columns were laid out between 1767 and 1774. The first house to be built, on the corner of Brock Street and the Royal Crescent, was Number 1 Royal Crescent. Having undergone substantial refurbishment in 2013, it has been reunited with its original servants' annex, and the museum now crystallizes a view of the English class system in the 18th century—status, wealth and elegance of the main house reflected in and contrasted with the servants' quarters and kitchen, set apart in the service wing. ⊠ *Royal Crescent* ☎ *01225/428126* ⊕ *www. bath-preservation-trust.org.uk* ☑ *£8.50* ☉ *Mid-Feb.–mid-Dec., Mon. 12–4:30, Tues.–Sun. 10:30–5:30; last admission 1 hr before closing.*

Pulteney Bridge. Florence's Ponte Vecchio inspired this 18th-century span, one of the most famous landmarks in the city and the only work of Robert Adam in Bath. It's unique in Great Britain because shops line both sides of the bridge. ⊠ *Between Bridge St. and Argyle St.*

Queen Square. Palatial houses and the Francis Hotel surround the garden in the center of this square designed by the older John Wood. An obelisk financed by Beau Nash celebrates the 1738 visit of Frederick, prince of Wales. ⊠ *South end of Gay St.*

Fodor's Choice ★ **Roman Baths and the Pump Room.** The hot springs have drawn people here since prehistoric times, so it's quite appropriate to begin an exploration of Bath at this excellent museum on the site of the ancient city's primary "watering hole." Roman patricians would gather to immerse themselves, drink the mineral waters, and socialize. With the departure of the Romans, the baths fell into disuse. When bathing again became fashionable at the end of the 18th century, this magnificent Georgian building was erected.

Almost the entire Roman bath complex was excavated in the 19th century, and the museum displays relics that include a memorable mustachioed, Celtic-influenced Gorgon's head, fragments of colorful curses invoked by the Romans against their neighbors, and information about Roman bathing practices. The **Great Bath** is now roofless, and the statuary and pillars belong to the 19th century, but much remains from the original complex, and the steaming, somewhat murky waters are undeniably evocative. Free tours take place hourly, and you can visit after 6:30 pm in July and August to experience the baths lighted by torches.

Adjacent to the Roman bath complex is the famed **Pump Room,** built in 1792–96, a rendezvous for members of 18th- and 19th-century Bath society. Here Catherine Morland and Mrs. Allen "paraded up and down for an hour, looking at everybody and speaking to no one," to quote from Jane Austen's *Northanger Abbey.* Today you can take in the elegant space—or you can simply, for a small fee, taste the fairly vile mineral water. Charles Dickens described it as tasting like warm flatirons. ▆ TIP ➙ The tourist office offers a £63.50 package that includes a visit to the Roman Baths, a three-course lunch or champagne afternoon tea, and a two-hour spa session. ✉ *Abbey Churchyard* ☎ *01225/477785* ⊕ *www.romanbaths.co.uk* ✎ *Roman Baths £12.75 (£13.25 in July and Aug.); £16.25 combined ticket includes the Fashion Museum and Assembly Rooms* ☉ *Mar.–June, Sept., and Oct., daily 9–6; July and Aug., daily 9 am–10 pm; Nov.–Feb., daily 9:30–5:30; last admission 1 hr before closing.*

QUICK BITES

Le Parisien. Tucked away in a quiet courtyard, Le Parisien is handy for coffee or a lunchtime baguette. Jacket potatoes, soups, quiches, and children's dishes also appear on the menu. ✉ *Milsom Pl., off Broad St.* ☎ *01225/447147.*

Pump Room. You can linger in the Pump Room for morning coffee or afternoon tea after seeing the Roman Baths. ✉ *Abbey Churchyard* ☎ *01225/444477.*

Thermae Bath Spa. The only place in Britain where you can bathe in natural hot-spring water, and in an open-air rooftop location as well, this striking complex designed by Nicholas Grimshaw consists of a Bath-stone building surrounded by a glass curtain wall. The only difficulty is in deciding where to spend more time—in the sleekly luxurious, light-filled Minerva Bath, with its curves and gentle currents, or in the smaller, open-air rooftop pool for the unique sensation of bathing with views of Bath's operatic skyline (twilight is atmospheric here). Two 18th-century thermal baths, the Cross Bath and the Hot Bath, are back in use, too (the latter for treatments only). End your session in the crisp third-floor café and restaurant. ▆ TIP ➙ It's essential to book spa treatments ahead. Towels, robes, and slippers are available for rent. Note that changing rooms are co-ed. Weekdays are the quietest time to visit. You must be 18 to book a spa treatment. A separate, free **Visitor**

Centre (April through October, Monday through Saturday 10–5, Sunday 11–4) opposite the entrance gives an overview of the project and provides audio guides (£2) for a brief tour of the exterior. ⊠ *Hot Bath St.* ☎ *0844/888–0844* ⊕ *www.thermaebathspa.com* ▤ *£26 for 2 hrs, £36 for 4 hrs, £56 all day* ⊙ *Daily 9 am–10 pm; last admission at 7.*

WORTH NOTING

American Museum in Britain. A 19th-century Greek Revival mansion in a majestic setting on a hill 2½ miles southeast of the city holds the only museum of American decorative arts outside the United States. Rooms are furnished in historical styles, such as a 17th-century keeping room from Massachusetts and a richly red New Orleans bedroom from the 1860s. Other galleries explore historical themes (the settlement of the West, the Civil War) or contain rugs and quilts, porcelain, and Shaker objects; a separate building is devoted to folk art. The parkland includes a reproduction of George Washington's garden at Mount Vernon. Take a bus headed to the University of Bath and get off at the Avenue, where signs point to the museum, half a mile away. The City Sightseeing bus also drops off here. ⊠ *Claverton Manor, off A36* ☎ *01225/460503* ⊕ *www.americanmuseum.org* ▤ *£9* ⊙ *Late Mar.–July, Sept., and Oct., Tues.–Sun. and national holidays noon–5; Aug., daily noon–5; late Nov.–mid-Dec., Tues.–Sun. and national holidays noon–4:30; last admission 1 hr before closing.*

Building of Bath Collection. This absorbing museum in the Georgian Gothic-style Countess of Huntingdon's Chapel is an essential stop on any exploration of Bath, particularly for fans of Georgian architecture. It illustrates the evolution of the city, with examples of everything from window design and wrought-iron railings to marbling and other interior decoration, while an informative film puts what you see into context. ⊠ *The Paragon* ☎ *01225/333895* ⊕ *www.bath-preservation-trust.org.uk* ▤ *£5; joint ticket with Number 1 Royal Crescent £10.50* ⊙ *Mid-Feb.–Nov., Tues.–Fri. 2–5, weekends 10.30–5; last admission 30 mins before closing.*

Herschel Museum of Astronomy. In this modest Bath town house, using a handmade telescope of his own devising, William Herschel (1738–1822) identified the planet Uranus. This small museum devoted to his studies and discoveries contains his telescopes, the workshop where he cast his speculum metal mirrors, musical instruments of his time (Herschel was the organist at Bath's Octagon Chapel), and the tiny garden where he made his discovery. ⊠ *19 New King St.* ☎ *01225/446865* ⊕ *www.bath-preservation-trust.org.uk* ▤ *£6* ⊙ *Weekdays 1–5, weekends and national holidays 11–5; last admission at 4:30.*

Museum of Bath at Work. The core of this industrial-history collection, which gives a novel perspective on the city, is an engineering works and fizzy drinks factory. This building once belonged to Bath entrepreneur Jonathan Bowler, who started his many businesses in 1872. The collection includes the original clanking machinery and offers glimpses into Bath's stone industry and cabinetmaking. ⊠ *Julian Rd.* ☎ *01225/318348* ⊕ *www.bath-at-work.org.uk* ▤ *£5 including audio-guide* ⊙ *Apr.–Oct., daily 10:30–5; Nov. and Jan.–Mar., weekends 10:30–5; last admission at 4.*

A GOOD WALK IN BATH

For an hour-long stroll that takes in Bath's architectural showpieces, start in the traffic-free Abbey Churchyard, a lively piazza (often filled with musicians and street artists) dominated by Bath Abbey and the Roman Baths complex. Work your way east to Grand Parade and look out over flower-filled gardens and the River Avon, crossed by the graceful, Italianate Pulteney Bridge.

Stroll over the shop-lined bridge to gaze up the broad thoroughfare of Great Pulteney Street; then cross back over the bridge and head east up Bridge Street, turning right at High Street to follow up Broad Street and its northern extension, Lansdown Road. Turn left onto Bennett Street, passing the 18th-century Assembly Rooms and the

Fashion Museum. Bennett Street ends at the Circus, an architectural tour de force compared by some to an inverted Colosseum.

The graceful arc of Bath's most dazzling terrace, the Royal Crescent, embraces a swath of green lawns at one end of Brock Street. Return to the Circus and walk south down Gay Street, which brings you past dignified Queen Square, with its obelisk, to the Theatre Royal. Wander east from here along tiny alleys packed with stores, galleries, and eating places, back to your starting point at Abbey Churchyard, where you could have a well-earned sit-down and tea at the Pump Room. Alternatively, end your perambulation with a soak at Thermae Bath Spa.

Museum of East Asian Art. Intimate galleries on three floors display ancient and modern pieces, mostly from China but with other exhibits from Japan, Korea, and Southeast Asia. Highlights are the Chinese jade figures, Buddhist objects, and Japanese lacquerware and prints. ⊠ *12 Bennett St.* 🕾 *01225/464640* ⊕ *www.meaa.org.uk* 🖼 *£5* ☉ *Tues.–Sat. 10–5, Sun. noon–5; last admission at 4:30.*

Prior Park. A vision to warm Jane Austen's heart, Bath's grandest house lies a mile or so southeast of the center, with splendid views over the Georgian townscape. Built around 1738 by John Wood the Elder of honey-color limestone, the Palladian mansion was the home of quarry owner and philanthropist Ralph Allen (1693–1764), whose guests included such luminaries as poet Alexander Pope and novelists Henry Fielding and Samuel Richardson. Today it's a school and the interior is not open to the public, but you may wander through the beautiful grounds, designed by Capability Brown and embellished with a Palladian bridge and lake. A leisurely circuit of the park should take around an hour. ■ TIP➡ The parking here is reserved for people with disabilities, so take a taxi or bus from the center. The City Sightseeing bus also calls here. ⊠ *Ralph Allen Dr.* 🕾 *01225/833422* ⊕ *www.nationaltrust. org.uk* 🖼 *£5.65* ☉ *Late Mar.–Oct., daily 10–5:30; early Nov.–mid-Mar., weekends 10–5:30; last admission 1 hr before closing.*

FAMILY **Royal Victoria Park.** Originally designed as an arboretum, this tidy expanse of lawns and shady walks just west of the Royal Crescent provides the perfect setting for pleasant strolls and leisurely picnics. The park has a pond, a **Botanic Garden,** and an adventure playground with plenty for kids. Hot-air balloon launches and open-air shows at festival time enliven the atmosphere. ⊠ *Upper Bristol Rd.* 🔳 *Free* ⊗ *Daily 24 hrs.*

WHERE TO EAT

$$ ╳ **Casanis.** Dappled sunlight on the stripped wood floor, small tables

FRENCH covered with white linens, and Provençal antiques and bottles of pastis make this place seem like a chic corner of France. Chef Laurent Couvreur puts his stamp on the beautifully presented and amiably served classic dishes, including goat's cheese with pear and pickled mushrooms, quail with lentil ragout, and an apple or chocolate tart. Round off your meal with a selection of tasty cheeses. The £16 two-course lunch menu is a steal. $ *Average main: £16* ⊠ *4 Saville Row* ☎ *01225/780055* ⊕ *www.casanis.co.uk* ⊗ *Closed Sun.*

$$ ╳ **Circus Cafe and Restaurant.** You could linger all day in this sophisti-

MODERN BRITISH cated eatery on the corner of the Circus. There's always a good crowd for morning coffee, elevenses (brunch), afternoon tea, and cocktails, let alone lunch and dinner, all of which are dispensed with efficient cordiality. If you can take your attention off the crumpets with Marmite, the spinach and sorrel soup, or the Wiltshire lamb under a marjoram crust, you can discuss the colorful modern art on the walls. Desserts include nutmeg crème brûlée with sherry-soaked raisins. Ingredients are locally sourced and wines come from small growers. $ *Average main: £16* ⊠ *34 Brock St.* ☎ *01225/466020* ⊕ *www.thecircuscafeandrestaurant. co.uk* ⊗ *Closed Sun.*

$ ╳ **Eastern Eye.** Delicious Indian dishes are the main draw, but the three

INDIAN magnificent glass domes of the large Georgian interior, the arresting South Asian murals, and the peppering of celebrities mean that a meal here becomes an event. Specialties of the house include *mughlai* chicken (flavored with egg, ginger, and garlic and fried in a sauce of yogurt, coconut, and poppy seeds) and salmon *bhaja* (pan-fried with Bengali spices and served with diced potatoes). All the classic dishes are on the capacious menu and are easy on the wallet. $ *Average main: £12* ⊠ *8a Quiet St.* ☎ *01225/422323.*

$ ╳ **Jamie's Italian.** Part of a chain owned by celebrity chef Jamie Oliver,

ITALIAN this buzzing brasserie is a cheerful counterpoint to Bath's predominantly sedate tone. The dining areas, spread over two floors and including a rooftop terrace, have a contemporary, slightly industrial feel. Expect dishes typical of Oliver's straightforward Italian rustic style, such as bruschetta, crispy polenta chips, or wild rabbit tagliolini. Desserts include ice creams with a variety of toppings. It can get busy, but you can take advantage of the all-day service by coming during off-peak hours. $ *Average main: £13* ⊠ *10 Milsom Pl.* ☎ *01225/432340* ⊕ *www. jamieoliver.com.*

$ ╳ **Jazz Café.** Snack to a background of jazz classics in this cramped

ECLECTIC but cozy café. Famous for its all-day breakfasts, the café is also a good spot for a quick lunch, with soups, salads, sandwiches, and fine mezes. Daily specials might include spicy beef chili, chicken and leek pie, or Moroccan pork. Get here early, as the place closes at 5 pm (4 on Sunday). $ *Average main: £7* ⊠ *Kingsmead Sq.* ☎ *01225/329002* ⊕ *www. bathjazzcafe.co.uk* ⊗ *No dinner.*

CLOSE UP

Bath's Georgian Architecture

Bath wouldn't be Bath without its distinctive 18th-century Georgian architecture, much of which was conceived by John Wood the Elder (1704–54), an antiquarian and architect. Wood saw Bath as a city destined for almost mythic greatness. Arriving in Bath in 1727, he sought a suitable architectural style, and found it in the Palladian style, made popular in Britain by Inigo Jones.

ELEMENTS OF STYLE

Derived from the Italian architect Andrea Palladio (1508–80), who in turn was inspired by ancient Roman architecture, Palladianism accentuated symmetry and proportion. The plain facades of buildings, dignified with columns, pilasters, and pediments over doors and windows, often contrasted with rich interiors. The Building of Bath Collection has more information.

BUILDINGS TO SEE

Wood created a harmonious city, building graceful terraces (row houses), crescents (curving rows of houses), and villas of the same golden local limestone used by the Romans. Influenced by nearby ancient stone circles as well as round Roman temples, Wood broke from convention in his design for Bath's Circus, a circle of houses broken only three times for intersecting streets.

After the death of Wood the Elder, John Wood the Younger (1728–82) carried out his father's plans for the Royal Crescent, a regal crescent of 30 houses. Today you can stop in at Number 1 Royal Crescent for a look at one of these homes—it's like eavesdropping on the 18th century. He also built the Assembly Rooms, which are open to the public.

7

$ ✕ **Pump Room.** The 18th-century Pump Room, with views over the
BRITISH Roman Baths, serves morning coffee, substantial lunches, and afternoon tea, to music by a pianist or string trio who play every day. The stately setting is the selling point rather than the food, but do sample the West Country cheese board and the homemade cakes and pastries. There's a fixed-price menu at lunchtime, and the place is usually open for dinners in July, August, and December and during the major festivals (reservations are essential). Be prepared to wait in line for a table during the day. $ *Average main: £12* ✉ *Abbey Churchyard* ☎ *01225/444477* ⊕ *www.romanbaths.co.uk* ⊗ *No dinner Jan.–June and Sept.–Nov.*

$ ✕ **Rustico.** Favorite places to sit in this traditional and cozy corner of
ITALIAN Cotswold Italy are among the scatter of cushions in the window or, on a sunny day, outside on the pavement. The welcoming staff gladly serve you, as the name might imply, with good old-fashioned country fare—homemade pastas like grandma used to make, lashings of seafood casserole, handsome steaks, and pork in creamy white wine sauce for instance. Leave room for a light and fluffy tiramisu. $ *Average main: £12* ✉ *2 Margaret's Bldgs., Cheltenham* ☎ *01225/310064* ⊕ *www. rusticobistroitaliano.co.uk* ⊗ *Closed Mon.*

$ ✕ **Sally Lunn's.** Small and slightly twee, this tourist magnet near Bath
BRITISH Abbey occupies the oldest house in Bath, dating to 1482. It's famous for the Sally Lunn bun, actually a semisweet bread served here since 1680. You can choose from more than 30 sweet and savory toppings

to accompany your bun, or turn it into a meal with such dishes as duck with orange-and-cinnamon sauce. There are also economical lunch and early-evening menus. Daytime diners can view the small kitchen museum in the cellar (30p for nondining visitors). $ *Average main: £12* ✉ *4 N. Parade Passage* ☎ *01225/461634* ⊕ *www.sallylunns.co.uk.*

$$ ✕ **Tilleys Bistro.** This intimate, bow-windowed French eatery presents

FRENCH   alluring meat, vegan, and vegetarian dishes offered in small, medium, and large portions. Choices include medallions of pork *à la dijonnaise* (fried tenderloin and mushrooms in a brandy, cream, and mustard sauce), roasted *aubergine à la Tunisienne* (eggplant cooked with chickpeas, dates, and apricots), and smoked haddock with a Cheddar cheese sauce. Pretheater meals are available weekdays between 6 and 7 pm. $ *Average main: £16* ✉ *3 N. Parade Passage* ☎ *01225/484200* ⊕ *www. tilleysbistro.co.uk* ☾ *No lunch Sun.*

WHERE TO STAY

For expanded hotel reviews, visit Fodors.com.

$ 📷 **Albany Guest House.** Homey and friendly, this Edwardian house close

B&B/INN   to the Royal Crescent has simply furnished rooms decorated with neutral shades of beige and cream. **Pros:** spotless rooms; convenient location; excellent breakfasts. **Cons:** some rooms are very small; limited parking. $ *Rooms from: £85* ✉ *24 Crescent Gardens* ☎ *01225/313339* ⊕ *www.albanybath.co.uk* ↙ *5 rooms* ⊖ *Breakfast.*

$$ 📷 **Bath Paradise House.** Don't be put off by the 10-minute uphill walk

B&B/INN   from the center of Bath—you'll be rewarded by a wonderful view of the city from the garden and upper stories of this Georgian guesthouse. **Pros:** great attention to detail; spectacular views from some rooms. **Cons:** uphill walk; books up far in advance. $ *Rooms from: £130* ✉ *88 Holloway* ☎ *01225/317723* ⊕ *www.paradise-house.co.uk* ↙ *11 rooms* ⊖ *Breakfast.*

$ 📷 **Cranleigh.** On a quiet hilltop above the city center, this Victorian

B&B/INN   guesthouse has wonderful views of the Avon Valley. **Pros:** quiet rooms; period furnishings; many choices at breakfast. **Cons:** far from center; along a busy road; steps to climb. $ *Rooms from: £90* ✉ *159 Newbridge Hill* ☎ *01225/310197* ⊕ *www.cranleighguesthouse.com* ↙ *9 rooms* ⊖ *Breakfast.*

$$ 📷 **Dukes Hotel.** True Georgian grandeur is evident in the refurbished

HOTEL   rooms of this Palladian-style mansion–turned–elegant small hotel. **Pros:** excellent central location; superb restaurant; friendly and helpful service. **Cons:** some rooms are small; steps to climb. $ *Rooms from: £120* ✉ *53–54 Great Pulteney St., entrance on Edward St.* ☎ *01225/787960* ⊕ *www.dukesbath.co.uk* ↙ *11 rooms, 6 suites* ⊖ *Breakfast.*

$$ 📷 **Harington's Hotel.** It's rare to find a compact hotel in the cobblestone

HOTEL   heart of Bath, and this informal three-story lodging converted from a group of Georgian town houses fits the bill nicely. **Pros:** good breakfasts; helpful staff. **Cons:** occasional street noise from revelers; steps to climb; many small rooms. $ *Rooms from: £145* ✉ *Queen St.* ☎ *01225/461728* ⊕ *www.haringtonshotel.co.uk* ↙ *13 rooms* ⊖ *Breakfast.*

$$ 📷 **Marlborough House.** A warm, informal welcome greets all who stay

B&B/INN   at this Victorian establishment not too far from the Royal Crescent, where each room charms with period furniture, fresh flowers, and antique beds. **Pros:** obliging and helpful hosts; immaculate rooms. **Cons:** walk to the center is along a busy road. Ⓢ *Rooms from: £125* ✉ *1 Marlborough La.* ☎ *01225/318175* ⊕ *www.marlborough-house. net* ⤴ *6 rooms* ⏐◎⏐ *Breakfast.*

$$$ ⚟ **Queensberry Hotel.** Intimate and elegant, this boutique hotel in a resi-
HOTEL   dential street near the Circus occupies three 1772 town houses built by John Wood the Younger for the marquis of Queensberry; it's a perfect marriage of chic sophistication, homey comforts, and attentive service. **Pros:** efficient service; tranquil ambience; valet parking. **Cons:** occasional street noise; no tea/coffee-making facilities in rooms; breakfast extra. Ⓢ *Rooms from: £165* ✉ *7 Russel St.* ☎ *01225/447928* ⊕ *www. thequeensberry.co.uk* ⤴ *26 rooms, 3 suites* ⏐◎⏐ *No meals.*

$$ ⚟ **Three Abbey Green.** Just steps from Bath Abbey, a gorgeous square
B&B/INN   dominated by a majestic plane tree is home to this welcoming B&B. **Pros:** superb location; airy rooms. **Cons:** some noise from pub goers; only two suites have bathtubs; no parking. Ⓢ *Rooms from: £120* ✉ *3 Abbey Green* ☎ *01225/428558* ⊕ *www.threeabbeygreen.com* ⤴ *7 rooms* ⏐◎⏐ *Breakfast.*

NIGHTLIFE AND THE ARTS

BARS AND   **Porter.** The city's only vegetarian pub (now with one meat dish on offer as
PUBS   well), the Porter features nightly music performances, from folk to funk, in its grungy cellar bar. ✉ *2 Miles's Bldgs., George St.* ☎ *01225/424104.*

Raven. Pub aficionados will relish the friendly, unspoiled ambience of the Raven, a great spot for a pint. There are regular poetry readings, science and storytelling nights upstairs. ✉ *Queen St.* ☎ *01225/425045.*

FESTIVALS   **Bath Comedy Festival.** Running for 10 days, April's Bath Comedy Festival features comedy events at venues throughout the city. ✉ *Bath Box Office, Abbey Chambers, Abbey Courtyard* ☎ *01225/463362* ⊕ *www. bathcomedy.com.*

Fodor'sChoice   **Bath International Music Festival.** Held over 12 days in May and June, the
★   Bath International Music Festival presents classical, jazz, and world-music concerts, dance performances, and exhibitions in and around Bath, many in the Assembly Rooms and Bath Abbey. ✉ *Bath Box Office, Abbey Chambers, Abbey Churchyard* ☎ *01225/463362* ⊕ *www. bathfestivals.org.uk.*

Bath Literature Festival. The 10-day Bath Literature Festival in early March features readings and talks by writers, mostly in the 18th-century Guildhall on High Street. ✉ *Bath Box Office, Abbey Chambers, Abbey Churchyard* ☎ *01225/463362* ⊕ *www.bathfestivals.org.uk.*

Jane Austen Festival. Celebrating the great writer with films, plays, walks, and talks over nine days in mid-September, the Jane Austen Festival is a feast for Janeites. ☎ *01225/443000* ⊕ *www.janeausten.co.uk/festival.*

THEATER   **Theatre Royal.** A gemlike Regency playhouse from 1805, the Theatre Royal has a year-round program that often includes pre- or post-London tours. You must reserve the best seats well in advance, but you can line up for same-day standby seats or standing room. Tours costing £4 usually take place at 11 am on alternate Saturdays: call first to check. ▮▮**TIP→** Take care with your seat location—sight lines can be poor. ✉ *Box Office, Saw Close* ☎ *01225/448844* ⊕ *www.theatreroyal.org.uk.*

SHOPPING

Bath has excellent small, family-run, and specialty shops; many close Sunday. The shopping district centers on Stall and Union streets and the SouthGate shopping center near the train station (modern stores), Milsom Street (traditional stores), and Walcot Street (arts and crafts). Leading off these main streets are alleyways and passages lined with galleries and antiques shops.

Bartlett Street Antiques Centre. This place has more than 50 showcases and stands selling every kind of antique imaginable, including silver, porcelain, and jewelry. ⊠ *Bartlett St.* ☎ *01225/469785.*

Bath Christmas Market. For 18 days in late November and early December, the outdoor Bath Christmas Market sells gift items—from handcrafted toys to candles, cards, and edible delights—in 130 chalet-style stalls concentrated in the area just south of the abbey. ⊠ *York St.* ☎ *0844/847–5257* ⊕ *www.bathchristmasmarket.co.uk.*

Bath Sweet Shop. The city's oldest candy store, Bath Sweet Shop boasts of stocking some 350 different varieties, including traditional licorice torpedoes, pear drops, and aniseed balls. Sugar-free treats are available. ⊠ *8 N. Parade Passage* ☎ *01225/428040.*

Beaux Arts Ceramics. This shop carries the work of prominent potters, sculptors, painters, and printmakers. ⊠ *12–13 York St.* ☎ *01225/464850* ⊕ *www.beauxartsbath.co.uk.*

Guildhall Market. The covered Guildhall Market, open Monday through Saturday 9–5, is the place for everything from jewelry and gifts to delicatessen food, secondhand books, bags, and batteries. There's a café, too. ⊠ *Entrances on High St. and Grand Parade* ⊕ *www. bathguildhallmarket.co.uk.*

SPORTS AND THE OUTDOORS

Bath Boating Station. To explore the River Avon by rented skiff, punt, or canoe, head for the Bath Boating Station, behind the Holburne Museum. It's open Easter to September. ⊠ *Forester Rd.* ☎ *01225/312900* ⊕ *www. bathboating.co.uk.*

CASTLE COMBE

12 miles northeast of Bath, 5 miles northwest of Chippenham.

Fodor's Choice ★ This Wiltshire village lived a sleepy existence until 1962, when it was voted the "prettiest village" in England—without any of its inhabitants knowing that it had even been a contender. The village's magic is that it's so toylike, so delightfully all-of-a-piece: you can see almost the whole town at one glance from any one position. Castle Combe consists of little more than a brook, a pack bridge, a street (which is called the Street) of simple stone cottages, a market cross from the 13th century, and the Perpendicular-style church of St. Andrew. The grandest house in the village (on its outskirts) is the Upper Manor House, built in the 15th century by Sir John Fastolf, and is now the Manor House Hotel.

GETTING HERE AND AROUND

Regular buses and trains go to Chippenham, where you can pick up a bus for Castle Combe, but it's easier to drive or join a tour.

The charm of tiny Castle Combe, with its one main street of stone cottages, far exceeds its size.

WHERE TO STAY

For expanded hotel reviews, visit Fodors.com.

$$$$ HOTEL Fodor's Choice ★ **Manor House Hotel.** Secluded in a 23-acre park on the edge of the village, this partly 14th-century manor house has guest rooms—some in mews cottages—that brim with antique character. **Pros:** romantic getaway; rich historical setting; good golf course. **Cons:** some rooms outside of main house. [$] *Rooms from: £230* ☎ *01249/782206* 🌐 *www.manorhouse.co.uk* 🛏 *48 rooms.*

LACOCK

8 miles southeast of Castle Combe, 12 miles east of Bath.

Fodor's Choice ★ Owned by the National Trust, this lovely Wiltshire village is the victim of its own charm, its unspoiled gabled and stone-tile cottages drawing tour buses aplenty. Off-season, however, Lacock slips back into its profound slumber, the mellow stone and brick buildings little changed in 500 years and well worth a wander. Besides Lacock Abbey, there's the handsome church of St. Cyriac (built with money earned in the wool trade) and a 14th-century tithe barn, and, in the village, a few antiques shops and a scattering of pubs that serve bar meals in atmospheric surroundings.

GETTING HERE AND AROUND

All buses from Bath to Lacock involve a change and take 60 to 110 minutes, so it's best to drive or join a tour.

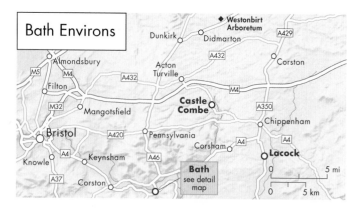

EXPLORING

Lacock Abbey. Well-preserved Lacock Abbey reflects the fate of many religious establishments in England—a spiritual center became a home. The abbey, at the town's center, was founded in the 13th century and closed down during the dissolution of the monasteries in 1539, when its new owner, Sir William Sharington, demolished the church and converted the cloisters, sacristy, chapter house, and monastic quarters into a private dwelling. The house passed to the Talbot family, the most notable descendant of whom was William Henry Fox Talbot (1800–77), who developed the world's first photographic negative. You can see the oriel window, the subject of this photograph in the upper rooms of the abbey, along with the rare 16th-century purpose-built strong room in the octagonal tower. The last descendant, Matilda Talbot, donated the property as well as Lacock itself to the National Trust in the 1940s. The abbey's grounds and Victorian woodland are also worth a wander. Harry Potter fans, take note: Lacock Abbey was used for some scenes at Hogwarts School in the film *Harry Potter and the Sorcerer's Stone.*

The **Fox Talbot Museum,** in a 16th-century barn at the gates of Lacock Abbey, commemorates the work of Fox Talbot as well as other pioneers and contmeporary artists in this field. ⊠ *High St.* ☎ *01249/730459* ⊕ *www.nationaltrust.org.uk* 🗍 *£10.80; excluding Abbey rooms £8.10* ☉ *Abbey rooms mid-Feb.–Oct., Wed.–Mon. 11–5; early Nov.–mid-Feb., weekends noon–4. Cloister, museum, and grounds mid-Feb.–Oct., daily 10:30–5:30; Nov.–mid-Feb., daily 11–4. Last admission 30 mins before closing.*

WHERE TO EAT

$$
BRITISH

✕ **Sign of the Angel.** An inn since the 15th century, this atmospheric restaurant is known for its roasts, steak, and kidney pies, and specialties like Stilton and walnut pâté with apple jelly. Don't pass up the homemade meringues, ice creams, and sorbets. Fixed-price menus are good value. If you tread the creaky boards you'll find six antiques-filled rooms in which to stay. $ *Average main: £18* ⊠ *6 Church St.* ☎ *01249/730230* ⊕ *www.lacock.co.uk* ☉ *Closed last wk of Dec.*

THE COTSWOLDS

A gently undulating area of limestone uplands, the Cotswolds are among England's best-preserved rural districts, and the quiet but lovely grays and ambers of the stone buildings here are truly unsurpassed. Much has been written about the area's age-mellowed towns, but the architecture of the villages actually differs little from that of villages elsewhere in England. Their distinction lies in their surroundings: the valleys are lush and rolling, and cozy hamlets appear covered in foliage from church tower to garden gate. Beyond the town limits, you can explore, on foot or by car, the "high wild hills and rough uneven ways" that Shakespeare wrote about.

Over the centuries, quarries of honey-color stone have yielded building blocks for many Cotswold houses and churches and have transformed little towns into realms of gold. Make Chipping Campden, Moreton-in-Marsh, or Stow-on-the-Wold your headquarters and wander for a few days. Then ask yourself what the area is all about. Its secret seems shared by two things—sheep and stone. These were once the great sheep-rearing areas of England, and during the peak of prosperity in the Middle Ages, Cotswold wool was in demand the world over. This made the local merchants rich, but many gave back to the Cotswolds by restoring old churches (the famous "wool churches" of the region) or building rows of almshouses of limestone now seasoned to a glorious golden-gray. These days the wool merchants have gone but the wealth remains—the region includes some of the most exclusive real estate in the country.

One possible route is to begin with Cheltenham—the largest town in the area and a gateway to the Cotswolds, but slightly outside the boundaries and more of a small city in atmosphere—then move on to the beauty spots in and around Winchcombe. Next are Sudeley Castle, Stanway House, and Snowshill Manor, among the most impressive houses of the region; the oversold village of Broadway; Chipping Campden—the Cotswold cognoscenti's favorite; and Hidcote Manor, one of the most spectacular gardens in England. Then circle back south, down through Moreton-in-Marsh, Stow-on-the-Wold, Upper Slaughter, Lower Slaughter, and Bourton-on-the-Water, and end with Bibury and Tetbury. This is definitely a region where it pays to go off the beaten track to take a look at that village among the trees.

CHELTENHAM

50 miles north of Bath, 13 miles east of Gloucester, 99 miles west of London.

Although Cheltenham has acquired a reputation as snooty—the population (around 110,000) is generally well-heeled and conservative—it's also cosmopolitan. The town has excellent restaurants and bars, fashionable stores, and a thriving cultural life. Its primary claim to renown, however, is its architecture, rivaling Bath's in its Georgian elegance, with wide, tree-lined streets, crescents, and terraces with row houses, balconies, and iron railings.

Like Bath, Cheltenham owes part of its fame to mineral springs. By 1740 the first spa was built, and after a visit from George III and Queen Charlotte in 1788, the town dedicated itself to idleness and enjoyment. "A polka, parson-worshipping place"—in the words of resident Lord Tennyson—Cheltenham gained its reputation for snobbishness when stiff-collared Raj majordomos returned from India to find that the springs—the only purely natural alkaline waters in England—were the most effective cure for their "tropical ailments."

Great Regency architectural set pieces—Lansdown Crescent, Pittville Spa, and the Lower Assembly Rooms, among them—were built solely to adorn the town. The Rotunda building (1826) at the top of Montpellier Walk—now a bank—contains the spa's original "pump room," in which the mineral waters were on tap. More than 30 statues adorn the storefronts of Montpellier Walk. Wander past Imperial Square, with its ironwork balconies, past the ornate Neptune's Fountain, and along the Promenade. In spring and summer lush flower gardens enhance the town's buildings, attracting many visitors.

GETTING HERE AND AROUND

Trains from London Paddington and buses from London Victoria head to Cheltenham. The train station is west of the center, and the bus station is centrally located off Royal Well Road. Drivers should leave their vehicles in one of the numerous parking lots. The town center is easily negotiable on foot. Cheltenham's tourist office (which will likely move to the Cheltenham Art Gallery by mid-2013) arranges walking tours (£5) of the town at 11 on Saturday from April until mid-November.

EXPLORING

Cheltenham Art Gallery and Museum. Now housed in a brand-new building, completed in 2013, the museum and art gallery demonstrates that from the 1880s onward Cheltenham was at the forefront of the Arts and Crafts movement. There are fine displays of William Morris textiles, furniture by Charles Voysey, and wood and metal pieces by Ernest Gimson. Decorative arts, such as Chinese ceramics, are also represented, and British artists, including Stanley Spencer and Vanessa Bell, make their mark. Other exhibits focus on local archaeology and history; one is devoted to Edward Wilson, who traveled with Robert Scott to the Antarctic on Scott's ill-fated 1912 expedition. ✉ *Clarence St.* ☎ *01242/237431* 🌐 *www.cheltenhammuseum.org.uk* 🎫 *Free* 🕒 *Daily: Apr.–Oct. 10–5; Nov.–Mar. 10–4.*

QUICK BITES

Well Walk Tea Room. Squeeze past all the antiques and knickknacks in this pretty bow-fronted shop and tearoom for a soup, pasta, or sandwich lunch, or treat yourself to an afternoon tea with crumpets and cakes. Along with traditional English Breakfast and Earl Grey, you can sample nettle and sweet fennel, jasmine, green, and white tea. In summer ask for a refeshing homemade lemonade. [$] *Average main: £3* ✉ *5–6 Well Walk, Cheltenham* ☎ *01242/574546* 🌐 *www.wellwalktearoom.co.uk* 🕒 *Closed Mon. No dinner.*

A tour of Gloucester Cathedral provides a visual lesson in architectural styles from Norman through Perpendicular Gothic.

OFF THE
BEATEN
PATH

Gloucester Cathedral. In the center of Gloucester, magnificent Gloucester Cathedral, with its soaring, elegant exterior, was originally a Norman abbey church, consecrated in 1100. Reflecting different periods, the cathedral mirrors perfectly the slow growth of ecclesiastical taste and the development of the Perpendicular style. The interior has largely been spared the sterilizing attentions of modern architects and is almost completely Norman, with the massive pillars of the nave left untouched since their completion. The fan-vaulted roof of the 14th-century cloisters is the finest in Europe, and the cloisters enclose a peaceful garden (used in the filming of *Harry Potter and the Sorcerer's Stone*). ▥ TIP➜ Don't miss the Whispering Gallery, which has a permanent exhibition devoted to the splendid, 14th-century stained glass of the Great East Window. Tours of the tower (269 steps up) are available, as are guided tours. Gloucester is 13 miles southwest of Cheltenham and reachable from there on frequent buses and trains. ✉ *Westgate St.* ☎ *01452/528095* ⊕ *www.gloucestercathedral.org.uk* 💷 *£5 requested donation, photography permit £3, tower tours £4, Whispering Gallery £2* ⊙ *Daily 7:30–6, except during services. Tower tours Apr.–Oct., Wed.–Fri. 2:30, Sat. 1:30 and 2:30, national holidays 11:30, 1:30, and 2:30; also Mon. and Tues. at 2:30 during school vacations. Whispering Gallery Apr.–Oct., weekdays 10:30–4, Sat. 10:30–3:30.*

Pittville Pump Room. The grandest of the remaining spa buildings, the pump room is set amid parkland, a 20-minute walk from the town center. The classic Regency structure, built in the late 1820s, now serves mainly as a concert hall and a theatrical venue but still offers its musty mineral waters to the strong of stomach. ✉ *E. Approach Dr., Pittville* ☎ *0844/576–2210* ⊕ *www.cheltenhamtownhall.org.uk* 💷 *Free* ⊙ *Wed.–Sun. 10–4.*

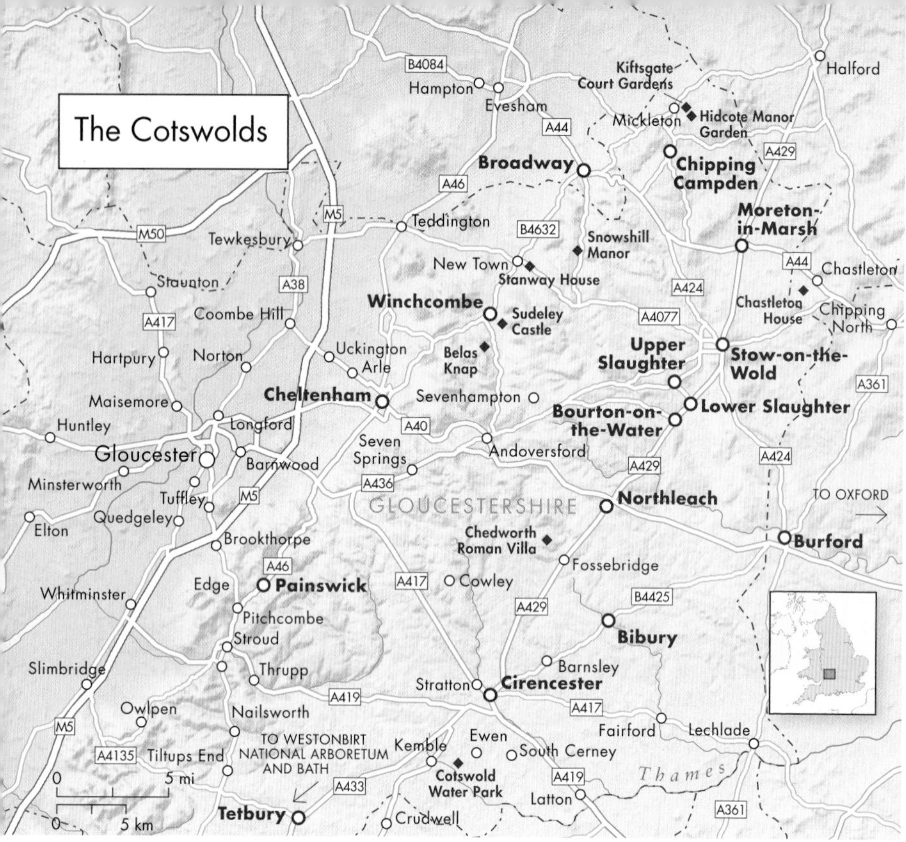
The Cotswolds
B4084
Hampton
Evesham
Kiftsgate Court Gardens
Mickleton
Hidcote Manor Garden
Halford
A44
A429
Broadway
Chipping Campden
A46
M5
Teddington
B4632
Moreton-in-Marsh
M50
Tewkesbury
Snowshill Manor
New Town
Stanway House
A44
Chastleton
Staunton
A38
A424
Chastleton House
Chipping North
Winchcombe
Sudeley Castle
A4077
A417
Coombe Hill
Upper Slaughter
Stow-on-the-Wold
Hartpury
Norton
Uckington
Arle
Belas Knap
A361
Maisemore
Cheltenham
Sevenhampton
Lower Slaughter
Huntley
Longford
A40
Bourton-on-the-Water
Gloucester
Barnwood
Seven Springs
Andoversford
A424
Minsterworth
A429
A436
Tuffley
M5
GLOUCESTERSHIRE
Northleach
TO OXFORD
Elton
Quedgeley
Chedworth Roman Villa
Burford
Brookthorpe
Fossebridge
A46
Whitminster
Edge
Painswick
A417
Cowley
B4425
A429
Pitchcombe
Bibury
Stroud
Slimbridge
Thrupp
Barnsley
Stratton
Cirencester
A419
Owlpen
Nailsworth
A417
M5
Fairford
Lechlade
TO WESTONBIRT NATIONAL ARBORETUM AND BATH
Ewen
Kemble
South Cerney
A4135
Tiltups End
0
5 mi
Cotswold Water Park
A419
Thames
A433
Latton
0
5 km
Tetbury
Crudwell
A361

WHERE TO EAT

$$ BISTRO 🍴 **Bistrot Coco.** Stone steps lead down to this intimate basement bistro where red lamps fringed with tassles, a wood-burning stove, and a little bar with a ceiling papered with French icons like the Eiffel Tower are the backdrop for classic French dishes. You might expect a warm goat's cheese salad, navarin of lamb, snails or frogs' legs, which you can accompany with a glass or two from the carefully selected wine list. There's a sheltered courtyard for warm days and a two-course lunch for £10. [$] *Average main: £15* ✉ *30 Cambray Pl.* ☎ *01242/534000.*

$$ MODERN BRITISH 🍴 **The Daffodil.** This restaurant proves that turning up the wow quotient doesn't always mean a drop in culinary standards. Housed in a former art deco cinema, the place is themed along 1920s lines. It's dimly lighted, with sweeping staircases and an open kitchen where the screen once stood; the best view is from the Circle Bar. The menu features twice-baked Double Gloucester soufflé, oxtail pudding with beef fillet, and slow-roasted pork belly. Afterward, indulge in a popcorn pannacotta, or a platter of cheeses with quince chutney. There's live jazz on Monday evening and at lunchtime on Saturday. Early-evening and lunch menus are a good deal. [$] *Average main: £15* ✉ *18–20 Suffolk Parade* ☎ *01242/700055* 🌐 *www.thedaffodil.com* ✍ *Reservations essential* 🕐 *Closed Sun.*

$$ MODERN BRITISH 🍴 **Purslane.** Daughters treating their mothers, ladies who shop, and gentlemen cutting a dash all come here, lured by the imaginative and well-presented menu and cool, unfussy surroundings. The freshest of Cornish fish, smoked eel from the River Severn, and Dorset oysters are accompanied by unusual, but delicious vegetables like wild garlic, alexanders, and radish shoots. The accent is on fish, but you will also find Gloucestershire chorizo and hay-baked rabbit, and plenty of local cheeses. Service is friendly and knowledgeable. [$] *Average main: £16* ✉ *16 Rodney Rd., Cheltenham* ☎ *01242/321639* 🌐 *www.purslane-restaurant.co.uk* ⏲ *Closed Sun and Mon.*

WHERE TO STAY

For expanded hotel reviews, visit Fodors.com.

$$$ HOTEL 🏨 **Cowley Manor.** Good-bye, floral prints: this Georgian mansion on 55 acres brings country-house style into the 21st century with a mellow atmosphere and modern fabrics and furnishings. **Pros:** beautiful grounds; excellent spa facilities; relaxed vibe. **Cons:** slightly corporate feel; some hitches with service. [$] *Rooms from: £185* ✉ *Off A435, Cowley* ☎ *01242/870900* 🌐 *www.cowleymanor.com* 🛏 *30 rooms* 🍽 *Breakfast.*

$$ B&B/INN 🏨 **Hanover House.** Centrally located, this family-run guesthouse dating from 1848 brims with character, and richly colored cushions, vases of flowers, and myriad books enliven the bright and airy rooms. **Pros:** fun; convenient location; award-winning breakfasts. **Cons:** not for those who wish to remain anonymous; all guests share one large table at breakfast. [$] *Rooms from: £100* ✉ *65 St. George's Rd.* ☎ *01242/541297* 🌐 *www.hanoverhouse.org* 🛏 *3 rooms* 🍽 *Breakfast.*

$ B&B/INN 🏨 **Lypiatt House.** A short walk from the center of Cheltenham in the chic Montpellier area, this splendid Victorian villa offers attentive service in elegant surroundings. **Pros:** clean and elegant; capacious parking; excellent breakfasts. **Cons:** slight traffic noise. [$] *Rooms from: £95* ✉ *Lypiatt Rd.* ☎ *01242/224994* 🌐 *www.lypiatt.co.uk* 🛏 *10 rooms* 🍽 *Breakfast.*

NIGHTLIFE AND THE ARTS

Cheltenham Jazz Festival. Held over a week in late April and early May, the Cheltenham Jazz Festival presents noted musicians from around the world. ☎ *01242/511211 inquiries, 0844/880–8094 box office* 🌐 *www.cheltenhamfestivals.com.*

Everyman Theatre. The late-Victorian Everyman Theatre is an intimate venue for opera, dance, concerts, and plays. **TIP→ You can often catch pre- or post-West End productions here, at a fraction of big-city prices.** ✉ *Regent St.* ☎ *01242/572573.*

Festivals Box Office. For information on the town's ambitious lineup of festivals, contact the Festivals Box Office. ✉ *Regent Arcade, High St.* ☎ *01242/511211 inquiries, 0844/880–8094 box office* 🌐 *www.cheltenhamfestivals.com.*

Fodor's Choice ★ **Literature Festival.** The 10-day Literature Festival in October brings together world-renowned authors, actors, and critics for hundreds of readings, lectures, and other events. ☎ *01242/511211 inquiries, 0844/880–8094 box office* 🌐 *www.cheltenhamfestivals.com.*

7

October's Literature Festival brings plenty of authors—and their books—to Cheltenham.

Music Festival. Cheltenham's famous Music Festival, held over 10 days in early July, highlights new compositions, often conducted by the composers themselves, plus a wide variety of choral and instrumental classical pieces. ☎ *01242/511211 inquiries, 0844/880–8094 box office* ⊕ *www.cheltenhamfestivals.com.*

Science Festival. For five days in early June, the Science Festival attracts leading scientists and writers. ☎ *01242/511211 inquiries, 0844/880–8094 tickets* ⊕ *www.cheltenhamfestivals.com.*

SHOPPING

This is serious shopping territory. A stroll along Montpellier Walk and then along the flower-bedecked Promenade brings you to high-end specialty stores and boutiques. A bubble-blowing Wishing Fish Clock, designed by Kit Williams, dominates the Regent Arcade, a modern shopping area behind the Promenade. A farmers' market enlivens the Promenade on the second and last Friday of the month.

Cavendish House. This high-end department store stocks designer fashions. ✉ *32–48 The Promenade* ☎ *01242/521300.*

Feva. Eye-catching women's clothing in bright, splashy colors, as well as accessories like shoes, belts, and handbags, are on display at Feva. More formal wear is sold on the upper floor. ✉ *20 Regent St.* ☎ *01242/222998.*

Martin. This shop carries a good stock of classic and modern jewelry. ✉ *19 The Promenade* ☎ *01242/522821.*

Q and C Militaria. A treasure trove for military buffs, Q and C Militaria offers badges and medals, breastplates, helmets, coats of arms, and books. It's run by ex-soldiers. ⊠ *22 Suffolk Rd.* ☎ *01242/519815.*

SPORTS

Cheltenham Racecourse. Important steeplechase races take place at Cheltenham Racecourse, north of the town center. The Gold Cup awards crown the last day of the National Hunt Festival in mid-March. ⊠ *Prestbury Park* ☎ *0844/579–3003 ticket line, 01242/513014 tickets and inquiries* ⊕ *www.cheltenham.co.uk.*

WINCHCOMBE

7 miles northeast of Cheltenham.

Fodor's Choice ★ The sleepy, unspoiled village of Winchcombe (population 4,500), once the capital of the Anglo-Saxon kingdom of Mercia, has some attractive half-timber and stone houses, as well as a clutch of appealing old inns serving food. A good place to escape the crowds, it's near Sudeley Castle and is also on several walking routes: the Cotswold Way; the Warden's Way and Windrush Way, both linking Winchcombe with Bourton-on-the-Water; and the Winchcombe Way, a 42-mile figure-eight trail around the northern Cotswolds. A three-day walking festival (⊕ *www.winchcombewelcomeswalkers.com*) takes place here in mid-May.

GETTING HERE AND AROUND
Hourly Castleways buses take 20 minutes to get to Winchcombe from Cheltenham (no Sunday service). By car, take B4632, leading over the steep and panoramic Cleeve Hill.

ESSENTIALS
Visitor Information Winchcombe Tourist Information Centre ⊠ *Town Hall, High St.* ☎ *01242/602925* ⊕ *www.visitcotswoldsandsevernvale.gov.uk.*

EXPLORING

Belas Knap Long Barrow. A bracing 2-mile walk south of Winchcombe on the Cotswold Way, one of Britain's national walking trails, leads to the hilltop site of Belas Knap, a Neolithic long barrow, or submerged burial chamber, above Humblebee Wood. ■TIP➔ **The site isn't much to see, but you hike through one of the most enchanting natural domains in England, with views stretching over to Sudeley Castle.** ☎ *0870/333–1181* ⊕ *www.english-heritage.org.uk/daysout/properties/belas-knap-long-barrow.*

FAMILY **Gloucestershire and Warwickshire Railway.** Less than a mile north of Winchcombe at Greet, this steam-hauled train chugs its way along the foot of the Cotswolds connecting Winchcombe with Toddington and Cheltenham Racecourse. From Cheltenham the round trip is 25 miles, but you can take a shorter trip from Winchcombe to Toddington. ⊠ *Winchcombe Station, Greet Rd., Greet* ☎ *01242/621405* ⊕ *www.gwsr.com* 🎫 *£12 return to Cebeltenham, £10 to Toddington* ☉ *June–Sept., Tues.–Thurs. and weekends 10–5; Apr.–Oct., Tues., Wed., and weekends 10–5; Feb. and Dec., weekends 10–5.*

St. Peter's Church. Almost 40 outlandish gargoyles adorn this mid-15th-century Perpendicular-style building, a typical Cotswold wool church full of light. The interior displays an embroidered altar frontal said to have been worked by Catherine of Aragon, first wife of King Henry VIII. Look for the Winchcombe Imp, an unusual figure for a rood screen, now at the back of the church. ✉ *Gloucester St.* ☎ *01242/602067.*

Sudeley Castle. One of the grand showpieces of the Cotswolds, Sudeley Castle was the home and burial place of Catherine Parr (1512–48), Henry VIII's sixth and last wife, who outlived him by one year. Here Catherine undertook, in her later years, the education of the ill-fated Lady Jane Grey and the future queen, Princess Elizabeth. Sudeley, for good reason, has been called a woman's castle. The term "castle" is misleading, though, for it looks more like a Tudor-era palace, with a peaceful air that belies its turbulent history. In the 17th century Charles I took refuge here, causing Oliver Cromwell's army to besiege the castle. It remained in ruins until the Dent-Brocklehurst family stepped in with a 19th-century renovation.

The 14 acres of gardens, which include the spectacular roses of the Queen's Garden and a Tudor knot garden, are the setting for Tudor fun days in summer. Inside the castle, visitors see only the West Wing, with the Long Room where exhibitions, such as very fine textiles or the Romans, illustrate the castle's history. The private apartments of Lord and Lady Ashcombe, where you can see paintings by Van Dyck, Rubens, Turner, and Reynolds, are viewable only on £18 Connoisseur Tours on Tuesday, Wednesday, and Thursday. The 11 cottages and appartments on the grounds are booked for a minimum of three-night stays. The castle is a mile southeast of Winchcombe. ✉ *Off B4632* ☎ *01242/602308, 01242/609481 Cottages* 🌐 *www.sudeleycastle.co.uk* 🎫 *£12; gardens £8* 🕓 *Apr.–Oct., daily 10:30–5.*

WHERE TO EAT

$$ MODERN BRITISH 🍴 **Wesley House.** Wooden beams and stone walls distinguish this 15th-century half-timber building, where the elegant dining room and sunny conservatory make a fine backdrop for superior Modern British dishes. The seasonal menu might include cured salmon with pea blini, lemon and thyme mascarpone as a starter, and roast guinea fowl with toasted hazelnut to follow. Fixed-price lunch and evening menus are a good value. You can eat and drink less formally in the adjoining snug or bar and grill, where sharing platters of cheeses, cured meats, or fish lets you sample a bit of everything. Upstairs, five small guest rooms have twisted beams and sloping ceilings, including the Preacher's Room, where John Wesley used to stay. [$] *Average main: £18* ✉ *High St.* ☎ *01242/602366* 🌐 *www.wesleyhouse.co.uk* 🕓 *No dinner Sun.*

BROADWAY

8 miles north of Winchcombe, 17 miles northeast of Cheltenham.

The Cotswold town to end all Cotswold towns, Broadway has become a favorite of day-trippers. William Morris first discovered the delights of this village, and J. M. Barrie, Vaughan Williams, and Edward Elgar soon followed. Today you may want to avoid Broadway in summer, when it's clogged with cars and buses. Named for its handsome, wide main street (well worth a stroll), the village includes numerous antiques shops, tea parlors, and boutiques. Step into Broadway's back-roads and alleys and you can discover any number of honey-color houses and colorful gardens.

GETTING HERE AND AROUND

Broadway can be reached by car via A44; park in one of the parking lots signposted from the main street. Johnson's Coaches connects the town with Stratford-upon-Avon, Chipping Campden, and Moreton-in-Marsh; Castleways connects Broadway with Winchcombe and Cheltenham. No buses run on Sunday. You'll need a car to reach Broadway Tower, Stanway House, and Snowshill Manor.

ESSENTIALS

Visitor Information Broadway Tourist Information Centre ⊠ *Russell Sq.* ☎ *01386/852937* ⊕ *www.beautifulbroadway.com.*

EXPLORING

Broadway Tower Country Park. Among the attractions of this park on the outskirts of town is its crenelated tower, an 18th-century "folly" built by the sixth earl of Coventry and later used by William Morris as a retreat. The panoramic view from the top takes in three counties and looks over peaceful countryside and wandering deer. There are plenty of nature trails and good spots for picnics. Wall panels on the three floors inside describe the tower's connection with the local Arts and Crafts movement and World War II. Note that the spiral staircase is narrow and steep. A nuclear bunker is open on weekends during the summer. ⊠ *Off A44* ☎ *01386/852390* ⊕ *www.broadwaytower. co.uk* ☞ *Park free, tower £4.80, bunker £3.50* ☉ *Daily 10.30–5, or dusk in winter.*

FAMILY
Fodor's Choice
★

Snowshill Manor. Three miles south of Broadway and 13 miles northeast of Cheltenham, Snowshill is one of the most unspoiled of all Cotswold villages. Snuggled beneath Oat Hill, with little room for expansion, the hamlet is centered on an old burial ground, the 19th-century St. Barnabas Church, and Snowshill Manor, a splendid 17th-century house that brims with the collections of Charles Paget Wade, gathered between 1919 and 1956. Over the door of the house is Wade's family motto, *Nequid pereat* ("Let nothing perish"). The rooms are bursting with Tibetan scrolls, spinners' tools, ship models, Persian lamps, and bric-a-brac; the Green Room displays 26 suits of Japanese samurai armor. Children love the place. Outside, an imaginative terraced garden provides an exquisite frame for the house. ■ TIP➔ **Admission is by timed tickets issued on a first-come, first-served basis, so arrive early in peak season.** ⊠ *Off A44, Snowshill* ☎ *01386/852410* ⊕ *www. nationaltrust.org.uk* ☞ *£9.40; garden only £5* ☉ *House Apr.–June, Oct., Sept., Wed.–Sun. and national holidays noon–5; July and Aug., Tues.–Sun. 11:30–4:30; garden mid-Mar.–June, Sept., Oct., Wed.–Sun. and national holidays 11–5:30; July and Aug. 11:30–5. Last admission 1 hr before closing.*

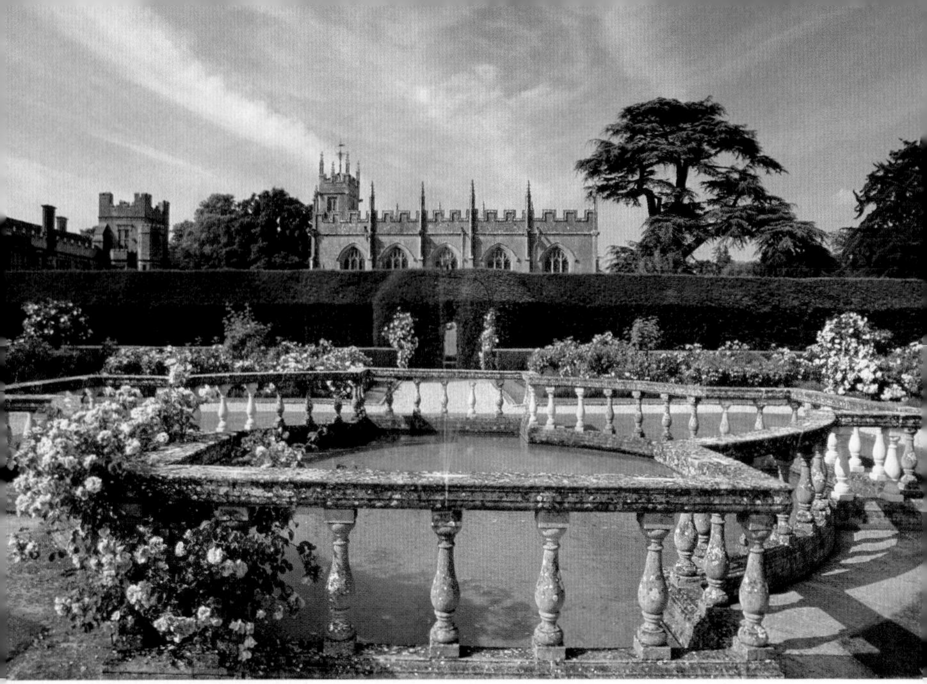

As enchanting as the house, the gardens at Sudeley Castle provide a perfect backdrop for outdoor events in summer.

Stanway House. This perfect Cotswold manor of glowing limestone, Stanway House dates from the Jacobean era. Its triple-gabled gatehouse is a Cotswold landmark, and towering windows dominate the house's Great Hall. They illuminate a 22-foot-long shuffleboard table from 1620 and an 18th-century bouncing exercise machine. The other well-worn rooms are adorned with family portraits, tattered tapestries, vintage armchairs, and, at times, Lord or Lady Neidpath themselves, the current owners. The partly restored baroque water garden has a modern fountain that shoots up 300 feet. The tallest in Britain, it shoots at 2:45 and 4. To get to Stanway, about 5 miles south of Broadway, take B4632 south from town, turning left at B4077. ✉ *Off B4077, Stanway* ☎ *01386/584469* 🌐 *www.stanwayfountain.co.uk* 🎟 *House and fountain £7; fountain only, £4.50* 🕓 *June–Aug., Tues. and Thurs. 2–5.*

WHERE TO EAT

$$$ MODERN BRITISH 🍴 **Russell's.** With a courtyard at the back and a patio at the front, this chic "restaurant with rooms" is perfect for a light lunch at midday or a full meal in the evening. The restaurant, in a former furniture factory belonging to local designer George Russell, is modern, airy, and stylish. Menus concentrate on Modern British dishes, with such temptations as Warwickshire lamb with herb crust and wild mushrooms, mandarin soufflé, and peach melba with coriander cress. The less expensive fixed-price menu is just as tempting, and there's also an attached fish-and-chip shop. Seven boutique-style rooms upstairs are very sleek. [$] *Average main: £20* ✉ *20 High St.* ☎ *01386/853555* 🌐 *www.russellsofbroadway.co.uk* 🕓 *No dinner Sun.*

$
MODERN BRITISH
✕ **The Swan.** In the center of Broadway, this pub-restaurant makes a handy stop for a snack, lunch, a drink, or something more substantial. Service may be occasionally slapdash and the place can get congested, but on a weekday it's cozy and convivial, with an open fire in winter and comfortable seating. The imaginative decor blends the traditional and trendy with large mirrors, log-studded walls, and eye-catching knickknacks. Among the hot dishes you're likely to find marinated sticky chicken with lemon, honey, and chili sauce, or duck breast in an orange sauce; tapots (small British tapas-style dishes) and tasting platters are a popular alternative. There's a good wine cellar and plenty of cask ales, as well as a childrens' menu. **$** *Average main: £14* ✉ *2 The Green* ☎ *01386/852278* ⊕ *www.theswanbroadway.co.uk.*

> ### SEEKING SHAKESPEARE
>
> The country delights of the area lure you to linger, but keep in mind that in the northern part of the Cotswolds, you're less than 15 miles from Stratford-upon-Avon. It's easy to detour to visit the Shakespeare sights or even see a play at the Royal Shakespeare Theatre.

WHERE TO STAY

For expanded hotel reviews, visit Fodors.com.

$$$$
HOTEL
▦ **Buckland Manor.** As an alternative to the hustle and bustle of Broadway, you can travel the 2 miles to the idyllic hamlet of Buckland and splurge at this exceptional traditional country house, which has more of a feel of a genteel family home than a hotel. **Pros:** beautiful setting; elegant guest rooms; large bathrooms with high-quality toiletries. **Cons:** some rooms are small; restaurant quite formal; steep prices. **$** *Rooms from: £305* ✉ *Off B4632, Buckland* ☎ *01386/852626* ⊕ *www.bucklandmanor.co.uk* ⤳ *13 rooms* ❙◉❙ *Breakfast.*

$$$
B&B/INN
▦ **Mill Hay House.** If the rose garden, trout-filled pond, and sheep on the hill at this 18th-century Queen Anne house aren't appealing enough, then the stone-flagged floors, leather sofas, and grandfather clocks should satisfy. **Pros:** delightful owners; beautifully landscaped gardens; gourmet breakfasts. **Cons:** books up quickly; no young children admitted. **$** *Rooms from: £175* ✉ *Snowshill Rd.* ☎ *01386/852498* ⊕ *www.millhay.co.uk* ⤳ *2 rooms, 1 suite* ❙◉❙ *Breakfast.*

$
B&B/INN
▦ **The Olive Branch.** Right on the main drag, this 16th-century cottage has authentic period charm and is strewn with antique knickknacks: a brass wind-up gramophone has pride of place. **Pros:** cottage character; central location; hospitable hosts. **Cons:** small bathrooms; narrow stairs; low ceilings. **$** *Rooms from: £98* ✉ *78 High St.* ☎ *01386/853440* ⊕ *www.theolivebranch-broadway.com* ⤳ *8 rooms* ❙◉❙ *Breakfast.*

Continued on page 467

GLORIOUS ENGLISH GARDENS
by Kate Hughes

The English have been masters of the garden for centuries; gardening is in the blood. No one, from the owner of vast acres in the country to a town dweller with a modest window box, is able to resist this pull. Since the 18th century they have also been inveterate garden visitors, with people from around the world following in their wake. Here's how to make the most of your garden visit, from the variety of styles you'll see to the best bets for all tastes around England.

Magnificent vista of the Pantheon and lake at Stourhead

For many people the quintessential English garden conjures up swaths of close-clipped lawns (the landscape garden), beds of roses, or colorful flowers (the herbaceous border) lining a path to a cottage door framed with honeysuckle.

This is not the whole story, however. Cathedrals and colleges yield up their sequestered cloister gardens; grand houses their patterned beds of flowers by the thousand; manor houses their amusing topiary shapes, orchards, and wildflower meadows; sweeping landscaped parks their classical temples and serpentine lakes; a Cornish ravine its jungle tumbling down to the sea. And this is not to mention the magnificent glasshouses and biomes of the botanical gardens housing spectacular plant treasures. Around the country, gardens large and small invite exploration.

GARDEN STYLES THROUGH THE AGES

In the gardens you'll be visiting, one theme remains constant no matter the style: the combination of usefulness and beauty. Gardens were larders as well as ornaments; plants were grown and birds and animals kept both for decoration and for eating. Behind each great garden was wealth, and gardens became as great a status symbol as the houses they surrounded. Growing the best pineapple, building the most elaborate terraces, flooding a valley to make a lake were all signs that you had made it in the world.

Clockwise from top left: Stowe Landscape Gardens; Chatsworth; Hidcote Manor Garden; Hampton Court Palace (formal Privy Garden)

SYMBOLS AND PATTERNS: TUDOR GARDENS

Since Tudor times the rose has been the emblem of England, and it still is the most loved English flower. Musk roses entwine the arbors in the garden created to impress Queen Elizabeth I on her visit to Kenilworth Castle in 1575, now magnificently restored. Here the formal arrangement of trellises, obelisks, fountain, statues, and aviary set in gravel paths and overlooked by a viewing platform exemplify gardens of the time. Also here is the first uniquely English garden feature—the knot garden. Low evergreen hedges, most famously planted with box, were interlaced in geometric patterns, the spaces filled with flowers and herbs. Good examples of knot gardens can be found at Hampton Court Palace and Hatfield House.

See it: *Hampton Court Palace* (Ch. 2), *Hatfield House* (Ch. 6), *Kenilworth Castle* (Ch. 8)

WEALTH AND POWER: THE 17TH-CENTURY FORMAL GARDEN

Landed gentry with time on their hands took gardening to their hearts. After the ravages of the Civil War (1642–49) and the Great Fire of London (1666) they felt the lure of the rural idyll, and country houses with small estates proliferated. The garden rectangle in front of the house was divided into smaller rectangles—the forerunner of garden "rooms" as at Sissinghurst and Hidcote Manor—and filled with formal walkways, fishponds, and fountains. Topiary gardens (Levens Hall and Packwood House) became popular, and an increase in foreign travel led to the introduction of a greater variety of bulbs and flowers. In 1621 the first botanic garden was set up in Oxford.

See it: *Hidcote Manor* (Ch. 7), *Levens Hall* (Ch. 10), *Packwood House* (Ch. 8), *Sissinghurst* (Ch. 3), *University of Oxford Botanic Garden* (Ch. 6)

Knot garden at Hatfield House

GEOMETRY TO LANDSCAPE: THE 18TH CENTURY

Gradually the formal approach gave way. One product of the fashionable Grand Tour, when aristocratic young bloods were exposed to new landscapes and ideas, was William Kent (1685–1748), the "father of modern gardening." His innovative genius was his English take on the Italian garden, converting the natural landscape into a pleasure ground for the rich, dotting it with statues, obelisks, and classical temples and ornamenting it with trees and serpentine lakes (Rousham and Stowe).

Kent was eclipsed by Lancelot "Capability" Brown (1715–83), who created 100 gardens between 1750 and 1780 (Stowe, Stourhead, Petworth, Kew Gardens). He brought the landscape right to the front door and created lakes and parkland that also provided timber, cover for game, and grazing for sheep and deer.

See it: *Kew Gardens* (Ch. 2), *Petworth* (Ch. 3) *Rousham and Stowe* (Ch. 6), *Stourhead* (Ch. 4)

SHOW AND TECHNOLOGY: THE VICTORIAN PERIOD

This was an age of new technology, variety, and the return of flowers. Wealthy industrialists could afford to move out of town and create rose gardens, ferneries, and rockeries, and display showier flowers such as chrysanthemums, dahlias, and rhododendrons. The invention of the lawn mower in 1830 made the English obsession with close-clipped lawns accessible to all. Bedding schemes and patterns reappeared in the new public parks of the 1830s and 1840s. One spectacular scheme is the parterre (ornamental flower garden with paths) at Waddesdon Manor, planted with lavish displays each spring and summer. Joseph Paxton (1803–1865) head gardener at Chatsworth, created the first greenhouse, which started a fashion for conservatories and the growing of exotic fruit such as figs and peaches.

See it: *Chatsworth* (Ch. 9), *Waddesdon Manor* (Ch. 6)

ARTS AND CRAFTS: INTO THE 20TH CENTURY

The Arts and Crafts movement drew inspiration from medieval romance and nature and preferred the informal cottage garden look, seen particularly in the Cotswolds (Hidcote Manor, Kiftsgate, Rodmarton Manor). Female gardeners came to the fore. Gertrude Jekyll (pronounced Jee-kill; 1843–1932), often working with the architect Edwin Lutyens (1869–1944), set the fashion for using drifts of single color, and Vita Sackville West (1892–1962) created the enduringly romantic Sissinghurst.

See it: *Hidcote Manor, Kiftsgate,* and *Rodmarton Manor (Ch. 7), Sissinghurst* (Ch. 3)

ANYTHING GOES: MODERN TIMES

The reaction to the drab years of the Second World War was to create garden cities and increasingly versatile gardens using all modern materials available. The bold approach and strong colors of Christopher Lloyd (1921–2006) at

Great Dixter has remained influential. Ripples were caused when gnomes, derided by many, were permitted in the 2013 Chelsea Flower Show. Environmental awareness has led to more educational gardens, such as the spectacular Eden Project in Cornwall.

See it: *Great Dixter* (Ch. 3), *Eden Project* (Ch. 5)

Overview of part of Sissinghurst (top); house and garden at Great Dixter (bottom)

BEST IN SHOW AROUND THE COUNTRY

Rousham Park

Practically every house or stately home you visit will be surrounded by a lovingly tended garden, but you will find a profusion of outstanding examples in the Cotswolds (Oxfordshire and Gloucestershire), Kent, and Cornwall. Kent is known as the "Garden of England" for its abundance of orchards and hop gardens; Cornwall's mild climate produces lush gardens, many by the sea; and the mellow honey-colored stone of the Cotswolds makes a perfect backdrop for floral ornament.

FLOWER GARDENS

The first three gardens, created in the 20th century, come top of the garden-visiting league. All show flair for harmonious planting in choice of color, form, and texture within a strong framework. Here flowers hold court.

❶ Hidcote Manor Garden (Bath and the Cotswolds). The pioneer of "garden rooms" and influential ever since, this garden blends the scent of old roses, long avenues with vistas, and the famous Red Border, especially vibrant from July.

❷ Sissinghurst (Southeast). Inspired by Hidcote Manor, it's divided into themed spaces: the Purple Border, the Rose Garden, the Cottage Garden, and, most famously, the White Garden.

❸ Great Dixter (Southeast). Vibrant color combinations surround the delightful 16th-century, half-timbered manor

house, also open. The Exotic Garden is at its best in late summer and early autumn.

❹ Rose Garden in the Savill Garden at Windsor (Thames Valley). The very contemporary Rose Garden (2010) has a viewing promontory for the 2,500 headily scented roses in their swaths of pinks, yellows, and reds.

BOTANIC AND TEACHING GARDENS

If you're thinking endless paths of plants and reading labels, think again. These gardens share their expertise through stunning architecture, hands-on activities, and fantastic displays.

❺ Kew Gardens (London). An 18th-century Chinese Pagoda is the landmark for Kew Gardens and its magnificent 19th-century greenhouses, housing a tropical rain forest and the world's tallest plant. There's also a treetop walkway.

❻ Eden Project (West Country). Cornwall's "global garden" explores man's relationship with plants with great imagination and a sense of fun. Huge biomes, like see-through golf balls, contain different plants from all climates.

❼ Wisley (Southeast). Flagship garden for the Royal Horticultural Society, it has a huge modern, elegant glasshouse, full of plants from around the world, plus flower and vegetable gardens and a unique interactive Root Zone.

Kew Gardens

Stourhead

LANDSCAPE GARDENS

The 18th-century English landscape garden has much more to offer than sweeping Capability Brown parkland. Adopt an aristocratic air and give yourself time to walk and admire the vistas.

8 Stowe Landscape Gardens (Thames Valley). The grandest stop on the garden visiting circuit for over 200 years, it has no less than 40 temples, enormous grand avenues, a serpentine lake, and even Elysian Fields.

9 Stourhead (South). Quite simply, this masterpiece of a garden set in a valley encompassing a lake is one of the finest landscape gardens in the world. Summer rhododendrons and trees in the fall add to the picture.

10 Rousham Park (Thames Valley). More intimate than Stowe or Stourhead, it makes for an idyllic walk. The walled garden blooms with flowers.

FAMILY FAVORITES

For kids, choose the bigger gardens; they will have special attractions and activities for them. The Eden Project and Kew Gardens are also family friendly.

11 Alnwick Garden (Northeast). This contemporary garden was created with families in mind. Kids will be fascinated by the poison garden, water jets, and Bamboo Maze, and won't forget eating in the wooden Treehouse Café.

12 Chatsworth (Lancashire and the Peaks). The grand water Cascade falling the 200-foot length of the steps and the Emperor Fountain shooting 300 feet into the sky provide entertainment, along with the maze, farmyard, and woodland adventure playground.

13 Westonbirt National Arboretum (Bath and the Cotswolds). Play zones are hidden throughout the arboretum. Kids can make dens, balance on logs, build nests, and, of course, climb trees.

Alnwick 270mi **11**
Newcastle
Sunderland
Penrith
Hartlepool
Darlington
Middlesbrough
Kendal
Lancaster
York
Leeds
Bradford
Manchester
Sheffield
Chester
12 Bakewell 135mi
Stoke
Nottingham
Boston
The Wash
Newcastle
Grantham
Shrewsbury
Leicester
Norwich
Wolverhampton
King's Lynn
Lowestoft
Birmingham
Peterborough
Stratford upon-Avon
Coventry **ENGLAND**
Ipswich
Hidcote Bartrim 1 85mi
10
8 Buckingham 45mi
Colchester
Cheltenham
Rousham 60mi
Luton
Harwich
Gloucester
Oxford
Kew 5 10mi
13 Tetbury 95mi
Englefield Green 4 .13 mi
7
★ LONDON 0mi
Bristol
Reading
Canterbury
Bath
Woking 20mi
Maidstone
Cranbrook 2 35mi
9
Salisbury
Northiam 3 50mi
Dover
Stourton 100mi
Southampton
Brighton
Rye
Bournemouth
Portsmouth
Weymouth
Isle of Wight
English Channel

* Approximate travel distance from London

Dieppe
FRANCE

MAKING THE MOST OF YOUR GARDEN VISIT

SEASONAL SPLENDOR

The best gardens will have something of interest year-round, though many close in winter. Spring through September yield the most rewards, and each season will have its special offerings: early spring offers snowdrops, followed by daffodils and bluebells. May is the month for azaleas and rhododendrons, roses are in full bloom in June, and by July herbaceous borders of lupins, delphiniums, and foxgloves are showing their true colors. August sees hydrangeas and dahlias coming to the fore, while in September there's a second flowering of roses. The oranges and reds of the fall last through October.

Eden Project

TOURING TIPS

The bigger houses have separate, often less expensive tickets for the gardens and the grounds only, so do ask. Depending on your itinerary, buying an English Heritage (⊕ www.english-heritage.org.uk) or National Trust (⊕ www.nationaltrust.org.uk) pass or joining the National Trust may save you money on garden admissions.

A car is preferable, as many places are not accessible by train or bus; Web sites often have information on public transportation options if they are available. The most popular gardens, such as Sissinghurst, get very crowded, especially on weekends, so come early or late in the day for a more peaceful visit. Most gardens have a café or restaurant, and nothing is more delightful than a cream tea in an English country garden in June.

Gardens associated with the National Trust are closed in winter, but their grounds remain open.

GOING DEEPER

The indispensable Yellow Book (£9.99) is published annually by the National Gardens Scheme (⊕ www.ngs.org.uk);

it is also available in sections by county (free, with donation). The directory lists public and private gardens that are normally closed to the public but have open days for charity throughout the year. Many of them offer teas as well.

FLOWER SHOWS

London claims the two main flower shows, both knockouts that last several days. The Chelsea Flower Show, five days in late May (£55; no kids under 5), and, outside the city, Hampton Court Palace Flower Show, six days in early July (£29.50), represent the cutting edge of design and cover every aspect of gardening (☎ 0121/767–4063 or ☎ 0844/338–7506, ⊕ www.rhs.org.uk).

MORE RESOURCES

Two useful Web sites are ⊕ www.gardenvisit.org, a mine of information on gardens by county, garden hotels, tours self-guided and led, and garden history; and ⊕ www.greatbritishgardens.co.uk, which has a good directory of gardens.

Good books to read are *The Gardens of Britain and Ireland* by Patrick Taylor (Dorling Kindersley), *The Good Gardens Guide*, edited by Katherine Lambert (Readers Digest), and *Great Gardens to Visit* by Tony Russell (Amberley Publishing).

CHIPPING CAMPDEN

4 miles east of Broadway, 18 miles northeast of Cheltenham.

Fodor'sChoice ★ Undoubtedly one of the most beautiful towns in the area, Chipping Campden, with its population of about 2,500, is the Cotswolds in a microcosm. It has St. James, the region's most impressive church; frozen-in-time streets; a silk mill that was once the center of the Guild of Handicraft; and pleasant, untouristy shops. One of the area's most seductive settings unfolds before you as you travel on B4081 through sublime English countryside and happen upon the town, tucked in a slight valley. North of town is lovely Hidcote Manor Garden. ▦TIP➡ Chipping Campden can easily be reached on foot along a level section of the Cotswold Way from Broadway Tower, outside Broadway; the walk takes about 75 minutes.

GETTING HERE AND AROUND

By car, Chipping Campden can be reached on minor roads from A44 or A429. There's a small car park in the center and spaces on the outskirts of the village. By bus, take Johnson's Coaches from Stratford-upon-Avon, Broadway, and Moreton-in-Marsh, or Pulham's Coaches from Bourton-on-the-Water and Cheltenham, changing at Moreton-in-Marsh (no Sunday service).

ESSENTIALS

Visitor Information **Chipping Campden Tourism Information Centre** ✉ *The Old Police Station, High St.* ☎ *01386/841206* ⊕ *www.chippingcamdenonline.org.*

EXPLORING

TOP ATTRACTIONS

Fodor'sChoice ★ **Hidcote Manor Garden.** Laid out around a Cotswold manor house, Hidcote Manor Garden is arguably the most interesting and attractive large garden in Britain. Crowds are large at the height of the season, but it's worthwhile anytime. A horticulturist from the United States, Major Lawrence Johnston, created the garden in 1907 in the Arts and Crafts style. Johnston was an imaginative gardener and avid traveler who brought back specimens from all over the world. The formal part of the garden is arranged in "rooms" separated by hedges and often with fine topiary work and walls. Besides the variety of plants, what's impressive are the different effects created, from calm open spaces to areas packed with flowers. ▦TIP➡ Look for one of Johnston's earliest schemes, the red borders of dahlias, poppies, fuchsias, lobelias, and roses; the tall hornbeam hedges; and the Bathing Pool garden, where the pool is so wide there's scarcely space to walk. The White Garden was probably the forerunner of the popular white gardens at Sissinghurst and Glyndebourne. If you have time, explore the tiny village of Hidcote Bartrim with its thatched stone houses; it borders the garden and fills a storybook dell. The garden is 4 miles northeast of Chipping Campden. ✉ *Off B4081, Hidcote Bartrim* ☎ *01386/438333* 🎫 *£9.50* 🕙 *Mid-Mar.–Apr. and Sept., Mon.–Wed. and weekends 10–6; May–Aug., daily 9–7; Oct.–early Nov., Mon.–Wed. and weekends 10–5; early Nov.–mid-Dec., weekends 11–4; last admission 1 hr before closing.*

7

St. James. The soaring pinnacled tower of St. James, a prime example of a Cotswold wool church (it was rebuilt in the 15th century with money from wool merchants), announces Chipping Campden from a distance; it's worth stepping inside to see the lofty nave. The church recalls the old saying, which became popular because of the vast numbers of houses of worship in the Cotswolds, "As sure as God's in Gloucestershire." ✉ *Church St.* ☎ *01386/841927* 🌐 *www.stjameschurchcampden.co.uk* 🎫 *£3 donation suggested* 🕒 *Mar.–Oct., Mon.–Sat. 11–5, Sun. 2–5:45; Nov.–Feb., Mon.–Sat. 11–3 Sun. 2–3.*

WORTH NOTING

Court Barn Museum. Near the church of St. James, this museum occupies an old agricultural building that has been smartly renovated to showcase the area's prominence in the fields of craft and design. You can admire examples of silverware, bookbinding, printing, woodcarving, and jewelry. Opposite the barn is an important row of almshouses dating from the reign of King James I. ✉ *Church St.* ☎ *01386/841951* 🌐 *www.courtbarn.org.uk* 🎫 *£4* 🕒 *Apr.–Sept., Tues.–Sun. 10–5; Oct.–Mar., Tues.–Sun. 10–4.*

Guild of Handicraft. In 1902 the Guild of Handicraft took over this former silk mill. Arts and Crafts evangelist Charles Robert Ashbee (1863–1942) brought 150 acolytes from London, including 50 guildsmen, to revive and practice such skills as cabinetmaking and bookbinding. The operation folded in 1920, but the refurbished building now houses the intriguing and very full workshop of a silversmith, and has a café and gallery on the ground floor. ✉ *Sheep St.* ☎ *0787/041–7144* 🎫 *Free* 🕒 *Workshops weekdays 9–5, Sat. 9–1; gallery daily 10–5.*

Kiftsgate Court Gardens. While not so spectacular as Hidcote Manor Garden, this intimate, privately owned garden, just a five-minute stroll away, still captivates. It's skipped by the majority of visitors to Hidcote, so you won't be jostled by the crowds. The interconnecting flower beds present harmonious arrays of color, and the contemporary formal water garden adds an elegant contrast. Don't miss the prized Kiftsgate rose, supposed to be the largest in England, flowering gloriously in mid-July. ✉ *Off B4081, Mickleton* ☎ *01386/438777* 🌐 *www.kiftsgate.co.uk* 🎫 *£7.50* 🕒 *Apr. and Sept., Mon., Wed., and Sun. 2–6; May–July, Sat.–Wed. noon–6; Aug., Sat.–Wed. 2–6.*

Market Hall. The broad High Street, lined with stone houses and shops, follows a captivating curve; in the center, on Market Street, is the Market Hall, a gabled Jacobean structure built by Sir Baptiste Hycks in 1627 "for the sale of local produce." ✉ *Market St.*

WHERE TO EAT

$$ MODERN BRITISH

🍴 **Churchill Arms.** In this small country pub just outside Chipping Campden, plain wooden tables and benches, a flagstone floor, and a roaring fire provide the backdrop for excellent food. In summer there's a small outside space as well. Crispy squid with chili dip, Ceasar salad with poached chicken, and sticky toffee pudding with ice cream appear on the menu. If you feel like staying overnight, upstairs are four bedrooms furnished in a contemporary style. [$] *Average main: £15* ✉ *Off B4035, Paxford* ☎ *01386/594000* 🌐 *www.thechurchillarms.com.*

Arts and Crafts in the Cotswolds

The Arts and Crafts movement flourished throughout Britain in the late-19th and early-20th centuries, but the Cotswolds are most closely associated with it. The godfather of the movement was designer William Morris (1834–96), whose home for the last 25 years of his life, Kelmscott Manor in Gloucestershire, became the headquarters of the school. A lecture by Morris, "The Beauty of Life," delivered in Birmingham in 1880, included the injunction that became the guiding principle of the movement: "Have nothing in your houses which you do not know to be useful or believe to be beautiful."

Driven by the belief that the spirit of medieval arts and crafts was being degraded and destroyed by the mass production and aggressive capitalism of the Victorian era, and aided by a dedicated core of artisans, Morris revolutionized the art of house design and decoration. His work with textiles was particularly influential.

WHERE TO SEE IT

Many of Morris's followers were influenced by the Cotswold countryside, such as the designer and architect Charles Robert Ashbee, who transferred his Guild of Handicraft from London to Chipping Campden in 1902. The village holds the small Court Barn Museum dedicated to local craftwork, including a permanent exhibition of pieces by the original group and those who followed in their wake.

Their work can also be seen at the Cheltenham Art Gallery and Museum (reopening after renovations in 2013), and, in its original context, at Rodmarton Manor outside Tetbury—which Ashbee declared the finest application of the movement's ideals. (Farther afield, Blackwell in the Lake District is a notable Arts and Crafts house.)

To see the Arts and Crafts ethic applied to horticulture, visit Hidcote Manor Garden, near Chipping Campden.

7

$ ✕ **Eight Bells.** Close to St. James Church, this traditional tavern has
BRITISH   low beams, a flagstone floor, and a small courtyard. The long menu includes such enticing dishes as wild mushroom and spinach risotto, chicken, leek and gammon pie, and baked fillet of sea trout. Fixed-price menus at lunchtime are easy on the wallet. The service is swift, and the good local ales are worth a taste. $ *Average main: £14* ⊠ *Church St.* ☎ *01386/840371* ⊕ *www.eightbellsinn.co.uk.*

WHERE TO STAY
For expanded hotel reviews, visit Fodors.com.

$ ⊡ **Badgers Hall.** Expect a friendly welcome at this antique B&B above
B&B/INN   a tearoom just across from the Market Hall, where the spacious, spotless rooms have beamed ceilings and exposed stonework. **Pros:** atmospheric building; attentive hosts; delicious breakfasts. **Cons:** low ceilings; entrance is through tea shop. $ *Rooms from: £98* ⊠ *High St.* ☎ *01386/840839* ⊕ *www.badgershall.com* ⊅ *3 rooms* ⦿ *Breakfast.*

$$$ ⊡ **Charingworth Manor.** Views of the countryside are limitless from this
HOTEL   14th-century manor house hotel where mullioned windows and oak beams enhance the sitting room. **Pros:** helpful and friendly staff; great

breakfasts; lots of amenities. **Cons:** some low beams in bedrooms; birds leave messages on cars. [$] *Rooms from: £180* ✉ *Off B4035, Charingworth* ☎ *01386/593555* 🌐 *www.classiclodges.co.uk* 🛏 *23 rooms, 3 suites* 🍴 *Breakfast.*

$$$ HOTEL 🏨 **Cotswold House.** This luxury hotel in the heart of Chipping Campden injects contemporary design into a stately 18th-century manor house, and from the swirling staircase in the entrance to the guest rooms studded with contemporary art and high-tech gadgetry, it's a winning formula. **Pros:** plenty of pampering; pleasant garden. **Cons:** some bathrooms are small. [$] *Rooms from: £185* ✉ *The Square* ☎ *01386/840330* 🌐 *www.cotswoldhouse.com* 🛏 *21 rooms, 7 suites* 🍴 *Breakfast.*

$$$ HOTEL 🏨 **Noel Arms Hotel.** Dating to the 14th century, Chipping Campden's oldest inn was built to accommodate foreign wool traders, and even though it's been enlarged, the building retains its exposed beams and stonework. **Pros:** traditional character; friendly staff. **Cons:** rooms can be noisy and overheated; annex overlooks car park. [$] *Rooms from: £185* ✉ *High St.* ☎ *01386/840317* 🌐 *www.noelarmshotel.com* 🛏 *27 rooms* 🍴 *Breakfast.*

SHOPPING

Hart. Descendants of an original member of the Guild of Handicraft specialize in fashioning lovely items from silver at this shop. ✉ *Guild of Handicrafts, Sheep St.* ☎ *01386/841100.*

Stuart House Antiques. This shop has windows filled with silverware and copperware, porcelain, Doulton figurines, and Staffordshire figures, and there's plenty more inside. ✉ *High St.* ☎ *01386/840995.*

MORETON-IN-MARSH

5 miles south of Chipping Campden, 18 miles northeast of Cheltenham, and 5 miles north of Stow-on-the-Wold.

In Moreton-in-Marsh, the houses have been built not around a central square but along a street wide enough to accommodate a market. The village has fine views across the hills. One local landmark, St. David's Church, has a tower of honey-gold ashlar. This town of about 3,500 also possesses one of the last remaining curfew towers, dated 1633; curfew dates to the time of the Norman Conquest, when a bell was rung to "cover-fire" for the night against any invaders.

GETTING HERE AND AROUND

Moreton-in-Marsh is on the A429 north of Cirencester. Park along the main street or in the lot on Station Road. The town has a train station with frequent connections to London Paddington. Pulham's Coaches arrive here from Cirencester or Cheltenham (neither on Sunday). There's also service to and from Stratford-upon-Avon, Stow-on-the-Wold, and Bourton-on-the-Water. For Sezincote, a car is necessary.

ESSENTIALS

Visitor Information **Moreton-in-Marsh Visitor Information Centre** ✉ *Moreton Area Centre, High St.* ☎ *01608/650881* 🌐 *www.cotswolds.com.*

EXPLORING

Sezincote. It comes as somewhat of a surprise to see the blue onion domes and miniature minarets of Sezincote, a mellow stone house and garden tucked into a valley near Moreton-in-Marsh. Created in the early 19th century, Sezincote (pronounced *see*-zinct) was the vision of Sir Charles Cockerell, who made a fortune in the East India Company. He employed his architect brother, Samuel Pepys Cockerell, to "Indian-ize" the residence with Hindu and Muslim motifs. Note the peacock-tail arches surrounding the windows of the first floor. The exotic garden, Hindu temple folly, and Indian-style bridge were favorites of the future George IV, who was inspired to create that Xanadu of Brighton, the Royal Pavilion. If you come in spring, glorious aconites and snowdrops greet you. Note that children are allowed inside only at the owners' discretion. ✉ *Off A44* ☎ *01386/700444* 🌐 *www.sezincote.co.uk* 🎟 *House and grounds £10; grounds only, £5* 🕒 *House May–Sept., Thurs., Fri., and national holidays 2:30–5:30; grounds Jan.–Nov., Thurs. and Fri. and national holidays 2–6 or dusk.*

Tuesday Market. Supposed to be the largest street market in the Cotswolds, the Tuesday Market takes over the center of the main street between 8 am and 2:30 pm, with a mix of household goods, fruits and vegetables, and some arts-and-crafts and jewelry stalls. Check out this market, which is no newcomer: it was chartered in 1227. ✉ *High St.*

7

WHERE TO EAT AND STAY

For expanded hotel reviews, visit Fodors.com.

$$ MODERN BRITISH 🍴 **Horse and Groom.** The squash in the car park tells you of the popularity of this pub situated between Broadway and Moreton-in-Marsh. Inside there is a scattering of small wooden tables and assortment of chairs, open fire, and service with a smile. The chalk board gives you the dishes of the day, which might be Dexter beef with red onion marmalade and horseradish mayonnaise or spiced lamb with harissa and chick peas, coriander, and yogurt. Tarts come as simple lemon, or made with banana, coffee, caramel, and peanuts. [$] *Average main: £15* ✉ *Bourton-on-the-Hill, Moreton-in-Marsh* ☎ *01386/700413* 🌐 *www.horseandgroom.info.*

$$ HOTEL 🏨 **Manor House Hotel.** Secret passageways and a priest's hole testify to the age of this 16th-century building, where the mullioned windows, original stonework, and log fires in winter are tastefully balanced by smart, contemporary furnishings in the public areas. **Pros:** accommodating staff; historical ambience; set back from the main road. **Cons:** smallish rooms; lots of stairs, some noise intrusion. [$] *Rooms from: £160* ✉ *High St.* ☎ *01608/650501* 🌐 *www.cotswold-inns-hotels.co.uk* 🛏 *35 rooms* 🍽 *Breakfast.*

STOW-ON-THE-WOLD

5 miles south of Moreton-in-Marsh, 15 miles east of Cheltenham.

At an elevation of 800 feet, Stow is the highest town in the Cotswolds—"Stow-on-the-Wold, where the wind blows cold" is the age-old saying. Built around a wide square, Stow's imposing golden stone houses have been discreetly converted into high-quality antiques stores, shops, and tea parlors. The Square, as it's known, has a fascinating history. In the 18th century Daniel Defoe wrote that more than 20,000 sheep could be sold here on a busy day; such was the press of livestock that sheep runs, known as "tures," were used to control the sheep, and these narrow streets still run off the main square. Today pubs and antiques shops fill the area.

Also here are St. Edward's Church and the Kings Arms Old Posting House, its wide entrance still seeming to wait for the stagecoaches that used to stop here on their way to Cheltenham.

GETTING HERE AND AROUND

Stow-on-the-Wold is well connected by road (A429, A424, and A436) and bus (from Moreton-in-Marsh, Bourton-on-the-Water, Northleach, Cirencester, and Cheltenham). There are car parks off Sheep Street and Fosseway (A429). Chastleton House is only reachable by car.

ESSENTIALS

Visitor Information **Stow-on-the-Wold Visitor Information Centre** ✉ *12 Talbot Ct., off Sheep St.* ☎ *01451/870150* 🌐 *www.go-stow.co.uk.*

EXPLORING

Chastleton House. One of the most complete Jacobean properties in Britain opts for a beguilingly lived-in appearance, taking advantage of almost 400 years' worth of furniture and trappings accumulated by many generations of the single family that owned it until 1991. The house was built between 1605 and 1612 for William Jones, a wealthy wool merchant, and has an appealing authenticity: bric-a-brac is strewn around, wood and pewter are unpolished, upholstery is uncleaned. The top floor is a glorious, barrel-vaulted long gallery, and throughout the house you can see exquisite plasterwork, paneling, and tapestries. The gardens include rotund topiaries and the first croquet lawn (the rules of croquet were codified here in 1865). **TIP→ Admission is by timed ticket on a first-come, first-served basis, so it's a good idea to arrive early.** Note that there is no tearoom or shop here. Chastleton is 6 miles northeast of Stow, signposted off A436 between Stow and A44. ✉ *Off A436, Moreton-in-Marsh* ☎ *01608/674981, 01494/755560 (info line)* 🌐 *www.nationaltrust.org.uk* 🎟 *£8.50; garden only £3.50* 🕒 *Mar. and Oct., Wed.–Sun. 1–4; Apr.–Sept., Wed.–Sun. 1–5.*

WHERE TO EAT AND STAY

For expanded hotel reviews, visit Fodors.com.

$ BRITISH 🍴 **Queen's Head.** An excellent and convivial stopping-off spot for lunch or dinner, this pub has a courtyard out back that's a quiet retreat on a summer day. Expect to rub shoulders with the local painters and decorators as well as passing tourists. Besides standard pub grub, including sandwiches, baguettes, and sausage and mash, there are daily specials such as homemade fish pie, and liver and bacon with onion gravy. Opposite on the green are some working stocks that you can try out. [$] *Average main: £9* ✉ *The Square* ☎ *01451/830563.*

$ B&B/INN 🏨 **Number Nine.** Beyond the traditional Cotswold stone exterior of this former coaching inn—now a bed-and-breakfast—are unfussy, spacious bedrooms done in soothing white and pale colors. **Pros:** helpful

Which Cotswold Garden Is Right for You?

Perhaps it's the sheer beauty of this area that has inspired the creation of so many superb gardens. Gardening is an English passion, and even nongardeners may be tempted by the choices large and small. Here's a guide to your options if time forces you to be selective.

Hidcote Manor Garden. The Arts and Crafts movement in Britain transformed not only interior design but also the world of gardening; in this large, influential, much-visited masterpiece of the style, hedges and walls set off vistas and surround distinct themed garden rooms.

Kiftsgate Court Gardens. Three generations of women gardeners created this intimate but charming garden that has traditional and modern features with harmonious colors.

Painswick Rococo Garden. This 18th-century garden, with its Gothic screen and other intriguing structures, has a pleasant intimacy; it's a rare survivor of the rococo style.

Rodmarton Manor. Here you can tour an Art and Crafts–style house and notable garden rooms that reflect this style.

Sezincote. England wouldn't be England without a touch of eccentricity, and in the Cotswolds the garden at this Indian-style manor, with its temple to a Hindu god, supplies a satisfying blend of the stately and the exotic.

Sudeley Castle. In England, gardens often complement a stately home and deserve as close a look as the house. At the home of Catherine Parr (Henry VIII's last wife), the 19th-century Queen's Garden is beloved for its roses.

Westonbirt National Arboretum. The magnificent collection of trees here spreads over 600 acres; late spring and fall are colorful.

and amiable hosts; close to pubs and restaurants. **Cons:** two bathrooms have tubs, not showers; low ceilings; steps to climb. $ *Rooms from: £80* ⊠ *9 Park St.* ☎ *01451/870333* ⊕ *www.number-nine.info* ↝ *3 rooms* ⦿ *Breakfast.*

$$ ⊞ **Stow Lodge.** A former rectory, this stately, family-run hotel couldn't be

HOTEL better placed, separated from Stow's main square by a tidy garden. **Pros:** central location; hospitable service; good breakfasts. **Cons:** chiming church clock can be disturbing; steep steps to top-floor rooms. $ *Rooms from: £130* ⊠ *The Square* ☎ *01451/830485* ⊕ *www.stowlodgehotel. co.uk* ↝ *19 rooms, 1 suite* ⦿ *Breakfast.*

SHOPPING

Stow-on-the-Wold is the leading center for antiques stores in the Cotswolds, with more than 40 dealers centered on the Square, Sheep Street, and Church Street.

Baggott Church St. Limited. This shop displays fine old furniture, portraits and landscape paintings, silver, and toys, their price tags tied on with ribbon. ⊠ *Church St.* ☎ *01451/830370.*

Cotswold shopping isn't just fancy antiques: towns such as Bourton-on-the-Water sell some quirky collectibles as well.

Durham House Antiques. Showcases of jewelry, silver items, and ceramics, along with antiquarian books, and period furniture are on display over two floors. It's open daily. ⊠ *Sheep St.* ☎ *01451/870404.*

Roger Lamb Antiques. Specializing in objets d'art and small furnishings from the Georgian and Regency periods, Roger Lamb Antiques counts lighting fixtures, bronze pieces, and Imari porcelain as particular fortes. ⊠ *The Square* ☎ *01451/831371.*

BOURTON-ON-THE-WATER

4 miles southwest of Stow-on-the-Wold, 12 miles northeast of Cheltenham.

Off A429 on the eastern edge of the Cotswolds, Bourton-on-the-Water is deservedly famous as a classic Cotswold village. Like many others, it became wealthy in the Middle Ages because of wool. The little River Windrush runs through Bourton, crossed by low stone bridges; it's as pretty as it sounds. This village makes a good touring base and has a collection of quirky small museums, but in summer it can be overcrowded. A stroll through Bourton takes you past stone cottages, many converted to small stores and fish-and-chip and tea shops.

GETTING HERE AND AROUND

Bourton-on-the-Water is served by Pulham's Coaches from Stow-on-the-Wold, Moreton-in-Marsh, Cirencester, and Cheltenham. By car, take A40 and A436 from Cheltenham. You may find parking in the center, but if not use the lot outside the village.

ESSENTIALS

Visitor Information Bourton-on-the-Water Visitor Information Centre
✉ *Victoria St.* ☎ *01451/820211* ⊕ *www.bourtoninfo.com.*

EXPLORING

FAMILY **Cotswold Motoring Museum and Toy Collection.** Housed in an old mill, this museum has seven rooms crammed to the rafters with more than 50 shiny vintage and classic cars, delightful caravans from the 1920s and 1960s, ancient motorbikes and bicycles, road signs from past times and a shepherd's hut on wheels. If this and the assortment of motoring memorabilia is not enough, there are also children's toys, pedal cars, models, and board games. ✉ *The Old Mill, Sherborne St.* ☎ *01451/821255* ⊕ *www.cotswoldmotoringmuseum.co.uk* ✆ *£4.75* ⊙ *Mid-Feb.–Oct., daily 10–6.*

FAMILY **Model Village.** Built in 1937, this knee-high model of Bourton-on-the-Water took five years to complete. As you walk down its tiny lanes, you'll see how little has changed over the past decades. The small exhibition at Miniature World shows miniature scenes and rooms; some you can make come to life. ✉ *Old New Inn, High St.* ☎ *01451/820467* ⊕ *www.theoldnewinn.co.uk* ✆ *£3.60; Miniature World £1* ⊙ *Late Mar.–Oct., daily 10–6; Nov.–late Mar., daily 10–4; last admission 15 mins before closing.*

WHERE TO EAT AND STAY

For expanded hotel reviews, visit Fodors.com.

$ ✕ **Rose Tree.** Plain wooden tables and understated decor are the setting
BRITISH for the wholesome British dishes served in this traditional restaurant beautifully sited on the banks of the Windrush. Try the chicken liver and mushroom pâté for starters, moving on to lemon sole with caper butter or steak and kidney pie. Desserts include raspberry pavlova, and lemon meringue pie. Candlelight adds atmosphere in the evenings. Sip a cocktail on the riverside terrace while you wait for your order. $ *Average main: £13* ✉ *Victoria St.* ☎ *01451/820635.*

$ 🏨 **Chester House Hotel.** Just steps from the River Windrush, this tradi-
HOTEL tional stone building has been tastefully adapted with contemporary fittings and style. **Pros:** friendly staff; stylish rooms. **Cons:** busy on weekends; coach house rooms overlook car park. $ *Rooms from: £95* ✉ *Victoria St.* ☎ *01451/820286* ⊕ *www.chesterhousehotel.com* ⬎ *22 rooms* ⦿ *Breakfast.*

SHOPPING

Cotswold Perfumery. This shop carries many perfumes that are manufactured here, and also stocks perfume bottles and jewelry. You can exercise your olfactory skills in the Perfumed Garden, part of a prebooked tour that takes in the laboratory, compounding room, and bottling process. ✉ *Victoria St.* ☎ *01451/820698* ⊕ *www.cotswold-perfumery.co.uk* ✆ *Factory tour £5* ⊙ *Mon.–Sat. 9:30–5, Sun. 10:30–5. Factory tours Mon.–Sat. at 11:30 and 2:30, Sun. at 2:30, but advisable to call first.*

Antiques and Markets in the Cotswolds

The Cotswolds contain one of the largest concentrations of art and antiques dealers outside London. The famous antiques shops here are, it's sometimes whispered, "temporary storerooms" for the great families of the region, filled with tole-ware, treen, faience firedogs, toby jugs, and silhouettes, plus country furniture, and ravishing 17th- to 19th-century furniture.

The center of antiquing is Stow-on-the-Wold, in terms of volume of dealers. Other towns that have a number of antiques shops are Broadway, Burford, Cirencester, Tetbury, and Moreton-in-Marsh. The Cotswolds have few of those "anything in this tray for £10" shops, however. The **Cotswold Antique Dealers' Association** (☎ *07831/850544* ⊕ *www.cotswolds-antiques-art.com*) represents 50 or so dealers in the area.

As across England, many towns in the region have market days, when you can purchase local produce (including special treats ranging from Cotswold cheeses to fruit juices), crafts, and items such as clothes, books, and toys. Moreton-in-Marsh has a market on Tuesday, while Cirencester is busy on Friday and some Saturdays. Attending a farmers' market or a general market is a great way to mingle with the locals and perhaps find a special treasure or a tasty treat.

LOWER SLAUGHTER AND UPPER SLAUGHTER

2 miles north of Bourton-on-the-Water, 15 miles east of Cheltenham.

Fodor's Choice ★ To see the quieter, more typical Cotswold villages, seek out the evocatively named Lower Slaughter and Upper Slaughter (the names have nothing to do with mass murder, but come from the Saxon word *sloh*, which means "a marshy place"). Lower Slaughter is one of the "water villages," with Slaughter Brook running down the center road of the town. Little stone footbridges cross the brook, and the town's resident gaggle of geese can often be seen paddling through the sparkling water. Nearby, Lower and Upper Swell are two other quiet towns to explore.

GETTING HERE AND AROUND

There's only a once-weekly bus service linking the Slaughters with the rest of the world; drivers should follow indications from A429 or B4068.

EXPLORING

Warden's Way. Connecting the two Slaughters is the Warden's Way, a mile-long pathway that begins in Upper Slaughter at the town-center parking lot and passes stone houses, green meadows, ancient trees, and a 19th-century corn mill with a waterwheel and brick chimney. The Warden's Way continues south to Bourton-on-the-Water; the full walk from Winchcombe to Bourton is 14 miles. You can pick up maps from local tourist offices.

Blue skies, stone buildings, a peaceful brook: villages such as Upper Slaughter demonstrate the enduring appeal of the Cotswolds.

WHERE TO STAY

For expanded hotel reviews, visit Fodors.com.

$$$
HOTEL

⊞ **Lords of the Manor Hotel.** You'll find refinement and a warm welcome in this rambling 17th-century manor house with Victorian additions, tucked away in a quintessential Cotswold village. **Pros:** heavenly setting; understated elegance; outstanding food. **Cons:** some rooms on the small side; limited Wi-Fi. ⓈRooms from: £200 ✉ Off A429, Upper Slaughter ☎ 01451/820243 ⊕ www.lordsofthemanor.com ⤵ 26 rooms ❘❍❘ Breakfast.

NORTHLEACH

7 miles southwest of Lower and Upper Slaughter, 14 miles southeast of Cheltenham.

Just off the Fosse Way (and bypassed by the busy A40), little Northleach—population around 2,000—has remained one of the least spoiled of Cotswold towns. Trim cottages, many with traditional stone-tile roofs, line the streets that converge on the spacious central square. By the 13th century Northleach had acquired substantial wealth thanks to the wool trade. The wool of the local Cotswold Lion sheep (so called because of their thick, manelike fleece) was praised above all others by weavers in Flanders, to whom it was exported.

GETTING HERE AND AROUND

Pulham's Coaches links Northleach with Bourton-on-the-Water and Cheltenham. It's an out-of-the-way village—signposted from A40 and A429—where you should be able to park near the central square and walk to the sights.

EXPLORING

Keith Harding's World of Mechanical Music. At this shop, the diverting tour lets you hear pianolas, music boxes, and other mechanical instruments from times past. You can even listen to the maestros Grieg, Paderewski, Rachmaninov, and Gershwin on piano rolls. The well-stocked shop stocks antique and modern music boxes, mechanical toys, piano rolls, books, and more. ⊠ *The Oak House, High St.* ☎ *01451/860181* ⊕ *www.mechanicalmusic.co.uk* 🎫 *£8* ☉ *Daily 10–5; last tour at 4.*

St. Peter and St. Paul. Besides its soaring pillars and clerestory windows, this 15th-century church, known as the cathedral of the Cotswolds, contains notable memorial brasses, monuments to the merchants who endowed the church. Each merchant has a wool sack and sheep at his feet. ⊠ *Mill End* ☎ *01451/860314* 🎫 *Free* ☉ *Daily 10–dusk.*

WHERE TO EAT AND STAY

For expanded hotel reviews, visit Fodors.com.

$$
MODERN BRITISH
✕ **Wheatsheaf Inn.** This pub, traditional on the outside, comfortably comtemporary and stylish on the inside, offers a snug coffee lounge and adjoining restaurant, which specializes in Modern British fare. On the menu you might see such light dishes as smoked Bibury trout, deviled whitebait, or wild boar prosciutto with figs. More substantial fare might include steaks with sauces, wild sea bass with truffle mash. In summer the courtyard garden makes an ideal spot for an elderfower and mint cocktail and alfresco dining. The inn also offers 13 stylish, uncluttered bedrooms and a spa. $ *Average main: £15* ⊠ *West End* ☎ *01451/860244* ⊕ *www.cotswoldswheatsheaf.com.*

$
B&B/INN
⛺ **Yew Tree Cottage.** For a peaceful stay in a traditional Cotswold cottage, you can't beat this guesthouse. **Pros:** full of character; charming hostess. **Cons:** a bit remote; dogs in the house. $ *Rooms from: £85* ⊠ *Off A429, Turkdean* ☎ *01451/860222* ⊕ *www.bestcotswold.com* 🛏 *2 rooms* ⵙ *Breakfast.*

BURFORD

9 miles east of Northleach, 18 miles north of Swindon, 18 miles west of Oxford.

Burford's broad main street leads steeply down to a narrow bridge across the River Windrush. The village served as a stagecoach stop for centuries and has many historic inns; it's now a popular stop for tour buses and seekers of antiques.

GETTING HERE AND AROUND

Burford can be easily reached by bus from Oxford—you may need to change at Witney—and Northleach. Once here, it's easy to stroll around. Drivers should park as soon as possible; there are possibilities on and off the High Street.

ESSENTIALS

Visitor Information Burford Visitor Information Centre ⊠ *33a High St.* ☎ *01993/823558* ⊕ *www.oxfordshirecotswolds.org.*

EXPLORING

St. John the Baptist. Hidden away at the end of a lane at the bottom of High Street is the splendid parish church of St. John the Baptist, its interior a warren of arches, chapels, and shrines. The church was remodeled in the 15th century from Norman beginnings. Among the monuments is one dedicated to Henry VIII's barber, Edmund Harman, that depicts four Amazonian Indians; it's said to be the first depiction of native people from the Americas in Britain. Look also for the elaborate Tanfield monument and its poignant widow's epitaph. ⊠ *Lawrence La.* ☎ *01993/823788* ⊕ *www.burfordchurch.org* ☜ *Free* ☉ *Mon.–Sat. 9–5, Sun. 9–10 and 1–5.*

WHERE TO EAT AND STAY

For expanded hotel reviews, visit Fodors.com.

$$ ✕ **The Angel at Burford.** At this informal eatery in a 16th-century coach-
MODERN BRITISH ing inn, the farmhouse-style tables are filled with contemporary dishes like rainbow trout with beetroot and carrot coleslaw, or cauliflower and roast garlic risotto. A secluded, sunny garden is a perfect place for a lunchtime baguette. Upstairs, the three delightful guest rooms are furnished in different styles: Indian in rich reds, French with a wooden sleigh bed, and cool-green contemporary Italian. ⓢ *Average main: £15* ⊠ *14 Witney St.* ☎ *01993/822714* ⊕ *www.theangelatburford.co.uk.*

$$$ ⬚ **Burford House.** Family photographs, old books, and toys scattered
HOTEL throughout this 17th-century building make it feel more like home than a hotel. **Pros:** friendly, unobtrusive service; comfortable public rooms; great dinners. **Cons:** rooms at front subject to traffic noise; parking diificult at peak times; piped music. ⓢ *Rooms from: £170* ⊠ *99 High St.* ☎ *01993/823151* ⊕ *www.burford-house.co.uk* ⬎ *8 rooms* ⎮☉⎮ *Breakfast.*

BIBURY

10 miles southwest of Burford, 6 miles northeast of Cirencester, 15 miles north of Swindon.

The tiny town of Bibury, with a population of less than 1,000, sits idyllically beside the little River Coln on B4425; it was famed Arts and Crafts designer William Morris's choice for Britain's most beautiful village. Fine old cottages, a river meadow, and the church of St. Mary's are some of the delights here.

GETTING HERE AND AROUND

There are buses to Bibury operated on weekdays only by Cotswold Green from Cirencester; otherwise public transport links are sparse. You'll need a car to reach Chedworth Roman Villa.

EXPLORING

Arlington Row. The town has a famously pretty and much-photographed group of 17th-century weavers' cottages made of stone.

FAMILY **Chedworth Roman Villa.** The remains of a mile of walls are what's left of one of the largest Roman villas in England, beautifully set in a wooded valley on the eastern fringe of the Cotswolds. Thirty-two rooms, including two complete bath suites, have been identified, and covered walkways take you over the colorful mosaics, some of the most complete in England. Audio guides are available, and there's a small museum. Look out for the rare large snails, fattenened on milk and herbs during Roman times, in the grounds. There's a café here, but it's also ideal place for a picnic. **TIP→ Look carefully for the signs for the villa: from Bibury, go across A429 to Yanworth and Chedworth. The villa is also signposted from A40. Roads are narrow.** The site is 6 miles northwest of Bibury and 10 miles southeast of Cheltenham. ✉ *Off A429, Yanworth* ☎ *01242/890256* 🌐 *www.nationaltrust.org.uk* 🎫 *£8.80* 🕒 *Mid-Feb.–late Mar., Nov., and Dec., daily 10–4; late Mar.–Oct., daily 10–5.*

WHERE TO STAY

For expanded hotel reviews, visit Fodors.com.

$$$ HOTEL 🏨 **Swan Hotel.** Few inns can boast of a more idyllic setting than this mid-17th-century coaching inn, originally a row of cottages on the banks of the gently flowing River Coln. **Pros:** idyllic spot; helpful staff. **Cons:** busy with day-trippers, and wedding parties on weekends; most standard rooms lack views. [$] *Rooms from: £170* ✉ *B4425* ☎ *01285/740695* 🌐 *www.cotswold-inns-hotels.co.uk* 🛏 *18 rooms, 4 suites* 🍴 *Breakfast.*

CIRENCESTER

6 miles southwest of Bibury, 9 miles south of Chedworth, 14 miles southeast of Cheltenham.

A hub of the Cotswolds since Roman times, when it was called Corinium, Cirencester (pronounced *sirensester*) was second only to London in importance. Today this old market town is the area's largest, with a population of 19,000. It sits at the intersection of two major Roman roads, the Fosse Way and Ermin Street (now A429 and A417). In the Middle Ages Cirencester grew rich on wool, which funded its 15th-century parish church. It preserves many mellow stone buildings dating mainly from the 17th and 18th centuries, and bow-fronted shops that still have one foot in the past.

GETTING HERE AND AROUND

Cirencester has hourly bus service from Cheltenham, and less frequent service from Moreton-in-Marsh, Tetbury, and Kemble (for rail links). By road, the town can be accessed on A417, A419, and A429. Its compact center is easily walkable.

ESSENTIALS

Visitor Information Cirencester Visitor Information Centre ✉ *Corinium Museum, Park St.* ☎ *01285/654180* 🌐 *www.cotswold.gov.uk.*

EXPLORING

FAMILY Fodor's Choice ★ **Corinium Museum.** Not much of the Roman town remains visible, but the museum displays an outstanding collection of Roman artifacts, including jewelry and coins, as well as mosaic pavements and full-scale reconstructions of local Roman interiors. Spacious and light-filled galleries that explore the town's history in Roman and Anglo-Saxon times and in the 18th century include plenty of hands-on exhibits for kids. ✉ *Park St.* ☎ *01285/655611* 🌐 *www.coriniummuseum.org* 🎟 *£4.95* 🕓 *Apr.–Oct., Mon.–Sat. 10–5, Sun. 2–5; Nov.–Mar., Mon.–Sat. 10–4, Sun. 2–4.*

St. John the Baptist. At the top of Market Place is this magnificent Gothic parish church, known as the cathedral of the "woolgothic" style. Its elaborate, three-tier, three-bay south porch, now gleaming gold after a renovation, is the largest in England and once served as the town hall. The chantry chapels and many coats of arms bear witness to the importance of the wool merchants as benefactors of the church. A rare example of a delicate 15th-century wineglass pulpit sits in the nave. ✉ *Market Pl.* ☎ *01285/659317* 🌐 *www.cirenparish.co.uk* 🎟 *£3 donation suggested* 🕓 *Mon.–Sat. 10–4:45 (10–4 in winter), Sun. 2–5.*

QUICK BITES

Made by Bob. The energy and buzz of this plate-glass and chrome eatery, situated right by the Corn Hall in the center of town, will set you up as much as the coffee and pastry, afternoon tea and a bun, or a soup and focaccia lunch. You can always pick something up from the delicatessen for a picnic if you prefer. [$] *Average main: £10* ✉ *Unit 6 The Cornhall, 26 Market Place, Cirencester* ☎ *01285/641818* 🕓 *Closed Sun.*

WHERE TO EAT AND STAY

For expanded hotel reviews, visit Fodors.com.

$$$ MODERN BRITISH 🍴 **Jesse's.** The fish is chilling on the counter and the charcoal is glowing in the oven as you sit at your mosaic-topped table and watch the chefs at work. The bistro, tucked away in a little courtyard is intimate yet roomy, bustling yet snug. Treat yourself to a chilled sherry, then be tempted by soft-shell crab in a sushi roll, local Gatcombe lamb or fish straight up from Cornwall. You'll be spoiled for choice by the excellent choices on the British cheese board. [$] *Average main: £20* ✉ *The Stableyard, Black Jack Street, Cirencester* ☎ *01285/641497* 🌐 *www.jessesbistro.co.uk* 🕓 *Closed Sun. No dinner Mon.*

$$$$ HOTEL 🏨 **Barnsley House.** A honey-and-cream Georgian mansion, the former home of garden designer Rosemary Verey has been discreetly modernized and converted into a luxurious retreat without sacrificing its essential charm.**Pros:** romantic setting; great attention to detail. **Cons:** some rooms at the top of three flights of stairs. [$] *Rooms from: £280* ✉ *B4425, Barnsley* ☎ *01285/740000* 🌐 *www.barnsleyhouse.com* 🛏 *9 rooms, 9 suites* 🍽 *Breakfast.*

$ B&B/INN 🏨 **Ivy House.** Delicious breakfasts, hospitable owners, and reasonable rates enhance a stay at this stone Victorian house, close to the center of town. **Pros:** homemade granola at breakfast; child-friendly atmosphere. **Cons:** on a main road; some rooms on the small side. [$] *Rooms from: £77* ✉ *2 Victoria Rd.* ☎ *01285/656626* 🌐 *www.ivyhousecotswolds.com* 🛏 *4 rooms* 🍽 *Breakfast.*

NIGHTLIFE AND THE ARTS

New Brewery Arts. A theater, an exhibition space, and a café are found in New Brewery Arts. ⊠ *Brewery Ct.* ☎ *01285/657181.*

SHOPPING

Corn Hall. This is the venue for a food market on Monday, Wednesday, and Thursday, an antiques market on Friday, and a crafts market on Saturday. ⊠ *Market Pl.* ⊕ *www.cornhallcirencester.com.*

Makers and Designers Emporium. Better known as MADE, this shop is a cornucopia of unusual designer items, including stationery, textiles, housewares, and jewelry. ⊠ *9 Silver St.* ☎ *01285/658225* ⊕ *www.made-gallery.com.*

Market Place. Every Monday and Friday, Cirencester's central Market Place is packed with stalls selling a motley assortment of goods, mainly household items but some local produce and crafts, too. A farmers' market takes place here every second and fourth Saturday of the month.

William H. Stokes. This shop specializes in oak furniture from the 16th and 17th centuries. ⊠ *6–8 Dollar St.* ☎ *01285/653907.*

SPORTS AND THE OUTDOORS

FAMILY **Cotswold Water Park.** You can indulge in water sports such as waterskiing and windsurfing at the Cotswold Water Park, 4 miles south of Cirencester. This group of 150 lakes covers 40 square miles and has multiple entrances. There's swimming May through September, and plenty to do for walkers, cyclists, and kayakers as well. You pay individual charges for the activities, and you can rent equipment on-site. ⊠ *B4696, South Cerney* ☎ *01793/752413* ⊕ *www.waterpark.org* ✉ *Free* ☉ *Individual operators have varying opening hrs.*

PAINSWICK

16 miles northwest of Cirencester, 8 miles southwest of Cheltenham, 5 miles south of Gloucester.

Fodor's Choice
★ An old Cotswold wool town of around 2,000 inhabitants, Painswick has become a chocolate-box picture of quaintness, attracting day-trippers and tour buses. But come during the week and you can discover the place in relative tranquillity. The huddled gray-stone houses and inns date from as early as the 14th century and include a notable group from the Georgian era. It's worth a stroll through the churchyard of St. Mary's, renowned for its table tombs and monuments and its 100 yew trees planted in 1792. The Cotswold Way passes near the center of the village, making it easy to take a pleasant walk in the countryside.

GETTING HERE AND AROUND

Painswick is on A46 between Stroud and Cheltenham. The village has hourly bus connections with Stroud (15 minutes) and Cheltenham (35 minutes), with reduced service on Sunday.

ESSENTIALS

Visitor Information Painswick Visitor Information Centre ⊠ *Town Hall, Victoria St.* ☎ *01452/813552* ⊕ *www.visitthecotswolds.org.uk.*

EXPLORING

Painswick Rococo Garden. Half a mile north of town, this delightful garden is a rare survivor from the exuberant rococo period of English garden design (1720–60). After 50 years in its original form, the 6-acre garden became overgrown. After the rediscovery of a 1748 painting of the garden by Thomas Robins, the garden was restored beginning in 1984. Now you can view the original structures—such as the pretty Gothic Eagle House and curved Exedra—take in the asymmetrical vistas, and try the modern maze, which, unusually, has three goals you can discover. There's also a restaurant and a shop. ✉ *B4073* ☎ *01452/813204* 🌐 *www.rococogarden.org.uk* 🎟 *£6.50* 🕒 *Mid-Jan.–Oct., daily 11–5; last admission at 4.*

SPECIAL DAYS

Painswick's annual Clypping Ceremony, on the first Sunday after September 19, has nothing to do with topiaries—the name derives from the Anglo-Saxon word "clyppan," meaning "encircle." Children with garlands make a ring around the parish church as traditional hymns are sung. The idea is to affirm the church and the faith it stands for. Another good time to visit is the town's Victorian Market Day in early July.

WHERE TO EAT AND STAY

For expanded hotel reviews, visit Fodors.com.

$ BRITISH 🍴 **Falcon Inn.** With views of the church of St. Mary's, this pub dating from 1554 offers a reassuringly traditional milieu for food and refreshment. Light meals are available at lunchtime, teas in the afternoon, and for the evening meal you might start with pigeon breast with pickled beetroot, then try lamb with a mustard and rosemary crust for your main course. The "spotted dick" (warm sponge pudding with dried fruit and custard) is the perfect end to the meal. The inn's grounds hold what is claimed to be the world's oldest bowling green. There are 11 well-furnished bedrooms upstairs. [$] *Average main: £14* ✉ *New St.* ☎ *01452/814222* 🌐 *www.falconinn-cotswolds.co.uk.*

$$ HOTEL 🏨 **Cardynham House.** In the heart of the village, this 15th- to 16th-century former wool merchant's house, which retains its beamed ceilings, Jacobean staircase, and Elizabethan fireplace, has four-poster beds in almost all of its rooms. **Pros:** romantic and quirky; great food in restaurant. **Cons:** some low ceilings; mainly small bathrooms. [$] *Rooms from: £100* ✉ *The Cross, Tibbiwell St.* ☎ *01452/814006, 01452/810030 restaurant* 🌐 *www.cardynham.co.uk* 🛏 *9 rooms* 🍽 *Breakfast.*

TETBURY

12 miles south of Painswick, 8 miles southwest of Cirencester.

With about 5,300 inhabitants, Tetbury claims royal connections. Indeed, the soaring spire of the church that presides over this Elizabethan market town is within sight of Highgrove House, the Prince of Wales's abode. The house isn't open to the public, but you can book well in advance for a tour of the gardens. Tetbury is known as one of the area's antiques centers.

With its majestic trees, Westonbirt National Arboretum is the perfect place to take in fall's splendor.

GETTING HERE AND AROUND

Tetbury is well connected to Cirencester by buses operated by Cotswold Green. There are no Sunday services. It's easy to stroll around the compact town.

ESSENTIALS

Visitor Information Tetbury Tourist Information Centre ✉ *33 Church St.* ☎ *01666/503552* ⊕ *www.visittetbury.co.uk.*

EXPLORING

Fodor's Choice
★

Highgrove House. Prince Charles and the late Princess Diana made their home at Highgrove House, 1½ miles southwest of Tetbury. Charles set about making the 37-acre estate his personal showcase for traditional and organic growing methods and conservation of native plants and animals. Here you can appreciate the amazing industry on the part of the royal gardeners who have created the orchards, kitchen garden, and woodland garden almost from nothing. Look for the stumpery, the immaculate and quirky topiaries, and the national collection of hostas. You can sample the estate's produce in the restaurant and shop, or from its retail outlet in Tetbury. Tickets go on sale in February and sell out quickly, so make sure to book well ahead. Allow three to four hours for a visit to the house. Those under 12 aren't permitted. ✉ *Off A433, Doughton* ☎ *020/7766–7310 book tours* ⊕ *www.highgrovegardens.com* ✉ *£22.50, prebooked only* ⊗ *Early Apr.–late Oct., weekdays plus occasional weekends.*

Market House. In the center of Tetbury, look for the eye-catching Market House, dating from 1655. Constructed of white-painted stone, it's built up on rows of Tuscan pillars. Various markets are held here during the week. ✉ *Market Sq.*

Rodmarton Manor. One of the last English country houses constructed using traditional methods and materials, Rodmarton Manor (built 1909–29) is furnished with specially commissioned pieces in the Arts and Crafts style. Ernest Barnsley, a follower of William Morris, worked on the house and gardens. The notable gardens—wild, winter, sunken, and white—are divided into "rooms" bounded by hedges of holly, beech, and yew. The manor is 5 miles northeast of Tetbury. ⊠ Off A433, Rodmarton ☎ 01285/841442 ⊕ www.rodmarton-manor.co.uk ⊠ £8; garden only, £5 ☉ May–Sept., Wed., Sat., and national holidays 2–5.

> ### WORD OF MOUTH
>
> "For a nice half or full day out, I can recommend Tetbury: it has several tea shops. In Tetbury there are lots of nice (though quite expensive) shops, an ancient Butterwalk and quaint little streets, and the church. Farther afield there is Westonbirt Arboretum, a lovely place for an afternoon's stroll among the trees."
> —annhig

St. Mary the Virgin. This church, in 18th-century neo-Gothic style, has a galleried interior with pews. ⊠ Church St. ☎ 01666/500088.

QUICK BITES

Snooty Fox. Just steps from Market House and at the heart of village life, the Snooty Fox is a bustling inn and restaurant with leather armchairs and an open fire in winter and a patio to use in summer. Real ales and local ciders are served at the bar, and teas, coffees, and hot and cold meals are available all day. ⊠ Market Pl. ☎ 01666/502436 ⊕ www.snooty-fox.co.uk.

FAMILY **Westonbirt National Arboretum.** Spread over 600 acres, this arboretum contains one of the most extensive collections of trees and shrubs in Europe. A lovely place to spend an hour or two, it's 3 miles southwest of Tetbury and 10 miles north of Bath. The best times to come for color are in late spring, when the rhododendrons, azaleas, and magnolias are blooming, and in fall, when the maples come into their own. Open-air concerts take place in summer, and there are exhibitions throughout the year. A gift shop, café, and restaurant are on the grounds. ⊠ Off A433 ☎ 01666/880220 ⊕ www.forestry.gov.uk/westonbirt ⊠ £8 Mar.–Sept.; £9 Oct. and Nov.; £5 Dec.–Feb. ☉ Apr.–Aug., daily 9–8; Sept.–Mar., daily 9–6.

WHERE TO EAT AND STAY
For expanded hotel reviews, visit Fodors.com.

$$ ✕ **The Chef's Table.** On Tetbury's Antiques Alley, this trendy eatery is a
BRITISH blend of farmhouse kitchen and designer chic, with a few tables and chairs next to an open kitchen. You can come for breakfast, a light lunch, or dinner with more substantial choices like chicken Kiev with garlic and parsley butter, perhaps followed by a delicious banana cake with rum and muscavado jelly. Reserve ahead because of the limited dining space. If you can't get a seat, don't despair—all dishes are available for a takeout lunch, and cheeses, hams, and organic bread are sold at the downstairs delicatessen. $ Average main: £17 ⊠ 49 Long St. ☎ 01666/504466 ⊕ www.thechefstable.co.uk ☉ Closed Sun. and Mon. No dinner Tues.

$$$$ HOTEL FAMILY Fodor's Choice ★

🏨 **Calcot Manor.** In an ideal world everyone would sojourn in this oasis of opulence at least once; the luxury never gets in the way of the overall air of relaxation, however, a tribute to the warmth and efficiency of the staff. **Pros:** delightful rural setting; excellent spa facilities; children love it. **Cons:** all but 12 rooms are separate from main building; not all rooms have separate shower units; steep prices. [$] *Rooms from: £280* ✉ *A4135* ☎ *01666/890391* 🌐 *www.calcotmanor.co.uk* 🛏 *26 rooms, 9 suites* 🍴 *Breakfast.*

SHOPPING

Tetbury is home to more than 30 antiques shops, some of which are incorporated into small malls.

Highgrove Shop. This pleasant, though pricey, shop sells organic products and gifts inspired by Prince Charles's gardens. ✉ *10 Long St.* ☎ *0845/521–4342* 🌐 *www.highgroveshop.com.*

House of Cheese. Farm-produced cheeses, all wonderfully fresh and flavorsome, are on offer at the House of Cheese. Pâtés and preserves are other goodies at this tiny shop. ✉ *13 Church St.* ☎ *01666/502865* 🌐 *www.houseofcheese.co.uk.*

Long Street Antiques. More than 40 dealers specialize in everything from jewelry and kitchenalia to oak and mahogany furniture. ✉ *14 Long St.* ☎ *01666/500850* 🌐 *www.longstreetantiques.com.*

8

STRATFORD-UPON-AVON AND THE HEART OF ENGLAND

WELCOME TO STRATFORD-UPON-AVON AND THE HEART OF ENGLAND

TOP REASONS TO GO

★ **The city of Birmingham:** The revamped city center shows off its superb art collections and cultural facilities, international cuisine, and renowned Jewellery Quarter.

★ **Half-timber architecture:** Black-and-white half-timber houses are a mark of pride throughout the region; there are concentrations of buildings from medieval times to the Jacobean era in Chester, Shrewsbury, and Ludlow.

★ **Ironbridge Gorge:** Recall the beginnings of England's Industrial Revolution at this fine complex of industrial-heritage museums.

★ **Shakespeare in Stratford:** To see a play by Shakespeare in the town where he was born—and perhaps after you've visited his birthplace or other sites—is a magical experience.

★ **Warwick Castle:** Taking in the history—and some modern kitsch—at this sprawling medieval castle is a fun day out and great for the whole family.

1 **Stratford-upon-Avon.** The birthplace of Shakespeare, the bustling historic town of Stratford-upon-Avon is liberally dotted with 16th-century buildings the playwright would recognize.

2 **Around Shakespeare Country.** Warwickshire—the county of which Stratford is the southern nexus—has sleepy villages and thatch-roof cottages, as well as stately homes and sprawling Warwick Castle.

3 **Birmingham.** Britain's second-largest city, once known as "the city of 1,001 trades," now makes the most of its industrial past through some outstanding museums and the biggest canal network outside Venice. There's also buzzing nightlife, and an excellent restaurant scene.

4 **Great Malvern, Hereford, and Environs.** This region includes the cathedral town of Hereford and bucolic villages set amid lush orchards. Providing a backdrop to it all are the volcanic ridges of the Malvern Hills, where you'll find genteel Great Malvern and Ledbury.

5 **Shrewsbury, Chester, and Environs.** The northern, most varied part of the region, studded with its characteristic half-timber buildings, embraces the World Heritage Site of Ironbridge Gorge, the Shropshire hills, and ancient Shrewsbury and Chester, as well as Ludlow with its gastronomic delights.

GETTING ORIENTED

Stratford-upon-Avon is northwest of London in the midland county of Warwickshire, known as Shakespeare Country. Tiny villages surround it; to the north are two magnificent castles, Warwick and Kenilworth. A little farther northwest is the region's main city, Birmingham. To the southwest, along the Malvern Hills, lie the peaceful spa town of Great Malvern and the prosperous agricultural city of Hereford. The western part of the region, bordering Wales, is hugged by the River Severn. The small city of Shrewsbury is here, close to Ironbridge with its industrial-heritage museums. To its south lies Ludlow, an architectural and culinary hot spot; at the northwestern edge of the region is the ancient city of Chester.

8

GREAT INDIAN FOOD IN ENGLAND

"Going for an Indian" or "going for a curry"—the two are synonymous—is part of English life. On any self-respecting town's main street there's at least one Indian restaurant or take-out place, from inexpensive to high-end.

(above) Chilis add heat to Indian food; you can cool things down with some bread; (right, top) *Rogan josh,* a spicy choice; (right, below) Chicken tikka masala, a favorite

British trade with, and subsequent rule over, India for the two centuries before 1947 has ensured an enduring national appetite for spices. The town of Cheltenham used to be known as an Anglo-Indian paradise because so many "curry-eating colonels" used to retire there. Immigration from Pakistan and Bangladesh in the mid-20th century led to a concentration of restaurants in Birmingham, Manchester, and London. Today you can also find South Indian, Nepalese, and Sri Lankan establishments. The exotic mix of herbs and spices gives Indian food its distinctive appeal. Typically, ginger, garlic, cilantro, cumin, cardamom, fenugreek, and cayenne enhance fresh vegetables and meat (chicken or lamb), fish, or cheese (paneer). Fresh cilantro is a common garnish. But it's the addition of chili that makes things hot: feel free to ask advice when ordering.

ACCOMPANIMENTS

Starters include lime pickle, mango chutney, and *raita* (diced cucumber in minty yogurt), all scooped up with *pappadams* (crispy, thin, fried tortillalike disks made from chickpea flour). For the main course, there's plain or pilaf Basmati rice, *naan* bread from the tandoor, or *chapatis* (flat bread). Side dishes include onion or eggplant *bhajis* (spiced fritters), and *sag aloo* (potato with spinach). Try Indian beer, too.

Curry is a general term for dishes with a hot, spicy sauce. The strength of each dish is given in italics after the description.

BALTI
Literally meaning "bucket," a *balti* dish is a popular Birmingham invention dating to the 1970s. Different combinations of meat, spices, and vegetables are stir-fried and served at the table in a small wok with handles. Naan bread or chapatis are accompaniments. *Mild to Medium.*

BIRYANI
Made with stir-fried chicken or lamb, almonds, and golden raisins, this rice-based dish has a dry texture. It can be served with a vegetable curry. *Medium.*

CHICKEN TIKKA MASALA
A British-Bangladeshi invention, this is reputedly the nation's favorite dish. Boneless chunks of chicken breast are marinated in yogurt and *garam masala* (dry-roasted spices), threaded on a skewer, and cooked in a tandoor. The accompanying creamy, tomato-based sauce is either orange-red from turmeric and paprika, or deep red from food coloring. *Mild.*

DHANSAK
Meat or prawns are combined with a thick sweet-and-sour sauce and a red or yellow *dal* (lentil stew) in a dish that originated in Persia. *Medium to hot.*

DOPIAZA
The name means two or double onions, so expect lots of onions, mixed with green bell peppers. The sauce is reduced, producing concentrated flavors. *Medium hot.*

JALFREZI
This dish derived from British rule in India, when the Indian cook would heat up leftover cold roast meat and potatoes. Fresh meat is cooked with green bell peppers, onions, and plenty of green chilis in a little sauce. *Hot.*

KORMA
Mild and sweet, this curry is very popular. Chicken or lamb is braised in a creamy or yogurt-based sauce to which almonds and coconut are added. *Mild.*

ROGAN JOSH
A staple dish, rogan josh is quite highly spiced. Its deep red color originally came from dried red Kashmiri chilis, but now red bell peppers and tomatoes are used. *Medium hot.*

TANDOORI CHICKEN
Chicken pieces are marinated in a yogurt and spice paste, and then cooked in a *tandoor* (barrel-shape clay oven). The red color comes from cayenne pepper, chili powder, or food coloring. It's served dry with slices of lemon or lime, naan bread, and salad. *Mild.*

–by Kate Hughes

8

Updated by Kate Hughes and Jack Jewers

The lyricism of England's geographical heartland is found in the remote, half-timber market towns of Herefordshire, Worcestershire, and Shropshire, and in the bucolic villages of Warwickshire. It melts away around the edges of Birmingham—England's second largest city, often maligned by Brits as a grubby postindustrial metropolis, but forging a new identity for itself as a cultural hub.

However, it's the countryside around here that does most to invoke the England of our imaginations—nowhere more so than Stratford-upon-Avon, birthplace of perhaps the nation's most famous son, William Shakespeare. You get new insight into the great playwright when you visit the stretch of country where he was born and raised. The sculpted, rolling farmland of Warwickshire may look nothing like the forested countryside of the 16th century, but plenty of sturdy Tudor buildings that Shakespeare knew survive to this day (including his birthplace). There's beauty in this—but also the possibility of tourist overkill. Stratford itself, with its Shakespeare sites and the theaters of the Royal Shakespeare Company, sometimes can get to feel like "Shakespeare World."

Still, there's much more to see—magnificent castles, bucolic churches, and gentle countryside—in this famously lovely part of England. Stop in at Charlecote, a grand Elizabethan manor house, and Baddesley Clinton, a superb example of late-medieval domestic architecture. The huge fortresses of Warwick Castle and Kenilworth Castle provide glimpses into the past.

To the west, some of England's prettiest countryside lies along the 108-mile border with Wales in the counties of Herefordshire, Worcestershire, and Shropshire. The Welsh borders are remote and tranquil, dotted with small villages and market towns full of 13th- and 14th-century black-and-white, half-timber buildings, the legacy of a forested countryside. The Victorians were responsible for the more recent fashion of painting these structures black and white. The more elaborately decorated half-timber buildings in market towns such as Shrewsbury and Chester are monuments to wealth, dating mostly from the early 17th century. More half-timbered structures are found in Ludlow, now a culinary center nestled in the lee of its majestic ruined castle.

In the 18th century, in a wooded stretch of the Severn Gorge in Shropshire, the coke blast furnace was invented and the first iron bridge was erected (1779), heralding the birth of the Industrial Revolution. You can get a sense of this history at the museums at Ironbridge Gorge.

The ramifications of that technological leap are what led to the rapid growth of Birmingham, the capital of the Midlands. Its industrial center, which suffered decades of decline in the 20th century, inspired culture as diverse as the heavy metal sound of Black Sabbath and the dark realm of Mordor in J.R.R. Tolkien's *The Lord of the Rings*. Today an imaginative makeover and active, varied cultural life are draws for anyone interested in the rebirth of modern urban Britain.

STRATFORD-UPON-AVON AND THE HEART OF ENGLAND PLANNER

WHEN TO GO

The Shakespeare sights get very crowded on weekends and school vacations; Warwick Castle usually brims with visitors, so arrive early in the day. Throughout the region, some country properties fill up quickly on weekends. Most rural sights have limited opening hours in winter, and the majority of attractions close at 5. Some stately homes have limited hours even in summer, which is when the countryside is at its most appealing. The open-air performances at Ludlow Castle take place at the end of June; the Autumn in Malvern Festival happens on weekends in October.

PLANNING YOUR TIME

Stratford-upon-Avon is ideal for day visits from London or as a base for exploring nearby; depending on your love of Shakespeare, you probably won't need more than a day or two here. Warwick can be explored in an hour or two, but castle lovers could spend half a day in the many lines at busy Warwick Castle. A drive through the area's country lanes is a pleasant way to spend a day; a stop at any stately home (check hours) will take a few hours. You're also near the northern Cotswolds if you want to explore the countryside further.

The museums and major sights of Birmingham can be covered in a day, and it's a good city for modern, budget hotels. However, the smaller cities of Hereford, Shrewsbury, and Chester, have more obvious charms. If you want to walk the hills, Great Malvern or Ledbury are good gateways for the Malvern Hills. In the north of the region, Ironbridge Gorge and Chester demand a full day each. Ludlow and Shrewsbury take less time, though it would be a shame to leave Ludlow without sampling its exceptionally fine dining. Once you've gone as far north as this, you might consider going on to Liverpool, if the Beatles and maritime history have any appeal, or hopping across the border to North Wales.

GETTING HERE AND AROUND

AIR TRAVEL

The region is served by Birmingham International Airport, 6 miles east of the city center. It has connections to all of Britain's major cities, and limited service to the United States.

Contacts **Birmingham International Airport** ⊠ *A45, off M42, Birmingham* ☎ *0870/222–0072* ⊕ *www.bhx.co.uk.*

BUS TRAVEL

The cheapest way to travel is by bus, and National Express serves the region from London's Victoria Coach Station. You can reach Birmingham in less than three hours; Hereford and Shrewsbury take between four and five hours. It also operates services from London's Heathrow (2¾ hours) and Gatwick (4 hours) airports to Birmingham.

Stagecoach serves local routes throughout the Stratford and Birmingham areas. Megabus, a budget service booked online, runs double-decker buses from Victoria Station in London to Birmingham. The First bus company has service between Birmingham, Hereford, and Ludlow.

Contacts **First** ☎ *0871/200–2233* ⊕ *www.firstgroup.com.*
Megabus ☎ *0871/266–3333 inquiries, 0900/160–0900 booking line; calls cost 61p per minute* ⊕ *www.megabus.com.* **National Express** ☎ *0871/781–8181* ⊕ *www.nationalexpress.com.* **Stagecoach** ☎ *0845/600–1314* ⊕ *www.stagecoachbus.com.*

CAR TRAVEL

To reach Stratford (100 miles), Birmingham (120 miles), Shrewsbury (150 miles), Ludlow (140 miles), and Chester (180 miles) from London, take M40. For the farther areas, keep on it until it becomes M42, or take M1/M6. M4 and then M5 from London take you to Hereford in just under three hours. Driving can be difficult in the region's western reaches—especially in the hills and valleys west of Hereford, where steep, twisting roads often narrow down into mere trackways.

Around Stratford, one pleasure of this rural area is driving the smaller "B" roads, which lead deep into the countryside. Local public bus service isn't sufficient for most sightseeing journeys around Warwickshire. Renting a car or taking a tour bus are the two best options, although trains serve the major towns.

TRAIN TRAVEL

Stratford has good train service and can be seen as a day trip from London if your time is limited (a matinee is your best bet if you want to squeeze in a play). Chiltern Railways trains leave from London Marylebone Station and also go to Warwick, and they offer a one-day (£35) or four-day (£50) Shakespeare Explorer ticket for the region. London Midland serves the area from Birmingham (about 40 miles from Stratford). From London, First Great Western, and Arriva trains serve Birmingham and the western parts of the region from Paddington Station, and Virgin, London Midland, and Silverlink trains leave from Euston (call National Rail Enquiries for information). Travel times are Paddington to Hereford and Ludlow, 3 hours (both changing at Newport); Euston to Birmingham, 1½ hours; Euston to Shrewsbury, with a change at Crewe or Birmingham, 2¾ hours; or to Chester, with a change at Crewe, 2¾ hours. West Midlands Day Ranger tickets (£22.50) and three- and seven-day Heart of England Rover tickets (£72.50 and £94) allow unlimited travel on trains throughout the region.

Contacts Chiltern Railways ☎ *0845/600–5165* ⊕ *www.chilternrailways.co.uk.* **London Midland** ☎ *0121/634–2040, 0844/811–0133* ⊕ *www.londonmidland. com.* **National Rail Enquiries** ☎ *0845/748–4950* ⊕ *www.nationalrail.co.uk.*

RESTAURANTS

Stratford has many reasonably priced bistros and unpretentious eateries offering a broad choice of international fare; Warwick and Kenilworth both have good restaurant options. Birmingham has good international restaurants but is probably most famous for its Indian and Pakistani "curry houses"; you'll find good choices both in the city center and out of town. The city hosts the annual Taste of Birmingham Festival in July. In the rest of the Midlands, casual spots dominate, although Ludlow is a culinary center. *Prices in the reviews are the average cost of a main course at dinner or, if dinner isn't served, at lunch.*

HOTELS

Stratford and Warwick have accommodations to fit every wallet. Because Stratford is *so* popular with theatergoers, book well ahead. Most hotels offer discounted two- and three-day packages. Near Stratford, a number of top-notch country hotels guarantee discreet but attentive service—at fancy prices. Birmingham's hotels, geared to the convention crowd and often booked well in advance, are mostly bland and impersonal, but a few are sophisticated; look for weekend discounts. In the countryside, many ancient inns and venerable Regency-style houses have been converted into hotels. *Prices in the reviews are the lowest cost of a standard double room in high season, including 20% V.A.T.*

VISITOR INFORMATION

Traveline can field all general transportation inquiries. Local tourist offices can recommend day or half-day tours of the region and will have the names of registered Blue Badge guides.

Contacts Heart of England Tourist Board ☎ *01905/887690* ⊕ *www.visittheheart.co.uk.* **Shakespeare Country** ☎ *0871/978–0800* ⊕ *www.shakespeare-country.co.uk.* **Traveline** ☎ *0871/200–2233* ⊕ *www.traveline.info.*

STRATFORD-UPON-AVON

Even under the weight of busloads of visitors, Stratford, on the banks of the slow-flowing River Avon, has somehow hung on to much of its ancient character and can, on a good day, still feel like an English market town. It doesn't take long to figure out who's the center of attention here. Born in a half-timber, early-16th-century building in the center of Stratford on April 23, 1564, William Shakespeare died on April 23, 1616, his 52nd birthday, in a more imposing house at New Place. Although he spent much of his life in London, the world still associates him with "Shakespeare's Avon."

With its thatch roof, half-timbering, and countryside setting, Anne Hathaway's Cottage is a vision from the past.

Here, in the years between his birth and 1587, he played as a young lad, attended grammar school, and married Anne Hathaway; and here he returned, as a prosperous man. You can see Shakespeare's whole life here: his birthplace on Henley Street; his burial place in Holy Trinity Church; Anne Hathaway's Cottage; the home of his mother, Mary Arden, at Wilmcote; New Place; and the neighboring Nash's House, home of Shakespeare's granddaughter.

By the 16th century, Stratford was a prosperous market town with thriving guilds and industries. Half-timber houses from this era have been preserved, and they're set off by later architecture, such as the elegant Georgian storefronts on Bridge Street, with their 18th-century porticoes and arched doorways.

Most sights cluster around Henley Street (off the roundabout as you come in on the A3400 Birmingham road), High Street, and Waterside, which skirts the public gardens through which the River Avon flows. Bridge and Sheep streets (parallel to Bridge) are Stratford's main thoroughfares and the site of most banks, shops, and eateries. Bridgefoot, between the canal and the river, is next to Clopton Bridge—"a sumptuous new bridge and large of stone"—built in the 15th century by Sir Hugh Clopton, once lord mayor of London and one of Stratford's richest and most philanthropic residents.

GETTING HERE AND AROUND
Stratford lies about 100 miles northwest of London; take M40 to Junction 15. The town is 37 miles southeast of Birmingham by A435 and A46 or by M40 to Junction 15.

Chiltern Railways serves the area from London's Marylebone Station. Six direct trains a day take just over two hours to reach Stratford; other trains require changing at Birmingham. London Midland operates direct routes from Birmingham's Snow Hill Station (journey time under an hour). Stratford has two stations, Stratford Parkway, northwest of the centre at Bishopston, and Stratford at the edge of the town center on Alcester Road, from which you can take a taxi or walk the short distance into town.

Stratford's center is small and easily walkable—it's unlikely you'd need to use the local bus service. City Sightseeing runs hop-on, hop-off guided tours of Stratford (£12.50), and you can combine the tour (about an hour with no stops) with entry to either three (£25.50) or five (£29) Shakespeare houses. In summer, the same company's Heart of Warwickshire tour includes Compton Verney, Charlecote Park, and Warwick (four trips on weekends from April through July, daily in August). The Stratford Town Walk runs all year and also offers ghost-themed walks and cruises.

The Shakespeare Birthplace Trust runs the main places of Shakespearean interest: Anne Hathaway's Cottage, Hall's Croft, Mary Arden's House, Nash's House and New Place, Shakespeare's Birthplace, and Shakespeare's Grave. ■TIP→ **Buy a money-saving combination ticket to all five properties for £22.50, or pay separate entry fees if you're visiting only one or two. Family tickets are an option, too. Advance booking online gives you a 10% saving.** Tickets for Hall's Croft and Nash's House and New Place are available only as a rather pricey (£14.95) joint ticket that includes the birthplace and grave.

PLANNING YOUR TIME

If you have only a day here, arrive early and confine your visit to two or three Shakespeare Birthplace Trust properties, a few other town sights, a pub lunch, and a walk along the river, capped off by a stroll to the cottage of Anne Hathaway. If you don't like crowds, avoid visiting on weekends and school vacations, and take in the main Shakespeare shrines in the early morning to see them at their least frenetic. One high point of Stratford's calendar is the Shakespeare Birthday Celebrations, usually on the weekend nearest to April 23.

ESSENTIALS

Tour Information **City Sightseeing** ☎ 01789/412680
⊕ www.city-sightseeing.com. **Shakespeare Birthplace Trust** ☎ 01789/204016
⊕ www.shakespeare.org.uk. **Stratford Town Walk** ☎ 01789/292478,
0785/576–0377 ⊕ www.stratfordtownwalk.co.uk.

Visitor Information **Stratford-upon-Avon Tourist Information Centre**
✉ Bridgefoot ☎ 01789/264293 ⊕ www.shakespeare-country.co.uk.

8

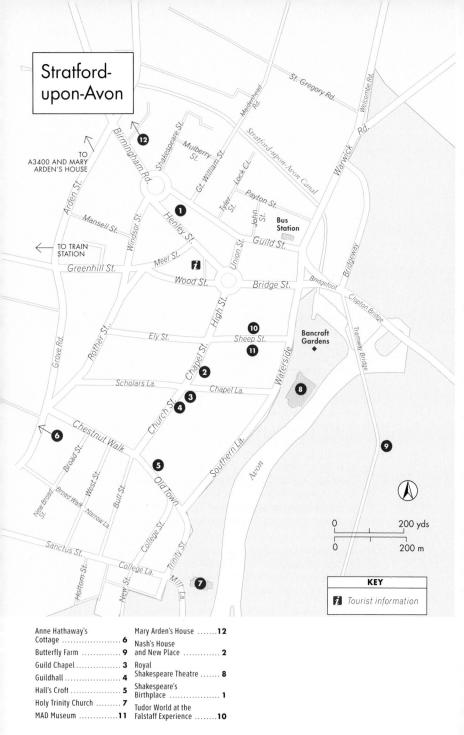

Stratford-upon-Avon

TO A3400 AND MARY ARDEN'S HOUSE

TO TRAIN STATION

St. Gregory Rd.

Welcombe Rd.

Warwick Rd.

Maidenhead Rd.

Stratford-upon-Avon Canal

Birmingham Rd.

Shakespeare St.

Mulberry St.

Gt. William St.

Lock Cl.

Tyler St.

John St.

Payton St.

Bus Station

Guild St.

Arden St.

Mansell St.

Windsor St.

Henley St.

Union St.

Meer St.

Greenhill St.

Wood St.

Bridge St.

Bridgefoot

Bridgeway

Clopton Bridge

Grove Rd.

Rother St.

Ely St.

High St.

Chapel St.

Sheep St.

Bancroft Gardens

Waterside

Tramway Bridge

Scholars La.

Chapel La.

Church St.

Southern La.

Avon

Chestnut Walk

Broad St.

West St.

Butt St.

Old Town

New Broad St.

Broad Walk

Narrow La.

College St.

Sanctus St.

College La.

Trinity St.

Mill La.

Hottom St.

New St.

1
2
3
4
5
6
7
8
9
10
11
12

0 — 200 yds
0 — 200 m

KEY

i *Tourist information*

EXPLORING

TOP ATTRACTIONS

Fodor's Choice ★ **Anne Hathaway's Cottage.** The most picturesque of the Shakespeare Trust properties, on the western outskirts of Stratford, was the family home of the woman Shakespeare married in 1582. The "cottage," actually a substantial Tudor farmhouse, has latticed windows and a grand thatch roof. Inside is period furniture, including the settle where Shakespeare reputedly conducted his courtship, and a rare carved Elizabethan bed; outside is a garden planted in lush Victorian style with herbs and flowers. A stroll through the adjacent orchard takes you to willow cabins where you can listen to sonnets, view sculptures with Shakespearean themes, and try a yew and a heart-shaped lavender maze. ■ TIP→ The best way to get here is on foot, especially in late spring when the apple trees are in blossom. The signed path runs from Evesham Place (an extension of Grove Road) opposite Chestnut Walk. Pick up a leaflet with a map from the tourist office; the walk takes a good half hour. ⌂ *Cottage La., Shottery* ☎ *01789/295517* ⊕ *www. shakespeare.org.uk* ⟟ *£9; £22.50 with the Five House Pass which includes Anne Hathaway's Cottage & Gardens, Hall's Croft, Mary Arden's Farm, Nash's House & New Place, Shakespeare's Birthplace, Shakespeare's Grave* ⊗ *Apr.–Oct., daily 9–5; Nov.–Mar., daily 10–4; last admission 30 mins before closing.*

Charlecote Park. A celebrated house in the village of Hampton Lucy, Charlecote Park was built in 1572 by Sir Thomas Lucy to entertain Queen Elizabeth I (in her honor, the house is shaped like the letter "E"). Shakespeare knew the house and may even have poached deer here. Overlooking the River Avon, the redbrick manor is striking and sprawling. It was renovated in neo-Elizabethan style by the Lucy family, represented here by numerous portraits, during the mid-19th century; a carved ebony bed is one of many spectacular pieces of furniture. The Tudor gatehouse is unchanged since Shakespeare's day, and a collection of carriages, a Victorian kitchen, and a small brewery occupy the outbuildings. Indulge in a game of croquet near the quirky, thatched, Victorian-era summer hut, or explore the deer park landscaped by Capability Brown. Interesting themed tours and walks take place in summer—call in advance to find out what's on offer. From Stratford by car take the B4086, or sign up there for City Sightseeing's Heart of Warwickshire tour. The house is 6 miles northeast of Stratford. ⌂ *B4086, off A429, Hampton Lucy* ☎ *01789/470277* ⊕ *www.nationaltrust.org. uk* ⟟ *£9.35, £5.90 in winter; grounds only £5* ⊗ *House Mar.–Oct., Thurs.–Tues. 11–4:30; Nov.–Dec., weekends noon–3:30; mid- to late Feb., Thurs.–Tues. noon–3:30. Park and gardens daily 10:30–5:30 or dusk. Last entry 30 mins before closing.*

Holy Trinity Church. The burial place of William Shakespeare, this 13th-century church sits on the banks of the Avon, with a graceful avenue of lime trees framing its entrance. Shakespeare's final resting place is in the chancel, rebuilt in 1465–91 in the late Perpendicular style. He was buried here not because he was a famed poet but because he was a lay rector of Stratford, owning a portion of the township tithes. On the north wall of

8

the sanctuary, over the altar steps, is the famous marble bust created by Gerard Jansen in 1623 and thought to be a true likeness of Shakespeare. The bust offers a more human, even humorous, perspective when viewed from the side. Also in the chancel are the graves of Shakespeare's wife, Anne; his daughter Susanna; his son-in-law John Hall; and his granddaughter's husband, Thomas Nash. Nearby, the Parish Register is displayed, containing Shakespeare's baptismal entry (1564) and his burial notice (1616). ☒ *Trinity St.* ☎ *01789/266316* ⊕ *www.stratford-upon-avon.org* ✉ *£2 for chancel* ☉ *Mar. and Oct., Mon.–Sat. 9–5, Sun. 12:30–5; Apr.–Sept., Mon.–Sat. 8:30–6, Sun. 12:30–5; Nov.–Feb., Mon.–Sat. 9–4, Sun. 12:30–5; last admission 20 mins before closing.*

> ### SHAKESPEARE FOR SALE
>
> In 1847 two widowed ladies were maintaining Shakespeare's birthplace in a somewhat ramshackle state. With the approach of the tercentennial of the playwright's birth, and in response to a rumor that the building was to be purchased by P. T. Barnum and shipped across the Atlantic, the city shelled out £3,000 for the relic. It was tidied up and opened to a growing throng of Shakespeare devotees.

FAMILY **MAD Museum.** Push buttons and pedals to your heart's content to make the two floors of the Museum of Mechanical Art and Design come alive. Witty, beautiful, and intricate automata and examples of kinetic art will clank, whirr, and rattle away. Marbles and Ping-Pong balls thread and bounce through looping runs, long metal arms give startling claps, and a train chuffs around high up on the walls. There are outside sculptures, too, and a shop full of weird and wonderful things to buy. ☒ *Sheep St., Stratford-upon-Avon* ☎ *01789/269356* ⊕ *www.theMADmuseum.co.uk* ✉ *£6.80* ☉ *Apr.–Sept. 11–5; Oct.–Mar. 10:30–5:30.*

FAMILY **Mary Arden's Farm.** A working farm, where food is grown using methods common in the 16th century, is the main attraction at Mary Arden's House (the childhood home of Shakespeare's mother) and Palmer's Farm. This bucolic stop is great for kids, who can try their hand at basket weaving and gardening, listen as the farmers explain their work in the fields, and watch the cooks prepare food in the Tudor farmhouse kitchen. It all brings the past to life. There are crafts exhibits, a café, and a garden. The site is 3 miles northwest of Stratford; you need to walk or drive here, or else go with a tour. ☒ *Off A3400, Wilmcote* ☎ *01789/293455* ⊕ *www.shakespeare.org.uk* ✉ *£9.95; £22.50 with the Five House Pass which includes Anne Hathaway's Cottage & Gardens, Hall's Croft, Mary Arden's Farm, Nash's House & New Place, Shakespeare's Birthplace, Shakespeare's Grave* ☉ *Apr.–Oct. daily 10–5.*

Fodor'sChoice **Royal Shakespeare Theatre.** Set amid gardens along the River Avon, the ★ Stratford home of the world-renowned Royal Shakespeare Company has a viewing tower and well-regarded rooftop restaurant among its amenities. The company, which presents some of the world's finest productions of Shakespeare's plays, has existed since 1879. Shows are also staged in the Swan. ■TIP→ Book ahead for the popular backstage tour. ☒ *Waterside* ☎ *0844/800–1110 ticket hotline* ⊕ *www.rsc.org.uk* ✉ *Backstage tour £7.50, front of house tour £5, open-air tour £6.50, tower visit £2.50.*

Shakespeare's Birthplace. A half-timber house typical of its time, the playwright's birthplace is a much-visited shrine that has been altered and restored since he lived here. Entering through the modern visitor center, you are immersed in an entertaining but basic introduction to Shakespeare through a "Life, Love, and Legacy" visual and audio exhibition; this can be crowded. You can see a First Folio and what is reputedly Shakespeare's signet ring, listen to the sounds of the Forest of Arden, and watch snippets of contemporary Shakespearean films. The house itself is across the garden from this large modern center. Colorful wall decorations and the furnishings in the actual house reflect comfortable, middle-class Elizabethan domestic life. Shakespeare's father, John, a glove maker and wool dealer, purchased the house; a reconstructed workshop shows the tools of the glover's trade. Mark Twain and Charles Dickens were earlier pilgrims here, and you can see the signatures of Thomas Carlyle and Walter Scott scratched into Shakespeare's windowpanes. In the garden, actors present excerpts from the plays. There's also a cafe and bookshop on the grounds. ⊠ *Henley St.* ☎ *01789/201822* ⊕ *www.shakespeare.org.uk* ⊠ *£14.95, includes entry to Hall's Croft and Nash's House* ⊙ *Apr.–June and Sept.–Oct., daily 9–5; July and Aug. daily 9–6; Nov.–Mar., daily 10–4.*

QUICK BITES

Hobsons Patisserie. Visitors and locals alike head for the half-timber Hobsons Patisserie to indulge in the famous savory pies or scrumptious afternoon teas. ⊠ **1 Henley St.** ☎ **01789/293330.**

WORTH NOTING

FAMILY **Butterfly Farm.** Europe's largest displays of exotic butterflies, spiders, caterpillars, and insects from all over the world are housed in a tropical greenhouse, a two-minute walk past the Bridgefoot footbridge. Kids can watch as butterflies emerge from pupae or take a look at the toxic black widow spider. ⊠ *Swan's Nest La.* ☎ *01789/299288* ⊕ *www.butterflyfarm.co.uk* ⊠ *£6.25* ⊙ *Apr.–Sept., daily 10–6; Oct.–Mar., daily 10–dusk.*

Compton Verney. A neoclassical country mansion remodeled in the 1760s by Robert Adam has been repurposed by the Peter Moores Foundation as an art museum with more than 800 works. The house is set in 120 acres of rolling parkland and lake landscaped by Capability Brown. The works of art are intriguingly varied and beautifully displayed in restored rooms: British folk art and portraits, textiles, Chinese pottery and bronzes, southern Italian art from 1600 to 1800, and German art from 1450 to 1600 are the main focus. Daily tours take place at noon and 2:30. From Stratford by car, take the B4086, or sign up in Stratford for City Sightseeing's Heart of Warwickshire tour; it's 9 miles east of Stratford. ⊠ *Off B4086, near Kineton* ☎ *01926/645500* ⊕ *www.comptonverney.org.uk* ⊠ *£5.40; extra charge for exhibitions* ⊙ *Late Mar.–mid-Dec., Tues.–Sun. and national holidays 11–5. Last entry 30 mins before closing.*

Guild Chapel. This chapel is the noble centerpiece of Stratford's Guild buildings, including the Guildhall, the Grammar School, and the almshouses—all well-known to Shakespeare. The ancient structure was rebuilt in the late Perpendicular style in the first half of the 15th century, thanks to the largesse of Stratford resident Hugh Clopton. Its otherwise plain interior includes fragments of a remarkable medieval fresco of the Last Judgment painted over in the 16th century and uncovered in a 20th-century reconstruction. The bell, also given by Sir Hugh, still rings as it did to tell Shakespeare the time of day. ⌂ *Chapel La., at Church St.* ☎ *01789/207111* ☛ *Free, donations welcome* ⊙ *Daily 10–4.*

Guildhall. Dating back to 1416, the Guildhall is occupied by King Edward's Grammar School, which Shakespeare probably attended as a boy; it's still used as a school. On the first floor is the Guildhall proper, where traveling acting companies performed. Many historians believe that it was after seeing the troupe known as the Earl of Leicester's Men in 1587 that Shakespeare got the acting bug and set off for London. You can usually visit during school vacations. Immediately beyond the Guildhall on Church Street is a row of 15th-century timber-and-daub almshouses, built for the poor and now serving as housing for pensioners. ⌂ *Church St..*

Hall's Croft. One of the finest surviving Jacobean (early 17th-century) town houses, this impressive residence has a delightful walled garden. Hall's Croft was the home of Shakespeare's elder daughter, Susanna, and her husband, Dr. John Hall, a physician who, by prescribing an herbal cure for scurvy, was well ahead of his time. His consulting room and medical dispensary are on view along with the other rooms, all containing Jacobean furniture of heavy oak and some 17th-century portraits. The café serves light lunches and afternoon teas. ⌂ *Old Town* ☎ *01789/292107* ⊕ *www.shakespeare.org.uk* ☛ *£14.95, includes admission to Shakespeare's Birthplace and New Place* ⊙ *Apr.–Oct., daily 10–5; Nov.–Mar., daily 11–4.*

Nash's House. This heavily restored house was the residence of Thomas Nash, who married Shakespeare's last direct descendant, his granddaughter Elizabeth Hall. It has been furnished in 17th-century style and contains a museum containing finds from the excavations of **New Place,** the house in which Shakespeare died in 1616. Built in 1483 "of brike and tymber" for a lord mayor of London, New Place was Stratford's grandest piece of real estate when Shakespeare bought it in 1597 for £60. It was torn down in 1759 by the Reverend Francis Gastrell, who was angry at the hordes of Shakespeare-related sightseers. You can see an Elizabethan knot garden in the gardens. ⌂ *Chapel St.* ☎ *01789/292325* ⊕ *www.shakespeare.org.uk* ☛ *£14.95, includes admission to Shakespeare's Birthplace and Hall's Croft* ⊙ *Apr.–Oct., daily 10–5; Nov.–Mar., daily 11–4.*

FAMILY **Tudor World at the Falstaff Experience.** Designed like a traditional Victorian museum, this place is G-rated except for the claim that the building is haunted—which is most of the draw. Tudor World is a dimly lighted and quirky maze of displays exploring aspects of the 16th century— the plague years, early medicine, bearbaiting, punishment, and alleged ghosts. At night, adults-only "ghost tours" (£7.50; nightly at 6) explore the house's paranormal history in spooky detail. ⌂ *The Shrieves House Barn, 40 Sheep St.* ☎ *0870/350–2770* ⊕ *www.falstaffexperience.co.uk* ☛ *£5.50* ⊙ *Daily 10:30–5:30.*

Stratford-upon-Avon has plenty of pubs and restaurants when you need a break from the Shakespeare trail.

WHERE TO EAT

$
BRITISH
Fodor'sChoice
★

✕ **The Black Swan/The Dirty Duck.** The only pub in Britain to be licensed under two names (the more informal one came courtesy of American GIs who were stationed here during World War II), this is one of Stratford's most celebrated pubs—it's attracted actors since the 18th-century thespian David Garrick's days. A little veranda overlooks the theaters and the river here. Along with your pint of bitter, you can choose from the extensive menu of daily specials, wraps, ciabattas, steaks, burgers, and grills. Few people come here for the food, though you will need to book ahead for dinner: the real attraction is the ambience and your fellow customers. $ *Average main: £10* ⊠ *Waterside* ☎ *01789/297312* ⊕ *www.dirtyduck-pub-stratford-upon-avon.co.uk.*

$$
MODERN BRITISH

✕ **Church Street Town House.** Theatergoers tucking into an early supper to the strains of the grand piano in the Blue Bar, grandmothers enjoying afternoon tea in the Library, and couples lingering over their candlelit suppers can all happily be found here. Plush armchairs, red drapes, oil paintings, and bookshelves add to the intimacy and refinement of this 18th-century town house. The chef aims to keep flavors to the fore and uses local produce in such dishes as baked Camembert with chutney, sea bass with fennel, butterbean and chickpea cassoulet, and peach and almond trifle. A dozen bedrooms replete with silvered French furniture are available should you wish to linger. $ *Average main: £15* ⊠ *16 Church St.* ☎ *01789/262222* ⊕ *www.churchstreettownhouse.com.*

$
BRITISH

✕ **Lambs of Sheep Street.** Sit downstairs to appreciate the hardwood floors and oak beams of this local epicurean favorite; upstairs, the look is a bit more contemporary. The updates of tried-and-true dishes include salmon cakes with sorrel sauce, and Cotswold lamb shank with creamed potatoes. Desserts are fantastic here, and daily specials keep the menu seasonal. The two- and three-course fixed-price menus (£13.50 and £17) for lunch or pretheater dining on weekdays are good deals. $ Average main: £14 ⊠ 12 Sheep St. ☎ 01789/292554 ⊕ www.lambsrestaurant. co.uk ⚑ Reservations essential ⊗ No lunch Mon. and Tues.

$

FRENCH

✕ **Le Bistrot Pierre.** There's always a satisfied hum in the air at this large, modern, and bustling bistro, part of a small chain, that's close to the river. It's French and make no mistake about it: olives from Provence, Alsace bacon, pâtés, free-range chickens from the Janzé region of Brittany, 21-day aged Scottish beef cooked overnight in Bordeaux wine, and rustic cheeses all appear on the menu. Croque Monsieur (toasted ham and cheese sandwich) is a popular lunchtime dish. Vegetarians are well catered to, and the service is amicable and attentive. $ Average main: £13 ⊠ Swan's Nest La. ☎ 01789/264804 ⊕ www.lebistrotpierre.co.uk.

$

MODERN BRITISH

✕ **Opposition.** Hearty, warming meals are offered at this informal, family-style restaurant in a 16th-century building on the main dining street near the theaters. The English and international dishes—chicken roasted with banana and served with curry sauce and basmati rice, for instance—win praise from the locals. There's a good range of lighter and vegetarian options and fixed-price menus as well. Make reservations a month ahead in summer. $ Average main: £14 ⊠ 13 Sheep St. ☎ 01789/269980 ⊕ www.theoppo.co.uk ⊗ Closed Sun.

$$

ITALIAN

✕ **Sorrento.** Family-run, this Italian restaurant takes a respectable, old-fashioned approach to service. Upon arrival, sip an aperitif in the lounge before you're escorted to your table for a silver-service, white-tablecloth meal. The menu of traditional favorites is cooked from family recipes, and includes a starter of cured beef with rocket and flakes of Parmesan, and main dishes of deep-fried calamari or black linguine with crab and scallops. There's also a hearty risotto of the day. Pretheater dinners are a good value. $ Average main: £17 ⊠ 8 Ely St. ☎ 01789/297999 ⊕ www. sorrentorestaurant.co.uk ⊗ Closed Sun. No lunch Mon.

$

THAI

✕ **Thai Boathouse.** Make for a window seat and you'll have the best inside view of the river, boats, and swans in Stratford, though the furnishings at this informal spot give you a small taste of Thailand. If the chicken, pork, or duck dishes don't grab you, try the king prawns or the sea bass; all are served with a judicious mix of exotic herbs and spices or a creamy curry sauce. $ Average main: £12 ⊠ Swan's Nest La. ☎ 01789/297733 ⊕ www.thaigroup.co.uk ⊗ No lunch Sat.

$

INDIAN

✕ **Thespian's Indian Restaurant.** A buzzing crowd of regulars frequents this casual Indian restaurant, drawn by its extensive menu of spicy dishes from the subcontinent and its friendly atmosphere. Along with dishes like the creamy lamb saqi (barbecued lamb simmered in coconut milk with ginger and mint), there are baltis, tandooris, and fish specials. It's an excellent option when you're bored with meat and potatoes. $ Average main: £9 ⊠ 26 Sheep St. ☎ 01789/267187.

$

BISTRO

✕ **The Vintner.** The imaginative, bistro-inspired menu varies each day at this café and wine bar. Pork fillet with caper butter is a popular main course, as is the steak; a children's menu is available. To dine before curtain time, arrive early or make a reservation. The building, largely unaltered since the late 1400s, has lovely flagstone floors and oak beams. $ *Average main: £14 ⊠ 5 Sheep St. ☎ 01789/297259 ⊕ www. the-vintner.co.uk.*

WHERE TO STAY

For expanded hotel reviews, visit Fodors.com.

$$$
HOTEL

Arden Hotel. Bedrooms are spacious and discreet with splashes of green, violet, and dark crimson in this redbrick boutique hotel across the road from the Royal Shakespeare Theatre. **Pros:** convenient to the Shakespeare theater; crisp and modern style; large bathrooms. **Cons:** gets booked up quickly; plastic, not real, orchids. $ *Rooms from: £170 ⊠ Waterside ☎ 01789/298682 ⊕ www.theardenhotelstratford. com ⤳ 45 rooms ¶⊙¶ Breakfast.*

$$
B&B/INN

The Bell. Just a few miles south of Stratford, this "pub with rooms" oozes imagination and individuality. **Pros:** rural setting; excellent food; friendly service. **Cons:** on a main road. $ *Rooms from: £125 ⊠ Alderminster ☎ 01789/450414 ⊕ www.thebellald.co.uk ⤳ 8 rooms, 1 suite ¶⊙¶ Breakfast.*

$$
B&B/INN

Cherry Trees. Although it's nothing fancy from the outside, this modern house near the river offers three beautifully and individually furnished suites in a tranquil location with chic rear garden. **Pros:** welcoming hosts; great breakfasts; convenient to in-town sights. **Cons:** too small for some. $ *Rooms from: £110 ⊠ Swan's Nest La. ☎ 01789/292989 ⊕ www.cherrytrees-stratford.co.uk ⤳ 3 suites ¶⊙¶ Breakfast.*

$$
HOTEL

Ettington Park Hotel. Built on land owned by the Shirley family since the 12th century, this Victorian Gothic mansion is a soothing retreat for theatergoers who don't want to cope with Stratford's crowds. **Pros:** gorgeous building; spacious rooms; relaxing lounge. **Cons:** a bit too formal for some; well outside Stratford; many wedding guests at weekends. $ *Rooms from: £140 ⊠ Off A3400, Alderminster ☎ 0845/072–7454 ⊕ www.handpickedhotels.co.uk ⤳ 42 rooms, 6 suites ¶⊙¶ Breakfast.*

$
B&B/INN

Heron Lodge. Just a mile outside Stratford town center, this B&B combines budget accommodation in a family home with high-quality service and breakfasts to match. **Pros:** welcoming and relaxing place; excellent service. **Cons:** outside town. $ *Rooms from: £65 ⊠ 260 Alcester Rd. ☎ 01789/299169 ⊕ www.heronlodge.com ⤳ 4 rooms, 1 suite ¶⊙¶ Breakfast.*

$$
HOTEL
FAMILY

Holiday Inn Stratford-upon-Avon. This good-value hotel's selling points are an excellent location near the center of the historic district and views across the river. **Pros:** good location; handy for families; free accommodation and dinners for kids under 13. **Cons:** modern and featureless; big and impersonal. $ *Rooms from: £130 ⊠ Bridgefoot ☎ 0871/942–9270 ⊕ www.holidayinn.com ⤳ 259 rooms, 2 suites ¶⊙¶ Breakfast.*

$$
HOTEL

Legacy Falcon Hotel. Licensed as an alehouse since 1640, this black-and-white timber-frame hotel in the center of town has an excellent location as well as a light, airy interior that looks out to a pleasant garden. **Pros:** great location; old portion of the building is charming; free parking. **Cons:** some rooms are a bit cramped; rooms can be a bit

8

hot. $ *Rooms from: £160* ✉ *Chapel St.* ☎ *0844/411–9005* ⊕ *www.legacy-hotels.co.uk* ⤳ *83 rooms* ⊙| *Breakfast.*

$$ 🛏 **Macdonald Alveston Manor.** This
HOTEL redbrick Elizabethan manor house across the River Avon has plenty of historic details, as well as a modern spa with a long list of treatments. **Pros:** nice mix of historic and modern; you can warm yourself by a fire in winter. **Cons:** modern rooms are less interesting; there's no elevator and lots of stairs; parking fee. $ *Rooms from: £120* ✉ *Clopton Bridge* ☎ *0844/879–9138* ⊕ *www.macdonald-hotels.co.uk* ⤳ *110 rooms, 3 suites* ⊙| *Breakfast.*

$$$ 🛏 **Menzies Welcombe Hotel Spa & Golf Club.** With its mullioned bay win-
HOTEL dows, gables, and tall chimneys, this hotel in an 1886 neo-Jacobean-style building evokes the luxury of bygone days. **Pros:** great for golfers; good spa facilities; gorgeous grounds and gardens. **Cons:** dining too formal for some; need a car to get here. $ *Rooms from: £180* ✉ *Warwick Rd.* ☎ *01789/295252* ⊕ *www.menzies-hotels.co.uk* ⤳ *78 rooms* ⊙| *Breakfast.*

$$ 🛏 **Mercure Shakespeare Hotel.** Built in the 1400s, this Elizabethan town
HOTEL house in the heart of town is a vision right out of *The Merry Wives of Windsor,* with its nine gables and long, stunning, black-and-white half-timber facade. **Pros:** historic building; relaxing lounge. **Cons:** some very small bedrooms; charge for parking. $ *Rooms from: £130* ✉ *Chapel St.* ☎ *01789/294997* ⊕ *www.mercure.com* ⤳ *63 rooms, 10 suites* ⊙| *Breakfast.*

$$ 🛏 **The Stratford.** Although this modern hotel may lack the period charm
HOTEL of older hotels, its up-to-date facilities, spacious rooms, and ample grounds make it a good option if Tudor beamed ceilings aren't a must. **Pros:** friendly; handy location very near train station; lots of modern conveniences. **Cons:** largely used as a conference hotel; rooms lack personality; parking charge. $ *Rooms from: £120* ✉ *Arden St.* ☎ *01789/271000* ⊕ *www.qhotels.co.uk* ⤳ *102 rooms* ⊙| *Breakfast.*

$ 🛏 **Victoria Spa Lodge.** This good-value B&B lies 1½ miles outside town,
B&B/INN within view of the Stratford Canal; the grand, clematis-draped building dates from 1837. **Pros:** beautiful building; full of character; family friendly. **Cons:** away from the town center. $ *Rooms from: £70* ✉ *Bishopton La., Bishopton* ☎ *01789/267985* ⊕ *www.victoriaspa.co.uk* ⤳ *7 rooms* ⊙| *Breakfast.*

$$ 🛏 **White Swan.** None of the character of this black-and-white timbered
HOTEL hotel, which claims to be the oldest building in Stratford, has been lost
Fodor's Choice in its swanky, but sympathetic update. **Pros:** antiquity; generous bath-
★ rooms; friendly service. **Cons:** tricky to stop with car; no parking onsite; stripey carpet may cause dizziness. $ *Rooms from: £150* ✉ *Rother St.* ☎ *01789/297022* ⊕ *www.white-swan-stratford.co.uk* ⤳ *37 rooms, 4 suites* ⊙| *Breakfast.*

THE PUB'S THE THING

Take a break from Shakespeare. Having a pint of ale or a bite to eat at the **Old Thatch,** on Greenhill Street, on a cool night when the fires are lighted and the mood is jovial, is a true English experience. You never know which direction the conversation will turn. Or stop by another of Stratford's pubs, such as the **Garrick** on the High Street, reputedly the oldest in town.

NIGHTLIFE AND THE ARTS

FESTIVALS

Shakespeare Birthday Celebrations. These festivities take place on and around the weekend closest to April 23. The events, spread over several days, include lectures, free concerts, processions, and impromptu performances. ☎ *01789/264293 ⊕ www.shakespearesbirthday.org.uk.*

THEATER

Fodor's Choice
★
Royal Shakespeare Company. One of the finest repertory troupes in the world and long the backbone of the country's theatrical life, the company performs plays year-round in Stratford and at venues around Britain. The stunning Royal Shakespeare Theatre, home of the RSC, has a thrust stage based on the original Globe Theater in London. The Swan Theatre, part of the theater complex and also built in the style of Shakespeare's Globe, stages plays by Shakespeare and contemporaries such as Christopher Marlowe and Ben Jonson, as well as works by contemporary playwrights. Prices usually are £14 to £60. ■ TIP→ Seats book up fast, but day-of-performance and returned tickets are often available. ✉ *Waterside* ☎ *0844/800–1110 ticket hotline ⊕ www.rsc.org.uk.*

SHOPPING

Chain stores and shops sell tourist junk, but this is also a good place to shop for high-quality (and high-price) silver, jewelry, and china. There's an open **market** (great for bargains) every Friday in the Market Place at Greenhill and Meer streets.

Antiques Centre. This building contains 50 stalls displaying jewelry, silver, linens, porcelain, and memorabilia. ✉ *60 Ely St..*

B&W Thornton. Above Shakespeare's Birthplace, B&W Thornton stocks Moorcroft pottery and glass. ✉ *23 Henley St.* ☎ *01789/269405.*

Chaucer Head Bookshop. This is the best of Stratford's many secondhand bookshops. ✉ *21 Chapel St.* ☎ *01789/415691.*

Lakeland. A great range of kitchen and home wares are available at Lakeland. ✉ *4/5 Henley St.* ☎ *01789/262100.*

Shakespeare Bookshop. Run by the Shakespeare Birthplace, the Shakespeare Bookshop carries Elizabethan plays, Tudor history books, children's books, and general paraphernalia. ✉ *Shakespeare's Birthplace, Henley St.* ☎ *01789/292176.*

SPORTS AND THE OUTDOORS

Avon Boating. From Easter to October, Avon Boating rents boats and punts and runs half-hour river excursions (£5.50). A Venetian gondola can be rented for £100 for 40 minutes. ✉ *The Boatyard, Swan's Nest La.* ☎ *01789/267073 ⊕ www.avon-boating.co.uk.*

Bancroft Cruisers. A family-run business, Bancroft Cruises runs regular 45-minute guided excursions along the Avon (£5.50). ✉ *Moathouse, Bridgefoot* ☎ *01789/269669 ⊕ www.bancroftcruisers.co.uk.*

AROUND SHAKESPEARE COUNTRY

This section of Warwickshire is marked by gentle hills, green fields, slow-moving rivers, quiet villages, and time-burnished halls, churches, and castles (Warwick and Kenilworth are the best examples, and well worth visiting). Historic houses such as Baddesley Clinton and Packwood House Court are another reason to explore. All the sights are close enough to Stratford-upon-Avon that you can easily use the town as a base if you wish.

HENLEY-IN-ARDEN

8 miles northwest of Stratford.

A brief drive out of Stratford will take you under the Stratford-upon-Avon Canal aqueduct to pretty Henley-in-Arden, whose wide main street is an architectural pageant of many periods. This area was once the Forest of Arden, where Shakespeare set one of his greatest comedies, *As You Like It.* Among the buildings to look for are the former Guildhall, dating from the 15th century, and the White Swan pub, built in the early 1600s. Near Henley-in-Arden are two stately homes worth a stop, Packwood House and Baddesley Clinton.

GETTING HERE AND AROUND

The town is on the A3400. London Midland trains for Henley-in-Arden depart every hour from Stratford; the journey takes about 15 minutes. Train service from Birmingham New Street takes about 45 minutes, and trains leave every hour. The town heritage center is open Easter through October.

ESSENTIALS

Visitor Information Henley-in-Arden Heritage and Visitors Center ⊠ *Joseph Hardy House, 150 High St.* ☎ *01564/795919* ⊕ *www.heritagehenley.org.uk.*

EXPLORING

Fodor's Choice ★ **Baddesley Clinton.** The eminent architectural historian Sir Nikolaus Pevsner described this as "the perfect late medieval manor house. The entrance side of grey stone, the small, creeper-clad Queen Anne brick bridge across the moat, the gateway with a porch higher than the roof and embattled—it could not be better." Set off a winding back-road, this grand manor dating from the 15th century retains its great fireplaces, 17th-century paneling, and three priest holes (secret chambers for Roman Catholic priests, who were hidden by sympathizers when Catholicism was banned in the 16th and 17th centuries). The café is an idyllic spot. Admission to the house is by timed ticket; Baddesley Clinton is 2 miles east of Packwood House and 15 miles north of Stratford-upon-Avon. ⊠ *Rising La., off A4141 near Chadwick End* ☎ *01564/783294* ⊕ *www.nationaltrust.org.uk* ☞ *£9.35; garden only £6.10; £14.10 combined ticket with Packwood House* ⊙ *House and grounds mid-Feb.–Oct., daily 11–5; Nov.–mid-Feb., daily 11–4; last admission 30 mins before closing.*

Packwood House. Garden enthusiasts are drawn to Packwood's recreated 17th-century gardens, highlighted by an ambitious topiary Tudor garden in which yew trees depict Jesus's Sermon on the

Mount. With tall chimneys, the house combines redbrick and half-timbering. Exquisite collections of 16th-century furniture and textiles in the interior's 20th-century version of Tudor architecture make this one of the area's finest historic houses open to the public. It's 5 miles north of Henley-in-Arden and 12 miles north of Stratford-upon-Avon. ⊠ *Off B4439, 2 miles east of Hockley Heath* ☎ *01564/782024* ⊕ *www.nationaltrust.org.uk* 💷 *£8.60; garden only £4.95; £14.10 combined ticket with Baddesley Clinton* ⊙ *House and garden mid-Feb.–mid-July, Sept., and Oct., Tues.–Sun. 11–5; mid-July and Aug. daily 11–5; last admission 30 mins before closing.*

COUNTRY WALKS

The gentle countryside rewards exploration on foot. Ambitious walkers can try the 26-mile Arden Way loop that takes in Henley-in-Arden and the Forest of Arden. On the 3-mile walk from Stratford to Wilmcote and Mary Arden's House, you can see beautiful scenery. Parkland with trails surrounds stately homes such as Charlecote Park. Even Stratford can be the base for easy walks along the River Avon or on the path bordering the Stratford-upon-Avon Canal. Stratford's Tourist Information Centre has pamphlets with walks.

WARWICK

8 miles east of Henley-in-Arden, 4 miles south of Kenilworth, 9 miles northeast of Stratford-upon-Avon.

Most famous for Warwick Castle—that vision out of the feudal ages—the town of Warwick (pronounced *war*-ick) is an interesting architectural mix of Georgian redbrick and Elizabethan half-timbering.

GETTING HERE AND AROUND

Frequent trains from London to Warwick leave London's Marylebone Station; travel time is about 90 minutes. The journey between Stratford-upon-Avon and Warwick takes around 30 minutes by train or bus. Stagecoach bus 16 is more frequent, running every hour.

ESSENTIALS

Visitor Information Warwick Tourist Information Centre ⊠ *Court House, Jury St.* ☎ *01926/492212* ⊕ *www.visitwarwick.co.uk.*

EXPLORING

Collegiate Church of St. Mary. Crowded with gilded, carved, and painted tombs, the **Beauchamp Chapel** of this church is the essence of late-medieval and Tudor chivalry—although it was built (1443–64) to honor the somewhat-less-than-chivalrous Richard Beauchamp, who consigned Joan of Arc to the flames. Alongside his impressive effigy in gilded bronze lie the fine tombs of Robert Dudley, earl of Leicester, adviser and favorite of Elizabeth I, and Leicester's brother Ambrose. The church's chancel, distinguished by its flying ribs, a feature unique to a parish church, houses the alabaster table tomb of Thomas Beauchamp and his wife; the adjacent tiny Dean's chapel has exquisite miniature fan vaulting. In the Norman crypt, look for the rare ducking stool (a chair in which people were tied for public punishment). There's a brass-rubbing

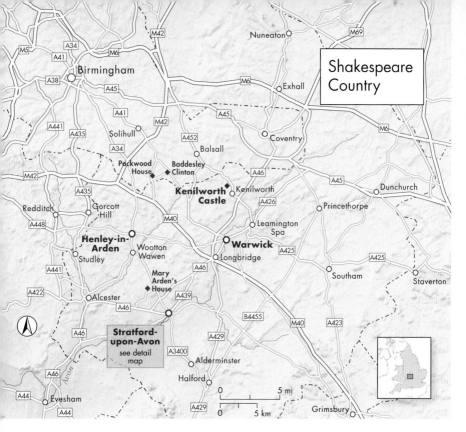

Shakespeare Country

center, and you can climb the tower in summer. It's a five-minute walk from Warwick Castle. ⊠ *Old Sq., Church St.* ☏ *01926/403940* ⊕ *www. stmaryswarwick.org.uk* ✉ *£2 donation suggested; tower £2.50* ⊙ *Apr.–Oct., daily 10–6; Nov.–Mar., daily 10–4:30.*

Lord Leycester Hospital. Unattractive postwar development has spoiled much of Warwick's town center, but look for the 15th-century half-timber Lord Leycester Hospital, a home for old soldiers since the earl of Leicester dedicated it to that purpose in 1571. Within the complex are a chapel, an impressive beamed hall containing a small museum, and a fine courtyard with a wattle-and-daub balcony and 500-year-old gardens with a pineapple pit. Try a cream tea in the Brethren's Kitchen. ⊠ *High St.* ☏ *01926/491422* ⊕ *www.lordleycester.com* ✉ *£4.90* ⊙ *Apr.–Sept., Tues.–Sun. 10–5; Oct.–Mar., Tues.–Sun. 10.*

FAMILY **St. John's House.** Kids as well as adults appreciate the well-thought-out St. John's House, a Jacobean building near the castle; beautiful gardens surround it. Inside are period costumes and scenes of domestic life, as well as a Victorian schoolroom and kitchen. ⊠ *Smith St.* ☏ *01926/412132* ✉ *Free* ⊙ *Apr.–Sept., Tues.–Sat. 10–5; Oct.–Mar., Tues.–Sat. 10–4.*

FAMILY
Fodor's Choice
★

Warwick Castle. The vast bulk of this medieval castle rests on a cliff overlooking the Avon—"the fairest monument of ancient and chivalrous splendor which yet remains uninjured by time," to use the words of Sir Walter Scott. Today the company that runs the Madame Tussauds wax museums owns the castle, and the exhibits and diversions can occupy a full day. Warwick is a great castle experience for kids, though it's pricey (there are family rates).

Warwick's two soaring towers, bristling with battlements, can be seen for miles: the 147-foot-high Caesar's Tower, built in 1356, and the 128-foot-high Guy's Tower, built in 1380. The castle's most powerful commander was Richard Neville, earl of Warwick, known during the 15th-century Wars of the Roses as the Kingmaker. Warwick Castle's monumental walls enclose an impressive armory of medieval weapons, as well as state rooms with historic furnishings and paintings by Peter Paul Rubens, Anthony Van Dyck, and other old masters. Twelve rooms are devoted to an imaginative wax exhibition, "A Royal Weekend Party—1898." Other exhibits display the sights and sounds of a great medieval household as it prepares for an important battle, and of a princess's fairy-tale wedding; in the Dragon Tower, Merlin and a talking dragon breathe life into the Arthurian legend. At the Mill and Engine House you can see the turning water mill and the engines used to generate electricity early in the 20th century. In the spooky dungeon exhibit you can wander by wax re-creations of decaying bodies, chanting monks, witches, executions, and "the labyrinth of lost souls"—a modern mirror maze. Elsewhere, a working trebuchet (a kind of catapult), falconry displays, and rat-throwing (stuffed, not live) games add to the atmosphere. Below the castle strutting peacocks patrol the 60 acres of grounds elegantly landscaped by Capability Brown in the 18th century. ■ TIP➜ Arrive early to beat the crowds. If you book online, you save on ticket prices. Lavish medieval banquets (extra charge) and special events, including festivals, jousting tournaments, and a Christmas market, take place throughout the year, and plenty of food stalls serve lunches. ⊠ *Castle La., off Mill St.* ☎ *01926/495421, 0871/265–2000 24-hr information line* ⊕ *www. warwick-castle.com* ⊠ *Castle, Dragon Tower and Dungeon £30.60, Castle and Dungeon £28.20, Castle £22.80; parking £6* ⊗ *Late July and Aug., daily 10–6; mid-Sept.–mid-July, daily 10–5; last admission 30 mins before closing.*

QUICK
BITES

Undercroft. After a vigorous walk around the ramparts at Warwick Castle you can drop by the cream-, crimson-, and gold-vaulted 14th-century Undercroft for a spot of tea or a hot meal from the cafeteria. ☎ *01926/495421.*

8

Now in impressive ruins, mighty Kenilworth Castle once hosted Queen Elizabeth I. Today it has gardens, exhibitions, and a great setting.

WHERE TO EAT AND STAY

For expanded hotel reviews, visit Fodors.com.

$ ✕ **The Art Kitchen.** You are encouraged to share the creative Thai dishes
THAI sold by "bytes" (small plates and larger portions) at this chic and contemporary restaurant. The green and red curries are favorites, especially the chicken or lamb Masaman curry. Also consider the prawn-and-coriander dumplings on lemongrass. The service is always courteous, and the art that peppers the walls is for sale. $ *Average main: £14* ✉ *7 Swan St.* ☎ *01926/494303* ⊕ *www.theartkitchen.com* ⊘ *Closed Sun.*

$ ✕ **Rose & Crown.** Stripped pine floorboards, red walls, big wooden tables,
MODERN BRITISH and solidly good food and drink set the tone at this contemporary gastro-pub with rooms on the town's main square. It's popular with locals, and the owners take pride in offering seasonal food that mixes British and international influences. There's a different roast every day and specials might include rose veal, pork with buttered leaks, or rabbit pie. Five moderately priced bedrooms provide simple but modern lodging. $ *Average main: £13* ✉ *30 Market Pl.* ☎ *01926/411117* ⊕ *www. roseandcrownwarwick.co.uk.*

$$ ⊤ **Mallory Court Hotel.** This elegant country-house hotel 6 miles southeast
HOTEL of Warwick makes a quiet, luxurious getaway; it has 30 rooms but still manages to feel as if you're just visiting wealthy friends. **Pros:** good for pampering; excellent restaurant. **Cons:** outside town; lots of weekend weddings. $ *Rooms from: £160* ✉ *Harbury La., Bishops Tachbrook* ☎ *01926/330214* ⊕ *www.mallory.co.uk* ⇆ *31 rooms* ⦿ *Breakfast.*

KENILWORTH CASTLE

5 miles north of Warwick.

GETTING HERE AND AROUND

The local Stagecoach company offers bus services to and from Stratford and Warwick on the 16 and X17 route. The castle is 1½ miles from the town center.

ESSENTIALS

Visitor Information **Kenilworth Library and Information Centre** ✉ *Kenilworth Library, 11 Smalley Pl.* ☎ *0300/555–8171* 🌐 *www.warwickshire.gov.uk/kenilworthlibrary.*

EXPLORING

Fodor's Choice ★ **Kenilworth Castle.** The sprawling, graceful red ruins of the castle loom over the green fields of Warwickshire, surrounded by the low grassy impression of what was once a lake that surrounded it completely. The top of the keep (central tower) has commanding views of the countryside, one good indication of why this was such a formidable fortress from 1120 until it was dismantled by Oliver Cromwell after the Civil War in the mid-17th century. Still intact are its keep, with 20-foot-thick walls; its great hall built by John of Gaunt in the 14th century; and its curtain walls, the low outer walls forming the castle's first line of defense. Even more than Warwick Castle, these ruins reflect English history. In 1326 King Edward II was imprisoned here and forced to renounce the throne, before he was transferred to Berkeley Castle and allegedly murdered with a red-hot poker. Here the ambitious Robert Dudley, earl of Leicester, one of Elizabeth I's favorites, entertained her four times, most notably in 1575 with 19 days of revelry. An excellent exhibition in the restored gatehouse discusses the relationship between Leicester and Elizabeth, and a stunning re-created Elizabethan garden with arbors, aviary, and an 18-foot high Cararra marble fountain provides further interest for a visit for an hour or two. This is a good place for a picnic and contemplation of the passage of time. The fine gift shop sells excellent replicas of tapestries and swords. ✉ *Off A452* ☎ *01926/852078* 🌐 *www.english-heritage.org.uk* 🎟 *£9* 🕐 *Apr.–Oct., daily 10–5; Nov.–Mar., weekends 10–4.*

WHERE TO EAT

$ BRITISH 🍴 **Clarendon Arms.** A location close to Kenilworth Castle helps make this pub a good spot for lunch and some good hand-pulled ales. You can order fine home-cooked food, including steaks and grills from the bar. Another option is to sample more upmarket fare with an international slant at the next-door Harrington's restaurant, under the same management. [$] *Average main: £9* ✉ *44 Castle Hill* ☎ *01926/852017* 🌐 *www.clarendonarmspub.co.uk.*

8

BIRMINGHAM

Though not the U.K.'s most visually appealing city—thanks to decline of heavy industry, bombing during World War II and some drab civic architecture in the decades afterwards—21st-century Birmingham is a vibrant and diverse metropolis, in the midst of a major cultural rebirth.

The city first flourished in the boom years of the 19th-century's Industrial Revolution. Its inventive citizens accumulated enormous wealth, and at one time the city had some of the finest Victorian buildings in the country. It still has some of the most ravishingly beautiful Pre-Raphaelite paintings, on view in the Birmingham Museum and Art Gallery.

Today art galleries, theater, museums, ballet, and a symphony orchestra all thrive here. Creative redevelopment and public art are increasingly making areas more attractive, too. The redeveloped Bullring shopping center, part of which has a striking, curving facade of 15,000 aluminum disks, has won widespread critical acclaim.

The city has a distinctive, almost singsong local accent—known as "Brummie"—that's often the butt of unfair jokes in the U.K. In 2008 the London *Times* reported a survey finding it to be the accent Brits most associated with stupidity, even more so than being unable to speak at all. A favorite local rebuttal is to point out that Shakespeare, born and raised just 25 miles away, would have had a Brummie accent.

Birmingham, with a metropolitan area population of 2.6 million, lies 25 miles north of Stratford-upon-Avon and 120 miles northwest of London.

GETTING HERE AND AROUND

Bus 900 runs from the airport to the city center every 20 minutes; a taxi will cost you around £25. Try to avoid the city's convoluted road network. Drivers are often surprised that Birmingham's inner ring road twists through the city center. Parking in the center is free from 6 pm to 8 am.

New Street train station is right in the center of the city, close to the Bullring shopping center. The bus station is at Oxford Street, a few minutes' walk from the Bullring.

Most of the central sights, which are well signposted, form a tight-knit group. The easiest way to get around the city is on foot, though you'll need a bus for the Barber Institute and Cadbury World, and a short Metro (tram) trip for the Jewellery Quarter. A Daytripper ticket covering bus, train, and Metro travel costs £6. The tourist information center, the best place to pick up a map, is close to the public bus and rail stations. It has details of heritage walks.

PLANNING YOUR TIME

A full day gives you time to linger in the Jewellery Quarter and browse the art museums. Much of Birmingham is now pedestrian-friendly, the downtown shopping area transformed into arcades and buses-only streets. You can also explore restored canals and canal towpaths.

ESSENTIALS

Visitor Information Birmingham Tourist Information Centre ✉ *The Rotunda, 150 New St.* ☎ *0844/888–3883* ⊕ *www.visitbirmingham.com.*

EXPLORING

TOP ATTRACTIONS

Fodor'sChoice ★ **Barber Institute of Fine Art.** Part of the University of Birmingham, the museum has a small but astounding collection of European paintings, prints, drawings, and sculpture, including works by Botticelli, Van Dyck, Gainsborough, Turner, Manet, Monet, Degas, Van Gogh, and Magritte. The museum is 3 miles from the city center; to get here, take a train from New Street Station south to University Station, or Bus 61, 63, or 98 from the city center. ⊠ *Off Edgbaston Park Rd., near East Gate, Edgbaston* ☎ *0121/414–7333* ⊕ *www.barber.org.uk* ◻ *Free* ⊙ *Mon.–Sat. 10–5, Sun. 11–5.*

Birmingham Back to Backs. Of the 20,000 courts of back-to-back houses (constructed around a courtyard and thus backing onto each other) built in the 19th century for the city's expanding working-class population, this is the only survivor. Three houses tell the stories of families, headed by a watchmaker, a locksmith, and a glassworker, who lived here between the 1840s and the 1930s. A few houses are available for overnight stays. Admission is by timed ticket, booked in advance; allow one hour for the tour and be prepared for steep stairs. ⊠ *55–63 Hurst St., City Centre* ☎ *0121/666–7671* ⊕ *www.nationaltrust.co.uk* ◻ *£7 (booking essential)* ⊙ *Feb.–mid-July and Sept.–mid-Dec., Fri.–Sun. 10–5, Tues.–Thurs. 1–5; mid.-July–Aug., Tues.–Sun., 10–5. Also public holidays 10–5 (but closed next day).*

Fodor'sChoice ★ **Birmingham Museum and Art Gallery.** Vast and impressive, this museum holds a magnificent collection of Victorian art and is known internationally for its works by the Pre-Raphaelites. All the big names are here—among them Rubens, Renoir, Constable, and Francis Bacon—reflecting the enormous wealth of 19th-century Birmingham and the aesthetic taste of its industrialists. Galleries of metalwork, silver, and ceramics reveal some of the city's history, and works from the Renaissance, the Arts and Crafts movement, and the present day are also well represented. Also on view is part of the incredible **Staffordshire Hoard,** the greatest haul of Anglo-Saxon treasure ever discovered. Items on display from the 3,500-strong haul, which was unearthed in a field 16 miles north of Birmingham in 2009, include helmets, gold, jewelry, and metalwork. The hoard's permanent home is likely to be an even split between here and Potteries Museum in Stoke, although the current display is scheduled to run through 2014. ⊠ *Chamberlain Sq., City Centre* ☎ *0121/303–2834* ⊕ *www.bmag.org.uk* ◻ *Free* ⊙ *Mon.–Thurs. and Sat. 10–5, Fri. 10:30–5, Sun. 12:30–5.*

FAMILY Fodor'sChoice ★ **Black Country Living Museum.** It was in the town of Dudley, in the 17th century, that coal was first used for smelting iron. The town became known as the capital of the Black Country, a term that arose from the resulting air pollution. This 26-acre museum consists of an entire village made up of buildings from around the region, including a chain maker's workshop; a trap-works where animal snares were fashioned; his-and-hers hardware stores (pots and pans for women, tools and sacks for men); a druggist; and a general store where costumed women describe life in a poor industrial community in the 19th century. You can also

8

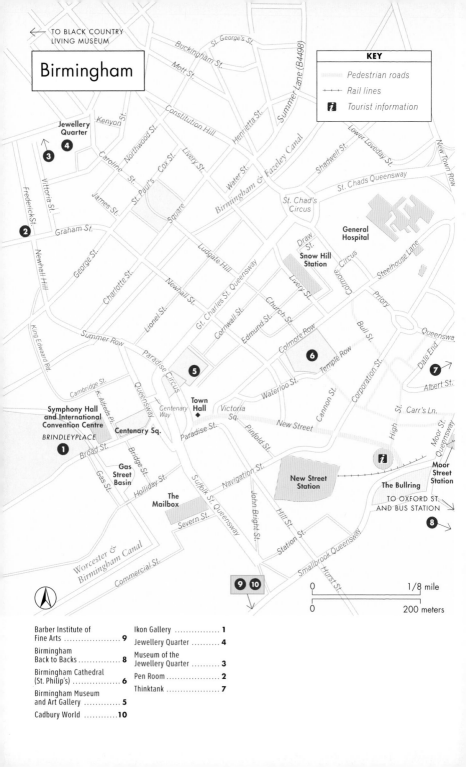

KEY

Pedestrian roads
Rail lines
ℹ️ Tourist information

← TO BLACK COUNTRY LIVING MUSEUM

Birmingham

Jewellery Quarter **4**

3

2

1 BRINDLEYPLACE

Symphony Hall and International Convention Centre

Centenary Sq.

5 Birmingham Museum and Art Gallery

Town Hall

Victoria Sq.

6

7

Snow Hill Station

St. Chad's Circus

General Hospital

Gas Street Basin

The Mailbox

New Street Station

ℹ️

The Bullring

Moor Street Station

TO OXFORD ST. AND BUS STATION

8

9 **10**

0   1/8 mile
0   200 meters

sit on a hard bench and watch Charlie Chaplin in the 1920s cinema, peer into the depths of a mine, or ride on a barge through a tunnel to experience the canal travel of yesteryear. For sustenance there are two cafés, the 1930s-era Fried Fish Shop that serves fish-and-chips cooked in beef drippings, and the Bottle & Glass pub for ales and drinks. ▮TIP→ To avoid the numerous school parties, visit on the weekend or during school vacations. The museum, 3 miles from the M5, is best reached by car. Leave M5 at Junction 2 by A4123, and then take A4037 at Tipton. Trains from Birmingham New Street to Tipton Station take 16 minutes; buses from the train station run past the museum, which is 1 mile away. ⊠ *Tipton Rd., Dudley* ☎ *0121/557–9643* ⊕ *www.bclm. co.uk* ☏ *£15.50; barge trip £6; parking £2.50* ☉ *Apr.–Oct., daily 10–5; Nov.–Mar., Wed.–Sun. 10–4.*

Jewellery Quarter. For more than two centuries, jewelers have worked in the district of Hockley, northwest of the city center; today around 200 manufacturing jewelers continue the tradition in the Jewellery Quarter, producing more than a third of the jewelry made in Britain. ▮TIP→ A free booklet from the tourist office gives you the lowdown shopping in the area. The city's Assay Office hallmarks 12 million items each year with the anchor symbol denoting Birmingham origin. The ornate green and gilded Chamberlain Clock, at the intersection of Vyse Street, Warstone Lane, and Frederick Street, marks the center of the district. Shops are closed Sunday. The quarter is two stops along Metro Line 1 from Snow Hill Station. ⊠ *Hockley* ⊕ *www.the-quarter.com.*

Museum of the Jewellery Quarter. The museum is built around the workshops of Smith & Pepper, a firm that operated here for more than 80 years. Little had changed here since the early 1900s when they finally closed their doors in 1981. A factory tour (about an hour) and exhibits explain the history of the neighborhood and the jeweler's craft, and you can watch demonstrations of jewelry being made in the traditional way. ⊠ *75–79 Vyse St., Jewellery Quarter* ☎ *0121/554–3598* ⊕ *www.bmag. org.uk* ☏ *£5* ☉ *Tues.–Sat. and national holidays 10:30–5; last admission 1 hr before closing.*

Sherborne Wharf. Birmingham has around 100 miles of navigable canals, and you can take a ride on a barge from Sherborne Wharf. Trips leave daily April through October at 11:30, 1, 2:30, and 4, and on weekends the rest of the year, departing from the International Convention Centre Quayside. An hour-long trip costs £8. ⊠ *Sherborne St., City Centre* ☎ *0121/455–6163* ⊕ *www.sherbornewharf.co.uk.*

FAMILY **Thinktank.** This interactive museum in the state-of-the-art Millennium Point center allows you to explore science and the history of Birmingham over four floors of galleries. You can watch giant steam engines at work, explore deep space, program a robot to play the drums, and help perform a hip operation; it's great for families. The IMAX cinema and planetarium put on shows throughout the day. The museum is a 10-minute walk from Moor Street railway station. ⊠ *Curzon St., Digbeth* ☎ *0121/202–2222* ⊕ *www.thinktank.ac* ☏ *£12.30; IMAX cinema £4–£13; planetarium £1.50–£3* ☉ *Daily 10–5; last admission 1 hr before closing.*

8

CLOSE UP

Cruising Birmingham's Canals

Canal near the Gas Street Basin

With eight canals and 34 miles of waterways, Birmingham has more canals in its center than Venice. The city is at the heart of a system of waterways built during the Industrial Revolution to connect inland factories to rivers and seaports—by 1840 the canals extended more than 4,000 miles throughout the British Isles. These canals, which carried 9 million tons of cargo a year in the late 19th century and helped make the city an industrial powerhouse, have undergone extensive cleanup and renovation, and are now a tourist attraction.

A walk along the Birmingham Canal Main Line near the Gas Street Basin will bring you to modern shops, restaurants, and more developments such as Brindleyplace in one direction and the Mailbox in the other, and you can see the city from an attractive new perspective. Contact the city tourist offices for maps of pleasant walks along the towpaths and canal cruises on colorfully painted barges.

WORTH NOTING

Birmingham Cathedral. The early-18th-century Cathedral of St. Philip, a few blocks from Victoria Square, contains some lovely plasterwork in its elegant, gilded Georgian interior. The stained-glass windows behind the altar, designed by the Pre-Raphaelite Edward Burne-Jones (1833–98) and executed by William Morris (1834–96), glow with sensuous hues. ⊠ *Colmore Row, City Centre* ☎ *0121/262–1840* ⊕ *www. birminghamcathedral.com* 🖾 *Free; suggested donation £2* ☉ *Weekdays 7:30–6:30 (closes 5 late July–early Sept., and for 1 wk after Christmas and Easter); weekends 8:30–5.*

FAMILY **Cadbury World.** The village of Bournville (4 miles south of the city center) contains this museum devoted to—what else?—chocolate. In 1879 the Quaker Cadbury brothers moved the family business from the city to this "factory in a garden." The museum traces the history of the cocoa bean and the Cadbury dynasty. The rain-forest walk, Cadabra ride, and exhibits, may seem kitschy, but Cadbury World is extremely popular. You can watch (and smell) chocolates being made by hand, enjoy free samples, and then stock up from the cut-price shop. The restaurant has specialty chocolate cakes as well as lunches. ⊠ *Off A38, Bournville* ☎ *0844/880–7667* ⊕ *www.cadburyworld.co.uk* 🖾 *£15* ☉ *Feb.–Nov., daily; mid–late Jan., Wed., Thurs. and weekends; Dec., Tues.–Thurs. and weekends; times vary by wk but generally 10–3 weekdays, 10–4 weekends in summer; reservations strongly advised, and essential at busy times.*

Ikon Gallery. Converted from a Victorian Gothic–style school, this gallery serves as the city's main venue for exhibitions of contemporary art from Britain and abroad. The bright, white interior is divided into comparatively small display areas, making the shows easily digestible. If you need fortifying, however, try the attached Opus Café. ✉ *1 Oozells Sq., Brindleyplace, City Centre* ☎ *0121/248–0708* 🌐 *www.ikon-gallery.co.uk* 🎟 *Free* 🕓 *Tues.–Sun. and national holiday Mon. 11–6.*

QUICK BITES

Malt House. The balcony of the redbrick Malt House is just the place to linger over a drink as you watch canal life go by. ✉ ***75 King Edward's Rd.*** ☎ ***0121/633–4171.***

Pen Room. During the 19th century, Birmingham was the hub of the world pen trade. This compact museum in a former factory illustrates that heyday through an overwhelming and decorative array of nibs, quills, fountain pens, inks, and all the paraphernalia of the pre-ballpoint era. You can try your hand at calligraphy and make your own nib. ✉ *Unit 3, the Argent Centre, 60 Frederick St., Jewellery Quarter* ☎ *0121/236–9834* 🌐 *www.penroom.co.uk* 🎟 *Free* 🕓 *Mon.–Sat. 11–4, Sun. 1–4.*

WHERE TO EAT

$ INDIAN Fodor's Choice ★

🍴 **Itihaas.** Birmingham has some of the country's finest Indian restaurants, and this is one upbeat choice. The style is traditional and colonial; potted palms and portraits rub shoulders with Raj-style antiques. The cooking concentrates on north Indian dishes, and some good choices are *koila murgh* (chicken marinated in yogurt and seared over charcoal) or *hara bara gosth* (a casserole of lamb cooked with garlic, chili, and spinach). The weekday lunchtime tapas menu is a deal at £8.95. [$] *Average main: £11* ✉ *18 Fleet St., City Centre* ☎ *0121/212–3383* 🌐 *www.itihaas.co.uk* 🕓 *No lunch weekends.*

$$$$ MODERN BRITISH

🍴 **Love's.** Overlooking a spruced-up stretch of canal bobbing with barges, this contemporary eatery takes you on an imaginative journey through the British culinary landscape. Chef Steve Love accompanies his Gloucestershire braised pig's head with crispy ear and smoked bacon relish, while his fillet of Cornish hake comes with broccoli quinoa. All menus are fixed-price; the three-course *prixe fixe* menu (Friday and Saturday lunch, Wednesday and Thursday evening) offers good value at £25; the tasting menu is £68. [$] *Average main: £32* ✉ *3 Canal Sq., City Centre* ☎ *0121/454–5151* 🌐 *www.loves-restaurant.co.uk* 🕓 *Closed Sun. and Mon.*

$$$ MODERN BRITISH

🍴 **Opus.** This stylish, modern restaurant specializes in local, seasonal British flavors. The accent is on local and British, so expect venison with braised red cabbage, or perhaps steamed turbot with, pink fur apple gnocchi. Meat is free range and fish is freshly caught. Adventurous diners may want a seat at the chef's table, right in the heart of the kitchen. After establishing how much interaction you're comfortable with, the kitchen staff will either chat to you as they prepare the food, or just leave you to enjoy the special five-course meal (£75) while you observe the action. [$] *Average main: £21* ✉ *54 Cornwall St., City Centre* ☎ *0121/200–2323* 🌐 *www.opusrestaurant.co.uk* 🕓 *Closed Sun.*

$$$$ MODERN BRITISH 🍴 **Purnell's.** Business moguls and sophisticated foodies can be found sampling an aperitif in a comfy armchair before moving to the sleek, slate-floor dining room at Purnell's. This high spot in the business district, in a Victorian terra-cotta and redbrick building, is where chef Glyn Purnell creates his adventurous Modern British fare. Devonshire crab comes with an apple and celeriac puree and smoked paprika honeycomb, while the wreck fish is accompanied by a "risotto" of coconut and cauliflower. Menus are designed to be shared by the whole table. **TIP→ Prices at lunchtime are half what they are in the evening.** [$] *Average main: £60* ✉ *55 Cornwall St., City Centre* ☎ *0121/212–9799* 🌐 *www.purnellsrestaurant.com* 🕒 *Closed Sun. and Mon. No lunch Sat.*

EAT BALTI IN BRUM

Birmingham is home to the *balti,* a popular cuisine created in the mid-1970s by the Pakistani community. The food is cooked and brought to the table in a woklike dish and eaten with naan bread, not rice. Curry and other spices season the meat and vegetables. There are more than 30 restaurants in the "Balti Triangle" of the Moseley and Sparkbrook districts. Here's one that is highly rated:

Al Frash ✉ *186 Ladypool Rd., Sparkhill* ☎ *0121/753–3120* 🌐 *www.alfrash.com.*

Buses 6, 12, 13, and 37 go to this area a few miles south of the center.

$ INDIAN Fodor's Choice ★ 🍴 **Pushkar.** A vogueish dining room is the perfect setting for the inventive Punjabi cuisine at this popular curry palace and cocktail bar on bustling Broad Street. Try seared fillet of sea bass on a bed of spiced mash with mango, ginger, and coconut, or perhaps the slow-braised lamb with spinach, garlic, and cumin, and you'll find out why Pushkar is a rich part of the superb Birmingham curry scene. [$] *Average main: £13* ✉ *245 Broad St., City Centre* ☎ *0121/643–7978* 🌐 *www.pushkardining.com.*

$$$ FRENCH Fodor's Choice ★ 🍴 **Simpsons.** Choose between the conservatory with garden views or the inner dining space of this elegant and gleaming Georgian villa known for French-influenced cuisine. Either way, the light and immaculate surroundings and assured and welcoming service make it easy to savor specialties such as wood pigeon with a lemon-and-date puree or beef fillet with potato pancetta terrine. There are four luxurious themed guest rooms for those who wish to stray no farther, and a cooking school. It's a mile south of the city center. [$] *Average main: £23* ✉ *20 Highfield Rd., Edgbaston* ☎ *0121/454–3434* 🌐 *www.simpsonsrestaurant.co.uk* 🕒 *No dinner Sun.*

$ THAI 🍴 **Thai Edge.** This elegant, contemporary eatery is perfectly at home in fashionable Brindleyplace. Dishes such as *goong gaeng keow waan* (green coconut-milk prawn curry with eggplant, lime leaves, and basil) and sea bass in banana leaves are excellent. Lunches are a good value. [$] *Average main: £9* ✉ *7 Oozells Sq., City Centre* ☎ *0121/643–3993* 🌐 *www.thaiedge.co.uk.*

WHERE TO STAY

For expanded hotel reviews, visit Fodors.com.

$ **The Bloc Hotel.** There are few frills, and even less space at this brand
HOTEL new budget hotel in the Jewellery Quarter, with its tiny "pod"-style bedrooms; but there's no shortage of designer touches. **Pros:** comfortable rooms; unbeatable price; well designed. **Cons:** absolutely no storage space aside from a couple of hooks and a space under the bed; breakfast costs extra and is not available on weekends. $ *Rooms from: £55* ✉ *Caroline St., City Centre, Birmingham* ☎ *0121/212–1223* ⊕ *www. blochotels.com* ⤳ *73 rooms* ❖ *Breakfast.*

$ **Eaton Hotel.** Fronted by an elegant, gleaming white facade, this mansion in leafy Edgbaston provides a peaceful, cozy stay two miles from
HOTEL the bustle of Birmingham's center. **Pros:** complimentary parking; good breakfasts; frequent buses to center. **Cons:** not in center. $ *Rooms from: £70* ✉ *279 Hagley Rd., Edgbaston* ☎ *0121/454–3311* ⊕ *www. eatonhotel.co.uk* ⤳ *54 rooms* ❖ *Breakfast.*

$ **Hilton Garden Inn.** An excellent central location near the waterside
HOTEL nightlife scene is a perk to staying at this smoothly run hotel. **Pros:** free Wi-Fi; windows open to catch the breeze. **Cons:** mostly for business travelers. $ *Rooms from: £69* ✉ *1 Brunswick Sq., Brindleyplace, City Centre* ☎ *0121/643–1003* ⊕ *hiltongardeninn3.hilton.com* ⤳ *238 rooms* ❖ *No meals.*

$$ **Hotel du Vin & Bistro.** A Victorian hospital in the city center got a
HOTEL makeover from this super-hip chain, but retains such original details as
Fodor's Choice the ironwork double stairway and marble columns. **Pros:** chic and comfortable; central location. **Cons:** expensive valet parking; breakfast costs
★ extra. $ *Rooms from: £100* ✉ *25 Church St., City Centre* ☎ *0121/200–0600* ⊕ *www.hotelduvin.com* ⤳ *56 rooms, 10 suites* ❖ *No meals.*

$ **Macdonald Burlington Hotel.** Housed in one of the city's grand Victorian buildings, this traditional hotel is a surprisingly good value option
HOTEL in the center of Birmingham. **Pros:** close to New Street Station and shops; very good weekend rates. **Cons:** attracts a mainly business clientele. $ *Rooms from: £72* ✉ *Burlington Arcade, 126 New St., City Centre* ☎ *0844/879–9019* ⊕ *www.burlingtonhotel.com* ⤳ *112 rooms* ❖ *Breakfast.*

$ **Malmaison.** Retail therapy is on your doorstep at this chic hotel in the
HOTEL Mailbox shopping center. **Pros:** handy for shopping and dining; near canal-side attractions; in-hotel spa. **Cons:** drab views; expensive parking (cheaper alternatives are close by); breakfast not included. $ *Rooms from: £80* ✉ *1 Wharfside St., City Centre* ☎ *0121/246–5000* ⊕ *www. malmaison.com* ⤳ *189 rooms, 10 suites* ❖ *No meals.*

$$ **Staying Cool at the Rotunda.** The 19th and 20th floors of the Rotunda,
RENTAL an iconic, cylindrical office building from 1965, now contain spacious
Fodor's Choice one- and two bedroom apartments, designed to the hilt in sleek mid-
★ century style. **Pros:** well-stocked kitchens; dreamy beds; Apple Mac entertainment systems with free Wi-Fi. **Cons:** no designated parking. $ *Rooms from: £139* ✉ *150 New St., City Centre* ☎ *0121/285–1250* ⊕ *www.stayingcool.com* ⤳ *15 apartments* ❖ *No meals.*

8

NIGHTLIFE AND THE ARTS

NIGHTLIFE

The city's thriving nightlife scene is concentrated around Broad Street and Hurst Street, as well as the Brindleyplace and Mailbox areas.

Asha's. Colorful Asha's, a bar and restaurant, has superb fresh fruit cocktails and Asian cuisine. ⊠ *12–22 Newhall St., City Centre* ☎ *0121/200–2767* ⊕ *www.ashasrestaurants.com/birmingham* ⊘ *No lunch weekends.*

Bar Epernay. This champagne bar and brasserie has a revolving piano and a warming brazier, making it perfect for relaxing after a day's sightseeing. ⊠ *171 Wharfside St., City Centre* ☎ *0121/632–1430* ⊕ *www.bar-epernay.co.uk.*

The Fighting Cocks. This handsome, trendy pub is full of polished wood tables, colorful cushions, and stained-glass windows. The beer selection is huge and the high-class pub food is delicious. This place gets rammed to the rafters for the traditional "roasts"—beef, pork, lamb, chicken, or nut—on Sunday at lunchtime. ⊠ *1 St. Mary's Row, Moseley, Birmingham* ☎ *0121/449–0811* ⊕ *www.thefightingcocksmoseley.co.uk.*

Jam House. This excellent drinking, dining, and dancing venue has live jazz, soul, or funk nightly. ⊠ *3–5 St. Paul's Sq., Jewellery Quarter* ☎ *0121/200–3030* ⊕ *www.thejamhouse.com/birmingham.*

Vaults. The bar at the Vaults is perfect for an intimate drink. Another option is to reserve your own private, brick-vaulted booth, draw the curtain, adjust the music, and relax. ⊠ *Newhall Pl., Jewellery Quarter* ☎ *0121/212–9837* ⊕ *www.vaultsbirmingham.com.*

THE ARTS

Birmingham's performing arts companies are well regarded throughout the country. Catch a performance if you can.

BALLET **Birmingham Royal Ballet.** The second company of the Royal Ballet, the Birmingham Royal Ballet is based at the Hippodrome Theatre, which also plays host to visiting companies such as the Welsh National Opera. ⊠ *Thorp St., City Centre* ☎ *0844/338–5000* ⊕ *www.brb.org.uk.*

CONCERTS **National Exhibition Centre.** The top names in rock and pop play at the National Exhibition Centre. The venue is close to the airport. ⊠ *M42* ☎ *0121/780–4141 box office, 0844/338–8000 information line* ⊕ *www.thenec.co.uk.*

Symphony Hall. This is the home of the distinguished City of Birmingham Symphony Orchestra and a venue for jazz, pop, and classical concerts. ⊠ *International Convention Centre, Broad St., City Centre* ☎ *0121/345–0600* ⊕ *www.thsh.co.uk.*

Town Hall Birmingham. The splendidly refurbished neoclassical Town Hall Birmingham holds a wide range of events, including organ recitals, opera, and folk concerts. ⊠ *Paradise St., City Centre* ☎ *0121/345–0600* ⊕ *www.thsh.co.uk.*

THEATER **New Alexandra Theatre.** The New Alexandra Theatre welcomes touring companies on their way to or from London's West End. ⊠ *Station St., City Centre* ☎ *0844/871–3011* ⊕ *www.alexandratheatre.org.uk.*

Birmingham Repertory Theatre. Founded in 1913, the Birmingham Repertory Theatre is equally at home with modern or classical works. It's one of England's oldest and most esteemed theater companies. ⊠ *Centenary Sq., Broad St., City Centre* ☎ *0121/236–4455* ⊕ *www.birmingham-rep. co.uk.*

FILM **Electric Cinema.** The Electric Cinema is a true art deco survivor and a class act. Sofas and waiter service enhance the decadent viewing experience. ⊠ *47–49 Station St., City Centre* ☎ *0121/643–7879* ⊕ *www. theelectric.co.uk.*

SHOPPING

SHOPPING CENTERS **Bullring.** The glass-roof Bullring has three floors of retail enticement, including two department stores, Debenhams and the stunningly curved Selfridges, covered with aluminum disks. Don't miss Selfridges's awesome Food Hall. ⊠ *Between New St. and High St., City Centre* ☎ *0121/632–1526.*

The Mailbox. Once a Royal Mail sorting office, the Mailbox entices with trendy shops and designer outlets such as Harvey Nichols and Armani, as well as some fine restaurants. ⊠ *150 Wharfside St., City Centre* ☎ *0121/632–1000* ⊕ *www.mailboxlife.com.*

JEWELLERY QUARTER **Crescent Silver.** This shop sells a range of interesting silver jewelry and gifts. ⊠ *83–85 Spencer St., Jewellery Quarter* ☎ *0121/236–9006.*

St. Paul's Gallery. An entertaining treasure trove, St. Paul's Gallery specializes in hand-signed fine-art prints of album covers, past and present. ⊠ *94–108 Norwood St., Jewellery Quarter* ☎ *0121/236–5800.*

8

GREAT MALVERN, HEREFORD, AND ENVIRONS

In the arc of towns to the west of Birmingham and around the banks of the River Wye to the south, history and tradition rub up against deepest rural England. Great Malvern or the cathedral town of Hereford are great bases from which to soak up the bucolic flavor of the Malvern Hills and Elgar country, or to view the spectacular swing of the Wye at Symonds Yat.

GREAT MALVERN

47 miles southwest of Birmingham, 18 miles northeast of Hereford.

Great Malvern feels a bit like a seaside resort, though instead of the ocean your eyes plunge into an expanse of green meadows rolling away into the Vale of Evesham. Off the A449, this attractive Victorian spa town's architecture has changed little since the mid-1800s. Its Winter Gardens complex with a theater, cinema, and gardens makes Great Malvern a good base for walks in the surrounding Malvern Hills. These hills, with their long, low, purple profiles rising from the surrounding plain, inspired much of the music of Sir Edward Elgar (1857–1934), who composed "Pomp and Circumstance." They also inspired his remark that "there is music in the air, music all around us."

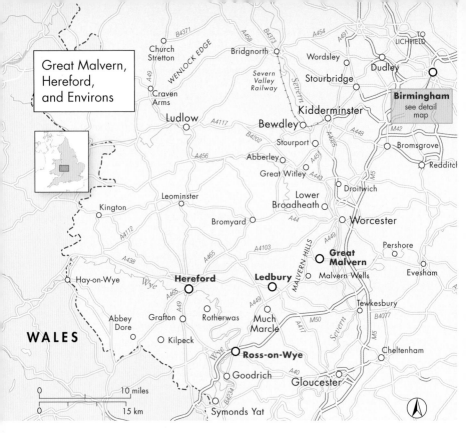

Great Malvern,
Hereford,
and Environs

GETTING HERE AND AROUND

To get here from Hereford will take 30 minutes or so by car. There are also frequent trains and buses run by First (30 minutes by train, one hour by bus). Birmingham is an hour away by car and rail.

ESSENTIALS

Visitor Information Malvern Tourist Information Centre ⊠ *21 Church St.* ☎ *01684/892289* ⊕ *www.visitthemalverns.org.*

EXPLORING

Great Malvern Priory. A solidly built early-Norman Benedictine abbey with later Perpendicular elements, the Priory dominates the steep streets downtown. The fine glass spans from the 15th century—including a magnificent east window and the vibrantly blue Magnificat window in the north transept—to the evocative Millennium Windows. There's a splendid set of misericords (the elaborately carved undersides of choir seats). ⊠ *Church St.* ☎ *01684/561020* ⊕ *www.greatmalvernpriory. uk* ⊠ *Free* ⊙ *Daily 9–5.*

<table>
<tr><td>OFF THE
BEATEN
PATH</td><td>**Worcester Cathedral.** There are few more quintessentially English sights than that of Worcester Cathedral, its towers overlooking the green expanse of the county cricket ground, and its majestic image reflected in the swift-flowing waters of the River Severn. A cathedral has stood on this site since 680, and much of what remains dates from the 13th</td></tr>
</table>

and 14th centuries. Notable exceptions are the Norman crypt (built in the 1080s), the largest in England, and the ambulatory, a cloister built around the east end. The most important tomb in the cathedral is that of King John (1167–1216), one of the country's least-admired monarchs, who alienated his barons and subjects through bad administration and heavy taxation and in 1215 was forced to sign that great charter of liberty, the Magna Carta. **TIP→ Don't miss the beautiful decoration in the vaulted chantry chapel of Prince Arthur, Henry VII's elder son, whose body was brought to Worcester after his death at Ludlow in 1502.**

The medieval library (accessible by pre-booked tour only) holds around 300 medieval manuscripts, dating from the 10th century onward. Worcester is 7 miles north of Great Malvern. ✉ *College Yard, at High St., Worcester* ☎ *01905/732900, 01905/732922 library tour bookings* 🌐 *www.worcestercathedral.co.uk* 🎟 *Free; Cathedral tours £4; library tours £5* 🕒 *Daily 7:30–6; tower Mar.–mid-July, Sept., and Oct., Sat. 11–5 (last entry 4:30), mid-July–Aug., school and bank holidays daily 11–5 (last entry 4:30); tours Apr.–Nov., Mon.–Sat. 11 and 2:30; Dec.–Mar., Sat. 11 and 2:30.*

WHERE TO STAY

For expanded hotel reviews, visit Fodors.com.

$ HOTEL 🏨 **Cottage in the Wood.** On shady grounds, this family-run hotel sits high up the side of the Malvern Hills, with splendid views of the landscape. **Pros:** tremendous views; good food; free Wi-Fi. **Cons:** three separate buildings; steep and narrow approach; cheaper rooms don't have the best views. [$] *Rooms from: £84* ✉ *Holywell Rd.* ☎ *01684/588860* 🌐 *www.cottageinthewood.co.uk* 🛏 *30 rooms* 🍴 *Multiple meal plans.*

$ B&B/INN 🏨 **Sidney House.** In addition to having stunning views, this dignified early 19th-century bed-and-breakfast, run by a friendly husband-and-wife team, sits near the town center. **Pros:** great views; easy access to Malvern Hills. **Cons:** on busy road, so ask for room at the back. [$] *Rooms from: £58* ✉ *40 Worcester Rd.* ☎ *01684/574994* 🌐 *www.sidneyhouse.co.uk* 🛏 *8 rooms* 🍴 *Breakfast.*

NIGHTLIFE AND THE ARTS

Malvern has links with Sir Edward Elgar as well as with George Bernard Shaw, who premiered many of his plays here.

Autumn in Malvern Festival. The Autumn in Malvern Festival takes place on weekends throughout October and concentrates on classical music, including Elgar, as well as literary events. ☎ *01684/892277, 01684/892289* 🌐 *www.malvernfestival.co.uk.*

LEDBURY

10 miles southwest of Great Malvern on A449.

Among the black-and-white half-timber buildings that make up the market town of Ledbury, take special note of two late-16th-century ones: the Feathers Hotel and the Talbot Inn. The cobbled Church Lane, almost hidden behind the 17th-century market house, is crowded with medieval half-timber buildings and leads to St. Michael's Church.

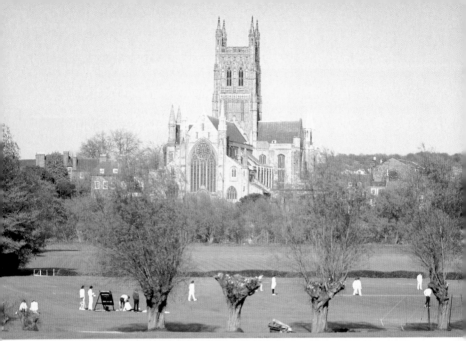

Worcester Cathedral has a blissfully English setting near the River Severn and the county cricket ground.

GETTING HERE AND AROUND

If you're driving, Ledbury is 25 minutes from Hereford via the A438, and 15 minutes from Great Malvern via the A449. There are local buses from both Hereford and Great Malvern, which has rail links with the rest of the country.

ESSENTIALS

Visitor Information Ledbury Tourist Information Centre ⊠ *Ice Bytes, 38 The Homend* ☎ *0844/567–8650* ⊕ *www.visitherefordshire.co.uk.*

EXPLORING

FAMILY **Eastnor Castle.** Completed in 1820, Eastnor Castle, a turreted Norman Revival extravaganza on the eastern outskirts of Ledbury, includes some magnificent neo-Gothic salons designed by 19th-century architect Augustus Pugin. The Hervey-Bathurst family has restored other grand rooms, full of tapestries, gilt-framed paintings, Regency chandeliers, old armchairs, and enormous sofas, making Eastnor a must-see for lovers of English interior decoration. In the Little Library, look out for the rare game of Life Pool, originally played on the billiards table. In the grounds there's a knight's maze and adventure playground to keep kids amused. Eastnor hosts the innovative Big Chill arts festival each August. ⊠ *A438* ☎ *01531/633160* ⊕ *www.eastnorcastle.com* 🖃 *House and grounds £9.50; grounds only, £6* ⊙ *Mid-July and Aug., Sun.–Thurs. 11–4:30; June and Sept., Sun. and bank holiday Mon. 11–4:30; Easter weekend, Fri.–Mon., 11–4:30; May bank holiday weekends (first and last wk), Sun. and Mon. 11–4:30; last admission 30 mins before closing.*

EATING WELL IN THE HEART OF ENGLAND

"The Malvern water," said John Wall in 1756, "is famous for containing nothing at all." The famously pure water is still bottled in the town and exported worldwide; it's said that the Queen never travels without it.

Outside Birmingham, this area is rich farming country where the orchards have produced succulent fruit, especially apples and plums. Hereford cider is popular because it tastes much sweeter than the cider brewed farther south in Devon.

The meat and milk products, which come from the local red-and-white Hereford breed of cattle, are second to none. Cheshire cheese, one of the country's oldest cheeses, is noted for its rich, crumbly texture; blue-veined Shropshire cheese is more unusual and worth trying. Ludlow produces a formidable assortment of local meat products and is noted for its sausages.

Fodor's Choice ★ **Hellens.** Just outside the village of Much Marcle, 4 miles southwest of Ledbury, lies the beautiful 17th-century manor of Hellens, kept like a time capsule in virtually unspoiled condition. The gloom and dust are part of the experience of visiting; candles illuminate the interior and there's no central heating. Part of the house dates from the 13th century and contains fine old-master paintings. Take a walk in the gardens and, if you have time, also check out the 13th-century village church. The house is ½ mile east of A449. ⊠ *Off B4024 and Monks Walk, Much Marcle* 🕾 *01531/660504* ⊕ *www.hellensmanor.com* 🖃 *£7* 🕙 *Apr.–Sept., Wed., Thurs., Sun., and bank holiday Mon., guided tours at 2, 3, and 4.*

Ledbury Heritage Centre. In the old grammar school, this museum traces the history of the building, town, railroad, and canal, mostly through local postcards. It also has displays on two literary celebrities linked to the area, John Masefield and Elizabeth Barrett Browning. ⊠ *Church La.* 🕾 *01531/635680* 🖃 *Free* 🕙 *Easter–Oct., daily 10:30–4.*

WHERE TO STAY
For expanded hotel reviews, visit Fodors.com.

$$ HOTEL 🖵 **Feathers Hotel.** You can't miss the striking black-and-white facade of this centrally located hostelry, which dates from the 16th century; its interior has a satisfyingly antique flavor, with wooden beams, creaking staircases, and ancient floorboards, and some rooms have four-posters. **Pros:** guest rooms retain a period feel; indoor heated pool. **Cons:** some guest rooms on the small side; some steps to climb. 🅂 *Rooms from: £140* ⊠ *High St.* 🕾 *01531/635266* ⊕ *www.feathers-ledbury.co.uk* 🛏 *22 rooms* 🍽 *Breakfast.*

8

ROSS-ON-WYE

10 miles southwest of Ledbury.

Perched high above the River Wye in the Malvern Hills, Ross-on-Wye seems oblivious to modern-day intrusions and remains at heart a small market town. Its steep streets come alive on Thursday and Saturday—market days—but they're always a happy hunting ground for antiques. Nearby towns have sights from a castle to a scenic overlook on the river.

GETTING HERE AND AROUND

A449 connects Ross-on-Wye with Great Malvern and Ledbury, and M50 leads directly to Ross from Junction 8 of M5. Stagecoach buses run from Ledbury (30 minutes) and have frequent connections with Hereford (50 minutes) and Gloucester (45 minutes).

ESSENTIALS

Visitor Information Ross-on-Wye Tourist Information Centre ⊠ *Swan House, Edde Cross St.* ☎ *01989/562768* ⊕ *www.visitherefordshire.co.uk.*

> ### WALKS AND DRIVES IN THE MALVERNS
>
> The Malvern Hills have climbs and walks of varying length and difficulty; the seasonal Malvern Hills Hopper bus gives useful access on weekends April through August. The best places to start are Great Malvern and Ledbury. The Elgar Route, a drive, extends for 45 miles and touches on Malvern and Worcester as it threads through the Malverns. The hilltop vistas across the countryside are spectacular—isolated hills rise up from the fairly flat plain. The area around Ross-on-Wye has ideal walks with scenic river views. For information on hiking the Malverns, contact the Malvern or Ross-on-Wye tourist office.

EXPLORING

Goodrich Castle. Looming dramatically over the River Wye at Kerne Bridge, the castle from the south looks like a fortress from the Rhineland amid the green fields; you quickly see its grimmer face from the battlements on its north side. Dating from the late 12th century, the red sandstone castle is surrounded by a deep moat carved out of solid rock, from which its walls appear to soar upward. Built to repel Welsh raiders, it was destroyed in the 17th century during the Civil War. The town of Goodrich is 3 miles south of Ross-on-Wye on the B4234. ⊠ *Castle La., Goodrich* ☎ *01600/890538* ⊕ *www.english-heritage.org.uk* ⌚ *£6.40* ⊙ *Mar.–June and Sept.–early Nov., daily 10–5; July and Aug., daily 10–6; mid-Nov.–Feb., weekends 10–4.*

Symonds Yat. Six miles south of Ross-on-Wye, outside the village of Symonds Yat ("gate"), the 473-foot-high Yat Rock commands superb views of the River Wye as it winds through a narrow gorge and swings around in a great 5-mile loop. It's best approached from the south on B4432, from which it's a short walk. A small ferry takes passengers across the river (£1). About a mile northeast of Symonds Yat is **King Arthur's Cave**; although any link to the legendary monarch is, well, just a legend, several important Paleolithic finds have been made in the cave, including flint tools and the bones of a woolly mammoth and a sabre-tooth cat. Today it is home to a colony of bats. To find the cave, take the exit marked Symonds Yat West from the A40. Park at the rest area just before Downard Park camp site and follow the track a short way into the woods.

SPORTS AND THE OUTDOORS

Symonds Yat Canoe Hire. This well-regarded company rents canoes and kayaks by the day or half day. It's a popular way to experience the River Wye. Prices start at £23 for a two-person canoe. (No credit cards.) ✉ *Leisure Park, off A40, Symonds Yat West* ☎ *01600/891069, 07860/848136* 🌐 *www.canoehire.com.*

WHERE TO STAY

For expanded hotel reviews, visit Fodors.com.

$$ HOTEL 🏨 **Chase Hotel.** The public areas in this nicely renovated Georgian-style country house retain some original elements. **Pros:** 11 acres of peaceful grounds; country-house appeal. **Cons:** conventional furnishings. [$] *Rooms from: £125* ✉ *Gloucester Rd.* ☎ *01989/763161* 🌐 *www.chasehotel.co.uk* 🛏 *36 rooms* 🍴 *Breakfast.*

HEREFORD

9 miles northwest of Ross-on-Wye, 56 miles southwest of Birmingham, 54 miles northeast of Cardiff.

Before 1066 Hereford was the capital of the Anglo-Saxon kingdom of Mercia and, earlier still, the site of Roman, Celtic, and Iron Age settlements. Today people come primarily to see the massive Norman cathedral, but quickly discover the charms of this busy country town. Hereford is the center of a wealthy agricultural area known for its cider, fruit, and cattle—the white-faced Hereford breed has spread across the world.

8

GETTING HERE AND AROUND

The bus and train stations are about half a mile northeast of the center. A train from Birmingham will take around 1¾ hours. Traveling by car, take M50 at Junction 8 of M5, then A417 and A438 to Hereford. First buses cover the local area, and the city is compact enough to cover on foot.

ESSENTIALS

Visitor Information Hereford Tourist Information Centre ✉ *1 King St.* ☎ *01432/268430* 🌐 *www.visitherefordshire.co.uk.*

EXPLORING

Cider Museum. A farm's cider house (the alcoholic, European kind) and a cooper's workshop have been re-created at the Cider Museum, where you can tour ancient cellars with huge oak vats. Cider brandy is made here, and the museum sells its own brand, along with other cider products. ✉ *Pomona Pl., at Whitecross Rd.* ☎ *01432/354207* 🌐 *www.cidermuseum.co.uk* 🎟 *£5.50* ⏲ *Apr.–Oct., Tues.–Sat. and bank holiday Mon. 10–5; Nov.–Mar., Tues.–Sat. 11–3; last admission 45 mins before closing.*

Fodor's Choice ★ **Hereford Cathedral and Mappa Mundi.** Built of local red sandstone, Hereford Cathedral retains a large central tower and some fine 11th-century Norman carvings, although most of the interior is 19th century. There are also some exquisite contemporary stained-glass windows in the Audley Chapel. However, its main attractions are two great treasures: a 12th-century chair, to the left of the high altar, one of the earliest pieces of furniture in the country and reputedly used by King Stephen; and the **Mappa Mundi,** the largest medieval map of the world still in existence. Drawn in about 1300, it's a fascinating glimpse of how the medieval mind viewed the world: Jerusalem is shown dead center, the Garden of Eden at the edge, Europe and Africa are the wrong way round—and, of course, there are no Americas. In addition to land masses, the map details 500 individual drawings, including cities, Biblical stories, mythical creatures and images of how people in different corners of the globe were thought to look—the last two frequently overlapping in wildly imaginative fashion. The map is held inside a chained library, containing some 1,500 books, among them an 8th-century copy of the Four Gospels. Chained libraries, in which books were attached to cupboards to discourage theft, are extremely rare: they date from medieval times, when books were as precious as gold. Tours of the cathedral (without the library), tower and garden run through summer; call to confirm times. ✉ *Cathedral Close* ☎ *01432/374200* 🌐 *www.herefordcathedral.org* 🎟 *Mappa Mundi and chained library exhibition £6; cathedral tours £4; tower tours £4; garden tours £5* 🕒 *Cathedral Mon.–Sat. 9:15–5:30, Sun. 9:15–3:30; Mappa Mundi and chained library exhibition Apr.–Oct., Mon.–Sat. 10–5, Nov.–Mar., Mon.–Sat. 10–4; cathedral tours Mon.–Sat., 11 and 2; tower tours Apr.–Oct., Wed. and Thurs. 11:30–2:30; garden tours June–Sept., Wed. and Sat. 2:30.*

Old House. The half-timber Old House is a fine example of domestic Jacobean architecture, furnished in 17th-century style on three floors. You can see a kitchen, dining hall, parlor, and bedrooms. Look for the dog's door between the nursery and master bedroom. ✉ *High Town* ☎ *01432/260694* 🌐 *www.herefordshire.gov.uk* 🎟 *Free* 🕒 *Apr.–Sept., Tues.–Sat. 10–5, Sun. and bank holiday Mon. 10–4; Oct.–Mar., Tues.–Sat. 10–5.*

WHERE TO EAT AND STAY

For expanded hotel reviews, visit Fodors.com.

$ BRITISH 🍴 **Café @ All Saints.** A good spot for lunch, this coffee bar and restaurant occupies the western end and gallery of this community-minded church, granting a rare opportunity to indulge body and spirit at one sitting. The imaginative menu is worth every penny, and the shepherd's pie is a winner. For something lighter, try the tasty sandwiches (roast mushroom and tofu, for example), salads, cakes, and local ice creams. Breakfasts are good here, too. [$] *Average main: £8* ✉ *High St.* ☎ *01432/370415* 🌐 *www.cafeatallsaints.co.uk* 🕒 *Closed Sun. No dinner.*

$$ HOTEL 🏨 **Castle House.** These conjoined Georgian villas next to the moat (all that remains of Hereford Castle) offer luxurious lodgings, a warm welcome, and good food. **Pros:** close to cathedral; quiet setting; lovely garden. **Cons:** cost a little high for what you get. [$] *Rooms from: £130* ✉ *Castle St.* ☎ *01432/356321* 🌐 *www.castlehse.co.uk* 🛏 *10 suites, 5 rooms* 🍽 *Breakfast.*

$ ⚉ **Sink Green Farm.** The benefits of staying at this informal working farm,
HOTEL which dates back to the 16th century, include views of the Wye Valley
and use of a hot tub in a summerhouse. **Pros:** friendly and casual; lovely
garden, river walks. **Cons:** car needed to get around. $ *Rooms from:
£64* ⊠ *The Straight Mile(B4399), Rotherwas* ☎ *01432/870223* ⊕ *www.
sinkgreenfarm.co.uk* ⤳ *4 rooms* ▤ *No credit cards* ❙⊙❙ *Breakfast.*

SHOPPING

Hereford has a market for livestock on Wednesday and for general
retail on Saturday.

Capuchin Yard. The stores in Capuchin Yard display handmade items
ranging from shoes to hats to knitwear. Other outlets feature fine ceramics. ⊠ *29 Church St..*

SHREWSBURY, CHESTER, AND ENVIRONS

Rural Shropshire, one of the least populated English counties, is far
removed from most people's preconceptions of the industrial Midlands.
Within its spread are towns long famed for their beauty, such as Ludlow.
Two important cities of the region, Shrewsbury and Chester, are both
renowned for their medieval heritage and their wealth of half-timber
buildings. The 6-mile stretch of the Ironbridge Gorge, however, gives
you the chance to experience the cradle of the Industrial Revolution
with none of the reeking smoke that gave this region west of Birmingham its name—the Black Country—during the mid-19th century. Now
taken over by the Ironbridge Gorge Museum Trust, the bridge, the first
in the world to be built of iron and opened in 1781, is the centerpiece
of this vast museum complex.

8

SHREWSBURY

*55 miles north of Hereford, 46 miles south of Chester, 48 miles north-
west of Birmingham.*

One of England's most important medieval towns, Shrewsbury (pronounced *shrose*-bury), the county seat of Shropshire, lies within a great
horseshoe loop of the Severn. It has numerous 16th-century half-timber buildings—many built by well-to-do wool merchants—plus elegant
ones from later periods. Today the town retains a romantic air (indeed,
there are many bridal shops, along with churches), and it can be a lovely
experience to stroll the Shrewsbury "shuts." These narrow alleys over-
hung with timbered gables lead off the central market square, which
was designed to be closed off at night to protect local residents. You
can also relax in Quarry Park on the river.

A good starting point for exploring the city is the small square between
Fish Street and Butcher Row. These streets are little changed since medieval times, when some of them took their names from the principal
trades carried on there, but Peacock Alley, Gullet Passage, and Grope
Lane clearly got their names from somewhere else.

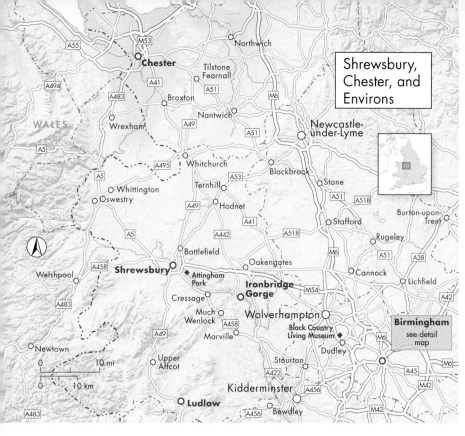

GETTING HERE AND AROUND

The train station is at the neck of the river that loops the center, a little farther out than the bus station on Raven Meadows. A direct train service runs here from Hereford (50 minutes) and Birmingham (one hour). If you're coming from London by car, take M40 and M42 north, then M6 and M54, which becomes A5 to Shrewsbury; the trip is 150 miles. The streets are full of twists, but it's small enough not to get lost. Walking tours of Shrewsbury depart from the tourist office at 2:30 Monday to Saturday, May through September (also 11 on Sunday); Monday to Saturday in October; and Saturday only in November (£4.50).

ESSENTIALS

Visitor Information Shrewsbury Visitor Information Centre ⊠ *Rowley's House, Barker St.* ☎ *01743/258888* ⊕ *www.visitshrewsbury.com.*

EXPLORING

TOP ATTRACTIONS

Attingham Park. Built in 1785 by George Steuart (architect of the church of St. Chad in Shrewsbury) for the first Lord Berwick, this elegant stone mansion has a three-story portico, with a pediment carried on four tall columns. The building overlooks a sweep of parkland, including a deer park landscaped by Humphrey Repton (1752–1818). Inside the house are painted ceilings and delicate plasterwork, a fine picture gallery designed by John Nash (1752–1835), and 19th-century Neapolitan furniture. Attingham Park is 4 miles southeast of Shrewsbury. ⊠ *B4380, off A5, Shrewsbury* ☎ *01743/708123* ⊕ *www.nationaltrust. org.uk* ✆ *£9.60; park and grounds only, £4.70* ⊘ *House Apr.–early Nov., Thurs.–Tues. daily 12:30–5:30; last admission 1 hr before closing. Park and grounds daily 9–6.*

Shrewsbury Abbey. Now unbecomingly surrounded by busy roads, the abbey was founded in 1083 and later became a powerful Benedictine monastery. The abbey church has survived many vicissitudes and retains a 14th-century west window above a Norman doorway. A more recent addition is a memorial to the World War I poet Wilfred Owen. To reach the abbey from the center, cross the river by the English Bridge. ⊠ *Abbey Church, Abbey Foregate* ☎ *01743/232723* ⊕ *www.shrewsburyabbey. com* ✆ *Free* ⊘ *Apr.–Oct., daily 10–4; Nov.–Mar., daily 10:30–3; last entry 15 mins before closing.*

Shrewsbury Castle. Guarding the northern approaches to the town, the sandstone castle rises over the River Severn at the bottom of Pride Hill. Originally Norman, it was dismantled during the Civil War and later rebuilt by Thomas Telford, the Scottish engineer who designed many notable buildings and bridges in the early 19th century. The castle holds the **Shropshire Regimental Museum,** containing enough social history to engage the non–military buff. ■**TIP**➔ **The numerous benches in the gardens are good for a quiet sit-down.** ⊠ *Castle Gates* ☎ *01743/358516* ⊕ *www.shrewsburymuseums.com* ✆ *£2.50* ⊘ *Late May–mid-Sept., Mon.–Wed., Fri. ,and Sat. 10:30–5, Sun. 10:30–4; mid-Sept.–mid-Dec., Mon.–Wed., Fri., and Sat. 10:30–4; mid-Dec.–mid-Feb. grounds only daily 9–5; mid-Feb.–late May Mon.–Wed., Fri., and Sat., and Easter Sun. 9:30–4.*

St. Chad. On a hilltop west of the town center, this church designed by George Steuart, the architect of Attingham Park, is one of England's most original ecclesiastical buildings. Completed in 1792, the round Georgian church is surmounted by a tower that is in turn square, octagonal, and circular—and finally topped by a dome. When being built, it provoked riots among townsfolk averse to its radical style. The interior has a fine Venetian east window and a brass Arts and Crafts pulpit. ⊠ *St. Chad's Terr.* ☎ *01743/365478* ✆ *Free* ⊘ *Apr.–Oct., daily 8–5; Nov.–Mar., daily 8–1.*

WORTH NOTING

Shrewsbury Museum and Art Gallery. Newly expanded and moved to a new site in the town's former Music Hall in 2013, this museum holds Shropshire pottery and ceramics, as well as artifacts of local history and Roman finds, such as a unique silver mirror from nearby Wroxeter. Other displays explore the life of Shrewsbury's famous son, Charles Darwin. ⊠ *Market St.* ☎ *01743/258885* ⊕ *www.shrewsburymuseums. com* ✆ *Free* ⊘ *May–Sept., Mon.–Sat. 10–5, Sun. 10–4; Oct.–Apr., Mon.–Sat. 10–5.*

The sprawling Ironbridge Gorge Museum interprets the country's industrial history and includes a re-created Victorian town.

WHERE TO EAT

$$ MODERN BRITISH 🍴 **Draper's Hall.** The dark-wood paneling, antique furniture, and intimate lighting of this 16th-century hall make this a distinctive dining spot for up-to-date modern British cuisine. You might try the beef fillet wrapped in Parma ham, or Cornish black bream with braised fennel. Another option is the lighter brasserie menu. The establishment also has four guest rooms. [$] *Average main: £17* ✉ *10 St. Mary's Pl.* ☎ *01743/344679* 🌐 *www.drapershallrestaurant.co.uk* 🕒 *No dinner Sun.*

$$ BRITISH 🍴 **Mad Jack's.** Whether you eat in the sleek, dark-wood restaurant or the foliage-filled courtyard, you'll be tucking into good local and seasonal produce. Look out for the Shropshire lamb and, in winter, local venison sausages with Shropshire blue cheese mash. It's a good spot for plump sandwiches at lunchtime, or afternoon tea or cocktails later in the day. Four contemporary rooms are available should you wish to linger longer. [$] *Average main: £15* ✉ *15 St. Mary's St.* ☎ *01743/358870* 🌐 *www.madjacks.uk.com* 🕒 *No dinner Sun.*

WHERE TO STAY

For expanded hotel reviews, visit Fodors.com.

$$ HOTEL 🏨 **Albright Hussey Hotel.** Lovely gardens surround this Tudor manor house, originally the home of the Hussey family, which dates back to 1524; black-and-white half-timbering combines with a later red-brick-and-stone extension. **Pros:** friendly service; fine food; beautiful grounds. **Cons:** popular venue for weddings; could do with a face-lift; newer rooms less attractive. [$] *Rooms from: £125* ✉ *Ellesmere Rd.* ☎ *01939/290523* 🌐 *www.albrighthussey.co.uk* 🛏 *22 rooms, 4 suites* 🍽 *Breakfast.*

$ HOTEL **The Lion Hotel.** The myriad corridors of this famous coaching inn in the heart of town creak with more than 600 years of history; rooms are small and traditionally furnished, but the glorious lounge, with its high ceiling, oil paintings, and carved-stone fireplace, sets the Lion apart. **Pros:** historic appeal; good breakfasts. **Cons:** prone to wedding parties on weekends; unlike the public rooms, many guest rooms have tired decor in need of an upgrade. [$] *Rooms from: £108* ✉ *Wyle Cop* ☎ *01743/353107* 🌐 *www.thelionhotelshrewsbury.co.uk* 🛏 *59 rooms* 🍴 *Breakfast.*

NIGHTLIFE AND THE ARTS

Theatre Severn. This theater covers all the lively arts: classical and popular music, dance, and drama. ✉ *Frankwell Quay* ☎ *01743/281281* 🌐 *www.theatresevern.co.uk.*

SHOPPING

Parade. Behind St. Mary's church, this shopping center is in a neoclassical building from 1830 that once held the Royal Infirmary. One of the most appealing malls in England, it has 30 attractive boutiques, a coffee shop, and a river terrace. ✉ *St. Mary's Pl.* ☎ *01743/343178* 🌐 *www.paradeshops.co.uk.*

IRONBRIDGE GORGE

4 miles east of Much Wenlock, 15 miles east of Shrewsbury, 28 miles northwest of Birmingham.

Fodor's Choice ★ The River Severn and its tree-cloaked banks make an attractive backdrop to this cluster of villages; within a mile of the graceful span of the world's first iron bridge are a cluster of fascinating museums exploring the area's industrial past and the reasons why it's been described as the "cradle of the Industrial Revolution."

8

GETTING HERE AND AROUND

To drive here from Shrewsbury, take the A5 east, the A442 south, and then the A4169 west before following the brown signs for Ironbridge. On weekends and bank holidays from Easter to late October, the Gorge Connect Bus shuttles passengers between Ironbridge's museums every 30 minutes; it's free of charge to museum passport holders.

ESSENTIALS

Visitor Information **Ironbridge Visitor Information** ✉ *Toll House, The Wharfage* ☎ *01952/433424* 🌐 *www.ironbridge.org.uk.*

EXPLORING

FAMILY Fodor's Choice ★ **Ironbridge Gorge Museum.** The 10 sites that make up the Ironbridge Gorge Museum—a World Heritage Site, spread over 6 square miles—preserve the area's fascinating industrial history in spectacular fashion. ■ TIP→ **Allow at least a full day to appreciate all the major sights, and perhaps to take a stroll around the famous iron bridge or hunt for Coalport china in the stores clustered near it.** On weekends and national holidays from April through October, a shuttle bus takes you between sites. The best starting point is the **Museum of the Gorge,** which has a good selection of literature and an audiovisual show on the gorge's history. In nearby Coalbrookdale, the **Museum**

of Iron explains the production of iron and steel. You can see the blast furnace built by Abraham Darby, who developed the original coke process in 1709. The adjacent **Enginuity** exhibition is a hands-on, feet-on, interactive exploration of engineering; it's good for kids. From here, drive the few miles along the river until the arches of the **Iron Bridge** come into view. Designed by T.F. Pritchard, smelted by Darby, and erected between 1777 and 1779, this graceful arch spanning the River Severn can best be seen—and photographed or painted—from the towpath, a riverside walk edged with wildflowers and shrubs. The tollhouse on the far side houses an exhibition on the bridge's history and restoration.

A mile farther along the river is the **Jackfield Tile Museum,** a repository of decorative tiles from the 19th and 20th centuries. Another half mile brings you to the **Coalport China Museum.** Exhibits show some of the factory's most beautiful wares, and craftspeople give demonstrations; visit the restrooms for the unique communal washbasins. Above Coalport is **Blists Hill Victorian Town,** where you can see old mines, furnaces, and a wrought-iron works. But the main draw is the re-creation of the "town" itself, with its doctor's office, bakery, grocer's, candle maker's, sawmill, printing shop, and candy store. At the entrance you can change some money for specially minted pennies and make purchases from the shops. Shopkeepers, the bank manager, and the doctor's wife are on hand to give you advice. If you don't fancy the refreshments at the Fried Fish shop, you could drop into the **New Inn** pub (in Blists Hill) for a traditional ale or ginger beer, and join one of the sing-alongs around the piano that take place a couple of times every afternoon; or, for something more formal, try the **Club Room** restaurant next door. ✉ *B4380* ☎ *01952/433424* 🌐 *www.ironbridge.org.uk* 🎟 *Passport ticket (all attractions, valid 1 year) £24. Individual sites: Blists Hill £16; Enginuity £8.50; Coalport China Museum £8.50; Jackfield Tile Museum £8.50; Museum of Iron £8.25; Darby Houses £5; Museum of Iron and Darby Houses £9; Broseley Pipeworks £5; Museum of the Gorge £4; Tar Tunnel £3.* 🕒 *Daily 10–5; Blists Hill Apr.–Oct., daily 10–5; Nov.–Mar., daily 10–4; Tar Tunnel Apr.–Oct., daily 10:30-4; (tunnel closed Nov.–Mar).*

WHERE TO EAT AND STAY

For expanded hotel reviews, visit Fodors.com.

$$$ MODERN BRITISH Fodor's Choice ★

🍴 **Restaurant Severn.** This discreet restaurant, set back from the main road in the center of Ironbridge, delivers fine-quality food prepared with care and attention. Chefs Beb and Eric Bruce prepare delicious fixed-price dinner menus of updated English fare; fillets of sole and sea bass with sorrel and vermouth, perhaps, or king scallops with bacon. You may round off the meal with a lemon meringue cheesecake with lavender and honey ice cream, or a damson and almond tart. [$] *Average main: £24* ✉ *33 High St., Ironbridge* ☎ *01952/432233* 🌐 *www.restaurantseven.co.uk* 🕒 *Closed Mon. and Tues. No dinner Sun. No lunch Wed.–Sat.*

$ HOTEL

🏨 **Hundred House Hotel.** The low beams, stained glass, wood paneling, and patchwork cushions that greet you as you enter this Georgian inn set the tone for the whimsical guest rooms. **Pros:** full of nooks and corners; good food. **Cons:** not for those who favor the plain and simple. $ *Rooms from: £75* ⊠ *Bidgnorth Rd. (A442), Norton* ☎ *01952/580240* ⊕ *www.hundredhouse.co.uk* ➴ *10 rooms* ⦿ *Breakfast.*

$

B&B/INN

🏠 **Library House.** At one time the village's library, this small guesthouse on the hillside near the Ironbridge museums (and a few steps from the bridge) has kept its attractive Victorian style while allowing for more modern luxuries—a DVD library, for instance. **Pros:** welcoming hosts; good location; free parking passes for the town. **Cons:** not for families with young children; no restaurant. $ *Rooms from: £90* ⊠ *11 Severn Bank* ☎ *01952/432299* ⊕ *www.libraryhouse.com* ➴ *4 rooms* ⦿ *Breakfast.*

LUDLOW

22 miles south of Ironbridge Gorge, 29 miles south of Shrewsbury, 24 miles north of Hereford.

Fodor's Choice

★

Medieval, Georgian, and Victorian buildings jostle for attention in pretty Ludlow, which has a finer display of black-and-white half-timber buildings than even Shrewsbury. Dominating the center is the Church of St. Lawrence, its extravagant size a testimony to the town's prosperous wool trade. Cross the River Teme and climb Whitcliffe for a spectacular view of the church and the Norman castle.

Several outstanding restaurants have given the town of just 10,000 a reputation as a culinary hot spot. Ludlow is now the national headquarters of the Slow Food movement, which focuses on food traditions and responsible production.

GETTING HERE AND AROUND

Ludlow has good train connections. From London Paddington, the journey time is 3¼ hours (changing at Newport), from Birmingham 1¾ hours, and from Shrewsbury 30 minutes. The train station is a 15-minute walk southwest to the center. Driving from London, take M40, M42, and then A448 to Kidderminster, A456, and A4117 to Ludlow. The town has good parking and is easily walkable.

ESSENTIALS

Visitor Information Ludlow Visitor Information Centre ⊠ *Castle St.* ☎ *01584/875053* ⊕ *www.ludlow.org.uk.*

EXPLORING

Ludlow and the Marches Food Festival. The festival takes place over a weekend in mid-September and has demonstrations and tastings of local sausages, ale, and cider. ☎ *01584/873957* ⊕ *www.foodfestival.co.uk.*

Ludlow Castle. The "very perfection of decay," according to author Daniel Defoe, the ruins of this red sandstone castle date from 1085. No wonder the massive structure dwarfs the town: it served as a vital stronghold for centuries and was the seat of the Marcher Lords who ruled "the Marches," the local name for the border region. The two sons of Edward IV—the little princes of the Tower of London—spent time here before being dispatched to London and their death in 1483. Follow the terraced walk around the castle for a lovely view of the countryside. ⊠ *Castle Sq.* ☎ *01584/873355* ⊕ *www.ludlowcastle.com* ⊠ *£5*

🕐 *Jan.–mid-Feb., weekends 10–4; mid-Feb.–Mar. and Oct.–Dec., daily 10–4; Apr.–July and Sept., daily 10–5; Aug. daily 10–6; last admission 30 mins before closing. Closed approx. 7 days in Sept. and Nov. and certain days in summer; call to confirm.*

OFF THE BEATEN PATH

Stokesay Castle. This 13th-century fortified manor house built by a wealthy merchant is arguably the finest of its kind in England. Inside the main hall, the wooden cruck roof and timber staircase (a rare survival) demonstrate state-of-the-art building methods of the day. Outside, the cottage-style garden creates a bewitching backdrop for the magnificent Jacobean timber-frame gatehouse. The castle is 7 miles northwest of Ludlow. ⊠ *Off A49, Craven Arms* ☎ *01588/672544* ⊕ *www.english-heritage.org.uk* 🔳 *£6.50* 🕐 *Apr.–Oct., daily 10–5; Nov.–Mar., weekends 10–4.*

WHERE TO EAT

Ludlow is known for some pricier fine-dining establishments, but options from excellent tearooms to pubs and ethnic restaurants are also available.

$$$$
FRENCH
Fodor's Choice
★

✕ **La Bécasse.** Dip into the past—the intimate building dates to 1349, the warm oak paneling merely to the 17th century—as you savor a fixed-price menu (£54–£65) of French food that's bang up to the minute. Rose-color glass chargers on crisp white table linens set the tone for such dishes as beef sirloin with Shropshire blue cheese dauphinoise, or crab with spiced fish cakes and papaya salsa. Vegetarians are well served with a separate menu. The two-course lunch menu is great value at £26. Reservations are essential on weekends. 🟨 *Average main: £54* ⊠ *17 Corve St.* ☎ *01584/872325* ⊕ *www.labecasse.co.uk* 🕐 *Closed Mon. No dinner Sun. No lunch Tues.*

$$$$
MODERN BRITISH
Fodor's Choice
★

✕ **Mr. Underhill's.** Occupying a converted mill building beneath the castle, this secluded establishment looks onto the wooded River Teme and is stylish, light, and informal. The superb Modern British, fixed-price menus take advantage of fresh seasonal ingredients. The daily changing menu could include roast duck breast with orange zest and peppercorn jus, or lemon sole with pistachio crust and smoked almond. Book well ahead, especially on weekends; rooms and suites are available should you want to make a night of it. 🟨 *Average main: £56* ⊠ *Dinham Weir* ☎ *01584/874431* ⊕ *www.mr-underhills.co.uk* 🔺 *Reservations essential* 🕐 *Closed Mon. and Tues. No lunch.*

WHERE TO STAY

For expanded hotel reviews, visit Fodors.com.

$$
HOTEL

🔲 **The Feathers.** Even if you're not staying here, take time to admire the extravagant half-timber facade of this hotel, built in the early 17th century and described by the historian Jan Morris in the *New York Times* as "the most handsome inn in the world." **Pros:** ornate plasterwork; unpretentious feel. **Cons:** most guest rooms lack the old-fashioned feel. 🟨 *Rooms from: £115* ⊠ *The Bull Ring* ☎ *01584/875261* ⊕ *www.feathersatludlow.co.uk* 🛏 *40 rooms* 🍴 *Multiple meal plans.*

$
B&B/INN
Fodor'sChoice
★
Fishmore Hall. Saved from dereliction in 2008, Fishmore Hall has been beautifully converted from a crumbling old mansion into a relaxing, contemporary place to stay. **Pros:** lovely location; well-designed rooms; beautiful views. **Cons:** restaurant is pricey; a little out of town. $ *Rooms from: £99* ✉ *Fishmore Rd., Ludlow* ☎ *01584/875148* ⊕ *www.fishmorehall.co.uk* ⤳ *15 rooms.*

$
B&B/INN
FAMILY
Timberstone. The Read family has made a rambling stone cottage in the Clee Hills into a welcoming haven. **Pros:** relaxing and hospitable; geared to families; great food. **Cons:** out of center of Ludlow; twisty lanes. $ *Rooms from: £90* ✉ *B4363, Clee Stanton* ☎ *01584/823519* ⊕ *www.timberstoneludlow.co.uk* ⤳ *4 rooms* ⊚ *Multiple meal plans.*

NIGHTLIFE AND THE ARTS

Ludlow Festival. The two-week Ludlow Festival, starting in late June, includes Shakespeare performed near the ruined castle, and opera, dance, and concerts around town. ☎ *0844/248–5165* ⊕ *www. ludlowfestival.co.uk.*

CHESTER

75 miles north of Ludlow, 46 miles north of Shrewsbury.

Cheshire's thriving center is Chester, a city similar in some ways to Shrewsbury, though it has many more black-and-white half-timber buildings (some built in Georgian and Victorian times), and its medieval walls still stand. History seems more tangible in Chester than in many other ancient cities, and modern buildings haven't been allowed to intrude on the center. A negative result of this perfection is that Chester has become a favorite bus-tour destination, with gift shops, noise, and crowds.

Chester has been a prominent city since the late 1st century, when the Roman Empire expanded north to the banks of the River Dee. The original Roman town plan is still evident: the principal streets, Eastgate, Northgate, Watergate, and Bridge Street, lead out from the Cross—the site of the central area of the Roman fortress—to the four city gates. The partly excavated remains of what is thought to have been the country's largest Roman amphitheater lie to the south of Chester's medieval castle.

GETTING HERE AND AROUND

There's a free shuttle bus to the center if you arrive by train, and buses pull up at Vicar's Lane in the center (Monday to Saturday). Chester is 180 miles from London, and about 2¾ hours by train (change at Crewe). If you're driving and here for a day only, use the city's Park and Ride lots, as central parking lots fill quickly, especially in summer.

Guided walks leave the town hall daily at 10:30, with an additional tour at 11:30 from May to October (£6). City Sightseeing operates daily tours in open-top buses from May to September.

ESSENTIALS

Visitor and Tour Information Chester Tourist Information Centre ✉ *Town Hall, Northgate St.* ☎ *0845/647–7868* ⊕ *www.visitchester.com.* **City Sightseeing** ☎ *0845/6477868, 01244/381461 weekdays only* ⊕ *www.city-sightseeing.com.*

8

Lined with handsome brick, stone, and half-timber buildings, Chester's compact center is perfect for shopping and strolling.

EXPLORING

TOP ATTRACTIONS

Chester Cathedral. Tradition has it that a church of some sort stood on the site of what is now Chester Cathedral in Roman times, but records indicate construction around AD 900. The earliest work traceable today, mainly in the north transept, is that of the 11th-century Benedictine abbey. After Henry VIII dissolved the monasteries in the 16th century, the abbey church became the cathedral church of the new diocese of Chester. The misericords (kneeling benches) in the choir stalls reveal carved figures of people and animals, both real and mythical, and above is a gilded and colorful vaulted ceiling. There are free guided tours daily at 2:30; meet inside under the big blue stained-glass window. ⊠ *St. Werburgh St., off Market Sq.* ☎ *01244/324756* ⊕ *www.chestercathedral.com* ☞ *Free; £3 suggested donation; audio guides £1* ⊙ *Mon.–Sat. 9–5, Sun. 1–4.*

City walls. Accessible from several points, the city walls provide splendid views of Chester and its surroundings. The whole circuit is 2 miles, but if your time is short, climb the steps at Newgate and walk along toward Eastgate to see the great ornamental **Eastgate Clock,** erected to commemorate Queen Victoria's Diamond Jubilee in 1897. Lots of small shops near this part of the walls sell old books, old postcards, antiques, and jewelry. Where the **Bridge of Sighs** (named after the enclosed bridge in Venice that it closely resembles) crosses the canal, descend to street level and walk up Northgate Street into Market Square.

Rows. Chester's unique Rows, which originated in the 12th and 13th centuries, are essentially double rows of stores, one at street level and the other on the second floor with galleries overlooking the street. The

Rows line the junction of the four streets in the old town. They have medieval crypts below them, and some reveal Roman foundations. ■TIP→ You can view some Roman foundations in the basement of fast-food restaurant Spudulike at 39 Bridge Street.

WORTH NOTING

ChesterBoat. This company runs excursions on the River Dee every 30 minutes daily (late March through October) and hourly on weekends (November through March). Saturday evening cruises in summer feature discos. ⊠ *Boating Station, Souters La.* ☎ *01244/325394* ⊕ *www. chesterboat.co.uk* ⊿ *£6.50.*

FAMILY **Chester Zoo.** Well-landscaped grounds and natural enclosures make the 80-acre zoo one of Britain's most popular, as well as the largest. Highlights include Chimpanzee Island, the jaguar enclosure, and the Islands in Danger tropical habitat. Baby animals are often on display. Eleven miles of paths wind through the zoo, and you can use the waterbus boats or the overhead train to tour the grounds. Fun, 10-minute animal talks, aimed at kids, take place at various locations around the zoo throughout the day. The zoo is 2 miles north of Chester. ⊠ *A41* ☎ *01244/380280* ⊕ *www.chesterzoo.org* ⊿ *Apr.–Oct. £18, Nov.–Mar. £14.50; waterbus £2, monorail £2* ⊗ *Daily 10–dusk.*

Grosvenor Museum. Start a visit to this museum with a look at the Roman Stones Gallery, which displays Roman-era tombstones previously used to repair city walls. (Keep an eye out for the wounded barbarian.) Afterward you can skip a few centuries to explore the period house for a tour from 1680 to the 1920s. ⊠ *27 Grosvenor St.* ☎ *01244/972197* ⊕ *www. grosvenormuseum.co.uk* ⊿ *Free* ⊗ *Mon.–Sat. 10:30–5, Sun. 1–4.*

WHERE TO EAT

$
BRITISH
✗ **Albion.** You feel as if you're stepping back in time at this Victorian pub; the posters, advertisements, flags, and curios tell you the idiosyncratic landlord keeps it as it would have been during World War I. The candlelit restaurant forms one of the three snug rooms and, unsurprisingly, serves up such traditional fare as corned beef hash, Staffordshire oatcakes, and gammon (thick-sliced ham) with pease pudding. You can stay overnight here as well. $ *Average main: £9* ⊠ *Park St.* ☎ *01244/340345* ⊕ *www.albioninnchester.co.uk* ▭ *No credit cards* ⊗ *No dinner Sun.*

$
BISTRO
✗ **Chez Jules.** Once a fire station, this bustling bistro is now unashamedly French and rustic, with red-and-white-check tablecloths and a menu chalked up on the blackboard. Start perhaps with a chicken liver parfait, followed by grilled sea bass with warm artichoke and pea salad, or perhaps a classic rib-eye steak. The two-course early-bird menu is great value at £12. $ *Average main: £13* ⊠ *71 Northgate St.* ☎ *01244/400014* ⊕ *www.chezjules.com.*

$$$$
FRENCH
Fodor'sChoice
★
✗ **Simon Radley at the Chester Grosvenor.** Named for its noted chef, this restaurant has a sophisticated panache and prices to match. Expect the seasonal but not the usual, including named dishes: Herdwick is mutton with wild garlic, spearmint jelly, and ewe's curd, while Millionaire is a rich dessert made with several types of chocolate. There's a fixed-price dinner (£69) as well as a daily tasting menu (£90). The wine cellar has

8

more than 1,000 bins. Reservations are essential on weekends, and children must be at least 12. [$] *Average main: £69* ✉ *Chester Grosvenor Hotel, Eastgate St.* ☎ *01244/324024* 🌐 *www.chestergrosvenor.com* ✍ *Reservations essential* ⏲ *No dinner Mon. and Sun. Closed 1st 3 wks in Jan.*

WHERE TO STAY

For expanded hotel reviews, visit Fodors.com.

$ HOTEL Fodor's Choice ★ 🏨 **ABode.** Perched on a busy traffic intersection on the edge of Chester's old town, this gleaming new hotel from the trendy ABode chain may not occupy the city's most romantic spot, but it's well run and comfortable. **Pros:** modern and comfortable; good food; great bar. **Cons:** lacks historic charm of older hotels; parking lot is hard to find (take the almost-hidden exit from the roundabout that looks like it's just for deliveries). [$] *Rooms from: £89* ✉ *Grosvenor Rd.* ☎ *01244/347000* 🌐 *www.abodehotels.co.uk/chester* 🛏 *85 rooms.*

$ B&B/INN 🏨 **Chester Recorder House.** This Georgian redbrick house has the perfect location right on the city wall and overlooking the River Dee. **Pros:** within easy reach of the center; excellent breakfasts. **Cons:** no elevator. [$] *Rooms from: £80* ✉ *19 City Walls* ☎ *01244/326580* 🌐 *www.recorderhotel.co.uk* 🛏 *11 rooms* 🍴 *Breakfast.*

$$ HOTEL 🏨 **Frogg Manor.** Leave the modern world behind while you dance foxtrots after dinner in the party room and sleep in sumptuous tranquillity. **Pros:** English eccentricity at its best; frills and furbelows. **Cons:** not for minimalists; inconsistent housekeeping; outside town. [$] *Rooms from: £101* ✉ *Nantwich Rd., Broxton* ☎ *01829/782238* 🌐 *www.froggmanorhotel.co.uk* 🛏 *8 rooms* 🍴 *Breakfast.*

$$$ HOTEL Fodor's Choice ★ 🏨 **Green Bough Hotel.** This friendly little hotel, furnished with antiques including cast-iron beds, is in Chester's leafy outskirts, about a mile from the center. **Pros:** attentive service; well-designed rooms. **Cons:** no young children allowed. [$] *Rooms from: £185* ✉ *60 Hoole Rd.* ☎ *01244/326241* 🌐 *www.greenbough.co.uk* 🛏 *8 rooms, 7 suites* 🍴 *Breakfast.*

NIGHTLIFE AND THE ARTS

Oddfellows. This is the swankiest bar in town. Sip champagne cocktails or afternoon tea and admire the big wallpaper and big candelabra. You can dine (and stay) here, too. ✉ *20 Lower Bridge St.* ☎ *01244/895700.*

SHOPPING

Bluecoat Books. This book emporium specializes in travel, art, architecture, and history. ✉ *1 City Walls* ☎ *01244/318752.*

Chester Market. This indoor market, near the Town Hall, in open every day except Sunday. ✉ *6 Princess St.* 🌐 *www.chestermarket.com.*

LANCASHIRE AND THE PEAKS

WELCOME TO LANCASHIRE AND THE PEAKS

TOP REASONS TO GO

★ **Walking in the Peak District:** Even a short hike in Edale or High Peak reveals the craggy, austere beauty for which the area is famous.

★ **Liverpool culture, old and new:** The Beatles' home city is already a must-see for fans of the Fab Four, but this once-rundown Victorian city has spent a decade reinventing itself as a cultural hub.

★ **Manchester nightspots:** Catch the city at night in any of its humming café-bars and pubs; or just enjoy a good beer in an ornate Victorian-era pub.

★ **Chatsworth House and Haddon Hall:** Engage the past and imagine yourself as a country landowner roaming the great pile that is Chatsworth, or as a Tudor noble strolling through the grounds of the quintessentially English Haddon Hall

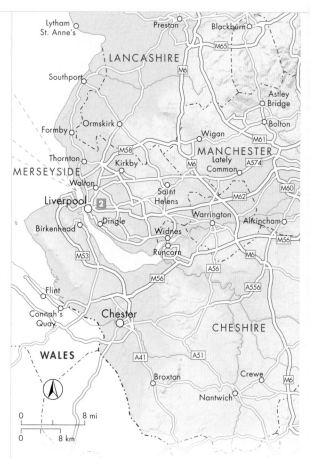

1 Manchester. The skies may be gray, but the vibrant city of Manchester is known for its modern urban design and its thriving music and club scenes. Great museums justify its status as the leading city of the northwest.

2 Liverpool. Now in the midst of a postindustrial rebirth, this city is more than the Beatles. The imposing waterfront, the pair of cathedrals, and the grand architecture make this clear. Even so, the museums don't forget to mention the city's place in rock-and-roll history.

GETTING ORIENTED

Manchester lies at the heart of a tangle of motorways in the northwest of England, about a half hour across the Pennines from Yorkshire. It's 70 miles from the southern edge of the Lake District. The city spreads west toward the coast and the mouth of the River Mersey, where Liverpool is still centered on its busy port. To see any great natural beauty, however, you must head east to the Peak District, a national park less than an hour's drive southeast of Manchester. It's also where you'll find two of the grandest and best-preserved historic homes in all of Britain: Chatsworth and Haddon Hall.

9

3 **The Peak District.**
Britain's first national park, the Peak District is studded with an array of stately homes, the most impressive being Chatsworth House. Dramatic moors, sylvan dales, and atmospheric limestone caverns just demanding to be explored.

THE BEATLES IN LIVERPOOL

This distinctive northern English city was the birthplace of the Beatles, who changed rock music forever using recording techniques unheard of at the time. The Fab Four became counterculture icons who defined the look and sound of the 1960s; but despite their international success, they remained true sons of Liverpool.

Reinvigorated over the past decade, the city remains a site of pilgrimage for fans more than half a century after the Beatles' early gigs here. Liverpool may no longer be the rough, postwar city the Beatles grew up in, but it makes the most of its connections to Paul McCartney, John Lennon, George Harrison, and Ringo Starr. John's and Paul's childhood homes, Mendips and 20 Forthlin Road, are in south Liverpool; both are National Trust sites. You can take in a show at Mathew Street's (re-created) Cavern Club, where the band played in its early days, or tour Penny Lane, Strawberry Fields, and other mop-top nostalgia spots. On the waterfront at Albert Dock, the Beatles Story museum provides a state-of-the-art overview of the group's career.

(above) The Beatles' music and style—and their haircuts—rocked the 1960s; (right, top) Mendips, John's childhood home and now a National Trust site; (right, bottom) The rebuilt Cavern

THEIR WORDS

"I knew the words to 25 rock songs, so I got in the group. 'Long Tall Sally' and 'Tutti Frutti,' that got me in. That was my audition."
—Paul McCartney

"Paul wasn't quite strong enough, I didn't have enough girl appeal, George was too quiet, and Ringo was the drummer. But we thought that everyone would be able to dig at least one of us, and that's how it turned out."
—John Lennon

FOLLOW IN THE FOOTSTEPS

SEE THE MAIN SIGHTS
The three key shrines of Beatle-dom in Liverpool are John's and Paul's childhood homes in south Liverpool, and the legendary Cavern Club on Mathew Street downtown where the Beatles were discovered by their future manager Brian Epstein in 1961. A combined ticket for both Beatle homes includes a bus between the city center and the two sites.

CHECK OUT THE BEATLES STORY
At this attraction in the Albert Dock, entertaining scenes re-create stages in the Fab Four's lives, from early gigs in Germany and the Cavern Club to each member's solo career, with 3-D computer animations, band artifacts, and more.

CHOOSE THE RIGHT TOUR
The two-hour Magical Mystery Tour departing from the Albert Dock Visitor Centre is a great way to zoom around Penny Lane, Strawberry Field, and other landmarks it would otherwise be difficult to find. Liverpool Beatles Tours can cram in every Beatles haunt on four-hour or full-day tours. Other options are private guides or personalized tours.

SLEEP WITH THE BEATLES . . . AND SHOP, TOO
Within earshot of the Cavern on the corner of Mathew Street is the Hard Day's Night Hotel, with Lennon- and McCartney-themed suites, Yellow Submarine jukeboxes, and an inviting bar. It's done with pizzazz. At 31 Mathew Street the Beatles Shop packs in memorabilia and souvenirs from vintage posters and vinyls to mugs.

GO TO BEATLES WEEK
The annual **International Beatle Week** (⊕ *www.cavernclub. org*) is usually held the last week in August. Attend John and Yoko fancy-dress parties, listen to Beatles tribute bands, and attend record fairs, exhibitions, and conventions.

TAKING STOCK

When these four local rapscallions appeared on the Liverpool pop circuit in the early 1960s, they were just another group of lads struggling to get gigs on the city's "Merseybeat" scene. What followed was extraordinary: Beatlemania swept over fans around the world, including the United States, which the group first visited in 1964. Before their 1969 breakup, the Beatles achieved phenomenal commercial and creative success, bringing bohemianism to the masses and embodying a generation's ideals of social liberation and peace. They reinvented pop music, bridging styles and genres as diverse as Celtic folk, psychedelia, and Indian raga, starring in epoch-making movies such as *A Hard Day's Night* and *Help!*, and causing such hysteria they couldn't even hear their own guitars on stage. Though adulation followed them everywhere, the Beatles remained obstinate "Scousers," showing a grounded charm and irreverent humor characteristic of their native city.

9

Updated by
Jack Jewers

For those looking for the postcard England of little villages, the northwest region of England might not appear at the top of a sightseeing list. Manchester, Britain's third-largest city, bustles with redevelopment, and Liverpool is undergoing significant revitalization. However, the 200 years of smoke-stack industry that abated only in the 1980s have taken a toll on the east Lancashire landscape. The region does have lovely scenery inland, in Derbyshire (pronounced *Dar*-be-sheer)—notably the spectacular Peak District, a national park at the southern end of the Pennine range.

Manchester and Liverpool, the economic engines that propelled Britain in the 18th and 19th centuries, are sloughing off their mid-20th-century decline and celebrating their rich industrial and maritime heritage in excellent museums—in imposing Victorian edifices, or, in Manchester's case, in strikingly modern buildings.

The cities, each with a population of about 450,000, have reestablished themselves as centers of sporting and musical excellence, and as nightlife hot spots. Since 1962 the Manchester United, Everton, and Liverpool football (soccer in the United States) clubs have won everything worth winning in Britain and Europe. The Beatles launched the Mersey sound of the '60s; contemporary Manchester groups still punch above their weight on both sides of the Atlantic. On the classical side of music, Manchester is also the home of Britain's oldest leading orchestra, the Hallé (founded in 1857)—just one legacy of 19th-century industrialists' investments in culture.

The Peak District is a wilder part of England, a region of crags that rear violently out of the plains. The Pennines, a line of hills that begins in the Peak District and runs as far north as Scotland, are sometimes called the "backbone of England." In this landscape of rocky outcrops and undulating meadowland you'll see nothing for miles but sheep, dry-stone (without mortar) walls, and farms, interrupted—spectacularly—by 19th-century villages and stately homes. In and around this area are Victorian-era spas such as Buxton, pretty towns such as Bakewell, and magnificent houses such as Chatsworth, Hardwick Hall, and Haddon Hall. The delight of the Peak District is being able to ramble for days in rugged countryside but still enjoy the pleasures of civilization.

LANCASHIRE AND THE PEAKS PLANNER

WHEN TO GO
Manchester has a reputation as one of the wettest cities in Britain, and visiting in summer won't guarantee fine weather. Nevertheless, wet or cold weather shouldn't spoil a visit because of the many indoor sights and cultural activities here and in Liverpool. Summer is the optimum time to see the Peak District, especially because traditional festivities take place in many villages. The *only* time to see the great houses of Derbyshire's Wye Valley is from spring through fall.

PLANNING YOUR TIME
It's possible to see the main sights of Manchester or Liverpool in a day, but you'd have to take the museums at a gallop. In Manchester the Museum of Science and Industry and the Imperial War Museum could easily absorb a day, as could the Albert Dock and waterfront area of Liverpool, where the Beatles Story, Tate Liverpool, Merseyside Maritime, and International Slavery museums, as well as the Museum of Liverpool, all vie for your attention. In Liverpool an additional half day is needed to see the homes of John Lennon and Paul McCartney. The buzzing nightlife of each city demands at least an overnight stay. You can explore the Peak District on a day trip from Manchester in a pinch, but allow longer to visit the stately homes or to hike.

GETTING HERE AND AROUND

AIR TRAVEL
Both Manchester and Liverpool are well served by their international airports. Manchester, the third-largest airport in the country, has the greater number of flights, including some from the United States.

Airports Liverpool John Lennon Airport ☏ *0871/521–8484* ⊕ *www.liverpoolairport.com.* **Manchester Airport** ☏ *0871/271–0711* ⊕ *www.manchesterairport.co.uk.*

BUS TRAVEL
National Express buses serve the region from London's Victoria Coach Station. Average travel time to Manchester or Liverpool is five hours. To reach Matlock, Bakewell, and Buxton you can take a bus from London to Derby and change to the TransPeak bus service, though you might find it more convenient to travel first to Manchester.

Bus Contacts National Express ☏ *08717/818178* ⊕ *www.nationalexpress.com.* **TransPeak** ☏ *01773/712265* ⊕ *www.trentbarton.co.uk.* **Traveline** ☏ *0871/200–2233* ⊕ *www.traveline.org.uk.*

CAR TRAVEL

If you're traveling by road, expect heavy traffic out of London on weekends. Travel time to Manchester or Liverpool from London via the M6 is 3 to 3½ hours. Although a car may not be an asset in touring the centers of Manchester and Liverpool, it's helpful in getting around the Peak District. Bus service there is quite good, but a car allows the most flexibility.

Roads within the region are generally very good. In Manchester and Liverpool, try to sightsee on foot to avoid parking problems. In the Peak District, park in signposted parking lots whenever possible. In summer, Peak District traffic is very heavy; watch out for speeding motorbikes, especially on the A6. In winter, know the weather forecast, as moorland roads can quickly become impassable.

TRAIN TRAVEL

Virgin Trains serves the region from London's Euston Station. Direct service to Manchester and Liverpool takes between 2 and 2½ hours. There are trains between Manchester's Piccadilly Station and Liverpool's Lime Street roughly three times an hour during the day; the trip takes 50 minutes. Get schedules and other information through National Rail Enquiries.

To reach Buxton, in the Peak District, from London, take the Manchester train; switch at Stockport. Local service—one train an hour—from Manchester to Buxton takes one hour. Call National Rail Enquiries for timetable information.

Train Contacts National Rail Enquiries ☎ *0845/748–4950*
🌐 *www.nationalrail.co.uk.*

TRANSPORTATION DISCOUNTS AND DEALS

A Wayfarer ticket (£10), which covers a day's travel on all forms of transport in Manchester and the Peak District, is a good deal. Contact National Rail Enquiries for information.

RESTAURANTS

Dining options in Manchester and Liverpool vary from smart cafés offering Modern British and Continental fare to excellent international restaurants. Manchester has one of Britain's biggest Chinatowns, and locals also favor the 40-odd Bangladeshi, Pakistani, and Indian restaurants along Wilmslow Road in Rusholme, a mile south of the city center, known as Curry Mile.

One local dish that has survived is Bakewell pudding (*never* called "tart" in these areas, as its imitations are elsewhere in England). Served with custard or cream, the pudding—a pastry covered with jam and a thin layer of almond-flavor filling—is the joy of Bakewell. Another regional creation is Lancashire hot pot, a hearty meat stew. *Prices in the reviews are the average cost of a main course at dinner or, if dinner isn't served, at lunch.*

HOTELS

Because the larger city-center hotels in Manchester and Liverpool rely on business travelers during the week, they may markedly reduce their rates on weekends. Smaller hotels and guesthouses abound in nearby suburbs, many just a short bus ride from downtown. The Manchester and Liverpool visitor centers operate room-booking services. Also worth investigating are serviced apartments, which are becoming more popular in the cities. The Peak District has inns, bed-and-breakfasts, and hotels, as well as a network of youth hostels. Local tourist offices have details; reserve well in advance for Easter and summer. *Prices in the reviews are the lowest cost of a standard double room in high season, including 20% V.A.T.*

VISITOR INFORMATION

Contacts **England's Northwest** ⊕ *www.visitenglandsnorthwest.com.*

MANCHESTER

Today Manchester's center hums with the vibe of cutting-edge popular music and a swank café culture. The city's once-grim industrial landscape, redeveloped since the late 1980s, includes tidied-up canals, cotton mills transformed into loft apartments, and stylish contemporary architecture that has pushed the skyline ever higher. Beetham Tower, the ninth-tallest building in Britain (and the tallest outside London), can't be overlooked. Bridgewater Hall and the Lowry, as well as the Imperial War Museum North, are outstanding cultural facilities. Sure, it still rains here, but the rain-soaked streets are part of the city's charm, in a bleak, northern kind of way.

The now-defunct Haçienda Club marketed New Order to the world, and Manchester became the clubbing capital of England. Joy Division, the Smiths, Stone Roses, Happy Mondays, and Oasis rose to the top of the charts. The extraordinary success of the Manchester United football club (which now faces a stiff challenge from its newly rich neighbor, Manchester City, owing to a stupendous injection of cash from its oil-rich Middle Eastern owners) has kept the eyes of sports fans fixed firmly on Manchester.

GETTING HERE AND AROUND

Manchester Airport has many international flights, so you might not even have to travel through London. There are frequent trains from the airport to Piccadilly Railway Station (15–20 minutes) and buses to Piccadilly Gardens Bus Station (one hour). A taxi from the airport to Manchester city center costs around £20. For details about public transportation in Manchester, call the Greater Manchester Passenger Transport Executive information line.

Driving to Manchester from London (3 to 3½ hours), take M1 north to M6, then the M62 east, which becomes M602 as it enters Greater Manchester. Trains from London's Euston Station drop passengers at the centrally located Piccadilly Railway Station. The journey takes just over two hours. Chorlton Street Coach Station, a few hundred yards west of Piccadilly Railway Station, is the main bus station for regional and long-distance buses.

Most local buses leave from Piccadilly Gardens Bus Station, the hub of the urban bus network. Metroshuttle operates three free circular routes around the city center; service runs every 5 to 10 minutes Monday to Saturday, from 7 to 7 and Sunday from 10 to 6.

Metrolink electric tram service runs through the city center and out to the suburbs. The Eccles extension has stops for the Lowry (Harbour City) and for the Manchester United Stadium (Old Trafford). Buy a ticket from the platform machine before you board. SystemOne Travelcards, which allow unlimited travel on buses, trains and trams after 9:30 am, cost £7; buy from the driver or any ticket machine.

Blue Badge Guides can arrange dozens of different tours of the city, and City Centre Cruises (☎ 0161/902–0222 ⊕ *www.citycentrecruises. co.uk*) offer a three-hour Sunday lunch round-trip on a barge to the Manchester Ship Canal.

ORIENTATION

Manchester is compact enough that you can easily walk across the city center in 40 minutes. Deansgate and Princess Street, the main thoroughfares, run roughly north–south and west–east; the lofty terra-cotta Victorian **Town Hall** sits in the middle, close to the visitor center and the fine **Manchester Art Gallery.** Dominating the skyline at the southern end of Deansgate is Manchester's highest building, Beetham Tower, which houses a Hilton Hotel and marks the beginning of the **Castlefield Urban Heritage Park,** with the Museum of Science and Industry and the canal system. The **Whitworth Art Gallery** is a bus ride from downtown; otherwise, all other central sights are within easy walking distance of the Town Hall. Take a Metrolink tram 2 miles south for the Salford Quays dockland area, with the **Lowry** and the **Imperial War Museum**; you can spend half a day or more in this area. ■ TIP→ Keep in mind that the museums are both excellent and free.

ESSENTIALS

Transportation Contacts Greater Manchester Passenger Transport Executive ☎ *0161/244–1000* ⊕ *www.gmpte.com.* **Metrolink** ☎ *0161/205–2000* ⊕ *www.metrolink.co.uk.* **Metroshuttle** ☎ *0161/244–1000* ⊕ *www.tfgm.com/ buses/Pages/metroshuttle.aspx.*

Tour Information Blue Badge Guides ☎ *0161/864–2640* ⊕ *www.britainsbestguides.org.* **City Centre Cruises** ☎ *0161/902–0222* ⊕ *www.citycentrecruises.co.uk.*

Visitor Information Manchester Visitor Information Centre ✉ *40-50 Piccadilly Plaza, Portland St., City Centre* ☎ *0871/222–8223* ⊕ *www.visitmanchester.com.*

EXPLORING

TOP ATTRACTIONS

Castlefield Urban Heritage Park. Site of an early Roman fort, the district of Castlefield was later the center of the city's industrial boom, which resulted in the building of Britain's first modern canal in 1764 and the world's first railway station in 1830. It has been beautifully restored into an urban park with canal-side walks, landscaped open spaces, and refurbished warehouses. The 7-acre site contains the reconstructed gate to the Roman fort of Mamucium, the buildings of the **Museum of Science and Industry,** and several of the city's hippest bars and restaurants. You can spend half a day here. ✉ *Off Liverpool Rd., Castlefield* ☎ *0161/834-4026.*

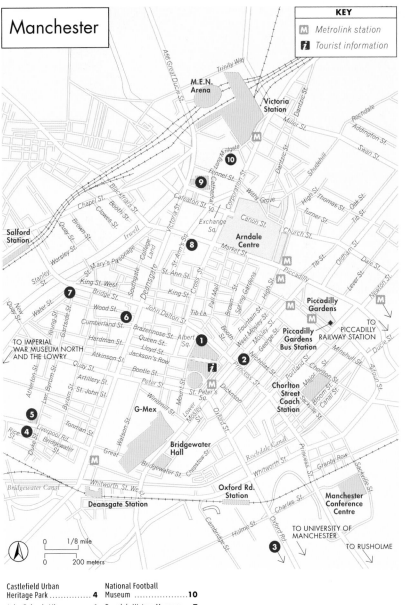

Manchester

KEY

Ⓜ Metrolink station

🛈 Tourist information

Manchester was an industrial powerhouse; learn all about this history at the engaging Museum of Science and Industry.

Imperial War Museum North. The thought-provoking exhibits in this striking, aluminum-clad building, which architect Daniel Libeskind described as representing three shards of an exploded globe, present the reasons for war and show its effects on society. Three Big Picture audiovisual shows envelop you in the sights and sounds of conflicts from 1914 to the present, and a storage system has trays of objects to examine, including artifacts from the 2003 war in Iraq. The Air Shard, a 100-foot viewing platform, gives a bird's-eye view of the city. The museum is on the banks of the Manchester Ship Canal in Salford Quays, across the footbridge from the Lowry. It's a 10-minute (often breezy) walk from the Harbour City stop of the Metrolink tram. ⊠ *Trafford Wharf Rd., Salford Quays* ☎ *0161/836–4000* ⊕ *www.iwm.org.uk* ☎ *Free* ⊙ *Daily 10–5; last admission 30 mins before closing.*

The Lowry. Clad in perforated steel and glass and fronted by an illuminated canopy, this impressive arts center in Manchester is one of the highlights of the Salford Quays waterways. L. S. Lowry (1887–1976) was a local artist, and one of the few who painted the industrial landscape. Galleries showcase Lowry's and other contemporary artists' work. The theater, Britain's largest outside London, presents an impressive lineup of touring companies. The nearest Metrolink tram stop is Harbour City, a 10-minute walk from the Lowry. ⊠ *Pier 8, Salford Quays* ☎ *0843/208–6000* ⊕ *www.thelowry.com* ☎ *Free, tours £5* ⊙ *Mon.–Sat. 10–8 (closes 6 on nights with no performance); Sun. and bank holiday Mon. 10–6. Galleries: Sun.–Fri. 11–5, Sat. 10–5.*

Manchester Art Gallery. Behind its impressive classical portico, this splendid museum presents its collections in both a Victorian and contemporary setting. Don't miss the outstanding collection of paintings by the Pre-Raphaelites and their circle, notably Ford Madox Brown's masterpiece *Work*, Holman Hunt's *The Hireling Shepherd*, and Dante Gabriel Rossetti's *Astarte Syriaca*. British artworks from the 18th and the 20th centuries are also well represented. The second-floor Craft and Design Gallery shows off the best of the decorative arts in ceramics, glass, metalwork, and furniture. ⊠ *Mosely St., City Centre* ☎ *0161/235–8888* ⊕ *www.manchestergalleries.org.uk* 🔖 *Free* ⊙ *Fri.–Wed. 10–5; Thurs. 10–9; last admission 30 mins before closing.*

FAMILY **Museum of Science and Industry.** The museum's five buildings, one of
Fodor's Choice which is the world's oldest passenger rail station (1830), hold marvel-
★ ous collections relating to the city's industrial past and present. You can walk through a reconstructed Victorian sewer, be blasted by the heat and noise of working steam engines, see cotton looms whirring in action, and watch a planetarium show. The Air and Space Gallery fills a graceful cast-iron-and-glass building, constructed as a market hall in 1877. ▪TIP➔ **Allow at least half a day to get the most out of all the sites.** ⊠ *Castlefield Urban Heritage Park, Liverpool Rd., main entrance on Lower Byrom St., Castlefield* ☎ *0161/832–2244* ⊕ *www.mosi.org. uk* 🔖 *Free, charges vary for special exhibits* ⊙ *Daily 10–5.*

FAMILY **People's History Museum.** Not everyone in 19th-century Manchester owned a cotton mill or made a fortune on the trading floor. This museum recounts powerfully the struggles of working people in the city since the Industrial Revolution. Displays include the story of the 1819 Peterloo Massacre—when the army attacked a crowd of civil rights protesters in Manchester's St. Peter's Square, killing 15 and almost sparking revolution—together with an unrivaled collection of trade-union banners, tools, toys, utensils, and photographs, all illustrating the working lives and pastimes of the city's people. ⊠ *Left Bank, City Centre* ☎ *0161/838–9190* ⊕ *www.phm.org.uk* 🔖 *Free* ⊙ *Daily 10–5.*

NEED A BREAK?

Mark Addy. The brick-vaulted Mark Addy pub is a good spot to have a drink and sample an excellent spread of pâtés, cheeses, and jazzed-up traditional workmen's favorites such as cheese and onion pie with spiced baked beans or roast pheasant with bacon and black pudding. The waterside pub is named for the 19th-century boatman who rescued more than 50 people from the River Irwell. ⊠ *Stanley St., off Bridge St., City Centre* ☎ *0161/832–4080* ⊕ *www.markaddy.co.uk.*

Royal Exchange. Throughout the city's commercial heyday, the most important building was the cotton market. Built with Victorian exuberance in 1874, the existing structure accommodated 7,000 traders. The giant glass-dome roof was restored after a 1996 IRA bombing. Visit to see the lunar module–inspired Royal Exchange Theatre, have a drink in the café, and browse the crafts shop or the clothes outlets in the arcade. ⊠ *St. Ann's Sq., City Centre* ☎ *0161/833–9833 (Theatre)* ⊕ *www.royalexchange.co.uk.*

Town Hall. Manchester's imposing Town Hall, with its 280-foot-tall clock tower, speaks volumes about the city's 19th-century sense of self-importance. Alfred Waterhouse designed the Victorian Gothic building (1867–76); extensions were added just before World War II. Over the main entrance is a statue of Roman general Agricola, who founded Mamucium in AD 79. Just inside the entrance, the Sculpture Hall has a magnificent low vaulted ceiling; now used as a café, the walls are lined with Gothic-style alcoves and statues of famous Mancunians. The Great Hall is decorated with murals of the city's history, painted between 1852 and 1865 by the Pre-Raphaelite Ford Madox Brown. You can view the murals for free, so long as the room isn't being used; call ahead to check. ⊠ *Albert Sq., public entrance on Lloyd St., City Centre* ☎ *0161/234–5000* 🎫 *Free* ☉ *Weekdays 9–5; Sculpture Hall also 11–4 Sat.*

Whitworth Art Gallery. This University of Manchester–run art museum has strong collections of British watercolors, old-master drawings, and postimpressionist works, as well as wallpapers. The excellent textile gallery—befitting a city built on textile manufacture—demonstrates the meaning and power of clothing in such items as a 16th-century Spanish funeral cope, 18th-century babies' vests, and a modern-day Turkish circumcision suit. There's also a good bistro and a gift shop. To get to the museum, catch any southbound bus with a number in the 40s (except 47) on Oxford Road, or from St. Peter's Square or Piccadilly Gardens. ⊠ *University of Manchester, Oxford Rd., University Quarter* ☎ *0161/275–7450* ⊕ *www.whitworth.manchester.ac.uk* 🎫 *Free* ☉ *Mon.–Sat. 10–5, Sun. noon–4.*

WORTH NOTING

John Rylands Library. Owned by the University of Manchester, this Gothic Revival masterpiece designed by Alfred Waterhouse was built by Enriqueta Augustina Rylands as a memorial to her husband, a cotton magnate. Constructed of red sandstone in the 1890s, the library resembles a cathedral and contains outstanding collections of illuminated manuscripts and personal papers of famous writers. ⊠ *150 Deansgate, City Centre* ☎ *0161/306–0555* ⊕ *www.library.manchester.ac.uk* 🎫 *Free* ☉ *Tues.– Sat. 10–5, Sun. and Mon. noon–5; last entry 30 mins before closing.*

Manchester Cathedral. The city's sandstone cathedral, set beside the River Irwell and originally a medieval parish church dating in part from the 15th century, is unusually broad for its length and has the widest medieval nave in Britain. Inside, angels with gilded instruments look down from the roof of the nave, and misericords (the undersides of choristers' seats) in the early-16th-century choir stalls reveal intriguing carvings. The octagonal chapter house dates from 1485. ⊠ *Victoria St., Millennium Quarter* ☎ *0161/833–2220* ⊕ *www.manchestercathedral.org* 🎫 *Free* ☉ *Weekdays 8:30–7, Sat. 8:30–5, Sun. 8:30–7:30.*

National Football Museum. Opened in 2012, this huge museum is devoted to one of the biggest British exports of all time—football (soccer), the English national sport, and the most popular team game in the world. This striking, glass-skinned triangle of a building includes a galaxy of footballing memorabilia, from historic trophies, souvenirs, and shirts (many of them signed by legends of the sport) to such near-sacred items

CLOSE UP

Manchester's History: Cottonopolis

Manchester's spectacular rise from a small town to the world's cotton capital—with the nickname Cottonopolis—in only 100 years began with the first steam-powered cotton mill, built in 1783. Dredging made the rivers Irwell and Mersey navigable to ship coal to the factories. The world's first passenger railway opened in 1830, and construction of the Manchester Ship Canal in 1894 provided the infrastructure for Manchester to dominate the industrial world. Check out 🌐 *www.modernhistory.co.uk* for information about seeing more of this industrial heritage.

A few people acquired great wealth, but factory hands worked under appalling conditions. Working-class discontent came to a head in 1819 in the Peterloo Massacre, when soldiers killed 15 workers at a protest meeting. The conditions under which factory hands worked were later recorded by Friedrich Engels (co-author with Karl Marx of the *Communist Manifesto*), who managed a cotton mill in the city. More formal political opposition to the government emerged in the shape of the Chartist movement (which campaigned for universal suffrage) and the Anti-Corn Law League (which opposed trade tariffs), forerunners of the British trade unions. From Victorian times until the 1960s, daily life for the average Mancunian was so oppressive that it bred the desire to escape, although most stayed put and endured the harsh conditions.

as the ball from the 1966 World Cup–the last time England won the sport's ultimate prize. Other exhibits explore football's role in British popular culture. In the interactive Football Plus zone you can pick up a microphone and develop your commentary style or test your ball skills in a range of activities, including a tense penalty shoot-out. ✉ *Urbis Bldg., Cathedral Gardens, Millennium Quarter* ☎ *0161/605–8200* 🌐 *www.nationalfootballmuseum.com* 🎟 *Free* 🕒 *Mon.–Sat. 10–5, Sun. 11–5.*

9

WHERE TO EAT

The city's dining scene, with everything from Indian (go to Rusholme) to Modern British fare, is lively. The Manchester Food and Drink Festival, held in late September or early October, showcases the city's chefs and regional products with special events. The city's pubs are also good options for lunch or dinner.

$ INDIAN 🍴 **Akbar's.** Locals line up for this big, bright, and buzzing contemporary restaurant just opposite the Museum of Science and Industry. If they're not tucking into sizzling, stir-fried balti dishes (a don't-miss), they might be enjoying a mild and creamy korma, *rogan josh* (with tomatoes and coriander), or a sweet-and-sour *dhansak* (with pineapple and lentils)—all popular staples. Vegetarians have plenty of choices, too. Be prepared to wait at busy times. [$] *Average main: £9* ✉ *73–83 Liverpool Rd., Castlefield* ☎ *0161/834–8444* 🌐 *www.akbars.co.uk* ✍ *Reservations not accepted* 🕒 *No lunch.*

$$
BRITISH

✕ **Albert's Shed.** A relaxed canalside setting and an alluring contemporary interior with large plate-glass windows compensate for the uninspiring, brick box facade of this traditional Castlefield restaurant. Most of the dishes, which use produce from Lancashire farms, hark back to the English country-manor table: roast venison loin topped with Stilton cheese and a port and blackberry jus, for example. Other dishes, like gnocchi with a rabbit and pancetta sauce, bring a scent of the Mediterranean. There's also a wide selection of pizzas. An excellent-value two-course lunch menu is served until 5 pm. [$] *Average main: £16* ✉ *20 Castle St., Castlefield* ☎ *0161/839–9818* ⊕ *www.albertsshed.com.*

> ## CHINATOWN
>
> The large red-and-gold Imperial Chinese Arch, erected in 1987, marks Manchester's Chinatown, one of the largest Chinese communities outside London. Bordered by Portland Street, Mosley Street, Princess Street, and Charlotte Street, the area is bustling on Sunday, when traders from all over the country stock up from the supermarkets, food stalls, herbalists, and gift shops. The restaurants offer excellent choices of authentic Cantonese cooking, so consider a stop here when your shopping energies run low.

$$
MODERN BRITISH

✕ **The Lime Tree.** Chef Patrick Hannity's unstuffy restaurant offers a seductive British menu with a hint of northern bohemia in the leafy suburb of West Didsbury. Expect Cheshire lamb in the exotic company of moussaka, couscous, and mint yogurt, or Morecambe Bay scallops in cannelloni. If you don't mind eating between 5:30 and 6:30 pm, the early-evening three-course menu is superb value at £15.95. Wine can be ordered by the glass to suit each dish. You might need to book a week in advance. [$] *Average main: £17* ✉ *8 Lapwing La., West Didsbury* ☎ *0161/445–1217* ⊕ *www. thelimetreerestaurant.co.uk* ⟐ *Reservations essential.*

$
BRITISH

✕ **Mr. Thomas's Chophouse.** The city's oldest restaurant, dating from 1872, dishes out good old British favorites such as brown onion soup, corned beef hash, Lancashire hot pot, and spotted dick pudding to crowds of city dwellers and shoppers. This hearty food is served in a Victorian-style room with a black-and-white-checked floor and green tiling. The wine list is exceptional. Mr. Sam's Chophouse in Chapel Walks serves similar fare. [$] *Average main: £14* ✉ *52 Cross St., City Centre* ☎ *0161/832–2245* ⊕ *www.tomschophouse.com.*

$
INDIAN

✕ **Mughli Restaurant and Charcoal Pit.** Take your seat by the open charcoal pit and be seduced by one of the sizzling tandoori or tikka dishes in this fast-paced Indian restaurant on Rusholme's "Curry Mile." Specializing in Mughlai (northern Indian and Pakistani) cuisine, the restaurant has a capacious, mood-lit interior with striking Indonesian murals and Bollywood posters. It's been a local fixture for over 20 years. [$] *Average main: £9* ✉ *28–32 Wilmslow Rd., Rusholme* ☎ *0161/248–0900* ⊕ *www.mughli.com.*

$$
JAPANESE
Fodor's Choice
★

✕ **Sapporo Teppanyaki.** The emphasis is on riotous good fun at this modern Japanese restaurant in Castlefield. Take your place around the chef's iron griddle and the theater begins; once you've had potato fritters tossed into your mouth and seen other morsels caught and balanced on the chef's spatula, you can enjoy a delicious and creative *teppanyaki* (main courses served on an iron plate) of duck in raspberry sauce or sole with lemon, ginger and coriander. For a quieter, lighter meal, take a private table and peruse the sushi menu. Curiosity might tempt you to try a Manchester roll, made of smoked swordfish with Lancashire cheese, carrots, and crabmeat. $ *Average main: £17* ✉ *91–93 Liverpool Rd., Castlefield* ☎ *0161/979–0578* ⊕ *www.sapporo.co.uk.*

$ ✕ **Sweet Mandarin.** Warm neon lights and floor-to-ceiling windows invite you into this contemporary Chinese restaurant from the hip streets of the Northern Quarter. Deliciously simple family recipes have earned it a growing reputation; locals flock here to enjoy the famous salt-and-pepper ribs, clay-pot chicken, Lily Kwok's curry, and crispy Szechuan beef, all of which come on the fixed-price banquet menu at £20 per head. On the à la carte menu, try General Tse's sweet-and-sour chicken, named after an uncle of the owner, whose protection of his secret recipe virged on militant. $ *Average main: £11* ✉ *19 Copperas St., Northern Quarter* ☎ *0161/832–8848 after 5 pm, 0776/783–4583 daytime* ⊕ *www.sweetmandarin.com* ☾ *Closed Mon.*

CHINESE

$ ✕ **Umezushi.** A short walk from Manchester's Victoria train station, this tiny restaurant may not look like much from the outside—among a row of industrial units inside converted railway arches—but it serves some of the most exceptional sushi in Manchester. Traditional maki and tempura are beautifully prepared, or you could opt for one of the more experimental daily specials, such as stir-fried spaghetti with chili and garlic, or Gressingham duck served with garlic and saki sauce. $ *Average main: £10* ✉ *Unit 4, Mirabel St., City Centre* ☎ *0161/832–1852* ⊕ *www.umezushi.co.uk.*

JAPANESE

WHERE TO STAY

For expanded hotel reviews, visit Fodors.com.

$ ⊡ **Arora.** Opposite the Manchester Art Gallery, the centrally located Arora Hotel occupies one of the city's grand Victorian buildings; its interior design, however, is minimalist modern. **Pros:** fun theme rooms; good deals on weekends. **Cons:** no parking; smallish rooms. $ *Rooms from: £80* ✉ *18–24 Princess St., City Centre* ☎ *0161/236–8999* ⊕ *www. arorainternational.com* ⤶ *141 rooms* ⧖ *No meals.*

HOTEL

$ ⊡ **Castlefield Hotel.** This popular modern hotel near the water's edge in the Castlefield Basin, opposite the Museum of Science and Industry, has cheery and traditional public rooms. **Pros:** excellent leisure facilities; reasonable rates. **Cons:** gym can get very busy; walls a little thin. $ *Rooms from: £99* ✉ *Liverpool Rd., Castlefield* ☎ *0161/832–7073* ⊕ *www.castlefield-hotel.co.uk* ⤶ *48 rooms* ⧖ *Breakfast.*

HOTEL

$$$$ ⊡ **Great John Street.** Once a Victorian schoolhouse, this plush boutique hotel next to the Granada TV studios now attracts well-heeled business executives, television stars, and anyone seeking something truly special. **Pros:** luxurious rooms; unique design. **Cons:** expensive valet parking. $ *Rooms from: £238* ✉ *Great John St., City Centre* ☎ *0161/831–3211* ⊕ *www.greatjohnstreet.co.uk* ⤶ *14 rooms, 16 suites* ⧖ *No meals.*

HOTEL

Fodor's Choice

★

$$ **The Lowry Hotel.** The strikingly modern design of this glass edifice
HOTEL   overlooking the River Irwell and Santiago Calatrava's Trinity Bridge
exudes luxury and spaciousness. **Pros:** luxury at every turn; spacious
rooms. **Cons:** rather bleak views in rooms facing Chapel Street; cheap-
est rates don't include breakfast. $ *Rooms from: £118* ⊠ *50 Dearman's
Pl., City Centre* ☎ *0161/827–4000* ⊕ *www.thelowryhotel.com* ➘ *157
rooms, 7 suites* ❑ *Multiple meal plans.*

$$ **The Midland Hotel.** The Edwardian splendor of the hotel's public rooms
HOTEL   manages to shine through a contemporary makeover, evoking the days
when this was the city's main railway station hotel. **Pros:** central location, close to Town Hall and a Metrolink stop; superb restaurant; good
for business travelers. **Cons:** impersonal feel; rooms facing road can be
noisy. $ *Rooms from: £119* ⊠ *Peter St., City Centre* ☎ *0161/236–3333*
⊕ *www.qhotels.co.uk* ➘ *298 rooms, 14 suites* ❑ *Breakfast.*

$ **The Oxnoble at Potato Wharf.** At the southern end of the city center
HOTEL   opposite the Museum of Science and Industry, this friendly and relaxed
gastro-pub comes with guestrooms that are simple, creamy cool, and
modern in style. **Pros:** friendly staff; bargain prices. **Cons:** no-frills
decor; noise from the bar reaches some of the rooms. $ *Rooms from:
£50* ⊠ *71 Liverpool Rd., Castlefield* ☎ *0161/839–7760* ⊕ *www.theox.
co.uk* ➘ *9 rooms* ❑ *No meals.*

$ **RoomZZZ.** Although the stylishly modern serviced apartments in this
RENTAL   old cotton warehouse are all about self-contained autonomy, the lobby
and corridors have the jazzed-up feel of a boutique hotel. **Pros:** bang
in the center of town; on Chinatown's doorstep; smoothly run. **Cons:**
bathrooms have glass doors; location can be noisy. $ *Rooms from:
£79* ⊠ *36 Princess St., Chinatown* ☎ *0844/248–8075* ⊕ *www.roomzzz.
co.uk* ➘ *48 apartments* ❑ *No meals.*

NIGHTLIFE AND THE ARTS

Manchester vies with London as Britain's capital of youth culture, but
has vibrant nightlife and entertainment options for all ages. Spending
time at a bar, pub, or club is definitely an essential part of any trip. For
event listings, check out the free *Manchester Evening News* or *Manchester Metro News,* both widely available.

NIGHTLIFE

The action after dark centers on the Deansgate and Northern Quarter
areas.

CAFÉ-BARS

Cloud 23. This swanky bar has a stunning 360-degree view of the city
that's not for the vertiginous. It's popular, so book well ahead. ⊠ *Hilton
Manchester Deansgate, 303 Deansgate, City Centre* ☎ *0161/870–1600*
⊕ *www.cloud23bar.com.*

Dry Bar. The Northern Quarter's original café-bar opened by Factory
Records, Dry Bar is full of young people dancing and drinking. ⊠ *28–30
Oldham St., Northern Quarter* ☎ *0161/236–9840* ⊕ *www.drybar.co.uk.*

Kosmonaut. This funky new bar in the Northern Quarter has attracted
a legion of fans since it opened in 2012. The stripped-down decor fits
the hipster mood; exposed brick walls, leather benches, and the odd

Manchester's pubs and café-bars, whether Victorian or modern, are well worth a stop.

wry touch such as old barber chairs that form an intimate nook by the window. The wine list and beer selection are good, although the cocktail menu draws the biggest crowd. ✉ *10 Tariff St., Northern Quarter* ☎ *0161/236–7171* ⊕ *www.kosmonaut.co.*

Living Room. For something a little more glamorous and intimate, the Living Room is one of city's top spots; a pianist plays on the gorgeous white piano in the early evening. Book ahead. ✉ *80 Deansgate, City Centre* ☎ *0161/832–0083* ⊕ *www.thelivingroom.co.uk.*

The Molly House. This lively bar has an outstanding selection of beers from around the world, in addition to good wine and cocktail lists. The tapas nibbles are delicious and surprisingly inexpensive. ✉ *26 Richmond St., Northside* ☎ *0161/237–9329* ⊕ *www.themollyhouse.com.*

PUBS

Britons Protection. You can sample more than 230 whiskies and bourbons at this gorgeous pub with stained-glass windows, cozy back rooms, and a mural of the Peterloo Massacre. ✉ *50 Great Bridgewater St., Peter's Fields* ☎ *0161/236–5895* ⊕ *www.britonsprotection.co.uk.*

Dukes 92. This spot has a great canal-side setting for a summer pub lunch or drink. ✉ *18 Castle St., Castlefield* ☎ *0161/839–3522* ⊕ *www.dukes92.com.*

Peveril of the Peak. A throwback Victorian pub with a green-tile exterior, Peveril of the Peak draws a crush of locals to its tiny rooms. ✉ *127 Great Bridgewater St., Peter's Fields* ☎ *0161/236–6364.*

Sinclair's Oyster Bar. In a half-timber pub built in the 17th century, Sinclair's Oyster Bar specializes in fresh oyster dishes. ⊠ *2 Cathedral Gates, Millennium Quarter* ☎ *0161/834–0430.*

DANCE CLUBS

42nd Street. Off Deansgate, 42nd Street plays retro, indie, sing-along anthems, and classic rock, with Manchester's proud musical heritage to the fore. ⊠ *2 Bootle St., City Centre* ☎ *0161/831–7108* ⊕ *www.42ndstreetnightclub.co.uk.*

Sankey's. Electro, techno, and hard-core music draw crowds of young people to Sankey's. ⊠ *Beehive Mill, Jersey St., Ancoats* ☎ *0161/236–5444* ⊕ *www.sankeys.info.*

GAY CLUBS

Gay Village. The Gay Village, which came to television in the British series *Queer as Folk,* has stylish bars and cafés along the Rochdale Canal; Canal Street is its heart. The area is not only the center of Manchester's good-size gay scene but also the nightlife center for the young and trendy.

Lammars. With colored-glass chandeliers, a mirrored grand piano, and other kitschy furnishings, the popular Lammars has stand-up comedy and live music. It's open late on weekends with a DJ playing Motown, soul, and disco classics. ⊠ *57 Hilton St., Northern Quarter* ☎ *0161/237–9058* ⊕ *www.lammars.co.uk.*

LIVE MUSIC

O2 Apollo Manchester. Housed in an art deco structure, the 3,500-seat venue (known by locals as just 'the Apollo') showcases live rock and comedy acts before a mixed-age crowd. ⊠ *Stockport Rd., Ardwick Green* ☎ *0844/477–7677* ⊕ *www.o2apollomanchester.co.uk.*

Band on the Wall. A famous venue recently revamped, Band on the Wall has a reputation for hosting both established and pioneering music groups. Past performers include Joy Division, Simply Red, and Björk. ⊠ *25 Swan St., Northern Quarter* ☎ *0845/250–0500* ⊕ *www. bandonthewall.org.*

Manchester Arena. Major rock and pop stars appear at the Manchester Arena. ⊠ *21 Hunt's Bank, Hunt's Bank* ☎ *0844/847–8000 box office, 0161/950–5000 recorded information* ⊕ *www.men-arena.com.*

Roadhouse. An intimate venue for live bands, the Roadhouse hosts funk and indie nights. ⊠ *8 Newton St., City Centre* ☎ *0161/237–9789* ⊕ *www.theroadhouselive.co.uk.*

THE ARTS

PERFORMING ARTS VENUES

Bridgewater Hall. Dramatically modern Bridgewater Hall has concerts by Manchester's renowned Hallé Orchestra and hosts both classical music and a varied light-entertainment program. ⊠ *Lower Mosley St., Peter's Fields* ☎ *0161/907–9000* ⊕ *www.bridgewater-hall.co.uk.*

Opera House. The elegant Opera House is a venue for West End musicals, opera, and classical ballet. ⊠ *3 Quay St., City Centre* ☎ *0844/871-3018* ⊕ *www.manchesteroperahouse.org.uk.*

Palace Theatre. One of the city's largest houses, the Palace Theatre presents touring shows—plays, ballet, and opera. ✉ *Oxford St., City Centre* ☎ *0844/871–3019* ⊕ *www.atgtickets.com.*

Royal Northern College of Music. Classical and contemporary music concerts—everything from opera to jazz—are on the bill at the Royal Northern College of Music. ✉ *124 Oxford Rd., University Quarter* ☎ *0161/907–5200* ⊕ *www.rncm.ac.uk.*

THEATER

Royal Exchange Theatre. This futuristic glass-and-metal structure, cradling a theater-in-the-round space, serves as the city's main venue for innovative contemporary theater. ✉ *St. Ann's Sq., City Centre* ☎ *0161/833–9833* ⊕ *www.royalexchange.co.uk.*

SHOPPING

The city is nothing if not fashion conscious; take your pick from glitzy department stores, huge retail outlets, designer shops, and idiosyncratic boutiques. Famous names are centered on Exchange Square, Deansgate, and King Street; the Northern Quarter provides style for younger trendsetters.

Afflecks Palace. Young Mancunians head to Afflecks Palace for four floors of bohemian glam, ethnic crafts and jewelry, and innovative gift ideas. ✉ *52 Church St., Northern Quarter* ☎ *0161/839–0718* ⊕ *www.afflecks.com.*

Barton Arcade. Inside a lovely Victorian arcade, Barton Arcade has plenty of specialty shopping. ✉ *51–63 Deansgate, City Centre* ⊕ *www.bartonarcade.com.*

Harvey Nichols. An outpost of London's chic luxury department store, Harvey Nichols is packed with designer goods and has an excellent second-floor restaurant and brasserie. ✉ *21 New Cathedral St., City Centre* ☎ *0161/828–8888* ⊕ *www.harveynichols.com/manchester.*

Lowry Designer Outlet. With 80 stores, the Lowry Designer Outlet has good discounts on top brands at stores such as Nike and Karen Millen. ✉ *11 The Quays, Salford Quays* ☎ *0161/848–1850* ⊕ *www.lowryoutletmall.com.*

Manchester Craft and Design Centre. Two floors of workshop-cum-retail outlets are found at the Manchester Craft and Design Centre. ✉ *17 Oak St., Northern Quarter* ☎ *0161/832–4274* ⊕ *www.craftanddesign.com.*

Oldham Street. In the Northern Quarter, Oldham Street is littered with urban hip-hop boutiques and music shops.

Corn Exchange. A stylish mall in the Victorian Corn Exchange, the Triangle has more than 30 stores, including independent designer shops. ✉ *Longridge Pl., Millennium Quarter* ☎ *0161/834–8961* ⊕ *www.thetriangle.co.uk.*

FOOTBALL

Football (soccer in the United States) is *the* reigning passion in Manchester. Locals support the local club, Manchester City, and glory seekers come from afar to root for Manchester United, based in neighboring Trafford. Matches for both clubs are usually sold out months in advance, though you have more of a chance with Manchester City.

Manchester City. This football club, a favorite with locals, plays at the City of Manchester Stadium. ⊠ *Rowsley St., SportCity* ☎ *0161/444–1894* ⊕ *www.mcfc.co.uk.*

Manchester City Museum and Stadium Tours. Here you can see club memorabilia, visit the changing rooms, and go down the tunnel to pitch side. Excluding match days, there are three tours daily Monday through Saturday, and two on Sunday. ⊠ *Rowsley St., SportCity* ☎ *0161/444–1894* ⊕ *www.mcfc.co.uk* 🖃 *£13.*

Manchester United. One of the biggest clubs in Soccer (and the world's richest sports team), Manchester United has home matches at Old Trafford. ⊠ *Sir Matt Busby Way, Trafford Wharf* ☎ *0161/868–8000* ⊕ *www.manutd.com.*

Manchester United Museum and Tour. You can take a trip to the Theatre of Dreams at the Manchester United Museum and Tour, which tells the history of the football club. It's best to prebook the tour, which takes you behind the scenes, into the changing rooms and players' lounge, and down the tunnel. Take the tram to the Old Trafford stop and walk five minutes. ⊠ *Sir Matt Busby Way, Trafford Wharf* ☎ *0161/868–8000* ⊕ *www.manutd.com* 🖃 *£16* ⊙ *Daily 9:30–5, except game days.*

LIVERPOOL

A city lined with one of the most famous waterfronts in England, celebrated around the world as the birthplace of the Beatles, and still the place to catch that "Ferry 'Cross the Mersey," Liverpool reversed a downturn in its fortunes with developments in the late 1980s, such as the impressively refurbished Albert Dock area and Tate Liverpool. Its stint as the European Union's Capital of Culture in 2008, when £3 billion was invested in the city, acted as a catalyst for further regeneration. UNESCO named six historic areas in the city center a World Heritage Site, in recognition of the city's maritime and mercantile achievements during the height of Britain's global influence. This heritage, together with the renowned attractions and a legacy of cultural vibrancy, now draws in an ever-increasing number of visitors.

The 1960s produced Liverpool's most famous export: the Beatles. The group was one of hundreds that copied the rock and roll they heard from visiting American GIs and merchant seamen in the late 1950s, and one of many that played local venues such as the Cavern (demolished but rebuilt nearby). All four Beatles were born in Liverpool, but the group's success dates from the time they left for London. Nevertheless, the city has milked the group's Liverpool connections for all they're worth, with a multitude of local attractions such as Paul McCartney's and John Lennon's childhood homes.

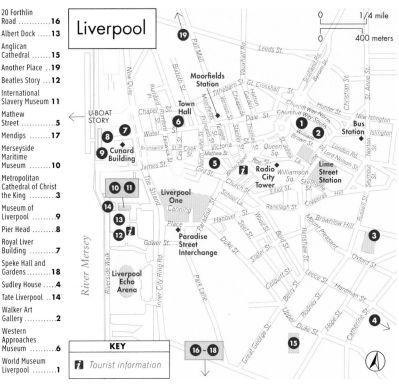

GETTING HERE AND AROUND

Liverpool John Lennon Airport, about 8 miles southeast of the city, receives mostly domestic and European flights. The Airlink 500 bus service runs to the city center every 30 minutes, and a taxi to the center of Liverpool costs around £15.

Long-distance National Express buses, including service from London, use the Norton Street Coach Station, and local buses depart from Sir Thomas Street, Queen Square, and the Paradise Street Interchange. Traveline has information on long-distance and local routes. Train service on Virgin Trains from London's Euston Station takes 2½ hours.

If you're walking (easier than driving), you'll find the downtown sights well signposted. Take care when crossing the busy inner ring road separating the Albert Dock from the rest of the city. The circular C4 bus ("Cumfybus") links Queen Square bus station with the Albert Dock (Gower Street stop).

TOURS

Blue Badge Guides can arrange dozens of different tours, which can be booked through the tourist office. Cavern City Tours (⊕ *www. cavernclub.org/beatles-tours*) offers a Beatles Magical Mystery Tour of Liverpool, departing from the Albert Dock visitor center. The two-hour bus tour, which costs £16, runs past Penny Lane, Strawberry Field, and other mop-top landmarks. Liverpool Beatles Tours has personalized tours of Beatles sites from two hours to all day. Yellow Duckmarine (⊕ *www.theyellowduckmarine.co.uk*) runs daily tours on amphibious vehicles from World War II. The trips, which cost between £12 and £16, depart from the Gower Street bus stop in Albert Dock.

ORIENTATION

Liverpool has a fairly compact center, and you can see most of the city highlights on foot. The skyline helps with orientation: the Radio City tower on **Queen Square** marks the center of the city. The Liver Birds, on top of the **Royal Liver Building,** signal the waterfront and River Mersey. North of the Radio City tower lie Lime Street Station and William Brown Street, a showcase boulevard of municipal buildings, including the outstanding **Walker Art Gallery** and **World Museum Liverpool.** The city's other museums, including the dazzling Museum of Liverpool and the **Beatles Story,** are concentrated westward on the waterfront in the **Albert Dock** area, a 20-minute walk or 5-minute bus ride away. **Hope Street,** to the east of the center, connects the city's two cathedrals, both easily recognizable on the skyline. On nearby Berry Street the red, green, and gold **Chinese Arch,** the largest multiple-span arch outside China, marks the small Chinatown area. ■ TIP➔ Allow extra time to tour the childhood homes of Paul McCartney and John Lennon, as they lie outside the city center.

ESSENTIALS

Bus Contacts Airlink 500 ☏ *0871/200–2233* ⊕ *www.arrivabus.co.uk.* **Traveline** ☏ *0871/200–2233* ⊕ *www.traveline.org.uk.*

Tour Contacts Blue Badge Guides ☏ *0794/093–3073 MerseyGuides Association* ⊕ *www.blue-badge-guides.com.* **Cavern City Tours** ✉ *Mathew St., City Centre* ☏ *0151/236–9091* ⊕ *www.cavernclub.org.* **Liverpool Beatles Tours** ✉ *25 Victoria St., City Centre* ☏ *0151/281–7738* ⊕ *www.beatlestours.co.uk.* **Yellow Duckmarine** ☏ *0151/708–7799* ⊕ *www.theyellowduckmarine.co.uk.*

Visitor Information Visit Liverpool ✉ *John Lennon Airport, South Terminal, Arrivals Hall* ☏ *0151/907–1057* ⊕ *www.visitliverpool.com* ✉ *Albert Dock, Anchor Courtyard, Waterfront* ☏ *0151/707–0729* ⊕ *www.visitliverpool.com.*

EXPLORING LIVERPOOL

TOP ATTRACTIONS

20 Forthlin Road. From 1955 to 1964, Paul McCartney lived with his family in this modest 1950s council house (a building rented from the local government). A number of the Beatles' songs, including "Love Me Do" and "When I'm Sixty-Four," were written here. The house is viewable only on a tour, leaving from the Jurys Inn next to Albert Dock or Speke Hall. ✉ *20 Forthlin Rd., Allerton* ☏ *0844/800–4791* ⊕ *www.nationaltrust.org.uk* 🎟 *£20, includes Mendips and Speke Hall gardens* ⊗ *Mid-Mar.–Oct., Wed.–Sun. and bank holiday Mon., Jury's Inn departure 10, 11, 2:15, Speke Hall departure 3; early Mar. and Nov., Wed.–Sun., Jury's Inn departure, 10, 11 and 2:15.*

Once a major shipping center and now transformed with museums, restaurants, and shops, the Albert Dock has views of the green dome of the Royal Liver Building.

Albert Dock. To understand the city's prosperous maritime past, head for waterfront Albert Dock, 7 acres of restored warehouses built in 1846. Named after Queen Victoria's consort, Prince Albert, the dock provided storage for silk, tea, and tobacco from the Far East until it was closed in 1972. The fine colonnaded brick warehouse buildings contain the **Merseyside Maritime Museum,** the **International Slavery Museum, Tate Liverpool,** and the **Beatles Story.** When weather allows, you can sit at an outdoor café overlooking the dock or take a boat trip through the docks and onto the river. For a bird's-eye view of the Albert Dock area, take the rotating Echo Wheel—Liverpool's 60-meter-tall version of the London Eye—which has 42 capsules seating up to eight passengers. ■ TIP→ Much of the pedestrian area of the Albert Dock and waterfront area is cobblestone, so wear comfortable shoes. ⊠ *Off Strand St. (A5036), Waterfront* ☎ *0151/707–0729 visitor center* ⊕ *www.albertdock.com.*

Beatles Story. You can follow in the footsteps of that most legendary of British bands at one of the more popular attractions in the Albert Dock complex. Entertaining scenes re-create stages in the Beatles' story (and their later careers as solo artists), from the enthusiastic early days in Germany and the Cavern Club to the White Room, where "Imagine" seems to emanate from softly billowing curtains. Artifacts include the glasses John Lennon wore when he composed "Imagine" and the blue felt bedspread used in the famous "Bed-in" in 1969. ■ TIP→ Avoid the crowds of July and August by visiting in the late afternoon. Purchase tickets, good for two days, online in advance. A shop sells every conceivable kind of souvenir a Fab Four fan could wish for. Included in the price is admission to a second location at the Mersey Ferries Terminal at Pier Head: *Fab4D*, a 3-D show with computer animation. Fans will Twist and Shout with delight. ⊠ *Albert Dock, Britannia Vaults, Waterfront* ☎ *0151/709–1963* ⊕ *www.beatlesstory.com* ✉ *£16* ۞ *Apr.–Oct., daily 9–7 (last admission 5); Nov.–Mar., daily 10–6 (last admission 5). Closed Dec. 25-26.*

International Slavery Museum. On the third floor of the Maritime Museum, this museum's three dynamic galleries recount the history of transatlantic slavery and trace its significance in contemporary society. "Life in West Africa" reproduces a Nigerian Igbo compound; life aboard slaveships bound for the Americas is revealed in the "Enslavement and the Middle Passage" section; and "Legacies of Slavery" examines the effect of the African diaspora on contemporary society. ⊠ *Albert Dock, Hartley Quay, off A5036, Waterfront* ☎ *0151/478–4499* ⊕ *www. liverpoolmuseums.org.uk* ✉ *Free* ۞ *Daily 10–5.*

Mendips. The National Trust maintains the 1930s middle-class, semidetached house that was the home of John Lennon from 1946 to 1963—a must-see for Beatles pilgrims. After his parents separated, John joined his aunt Mimi here; she gave him his first guitar but banished him to the porch, saying, "The guitar's all very well, John, but you'll never make a living out of it." The house can be seen only on a tour, leaving from the Jury's Inn next to Albert Dock (mornings) or Speke Hall (afternoons). ⊠ *251 Menlove Ave., Woolton* ☎ *0844/800–4791* ⊕ *www. nationaltrust.org.uk* ✉ *£20, includes 20 Forthlin Rd. and Speke Hall gardens* ۞ *Mid-Mar.–Oct., Wed.–Sun. and bank holiday Mon., Jury's Inn departure 10, 11, 2:15, Speke Hall departure 3; early Mar. and Nov., Wed.–Sun., Jury's Inn departure, 10, 11, and 2:15.*

FAMILY
Fodor's Choice
★

Merseyside Maritime Museum. Part of the Albert Dock complex, this is a wonderful place to explore the role of the sea in the life of the city. The museum captures the triumphs and tragedies of Liverpool's seafaring history over five floors. Besides exhibits of maritime paintings, models, ceramics, and ships in bottles, the main museum brings to life the ill-fated stories of the *Titanic* and *Lusitania*, the Battle of the Atlantic, and the city's role during World War II. The basement is home to the Customs and Excise National Museum, which explores the heroes and villains of the world of smuggling, together with the story of mass emigration from the port in the 19th century. In summer full-size vessels are on display. ⊠ *Albert Dock, Hartley Quay, off A5036, Waterfront* ☎ *0151/478–4499* ⊕ *www.liverpoolmuseums.org.uk* ✉ *Free* ۞ *Daily 10–5.*

Pier Head. Here you can take a ferry across the River Mersey to Birkenhead and Seacombe. Mersey Ferries depart regularly and offer fine views of the city—a journey celebrated in "Ferry 'Cross the Mersey," Gerry and the Pacemakers' 1964 hit song. It was from Pier Head that 9 million British, Irish, and other European emigrants set sail between 1830 and 1930 for new lives in North America, Australia, and Africa. ■ TIP➔ The ferry terminal is home to the Beatles Story, so you might want to make this the last stop on your Beatles tour. ⊠ *Pier Head Ferry Terminal, off A5036, Waterfront* ☎ *0151/330–1444* ⊕ *www.merseyferries.co.uk* ✉ *£4 round-trip, cruises £8; with U-Boat Story £12.* ۞ *Ferries every 20 mins weekdays 7:20–9:40 and 4:10–7:05; cruises hourly weekdays 10–3, weekends 10–6.*

CLOSE UP

Liverpool's History: Shipping Center

Liverpool, on the east bank of the Mersey River estuary, at the point where it merges with the Irish Sea, developed from the 17th century through the slave trade. It became Britain's leading port for ferrying Africans to North America and for handling sugar, tobacco, rum, and cotton, which began to dominate the local economy after the abolition of the slave trade in 1807.

Because of its proximity to Ireland, the city was also the first port of call for those fleeing famine, poverty, and persecution in that country. Similarly, Liverpool was often the last British port of call for thousands of mostly Jewish refugees fleeing Eastern Europe.

Many of the best-known liner companies were based in Liverpool, including Cunard and White Star, whose best-known vessel, the *Titanic*, was registered in Liverpool. The city was dealt an economic blow in 1894 with the opening of the Manchester Ship Canal, which allowed traders to bypass Liverpool and head to Manchester, 35 miles east. Britain's entry into the European Common Market saw more trade move from the west coast to the east, and the postwar growth of air travel diverted passengers from the sea. But as a sign of the city's revival, oceangoing liners returned to the city in 2008 after the building of a new cruise liner terminal at the Pier Head.

Royal Liver Building. Best seen from the ferry, the 322-foot-tall Royal Liver (pronounced *lie-ver*) Building with its twin towers is topped by two 18-foot-high copper birds. They represent the mythical Liver Birds, the town symbol; local legend has it that if they fly away, Liverpool will cease to exist. For decades Liverpudlians looked to the Royal Liver Society for assistance—it was originally a burial club to which families paid contributions to ensure a decent send-off. ⊠ *Water St., off A5036, Waterfront.*

Fodor's Choice ★ **Tate Liverpool.** A handsome conversion of Albert Dock warehouses by the late James Stirling, one of Britain's leading 20th-century architects, hosts an offshoot of the London-based art galleries of the same name. There is no permanent collection; challenging exhibitions of modern art change every couple of months. A free introductory tour begins daily at 2:40. There's an excellent shop, a children's play area, and a dockside café-restaurant. ⊠ *Albert Dock, The Colonnades, Waterfront* ☏ *0151/702–7400* ⊕ *www.tate.org.uk* 🔁 *Free; charges for special exhibitions vary* ☉ *Apr.–Sept., daily 10–5:50; Oct.–Mar., Tues.–Sun. 10–5:50; last admission 5.*

Fodor's Choice ★ **Walker Art Gallery.** With a superb display of British art and some outstanding Italian and Flemish works, the Walker maintains its reputation as one of the best British art collections outside London. Don't miss the unrivaled collection of paintings by 18th-century Liverpudlian equestrian artist George Stubbs, and works by J.M.W. Turner, John Constable, Sir Edwin Henry Landseer, and the Pre-Raphaelites. Modern artists are included, too; on display is one of David Hockney's typically Californian pool scenes. Other excellent exhibits showcase china, silver, and furniture that once adorned the mansions of Liverpool's industrial barons. The Tea Room holds center stage in the airy museum lobby. ⊠ *William Brown St., City Centre* ☎ *0151/478–4199* ⊕ *www. liverpoolmuseums.org.uk* ⊠ *Free* ⊙ *Daily 10–5.*

FAMILY **World Museum Liverpool.** You can travel from the prehistoric to the space age through stunning displays in these state-of-the-art galleries. Ethnology, the natural and physical sciences, and archaeology all get their due on five floors. Highlights include a collection of Egyptian mummies in the Ancient World Gallery, and a beautiful assemblage of Javanese shadow puppets in the World Culture Gallery. There's plenty to keep kids amused, from monster bugs in the Bug House, to life-size casts of prehistoric monsters in the Dinosaurs Gallery. ⊠ *William Brown St., City Centre* ☎ *0151/478–4393* ⊕ *www.liverpoolmuseums.org.uk* ⊠ *Free* ⊙ *Daily 10–5.*

WORTH NOTING

Anglican Cathedral. The largest church in northern Britain overlooks the city and the River Mersey. Built of local sandstone, the Gothic-style cathedral was begun in 1903 by architect Giles Gilbert Scott; it was finally finished in 1978. A custom-built theater shows "the Great Space," a 10-minute panoramic film on the history of the Cathedral. The 331-foot-tall tower is a popular climb; two elevators and 108 steps take you to breathtaking views. From February to October you can book special "Twlight Tower" tickets, allowing you a spectacular view of sunset over the city, as seen from the top. ⊠ *St. James Mount, City Centre* ☎ *0151/709–6271* ⊕ *www.liverpoolcathedral.org.uk* ⊠ *£3 suggested donation; £5 combined ticket for film, tower, and audio tour; Twlight Tower £5 (booking essential)* ⊙ *Daily 8–6. Tower weekdays 10–4:30, Sat. 9–4:30, Sun. around 11:45–3:30. Twlight Tower times according to sunset.*

Another Place. A hundred naked, life-size, cast-iron figures by sculptor Antony Gormley stand proudly on the 2 miles of foreshore at Crosby Beach, weathered by sand and sea. Unlike most other statues, you are permitted to interact with these and even clothe them as you wish. Check tide times before you go and be aware that it's not safe to walk out to the farthest figures. The site is 6 miles north of downtown Liverpool; to get here, take the Merseyrail train to Waterloo from Moorfields Station. A taxi will cost around £20. ⊠ *Crosby Beach, Mariners Rd., Crosby Beach* ☎ *01704/533333 for tide times* ⊕ *www.visitsouthport. com* ⊠ *Free.*

Mathew Street. It was at the Cavern on this street that Brian Epstein, the Beatles' manager, first heard the group in 1961. The Cavern had opened at No. 10 as a jazz venue in 1957, but beat groups, of whom the Beatles were clearly the most talented, had taken it over. Epstein became their manager a few months after first visiting the club, and within two years the group was the most talked-about phenomenon in music. The club was demolished in 1973; it was rebuilt a few yards from the original site. At No. 5 is the Cavern Pub, opened in 1994, with Beatles memorabilia and plenty of nostalgia. ■ TIP➔ **At No. 31, check out the well-stocked Beatles Shop.**

QUICK
BITES

Delifonseca. Not far from Mathew Street, Delifonseca offers reviving coffee and cake, as well as excellent sandwiches and salads, English breakfasts, and Sunday roasts. You could also stock up on munchies from the capacious downstairs deli. ⊠ *12 Stanley St., City Centre* ☏ *0151/255–0808* ⊕ *www.delifonseca.co.uk.*

Metropolitan Cathedral of Christ the King. Consecrated in 1967, this Roman Catholic cathedral is a modernistic, funnel-like structure of concrete, stone, and mosaic, topped with a glass lantern. Long, narrow, blue-glass windows separate chapels, each with modern works of art. An earlier design by classically inspired architect Edwin Lutyens was abandoned when World War II began (the current design is by Frederick Gibberd), but you can still take a look at Lutyen's vast brick-and-granite crypt and barrel-vaulted ceilings. ⊠ *Mount Pleasant, City Centre* ☏ *0151/709– 9222* ⊕ *www.liverpoolmetrocathedral.org.uk* 🎫 *£2.50 suggested donation; £3 Crypt and Treasury* ⊗ *Apr.–Oct., daily 7:30–6; Nov.–Mar., Mon.–Sat 7:30–6, Sun. 7:30–5.*

Museum of Liverpool. Clad in Jura stone and shaped like a ship, with a spectacular spiral staircase running from the atrium to each floor, this ambitious museum opened in 2011 on the waterfront at Pier Head. It tells the story of the city from its earliest settlement in the Neolithic Age. Highlights include an extraordinary 3-D map with different perspectives of the city as you move around it, an engrossing film about soccer culture, and an interactive time line peeling away layers of Liverpool's history. ⊠ *Pier Head, Waterfront* ☏ *0151/478–4545* ⊕ *www. liverpoolmuseums.org.uk* 🎫 *Free* ⊗ *Daily 10–5.*

Speke Hall and Gardens. This black-and-white mansion 6 miles from downtown Liverpool is one of the best examples of half-timbering in Britain. Built around a cobbled courtyard, the great hall dates to 1490; an elaborate western bay with a vast chimneypiece was added in 1560. The house, owned by the National Trust, was heavily restored in the 19th century, though a Tudor priest hole and Jacobean plasterwork remain intact. The Victorian landscaped gardens enjoy views over the Mersey toward North Wales. Speke Hall is on the east side of the airport; the Airlink 500 bus drops you a pleasant 10-minute walk away. ⊠ *The Walk, Speke* ☏ *0151/427–7231* ⊕ *www.nationaltrust. org.uk* 🎫 *£8.60; gardens only £5.25* ⊗ *Mid-Mar.–Oct., Wed.–Sun. and bank holiday Mon. 11–5; Nov.–early Dec., weekends 11–4:30; entry to house by guided tour only until 12:30; last admission 30 mins before closing.*

Sudley House. This handsome 19th-century mansion next to Liverpool John Moore's University contains the extraordinary art collection amassed by shipping magnate George Holt (1825–96). Paintings on display include works by J.M.W. Turner, Thomas Gainsborough, Dante Gabriel Rossetti, and Joshua Reynolds. The interior of the building itself is an immaculately maintained example of high Victorian domestic style. Permanent displays around the house include a collection of historic children's toys and women's fashion from the 18th century to the present day. Sudley House is about 5 miles southeast of the city center.

9

To drive, take the A5036 along the river heading south; alternatively, Bus No. 61 to Elmswood Road, 80 or 80A to Rose Lane, or 82 to Aigburth Road. ⊠ *Mossley Hill Rd., Aigburth* ☏ *0151/478–4016* ⊕ *www. liverpoolmuseums.org.uk* 🎟 *Free* ⊙ *Daily 10–5.*

U-Boat Story. Explore the claustrophobic world of life onboard a German World War II submarine, one of only four left in the world. Sunk in 1945 by RAF depth charges, U-534 was hauled off the sea bed in 1993. Now she's docked at Birkenhead, beside the Woodside Ferry Terminal. As well as listening to interviews with crew members, you can decode enemy messages on an Enigma machine and take charge of a model submarine. There are free guided tours each day at 2. ⊠ *Woodside Ferry Terminal, off A41, Birkenhead* ☏ *0151/300–1000* ⊕ *www.u-boatstory. co.uk* 🎟 *£6; combined ticket with River Cruise £12* ⊙ *Daily 10–5:30; last admission 5.*

Western Approaches: the Liverpool War Museum. Winston Churchill said that the threat of a U-Boat attack from the Atlantic was his greatest fear during World War II. At this evocative war museum you can explore the warren of rooms under the city streets that served the top-secret "Western Approaches Command HQ" frp, 1941–45. The lofty Operations Room, full of the state-of-the-art technology of the time, is especially interesting. ⊠ *1–3 Rumford St., off Chapel St., City Centre* ☏ *0151/227–2008* ⊕ *www.liverpoolwarmuseum.co.uk* 🎟 *£6* ⊙ *Mar.–Oct., Mon.–Thurs. and Sat. 10:30–4:30; last admission 1 hr before closing.*

WHERE TO EAT

$$$
MODERN BRITISH

✕ **60 Hope Street.** The combination of a ground-floor restaurant and a more informal basement bistro makes this a popular choice. A light, polished-wood floor and blue-and-cream walls help create an uncluttered backdrop for updated British dishes; baked lemon sole with saffron potatoes and crispy capers, for example, or braised ox cheek with celeriac puree and wood blewitts. For dessert you could try a rich chocolate fondant, or embrace the slightly mischevous spirit of the place with a deep-fried jam sandwich. 💲 *Average main: £21* ⊠ *60 Hope St., City Centre* ☏ *0151/707–6060* ⊕ *www.60hopestreet.com* ⊙ *Closed Sun. No lunch Sat. in restaurant.*

$
JAPANESE

✕ **Etsu.** Minimalist decor, a friendly staff, and a polished Japanese menu greet you at this inconspicuous street-corner locale just off the Strand. Along with the traditional sushi, noodle soups, and tempuras, all served with the freshest ingredients, are some witty East-meets-West creations, including sushi pizzas and tuna burgers made of rice blocks. The bento box meals provide great value at lunchtime in between museum visits. Make sure you try a *shochu*, a stronger version of sake, served neat or with oolong tea. 💲 *Average main: £14* ⊠ *25 The Strand, entrance on Brunswick St., City Centre* ☏ *0151/236–7530* ⊕ *www.etsu-restaurant. co.uk* ⊙ *Closed Mon. No lunch Wed. and weekends.*

$
ASIAN

✕ **Matou.** Expansive views of the historic waterfront are joined by the scent of Eastern spices at this popular spot on the second floor of the Mersey Ferry Terminal. The menu sticks to pan-Asian classics, such as Thai green curry, crispy aromatic lamb, and stir-fried beef in a black-bean sauce. Contemporary dark-wood furnishings sit beside huge slanting windows in the dining room. $ *Average main: £11* ⊠ *Mersey Ferry Terminal, Georges Parade, Pier Head* ☎ *0151/236–2928* ⊕ *www.matou.co.uk.*

$$$

MODERN
EUROPEAN

Fodor's Choice
★

✕ **Panoramic 34.** Watch the city lights glitter beyond the sweeping windows of this 34th-floor restaurant overlooking the waterfront. The boundless views and sleek decor are matched by head chef Parth Bhatt's voguish European menu. Fillet of halibut might be stewed with chorizo and clams; lamb could appear with sweetbreads, dauphinoise potatoes, and almond puree. Even if you're dining elsewhere, enjoy a cocktail here, especially at sunset. $ *Average main: £20* ⊠ *West Tower, Brook St., 34th fl., Waterfront* ☎ *0151/236–5534* ⊕ *www.panoramicliverpool. com* ☻ *Closed Mon.*

$$

INTERNATIONAL

✕ **The Restaurant Bar and Grill.** An alluring cocktail bar beneath a glass-domed ceiling provides a glitzy habitat for local celebrities and high-fliers in this former banking house in the commercial district. Served in a dining room lined with wine racks and coffee-color leather seating, you can choose from international favorites, from Thai curries to Indian tandoori dishes, or perhaps just a simple rib-eye steak. Desserts include a delicious range of homemade sorbets. $ *Average main: £18* ⊠ *Halifax House, Brunswick St., City Centre* ☎ *0151/236–6703* ⊕ *www.therestaurantbarandgrill.co.uk.*

$$

BRITISH

✕ **Side Door.** You'll often find couples enjoying a meal before a play or concert at this intimate and unpretentious bistro. The menu changes every week, but there are always plenty of fish choices, such as cod fillet with olive mash and *caponata*—a Sicilian eggplant and caper sauce—or brown trout with roast pepper and courgette. Sticky toffee pudding is a don't-miss dessert. The service is attentive, and the early evening fixed-price meals are a good value. $ *Average main: £16* ⊠ *29A Hope St., City Centre* ☎ *0151/707–7888* ⊕ *www.thesidedoor.co.uk* ☻ *Closed Sun.*

$

CAFÉ

✕ **Tate Café.** The Tate Liverpool's café is a winner for daytime sustenance whenever you're visiting the Albert Dock area—especially on warm summer days when you can request dockside seating. Choose from among the salads and open sandwiches including steak with Wirral watercress, as well as main dishes such as spinach and feta pattie with butterbean and chickpea stew. Fruit scones with jam and cream also make an appearance. $ *Average main: £8* ⊠ *Albert Dock, The Colonnades, Waterfront* ☎ *0151/702–7581* ⊕ *www.tate.org.uk* ☻ *Closed Mon. in winter. No dinner.*

WHERE TO STAY

For expanded hotel reviews, visit Fodors.com.

$

HOTEL

🏨 **Crowne Plaza Liverpool City Centre.** Many of the city's main sights are at the doorstep of this handsome brick building, located on the waterfront next to the Royal Liver Building. **Pros:** on waterfront; friendly staff; plenty of activities. **Cons:** chain-hotel furnishings; no Wi-Fi in rooms. $ *Rooms from: £84* ⊠ *St. Nicholas Pl., off A5036, Waterfront* ☎ *0151/243–8000* ⊕ *www.cpliverpool.com* ⇆ *159 rooms* ⍗ *Multiple meal plans.*

$$ HOTEL **Hard Day's Night Hotel.** A marble-columned former office block on the corner of Mathew Street has been transformed into a giant homage in hotel form to Liverpool's most famous musical export. **Pros:** welcoming staff; sophisticated rooms; close to Beatles attractions. **Cons:** can't escape the gimmicky feel; street noise can be very loud in some rooms; no parking. [$] *Rooms from: £100* ✉ *Central Bldgs., N. John St., City Centre* ☎ *0151/236–1964* 🌐 *www.harddaysnighthotel.com* 🛏 *108 rooms, 2 suites* 🍴 *No meals.*

$ HOTEL **Hope Street Hotel.** Liverpool's first boutique hotel is in a converted carriage warehouse built in the style of a Venetian palazzo. **Pros:** beautiful design; plenty of space; attentive staff. **Cons:** rooms face a busy street. [$] *Rooms from: £94* ✉ *40 Hope St., City Centre* ☎ *0151/709–3000* 🌐 *www.hopestreethotel.co.uk* 🛏 *89 rooms* 🍴 *No meals.*

$ HOTEL **Hotel Indigo.** Combining the designer feel of a boutique hotel with the facilities of an established chain, Hotel Indigo is a slick option in the commercial district. **Pros:** talked-about restaurant; up-to-the-minute design; good location near Pier Head. **Cons:** not the most spacious rooms. [$] *Rooms from: £75* ✉ *10 Chapel St., City Centre* ☎ *0151/559–0111* 🌐 *www.hotelindigoliverpool.co.uk* 🛏 *151 rooms* 🍴 *Multiple meal plans.*

$ HOTEL **Malmaison.** The only purpose-built hotel in this chic chain—most are in renovated older buildings—the Malmaison combines glamourous funishings with sleek industrial design and a great sense of space. **Pros:** buzzy atmosphere; rich decor. **Cons:** dark guest rooms; no parking; views to the back are disappointing. [$] *Rooms from: £69* ✉ *Princes Dock, Waterfront* ☎ *0151/229–5000* 🌐 *www.malmaison.com* 🛏 *128 rooms, 2 suites* 🍴 *Multiple meal plans.*

$ RENTAL **Staybridge Apartments.** These up-to-the-minute and well-equipped apartments close to the Liverpool Echo Arena make for a great stay on the waterfront. **Pros:** upbeat atmosphere; complimentary receptions on weekday evenings; public spaces for socializing. **Cons:** limited parking; no nice views. [$] *Rooms from: £77* ✉ *21 Keel Wharf, Waterfront* ☎ *0151/703–9700 front desk, 0871/423–4942 central reservations* 🌐 *www.staybridge.co.uk* 🛏 *132 apartments* 🍴 *Breakfast.*

NIGHTLIFE AND THE ARTS

NIGHTLIFE

The many bars, clubs, and pubs of Liverpool are an experience in themselves, from the trendy to the traditional.

Fodor's Choice ★ **Alma de Cuba.** A church transformed into a luxurious bar, Alma de Cuba uses a huge mirrored altar and hundreds of dripping candles to great effect. ✉ *Seel St., City Centre* ☎ *0151/702–7394* 🌐 *www.alma-de-cuba.com.*

Cavern Club. Despite not being the original venue—that was demolished years ago—the Cavern Club still draws in rock and roll fans with its Beatles tribute bands and other live acts on weekends. ✉ *8–10 Mathew St., City Centre* ☎ *0151/236–1965* 🌐 *www.cavernclub.org.*

Liverpool claims its share of stylish bars and restaurants such as Alma de Cuba, housed in a converted church.

Heebie Jeebies. A frequently changing roster of local indie bands and talented DJs makes this two-story club a top option with the young alternative crowd. ✉ *80–82 Seel St., City Centre* ☎ *0151/709–3678.*

Philharmonic Dining Rooms. Opposite Philharmonic Hall, the Philharmonic (commonly know as "The Phil") is a Victorian-era extravaganza decorated in rich woods and colorful marble. Choose a comfy spot in one of the dining rooms and order one of the award-winning ales and perhaps such pub grub as hand-battered fish-and-chips, which here is raised to a whole new level. ✉ *36 Hope St., City Centre* ☎ *0151/707– 2837* ⊕ *www.nicholsonspubs.co.uk.*

Ye Cracke. One of the city's oldest pubs, Ye Cracke was much visited by John Lennon and his first wife, Cynthia, when they were at art school together. ✉ *13 Rice St., off Hope St., City Centre* ☎ *0151/709–4171.*

THE ARTS

FILM
FACT Centre. Part of the Foundation for Art and Creative Technology, this theater shows art-house and independent films on three screens. Galleries display experimental film, video, and new media. ✉ *88 Wood St., City Centre* ☎ *0151/707–4464 information, 0871/902–5737 cinema bookings* ⊕ *www.fact.co.uk.*

PERFORMING ARTS VENUES
Bluecoat. Contemporary visual and performing arts come together at the Bluecoat. ✉ *School La., City Centre* ☎ *0151/702–5324* ⊕ *www. thebluecoat.org.uk.*

Liverpool Empire. This theater presents major ballet, opera, drama, and musical performances. ✉ *Lime St., City Centre* ☎ *0844/847–3017* ⊕ *www.liverpoolempire.org.uk.*

Philharmonic Hall. The well-regarded Royal Liverpool Philharmonic Orchestra plays its concert season at Philharmonic Hall. The venue also hosts contemporary music, jazz, and world concerts, and shows classic films. ✉ *Hope St., City Centre* ☎ *0151/709–3789* ⊕ *www.liverpoolphil.com.*

THEATER

Everyman Theatre. The Everyman Theatre focuses on works by British playwrights as well as experimental productions from around the world. Productions here frequently attract national attention. At this writing a two-year renovation was scheduled to be completed by the end of 2013. A second theater, the Everyman Playhouse in Williamson Square, stages more mainstream productions. ✉ *5–9 Hope St., City Centre* ☎ *0151/709–4776 box office (both theaters).*

SHOPPING

Circa 1900. This shop specializes in authentic art nouveau and art deco pieces, from ceramics and glass to furniture, in an upmarket marble shopping arcade within the historic India Buildings. ✉ *Holts Arcade, Water St., City Centre* ☎ *0151/236–1282* ⊕ *www.classicartdeco.co.uk.*

The Beatles Shop. All the mop-top knickknacks of your dreams are available at this hugely popular, official Beatles souvenir shop. ✉ *31 Mathew St., City Centre* ☎ *0151/236–8066* ⊕ *www.thebeatleshop.co.uk.*

Liverpool One. The city's largest shopping complex, Liverpool One has more than 160 stores, including John Lewis. ✉ *Paradise St., City Centre* ☎ *0151/232–3100* ⊕ *www.liverpool-one.com.*

Metquarter. With more than 40 stores, Metquarter is the place for upmarket boutiques, designer names, and the latest fashions. ✉ *35 Whitechapel, City Centre* ☎ *0151/224–2390* ⊕ *www.metquarter.com.*

SPORTS AND THE OUTDOORS

FOOTBALL

Football matches are played on weekends and, increasingly, weekdays. Tickets for Liverpool are sold out months in advance, but you should have more luck with Everton.

Everton Football Club. One of Liverpool's two great football teams, Everton plays at Goodison Park. ✉ *Goodison Park, Goodison Rd.* ☎ *0871/663–1878* ⊕ *www.evertonfc.com.*

Liverpool Football Club. One of England's top teams, Liverpool plays at Anfield, 2 miles north of the city center. ✉ *Anfield Rd., Anfield* ☎ *0844/844–0844* ⊕ *www.liverpoolfc.tv.*

Liverpool Museum and Stadium Tour. This trip into the dressing rooms and down the tunnel of Anfield Football Stadium gives you a sense of match day for the Liverpool Football Club. There are no tours on days that games are scheduled. ✉ *Anfield Rd., Anfield* ☎ *0151/260–6677* ⊕ *www.liverpoolfc.tv* 💷 *£16* ⊙ *Daily 10–3.*

HORSE RACING

Aintree Racecourse. Britain's most famous horse race, the Grand National Steeplechase, has been run at Liverpool's Aintree Racecourse almost every year since 1839. The race is held in March or April; book well ahead. Admission on most race days is around £20. ⌧ *Ormskirk Rd., Aintree* ☏ *0844/579–3001* ⊕ *www.aintree.co.uk.*

THE PEAK DISTRICT

Heading southeast, away from the urban congestion of Manchester and Liverpool, it's not far to the southernmost contortions of the Pennine Hills. Here, about an hour from Manchester, sheltered in a great natural bowl, is the spa town of Buxton: at an elevation of more than 1,000 feet, it's the second-highest town in England. Buxton makes a convenient base for exploring the 540 square miles of the Peak District, Britain's oldest—and, its fans say, most beautiful—national park. About 38,000 people live in the towns throughout the park.

"Peak" is perhaps misleading; despite being a hilly area, it contains only gentle rises that don't reach much higher than 2,000 feet. Yet a trip around destinations such as Bakewell, Matlock, Castleton, and Edale, and the grand estates of Chatsworth House, Haddon Hall, and Hardwick Hall involves negotiating fairly perilous country roads, each of which repays the effort with enchanting views. Outdoor activities are popular in the Peaks, particularly caving (or "potholing"), walking, and hiking. Bring all-weather clothing and waterproof shoes.

BUXTON

25 miles southeast of Manchester.

Buxton makes a good base for Peak District excursions, but it has its own attractions as well. The town's spa days left a notable legacy of 18th- and 19th-century buildings, parks, and open spaces that give the town an air of faded grandeur. The Romans arrived in AD 79 and named Buxton Aquae Arnemetiae, loosely translated as "Waters of the Goddess of the Grove." The mineral springs, which emerge from 3,500 to 5,000 feet below ground at a constant 82°F, were believed to cure assorted ailments; in the 18th century the town became established as a popular spa, a minor rival to Bath. You can still drink water from the ancient St. Anne's Well, and it's also sold throughout Britain.

GETTING HERE AND AROUND

Both the National Express and TransPeak bus services from Manchester stop at Buxton. There are departures every two to three hours from Manchester's Chorlton Street Bus Station. If you're driving from Manchester, take A6 southeast to Buxton. The journey takes one hour. The hourly train from Manchester to Buxton takes an hour.

ESSENTIALS

Visitor Information Buxton Tourist Information Centre ⌧ *Pavilion Gardens, St. John's Rd.* ☏ *01298/25106* ⊕ *www.visitpeakdistrict.com.*

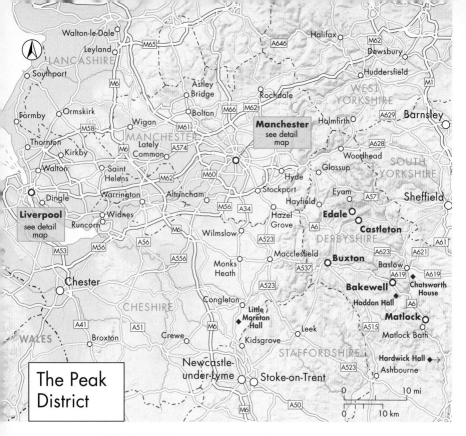

The Peak District

EXPLORING

TOP ATTRACTIONS

The Crescent. Almost all out-of-town roads lead toward this central green with its curving semicircle of buildings. The Georgian-era Crescent, with its arches, colonnades, and 378 windows, was built in 1780 by fashionable architect John Carr for the fifth duke of Devonshire (of nearby Chatsworth House). The thermal baths at the end of the Crescent now house a shopping center. It's near where Terrace Road meets St. Johns Road. ⊠ *Off Terrace Rd.*

OFF THE
BEATEN
PATH

Little Moreton Hall. In some ways the epitome of "magpie" black-and-white half-timber buildings, Little Moreton Hall was built by the Moreton family between 1450 and 1580. The exterior is covered with an intricate plethora of zigzags, crosses, and lozenge shapes, crafted of timber and daub. The long gallery and colorful Tudor-era wall paintings are spectacular. Costumed guides add a little liveliness for kids. There's also a tearoom serving sandwiches, cakes, and light meals. Little Moreton Hall lies to the west of the Peak District; to get here from Liverpool, take the M6 to the A534 east to Congleton. The house is 20 miles southwest of Buxton. ⊠ *A34, Congleton* ☎ *01260/272018* ⊕ *www.nationaltrust. org.uk* ✉ *£7.50* ⊘ *Early–mid-Mar., Nov. and Dec., weekends 11–4; late Mar.–Oct., Wed.–Sun. 11–5.*

Pavilion Gardens. Surrounded by 25 acres of pretty gardens, the Pavilion, with its ornate iron-and-glass roof, was originally a concert hall and ballroom. Erected in the 1870s, it remains a lively place that hosts local events, and also has a plant-filled conservatory, two cafés, and a restaurant. The Pavilion is adjacent to the Crescent and the Slopes on the west; the tourist office is here, too, with a food-and-crafts shop. ✉ *St. John's Rd.* ☎ *01298/23114* 🌐 *www.paviliongardens.co.uk.*

WORTH NOTING

Buxton Museum and Art Gallery. On the eastern side of the Slopes, this museum contains a collection of Blue John stone, a semiprecious mineral found only in the Peak District, as well as displays of local archaeological finds and pieces made from Derbyshire black marble. There's also a small art gallery. ✉ *Terrace Rd.* ☎ *01629/533540* 🌐 *www.derbyshire.gov.uk/leisure/buxton_museum* 🎟 *Free* 🕒 *Oct.–Mar., Tues.–Fri. 9:30–5:30, Sat. 9:30–5; Apr.–Sept., Tues.–Fri. 9:30–5:30, Sat. 9:30–5, Sun. 10:30–5.*

Buxton Opera House. Built in 1903, the opera house is one of the most architecturally exuberant structures in town. Its marble bulk, bedecked with carved cupids, is even more impressive inside. The varied program of events includes classical music recitals, jazz, ballet, theater, and standup comedy. ✉ *Water St.* ☎ *0845/127–2190* 🌐 *www.buxtonoperahouse.org.uk.*

Poole's Cavern. The Peak District's extraordinary geology can be seen up close at this large limestone cave far beneath the 100 wooded acres of Buxton Country Park. The cave was inhabited in prehistoric times and contains, in addition to the standard stalactites and stalagmites, the source of the River Wye, which flows through Buxton. Admission includes a guided tour lasting nearly an hour. ✉ *Green La.* ☎ *01298/26978* 🌐 *www.poolescavern.co.uk* 🎟 *£8.80* 🕒 *Mar.–Oct., daily 9:30–5 (tours every 20 mins, last tour 4:30); Nov.–Feb., weekends 10–4 (tours every 20 mins, last tour 3:30), weekends tours at 10:30, 12:30, and 2:30 only.*

9

WHERE TO EAT

$$ MODERN BRITISH 🍴 **Columbine.** The husband-and-wife team behind Columbine are known for their fine use of local ingredients and flavors, from pork tenderloin with a Derby sage cheese glaze, to duck braised in port with wild mushrooms. The cozy venue, with upstairs and downstairs seating, is a good spot for pre- and posttheater meals. [$] *Average main: £16* ✉ *7 Hall Bank* ☎ *01298/78752* 🌐 *www.columbinerestaurant.co.uk* 🕒 *Closed Sun. Closed Tues. Nov.–Apr. No lunch Aug.–June.*

WHERE TO STAY

For expanded hotel reviews, visit Fodors.com.

$ B&B/INN 🏨 **Buxton Victorian Guesthouse.** One of a group of row houses built by the duke of Devonshire in 1860, this handsomely decorated house stands in the center of Buxton. **Pros:** peaceful location on Pavilion Gardens; free Wi-Fi; delightful hosts. **Cons:** many stairs to climb. [$] *Rooms from: £94* ✉ *3A Broad Walk* ☎ *01298/78759* 🌐 *www.buxtonvictorian.co.uk* 🛏 *6 rooms, 1 suite* 🍽 *Breakfast.*

$$
B&B/INN
 Old Hall. In a refurbished 16th-century building rumored to have once accommodated Mary Queen of Scots, this hotel overlooks the ornate Buxton Opera House. **Pros:** unpretentious atmosphere; good dining choices. **Cons:** conventional furnishings; no private parking. $ *Rooms from: £100* ⊠ *The Square* ☎ *01298/22841* ⊕ *www.oldhallhotelbuxton. co.uk* ⤴ *38 rooms* ⦿| *Breakfast.*

$
B&B/INN
 Stoneridge. Built of stone, this Edwardian B&B has been richly restored. **Pros:** excellent food choices; secluded and tranquil garden. **Cons:** no tubs in bathrooms; two-night minimum at weekends. $ *Rooms from: £75* ⊠ *9 Park Rd.* ☎ *01298/26120* ⊕ *www.stoneridge. co.uk* ⤴ *4 rooms* ⊟ *No credit cards* ⦿| *Breakfast.*

NIGHTLIFE AND THE ARTS

Buxton Festival. The renowned Buxton Festival, held for two weeks during mid-July each year, includes opera, drama, and concerts. ⊠ *The Square* ☎ *0845/127–2190 box office* ⊕ *www.buxtonfestival.co.uk.*

SHOPPING

Buxton has many kinds of stores, especially around Spring Gardens, the main shopping street.

Cavendish Arcade. Stores in the beautifully tiled Cavendish Arcade, on the site of the old thermal baths, sell antiques, jewelry, fashions, and leather goods in stylish surroundings. ⊠ *The Crescent.*

EN ROUTE
As you head southeast from Buxton on the A6, you pass through the spectacular valleys of Ashwood Dale, Wyedale, and Monsal Dale before reaching Bakewell.

BAKEWELL

12 miles southeast of Buxton, 32 miles northeast of Little Moreton Hall.

In Bakewell, a medieval bridge crosses the winding River Wye in five graceful arches, and the 9th-century Saxon cross that stands outside the parish church reveals the town's great age. Narrow streets and houses built out of the local gray-brown stone also make the town extremely appealing. Ceaseless traffic through the streets can take the shine off—though there's respite down on the quiet riverside paths.

This market town is the commercial hub of the Peak District, for locals and visitors. The crowds are really substantial on market day (Monday), attended by area farmers. For a self-guided hour-long stroll, pick up a map at the tourist office, where the town trail begins. A small exhibition upstairs explains the landscape of the Peak District.

GETTING HERE AND AROUND

TransPeak offers bus services from Manchester's Chorlton Street Bus Station to Bakewell. National Express covers the same route, but only once a day at 6:40 am. By car, Bakewell is a one-hour, 30-minute drive southeast on the A6 from Manchester.

ESSENTIALS

Visitor Information Bakewell Visitor Centre ⊠ *Old Market Hall, Bridge St.* ☎ *01629/816558* ⊕ *www.visitpeakdistrict.com.*

CLOSE UP

Stoke-on-Trent: The Potteries

The area known as the Potteries, about 55 miles southeast of Liverpool, is still the center of Britain's ceramics industry, though production is increasingly being transferred overseas. There are, in fact, six towns, now administered as "the city of Stoke-on-Trent." Famous names such as Wedgwood, Royal Doulton, Spode, and Coalport carry on, though they've been taken over by other companies.

The most famous manufacturer, Josiah Wedgwood, established his pottery works at Etruria, near Burslem, in 1759, and created the cream-color ware (creamware), which so pleased Queen Charlotte that in 1762 she appointed him royal supplier of dinnerware. More recent innovators include the very collectible Clarice Cliff, who strove to brighten plain whiteware in the 1920s with her colorful geometric and floral designs. Also bold and colorful were the classic art deco pieces of Susie Cooper. Museums portray the history of this area, and there's still plenty of shopping, with good prices for seconds.

Emma Bridgewater. This highly successful local firm is known across Britain for its whimsical pottery designs. The 45-minute factory tour shows how Emma adapted 200-year-old techniques. Another highlight is a visit to the decorating studio, where you can try your hand at creating some designs of your own. There's also a gift shop and a little café. ⊠ Lichfield St., Hanley ☎ 01782/201328 ⊕ www.emmabridgewaterfactory. com ⌑ £2.50; refunded with anything bought in gift shop ☉ Mon.–Sat. 9:30–5:30, Sun. 10–4.

Gladstone Pottery Museum. The country's only remaining old-style Victorian pottery factory, the Gladstone Pottery Museum's traditional bottle kilns are surrounded by original workshops where you can watch the old skills of throwing, casting, and decorating in action. The Flushed with Pride galleries tell the story of the toilet from the 1840s onward. There are daily workshops, too. ⊠ Uttoxeter Rd., Longton ☎ 01782/237777 ⊕ www. stokemuseums.org.uk ⌑ £7.25 ☉ Apr.– Sept., daily 10–5; Oct.–Mar., daily 10–4; last admission 1 hr before closing.

Potteries Museum and Art Gallery. The modern Potteries Museum and Art Gallery displays a 5,000-piece ceramic collection of international repute, and is recognized worldwide for its unique Staffordshire pottery. Other highlights are an original World War II Spitfire plane and works by Picasso, Degas, and Dürer. ⊠ Bethesda St., Hanley ☎ 01782/232323 ⊕ www. stokemuseums.org.uk ⌑ Free ☉ Mon.– Sat. 10–5, Sun. 2–5.

Wedgwood Museum and Visitor Centre. At the Wedgwood Museum and Visitor Centre you can learn about the history of Wedgwood, and see samples of its finest pieces. The visitor center has craft demonstrations and also displays Doulton and Minton ware. Both the museum and visitor center have shops where you can buy firsts and seconds. There's also a buffet restaurant serving hot lunches and afternoon tea on— you guessed it—Wedgwood china. ⊠ Wedgewood Drive, Off A5035, Barlaston ☎ 01782/371919 ⊕ www. wedgwoodmuseum.org.uk ⌑ £6 museum, £10 museum and visitor center ☉ Weekdays 9–5, weekends 10–5.

9

EXPLORING

FAMILY

Fodor'sChoice

★

Chatsworth House. Glorious parkland leads to the ancestral home of the dukes of Devonshire and one of England's greatest country houses. The vast expanse of greenery, grazed by deer and sheep, sets off the Palladian-style elegance of "the Palace of the Peak." Originally an Elizabethan house, Chatsworth was conceived on a monumental scale. It was altered over several generations starting in 1686, and the architecture now has a hodgepodge look, though the Palladian facade remains untouched.

> **BAKEWELL PUDDING**
>
> Bakewell is the source of Bakewell pudding, said to have been created inadvertently when, sometime in the 19th century, a cook at the town's Rutland Arms Hotel (which is still in business) dropped some rich cake mixture over jam tarts and baked it. Every local bakery and tearoom claims an original recipe, so it's easy to spend a gustatory afternoon tasting rival puddings.

The house is surrounded by woods, elaborate gardens, greenhouses, rock gardens, and the most famous water cascade in the country—all designed by two great landscape artists: Capability Brown in the 18th century and, in the 19th, Joseph Paxton, an engineer as well as a brilliant gardener. The gravity-fed Emperor Fountain can shoot as high as 300 feet. ■TIP→ Plan on at least a half day to explore the grounds; avoid Sunday if you're allergic to heavy crowds. Inside are intricate carvings, Van Dyck portraits, superb furniture, and a few fabulous rooms, including the Sculpture Gallery, the library, and the Blue Drawing Room, where you can see two of the most famous portraits in Britain, Sir Joshua Reynolds's *Georgiana, Duchess of Devonshire, and Her Baby,* and John Singer Sargent's enormous *Acheson Sisters.* Chatsworth is 4 miles northeast of Bakewell. On the grounds are a farm with milking demonstrations at 3 and an adventure playground. ⊠ *Off B6012* ☎ *01246/565300* ⊕ *www.chatsworth.org* ⊡ *House, gardens, and farm £19; house and gardens £16; gardens only £10* ◯ *House daily 11–5:30; gardens daily 11–6, farmyard and adventure playground daily 10:30–5:30; last admission 1 hr before closing.*

Eyam. This tiny, idyllic, gray-stone village is synonymous with an extraordinary act of self-sacrifice that took place here in 1665. After a local tailor died of the plague, the villagers isolated themselves from the outside world rather than risk the spread of Black Death (the area had hitherto been spared the disease). They succeeded in containing the disease, but at huge cost: by the time it had run its course, most of the residents were dead. Their heroism is commemorated in a series of florid memorials in the village churchyard. For information see ⊕ www.eyamplaguevillage.co.uk. The small museum at the edge of the village on Hawkhill Road puts everything into context (open late March to October, Tuesday to Sunday, 10 to 4:30; admission £2.50). Eyam is 6 miles north of Bakewell off the A623 . ⊠ *Hawkwill Rd., Eyam* ☎ *01433/631371 (museum).*

The Emperor Fountain enhances the bucolic landscape at Chatsworth, one of England's most magnificent stately homes.

9

QUICK BITES

Eyam Tea Rooms. Surrounded by blooming pot plants in summer, this sweet little tea room, a stone's throw from the village church, serves afternoon tea and traditional lunches. ⊠ *The Square, Eyam* ☎ *01433/631274.*

Fodor's Choice
★

Haddon Hall. One of England's finest stately homes, and perhaps the most authentically Tudor of the great houses, Haddon Hall bristles with intricate period detail. Built between 1180 and 1565, the house passed into the ownership of the dukes of Rutland and remained largely untouched until the early 20th century, when the ninth duke undertook a superlative restoration. This revealed a series of early decorative 15th-century frescoes in the chapel. The finest of the intricate plasterwork and wooden paneling is best seen in the superb Long Gallery on the first floor. Baking is still done in the bread ovens in the well-preserved Tudor kitchen, using authentic Tudor methods. Here, too, is the unique collection of Gothic dole cupboards, some original to the house, which would have been filled with food and placed outside for those in need. Unsurprisingly the house is a popular filming location; its starring roles include *The Princess Bride* (1985), *Pride and Prejudice* (2005) and *The Other Boleyn Girl* (2008). ⊠ *A6* ☎ *01629/812855* ⊕ *www.haddonhall.co.uk* ⊠ *£9.50, parking £1.50* ⊙ *Apr. and Oct., Sat.–Mon. noon–5; May–Sept., daily noon–5 (closes 8 on Thurs., June and July; last admission 1 hr before closing.*

WHERE TO EAT AND STAY
For expanded hotel reviews, visit Fodors.com.

$$
MODERN BRITISH
Fodor'sChoice
★

✕**Devonshire Arms.** This stone 18th-century coaching inn, which counts Charles Dickens as one of its many famous visitors, is divided into a cozy bar area and a modern brasserie, both serving impressive homemade fare. Alongside old favorites like bangers and mash, the menu offers such imaginative creations as roast partridge with pinot noir potato puree, and Chatsworth estate venison with smoked aubergine (eggplant), churros, and chili chocolate sauce. For dessert, try the apple tarte tatin served with ice cream made from apple and bilberries—a native English fruit in the same family as (but different from) blueberries. The inn, 2 miles south of Chatsworth, also has eight bedrooms. $ *Average main: £15* ✉ *B6012, Beeley* ☎ *01629/733259* ⊕ *www.devonshirebeeley.co.uk.*

$$$$
MODERN BRITISH

✕**Fischer's.** The Fischer family bought this stately Edwardian manor on the edge of the Chatsworth estate, 4 miles north of Bakewell, to house their restaurant. Intimate and formal, the restaurant takes pride in using high-quality local products; on the fixed-price menus you'll find wild venison, Derbyshire pork and lamb, and Yorkshire rhubarb, all presented with care and aplomb. If you can't decide, there's a six-course tasting menu of specialty dishes (£72, or £120 with wines). With 11 elegant bedrooms here as well, you might consider staying the night. $ *Average main: £34* ✉ *Baslow Hall, Calver Rd., Baslow* ☎ *01246/583259* ⊕ *www.fischers-baslowhall.co.uk.*

$
BRITISH

✕**The Old Original Bakewell Pudding Shop.** Given the plethora of local rivals, it takes a bold establishment to claim its Bakewell puddings as "original," but there's certainly nothing wrong with those served here. A British favorite, the "pudding" in question is actually a dense, sugary pie with a jam and almond filling and a puff pastry crust, eaten cold or hot with custard or cream. A more common varient, the Bakewell tart, is made with shortcrust pastry, but aficionados consider the pudding to be more authentic. The oak-beam dining room also turns out commendable main courses of Yorkshireman (batter pudding with meat and vegetables) and steak-and-ale pie. $ *Average main: £8* ✉ *The Square* ☎ *01629/812193* ⊕ *www.bakewellpuddingshop.co.uk.*

$
B&B/INN

▦**Haddon House Farm.** This may be a working farm, but there's nothing workaday about the colourful and beautifully designed rooms (with themes such as Shakespeare and Monet's Garden) that the Nicholls husband-and-wife team have created. **Pros:** charming and obliging hosts; outdoor hot tub; easily accessible by bus. **Cons:** no credit cards; £10 surcharge for one-night stays. $ *Rooms from: £95* ✉ *Haddon Rd.* ☎ *01629/814024* ⊕ *www.great-place.co.uk* ⤳ *4 rooms* ▭ *No credit cards* ❑⃝ *Breakfast.*

MATLOCK

8 miles southeast of Bakewell, 5 miles south of Haddon Hall.

In the heart of the Derbyshire Dales, Matlock and its near neighbor Matlock Bath are former spa towns compressed into a narrow gorge on the River Derwent. Some surviving Regency buildings in Matlock testify to its former importance, although it's less impressive an ensemble

CLOSE UP

Well Dressing

Unique to the Peak District is the custom of well dressing, when certain wells or springs are decorated with elaborate pictures made of flowers. Frames up to 4 feet wide and 6 feet high, covered with a base of clay, are filled with a colorful mosaic of seeds, grasses, berries, and moss as well as flowers and flower petals, a process that involves a team of workers and takes about a week to complete. The designs usually incorporate religious themes such as biblical stories, though the origin of the custom is disputed; some say it's a Christian veneer over an ancient pagan rite;

others claim it started during the Black Death, when locals (mistakenly) believed that the purity of their water supply had spared them the worst ravages of the plague.

The well dressing and blessing ceremony, usually accompanied by a brass band, heralds the start of several days of festivities. Of the 70 or so towns and villages that continue this summertime tradition, Tissington (May), south of Matlock; Bakewell (early July); and, near Chatsworth, Eyam (late August) are among the most popular. Check with local tourist offices for information.

than that presented by Buxton. The surroundings, however, are particularly beautiful.

The Matlock River Illuminations, a flotilla of lighted boats, shimmers after dark on weekends between September and late October, along the still waters of the Derwent.

GETTING HERE AND AROUND

Matlock is served by National Express and TransPeak buses from Manchester's Chorlton Street Bus Station. The town is about a one-hour, 40-minute drive southeast on the A6 from Manchester.

ESSENTIALS

Visitor Information Matlock Visitor Information Point ⊠ Matlock Station, off A6 ☎ 01629/343666 ⊕ www.visitpeakdistrict.com.

EXPLORING

Fodor's Choice ★ **Hardwick Hall.** Few houses in England evoke the late Elizabethan era as vividly as Hardwick Hall, a beautiful stone mansion and treasure trove. The facade glitters with myriad windows, making it easy to see why the house came to be known as "Hardwick Hall, more glass than wall." ▀TIP➔ Choose a sunny day to see the rooms and their treasures at their best. The vast state apartments well befit their original chatelaine, Bess of Hardwick. By marrying a succession of four rich husbands, she had become second only to Queen Elizabeth in her wealth when work on this house began. She took possession in 1597, and four years later made an inventory of the important rooms and their contents—furniture, tapestries, and embroideries. Unique patchwork hangings, probably made from clerical copes and altar frontals taken from monasteries and abbeys, grace the entrance hall, and superb 16th- and 17th-century tapestries cover the walls of the main staircase and first-floor High Great Chamber. The collection of Elizabethan embroideries—table carpets, cushions, bed hangings, and pillowcases—is second to none. Outside, you can visit the walled gardens. The hall appeared as Malfoy Manor in the last two Harry Potter movies. Hardwick Hall is 10 miles east of Matlock. Access is signposted from Junction 29 of the M1 motorway. ✉ *Doe Lea, Chesterfield* ☎ *01246/850430* 🌐 *www.nationaltrust.org.uk* 🎫 *£11; gardens only, £5.50* 🕐 *House mid-Mar.–Oct., Wed.–Sun. noon–4:30. Gardens daily 9–6; last admission 30 mins before closing. Grounds daily 8–dusk.*

FAMILY **Heights of Abraham Country Park and Caverns.** At Matlock Bath, 2 miles south of Matlock, river and valley views unfold from the curving line of buildings that makes up the village. Aside from riverside strolls, the major attraction is the cable-car ride across the River Derwent that takes you to this park on the crags above, with a visitor center and café. The all-inclusive ticket allows access to the woodland walks and nature trails of the 60-acre park, as well as entry to a cavern and a guided descent into an old lead mine, where workers toiled by candlelight. ✉ *A6, Matlock Bath* ☎ *01629/582365* 🌐 *www.heightsofabraham.com* 🎫 *£13.50 cable car, park, exhibition, and caverns* 🕐 *Mid-Feb.–late Feb. and mid-Mar.–early Nov., daily 10–4:30; early to mid-Mar., weekends 10–4:30. Closes 5 at peak times.*

WHERE TO STAY

For expanded hotel reviews, visit Fodors.com.

$ RENTAL 🏨 **Riber Hall.** This early-17th-century lodging offers delightful serviced apartments in the sleepy hamlet of Riber, a mile south of Matlock. **Pros:** countryside on the doorstep; historical character; good value. **Cons:** no children allowed; car required. [$] *Rooms from: £59* ✉ *Riber Rd., Riber* ☎ *01629/580772* 🌐 *www.riberhall.com* 🛏 *10 apartments* 🍴 *No meals.*

SPORTS AND THE OUTDOORS

High Peak Trail. One of the major trails in the Peak District, High Peak Trail runs for 17 miles from Cromford (south of Matlock Bath) to Dowlow, following the route of an old railroad. 🌐 *www.peakdistrict.gov.uk.*

Red House Stables. Trips through the local countryside on horse-drawn antique carriages are offered by Red House Stables. An hour-long ride costs around £30. ✉ *Old Rd.* ☎ *01629/733583* 🌐 *www.workingcarriages.com.*

CASTLETON

24 miles northwest of Matlock, 10 miles northwest of Chatsworth, 9 miles northeast of Buxton.

The area around Castleton, in Hope Valley, contains the most famous manifestations of the geology of the Peak District. A number of caves and mines are open to the public, including some former lead mines and Blue John mines (amethystine spar; the unusual name is a corruption of the French *bleu-jaune*, meaning "blue yellow"). The limestone caverns attract many people, which means that pretty Castleton shows a certain commercialization. Summer brings the crowds, many of which poke around in the numerous shops displaying Blue John jewelry and wares.

GETTING HERE AND AROUND

Hope Rail Station, 1½ miles from the center of Castleton, is served by the Manchester–Sheffield railroad line. By car, Castleton is a one-hour drive southeast on the A6 from Manchester.

ESSENTIALS

Visitor Information **Castleton Visitor Centre** ✉ *Buxton Rd.* ☎ *01629/816558* 🌐 *www.visitpeakdistrict.com.*

EXPLORING

FAMILY **Peak Cavern.** Caves riddle the entire town and the surrounding area, and in the massive Peak Caverns, rope making has been done on a great ropewalk for more than 400 years. You can still see the remains of the 17th-century rope makers' village. Some trivia to keep kids amused: the Peak Caverns were historically called the "Devil's Arse," due to the flatulent noise that water makes when draining out of the caves. ✉ *Off Goosehill* ☎ *01433/620285* 🌐 *www.peakcavern.co.uk* 🎟 *£9 Peak Cavern; £15 joint ticket with Speedwell Caverns* 🕒 *Apr.–Oct., daily 10–5, tours hourly; Nov.–Mar., weekends and school holidays daily 10–5, tours hourly; weekdays tours 2 and 5.*

Peveril Castle. In 1176 Henry II added the square tower to this Norman castle, whose ruins occupy a dramatic crag above the town. The castle has superb views—from here you can still clearly see a curving section of the medieval defensive earthworks in the town center below. Peveril Castle is protected on its west side by a 230-foot-deep gorge formed by a collapsed cave. Park in the town center, from which it's a steep climb up. ✉ *Market Pl.* ☎ *01433/620613* 🌐 *www.english-heritage.org.uk* 🎟 *£4.60* 🕒 *Apr.–Oct., daily 10–5.*

FAMILY
Fodor's Choice ★
Speedwell Cavern. The area's most exciting cavern by far is Speedwell Cavern, where 105 slippery steps lead down to old lead-mine tunnels blasted out by 19th-century miners. Here you transfer to a small boat for the claustrophobic ¼-mile trip through an illuminated access tunnel to the cavern itself. At this point you're 600 feet underground, with views farther down to the so-called Bottomless Pit, a cavern entirely filled with water. An on-site shop sells items made of Blue John, a mineral found nowhere else in the world. Speedwell Cavern is at the bottom of Winnats Pass, 1 mile west of Castleton. ✉ *Winnats Pass* ☎ *01433/620512* 🌐 *www.speedwellcavern.co.uk* 🎟 *£9.50; £15 includes Peak Cavern* 🕒 *Apr.–Oct., daily 10–5; Nov.–Mar., daily 10–4; last tour 1 hr before closing.*

9

WHERE TO STAY

For expanded hotel reviews, visit Fodors.com.

$ B&B/INN 🏨 **Bargate Cottage.** Dating to 1650, this cottage below Peveril Castle is a sweet, cozy place to stay. **Pros:** peaceful location; great breakfasts; charming hosts. **Cons:** small rooms. [$] *Rooms from: £70* ✉ *Market Pl.* ☎ *01433/620201* 🌐 *www.bargatecottage.co.uk* 🛏 *3 rooms* 💳 *No credit cards* 🍴 *Breakfast.*

$ B&B/INN 🏨 **Underleigh House.** Peaceful is the word for the location of this creeper-clad cottage and barn at the end of a lane in beautiful hiking country. **Pros:** superb views; free Wi-Fi; ample breakfasts. **Cons:** minimum stays on weekends. [$] *Rooms from: £90* ✉ *Off Edale Rd., Hope* ☎ *01433/621372* 🌐 *www.underleighhouse.co.uk* 🛏 *3 rooms, 2 suites* 🍴 *Breakfast.*

EN
ROUTE

Winnats Pass. Heading northwest to Edale, the most spectacular driving route is over Winnats Pass, through a narrow, boulder-strewn valley. The name means "wind gate," due to the wind-tunnel effect of the peaks on each side. Beyond are the tops of Mam Tor (where there's a lookout point) and the hamlet of Barber Booth, after which you run into Edale.

EDALE

5 miles northwest of Castleton.

At Edale, an extremely popular hiking center, you're truly in the Peak District wilds. This sleepy, straggling village, in the shadow of Mam Tor and Lose Hill and the moorlands of the high plateau known as Kinder Scout (2,088 feet), lies among some of the most breathtaking scenery in Derbyshire. England can show little wilder scenery than Kinder Scout, with its ragged edges of grit stone and its interminable leagues of heather and peat.

GETTING HERE AND AROUND

Edale Rail Station has service to Manchester and Sheffield. By car, Edale is a one-hour drive southeast on the A6 from Manchester.

ESSENTIALS

Visitor Information The Moorland Centre ⊠ *Fieldhead* ☎ *01433/670207* ⊕ *www.visitpeakdistrict.com.*

EXPLORING

Old Nag's Head. This pub at the top of the village has marked the official start of the Pennine Way since 1965. Call in at the Hiker's Bar, sit by the fire, and tuck into hearty bar meals and hot toddies. On Monday and Tuesday in winter, when this pub is closed, the Ramblers' Inn, at the other end of the village, is open. ⊠ *Grinsbrook Booth* ☎ *01433/670291* ⊕ *www.the-old-nags-head.co.uk.*

SPORTS AND THE OUTDOORS

Pennine Way. The 250-mile-long Pennine Way starts in the village of Edale, 4 miles northeast of Castleton, and crosses Kinder Scout, a moorland plateau and nature reserve. If you plan to attempt this, seek local advice first, because bad weather can make the walk treacherous. However, several much shorter routes into the Edale Valley, like the 8-mile route west to Hayfield, give you a taste. ⊕ *www.nationaltrail.co.uk.*

THE LAKE
DISTRICT

WELCOME TO THE LAKE DISTRICT

TOP REASONS TO GO

★ **Hiking the trails:**
Whether it's a demanding trek or a gentle stroll, walking is the way to see the Lake District at its best.

★ **Messing about in boats:** There's nowhere better for renting a small boat or taking a cruise. The Coniston Boating Centre and Derwent Water Marina near Keswick are possible places to start.

★ **Literary landscapes:**
The Lake District has a rich literary history, in the children's books of Beatrix Potter, in the writings of John Ruskin, and in the poems of Wordsworth. Stop at any of the writers' homes to enrich your experience.

★ **Pints and pubs:**
A pint of real ale in one of the region's inns, such as the Drunken Duck near Hawkshead, may never taste as good as after a day of walking.

★ **Sunrise at Castlerigg:**
The stone circle at Castlerigg, in a hollow ringed by peaks, is a reminder of the region's ancient history.

1 The Southern Lakes. The southern lakes and valleys contain the park's most popular, and thus most overcrowded in summer, destinations. The region incorporates the largest body of water, Windermere, as well as most of the quintessential Lakeland towns and villages: Bowness, Ambleside, Grasmere, Elterwater, Coniston, and Hawkshead. To the east and west of this cluster of habitation, the valleys and fells climb to some beautiful upland country.

2 Penrith and the Northern Lakes. In the north, the landscape opens out across the bleaker fells to reveal challenging, spectacular walking country. Here, in the northern lakes, south of Keswick and Cockermouth, you have the best chance to get away from the crowds. This region's northwestern reaches are largely unexplored, while the northeast is home to Penrith, a bustling market town.

GETTING ORIENTED

The Lake District is in northwest England, some 70 miles north of the industrial belt that stretches from Liverpool to Manchester, and south of Scotland. The major gateway from the south is Kendal, and from the north, Penrith. Both are on the M6 motorway. Main-line trains stop at Oxenholme, near Kendal, with a branch linking Oxenholme to Kendal and Windermere. Windermere, in the south, is the most obvious starting point and has museums, cafés, and gift shops. But the farther (and higher) you can get from the southern towns, the more you'll appreciate the area's spectacular landscapes. The Lake District National Park breaks into two reasonably distinct sections: the gentler, rolling south and the craggier, wilder north.

10

CLASSIC ENGLISH DESSERTS

The English love to round off lunch or dinner with something sweet. British food is experiencing an ongoing revival that has cooks bringing back favorites such as fool, trifle, spotted dick, and sticky toffee pudding, and making the most of seasonal fruits and traditional spices.

(above) A dense texture and toffee sauce make sticky toffee pudding perfect for winter; (right, top) Trifle variation with strawberries and mascarpone; (right, bottom) Eton mess can use mixed berries.

"Sweet," "afters," and "pudding" all refer informally to dessert; "sweets" are simply candies, though. In England dessert is as likely to be a delicate creamy confection as a warming fruit pie or a rich, hearty pudding. Winter is the perfect time for steamed puddings, made with currants, dried fruits, and spices such as cinnamon, nutmeg, cloves, and ginger, or for hot fruit crumbles with custard. The warmer months bring an avalanche of fresh berries, and with them light, creamy desserts such as syllabub and fool come into their own. For many, the classic desserts such as sticky toffee pudding and spotted dick capture memories of growing up in the 20th century. Today dessert bars are becoming a trend in cities including London.

SPECIAL INGREDIENTS

Desserts may use wine and brandy, and other special items. These include **currants**—dried small black grapes—as well as dried fruits, candied fruit peel, and spices such as cinnamon, cloves, nutmeg, and ginger. **Quinces**, hard, applelike fruits, can be combined with apples in a crumble or turned into a paste to accompany cheese. **Damsons** are acidic plums, made into jams, jellies, or wine.

HOT STEAMED PUDDINGS

These puddings are cooked slowly over boiling water. Sticky toffee pudding is a dark sponge cake, made with finely chopped dates or prunes, and covered in a thick toffee sauce. The oddly named spotted dick is traditionally made with suet and steamed in a hot cloth, "spotted" with currants and other dried fruits, and served with custard. Another classic, Christmas pudding, dates from medieval times. Also known as plum pudding, it contains brandy, currants, and dried fruit, and is strong-flavored. Before the pudding steams for many hours, each family member stirs the mixture and makes a wish.

FRUIT CRUMBLES

Crumbles, similar to American crisps, were invented during wartime rationing when butter, flour, and sugar were too scarce to make pastry for pie. Tart Bramley apples native to England work well with cinnamon and cloves. Don't pass up rhubarb crumble, especially around February when the delicate bright pink forced variety of rhubarb from Yorkshire makes its brief appearance.

TRIFLE, FOOL, AND SYLLABUB

Dating from Tudor times, fool is simply a sharp fruit, usually gooseberry, swirled with whipped cream and a little sugar. Trifle evolved from fool, and begins with a layer of sponge cake (soaked

in port, sherry, or Madeira wine) and Jell-O or jam, topped with custard and whipped cream. Light but flavorful, syllabub is made from wine or brandy infused overnight with lemon and sugar, and whipped with cream.

ETON MESS

Invented at the famous Eton College, after, it's said, a Labrador dog accidentally sat on a picnic basket, Eton Mess is still served at the annual prize-giving ceremony. This unfussy summer dessert consists of strawberries mixed with whipped cream and crushed meringue.

SUMMER PUDDING

Fresh summer berries, bread, and a little sugar are all that should go into a summer pudding. Left for several hours so that the sweet and sharp flavors develop, the pudding turns out a deep red color, and is often served with a touch of cream.

MORE FAVORITES

Grasmere gingerbread from the Lake District is a dense spicy cake flavored with ginger and golden syrup. Eccles cakes, from Eccles in Lancashire, are round pastry cases, slashed three times for the Holy Trinity and filled with syrupy currants. Bakewell pudding or tart has a layer of jam and almond sponge, topped with flaked almonds or white icing.

10

Updated by
Julius Honnor

"Let nature be your teacher." Wordsworth's ideal comes true in this popular region of jagged mountains, waterfalls, wooded valleys, and stone-built villages. No mountains in Britain give a greater impression of majesty; deeper and bluer lakes can be found, but none that fit so readily into the surrounding scene. Outdoors enthusiasts flock to this region for boating or hiking, while literary types visit the homes of Beatrix Potter and other favorite writers.

In 1951 the Lake District National Park was created here from parts of the old counties of Cumberland, Westmorland, and Lancashire. The Lake District is a contour map come to life, covering an area of approximately 885 square miles and holding 16 major lakes and countless smaller stretches of water. The scenery is key to all the park's best activities: you can cross it by car in about an hour, but this is an area meant to be walked or boated or climbed. The mountains aren't high by international standards—Scafell Pike, England's highest peak, is only 3,210 feet above sea level—but they can be tricky to climb. In spring, many summits remain snowcapped long after the weather below has turned mild.

The poets Wordsworth and Coleridge, and other English writers, found the Lake District an inspiring setting for their work, and visitors have followed ever since, to walk, go boating, or just relax and take in the views. Seeing the homes and other sights associated with these writers can occupy part of a trip.

This area can be one of Britain's most appealing reservoirs of calm, though in summer the lakeside towns, however appealing, can lose their charm when cars and tour buses clog the narrow streets. Similarly, the walks and hiking trails that crisscross the region seem less inviting when you share them with a crowd. Despite the challenges of popularity, the Lake District has managed tourism and the landscape in a manner that retains the character of the villages and the natural environment. Explore beyond Windermere and Keswick to discover little farming communities eking out a living despite the occasionally harsh conditions.

Today, too, a new generation of hotel and restaurant owners is making more creative use of the local foods and other assets of the Lakeland fells, and chic modern or foodie-oriented establishments are springing up next to traditional tearooms and chintz-filled inns.

Off-season visits can be a real treat. All those inns and bed-and-breakfasts that turn away crowds in summer are eager for business the rest of the year (and their rates drop accordingly). It's not an easy task to find a succession of sunny days in the Lake District—some malicious statisticians allot to it about 250 rainy days a year—but when the sun breaks through and brightens the surfaces of the lakes, it's an away-from-it-all place to remember.

LAKE DISTRICT PLANNER

WHEN TO GO

The Lake District is one of the rainiest areas in Britain, but June, July, and August hold the best hope of fine weather and summer is the time for all the major festivals. You will, however, be sharing the lakes with thousands of other people. If you travel at this time, turn up early at popular museums and attractions, and expect to work to find parking. April and May, as well as September and October, are good alternatives. Later and earlier in the year there'll be even more space and freedom, but many attractions close, and from December to March, snow and ice can block roads and may preclude serious hill walking without heavy-duty equipment.

PLANNING YOUR TIME

You could spend months tramping the hills, valleys, and fells of the Lake District, or, in three days you could drive through the major towns and villages. The key is not to do too much in too short a time. If you're traveling by public transportation, many places will be off-limits. As a base, Windermere has the best transport links, but it can be crowded and it has less character than some of the smaller towns like Ambleside and Keswick, which also have plenty of sleeping and eating options. For a more intimate version of village life, try Coniston, Hawkshead, or Grasmere. Keep in mind that the northern and western lakes have the most dramatic scenery and offer the best opportunity to escape the summertime hordes.

The Lake District may be compact, but it's not a place to hurry. Allow plenty of time for walking: paths can be steep and rocky, and in any case you'll want to stop frequently to look at the great views. A good day's walking with a picnic can be done from nearly anywhere. Driving brings its own speed inhibitors, from sheep on the roads to slow tractors.

You're likely to be based down near lake level, but try to experience the hills, too. If you're short of time, a drive over one of the high passes such as Honister will give you a glimpse of the enormity of the landscape.

10

GETTING HERE AND AROUND

AIR TRAVEL

Manchester Airport has its own rail station with direct service to Carlisle, Windermere, and Barrow-in-Furness. Manchester is 70 miles from the southern part of the Lake District.

Contact Manchester Airport ✉ *M56, Near Junctions 5 and 6* ☎ *08712/710711* ⊕ *www.manchesterairport.co.uk.*

BOAT TRAVEL

Whether you rent a boat or take a ride on a modern launch or vintage vessel, getting out on the water is a fun (and often useful) way to see the Lake District. Windermere, Coniston Water, and Derwentwater all have boat rental facilities.

BUS TRAVEL

National Express serves the region from London's Victoria Coach Station and from Manchester's Chorlton Street Station. Average travel time to Kendal is just over 7 hours from London; to Windermere, 7½ hours; and to Keswick, 8¼ hours. From Manchester there's one bus a day to Windermere via Ambleside, Grasmere, and Keswick. There's direct bus service to the Lake District from Carlisle, Lancaster, and York.

Stagecoach in Cumbria provides local service between Lakeland towns and through the valleys and high passes. Bus service between main tourist centers is fairly frequent on weekdays, but much reduced on weekends and bank holidays. Don't count on reaching the more remote parts of the area by bus. Off-the-beaten-track touring requires a car or strong legs. A one-week Cumbria Goldrider ticket (£23.50), available on the bus, is valid on all routes. Explorer tickets (£10) are valid for a day on all routes. Contact Traveline for up-to-date timetables.

Contacts National Express ☎ *08717/818178* ⊕ *www.nationalexpress.com.* **Traveline** ☎ *0871/200–2233* ⊕ *www.traveline.info.*

CAR TRAVEL

A car is almost essential in the Lake District; bus service is limited and trains can get you to the edge of the national park but no farther. You can rent cars in Penrith and Kendal. Roads within the region are generally good, although minor routes and mountain passes can be steep and narrow. Warning signs are often posted if snow or ice has made a road impassable; check local weather forecasts in winter before heading out. In July and August and during the long public holiday weekends, expect heavy traffic. The Lake District has plenty of parking lots; use them to avoid blocking narrow lanes.

To reach the Lake District by car from London, take M1 north to M6, getting off either at Junction 36 and joining A590/A591 west (around the Kendal bypass to Windermere) or at Junction 40, joining A66 direct to Keswick and the northern lakes region. Travel time to Kendal is about four to five hours, to Keswick five to six hours. Expect heavy traffic out of London on weekends.

TRAIN TRAVEL

There are direct trains from Manchester and Manchester airport to Windermere. For schedule information, call National Rail Enquiries. Two train companies serve the region from London's Euston Station: take a Virgin or Northern Rail train bound for Carlisle, Edinburgh, or Glasgow and change at Oxenholme for the branch line service to Kendal and Windermere. Average travel time to Windermere (including the change) is 4½ hours. If you're heading for Keswick, you can either take the train to Windermere and continue from there by Stagecoach bus (Bus 554/555/556; 70 minutes), or stay on the main London–Carlisle train to Penrith Station (four hours), from which Stagecoach buses (Bus X5) also run to Keswick (45 minutes). Direct trains from Manchester depart for Windermere five times daily (travel time two hours). First North Western runs a local service from Windermere and Barrow-in-Furness to Manchester Airport. National Rail can handle all questions about trains.

Train connections are good around the edges of the Lake District, but you must take the bus or drive to reach the central Lakeland region. Trains are sometimes reduced, or nonexistent, on Sunday.

Contacts **National Rail Enquiries** ☎ 08457/484950 ⊕ www.nationalrail.co.uk. **Northern Rail** ☎ 0844/241–3454 ⊕ www.northernrail.org. **Virgin Trains** ☎ 08719/774222 ⊕ www.virgintrains.co.uk.

NATIONAL PARK

The Lake District National Park head office (and main visitor center) is at Brockhole, north of Windermere. It's closed November through mid-February. Helpful regional national-park information centers sell books and maps, book accommodations, and provide walking advice.

Contacts **Bowness Bay Information Centre** ⊠ Glebe Rd., Bowness-on-Windermere ☎ 015394/42895. **Keswick Information Centre** ⊠ Moot Hall, Main St., Keswick ☎ 017687/72645. **Lake District Visitor Centre** ⊠ Brockhole, Ambleside Rd., Windermere ☎ 015394/46601 ⊕ www.brockhole.co.uk. **Ullswater Information Centre** ⊠ Beckside Car Park, off Greenside Rd., Glenridding ☎ 017684/82414 ⊕ www.lakedistrict.gov.uk.

TOURS

Mountain Goat and Lakes Supertours provide minibus sightseeing tours with skilled local guides. Half- and full-day tours, some of which really get off the beaten track, depart from Bowness, Windermere, Ambleside, and Grasmere.

Walks range from gentle, literary-oriented strolls to challenging ridge hikes. The Lake District National Park or tourist information centers can put you in touch with qualified guides. Blue Badge Guides can provide experts on the area. English Lakeland Ramblers organizes single-base and inn-to-inn guided tours of the Lake District. Lake District Walker offers guided day hikes for different abilities.

Contacts **Cumbria Tourist Guides** ☎ 01228/562096 ⊕ cumbriatouristguides. co.uk. **English Lakeland Ramblers** ☎ 703/680–4276, 800/724–8801 ⊕ www.ramblers.com. **Lake District Walker** ☎ 0844/693–3389 ⊕ www.thelakedistrictwalker.co.uk. **Lakes Supertours** ⊠ 1 High St., Windermere ☎ 015394/42751 ⊕ www.lakes-supertours.com. **Mountain Goat** ⊠ Victoria St., Windermere ☎ 015394/45161 ⊕ www.mountain-goat.com.

10

RESTAURANTS

Lakeland restaurants increasingly reflect a growing British awareness of good food. Local sourcing and international influences are common, and even old Cumberland favorites are being creatively reinvented. Pub dining in the Lake District can be excellent—the hearty fare often makes use of local ingredients such as Herdwick lamb, and real ales are a good accompaniment. If you're going walking, ask your hotel or B&B about making you a packed lunch. Some local delicatessens also offer this service. *Prices in the reviews are the average cost of a main course at dinner or, if dinner isn't served, at lunch.*

HOTELS

Your choices include everything from small country inns to grand lakeside hotels; many hotels offer the option of paying a higher price that includes dinner as well as breakfast. The regional mainstay is the bed-and-breakfast, from the house on Main Street to an isolated farmhouse. Most country hotels and B&Bs gladly cater to hikers and can provide on-the-spot information. Wherever you stay, book well in advance for summer visits, especially those in late July and August. In winter many accommodations close for a month or two. On weekends and in summer it may be hard to get a reservation for a single night. Internet access is improving, and an increasing number of hotels and cafés offer Wi-Fi access. *Prices in the reviews are the lowest cost of a standard double room in high season, including 20% V.A.T.*

VISITOR INFORMATION

Contacts Cumbria Tourism ✉ *Windermere Rd., Staveley* ☎ *01539/822222* ⊕ *www.golakes.co.uk.*

THE SOUTHERN LAKES

Among the many attractions here are the small resort towns clustered around Windermere, England's largest lake, and the area's hideaway valleys, rugged walking centers, and monuments rich in literary associations. This is the easiest part of the Lake District to reach, with Kendal, the largest town, just a short distance from the M6 motorway. An obvious route from Kendal takes in Windermere, the area's natural touring center, before moving north through Ambleside and Rydal Water to Grasmere. Some of the loveliest Lakeland scenery is to be found by then turning south, through Elterwater, Hawkshead, and Coniston.

KENDAL

70 miles north of Manchester.

The southern gateway to the Lake District is the "Auld Gray Town" of Kendal, outside the national park and less touristy than the towns to the northwest. You may want to stay closer to the action, but the town has some worthwhile sights. Nearby hills frame Kendal's gray stone houses and provide some delightful walks; you can also explore the ruins of Kendal Castle. ■ TIP➔ Pack a slab of Kendal mint cake, the local peppermint candy that British walkers and climbers swear by. It's for sale around the region.

The design of the famous, fanciful topiary garden at Levens Hall dates back to the 17th century.

The town's motto, "Wool Is My Bread," refers to its importance as a textile center in northern England before the Industrial Revolution. It was known for manufacturing woolen cloth, especially Kendal Green, which archers favored. Away from the main road are quiet courtyards and winding medieval streets known as "ginnels." Wool merchants used these for easy access to the River Kent.

GETTING HERE AND AROUND

Kendal is just off the M6, about 70 miles north of Manchester. It has train service via a branch line from Oxenholme, and National Express bus service from London as well. It's the largest town in the area but is still plenty small enough to walk around.

ESSENTIALS

Visitor Information Kendal Tourist Information Centre ⊠ *Made in Cumbria, 25 Stramongate* ☎ *01539/735891* ⊕ *www.exploresouthlakeland.co.uk.*

EXPLORING

Fodor's Choice
★

Abbot Hall. The region's finest art gallery, Abbot Hall occupies a Palladian-style Georgian mansion built in 1759. In the permanent collection are works by Victorian artist and critic John Ruskin, who lived near Coniston, and by 18th-century portrait painter George Romney, who worked in Kendal. "The Great Picture," a grand 17th-century triptych of the life of Lady Ann Clifford, is attributed to Flemish painter Jan Van Belcamp. The gallery also owns some excellent contemporary art, including work by Barbara Hepworth, Ben Nicholson, Winifred Nicholson, and L.S. Lowry. There's also an excellent café. Abbot Hall is on the River Kent, next to the parish church. The **Museum of Lakeland Life**, with exhibits on blacksmithing and wheelwrighting and a

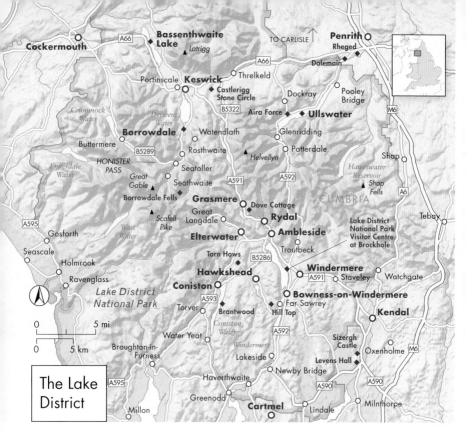

The Lake District

wonderful re-creation of a period pharmacy, is in the former stable block of the hall, on the same site. ⊠ *Off Highgate* ☎ *01539/722464* ⊕ *www.abbothall.org.uk* ⊠ *Abbot Hall £6.20; Museum of Lakeland Life £5; combined ticket £8* ⊙ *Mar.–Oct., Mon.–Sat. 10:30–5; Nov.– mid-Dec. and mid-Jan.–Feb., Mon.–Sat. 10:30–4.*

FAMILY **Levens Hall.** An Elizabethan house and the home of the Bagot family since 1590, Levens Hall is famous for its topiary garden, probably the most distinctive in the world. Laid out in 1694, the garden retains its original design, and the yew and beech hedges, cut into complex shapes that resemble enormous chess pieces, rise among a profusion of flowers. The house contains a stunning medieval hall with oak panel-ing, ornate plasterwork, Jacobean furniture, and Cordova goat-leather wallpaper. You can easily spend a couple of hours here admiring the place or getting lost in the living willow labyrinth. There's a play area for children. Levens Hall is 4 miles south of Kendal. ⊠ *Off A590, Levens* ☎ *015395/60321* ⊕ *www.levenshall.co.uk* ⊠ *£12.50; gardens only, £8.50* ⊙ *Mid-Apr.–mid-Oct., Sun.–Thurs., house noon–4:30, last admission at 4; gardens 10–5.*

Sizergh Castle. One of the Lake District's finest fortified houses, Siz-ergh Castle has a 58-foot-tall tower that dates from 1340, more than 1,600 acres of grounds, and the national fern collection. Expanded in Elizabethan times, the castle includes outstanding oak-paneled interiors with intricately carved chimneypieces and oak furniture. The estate has ancient woodland, and there are good walks here. Sizergh is 3½ miles south of Kendal. ✉ *Off A591, Sizergh* ☎ *015395/60951* 🌐 *www.nationaltrust.org.uk* 🎟 *£9.45; gardens only £5.85* ⏲ *Castle mid-Mar.–Oct., Sun.–Thurs. 1–5 (also noon–1 by guided tour); gardens mid-Mar.–Oct., Mon.–Sun. 11–5.*

WAINWRIGHT'S GUIDES

Alfred Wainwright (1907–91), an accountant, became one of travel writing's most famous authors. First published in the 1950s and 1960s, his handwritten, illustrated guides have sold more than 2 million copies; these classics are still sold in area bookstores. The gruff Wainwright seemed to want the hills to himself, yet he lovingly created 49 books that continue to introduce people to the Lakeland mountains.

WHERE TO EAT AND STAY

The Brewery Arts Centre has other good dining options in Kendal, including the Grain Store restaurant and the theatrical Warehouse Café.

For expanded hotel reviews, visit Fodors.com.

$$ MODERN BRITISH 🍴 **The New Moon.** Small but sleek, this restaurant with an open fire and artfully battered floorboards has won a good local reputation for high-quality dishes. The vegetarian selections are always worthwhile, and the sometimes adventurous Modern British cooking shows Mediterranean flourishes. Damson plum-and-pork sausages come with mashed potatoes and a red wine jus, and the fresh mussels are cooked in a curry sauce. Excellent lunches and the fixed-price early dinners (5:30–7 weekdays) are especially good value. [$] *Average main: £15* ✉ *129 Highgate* ☎ *01539/729254* 🌐 *www.newmoonrestaurant.co.uk* ⏲ *Closed Sun. and Mon.*

$ VEGETARIAN 🍴 **Waterside Wholefoods Café.** In summer, grab one of the outdoor picnic tables overlooking the River Kent and order from the delicious, filling vegetarian (and mostly organic) menu of soups, buckwheat burgers, curried green lentil pie, salads, and cakes and scones. Don't miss the moist chocolate, walnut, and pear tart. [$] *Average main: £6* ✉ *2 Kent View* ☎ *01539/729743* 🌐 *www.watersidewholefood.co.uk* ⏲ *Closed Sun. No dinner.*

$ B&B/INN 🏨 **Beech House.** Old-fashioned charm combines with modern luxuries like heated bathroom floors in this comfortable, ivy-clad town house. **Pros:** homey rooms; locally made toiletries; private parking. **Cons:** steep walk up the hill to get here; two-night minimum on weekends. [$] *Rooms from: £80* ✉ *40 Greenside* ☎ *01539/720385* 🌐 *www.beechhouse-kendal.co.uk* 🛏 *6 rooms* 🍽 *Breakfast.*

NIGHTLIFE AND THE ARTS

Brewery Arts Centre. A contemporary complex in a converted brewery, the Brewery Arts Centre includes a gallery, theater, cinemas, and workshop spaces. The Grain Store, overlooking lovely gardens, serves lunch and dinner, the Warehouse Café offers tasty toasted sandwiches and occasional live performances, and Vats Bar has good beer and wine. In November the Mountain Film Festival presents productions

10

aimed at climbers and walkers. ⊠ *Highgate* ☎ *01539/725133* ⊕ *www. breweryarts.co.uk* ☜ *Free* ☽ *Mon.–Sat. 9 am–11 pm.*

SHOPPING

Kendal has a pleasant mix of chains, factory outlet stores, specialty shops, and traditional markets. The most interesting stores are tucked away in the quiet lanes and courtyards around Market Place, Finkle Street, and Stramongate. There's been a **market** in Kendal since 1189, and outdoor market stalls still line the center of town along Stramongate and Market Place every Wednesday and Saturday.

Peter Hall & Son. This woodcraft workshop, 5 miles north of Kendal, sells finely honed furnishings, boxes, and bowls, among other items. ⊠ *Danes Rd., Staveley* ☎ *01539/821633* ⊕ *www.peter-hall.co.uk.*

WINDERMERE AND BOWNESS-ON-WINDERMERE

10 miles northwest of Kendal.

For a natural touring base for the southern half of the Lake District, you don't need to look much farther than Windermere, though it does get crowded in summer. The resort became popular in the Victorian era when the arrival of the railway made the remote and rugged area accessible. Wordsworth and Ruskin opposed the railway, fearing an influx of tourists would ruin the tranquil place. Sure enough, the railway terminus in 1847 brought with it Victorian day-trippers, and the original hamlet of Birthwaite was subsumed by the new town of Windermere, named after the lake.

Windermere has continued to flourish, despite being a mile or so from the water; the development now spreads to envelop the slate-gray lakeside village of Bowness-on-Windermere. Bowness is the more attractive of the two, but they're so close it doesn't matter where you stay.

GETTING HERE AND AROUND

Windermere is easily reached by car, less than a half hour off the M6. There's also a train station at the eastern edge of town; change at Oxenholme for the branch line to Kendal and Windermere.

Bus 599, leaving every 20 minutes in summer (hourly the rest of the year) from outside the Windermere train station, links the town with Bowness.

The Windermere Ferry, which carries cars and pedestrians, crosses from Ferry Nab on the Bowness side of the lake to reach Far Sawrey and the road to Hawkshead. With year-round ferry service between Ambleside, Bowness, Brockhole, and Lakeside, Windermere Lake Cruises is a pleasant way to experience the lake.

ESSENTIALS

Contacts **Windermere Ferry** ☎ 01228/227653 ⊕ www.cumbria.gov.uk ☜ £4.30 one-way for cars; 50p one-way for foot passengers ☽ Apr.–Oct., Mon.–Sat. 6:50 am–9:50 pm, Sun. 9:10 am–9:50 pm; Nov.–Mar., Mon.–Sat. 6:50 am–8:50 pm, Sun. 9:10 am–8:50 pm. Approx every 20 mins. **Windermere Lake Cruises** ⊠ Windermere ☎ 015394/43360 ⊕ www.windermere-lakecruises.co.uk.

Visitor Information **Windermere Tourist Information Centre** ⊠ Victoria St. ☎ 015394/46499 ⊕ www.exploresouthlakeland.co.uk.

Walk through an underwater tunnel and learn about the Lake District's fish, frogs, and otters at the Lakes Aquarium near Windermere.

EXPLORING

TOP ATTRACTIONS

Fodor's Choice ★ **Blackwell.** From 1898 to 1900, architect Mackay Hugh Baillie Scott (1865–1945) designed Blackwell, a quintessential Arts and Crafts house with carved paneling, delicate plasterwork, and a startling sense of light and space. Originally a retreat for a Manchester brewery owner, the house is a refined mix of modern style and the local vernacular. Lime-washed walls and sloping slate roofs make it fit elegantly into the landscape above Windermere, and the artful integration of decorative features into stained glass, stonework, friezes, and wrought iron gives the house a sleekly contemporary feel. Accessibility is wonderful here: nothing is roped off and you can even play the piano. Peruse the shop and try the honey-roast ham in the excellent tearoom. The grounds are also worth a visit: they often host contemporary sculpture installations. ✉ B5360 ☎ 015394/46139 ⊕ www.blackwell. org.uk ⬚£7.20; garden only £4 ⊗ Apr.–Oct., daily 10:30–5; Nov., Dec., and mid-Jan.–Mar., daily 10:30–4.

FAMILY Fodor's Choice ★ **Lakes Aquarium.** On the quayside at the southern end of Windermere, this excellent aquarium has wildlife and waterside exhibits. One highlight is an underwater tunnel walk along a re-created lake bed, complete with diving ducks and Asian short-clawed otters. Piranhas, rays, and tropical frogs also have their fans, and there are some unexpected extra treats such as marmosets, a caiman, and Cinder the boa constrictor. A friendly, knowledgeable staff is eager to talk about the animals. ▥TIP→ Animal handling takes place daily at 12:45 in the rain-forest areas. ✉ C5062, Lakeside ☎ 015394/30153 ⊕ www.lakesaquarium.

co.uk 🖱 *£8.95; £12.15 combined ticket with Lakeside & Haverthwaite Railway Company* ⊘ *Apr.–Oct., daily 9–6; Nov.–Mar., daily 9–5; last entry 1 hr before closing.*

OFF THE BEATEN PATH

Orrest Head. To escape the traffic and have a view of Windermere, set out on foot and follow the signs to the left of the Windermere Hotel to Orrest Head. The shady, uphill path winds through Elleray Wood, and after a 20-minute hike you arrive at a rocky little summit (784 feet) with a panoramic view that encompasses the Yorkshire fells, Morecambe Bay, and the beautiful Troutbeck Valley.

Windermere. No sights in Windermere or Bowness compete with that of Windermere itself. At 11 miles long, 1½ miles wide, and 220 feet deep, the lake is England's largest and stretches from Newby Bridge almost to Ambleside, filling a rocky gorge between thickly wooded hills. The cold waters are superb for fishing, especially for Windermere char, a rare lake trout. In summer, steamers and pleasure craft travel the lake, and a trip across the island-studded waters, particularly the round-trip from Bowness to Ambleside or down to Lakeside, is wonderful. Although the lake's marinas and piers have some charm, you can bypass the busier stretches of shoreline (in summer they can be packed solid) by walking beyond the boathouses. Here, from among the pine trees, are fine views across the lake. Windermere Lake Cruises offers a variety of excursions. ⊕ *www.windermere-lakecruises.co.uk.*

ARTS AND CRAFTS TRAIL

The Arts and Crafts movement of the late 19th century flourished in the Lake District, inspired by the landscape as well as the writings of John Ruskin, who lived here. The search for meaningful style produced many artistic gems in the area's houses, churches, and hotels. At Blackwell you can purchase an Arts and Crafts Trail map and explore the best of them. Blackwell's website, ⊕ *www.blackwell.org.uk,* has extensive information about trail sites.

WORTH NOTING

FAMILY **Brockhole.** A lakeside 19th-century mansion with 30 acres of terraced gardens sloping down to the water, Brockhole serves as the park's official visitor center and has exhibits about the local ecology, flora, and fauna. Impressive aerial photography is good for orientation and inspiration, making it a good stop at the start of your visit. The gardens, designed in the Arts and Crafts style by Thomas Mawson, are at their best in spring, when daffodils punctuate the lawns and azaleas burst into bloom. There's an adventure playground, croquet field, miniature golf course, and rowboats for hire, and an aerial walkway and zipline through the trees are being added. The bookstore carries hiking guides and maps, and you can picnic here or eat at the café-restaurant. Bus 555/559 goes to the visitor center from Windermere and boats from Waterhead stop at a pier. Windermere Lake Cruises has seasonal ferry service to Brockhole from Waterhead in Ambleside. ✉ *Ambleside Rd.* ☎ *015394/46601* ⊕ *www.brockhole.co.uk* 🖱 *Free* ⊘ *Mid-Feb.–Oct., daily 10–5. Gardens daily dawn–dusk.*

FAMILY **Lakeside & Haverthwaite Railway Company.** Vintage steam trains chug along on the 4-mile branch line between Lakeside and Haverthwaite, giving you a great view of the lake's southern tip. You can add on a lake cruise for another perspective on the region's natural beauty. Departures from Lakeside coincide with ferry arrivals from Bowness and Ambleside. ⊠ *A590, Haverthwaite* ☏ *015395/31594* ⊕ *www.lakesiderailway. co.uk* ⊑ *£6.40 round-trip; £12.15 combined ticket with Lakeside Aquarium* ⊙ *Apr.–Oct., daily 10:30–6.*

FAMILY **World of Beatrix Potter.** A touristy attraction aimed at kids interprets the author's 23 tales with three-dimensional scenes of Peter Rabbit and more. Skip it if you can and visit Potter's former home at Hill Top and the Beatrix Potter Gallery in Hawkshead. ⊠ *The Old Laundry, Crag Brow, Bowness-on-Windermere* ☏ *0844/504–1233* ⊕ *www.hopskip-jump.com* ⊑ *£6.95* ⊙ *Apr.–Sept., daily 10–5:30; Oct.–Mar., daily 10–4:30; closed 1 week end of Jan.*

WHERE TO EAT

$ ✕ **Angel Inn.** Up the steep slope from the water's edge in Bowness, this
BRITISH spacious, stylish pub serves good home-cooked fare as well as a fine collection of beers that includes its own Hawkshead brew. Specials, chalked on a board, might be grilled sole with crushed crab and charbroiled steak with thyme-roasted tomatoes. Leather sofas and open fires make the Angel a cozy place; service is low-key and friendly, and the decoration is bright, minimal, and contemporary, with wooden floors and off-white walls. Thirteen comfortable, good-value bedrooms complete the picture. $ *Average main: £14* ⊠ *Helm Rd., Bowness-on-Windermere* ☏ *015394/44080* ⊕ *www.theangelinnbowness.com.*

$$ ✕ **Giotto.** Set back from the town's main street, this smart Italian eat-
ITALIAN ery has an authentic wood-fired oven. There's a good choice of Italian dishes such as gnocchi and salmon with a Parmesan, pesto, and breadcrumb topping, but it's the crispy pizzas that are the real stars. Head for the outdoor seating in summer. The early evening menu is good value. $ *Average main: £15* ⊠ *Jester Court, Birch St., Grasmere* ☏ *015394/44854* ⊙ *Closed Mon. No lunch.*

$$ ✕ **Jerichos at the Waverley.** The area's most stylish restaurant occupies
MODERN BRITISH an 1870 Victorian building near the center of town and has 10 smart bedrooms upstairs; staying here means you'll also get a high-quality breakfast. An open kitchen, leather-backed chairs, bare wood, and candles give the place a contemporary look and make for a sophisticated evening out. Choices from the brief, frequently changing Modern British menu might include beef with a wine sauce or lamb on horseradish mash with buttered cabbage. $ *Average main: £18* ⊠ *College Rd.* ☏ *015394/42522* ⊕ *www.jerichos.co.uk* ⊙ *Closed Mon. and Thurs., last 2 wks of Nov., and 1st wk of Dec. No lunch.*

$ ✕ **Lazy Daisy's.** Wooden floors, a big window onto the main street,
BRITISH displays of hops, and the smell of homemade bread: it's a Lakeland kitchen with a contemporary twist. Try the daily roast, slow cooked with herbs, or great sandwiches such as melted Brie, bacon, and tomato, and homemade soup. Good all day are cakes such as "lumpy bumpy"—a caloric mix of peanuts, sugar, and chocolate. This friendly and cozy coffee shop also serves a full dinner menu, and there's Wi-Fi,

10

too. $ *Average main: £12* ✉ *31–
33 Crescent Rd.* ☎ *015394/43877*
⊕ *www.lazydaisyslakelandkitchen.
co.uk* ☽ *Sun.*

$$ ✕ **Queen's Head Hotel.** An unpre-
BRITISH tentious 17th-century inn in the
pretty little village of Troutbeck,
the Queen's Head serves innova-
tive pub food all through the day.
Dishes may include free-range duck
with cashews and watermelon or
fish-and-chips made with a vodka
batter. It's also noted for real ales served from what was once an Eliza-
bethan four-poster bed. The intimate dining rooms have oak beams,
flagged floors, and log fires. Lunches can be less hearty than the excellent
evening meals. If you want to stay overnight, the 15 guest rooms have
splendid views. $ *Average main: £15* ✉ *A592, 3 miles north of Winder-
mere, Troutbeck* ☎ *015394/32174* ⊕ *www.queensheadtroutbeck.co.uk.*

STAY ON A FARM

Sally's Cottages (⊕ *www.
sallyscottages.co.uk*) is a good
place to start checking out farm
stays. Go Lakes (⊕ *www.golakes.
co.uk*) has a wide range of less
luxurious options. Prices can be
reasonable, but you'll need a car
for most.

WHERE TO STAY

For expanded hotel reviews, visit Fodors.com.

$ ⛻ **1 Park Road.** On a quiet street, this upmarket boutique B&B has
B&B/INN spacious guest rooms with carefully chosen fabrics and contempo-
Fodor'sChoice rary touches such as iPod docking stations. **Pros:** welcoming and
★ stylish; collects guests from the station; good food, wine, and beer.
Cons: a 15-minute walk to the lake. $ *Rooms from: £84* ✉ *1 Park
Rd.* ☎ *015394/42107* ⊕ *www.1parkroad.com* ⇌ *6 rooms* ⅧⅠ *Breakfast.*

$ ⛻ **Archway Guesthouse.** A chef and a restaurant manager make a friendly
B&B/INN and well-qualified team running this excellent little guesthouse in a
Victorian building near the train station. **Pros:** great value; uncluttered
sitting area; rooms at front have good views. **Cons:** not as much space
as you might find elsewhere. $ *Rooms from: £75* ✉ *13 College Rd.*
☎ *015394/45613* ⊕ *www.the-archway.co.uk* ⇌ *4 rooms* ⅧⅠ *Breakfast.*

$$$$ ⛻ **Gilpin Lodge.** Hidden among 22 acres of grounds with meandering
HOTEL paths leading to sleek, spacious lodges, this rambling country-house
Fodor'sChoice hotel pampers you in a low-key way. **Pros:** plenty of pampering; notable
★ food; a policy of no weddings or conferences. **Cons:** a little out of the
way; expensive rates. $ *Rooms from: £310* ✉ *Crook Rd., 2 miles east
of Windermere, Bowness-on-Windermere* ☎ *015394/88818* ⊕ *www.
gilpinlodge.co.uk* ⇌ *26 rooms and suites* ⅧⅠ *Some meals.*

$ ⛻ **Ivy Bank.** One of Windermere's smartest bed-and-breakfasts, spotless
B&B/INN Ivy Bank is in a quiet, leafy part of town. **Pros:** bike storage; good walks
nearby, family room. **Cons:** most rooms have showers, but no tubs.
$ *Rooms from: £80* ✉ *Holly Rd.* ☎ *015394/42601* ⊕ *www.ivy-bank.
co.uk* ⇌ *5 rooms* ⅧⅠ *Breakfast.*

$$$ ⛻ **Miller Howe.** A lovely location, lake views, and superb service help set
HOTEL this luxurious Edwardian country-house hotel apart. **Pros:** more than 5
Fodor'sChoice acres of grounds; great lake views; staff that take care of the little extras.
★ **Cons:** sometimes closes for a couple of weeks in winter. $ *Rooms from:
£210* ✉ *Rayrigg Rd., Bowness-on-Windermere* ☎ *015394/42536*
⊕ *www.millerhowe.com* ⇌ *15 rooms* ⅧⅠ *Some meals.*

$$$
HOTEL
Fodor's Choice
★

Punch Bowl Inn. An outstanding inn and restaurant, the Punch Bowl is a stylish but down-to-earth retreat in the peaceful Lyth Valley, between Windermere and Kendal. **Pros:** contemporary design; relaxed atmosphere; excellent food. **Cons:** a little way from the area's main sights. $ *Rooms from: £165* ⊠ *Off A5074, Crosthwaite* ☎ *015395/68237* ⊕ *www.the-punchbowl.co.uk* ↳ *9 rooms* ⏐⊙⏐ *Breakfast.*

$$$$
HOTEL

The Samling. On its own sculpture-dotted 67 acres above Windermere, this place oozes exclusivity from every carefully fashioned corner. **Pros:** you'll feel like a star, and may sit next to one at breakfast, too. **Cons:** exclusivity doesn't come cheap. $ *Rooms from: £280* ⊠ *Ambleside Rd.* ☎ *01539/431922* ⊕ *www.thesamlinghotel.co.uk* ↳ *11 suites* ⏐⊙⏐ *Breakfast.*

SHOPPING

The best selection of shops is at the Bowness end of Windermere, on Lake Road and around Queen's Square: clothing stores, crafts shops, and souvenir stores of all kinds.

Fodor's Choice
★

More? The Artisan Baker. Between Kendal and Windermere, this bakery is the place to stop for mouthwatering, award-winning bread, cakes, and sandwiches. It also brews fine coffee. ⊠ *Mill Yard, Staveley* ☎ *015398/22297* ⊕ *www.moreartisan.co.uk.*

SPORTS AND THE OUTDOORS

BIKING

Country Lanes Cycle Hire. This shop rents a variety of bikes from £16 per day. ⊠ *Windermere Railway Station, off A591* ☎ *015394/44544* ⊕ *www.countrylaneslakedistrict.co.uk.*

BOATING

Windermere Lake Holidays. This company rents a wide range of vessels, from small sailboats to houseboats. ⊠ *Mereside, Ferry Nab, Bowness-on-Windermere* ☎ *015394/43415* ⊕ *www.lakewindermere.net.*

AMBLESIDE

7 miles northwest of Windermere.

Unlike Kendal and Windermere, Ambleside seems almost part of the hills and fells. Its buildings, mainly of local stone and many built in the traditional style that forgoes the use of mortar in the outer walls, blend perfectly into their setting. The small town sits at the northern end of Windermere along A591, making it a popular center for Lake District excursions. It has a better choice of restaurants than Windermere or Bowness, and the numerous outdoor shops are handy for fell walkers. Ambleside does, however, suffer from overcrowding in high season. Wednesday, when the local market takes place, is particularly busy.

10

GETTING HERE AND AROUND

An easy drive along A591 from Windermere, Ambleside can also be reached by ferry.

ESSENTIALS

Visitor Information Ambleside Tourist Information Centre
⊠ *The Hub, Central Bldgs., Market Cross, Rydal Rd.* ☎ *0844/225 0544* ⊕ *www.thehubofambleside.co.uk.*

EXPLORING

Armitt Museum. Ambleside's fine local-history gallery and library explores the town's past and its surroundings through the eyes of local people such as Beatrix Potter. A large collection of Beatrix Potter's natural-history watercolors and a huge number of photographic portraits can be viewed by appointment in the excellent library upstairs. Temporary exhibitions of art with a local connection are widely lauded. ✉ *Rydal Rd.* ☎ *015394/31212* 🌐 *www.armitt.com* 🎟 *£2.50* 🕐 *Mon.–Sat. 10–5; last admission at 4:30.*

Bridge House. This tiny 17th-century stone building, once an apple store, perches on an arched stone bridge spanning Stone Beck. It may have been built here to avoid land tax. This much-photographed building holds a shop and an information center. ✉ *Rydal Rd.* ☎ *015394/35599* 🎟 *Free* 🕐 *Easter–Oct., daily 10–5.*

QUICK BITES

Sheila's Cottage. Serving great homemade cakes and desserts, cozy Sheila's Cottage is a good place to gather the strength for a walk or to relax after one by the fire. Try a good-value afternoon tea with tea bread or, for full calorie replenishment, go for a hot chocolate loaded with cream. The place also sells wine and local beer. ✉ ***The Slack*** ☎ ***015394/33079*** 🌐 ***www.sheilascottage.co.uk.***

WHERE TO EAT

$ VEGETARIAN Fodor's Choice ★

🍴 **Fellinis.** Billing itself as "Vegeterranean" to reflect its Mediterranean culinary influences, Fellinis is one of Cumbria's finest foodie destinations. Upstairs is a plush studio cinema screening art-house releases, while downstairs the restaurant rustles up sumptuous concoctions for a sophisticated crowd. The menu's imaginative dishes might start with sweet potato galletes, then continue with herb and three-cheese phyllo-dough pastry topped with a spiced tomato and coriander sauce. The large, open dining room has soft seating, bold patterns, oversize lamp shades, and a chill, jazzy soundtrack. White tablecloths, contemporary art, and fresh flowers enhance the modern sensibility. [$] *Average main: £12* ✉ *Church St.* ☎ *01539/433845* 🌐 *www.fellinisambleside.com* 🕐 *No lunch.*

$ MODERN BRITISH

🍴 **Glass House.** A converted medieval mill with a working waterwheel is an atmospheric setting for this restaurant serving Modern British cuisine. Despite the name, wood predominates, with huge, thick beams and an open fire. Look for an international twist in dishes such as chicken liver parfait with toasted brioche or braised lamb with potatoes. You can have an elegant dinner, a good value lunch, or just sip a cappuccino in the courtyard beside the stream. [$] *Average main: £12* ✉ *Rydal Rd.* ☎ *015394/32137* 🌐 *www.theglasshouserestaurant.co.uk* ✍ *Reservations essential.*

$ BRITISH

🍴 **Lucy's on a Plate.** Ambleside's favorite informal eatery has survived various travails and remains a good spot to relax, whether with mushroom stroganoff for lunch, a chocolate almond torte for afternoon tea, or grilled char for dinner by candlelight. One room has scrubbed pine tables; a conservatory provides additional seating. Lucy's is famous for its wide selection of puddings (desserts), so make sure to save some room. [$] *Average main: £9* ✉ *Church St.* ☎ *015394/31191* 🌐 *www.lucysofambleside.co.uk.*

WHERE TO STAY

For expanded hotel reviews, visit Fodors.com.

$ **3 Cambridge Villas.** It's hard to find a more welcoming spot than this
B&B/INN lofty Victorian house right in the center of town, thanks to hosts who
know a thing or two about local walks. **Pros:** especially good value for
single travelers; warm family welcome; central location. **Cons:** some
rooms are a little cramped; can occasionally be noisy. $ *Rooms from:
£75 ✉ 3 Church St. ☎ 015394/32307 ⊕ www.3cambridgevillas.co.uk
⇨ 7 rooms, 5 with bath ⏐⊙⏐ Breakfast.*

$ **Rooms at the Apple Pie.** Converted from what were once the offices
B&B/INN of Beatrix Potter's solicitor husband, one of Ambleside's best cafés has
branched out into accommodations. **Pros:** scrumptious breakfasts; central location. **Cons:** not staffed 24 hours a day. $ *Rooms from: £80
✉ Rydal Rd., Keswick ☎ 015394/33679 ⊕ www.roomsattheapplepie.
co.uk ⇨ 8 rooms ⏐⊙⏐ Breakfast.*

SPORTS AND THE OUTDOORS

The fine walks in the vicinity include routes north to Rydal Mount or
southeast over Wansfell to Troutbeck. Each walk will take up to a half
day, there and back. Ferries from Bowness-on-Windermere dock at
Ambleside's harbor, called Waterhead. ▪▪TIP➜ To escape the crowds,
rent a rowboat at the harbor for an hour or two.

RYDAL

1 mile northwest of Ambleside.

The village of Rydal, on the small glacial lake called Rydal Water, is
rich with Wordsworthian associations.

EXPLORING

Dora's Field. One famous beauty spot linked with Wordsworth is Dora's
Field, below Rydal Mount next to the church of **St. Mary's** (where you
can still see the poet's pew). In spring the field is awash in yellow daffodils, planted by William Wordsworth and his wife in memory of their
beloved daughter Dora, who died in 1847. ✉ A591.

Rydal Mount. If there's one poet associated with the Lake District, it is
Wordsworth, who made his home at Rydal Mount from 1813 until his
death. Wordsworth and his family moved to these grand surroundings
when he was nearing the height of his career, and his descendants still
live here, surrounded by his furniture, his books, his barometer, and
portraits. You can see the study in which he worked, Dorothy's bedroom, and the 4½-acre garden, laid out by the poet himself, that gave
him so much pleasure. ▪▪TIP➜ Wordsworth's favorite footpath can be
found on the hill past White Moss Common and the River Rothay. Spend
an hour or two walking the paths and you may understand why the
great poet composed most of his verse in the open air. A tearoom in
the former saddlery provides cakes and drinks; in winter it moves into
the dining room. ✉ Off A591 ☎ 015394/33002 ⊕ www.rydalmount.
co.uk 🖘 £6.75; garden only £4.50 ⊗ Mar.–Oct., daily 9:30–5; Nov.,
Dec., and Feb., Wed.–Sun. 11–4.

10

WHERE TO STAY

For expanded hotel reviews, visit Fodors.com.

$$ B&B/INN **Cote How Organic Guest House.** Elegant, peaceful, and with a focus on organic and sustainable fare, Cote How is a cut above most of the B&Bs in the lakes. **Pros:** beautiful gardens; great organic food; spacious rooms. **Cons:** location is great for walks and privacy, less so if you want other amenities; no kids under 8. [$] *Rooms from: £140* ✉ *Off A591* ☎ *015394/32765* 🌐 *www.cotehow.co.uk* *3 rooms* 🍴 *Breakfast.*

GRASMERE

3 miles north of Rydal, 4 miles northwest of Ambleside.

Fodor's Choice ★ Lovely Grasmere, on a tiny, wood-fringed lake, is made up of crooked lanes in which Westmorland slate–built cottages hold shops and galleries. The village is a focal point for literary and landscape associations because this area was the adopted heartland of the Romantic poets, notably Wordsworth and Coleridge. The Vale of Grasmere has changed over the years, but many features Wordsworth wrote about are still visible. Wordsworth lived on the town's outskirts for almost 50 years and described the area as "the loveliest spot that man hath ever known."

GETTING HERE AND AROUND

On the main A591 between Ambleside and Keswick, Grasmere is easily reached by car.

ESSENTIALS

Visitor Information **Grasmere Tourist Information Centre** ✉ *Church Stile* ☎ *015394/35665* 🌐 *www.nationaltrust.org.uk/grasmere.*

EXPLORING

FAMILY Fodor's Choice ★ **Allan Bank.** Rope swings on the grounds, picnics in atmospheric old rooms, and walls you can write on: Allan Bank is unlike most other historic houses cared for by the National Trust. On a hill above the lake near Grasmere village, Allan Bank was once home to poet William Wordsworth. Seriously damaged by fire in 2011, it has been partially restored but also left deliberately undecorated. It offers a much less formal experience than other stops on the Wordsworth trail. There are frequent child-friendly activities. Red squirrels can be seen on the woodland walk through the grounds. ✉ *Off A591, Grasmere* 🌐 *www.nationaltrust.org.uk* 🎫 *£4.80* 🕐 *Mid-Mar.–Dec., daily 10–5.*

Dove Cottage and Wordsworth Museum. William Wordsworth lived in Dove Cottage from 1799 to 1808, a prolific and happy time for the poet. During this time he wrote some of his most famous works including, "Ode: Intimations of Immortality" and *The Prelude*. Built in the early 17th century as an inn, this tiny, dim, and, in some places, dank, house is beautifully preserved, with an oak-paneled hall and floors of Westmorland slate. It first opened to the public in 1891 and remains as it was when Wordsworth lived here with his sister, Dorothy, and wife, Mary. Bedrooms and living areas contain much of Wordsworth's furniture and many personal belongings. Coleridge was a frequent visitor, as was Thomas De Quincey, best known for his 1822 autobiographical masterpiece *Confessions of an English Opium-Eater*. De Quincey

One of the Lake District's literary landmarks, Dove Cottage near Grasmere was where poet William Wordsworth wrote many famous works.

moved in after the Wordsworths left. You visit the house on a timed guided tour, and the ticket includes admission to the spacious, modern Wordsworth Museum, which documents the poet's life and the literary contributions of Wordsworth and the Lake Poets. The museum includes space for major art exhibitions. The **Jerwood Centre,** open to researchers by appointment, houses 50,000 letters, first editions, and manuscripts. Afternoon tea is served at **Villa Colombina.** ⊠ *A591, south of Grasmere* ☎ *015394/35544* ⊕ *www.wordsworth.org.uk* ☜ *£7.50* ⊗ *Mar.–Oct., daily 9:30–5:30; Nov.–Feb., daily 9:30–4:30.*

QUICK BITES **Heidi's.** This bustling, cozy little café and deli is lined with jars of locally made jams and chutneys. Bang in the center of Grasmere, it's great for coffee and a homemade pastry or flapjack (bars made with syrup, butter, and oats). ⊠ *Red Lion Sq.* ☎ *015394/35248* ⊕ *www.heidisgrasmerelodge.co.uk.*

St. Oswald's. William Wordsworth, his wife Mary, his sister Dorothy, and four of his children are buried in the churchyard of this church on the River Rothay. The poet planted eight of the yew trees here. As you leave the churchyard, stop at the Gingerbread Shop, in a tiny cottage, for a special local treat. ⊠ *Stock La.* ⊕ *www.grasmereandrydal.org.uk.*

WHERE TO EAT

$$ ⨉ **The Jumble Room.** A small stone building dating to the 18th century, Grasmere's first shop is now a friendly, fashionable, and colorful place, with children's books, bold animal paintings, and hanging lamps. A dedicated local fan base means the place always buzzes, and the owners' enthusiasm is contagious. The food is an eclectic mix

BRITISH
Fodor's Choice
★

10

of international and traditional British: excellent fish-and-chips and beefsteak appear on the menu with polenta gnocchi with beetroot, pesto, and thyme-roasted pumpkin. Lunches are lighter and cheaper, with good soups and homemade puddings; bread is baked fresh every day. Note: hours change frequently, so call ahead. $\boxed{\$}$ *Average main: £15 ⌧ Langdale Rd. ☎ 015394/35188 ⊕ www.thejumbleroom.co.uk ⊗ Closed Mon. and Tues.*

$$ ✕ **Tweedies Bar.** One of the region's best gastro-pubs, Tweedies attracts
MODERN BRITISH many locals as well as visitors. Delicious updated British classics include
Fodor'sChoice pork stuffed with apricots and wrapped in prosciutto, and venison with
★ potato and beetroot dauphinoise. Everything is served in a smart, cozy, wood-filled contemporary pub with mellow music, flickering candles, a slate floor, and a fireplace. The Lodge Restaurant in the Dale Lodge Hotel next door serves the same menu in a more formal setting. Several of Cumbria's best beers are on tap alongside a good selection of world beers. $\boxed{\$}$ *Average main: £16 ⌧ Langdale Rd. ☎ 015394/35300 ⊕ www. tweediesbargrasmere.co.uk.*

WHERE TO STAY

For expanded hotel reviews, visit Fodors.com.

$ ▦ **Banerigg House.** A cozy family home less than a mile south of the vil-
B&B/INN lage, Banerigg House has unfussy, well-appointed rooms, most with lake views. **Pros:** very welcoming hosts; good value for single rooms; canoes available. **Cons:** a little out of town; the house has an awkward turn onto the busy road. $\boxed{\$}$ *Rooms from: £78 ⌧ Lake Rd. ☎ 015394/35204 ⊕ www.guesthouse-cumbria.co.uk ⇱ 6 rooms, 5 with bath ▭ No credit cards* ⦿❘ *Breakfast.*

$ ▦ **Heidi's Grasmere Lodge.** Small but sumptuous, this lodging has a dis-
B&B/INN tinctly feminine sensibility, with floral wallpaper, curly steel lamps,
Fodor'sChoice and painted woodwork. **Pros:** chic bathrooms with whirlpool tubs;
★ warm welcome. **Cons:** no children allowed; so pristine you may worry about your muddy boots. $\boxed{\$}$ *Rooms from: £89 ⌧ Red Lion Sq. ☎ 015394/35248 ⊕ www.heidisgrasmerelodge.co.uk ⇱ 6 rooms* ⦿❘ *Breakfast.*

$$$ ▦ **Moss Grove.** A Victorian building in the heart of Grasmere, the chic
B&B/INN and spacious Moss Grove has an emphasis on its environmental creden- tials. **Pros:** plenty of room; huge chunky furniture; modern design with a conscience. **Cons:** tight parking; not the place for a big fry-up break- fast. $\boxed{\$}$ *Rooms from: £179 ⌧ Red Lion Sq. ☎ 015394/35251 ⊕ www. mossgrove.com ⇱ 11 rooms* ⦿❘ *Breakfast.*

SHOPPING

Fodor'sChoice **Grasmere Gingerbread Shop.** The smells wafting across the churchyard
★ draw many people to the Grasmere Gingerbread Shop. Since 1854 Sarah Nelson's gingerbread has been sold from this cramped 17th- century cottage, which was once the village school. The delicious treats, still made from a secret recipe, are available in attractive tins for the journey home or to eat right away. ⌧ *Church Cottage ☎ 015394/35428 ⊕ www.grasmeregingerbread.co.uk.*

CLOSE UP

Poetry, Prose, and the Lakes

The Lake District's beauty has whetted the creativity of many a famous poet and artist over the centuries. Here's a quick rundown of some of the writers inspired by the area's vistas.

William Wordsworth (1770–1850), one of the first English Romantics, redefined poetry by replacing the mannered style of his predecessors with a more conversational style. Many of his greatest works, such as *The Prelude,* draw directly from his experiences in the Lake District, where he spent the first 20 and last 50 years of his life. Wordsworth and his work had an enormous effect on Coleridge, Keats, Shelley, Byron, and countless other writers. Explore his homes in Rydal and Grasmere, among other sites.

John Ruskin (1819–1900), writer, art critic, and early conservationist, was an impassioned champion of new ways of seeing. He defended contemporary artists such as William Turner and the Pre-Raphaelites. His five-volume masterwork, *Modern Painters,* changed the role of the art critic from that of approver or naysayer to that of interpreter. Stop by Coniston to see his home and the Ruskin Museum.

Thomas De Quincey (1785–1859) wrote essays whose impressionistic style influenced many 19th-century writers, including Poe and Baudelaire. His most famous work, *Confessions of an English Opium-Eater* (1822), is an imaginative memoir of his young life, which indeed included opium addiction. He settled in Grasmere in 1809.

Beatrix Potter (1866–1943) never had a formal education; instead, she spent her childhood studying nature. Her love of the outdoors, and Lakeland scenery in particular, influenced her delightfully illustrated children's books, including *The Tale of Peter Rabbit* and *The Tale of Jemima Puddle-Duck.* Potter also became a noted conservationist who donated land to the National Trust. The story of her life was made into the 2006 film *Miss Potter,* starring Renée Zellweger and Ewan McGregor. Today you can visit Hill Top, the writer-artist's home in Hawkshead.

10

SPORTS AND THE OUTDOORS

Loughrigg Terrace. The most panoramic views of lake and village are from the south of Grasmere, from the bare slopes of Loughrigg Terrace, reached along a well-signposted track on the western side of the lake or through the woods from parking lots on the A591 between Grasmere and Rydal Water. It's less than an hour's walk from the village, though your stroll can be extended by continuing around Rydal Water, passing Rydal Mount, detouring onto White Moss Common before returning to Dove Cottage and Grasmere, a 4-mile (three-hour) walk in total.

Continued on page 621

IN FOCUS HIKING IN THE LAKE DISTRICT

HIKING IN THE LAKE DISTRICT
by Julius Honnor

From easy strolls around lakes to mountain climbs, the Lake District has some of England's best hiking. The landscape is generally accessible but also spectacular, with crashing streams cascading from towering mountains into the rivers and lakes that define the region. The scenery that inspired Wordsworth and Ruskin, among many others, is best experienced on an exhilarating walk.

With its highest mountain topping out at just 3,209 feet, the Lake District has peaks that are sometimes sniffed at by hardcore hikers, but they provide a stunning and not always benevolent setting. In winter the peaks are often ice- and snow-bound, and even routes at lower levels can occasionally be impassable.

There is plenty of variety to suit all abilities and enthusiasms, and almost everywhere you go in the national park you'll come across wooden footpath signs pointing the way over stiles and across fields. Paths are usually well maintained and, especially in summer, the most popular trails can be busy with booted walking hordes. Many people don't venture far from their cars, however, and peace and solitude are usually only a hillside or two away.

Many lakes and tarns (small mountain lakes) have paths that skirt their edges, though to see the best of the region you should head upward into the fells (mountains) and valleys, where the landscape becomes increasingly grand. Some of the best routes combine a boat ride with a walk up a fellside. When your walk is over, be sure to reward yourself with a pint at the pub.

Above: View of Troutbeck Park, a farm near Troutbeck that writer Beatrix Potter left to the National Trust

CHOOSE YOUR BEST DAY HIKE

Trails are abundant in the Lake District: you can walk just about anywhere, but a little planning will be rewarded. It's worthwhile to buy a good Ordnance Survey map, too. The routes included here, from 90 minutes to 5 hours, all show the national park at its best, from the southern lakes to the wilder, bleaker northern lakes. A couple of the trails are fairly popular, well-trodden routes; others take you off the most beaten paths. Several include a boat trip for extra enjoyment— just don't miss the last boat home.

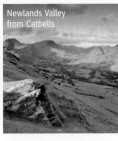

Newlands Valley from Catbells

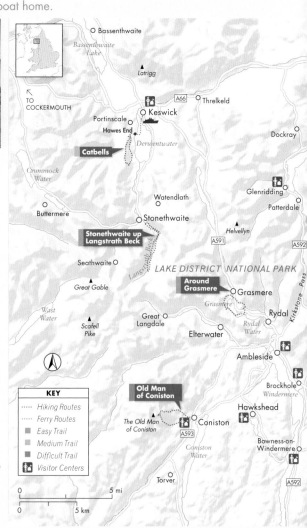

CATBELLS

Medium; 3.6 miles walking, plus boat ride to and from Keswick; 1 hour, 30 minutes walking
Starting point: Hawes End

This classic, popular Lakes route climbs the long, fairly gently sloping hill of Catbells, above Derwentwater. You'll need to catch the ferry from Keswick to the beginning of the route at Hawes End. The Keswick-on-Derwentwater Launch Co (☎ *017687/72263*, ⊕ *www. keswick-launch.co.uk*) runs a boat every hour in summer, less frequently in winter.

From the ferry landing stage, climb straight uphill before heading right (south) along the spine of the hill to the summit. From Catbells, the views over Derwentwater and beyond to the high fells of Skiddaw and

Borrowdale

On Pillar mountain, western Lake District

Blencathra are breathtaking. Take the lower path, nearer the lake, on the return in order to make this a circular route. The route can be shortened by catching a boat back from High Bran-delhow or Low Brandel-how (other landing stages) instead of Hawes End.

STONETHWAITE UP LANGSTRATH BECK
Easy; 6 miles; 2 hours, 30 minutes
Starting point: Stonethwaite

In the high valleys in the middle of the Lake District, rivers become streams and wind through a wonderfully wild, largely treeless land-scape away from the lakes themselves.. Running south from Derwentwater, Bor-rowdale is one of the most beautiful valleys around, but for even more spectacular walking country continue to the hamlet of Stonethwaite, from where the road becomes a track and then

red deer

a path as it leads up beside the beck, the valley opening out into moorland. At the bottom of the valley, the climb is a fairly gentle one. About 3 miles upstream, cross a bridge and return on the other side of the stream. The Langstrath Inn makes a good food and drink spot at the end of the walk.

TROUTBECK TO THORNTHWAITE CRAG
Difficult; 9.8 miles; 4–5 hours
Starting point: Troutbeck

Windermere is more known for its boating, but you can find great mountain routes. Starting in the village of Troutbeck, 3 miles north of Windermere, this walk drops down into the valley, fol-lowing the stream of Hagg Gill and climbing around a hill known as the Troutbeck Tongue. The trail then rises onto the ridge of Thorn-thwaite Crag, from where there are vertiginous views. Parts of this upper section are steep. For the return to Troutbeck, head west into the valley of the Trout Beck (stream) itself. Back in the village of Troutbeck, the Queen's Head Hotel is a great pub for food and drink.

10

Looking away from Martindale, toward Ullswater.

KENTMERE TO LONG SLEDDALE
Medium; 4.5 miles; 2 hours, 30 minutes
Starting point: Kentmere

Easily accessible from popular centers in the south of the region such as Windermere or Kendal, Kentmere and Long Sleddale are nevertheless in a part of the national park that many visitors bypass in their haste to get to the lakes—and that's a shame. These two valleys are beautiful examples of rural Cumbria, and the easy climb from one to another has some great views.

For a circular route, head south along the road from the village of Kentmere before heading left up the hill and across high moorland and down into the grand valley of Long Sleddale. The trail is a pleasant loop.

■ TIP→ Stop off at More? The Artisan Baker (⊕ www.moreartisan.co.uk), in Mill Yard in Staveley, to stock up on cakes and sandwiches to fortify you along the way. You have to pass through Staveley to get to the starting point of the walk.

HOWTOWN TO MARTINDALE
Medium; 7.6 miles plus optional boat ride from Pooley Bridge; 3 hours, 30 minutes plus 25-minute boat ride
Starting point: Howtown

To get to Howtown, you can drive the long, narrow road down the eastern side of Ullswater; but to arrive at this spot in style, catch an antique Ullswater Steamer (⊕ *www.ullswater-steamers.co.uk*) from Pooley Bridge at the lake's northern end.

Martindale is a magically hidden valley, enclosed on all sides by large fells. Climbing the steep switchback road up the bare hillside of Hallin Fell to the pass from the hamlet of Howtown, there is nothing to suggest the beautifully pastoral landscape beyond. Sheep graze at lower levels; higher up the steep sides of the valley are wild and rocky.

To turn this into a circular route, turn left at the top of the valley and return along the ridge of Beda Fell. In Howtown, the eponymous hotel serves food and drink and will make you a take-out lunch.

AROUND GRASMERE
Easy; 3.4 miles (can easily be extended to go around Rydal Water); 1 hour, 30 minutes
Starting point: Grasmere village

Rich with literary and artistic traditions, Grasmere is a bijou little lake easily walked around in an afternoon.

Starting in the village, where there is parking, head counter-clockwise around the lake, skirting the lower edge of Loughrigg Terrace. At the southeastern end of the lake, follow the stream through woods that link Grasmere to Rydal Water. If you want something a little longer, the walk can be extended around Rydal before you cross the A591 and return to Grasmere across White Moss Common.

Snow in the Lake District

View of the Langdale Fells

In Grasmere, Tweedies Bar is a good place for a post-stroll pint.

OLD MAN OF CONISTON

Difficult; 4.6 miles; 2 hours, 30 minutes to 3 hours
Starting point:
Coniston village

Of all the area's classic peaks, the Old Man of Coniston is one of the most accessible. Though it's a fairly steep route that can be difficult in winter, the paths are well-trodden and well-maintained and it doesn't require any climbing to reach the summit, 2,634 feet up. From the top on a clear day, there are extraordinary views down to Coniston Water and around and beyond the Furness Fells.

Set off from the center of the village of Coniston, where the Black Bull Inn offers good hearty food and some excellent ales. Multiple paths to the summit make it easy to turn the walk into a circular route.

PREPARING FOR YOUR HIKE

CHOOSING A HIKE

A glance at a map of the Lake District National Park (⊕ www.lakedistrict.gov.uk) reveals a lacework mesh of footpaths; stop your car at random on a country road and there will probably be a path somewhere nearby. In the Lake District meticulous planning is not necessarily required in order to go for a walk: possibilities for short strolls abound.

The walks suggested offer good options; for other choices and for maps, stop in any town visitor information office or at the Lake District National Park Visitor Centre at Brockhole.

There are trails from this visitor center. You can also join a guided hike. *(For more information on these offices, see the towns in this chapter and the Lake District Planner.)*

WHAT TO WEAR

Check the weather, but expect the unexpected. Good clothing, and clothing for rain, is essential: even at the height of summer, wet weather can roll in from the west and spoil a sunny day. Higher up, too, temperatures are noticeably colder than at lake level, and it's usually much breezier. Generally a good pair of walking boots will suffice, and for lakeside walks you'd probably get by with flat-soled shoes. For the highest routes, snow and ice in winter can linger until spring and a set of slip-on spikes can be useful. The national park is overflowing with shops selling walking clothes, maps, and equipment.

WHAT TO BRING

Carry plenty of water and lightweight, high-energy food—or whatever you want for a picnic. Kendal mint cake is a favorite snack. Don't forget sunscreen and insect repellent. Bring a map: Ordnance Survey maps, available in area bookstores and visitor centers, are the best.

10

A WALK TO THE PUB

Kirkstone Pass Inn

It sometimes feels as if the entire Lake District economy revolves around walkers and walking, and the national park's pubs are no exception. The area has some of the finest exponents of that most English of institutions, the hiker's pub. To get the true flavor of the Lake District, join the locals and drink up.

Most of these pubs offer a hot fire to warm your feet by in cool weather, and some calorie-rich sustenance to send you on your way or replenish energy when you return from your walk. Few have any frills, and the stone floors are meant to be walked on with muddy boots. All offer local Cumbrian ales (some even brew their own), which will never taste as good as after a long hard stride up a steep fell. These pubs usually have their own parking, making them good starting and finishing places for a Lake District walk.

Here's a guide to some of the best, and some of the best placed, pubs.

Britannia Inn. Facing onto the village green in Elterwater, the Britannia is a destination as much as a stopping-point for many ramblers, who spill out onto the terrace of this cozy old pub on sunny days. *Elterwater,* ⊕ *www. britinn.net*

Drunken Duck Inn. Too stylish to be considered an archetypal walkers' pub, the inn has a superb isolated setting and fantastic home-brewed beers that nevertheless make it a great stopping place. A terrace opposite the pub has great views of the central fells and attracts many walkers who might otherwise feel put off by the gastropub interior. *Barngates, near Hawkshead,* ⊕ *www.drunkenduckinn.co.uk*

Kirkstone Pass Inn. At around 1,500 feet above sea level, this old coaching inn is the highest in the Lake District, and well placed for a satisfying pint after a walk on one of the nearby fells. *A592, Kirkstone Pass,* ⊕ *www. kirkstonepassinn.com*

Old Dungeon Ghyll. Isolated at the top of Great Langdale, this 300-year old hotel serves homemade soup and flapjacks (a bar cookie) to waves of passing walkers. *Elterwater,* ⊕ *www.odg.co.uk*

Queen's Head Hotel. Troutbeck's best pub is an excellent all-rounder, serving delicious food in a comfortable atmosphere and good beers from a distinctive bar. It's handily placed for walks up the Troutbeck valley toward Thornthwaite Crag. *Troutbeck, near Windermere,* ⊕ *www.queensheadhotel.com*

ELTERWATER

2½ miles south of Grasmere, 4 miles west of Ambleside.

The delightful village of Elterwater, at the eastern end of the Great Langdale Valley on B5343, is a good stop for hikers. It's barely more than a cluster of houses around a village green, but from here you can choose from a selection of excellent circular walks.

WHERE TO EAT AND STAY

For expanded hotel reviews, visit Fodors.com.

$ BRITISH 🍴 **Britannia Inn.** At this 500-year-old pub, restaurant, and inn in the heart of superb walking country, antiques, comfortable chairs, and prints and oil paintings furnish the cozy, beamed public rooms. The whole family can relax with a bar meal and Cumbrian ale on the terrace while taking in the village green and the rolling scenery beyond. The hearty traditional British food—from grilled sea bass fillet to chicken and leek pie—is popular with locals, as are the many ales and whiskies. The nine smallish guest rooms are more modern in style, and include use of the nearby Langdale Spa's pool, sauna, and fitness room. [$] *Average main: £13* ✉ *B5343* ☎ *015394/37210* 🌐 *thebritanniainn.com.*

$ BRITISH 🍴 **Sticklebarn.** The National Trust owns other pubs, but Sticklebarn is the first one it has run. With its own water supply and hydro-electric power, the pub's aim is sustainability. The kitchen uses as much produce as possible from the immediate area, and makes its own gin and vodka. Most of the menu is traditional pub fare—burgers, macaroni and cheese, and lamb stew, for example—aimed at the Langdale walkers that fill the rustic, wood-beamed dining room. Tables spill out onto the terrace in sunny weather. There's also a wood-fired pizza oven. [$] *Average main: £11* ✉ *Great Langdale* ☎ *01539/437356* 🌐 *www.nationaltrust.org.uk.*

$$ HOTEL 🏨 **Old Dungeon Ghyll Hotel.** There's no more comforting stop after a day outdoors than the Hiker's Bar of this 300-year-old hotel at the head of the Great Langdale Valley. **Pros:** ideally situated for walking; wonderfully isolated; spectacular views all around. **Cons:** no-nonsense approach not to everyone's taste. [$] *Rooms from: £116* ✉ *Off B5343, Great Langdale* ☎ *015394/37272* 🌐 *www.odg.co.uk* 🛏 *12 rooms* 🍽 *Breakfast.*

SPORTS AND THE OUTDOORS

There are access points to Langdale Fell from several spots along B5343, the main road; look for information boards at local parking places. You can also stroll up the river valley or embark on more energetic hikes to Stickle Tarn or to one of the summits of the Langdale Pikes. Beyond the Old Dungeon Ghyll Hotel, the Great Langdale Valley splits in two around a hill known as the Band—a path up its spine has particularly good views back down over the valley and can be continued to the summit of Scafell Pike.

CONISTON

5 miles south of Elterwater.

This small lake resort and boating center attracts climbers to the steep peak of the **Old Man of Coniston** (2,635 feet), which towers above the slate-roof houses. It also has sites related to John Ruskin. Quieter than Windermere, Coniston is a good introduction to the pastoral and watery charms of the area, though the small town itself can get crowded in summer.

GETTING HERE AND AROUND

The Coniston Launch connects Coniston Pier with Ruskin's home at Brantwood and some other stops around the lake, offering hourly service (£10.50 for a day-long, "hop on and off" ticket; £17.15 including entry to Brantwood) on its wooden Ruskin and Ransome launches.

ESSENTIALS

Visitor Information Coniston Launch ⊠ *Coniston* ☎ *017687/75753* ⊕ *www.conistonlaunch.co.uk.* **Coniston Tourist Information Centre** ⊠ *Ruskin Ave.* ☎ *015394/41533* ⊕ *www.conistontic.org.*

EXPLORING

Fodor's Choice ★ **Brantwood.** On the eastern shore of Coniston Water, Brantwood was the cherished home of John Ruskin (1819–1900), the noted Victorian artist, writer, critic, and social reformer, after 1872. The rambling 18th-century house (with Victorian alterations) is on a 250-acre estate that stretches high above the lake. Here, alongside mementos such as his mahogany desk, are Ruskin's own paintings, drawings, and books. On display is art that this great connoisseur collected, and in cerebral corners such as the Ideas Room visitors are encouraged to think about meaning and change. Ruskin's Rocks explores his fascinations with stones and music with a brilliant bit of modern technology. A video on Ruskin's life shows the lasting influence of his thoughts, and the Severn Studio has rotating art exhibitions. Ruskin himself laid out the extensive grounds; take time to explore the gardens and woodland walks. Brantwood hosts a series of classical concerts on some Saturdays as well as talks, guided walks, and study days. ⊠ *Off B5285* ☎ *015394/41396* ⊕ *www.brantwood.org.uk* ⊡ *£7.20; gardens only £4.95* ⊘ *Mid-Mar.– mid-Nov., daily 10.30–5; mid-Nov.–mid-Mar., Wed.–Sun. 10.30–4.*

Coniston Water. The lake came to prominence in the 1930s when Arthur Ransome made it the setting for *Swallows and Amazons,* one of a series of novels about a group of children and their adventures. The lake is about 5 miles long, a tempting stretch that drew Donald Campbell here in 1959 to set a water-speed record of 260 mph. He was killed when trying to beat it in 1967. His body and the wreckage of *Bluebird K7* were retrieved from the lake in 2001. Campbell is buried in St. Andrew's church in Coniston, and a stone memorial on the village green commemorates him.

Ruskin Museum. This repository of fascinating and thought-provoking manuscripts, personal items, and watercolors by John Ruskin illuminates his thinking and influence. There is also a focus on speedboat racer Donald Campbell; the tail fin of his *Bluebird K7,* dragged up from Coniston Water, is here. Good local-interest exhibits include copper mining, geology, lace, and more. ⊠ *Yewdale Rd.* ☎ *015394/41164*

⊕ *www.ruskinmuseum.com*
🎫 *£5.25* ⊙ *Mid-Mar.–mid-Nov.,
daily 10–5:30; mid-Nov.–mid-Mar.,
Wed.–Sun. 10:30–3:30.*

Steam Yacht *Gondola*. The National
Trust's luxurious Victorian steam
yacht (originally launched in 1859
and restored in the 1970s) runs
between Coniston Pier, Brantwood,
and Park-a-Moor at the south end
of Coniston Water, daily from April
through October (£10.50). A stop
at Monk Coniston jetty connects
to the footpaths through the Monk
Coniston Estate, linking Coniston
Water to the beauty spot of Tarn
Hows. ▥ TIP→ **You get a 10% dis-
count if you book online.** ⊠ *Coniston Pier* ☎ *015394/41288* ⊕ *www.
nationaltrust.org.uk/gondola.*

> ### LAKE DISTRICT BIKING
>
> Cycling along the numerous bicy-
> cle paths and quiet forest roads in
> Cumbria is pleasurable and safe.
> Some flat paths are beside the
> lakes, but the best routes involve
> plenty of ups and downs. The
> Cumbria Cycle Way circles the
> county, and for local excursions
> guided bike tours are often avail-
> able, starting at about £25 per
> day. Contact local tourist offices
> or bike-rental places for details on
> cycle routes.

WHERE TO EAT

$ ╳ **Black Bull Inn.** Attached to the Coniston Brewing Company, whose ales
BRITISH are on tap here, the Black Bull is an old-fashioned pub in the heart of the
village. It's a good pick for simple, hearty food and exemplary beer. Old
photos of Donald Campbell's boat *Bluebird* decorate the walls, and there
are wooden beams and benches. The menu lists daily specials as well as
sandwiches for lunch or shrimp from Morecambe Bay. $ *Average main:
£10* ⊠ *Coppermines Rd.* ☎ *015394/41335* ⊕ *www.conistonbrewery.com.*

$ ╳ **Jumping Jenny's.** Named after Ruskin's beloved boat, the wood-
BRITISH beamed tearoom at Brantwood occupies the converted coach house. It
has an open-log fire and mountain views, and serves morning coffee,
lunch (sophisticated soups, pastas, sandwiches, and salads), and afternoon tea with homemade cakes. You can sit on the terrace in season for
a great view across Coniston Water. $ *Average main: £8* ⊠ *Off B5285*
☎ *015394/41715* ⊕ *www.jumpingjenny.net* ⊙ *No dinner.*

WHERE TO STAY

For expanded hotel reviews, visit Fodors.com.

$ ▦ **Bank Ground Farm.** Used by Arthur Ransome as the model for the
HOTEL setting for *Swallows and Amazons,* 15th-century Bank Ground is beau-
Fodor'sChoice tifully situated on the eastern shore of Coniston Water, opposite the
★ village of Coniston on the western shore. **Pros:** stunning lake views;
homey atmosphere; traditional welcome. **Cons:** a fair walk from the
village. $ *Rooms from: £90* ⊠ *Off B5285* ☎ *015394/41264* ⊕ *www.
bankground.com* ⊅ *7 rooms, 5 cottages* ◎ *Breakfast.*

$ ▦ **Lakeland House.** In the middle of Coniston, Lakeland House has
B&B/INN smart, modern rooms with bold wallpaper, beamed ceilings, and slate-
floored bathrooms. **Pros:** café downstairs means drinks and snacks are
never far away; good value. **Cons:** not as homey as a traditional B&B.
$ *Rooms from: £80* ⊠ *Tilberthwaite Ave., Keswick* ☎ *015394/41303*
⊕ *www.lakelandhouse.co.uk* ⊅ *6 rooms* ◎ *Breakfast.*

10

SHOPPING

Heritage Meats. Once owned by Beatrix Potter, Yew Tree Farm is nestled in some especially attractive hills. Owner Caroline Watson has a conservation-based approach to farming and sells great free-range meat. If you're staying nearby in a self-catering cottage, stock up on Herdwick chops or wild Lakeland game. ⊠ *A593, Coniston* ☎ *015394/41433* ⊕ *www.heritagemeats.co.uk.*

SPORTS AND THE OUTDOORS

BOATING

Coniston Boating Centre. Here you can rent launches, canoes, kayaks, and wooden rowboats, or even take a sailing lesson. Bikes are also available, and a picnic area and café are nearby. Rowboats are £10 an hour, while motorboats are £20 an hour. On weekends you can also walk on the water in a giant transparent plastic ball (£5). ⊠ *Lake Rd.* ☎ *015394/41366* ⊕ *www.conistonboatingcentre.co.uk.*

HIKING

Steep tracks lead up from the village to the **Old Man of Coniston.** The trail starts near the Sun Hotel on Brow Hill and goes past an old copper mine to the peak, which you can reach in about two hours. It's one of the Lake District's most satisfying hikes—not too arduous but high enough to feel a sense of accomplishment and get fantastic views (west to the sea, south to Morecambe Bay, and east to Windermere). Experienced hikers include the peak in a seven-hour circular walk from the village, also taking in the heights and ridges of Swirl How and Wetherlam.

HAWKSHEAD

3 miles east of Coniston.

In the Vale of Esthwaite, this small market town is a pleasing hodgepodge of tiny squares, cobbled lanes, and whitewashed houses. There's a good deal more history here than in most local villages, however. The Hawkshead Courthouse, just outside town, was built by the monks of Furness Abbey in the 15th century. Hawkshead later derived much wealth from the wool trade, which flourished here in the 17th and 18th centuries.

As a thriving market center, Hawkshead could afford to maintain the **Hawkshead Grammar School,** at which William Wordsworth was a pupil from 1779 to 1787; he carved his name on a desk inside, now on display. In the village, Ann Tyson's House claims the honor of having provided the young William with lodgings. The twin draws of Wordsworth and Beatrix Potter—apart from her home, Hill Top, there's a Potter gallery—conspire to make Hawkshead crowded year-round.

GETTING HERE AND AROUND

Hawkshead is east of Coniston on B5285 and south of Ambleside via B5286. An alternative route is to cross Windermere via the car ferry from Ferry Nab, south of Bowness. Local buses link the village to others nearby.

ESSENTIALS

Visitor Information Hawkshead Tourist Information Centre ⊠ *Main St.* ☎ *015394/36946* ⊕ *www.hawksheadtouristinfo.org.uk.*

Children's writer Beatrix Potter used details from her house at Hill Top, near Hawkshead, in the illustrations for her stories.

EXPLORING

FAMILY
Fodor'sChoice
★

Beatrix Potter Gallery. In the 17th-century solicitor's offices formerly used by Potter's husband, the Beatrix Potter Gallery displays a selection of the artist-writer's original illustrations, watercolors, and drawings. There's also information about her interest in conservation and her early support of the National Trust. The house looks almost as it would have in her day, though with touch screens in wooden frames and a children's play area upstairs. Admission is by timed ticket when the place gets busy. ✉ *Main St.* ☎ *015394/36355* ⊕ *www.nationaltrust.org.uk* 🎟*£4.80* ⊙ *Mid-Feb.–mid-Mar., Sat.–Thurs. 10:30–3:30; mid-Mar.–May, Sept., and Oct., Sat.–Thurs. 10:30–5; June–Aug., Sat.–Thurs. 10:30–5.*

Fodor'sChoice
★

Hill Top. Children's author and illustrator Beatrix Potter (1866–1943), most famous for her *Peter Rabbit* stories, called this place home. The house looks much the same as when Potter bequeathed it to the National Trust, and fans will recognize details such as the porch and garden gate, old kitchen range, Victorian dollhouse, and four-poster bed, which were depicted in the book illustrations. ■TIP➔ Admission to this often-crowded spot is by timed ticket; book in advance and avoid summer weekends and school vacations. Hill Top lies 2 miles south of Hawkshead by car or foot, though you can also approach via the car ferry from Bowness-on-Windermere. ✉ *Off B5285, Near Sawrey* ☎ *015394/36269* ⊕ *www.nationaltrust.org.uk* 🎟*£8.50* ⊙ *House mid-Feb.–Mar., Sat.–Thurs. 10:30–3:30; Apr., May, Sept., and Oct., Sat.–Thurs. 10:30–4:30; June–Aug., Sat.–Thurs. 10–5:30. Gardens mid-Feb.–Mar., daily 10:15–4; Apr., May, Sept., and Oct., daily 10–5; June–Aug., daily 9:45–5:45; Nov. and Dec., daily 10–4.*

10

Tarn Hows. Two miles northwest of Hawkshead (follow signs on B5285) is this small mountain lake, one of the Lake District's most celebrated beauty spots. Scenic overlooks let you drink it all in, or you can take an hour to putter along the paths. Easter through October, a free National Trust bus runs here from Hawkshead and Coniston on Sunday.

WHERE TO EAT

$

BRITISH

Fodor's Choice

★

✕ **Tower Bank Arms.** With a porch that appears in a Beatrix Potter story and a location just a rabbit's hop from the author's home, you might expect this pub to be something of a tourist trap. It's anything but. There's a slate floor, a crackling open fire, and a bar that stocks some of the best beers around, usually including some of the great ales from the nearby Barngates Brewery. There's a friendly welcome and the meals are tasty and copious, making use of local ingredients; the beef-and-ale stew is especially good. Four bedrooms upstairs (starting at £95) offer a good-value alternative to pricier lodgings. $ *Average main: £10* ⊠ *Off B5285, Near Sawrey* ☎ *015394/36334* ⊕ *www.towerbankarms.com.*

WHERE TO STAY

For expanded hotel reviews, visit Fodors.com.

$$

HOTEL

Fodor's Choice

★

⬚ **Drunken Duck Inn.** After four centuries, this friendly old coaching inn remains an outstanding place for both food and lodging. **Pros:** superchic rural style; excellent dining and drinking. **Cons:** hunting paraphernalia may put you off your beer; can feel isolated. $ *Rooms from: £140* ⊠ *Off B5286, Barngates* ☎ *015394/36347* ⊕ *www.drunkenduckinn.co.uk* ➷ *16 rooms* ❦*Some meals.*

$$$

B&B/INN

⬚ **Randy Pike.** Built in the 19th century as the shooting lodge for Wray Castle, Randy Pike is filled with stylish, imaginative, and playful touches. **Pros:** plenty of space; good food; big garden. **Cons:** a little out of the way; pricey rates. $ *Rooms from: £200* ⊠ *Off B5286, between Outgate and Clappersgate* ☎ *015394/36088* ⊕ *www.randypike.co.uk* ➷ *3 rooms* ❦*Breakfast.*

$

B&B/INN

Fodor's Choice

★

⬚ **Yewfield.** With the laid-back friendliness of a B&B and the sophisticated style of a country house, Yewfield is a very good value—especially if you can score one of the rooms at the front of the house with a great view across the valley. **Pros:** out-of-the-way location; pretty garden; apartments are great for weeklong stays. **Cons:** not good for families with young kids. $ *Rooms from: £98* ⊠ *Hawkshead Hill* ☎ *015394/36765* ⊕ *www.yewfield.co.uk* ➷ *10 rooms, 2 apartments* ☾ *Closed Dec. and Jan.* ❦*Breakfast.*

SPORTS AND THE OUTDOORS

Grizedale Forest Park. Stretching southwest from Hawkshead and blanketing the hills between Coniston and Windermere, Grizedale Forest Park has a thick mix of oak, pine, and larch woods crisscrossed with biking and walking paths. Fify permanent outdoor sculptures are scattered beside the trails. The **visitor center** has information, maps, a café, and an adventure playground. ⊠ *Off B5286* ☎ *01229/860010* ⊕ *www.forestry.gov.uk/grizedaleforestpark.*

The Grizedale Forest Park has adventures including the Go Ape aerial challenge—or you can just walk through the sculpture park.

Grizedale Mountain Bikes. If you have the urge to explore the trails of the national park, Grizedale Mountain Bikes rents all the right equipment from £26 per day. ⊠ *Grizedale Forest Park Visitor Centre, off B5286* ☏ *01229/860369* ⊕ *www.grizedalemountainbikes.co.uk.*

CARTMEL

17 miles south of Hawkshead.

The village of Cartmel is the southern Lakeland area's most attractive, set in a gentler Cumbrian landscape of hills and fields beyond the trees of Grizedale and the southern tip of Windermere. It comes alive when more than 20,000 people descend on Cartmel Racecourse for steeple-chasing on holiday weekends in May and August. Dominating the town is the ancient priory, now the village church. **Market Square** has pubs, bookshops, and the village shop, rightly famed for its delicious sticky toffee pudding. Helped by the L'Enclume restaurant, the town has a large and growing foodie reputation and some excellent gourmet shops, including a great cheese shop.

EXPLORING

Cartmel Priory. Founded in 1190, the huge Cartmel Priory survived the dissolution of the monasteries in the 16th century because it was also the village church. Four monks and 10 villagers were hanged, how-ever. The 25 wooden misericords are from 1440 and include a carved depiction of the Green Man, with a face made of leaves. ⊠ *Priest La., Cartmel* ☏ *015395/36261* ⊕ *www.cartmelpriory.org.uk* ✉ *Free; tours £2.50* ☉ *Daily 10–5:30. Tours Apr.–Oct., Wed. 11 and 2.*

CLOSE UP

What's Real About Real Ale?

The English can be passionate about their drink, as the growing interest in real ale shows. It differs from other beers by the use of natural ingredients and the fact that it's matured by fermentation in the barrel from which the ale is served. The process doesn't use carbon dioxide, so pure taste wins out over fizz.

The **Directory of U.K. Real Ale Breweries** (🌐 *www.quaffale.org.uk*) lists 34 operating real-ale breweries in Cumbria, of which the Coniston Brewing Company, Barngates Brewery (at the Drunken Duck Inn), and Hawkshead (in Staveley, between Kendal and Windermere) are three of the best. Most real ales are caramel in color and hoppy, malty, and slightly bitter to taste. A pint of ale is the usual quantity to be consumed, though a half is acceptable; you can also find it in bottles.

Most pubs in the Lake District offer some sort of local brew—the better ones take enormous pride in their careful tending of the beer, from barrel to glass. Interested in the subject, or just in the taste? Check out the website of the **Campaign for Real Ale** (🌐 *www.camra.org.uk*).

Holker Hall. The red sandstone towers of Holker Hall rise above elegant English gardens. The Cavendish family still lives in the house, which has a fine cantilevered staircase and a library with more than 3,000 books; much of the house was rebuilt in Elizabethan style after an 1871 fire. Topiaries, a labyrinth, and an enormous lime tree are the highlights of the 25 acres of gardens. The three-day Holker Festival in early June celebates the gardens and local culture and food. ✉ *Off A5278, 2 miles west of Cartmel, Cark-in-Cartmel* ☎ *015395/58328* 🌐 *www.holker.co.uk* 🎟 *House and gardens £11.50; gardens only, £7.50* 🕒 *House Apr.–Oct., Sun.–Fri. 11–4; gardens Mar.–Oct., Sun.–Fri. 10:30–5:30.*

WHERE TO EAT

$$$$ MODERN BRITISH Fodor's Choice ★

🍴 **L'Enclume.** The village of Cartmel has earned a place on England's culinary map with this ambitious restaurant with rooms. The restaurant is in what was once a forge, now converted to a bright, contemporary, and airy space with dark wooden beams, stark white walls, and splashes of color. Chef Simon Rogan's innovative food incorporates long-forgotten herbs and cutting-edge techinques. The set dinner (£95) comes with up to 12 courses; if that sounds like a bit much, go for the simpler lunch (£39). Dishes might include potatoes in onion ashes and lovage, or roast cauliflower with young squid and elderberry vinegar. Some things work better than others at this outpost of molecular gastronomy, but boredom is never a risk. Nearby Rogan and Company, run by the same team, has a slightly less elevated menu. The 18 elegant rooms (from £99) are in three different buildings around the village. [$] *Average main: £69* ✉ *Cavendish St.* ☎ *015395/36362* 🌐 *www.lenclume.co.uk* ✍ *Reservations essential* 🕒 *No lunch Mon. and Tues.*

SHOPPING

Cartmel Cheeses. A huge range of delcious cheeses, mostly British, can be purchased in this welcoming, pungent little shop. Free tasters are often available. ⊠ *1 Unsworth Yard, Cartmel* ☎ *015395/58623* ⊕ *www.cartmelcheeses.co.uk* ⊙ *Tues.–Sun. 10–5.*

Cartmel Village Shop. This fabulous delicatessen, famous for its deliciously rich sticky toffee pudding, is also a great place to purchase picnic provisions. ⊠ *The Square, Cartmel* ☎ *015395/36280* ⊕ *www.cartmelvillageshop.co.uk.*

PENRITH AND THE NORTHERN LAKES

The scenery of the northern lakes is considerably more dramatic—some would say bleaker—than much of the landscape to the south, a change that becomes apparent on your way north from Kendal to Penrith. A 30-mile drive on the A6 takes you through the wild and desolate Shap Fells, which rise to a height of 1,304 feet. This is one of the most notorious moorland crossings in the country: even in summer it's a lonely place to be, and in winter, snow on the road can be dangerous. From Penrith the road leads to Ullswater, possibly the grandest of all the lakes; then there's a winding route west past Keswick, south through the marvelous Borrowdale Valley, and on to Cockermouth. Outside the main towns such as Keswick, it can be easier to escape the summer crowds in the northern lakes.

PENRITH

30 miles north of Kendal.

The red-sandstone town of Penrith was the capital of old Cumbria, part of the Scottish kingdom of Strathclyde in the 9th and 10th centuries. It was rather neglected after the Normans arrived, and the Scots sacked it on several occasions. Penrith has been a thriving market town for centuries; the market still takes place on Tuesday, and it continues to be known for good shopping.

The tourist information center, in the Penrith Museum, has information about the historic town trail, which takes you through narrow byways to the plague stone on King Street, where food was left for the stricken, to St. Andrew's churchyard and its 1,000-year-old "hog back" tombstones (stones carved as stylized "houses of the dead"), and finally to the ruins of Penrith Castle.

10

GETTING HERE AND AROUND

Penrith is just off the M6, 30 miles north of Kendal and 100 miles north of Manchester. Both the M6 and the alternative A6 cross the Pennines spectacularly at Shap Fells. From Windermere you can reach Penrith by going over the Kirkstone Pass to Ullswater. There are some direct trains from Euston Station in London to Penrith; sometimes it's necessary to change.

ESSENTIALS

Visitor Information Penrith Tourist Information Centre ⊠ *Penrith Museum, Middlegate* ☎ *01768/867466* ⊕ *www.visiteden.co.uk.*

EXPLORING

TOP ATTRACTIONS

FAMILY
Fodor's Choice
★

Lowther Castle. On 130 acres of parkland and gardens, the 1806 Lowther Castle fell into disrepair during the second half of the 20th century. Once used as a chicken farm, this fairy-tale structure is currently being carefully restored. Its turrets can be seen from all over the grounds. which are carpeted with wildflowers, dotted with living willow sculptures, and filled with tree swings and other play areas for the kids. The gallery has ornate Italian plaster decoration, and the café is a fine spot for afternoon tea and cake. ⊠ *Off A6, Lowther* ☎ *01931/712192* ⊕ *www.lowthercastle.org* ✉ *£8* ⊙ *Daily 10–5.*

Fodor's Choice
★

The Watermill. This fully functioning stone-ground flour mill is well worth a visit for its delicious baked goods and for a tour of the fascinating workings of the mill itself. There's been a mill here since the 13th century, and the current struction was built in 1760. Tours are officially self-guided (take an information sheet), but the miller will probably take a break to show you around. Just up the road is the Bronze Age stone circle of Long Meg and her Daughters. According to folklore, the 51 stones (27 of which are still upright) were a coven of witches turned to stone by a Scottish wizard. ⊠ *Off A66, 6 miles northeast of Penrith, Little Salkeld* ☎ *01768/881523* ⊕ *www.organicmill.co.uk* ⊙ *Daily 10:30–5* ⊙ *£2.*

WORTH NOTING

Askham Hall. A part of the Lowther Estate, beautiful Askham Hall boasts spectacular gardens. There's a 230-foot long herbaceous border, secret paths, terraces, and views of the River Lowther. The café has a wood-fired pizza oven, which is lighted in summer months, and some very fine cakes. The place is about 10-minutes south of Penrith. ⊠ *Off A6, Askham* ☎ *01931/712348* ⊕ *www.askhamhall.co.uk.*

Dalemain. Home of the Hasell family since 1679, Dalemain began with a 12th-century peel tower built to protect the occupants from raiding Scots, and is now a delightful hodgepodge of architectural styles. An imposing Georgian facade of local pink sandstone encompasses a medieval hall and extensions from the 16th through the 18th century. Inside are a magnificent oak staircase, furniture dating from the mid-17th century, a Chinese drawing room, a 16th-century room with intricate plasterwork, and many fine paintings, including masterpieces by Van Dyck. The gardens are worth a look, too, and deer roam the estate. Dalemain is 3 miles southwest of Penrith. ⊠ *A592* ☎ *017684/86450* ⊕ *www.dalemain.com* ✉ *£10; gardens only £7* ⊙ *House Apr.–Sept., Sun.–Thurs. 11:15–4; Oct., Sun.–Thurs. 11:15–3. Gardens Apr.–Oct., Sun.–Thurs. 10:30–5; Nov.–mid-Dec., Sun.–Thurs. 11–3.*

Penrith Castle. The evocative remains of this 15th-century redbrick castle stand high above a steep, now-dry moat. Home of the maligned Richard, duke of Gloucester (later Richard III), who was responsible for keeping peace along the border, it was one of England's first lines of defense against the Scots. By the civil war the castle was in ruins, and the townsfolk used some of the fallen stones to build their houses. The ruins stand in a park, across from the town's train station. ⊠ *Off*

Castlegate ☎ *0870/333–1181* 🌐 *www.english-heritage.org.uk* 🎟 *Free* 🕒 *June–Sept., daily 7:30 am–9 pm; Oct.–May, daily 7:30–4:30.*

Penrith Museum. In a 16th-century building that served as a school from 1670 to the 1970s, this museum contains neolithic axe heads, interesting fossils, and an informative film about the Cumbrian fells and fell walking. The Penrith Tourist Information Centre is here. ✉ *Middlegate* ☎ *01768/865105* 🌐 *www.eden.gov.uk/museum* 🎟 *Free* 🕒 *Apr.–Oct., Mon.–Sat. 10–4, Sun. 11–4; Nov.–Mar., Mon.–Sat. 10–4.*

FAMILY **Rheged.** Named for the Celtic kingdom of Cumbria, Rheged is a modern, grass-covered visitor center with activities for kids and some interesting free exhibits about the history, culture, and other aspects of the Lake District. A gallery hosts rotating art and photography exhibits, and a massive theater shows 3-D and large-format movies. Shops showcase Cumbrian food and drink and crafts, and three different cafés offer drinks and light meals. Rheged is 2 miles southwest of Penrith and 1 mile west of Junction 40 on the M6. ✉ *A66* ☎ *01768/868000* 🌐 *www.rheged.com* 🎟 *Free; movie £6.50* 🕒 *Daily 10–5:30.*

WHERE TO EAT AND STAY

For expanded hotel reviews, visit Fodors.com.

$ BRITISH Fodor's Choice ★ 🍴 **George and Dragon.** This pub and restaurant makes good use of local produce for tasty traditional dishes, including wild mushroom and black pudding fricassee. Sausages come from the Eden Valley, brown trout from the River Lowther, and much of the greens are grown in the gardens at Askham Hall. The inn is also a well-tended spot for a pint of local beer, with handsome slate floors, roaring wood fires, and hanging hops. Bonnie Prince Charlie was once involved in a battle here, and the remains of 12 Scottish rebels were discovered in the pub's back garden. For an overnight stay, choose from 12 smart, individually designed guest rooms with furnishings from the Lowther family's collection. [$] *Average main: £13* ✉ *A6, south of Penrith, Clifton* ☎ *01768/865381* 🌐 *www.georgeanddragonclifton.co.uk* 🕒 *No lunch Mon.*

$ CAFÉ Fodor's Choice ★ 🍴 **No. 15.** Red walls and comfy sofas set the tone for this laid-back, spacious contemporary gallery and café. There's a large range of teas and coffees, as well as such dishes as homemade soups, savory pancakes, and huge slabs of chocolate cake. There's free Wi-Fi, as well as occasional live music in the evening. [$] *Average main: £6* ✉ *15 Victoria Rd.* ☎ *01768/867453.*

$ B&B/INN 🏨 **Brooklands.** The welcome is friendly, the breakfast is hearty (salmon cakes and omelets are among the options), and rooms have patterned wallpaper and heavy, luxurious fabrics at this Victorian terraced house. **Pros:** well-looked-after B&B; bathrobes in room; fancy toiletries. **Cons:** a drive from the spectacular Lakeland scenery. [$] *Rooms from: £78* ✉ *2 Portland Pl.* ☎ *01768/863395* 🌐 *www.brooklandsguesthouse.com* 🛏 *8 rooms* 🍽 *Breakfast.*

SHOPPING

Penrith is a diverting place to shop, with its narrow streets and arcades chockablock with family-run specialty shops. Major shopping areas include Devonshire Arcade, with its brand-name stores; the pedestrian-only Angel Lane and Little Dockray; and Angel Square.

James & John Graham of Penrith Ltd. Artisanal cheese and other local products are available at this great bakery and well-stocked deli. ⊠ *Market Sq.* ☏ *01768/862281* ⊕ *www.jjgraham.co.uk.*

Penrith Farmers' Market. The stalls of the outdoor market line Dockray, Corn Market, and Market Square on the third Tuesday of the month from 9:30 to 2:30, selling fine local produce and original crafts.

Toffee Shop. This shop, where the Queen buys her toffee, may also have England's best fudge. ⊠ *7 Brunswick Rd.* ☏ *01768/862008* ⊕ *www. thetoffeeshop.co.uk.*

ULLSWATER

6 miles southwest of Penrith.

Hemmed in by towering hills, Ullswater, the region's second-largest lake, is one of the least developed, drawing people for its calm waters and good access to the mountain slopes of Helvellyn. The A592 winds along the lake's pastoral western shore, through the adjacent hamlets of **Glenridding** and **Patterdale** at the southern end. Lakeside strolls, great views, tea shops, and rowboat rentals provide the full Lakeland experience.

ESSENTIALS

Visitor Information Ullswater Tourist Information Centre ⊠ *Beckside Car Park, off A592, Glenridding* ☏ *017684/82414* ⊕ *www.visiteden.co.uk.*

EXPLORING

Aira Force. A spectacular 65-foot waterfall pounds under a stone bridge and through a wooded ravine to feed into Ullswater. From the parking lot it's a 10-minute walk to the falls, with more serious walks on Gowbarrow Fell and to the village of Dockray beyond. ■ TIP→ Bring sturdy shoes, especially in wet or icy weather, when the paths can be treacherous. Just above Aira Force in the woods of Gowbarrow Park is the spot where, in 1802, William Wordsworth's sister Dorothy observed daffodils that, as she wrote, "tossed and reeled and danced and seemed as if they verily laughed with the wind that blew upon them." Two years later Wordsworth transformed his sister's words into the famous poem "I Wandered Lonely as a Cloud." And two centuries later, national park wardens patrol Gowbarrow Park in season to prevent tourists from picking the few remaining daffodils. ⊠ *A592, near A5091* ⊕ *www.nationaltrust.org.uk* 🚗 *Parking £3.50–£5.50.*

Helvellyn. West of Ullswater's southern end, the brooding presence of Helvellyn (3,118 feet), one of the Lake District's most formidable mountains and England's third highest, recalls the region's fundamental character. It's an arduous climb to the top, especially via the challenging ridge known as Striding Edge, and the ascent shouldn't be attempted in poor weather or by inexperienced hikers. Signposted paths to the peak run from the road between Glenridding and Patterdale and pass by **Red Tarn,** at 2,356 feet the highest small mountain lake in the region. ⊠ *Glenridding.*

The most expert climbers will attempt an ascent of Helvellyn along the perilously narrow Striding Edge even in winter.

Fodor's Choice ★ **Ullswater Steamers.** These antique vessels, including a 19th-century steamer that is said to be the oldest working passenger ship in the world, run the length of Ullswater between Glenridding in the south and Pooley Bridge in the north, via Howtown on the eastern shore. It's a pleasant tour, especially if you combine it with a lakeside walk. One-way trips start from £6.20, or you can sail the entire day for £13.20. ✉ *Pier House, off A592, Glenridding* ☎ *017684/82229* 🌐 *www.ullswater-steamers.co.uk.*

WHERE TO STAY

For expanded hotel reviews, visit Fodors.com.

$$$ HOTEL 🏨 **Howtown Hotel.** Near the end of the road on the isolated eastern side of Ullswater, this gloriously quiet family-run hotel is low-key and low-tech. **Pros:** exceptionally quiet; spectacular location; dinner included in price. **Cons:** not for those who must be plugged in; a bit remote, books up fast. [$] *Rooms from: £178* ✉ *Howtown Rd., Howtown* ☎ *017684/86514* 🌐 *www.howtown-hotel.com* 🛏 *12 rooms, 4 cottages* 💳 *No credit cards* 🕒 *Closed Nov.–Mar.* 🍴 *Some meals.*

$$$ HOTEL 🏨 **Sharrow Bay.** Sublime views and exceptional service and cuisine add distinction to this country house on the shores of Ullswater. **Pros:** great views across Ullswater; pretty garden; top-notch service. **Cons:** not for the faint of wallet; some distance from other facilities. [$] *Rooms from: £200* ✉ *Howtown Rd., Pooley Bridge* ☎ *017684/86301* 🌐 *www.sharrowbay.co.uk* 🛏 *16 rooms, 8 suites* 🍴 *Some meals.*

KESWICK

14 miles west of Ullswater.

The great mountains of Skiddaw and Blencathra brood over the gray slate houses of Keswick (pronounced *kezz*-ick), on the scenic shores of Derwentwater. The town is a natural base for exploring the rounded, heather-clad Skiddaw range to the north, while the hidden valleys of Borrowdale and Buttermere (the latter reached by stunning Honister Pass) take you into the rugged heart of the Lake District. Nearby, five beautiful lakes are set among the three highest mountain ranges in England. The tourist information center here has regional information and is the place to get fishing permits for Derwentwater.

Keswick's narrow, cobbled streets have a grittier charm compared to the refined Victorian elegance of Grasmere or Ambleside. However, it's the best spot in the Lake District to purchase mountaineering gear and outdoor clothing. There are also many hotels, guesthouses, restaurants, and pubs.

GETTING HERE AND AROUND

It's easily reached along A66 from Penrith, though you can get to Keswick more scenically via Grasmere in the south. Buses run from the train station in Penrith to Keswick. The town center is pedestrianized.

▥ **TIP→** Traffic can be horrendous in summer, so consider leaving your car in Keswick. The open-top Borrowdale bus service between Keswick and Seatoller (to the south) runs frequently, and the Honister Rambler minibus is perfect for walkers aiming for the high fells of the central lakes; it makes stops from Keswick to Buttermere. The Keswick Launch service on Derwentwater links to many walks as well as the Borrowdale bus service.

ESSENTIALS

Visitor Information Keswick Information Centre ✉ *Moot Hall, Market Sq.* ☎ *017687/72645* ⊕ *www.keswick.org.*

EXPLORING

Castlerigg Stone Circle. A Neolithic monument about 100 feet in diameter, this stone circle was built around 3,000 years ago on a hill overlooking St. John's Vale. The brooding northern peaks of Skiddaw and Blencathra loom to the north, and there are views of Helvellyn to the south. The 38 stones aren't large, but the site makes them particularly impressive. Wordsworth described them as "a dismal cirque of Druid stones upon a forlorn moor." The site, always open to visitors, is 4 miles east of Keswick. There's usually space for cars to park beside the road that leads along the northern edge of the site. ✉ *Off A66* ⊕ *www. english-heritage.org.uk* ▦ *Free.*

FAMILY **Cumberland Pencil Museum.** Legend has it that shepherds found graphite on Seathwaite Fell after a storm uprooted trees in the 16th century. The Derwent company still makes pencils here, and the museum contains the world's longest colored pencil (it takes 28 men to lift it), a pencil produced for World War II spies that contains a rolled-up map, and displays about graphite mining. There's a café and plenty of opportunities for kids to draw. ✉ *Southey Works, Carding Mill La.* ☎ *017687/73626* ⊕ *www. pencilmuseum.co.uk* ▦ *£4.25* ⊙ *Daily 9:30–5; last admission at 4.*

Festivals and Folk Sports

With everything from rushbearing to Westmorland wrestling to traditional music, the Lake District hosts some of Britain's most unusual country festivals as well as some excellent but more typical ones.

MAJOR EVENTS

Major festivals include the Keswick Film Festival (February), Words by the Water (a literary festival in Keswick, March), Keswick Jazz Festival (May), Cockermouth and Keswick carnivals (June), Ambleside and Grasmere rushbearing (August), and the Lake District Summer Music (regionwide, in August)—but there are many others. Horse racing comes to Cartmel over May and August bank holiday weekends.

SPECIAL ACTIVITIES

Rushbearing dates back to medieval times, when rushes covered church floors; today processions of flower-bedecked children and adults bring rushes to churches in a number of villages. Folk sports, often the highlights at local festivals, include Cumberland and Westmorland wrestling, in which the opponents must maintain a grip around each other's body. Fell running, a sort of cross-country run where the route goes roughly straight up and down a mountain, is also popular.

A calendar of events is available at tourist information centers or on the Cumbria Tourism website, ⊕ *www.golakes.co.uk.*

Derwentwater. To understand why Derwentwater is considered one of England's finest lakes, take a short walk from Keswick's town center to the lakeshore and past the jetty, and follow the **Friar's Crag** path, about a 15-minute level walk from the center. This pine-tree-fringed peninsula is a favorite vantage point, with its view of the lake, the ring of mountains, and many tiny islands. Ahead, crags line the **Jaws of Borrowdale** and overhang a mountain ravine—a scene that looks as if it emerged from a Romantic painting.

Keswick Launch Company. For the best lake views, take a wooden-launch cruise around Derwentwater. Between late March and November, cruises set off every hour in each direction from a dock at the shore; there's also a limited winter timetable. You can also rent a rowboat here. Buy a hop-on, hop-off Around the Lake ticket (£9.50) and take advantage of the seven landing stages around the lake that provide access to hiking trails, such as the two-hour climb up and down Cat Bells, a celebrated lookout point on the western shore of Derwentwater. ⊠ *Lake Rd.* ☎ *017687/72263* ⊕ *www.keswick-launch.co.uk.*

10

WHERE TO EAT

$

BRITISH

✕ **Café Bar 26.** A metropolitan bar in a town where cozy tearooms are more the norm, Café Bar 26 has wooden beams, mellow brick-color walls, flickering candlelight, an excellent coffee machine, and live music every Saturday. The wine list is on the short side, but there are tasty homemade pizzas and tapas. In the middle of the day, lunch options include potted shrimp, burgers, and fish cakes. The four spacious bedrooms upstairs are an excellent value for an overnight stop. $ *Average main: £6* ⊠ *26 Lake Rd.* ☎ *017687/80863* ⊕ *www.cafebar26.co.uk.*

$ ✕**Lakeland Pedlar.** With a contemporary design, this café and bike shop
VEGETARIAN   serves inspired vegetarian and vegan dishes from around the world,
including spanakopita (Greek feta and spinach pie), chickpea tagine,
and filling, homemade soups. You can use the Wi-Fi while choosing
from fresh juices, espresso, and homemade cakes; hearty breakfasts are
a specialty. Admire the fells from the outdoor tables, or take food with
you for the trail. $ *Average main: £8 ✉ Henderson's Yard, Bell Close*
☎ *017687/74492 ⊕ www.lakelandpedlar.co.uk ⊘ No dinner Sun.-Thu.
or Sept.–June.*

$$ ✕**Morrels.** One of the town's better eateries, Morrels has local art and
MODERN BRITISH   wooden floors that give a contemporary edge to the bar and dining
area. Updated British fare is the specialty at this mellow place: a tomato,
olive, and pine-nut compote complements the mackerel fillet, and the
fish cakes come spiced with a bean-and-corn salsa. The restaurant opens
afternoons at 5:30 for anyone going to the town's theater. A couple of
equally stylish apartments upstairs are available for short-term rentals.
$ *Average main: £15 ✉ 34 Lake Rd. ☎ 017687/72666 ⊕ www.morrels.
co.uk ⊘ Closed Mon. No lunch.*

WHERE TO STAY

For expanded hotel reviews, visit Fodors.com.

$ ☷ **Ferndene.** Exceptionally friendly, this spotless B&B is carefully tended
B&B/INN   by its kindly owners. **Pros:** family-focused; good value; bicycle storage.
FAMILY   **Cons:** lacks style of more expensive lodgings. $ *Rooms from: £72 ✉ 6
St. John's Terr. ☎ 017687/74612 ⊕ www.ferndene-keswick.co.uk ⤳ 6
rooms ⦿ Breakfast.*

$$ ☷ **Highfield Hotel.** Slightly austere on the outside but charming within,
HOTEL   this Victorian hotel overlooks the lawns of Hope Park and has accom-
modations with great character, including rooms in the turret and
the former chapel. **Pros:** good service; tasty food; great views. **Cons:**
some small downstairs bedrooms. $ *Rooms from: £100 ✉ The Heads
☎ 017687/72508 ⊕ www.highfieldkeswick.co.uk ⤳ 18 rooms ⊘ Closed
Jan.–mid-Feb. ⦿ Some meals.*

$$ ☷ **Howe Keld.** In a town that overflows with B&Bs, this comfortable
B&B/INN   town house stands out because of its contemporary flair and pamper-
Fodor'sChoice   ing touches. **Pros:** famously filling breakfasts; good ecological practices;
★   one room accessible for people with disabilities. **Cons:** a short distance
from the heart of town; backs onto a busy road. $ *Rooms from: £104
✉ 5–7 The Heads ☎ 017687/72417 ⊕ www.howekeld.co.uk ⤳ 14
rooms ⊘ Closed Jan. ⦿ Breakfast.*

$ ☷ **The Lookout.** Up the hill from the town center, this friendly and eco-
B&B/INN   nomical B&B lives up to its name, with balconies gazing out onto the
high fells. **Pros:** welcoming hosts; stylish rooms; great views. **Cons:** some
distance from Keswick's amenities. $ *Rooms from: £95 ✉ Chestnut
Hill ☎ 017687/80407 ⊕ www.thelookoutkeswick.co.uk ⤳ 3 rooms
⦿ Breakfast.*

The setting of the Castlerigg Stone Circle, ringed by stunning mountains, makes this Neolithic monument deeply memorable.

NIGHTLIFE AND THE ARTS

Keswick Film Club. With an excellent festival in February and a program of international and classic films, the Keswick Film Club lights up the old redbrick Alhambra Cinema on St. John's Street and the Theatre by the Lake. ☎ *017687/72195* ⊕ *www.keswickfilmclub.org.*

Keswick Jazz Festival. Held each May, the popular Keswick Jazz Festival consists of four days of music. Reservations are accepted as early as before Christmas. ☎ *017687/74411* ⊕ *www.keswickjazzfestival.co.uk.*

Theatre by the Lake. The company at the Theatre by the Lake presents classic and contemporary productions year-round. The Keswick Music Society season runs from September through January, and the Words on the Water literary festival takes place in March. ⊠ *Lake Rd.* ☎ *017687/74411* ⊕ *www.theatrebythelake.com.*

SHOPPING

Keswick has a good choice of bookstores, crafts shops, and wool-clothing stores tucked away in its cobbled streets, as well as excellent outdoor shops. Keswick's market is held Saturday.

George Fisher. The area's largest and best outdoor equipment store, George Fisher sells sportswear, travel books, and maps. Daily weather information is posted in the window. ⊠ *2 Borrowdale Rd.* ☎ *017687/72178* ⊕ *www.georgefisher.co.uk.*

Needle Sports. This company stocks all the best equipment for mountaineering and for rock and ice climbing. ⊠ *56 Main St.* ☎ *017687/72227* ⊕ *www.needlesports.com.*

10

Northern Lights Gallery. This well-lighted space carries a good selection of contemporary paintings, photography, sculpture, jewelry, and ceramics by around 80 local artists. ⊠ *22 St. John's St.* ☎ *01768/775402* ⊕ *www. northernlightsgallery.co.uk.*

Thomasons. A butcher and delicatessen, Thomasons sells some very good meat pies—just the thing for putting in your pocket before you climb a Lakeland fell. ⊠ *8–10 Station St.* ☎ *017687/80169.*

SPORTS AND THE OUTDOORS

BIKING

Keswick Bikes. This company rents bikes (from £20 per day) and provides information on all the nearby trails. In addition to this branch, there's another above the Lakeland Pedlar. Guided tours can be arranged with advance notice. ⊠ *133 Main St.* ☎ *017687/73355* ⊕ *www.keswickbikes.co.uk.*

WATER SPORTS

Derwent Water Marina. Rental boats in all shapes and sizes and instruction in canoeing, sailing, and windsurfing can be had at Derwent Water Marina. Other water-related activities include ghyll scrambling—the fine art of walking up or down a steep Lakeland stream. A two-day sailing or windsurfing course costs £185. ⊠ *Portinscale* ☎ *017687/72912* ⊕ *www.derwentwatermarina.co.uk.*

EN ROUTE The most scenic route from Keswick, B5289 south, runs along the eastern edge of Derwentwater, past turnoffs to natural attractions such as Ashness Bridge, the idyllic tarn of Watendlath, the Lodore Falls (best after a good rain), and the precariously balanced Bowder Stone. Farther south is the tiny village of **Grange**, a walking center at the head of Borrowdale, where there's a riverside café.

BORROWDALE

7 miles south of Keswick.

Fodor'sChoice
★

South of Keswick and its lake lies the valley of Borrowdale, whose varied landscape of green valley floor and surrounding crags has long been considered one of the region's most magnificent treasures. **Rosthwaite,** a tranquil farming village, and **Seatoller,** the southernmost settlement, are the two main centers (both are accessible by bus from Keswick), though they're little more than clusters of aged buildings surrounded by glorious countryside.

GETTING HERE AND AROUND

The valley is south of Keswick on B5289. The Borrowdale bus service between Keswick and Seatoller runs frequently.

EXPLORING

Fodor'sChoice
★

Borrowdale Fells. These steep fells rise up dramatically behind Seatoller. Get out and walk whenever inspiration strikes. Trails are well signposted, or you can pick up maps and any gear in Keswick.

Scafell Pike. England's highest mountain at 3,210 feet, Scafell (pronounced *scar*-fell) Pike is visible from Seatoller. One route up the mountain, for experienced walkers, is from the hamlet of Seathwaite, a mile south of Seatoller.

WHERE TO STAY

For expanded hotel reviews, visit Fodors.com.

$$ ⊞ **Langstrath Country Inn.** In the tranquil hamlet of Stonethwaite, the
HOTEL welcoming Langstrath was originally built as a miner's cottage in the
16th century but has expanded into a spacious inn with chunky wooden
tables and logs burning on a slate open fire. **Pros:** great walks right out
the door; children welcomed and looked after; wonderfully peaceful.
Cons: few other places to eat or shop nearby. $ *Rooms from: £106*
⊠ *Off B5289, Stonethwaite* ☎ *017687/77239* ⊕ *www.thelangstrath.*
com ↵ *8 rooms* ⊙ *Closed Dec. and Jan.* ⊚*Breakfast.*

EN   **Honister Pass.** Beyond Seatoller, B5289 turns westward through Honister
ROUTE Pass (1,176 feet) and Buttermere Fell. Boulders line the road, which is
one of the most dramatic in the region; at times it channels through
soaring rock canyons. The road sweeps down from the pass to the vil-
lage of Buttermere, sandwiched between its namesake lake and Crum-
mock Water at the foot of high, craggy fells. Just beyond the pass
toward Buttermere, Syke Farm sells fantastic ice cream. To the north,
Newlands Pass is an equally spectacular route back to Keswick.

COCKERMOUTH

15 miles northwest of Borrowdale, 14 miles northwest of Seatoller.

This small but bustling town, at the confluence of the rivers Derwent
and Cocker, has a maze of narrow streets that are a delight to wander.
It's a bit off the usual tourist path, and a bit bohemian. The ruined
13th-century castle is open only on special occasions. Over a weekend
in September the town holds the Taste Cumbria Food Festival.

GETTING HERE AND AROUND

The most straightforward access to the town is along the busy A66 from
Penrith. For a more scenic, roundabout route, head over the Whinlatter
or Honister passes from Keswick.

ESSENTIALS

Visitor Information Cockermouth Tourist Information Centre
⊠ *4 Kings Arms Ln.* ☎ *01900/822634* ⊕ *www.cockermouth.org.uk.*

EXPLORING

Fodor'sChoice **Castlegate House Gallery.** One of the region's best galleries, Castlegate
★   displays and sells an outstanding collection of contemporary works,
many by Cumbrian artists. Changing exhibitions focus on paintings,
sculpture, glass, ceramics, and jewelry. ⊠ *Castlegate* ☎ *01900/822149*
⊕ *www.castlegatehouse.co.uk* ⊙ *Mon. and Wed.–Sat. 10–5.*

Jennings Brewery. Learn how real ales are made on a tour that allows
you to see inside the fermentation casks, which hold up to 150 barrels
of beer. It finishes up in the bar for a tasting. There are usually one or
two tours a day in summer, less frequently the rest of the year. ⊠ *Cas-*
tle Brewery, off Castlegate ☎ *0845/1297190* ⊕ *www.jenningsbrewery.*
co.uk ↵ *£8 tour* ⊙ *Jan. and Feb., Mon.–Sat. 10–1; Mar.–Dec., Mon.–*
Sat. 10–4. Tours Apr.–Oct, Mon.–Sat noon and 2; Nov., Dec., and Mar.,
weekdays 2, Sat. noon and 2.

10

Wordsworth House. Cockermouth was the birthplace of William Wordsworth (and his sister Dorothy), whose childhood home was this 18th-century town house. You see it complete with clutter, costumed interpreters, and period cooking in the kitchen. Young visitors can also dress up in period costumes. Harpsichord recitals take place regularly. Wordsworth's father is buried in the All Saints' churchyard, and the church has a stained-glass window in memory of the poet. ✉ *Main St.* ☎ *01900/824805* 🌐 *www.nationaltrust.org.uk* 🎟 *£6.36* 🕓 *Mid-Mar.–Oct., Sat.–Thurs. 11–5; last admission at 4.*

WHERE TO EAT AND STAY

For expanded hotel reviews, visit Fodors.com.

$ BRITISH

🍴 **Bitter End.** Flocked floral wallpaper, old lamps, an open fire, and a handsome wooden floor set the tone at this appealing pub. Homey, intimate, and steadfastly independent, the pub serves big, tasty portions of traditional British food such as lamb cobbler and fish-and-chips and well-kept, locally brewed beer. Excellent Sunday lunches are especially popular with locals. [$] *Average main: £11* ✉ *15 Kirkgate* ☎ *01900/828993* 🌐 *www.bitterend.co.uk.*

$$ VEGETARIAN

🍴 **Quince & Medlar.** Sophisticated and imaginative vegetarian cuisine, served by candlelight, is the specialty at this refined, wood-paneled Georgian town house. You'll probably be offered a drink in the sitting room before being called to your table; you choose from at least six main courses, such as smoked Cumberland cheese and mushroom roulade, all served with seasonal vegetables. [$] *Average main: £15* ✉ *13 Castlegate* ☎ *01900/823579* 🌐 *www.quinceandmedlar.co.uk* ✍ *Reservations essential* 🕓 *Closed Sun. and Mon. No lunch.*

$ B&B/INN Fodor's Choice ★

🏨 **Six Castlegate.** After a day of exploring, relax in style at this elegant B&B in a Georgian town house. **Pros:** modern facilities and antique style blend nicely; near galleries and attractions; exceptional value. **Cons:** road noise in some rooms. [$] *Rooms from: £75* ✉ *6 Castlegate* ☎ *01900/826786* 🌐 *www.sixcastlegate.co.uk* 🛏 *6 rooms* 🍽 *Breakfast.*

$$ B&B/INN Fodor's Choice ★

🏨 **The Pheasant.** Halfway between Cockermouth and Keswick at the northern end of Bassenthwaite Lake, this traditional 18th-century coaching inn exudes English coziness without the usual Lakeland fussiness. **Pros:** atmosphere of a well-loved local inn; fantastic bar; great food. **Cons:** a little out of the way. [$] *Rooms from: £150* ✉ *Off A66, Bassenthwaite Lake* ☎ *017687/76234* 🌐 *www.the-pheasant.co.uk* 🛏 *15 rooms, 3 suites* 🍽 *Some meals.*

EAST ANGLIA

WELCOME TO EAST ANGLIA

TOP REASONS TO GO

★ **Cambridge:** A walk through the colleges is grand, but the best views of the university's colleges and immaculate lawns (and some famous bridges) are from a punt on the river.

★ **Constable country:** In the area where Constable grew up, you can walk or row downstream from Dedham straight into the setting of one of the English landscape painter's masterpieces at Flatford Mill.

★ **Lincoln's old center:** The ancient center of the city has a vast, soaring cathedral, a proper rampart-ringed castle, and winding medieval streets.

★ **Wild North Sea coast:** North Norfolk has enormous sandy beaches (great for walking) and opportunities to see seals and birdlife, especially on the salt marshes around Blakeney.

★ **Lavenham:** This medieval town is the most comely of the tight-knit cluster of places that did well from the wool trade, with architecture including timber-frame houses gnarled into crookedness by age.

1 Cambridge. The home of the ancient university is East Anglia's liveliest town. The city center is perfect for ambling around the colleges, museums, and King's College Chapel, one of England's greatest monuments.

2 Ely and Central Suffolk. The villages within a short drive of Cambridge remain largely unspoiled. Ely's lofty cathedral dominates the surrounding flatlands, and Sudbury, Long Melford, Lavenham, and Bury St. Edmunds preserve their rich historical flavor.

3 The Suffolk Coast. Idyllic villages such as Dedham and Flatford form the center of what's been dubbed "Constable Country," while the nearby Suffolk Coast includes such atmospheric seaside towns as Woodbridge and Aldeburgh.

11

GETTING ORIENTED

East Anglia, in southeastern England, can be divided into distinct areas for sightseeing: the central area surrounding the ancient university city of Cambridge and including Ely, with its magnificent cathedral rising out of the flatlands, and the towns of inland Suffolk; the Suffolk Heritage Coast, with its historic small towns and villages; and the northeast, with the region's capital, Norwich, the waterways of the Broads, and the beaches and salt marshes of the North Norfolk coast. Farther north, in Lincolnshire, are the city of Lincoln, landmarked by its tall, fluted cathedral towers, and the historic town of Stamford.

4 Norwich and North Norfolk. Sights in Norwich include its cathedral and castle. To the north and west you'll find the stately homes of Blickling Hall, Houghton Hall, and Sandringham, plus quiet coastal resorts such as Blakeney and Wells-next-the-Sea.

5 Stamford and Lincoln. On the western fringes of East Anglia, Lincoln is worth visiting for its Norman cathedral, whereas Stamford is best known for Burghley House, an impressive Elizabethan mansion.

EAST ANGLIA'S SEAFOOD BOUNTY

Perhaps unsurprisingly in an island nation, the harvest of the rivers and the sea forms an essential part of the British culinary tradition. Few regions are so closely associated with a love of good seafood as East Anglia.

(above) Fish-and-chips taste perfect during a day by the sea in East Anglia; (right, top) Cromer crab dressed with lemon mayonnaise; (right, bottom) Potted shrimp, a tasty appetizer

The coastlines of Essex, Suffolk, and Norfolk overflow with towns that specialize in one type of seaborne bounty or another. Shrimp, crab, and oysters are still caught using centuries-old methods; and lobsters, crabs, and mussels from Norfolk are sent to the top restaurants in London. Changing tastes tell a kind of social history of their own: oysters, now an expensive luxury, were once considered peasant food; and a new generation of chefs, eager to reconnect with forgotten ingredients and methods, is rediscovering old-fashioned flavors such as eel and samphire. Then there's that most famous of British seafood dishes—humble fish-and-chips. Some of the best in the country can be found in Suffolk towns such as Aldeburgh, where savvy fish-and-chip shop owners have installed webcams so customers can check how far the line stretches down the street.

SEA SALT

Evidence suggests that sea salt has been harvested in East Anglia for 2,000 years. It's popular today—but only one regional company still produces sea salt in the local style. Based in and named after the harbor town of Maldon in Essex, Maldon Crystal Salt Company uses a distinctive method that yields thin, flaky crystals with a delicate piquancy. Praised by chefs, Maldon salt is widely available at English supermarkets.

11

CHOOSING YOUR FISH-AND-CHIPS

The key word is simplicity: very fresh fish, deep-fried in batter, served immediately. Chips (slices of fried potato) must be thick cut and slightly soft, not crisp like fries, and sprinkled with salt and vinegar. The kind you get in fish-and-chips shops is almost always better than pub offerings. Cod, plaice, and haddock are the most popular choices, but the concern about cod overfishing means that you may see pollock, coley, or skate as alternatives.

CROMER CRAB

Known for their juicy flesh and higher-than-average white meat content, the best East Anglian crab comes from the area around Cromer in Norfolk. It's often served in salads and pasta dishes, or in savory crab cakes.

EEL

A staple of the East Anglian diet for centuries but long out of favor, the humble eel is making a comeback at fashionable restaurants. Eels are usually served smoked (on their own, or in soups or salads) or jellied in a flavored stock with the consistency of aspic.

MUSSELS

This type of small clam is particularly associated with the towns of Brancester and Stiffkey. Cheap and versatile, mussels can be served on their own; with other seafood; or in soups and stews.

OYSTERS

The Essex coast has been producing oysters since Roman times. A luxury item, oysters are usually served raw by the dozen, with few accompaniments, as a main course, or as a starter by the half dozen.

SAMPHIRE

A green sea vegetable that grows wild on shores and marshland, samphire is abundant in East Anglia, where it's an accompaniment to local seafood. Crisp and slightly salty, it's often described as "tasting like the sea."

SHERINGHAM LOBSTER

This well-regarded lobster is usually served with melted butter, or with fries as a kind of upper-class cousin of fish-and-chips. Lobster bisque—a rich, creamy soup—is also popular.

SHRIMP

Caught primarily off the coasts of Lancashire and East Anglia, the British shrimp is a type of shellfish similar to, but much smaller than, prawns. Potted shrimp is a traditional starter, made with butter, mace, and nutmeg.

YARMOUTH BLOATERS

A form of cured herring produced in Great Yarmouth, near Norwich, these fat, slightly salted fish aren't gutted before being smoked. This gives them a particularly strong, almost gamey flavor.

Updated by
Jack Jewers

One of those beautiful English inconsistencies, East Anglia has no spectacular mountains or rivers to disturb the storied, quiet land, full of rural delights. Occupying an area of southeastern England that pushes out into the North Sea, its counties of Essex, Norfolk, Suffolk, Lincolnshire, and Cambridgeshire feel cut off from the pulse of the country. Among its highlights is Cambridge, a lovely and ancient university city. East Anglia also has four of the country's greatest stately homes: Holkham Hall, Blickling Hall, Houghton Hall, and Sandringham—where the Queen spends Christmas.

In times past East Anglia was one of the most important centers of power in northern Europe. Towns like Lincoln were major Roman settlements, and the medieval wool trade brought huge prosperity to the higgledy-piggledy streets of tiny Lavenham. Thanks to its relative lack of thoroughfares and canals, however, East Anglia was mercifully untouched by the Industrial Revolution. The area is rich in idyllic, quintessentially English villages: sleepy, sylvan settlements in the midst of otherwise deserted lowlands. Even the towns feel small and manageable; the biggest city, Norwich, has a population of just 130,000. Cambridge, with its ancient university, is the area's most famous draw. There are incomparable cathedrals, at Ely and Lincoln particularly, and one of the finest Gothic buildings in Europe, King's College Chapel.

And yet, despite all of these treasures, the real joy of exploring East Anglia is making your own discoveries. Spend a couple of days exploring the hidden byways of the fens, or just taking in the subtle beauties of the many England-like-it-looks-in-the-movies villages. If you find yourself driving down a small country lane and an old church or mysterious, ivy-covered ruin peeks out from behind the trees, give in to your curiosity and look inside. Such hidden places are East Anglia's best-kept secret. There are real treasures to be found within those walls.

EAST ANGLIA PLANNER

WHEN TO GO

Summer and late spring are the best times to visit East Anglia. Late fall and winter can be cold, windy, and rainy, though this is England's driest region and crisp, frosty days here are beautiful. To escape crowds, avoid the popular Norfolk Broads in late July and August. You can't visit most of the Cambridge colleges during exam period (late May to mid-June), and the competition for hotel rooms heats up during graduation week (late June). The Aldeburgh Festival of Music and the Arts, one of the biggest events on the British classical music calendar, takes place in June.

PLANNING YOUR TIME

Cambridge is the region's most interesting city, and ideally you should allow two days to absorb its various sights. (In a pinch you could do it as a day trip from London, but only with an early start and a good pair of walking shoes.) You could easily use the city as a base for exploring Ely, Bury St. Edmunds, Lavenham, Long Melford, and Sudbury, although you'll also find accommodations in these towns. The Suffolk Coast offers enticing overnight stops in such small towns as Dedham and Aldeburgh. In the northern part of the region, Norwich makes a good place to stop for the night, and has enough sights to keep you interested for a day. If you're here to see the coast, you'd do better staying in villages such as Blakeney or Wells. Allow several hours to see the large houses such as Blickling Hall, near Norwich, and Burghley House, outside Stamford. Lincoln, notable for its cathedral, and Stamford are west and north of Norfolk if you want to work them into an itinerary.

GETTING HERE AND AROUND

AIR TRAVEL

Norwich International Airport serves a limited number of domestic and international destinations, though not the United States. London Stansted Airport, 30 miles south of Cambridge, is used mainly for European flights. The vast majority of travelers to the region arrive by train, car, or bus.

Airports London Stansted Airport ⊠ Bassingbourn Rd., Bishop's Stortford ☏ 0844/335–1803 ⊕ www.stanstedairport.com. **Norwich International Airport** ⊠ Amsterdam Way, off A140, Norwich ☏ 01603/411923 ⊕ www.norwichairport.co.uk.

BUS TRAVEL

National Express buses serve the region from London's Victoria Coach Station. Average travel times are 3 hours to Cambridge and Norwich, 2½ hours to Bury St. Edmunds, and 4½ hours to Lincoln.

Long-distance buses are useful for reaching the region and traveling between its major centers, but for smaller hops, local buses are best. First and Stagecoach buses cover the Cambridge, Lincolnshire, and Norwich areas. Information about local Norfolk service and county service is available from the Norfolk Bus Information Centre. Traveline can answer public transportation questions.

A FirstDay ticket from First for a day's unlimited bus travel around Norwich and the Norfolk coast costs £14, while a FirstWeek pass, good for seven days, costs £28. These tickets cover all buses except the Park and Ride shuttles that link parking lots with the town center. There are also various local passes that cost from £3.70 to £7 daily, £10 to £25 weekly. You can buy any of these tickets from the driver.

Bus Contacts First ☎ *0845/410–4444* ⊕ *www.firstgroup.com.* **National Express East Anglia** ☎ *0845/600–7245* ⊕ *www.nationalexpresseastanglia.com.* **Norfolk Bus Information Centre** ☎ *0845/300–6116.* **Stagecoach** ☎ *0871/834–0010* ⊕ *www.stagecoachbus.com/cambridge.* **Traveline** ☎ *0871/200–2233* ⊕ *www.traveline.org.uk.*

CAR TRAVEL

If you're driving from London, Cambridge (54 miles) is off M11. At Exit 9, M11 connects with A11 to Norwich (114 miles); A14 off A11 goes to Bury St. Edmunds. A12 from London goes through east Suffolk via Ipswich. For Lincoln (131 miles), take A1 via Huntingdon, Peterborough, and Grantham to A46 at Newark-on-Trent. A more scenic alternative is to leave A1 at Grantham and take A607 to Lincoln.

East Anglia has few fast main roads besides those mentioned here. Once off the A roads, traveling within the region often means taking country lanes that have many twists and turns, and going even just a few miles can take much longer than you think.

TRAIN TRAVEL

The entire region is well served by trains from London's Liverpool Street and King's Cross stations. The quality and convenience of these services varies enormously, however. Cambridge trains leave from King's Cross and Liverpool Street, take around one hour, and cost between £15 and £22. On the other hand, getting to Lincoln from King's Cross entails at least one transfer, takes two to three hours, and costs £26 to £87, depending on when you travel. ■ TIP➜ Tickets for trains between London and Lincoln can be a fraction of the price if you buy online in advance. A good way to save money on local trains in East Anglia is to buy an Anglia Plus Ranger Pass. It costs £17 for one day or £34 for three days, and allows unlimited rail travel in Norfolk, Suffolk, and part of Cambridgeshire. You can add up to four kids for an extra £2 each.

Train Contacts East Midlands Trains ☎ *0845/712–5678* ⊕ *www.eastmidlandstrains.co.uk.* **First Capital Connect** ☎ *0845/026–4700* ⊕ *www.firstcapitalconnect.co.uk.* **Greater Anglia** ☎ *0845/600–7245* ⊕ *www.greateranglia.co.uk.* **National Rail Enquiries** ☎ *0845/748–4950* ⊕ *www.nationalrail.co.uk.*

RESTAURANTS

In summer the coast gets so packed with people that reservations are essential at restaurants. Getting something to eat at other than regular mealtime hours isn't always possible in small towns; head to cafés if you want a midmorning or after-lunch snack. Look for area specialties, such as crab, lobster, duckling, Norfolk black turkey, hare, and partridge, on menus around the region. In Norwich there's no escaping the hot, bright-yellow Colman's mustard, which is perfect smeared gingerly on some sausage and mash. *Prices in the reviews are the average cost of a main course at dinner or, if dinner isn't served, at lunch.*

HOTELS

The region is full of centuries-old, half-timber inns with rooms full of roaring fires and cozy bars. Bed-and-breakfasts are a good option in pricey Cambridge. It's always busy in Cambridge and along the coast in summer, so reserve well in advance. *Prices in the reviews are the lowest cost of a standard double room in high season, including 20% V.A.T.*

VISITOR INFORMATION

Broads Authority ⊠ *Yare House, 62 Thorpe Rd., Norwich* ☎ *01603/610734* ⊕ *www.broads-authority.gov.uk.*

East of England Tourism ⊠ *Dettingen House, Dettingen Way, Bury St. Edmunds* ☎ *0333/3204202* ⊕ *www.visiteastofengland.com.*

CAMBRIDGE

Fodor'sChoice
★

With the spires of its university buildings framed by towering trees and expansive meadows, its medieval streets and passages enhanced by gardens and riverbanks, the city of Cambridge is among the loveliest in England. The city predates the Roman occupation of Britain, but there's confusion over exactly how the university was founded. The most widely accepted story is that it was established in 1209 by a pair of scholars from Oxford, who left their university in protest over the wrongful execution of a colleague for murder.

Keep in mind there's no recognizable campus: the scattered colleges *are* the university. The town reveals itself only slowly, filled with tiny gardens, ancient courtyards, imposing classic buildings, alleyways that lead past medieval churches, and wisteria-hung facades. Perhaps the best views are from the Backs, the green parkland that extends along the River Cam behind several colleges. This sweeping openness, a result of the larger size of the colleges and from the lack of industrialization in the city center, is what distinguishes Cambridge from Oxford.

This university town may be beautiful, but it's no museum. Well-preserved medieval buildings sit cheek-by-jowl next to the latest in modern architecture (for example, the William Gates building, which houses Cambridge University's computer laboratory) in this growing city dominated culturally and architecturally by its famous university (whose students make up around one-fifth of the city's 109,000 inhabitants), and beautified by parks, gardens, and the quietly flowing River Cam.

GETTING HERE AND AROUND

Good bus (three hours) and train (one hour) services connect London and Cambridge. The long-distance bus terminal is on Drummer Street, very close to Emmanuel and Christ's colleges. Several local buses connect the station with central Cambridge, including the frequent Citi 7 and 8 servicesalthough any bus listing City Centre or Emmanuel Street among its stops will do. The journey takes just under 10 minutes. If you're driving, don't attempt to venture very far into the center—parking is scarce and pricey. The center is amenable to explorations on foot, or you could join the throng by renting a bicycle.

Stagecoach sells Dayrider (£3.70) tickets for all-day bus travel within Cambridge, and Megarider tickets (£12.50) for seven days of travel within the city. You can extend these to cover the whole county of Cambridgeshire (£5.70 and £22.50, respectively). Buy any of them from the driver.

TOURS City Sightseeing operates open-top bus tours of Cambridge—the Backs, the colleges, the Imperial War Museum in Duxford, and the Grafton shopping center. Tours can be joined at marked bus stops in the city. Tickets are £13. Also ask the tourist office about tours.

TIMING

In summer and over the Easter and Christmas holidays Cambridge is devoid of students, its heart and soul. To see the city in full swing, visit from October through June. In summer there are arts and music festivals, notably the Strawberry Fair and the Arts Festival (both June) and the Folk Festival (late July to early August). The May Bumps, intercollegiate boat races, are, confusingly, held the first week of June. This is also the month when students celebrate the end of exam season, so expect to encounter some boisterous nightlife.

Visitor and Tour Information Cambridge University ☎ 01223/337733
⊕ www.cam.ac.uk. **City Sightseeing** ✉ Cambridge Train Station, Station Rd.
☎ 01223/423578 ⊕ www.city-sightseeing.com. **Visit Cambridge** ✉ Peas Hill
☎ 0871/226–8006 ⊕ www.visitcambridge.org.

EXPLORING

Exploring the city means, in large part, exploring the university. Each of the 25 oldest colleges is built around a series of courts, or quadrangles, framing manicured, velvety lawns. Because students and fellows (faculty) live and work in these courts, access is sometimes restricted, and at *all* times you're asked not to picnic in the quadrangles.

Visitors aren't normally allowed into college buildings other than chapels, dining halls, and some libraries; some colleges charge admission for certain buildings. Public visiting hours vary from college to college, depending on the time of year, and it's best to call or to check with the city tourist office. Colleges close to visitors during the main exam time, late May to mid-June. Term time (when classes are in session) means roughly October to December, January to March, and April to June; summer term, or vacation, runs from July to September. ∎TIP→ **Bring a pair of binoculars, as some college buildings have highly intricate details, such as the spectacular ceiling at King's College Chapel.** When the colleges are open, the best way to gain access is to join a walking tour led by an official Blue Badge guide—many areas are off-limits unless you do. The two-hour tours (£14 to £18.50) leave up to four times daily from the city tourist office. The other traditional view of the colleges is gained from a punt—the boats propelled by pole on the River Cam.

Cricket, anyone? Audley End, a 17th-century house, serves as an idyllic backdrop for a cricket match.

TOP ATTRACTIONS

OFF THE
BEATEN
PATH

Audley End House and Gardens. A famous example of early-17th-century architecture, Audley End was once owned by Charles II, who bought it as a convenient place to break his journey on the way to the Newmarket races. Although the palatial building was remodeled in the 18th and 19th centuries, the Jacobean style is still on display in the magnificent Great Hall. You can walk in the park, landscaped by Capability Brown in the 18th century, and the fine Victorian gardens. Two exhibits focus on the lives of domestic servants in the late 19th century. The Service Wing lets you look "below stairs" at the kitchen, scullery (where fish were descaled and chickens were plucked), and game larder (where pheasants, partridges, and rabbits were hung), while the Stable Yard gives kids the chance to see old saddles and tack, and don Victorian riding costumes. The house is in Saffron Waldon, 14 miles south of Cambridge. ⊠ *Off London Rd., Saffron Waldon* ☎ *01799/522842* ⊕ *www.english-heritage. org.uk* 🖅 *£13; Service Wing, Stable Yard, and gardens only £9* ⊙ *House Apr.–Sept., Wed.–Sun. noon–5; Oct., Wed.–Sun. 10–4. Service Wing, Stable Yard, and gardens Apr.–June, Wed.–Sun. 10–6; July–Sept., daily 10–6; Oct., Wed.–Sun. 10–5; Nov.–Mar, weekends 10–4.*

Emmanuel College. The master hand of architect Christopher Wren (1632–1723) is evident throughout much of Cambridge, particularly at Emmanuel, built on the site of a Dominican friary, where he designed the chapel and colonnade. A stained-glass window in the chapel has a likeness of John Harvard, founder of Harvard University, who studied here. The college, founded in 1584, was an early center of Puritan learning; a number of the Pilgrims were Emmanuel alumni,

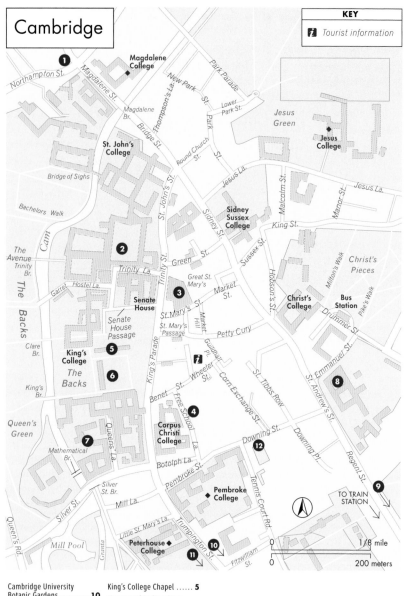

Cambridge

KEY
🛈 *Tourist information*

and they remembered their alma mater in naming Cambridge, Massachusetts. ✉ *St. Andrew's St.* ☎ *01223/334200* ⊕ *www.emma. cam.ac.uk* 🖼 *Free* ⊗ *Daily 9–6, except exam period.*

Fodor's Choice
★
Fitzwilliam Museum. In a Classical Revival building renowned for its grand Corinthian portico, the Fitzwilliam, founded by the seventh viscount Fitzwilliam of Merrion in 1816, has one of Britain's most outstanding collections of art and antiquities. Highlights include two large Titians, an extensive collection of French impressionist painting, and many paintings by Matisse and Picasso. The opulent interior

displays its treasures to marvelous effect, from Egyptian pieces such as inch-high figurines and painted coffins, to sculptures from the Chinese Han dynasty of the 3rd century BC. Other collections of note here are a fine assortment of medieval illuminated manuscripts and a fascinating room full of armor and muskets. ✉ *Trumpington St.* ☎ *01223/332900* ⊕ *www.fitzmuseum.cam.ac.uk* 🖼 *Free* ⊗ *Tues.–Sat. 10–5, Sun. noon–5.*

Great St. Mary's. Known as the "university church," Great St. Mary's has its origins in the 11th century, although the current building dates from 1478. The main reason to visit is to climb the 113-foot tower, which has a superb view over the colleges and marketplace. Also here is the Michaelhouse Centre, a small café, gallery, and performing arts venue with frequent free lunchtime concerts. Guided tours must be booked in advance. ✉ *Market Hill, King's Parade* ☎ *01223/462914* ⊕ *www.gsm.cam.ac.uk* 🖼 *Free, tower £3.50, guided tours £10* ⊗ *May–Aug., Mon.–Sat. 9:30–5, Sun. 12:30–5; Sept.–Apr., Mon.–Sat. 9:30–4, Sun. 12:30–4.*

OFF THE
BEATEN
PATH
Imperial War Museum Duxford. Europe's leading aviation museum houses a remarkable collection of 180 aircraft from Europe and the United States. The former airfield is effectively a complex of several museums under one banner. The **Land Warfare Hall** features tanks and other military vehicles. The striking **American Air Museum**, honoring the 30,000 Americans killed in action flying from Britain during World War II, contains the largest display of American fighter planes outside the U.S. **AirSpace** contains a vast array of military and civil aircraft in a 3-acre hangar. Directly underneath is the **Airborne Assault Museum,** which chronicles the history of airborne forces, such as the British Parachute Regiment, which played a pivotal role in the Normandy Landings. There are also hangars where you can watch restoration work on World War II planes and exhibitions on maritime warfare and the Battle of Britain. ✉ *A505, Duxford* ☎ *01223/835000* ⊕ *duxford. iwm.org.uk* 🖼 *£17.50* ⊗ *Mid-Mar.–late Oct., daily 10–6; late Oct.–mid-Mar., daily 10–4. Last admission 1 hr before closing.*

A must-see at Cambridge is King's College Chapel, a masterpiece of Perpendicular Gothic style.

King's College. Founded in 1441 by Henry VI, King's College has a magnificent late-15th-century chapel that is its most famous landmark. Other notable architecture is the neo-Gothic Porters' Lodge, facing King's Parade, which was a relatively recent addition in the 1830s, and the classical Gibbs building. ▨ TIP→ Head down to the river, from where the panorama of college and chapel is one of the university's most photographed views. Past students of King's College include the novelist E.M. Forster, the economist John Maynard Keynes, and the World War I poet Rupert Brooke. ⊠ *King's Parade* ☎ *01223/331100* ⊕ *www.kings. cam.ac.uk* ✉ *£7.50, includes chapel* ⊗ *Term time, weekdays 9:30–3:30, Sat. 9:30–3:15, Sun. 1:15–2:30; out of term, daily 9:30–4:30.*

Fodor's Choice
★

King's College Chapel. Based on Sainte-Chapelle, the 13th-century royal chapel in Paris, this house of worship is perhaps the most glorious flowering of Perpendicular Gothic in Britain. Henry VI, the king after whom the college is named, oversaw the work. From the outside, the most prominent features are the massive flying buttresses and the fingerlike spires that line the length of the building. Inside, the most obvious impression is of great space—the chapel was once described as "the noblest barn in Europe"—and of light flooding in from its huge windows. The brilliantly colored bosses (carved panels at the intersections of the roof ribs) are particularly intense, although hard to see without binoculars. An exhibition in the chantries, or side chapels, explains more about the chapel's construction. Behind the altar is *The Adoration of the Magi,* an enormous painting by Peter Paul Rubens. ▨ TIP→ The chapel, unlike the rest of King's College, stays open during exam periods. Every Christmas Eve a festival of carols is sung by the chapel's famous choir. To compete for the small number of tickets available, join the line at the college's main entrance early—doors open at 7 am. ⊠ *King's Parade* ☎ *01223/331212* ⊕ *www. kings.cam.ac.uk* ✍ *£7.50, includes college and grounds* ☉ *Term time, weekdays 9:30–3:30, Sat. 9:30–3:15, Sun. 1:15–2:30; out of term, daily 9:30–4:30. Chapel occasionally closed for services and private events; call or check online.*

Pickerel Inn. The 600-year-old Pickerel Inn, one of the city's oldest pubs, makes for a good stop for an afternoon pint of real ale and a bowl of doorstop-sized potato wedges. Watch for the low beams. ⊠ *30 Magdalene St.* ☎ *01223/355068.*

Fodor's Choice
★

Polar Museum. Beautifully designed, this museum at the university's Scott Polar Research Institute chronicles the history of polar exploration. There's a particular emphasis on the British expeditions of the 20th century, including the ill-fated attempt by Robert Falcon Scott to be the first to reach the South Pole in 1912. Norwegian explorer Roald Amundsen reached the pole first; Scott and his men perished on the return journey, but his story became legendary. There are also collections devoted to the indigenous people of northern Canada, Greenland, and Alaska. ⊠ *Scott Polar Research Institute, Lensfield Rd.* ☎ *01223/336540* ⊕ *www.spri. cam.ac.uk/museum* ✍ *Free* ☉ *Tues.–Sat. 10–4.*

Queens' College. One of the most eye-catching colleges, Queens' is named after Margaret, queen of Henry VI, and Elizabeth, queen of Edward IV. Founded in 1448, the college is tucked away on Queens' Lane, next to the wide lawns that lead down from King's College to the Backs. The secluded "cloister court" looks untouched since its completion in the 1540s. Queens' masterpiece is the **Mathematical Bridge,** the original version of which is said to have been built without any fastenings. The current bridge (1902) is securely bolted. The college is closed to visitors late May to late June. ⊠ *Queens' La.* ☎ *01223/335511* ⊕ *www.quns.cam.ac.uk* ✍ *£2.50* ☉ *Mid-Mar.–mid-May and late June–Sept., daily 10–4:30; Oct., weekdays 2–4, weekends 10–4:30; Nov.–mid-Mar., daily 2–4.*

Trinity College. Founded in 1546 by Henry VIII, Trinity replaced a 14th-century educational foundation and is the largest college in either Cambridge or Oxford, with nearly 700 undergraduates. In the 17th-century great court, with its massive gatehouse, is **Great Tom,** a giant clock that strikes each hour with high and low notes. The college's greatest masterpiece is Christopher Wren's **library,** colonnaded and seemingly constructed with as much light as stone. Among the things you can see here is A. A. Milne's handwritten manuscript of *The House at Pooh Corner.* Trinity alumni include Isaac Newton, William Thackeray, Lord Byron, Alfred Tennyson, and 31 Nobel Prize winners. ⊠ *St. John's St.* ☎ *01223/338400* ⊕ *www.trin.cam.ac.uk* ✍ *£1* ☉ *College and chapel daily 10–4, except exam period and event days; great court and library weekdays noon–2, Sat. in term time 10:30–12:30.*

WORTH NOTING

Cambridge University Botanic Gardens. Opened in 1846, these 40 acres contain rare specimens like the jade vine, greenhouses filled with orchids and other tropical beauties, and a rock garden with delicate plants from rocky regions all over the world. The gardens are a five-minute walk from the Fitzwilliam Museum. ✉ *Cory Lodge, Bateman St.* ☎ *01223/336265* 🌐 *www.botanic.cam.ac.uk* 🎟 *£4.50* 🕒 *Apr.–Sept., daily 10–6; Nov.–Jan., daily 10–4; Feb., Mar., and Oct., daily 10–5. Conservatories close ½ hr before gardens.*

Kettle's Yard. Originally a private house owned by a former curator of London's Tate galleries, Kettle's Yard contains a fine collection of 20th-century art, sculpture, furniture, and decorative arts, including works by Henry Moore, Barbara Hepworth, and Henri Gaudier-Brzeska. A separate gallery shows changing exhibitions of modern art and crafts, and weekly concerts and lectures attract an eclectic mix of enthusiasts. Ring the bell for admission. ✉ *Castle St.* ☎ *01223/748100* 🌐 *www.kettlesyard.co.uk* 🎟 *Free* 🕒 *House Apr.–late Sept., Tues.–Sun. 2–5; Oct.–Mar., Tues.–Sun. 2–4. Gallery Tues.–Sun. 1–5.*

Museum of Archaeology and Anthropology. The university maintains some fine museums in its research halls on Downing Street—the wonder is that they're not better known to visitors. At the recently renovated Museum of Archaeology and Anthropology, highlights include an array of objects brought back from Captain Cook's pioneering voyages to the Pacific; Roman and medieval-era British artifacts; and the oldest human-made tools ever discovered, from the African expeditions of British archeaologist Louis Leakey (1903–1972). ✉ *Downing St.* ☎ *01223/333516* 🌐 *maa.cam.ac.uk* 🎟 *Free* 🕒 *Tues.–Sat. 10:30–4:30.*

Whipple Museum of the History of Science. This rather delightful, dusty old cupboard of a museum contains all manner of scientific artifacts, instruments and doodads from the medieval period to the early 20th century. Most fun is the section on astronomy, including a beautiful 18th-century grand orrary—an elaborate three-dimensional model of the solar system, minus the planets that had yet to be discovered at the time. ✉ *Free School La.* ☎ *01223/330906* 🌐 *www.hos.cam.ac.uk/whipple* 🎟 *Free* 🕒 *Weekdays 12:30–4:30.*

WHERE TO EAT

$ ✕ **Jamie's Italian.** Run by celebrity chef Jamie Oliver, this is one of the
ITALIAN busiest restaurants in Cambridge. In truth, the long queues probably have more to do with his star power and the no-reservations policy, but the food also deserves praise. The menu is a combination of authentic Italian flavors and modern variations on the classics; you could opt for the pasta *arrabiata*, made with bread crumbs and fiery peppers, or fillet of sea bream with garlic, wine, capers, and plum tomatoes. The gorgeous building, a former library, is an attraction in itself. The atmosphere is relaxed and casual, and the prices are lower than you'd expect. [$] *Average main: £14* ✉ *Old Library, Wheeler St.* ☎ *01223/654094* 🌐 *www.jamieoliver.com/italian* ✍ *Reservations essential.*

11

$$ ✗ **Loch Fyne.** Part of a Scottish chain that harvests its own oysters, this
SEAFOOD airy, casual place across from the Fitzwilliam Museum is deservedly popu-
lar. The mussels and salmon are fresh and well prepared, and line-caught
tuna is served with a mint-and-caper salsa. Try the smoky, sweet Bradan
Rost smoked salmon flavored with Scotch whisky if it's on the menu. The
place is open for breakfast, lunch, and dinner. $ *Average main: £15* ⊠ *37
Trumpington St.* ☎ *01223/362433* ⊕ *www.lochfyne-restaurants.com.*

$$$$ ✗ **Midsummer House.** Beside the River Cam on the edge of Midsummer
FRENCH Common, this gray-brick building holds an elegant restaurant with a
comfortable conservatory and a handful of tables under fruit trees in a
lush, secluded garden. Fixed-price menus for lunch and dinner include
innovative French and Mediterranean dishes. Choices might include
roasted sea bass or venison with blue cheese and cocoa nibs. $ *Av-
erage main: £40* ⊠ *Midsummer Common* ☎ *01223/369299* ⊕ *www.
midsummerhouse.co.uk* ✍ *Reservations essential* ☉ *Closed Sun. and
Mon. No lunch Tues.*

$$ ✗ **The Oak.** This charming, intimate restaurant has fast become a local
BRITISH favorite. It's near an unpromisingly busy intersection, but the friend-
liness of the staff and classic bistro food more than make up for it.
Typical mains include linguini with crab and spiced tomato sauce, or
rib-eye steak with truffle butter and fries. Ask to be seated in the lovely
walled garden if the weather's fine. $ *Average main: £15* ⊠ *6 Lensfield
Rd.* ☎ *01223/323361* ⊕ *www.theoakbistro.co.uk.*

$$$$ ✗ **Restaurant 22 Chesterton Road.** Pretty stained-glass windows separate
BRITISH this sophisticated little restaurant from bustling Chesterton Road. The
setting, in a terrace of houses, is low-key, but the food is creative and
eye-catching. The fixed-price menu changes monthly and features such
dishes as pork belly with bubble and squeak (a traditional dish made
of fried potatoes and onions), and beef and chorizo stew with rosemary
dumplings. $ *Average main: £33* ⊠ *22 Chesterton Rd.* ☎ *01223/351880*
⊕ *www.restaurant22.co.uk* ☉ *Closed Sun. and Mon. No lunch.*

$$ ✗ **River Bar & Kitchen.** Across the river from Magdalene College, this pop-
MODERN BRITISH ular waterfront bar and grill serves delicious steak and burgers, plus spe-
cialties such as lobster macaroni and cheese and blackened salmon with
soy and ginger greens. Light lunches are served in the afternoon, and
the evening cocktail list is small but elegant. Try the French 75, which
is gin with lemon juice, sugar, and sparkling wine. $ *Average main: £17*
⊠ *Quayside, Thompsons Ln., off Bridge St.* ☎ *01223/307030* ⊕ *www.
riverbarsteakhouse.com* ✍ *Reservations essential.*

$$ ✗ **Three Horseshoes.** This early-19th-century pub-restaurant in a thatched
ITALIAN cottage has an elegant dining space in the conservatory and more casual
tables in the airy bar. The tempting, beautifully presented, and carefully sourced dishes are modern Italian with a British accent. Appetizers
might include beetroot risotto with creamed goat cheese and orange
oil, and among the main courses you might find beef shin with risotto,
or haunch of venison with blackened leeks and dauphinoise potatoes.
The wine list is enormous and predominantly Italian, but there are also
some good New World choices. It's 5 miles west of Cambridge, about
a 10-minute taxi ride. $ *Average main: £18* ⊠ *High St., Madingley*
☎ *01954/210221* ⊕ *www.threehorseshoesmadingley.co.uk.*

$$ **✕ The Willow Tree.** Plenty of Cambridge residents are happy to drive 20
MODERN BRITISH minutes to this stylish pub in the sleepy village of Bourn. The seasonal menu serves classic British and European dishes with a flourish. Typical dishes include sea bass with saffron sauce, or venison pie topped with creamed potatoes. There's also a selection of pizzas and tapas. For dessert try the chocolate and blueberry tart with Kahlúa mascarpone, or perhaps the "playful plate," a taster menu of traditional British candies. Best of all, the prices are reasonable. Bourn is 10 miles east of Cambridge; take the B1046 for the prettiest drive. $ *Average main: £15 ⊠ 29 High St., Bourn* ☎ *01954/719775* ⊕ *www.thewillowtreebourn.com.*

WHERE TO STAY

There aren't many hotels downtown. For more (and cheaper) options, consider one of the numerous guesthouses on the arterial roads and in the suburbs. These average around £30 to £80 per person per night and can be booked through the tourist information center.

For expanded hotel reviews, visit Fodors.com.

$$ **DoubleTree by Hilton.** This modern establishment makes the most of its
HOTEL peaceful riverside location, and many rooms have sweeping views of the surrounding area. **Pros:** central position; good facilities and service; spacious rooms. **Cons:** price fluctuates wildly over summer season. $ *Rooms from: £150 ⊠ Granta Pl. and Mill La.* ☎ *01223/259988* ⊕ *www. doubletreecambridge.com ⤳ 118 rooms, 4 suites* ⍩ *Multiple meal plans.*

$$ **Duke House.** Guest rooms at this beautifully converted town house
B&B/INN (home of the Duke of Glouchester when he was a student) look like they've
Fodor'sChoice been copied from the pages of a lifestyle magazine. **Pros:** beautiful house;
★ great location; suites are quite spacious. **Cons:** gets booked up fast; cheaper rooms are small. $ *Rooms from: £130 ⊠ 1 Victoria St.* ☎ *01223/314773* ⊕ *www.dukehousecambridge.co.uk ⤳ 4 rooms* ⍩ *Breakfast.*

$$ **Duxford Lodge.** A short drive from the Imperial War Museum in
HOTEL Duxford, this family-run hotel sits off the main road between Cambridge and Saffron Walden. **Pros:** off the beaten path; good food; family rooms are excellent value. **Cons:** need a car to get around; prices go up air show weekends. $ *Rooms from: £119 ⊠ Ickleton Rd., Duxford* ☎ *01223/836444* ⊕ *www.duxfordlodgehotel.co.uk ⤳ 11 rooms* ⍩ *Breakfast.*

$ **Finches Bed and Breakfast.** Although it's in a rather inauspicious build-
B&B/INN ing, the diminutive Finches is a well-run B&B with prices that make it excellent value. **Pros:** cheerful staff; quiet location; good level of service. **Cons:** away from the action; no tubs in bathrooms; no credit cards. $ *Rooms from: £70 ⊠ 144 Thornton Rd.* ☎ *01223/276653* ⊕ *www. finches-bnb.com ⤳ 3 rooms* ⊟ *No credit cards* ⍩ *Breakfast.*

$$ **Regent Hotel.** A rare small hotel in central Cambridge, this hand-
HOTEL some Georgian town house has wooden sash windows that look out over a tree-lined park called Parker's Piece. **Pros:** good view from top rooms; close to bars and restaurants. **Cons:** no parking; a tad scruffy; disappointing breakfasts. $ *Rooms from: £102 ⊠ 41 Regent St.* ☎ *01223/351470* ⊕ *www.regenthotel.co.uk ⤳ 22 rooms* ⍩ *Breakfast.*

$$$ HOTEL Fodor's Choice ★ **The Varsity.** This stylish boutique hotel with an adjoining spa has wide windows that flood the place with light. **Pros:** beautiful location; gorgeous views; stylish design. **Cons:** not such great views in the cheap rooms. [$] *Rooms from: £165* ✉ *Thompson's La., off Bridge St.* ☎ *01223/306030* 🌐 *www.thevarsityhotel.co.uk* 🛏 *48 rooms* 🍴 *Multiple meal plans.*

$ B&B/INN **Warkworth House.** The location of this sweet B&B could hardly be better, as the Fitzwilliam Museum and several of Cambridge's colleges are within a 15-minute walk. **Pros:** excellent location; lovely hosts; some free parking. **Cons:** few frills. [$] *Rooms from: £80* ✉ *Warkworth Terr.* ☎ *01223/363682* 🌐 *www.warkworthhouse.co.uk* 🛏 *5 rooms* 🍴 *Breakfast.*

NIGHTLIFE AND THE ARTS

NIGHTLIFE

The city's pubs provide the mainstay of Cambridge's nightlife and shouldn't be missed.

Eagle. This 16th-century coaching inn with a cobbled courtyard has lost none of its old-time character. It also played a minor role in scientific history when on February 28, 1953, a pair of excited Cambridge scientists announced to a roomful of rather surprised lunchtime patrons that they'd just discovered the secret of life: DNA. A plaque outside commemorates the event. ✉ *8 Benet St.* ☎ *01223/505020.*

Fort St. George. Overlooking the university boathouses, Fort St. George gets the honors for riverside views. ✉ *Midsummer Common* ☎ *01223/354327.*

Free Press. A favorite of student rowers, this small pub has an excellent selection of traditional ales. ✉ *7 Prospect Row* ☎ *01223/368337* 🌐 *www.freepresspub.co.uk.*

THE ARTS

CONCERTS Cambridge supports its own symphony orchestra, and regular musical events are held in many colleges, especially those with large chapels.

Cambridge Folk Festival. Spread over four days in late July or early August at Cherry Hinton Hall, the Cambridge Folk Festival attracts major international folk singers and groups. ☎ *01223/457555* 🌐 *www.cambridgefolkfestival.co.uk.*

Corn Exchange. The beautifully restored Corn Exchange presents classical and rock concerts, stand-up comedy, musicals, opera, and ballet. ✉ *Wheeler St.* ☎ *01223/357851* 🌐 *www.cornex.co.uk.*

King's College Chapel. During regular terms, King's College Chapel has evensong services Monday through Saturday at 5:30, Sunday at 3:30. **TIP→ Your best chance of seeing the full choir is Thursday to Sunday.** ✉ *King's Parade* ☎ *01223/769340* 🌐 *www.kings.cam.ac.uk.*

THEATER **ADC Theatre.** Home of the famous *Cambridge Footlights Revue*, the ADC Theatre hosts mainly student and fringe theater productions. ✉ *Park St.* ☎ *01223/300085* 🌐 *www.adctheatre.com.*

Arts Theatre. The city's main repertory theater, the Arts Theatre was built by economist John Maynard Keynes in 1936 and supports a full program of plays and concerts. It also has a good ground-floor bar and two restaurants. ⊠ *6 St. Edward's Passage* ☎ *01223/503333* ⊕ *www. cambridgeartstheatre.com.*

SHOPPING

Head to the specialty shops in the center of town, especially in and around Rose Crescent and King's Parade. Bookshops, including antiquarian stores, are Cambridge's pride and joy.

All Saints Garden Art & Craft Market. This market displays the wares of local artists outdoors on Saturday. It's also open Friday from June to August and Wednesday to Friday in December (weather permitting). ⊠ *Trinity St.* ⊕ *www.cambridge-art-craft.co.uk.*

Ryder & Amies. Need a straw boater? This shop carries official university wear, from hoodies to ties to cufflinks. ⊠ *22 King's Parade* ☎ *01223/350371* ⊕ *www.ryderamies.co.uk.*

BOOKS **Cambridge University Press Bookshop.** In business since at least 1581, the Cambridge University Press runs this store on Trinity Street. ⊠ *1 Trinity St.* ☎ *01223/333333* ⊕ *www.cambridge.org/uk/bookshop.*

G. David. Near the Arts Theatre, G. David sells antiquarian books. ⊠ *16 St. Edward's Passage* ☎ *01223/354619* ⊕ *www.gdavidbookseller.co.uk.*

Haunted Bookshop. This shop carries a great selection of old, illustrated books and British classics. And apparently it has a ghost, too. ⊠ *9 St. Edward's Passage* ☎ *01223/312913* ⊕ *www.sarahkeybooks.co.uk.*

Heffer's. With many rare and imported books, Heffner's boasts a particularly extensive arts section. ⊠ *20 Trinity St.* ☎ *01223/463200* ⊕ *book-shop.blackwell.co.uk.*

SPORTS AND THE OUTDOORS

BIKING

City Cycle Hire. This shop charges supercheap rates of £7 per half day, £10 per day, and £25 for a week. All bikes are mountain or hybrid bikes. Advance reservations are essential in July and August. ⊠ *61 Newnham Rd.* ☎ *01223/365629* ⊕ *www.citycyclehire.com.*

PUNTING

You can rent punts at several places, notably at Silver Street Bridge–Mill Lane, at Magdalene Bridge, and from outside the Rat and Parrot pub on Thompson's Lane on Jesus Green. Hourly rental costs £15 to £20. Chauffeured punting, usually by a Cambridge student, is also popular. It costs around £12 per person.

Scudamore's Punting Co. This company rents chauffeured and self-drive punts. It also offers various tours, ranging from a Ghost Tour to a Punt & Cream Tea Tour, for about £18.50 per person. Private tours can be booked for the same price, but there's quite a hefty minimum charge. ⊠ *Granta Place, Mill La.* ☎ *01223/359750* ⊕ *www.scudamores.com.*

11

CLOSE UP

Punting on the Cam

To punt is to maneuver a flat-bottom, wooden, gondolalike boat—in this case, through the shallow River Cam along the verdant Backs behind the colleges of Cambridge. One benefit of this popular activity is that you get a better view of the ivy-covered walls from the water. Mastery of the sport lies in your ability to control a 15-foot pole, used to propel the punt. With a bottle of wine, some food, and a few friends, you may find yourself saying things such as, "It doesn't get any better than this." One piece of advice: if your pole gets stuck, let go. You can use the smaller paddle to go back and retrieve it. Hang on to a stuck punt for too long and you'll probably fall in with it.

The lazier-at-heart may prefer chauffeured punting, with food supplied. Students from Cambridge often do the work, and you get a fairly informative spiel on the colleges. For a romantic evening trip, there are illuminated punts.

One university punting society once published a useful "Bluffer's Guide to Punting" featuring detailed instructions and tips on how to master the art. It has been archived online at ⊕ *duramecho.com/Misc/ HowToPunt.html.*

ELY AND CENTRAL SUFFOLK

This central area of towns and villages within easy reach of Cambridge is testament to the amazing changeability of the English landscape. The town of Ely is set in an eerie, flat, and apparently endless marsh, or fenland. (A medieval term, "the fens," is still used informally to describe the surrounding region.) Only a few miles south and east into Suffolk, however, all this changes to pastoral landscapes of gently undulating hills, and clusters of villages including pretty Sudbury and Lavenham.

ELY

16 miles north of Cambridge.

Known for its magnificent cathedral, Ely is the "capital" of the fens, the center of what used to be a separate county called the Isle of Ely (literally "island of eels"). Until the land was drained in the 17th century, Ely was surrounded by treacherous marshland, which inhabitants crossed wearing stilts. Today Wicken Fen, a nature reserve 9 miles southeast of town (off A1123), preserves the sole remaining example of fenland in an undrained state.

Enveloped by fields of wheat, sugar beets, and carrots, Ely is a small, dense town that fails to live up to the high expectations created by its big attraction, its cathedral. The shopping area and market square lie to the north and lead down to the riverside, and the medieval buildings of the cathedral grounds and the King's School (which trains cathedral choristers) spread out to the south and west. Ely's most famous resident was Oliver Cromwell, whose house is now a museum.

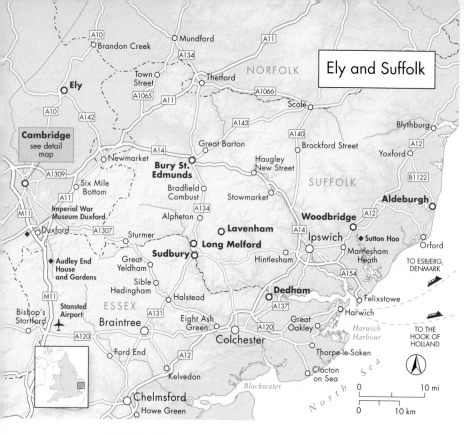

Ely and Suffolk

GETTING HERE AND AROUND

The 9 and 12 buses leave twice an hour from the Drummer Street bus station in Cambridge. The journey to Ely takes around an hour. To drive there from Cambridge, simply take the A10 road going north out of the city. Ely is quite small, so find somewhere to park and walk to the center. Trains from Cambridge to Ely leave three times an hour and take 15 minutes.

ESSENTIALS

Visitor Information Visit Ely ⊠ Oliver Cromwell's House, 29 St. Mary's St. ☎ 01353/662062 ⊕ visitely.eastcambs.gov.uk.

EXPLORING

Fodor's Choice ★

Ely Cathedral. Known affectionately as the Ship of the Fens, Ely Cathedral can be seen for miles, towering above the flat landscape on one of the few ridges in the fens. In 1083 the Normans began work on the cathedral, which stands on the site of a Benedictine monastery founded by the Anglo-Saxon princess Etheldreda in 673. In the center of the cathedral you see a marvel of medieval construction—the unique octagonal **Lantern Tower**, a sort of stained-glass skylight of colossal proportions, built to replace the central tower that collapsed in 1322. The cathedral's **West Tower** is even taller; the view from the top (if you can manage the 288 steps) is spectacular. Tours of both towers are daily between April and October and on weekends between November and March. The cathedral is also notable for its 248-foot-long **nave,** with its simple Norman arches and Victorian painted ceiling. Much of the decorative carving of the 14th-century **Lady Chapel** was defaced during the Reformation (mostly by knocking off the heads of the statuary), but enough traces remain to show its original beauty.

The cathedral houses a superior **Stained Glass Museum,** up a flight of 42 steps. Exhibits trace the history of stained glass from medieval to modern times. Ely Cathedral is a popular location for films; it doubled for Westminster Abbey in *The King's Speech* (2010). Guided tours

> ### DRAINING EAST ANGLIA
>
> Large areas of East Anglia were originally barely inhabited, swampy marshes. Drainage of the wetlands by the creation of waterways was carried out most energetically in the 17th and 18th centuries. The process was far from smooth. Locals, whose fishing rights were threatened, sometimes destroyed the work. Also, as the marshland dried out, it shrank and sank, requiring pumps to stop renewed flooding. Hundreds of windmills were used to pump water away; some of them can still be seen today.

begin daily at 10:45, 1, and 2, with an additional tour at 3 on weekends and also weekdays between April and October. ▮▮TIP→ Always call ahead about tours, as times are subject to change. ✉ *The Gallery* 📞 *01353/667735* ⊕ *www.elycathedral.org* 🎫 *£7 including tour; with Octagon Tower or West Tower £8.50; with Stained Glass Museum £10.20; combined ticket £16.20* ☉ *May–Oct., daily 7–6:30; Nov.–Apr., Mon.–Sat. 7:30–6:30, Sun. 7:30–5:30.*

Oliver Cromwell's House. This half-timber medieval building stands in the shadows of Ely Cathedral. During the 10 years he lived here, Cromwell (1599–1658) was leading the rebellious Roundheads in their eventually victorious struggle against King Charles I in the English Civil War. The house contains an exhibition about its controversial former occupant, who was Britain's Lord Protector from 1653 to 1658. It's also the site of Ely's tourist information center. ✉ *29 St. Mary's St.* 📞 *01353/662062* ⊕ *www.visitely.org.uk* 🎫 *£4.60* ☉ *Apr.–Oct., daily 10–5; Nov.–Mar., Sat. 10–5, Sun.–Fri. 11–4.*

WHERE TO EAT AND STAY

For expanded hotel reviews, visit Fodors.com.

$$
BRITISH
Fodor's Choice
★

✕ **Old Fire Engine House.** Scrubbed pine tables fill the main dining room of this converted fire station near Ely Cathedral. Another room, used when there's a crowd, has an open fireplace and a polished wood floor, and also serves as an art gallery. Among the English dishes are such traditional fenland recipes as pike baked in white wine, as well as eel pie and game in season. Desserts might include treacle pudding (a light, steamed cake) or homemade ice cream. Reserve ahead for afternoon tea (£19.25). 💲 *Average main: £16* ✉ *25 St. Mary's St.* 📞 *01353/662582* ⊕ *www.theoldfireenginehouse.co.uk* ☉ *Closed 2 wks at Christmas. No dinner Sun.*

$ ▦ **Cathedral House.** This Georgian house, full of such interesting period
HOTEL   details as an oriel window and a handsome staircase, makes a pleasant
overnight stop in Ely. **Pros:** heaps of character; steps from the cathedral;
free Wi-Fi; handy parking. **Cons:** small bathrooms; on a busy road; late
check-in time. $ *Rooms from: £80* ✉ *17 St. Mary's St.* ☎ *01353/662124*
⊕ *www.cathedralhouse.co.uk* ⤵ *3 rooms, 1 cottage* ⊟ *No credit cards*
†◯| *Breakfast.*

SUDBURY

32 miles southeast of Ely, 16 miles south of Bury St. Edmunds.

An early silk-weaving industry (still in existence, on a smaller scale) as
well as the wool trade brought prosperity to Sudbury, which has three
fine Perpendicular Gothic churches and some half-timber houses.

Thomas Gainsborough, one of the greatest English portrait and landscape painters, was born here in 1727; a statue of him holding his
palette stands on Market Hill. In Charles Dickens's first novel, *The
Pickwick Papers,* Sudbury was the model for the fictional Eatanswill,
where Mr. Pickwick stands for Parliament.

GETTING HERE AND AROUND

From Cambridge, driving to Sudbury requires a circuitous route that
takes about an hour. The A14 is slightly quicker, but the A3107 is
more picturesque. There are no practical bus or train connections from
Cambridge or Ely.

ESSENTIALS

Visitor Information Sudbury Tourist Information Centre ✉ *Town Hall,
Market Hill* ☎ *01787/881320* ⊕ *www.sudbury.org.uk.*

EXPLORING

Gainsborough's House. The birthplace and family home of Thomas Gainsborough (1727–88) contains many paintings and drawings by the artist
and his contemporaries. Although it presents a Georgian facade, with
touches of the 18th-century neo-Gothic style, the building is essentially
Tudor. The walled garden has a mulberry tree planted in 1620 and a
printmaking workshop. The entrance is through the café and shop
on Weavers Lane. ✉ *46 Gainsborough St.* ☎ *01787/372958* ⊕ *www.
gainsborough.org* 🎟 *£5* ⊗ *Mon.–Sat. 10–5.*

LONG MELFORD

2 miles north of Sudbury, 14 miles south of Bury St. Edmunds.

It's easy to see how this village got its name, especially if you walk the
full length of its 2-mile-long main street, which gradually broadens
to include green squares and trees, and finally opens into the large
triangular green on the hill. Long Melford grew rich on its wool trade
in the 15th century, and the town's buildings are an appealing mix,
mostly Tudor half-timber or Georgian. Many house antiques shops.
Away from the main road, Long Melford returns to its resolutely late-
medieval roots.

GETTING HERE AND AROUND

Long Melford is just off the main A134. If you're driving from Sudbury, take the smaller B1064; it's much quicker than it looks on the map. There are several bus connections with Sudbury, Bury St. Edmonds, and Ipswich. The nearest train station is in Sudbury.

EXPLORING

Holy Trinity Church. This largely 15th-century church, founded by the rich clothiers of Long Melford, stands on a hill at the north end of the village. Close up, the delicate flint flush-work (shaped flints set into a pattern) and huge Perpendicular Gothic windows that take up most of the church's walls have great impact, especially because the nave is 150 feet long. The Clopton Chapel, with an ornate (and incredibly rare) painted medieval ceiling, predates the rest of the church by 150 years. The beautiful Lady Chapel has an unusual cloister; the stone on the wall in the corner is an ancient multiplication table, used when the chapel served as a school in the 17th and 18th centuries. ✉ *Main St.* ☎ *01787/310845* 🌐 *www.longmelfordchurch.com* 🕒 *Apr.–Oct., daily 10–6; Nov.–Mar., daily 10–5.*

Melford Hall. Distinguished from the outside by its turrets and topiaries, Melford Hall is an Elizabethan house with its original banqueting room, a fair number of 18th-century additions, and pleasant gardens. Much of the porcelain and other fine pieces here come from the *Santissima Trinidad,* a ship loaded with gifts from the emperor of China and bound for Spain that was captured in the 18th century. Children's writer Beatrix Potter, related to the owners, visited often; there's a small collection of Potter memorabilia. ✉ *Off A134* ☎ *01787/376395* 🌐 *www.nationaltrust.org.uk* 🎟 *£7* 🕒 *Mar.–Oct., Wed.–Sun. 1–5.*

WHERE TO STAY

For expanded hotel reviews, visit Fodors.com.

$ HOTEL 🏨 **The Bull.** This half-timber Elizabethan building reveals its long history with stone-flagged floors, bowed and twisted oak beams, and heavy antique furniture. **Pros:** historic atmosphere; comfortable bedrooms; friendly staff. **Cons:** minimum stay on summer weekends; popular with wedding parties. [$] *Rooms from: £85* ✉ *Hall St.* ☎ *01787/378494* 🌐 *www.thebull-hotel.com* 🛏 *25 rooms* 🍴 *Some meals.*

LAVENHAM

4 miles northeast of Long Melford, 10 miles southeast of Bury St. Edmunds.

Fodor's Choice ★ Virtually unchanged since the height of its wealth in the 15th and 16th centuries, Lavenham is one of the most perfectly preserved examples of a Tudor village in England. The weavers' and wool merchants' houses occupy not just one show street but most of the town. The houses are timber-frame in black oak, the main posts looking as if they could last another 400 years, although their walls are often no longer entirely perpendicular to the ground. The town has many examples of Suffolk pink buildings, in hues from pale pink to apricot, and many of these house small galleries selling paintings and crafts.

GETTING HERE AND AROUND

Lavenham is on the A1141 and B1071. Take the latter if possible, as it's a prettier drive. There are hourly buses from Sudbury and Bury St. Edmunds and slightly less frequent buses from Ipswich. The nearest train station is in Sudbury.

ESSENTIALS

Visitor Information **Lavenham Tourist Information Centre** ✉ *Lady St.* ☎ *01787/248207* 🌐 *www.southandheartofsuffolk.org.uk* 🕒 *Mid-Mar.–Oct., daily 10–4:45; Nov.–Dec., daily 11–3; Jan.–mid-Mar., weekends 11–3.*

EXPLORING

Church of St. Peter and St. Paul. Set apart from the village on a hill, this grand 15th-century church was built between 1480 and 1520 by cloth merchant Thomas Spring. The height of its tower (141 feet) was meant to surpass those of the neighboring churches—and perhaps to impress rival towns. The rest of the church is perfectly proportioned, with intricately carved wood. ✉ *Church St.* ☎ *01787/247244* 🎟 *Free* 🕒 *Daily; hrs vary but usually 10–5.*

Lavenham Guildhall. Also known as the Guildhall of Corpus Christi, this higgledy-piggledy timber-frame building dating from 1529 dominates Market Place, an almost flawlessly preserved medieval square. Upstairs is a rather dull exhibition on local agriculture and the wool trade, although looking around the building itself is well worth the admission charge. ✉ *Market Pl.* ☎ *01787/247646* 🌐 *www.nationaltrust.org.uk* 🎟 *£4.85* 🕒 *Early–late Mar., Wed.–Sun. 11–4; late Mar.–Oct., daily 11–5; Nov., weekends 11–4.*

Little Hall. This timber-frame wool merchant's house (brightly painted on the outside, in the local custom) contains a display showing the building's progress from its creation in the 14th century to its subsequent "modernization" in the 17th century. It also has a beautiful garden at the back. ✉ *Market Pl.* ☎ *01787/247019* 🌐 *www.littlehall.org.uk* 🎟 *£3.50* 🕒 *Apr.–Oct., Wed., Thurs., and weekends 2–5:30, Mon. 10–1, bank holidays 11–5:30.*

QUICK BITES

Tickled Pink Tea Room. In a haphazardly leaning house built in 1532, the Tickled Pink Tea Room serves fresh cakes and tea as well as soup and sandwiches. ✉ ***17 High St.*** ☎ ***01787/249517.***

WHERE TO EAT

$$$ FRENCH Fodor's Choice ★

🍴 **Great House.** This excellent "restaurant-with-rooms" on the medieval market square serves modern British cuisine with a slight French twist; dishes could include pork belly confit or turbot with vanilla butter and a Jerusalem artichoke sauce. The five spacious guestrooms have sloping floors, beamed ceilings, well-appointed bathrooms, and antique furnishings. [$] *Average main: £21* ✉ *Market Pl.* ☎ *01787/247431* 🌐 *www.greathouse.co.uk* ✍ *Reservations essential* 🕒 *Closed Mon. and Jan. No dinner Sun. No lunch Mon. and Tues.*

$ INDIAN Fodor's Choice ★

🍴 **Memsaab.** In a town ready to burst with cream teas, it's a bit of a surprise to find an Indian restaurant, let alone such an exceptional one. Among the classics one would expect from a curry house—from mild kormas to spicy *madrases* and *jalfrezies* (traditional curries

Colorful and ancient, the timbered houses in pretty towns such as Lavenham recall the days when these buildings housed weavers and wool merchants.

made with chili and tomato)—are some finely executed specialties, including Nizami chicken (a fiery dish prepared with yogurt and fresh ginger) and duck *bhujon* (with orange and Madeira sauce). The menu also contains regional specialties from Goa and Hyderabad. [$] *Average main: £11* ✉ *2 Church St.* ☎ *01787/249431* 🌐 *www.memsaaboflavenham.co.uk.*

WHERE TO STAY

For expanded hotel reviews, visit Fodors.com.

$ B&B/INN 🏨 **Guinea House.** Still a private home after 600 years, Guinea House attracts travelers seeking more authenticity than your average B&B. **Pros:** quiet central location; intimate feel; one-of-a-kind atmosphere. **Cons:** low ceilings and hobbit-size doorways; no common areas. [$] *Rooms from: £75* ✉ *16 Bolton St.* ☎ *01787/249046* 🌐 *www.guineahouse.co.uk* 🛏 *2 rooms* 💳 *No credit cards* 🍴 *Breakfast.*

$$ B&B/INN 🏨 **Lavenham Priory.** You can immerse yourself in Lavenham's Tudor heritage at this sprawling house that dates back to the 13th century. **Pros:** historic ambience; charming rooms; lovely garden; free Wi-Fi. **Cons:** no locks on room doors; service can be surly; traffic noise in side rooms. [$] *Rooms from: £120* ✉ *Water St.* ☎ *01787/247404* 🌐 *www.lavenhampriory.co.uk* 🛏 *5 rooms, 1 suite* 🍴 *Breakfast.*

$$$ HOTEL 🏨 **Swan Hotel.** This half-timber 14th-century lodging has rambling public rooms, roaring fireplaces, and corridors so low that cushions are strategically placed on beams. **Pros:** lovely building; atmospheric rooms. **Cons:** creaky floors; lots of steps to climb. [$] *Rooms from: £195* ✉ *High St.* ☎ *01787/247477* 🌐 *www.theswanatlavenham.co.uk* 🛏 *47 rooms, 2 suites* 🍴 *Some meals.*

BURY ST. EDMUNDS

10 miles north of Lavenham, 28 miles east of Cambridge.

The Georgian streetscape helps make the town one of the area's prettiest, and the nearby Greene King Westgate Brewery adds the smell of sweet hops to the air. Robert Adam designed the town hall in 1774.

Bury St. Edmunds owes its name, and indeed its existence, to Edmund, the last king of East Anglia and medieval patron saint of England, who was hacked to death by marauding Danes in 869. He was subsequently canonized, and his shrine attracted pilgrims, settlement, and commerce. In the 11th century the erection of a great Norman abbey (now only ruins) confirmed the town's importance as a religious center. The tourist office has a leaflet about the ruins and can arrange a guided tour.

GETTING HERE AND AROUND
The 11 bus from Cambridge's Drummer Street bus station takes about an hour to reach Bury St. Edmunds. By car, the town is a short drive from either Lavenham or Cambridge. Trains from Cambridge to Bury St. Edmunds leave once or twice an hour and take about 40 minutes.

ESSENTIALS
Visitor Information Visit Bury St. Edmunds ✉ *6 Angel Hill* ☎ *01284/764667* ⊕ *www.visit-burystedmunds.co.uk.*

EXPLORING
TOP ATTRACTIONS
Abbey Ruins and Botanical Gardens. This is all that remains of the Abbey of Bury St. Edmunds, which fell during Henry VIII's dissolution of the monasteries. The Benedictine abbey's enormous scale is evident in the surviving Norman Gate Tower on Angel Hill; besides this, only the fortified Abbot's Bridge over the River Lark and a few ruins are left standing. There are explanatory plaques amid the ruins, which are now the site of the Abbey Botanical Gardens, with roses, elegant hedges, and rare trees, including a Chinese tree of heaven planted in the 1830s. There's also an aviary, a putting green, and a children's play area. ✉ *Angel Hill* ☎ *01284/764667* ⊕ *www.english-heritage.org.uk* 🎟 *Free* ⊙ *Mon.–Sat. 7:30–dusk, Sun. 9–dusk; Jan.–Mar., hrs vary.*

St. Edmundsbury Cathedral. Although the cathedral dates from the 15th century, its brilliant ceiling and gleaming stained-glass windows are the result of 19th-century restoration by architect Sir Gilbert Scott. Don't miss the memorial near the altar to an event in 1214, when the barons of England took an oath here to force King John to grant the Magna Carta. The cathedral's original Abbey Gate was destroyed in a riot, and it was rebuilt in the 14th century with defense in mind—you can see the arrow slits. From Easter to September, guided tours are available Monday to Saturday at 11:30. There's also a small but popular café. ✉ *Angel Hill* ☎ *01284/748720* ⊕ *www.stedscathedral.co.uk* 🎟 *Free, suggested donation £3* ⊙ *Daily 8:30–6.*

WORTH NOTING

Angel Hill. A walk here is a journey through the history of Bury St. Edmunds. Along one side, the Abbey Gate, Norman Gate Tower, and St. Mary's Church make up a continuous display of medieval architecture. Elegant Georgian houses line Angel Hill on the side opposite St. Mary's Church; these include the Athenaeum, an 18th-century social and cultural meeting place that has a fine Adam-style ballroom.

Angel Hotel. This splendid lodging is the scene of Sam Weller's meeting with Job Trotter in Dickens's *The Pickwick Papers*. Dickens stayed here while he was giving readings at the Athenaeum. ⊠ *3 Angel Hill* ☎ *01284/714000* ⊕ *www.theangel.co.uk.*

OFF THE BEATEN PATH

Ickworth House. The creation of the eccentric Frederick Hervey, fourth earl of Bristol and bishop of Derry, this unusual 18th-century home was owned by the Hervey family until the 1960s. Inspired by his travels, Hervey wanted an Italianate palace and gardens. Today the two wings around a striking central rotunda contain a hotel (east wing) and paintings by William Hogarth, Titian, and Gainsborough (west wing). Behind the house, the rose gardens and vineyards spread out to reach 1,800 acres of woods. A stroll over the hills gives the best vistas of the house, which is 7 miles southwest of Bury St. Edmunds. ⊠ *Off A143, Horringer* ☎ *01284/735270* ⊕ *www.nationaltrust.org.uk* ⊠ *£10.40; gardens and park only £4.50* ☉ *Rotunda Wing mid-Mar.–Oct., Thurs. noon–3, Fri.–Tues., 11–5; Nov.–mid-Dec., weekends 11–4. West Wing and Gardens Jan.–mid-Mar., Nov., and Dec., daily 10:30–4; mid-Mar.–Oct., daily 10:30–5. Park daily 8–8.*

Moyse's Hall Museum. This 12th-century building, probably the oldest extant building in East Anglia, is a rare surviving example of a Norman house. The rooms hold exhibitions on Suffolk throughout the ages. One macabre display relates to the Red Barn murder, a local case that gained notoriety in a 19th-century play. ⊠ *Cornhill* ☎ *01284/757160* ⊕ *www.moyseshall.org* ⊠ *£7.30, includes West Stow Anglo Saxon Village* ☉ *Mon.–Sat. 10–5, Sun noon–4.*

St. Mary's Church. Built in the 15th century, St. Mary's has a blue-and-gold embossed "wagon" (barrel-shape) roof over the choir. Mary Tudor, Henry VIII's sister and queen of France, is buried here. ⊠ *Angel Hill, at Honey Hill* ☎ *01284/754680* ⊕ *www.stmarystpeter.net* ☉ *Apr.–Oct., daily 10–4; Nov.–Mar., daily 10–3.*

FAMILY **West Stow Anglo Saxon Village.** This family-friendly museum past the outskirts of Bury St. Edmunds has indoor galleries displaying items from the Anglo-Saxon period (450–1066) as well as a reconstruction of a village from that period with thatched-roof houses. Costumed performers give demonstrations of traditional crafts, and there's also a small farm with rare breeds of pigs and chickens. Call ahead in winter, as the hours vary. ✉ *Icklingham Rd., West Stow* ☎ *01284/728718* 🌐 *www.weststow.org* 🎟 *£7.30, includes Moyse's Hall Museum* 🕑 *Daily 10–5.*

A HALF-PINT PUB?

Nutshell. While you're in Bury St. Edmunds, pop in for a pint of the local Greene King ale at the Nutshell, which claims to be Britain's smallest pub, measuring just 16 feet by 7½ feet. ✉ *17 The Traverse* ☎ *01284/764867* 🌐 *www.thenutshellpub.co.uk.*

WHERE TO EAT

$ CAFÉ 🍴 **Harriet's Café Tearooms.** In an elegant dining room, Harriet's brings back the tearooms of yesteryear. The staff, dressed in old-style uniforms, serve snacks, sandwiches, or full afternoon teas (£13–£25) while hits from the 1940s play in the background. [$] *Average main: £7* ✉ *57 Cornhill Bldgs.* ☎ *01284/756256* 🌐 *www.harrietscafetearooms.co.uk* 🕑 *No dinner.*

$$$ FRENCH Fodor's Choice ★ 🍴 **Maison Bleue.** This stylish French restaurant, with the same owners as the Great House in nearby Lavenham, specializes in locally caught seafood. Typical choices include wild halibut with English wild boar chorizo, or lobster tail with seaweed tagliatelle, in addition to meatier options like Suffolk lamb. [$] *Average main: £21* ✉ *31 Churchgate St.* ☎ *01284/760623* 🌐 *www.maisonbleue.co.uk* ✍ *Reservations essential* 🕑 *Closed Sun. and Mon.*

WHERE TO STAY

For expanded hotel reviews, visit Fodors.com.

$$ B&B/INN 🏨 **The Old Cannon Brewery.** This delightful old inn near the Bury St. Edmunds train station has a handful of bedrooms in its converted Victorian brewhouse.**Pros:** full of character; good food; friendly hosts. **Cons:** pub is noisy until closing time. [$] *Rooms from: £110* ✉ *86 Cannon St.* ☎ *01284/768769* 🌐 *www.oldcannonbrewery.co.uk* 🛏 *5 rooms* 🍽 *Multiple meal plans.*

$$ B&B/INN 🏨 **Ounce House.** Small and friendly, this Victorian B&B has a great deal of charm. **Pros:** spotlessly clean; spacious and comfortable rooms; generous breakfasts. **Cons:** fussy decor; booked up far in advance. [$] *Rooms from: £130* ✉ *Northgate St.* ☎ *01284/761779* 🌐 *www.ouncehouse.co.uk* 🛏 *4 rooms* 🍽 *Breakfast.*

NIGHTLIFE AND THE ARTS

Theatre Royal. Built in 1819, the Theatre Royal is an outstanding example of Regency design. Guided tours can be booked at the box office. ✉ *6 Westgate St.* ☎ *01284/769505* 🌐 *www.theatreroyal.org* 🎟 *£6* 🕑 *Guided tours Tues., Thurs., and Sat., call for hrs.*

THE SUFFOLK COAST

The 40-mile Suffolk Heritage Coast, which wanders northward from Felixstowe up to Kessingland, is one of the most unspoiled shorelines in the country. The lower part of the coast is the most impressive; however, some of the loveliest towns and villages, such as Dedham and the older part of Flatford, are inland. The best way to experience the countryside around here is to be willing to get lost along its tiny, ancient back roads. Try to avoid the coastal area between Lowestoft and Great Yarmouth; it has little to offer but run-down beach resorts.

DEDHAM

62 miles southeast of Cambridge, 15 miles southeast of Bury St. Edmund.

Fodor's Choice ★ Dedham is the heart of Constable country. Here gentle hills and the cornfields of Dedham Vale, set under the district's delicate, pale skies, inspired John Constable (1776–1837) to paint some of his most celebrated canvases. He went to school in Dedham, a picture-book village that did well from the wool trade in the 15th and 16th centuries and has retained a prosperous air ever since. The 15th-century church looms large over handsomely sturdy, pastel-color houses.

Nearby towns have several other sites of interest to Constable fans. About 2 miles from of Dedham is Flatford, where you can see Flatford Mill, one of the two water mills owned by Constable's father. Northeast of Dedham, off A12, the Constable trail continues in East Bergholt, where Constable was born in 1776. Although the town is mostly modern, the older part has some atmospheric buildings like the church of St. Mary-the-Virgin.

GETTING HERE AND AROUND

From the main A12, Dedham is easily reached by car via the B1029. Public transportation is extremely limited; there's no nearby train station.

EXPLORING

Bridge Cottage. On the north bank of the Stour, this 16th-century home in East Bergholt has a shop and an exhibition about Constable's life. You can also rent rowboats here. ⊠ *Off B1070, East Bergholt* ☎ *01206/298260* ⊕ *www.nationaltrust.org.uk* 🖭 *Free* ☉ *Mar., Wed.– Sun. 10:30–5; Apr. and Oct., daily 10:30–5; May–Sept., daily 10:30– 5:30; Nov. and Dec., Wed.–Sun., 10:30–3:30; Jan. and Feb., weekends 10:30–3:30.*

St. Mary-the-Virgin. One of the most remarkable churches in the region, St. Mary-the-Virgin was started just before the Reformation. The doors underneath the ruined archways outside (remnants of a much older church) contain a series of mysterious symbols—actually a coded message left by Catholic sympathizers of the time. The striking interior contains a host of treasures, including an ancient wall painting of the Virgin Mary in one of the rear chapels, a 14th-century chest, and an extraordinary series of florid memorial stones on the nave wall opposite the main entrance. ⊠ *Flatford Rd., East Bergholt* ☎ *01206/392646* 🖭 *Free* ☉ *Daily; hrs vary but usually 10–5.*

The area around Flatford is Constable Country: you may feel like you're in one of the artist's paintings as you explore the area in a rowboat.

Willy Lott's House. A five-minute stroll down the path from Bridge Cottage brings you to this 16th-century structure that is instantly recognizable from Constable's painting *The Hay Wain* (1821). Although the house itself is not open to the public, the road is a public thoroughfare, so you don't have to buy a ticket to see the famous—and completely unchanged—view for yourself. Just stand across from the two trees on the far bank, with the mill on your right, and look upstream. **TIP→ On the outside wall of the mill is a handy reproduction of the painting** to help you compose your own photo. ✉ *Off B1070, East Bergholt.*

WHERE TO EAT AND STAY

$$$$ BRITISH Fodor's Choice ★

🍴 **Le Talbooth.** This sophisticated restaurant is set in a Tudor house beside the idyllic River Stour. There are lighted terraces where food and drinks are served on warm evenings and where jazz and steel bands play on summer Sunday evenings. Inside, original beams, leaded-glass windows, and a brick fireplace add to the sense of history. The superb British fare at lunch and dinner may include filet of John Dory with crayfish and anchovies, duck breast with red cabbage and parsley root, or Dedham Vale beef with Madeira jus. [$] *Average main: £26* ✉ *Gun Hill* ☎ *01206/323150* 🌐 *www.milsomhotels.com/letalbooth* ✍ *Reservations essential* 🕒 *No dinner Sun. Nov.–May.*

$ BRITISH

🍴 **Marlborough Head.** This friendly, 300-year-old pub across from Constable's school in Dedham serves traditional pub grub with a flourish. Dishes such as venison pie and bangers and mash share the menu with fish-and-chips and burgers. There are also rooms available, one with a four-poster bed. [$] *Average main: £10* ✉ *Mill La.* ☎ *01206/323250* 🌐 *www.marlborough-head.co.uk* 🕒 *No dinner Sun.*

Continued on page 680

ENGLAND THROUGH THE AGES

English unflappability can cover up a multitude of dark deeds. A landscape, village scene, or ruined castle may present itself as a serene, untroubled canvas, but this is mere show. Trauma and passion are the underlying reality of history; dynastic ambitions, religious strife, and sedition are the subtext. Dig deeper, and what might appear to be a vast, nation-wide museum turns out to be a complex tapestry of narratives and personalities.

On a far-flung corner of Europe, England's geographical position can account for many things: its slowness in absorbing technological and cultural influences from the great Mediterranean civilizations, its speedy adaptation to the global explosion of trade in the early modern era, and its separate, rather aloof identity. But other factors have molded English history too, not least the waves of immigration, settlement and conquest, by Celts, Romans, Danes, and Normans among numerous others. Perhaps the greatest factor of all has been the unforeseen events, accidental meetings, and random coincidences that history delights in throwing up. The careful—sometimes over-zealous—custodianship of England's heritage may pretend otherwise, but behind every object and beneath every ruin lies a tangle of interconnected events. With some context, history is lifted out of the realm of show and into biting reality.

—*by Robert Andrews*

On stage at Shakespeare's Globe Theatre, London

| TIMELINE | 3000 BC First building of Stonehenge (later building 2400–1600 BC) | 55–54 BC Julius Caesar's exploratory expeditions to England | AD 410 Roman rule of Britain ends |

3000 BC | 1000 BC | 0 | AD 900

(clockwise from top left) Avebury Stone Circles in Wiltshire; Roman Baths, Bath; Illuminated manuscript, *Liber Vitae*, 1031; Iron Age coins from Yorkshire

5000 BC–55 BC

Early Arrivals

The British Isles had already assumed their current shape by 5000 BC, after the final thawing of the last ice age had resulted in a substantial northwestern promontory being detached from the rest of mainland Europe. However, the influx of different peoples and cultures from the east continued as before. It may have been one of these waves of immigrants that brought agriculture to the islands. Numerous burial sites, hill forts, and stone circles have survived from these early societies, notably in the soft chalk downs of southern England.

■ Visit: Stonehenge and Avebury (⇨ Ch. 4).

55 BC–AD 450

Roman Britain

The emperor Claudius declared Colchester Rome's first British colony soon after the invasion of AD 43, and legionary fortresses in the north were established by AD 75. Resistance included Queen Boudicca's uprising, during which Londinium (London) was razed. However, a Romano-British culture was forged with its northern limit at Hadrian's Wall, built in AD 128. To the south, Celtic Britain became integrated into the Roman Empire with the construction of villas, baths, fortifications, and roads.

■ Visit: Fishbourne Roman Palace (⇨ Ch. 3). Roman Baths, Bath (⇨ Ch. 7).

450–1066

Anglo-Saxons

Following the withdrawal of the Roman legions, Britain fell prey to invasions by Jutes, Angles, and Saxons from the mainland. The native Celts were pushed back to the fringes of Britain: Cornwall, Wales, northern England, and Scotland. Eventually seven Anglo-Saxon kingdoms emerged, all of which had adopted Christianity by 650. In the 8th century, the Anglo-Saxon kingdoms faced aggressive incomers from Scandinavia, halted only when Alfred the Great, king of Wessex, unified the English against the Viking invaders.

■ Visit: Bede's World (⇨ Ch. 13). Jorvik Viking Centre, York (⇨ Ch. 12).

597 St. Augustine arrives in Canterbury to Christianize Britain

1066 William of Normandy defeats King Harold at the Battle of Hastings

1086 Domesday Book completed, a survey of all taxpayers in England

1215 King John signs Magna Carta at Runnymede

AD 1000   AD 1100   AD 1200   AD 1300

11

IN FOCUS ENGLAND THROUGH THE AGES

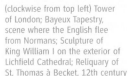

(clockwise from top left) Tower of London; Bayeux Tapestry, scene where the English flee from Normans; Sculpture of King William I on the exterior of Lichfield Cathedral; Reliquary of St. Thomas à Becket, 12th century

1066–1381 Middle Ages: Normans and Plantagenets

The course of England's history altered radically when William, duke of Normandy, invaded and became king of England in 1066. A Norman military and feudal hierarchy was established, French became the language of government, and the country became more centralized. Trading and dynastic links with Europe meant that military campaigns abroad consumed resources, while artistic innovations were more easily absorbed at home—for example, the introduction of Gothic architecture in England's churches and cathedrals. The Plantagenet dynasty came to power in 1154 with the accession of Henry II. A power struggle with the church led to the murder of Henry's archbishop Thomas à Becket in Canterbury Cathedral, which became a center for pilgrimage. The autocratic ambitions of Henry's son John were similarly stymied when he was forced to sign the Magna Carta, promulgating basic principles of English law: no taxation except through Parliament, trial by jury, and property guarantees. In 1348–49, the Black Death (bubonic plague) reduced Britain's population from 4.25 million to 2.5 million.

■ Visit: Tower of London (⇨ Ch. 2). Canterbury Cathedral (⇨ Ch. 3). Wells Cathedral (⇨ Ch. 5).

1381–1485 Twilight of the Middle Ages

English kings invested resources in the Hundred Years War, a struggle to increase their territories in France, but Henry V's gains at Agincourt in 1415 were reversed following the succession of the infant Henry VI. In the domestic Wars of the Roses, the House of York, with a white rose as emblem, triumphed over the House of Lancaster (red rose as emblem), when Edward IV seized the crown. But Edward's brother Richard III was defeated by Henry Tudor, who became Henry VII.

■ Visit: St. James, Chipping Campden (⇨ Ch. 7). King's College Chapel, Cambridge (⇨ Ch. 11).

| TIMELINE | 1485 Henry Tudor (Henry VII) defeats Richard III at the Battle of Bosworth | 1530s Dissolution of the monasteries under Henry VIII | 1588 Spanish Armada fails to invade England |

AD 1450   1500   1550   1600

(clockwise from top left) Hampton Court Palace; Elizabeth I; English ships and the Spanish Armada; Queen Mary I; Henry VIII

Tudor Renaissance

1485–1603

The Tudor era saw the political consolidation of the kingdom but a deep religious divide. Henry VIII's break with Rome in order to obtain a divorce from Catherine of Aragon coincided with the Reformation, and he pursued his attack on the church with the dissolution of the monasteries. Protestantism became further entrenched under the short reign of Henry's son, Edward VI, but Catholicism was again in the ascendant under Mary. Elizabeth I strove to heal the sectarian divisions while upholding the supremacy of a Protestant Church of England. Her position was further imperiled by the threat of invasion by Spain, which abated with the defeat of the Spanish Armada in 1588. Elizabeth encouraged piratical attacks on the Spaniards throughout the Atlantic, as well as voyages to the New World, with Walter Raleigh leading expeditions to Virginia in the 1580s. A major flourishing of arts and letters took place during the reign of Good Queen Bess, with such figures as Edmund Spenser and William Shakespeare. When Elizabeth died without an heir, her chief minister, Robert Cecil, invited the Stuart James VI of Scotland to occupy the throne as James I of England.

■ Visit: Hampton Court Palace (⇨ Ch. 2). Burghley House (⇨ Ch. 11). Longleat (⇨ Ch. 4).

Stuart England

1603–1660

The Stuarts' attempts to rule independently of Parliament led to disaster. Religious tensions persisted, and Puritans and other dissenters began to seek refuge in the New World. Those who stayed were persecuted under James's son Charles I, who alienated the gentry and merchant classes until war was declared between king and Parliament. The Civil War ended with Charles's trial and execution in 1649 and an interregnum in which Oliver Cromwell, the general who became Parliamentarian leader, was declared Lord Protector.

■ Visit: Banqueting House, London (⇨ Ch. 2).

| 1620 Pilgrims sail from Plymouth on the *Mayflower* | 1660 The Restoration: Charles II restored to the throne | 1689 Bill of Rights: Parliament established as England's primary governing body | 1795–1815 Napoleonic Wars: Britain and its allies defeat France |

1650   1700   1750   1800

11

IN FOCUS ENGLAND THROUGH THE AGES

(clockwise from top left) *The Great Fire of London* by Turner; George III; West front entrance of St. Paul's Cathedral; Charles II; Chippendale mahogany bonnet-top highboy, 1770s

1660–1714 Restoration

In an uneasy pact with Parliament, Charles I's son was invited back from exile to reign as Charles II. The Restoration led to a revival of the arts, especially in the fields of theater and literature, and a wave of church building. Old divisions resurfaced when Charles was succeeded by James II, whose conversion to Catholicism led to the Glorious Revolution (1688), when Parliament offered the English crown to William of Orange and Mary Stuart, James II's daughter. The thrones of England and Scotland were united in the Act of Union (1707).

■ Visit: St. Paul's Cathedral (⇨ Ch. 2). Blenheim Palace (⇨ Ch. 6).

1714–1837 Georgian England

With the death of Queen Anne, the Stuart monarchy came to an end and the succession of the new kingdom of Great Britain passed to the Protestant German House of Hanover. But real power now lay with Parliament. George I spent most of his reign in Germany; George II leaned heavily on Robert Walpole (the first "prime minister"); George III was intermittently mad; and George IV's life was marked by dissipation. However, despite losing the Thirteen Colonies in the American Revolution, Britain had by now become the leading European power in the Indian subcontinent.

It demonstrated martial supremacy over France in the wars that simmered throughout this period, finally ending in Britain's two victories against Napoleon at Trafalgar and Waterloo. The growing empire, combined with engineering and technical advances at home, helped bring about an early Industrial Revolution in Britain. The process accelerated urbanization, especially in the Midlands and north, and created an urban working class. Partly in response, a new sentimental view of rural England emerged, reflected in the building of stately homes with landscaped estates.

■ Visit: Bath (⇨ Ch. 7). Stourhead (⇨ Ch. 4).

(clockwise from top left) Queen Victoria in characteristic mourning clothes; Edward VII in coronation robes; Trellis wallpaper Arts and Crafts design by William Morris, 1862; British troops in France, World War I

Victorian Age of Empire

1837–1901

Victoria's reign coincided with the high-water mark of the British Empire, expanding into Africa and consolidating in India. Two parties dominated politics: the Liberals and the Conservatives. These parties supplied such prime ministers as Benjamin Disraeli (Conservative) and William Gladstone (Liberal), who left their mark in reformist measures relating to working conditions, policing, education, health, welfare provision, and the extension of suffrage—all areas highlighted in the literature of the time, notably in the works of Charles Dickens. A network of railways and a nationwide postal service

enhanced infrastructure and the growth of industry. In other spheres, the Victorian age harked back to the past, whether in art, as in the Arts and Crafts and Pre-Raphaelite movements, or in architecture, which revived old forms of building from classical to Gothic and Tudor. After Prince Albert's death in 1861, Victoria became a recluse in her Isle of Wight palace, Osborne House, though her golden and diamond jubilees restored her popularity while glorifying the achievements of her long reign.

■ Visit: Houses of Parliament (⇨ Ch. 2). Black Country Living Museum (⇨ Ch. 8). Osborne House (⇨ Ch. 4).

Edwardian England and World War I

1901–1918

Edward VII, Victoria's son, was a keen sportsman, gambler, and society figure who embodied the blinkered spirit of the country in the aftermath of the Victorian age. The election to Parliament of 29 members of the newly formed Labour Party in 1906 signaled a realignment of politics, though the eruption of World War I sidetracked domestic concerns. The intense fighting across Europe brought about huge loss of life and economic meltdown.

■ Visit: Royal Liver Building (⇨ Ch. 9). Great Dixter (⇨ Ch. 3).

1939–45 World War II	1952 Queen Elizabeth II accedes to the throne	1994 Channel Tunnel opened	2012 Olympics in London
1940	1965	1990	2015

11

IN FOCUS ENGLAND THROUGH THE AGES

(clockwise from bottom left) Winston Churchill; London Aquatics Centre for the 2012 Olympics; The Beatles; The wedding of Prince William and Catherine Middleton, April 2011 (their son, Prince George, was born in 2013)

1918–1945
Depression and World War II

The interwar period was one of social upheaval, and the unemployment caused by the Great Depression rose to 70% in some areas. At the start of World War II, Hitler's forces pushed the British army into the sea at Dunkirk. The aerial Blitz that followed devastated cities. Winston Churchill's rousing leadership and the support of United States and Commonwealth forces helped turn the tide, with Britain emerging triumphant—but bankrupt.

■ Visit: Imperial War Museum, London (⇨ Ch. 2). Manchester (⇨ Ch. 9), and Duxford (⇨ Ch. 11).

1945–PRESENT
To Present Day

Elected in 1945, the new Labour government introduced important reforms in welfare and healthcare and initiated the dismantling of the British empire, starting with independence for India and Pakistan in 1947. The years of austerity lasted until the late 1950s, but the following decade saw a cultural explosion that covered every field, from art (David Hockney and Peter Blake) to music (the Beatles and Rolling Stones at the forefront) to fashion (Twiggy, Mary Quant, and the Carnaby Street look), reflecting a new consumer confidence. British industry had never recovered its former, pre-war strength,

however, and inflation and industrial strife marked the 1970s. Britain's entry into the European Economic Community (later to become the European Union) in 1973 did not immediately slow the economic decline. Manufacturing was largely forsaken by Margaret Thatcher (Conservative) and Tony Blair (Labour) in favor of service industries, but Britain's heavy reliance on finance meant that the economy was hit hard by the crash of 2009. In 2010, the Conservative party established a coalition government with the Liberal Democrats.

■ Visit: Beatles attractions, Liverpool (⇨ Ch. 9). Tate Modern, London (⇨ Ch. 2). Angel of the North (⇨ Ch. 13).

$$$$
HOTEL
⊤ **Maison Talbooth.** Constable painted the rich meadowlands in which this luxurious Victorian country-house hotel is set. **Pros:** good food; lovely views over Dedham Vale; some private hot tubs. **Cons:** restaurant books up fast; perhaps a little snooty. $ *Rooms from: £300* ✉ *Stratford Rd.* ☎ *01206/322367* ⊕ *www.milsomhotels.com* ⇖ *10 rooms* ⊺⊙⊺ *Breakfast.*

SPORTS AND THE OUTDOORS

Boathouse Restaurant. From Dedham, on the banks of the River Stour, you can rent a rowboat from the Boathouse Restaurant. The cost is £14 per hour. ✉ *Mill La.* ☎ *01206/323153* ⊕ *www.dedhamboathouse.co.uk* ⊠ *£14 per hr* ⊙ *Easter–Sept., daily 10–5.*

WOODBRIDGE

18 miles northeast of Dedham.

One of the first good ports of call on the Suffolk Heritage Coast, Woodbridge is a town whose upper reaches center on a fine old market square, site of the 16th-century Shire Hall. Woodbridge is at its best around its old quayside, where boatbuilding has been carried out since the 16th century. The most prominent building is a white-clapboard mill, which dates from the 18th century and is powered by the tides.

GETTING HERE AND AROUND

Woodbridge is on A12. There are local buses, but they mostly serve commuters. By train, Woodbridge is 1½ hours from London, and just under 2 hours from Cambridge (with connections).

ESSENTIALS

Visitor Information Woodbridge Tourist Information Centre ✉ *Woodbridge Library, New St.* ☎ *01394/446510* ⊕ *www.suffolkcoastal.gov.uk/tourism/tics.*

EXPLORING

Sutton Hoo. The visitor center at Sutton Hoo tells the story of one of Britain's most significant Anglo-Saxon archaeological sites. In 1938 a local archaeologist excavated a series of earth mounds and discovered a 7th-century burial ship, probably that of King Raedwald of East Anglia. A replica of the 90-foot-long ship stands in the visitor center, which has artifacts and displays about Anglo-Saxon society—although the best finds have been moved to the British Museum in London. Trails around the 245-acre site explore the area along the River Deben. ✉ *Off B1083* ☎ *01394/389700* ⊕ *www.nationaltrust.org.uk* ⊠ *£7.50* ⊙ *Mar.–Nov., daily 10:30–5; Nov.–Mar., weekends 11–4.*

WHERE TO EAT AND STAY
For expanded hotel reviews, visit Fodors.com.

$
SEAFOOD
Fodor's Choice
★
✕ **Butley Orford Oysterage.** What started as a little café that sold oysters and cups of tea is now a bustling restaurant. It has no pretenses to grandeur but serves some of the best smoked fish you're likely to taste anywhere. The fish pie is legendary in these parts, and the traditional English desserts are exceptional. The actual smoking (of fish, cheese, and much else) takes place in the adjacent smokehouse, and products are for sale in a shop around the corner. $ *Average main: £7* ✉ *Market*

Hill, Orford ☎ *01394/450277* 🌐 *www.butleyorfordoysterage.co.uk* ⏲ *No dinner Sun.–Thurs., Nov.–Mar., and Sun.–Tues., Apr. and May.*

$$ B&B/INN Fodor's Choice ★ 🏨 **Crown and Castle.** Artsy, laid-back, and genuinely friendly, this little gem occupies an 18th-century building in the village of Orford, 10 miles east of Woodbridge. **Pros:** warm service; relaxed atmosphere; good restaurant. **Cons:** need a car to get around. [$] *Rooms from: £130* ✉ *Market Hill, Orford* ☎ *01394/450205* 🌐 *www.crownandcastle.co.uk* 🛏 *19 rooms* 🍴 *Multiple meal plans.*

$$$ HOTEL 🏨 **Seckford Hall.** The sense of history at this delightfully old-school hotel comes from more than just the magnificent Tudor architecture. **Pros:** antique charm; lovely setting; great atmosphere. **Cons:** no elevator; creaky old beds; minimum stay on weekends. [$] *Rooms from: £165* ✉ *Off A12* ☎ *01394/385678* 🌐 *www.seckford.co.uk* 🛏 *32 rooms* 🍴 *Multiple meal plans.*

ALDEBURGH

15 miles northeast of Woodbridge.

Aldeburgh (pronounced *orl*-bruh) is a quiet seaside resort, except in June, when the town fills with people attending the noted Aldeburgh Festival. Its beach is backed by a promenade lined with candy-color dwellings. The 20th-century composer Benjamin Britten lived here for some time. He was interested in the story of Aldeburgh's native son, poet George Crabbe (1754–1832), and turned his life story into *Peter Grimes,* a celebrated opera that perfectly captures the atmosphere of the Suffolk Coast.

GETTING HERE AND AROUND

You have little choice but to drive to Aldeburgh; turn off the A12 near Farnham and follow signs. There's no train station, and no bus service.

ESSENTIALS

Visitor Information Aldeburgh Tourist Information Centre ✉ *48 High St.* ☎ *01728/453637* 🌐 *www.visit-suffolkcoast.co.uk.*

EXPLORING

Aldeburgh Museum. The Elizabethan Moot Hall, built of flint and timber, stood in the center of a thriving 16th-century town when first erected. Now it's just a few steps from the beach, a mute witness to the erosive powers of the North Sea. It's the home of the Aldeburgh Museum, a low-key collection that includes finds from an Anglo-Saxon ship burial. ✉ *Market Cross Pl.* ☎ *01728/454666* 🌐 *www.aldeburghmuseumonline.co.uk* 🎟 *£2* ⏲ *Apr., May, Sept., and Oct., daily 2:30–5; June–Aug., daily noon–5.*

WHERE TO EAT AND STAY

$ BRITISH Fodor's Choice ★ 🍴 **Aldeburgh Fish and Chip Shop.** A frequent entry on "best fish-n-chips in Britain" lists, Aldeburgh's most celebrated eatery always has a long line of eager customers come frying time. The fish is fresh and local, the batter melts in your mouth, and the chips (from locally grown potatoes) are satisfyingly chunky. Upstairs you can bring your own wine or beer and sit at tables, but for the full experience, join the line and take out the paper-wrapped version. The nearby Golden Galleon, run by the same people, is a good alternative if this place is too crowded. [$] *Average main: £5* ✉ *226 High St.* ☎ *01728/452250* 🌐 *www.aldeburghfishandchips.co.uk* 💳 *No credit cards.*

$ MODERN BRITISH 🍴 **The Lighthouse.** An excellent value, this low-key brasserie with tightly packed wooden tables relies exclusively on local produce. The menu focuses on seafood, including oysters and Cromer crabs. All the contemporary British dishes are imaginatively prepared. Desserts, such as the Grand Marnier fudge cake, are particularly good. [$] *Average main: £13* ✉ *77 High St.* ☎ *01728/453377* 🌐 *www.lighthouserestaurant.co.uk.*

$ B&B/INN 🏨 **Dunan House.** A creative, friendly atmosphere pervades this pretty B&B, home to artists Ann Lee and Simon Farr, their cats, and their friendly dog. **Pros:** spacious rooms; delightful hosts; location near the beach. **Cons:** advance deposite required. [$] *Rooms from: £80* ✉ *41 Park Rd.* ☎ *01728/452486* 🌐 *www.dunanhouse.co.uk* 🛏 *3 rooms* 🍽 *Breakfast.*

$$ HOTEL 🏨 **Wentworth Hotel.** The Pritt family has owned and managed the Wentworth since 1920, and the attention shows. **Pros:** good restaurant; sea views. **Cons:** small bathrooms; service can be impersonal. [$] *Rooms from: £159* ✉ *Wentworth Rd.* ☎ *01728/452312* 🌐 *www.wentworth-aldeburgh.com* 🛏 *35 rooms* 🍽 *Breakfast.*

NIGHTLIFE AND THE ARTS

Fodor's Choice ★ **Aldeburgh Festival.** East Anglia's most important arts festival, and one of the best known in Britain, is the Aldeburgh Festival. It's held for two weeks in June in the small village of Snape, 5 miles west of Aldeburgh. Founded by Benjamin Britten, the festival concentrates on music but includes exhibitions, poetry readings, and lectures. A handful of events are aimed specifically at children. ✉ *Snape* ☎ *01728/687110* 🌐 *www.aldeburgh.co.uk.*

Snape Maltings. It's well worth a stop to take in the peaceful River Alde location of this cultural center. It includes art galleries and crafts shops in distinctive large brick buildings once used to malt barley. There are also a café, tearoom, and a pub, the Plough and Sail. There's a farmer's market on the first Saturday of the month, a major food festival in September, and a Benjamin Britten festival in October. Leisurely 45-minute river cruises (£7.50) leave from the quayside in summer. ✉ *Off B1069, Snape* ☎ *01728/688303* 🌐 *www.snapemaltings.co.uk* 🕒 *Late Mar.–July and Sept.–Nov., daily 10–5:30; Aug., daily 10–6; Dec.–late Mar., daily 10–5.*

NORWICH AND NORTH NORFOLK

Norwich, unofficial capital of East Anglia, is dominated by the 15th-century spire of its impressive cathedral. Norfolk's continuing isolation from the rest of the country, and its unspoiled landscape and architecture—largely bypassed by the Industrial Revolution—have proved to be a draw. Many of the flint-knapped (decorated with broken flint) houses in North Norfolk's newly trendy villages are now weekend or holiday homes. Windmills, churches, and waterways are the area's chief defining characteristics. A few miles inland from the Norfolk coast you reach the Broads, a national park made up of a network of shallow, reed-bordered lakes, many linked by wide rivers. Boating and fishing are great lures; rent a boat for a day or a week and the waterside pubs, churches, villages, and nature reserves are all within easy reach.

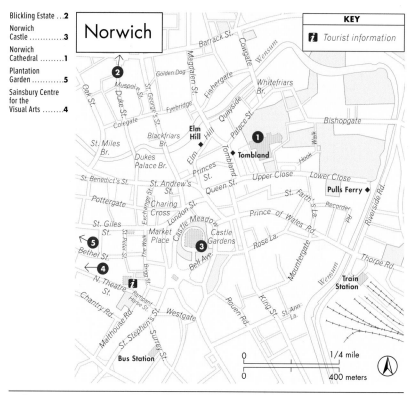

Norwich

KEY

🛈 *Tourist information*

NORWICH

63 miles northeast of Cambridge.

It used to be said that Norwich had a pub for each day of the year and a church in which to repent for every Sunday. Although this is no longer true, real ales and steeples (including that of its grand cathedral) are still much in evidence in this pleasant city of 130,000. The University of East Anglia brings a cosmopolitan touch, including a lively arts scene and a love of literature evident by the city's many independent bookstores. It's a good base from which to explore the Norfolk Broads and the coast.

Established by the Saxons because of its prime trading position on the rivers Yare and Wensum, the town sits in the triangle between the two waterways. The inner beltway follows the line of the old city wall, much of which is still visible. It's worth walking or driving around after dark to see the floodlit buildings. By the time of the Norman Conquest, Norwich was one of the largest settlements in England, although much was destroyed by the Normans to create a new town. You can see the old flint buildings as you walk down the medieval streets and alleyways. Despite some industrial sites and many modern shopping centers, the town remains engaging.

GETTING HERE AND AROUND

Two Norwich-bound trains per hour leave from London's Liverpool Street station; the journey takes two hours. Buses to Norwich leave London's Victoria Coach Station every couple of hours; the trip takes three hours. The bus and train stations are a 10- to 15-minute walk from the city center. If you're driving, leave your car in any of the numerous lots scattered around the center.

City Sightseeing operates 45-minute open-top bus tours of Norwich, leaving hourly (starting at 10) from Theatre Street. Tours cost £9.50.

ESSENTIALS

Visitor and Tour Information City Sightseeing ⊠ *Theatre St., across from Theatre Royal* ☎ *01263/587005* ⊕ *www.city-sightseeing.com.* **Visit Norwich** ⊠ *The Forum, Millennium Plain* ☎ *01603/213999* ⊕ *www.visitnorwich.co.uk.*

EXPLORING

Fodor'sChoice
★
Blickling Estate. Behind the wrought-iron entrance gate to Blickling Estate, two mighty yew hedges form a magnificent frame for this perfectly symmetrical Jacobean masterpiece. The redbrick mansion, 15 miles north of Norwich, has towers and chimneys, baroque Dutch gables, and, in the center, a three-story timber clock tower. The grounds include a formal flower garden and parkland with woods that conceal a temple, an orangery, and a pyramid. Blickling belonged to a succession of historic figures, including Sir John Fastolf, the model for Shakespeare's Falstaff; Anne Boleyn's family; and finally, Lord Lothian, ambassador to the United States at the outbreak of the World War II. The Long Gallery (127 feet) has an intricate plasterwork ceiling with Jacobean emblems. ⊠ *B1354, Blickling* ☎ *01263/738030* ⊕ *www.nationaltrust.org.uk/blickling-estate* 🎫 *£12.50; gardens only £9* ⊗ *House mid-Mar.–early Oct., Wed.–Mon. noon–5; mid-Feb.–mid-Mar., Nov., and Dec., weekends 11–3. Gardens mid-Feb.–Oct. daily 10:15–5:30; mid-Nov.–mid-Dec., Thurs.–Sun., 10:15–4; Jan.–mid-Feb., 10:15–3.*

FAMILY
Norwich Castle. The decorated stone facade of this castle, now a museum on the hill in the center of the city, makes it look like a children's-book illustration. Dating from 1130, the castle is Norman, but a stone keep replaced the original wooden bailey (wall). The thick walls and other defenses attest to its military function. Galleries contain a somewhat eclectic mix of artifacts and interactive displays, covering everything from ancient Egypt to Norman Norfolk and even the history of teapots. One gallery is devoted to the Norwich School of painters who, like John Constable, focused on the everyday landscape and seascape. ▇TIP➔ **Admission is £1 the last hour before closing and between noon and 1 on weekdays.** ⊠ *Castle Meadow* ☎ *01603/493625* ⊕ *www.museums. norfolk.gov.uk* 🎫 *£6.80; special exhibitions £3.50* ⊗ *Oct.–June, Mon.– Sat. 10–4:30, Sun. 1–4:30; July–Sept., Mon.–Sat. 10–5, Sun. 1–5.*

Fodor'sChoice
★
Norwich Cathedral. The grandest example of Norman architecture in Norwich has a towering 315-foot spire and the second-largest monastic cloisters in Britain (only Salisbury's are bigger). The cathedral was begun in 1096 by Herbert de Losinga, who had come from Normandy in 1091 to be its first bishop; his splendid tomb is by the high altar.

CLOSE UP

Experiencing Norfolk's Broads

11

Breathtakingly lovely, the Broads are a network of rivers and canals that stretch for about 150 miles across East Anglia, mostly in North Norfolk. It's a unique landscape of glassy waters, reed-covered marshlands, and impossibly photogenic windmills. At sunset, the whole area turns the color of honey.

The Broads can be seen fleetingly from your car window, but it's nothing compared to floating through them on a boat.

Broads Tours. Based in Wroxham, 7 miles northeast of Norwich, Broads Tours offers day cruises around the area, as well as cruiser boat rentals for a few days or a few weeks. ✉ *The*

Bridge, Wroxham ☎ *01603/782207* ⊕ *www.broads.co.uk.*

You can also see much of the Broads by bike.

Broadland Cycle Hire. Located 8 miles northeast of Norwich, Broadland Cycle Hire charges £15 per day for rental (with discounts for couples and families). The company can recommend several good bike routes. ✉ *Horning Rd., Hoveton* ☎ *07887/480331* ⊕ *www.norfolkbroadscycling.co.uk.*

For more information visit ⊕ *www.enjoythebroads.com*, where you can download a useful brochure from the tourist board.

The remarkable length of the nave is immediately impressive; the similarly striking height of the vaulted ceiling makes it a strain to study the delightful colored bosses, which illustrate Bible stories with great vigor and detail (binoculars are handy). The grave of Norfolk-born nurse Edith Cavell, the British World War I heroine shot by the Germans in 1915, is at the eastern end. There's also a medieval-style herb garden, a Japanese garden, a restaurant, and a coffee shop. Guided tours are offered Monday to Saturday at 11, noon, 1, 2, and 3. The Cathedral Close is one of the most idyllic places in Norwich; past the mixture of medieval and Georgian houses, a path leads down to the ancient water gate, Pulls Ferry. ■ TIP➔ Keep an eye out for peregrine falcons. They've been nesting in the spire since a breeding program began in 2011. ✉ *62 The Close* ☎ *01603/218300* 🖾 *Free* ⊗ *Cathedral daily 7:30–6:30; herb garden daily 9–5.*

Plantation Garden. Abandoned and overgrown for more than 40 years after World War II, these beautiful Victorian gardens have been painstakingly returned to their former glory by a team of volunteers. Originally planted in 1856, the 2-acre site, dotted with fanciful Gothic follies, includes original features like an Italianate terrace and a huge rockery. It's a particularly tranquil spot when the spring and summer flowers are in full bloom—bring a picnic if the weather's good, or have a bite in the café. The entrance is difficult to find; look for the little gate next to the Beeches Hotel. There's no car park, but you can use the lot at the nearby Black Horse Pub. ✉ *4 Earlham Rd.* ☎ *01603/621868* ⊕ *www.plantationgarden.co.uk* 🖾 *£2* ⊗ *Daily 9–6.*

To get the most from your visit to Blickling, a Jacobean mansion, take time to explore the gardens and grounds.

Sainsbury Centre for the Visual Arts. Designed by Norman Foster, this hangarlike building on the campus of the University of East Anglia holds the collection of the Sainsbury family. It includes a remarkable quantity of 20th-century works, including pieces by Pablo Picasso and Alberto Giacometti. Rotating exhibitions include big-name photography and art shows. Buses 22, 25A, X25 run from downtown Norwich. ✉ *University of East Anglia, Earlham Rd.* ☎ *01603/593199* 🌐 *www.scva.org.uk* 🎟 *Free* 🕒 *Tues.–Sun. 10–5.*

WHERE TO EAT AND STAY

For expanded hotel reviews, visit Fodors.com.

$ BRITISH 🍴 **Adam and Eve.** Said to be Norwich's oldest pub, this place dates back to at least 1249. From noon until 7, the kitchen serves such hearty pub staples as chicken-and-ham pie or cheese-and-ale soup from the short but solid bar menu. Theakston's and Adnams beer are available on tap, as is Aspall's cider. [$] *Average main: £7* ✉ *17 Bishopsgate* ☎ *01603/667423.*

$ BRITISH 🍴 **Britons Arms.** A converted pub, this cozy, thatched café and restaurant has famously good homemade cakes as well as pies and tarts. The building, which dates from 1347, has low ceilings, a garden that's open in summer, and a crackling fire in winter. [$] *Average main: £12* ✉ *9 Elm Hill* ☎ *01603/623367* 💳 *No credit cards* 🕒 *Closed Sun.*

$ BELGIAN FAMILY 🍴 **Waffle House.** The perfect antidote to all those heavy English breakfasts, this is the kind of place where walking through the door is enough to make you swoon. It's waffles, waffles, and more waffles on the menu, and the selection is imaginative. Breakfast choices include savory toppings such as smoked salmon; later in the day you can order waffles topped with anything from seared tuna with lime and chili, to hummus and avocado. Or you could skip to dessert and order yours topped with pecans and butterscotch or *banoffee* sauce (a heavenly mix of banana and toffee). [$] *Average main: £7* ✉ *39 St. Giles St.* ☎ *01603/612790* 🌐 *www.wafflehouse.co.uk.*

$$ HOTEL 🏨 **The Old Rectory.** This gorgeous, ivy-covered Georgian manor house overlooking manicured lawns and rolling hills is a real find. **Pros:** lovely old building; peaceful setting; friendly staff. **Cons:** away from the action; minimum stay some weekends. [$] *Rooms from: £130* ✉ *103 Yarmouth Rd., Thorpe St. Andrew* ☎ *01603/700772* 🌐 *www.oldrectorynorwich.com* 🛏 *7 rooms* 🍴 *Breakfast.*

NIGHTLIFE AND THE ARTS

Maddermarket Theatre. Patterned on the layout of Elizabethan theaters, the Maddermarket Theatre has been the base of amateur and community theater in Norwich since 1911. ✉ *St. John's Alley* ☎ *01603/620917* 🌐 *www.maddermarket.co.uk.*

Norwich Arts Centre. This eclectic venue hosts a busy program of live music, dance, and comedy. Its café has free Internet access. ✉ *St. Benedict's St.* ☎ *01603/660352* 🌐 *www.norwichartscentre.co.uk.*

Norwich Playhouse. This professional repertory group performs everything from Shakespeare to world premieres of new plays. ✉ *42-58 St. George's Street* ☎ *01603/598598* 🌐 *www.norwichplayhouse.org.uk.*

Theatre Royal. Norwich's biggest and best-known theater, the Theatre Royal hosts touring companies staging musicals, ballet, opera, and plays. ✉ *Theatre St.* ☎ *01603/630000* 🌐 *www.theatreroyalnorwich.co.uk.*

SHOPPING

The medieval lanes of Norwich, around Elm Hill and Tombland, contain the best antiques, book, and crafts stores.

Book Hive. Considered by many to be among the best bookstores in England, the Book Hive has a rounded glass facade that give you a hint of the treasures within. The three-story independent shop specializes in fiction, poetry, art and design, cookery, and children's books. Drop by and you might stumble onto a book reading, cooking class, or other event. ✉ *53 London St.* ☎ *01603/219268* 🌐 *www.thebookhive.co.uk.*

Colman's Mustard Shop. Paying homage to Colman's Mustard, an iconic local company founded in the early 19th century, this shop sells collectibles and more than 15 varieties of mustard. There's also a quirky little museum devoted to the history of the brand. ✉ *15 Royal Arcade* ☎ *01603/627889* 🌐 *www.mustardshopnorwich.co.uk.*

Norwich Market. Open Monday to Saturday, the city's main outdoor market has been the heart of the city's commerce for 900 years. 200 vendors sell everything from jewelry to clothing and food. ✉ *Market Pl.* ☎ *01603/213537* 🌐 *www.norwich.gov.uk.*

SPORTS AND THE OUTDOORS

City Boats. A summer trip down the River Yare gives a fresh perspective on Norwich. Longer trips are available down the rivers Wensum and Yare to the nearer parts of the Norfolk Broads. ✉ *Highcraft Marina, Griffin La.* ☎ *01603/701701, 07806/571337* 🌐 *www.cityboats.co.uk.*

BLAKENEY

28 miles northwest of Norwich.

The Norfolk coast begins to feel wild and remote near Blakeney, 14 miles west of Cromer. Driving the coast road from Cromer, you pass marshes, sandbanks, and coves, as well as villages. Blakeney is one of the most appealing, with harbors for small fishing boats and yachts. Once a bustling port town exporting corn and salt, it enjoys a quiet existence today, and a reputation for wildlife viewing at Blakeney Point.

GETTING HERE AND AROUND

A48 passes through the center of Blakeney. There are few bus connections, though the 46 and CH1 Coasthopper connect the town with Wells-next-the-Sea.

EXPLORING

Blakeney National Nature Reserve. The 1,000 acres of grassy dunes at Blakeney Point are home to nesting terns and about 500 common and gray seals. The 3½-mile walk here from Cley Beach is beautiful, but a boat trip from Blakeney or Morston Quay is fun and educational. An information center and a tearoom at Morston Quay are open according to tides and weather. ⊠ *Morston Quay, Quay Rd., Morston* ☎ *01263/740241* ⊕ *www.nationaltrust.org.uk/blakeney* ⊠ *Free.*

WHERE TO EAT AND STAY

For expanded hotel reviews, visit Fodors.com.

$ ✕ **Anchor Inn.** This delightful little gastro-pub in Morston, 1½ miles
SEAFOOD west of Blakeney, has a cozy, coastal atmosphere. Platters of mussels and oysters are popular, as are the outstanding servings of fish-and-chips. Less fishy options include local oxtail and venison stew, and roast Norfolk chicken with buttered kale, potatoes, and parsnips. $ *Average main: £13* ⊠ *22 The Street, Morston* ☎ *01263/741392* ⊕ *www.morstonanchor.co.uk.*

$$ ✕ **White Horse at Blakeney.** Traditional British food with an imaginative
MODERN BRITISH twist is the draw at this former coaching inn. You may find cod served with dauphinoise potatoes and sautéed brown shrimp, or braised beef brisket with horseradish mash and wilted spinach. You can dine in the bar, the airy conservatory, or the more intimate Long Room. There are also a few simply furnished guest rooms with sea views starting at £70. $ *Average main: £17* ⊠ *4 High St.* ☎ *01263/740574* ⊕ *www.blakeneywhitehorse.co.uk.*

$$ ⛵ **Byfords.** In a market town 5 miles southeast of Blakeney, Byfords epit-
HOTEL omizes the increasing trendiness of North Norfolk. **Pros:** plush rooms; amiable staff; relaxed atmosphere. **Cons:** minimum stay on weekends. $ *Rooms from: £145* ⊠ *1–3 Shirehall Plain, Holt* ☎ *01263/711400* ⊕ *www.byfords.org.uk* ⊷ *16 rooms* ❖❘ *Multiple meal plans.*

SPORTS AND THE OUTDOORS

Bishop's Boats. This company runs one- or two-hour seal-watching trips daily between February and early November for £9 per person. ⊠ *The Quay, at the end of High St.* ☎ *0800/074–0754* ⊕ *www.norfolksealtrips.co.uk.*

Norwich,
North Norfolk,
and Lincoln

Temples Seal Watching Trips. Temples Seal Watching Trips organizes two-hour boat trips out to Blakeney Point, where you can watch seals in their natural environment. Certain sailings drop you off at the Point for an hour before taking you back. Tours cost £9; there are usually two or three daily departures in high season. The ticket office is in Morston, 1½ miles west of Blakeney. ⊠ *Anchor Inn, 22 The Street, Morston* ☎ *01263/740791* ⊕ *www.sealtrips.co.uk.*

WELLS-NEXT-THE-SEA

10 miles west of Blakeney, 34 miles northwest of Norwich.

A quiet base from which to explore other nearby towns, the harbor town of Wells-next-the-Sea and the nearby coastline remain untouched, with many excellent places for bird-watching and walking on the sandy beaches of Holkham Bay, near Holkham Hall. Today the town is a mile from the sea, but in Tudor times, when it was closer to the ocean, it served as one of the main ports of East Anglia. The remains of a medieval priory point to the town's past as a major pilgrimage destination in the Middle Ages. Along the nearby beach a narrow-gauge steam train makes the short journey to Walsingham between Easter and October.

Walking Paths in East Anglia

East Anglia is a walker's dream, especially if a relatively flat trail appeals to you. The regional website ⊕ *www.visiteastofengland.com* has further details about these paths.

The long-distance footpath known as the **Peddars Way** follows the line of a pre-Roman road, running from near Thetford through heathland, pine forests, and arable fields, and on through rolling chalk lands to the Norfolk coast near Hunstanton.

The **Norfolk Coastal Path** then continues eastward along the coast, joining at Cromer with the delightfully varied **Weaver's Way**, which passes through medieval weaving villages and deeply rural parts of the Norfolk Broads on its 56-mile route from Cromer to Great Yarmouth. Anyone interested in birds should carry binoculars and a field guide, as both of these routes have abundant avian life—both local and migratory.

GETTING HERE AND AROUND

Wells-next-the-Sea is on the main A149 coastal road, but can also be reached via the B1105 from Fakenham. The nearest train station is about 16 miles away in Sheringham. There are regular buses from Sheringham, Fakenham, and Norwich.

ESSENTIALS

Visitor Information **Wells-next-the-Sea Tourist Information Centre**
⊠ *Staithe St.* ☎ *01328/710885* ⊕ *www.wells-guide.co.uk.*

EXPLORING

Fodor'sChoice
★ **Holkham Hall.** One of the most splendid mansions in Britain, Holkham Hall is the seat of the Coke family, the earls of Leicester. In the late 18th century, Thomas Coke went on a grand tour of the Continent, returning with art treasures and determined to build a house according to the new Italian ideas. Centered by a grand staircase and modeled after the Baths of Diocletian, the 60-foot-tall Marble Hall (mostly alabaster, in fact), may be the most spectacular room in Britain. Beyond are salons filled with works from Coke's collection of masterpieces, including paintings by Gainsborough, Van Dyck, Rubens, and Raphael. Surrounding the house is parkland landscaped by Capability Brown in 1762. You'd be hard-pressed to walk through it without spotting several deer. A good way to see the grounds is a half-hour-long lake cruise. The original walled kitchen gardens have been restored and once again provide produce for the estate. The **Bygones Museum,** in the old stable block, displays everything from gramophones to fire engines. ⊠ *Off A149* ☎ *01328/710227* ⊕ *www.holkham.co.uk* ☞ *Hall, museum, and gardens £12; museum and gardens only £7; park free* ⊙ *House late Mar.–Oct., Sun., Mon., and Thurs. noon–4. Museum and gardens late Mar.–Oct., daily 10–5. Park daily 7–7.*

Houghton Hall. Built in the 1720s by the first British prime minister, Sir Robert Walpole, this extraordinary Palladian pile has been carefully restored by its current owner, the seventh marquess of Cholmondeley (pronounced "Chumley"). The double-height Stone Hall and the sumptuous private quarters reveal designer William Kent's preference for gilt, stucco, plush fabrics, and elaborate carvings. Don't leave the grounds without viewing the beautiful medieval simplicity of St. Martin's Church. Houghton Hall is 14 miles southwest of Wells-next-the-Sea. ✉ *Off A148, King's Lynn* ☎ *01485/528569* 🌐 *www.houghtonhall.com* 🎟 *£18; park and grounds only £8* ⏱ *House mid-May–Sept., Wed.–Sun. 11–5.*

Sandringham House. Not far from the old-fashioned seaside resort of Hunstanton, Sandringham House is where the Royal Family traditionally spends Christmas. The redbrick Victorian mansion was clearly designed for enormous country-house parties, with a ballroom, billiard room, and bowling alley, as well as a shooting lodge on the grounds. The house and gardens close when the Queen is in residence (for about a week in late July), but the woodlands, nature trails, and museum of royal memorabilia in the old stables remain open, as does the church, which is medieval but in heavy Victorian disguise. Tours access most rooms but steer clear of personal effects of current royals. The house is 20 miles southwest of Wells-next-the-Sea. ✉ *Off B1440, Sandringham* ☎ *01485/545408* 🌐 *www.sandringhamestate.co.uk* 🎟 *House, gardens, and museum £12; gardens and museum only £8* ⏱ *House and museum: Easter–Oct., daily 11–5. Gardens Easter–Oct., daily 10:30–5.*

WHERE TO EAT AND STAY

For expanded hotel reviews, visit Fodors.com.

$$ MODERN BRITISH 🍴 **Hoste Arms.** You'll find this renowned gastro-pub in the village of Burnham Market, 6 miles west of Wells-next-the-Sea. The 17th-century former coaching inn offers such delights as baked cod with beetroot and goat cheese tortellini, and rack of lamb with minted potato croquettes and curly kale. Accompanying the meals is a good range of fine wines. The bar has an open fire, and there's a conservatory and a large terrace for alfresco lunches. Modern or traditional guest rooms are available from around £60. [$] *Average main: £18* ✉ *The Green, Burnham Market* ☎ *01328/738777* 🌐 *www.hostearms.co.uk.*

$$ HOTEL 🏨 **The Crown Hotel.** Overlooking a tiny park in the middle of Wells-next-the-Sea, this cozy little hotel and restaurant is owned by New Zealand-born TV chef Chris Coubrough. **Pros:** cozy atmosphere; great restaurant; wonderful beds. **Cons:** some rooms on the small side. [$] *Rooms from: £130* ✉ *The Buttlands* ☎ *01328/710209* 🌐 *www.thecrownhotelwells.co.uk* 🛏 *10 rooms, 2 suites* 🍽 *Breakfast.*

$$$ HOTEL FAMILY 🏨 **Victoria at Holkham.** A colorful, whimsical hideaway, this hotel on the Holkham Hall estate is more laid-back and family-friendly than the austere Victorian exterior suggests. **Pros:** original character; excellent location; outstanding food. **Cons:** minimum stay on weekends; extremely busy in summer; no elevator. [$] *Rooms from: £175* ✉ *Park Rd., Holkham* ☎ *01328/711008* 🌐 *www.holkham.co.uk/victoria* 🛏 *9 rooms, 1 suite, 4 self-contained lodges* 🍽 *Breakfast.*

SPORTS AND THE OUTDOORS

On Yer Bike Cycle Hire. For £14 per day, On Yer Bike Cycle Hire will deliver bikes to your local lodging. Reservations are required. ✉ *Nutwood Farm, The Laurels, Wighton* ☎ *01328/820719, 07799/647330* 🌐 *www.norfolkcyclehire.co.uk.*

STAMFORD AND LINCOLN

The fens of northern Cambridgeshire pass imperceptibly into the three divisions of Lincolnshire: Holland, Kesteven, and Lindsey are parts of the county, divided administratively. Holland borders the Isle of Ely and the Soke of Peterborough. This marshland spreads far and wide south of the Wash. The chief attractions are two towns: Stamford, to the southwest, and Lincoln, with its magnificent cathedral.

STAMFORD

48 miles northwest of Cambridge.

Serene, honey-hued Stamford, on a hillside overlooking the River Welland, has a well-preserved center, in part because in 1967 it was designated England's first conservation area. This unspoiled town, which grew rich from the medieval wool and cloth trades, has a delightful, harmonious mixture of Georgian and medieval architecture.

GETTING HERE AND AROUND

Stamford is on the A43 and A1. Trains from London (Kings Cross and St. Pancras stations) depart about every 30 minutes, and about every hour from Lincoln (all with connections). The journey from London takes between one and two hours, or between two and three from Lincoln due to connections.

ESSENTIALS

Visitor Information Stamford Tourist Information Centre ⊠ *27 St. Mary's St.* ☎ *01780/755611* ⊕ *www.southwestlincs.com.*

EXPLORING

FAMILY

Fodor's Choice ★

Burghley House. Considered one of the grandest houses of the Elizabethan age, this architectural masterpiece is celebrated for its rooftops bristling with pepper-pot chimneys and slate-roof towers. It was built between 1565 and 1587, to the design of William Cecil when he was Elizabeth I's high treasurer, and his descendants still occupy the house. The interior was remodeled in the late 17th century with treasures from Europe. On view are 18 sumptuous rooms, with carvings by Grinling Gibbons and ceiling paintings by Antonio Verrio (including the Heaven Room and the Hell Staircase—just as dramatic as they sound), as well as innumerable paintings and priceless porcelain. You can tour on your own or join a free 80-minute guided tour beginning daily at 3:30. In the 18th century Capability Brown landscaped the grounds (where deer roam and open-air concerts are staged in summer) and added the Gothic Revival orangery, where today you can take tea or lunch. A more contemporary addition is the Garden of Surprise, filled with imaginative sculptures, water jets, and a mirrored maze. In late August or early September, Burghley is host to the international Burghley Horse Trials. The house is a mile southeast of Stamford. ⊠ *Off A1* ☎ *01780/752451* ⊕ *www.burghley.co.uk* ⊡ *House and gardens £13.80; gardens only £8* ☉ *Mid-Mar.–early Nov., Sat.–Thurs. 11–5.*

LINCOLN

11

Fodor's Choice
★

53 miles north of Stamford, 93 miles northwest of Cambridge, 97 miles northwest of Norwich.

Celts, Romans, and Danes all had important settlements here, but it was the Normans who gave Lincoln its medieval stature after William the Conqueror founded Lincoln Castle as a stronghold in 1068. Four years later William appointed Bishop Remigius to run the huge diocese stretching from the Humber to the Thames, resulting in the construction of Lincoln Cathedral, the third-largest in England after York Minster and St. Paul's. Since medieval times Lincoln's status has declined. However, its somewhat remote location (there are no major motorways or railways nearby) has helped preserve its traditional character.

The cathedral is on the aptly named Steep Hill; to its south, narrow medieval streets cling to the hillside. Jew's House, on the Strait, dating from the early 12th century, is one of several well-preserved domestic buildings in this area. The name is almost as old as the house itself—it refers to a former resident, Belaset of Wallingford, a Jewish woman who was murdered by a mob in 1290, the same year the Jews were expelled from England. The River Witham flows unobtrusively under the incongruously named High Bridge, a low, vaulted Norman bridge topped by timber-frame houses from the 16th century. West from here you can rent boats, or, in summer, go on a river cruise.

GETTING HERE AND AROUND

There are direct buses (four to five hours) from London, but most rail journeys (two to three hours) involve changing trains. The bus and train stations are south of the center, and it's a steep walk uphill to the cathedral and castle. You can avoid the climb by taking the Walk & Ride electric bus service (£1.40) from the stop on St. Mary's Street. Purchase tickets on board. Drivers will find parking lots around the bus and train stations and in the center at the Lawn and Westgate.

ESSENTIALS

Visitor Information Lincoln Tourist Information Centre ✉ *9 Castle Hill* ☎ *01522/545458* ⊕ *www.visitlincolnshire.com.*

EXPLORING

Fodor's Choice
★

Lincoln Cathedral. Lincoln's crowning glory, the Cathedral of St. Mary was for centuries the tallest building in Europe. The Norman bishop Remigius began work in 1072. The Romanesque church he built was irremediably damaged, first by fire, then by earthquake. Today its most striking feature is the west front's strikingly tall towers, best viewed from the 14th-century Exchequer Gate in front of the cathedral, or from the castle battlements beyond. Inside, a breathtaking impression of space and unity belies the many centuries of building and rebuilding. The stained-glass window at the north end of the transept (known as the Dean's Eye) dates from the 13th century. ■TIP→ **Look for the Lincoln Imp on the pillar nearest St. Hugh's shrine; according to legend, an angel turned this creature to stone.**

DID YOU KNOW?

In the Heaven Room at Burghley House, 17th-century painter Antonio Verrio shows the classical gods and goddesses of Mount Olympus hard at play. Their frolicking looks almost three-dimensional. In the center of this opulence is a massive 18th-century silver wine cooler, an item the gods (and more earthly lords) might have found useful.

Through a door on the north side is the chapter house, a 10-sided building with one of the oldest vaulted ceilings in the world. It sometimes housed the medieval Parliament of England during the reigns of Edward I and Edward II. The cathedral library, designed by Christopher Wren (1632–1723), was built onto the north side of the cloisters after the original library collapsed. Separate guided tours of the cathedral, roof, and tower are included in the price. They are particularly popular, so book ahead. For safety reasons, children under 14 are not allowed on the roof or tower tours. ✉ *Minster Yard* ☎ *01522/561600* ⊕ *www.lincolncathedral.com* 🎫 *£6* ⊙ *July and Aug., weekdays 7:15 am–8 pm, weekends 7:15–6; Sept.–June, weekdays 7:15–6, weekends 7:15–5.*

QUICK
BITES

Pimento Tearooms. After climbing the aptly named Steep Hill, revive yourself with one of the 23 different teas or 15 coffees available here. Choose a cake or snack to go along with your pick-me-up. ✉ *26 Steep Hill* ☎ *01522/522677.*

FAMILY **Lincoln Castle.** Facing the cathedral across Exchequer Gate, this castle was built by William the Conqueror in 1068, incorporating the remains of Roman walls. The castle was used as a debtor's prison from 1787 to 1878. In the chapel you can see cagelike stalls where convicts heard sermons; they were designed this way so inmates couldn't tell who their fellow prisoners were, thus supposedly preserving a modicum of dignity. The castle's star exhibit is an original copy of **Magna Carta**, signed by King John in 1215. This is one of only four surviving copies, and one of few ever to have left the country—it was secretly moved to Fort Knox for safekeeping during World War II. ✉ *Castle Hill* ☎ *01522/511068* ⊕ *www.lincolnshire.gov.uk/lincolncastle* 🎫 *£6* ⊙ *Apr. and Sept., daily 10–5; May–Aug., daily 10–6; Oct.–Mar., daily 10–4; last entry 45 mins before closing.*

Medieval Bishop's Palace. On the south side of Minster Yard, this building has exhibits about the former administrative center of the diocese, plus a garden and working vineyard. ✉ *Minster Yard* ☎ *01522/527468* ⊕ *www.english-heritage.org.uk* 🎫 *£4.50* ⊙ *Apr.–Oct., Thurs.–Mon. 10–5; Nov.–Mar., weekends 10–4.*

Minster Yard. Surrounding the cathedral on three sides, Minster Yard contains buildings of different periods, including graceful Georgian architecture. A statue of Alfred, Lord Tennyson, who was born in Lincolnshire, stands on the green near the chapter house.

WHERE TO EAT AND STAY

For expanded hotel reviews, visit Fodors.com.

$ ✕ **Brown's Pie Shop.** More than you might imagine from the modest
BRITISH name, Brown's Pie Shop serves the best of old-school British cuisine: succulent beef, great desserts, and some very good, freshly made savory pies. There are also fish specials, steaks, and a small selection of vegetarian dishes. This restaurant, close to the cathedral, serves an economical early-evening menu. $ *Average main: £13* ✉ *33 Steep Hill* ☎ *01522/527330* ⊕ *www.brownspieshop.co.uk.*

$$ MODERN BRITISH Fodor's Choice ★ 🍴 **Jew's House.** This intimate restaurant is a much more sedate place than its colorful and sometimes dark history suggests (the name is medieval—check out the story while you're here). It's one of Lincoln's oldest buildings, a rare survivor of 12th-century Norman domestic architecture, and worth a visit to see even if the cosmopolitan menu weren't so outstanding. Typical main dishes include trout with dates and candied eggplant, or roast mallard with quince tatin and a green peppercorn sauce. [$] *Average main: £19* ✉ *15 The Strait* ☎ *01522/524851* 🌐 *www.jewshouserestaurant.co.uk* 🕓 *Closed Sun. and Mon.*

$ BRITISH 🍴 **Wig and Mitre.** This pub-café-restaurant serves everything from breakfast to full evening meals in its old-fashioned dining room. The produce comes from the local markets, and evening dishes may include pork collar with braised beans or fillet steak with bacon and thyme rösti. [$] *Average main: £14* ✉ *30–32 Steep Hill* ☎ *01522/535190* 🌐 *www.wigandmitre.com.*

$ B&B/INN 🏨 **Bailhouse & Mews.** In a 14th-century baronial hall near the cathedral, the welcoming Bailhouse & Mews is a beautifully converted little hotel with flagstone floors and wooden beams. **Pros:** good value; views of cathedral and castle; convenient parking. **Cons:** some street noise; beds are rather creaky. [$] *Rooms from: £84* ✉ *34 Bailgate* ☎ *01522/541000* 🌐 *www.bailhouse.co.uk* 🛏 *10 rooms, 3 cottages, 1 house* 🍽 *Breakfast.*

NIGHTLIFE AND THE ARTS

Theatre Royal. A fine Victorian auditorium, the Theatre Royal previews plays and musicals before their London runs and also hosts touring productions and comedy. ✉ *Clasketgate* ☎ *01522/519999* 🌐 *www.lincolntheatreroyal.com.*

SHOPPING

The best stores are on Bailgate, Steep Hill, and the medieval streets leading directly down from the cathedral and castle.

Cheese Society. Just off Steep Hill, this shop has a great selection of English and French cheeses, including the delicious local Lincoln Blue. There's also an attached café. ✉ *1 St. Martin's La.* ☎ *01522/511003* 🌐 *www.thecheesesociety.co.uk.*

Harding House Galleries. Steep Hill has good bookstores, antiques shops, and art galleries, including the delightful Harding House Gallery, a co-operative of contemporary visual artists. ✉ *Steep Hill* ☎ *01522/523537* 🌐 *www.hardinghousegallery.co.uk.*

YORKSHIRE

WELCOME TO YORKSHIRE

TOP REASONS TO GO

★ **York Minster:**
The largest Gothic cathedral in Northern Europe helps make York one of the country's most visited towns. The building's history is told in its crypt, brilliantly converted into a museum.

★ **North York Moors:**
There's enough space in this national park for walkers to experience isolation amid the heather-covered hills that glow crimson and purple in late summer and early fall.

★ **Rievaulx Abbey:**
Heading down the tiny lane that leads to the ruins of one of the great Cistercian abbeys only serves to make it all the more dramatic when its soaring arches appear out of the trees.

★ **Coastal towns:**
Seafront Whitby inspired Bram Stoker to write *Dracula*. Robin Hood's Bay, a village set in a ravine, has an outstanding beach.

★ **Haworth:** Looking as if it were carved from stone, this picture-perfect hillside town in the dales is a lovely place to learn about the Brontë sisters.

1 York. Still enclosed within its medieval city walls, this beautifully preserved city makes the perfect introduction to Yorkshire. Its towering Minster and narrow little streets entrance history buffs.

2 York Environs. This rural region contains the elegant Victorian spa town Harrogate, as well as charming villages like Knaresborough, tucked away in a steep valley. Baroque Castle Howard is also near York.

3 Leeds and Brontë Country. Rocky and bleak, this windswept stretch of country provides an appropriate setting for the dark, dramatic narratives penned by the Brontë sisters in Haworth. Former industrial powerhouse Leeds is being reinvented as a shopping and entertainment hub.

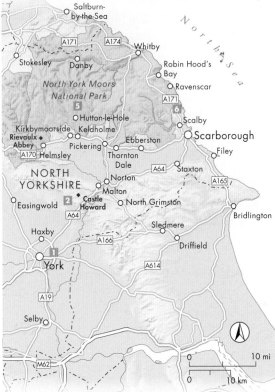

GETTING ORIENTED

Yorkshire is the largest of England's historic counties (and its proud inhabitants would say it's the only one worth visiting). At its heart is the ancient city of York, with its cathedral and medieval city walls. To the west is the bustling city of Leeds, while a few miles away are the wild hills that form what the tourist office calls Brontë Country—Haworth, where the Brontë family lived, and the valleys and villages of the Yorkshire Dales. North of York is the North York Moors National Park. Isolated stone villages, moorland walks, and Rievaulx Abbey are within easy reach. Along the east coast of Yorkshire, beaches and a fascinating history await you in the resort town of Scarborough, the former whaling port of Whitby, and Robin Hood's Bay.

4 The Yorkshire Dales. This hilly region, a bit off the beaten track, has windswept moors and peaceful valleys that offer extraordinary views. Gorgeous villages like Bolton Abbey and Grassington are well worth exploring.

5 The North York Moors. A short drive north from York, these heather-covered hills are the perfect place to hike. Hutton-le-Hole and Helmsley are pleasant towns, and the ruins of Rievaulx Abbey are nearby.

6 The North Yorkshire Coast. Along this part of the coast, tiny fishing villages cling to cliffs pounded by the surf of the cold North Sea. Scarborough and adorable Robin Hood's Bay make ideal getaways.

GREAT ENGLISH CHEESES

England's lush pastures yield more than 700 types of cheese, which the English eat at any time except breakfast. Smooth and creamy, nutty and tasty, or blue and smelly, cheese turns up in sandwiches and soups, on toast, as a topping, and on cheese boards at the end of a meal. Ask for advice before you choose.

(above) You can buy pieces of cheese both small and large around England; (right, top) Wensleydale cheese; (right, bottom) Strong-flavored Blue Stilton is a classic.

Cheeses come in three strengths: mild, medium, and mature. Young cheese is mild and crumbly; as it ages, the flavor gets sharper and the texture firmer. Protected Designation of Origin (PDO) applies to 14 cheeses that are produced in a designated area. An increasing number of small artisan makers produce distinctive and organic cheeses as well as those made from the milk of goats (Quickes) or sheep (Blacksticks); they aren't afraid to experiment. Cornish Yarg is covered with nettles, Stinking Bishop is washed in perry (an alcoholic drink made from pears), and White Stilton is often stuffed with fruit. Many pubs still serve local cheese as part of a "ploughman's lunch" served with crusty bread, relish, and pickled onion.

ACCOMPANIMENTS

For **ploughman's lunches,** look for fruit chutneys made from raisins, apples, onions, vinegar, and sugar. Branston pickle is a crunchy, spicy-sweet mix of chopped vegetables. Small pickled onions and gherkins are common; piccalilli consists of cauliflower florets pickled in a thick yellow spicy sauce. **Cheese boards** have three or four cheeses; grapes, apples, and pears; and biscuits and crackers.

These cheeses are made from cows' milk.

BLUE STILTON
This has been the king of English cheeses since the 18th century. With a strong taste and scent, it's now the cheese traditionally served at Christmas, often with port. Distinguished by blue veins and a crusty exterior, the whole cheeses are wheel-shape and become softer and creamier as they age. As a condition of its PDO status, it must be made in Nottinghamshire, Derbyshire, or Leicestershire. White Stilton is milder, younger, crumbly, and creamy; it's a good dessert cheese often combined with dried fruit.

CHEDDAR
Originally matured only in caves at Cheddar in Somerset, this is the best known of all English cheeses. Ranging from mild to extra-mature (nuttier), it's firm in texture. If you're looking for the best, aim for West Country Farmhouse Cheddar, which has PDO status when it's made traditionally in Devon, Cornwall, Somerset, and Dorset.

CHESHIRE
The oldest named English cheese has appeared on the menu since Roman times. Usually white in color, it has a crumbly texture and salty tang, and is sometimes colored with annatto, a derivative of the achiote tree that gives a yellow hue to orange color.

DOUBLE AND SINGLE GLOUCESTER
Both varieties have a smooth, dense texture and creamy flavor. Double is more common, and its buttery color is due to annatto. Single Gloucester has PDO status; this requires the cheese to be made in Gloucestershire, to be wheel-shaped, and to be natural in color.

LANCASHIRE
This cheese comes in three strengths according to age: creamy, crumbly, and tasty. The creamy, young cheese is ideal for cheese on toast (Welsh rarebit); the crumbly goes well with fruitcake or an apple, or is good in a salad. The rich, nutty tasty variety (matured longer) often turns up in a ploughman's lunch.

SHROPSHIRE BLUE
Contrary to expectation, this cheese has never been made in Shropshire. Now produced exclusively in the East Midlands, it's a soft, mellow, orange-color cheese with blue veins, created by injecting the *penicillum* mold.

WENSLEYDALE
Made all over the country, the cheese is traditionally made at Hawes in Wensleydale in Yorkshire. It has a white, crumbly texture and a salty taste; it's best eaten when young and fresh. Wensleydale is often served with fruitcake, fresh apples, or hot apple dishes.

—by Kate Hughes

Updated by
Ellin Stein

A hauntingly beautiful region, Yorkshire is known for its wide-open spaces and dramatic landscapes. The hills of the North York Moors and the Yorkshire Dales glow pink with heather in summer, turning to black in winter. Rugged fishing villages like Robin Hood's Bay cling to the edges of cliffs in one of England's last remaining wildernesses. Historic buildings line the narrow streets of towns like York, Whitby, and Harrogate, while ancient cathedrals, abbeys, and castles provide majestic backdrops to day-to-day life.

Some of the region's biggest attractions are the result of human endeavor: the towering cathedral designed by unknown geniuses in medieval York; Castle Howard, Vanbrugh and Hawksmoor's baroque masterpiece near York; and the rooms in the obscure hillside town of Haworth where the Brontë sisters changed literature.

The Yorkshire landscape, however, is just as compelling. The most rugged terrain is the North York Moors, a vast, wild, windswept area dotted with fluffy sheep that wander at will in summer. The West Yorkshire Pennines, with their moors and rocky crags punctuated by gray stone villages, is the landscape that inspired the Brontës. Farther to the north are the lush, green valleys known as the Yorkshire Dales, where the high rainfall produces luxuriant vegetation, swift rivers, and sparkling streams. These are wonderfully peaceful places, except in summer, when hundreds of hikers (or "ramblers," as they're known in England) appear over the hills, injecting life into the local economy.

The area isn't all green fields and perfect villages—there's also a gritty, urban aspect to the region. In West Yorkshire, once down-at-heels Leeds has remade itself with trendy restaurants and cafés, along with a buzzing music industry and nightlife scene.

YORKSHIRE PLANNER

WHEN TO GO

To see the heather at its most lush, visit in summer (but despite the season, be prepared for some chilly days). It's also the best time to see the coast, as colorful regattas and arts festivals are underway. York Minster makes a splendidly atmospheric focal point for the prestigious York Early Music Festival in early July. Spring and fall bring their own rewards: far fewer crowds and crisp, clear days, although there's an increased risk of rain and fog. The harsh winter is tricky: while the moors and dales are beautiful covered in snow and the coast sparkles on a clear, bright day, storms and blizzards can set in quickly. Then the moorland roads become impassable and villages can be cut off entirely. In winter, stick to York and the main towns.

PLANNING YOUR TIME

Yorkshire is a vast region, and difficult to explore in a short amount of time. If you're in a hurry, you could see the highlights of York or Leeds as a day trip from London; the fastest trains take just two hours. But it's an awful lot to pack into one day, and you're bound to leave out places you'll probably regret missing. Proper exploration—especially of the countryside—requires time and effort. In a few days you could explore York and some highlights such as Castle Howard and Studley Royal. You'd need the better part of a week to take in the small towns, abandoned abbeys, and inspiring moors and coast. It's well worth it: this is the path less traveled. The York Pass (⊕ *www.yorkpass.com*), good for one, two, or three days, can save you money on more than 30 attractions, but check it against your itinerary.

GETTING HERE AND AROUND

AIR TRAVEL

Leeds Bradford Airport, 11 miles northwest of Leeds, has frequent flights from other cities in England and Europe. Look for cheap fares on British Airways, flybe, Jet2, or Ryanair. Another good choice for this region is Manchester Airport, about 40 miles southwest of Leeds. This larger airport is well served by domestic and international carriers.

Airports Leeds Bradford International Airport ⊠ *A658, Yeadon* ☎ *0871/288–2288* ⊕ *www.leedsbradfordairport.co.uk.* **Manchester Airport** ⊠ *M56, near Junctions 5 and 6, Manchester* ☎ *0871/271–0711* ⊕ *www.manchesterairport.co.uk.*

BUS TRAVEL

National Express and Megabus both have numerous daily departures from London's Victoria Coach Station to major cities in Yorkshire. Average travel times are 4¼ hours to Leeds, 6 hours to York, and 8 hours to Scarborough. Once you're in the region, local bus companies take over the routes. There are Metro buses from Leeds and Bradford into the more remote parts of the Yorkshire Dales. Other companies are Harrogate & District for services to Ripon, Harrogate, and Leeds; Keighley & District to Haworth; Yorkshire Coastliner for Castle Howard, Scarborough, Whitby, Malton, and Leeds; Arriva for Whitby,

Scarborough, and Middlesbrough; and the volunteer-run Dalesbus for Hawes and other destinations in summer. In York the main local bus operator is Transdev. Traveline has route information.

Bus Contacts Arriva ☎ 0844/800–4411 ⊕ www.arrivabus.co.uk. **Dalesbus** ☎ 01756/749400 ⊕ www.dalesbus.org. **Harrogate & District** ☎ 01423/566061 ⊕ www.harrogatebus.co.uk. **Keighley & District** ☎ 01535/603284 ⊕ www.keighleyanddistrict.co.uk. **Megabus** ☎ 0900/160–0900 ⊕ uk.megabus.com. **MetroLine** ☎ 0113/245–7676 ⊕ www.wymetro.com. **National Express** ☎ 0871/781–8178 ⊕ www.nationalexpress.com. **Traveline** ☎ 0871/200–2233 ⊕ www.traveline.info. **Transdev York** ☎ 01904/633990 ⊕ www.yorkbus.co.uk. **Yorkshire Coastliner** ☎ 01653/692556 ⊕ www.yorkbus.co.uk.

CAR TRAVEL

If you're driving, the M1 is the principal route north from London. This major thoroughfare gets you to Leeds in about three hours. For York (204 miles) and the Scarborough areas, stay on M1 to Leeds (197 miles), and then take A64. For the Yorkshire Dales, take M1 to Leeds, then A65 north and west to Skipton. For the North York Moors, take the A64 and then the A169 north from York to Pickering, then continue north on the A169 to Whitby or west on the A170 Helmsley. The trans-Pennine motorway, the M62, between Liverpool and Hull, crosses the bottom of this region. North of Leeds, A1 is the major north–south road, although narrow stretches, roadworks, and heavy traffic make this route slow going at times.

Some of the steep, narrow roads in the countryside off the main routes are difficult drives and can be perilous (or closed altogether) in winter. Main roads often closed by snowdrifts are the moorland A169 and the coast-and-moor A171. If you plan to drive in the dales or moors in winter, check the weather forecast in advance.

TRAIN TRAVEL

East Coast trains travel to York and Leeds from London's King's Cross Station. Grand Central trains head to York and Thirsk. Average travel times from King's Cross are 2 hours to York and 2¼ hours to Leeds. Northern Rail trains operate throughout the region. Contact National Rail for train times, and to find out if any discounted Rover tickets are available for your journey.

Train Contacts East Coast ☎ 0845/722–5111 ⊕ www.eastcoast.co.uk. **Grand Central** ☎ 0844/811–0071 ⊕ www.grandcentralrail.com. **National Rail Enquiries** ☎ 0845/748–4950 ⊕ www.nationalrail.co.uk. **Northern Rail** ☎ 0845/000–0125 ⊕ www.northernrail.org.

RESTAURANTS

Yorkshire is known for hearty food, though bacon-based breakfasts and lunches of pork pies do tend to pale fairly quickly. Increasingly, the larger towns and cities, particularly Leeds, have developed a foodie scene of sorts. Indian restaurants (called curry houses) can be very good in northern cities. Out in the countryside, pubs are your best bet for dining. Many offer excellent home-cooked food and locally reared meat (especially lamb) and vegetables. Roast beef dinners generally come with Yorkshire pudding, the tasty, puffy, oven-baked dish made from egg batter known as a popover in the United States and Canada. It's generally served with lots of gravy. Be sure to sample local cheeses, especially Wensleydale, which has a delicate flavor and honey aftertaste. *Prices in the reviews are the average cost of a main course at dinner or, if dinner isn't served, at lunch.*

12

HOTELS

Traditional hotels are limited primarily to major towns and cities; those in the country tend to be guesthouses, inns, B&Bs, or pubs with rooms. Many of the better guesthouses are at the edge of town, but some proprietors will pick you up at the main station if you're relying on public transportation—verify before booking. Rooms fill quickly at seaside resorts in July and August, and some places in the moors and dales close in winter. Always call ahead to make sure a hotel is open and has space available. *Prices in the reviews are the lowest cost of a standard double room in high season, including 20% V.A.T.*

VISITOR INFORMATION

Contact **Welcome to Yorkshire** ☎ 0113/322–3500 ⊕ www.yorkshire.com.

YORK

Fodor'sChoice
★

For many people, the first stop in Yorkshire is the historic cathedral city of York. Much of the city's medieval and 18th-century architecture has survived, making it a delight to explore. It's one of the most popular short-stay destinations in Britain, and only two hours by train from London's King's Cross Station.

Named "Eboracum" by the Romans, York was the military capital of Roman Britain, and traces of garrison buildings survive throughout the city. After the Roman Empire collapsed in the 5th century, the Saxons built "Eoforwic" on the ruins of a fort, but were soon defeated by Vikings who called the town "Jorvik" and used it as a base from which to subjugate the countryside. The Normans came in the 11th century and emulated the Vikings by using the town as a military base. It was during Norman times that the foundations of York Minster, the largest medieval cathedral in England, were laid. The only changes the 19th century brought were large houses, built mostly on the outskirts of the city center.

GETTING HERE AND AROUND

If you're driving, take the M1 north from London. Stay on it to Leeds, and then take the A64 northeast for 25 miles to York. The journey should take around 3½ hours. Megabus coaches leave from St. Pancras International station three times a day (4½ hours), and National Express buses depart from London's Victoria Coach Station three times a day (5½ hours). Grand Central and c2c trains run from London's King's Cross Station about every 30 minutes during the week (2 hours). York Station, just outside the city walls, has a line of taxis out front to take you to your hotel. If you don't have bags, the walk to town takes eight minutes.

York's city center is mostly closed to traffic and is very walkable. The old center is a compact, dense web of narrow streets and tiny medieval alleys called "snicklaways." These provide shortcuts across the city center, but they're not on maps, so you never quite know where you'll end up, which in York is often a pleasant surprise.

TOURS City Sightseeing runs frequent hop on, hop off bus tours of York that stop at the Castle Museum, Clifford's Tower, and Jorvik Viking Centre. The York Association of Voluntary Guides arranges short walking tours around the city at least once a day. The tours are free, but tips are appreciated.

Ghost Creeper runs "bloodcurdling" tours weekend nights from November to late December and March to June, and nightly from July through Halloween. Tours start at 7:30 pm outside the Jorvik Viking Centre and cost £5 per person. Guides with Ghost Hunt take a slightly tongue-in-cheek approach to the ghouls. The tours start at 7:30 pm nightly in the Shambles and cost £5 per person. Old hands at exploring the city's spectral species, Ghost Trail of York guides take a straightforward approach to ghosts—telling you what other people have heard or seen, and what they've seen themselves. The hour-long tours commence at 7:30 pm by the Minster and cost £4 per person. The old-timer of ghost tours, the Original Ghost Walk of York presents the city's ghost tales as fascinating unexplained mysteries. The tours depart at 8 pm from in front of the King's Arms Pub on Ouse Bridge and cost £5 per person.

TIMING

In July and August tourists choke the narrow streets and form long lines at the Minster. April, May, June, and September are less crowded, but the weather can be unpredictable. April is also the time to see the embankments beneath the city walls rippling with pale gold daffodils.

ESSENTIALS

Tour Information **City Sightseeing** ☎ 01904/634296 ⊕ www.city-sightseeing.com. **Ghost Creeper** ☎ 07947/325239 ⊕ www.ghostcreeper.com. **Ghost Hunt** ☎ 01904/608700 ⊕ www.ghosthunt.co.uk. **Ghost Trail of York** ☎ 01904/633276 ⊕ www.ghosttrail.co.uk. **Original Ghost Walk of York** ☎ 01759/373090 ⊕ www.theoriginalghostwalkofyork.co.uk. **York Association of Voluntary Guides** ✉ 1 Museum St. ☎ 01904/550098 ⊕ www.visityork.org.

Visitor Information **York** ✉ 1 Museum St. ☎ 01904/550099 ⊕ www.visityork.org.

EXPLORING

TOP ATTRACTIONS

City walls. York's almost 3 miles of ancient stone walls are among the best preserved in England. A walk on the narrow paved path along the top leads you through 1,900 years of history, from the time the earthen ramparts were raised by the Romans and York's Viking kings to repel raiders, to their fortification by the Normans, to their current colorful landscaping by the city council. The walls are crossed periodically by York's distinctive "bars," or fortified gates: the portcullis on Monk's Bar on Goodramgate is still in working order, and Walmgate Bar in the east is the only gate in England with an intact barbican. It also has scars from the cannon balls hurled at it during the Civil War. Bootham Bar in Exhibition Square was the defensive bastion for the

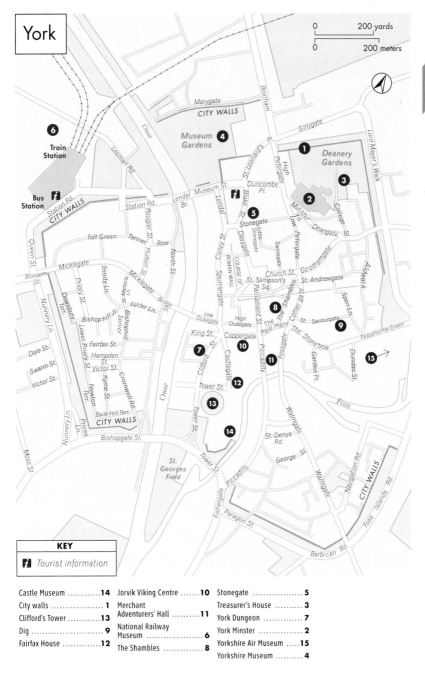

York

0 — 200 yards
0 — 200 meters

12

Train Station

Bus Station

KEY

🛈 *Tourist information*

The Shambles, a narrow medieval street in York, once held butchers' shops, but now has stores that serve the city's many shoppers and visitors.

north road, and Micklegate Bar, in the city's southwest corner, was traditionally the monarch's entrance. To access the path and the lookout towers, find a staircase at one of the many breaks in the walls. ✉ Free ☉ Daily 8 am–dusk.

FAMILY **Dig.** This venture from the people behind the Jorvik Viking Centre is a great way to get young people inspired about history and archaeology. It's a reproduction of an archaeological dig in and beneath an old church; kids, supervised by knowledgeable experts, dig in the dirt and "find" Roman or Viking artifacts. After your exploration, head to the lab to learn what archaeological finds discovered on the site reveal about former inhabitants. ✉ St. Saviour's Church, St. Saviourgate ☎ 01904/615505 ⊕ www.vikingjorvik.com ✉ £5.50; joint admission to Jorvik Viking Centre £13.25 ☉ Daily 10–5, last admission at 4.

FAMILY **Jorvik Viking Centre.** This kid-focused exhibition re-creates a 10th-century Viking village. A mixture of museum and carnival ride, you "travel through time" by climbing into a Disney-esque machine that propels you above straw huts and mannequins in Viking garb. Commentary is provided in 6 languages. Kids will get a lot out of it, but adults are unlikely to learn anything new. A small collection of Viking-era artifacts is on display at the end of the ride. ✉ Coppergate ☎ 01904/615505 ⊕ www.vikingjorvik.com ✉ £9.75; joint admission to Dig £13.25 ☉ Apr.–Oct., daily 10–5; Nov.–Mar., daily 10–4.

FAMILY **National Railway Museum.** A must for train-lovers, Britain's biggest railway museum houses part of the national collection of rail vehicles. Don't miss such gleaming giants of the steam era as the *Mallard*, holder of the world speed record for a steam engine (126 mph), and train-buff legend the *Flying Scotsman*. Passenger cars used by Queen Victoria are on display, as is the only Japanese bullet train to be seen outside Japan. You can climb aboard some of the trains and occasionally take a short trip on one. ⊠ *Leeman Rd.* ☎ *08448/153139* ⊕ *www.nrm.org. uk* 🎫 *Free* ☉ *Daily 10–6.*

The Shambles. York's best-preserved medieval street has shops and residences in half-timbered buildings with overhangs so massive you could almost reach across the narrow gap from one second-floor window to another. Once a hub of butchers (meat hooks are still fastened outside some of the doors), today it's mostly filled with independent shops and remains highly atmospheric.

WHERE ARE THE GATES?

The Viking conquerors of northern England who held the region for more than a century made York their capital. *Gate* was the Viking word for "street," hence street names such as Goodramgate and Micklegate. Adding to the confusion, the city's entrances, or gates, are called "bars," from an Old English term. As local tour guides like to say, "In York, our streets are called gates, our gates are called bars, and our bars are called pubs."

Stonegate. This narrow, pedestrian-only street lined with Tudor and 18th-century storefronts retains considerable charm. It's been in daily use for almost 2,000 years, when it was first paved during Roman times. Today it's a vibrant shopping strip lined with upscale boutiques, jewelers, and quirky one-offs like the Eye of Newt at 35, your one-stop shop for "tarot, spells, candles, crystal balls, potions, and wands." A passage just off Stonegate, at 52A, leads to the remains of a 12th-century Norman stone house attached to a more recent structure. You can see the old Norman wall and window. ■ TIP→ Look out for the little red "printer's devil" at No. 33, a medieval symbol of a printer's premises. At the intersection of Stonegate and High Petergate, Minerva reclines on a stack of books, indicating they were once sold inside.

QUICK BITES

Betty's. Betty's has been a York institution since 1937. The plate-glass windows with art nouveau stained glass, the dessert trollies, and solicitous white-aproned staff contribute to an impression of stepping back in time to when afternoon tea was a genteel ritual. The traditional dishes (like pork schnitzel and fried haddock) are so-so, but the tea and cakes are excellent. An in-house store sells a wide range of specialty coffees and teas plus pastries and old-fashioned sweets like rose and violet creams. There's also a smaller branch at 46 Stonegate. ⊠ *6–8 Helen's Sq., off Stonegate* ☎ *01904/659142.*

FAMILY **York Dungeon.** This place takes a tongue-in-cheek approach to exploring the more violent and gory aspects of York's history. Lurid lighting, lots of fake blood, and costumed actors enliven episodes from the careers of infamous residents like highwayman Dick Turpin, revolutionary Guy Fawkes, Viking king Eric Bloodaxe, and more, all to a soundtrack of wailing, screaming, and agonized moaning. As you might imagine, it's popular with kids, though not suitable for those under

10. ✉ *12 Clifford St.* ☎ *0871/423–2260* ⊕ *www.the-dungeons.co.uk/ york* ✉ *£15.60* ⊙ *Feb., Mar., Sept., and Oct., 10:30–4:30; Apr.–July, 10–5:30; Nov.–Jan., 11–4. Last admission 1 hr before closing.*

York Minster. *For information about the cathedral, see the feature York Minster: Gothic Grandeur.*

FAMILY **Yorkshire Air Museum.** Located on 20 acres of parkland, this is the country's largest World War II airbase open to the public. The independent museum showcases numerous historic aircraft, many of which are still in working condition and are certain to delight aviation enthusiasts. Planes range from early-20th-century biplanes and gliders to Spitfires and other World War II-era planes to contemporary fighter jets. There are also exhibits devoted to military vehicles, aircraft weaponry, and Royal Air Force uniforms. The museum is home to a memorial and gardens commemorating British and allied servicemembers who lost their lives in the conflict. ✉ *Halifax Way, Elvington* ☎ *01904/608595* ⊕ *www.yorkshireairmuseum.org* ✉ *£8* ⊙ *April–mid-Nov., 10–5; mid-Nov.–Mar., 10–4.*

WORTH NOTING

FAMILY **Castle Museum.** In an 18th-century building whose elegance belies its former purpose as a debtors' prison, this quirky museum of everyday items includes a Victorian street complete with a working water mill, as well as notable domestic interiors, a toy gallery, and an exhibition on World War I. You can also visit the cell where Dick Turpin, the 18th-century highwayman and folk hero, spent the night before his execution. ✉ *Eye of York* ☎ *01904/687687* ⊕ *www.yorkcastlemuseum. uk* ✉ *£8.50* ⊙ *Daily 9:30–5.*

Clifford's Tower. This rather battered-looking keep at the top of a steep mound is all that remains of the old York castle. Sitting on a grassy mound, this squat stone tower dates from the early 12th century. The Norman tower that preceded it, built in 1068 by William the Conquerer, was destroyed in 1190 when more than 150 Jews locked themselves inside to protect themselves from a violent mob. Trapped with no food or water, they committed mass suicide by setting their own prison aflame. From the top of the tower you have good views of the city. ✉ *Tower St.* ☎ *01904/646940* ✉ *£4.20* ⊙ *Apr.–Sept., daily 10–6; Oct., daily 10–5; Nov.–Mar., daily 10–4.*

Fairfax House. This 1762 Georgian town house is a museum of decorative arts. The house is beautifully decorated with period furniture, crystal chandeliers, and silk damask wallpaper. Entrance on Monday is restricted to guided tours at 11 and 2. ✉ *Castlegate* ☎ *01904/655543* ⊕ *www.fairfaxhouse.co.uk* ✉ *£6* ⊙ *Feb.–Dec., Tues.–Sat. 10–5, Sun. 12:30–4; Mon. by appt.; last admission 30 mins before closing.*

Merchant Adventurers' Hall. Built between 1357 and 1361 by a wealthy medieval guild, this is the largest half-timbered hall in York. Portraits, silver, and furniture are on display, and the house itself is much of the attraction. A riverfront garden lies behind the hall. ✉ *Fossgate* ☎ *01904/654818* ⊕ *www.theyorkcompany.co.uk* ✉ *£6* ⊙ *Mar.–Oct., Mon.–Thurs. 9–5, Fri. and Sat. 9–3:30, Sun. 11–4; Nov.–mid-Dec., Jan., and Feb., Mon.–Sat. 10–4.*

A WALK IN YORK

York is a fine city for walking, especially along the walls embracing the old center. Start at the Minster and head down Stonegate, a lane dating back to the Middle Ages now lined with shops that leads directly to Betty's celebrated tearooms. Eventually you'll come to a highly atmospheric shopping street known as the Shambles and further along the remains of the old castle. Take time to shop if you wish; York has both antiques shops and spots with plenty of contemporary items, and draws many local shoppers.

To get a sense of where you are at any point, climb the steps up to the top of the city walls (they are also good for a walk). The River Ouse is bordered in places by walking paths that make for a pleasant stroll.

Treasurer's House. Surprises await inside this large 17th-century house, the home from 1897 to 1930 of industrialist Frank Green. With a fine eye for texture, decoration, and pattern, Green re-created period rooms—including a medieval great hall—as a showcase for his collection of antique furniture. Delft tiles decorate the former kitchen (now a shop), copies of medieval stenciling cover the vibrant King's Room, and 17th-century stumpwork adorns the Tapestry Room. The cellar has displays about a ghostly Roman legion allegedly sighted there in the 1950s. ✉ *Minster Yard* ☎ *01904/624247* 🌐 *www.nationaltrust.org.uk* 🎟 *House and garden £6.50, attic tour £3, cellar tour £2.40* 🕒 *Mar.–Oct., Sat.–Thurs. 11–5; Feb. and Nov., Sat.–Thurs. 11–3, by guided tour only; last admission at 4:30.*

Yorkshire Museum. The natural and archaeological history of the county, including material on the Roman, Anglo-Saxon, and Viking aspects of York, is the focus of this museum on the site of the medieval St. Mary's Abbey. The museum is divided into themed galleries focusing on the different time periods. On display in the early 19th-century Greek Revival–style building with its massive Doric column is the 15th-century Middleham Jewel, a pendant gleaming with a large sapphire, and the extremely rare Copperplate Helmet, a 1,200-year-old Viking artifact discovered during excavations of the city. ✉ *Museum Gardens, Museum St.* ☎ *01904/687687* 🌐 *www.yorkshiremuseum.org.uk* 🎟 *£7.50* 🕒 *Daily 10–5.*

WHERE TO EAT

$$ MODERN BRITISH

🍴 **Blue Bicycle.** One of York's best restaurants is in a building that once served as a brothel, a past reflected in its murals featuring undraped women. Downstairs are four intimate walled booths, and at street level is a lively room lighted with candles. The menu changes with the seasons and concentrates on local seafood. Typical dishes include pan-seared scallops with horseradish puree, seared sea bass with truffled potatoes, or grilled local beef sirloin with pink peppercorn mash. The wine list is impressive, and the service couldn't be friendlier. The restaurant has six self-contained apartments—called the Blue Rooms—in a courtyard to the rear. [$] *Average main: £18* ✉ *34 Fossgate* ☎ *01904/673990* 🌐 *www.thebluebicycle.com* ✍ *Reservations essential.*

Continued on page 717

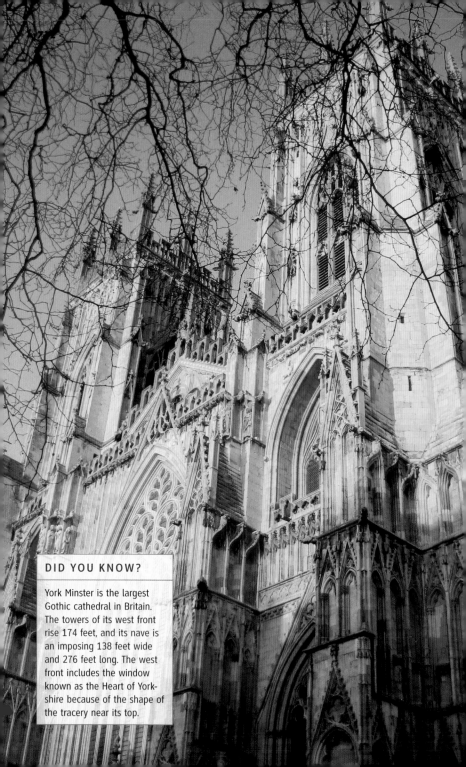

DID YOU KNOW?

York Minster is the largest Gothic cathedral in Britain. The towers of its west front rise 174 feet, and its nave is an imposing 138 feet wide and 276 feet long. The west front includes the window known as the Heart of Yorkshire because of the shape of the tracery near its top.

YORK MINSTER
GOTHIC GRANDEUR by Christi Daugherty

You can see this vast cathedral from 10 miles away, the tall Gothic towers rising over the flat horizon. The focal point of York, it encompasses centuries of the city's history, and its treasures include 128 dazzling medieval glass windows. The Minster today is a tranquil place, but over the centuries it has survived structural threats and political upheaval.

The present York Minster is the fourth attempt to build a church on this site. The first, a Saxon minster from the 7th century, was built of wood. In the 8th century it was rebuilt in stone. Norman invaders badly damaged the first stone church in 1069 as they conquered the recalcitrant north. They later rebuilt it in their own style, and you can see Norman elements—foundations, masonry, columns—in the undercroft. Marauding Vikings, however, damaged that build-

ing. Much of the limestone building you see is the result of the vision of one 13th-century archbishop, Walter de Gray. He wanted to build one of the world's greatest cathedrals, on the scale of Canterbury, with vaulted ceilings soaring hundreds of feet high. York Minster was finally completed in 1472. De Gray stayed with his beloved building beyond the end. He died in 1255, and his effigy lies atop his tomb inside the south transept near the main entrance.

(top left) York Minster interior, (top right) A stone gargoyle, (bottom right) Chapter House ceiling

MINSTER ORIENTATION AND HIGHLIGHTS

The Minster is designed in cruciform, meaning in the shape of a cross. As you walk through the main doors, you're entering the south transept, one of the arms of the cross. These transepts were built in Archbishop de Gray's time in the 13th century. Ahead of you, the grand, soaring, light-filled nave stretches out to your left and right, with massive stained-glass windows at both ends. Across the nave is the northern transept—the other arm of the cross—and off it a corridor leads to the octagonal Chapter House. The nave's ceiling is supported by flying buttresses on the exterior of the building. In the 13th and 14th centuries, this architectural feature was so experimental that the builders could not be certain the structure would not simply collapse.

Nave

❶ Nave. The 14th-century builders of the nave used painted wood for the nave's soaring ceilings out of practicality: they feared stone would be too heavy. A fire in 1840 destroyed the roof, but the vaulting and bosses are exact replicas. Giant stained-glass windows glow from each end: the Heart of Yorkshire to the west, and opposite it the great East Window. ⚠ The East Window is being restored.

❷ Great West Window. The heart-shaped tracery in the window that dominates the west end of the nave dates to 1338, and is remarkable both for its shape and its intricate design.

❸ Rose Window. This extraordinary stained-glass window in the south transept has 13th-century stonework, but it has early 16th-century glass in which white and red Tudor roses show the union of the houses of York and Lancaster. It was nearly lost when lightning struck the building in 1984, causing a fire.

❹ The Five Sisters. At the end of the north transept, these five tall, blade-shaped windows from around 1260 are rare pieces of medieval glass art made of more than 100,000 pieces of glass. Each blade is more than five feet wide and towers 52 feet high. All were painted on gray-tinged glass using a technique known as grisaille.

❺ Chapter House. With a beautifully painted and gilded ceiling (restored in 1845), the octagonal 13th-century Chapter House is a marvel, lined with exquisite stained glass and decorated with fanciful animals and gargoyles with human faces that could be caricatures of early monks.

❻ Choir Screen. Stretching along one section of the nave, an elegantly carved 15th-century stone panel, known as the choir screen, contains almost life-size sculptures of 15 kings of England from William the Conqueror to Henry VI.

The Rose Window

Choir Screen

1069 Normans destroy Saxon structure	**1220** Walter de Gray begins church	**1472** The Minster is consecrated	**1829** Arson attack damages choir	**1967** Tower is structurally threatened

| 1200 | 1400 | 1600 | 1800 | 2000 |

12

IN FOCUS YORK MINSTER: GOTHIC GRANDEUR

Stained-glass window

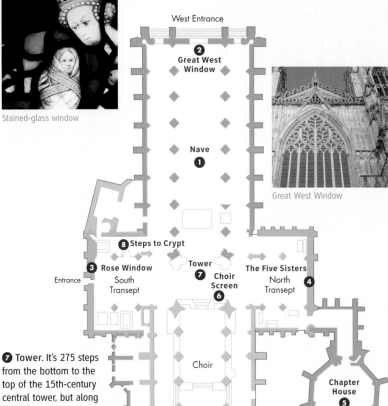

West Entrance

2
Great West Window

Nave
1

Great West Window

8 Steps to Crypt

3 Rose Window

Entrance

Tower
7 Choir Screen
6

South Transept

The Five Sisters

North Transept
4

7 Tower. It's 275 steps from the bottom to the top of the 15th-century central tower, but along the way you pass wonderful carvings and gargoyles. From the top you are rewarded with views of the city and surrounding countryside. Children under 8 are not allowed.

8 Crypt. Much older than the Minster building a level above, the crypt was mostly built in Norman times, in the 11th and 12th centuries. In the unique carving on the bases of the pillars you can see the marks left by the builders' chisels.

Choir

Chapter House
5

High Altar

Lady Chapel

East End

KEY: Gothic Styles
Early English, 1220-1260
Decorated, 1280-1350
Perpendicular, 1361-1472

MAKING THE MOST OF YOUR VISIT

Five Sisters

WHEN TO VISIT

The best time to visit is early or late in the day. The church is busiest between 11 am and 2 pm. If you can avoid weekends or holidays, do, as the church can be crowded. You may encounter choir practice in the early evening. Look for occasional evening concerts; attending Evensong service can also be lovely. The building sometimes closes for church events and meetings, and it is closed to visitors (except those attending services) on most major religious holidays.

WHAT TO WEAR AND BRING

The church is enormous, so wear comfortable shoes. Bring binoculars to see the glass and higher carvings. The stone walls keep it cool inside year-round. There are no restrictions on attire. You may want to bring a bottle of water; there's no tea shop.

PLANNING YOUR TIME

A thorough visit, including the crypt, undercroft, and central tower, can take two hours, and could take longer for those who read all the displays or study the stained glass. The Orb exhibit shows some glass at eye level.

FOR FREE

The church is always free for worshippers or those who wish to pray.

TOURS

Free tours may be available without reservations. There are also tours of the stained-glass conservation studio or "Hidden Minster" tours some days, but call ahead to book; fees are £8.50.

VISITOR INFORMATION

✉ *Duncombe Pl.* ☎ *0844/939–0011* ⊕ *www.yorkminster.org* ✈ *Minster £10, Minster and Tower £15* ☉ *Mon.– Sat. 9–5, Sun. noon–5; weather may affect Tower hours.* Entrance fee includes the crypt, undercroft, and treasury. Services are held daily throughout the day.

WALKING THROUGH HISTORY: THE UNDERCROFT

One of the must-see sections of York Minster isn't in the Gothic building at all, but underneath it. The undercroft was excavated in the late 1960s and early 1970s after a survey found that the central tower was near collapse. While working frantically to shore up the foundations, builders uncovered extensive remains of previous structures on this site. Now the ruins and remnants they uncovered form the basis for the excellent Undercroft Museum. You walk past Norman pillars and stonework, Viking gravestones, Saxon carvings and coffins, and the remains of a Roman ba-

silica. The displays put all that you are seeing into the context of the region's history.

York Minster crypt

$ 🍴 **Café Concerto.** Music is the theme at this relaxed, intimate bistro in sight
BRITISH of York Minster where sheet music serves as wallpaper. The kitchen serves British classics with an emphasis on local ingredients. Dinner favorites include braised lamb shank with caramelized onion mash, panfried pork fillet with a Madeira cream sauce, or sirloin steak with field mushrooms and roast potatoes. Lunch is mostly soups, salads, and sandwiches, and you can always pop in for tea and cake. [$] *Average main: £14* ✉ *21 High Petergate* ☎ *01904/610478* 🌐 *www.cafeconcerto.biz.*

$$ 🍴 **Le Langhe.** So popular that it has already moved twice to larger prem-
ITALIAN ises, this combination café/restaurant/upscale deli has an emphasis on Italian, particularly Piedmontese, meats and cheeses. The deli sells take-out sandwiches incorporating a variety of both, as well as small-producer olive oils, wines, and other items sourced by the owners. The glass-roofed café offers a variety of house-made pastas, such as pasta with Whitby crab with shallots and potatoes. Entreés change daily and might include slow-cooked pork belly, lemon sole, or venison. There's a tasting menu at dinner, and fixed-price lunch menus. The upstairs restaurant serves dinner on Friday and Saturday. [$] *Average main: £18* ✉ *The Old Coach House, Peasholme Green* ☎ *01904/622584* 🌐 *www.lelanghe.co.uk* ✍ *Reservations essential.*

$$ 🍴 **Melton's.** A converted Victorian shop, this unpretentious restaurant
MODERN BRITISH has work by local artists on the walls, but you'll more likely be trying to catch a glimpse of the open kitchen beyond a glass door. The excellent seasonal menus are highly imaginative takes on modern British dishes using regional produce, such as chicken with apples and parsley mashed potatoes, venison in a red-wine sauce with fondant potatoes, or fish-and-mussel stew with potatoes and fennel. There's also a five-course "Yorkshire Tasting Menu" for £38. Melton's is a 10-minute walk from Clifford's Tower. There's an offshoot bar-bistro called Melton's Too on neaby Walmsgate. [$] *Average main: £18* ✉ *7 Scarcroft Rd.* ☎ *01904/634341* 🌐 *www.meltonsrestaurant.co.uk* ✍ *Reservations essential* 🕒 *Closed Sun. and Mon. and 3 wks at Christmas.*

$ 🍴 **Spurriergate Centre.** Churches aren't just for services, as this 15th-cen-
CAFÉ tury house of worship proves. Resurrected as a cafeteria (there's also a café on the upper floor), St. Michael's is a favorite spot for both tourists and locals to refuel spiritually (you can request use of the prayer room upstairs) as well as physically. You may end up eating beef casserole on the spot where John Wesley prayed in 1768. Don't pass up the cream scones. [$] *Average main: £7* ✉ *Spurriergate* ☎ *01904/629393* 🌐 *www.thespurriergatecentre.com* 🕒 *Closed Sun. No dinner.*

WHERE TO STAY

For expanded hotel reviews, visit Fodors.com.

$$ 🏨 **Cedar Court Grand Hotel and Spa.** This handsome, comfortable hotel is
HOTEL near the train station—not surprising, considering it was formerly the headquarters of the regional railroad. **Pros:** beautiful building; spacious rooms; good location. **Cons:** continental breakfast only average; unceasing soft rock in restaurant. [$] *Rooms from: £155* ✉ *Station Rise* ☎ *01904/380038* 🌐 *www.cedarcourtgrand.co.uk* 🛏 *107 rooms, 13 suites* 🍽 *Breakfast.*

HAUNTED YORK

Given its lengthy history, dark streets, and atmospheric buildings, it's no surprise that York feels as if it could be haunted. Indeed, a body called the Ghost Research Foundation International has determined that, with 500 recorded cases of ghostly encounters, York is the most haunted city in England, and one of the most haunted in the world.

Not everybody believes in earth-bound spirits, but that hasn't stopped the local tourism industry from assuming many do. Should you choose to explore the town's spookier side, try Ghost Creeper, Ghost Hunt, Ghost Trail of York, or the Original Ghost Tour of York.

$
B&B/INN
☷ Dairy Guest House. Victorian stained glass, fine woodwork, and intricate plaster cornices are original features of this former dairy near the city walls. **Pros:** nice period details; comfortable rooms. **Cons:** a bit of a walk to the center; minimum stay required in summer; few amenities. $ *Rooms from: £60 ☒ 3 Scarcroft Rd. ☎ 01904/639367 ⊕ www. dairyguesthouse.co.uk ⤳ 6 rooms ☉ Breakfast.*

$$
HOTEL
☷ Grange Hotel. Built in the early 19th century as a home for a wealthy member of the York clergy, this luxurious boutique hotel is reminiscent of a grand country house. **Pros:** spacious rooms; lovely decor; good food. **Cons:** can feel a bit fussy; restaurant service uneven. $ *Rooms from: £115 ☒ 1 Clifton ☎ 01904/644744 ⊕ www.grangehotel.co.uk ⤳ 36 rooms ☉ Breakfast.*

$
B&B/INN
☷ The Hazelwood. These two tall, elegant Victorian town houses retain many of their original features and stand in a peaceful cul-de-sac; they're away from the hustle and bustle despite being a short walk from York Minster. **Pros:** good service; lovely building; convenient parking. **Cons:** thin walls; poor water pressure on upper floors. $ *Rooms from: £80 ☒ 24–25 Portland St. ☎ 01904/626548 ⊕ www.thehazelwoodyork. com ⤳ 14 rooms ☉ Breakfast.*

$$
HOTEL
☷ Hotel Du Vin. A 19th-century orphanage, this historic building has been converted into a swanky hotel that preserves the original exposed brick walls and arched doorways. **Pros:** makes great use of the space; friendly staff; comfortable beds. **Cons:** high parking charges; low bathroom lighting. $ *Rooms from: £129 ☒ 89 The Mount ☎ 01904/557350 ⊕ www.hotelduvin.com ⤳ 44 rooms ☉ Breakfast.*

$$$
HOTEL
☷ Middlethorpe Hall & Spa. Aimed at those who prize period details like oak-paneled walls, four-poster beds, carved wood bannisters, and window seats and whose idea of luxury is a bowl of fresh daffodils, this splendidly restored Queen Anne-style mansion feels less like a country-house hotel than an actual country house.**Pros:** period luxury; gorgeous grounds; attentive staff. **Cons:** water pressure; outside the city center. $ *Rooms from: £199 ☒ Bishopthorpe Rd. ☎ 01904/641241 ⊕ www. middlethorpe.com ⤳ 18 rooms, 11 suites ☉ Breakfast.*

$$
HOTEL
☷ Mount Royale Hotel. This hotel has the feel of a relaxing country house despite being close to the city center in an upscale residential

The Vikings occupied York, and the city recalls this era enthusiastically during the Viking Festival each February.

neighborhood. **Pros:** large rooms; lovely pool and garden; good service. **Cons:** well outside the town center; some rooms dated. $ *Rooms from: £125* ✉ *117–119 The Mount* ☎ *01904/628856* ⊕ *www.mountroyale. co.uk* ⇋ *14 rooms, 10 suites* ⍩*Breakfast.*

NIGHTLIFE AND THE ARTS

NIGHTLIFE
York is full of historic pubs where you can while away an hour over a pint.

Black Swan. In a 14th-century Tudor building complete with flagstone floors and oak paneling, this pub serves home-cooked bar food and hosts a roster of local folk musicians. ✉ *Peasholme Green* ☎ *01904/679131* ⊕ *www.blackswanyork.com.*

Old White Swan. Spreading across five medieval, half-timbered buildings on busy Goodramgate, the Old White Swan is known for good pub lunches and its ghosts—it claims to have more than the equally venerable Black Swan. ✉ *80 Goodramgate* ☎ *01904/540911* ⊕ *www. nicholsonspubs.co.uk.*

Snickleway Inn. The 15th-century setting, complete with open fireplaces, gives the Snickleway Inn a real sense of history. ✉ *Goodramgate* ☎ *01904/656138.*

THE ARTS
Early Music Festival. Featuring songs written before the 18th century, the Early Music Festival is held each July. There's also a Christmas version in early December. ☎ *01904/658338* ⊕ *www.ncem.co.uk.*

Viking Festival. Held every February, these celebrations include a parade and long-ship regatta. It ends with the Jorvik Viking combat reenactment, when Norsemen confront their Anglo-Saxon enemies. ⊠ *Jorvik Viking Centre, Coppergate* ☎ *01904/543400* ⊕ *www.vikingjorvik.com.*

York Theatre Royal. In a lovely 18th-century building, the York Theatre Royal hosts theater, dance, music, and comedy performances, as well as readings, lectures, and children's entertainment. ⊠ *St. Leonard's Pl.* ☎ *01904/623568* ⊕ *www.yorktheatreroyal.co.uk.*

SHOPPING

Stonegate is the city's main shopping street. Winding down from the Minster toward the river, it's lined with a mix of unique shops and boutiques. Another good shopping street is Petergate, which has mostly chain stores. The Shambles is another prime shopping area, with an eclectic mix of shops geared towards locals and tourists.

Minster Gate Bookshop. This shop sells secondhand books, old maps, and prints. ⊠ *8 Minster Gate* ☎ *01904/621812* ⊕ *www. minstergatebooks.co.uk.*

Mulberry Hall. This store sells fine bone china from big names ranging from Royal Doulton to Donna Karan Lenox and glittering crystal from the likes of Baccarat and Lalique. There are also elegant ornaments, cookware, and kitchen essentials. An upstairs traditional tea room serves light lunches and snacks on Wedgwood china. ⊠ *Stonegate* ☎ *01904/620736* ⊕ *www.mulberryhall.co.uk.*

YORK ENVIRONS

West and north of York a number of sights make easy, appealing day trips from the city: the spa town of Harrogate, atmospheric Knaresborough, the ruins of Fountain Abbey, the market town of Ripon, and nearby Newby Hall. If you're heading northwest from York to Harrogate, you might take the less direct B1224 across Marston Moor, where, in 1644, Oliver Cromwell won a decisive victory over the Royalists during the English Civil War. A few miles beyond, at Wetherby, you can cut northwest along the A661 to Harrogate. Also nearby toward the northeast is Castle Howard, a magnificent stately home.

HARROGATE

21 miles west of York, 11 miles south of Ripon, 16 miles north of Leeds.

During the Regency and early-Victorian periods, it became fashionable for the aristocratic and wealthy to "take the waters" at British spa towns, combining the alleged health benefits with socializing. In Yorkshire the most elegant spa destination was Harrogate, where today its mainly Victorian buildings, parks, and spas still provide a relaxing getaway.

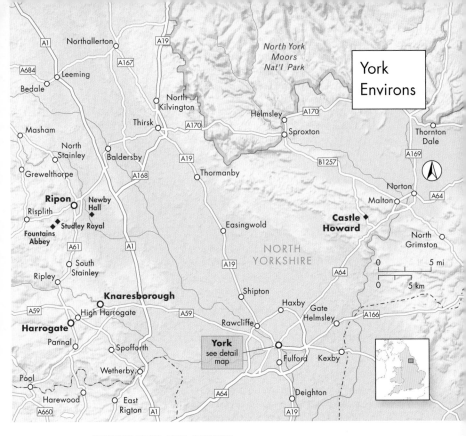

York Environs

GETTING HERE AND AROUND

Trains from York leave every hour or so, and the journey takes about 30 minutes. There's one direct train daily from London. National Express buses leave from York every hour most days; the journey takes about 40 minutes. By car, Harrogate is off A59, and is well marked. It's a walkable town, so you can park in one of its central parking lots and explore on foot.

Within and around Harrogate, the Harrogate and District bus company provides area services, and taxis are plentiful.

ESSENTIALS

Visitor Information Harrogate Tourist Information Centre ⊠ *Royal Baths, Crescent Rd.* ☎ *01423/537300* ⊕ *www.enjoyharrogate.com.*

EXPLORING

Royal Pump Room Museum. This octagonal structure was built in 1842 over the original sulfur well that brought great prosperity to the town. You can still sniff the evil-smelling spa waters here. The museum displays some equipment of spa days gone by, alongside a somewhat eccentric collection of fine 19th-century china, clothes, and bicycles. ⊠ *Crown Pl.* ☎ *01423/556188* ⊕ *www.harrogate.gov.uk* ⊠ *£3.80* ☉ *Apr.–Oct., Mon.–Sat. 10:30–5, Sun. 2–5; Nov.–Mar., Mon.–Sat. 10:30–4, Sun. 2–4.*

The Stray. At the edge of the town center, this 200-acre grassy parkland is a riot of color in spring. It contains many of the mineral springs that first made Harrogate famous. ⊕ *www.harrogate.gov.uk.*

Turkish Baths and Health Spa. Dating from 1897, the exotic and fully restored Turkish Baths allow you to experience what brought so many Victorians to Harrogate. After changing into your bathing suit, you can relax on luxurious lounge chairs in the stunning mosaic-tile warming room. Move on to increasingly hot sauna rooms, and then soak up eucalyptus mist in the steam room before braving the icy plunge pool. You can also book a massage or facial. Open hours are divided into women-only and mixed nights, so book in advance. ⊠ *Parliament St.* ☎ *01423/556746* ⊕ *www.turkishbathsharrogate.co.uk* £15–£20.50 *per session* ☽ *Daily; call for schedule.*

Valley Gardens. Southwest of the town center, these 17-acres of formal gardens include a children's boating lake, tennis courts, skate park, and a little café. ⊠ *Valley Dr.* ⊕ *www.harrogate.gov.uk.*

WHERE TO EAT AND STAY
For expanded hotel reviews, visit Fodors.com.

$
CAFÉ
✕ **Betty's Cafe Tea Rooms.** This celebrated Yorkshire tearoom began life in Harrogate in 1919, when a Swiss restaurateur brought his Alpine pastries and chocolates to England. The welcoming decor has changed little since then, and the extensive array of teas not at all. In addition to omelets, quiches, sandwiches, and traditional cakes and pastries, the menu ranges from the Dales (sausages) to the Alps (rösti). A pianist plays nightly. Reservations are accepted only for afternoon tea served in the Imperial Room on weekends. $ *Average main: £11* ⊠ *1 Parliament St.* ☎ *01423/814070* ⊕ *www.bettys.co.uk.*

$$$$
INTERNATIONAL
Fodor's Choice
★
✕ **The Yorke Arms.** The peaceful rural location of this "restaurant with rooms" belies the sophistication of its distinctive cooking. With an emphasis on seasonal ingredients, creative combinations of flavors, and elegant presentations, the kitchen turns out such appetizers as wild garlic tarts with artichoke and apple, or truffled rabbit and smoked chicken with persimmons. Main courses might include honeyed quail with polenta and marjoram or John Dory with scallops. The dessert selection is fabulous, so save room. The dinner menu is pricey, but the £35 set menu at lunch is good value. The restaurant is housed in a medieval building that dates back to the 11th century (the monks of nearby Fountains Abbey made cheese in the cellar), and the 11 rooms are spacious and charming. There are also four modern courtyard rooms. $ *Average main: £35* ⊠ *Ramsgill-in-Nidderdale, Pateley Bridge* ☎ *01423/755423.*

$$
HOTEL
⊞ **Hotel du Vin.** This hip hotel sprawls through eight Georgian houses, with stripped-wood floors, clubby leather armchairs, and a purple billiard table setting the tone. **Pros:** tasty food; wonderful wine list; helpful staff; modern vibe. **Cons:** some rooms dark; housekeeping uneven; the bar can take over the lounge. $ *Rooms from: £145* ⊠ *Prospect Pl.* ☎ *01423/856800* ⊕ *www.hotelduvin.com* 40 *rooms, 8 suites* ⊚ *No meals.*

You can paddle on the River Nidd in the pretty town of Knaresborough.

NIGHTLIFE AND THE ARTS

Harrogate Festival. This annual celebration of ballet, contemporary dance, music, film, comedy, street theater, and more takes place throughout July. ☎ *01423/562303* ⊕ *www.harrogate-festival.org.uk.*

KNARESBOROUGH

3 miles northeast of Harrogate, 17 miles west of York.

At the bottom of a precipitously deep rocky gorge along the River Nidd, the little town of Knaresborough could hardly be more photogenic. It's best seen from a train, crossing the high Victorian viaduct above. In summer you can rent a boat and row down the slow-moving river, or stroll through the town's square, site of a market since the early 14th century. On the top of the hill are the ruins of the castle where Richard II was imprisoned for a night in 1399.

GETTING HERE AND AROUND

Northern Rail trains leave from Leeds every 30 minutes (a 45-minute trip) and from York every hour or so (a 30-minute trip). Local buses travel here from nearby towns, but they're less frequent. By car, the village is on A59, and well signposted.

The village lies on a precipitous hill. The town is easily walkable, although it helps to be in good shape. There are clearly marked public parking areas.

EXPLORING

FAMILY **Mother Shipton's Cave.** Across the river from the center of town, this tour-ist attraction is tucked away in a pleasant park. According to local lore, the cave is the birthplace of the titular 16th-century alleged prophet-ess, who supposedly foretold such events as the defeat of the Spanish Armada. The mineral-rich well beside her cave is famed for its ability to turn most objects to stone in four months. Call ahead in winter. ⊠ *Pro-phesy Lodge, High Bridge* ☎ *01423/864600* ⊕ *www.mothershipton. co.uk* ☞ *£6* ☉ *Apr.–Oct., daily 10–5:30; Feb., weekends 10–4:30.*

RIPON

12 miles north of Knaresborough, 24 miles northwest of York.

Said to be England's second-oldest city and still one of its smallest, Ripon has been the site of a market since the 10th century, and prob-ably before. A basilica was built here in the 7th century, and its chapel remains within the existing building, which is a mostly 12th-century minster. The church was designated a cathedral in the mid-19th century, making Ripon technically a city despite its population of only about 16,000. Don't miss the Hornblower announcing he's on duty by blow-ing his horn at 9 pm every evening in the town square, an unbroken tradition that goes back 900 years. Market day, Thursday, is probably the best day to stop by.

GETTING HERE AND AROUND

Ripon is just off A1 via the A61, 12 miles north of Harrogate. There's no train service to Ripon, but local buses run from Harrogate several times a day.

EXPLORING

FAMILY **Newby Hall.** An early-18th-century house redecorated later in the same century by Robert Adam for his patron William Weddell, Newby Hall contains fine decorative art of its period, particularly ornamental plas-terwork and Chippendale furniture. The domed Sculpture Hall, devoted to Roman statuary, and the Tapestry Hall, boasting priceless Gobelin tapestries, are gorgeous. The 25 acres of gardens are justifiably famous; a double herbaceous border, which runs down to the river, separates garden "rooms," each flowering during a different season. A miniature railroad, playground, and pedal boats amuse kids. The house is 5 miles southeast of Ripon. Entry to the house is restricted to guided tours, offered April to September. ⊠ *Off A1, Skelton-on-Ure* ☎ *0845/450–4068* ⊕ *www.newbyhall.com* ☞ *£14; gardens only, £9.70* ☉ *Apr.–June and Sept., Tues.–Sun. and holiday Mon., 11–5:30; July and Aug. daily 11–5:30; last admission 30 mins before closing.*

Ripon Cathedral. Successive churches here were destroyed by the Vikings and the Normans. The current cathedral, dating from the 12th and 13th centuries, is notable for its finely carved choir stalls. The Saxon crypt (AD 672) used to house sacred relics but is now a series of empty chambers. ⊠ *Minster Rd.* ☎ *01765/603462* ⊕ *www.riponcathedral.org. uk* ☞ *Free; £5 donation suggested for guided tour* ☉ *Daily 8:30–6.*

12

Fodor's Choice ★ **Studley Royal Water Garden & Fountains Abbey.** You can easily spend a day at this UNESCO World Heritage Site, an 822-acre complex made up of an 18th-century water garden and deer park, a Jacobean mansion, and, on the banks of the River Skell, Fountains Abbey, the largest monastic ruins in Britain. Here a neoclassical vision of an ordered universe—with spectacular terraces, classical temples, and a grotto—blends with the majestic Gothic abbey, which was founded in 1132 and completed in the early 1500s. It housed Cistercian monks, called "White Monks" for the color of their robes, who devoted their lives to silence, prayer, and work. Of the surviving buildings, the lay brothers' echoing refectory and dormitory are the most complete. The 12th-century Fountains Mill, perhaps the best-preserved in England, displays reconstructed machinery (wool was the abbey's profitable business). The 17th-century Fountains Hall is partially built with stones taken from the abbey. The water garden and Fountains Abbey are 9 miles northwest of Knaresborough, 4 miles southwest of Ripon. ✉ *Off B6265* ☎ *01765/608888* 🌐 *www.nationaltrust.org.uk/fountainsabbey* 🎟 *£9.50* 🕓 *Apr.–Sept., daily 10–5; Oct. and Mar., daily 10–4; Nov.–Jan., Sat.–Thurs. 10–4.*

WHERE TO EAT AND STAY

For expanded hotel reviews, visit Fodors.com.

$$ BRITISH 🍴 **Lockwood's.** This family-run eatery with a bistro atmosphere (stripped-brick walls, wood floor, zinc-topped bar) serves breakfast, lunch, and dinner, specializing in simple classics made with local ingredients. Lunch ranges from sandwiches to salads; frequently changing dinner options include sea bass with shrimp and pureed Jerusalem artichokes, or pan-fried chicken with pigs in blankets. [$] *Average main: £15* ✉ *83 North St.* ☎ *01765/607555* 🌐 *www.lockwoodsrestaurant.co.uk* 🕓 *Closed Sun. and Mon.*

$$$ HOTEL Fodor's Choice ★ 🏨 **Swinton Park.** If you've ever wanted to experience the *Downton Abbey* lifestyle, head for this luxury hotel situated in a castle complete with battlements, a tower, and a turret. **Pros:** eye-popping castle; gorgeous rooms; attentive service. **Cons:** some rooms have better views than others; atmosphere is fairly formal. [$] *Rooms from: £195* ✉ *Swinton Park, Off A1, Masham* ☎ *01765/680900* 🌐 *www.swintonpark.com* 🛏 *25 rooms, 6 suites* 🍽 *Breakfast.*

CASTLE HOWARD

15 miles northeast of York, 12 miles southeast of Helmsley.

The Baroque grandeur of Castle Howard is without equal in northern England. The grounds, enhanced by groves of trees, a twinkling lake, and a perfect lawn, add to the splendor.

GETTING HERE AND AROUND

There's a daily scheduled bus service between Malton and Castle Howard, which is well outside any town and several miles off any public road. The nearest train stop is Malton, and you can take a taxi from there. By car, follow signs off A64 from York.

At Castle Howard, a baroque masterpiece, the splendor of the grounds matches the opulence of the sprawling house.

EXPLORING

FAMILY
Fodor's Choice
★

Castle Howard. Standing in the Howardian Hills to the west of Malton, Castle Howard is an outstanding example of English Baroque, with a distinctive roofline punctuated by a magnificent central dome. It served as Brideshead, the home of the fictional Flyte family in Evelyn Waugh's tale of aristocratic woe, *Brideshead Revisited,* in both the 1981 TV and 2008 film adaptations. The house was the first commission for playwright-turned-architect Sir John Vanbrugh, who, assisted by Nicholas Hawksmoor, designed it for the 3rd earl of Carlisle, a member of the Howard family. Started in 1701, the central portion took 25 years to complete, with a Palladian wing added subsequently, but the end result was a stately home of audacious grandeur.

A spectacular central hallway with soaring columns supporting a hand-painted ceiling dwarfs all visitors, and there's no shortage of spendor elsewhere: vast family portraits, intricate marble fireplaces, immense tapestries, Victorian silver on polished tables, and a great many marble busts. Outside, the neoclassical landscape of carefully arranged woods, lakes, and lawns led 18th-century *bon vivant* Horace Walpole to comment that a pheasant at Castle Howard lived better than a duke elsewhere. Hidden throughout the 1,000 acres of formal and woodland gardens are temples, statues, fountains, and a grand mausoleum—even a fanciful children's playground. Hourly tours of the grounds, included in the admission price, fill you in on more background and history. ⊠ *Off A64 and B1257, Malton, York* ☎ *01653/648333* ⊕ *www.castlehoward.co.uk* ✉ *£14; gardens only £9.50* ☉ *House late Mar.–Oct., daily 11–5:30; last admission at 4. Grounds daily 10–6:30 or dusk; last admission at 4:30.*

LEEDS AND BRONTË COUNTRY

The busy city of Leeds provides an obvious starting point for a tour of West Yorkshire. From here you can strike out for the traditional wool towns, such as Saltaire, a UNESCO-protected gem, and the Magna museum at Rotherham, which draws long lines for its surprisingly interesting exploration of steel production. But the main thrust of many visits to West Yorkshire is to the west of Leeds, where the stark hills north of the Calder Valley and south of the River Aire form the district immortalized in the equally unsparing novels of the Brontë sisters. Haworth, a gray-stone village, might have faded into obscurity were it not for the enduring fame of the literary sisters. Every summer, thousands toil up the steep main street to visit their former home, but to truly appreciate the setting that inspired their books you need to go farther afield to the ruined farm of Top Withins, which in popular mythology, if not in fact, was the model for Wuthering Heights.

LEEDS

25 miles southwest of York, 43 miles northeast of Manchester.

Once an industrial powerhouse, Leeds has reinvented itself as a vibrant dining, drinking, and shopping destination with numerous cafés with outdoor tables defying the northern weather, trendy restaurants, and sleek bars. A large student population keeps the town young and hip, supporting the city's good music shops and funky boutiques.

The 20th century was not kind to Leeds: World War II air raids destroyed the city's most distinguished landmarks, and in the 1960s urban planners replaced much of what was left with undistinguished modern buildings. The city is currently restoring its surviving Victorian buildings and is converting riverfront factories and warehouses into pricey loft apartments and offices buildings.

GETTING HERE AND AROUND

Leeds Bradford Airport, 8 miles northwest of the city, is the main gateway to this part of the country. National Express and Megabus have frequent buses here from London's Victoria Coach Station. The journey takes about four hours. East Coast trains depart from London's King's Cross Station to Leeds Station about every 30 minutes during the week. The trip takes about 2¼ hours. Leeds Station is in the middle of central Leeds and usually has a line of taxis waiting out front.

A city of nearly 750,000 people, Leeds has an efficient local bus service. Most visitors will never use it, as most sights are in the easily walkable downtown.

ESSENTIALS

Visitor Information Leeds Visitor Centre ⊠ *Leeds City Station* ☎ *0113/242–5242* ⊕ *www.visitleeds.co.uk.*

EXPLORING

TOP ATTRACTIONS

The Calls. East of Granary Wharf, the Calls has converted some of the old riverfront warehouses into snazzy bars and restaurants that enliven the cobbled streets. The best have pleasant terraces overlooking the river.

Harewood House. The home of the earl of Harewood, a cousin of the Queen, Harewood House (pronounced *har*-wood) is a spectacular neoclassical mansion built in 1759 by John Carr of York. Highlights include Robert Adam interiors, important paintings and ceramics, and a large, ravishingly beautiful collection of Chippendale furniture (Chippendale was born in nearby Otley), notably the magnificent State Bed. The Old Kitchen and Below Stairs exhibition illustrates life from the servants' point of view. Capability Brown designed the handsome grounds, and Charles Barry created a notable Italian garden with fountains in the 1840s. Also here are a bird garden with numerous rare and endangered species, and a playground. The house is 7 miles north of Leeds; you can take Harrogate & District Bus 36. ⊠ *Junction of A61 and A659, Harewood* ☎ *0113/218–1010* ⊕ *www.harewood. org* ☑ *£14* ⊗ *House Apr.–Oct., daily 11–4. Last admission 30 mins before closing. Gardens Apr.–Oct., daily 10–6; Nov., Feb., and Mar., daily 10–4.*

Leeds Art Gallery. Next door to the Victorian Town Hall, Yorkshire's most impressive art museum has a strong core collection of works by Courbet, Sisley, Constable, Crome, and the internationally acclaimed Yorkshire sculptor Henry Moore, who studied at the Leeds School of Art. The graceful statue on the steps outside the gallery is Moore's *Reclining Woman.* More works by Moore are at the adjacent **Henry Moore Institute,** which also has regular exhibitions of modern sculpture. The **Craft Centre and Design Gallery,** also in the museum, exhibits and sells fine contemporary crafts. ⊠ *The Headrow* ☎ *0113/247–8256* ⊕ *www.leeds.gov.uk/artgallery* ☑ *Free* ⊗ *Mon., Tues., and Thurs.–Sat. 10–5, Wed. noon–5, Sun. 1–5.*

QUICK BITES

New Conservatory. Step into to the cozy, book-lined New Conservatory for fresh sandwiches, hot dishes, and cakes. You can also sit and relax with a cup of tea or a glass of wine. ⊠ *The Albions, Albion Pl., off Briggate* ☎ *0113/246–1853.*

Fodor's Choice
★

Temple Newsam. One of Britain's great country houses, this huge Elizabethan and Jacobean building contains an impressive collections of furniture, paintings, and ceramics belonging to the city of Leeds. As the birthplace of Lord Darnley (1545–67), the doomed husband of Mary, Queen of Scots, it's rich in historical significance. Surrounding the house are 1,500 acres of parkland, farmland, lakes, and gardens, along with miles of woodland walks. The park and gardens were created by noted 18th-century landscape designer Capability Brown. Temple Newsam is 4 miles east of Leeds on A63; Buses 19, 40, and 163 leave from Leeds Central Bus Station every 30 minutes and stop at the Lidl Supermarket, a 25-minute walk from the house. ⊠ *Off Selby*

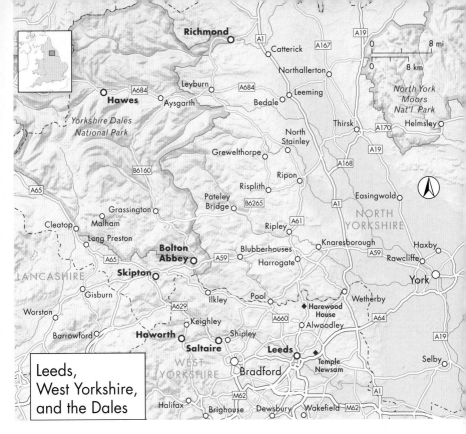

Leeds,
West Yorkshire,
and the Dales

Rd. ☎ 0113/264-7321 ⊕ *www.leeds.gov.uk/templenewsam* ✉ *House £3.70, farm £3.30, joint ticket £6.20* ☉ *House Apr.–Oct., Tues.–Sun. 10:30–5; Nov.–Mar., Tues.–Sun. 10:30–4; farm Apr.–Oct., 10–5; Nov.–Mar., 10–4. Last admission 45 mins before closing.*

WORTH NOTING

Granary Wharf. Once at the heart of Leeds's decaying industrial zone, this regenerated development in the Canal Basin along the River Aire is now a trendy hub of chic bars and pleasant cafés. Granary Wharf is reached via the Dark Arches where the River Aire flows under City Station.

Hepworth Wakefield. The largest purpose-built British gallery outside of London focuses on 20th-century British art, notably sculptors Henry Moore and Barbara Hepworth, with important works by both. The unique design of slightly skewed concrete building blocks, combined with the powerful permanent collection and exhibitions devoted to contemporary artists, has attracted interest from art lovers around the world. It's in the workaday West Yorkshire town of Wakefield, 12 miles south of Leeds off M1. ✉ *Gallery Walk, Wakefield* ☎ *01924/247360* ⊕ *www.hepworthwakefield.org* ✉ *Free* ☉ *Tues.–Sun. 10–5.*

OFF THE BEATEN PATH

Magna. A 45-minute drive south from Leeds to Rotherham brings Yorkshire's industrial past squarely into view in the form of Magna, a widely respected science museum housed in a former steelworks. Smoke, flames, and sparking electricity bring one of the original six arc furnaces roaring to life in a sound-and-light show. Four pavilions engagingly illustrate the use of fire, earth, air, and water in the production of steel. ✉ *Sheffield Rd., Junction 33 or 35 off M1, Rotherham* ☎ *01709/720002* 🌐 *www.visitmagna.co.uk* 🎫 *£11* 🕒 *Daily 10–5.*

FAMILY **Royal Armouries.** Much of the legendary arms and armor originally collected in the Tower of London fills the Royal Armouries, which occupies a redeveloped 13-acre dockland site 15 minutes from the city center. Five themed galleries—War, Tournament, Self-Defense, Hunting, and Arms and Armor of the Orient—trace the history of weaponry. The state-of-the-art building is stunningly designed: expect a full-size elephant in armor, models of warriors on horseback, and floor-to-ceiling tents, as well as spirited interactive displays and live demonstrations. Shoot a crossbow, direct operations on a battlefield, or, around Easter and the end of August, experience an Elizabethan joust. ✉ *Armouries Dr., off M1 or M621* ☎ *0113/220–1999* 🌐 *www.armouries.org.uk* 🎫 *Free* 🕒 *Daily 10–5.*

Yorkshire Sculpture Park. In the nearby town of Wakefield, this outdoor gallery sprawls across more than 500 acres of an 18th-century estate. The park and garden are filled with a carefully curated collection including works by Henry Moore and Barbara Hepworth, as well other respected artists such as Antony Gormley, Anthony Caro, and David Nash. You can get here easily from Leeds by train or car. ✉ *West Bretton, Wakefield* ☎ *01924/832631* 🌐 *www.ysp.co.uk* 🎫 *Free* 🕒 *Galleries Mar.–Oct., daily 10–5; Nov.–Feb., daily 10–4; grounds Mar.–Oct., daily 10–6; Nov.–Feb., daily 10–5:30.*

WHERE TO EAT

$$$ MODERN BRITISH 🍴 **Anthony's.** This is actually three eateries in one. Anthony's, the fine-dining restaurant, is in an art gallery-like space on the ground floor of the Corn Exchange. The chef takes many chances, and the results are hugely rewarding to lovers of creative cuisine. Main courses change frequently but can include rib-eye steak with baby squid and baby gem lettuce or a palate cleanser of black sesame-seed ice cream. There are fixed-price menus for lunch (three courses, £22.50) and dinner (six courses, £45). In the courtyard outside is a less formal cafe that serves sandwiches and salads, as well as fabulous homemade cupcakes with "infusions" of cappucino or lemon fizz. Upstairs there's a brasserie called Piazza by Anthony that serves grills and gastropub favorites and a patisserie in the Victoria Quarter shopping arcade. [$] *Average main: £25* ✉ *Corn Exchange, Call La.* ☎ *0113/245–5922* 🌐 *www.anthonysrestaurant.co.uk* 🕒 *Closed Sun. and Mon.*

$$ MODERN BRITISH 🍴 **Brasserie Forty 4.** This Brasserie is modern and buzzy, with friendly service and tasty food. There are two dining rooms, one with wood tables and terra-cotta walls, the other more formal with white tablecloths. Both have arched windows overlooking the river and in summer there's a deck for alfresco dining. The often-changing menu usually features appetizers like oxtail risotto with white truffle oil

12

or seared king scallops with cauliflower puree. Elegant main courses include chicken breast with wild mushrooms and leeks, or venison haunch and spinach in a black truffle sauce. On weekdays there's a three-course fixed-price menu for £23.95 that includes a bottle of wine. $ *Average main: £16* ⊠ *44 The Calls* ☎ *0113/234–3232* ⊕ *www. brasserie44.com.*

$ ✕ **The Cross Keys.** A former watering hole for foundry workers, this
BRITISH lovely old inn is now a warm gastropub with exposed brick and wood beams. The food is unfussy and reliably good, noted for its use of fresh, local ingredients. The menu inclines towards old favorites done right, like chicken breast in a red wine sauce, wild boar sausages and mashed potatoes, or beer-battered fish with fries. In summer, you can sit in a sunny courtyard with a glass of wine from the varied wine list or a pint of local ale. Best of all, the prices make it a good value. $ *Average main: £11* ⊠ *107 Water La.* ☎ *0113/243–3711* ⊕ *www. the-crosskeys.com.*

$ ✕ **Whitelocks.** Formally known as Whitelocks First City Luncheon Bar,
BRITISH this place claims to date back to 1718. Tucked away in a quiet alley off bustling Briggate, the narrow, atmospheric bar retains original features like beveled mirrors, thick wood beams, copper-topped tables, and mosaic tiles. It serves superior pub food with an emphasis on the local and seasonal, like pork terrine with pale-ale chutney or roast topside of local beef. Beers from local microbreweries are featured, and the prices are friendly. $ *Average main: £10* ⊠ *6–8 Turks Head Yard, off Briggate* ☎ *0113/245–3950.*

WHERE TO STAY

For expanded hotel reviews, visit Fodors.com.

$$ ⛨ **42 The Calls.** This high-tech, high-concept hotel in the trendy water-
HOTEL front area occupies a coverted 18th-century corn mill overlooking the river. **Pros:** riverside location; comfortable rooms; clever use of space. **Cons:** some find it too trendy; street noise on weekends. $ *Rooms from: £150* ⊠ *42 The Calls* ☎ *0113/244–0099* ⊕ *www.42thecalls.co.uk* ⥌ *41 rooms* ⦿*Breakfast.*

$$ ⛨ **Malmaison.** Once the headquarters of the local tram company, this
HOTEL Edwardian building has been reinvented as a funky hotel. **Pros:** friendly service; tasty restaurant; comfortable beds. **Cons:** some rooms on small side; front rooms may get street noise on weekends; worn public areas. $ *Rooms from: £100* ⊠ *1 Swinegate* ☎ *0113/398–1000* ⊕ *www. malmaison.com* ⥌ *100 rooms* ⦿*Breakfast.*

$ ⛨ **Quebecs.** This boutique hotel is full of elegant Victorian touches,
HOTEL especially the sweeping oak staircase illuminated by tall stained-glass windows. **Pros:** gorgeous building; stylish rooms; friendly service. **Cons:** limited parking; some rooms have drab outlooks. $ *Rooms from: £80* ⊠ *9 Quebec St.* ☎ *0113/244–8989* ⊕ *www.quebecshotel.co.uk* ⥌ *44 rooms, 7 suites* ⦿*Breakfast.*

NIGHTLIFE AND THE ARTS
NIGHTLIFE

At fashionable café-bars all over Leeds you can grab a bite or enjoy cappuccinos or designer beers until late into the night. There's no shortage of clubs, either: Leeds has one of the best party scenes outside London.

Mojo. This is a real rock-and-roll bar, with the music and the look to match. ⊠ *18 Merrion St.* ☎ *0845/611-8643* ⊕ *www.mojobar.co.uk.*

Norman Bar. This place has won over the local in-crowd with its weird and wonderful design incorporating curved walls. Thai food is another of the draws. ⊠ *36 Call La.* ☎ *0113/234–3988* ⊕ *www.normanbar.co.uk.*

The Ship. A tavern for 300 years, this is a friendly place to stop in for a quick drink or a tasty pub lunch. ⊠ *71A Briggate* ☎ *0113/246–8031* ⊕ *www.theshipleeds.co.uk.*

THE ARTS

Grand Theatre. A leading regional opera company, Opera North is based in Leeds at the Victorian-era Grand Theatre. Besides opera, the lavish neo-Gothic auditorium also plays host to touring musicals, ballet, and plays. ⊠ *Grand Theatre, 46 New Briggate* ☎ *0844/848–2700* ⊕ *www. leedsgrandtheatre.com.*

Town Hall. The Victorian Town Hall hosts an international concert season (October through May) that attracts top performers and conductors. ⊠ *The Headrow* ☎ *0113/224–3801* ⊕ *www.leedsconcertseason.com.*

West Yorkshire Playhouse. In the heart of Leed's cultural quarter, this ultramodern theater's adaptable space makes it eminently suitable for staging both new works and classics. ⊠ *Playhouse Sq., Quarry Hill* ☎ *0113/213–7700* ⊕ *www.wyp.org.uk.*

SHOPPING

Corn Exchange. Housed in a converted 19th-century mercantile exchange, this glass-roofed shopping mall has independent boutiques, laid-back restaurants, and specialty stores on three levels. ⊠ *Call La.* ☎ *0113/234–0363.*

Kirkgate Market. The city has some excellent markets, notably Kirkgate Market, an Edwardian beauty that's the largest in the north of England. ⊠ *34 George St.* ☎ *0113/378–1950* ⊗ *Closed Sun.*

Victoria Quarter. Notable for the soaring glass-covered arches of its beautiful-turn-of-the-century shopping arcades, the spiffy Victoria Quarter combines 19th-century design and 21st-century style. ⊠ *Briggate* ☎ *0113/245–5333.*

SALTAIRE

12 miles east of Leeds, 8 miles east of Haworth.

GETTING HERE AND AROUND

An old wool-market town, Saltaire has regular bus and train services from the nearby town of Bradford. Drivers should take A650 from Bradford and follow the signs.

ESSENTIALS

Visitor Information Saltaire Visitor Information Centre ✉ *Salt's Mill, Victoria Rd.* ☎ *01274/437942* ⊕ *www.visitsaltaire.com.*

EXPLORING

Fodor'sChoice **Saltaire.** A UNESCO World Heritage Site, the former model village of
★ Saltaire was built in the mid-19th century by textile magnate Sir Titus Salt. When he decided to relocate his factories from the dark mills of Bradford to the countryside, he hoped to create an ideal industrial community in which his workers would be happy. The Italianate village is remarkably well preserved, its former mills and houses now turned into shops, restaurants, and galleries. Part of Salt's Mill, built in 1853, resembles a palazzo. The largest factory in the world when it was built, today it holds an art gallery, along with crafts and furniture shops. One-hour guided tours (£4) of the village depart weekends and some holiday Mondays at 2 pm from the tourist information center. ✉ *A657.*

1853 Gallery. This gallery is devoted to a remarkable exhibition of some 400 works by Bradford-born artist David Hockney. There are two restaurants on-site. ✉ *Salt's Mill, Victoria Rd.* ☎ *01274/531163* 🔁 *Free* ☾ *Weekdays 10–5:30, weekends 10–6.*

OFF THE
BEATEN
PATH

National Media Museum. Bradford, 10 miles west of Leeds, is known for this renowned museum, which traces the history of photographic media. It's a huge and hugely entertaining place, with seven galleries displaying the world's first photographic negative, the latest digital imaging, an Imax theater, and everything between. ■TIP➔ It's popular with children, so come early or late in the day. ✉ *Pictureville, off Prince's Way, Bradford* ☎ *01274/202030, 0870/701–0200* ⊕ *www. nationalmediamuseum.org.uk* 🔁 *Free* ☾ *Daily 10–6.*

HAWORTH: HEART OF BRONTË COUNTRY

8 miles west of Saltaire.

Whatever Haworth might have been in the past, today it's Brontë country. This old stone-built textile village on the edge of the Yorkshire Moors long ago gave up its own personality and allowed itself to be taken over by the literary sisters, their powerful novels, and their legions of fans. In 1820, when Anne, Emily, and Charlotte were very young, their father relocated them and their other three siblings away from their old home in Bradford to Haworth. The sisters—Emily (author of *Wuthering Heights*, 1847), Charlotte (*Jane Eyre*, 1847), and Anne (*The Tenant of Wildfell Hall*, 1848) were all affected by the stark, dramatic countryside.

These days, it seems that every building they ever glanced at has been turned into a memorial, shop, or museum. The Haworth Visitor Center has good information about accommodations, maps, books on the Brontës, and inexpensive leaflets to help you find your way to such outlying *Wuthering Heights* sites as Ponden Hall (Thrushcross Grange) and Ponden Kirk (Penistone Crag).

The streets and houses of Haworth look much as they did when the Brontë sisters lived and wrote their famous novels in this village near the moors.

GETTING HERE AND AROUND

To reach Haworth by bus or train, buy a Metro Day Rover for bus and rail (£7.50) and take the Metro train from Leeds train station to Keighley, where you change to a Keighley & District bus to Haworth. On weekends you can opt to take the Keighley and Worth Valley Railway to continue on to Haworth.

By car, Haworth is an easy 25-mile drive on A629 from Leeds; it's well signposted, and there's plenty of cheap parking in town.

ESSENTIALS

Visitor Information Haworth Visitor Information Centre ⊠ *2–4 Westlane* ☎ *01535/642329.*

EXPLORING

Fodor'sChoice
★

Brontë Parsonage Museum. The best of Haworth's Brontë sights is this somber Georgian house where the sisters grew up. It displays original furniture (some bought by Charlotte after the success of *Jane Eyre*), portraits, and books. The Brontës moved here when the Reverend Patrick Brontë was appointed to the local church, but tragedy soon struck—his wife, Maria, and their two eldest children died within five years. The museum explores the family's tragic story, bringing it to life with a strong collection of enchanting mementos of the four children. These include tiny books they made when they were still very young; Charlotte's wedding bonnet; and the sisters' spidery, youthful graffiti on the nursery wall. Branwell, the Brontës' only brother, painted several of the portraits on display. ⊠ *Church St.* ☎ *01535/642323* ⊕ *www.bronte. org.uk* ⊠ *£7* ⊙ *Apr.–Sept., daily 10–5:30; Oct.–Mar., daily 11–5; last admission 30 mins before closing.*

12

LANDSCAPE AS MUSE

The rugged Yorkshire Moors helped inspire Emily Brontë's 1847 *Wuthering Heights*; if ever a work of fiction grew out of the landscape in which its author lived, it was surely this. "My sister Emily loved the moors," wrote Charlotte. "Flowers brighter than the rose bloomed in the blackest of the heath for her; out of a sullen hollow in a livid hillside her mind could make an Eden. She found in the bleak solitude many and dear delights; and not the least and best loved was liberty."

Brontë Waterfall. If you have the time, pack a lunch and walk for 2¾ miles or so from Haworth along a field path, a lane, and a moorland track to the lovely, isolated waterfall that has, inevitably, been renamed in honor of the sisters. It was one of their favorite haunts, which they wrote about in poems and letters.

FAMILY **Keighley and Worth Valley Railway.** On this gorgeous 5-mile-long branch line, Haworth is one stop along the route on which handsome steam engines carry passengers between Keighley and Oxenhope. On special days, family fairs en route add to the fun. ✉ *Haworth Station, Station Rd.* ☎ *01535/645214* 🌐 *www.kwvr.co.uk* 🎫 *£10 round-trip, £15 Day Rover ticket* 🕒 *Sept.–May, weekends; June–Aug., daily.*

Main Street. Haworth's steep, cobbled high street has changed little in outward appearance since the early 19th century, but it now acts as a funnel for crowds heading for points of interest: the **Black Bull** pub, where the reprobate Branwell Brontë drank himself into an early grave; the former **post office** (now a bookshop) from which Charlotte, Emily, and Anne sent their manuscripts to their London publishers; and the **church**, with its atmospheric graveyard (Charlotte and Emily are buried in the family vault inside the church; Anne is buried in Scarborough).

Top Withins. A ruined, gloomy mansion on a bleak hilltop farm 3 miles from Haworth, Top Withins is often taken to be the inspiration for the fictional Wuthering Heights. Brontë scholars say it probably isn't; even in its heyday, the house never fit the book's description of Heathcliff's lair. Still, it's an inspirational walk across the moors. There and back from Haworth is a 3½-hour walk along a well-marked footpath that goes past the Brontë waterfall. **TIP→ If you've read *Wuthering Heights*, you don't need to be reminded to wear sturdy shoes and protective clothing.**

WHERE TO STAY

For expanded hotel reviews, visit Fodors.com.

$ B&B/INN 🏨 **Aitches.** In a 19th-century stone house very close to the Brontë Parsonage, this intimate B&B has cozy guest rooms decorated with pine furnishings and colorful quilts. **Pros:** excellent food; friendly staff. **Cons:** the traditional decor won't appeal to everyone. [$] *Rooms from: £60* ✉ *11 West La.* ☎ *01535/642501* 🌐 *www.aitches.co.uk* 🛏 *5 rooms* 🍴 *Breakfast.*

$ B&B/INN 🏨 **Ashmount Country House.** A short walk from the Parsonage, this charming stone building was once home to the Brontë sisters' physician, Amos Ingham. **Pros:** lovely period building; ideal location; great views. **Cons:** books up in advance. [$] *Rooms from: £95* ✉ *Mytholmes La.* ☎ *01535/645726* 🌐 *www.ashmounthaworth.co.uk* 🛏 *12 rooms* 🍴 *Breakfast.*

THE YORKSHIRE DALES

To the west of the North York Moors, this landscape has been shaped by limestone: lush green valleys (known as *dales*, the Viking word for valley) lie between white limestone scars (cliffs), while broad uplands are punctuated with dark fells (crags). The limestone cliffs, filled with caves, invite exploration.

As well as dramatic landscapes like the spectacular cliffs and gorges at Malham Cove and Gordale Scar, the area has some breathtaking waterfalls. Ruined priories, narrow roads, drystone walls made without mortar, and babbling rivers make for a quintessentially English landscape, full of paths and trails to explore.

BOLTON ABBEY

12 miles north of Haworth, 24 miles northwest of Leeds.

A leafy, picturesque village amid the rolling hills of the Yorkshire Dales, Bolton Abbey is a famously attractive town with a stone church and an evocative ruined priory. Much of the area is still technically owned by the duke of Devonshire, who has a huge estate nearby—a lingering reminder of the country's feudal past.

GETTING HERE AND AROUND

Bolton Abbey, off the A59 between Skipton and Harrogate, is best reached by car.

EXPLORING

Bolton Priory. Some of the loveliest Wharfedale scenery comes into view around Bolton Priory, the 13th-century ruins of an Augustinian priory that sit on a grassy embankment over a great curve of the River Wharfe. The ruins were immortalized by J.M.W. Turner, who was inspired to create a number of watercolors of the abbey and nearby sites. Close to Bolton Priory, surrounded by romantic woodland scenery, the River Wharfe plunges through a narrow chasm in the rocks (called the Strid) before reaching **Barden Tower**, a medieval hunting lodge. This lodge is now a ruin and can be visited just as easily as Bolton Priory, in whose grounds it stands. The priory is just a short walk or drive from the village of Bolton Abbey. You can visit the priory church on the Bolton Abbey estate, which is owned by the duke of Devonshire. ⊠ *B6160, off A59* ☏ *01756/718009* ⊕ *www.boltonabbey.com* ✉ *Free* ⊙ *Daily 9–dusk.*

Embsay and Bolton Abbey Steam Railway. You can take a ride on this scenic railway, which has a station in Bolton Abbey. Hours vary greatly, so it's best to call ahead. ⊠ *Bolton Abbey Station, off A59* ☏ *01756/710614, 01756/795189 recorded timetable* ⊕ *www.embsayboltonabbeyrailway. org.uk* ✉ *£10* ⊙ *Mar., and early-mid. Nov., Sun. only; Apr.–July, Sept., and Oct., Tues. and weekends; Aug., daily; Dec., weekends only.*

WHERE TO STAY

For expanded hotel reviews, visit Fodors.com.

$$$$ 🍽 **Devonshire Arms Country House Hotel & Spa.** Originally an 18th-century
HOTEL   coaching inn, this luxurious country-house hotel sits near the River Wharfe, an easy walk from Bolton Abbey. **Pros:** one of the region's

The imposing ruins of Bolton Priory provide a scenic backdrop for a walk along the River Wharfe.

best hotels; real country-house atmosphere. **Cons:** you pay for all that charm; some new-wing rooms small. [$] *Rooms from: £250* ✉ *B6160, off A59* ☎ *01756/710441* 🌐 *www.thedevonshirearms.co.uk* 🛏 *37 rooms, 3 suites* 🍴 *Breakfast.*

SKIPTON

6 miles west of Bolton Abbey, 12 miles north of Haworth, 22 miles west of Harrogate.

Skipton in Airedale, capital of the limestone district of Craven, is a country market town with as many farmers as visitors milling in the streets. There are markets Monday, Wednesday, Friday, and Saturday, with a farmers' market on Sunday, and shops selling local produce predominate.

GETTING HERE AND AROUND

Skipton is off A59 and A65 at the southern edge of the Yorkshire Dales National Park. From Leeds, First Leeds buses run regularly to Skipton. Little Red Bus buses depart once a day on Saturdays from Harrogate. There are regular trains from Leeds; the journey takes about 40 minutes.

ESSENTIALS

Visitor Information Skipton Tourist Information Centre ✉ *Town Hall, High St.* ☎ *01756/792809* 🌐 *www.skiptononline.co.uk* 🕒 *Daily 9:30–4.*

EXPLORING

Grassington National Park Centre. This visitor center 10 miles north of Skipton has guidebooks, maps, and bus schedules to help you enjoy a day in the Yorkshire Dales National Park. Grassington is deep in the Dales on the tiny B6265, also known as the Grassington Road; buses travel here from nearby towns. A small stone village, it makes a good base for exploring Upper Wharfedale. The Dales Way footpath passes through the village, where there are stores, pubs, and cafés. In summer it becomes overwhelmed by day-trippers and hikers, but you can escape them on the many local walks. ✉ *Colvend, Hebdon Rd., Grassington* ☎ *01756/751690* 🌐 *www.yorkshiredales.org.uk* 🕒 *Apr.–Oct., daily 10–5; Nov.–Dec., Feb.–Mar., Sat.–Sun. 10–4; Closed Jan.*

Skipton Castle. Built by the Normans in 1190 and largely unaltered since the 17th century, Skipton Castle is a remarkably well-preserved medieval castle. After the Battle of Marston Moor during the Civil War, it remained the only Royalist stronghold in the north of England. So sturdy was the squat little fortification with its rounded battlements (in some places the walls are 12 feet thick) that Oliver Cromwell ordered that the roof be removed, as it had survived one bombardment after another during a three-year siege. After the war the castle's owner, Lady Anne Clifford, asked if she could replace the roof, so Cromwell passed an Act of Parliament to allow her do so, stipulating the roof couldn't be strong enough to withstand cannon fire. The Act was finally repealed in the 1970s in order for the roof to be repaired. In the central courtyard a yew tree planted more than 300 years ago by Lady Anne herself, to mark the castle's recovery from its Civil War damage, is still flourishing. ✉ *The Bailey* ☎ *01756/792442* 🌐 *www.skiptoncastle.co.uk* 🎟 *£7* 🕒 *Mar.–Sept., Mon.–Sat. 10–6, Sun. noon–6; Oct.–Feb., Mon.–Sat. 10–4, Sun. noon–4.*

WHERE TO EAT AND STAY

For expanded hotel reviews, visit Fodors.com.

$$ MODERN BRITISH 🍴 **Angel Inn.** The hidden-away hamlet of Hetton is often filled with cars belonging to diners at the Angel Inn, such is the attraction of this casual brasserie and more formal restaurant. Both specialize in locally sourced seasonal food, such as beautifully prepared roast lamb, beef, and seafood. Two-course set-price menus are £15.95, three courses are £19.95. The ancient stone barn across the road has five well-equipped guest rooms decorated in an unfussy country style (£150) with another four contemporary bedrooms in a more modern building. The inn is 5 miles north of Skipton. [$] *Average main: £15* ✉ *Off B6265, Hetton* ☎ *01756/730263* 🌐 *www.angelhetton.co.uk.*

$ BRITISH 🍴 **Devonshire Hotel.** This traditional inn makes a comfortable rural dining spot, with its oak-paneled dining room aglow with flickering candles. Local lamb, beef, and dishes such as creamy fish pie appear on the menu with fresh local vegetables. There are also seven beautifully decorated rooms and one suite with a mix of antiques and modern furniture (£75). The inn is 10 miles north of Skipton in the town of Grassington. [$] *Average main: £12* ✉ *27 Main St., Grassington* ☎ *01756/752525* 🌐 *www.thedevonshirehotel.co.uk.*

$ B&B/INN 🏨 **Ashfield House.** Three converted 17th-century stone cottages, once the homes of Grassington lead miners, make up this well-run small hotel off the main street. **Pros:** charming cottages; gorgeous gardens; warm service. **Cons:** decor on the fussy side; not a lot of amenities; parking can be tricky. [$] *Rooms from: £50* ✉ *3 Summers Fold, Grassington* ☎ *01756/752584* 🌐 *www.ashfieldhouse.co.uk* 🛏 *7 rooms, 1 suite* 🍽 *Breakfast.*

$$$ B&B/INN 🏨 **The Devonshire Fell.** This more casual sister property of the Devonshire Arms down the road (guests have access to the larger property's spa and hiking trails) boasts outstanding views over a particularly lovely part of the Yorkshire Dales. **Pros:** lovely views; excellent location; tasty restaurant. **Cons:** skimpy complimentary breakfast; casual service; poor cell phone service. [$] *Rooms from: £169* ✉ *Off B6160, Burnsall* ☎ *01756/729000* 🌐 *www.devonshirefell.co.uk* 🛏 *12 rooms.*

SPORTS AND THE OUTDOORS

Avid summer hikers descend in droves on Malham, 12 miles northwest of Skipton, to tour the remarkable limestone formations. Malham Cove, a huge, 260-foot-high natural rock amphitheater, is a mile north of the village and provides the easiest local walk. Taking the 420 steps up to the top is a brutal climb, though you'll be rewarded by magnificent views.

At Gordale Scar, a deep natural chasm between overhanging limestone cliffs, the white waters of a moorland stream plunge 300 feet. It's a mile northeast of Malham by a lovely riverside path.

A walk of more than 3 miles north leads to Malham Tarn, an attractive lake on a slate bed in windswept isolation.

Malham National Park Centre. With informative displays, Malham's National Park Centre gives you some ideas for what to see and do, both in town and in the Yorkshire Dales National Park. You can also get a list of bed and breakfasts and pub accommodations. ✉ *Chapel Gate, Malham* ☎ *01729/833201* 🌐 *www.yorkshiredales.org.uk* 🕒 *Apr.–Oct., daily 10–5; Nov.–Mar., hrs vary.*

HAWES

30 miles north of Skipton.

The best time to visit the so-called cheesiest town in Yorkshire is on Tuesday, when farmers crowd into town for the weekly market. Crumbly, white Wensleydale cheese has been made in the valley for centuries, and it's sold in local stores and at the market. Allow time to explore the cobbled side streets, some of which are filled with antiques shops and tearooms.

GETTING HERE AND AROUND

Hawes is high in the moors on A684. To get here from Grassington, take the B6160 north for 23 miles. There's no train service, but buses travel from Leeds throughout the day on summer weekends.

EXPLORING

Dales Countryside Museum. In the same old train station as the Hawes National Park Information Centre, this museum traces life in the dales past and present. A traditional rope-making shop opposite also welcomes visitors. ✉ *Station Yard, Burtersett Rd.* ☎ *01969/667494* 🌐 *www.yorkshiredales.org.uk* 🎫 *Museum £4* 🕒 *Apr.–Oct., daily 10–5; Nov.–Dec. and Feb., daily 10–4. Last entry 1 hr before closing.*

Wensleydale Creamery. In a working dairy, this museum tells the story of the famed local cheese so beloved by the popular animated characters Wallace and Gromit. You can watch production (best seen between 10 and 2) from the viewing gallery, and then taste (and buy) the output in the excellent cheese shop. A restaurant offers plenty of samples—try Wensleydale smoked, with ginger, or with apple pie. ⊠ *Gayle La.* ☎ *01969/667664* ⊕ *www.wensleydale.co.uk* ⊡ *Tour £2.50* ⊘ *Museum daily 10-4; shop daily 10–5.*

RICHMOND

24 miles northeast of Hawes.

Tucked into a bend above the foaming River Swale, Richmond has a picturesque network of narrow Georgian streets and terraces opening onto a large cobbled marketplace that dates back to medieval times. The town's history can be traced to the late 11th century, when the Normans swept in, determined to subdue the local population and establish their rule in the north. They built the mighty castle whose massive keep still dominates the skyline.

GETTING HERE AND AROUND

East Coast Trains run regularly from Leeds and from London's King's Cross to the nearest station, Darlington. From here take the No. 27 bus that runs every 30 minutes. The journey from London takes around 2½ hours, from Leeds it takes about 1½ hours. By car, Richmond is on the rural B6274—follow signs off A1.

ESSENTIALS

Visitor Information Richmond Tourist Information Centre ⊠ *Friary Gardens, Victoria Rd.* ☎ *01748/823316* ⊕ *www.northyorks.gov.uk.*

EXPLORING

Georgian Theatre Royal. A jewel box built in 1788 and still an active community playhouse, this Georgian theatre/museum retains original features such as the wooden seating from which patrons watched 18th century Shakespearean actor David Garrick. During the hourly tours from Monday to Saturday between 10 and 4 (except January), you can see Britain's oldest painted scenery dating back to 1836 and try on theatrical costumes. ⊠ *Victoria Rd.* ☎ *01748/823710* ⊕ *www. georgiantheatreroyal.co.uk* ⊡ *£3.50 suggested donation* ⊘ *Museum early-Feb.–Dec., Mon.–Sat. 10–4:30.*

Richmond Castle. The 12th-century great keep of this castle, considered to be one of the finest examples of a Norman fortress in England, towers 100 feet above the river. There are excellent views of the countryside, once you climb the 130 steps to the top. Originally built around 1071 by the first earl of Richmond, the castle retains much of its curtain wall and three chapels. There's also an even earlier, two-story structure known as Scolland's Hall, which was built in the 11th century and is believed to be the oldest great hall in England. During World War I, conscientious objectors were imprisoned in the castle, and you can still see their graffiti. A path along the river leads to the ruins of golden-stone Easby Abbey. One historical note: when Henry Tudor (son of the earl of Richmond) became Henry VII in 1485, he began calling his palace in southwest London after the site of his family seat, leading to that part of the city becoming known as Richmond. ✉ *Riverside Rd.* ☎ *01748/822493* 🌐 *www.english-heritage.org.uk* 🎫 *£4.80* ⏲ *Apr.–Sept., daily 10–6; Oct.–Mar., Thurs.–Mon. 10–4.*

WHERE TO EAT AND STAY

For expanded hotel reviews, visit Fodors.com.

$$ BRITISH 🍴 **Shoulder of Mutton Inn.** In an18th-century inn on the outskirts of an unspoiled country village, this cozy restaurant has sweeping views of the Dales. Exposed stone walls, open fireplaces, and original oak beams contribute to an atmosphere that is traditional but not fusty, a theme continued in the satisfying food. Incorporating local ingredients whenever possible, main courses include grilled cod with a crab, lime, and coconut crust and Gressingham duck breast in a Madeira sauce. A lighter bar menu lists dishes such as fish cakes and a vegetarian pot pie. Dinner is served between 6:30 and 8:45. The inn's five rooms (from £65) are simple but comfortable. (Just to confuse things, there's a Shoulder of Mutton pub in Middleton Tyas, also outside Richmond, that serves highly-regarded pub food.) [$] *Average main: £15* ✉ *Kirby Hill* ☎ *01748/822772* 🌐 *www.shoulderofmutton.net* ⏲ *Restaurant closed Mon. and Tues. No lunch weekdays.*

$$ HOTEL 🏨 **Frenchgate.** This three-story Georgian town house on a quiet cobbled street has a bright and welcoming interior and a secluded walled garden for summer days. **Pros:** lovely gardens; good food; luxurious bathrooms. **Cons:** some bedrooms not as nice as others. [$] *Rooms from: £118* ✉ *59–61 Frenchgate* ☎ *01748/822087* 🌐 *www.thefrenchgate.co.uk* 🛏 *9 rooms* 🍽 *Breakfast.*

$$ B&B/INN 🏨 **Millgate House.** This 18th-century house in the center of Richmond has been beautifully restored, as you'll note from the elegant dining room and sitting room. **Pros:** central location; elegant atmosphere; plenty of privacy. **Cons:** rooms can be a bit chilly. [$] *Rooms from: £110* ✉ *3 Millgate* ☎ *01748/823571* 🌐 *www.millgatehouse.com* 🛏 *3 rooms, 2 apartments.* 🍽 *Breakfast.*

THE NORTH YORK MOORS

The North York Moors are a dramatic swath of high moorland starting 25 miles north of the city of York and stretching east to the coast and west to the Cleveland Hills. Only a few pockets remain of the dense forest that once covered the area. The transformation began during the Middle Ages, when the monks of Rievaulx and Whitby abbeys began raising huge flocks of sheep. Over the course of centuries, the sheep have kept the moors deforested, which ensures that the pink heather on which they feed spreads lushly across the hills. A series of isolated, medieval "standing stones" that once served as signposts on the paths between the abbeys are still handy for hikers.

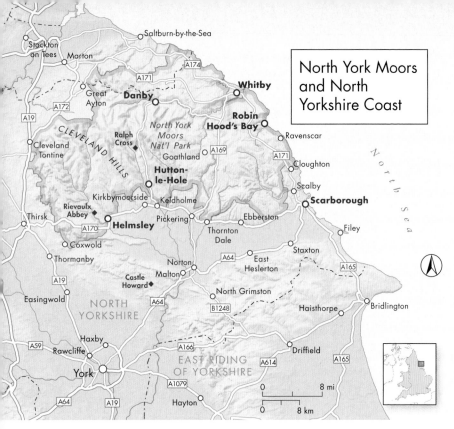

For more than four decades the area has been a national park, ensuring the protection of the bleak moors and grassy valleys that shelter brownstone villages and hamlets. Minor roads and tracks crisscross the hills, but there's no single, obvious route through the region. You can approach from York; another approach is from the coast at Whitby, along the Esk Valley to Danby, which is also accessible on the Esk Valley branch-train line running between Middlesbrough and Whitby. From Danby, minor roads run south over the high moors reaching Hutton-le-Hole, beyond which main roads lead to such interesting market towns as Helmsley, on the moors' edge. Completing the route in this direction leaves you with an easy side trip to Castle Howard before returning to York.

DANBY

49 miles northeast of York, 15 miles west of Whitby.

The old stone village of Danby nestles in the green Esk valley, a short walk from the summit of the moors. It's been settled since Viking times—Danby means "village where the Danes lived"—and these days it's home to the main information center for Moors National Park. There's also a pub and a cozy bakery with a tearoom. Bring hiking boots and within 10 minutes you can be surrounded by moorland looking down on the village below.

GETTING HERE AND AROUND

From York, take A64 to A169 and then follow the signs across the moor. Northern Rail travels to Danby station throughout the day from nearby towns. To get here from Whitby, take A171 west and turn north for Danby after 12 miles, after which it's a 3-mile drive over Danby Low Moor to the village.

EXPLORING

Moors National Park Centre. In a house on the eastern outskirts of Danby, the North York Moors National Park Centre interests gardeners with its extensive displays of local flora and fauna. There's a tearoom, a picnic area, a gallery of changing exhibits of work by local artists, and a beautiful play area for kids. ⊠ *Danby Lodge, Lodge La.* ☎ *01439/772737* ⊕ *www.northyorkmoors.org.uk* ✆ *Free* ☉ *Jan. and Feb., weekends 11–4; Mar., Nov., and Dec., daily 11–4; Apr.–Oct., daily 10–5.*

EN ROUTE From Danby take the road due west for 2 miles to Castleton, and then turn south over the top of the moors toward Hutton-le-Hole. The narrow road offers magnificent views over Moors National Park, especially at the old stone **Ralph Cross** (5 miles), which marks the park's highest point. Drive carefully: sheep dodging is a necessary skill.

HUTTON-LE-HOLE

13 miles south of Danby.

Sleepy Hutton-le-Hole is a charming little place based around a wide village green, with fluffy sheep snoozing in the shade of stone cottages. Unfortunately, it can be unbearably crowded in summer. You can always keep driving to either the charming nearby village of Thorton-le-Dale or to the medieval market towns of Helmsley or Pickering.

GETTING HERE AND AROUND

Hutton-le-Hole is on the moors off A170. It has no train station, and is only accessible by bus in summer when the Yorkshire Coastliner travels between the small towns in the region.

EXPLORING

Ryedale Folk Museum. The excellent open-air Ryedale Folk Museum lets you wander among more than 20 historic buildings, including a medieval crofter's cottage, a Tudor manor house, a 16th-century glass kiln, a 19th-century blacksmith's forge, and other agricultural and craft-related structures. There are also interesting craft demonstrations. ⊠ *Off A170* ☎ *01751/417367* ⊕ *www.ryedalefolkmuseum.co.uk* ✆ *£7* ☉ *Mid-Jan.–mid-Dec., daily 10–5:30 or dusk.*

HELMSLEY

8 miles southwest of Hutton-le-Hole, 27 miles north of York.

The market town of Helmsley, with its flowering window boxes, stone cottages, churchyard, and arched bridges leading across streams, is the perfect place to spend a relaxing afternoon. You can while away a few hours lingering in its tea shops and tiny boutiques or exploring the craggy remains of its Norman castle. Market day is Friday. Nearby are the impressive ruins of Rievaulx Abbey.

GETTING HERE AND AROUND

There's no train station in Helmsley, but it's served by bus from Scarborough. By car, Helmsley is on A170.

ESSENTIALS

Visitor Information Helmsley Tourist Information Centre ✉ *Castle Gate* ☎ *01439/770173* ⊕ *www.ryedale.gov.uk* ⊘ *Daily 10–5.*

EXPLORING

Fodor'sChoice
★
Rievaulx. The perfect marriage of architecture and countryside, Rievaulx (pronounced ree-*voh*) Abbey has a dramatic setting 2 miles northwest of Helmsley, its soaring arches built to precisely frame a forested hillside rushing down to the River Rye. A French Cistercian sect founded this abbey in 1132, and the monks' life of isolation didn't prevent them from being active in the wool trade. By the end of the 13th century the abbey was massively wealthy and the evocative ruins give a good indication of how vast it once was. Medieval mosaic tiling can still be seen here and there, and large parts of the symmetrical cloisters remain. At the entrance to the Chapter House is the original shrine of the first abbot, William.

By the time of Henry VIII, the abbey had shrunk dramatically; only 20 or so monks lived here when the king's soldiers arrived to destroy the building in 1538. After that, the earl of Rutland owned Rievaulx, and he did his best to demolish what was left, with villagers carting away stones from the abbey to build their houses. What remains is a beautiful ghost of the magnificent building that once stood here. From Rievaulx Abbey it's a short climb or drive up to the hill to Rievaulx Terrace, an 18th-century escarpment with a magnificent view of the abbey. At either end of the woodland walk are two mid-18th-century follies in the style of small Palladian temples. ✉ *Off B1257* ☎ *01439/798228* ⊕ *www.english-heritage.org.uk* ⊠ *£6* ⊘ *Apr.–Sept., daily 10–6; Oct., daily 10–5; Nov.–Mar., weekends 10–4.*

Shandy Hall. The Brontës aren't the only literary lions to emerge from this part of Yorkshire. With his eccentric, satirical book *The Life and Opinions of Tristam Shandy, Gentleman,* Laurence Sterne experimented with style even as the modern novel was still emerging as a literary form. Working as the local parson (despite the book's bawdy humor), Sterne lived and wrote in this delightful 15th-century house with 18th-century additions and is buried in the local church. Restored in the 1990s, it contains the world's largest collection of Sterne's work. There are also two acres of grounds, including a walled rose garden. ✉ *Off A19, Coxwold* ☎ *01347/866465* ⊕ *www.laurencesternetrust.*

The ruins of Rievaulx Abbey, which was enormously wealthy in medieval times because of the wool trade, show how large the abbey was.

org.uk ✉*£4.50* ⊗ *House: May–Sept., Wed., 2–4:30, Sun. 2:30–4:30. Gardens: May–Sept., Sun.–Fri., 11–4:30.*

WHERE TO STAY

For expanded hotel reviews, visit Fodors.com.

$$ ⚐ **Black Swan Hotel.** A splendid base for exploring the area, this ivy-cov-
HOTEL ered property sits on the edge of Helmsley's market square. **Pros:** historic charm; great location. **Cons:** decor is a bit old-fashioned; bathrooms on small side. $ *Rooms from: £144* ⊠ *Market Pl.* ☎*01439/770466* ⊕ *www.blackswan-helmsley.co.uk* ⤳*45 rooms* ⦿*Breakfast.*

$ ⚐ **No. 54.** Tea and cakes provide a tasty welcome at this B&B in a stone
B&B/INN cottage just off the market square. **Pros:** tasty treats on arrival; comfy beds; pretty courtyard. **Cons:** small rooms; some noise between rooms. $ *Rooms from: £90* ⊠ *54 Bondgate* ☎*01439/771533* ⊕ *www.no54. co.uk* ⤳*3 rooms* ⦿*Breakfast.*

SPORTS AND THE OUTDOORS

Cleveland Way. On the southern edge of the moors, Helmsley is the starting point of the long-distance moor-and-coastal footpath known as the Cleveland Way. Boots go on at the old cross in the market square, then it's 50 miles or so across the moors to the coast, followed by a similar distance south to Filey along the cliffs. The footpath is 110 miles long and takes around nine days start to finish. The trail passes close to Rievaulx Abbey, a few miles outside town. ⊕*www. nationaltrail.co.uk.*

Visiting Yorkshire's Monastic Past

Today the ruined abbeys at Fountains, Rievaulx, and Whitby are top attractions where you can learn about the religious life and business activities of Yorkshire's great monasteries, and the political machinations that destroyed them. They vividly evoke daily life during the Middle Ages.

THE FALL OF THE MONASTERIES
The sheer number of what were once richly decorated monastic buildings is a testament to the power of the Catholic monks of medieval Yorkshire. They became some of the richest in Europe by virtue of the international wool trade that they

conducted from these vast estates with the help of lay workers. The buildings are now mostly romantic ruins, a result of the dissolution of the monasteries during the 16th century following Henry VIII's establishment of the Church of England (with himself as its head) in 1534. This was both retaliation against the Catholic Church for denying him a divorce (and thus, in his view, a male heir) and a way of appropriating the monasteries' wealth. By 1540 no monasteries remained in England; the king confiscated all their property, redistributed their land, and destroyed or gave away many buildings.

THE NORTH YORKSHIRE COAST

The coastline of the North York Moors offers a dramatic view of spectacular white cliffs covered in pink heather, which plummet down to the dark sea hundreds of feet below. The red roofs of Robin Hood's Bay, the sharply curved bay at Whitby, and the gold-and-white buildings of Scarborough capture the imagination at first sight. Most coastal towns still support an active fishing industry, and every harbor offers fishing and leisure trips throughout summer. Beaches at Scarborough and Whitby have patrolled areas: swim between the red-and-yellow flags, and don't swim when a red flag is flying. All the North Sea beaches are ideal for fossil hunting and seashell collecting.

SCARBOROUGH

44 miles northeast of York.

There's no Scarborough Fair, and historians are divided on whether there ever was one, but don't let that stop you from heading to this classic English seaside resort on the North Sea. The liveliest tourist action is on South Bay, a riot of tacky arcades, ice-cream stands, and stores selling "rock" (luridly colored hard candy). Above the former spa are the lemon-hued Victorian and Regency terraces of the genteel South Cliff Promenade, with its views across Cayton Bay and a Victorian funicular linking it to the South Sands below. The South Bay and quieter North Bay are divided by a rocky headland on which sits the ruins of an 11th-century castle. The huddle of streets, alleyways, and red-roof cottages around the harbor gives an idea of what the town was like before it became a resort.

A former smuggling center, the village of Robin's Hood Bay is known for its red-roof cottages as well as its beach.

GETTING HERE AND AROUND

Scarborough is difficult to reach by public transportation. There are no direct trains from London, and a bus from London takes all day. Transpennine Express trains leave from York every hour or so; the journey takes just under an hour. The journey from Leeds by National Express bus takes about three hours. By car, Scarborough is on the coastal A165 road.

ESSENTIALS

Train Information Transpennine Express ☎ 0845/748–4950 | ⊕ www.tpexpress.co.uk.

Visitor Information Scarborough Tourist Information Centre ✉ Brunswick Shopping Centre, Westborough ☎ 01723/383636 ⊕ www.discoveryorkshirecoast.com.

EXPLORING

Rotunda Museum. One of the country's first purpose-built museums, this extraordinary cylindrical building was constructed in 1829 to house Jurassic fossils and minerals collected nearby. Designed by William Smith, known as "the father of English geology," it now displays important archaeological finds and local history collections. One exhibit showcases evidence of local dinosaurs, such as bones and footprints. ✉ Vernon Rd. ☎ 01723/353765 ⊕ www.rotundamuseum.org.uk ✉ £4.50 ☉ Tues.–Sun. 10–5.

Scarborough Castle. There's been a clifftop stone fortress on this promontory between the North and South bays since 1136, when it was built by the Earl of Albemarle. Some stonework remains from a 4th century Roman signaling station on the site, and archaeological digs have uncovered evidence that prehistoric fortifications existed here as far back as 500 BC. In 1158 Henry II added the massive keep that dominates the existing ruins, along with the massive curtain walls that made the castle virtually impregnable. It remained largely unscathed until Cromwell's cannons did their worst during the Civil War. Further demolition came in 1914 when German warships shelled the town, and in 2012 when local vandals significantly damaged the Roman stonework. **TIP→ The castle has a spectacular panoramic view of the coast.** ✉ *Castle Rd.* ☎ *01723/372451* 🌐 *www.english-heritage.org.uk* 🎟 *£5* 🕒 *Apr.–Sept., daily 10–6; Oct.–early Nov., Thurs.–Mon. 10–4; early Nov.–Mar., weekends 10–4.*

A SPA IS BORN

In 1626 Elizabeth Farrow came upon a stream of acidic water running from a cliff south of Scarborough. This led to the town's becoming a hugely popular spa on a par with Harrogate. By the 18th century, when icy sea bathing came into vogue, no beaches were busier than Scarborough's. Donkeys and horses drew wheeled cabins called bathing machines into the surf to enable ladies to change into bathing costumes while preserving their modesty. The city's prosperity manifested itself in the handsome Regency and early Victorian residences and hotels you see today.

FAMILY **Scarborough Sea Life Centre and Marine Sanctuary.** This aquarium and marine sanctuary is a great—if rather expensive—way to entertain the kids for an afternoon. Marine habitats and creatures from around Britain and further afield are represented, with otters, penguins, loggerhead turtles, octopuses, and rescued seal pups being particularly popular. ✉ *Scalby Mills, North Bay* ☎ *01723/373414* 🌐 *www.visitsealife.com* 🎟 *£16.20* 🕒 *Late Apr.–late July, daily 10–5; late July–early Sept., daily 10–6; early Sept.–late Nov., daily 10–5; early Nov.–Mar., daily 10–4.*

St. Mary's. Most visitors to this little medieval church near the castle are attracted by the churchyard's most famous occupant: Anne, the youngest Brontë sister. As a governess, Anne accompanied her employers to Scarborough for five summers. Shortly before her death from tuberculosis in 1849, she returned here in the hope the sea air would stimulate a recovery. Her sister Charlotte decided to "lay the flower where it had fallen" and buried Anne above the bay she'd loved. ✉ *Castle Rd.* ☎ *01723/500541* 🌐 *www.scarborough-stmarys.org.uk.*

WHERE TO EAT AND STAY

For expanded hotel reviews, visit Fodors.com.

$ BRITISH 🍴 **The Golden Grid.** Everyone has to have fish-and-chips at least once in Scarborough, and this harbor-front spot is a classic of its kind. Choose an upstairs window table and tuck into freshly fried cod or haddock. Lobster, shellfish platters, and traditional roasts are also available. [$] *Average main: £10* ✉ *4 Sandside* ☎ *01723/360922* 🌐 *www.goldengrid.co.uk.*

$$ ITALIAN 🍴 **Lanterna.** This unpretentious restaurant prides itself on *not* being trendy. Instead, the family-run eatery offers acclaimed northern Italian dishes, including homemade spaghetti with local velvet crab, as well as seafood chosen fresh off the boats in the harbor. Opt for seasonal specials using white truffles (October to January) or locally sourced vegetables. With only 30 seats, it books up quickly. [$] *Average main: £20* ✉ *33 Queen St.* ☎ *01723/363616* 🌐 *www.lanterna-ristorante.co.uk* ✍ *Reservations essential* 🕒 *Closed Sun. and 2 wks late Oct. No lunch.*

$ HOTEL 🏨 **Crown Spa Hotel.** The centerpiece of the Regency Esplanade, this grand 19th century hotel was built to accommodate fashionable visitors and overlooks South Bay. **Pros:** Victorian grandeur; modern amenities; free access to health club. **Cons:** inconsistent service. [$] *Rooms from: £83* ✉ *The Esplanade, South Cliff* ☎ *01723/357426* 🌐 *www.crownspahotel.com* 🛏 *115 rooms* 🍽 *Breakfast.*

NIGHTLIFE AND THE ARTS

Stephen Joseph Theatre. Scarborough is firmly on Britain's theater map, largely thanks to the presence of local resident and noted playwright Alan Ayckbourn, who was for many years the artistic director of this theater and premiered most of his plays here. With a commitment to new writing and a strong summer repertory season, it has two stages, plus a cinema, restaurant, and bar. ✉ *Westborough* ☎ *01723/370541* 🌐 *www.sjt.uk.com.*

ROBIN HOOD'S BAY

15 miles northwest of Scarborough, 7 miles south of Whitby.

With red-roof cottages and cobbled roads squeezed into a narrow ravine, this tiny fishing village is considered by many to be the prettiest on the Yorkshire coast. Its winding stone staircases eventually bring you to the headland. Despite its name, the village has no connection to the famous medieval outlaw, beyond a historic association with illegal activity. It was once a smuggling center, with contraband passed up the streambed beneath cottages, which are linked to one another by secret passages. On the beach the rocks exposed at low tide are a good hunting ground for Jurassic fossils. **TIP→ Park in the pay lots at the top of the hill. Do not attempt to drive down the hill.**

GETTING HERE AND AROUND

Park in the public lots at the top of the hill. Robin Hood's Bay has no train station, but buses arrive from Scarborough and Whitby throughout the day.

EXPLORING

Robin Hood's Bay Beach. The beach is lovely but deceptive—the tide rushes in quickly, so take care not to get cut off. Provided the tide is out, you can stroll for a couple of hours south from the town along a rough stone shore full of rock pools, inlets, and sandy strands. A few stretches of sand are suitable for sunbathers. To the south, at the curiously named **Boggle Hole,** an old water mill nestles in a ravine. Farther south is **Ravenscar,** a Victorian village that currently consists of little more than a hotel, which can be reached by walking up the cliff along a hazardous but exhilarating path.

The ruins of Whitby Abbey rise above the pretty town of Whitby and the River Esk.

WHERE TO EAT AND STAY

For expanded hotel reviews, visit Fodors.com.

$ ✕ **Bay Hotel.** The village's most favored pub is this friendly Victorian
BRITISH   retreat, perfectly positioned at the bottom of the village. It's atop a sea-
wall on the edge of the North Sea, so there are dramatic views (if you
can get a coveted window table). In winter, a roaring fire warms all comers. Whitby scampi and savory meat pies are often on the menu, which
leans toward well-prepared traditional pub grub. **$** *Average main: £12*
✉ *The Dock* ☎ *01947/880278.*

$ ⚏ **Raven Hall Hotel.** With 100 acres of landscaped grounds, this Geor-
RESORT   gian country-house hotel dramatically perched 600 feet above sea level
on the Ravenscar headlands in the North York Moors National Park
offers lovely views from most rooms. **Pros:** breathtaking coastal views;
great for outdoorsy types; relaxing atmosphere. **Cons:** some areas tired;
food variable. **$** *Rooms from: £75* ✉ *The Avenue, off Station Rd.,
Ravenscar* ☎ *01723/870353* ⊕ *www.ravenhall.co.uk* ⇲ *52 rooms, 8
lodges* ⦿| *Breakfast.*

SPORTS AND THE OUTDOORS

Several superb long-distance walks start at, finish in, or run through
Robin Hood's Bay.

Coast-to-Coast Walk. The village marks one end of the 190-miles Coast-
to-Coast Walk; the other is at St. Bee's Head on the Irish Sea. Walkers
finish at the Bay Hotel, overlooking the harbor.

Lyke-Wake Walk. The across-the-moors Lyke-Wake Walk finishes 3 miles
from Robin Hood's Bay at Ravenscar. ⊕ *www.lykewakewalk.co.uk.*

WHITBY

7 miles northwest of Robin Hood's Bay, 20 miles northeast of Pickering.

Fodor's Choice ★ A fishing port with a Gothic edge, Whitby is a busy tourist hub, but it handles the crowds so well you might not notice (except at dinnertime, when it's hard to get a seat in a restaurant). Set in a ravine at the mouth of the River Esk, Whitby's narrow streets climb from the curved harbor up cliffs surmounted by the dramatic ruins of a 13th-century abbey. Fine Georgian houses dominate the west side of the river (known as West Cliff), and on the other side of an Edwardian swing bridge are the smaller 17th-century buildings of the old town (known as East Cliff). Here cobbled Church Street is packed in summer with people exploring the shop-lined alleyways.

Whitby came to prominence as a whaling port in the mid-18th century. Whaling brought wealth, and shipbuilding made it famous: Captain James Cook (1728–79), explorer and navigator, sailed on his first ship from Whitby in 1747, and all four of his subsequent discovery vessels were built here. A scaled-down replica of Cook's ship *Endeavour* offers tours of the Yorkshire coast.

GETTING HERE AND AROUND

A car is a must, as there are no direct buses or trains from London. National Express and Megabus serve the region, but you must change at least once, and the journey can take up to 10 hours. National Express trains from London's King's Cross Station go to Leeds, where you can change to a local train. Alternatively, you can go from King's Cross to Middlesborough and from there take a scenic train ride to Whitby. The entire journey takes around six hours.

Whitby has a small town center, and it's easily walkable. The train station is in the town center, between its two cliffs. If you're looking for a taxi, they tend to line up outside the station.

ESSENTIALS

Visitor Information Whitby Tourist Information Centre ⊠ *Langborne Rd.* ☎ *01723/383636* ⊕ *www.discoveryorkshirecoast.com.*

EXPLORING

TOP ATTRACTIONS

St. Mary. On top of the East Cliff—reached by climbing 199 stone steps—this Norman church overlooks the town, while it in turn is watched over by the striking ruins of Whitby Abbey. Bram Stoker lived in Whitby briefly and later said the image of pallbearers carrying coffins up the church's long stone staircase inspired him to write *Dracula*. The unusual-looking church with its ship's-deck roof, triple-decker pulpit, and enclosed box pews dates from the 12th century, although almost everything else you see today is the result of 19th- and 20th-century renovations. The churchyard is filled with the weather-beaten gravestones of former mariners and fishermen. ■ **TIP➡ Rather than walking, you can drive to the hilltop and park in the abbey's lot for a small fee. Or take the hourly Esk Valley Bus 97.** ⊠ *Church Ln.* ☎ *01947/603421* ☜ *Free. £1 suggested donation* ☼ *Apr., daily 10–3; May–June., daily 10–3:30; June–Aug., 10–4; Sept. and Oct., daily 10–3; Nov.–Mar., daily 10–2.*

Whitby Abbey. Set high on the East Cliff, the glorious ruins of the once grand church can be seen from the hills of the moors miles away. The abbey was founded in AD 657 by St. Hild; it's one of very few founded by a woman and operated with a mixed population of monks and nuns. Sacked by the Vikings in the 9th century, the monastery was refounded in the 11th century. Enlarged in the 13th century, it flourished until it

was destroyed by Henry VIII. The excellent visitor center has exhibits on Hild and *Dracula* author Bram Stoker, artifacts from the site, and interactive displays on the medieval abbey. ⊠ *Abbey La.* ☎ *01947/603568* ⊕ *www.english-heritage.org.uk* 🔖 *£6.40* ⊗ *Apr.–Sept., daily 10–6; Oct., Thurs.–Mon. 10–5; Nov., daily 10–5; late-Feb.–Mar., weekends 10–4.*

WORTH NOTING

FAMILY **Bark *Endeavour*.** This scaled-down replica of Captain Cook's ship was built by local craftspeople using original drawings and specifications, and it includes hardwood decks, detailed rigging, and carved timber mouldings. The ship offers half-hour tours of Whitby harbor and excursions along North Yorkshire's Jurassic coast as far as Sandsend, accompanied by commentary on Cook's life and Whitby sights. ⊠ *Fish Quay, Pier Rd.* ☎ *01723/364100* ⊕ *www.endeavourwhitby.com* 🔖 *£3* ⊗ *Apr.–Oct., daily 10:30–dusk, weather permitting.*

Captain Cook Memorial Museum. Filled with exhibits documenting the life of the famous explorer and those who sailed with him, this museum is in the 17th-century house that belonged to ship owner John Walker. This is where Cook lodged as an apprentice seaman from 1746 to 1750. On display are mementos of Cook's epic expeditions, including maps, diaries, and drawings. ⊠ *Grape La.* ☎ *01947/601900* ⊕ *www. cookmuseumwhitby.co.uk* 🔖 *£4.80* ⊗ *Mar., daily 11–3; Apr.–Oct., daily 9:45–5; Nov.–Feb. by appointment.*

OFF THE BEATEN PATH **Goathland.** This moorland village, 8 miles southwest of Whitby, has a charming 1865 train station that was the location for Hogsmeade Station, where students bound for Hogwarts disembarked in the film *Harry Potter and the Sorcerer's Stone.*

North Yorkshire Moors Railway. The 18-mile-long North Yorkshire Moors Railway, between Grosmont and Pickering, passes through picturesque towns and moorland. The route of the steam-powered trains sometimes extends to Whitby. ⊠ *Pickering Station, Park St., Pickering* ☎ *01751/472508* ⊕ *www.nymr.co.uk* 🔖 *£24* ⊗ *Late Mar.–early Nov., daily; early Nov.–Feb., some weekends and holidays*

Whitby Museum. Exhibits in this quirky museum range from local geology and natural history to archaeology, whaling, and trade routes in Asia. It's notable for its traditional approach—displays use handwritten cards. ⊠ *St. Hilda's Terr.* ☎ *01947/602908* ⊕ *www.whitbymuseum.org. uk* 🔖 *£5* ⊗ *Tues.–Sun. 9:30–4:30.*

All aboard! You can take North Yorkshire Moors Railway steam trains to stations including Goathland.

WHERE TO EAT

$$ ✕ **Greens of Whitby.** Specializing in local meat and seafood, Greens is
BRITISH actually two eateries sharing the same menu but with different atmo-
spheres: downstairs is a buzzy bistro, while upstairs a quieter, more
intimate restaurant. The selections might include mussels with white
wine and herbs, beer-battered haddock and fries, or Yorkshire beef with
Wensleydale and Yorkshire blue cheeses, plus a constantly changing
catch of the day. The restaurant also rents two stylish boutique apart-
ments. $ *Average main: £16* ⊠ *13 Bridge St.* ☎ *01947/600284* ⊕ *www.
greensofwhitby.com.*

$ ✕ **Magpie Café.** Seafood is the draw here, and the long menu includes
SEAFOOD freshly caught salmon, haddock, halibut, and cod, all of which can be
served grilled or poached. But the crowds come for the outstanding
traditional fish-and-chips. The food is good and fans say it's worth the
wait, which can stretch to an hour on busy nights. $ *Average main: £12*
⊠ *14 Pier Rd.* ☎ *01947/602058* ⊕ *www.magpiecafe.co.uk* ⌣ *Reserva-
tions not accepted* ☉ *Closed Jan.*

WHERE TO STAY

For expanded hotel reviews, visit Fodors.com.

$ 🏠 **Broom House.** Tucked away in the tiny village of Egton Bridge, about 5
B&B/INN miles outside Whitby, this two-story stone house sits beneath some for-
ested hills. **Pros:** gorgeous setting; lovely rooms; friendly staff. **Cons:** far
from Whitby; need a car to get around. $ *Rooms from: £83* ⊠ *Broom
House La.* ☎ *01947/895279* ⊕ *www.egton-bridge.co.uk* ⌣ *8 rooms*
◦⊙ *Breakfast.*

$$ HOTEL **Dunsley Hall Hotel.** Originally a shipping magnate's residence, this Victorian-era country house sits 4 miles west of Whitby on 4 acres of gardens and grounds, with views of the sea in the distance. **Pros:** gardens; attentive staff. **Cons:** modern rooms not as charming; poor Internet signal. [$] *Rooms from: £159* ✉ *Dunsley Rd., Dunsley* ☎ *01947/893437* 🌐 *www.dunsleyhall.com* 🛏 *26 rooms* 🍴 *Breakfast.*

$ B&B/INN **Shepherd's Purse.** This charming little complex in the cobbled old town consists of shabby-chic guest rooms surrounding a courtyard. **Pros:** quirky, romantic style; comfortable rooms. **Cons:** some rooms are quite small; no breakfast; noise between rooms. [$] *Rooms from: £65* ✉ *95 Church St.* ☎ *01947/820228* 🌐 *www.theshepherdspurse.com* 🛏 *7 rooms, 5 with bath* 🍴 *No meals.*

NIGHTLIFE AND THE ARTS

Whitby Folk Week. Music, traditional dance, and storytelling dominate Whitby Folk Week, usually held the week before the late-August bank holiday. Pubs, halls, and sidewalks become venues for more than 600 traditional folk events by British performers. ☎ *01274/833669* 🌐 *www.whitbyfolk.co.uk.*

Whitby Regatta. Held each August, the Whitby Regatta is a three-day jamboree of rowing races, vintage car rallies, naval displays, military flybys, fireworks, music, and more. 🌐 *www.whitbyregatta.co.uk.*

THE NORTHEAST

WELCOME TO THE NORTHEAST

TOP REASONS TO GO

★ **Hadrian's Wall:**
The ancient Roman wall is a wonder for the wild countryside around it as well as its stones and forts, such as Housesteads and Vindolanda.

★ **Castles, castles, castles:** Fought over by the Scots and the English, and prey to Viking raiders, the Northeast was heavily fortified. Durham, Alnwick, and Dunstanburgh castles are spectacular remnants of this history.

★ **Medieval Durham:**
A splendid Norman cathedral that dates back to the 11th century is just one of the city's charms. Take a stroll on its ancient winding streets.

★ **Lindisfarne (Holy Island):** To get to this historic island, you drive across a causeway that floods at high tide. This remote spot includes the ruins of Lindisfarne Priory.

★ **Alnwick Castle and Gardens:** The inland seat of the dukes of Northumberland is fascinating with its formidable walls, luxurious interiors, and gardens.

1 Durham, Newcastle, and Environs. The historic city of Durham, set on a rocky spur, has a stunning castle and cathedral. South and west are scenic towns with castles and industrial heritage sites. Newcastle, to the north, is a sprawling metropolis with a lively regional arts scene.

2 Hadrian's Wall Country. England's wildest countryside is traversed by the remains of the wall that marked the northern border of the Roman Empire. Hexham is a useful base, and Housesteads Roman Fort is a key site. It's stunning country for walking or biking.

3 The Far Northeast Coast. In this dramatic landscape rocky hillsides plunge into the sea. The ruins of castle towers such as Dunstanburgh and Bamburgh stand guard over windswept beaches, and Lindisfarne has a long religious history. Alnwick, inland, has spectacular gardens.

Cornhill-on-Tweed
Cro

Rochester
Elishaw

West Woodburn

Northumberland National Park

Hadrian's Wall **2**
Greenhead   Henshaw   Hexham
Broon

Ireshopeburn

0   10 mi
0   10 km

GETTING ORIENTED

The historic cathedral city of Durham, one of the region's top attractions, sits to the east of the wooded foothills of the Pennines mountain range, in the southern part of the region. Farther north, busy Newcastle straddles the region's main river, the muddy Tyne. West of Newcastle, the remains of Hadrian's Wall snake through rugged scenery. Head northwest of the wall for the wilderness of Northumberland National Park. Along the far Northeastern coast, towering castles and misty islands punctuate the stunning, final miles of England's eastern shoreline.

Lindisfarne
FARNE ISLANDS
Crookham
Bamburgh
Wooler
Belford
Beadnell
High-Newton -by-the-Sea
Dunstanburgh Castle
Craster
Powburn
Alnwick
Alnmouth
NORTHUMBERLAND
Warkworth
Longframlington
North Sea
Morpeth
Blyth
Belsay
Hartley
Newcastle upon Tyne
Wallsend
North Shields
Tyne
Wylam
Gateshead
South Shields
omhaugh
Sunniside
Sunderland
Washington
Chester-le-Street
Castleside
Seaham
Durham
Peterlee
Frosterley
Wear
Hartlepool
Bishop Auckland
DURHAM
Staindrop
Stockton
Barnard Castle
Middlesbrough
Darlington

North York Moors National Park

HADRIAN'S WALL

Winding through the wild and windswept Northumberland countryside, Hadrian's Wall is Britain's most important Roman relic. It once formed the northern frontier of the Roman Empire—its most remote outpost and first line of defense against raiders from the north. Even today, as a ruin, the wall is an awe-inspiring structure.

(above) The wall is a dramatic sight in the countryside; (right, top) Roman writing tablet from Vindolanda; (right, bottom) Remains of a fort near Housesteads

One of the most surprising things about visiting the 73-mile-long wall is its openness and accessibility. Although many of the best-preserved sections are within managed tourist sites, Hadrian's Wall is also part of the landscape, cutting through open countryside. Signposted trails along the entire route allow you to hike or cycle along most of the wall for free. The area around the wall is also rich in archaeological treasures that paint a picture of a thriving, multicultural community. The soldiers and their families who were stationed here came from as far away as Spain and North Africa, and recent discoveries give us an insight into their daily lives. Artifacts displayed at the wall's museums provide fascinating perspective.

POSTCARDS FROM THE PAST

"Oh, how much I want you at my birthday party. You'll make the day so much more fun. Good-bye, sister, my dearest soul."

"I have sent you two pairs of sandals and two pairs of underpants. Greet all your messmates, with whom I pray you live in the greatest good fortune."

—From 1st-century writing tablets unearthed at Vindolanda

SEEING THE WALL'S HIGHLIGHTS

Hadrian's Wall has a handful of Roman-era forts, the best of which are concentrated near Housesteads, Vindolanda, and Chesters. Housesteads is the most complete, although getting there involves a quarter-mile walk up a hill; Chesters and Vindolanda have excellent museums. The separate Roman Army Museum near Greenhead offers a good overview of the wall's history and is near one of the best sections in open country-side, at Walltown Crags.

WHEN TO GO

The best time to visit is midsummer, when the long hours of daylight allow time to see a few of the wall's major attractions and fit in a short hike on the same day. Winter brings icy winds; not all the forts and museums stay open, but those that do can be all but deserted. The weather can change suddenly at any time of year, so always bring warm clothes.

GETTING AROUND BY CAR OR BUS

The tiny, winding B6318 road passes within a stone's throw of most of the forts. It's a true back road, so don't expect to get anywhere fast. Public transport is limited; the special AD 122 bus covers the highlights (but only during summer), and several local buses follow parts of the same route.

EXPLORING BY FOOT OR BIKE

Hadrian's Wall Path meanders along the wall's entire length; it's a seven-day hike. Joining it for a mile or so is a great way to see the wall and stunning scenery. Try the section around Walltown, or near Corbridge, where the path goes by the remains of a Roman garrison town. Hadrian's Cycleway, for bicyclists, follows roughly the same route.

SIGHTSEEING RESPONSIBLY

The wall is accessible, but vulnerable. Don't climb on it, and never break off or remove anything. In muddy weather you're encouraged not to stand directly next to the wall, as over time this can make the soil unstable.

WALL TIMELINE

13

55 BC Julius Caesar invades what's now southern England, but doesn't stay. He names the island Britannia.

AD 41–50 Full-scale invasion. The Romans establish fortified towns across the south, including Londinium (London).

75–79 The conquest of northern England is completed—but the Romans fail to take Caledonia (Scotland).

122 Emperor Hadrian orders the construction of a defensive wall along the territory's northern border.

208 After the Romans make another disastrous attempt to invade Caledonia, Hadrian's Wall is expanded.

410 The Romans leave Britain. Local tribes maintain the wall for at least a century.

1700s Stones from the ruined wall are plundered for road building.

1830s Local philanthropist John Clayton buys land around the wall to save it from further destruction.

1973 First Vindolanda tablets are found.

1987 Hadrian's Wall becomes a UNESCO World Heritage Site.

Updated by
Jack Jewers

For many Britons the words "the Northeast" provoke a vision of near-Siberian isolation. But although there are wind-hammered, wide-open spaces and empty roads threading the wild high moorland, the Northeast also has simple fishing towns, small villages of remarkable charm, and historic abbeys and castles that are all the more romantic for their often-ruinous state. This is also where you'll find two of England's most iconic sights: the medieval city of Durham and the stark remains of Hadrian's Wall.

Even the remoteness can be relative. Suddenly, around the next bend of a country road, you may come across an imposing church, a tall monastery, or a Victorian country house. The value found in the shops and accommodations, the uncrowded beaches ideal for walking, and the friendliness of the people add to the appeal. Still, outside of a few key sights, the Northeast is off the well-trodden tourist path.

Mainly composed of the two large counties of Durham and Northumberland, the Northeast includes English villages adjacent to the Scottish border area, renowned in ballads and romantic literature for feuds, raids, and battles. Fittingly, Durham Cathedral, the seat of bishops for nearly 800 years, was once described as "half church of God, half castle 'gainst the Scot." Hadrian's Wall, which marked the northern limit of the Roman Empire, stretches across prehistoric remains and moorland. Not far north of Hadrian's Wall are some of the most interesting parts of Northumberland National Park. Steel, coal, railroads, and shipbuilding made prosperous towns such as Newcastle upon Tyne, which is now re-creating itself as a cultural center.

The region's 100 miles of largely undeveloped coast is one of the least visited and most dramatic shorelines in all Europe. Several outstanding castles perch on headlands and promontories along here, including Bamburgh, which according to legend was the site of Joyous Garde, the castle of Sir Lancelot of the Round Table.

NORTHEAST PLANNER

WHEN TO GO

The best time to see the Northeast is in summer. This ensures that the museums—and the roads—will be open, and you can take advantage of the countryside walks that are one of the region's greatest pleasures. Rough seas and inclement weather make it dangerous to swim at any of the beaches except in July and August; even then, don't expect warm water. At the end of June, Alnwick hosts its annual fair, with a medieval market, art shows, and concerts. The Durham Regatta also takes place in June. The Northumberland Traditional Music Festival runs over two weeks in October. Winter here isn't for the fainthearted. The weather is terrible, but there are few places in England so beautiful and remote.

PLANNING YOUR TIME

If you're interested in exploring Hadrian's Wall and the Roman ruins, you'll probably want to base yourself at a guesthouse in or around Hexham. From there you can easily take in Housesteads and the other local landmarks. Anywhere in this area is within easy reach of Durham, with its lovely ancient buildings, or Newcastle, with its excellent museums. Romantics will want to spend a day or two driving up the coast to take in the incredible views.

GETTING HERE AND AROUND

AIR TRAVEL

Newcastle's airport (a 15-minute drive from the city center) has flights from British and European cities.

Contacts Newcastle Airport ⊠ *Off A696, Woolsington, Newcastle upon Tyne* ☎ *0871/882–1121* ⊕ *www.newcastleairport.com.*

BUS TRAVEL

National Express and Megabus (book online to avoid premium telephone charges) travel to Durham and Newcastle and leave from London's Victoria Coach Station, but the journey takes between six and eight hours, more than twice the time it takes by train. (Though it can be considerably cheaper, especially if you book months in advance.) Connecting services to other parts of the region leave from those cities. Traveline has information. The Explorer Northeast Pass (£9) allows unlimited one-day travel on most local bus and Metro train services in the region and is available from the bus driver or local bus or Metro stations.

Contacts Explorer Northeast Pass ⊕ *www.explorernortheast.co.uk.* **Megabus** ☎ *0900/160–0900* ⊕ *www.megabus.com/uk.* **National Express** ☎ *0871/781–8178* ⊕ *www.nationalexpress.com.* **Traveline** ☎ *0871/200–2233* ⊕ *www.traveline.org.uk.*

CAR TRAVEL

If you're headed to small villages, remote castles, or Hadrian's Wall, traveling by car is the best alternative. The A1 highway links London and Newcastle (five to six hours). The scenic route is the A697, which branches west off A1 north of Morpeth. For the coast, leave the A1 at Alnwick and follow the minor B1340 and B1339 for Craster, Seahouses, and Bamburgh. Holy Island is reached from the A1.

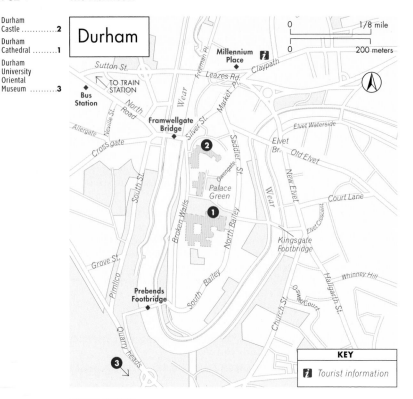

TRAIN TRAVEL

Within England, the train is still the best way to reach this region. East Coast runs the train service from London to the Northeast. The average travel times from London are three hours to Durham and Newcastle. From Newcastle you can catch local trains to Alnwick, Corbridge, Hexham, and Carlisle; these journeys take about 30 minutes. National Rail Enquiries has information.

Contacts East Coast ☎ *0845/722–5333* ⊕ *www.eastcoast.co.uk.*
National Rail Enquiries ☎ *0845/748–4950* ⊕ *www.nationalrail.co.uk.*

RESTAURANTS

Make sure to sample fine local meats and produce. Look for restaurants that serve game from the Kielder Forest, local lamb from the hillsides, salmon and trout from the rivers, and shellfish, crab, and oysters from the coast. Outside the cities, the region lags somewhat behind other parts of England in terms of good places to eat, although there are special spots to be found. Aside from the ubiquitous chains, the best bets are often small country pubs that serve the traditional, hearty fare associated with the region. Don't wait until 9 pm to have dinner, though, or you may have a hard time finding a place that's still serving. *Prices in the reviews are the average cost of a main course at dinner or, if dinner isn't served, at lunch.*

HOTELS

The large hotel chains don't have much of a presence in the North-east, outside the few cities. Instead, you can expect to find country houses converted into welcoming hotels, old coaching inns that still greet guests after 300 years, and cozy bed-and-breakfasts convenient to hiking trails. Many budget accommodations close in winter. *Prices in the reviews are the lowest cost of a standard double room in high season, including 20% V.A.T.*

VISITOR INFORMATION

Contacts **Hadrian's Wall Country** ☎ *01434/322002* ⊕ *www.hadrians-wall.org.*

13

DURHAM, NEWCASTLE, AND ENVIRONS

Durham—the first major Northeastern town on the main road up from London—is by far the region's most interesting historic city. Its cobble-stone streets and towering cathedral make it a charming place to visit. The city is surrounded on all sides by scenic countryside, ruined castles, and isolated villages. Newcastle, though, is the region's biggest, liveli-est, and most cosmopolitan city. Most other towns in the area made their fortunes during the Industrial Revolution and have since subsided into slow decline.

DURHAM

250 miles north of London, 15 miles south of Newcastle.

The great medieval city of Durham, seat of County Durham, stands dramatically on a rocky spur, overlooking the countryside. Its cathedral and castle, a World Heritage Site, rise together on a wooded penin-sula almost entirely encircled by the River Wear (rhymes with "beer"). For centuries these two ancient structures have dominated Durham—a thriving university town, the Northeast's equivalent of Oxford or Cam-bridge. Steep, narrow streets overlooked by perilously angled medieval houses and 18th-century town houses make for fun exploring. In the most attractive part of the city, near the Palace Green and along the river, people go boating, anglers cast their lines, and strollers walk along the shaded paths. For great views, take a short stroll along the River Wear and cross the 17th-century Prebends Footbridge. You can return to town via the 12th-century Framwellgate Bridge.

Despite the military advantages of its location, Durham was founded surprisingly late, probably in about the year 1000, growing up around a small Saxon church erected to house the remains of St. Cuthbert. It was the Normans, under William the Conqueror, who put Durham on the map, building the first defensive castle and beginning work on the cathedral. From here Durham's prince-bishops, granted almost dictato-rial local powers by William in 1072, kept a tight rein on the county, coining their own money and maintaining their own laws and courts; not until 1836 were these rights finally restored to the English Crown.

Rounded arches and columns with zigzag patterns are hallmarks of the Romanesque style at Durham Cathedral.

GETTING HERE AND AROUND

East Coast trains from London's King's Cross Station arrive at the centrally located Durham Station once an hour during the day. The journey takes about three hours. Trains from York arrive three to four times an hour; that journey takes roughly 50 minutes. A handful of National Express and Megabus buses make the seven-hour trip from London daily. The Durham Cathedral Bus (route 40) links parking lots and the train and bus stations with the cathedral, castle, and university. Between 10 and 4 Monday through Saturday, cars are charged £2 (on top of parking charges) to enter the Palace Green area. You pay the charge at an automatic tollbooth on exiting. ▥ **TIP→ If you don't have change for the tollbooth, press the button and an attendant will take down your information. Pay later, in person or over the phone, at the Parking Shop. Don't forget or you'll be fined.**

ESSENTIALS

Visitor Information Durham Visitor Contact Centre ✉ *Claypath* ☎ *03000/262–626* ⊕ *www.thisisdurham.com.* **Parking Shop** ✉ *Forster House, Finchdale Rd.* ☎ *0191/384–6633* ⊕ *www.durham.gov.uk.*

EXPLORING

Durham Castle. Facing the cathedral across Palace Green, Durham's stately, manorlike castle commands a strategic position above the River Wear. For almost 800 years the castle was the home of the enormously powerful prince-bishops; from here they ruled large tracts of the countryside and acted as the main line of defense against Scottish raiders from the north. Henry VIII was the first to curtail the bishops' autonomy, although it wasn't until the 19th century that they finally had their powers annulled. The castle was given over to University College, part of the University of Durham (founded 1832), the oldest in England after Oxford and Cambridge. You can visit the castle only on a 45-minute guided tour. Times can vary, especially on summer afternoons, so call ahead. ⊠ *Palace Green* ☎ *0191/334–2932* ⊕ *www.dur.ac.uk/university.college* ⌹ *£5* ☯ *Early Oct.–late June, weekdays at 2, 3, and 4; late June–early Oct., weekdays at 10, 11, noon, 2, and 5.*

13

QUICK BITES

9 Altars Café. Down a narrow alleyway between the castle and the river, the tiny 9 Altars Café is an excellent spot for coffee and sandwiches. Eat on the river terrace if the weather's good—and you're lucky enough to get a seat. ⊠ *River St.* ☎ *0191/374–1120* ⊕ *www.9altars.com.*

Fodor's Choice
★

Durham Cathedral. A Norman masterpiece in the heart of the city, the cathedral is an amazing vision of solidity and strength, a far cry from the airy lightness of later Gothic cathedrals. Construction began about 1090, and the main body was finished about 1150. The round arches of the nave and the deep zigzag patterns carved into them typify the heavy, gaunt style of Norman, or Romanesque, building. The technology of Durham, however, was revolutionary. This was the first European cathedral to be given a stone, rather than a wooden, roof. When you consider the means of construction available to its builders—the stones that form the ribs of the roof had to be hoisted by hand and set on a wooden structure, which was then knocked away—the achievement seems staggering.

The story of the Cathedral actually goes back 200 years before the first stones were laid. After a Viking raid on the monastery at Lindisfarne in 875, a group of monks smuggled away the remains of St. Cuthbert, patron saint of Northumbria. The remains were were eventually interred in a shrine on this spot, which became a hugely popular destination for pilgrims. The wealth this brought the town was more than enough to pay for the building of the cathedral. Today Cuthbert's shrine is a relatively humble marble slab, although the enormous painting suspended from the ceiling is what the spectacular medieval coffin covering is thought to have looked like.

Note the enormous bronze **Sanctuary Knocker,** shaped like the head of a ferocious mythological beast, mounted on the massive northwestern door. By grasping the ring clenched in the animal's mouth, medieval felons could claim sanctuary; cathedral records show that 331 criminals sought this protection between 1464 and 1524. An unobtrusive tomb at the western end of the cathedral, in the Moorish-influenced **Galilee Chapel,** is the final resting place of the Venerable Bede, an 8th-century Northumbrian monk whose contemporary account of the English people made him the country's first reliable historian. In good weather you can climb the tower, which has spectacular views of Durham. From April to October, guided tours of the cathedral are offered daily at 10:30, 11, and 2.

After a two-year refurbishment, the excellent **museum** is due to reopen in late 2013. The collection includes the cathedral's beautiful illuminated manuscripts. There's also a decent restaurant and a lovely shop on the premises. A choral evensong service takes place Tuesday to Saturday at 5:15 and Sunday at 3:30. ✉ *Palace Green* ☎ *0191/386–4266* 🌐 *www.durhamcathedral.co.uk* 🎫 *£5; tower £5; guided tours £5* ⏲ *Cathedral mid-July–Aug., daily 7:30 am–8 pm; Sept.–mid-July, Mon.–Sat. 7:30–6, Sun. 7:45–5:30. Tower Apr.–Sept., Mon.–Sat. 10–4; Oct.–Mar., Mon.–Sat. 10–3.*

DURHAM'S REGATTA

The pretty River Wear winds through Durham, curving beneath the cathedral and castle. In mid-June each year the city hosts the prestigious Durham Regatta, Britain's oldest rowing event. Three hundred racing crews compete in events, including races for single sculls and teams of eight.

Durham University Oriental Museum. A 15-minute walk from the cathedral, this museum displays fine art and craftwork from all parts of Asia and the Middle East. Galleries are ordered by culture, including Ancient Egypt, China, and Korea. Among the highlights are beautiful Qing dynasty jade and laquer ornaments, and a collection of Japanese woodblock prints from the Edo period. ✉ *Elvet Hill, off South Rd.* ☎ *0191/334–5694* 🌐 *www.dur.ac.uk/oriental.museum* 🎫 *£1.50* ⏲ *Weekdays 10–5, weekends noon–5.*

WHERE TO EAT

$$ FRENCH 🍴 **Bistro 21.** This fashionable restaurant, a few miles northwest of the center, is known for its eclectic menu of French classics with a modern twist. Signature dishes include rib-eye steak with tarragon and mustard butter, herb-encrusted salmon with creamed leeks, and black truffle gnocchi with wild mushrooms and Madeira cream. Get here by taxi, or take Bus 43 to Durham Hospital and walk five minutes. [$] *Average main: £17* ✉ *Aykley Heads* ☎ *0191/384–4354* 🌐 *www.bistrotwentyone.co.uk* ⏲ *No dinner Sun.*

$$ BRITISH 🍴 **Oldfields.** At this convivial restaurant, cheerful raspberry walls and unfussy walnut furnishings create a nicely laid-back vibe that complements the excellent food. Organic vegetables and free-range meat, sourced mostly from the surrounding region, are a specialty. The seasonal menu features such dishes as deviled kidneys with cauliflower, roasted chicken with garlic butter, and haddock and crab *kedgeree* (a rice dish with parsley and butter or cream). [$] *Average main: £16* ✉ *18 Clay Path* ☎ *0191/370–9595* 🌐 *www.oldfieldsrealfood.co.uk.*

$$ THAI 🍴 **Zen.** This popular restaurant mainly serves Thai food, but the menu is also scattered with Japanese, Chinese, and Indonesian dishes. This rather dizzying trip around the Far East can take you from Thai green curry to Mongolian lamb, or perhaps teriyaki beef or cod fillet wrapped in banana leaves served with chili and lime. Or, if you're feeling less adventurous, there's steak. [$] *Average main: £16* ✉ *Court La.* ☎ *0191/384–9588* 🌐 *www.zendurham.co.uk.*

WHERE TO STAY

For expanded hotel reviews, visit Fodors.com.

$ 🏠 **Georgian Town House.** At the top of a cobbled street overlooking the
B&B/INN   cathedral and castle, this family-run guesthouse has small, snug bedrooms with pleasant city views. **Pros:** great location; jovial owners;
good-value rooms. **Cons:** most rooms are small; decor won't please
everyone. $Rooms from: £75 ⊠ 11 Crossgate 🕾 0191/386–8070
⊕ www.thegeorgiantownhouse.co.uk ⤳ 8 rooms ▬ No credit cards
☾ Closed last wk of Dec. ◉ Breakfast.

$$ 🏠 **Lumley Castle Hotel.** This is a real Norman castle, right down to
HOTEL   the dungeons and maze of dark flagstone corridors. **Pros:** great for
Fodor's Choice   antiques lovers; festive meals; good online deals. **Cons:** it's easy to
★   get lost down the winding corridors. $Rooms from: £100 ⊠ B1284,
Chester-le-Street 🕾 0191/389–1111 ⊕ www.lumleycastle.com ⤳ 59
rooms ◉ Multiple meal plans.

$ 🏠 **Seven Stars Inn.** This early-18th-century coaching inn is cozy and
HOTEL   surprisingly affordable. **Pros:** cozy lounge; reasonable rates; pleas-
ant staff. **Cons:** on a main road; minimum two-night stay at peak
times; very strict midnight curfew. $Rooms from: £85 ⊠ High St.
N, Shincliffe Village 🕾 0191/384–8454 ⊕ www.sevenstarsinn.co.uk
⤳ 8 rooms ◉ Breakfast.

$ 🏠 **Victoria Inn.** An authentically Victorian air pervades at this cozy pub
B&B/INN   near Durham Cathedral, considered one of the country's best B&Bs.
Pros: step-back-in-time atmosphere; lovely hosts; free Wi-Fi. **Cons:** few
amenities; pub doesn't serve full meals. $Rooms from: £70 ⊠ 86 Hall-
garth St. 🕾 0191/386–5269 ⊕ www.victoriainn-durhamcity.co.uk ⤳ 6
rooms ◉ Breakfast.

NIGHTLIFE AND THE ARTS

Durham's nightlife is geared to university students.

Half Moon. This handsome old pub is as popular for its excellent range
of traditional ales as for its one-of-a-dying-breed atmosphere. ⊠ New
Elvet 🕾 0191/374–1918.

SHOPPING

Bramwells Jewellers. The specialty here is a pendant copy of the gold-
and-silver cross of St. Cuthbert. ⊠ 24 Elvet Bridge 🕾 0191/386–8006.

Durham Indoor Market. The food and bric-a-brac stalls in Durham Indoor
Market, a Victorian arcade, are open Monday through Saturday 9–5.
An excellent farmers' market is held on the third Thursday of every
month. ⊠ Market Pl. 🕾 0191/384–6153 ⊕ www.durhammarkets.co.uk.

SPORTS AND THE OUTDOORS

Brown's Boat House. At the downtown Brown's Boat House, you can rent
rowboats April through early November. You can also take short cruises
from April to October. ⊠ Elvet Bridge 🕾 0191/386–3779.

13

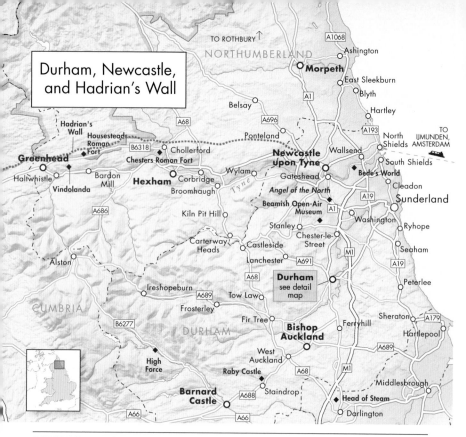

BISHOP AUCKLAND

10 miles southwest of Durham.

For 700 years, between the 12th and 19th century, the powerful prince-bishops of Durham had their country residence in Auckland Castle, in the town of Bishop Auckland. When finally deprived of their powers in 1836, the bishops left Durham and made Bishop Auckland their official home. You can tour the house as well as nearby Raby Castle.

GETTING HERE AND AROUND

Bishop Auckland is just off the A1 motorway from London (260 miles) or Durham (13 miles). There's no direct train service here from London or Durham. However, you can take a train from either city to Darlington and change. The journey takes about three hours from London and one hour from Durham.

ESSENTIALS

Visitor Information Bishop Auckland Tourist Information Centre
⊠ *Town Hall, Market Pl.* ☎ *0300/026–2626* ⊕ *www.thisisdurham.com.*

EXPLORING

Auckland Castle. Arguably the greatest of the prince-bishops of Durham's properties is this episcopal palace, which you enter through an elaborate stone arch. Much of what's on view today dates from the 16th century, although the limestone-and-marble chapel, with its dazzling stained-glass windows, was built in 1665 from the ruins of a 12th-century hall. ■TIP→ Don't miss the extraordinary paintings of Jacob and his 12 sons by the 17th-century Spanish artist Francisco de Zurbarán, in the Long Dining Room. Call ahead to confirm opening times. ⊠ *Off Market Pl.* ☏ *01388/601627* ⊕ *www.auckland castle.org* ➡ *£5* ⊙ *Easter–June and Sept., Mon. and Sun. 2–5; July and Aug., Mon. and Wed. 11–5, Sun. 2–5; park daily 7 am–sunset.*

UPSTAIRS, DOWNSTAIRS

Gorgeous Raby Castle acts as a living museum for castle life through the centuries. It's especially good at juxtaposing life as a servant with life as a lord. In the lord's dining room, rich red carpets and patterned silk wallpaper glow under a soaring, intricately carved ceiling. Downstairs, the servants had their meals in the bare, low-ceilinged medieval servants' hall, sitting at a rough pine table on hard wooden benches.

FAMILY
Fodor's Choice
★
Head of Steam. A family-friendly museum in nearby Darlington tells the story of the early days of rail travel. The town gained fame in 1825, when George Stephenson piloted his steam-powered *Locomotion No. 1* along newly laid tracks the few miles to nearby Stockton, thus kick-starting the railway age. Set in an abandoned 1842 train station, the museum has interactive exhibits and big steam trains that are great for kids; antique engines and scale models help bring history to life. There's also a café and children's activity room. ■TIP→ A ticket for families with up to four kids costs £10. Darlington is 13 miles southeast of Bishop Auckland, on A68. Train connections run roughly every two hours. ⊠ *North Road Station, Station Rd., Darlington* ☏ *01325/460532* ⊕ *www.head-of-steam.co.uk* ➡ *£5* ⊙ *Apr.–Sept., Tues.–Sun. 10–4; Oct.–Mar., Wed.–Sun. 11–3:30.*

Fodor's Choice
★
Raby Castle. The stone battlements and turrets of moated Raby Castle, once the seat of the powerful Nevills and currently the home of the 11th baron Barnard, stand amid a 200-acre deer park and ornamental gardens. Charles Nevill supported Mary, Queen of Scots in the 1569 uprising against Elizabeth I; when the Rising of the North failed, the estate was confiscated. Dating mostly from the 14th century (using stone plundered from Barnard Castle) and renovated in the 18th and 19th centuries, the luxuriously furnished castle has displays of art and other treasures. Rooms in wonderfully elaborate Gothic Revival, Regency, and Victorian styles are open for viewing. In May, June, and September you can only visit by guided tour, except on Sunday when you're free to wander around (as you can every day in July and August). Raby Castle is 7 miles southwest of Bishop Auckland and 1 mile north of Staindrop. ⊠ *A688, Staindrop* ☏ *01833/660202* ⊕ *www.rabycastle. com* ➡ *£10; park and gardens £6* ⊙ *Castle July and Aug., Sun.–Fri. 1–4:30; May, June, and Sept., Sun. 1–4:30; Mon.–Wed. tours only, 1–3:20 (last tour). Park and gardens July and Aug., Sun.–Fri. 11–5; May, June, and Sept., Sun.–Wed. 11–5.*

The 18th-century mechanical silver swan at the Bowes Museum swallows a silver fish each day.

BARNARD CASTLE

14 miles south of Bishop Auckland, 25 miles southwest of Durham.

The handsome market town of Barnard Castle has sights of its own and can also serve as a base for venturing into the Teesdale Valley to the northwest. Its unusual butter-market hall (known locally as Market Cross), surmounted by an old fire-alarm bell, marks the junction of the streets Thorngate, Newgate, and Market Place. Stores, pubs, and cafés line these thoroughfares. In 1838 Charles Dickens stayed at the **King's Head Inn** here while doing research for his novel *Nicholas Nickleby*. The local tourist office has a free "In the Footsteps of Charles Dickens" leaflet.

GETTING HERE AND AROUND

Barnard Castle is about a 20-minute drive from Bishop Auckland on A688. You can make the journey by local buses, but it takes more than an hour and involves a change in Darlington.

ESSENTIALS

Visitor Information Barnard Castle Visitor Information Point ⊠ *Flatts Rd.* 📠 *0300/026–2626* ⊕ *www.teesdalediscovery.com.*

EXPLORING

Barnard Castle. The substantial ruins of Barnard Castle, which gave the town its name, cling to an aerie overlooking the River Tees. From the outside it looks satisfyingly complete from the right angle; inside it's mostly just a shell. You can see parts of the 14th-century Great Hall and the cylindrical, 13th-century tower. Look for the figure of a carved boar high on the wall of the inner courtyard—it was the family emblem of King Richard III (1452–85), placed there during his reign in honor of the elevated status he bestowed upon the castle. ⊠ *Off Galgate* ☎ *01833/638212* ⊕ *www.english-heritage.org.uk* 🗐 *£4.50* 🕙 *Apr.–Sept., daily 10–6; Oct.–Mar., weekends 10–4.*

Fodor's Choice
★

Bowes Museum. This vast French-inspired château a mile west of the town center was built between 1862 and 1875. Highlights include paintings by Canaletto, El Greco, Francisco Goya, and François Boucher, in addition to beautiful collections of ceramics and glass, 18th-century French furniture, and 19th- and 20th-century fashion. ▮▮ TIP➔ **Don't miss the amazing 18th-century mechanical swan, which catches and swallows a silver fish every day at 2.** The café serves light meals and afternoon tea. ⊠ *Newgate* ☎ *01833/690606* ⊕ *www. thebowesmuseum.org.uk* 🗐 *£9* 🕙 *Daily 10–5.*

High Force. The Upper Teesdale Valley's elemental nature shows its most volatile aspect in the sprays of England's highest waterfall, the 72-foot High Force. From the roadside parking lot it's a 10-minute walk through woodland to the massive rocks over which the water tumbles. Access is sometimes closed in bad weather. The waterfall is 15 miles northwest of Barnard Castle. ⊠ *Off B6277* ☎ *01833/622209* 🗐 *£1.50; parking £2* 🕙 *Easter–Oct., daily 9:30–5; Nov.–Easter, open but unattended.*

NEWCASTLE UPON TYNE

16 miles north of Durham, 42 miles northeast of Barnard Castle.

Durham may have the glories of its castle, cathedral, and university, but the liveliest city of the Northeast is Newcastle, currently reinventing itself as a regional center for culture and modern architecture after years of decline. Settled since Roman times on the River Tyne, the city made its fortune twice—first by exporting coal and later by shipbuilding. As a 19th-century industrial center, Newcastle had few equals in Britain, showing off its wealth in grand Victorian buildings lining the broad streets. Some of these remain, particularly on Grey Street. The cluster of bridges (older and newer) crossing the Tyne is a quintessential city sight.

Much of the regeneration since the early 1990s has been based around the Gateshead Quays. Here the Baltic Centre for Contemporary Art and the pedestrian-only Millennium Bridge—the world's first tilting bridge, which opens and shuts like an eyelid—have risen from industrial wasteland.

GETTING HERE AND AROUND

Newcastle Airport, a 15-minute drive from the city center, has flights from British and European cities. Metro trains connect to the center. The A1 highway links London and Newcastle (five to six hours).

East Coast trains from London's King's Cross take about three hours. National Express and Megabus have service from London's Victoria Coach Station several times a day for the six- to eight-hour trip.

Newcastle has a good public transportation system. Its Metro light-rail network is easy to use, well signposted, and has stops near most sights. Buses go all the places Metro doesn't reach.

ESSENTIALS

Visitor Information **Newcastle upon Tyne Tourist Information Centre** ⊠ *8–9 Central Arcade, Market St.* ☎ *0191/277–8000* ⊕ *www.newcastlegateshead.com.*

EXPLORING
TOP ATTRACTIONS

Angel of the North. South of Newcastle, near the junction of A1 and A1(M) at Gateshead, stands England's largest—and one of its most popular—sculptures, the *Angel of the North.* Created by Antony Gormley in 1998, the rust-color steel sculpture is a sturdy, abstract human figure with airplane-like wings rather than arms. It stands 65 feet tall and has a horizontal wingspan of 175 feet. There's parking nearby, signposted on A167. ⊠ *A167, Gateshead* ☜ *Free.*

Baltic Centre for Contemporary Art. Formerly a grain warehouse and now the country's largest national gallery for contemporary art outside London, the Baltic Centre for Contemporary Art presents intriguing changing exhibitions. There's also a café and a rooftop restaurant. ⊠ *Gateshead Quays, S. Shore Rd.* ☎ *0191/478–1810* ⊕ *www.balticmill. com* ☜ *Free* ⊗ *Tues. 10:30–6, Wed.–Mon. 10–6.*

FAMILY **Beamish Open-Air Museum.** Made up of buildings moved from elsewhere in the region, this sprawling complex explores the way people in the Northeast lived and worked from the early 1800s to the early 1900s. A streetcar takes you around the site and to a reconstructed 1920s shopping street with a dentist's office, pub, and grocery store, staffed by costumed volunteers. Other attractions include a small manor house, a railroad station, and a coal mine. In summer, a steam train makes a short run. ▮TIP➔ **Allow at least a half day if you come in summer, less in winter.** The museum is about 8 miles south of Newcastle. ⊠ *Off A693, Beamis* ☎ *0191/370–4000* ⊕ *www.beamish.org.uk* ☜£*18* ⊗ *Apr.–Oct., daily 10–5; Nov.– Mar., Tues.–Thurs. and weekends 10–4; last admission 1 hr before closing.*

FAMILY **Great North Museum.** An amalgam of several collections belonging to
Fodor'sChoice Newcastle University, this beautifully renovated museum contains an
★ impressive array of ancient archaeological finds, plus galleries on natural history and astronomy. Highlights include artifacts left behind by the Roman builders of Hadrian's Wall; ancient Egyptian mummies; and a reconstruction of the 1st-century Temple of Mithras at Carrawburgh. This place isn't designed for kids, but there's plenty here to amuse them, including a planetarium and a life-size model of a T-Rex. A short walk takes you to the smaller **Hatton Gallery,** which holds artwork by Francis Bacon and Kurt Schwitters. It includes a masterpiece by the latter called *Merzbarn Wall,* commissioned by New York's Museum of Modern Art after World War II to replace an earlier version destroyed in Germany. The museum is just off the Great North Road, and five minutes from the Haymarket Metro station. ⊠ *Barras Bridge* ☎ *0191/222–6765* ⊕ *www.twmuseums.org.uk/ greatnorthmuseum* ☜ *Free* ⊗ *Mon.–Sat. 10–5, Sun. 1–5.*

Sir Norman Foster designed the Sage Gateshead performance venue, an emblem of Newcastle's revival.

QUICK
BITES

Tyneside Coffee Rooms. The 70-year-old art-deco Tyneside Coffee Rooms, on the second floor above the Tyneside Cinema, makes an intriguing place to stop for tea, coffee, and a good, unfussy lunch. The popular place is open daily until 10 pm (11 pm on Sunday). ✉ *10 Pilgrim St.* ☎ *0191/227–5520* ⊕ *www.tynesidecinema.co.uk.*

WORTH NOTING

FAMILY **Bede's World.** Four miles east of Newcastle, this site holds substantial monastic ruins, the church of St. Paul, and a small museum reflecting the long tradition of religion and learning that began here in AD 681, when the first Saxon church was established on the site. The Venerable Bede, deemed to be England's earliest historian, moved into the monastery as a child and remained until his death. You can gain a sense of medieval life from the farm buildings, reconstructed by modern historians using traditional methods, and the rare breeds of pigs and cattle on the 11-acre Anglo-Saxon farm. There's also a shop and a café. To get here, take Bus 526 or 527, or the Metro to the Bede/Jarrow station (20-minute walk). ✉ *Church Bank, Jarrow* ☎ *0191/489–2106* ⊕ *www. bedesworld.co.uk* ✉ *£6* ⊙ *Apr.–Sept., daily 10–5:30; Oct.–Mar., daily 10–4:30; last admission 1 hr before closing.*

Corbridge Roman Town. The foundations of this important Roman garrison town (the farthest north in the entire Roman Empire) are brought to life with a lively audio commentary, plus occasional reenactments during the summer. The small museum houses the Corbridge Hoard, a surprisingly well-preserved collection of tools and personal possessions left behind by Roman soldiers in the 2nd century. ■TIP→ **The**

site is often closed in bad weather, so call ahead. ✉ *Corchester La., Corbridge, Northumberland* ☎ *01434/632–349* 🌐 *www.english-heritage.org.uk* 🎟 *£5* 🕒 *Apr.–Sept., daily 10–5:30; Oct.–early Nov., daily 10–4; early Nov.–Mar., weekends 10–4.*

WHERE TO EAT

For expanded hotel reviews, visit Fodors.com.

$$ MODERN BRITISH 🍴 **Café 21.** A Newcastle classic, this sleek brasserie is a local favorite for romantic dinners. Warm wood, leather banquettes, and crisp white table linens lend a polished look. The menu focuses on modern versions of classic British cuisine, peppered with European influences; try the grilled halibut with truffled lentils, or the shoulder of lamb with Provençal vegetables, garlic, and rosemary. Desserts such as iced lemon curd parfait are excellent. [$] *Average main: £19* ✉ *Trinity Gardens, Quayside* ☎ *0191/222–0755* 🌐 *www.cafetwentyone.co.uk.*

$ SOUTH INDIAN Fodor's Choice ★ 🍴 **Rasa.** The only branch of this super-hip minichain outside London, Rasa serves surprisingly authentic, exceptionally delicious Indian cuisine. The menu is short, focusing entirely on specialties from India's Kerala region; meat is used sparingly, but there are plenty of fish and vegetarian options. Try the *kappayum meenum vevichathu*, which mixes king fish and tamarind in a spicy, fragrant sauce, or the *chemmeen masala*, prawns prepared with a tangy tomato and chili reduction. A shared *dosa* is the ideal way to mop up the last of those heavenly sauces—they're light-as-a-feather flatbreads, stuffed with vegetables or curried potatoes. [$] *Average main: £8* ✉ *27 Queen St.* ☎ *0191/232–7799* 🌐 *www.rasarestaurants.com* 🕒 *No lunch Sun.*

WHERE TO STAY

For expanded hotel reviews, visit Fodors.com.

$$ HOTEL 🏨 **Jesmond Dene House.** Occupying a sprawling 19th-century mansion in the northeastern part of the city, this hotel is surrounded by lush gardens and filled with polished oak floors, huge windows, and wandering staircases. **Pros:** beautiful light-filled rooms; lovely gardens; free Wi-Fi. **Cons:** the restaurant is popular, so you need to book in advance. [$] *Rooms from: £120* ✉ *Jesmend Dene Rd.* ☎ *0191/212–3000* 🌐 *www.jesmonddenehouse.co.uk* 🛏 *40 rooms* 🍽 *Breakfast.*

$ HOTEL 🏨 **Malmaison.** Converted from an old riverside warehouse, this glamorous, design-conscious hotel sits beside the pedestrian Millennium Bridge. **Pros:** spacious and quiet rooms; relaxing spa; good restaurant. **Cons:** unreliable Wi-Fi. [$] *Rooms from: £90* ✉ *Quayside* ☎ *0191/245–5000* 🌐 *www.malmaison.com* 🛏 *116 rooms* 🍽 *Multiple meal plans.*

NIGHTLIFE AND THE ARTS

Theatre Royal. The region's most established performing arts center, the Theatre Royal stages high-quality productions and is also a venue for touring musicals and dance. ✉ *Grey St.* ☎ *0844/811–2121* 🌐 *www.theatreroyal.co.uk.*

HADRIAN'S WALL COUNTRY

A formidable line of Roman fortifications, Hadrian's Wall was the Romans' most ambitious construction in Britain. The land through which the old wall wanders is wild and inhospitable in places, but that seems only to add to the powerful sense of history it evokes. Museums and information centers along the wall make it possible to learn as much as you want about the Roman era.

13

HADRIAN'S WALL

73 miles from Wallsend, north of Newcastle, to Bowness-on-Solway, beyond Carlisle.

The most important Roman relic in Britain extends across the countryside and can be accessed in many ways. In Northumberland National Park, about half a mile north of Vindolanda, the Once Brewed National Park Visitor Centre has informative displays about Hadrian's Wall and can advise about local walks.

GETTING HERE AND AROUND

The A69 roughly follows Hadrian's Wall, although sometimes it's a few miles in either direction. The best sections of the wall are near the narrower B6318, including Vindolanda, Housesteads Roman Fort, and Chesters Roman Fort. There's a small railway station at Hexham, with frequent trains from Newcastle.

A special Hadrian's Wall Bus offers day passes (£9.50) for service between Wallsend and Carlisle, stopping at Newcastle, Hexham, and the major Roman forts. The aptly named AD122 public bus runs between Newcastle and Carlisle during the summer months, stopping near all the major destinations along the way. Buses 10, 74, 93, 185, 685, 689, and 880 also pass parts of the wall.

ESSENTIALS

Visitor Information Hadrian's Wall Country Bus ☎ *01434/322002* ⊕ *www.hadrians-wall.org.*

EXPLORING

Fodor'sChoice ★ **Hadrian's Wall.** Dedicated to the Roman god Terminus, the massive span of Hadrian's Wall once marked the northern frontier of the Roman Empire. Today remnants of the wall wander across pastures and hills, stretching 73 miles from Wallsend in the east to Bowness-on-Solway in the west. The wall is a World Heritage Site, and excavating, interpreting, repairing, and generally managing the Roman remains a Northumbrian growth industry. ■TIP→ **Chesters, Housesteads, Vindolanda, and the Roman Army Museum near Greenhead give you a good introduction to the life led by Roman soldiers.** In summer there are talks, plays, and festivals; local tourist offices have details.

At Emperor Hadrian's command, three legions of soldiers began building the wall in AD 122, and finished it in four years. It was constructed by soldiers and masons after repeated invasions by troublesome Pictish tribes from what is now Scotland. During the Roman era it was the most heavily fortified wall in the world, with walls 15 feet high and 9 feet thick; behind it lay the vallum, a ditch about 20 feet wide and 10 feet deep. Spaced at 5-mile intervals along the wall were massive forts (such as those at Housesteads and Chesters), which could house up to 1,000 soldiers. Every mile was marked by a thick-walled milecastle (a fort that housed about 30 soldiers), and between each milecastle were two turrets, each lodging four men who kept watch. For more than 250 years the Roman army used the wall to control travel and trade and to fortify Roman Britain against the barbarians to the north.

During the Jacobite Rebellion of 1745, the English dismantled much of the Roman wall and used the stones to pave what is now the B6318 highway. The most substantial stretches of the remaining wall are between Housesteads and Birdoswald (west of Greenhead). Running through the southern edge of Northumberland National Park and along the sheer escarpment of Whin Sill, this section is also an area of dramatic natural beauty. The ancient ruins, rugged cliffs, dramatic vistas, and spreading pastures make it a great area for hiking.

SPORTS AND THE OUTDOORS

BIKING

Bike Shop. Daily rentals in the Bike Shop begin at £15. ⊠ *16–17 St. Mary's Chare, off St. Mary's Wynd, Hexham* ☎ *01434/601032.*

Purple Mountain Bike Centre. Mountain bike rentals start at £20 per day at Purple Mountain Bike Centre. ⊠ *Kielder Castle, Kielder* ☎ *01434/250532* ⊕ *www.purplemountain.co.uk.*

Hadrian's Cycleway. Between Tynemouth and Whitehaven, Hadrian's Cycleway follows the River Tyne from the east coast until Newcastle, where it traces the entire length of Hadrian's Wall. It then continues west to the Irish Sea. Maps and guides are available at the Tourist Information Centre in Newcastle. ⊕ *www.cycle-routes.org/hadrianscycleway.*

HIKING

Hadrian's Wall Path. One of Britain's national trails, Hadrian's Wall Path runs the entire 73-mile length of the wall. If you don't have time for it all, take one of the less challenging circular routes. One of the most scenic but also most difficult sections is the 12-mile western stretch between Sewingshields and Greenhead. ⊕ *www.nationaltrail.co.uk/hadrianswall.*

HEXHAM

22 miles west of Newcastle, 31 miles northwest of Durham.

The area around the busy market town of Hexham is a popular base for visiting Hadrian's Wall. Just a few miles from the most significant remains, it's a bustling working town, but it has enough historic buildings and winding medieval streets to warrant a stop in its own right. First settled in the 7th century, around a Benedictine monastery, Hexham later became a byword for monastic learning, famous for its book painting, sculpture, and singing.

GETTING HERE AND AROUND

The A1 highway links London and the region (five to six hours). No major bus companies travel here, but the AD122 tourist bus from Newcastle and Carlisle does. East Coast trains take about three hours to travel from London's King's Cross to Newcastle. From there, catch a local train.

Hexham is a small, walkable town. It has infrequent local bus service, but you're unlikely to need it. If you're driving, park in the lot by the tourism office and walk into town. The tourism office has free maps and will point you in the right direction.

13

ESSENTIALS

Visitor Information **Hexham Tourism Information Centre** ⊠ *Wentworth Car Park, Wentworth Pl.* ☎ *01434/652220* ⊕ *www.visitnortheastengland.com.*

EXPLORING

Birdoswald Roman Fort. Beside the longest unbroken stretch of Hadrian's Wall, Birdoswald Roman Fort reveals the remains of gatehouses, a granary, and a parade ground. You can also see the line of the original turf wall, later rebuilt in stone. Birdoswald has a unique historical footnote: unlike other Roman forts along the wall, it was maintained by local tribes long after being abandoned by the Romans. The small visitor center has artifacts discovered at the site, a full-scale model of the wall, and a good café. ⊠ *Wallace Dr., Ravenglass, Cumbria* ⊕ *www.hadrians-wall.org* ⌨*£5.50* ⊙ *Nov.–Mar., weekends 10–4; Apr.–Sept., daily 10–5:30; Oct., daily 10–4.*

Chesters Roman Fort. In a wooded valley on the banks of the North Tyne River, this cavalry fort was known as Cilurnum in Roman times, when it protected the point where Hadrian's Wall crossed the river. Although the site cannot compete with Housesteads for its setting, the museum holds a fascinating collection of Roman artifacts, including statues of river and water gods, altars, milestones, iron tools, weapons, and jewelry. The military bathhouse by the river is supposedly the best-preserved Roman structure of its kind in the British Isles. The fort is 4 miles north of Hexham. ⊠ *B6318, Chollerford* ☎ *01434/681379* ⊕ *www.english-heritage. org.uk* ⌨*£5.50* ⊙ *Apr.–Oct., daily 10–6; Nov.–Mar., weekends 10–4.*

Hexham Abbey. A site of Christian worship for more than 1,300 years, ancient Hexham Abbey forms one side of the town's main square. Inside, you can climb the 35 worn stone "night stairs," which once led from the main part of the abbey to the canon's dormitory, to overlook the whole ensemble. Most of the current building dates from the 12th and 13th centuries, and much of the stone, including that of the Anglo-Saxon crypt, was taken from the Roman fort at Corbridge. Note the portraits on the 16th-century wooden rood screen and the four panels from a 15th-century *Dance of Death* in the sanctuary. In September the abbey hosts the renowned Festival of Music and the Arts, which hosts classical musicians from around the world. ⊠ *Beaumont St.* ☎ *01434/602031* ⊕ *www.hexhamabbey.org.uk* ⌨*£3* ⊙ *Daily 9:30–5.*

Market Place. Since 1239 this has been the site of a weekly market, held each Tuesday (although there are usually a handful of sellers during the rest of the week, aside from Sunday). Crowded stalls are set out under the long slate roof of the Shambles; others, protected only by bright awnings, take their chances with the weather.

FAMILY **Old Gaol.** Dating from 1330, Hexham's Old Gaol houses fascinating exhibits about the history of the borderlands, including tales of the terrifying "reavers" and their bloodthirtsty raids into Northumberland from Scotland during the 16th and 17th centuries. Photographs, weapons, and a reconstructed house interior give a full account of what the region was like in medieval times. A glass elevator takes you to four floors, including the dungeon. ✉ *Hallgate* ☎ *01434/652439* 🎟 *£4* ⏲ *Apr.–June and Sept., Tues.–Sat. 11–4:30; July and Aug., Mon.–Sat. 11–4:30; Feb., Mar., Oct., and Nov., Tues. and Sat. 11–4:30.*

WHERE TO EAT AND STAY

For expanded hotel reviews, visit Fodors.com.

$$$$ BRITISH 🍴 **Langley Castle.** This lavish 14th-century castle with turrets and battlements offers an elegant fine-dining experience. The baronial dining room is romantic, with little candlelit alcoves draped in rich fabric. Choose from an excellent five-course prix-fixe menu of traditional English dishes—perhaps the beef shin and pheasant breast served with oyster mushrooms and Madeira jus, or the Dover sole with parsley and caper butter. There's also a lighter (and cheaper) snack menu. If you're really taken with the place, rooms start at around £160 per night. Langley Castle is 6 miles west of Hexham. [$] *Average main: £40* ✉ *A686, Langley-on-Tyne* ☎ *01434/688888* 🌐 *www.langleycastle.com.*

$ B&B/INN 🏨 **Battlesteads Hotel.** On the outer edge of Hexham, this delightful old inn combines three virtues: good food, cozy rooms, and eco-friendly credentials, with a string of awards to prove it (including "Green Pub of the Year" in 2010). **Pros:** lovely staff; good food; green ethos. **Cons:** some rooms on the small side; no mobile phone reception. [$] *Rooms from: £90* ✉ *Wark on Tyne* ☎ *01434/230209* 🌐 *www.battlesteads.com* 🛏 *17 rooms* 🍽 *Breakfast.*

$ B&B/INN 🏨 **Dene House.** This former farmhouse on 9 acres of lovely countryside has beamed ceilings and homey rooms with pine pieces and colorful quilts. **Pros:** tasty breakfasts; warm atmosphere; reasonable rates. **Cons:** no restaurant. [$] *Rooms from: £70* ✉ *B6303, Juniper* ☎ *01434/673413* 🌐 *www.denehouse-hexham.co.uk* 🛏 *3 rooms, 1 with bath* 🍽 *Breakfast.*

NIGHTLIFE AND THE ARTS

Queen's Hall Arts Centre. Theater, dance, and art exhibitions are on the bill at the Queen's Hall Arts Centre. ✉ *Beaumont St.* ☎ *01434/652477* 🌐 *www.queenshall.co.uk.*

GREENHEAD

18 miles west of Hexham, 49 miles northwest of Durham.

In and around tiny Greenhead you'll find a wealth of historical sites related to Hadrian's Wall, including the fascinating Housesteads Roman Fort, the Roman Army Museum, and Vindolanda. In Northumberland National Park, about half a mile north of Vindolanda, the Once Brewed National Park Visitor Centre has informative displays about Hadrian's Wall and can advise about local walks.

The rose displays at Alnwick Garden have a romantic view of nearby Alnwick Castle.

GETTING HERE AND AROUND

Greenhead is on the A69 and B6318. The nearest train station is 3 miles east, in Haltwhistle.

ESSENTIALS

Visitor Information Once Brewed National Park Visitor Centre
✉ *Northumberland National Park, Military Rd., Bardon Mill, Once Brewed*
☎ *01434/344396* ⊕ *www.northumberlandnationalpark.org.uk* ⊘ *Apr.–Oct.,*
daily 9:30–5; Nov.–Mar., weekends 10–3.

EXPLORING

Fodor'sChoice
★

Housesteads Roman Fort. If you have time to visit only one Hadrian's Wall site, Housesteads Roman Fort, Britain's most complete example of a Roman fort, is your best bet. It includes long sections of the wall, an excavated fort, and a new visitor center with a collection of artifacts discovered at the site and computer-generated images of what the fort originally looked like. The fort itself is a 10-minute walk uphill from the parking lot (not for those with mobility problems), but the effort is worth it to see the surprisingly extensive ruins, dating from around AD 125. Excavations have revealed the remains of granaries, gateways, barracks, a hospital, and the commandant's house. ▐TIP➔ **The northern tip of the fort, at the crest of the hill, has one of the best views of Hadrian's Wall, passing beside you before disappearing over hills and crags in the distance.** ✉ *B6318, Haydon Bridge* ☎ *01434/344363* ⊕ *www.english-heritage.org.uk* ✉ *£6.50* ⊘ *Apr.–Oct., daily 10–6; Nov.–Mar., weekends 10–4.*

FAMILY **Roman Army Museum.** At the garrison fort of Carvoran, this museum makes an excellent introduction to Hadrian's Wall. Full-size models and excavations bring this remote outpost of the empire to life; authentic Roman graffiti adorns the walls of an excavated barracks. There's a well-designed museum with Roman artifacts and a 3D film that puts it all into historical context. Opposite the museum, at Walltown Crags on the Pennine Way (one of Britain's long-distance national hiking trails), are 400 yards of the best-preserved section of the wall. The museum is 1 mile northeast of Greenhead. ⊠ *Off B6318* ☎ *01697/747485* ⊕ *www. vindolanda.com* ⊑ *£5; £10 with admission to Vindolanda* ☉ *Mid-Feb–Mar. and Oct., daily 10–5; Apr.–Sept., daily 10–6; Nov.–mid-Feb., weekends 10–4.*

Vindolanda. About 8 miles east of Greenhead, this archaeological site holds the remains of eight successive Roman forts and civilian settlements, providing an intriguing look into the daily life of a military compound. Most of the visible remains date from the 2nd and 3rd centuries, and new excavations are constantly under way. A reconstructed Roman temple, house, and shop provide context, and the museum displays rare artifacts, such as a handful of extraordinary wooden tablets with messages about everything from household chores to military movements. A full-size reproduction of a section of the wall gives a sense of its massiveness. The site is sometimes closed in bad weather. ⊠ *Off B6318, Bardon Mill* ☎ *01434/344277* ⊕ *www.vindolanda.com* ⊑ *£6.50; £10 includes admission to Roman Army Museum* ☉ *Mid-Feb.–Mar. and Oct., daily 10–5; Apr.–Sept., daily 10–6; Nov.–mid-Feb., weekends 10–4.*

WHERE TO EAT AND STAY
For expanded hotel reviews, visit Fodors.com.

$ ✕ **Milecastle Inn.** The snug bar and restaurant of this remote, peaceful BRITISH 17th-century pub make an excellent place to dine. Fine local meat goes into its famous pies; take your pick from wild boar and duckling. The unfussy menu also features such staples as fish-and-chips or lasagne with garlic bread. Two cottages are available for rent. The inn is on the north side of Haltwhistle on B6318. $ *Average main: £11* ⊠ *Military Rd., Haltwhistle* ☎ *01434/321372* ⊕ *www.milecastle-inn.co.uk.*

$ ⌂ **Holmhead Guest House.** Talk about a feel for history—this former B&B/INN farmhouse in open countryside, graced with stone arches and exposed beams, is not only built *on* Hadrian's Wall but also partly *from* it. **Pros:** full of atmosphere; close to Hadrian's Wall; reasonable rates. **Cons:** rooms are a bit of a squeeze; you need a car out here. $ *Rooms from: £68* ⊠ *Off A69* ☎ *01697/747402* ⊕ *www.bandbhadrianswall.com* ⇆ *4 rooms, 8 beds, 1 apartment* ⦿*Breakfast.*

MORPETH

15 miles north of Newcastle, 20 miles south of Alnwick.

Surrounded by idyllic pastures and tiny lanes, the hilly medieval market town of Morpeth is the closest thing this part of Northumberland comes to bustling. It's an ideal stop while visiting some of the region's more hidden-away sights to the north of Newcastle.

GETTING HERE AND AROUND

Just off the A1, Morpeth is easily reached by car. Trains leave Newcastle every hour and take 22 minutes. Buses X14, X15, X18, and 44A connect Newcastle and Morpeth, and the journey takes around 40 minutes.

ESSENTIALS

Visitor Information **Morpeth Tourist Information Centre** ⊠ *The Chantry, Bridge St.* ☎ *01670/623455* ⊕ *www.visitnorthumberland.com.*

EXPLORING

Brinkburn Priory. A fine historical anecdote concerns this idyllic Augustinian priory, founded in the early 12th century. A group of Scottish "reivers" came looking for the place in order to raid and loot it, but because it was entirely hidden by forest, they were unable to find it and gave up. The monks were so happy that they sounded the bells in celebration—revealing the location, so the Scots promptly returned and sacked the place. Most of the beautiful, light-filled building is the result of a Victorian restoration, though elements of the original remain. On the same site are a mill and a 19th-century manor house, which incorporates the undercroft from the former monk's refectory. Classical music concerts are held here throughout the year. ▇ TIP➔ **The walk from the car park takes 10 minutes, but those with mobility problems can drive all the way down.** ⊠ *Off B6344* ☎ *01665/570628* ⊕ *www. english-heritage.org.uk* 🎫 *£3.50* ⊗ *Apr.–Sept., Thurs.–Mon. 11–4.*

FAMILY

Fodor's Choice

★

Cragside. The turrets and towers of Tudor-style Cragside, a Victorian country house, look out over the edge of a forested hillside. It was built between 1864 and 1895 by Lord Armstrong, an early electrical engineer and inventor, and designed by Richard Norman Shaw, a well-regarded architect. Among Armstrong's contemporaries Cragside was called "the palace of a modern magician" because it contained so many of his inventions. This was the first house in the world to be lighted by hydroelectricity; the grounds also hold an energy center with restored mid-Victorian machinery. There are Pre-Raphaelite paintings and an elaborate mock-Renaissance marble chimneypiece. The gardens, including a huge rock garden and a sculpture trail, are as impressive as the house; in June rhododendrons bloom in the 660-acre park surrounding the mansion. There's also a children's adventure playground. ▇ TIP➔ **Paths around the grounds are steep and distances can be long, so wear comfortable shoes.** ⊠ *Off A697 and B6341, Rothbury* ☎ *01669/620333* ⊕ *www.nationaltrust.org.uk* 🎫 *Grounds and house £14; grounds only £9* ⊗ *House Mar.–mid-July and Sept.–late Oct., Tues.–Fri. 1–5; weekends 11–5; mid-July–Aug., daily 11–5. Grounds Mar.–Oct., Tues.–Sun. 10–7; Nov.–late Dec., Fri.–Sun. 11–4.*

WHERE TO EAT AND STAY

For expanded hotel reviews, visit Fodors.com.

$

DELI

✕ **Central Bean Coffee House.** There's a distinct Pacific Northwest vibe at this funky little independent eatery in central Morpeth. Locals flock to the place for fresh sandwiches, panini, or cakes, or just a fine cup of joe. $ *Average main: £6* ⊠ *21 Sandersone Arcade* ☎ *01670/512300* ⊕ *www.centralbean.co.uk* ⊗ *No dinner.*

13

$$ ⬛ **Shieldhall Guesthouse.** This lovely 19th-century farmhouse was once
B&B/INN   home to the family of the legendary landscaper Capability Brown. **Pros:**
Fodor's Choice   lots of peace and quiet; dinners are exceptional. **Cons:** well outside
★   town; need a car to get around. $ *Rooms from: £100 ⊠ Off B6342,
Wallington ☎ 01830/540387 ⊕ www.shieldhallguesthouse.co.uk ⤵ 3
rooms* ❙◎❙ *Breakfast.*

$ ⬛ **Thistleyhaugh.** This ivy-covered stone farmhouse sits at the center
B&B/INN   of a 720-acre organic farm. **Pros:** idyllic farmhouse location; wonder-
ful hosts; excellent food. **Cons:** isolated location means you can't get
around without a car. $ *Rooms from: £90 ⊠ Off A697, Longframling-
ton ☎ 01665/570629 ⊕ www.thistleyhaugh.co.uk ⤵ 5 rooms* ☉ *No
dinner Sun.* ❙◎❙ *Breakfast.*

THE FAR NORTHEAST COAST

Extraordinary medieval fortresses and monasteries line the final 40
miles of the Northeast coast before England gives way to Scotland.
Northumbria was an enclave where the flame of learning was kept
alive during Europe's Dark Ages, most notably at Lindisfarne, home of
saints and scholars. Castles abound, including the spectacularly sited
Bamburgh and the desolate Dunstanburgh. The region also has some
magnificent beaches, though because of the cold water and rough seas
they're far better for walking than swimming. The 3-mile walk from
Seahouses to Bamburgh gives splendid views of the Farne Islands, and
the 2-mile hike from Craster to Dunstanburgh Castle is unforgettable.
A bit inland are a few other pretty towns and other castles.

ALNWICK

30 miles north of Newcastle, 46 miles north of Durham.

Dominated by a grand castle, the little market town of Alnwick (pro-
nounced *ahn*-ick) is the best base from which to explore the dramatic
coast and countryside of northern Northumberland.

GETTING HERE AND AROUND

If you're driving, Alnwick is just off the A1. Buses 501, 505, and 518
connect Alnwick with Newcastle, Berwick, and Morpeth. The nearest
train station is 4 miles away in Alnmouth; trains travel between here
and Newcastle roughly every hour and take 25 minutes.

ESSENTIALS

Visitor Information Visit Alnwick ⊠ *2 The Shambles* ☎ *01665/511333*
⊕ *www.visitalnwick.org.uk.*

EXPLORING

FAMILY   **Alnwick Castle.** Sometimes called the "Windsor of the North," the impos-
Fodor's Choice   ing Alnwich Castle is more familiar to many as a location in the Harry
★   Potter movies. (The castle grounds appear as the exterior of Hogwarts
School.) The building is still home to the dukes of Northumberland,
whose family, the Percys, dominated in the Northeast for centuries.
Family photos and other knickknacks are scattered around the lavish
staterooms, a subtle reminder that this is a family home rather than a

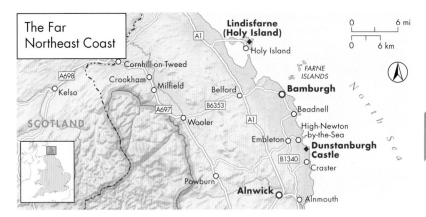

The Far
Northeast Coast

museum. Highlights include the extraordinary gun room, lined with hundreds of antique pistols in swirling patterns; the formal dining room, its table set as if guests are due at any minute; and the magnificent galleried library, containing 14,000 books in floor-to-ceiling cases.

There's plenty here for younger visitors: **Knights' Quest** lets kids dress up and complete interactive challenges; **Dragon's Quest** is a labyrinth designed to teach a bit of medieval history; and for the very young there are Harry Potter–style **Broomstick Lessons,** on the exact spot used in the movie. Spooky ghost stories are told by costumed actors in the **Lost Cellars.** In addition, the staff hides a toy owl somewhere in each room of the castle, and kids get a certificate if they spot them all. ■TIP➔ Tickets are valid for one year, so you can come back if you don't see everything in a day. ✉ *Narrowgate* ☎ *01665/511350* ⊕ *www.alnwickcastle.com* 🎫 *£14; combined ticket with Alnwick Gardens £23* ☉ *Late Mar.–late Oct., castle daily 11–5; grounds daily 10–6. Last admission at 4:15.*

FAMILY
Fodor's Choice
★

Alnwick Garden. A marvelous flight of fancy, Alnwick Garden was designed by Capability Brown in 1750. Centering on modern terraced fountains by Belgian designers Jacques and Peter Wirtz, the gardens include traditional features (shaded woodland walks, a rose garden) and funkier, kid-appealing elements such as a Poison Garden and a labyrinth of towering bamboo. ■TIP➔ You can buy clippings of the unique varieties of roses in the shop. This is the location of one of the area's most unusual restaurants, the Treehouse. ✉ *Denwick La.* ☎ *01665/511350* ⊕ *www.alnwickgarden.com* 🎫 *£12; combined ticket with Alnwick Castle £24* ☉ *Apr.–Oct., daily 10–6; Nov.–Mar., Mon.–Sat. 10–3, Sun. 11–5. Closed 3rd wk in Jan. Last admission 45 mins before closing.*

WHERE TO EAT AND STAY
For expanded hotel reviews, visit Fodors.com.

$$
BRITISH
Fodor's Choice
★

✕ **The Treehouse.** You don't have to visit Alnwick Garden to eat at this extraordinary restaurant set among the treetops. The location may sound gimmicky, but the effect is quite magical, especially when the place is lit up at night. The Modern British fare is excellent—honey glazed duck in a peppercorn and brandy sauce, perhaps, or roasted cod with tomato and chorizo gnocchi. From July to September, the kitchen only serves prix-fixe menus at night; the rest of the year there's an à la carte selection. You can grab a light lunch or tea and cake at the Potting Shed bar, which is also open for predinner drinks. [$] *Average main: £18* ✉ *Alnwick Garden, Denwick La.* ☎ *01665/511852* 🌐 *www.alnwickgarden.com/eat* ⏲ *No dinner Mon.–Wed.*

$ HOTEL 🏨 **The Tower.** More of a "restaurant with rooms" than a guesthouse, this charming place around the corner from Alnwick Castle is a great find. **Pros:** relaxed atmosphere; sweet hosts; good restaurant. **Cons:** double rooms are on the small side. [$] *Rooms from: £60* ✉ *10 Bondgate Within* ☎ *01665/603888* 🌐 *www.thetoweralnwick.com* 🛏 *5 rooms* 🍴 *Breakfast.*

DUNSTANBURGH CASTLE

8 miles northeast of Alnwick.

More than worth the effort it takes to get here (this is not the kind of place where you can just drive up to the front gate) Dunstanburgh is as dramatic an old ruin as they come.

GETTING HERE AND AROUND

The castle is accessible only by footpaths from the villages of Craster or Embleton off the B1339 rural road. Follow the signs to the castle. To get here you'll need a car—there's no public transportation to or near the site.

EXPLORING

Dunstanburgh Castle. Perched romantically on a cliff 100 feet above the shore, these castle ruins can be reached along a windy, mile-long coastal footpath that heads north from the tiny fishing village of Craster. Built in 1316 as a defense against the Scots, and later enlarged by John of Gaunt, the powerful Duke of Lancaster who virtually ruled England in the late 14th century, the castle is known to many from the popular paintings by 19th-century artist J.M.W. Turner. The castle is a signposted 1.3 mile walk from the nearest parking lot in Craster, on the outskirts of Alnwick. ✉ *Windside Hill, Alnwick* ☎ *01665/576231* 🌐 *www.english-heritage.org.uk* 🎟 *£4.50* ⏲ *Apr.–Sept., daily 10–5; Oct.–early Nov., daily 10–4; early Nov.–Mar., weekends 10–4.*

BAMBURGH

14 miles north of Alnwick.

Tiny Bamburgh has a splendid castle, and several beaches are a few minutes' walk away.

GETTING HERE AND AROUND

Bamburgh can be reached by car on B3140, B3141, or B3142. Buses run from Alnwick to Bamburgh every two hours at quarter to the hour. The nearest train station is in Chathill, about 7 miles away.

It's worth the scenic coastal walk to see the remote cliff-top ruins of Dunstanburgh Castle.

EXPLORING

Fodor's Choice ★ **Bamburgh Castle.** You'll see Bamburgh Castle long before you reach it: a solid, weatherbeaten clifftop fortress that dominates the coastal view for miles around. A fortification of some kind has stood here since the 6th century, but the Norman castle was damaged during the 15th century and the central tower is all that remains intact. Much of the structure—the home of the Armstrong family since 1894—was restored during the 18th and 19th centuries. The interior is mostly late Victorian (most impressively, the Great Hall), although a few rooms, such as the small but alarmingly well-stocked armory, have a more authentically medieval feel. The breathtaking view across the North Sea is worth the trip much as anything else; bring a picnic if the weather's good (or order to-go sandwiches at the café). ✉ *Off B1340* ☎ *01668/214515* 🌐 *www.bamburghcastle.com* 🎟 *£10* 🕒 *Mid-Feb.–Oct., daily 10–5; Nov.–mid-Feb., weekends 11–4:30; last admission 1 hr before closing.*

WHERE TO EAT AND STAY

For expanded hotel reviews, visit Fodors.com.

$$$$ BRITISH 🍴 **Waren House.** Six acres of woodland surround this Georgian house on a quiet bay between Bamburgh and Holy Island. The crisply elegant restaurant has romantic views of Holy Island when the trees are bare; three-course fixed-price dinners might include beef oysters with onion compote and horseradish potato puree, or sea bass with citrus-steamed chard, perhaps followed by apple, plum, and walnut crumble. The public areas are comfortably furnished in period style, and there are guest rooms (£100, including dinner) if you want to linger overnight. [$] *Average main: £37* ✉ *B1342, Waren Mill* ☎ *01668/214581* 🌐 *www.warenhousehotel.co.uk.*

$$ HOTEL **Lord Crewe Hotel.** This cozy, stone-walled inn with oak beams sits in the heart of the village, close to Bamburgh Castle. **Pros:** in the center of the village; good restaurant. **Cons:** pub can get quite crowded. [$] *Rooms from: £115* ✉ *Front St.* ☎ *01668/214243* 🌐 *www.lordcrewe.co.uk* 🛏 *18 rooms* 🍴 *Breakfast.*

LINDISFARNE (HOLY ISLAND)

6 miles north of Bamburgh off the A1, 22 miles north of Alnwick.

Cradle of northern England's Christianity and home of St. Cuthbert, Lindisfarne (or Holy Island) has a religious history that dates from AD 635, when St. Aidan established a monastery here. Under its greatest abbot, the sainted Cuthbert, Lindisfarne became one of the foremost centers of learning in Christendom. Today you can explore the atmospheric ruined priory and a castle.

GETTING HERE AND AROUND

By car the island is reached from the mainland via a long drive on a causeway that floods at high tide, so check when crossing is safe. The times, which change daily, are displayed at the causeway and printed in local newspapers. Traffic can be heavy; allow at least a half hour for your return trip. The only public transportation to Holy Island is run by Perryman's Buses. Bus 477 has limited service (two buses a day, and not every day) from Berwick-upon-Tweed railway station to the island.

ESSENTIALS

Bus Contacts **Perryman's Buses** ☎ *01289/308719* 🌐 *www.perrymansbuses.co.uk.*

EXPLORING

Lindisfarne Castle. Reached during low tide via a causeway from the mainland, this castle appears to grow out of the rocky pinnacle on which it was built 400 years ago, looking for all the world like a fairy-tale illustration. In 1903 architect Sir Edwin Lutyens converted the former Tudor fort into a private home that retains the original's ancient features. Across several fields from the castle is a walled garden designed by Gertrude Jekyll. Call ahead for times, as they change with the tides. ✉ *Marygate, Lindisfarne, Berwick-upon-Tweed* ☎ *01289/389244* 🌐 *www.nationaltrust.org.uk* 🎫 *£7* 🕒 *Castle Mar.–Oct., Tues.–Sun. (also Mon. in Aug.) 10–3 or noon–5; Nov.–early Dec., alternate weekends 10–3. Last admission 30 mins before closing.*

Lindisfarne Priory. In the year 875, Vikings destroyed the Lindisfarne community; only a few monks escaped, carrying with them Cuthbert's bones, which were reburied in Durham. The sandstone Norman ruins of Lindisfarne Priory, reestablished in the 11th century, remain impressive and beautiful. A museum here displays Anglo-Saxon carvings. ✉ *Prior La.* ☎ *01289/389200* 🌐 *www.english-heritage.org.uk* 🎫 *£5* 🕒 *Apr.–Sept., daily 9:30–5; Oct.–early Nov., daily 9:30–4; early Nov.–Mar., weekends 10–4.*

WALES

WELCOME TO WALES

TOP REASONS TO GO

★ **Castle country:**
Wales doesn't quite have a castle in each town, but there is a greater concentration than almost anywhere else in Europe—more than 600 in all.

★ **The Gower Peninsula:**
This stretch of coastland near Swansea includes some of the region's prettiest beaches, as well as spectacular coastal views and medieval ruins.

★ **Snowdonia:** The biggest of the country's three national parks contains its highest mountain, Snowdon, as well as villages that recall the past.

★ **Brecon Beacons:**
Moorlands, mountains, and valleys make up this rough and wild stretch of the Welsh midlands, as popular with hikers as it is with those who are just happy to take in the stunning views from the road.

★ **Hay-on-Wye:**
This pretty village on the Welsh-English border has become world famous as a book lover's paradise; every street is lined with secondhand bookstores.

1 South Wales. Cardiff, the lively young capital city, is here, as are two very different national parks: the green, swooping hills of the Brecon Beacons and, in the far west, the sea cliffs, beaches, and estuaries of the Pembrokeshire Coast. Both are excellent for outdoor activities such as walking and mountain biking. Pembrokeshire has some of the region's best beaches.

2 Mid-Wales. The quietest part of Wales is home to scenic countryside, from rolling hills to more rugged mountains. Aberystwyth is a Victorian resort town on the coast, and Hay-on-Wye is a magnet for lovers of antiquarian bookstores.

3 North Wales. Wales's most famous castles are in its northern region. The cream of the crop is Caernarfon, a medieval palace dominating the waterfront on the Menai Strait. Conwy (castle and town) is popular, too. Snowdonia's mountains are a major draw, as is the quirky, faux-Italian village of Portmeirion.

GETTING ORIENTED

Wales has three main regions: South, Mid-, and North. South Wales is the most varied and in just a few miles you can travel from Wales's bustling and cosmopolitan capital city, Cardiff, to the most enchanting old villages and historical sights. Mid-Wales is almost entirely rural (its largest town has a population of just 16,000), and it's fringed on its western shores by the arc of Cardigan Bay. Here you'll find mountain lakes, quiet roads, hillside sheep farms, and traditional market towns. North Wales is a mixture of mountains, popular sandy beaches, and coastal hideaways. Although dominated by the rocky Snowdonia National Park, the north has a gentler, greener side along the border with England.

14

CASTLES IN WALES

You can't go far in Wales without seeing a castle: there are more than 600 of them. From crumbling ruins in fields to vast medieval fortresses with rich and violent histories, these castles rank among the most impressive in the world.

(above) The marquess of Bute transformed Cardiff Castle into a Victorian extravaganza; (right, top) Caerphilly Castle's romantic moat; (right, bottom) Raglan Castle's impressive ruins

The first great wave of castle building arrived in England with the Norman Conquest in 1066. When the descendants of those first Anglo-Norman kings invaded Wales 200 years later, they brought with them their awesome skill and expertise. Through deviousness and brutal force, King Edward I (1239–1307) won control over the Welsh lords in the north and wasted no time in building mighty castles, including Caerphilly and Conwy, to consolidate his power. These became known as his "ring of iron." Wars came and went over the next few centuries, until, rendered obsolete by gunpowder and the changing ways of warfare, castles were destroyed or fell into disrepair. Only in the Victorian age, when castles became hugely fashionable, was there widespread acceptance of how important it was to save these historic structures for the nation.

CASTLE GLOSSARY

Bailey: open grounds within a castle's walls.

Battlements: fortified ledge atop castle walls.

Keep: largest, most heavily defended castle building.

Moat: water-filled ditch around castle.

Motte: steep man-made hill on which a castle was often built.

Portcullis: iron drop-gate over entrance.

With such a dizzying array of castles, it can be hard to know where to start. Here are six of the best to help you decide. At the larger sites, buy a guidebook or take an audio or other tour so that you can best appreciate the remains of a distant era.

CAERNARFON CASTLE

Welsh naturalist Thomas Pennant (1726–98) called Caernarfon Castle "that most magnificent badge of our subjection." Built in 1283 on the site of an earlier castle, it's the most significant symbol of Edward I's conquest of Wales. It's also the best preserved of his "ring of iron" and, along with Edward's Beaumaris, Harlech, and Conwy castles in North Wales, is a UNESCO World Heritage Site. *North Wales*

CAERPHILLY CASTLE

Near Cardiff, this is the largest castle in Wales, and the second largest in Britain after Windsor Castle. Caerphilly's defenses included a man-made island and two huge lakes. The castle was ruined by centuries of warfare, although modern renovations have recaptured much of its former glory. Kids love it. *South Wales*

CARDIFF CASTLE

Though the capital's titular castle has medieval sections, most of it is, in fact, a Victorian flight of fancy. Its most famous occupant, the third marquess of

Bute (1847–1900), was once the richest man in the world, and his love of the exotic led to the bizarre mishmash of styles. *South Wales*

CARREG CENNEN CASTLE

The great views over the countryside are worth the steep hike to this bleak, craggy cliff-top fortress in the Brecon Beacons. This medieval stronghold was partially destroyed during the Wars of the Roses in the 15th century. Some interior rooms, hollowed out from the mountain itself, survive intact. *South Wales*

CONWY CASTLE

Imposing, if partially ruined, Conwy Castle with its eight towers captures like no other the feeling of sheer dominance that Edward I's citadels must have had over the landscape. The approach by foot over the River Conwy, along a 19th-century suspension bridge designed by Thomas Telford, makes for an awesome view. You can walk the ancient walls of Conwy town, which has places to eat and shop. *North Wales*

RAGLAN CASTLE

The boyhood home of Henry VII, the first Tudor king, Raglan is a small but impressive 15th-century castle, surrounded by a steep moat (one of the few in Wales that's still filled with water). Largely a ruin, it's relatively complete from the front, making for some irresistible, fairy-tale photo ops. *South Wales*

Updated by
Jack Jewers

Not as famous as Ireland, or as feted as Scotland, Wales isn't high on many people's itineraries when they first visit this region. And what a shame that is, for Wales is a land of dramatic national parks, such as the Brecon Beacons and Snowdonia; plunging, unspoiled coastlines, such as the Gower Peninsula and Cardigan Bay; and a host of awe-inspiring medieval castles. You won't encounter hordes of travelers, which is a big part of its appeal.

Vast swaths of Wales were untouched by the industrial boom of the 19th century. Although pockets of the country were given over to industries such as coal mining and manufacturing (both of which have all but disappeared), most of Wales remained unspoiled. The country is largely rural, and there are more than 10 million sheep—but only 3 million people. It has a Britain-as-it-used-to-be feel that can be hugely appealing.

Now is a great time to visit Wales. The country is reveling in a new political autonomy, little more than a decade old, that's brought with it a flourish of optimism and self-confidence. Wales loves being Wales, and that enthusiasm is infectious to the visitor. It also means that the tourism industry has grown in leaps and bounds, including some truly unique and special places to stay.

Although Wales is a small country—on average, about 60 miles wide and 170 miles north to south—looking at it on a map is deceptive. It's quite a difficult place to get around, with a distinctly old-fashioned road network and poor public transportation connections. To see it properly, you really need a car. The good news is that along the way you'll experience some beautiful drives. There are rewards to be found in the gentle folds of its valleys and in the shadow of its mountains.

Were some of the more remote attractions in Wales in, say, the west of Ireland, they'd be world famous, and overrun with millions of visitors. Here, if you're lucky, you can almost have them to yourself.

WALES PLANNER

WHEN TO GO

The weather in Wales, as in the rest of Britain, is a lottery. It can be hot in summer or never stop raining. Generally it's cool and wet in spring and autumn, but could also be surprisingly warm and sunny. The only surefire rule is that you should be prepared for the unexpected.

Generally speaking, southwest Wales tends to enjoy a milder climate than elsewhere in Britain, thanks in part to the moderating effects of the Gulf Stream. In contrast, mountainous areas like Snowdonia and the Brecon Beacons can be chilly at any time of the year. Book far ahead for major festivals such as the literary Hay Festival, Brecon Jazz, and the Abergavenny Food Festival.

PLANNING YOUR TIME

First-time visitors often try to cover too much ground in too little time. It's not hard to spend half your time traveling between points that look close on the map, but take the better part of a day to reach. From Cardiff, it's easy to visit the Wye Valley, Brecon Beacons, and the Gower Peninsula. Along the North Wales coast, Llandudno and Lake Vyrnwy make good bases for the Snowdonia National Park.

The location of Wales lends itself to a border-hopping trip—in both directions. Well-known locations like Bath (near South Wales) and Chester (near North Wales) are no more than an hour from the Welsh border, and you can even take a ferry to Ireland if you want to go farther afield.

GETTING HERE AND AROUND

AIR TRAVEL

If you're arriving from the United States, London's Heathrow and Gatwick airports are generally the best options because of their large number of international flights. Heathrow (2 hours) is slightly closer than Gatwick (2½ hours), but both have excellent motorway links with South Wales. For North Wales, the quickest access is via Manchester Airport, with a travel time of less than an hour to the Welsh border.

Cardiff International Airport, 19 miles from downtown Cardiff, is the only airport in Wales with international flights, but these are mostly from Europe and Canada. A bus service runs from the airport to Cardiff's central train and bus stations.

Airports Cardiff International Airport ✉ *A4226, Rhoose* ☎ *01446/711111* ⊕ *www.cwlfly.com.* **Manchester Airport** ✉ *M56, Near Junctions 5 and 6* ☎ *08712/710711* ⊕ *www.manchesterairport.co.uk.*

BUS TRAVEL

Most parts of Wales are accessible by bus, but long-distance bus travel takes a long time. National Express travels to all parts of Wales from London's Victoria Coach Station and also direct from London's Heathrow and Gatwick airports. The company also has routes into Wales from many major towns and cities in England and Scotland. Average travel times from London are 3½ hours to Cardiff, 4 hours to Swansea, 7 hours to Aberystwyth, and 4½ hours to Llandudno.

Wales's three national parks run summer bus services. In the North, the excellent Snowdon Sherpa runs into and around Snowdonia and links with main rail and bus services. The Pembrokeshire Coastal Bus Service operates in the Pembrokeshire Coast National Park, and the Beacons Bus serves the Brecon Beacons National Park.

Bus Contacts **Beacons Bus** ☎ *0871/200–2233* ⊕ *www.travelbreconbeacons.info.* **National Express** ☎ *0871/781–8178* ⊕ *www.nationalexpress.com.* **Pembrokeshire Coastal Bus** ☎ *0845/345–7275* ⊕ *www.pembrokeshirecoast. org.uk.* **Snowdon Sherpa** ☎ *01286/870880* ⊕ *www.gwynedd.gov.uk.*

CAR TRAVEL

To explore the Welsh heartland properly, you really need a car. Be prepared to take the scenic route: there are no major highways north of Swansea (which means virtually all of Wales). For the most part it's all back roads, all the way. There are some stunning routes to savor: the A487 runs along or near most of the coastline, while the A44 and A470 both wind through mountain scenery with magnificent views.

FERRY TRAVEL

Two ferry ports that connect Britain with Ireland are in Wales. Regular daily ferries with Stena Line and Irish Ferries sail from Fishguard, in the southwest, and Holyhead, in the northwest. Celtic Link runs some ferries between Rosslare and Cherbourg in France.

Ferry Contacts **Celtic Link** ⊕ *www.celticlinkferries.com.* **Irish Ferries** ☎ *0818/300–400* ⊕ *www.irishferries.com.* **Stena Line** ☎ *0844/770–7070* ⊕ *www.stenaline.co.uk.*

TRAIN TRAVEL

Travel time on the First Great Western rail service from London's Paddington Station is about two hours to Cardiff and three hours to Swansea. Trains connect London's Euston Station with Mid-Wales and North Wales, often involving changes in cities such as Birmingham. Travel times average between three and five hours. Regional train service covers much of South and North Wales but, frustratingly, there are virtually no direct connections between these regions. For example, to make the 73-mile trip between Cardiff and Aberystwyth you have to make a connection in Shrewsbury, lengthening the trip to 147 miles. North Wales has a cluster of steam railways, but these are tourist attractions rather than a practical way of getting around. The mainline long-distance routes can be very scenic indeed, such as the Cambrian Coast Railway, running between Machynlleth and Pwllheli, and the Heart of Wales line, linking Swansea with London, Bristol, and Manchester.

Train Contacts **National Rail Enquiries** ☎ *0845/748–4950* ⊕ *www.nationalrail.co.uk.*

DISCOUNTS AND DEALS

For travel within Wales, ask about money-saving unlimited-travel tickets (such as the Freedom of Wales Flexi Pass, the North and Mid-Wales Rover, and the South Wales Flexi Rover), which include the use of bus services. A discount card offering a 20% reduction on each of the steam-driven Great Little Trains of Wales is also available. It costs £10 and is valid for 12 months.

The Cadw/Welsh Historic Monuments Explorer Pass is good for unlimited admission to most of Wales's historic sites. The seven-day pass costs £20 per person, £32 per couple, or £39 per family; the three-day pass costs £13.50, £20.50, and £28.30, respectively. Passes are available at any site covered by the Cadw program. All national museums and galleries in Wales are free.

Discount Information Cadw/Welsh Historic Monuments ⊠ *Plas Carew, Unit 5–7 Cefn Coed, Parc Nantgarw, Treforest* ☎ *01443/336000* ⊕ *www.cadw. wales.gov.uk.* **Flexi Pass information** ☎ *0845/606–1660* ⊕ *www.nationalrail. co.uk.* **Great Little Trains of Wales** ⊕ *www.greatlittletrainsofwales.co.uk.* **National Museums and Galleries of Wales** ⊕ *www.museumwales.ac.uk.*

TOURS

In summer there are all-day and half-day tour-bus excursions to most parts of the country. In major resorts and cities, ask for details at a tourist information center or bus station.

The Wales Official Tourist Guide Association (WOTGA) uses only guides recognized by VisitWales and will create tailor-made tours. You can book a driver-guide or someone to accompany you as you drive.

Tour Information Wales Official Tourist Guide Association ☎ *01633/774796* ⊕ *www.walestourguides.com.*

RESTAURANTS

Wales has developed a thriving restaurant scene over the last decade or so, and not just in major towns. Some truly outstanding food can be found in rural pubs and hotel restaurants. More and more restaurants are creating dishes using fresh local ingredients—Welsh lamb, Welsh Black beef, Welsh cheeses, and seafood from the Welsh coast—that show off the best of the region's cuisine. *Prices in the reviews are the average cost of a main course at dinner or, if dinner isn't served, at lunch.*

HOTELS

A 19th-century dictum, "I sleeps where I dines," still holds true in Wales, where good hotels and good restaurants often go together. Castles, country mansions, and even disused railway stations are being transformed into interesting hotels and restaurants. Traditional inns with low, beamed ceilings, wood paneling, and fireplaces are often the most appealing places to stay. The best ones tend to be off the beaten track. Cardiff and Swansea have some large chain hotels, and, for luxury, some excellent spas have cropped up in the countryside. An added bonus is that prices are generally lower than they are for equivalent properties in the Cotswolds, Scotland, or southeast England. *Prices in the reviews are the lowest cost of a standard double room in high season, including 20% V.A.T.*

VISITOR INFORMATION

Contacts VisitWales Centre ☎ *08708/300306* ⊕ *www.visitwales.com.* **Wales in Style** ⊕ *www.walesinstyle.com.*

Castell Coch looks medieval but don't be fooled: it's a delightful Victorian-Gothic fantasy.

SOUTH WALES

The most diverse of Wales's three regions, the south covers the area around Cardiff that stretches southwest as far as the rugged coastline of Pembrokeshire. It's the most accessible part of the country, as the roads are relatively good and the rail network is more extensive than it is elsewhere in Wales. Pleasant seaside towns such as Tenby are within a four- to five-hour drive of London; from Cardiff and Swansea you're never more than a half hour away from some gorgeous small villages.

Cardiff has had limited success in reinventing itself as a cultured, modern capital, but Swansea and neighboring Newport have struggled to find their place in this postindustrial region. With a few exceptions, it's better to stick to the countryside in South Wales. The heart-stopping Gower Peninsula stretches along 14 miles of sapphire-blue bays and rough-hewn sea cliffs, and the Brecon Beacons National Park is an area of grassy mountains and craggy limestone gorges.

CARDIFF CAERDYDD

20 miles southwest of the Second Severn Bridge.

With a population of around 330,000, Cardiff is the largest and most important city in Wales. It's also one of the youngest capitals in Europe: although a settlement has existed here since Roman times, Cardiff wasn't declared a city until 1905, and didn't become the capital until 50 years later. This is an energetic, youthful place, keen to show its newfound cosmopolitanism to the world. Cardiff is experiencing something of a cultural renaissance with the opening of the Wales Millennium Centre in Cardiff Bay.

For all its urban optimism, however, Cardiff is still a rather workaday town, with little to detain you for more than a day. See Cardiff Castle and the National Museum, wander Cardiff Bay, and maybe catch a show. Otherwise, it's a convenient base for exploring the nearby countryside.

GETTING HERE AND AROUND

The capital is a major transportation hub with good connections to other parts of South Wales and with England. Getting to Mid-Wales and North Wales is more difficult, as there's no direct north–south train route (you'll have to connect in Bristol or Shrewsbury) and north–south buses are painfully slow. From London, trains from Paddington to Cardiff Central take about two hours; National Express coaches take about three hours. Cardiff is easily accessible by the M4 motorway. You must pay a £6.20 toll to cross the Severn Bridge between England and Wales (though crossing back is free).

TIMING

If you don't like crowds, avoid Cardiff during international rugby tournaments or other major sporting events.

ESSENTIALS

Visitor and Tour Information Cardiff Bay Visitor Centre ⊠ *Wales Millennium Centre, Bute Pl.* ☎ *029/2087–3573* ⊕ *www.visitcardiff.com.* **Cardiff Tourist Information Centre** ⊠ *The Old Library, The Hayes* ☎ *029/2087–3573* ⊕ *www.visitcardiff.com.*

EXPLORING
TOP ATTRACTIONS

FAMILY

Fodor's Choice

★

Caerphilly Castle. One of the largest and most impressive fortresses in Wales, Caerphilly was remarkable at the time of its construction in the 13th century. Built by an Anglo-Norman lord, the concentric fortification contained powerful inner and outer defenses. It was badly damaged during the English Civil War, although extensive 20th-century renovations have restored much of its former glory. The original Great Hall is still intact, and near the edge of the inner courtyard there's a replica of a trebuchet—a giant catapult used to launch rocks and other projectiles at the enemy. Kids love exploring this castle, which is 7 miles north of Cardiff. ⊠ *Castle St., Caerphilly* ☎ *029/2088–3143* ⊕ *www.cadw.wales. gov.uk* 🎫 *£4* ☉ *Mar.–June, Sept., and Oct., daily 9:30–5; July and Aug., daily 9:30–6; Nov.–Feb., Mon.–Sat. 10–4, Sun. 11–4. Last admission 30 min before closing.*

Cardiff Bay. Perhaps the most potent symbol of Cardiff's 21st-century rebirth, this upscale district is a 10-minute cab ride from Cardiff Central Station. Its museums and other attractions are clustered around the bay itself. The area can seem rather tranquil during the day, but buzzes with activity at night.

Techniquest. A large science-discovery center for children, Techniquest has 160 interactive exhibits, a planetarium, and a science theater. ⊠ *Stuart St., Cardiff Bay* ☎ *029/2047–5475* ⊕ *www.techniquest.org* 🎫 *£7; planetarium £1.30* ☉ *Jan.–mid-July and Sept.–Dec., weekends 9:30–4:30; mid-July–Aug., daily 10–5*

Wales Millennium Centre. Inviting comparisons to Bilbao's Guggenheim, Cardiff's main arts complex (known locally as "The Armadillo" for its coppery, shingled exterior) is an extraordinary building, inside and out. The materials used in the construction are intended to represent "Welshness." (Slate is for the rocky coastline, for example, while wood is for its ancient forests.) The massive words carved into the curving facade read "In These Stones Horizons Sing" in English and Welsh. Inside there's a maritime feel, from the curving wooden stairs to balconies evoking the bow of a ship. A broad range of cultural programs take place on the various stages, from ballet and opera to major touring shows. Guided tours (£5.50) depart about every hour. ⊠ *Bute Pl., Cardiff Bay* ☎ *029/2063–6464* ⊕ *www.wmc.org.uk*

Fodor's Choice
★

Cardiff Castle. A higgledy-piggledy mishmash of styles, from austere Norman keep to over-the-top Victorian mansion, Cardiff Castle is an odd but beguiling place, located right in the middle of the city. Take the tour of the Victorian portion to discover the castle's exuberant side. William Burges (1827–81), an architect obsessed by the Gothic period, transformed the castle into an extravaganza of medieval color for the third marquess of Bute. The result was the Moorish-style ceiling in the Arab Room, the intricately carved shelves lining the Library, and gold leaf murals everywhere. Look for the painting of the Invisible Prince in the Day Nursery; on first glance it's just a tree, but stare long enough and a man takes shape in the branches. Note the not-so-subtle rejection of Darwin's theory of evolution, represented by monkeys tearing up his book around the library's doorway. The vast grounds, which include beautiful rhododendron gardens and a habitat for owls and falcons, are sometimes the setting for jousting in summer. ⊠ *Castle St.* ☎ *029/2087–8100* ⊕ *www.cardiffcastle.com* 🎫 *£11, £14 with guided tour* ⊗ *Mar.–Oct., daily 9–6; Nov.–Feb., daily 9–5. Last admission 1 hr before closing.*

Castell Coch. Perched on a hillside is this fairy-tale castle. The turreted Red Castle was built on the site of a medieval stronghold in the 1870s, about the time that the "Fairytale King" Ludwig II of Bavaria was creating his castles in the mountains of Germany. This Victorian fantasy wouldn't look out of place among them. The castle was another collaboration of the third marquess of Bute and William Burges, who transformed Cardiff Castle. Burges created everything, including the whimsical furnishings and murals, in a remarkable exercise in Victorian-Gothic whimsy. ⊠ *A470, 4 miles north of Cardiff, Tongwynlais* ☎ *029/2081–0101* ⊕ *www.cadw.wales.gov.uk* 🎫 *£3.80* ⊗ *Mar.–June, Sept., and Oct., daily 9:30–5; July and Aug., daily 9:30–6; Nov.–Feb., Mon.–Sat. 10–4, Sun. 11–4; last admission 30 min before closing.*

FAMILY

Doctor Who Experience. The phenomenally popular BBC TV series—which has been made in Wales since 2005—marked its 50th anniversary in 2013, and this suitably high-tech exhibit celebrates its weird and wonderful charms. There are interactive displays, specially recreated sets, and a huge collection of costumes and props from the show, plus an exceedingly well-stocked gift shop. Fans will be in heaven. Entry is by timed ticket, so try to book ahead. ▇ TIP → Reserve online and save more than £10 on family tickets. Kids get a

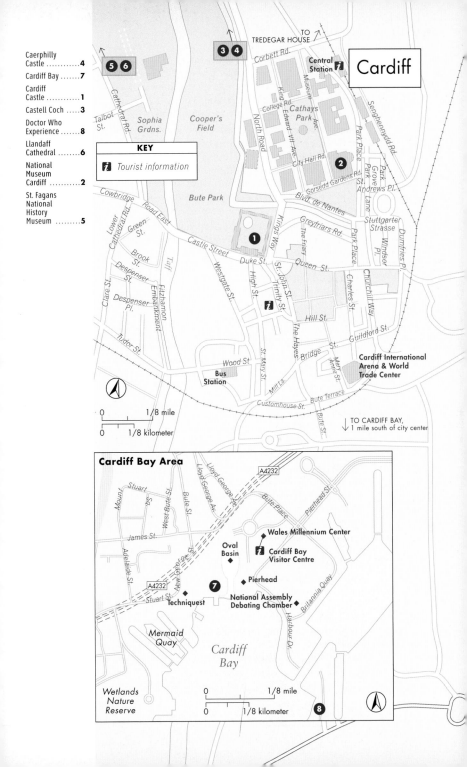

Cardiff

KEY

i *Tourist information*

TO
TREDEGAR HOUSE

Corbett Rd.

Central Station

Cathedral Rd.
Talbot St.
Sophia Grdns.
Cooper's Field

College Rd.
Cathays Park
North Road
King Edward VII Ave.
Museum Ave.

Senghennydd Rd.

City Hall Rd.

Gorsedd Gardens Rd.

Park Place
Park Grove
Park Lane
St. Andrews Pl.

Cowbridge Road East

Bute Park

Blvd. de Nantes

Stuttgarter Strasse

Lower Cathedral Rd.
Green St.
Brook St.
Despenser St.
Despenser Pl.
Clare St.
Taff
Fitzhamon Embankment

Castle Street
Duke St.
Westgate St.
High St.
Kings Way
St. John St.
Trinity St.

Greyfriars Rd.
The Friary
Queen St.
Park Place
Charles St.
Churchill Way
Windsor Pl.
Dumfries Pl.

Hill St.

The Hayes
Bridge St.
Guildford St.

Tudor St.
Wood St.
Bus Station
St. Mary St.
Mill La.
Mary Anne St.

Cardiff International Arena & World Trade Center

Customhouse St.
Bute Terrace
Bute St.

0   1/8 mile
0   1/8 kilometer

↓ TO CARDIFF BAY,
1 mile south of city center

Cardiff Bay Area

A4232

Mount Stuart Sq.
West Bute St.
Bute St.
Lloyd George Av.
Bute Place
Pierhead St.

James St.

New George St.

Oval Basin

Wales Millennium Center

Cardiff Bay Visitor Centre

Adelaide St.

A4232

Stuart St.
Techniquest

Pierhead

National Assembly
Debating Chamber

Britannia Quay

Harbour Dr.

Mermaid Quay

Cardiff Bay

Wetlands Nature Reserve

0   1/8 mile
0   1/8 kilometer

pack of Dr. Who-related goodies, too. ⊠ *Discovery Quay, Butetown* ☎ *0844/801–2279 box office, 0844/801–3663 information* ⊕ *www. doctorwhoexperience.com* ☒ *£13* ⊘ *Mar.–mid-July and Sept.–Jan., Wed.–Mon. 10–5; mid-July–Aug., daily 10–5; Feb., Thurs.–Mon. 10–5; last admission 90 mins before closing.*

National Museum Cardiff. At this splendid museum you can learn about the story of Wales through its archaeology, art, and industry. The Evolution of Wales gallery uses inventive robotics and audiovisual effects. There's a fine collection of modern European art, including works by Daumier, Renoir, Van Gogh, and Cézanne. ⊠ *Cathays Park* ☎ *029/2057–3000* ⊕ *www.museumwales.ac.uk* ☒ *Free* ⊘ *Tues.–Sun. and holidays 10–5.*

Tredegar House. One of the grandest stately homes in Wales, Tredegar House was bought by the National Trust in 2011 and opened its doors to visitors in 2013. Highlights of the self-guided tour include the grand baroque Jacobean New Hall and the enormous Victorian kitchens, both restored to their former glory. Don't miss the lavish Victorian Side Hall, lined with portraits of the Morgan family, which owned Tredegar until the 1950s. The grounds include immaculately laid-out formal gardens and an orangery. Tredegar is just outside Newport, 12 miles northwest of Cardiff. ⊠ *Tredegar House Dr., off A48, Newport* ☎ *01633/815880* ⊕ *www.nationaltrust.co.uk* ☒ *£6.80* ⊘ *House Mar.–Oct., weekends 11–5; mid–late Feb., weekends 11–4:30. Gardens Mar.–Oct., weekends 10:30–5, mid–late Feb., weekends 11–4:30.*

WORTH NOTING

Llandaff Cathedral. In a suburb that retains its village feeling, you can visit this cathedral, which was repaired after serious bomb damage in World War II. The cathedral includes the work of a number of Pre-Raphaelites as well as *Christ in Majesty,* a 15-foot-tall aluminum figure by sculptor Jacob Epstein (1880–1959). From Cardiff, cross the River Taff and follow Cathedral Road for about 2 miles. Guided tours are available by arrangement. ⊠ *Cathedral Close, Llandaff* ☎ *029/2056–4554* ⊕ *www. llandaffcathedral.org.uk* ☒ *Free* ⊘ *Mon., Fri. and Sat., 9–7; Tues. and Thurs., 7–7; Wed., 7–8; Sun., 7–7:30.*

FAMILY **St. Fagans National History Museum.** On 100 acres of gardens, this excellent open-air museum celebrates the region's architectural history with a collection of farmhouses, cottages, shops, chapels, a school, and a 16th-century manor house. All but two of the structures were brought here from around Wales. Of special note are the ironworkers' cottages; a string of attached structures each reflecting a different era from 1805, 1855, 1925, 1955, and 1985 from the decor to the technology to the gardening methods. Galleries display clothing and other articles from daily life, and special events highlight local customs. ⊠ *Off A4232, St. Fagans* ☎ *029/2057–3500* ⊕ *www.museumwales. ac.uk* ☒ *Free* ⊘ *Daily 10–5.*

WALES: COUNTRY WITHIN A COUNTRY

Is Wales a nation, a state, or a country? The answer—confusingly—is yes, kind of, and yes and no. This requires some untangling.

Wales is a country within the United Kingdom, the same as Scotland and England. It has its own language—which you'll see on every signpost, though everybody also speaks English—its own flag, and sends its own teams to international sporting events like soccer's World Cup (but not the Olympics).

While Wales has the right to pass some of its own laws, it isn't a sovereign nation. It shares the same head of state and has the same central government as England, Scotland, and Northern Ireland. It uses the same currency, and there are no restrictions for travelers who cross the English border.

In medieval times Wales was an independent nation, but lacked a single government or ruler. It was slowly annexed by England in a drawn-out series of wars and skirmishes. Although the Welsh retained a strong sense of their own national identity, by the middle of the 16th century their land was effectively part of England.

This was the case until 1997, when Tony Blair was elected prime minister on a platform that included semiautonomous legislatures for Wales and Scotland. Two years later, the Welsh Assembly passed the first laws made solely by and for Wales in more than 400 years.

You should always refer to Wales as a separate country. Be respectful of the fact that when you cross the border you're entering a place with a rich and proud history of its own.

14

WHERE TO EAT

$$ FRENCH 🍴 **Bayside Brasserie.** With its gorgeous view over Cardiff Bay, this undeniably romantic restaurant is one of the most popular in Cardiff. The classic bistro menu has few surprises, but the kitchen serves up some tasty fare. Fish is a particular specialty—start with an appetizer of mussels, scallops, or smoked salmon before moving on to fillet of sea bass stuffed with citrus fruit, or a simple Welsh sirloin from the grill. The extensive wine list includes organic and fair-trade labels. [$] *Average main: £16* ✉ *Mermaid Quay, Bute Pl.* ☎ *029/2035–8444* 🌐 *www.baysidebrasserie.com.*

$ BRITISH 🍴 **The Clink.** Well, this is unusual: a trendy new restaurant in which all the food is prepared by prisoners. The idea behind the Clink (British slang for jail) is that those serving time for minor crimes are given the chance to turn their lives around by gaining experience as gourmet chefs. The restaurant (just outside the prison grounds) is a bright, modern space, and the Modern British food is genuinely delicious. You might try shoulder of lamb with lemon, olive, and caper tapenade, or the wild boar and venison ragout with grilled polenta. At the time of writing, the restaurant is open for lunch all week, plus a single dinner sitting on Wednesday. This is likely to change, however. [$] *Average main: £10* ✉ *Knox Rd., in front of Cardiff Prison* ☎ *029/2092–3130* 🌐 *www.theclinkcharity.com/cardiff.*

$$ BRITISH Fodor's Choice ★ 🍴 **The Potted Pig.** Vaulted ceilings and exposed brick walls provide a dramatic backdrop to this restaurant down the block from Cardiff Castle. Formerly a bank vault, the Potted Pig turns out superb Welsh dishes. Starters like duck hash with fried egg and entrees such as Devonshire brown crab with chips and mayonnaise keep diners satisfied. Popular desserts like the jelly roll can run out by the end of the night. Servers are warm and attentive and knowledgeable about wine. The underground atmosphere and candlelight make this a romantic dinner choice. [$] *Average main: £17* ✉ *27, High St.* ☎ *029/2022–4817* 🌐 *www.thepottedpig.com* 🕒 *Closed Mon. No dinner Sun.*

$ PIZZA 🍴 **Restaurant Minuet.** A longtime favorite with locals, Restaurant Minuet serves simple, fresh Italian lunches at decidedly ungourmet prices. The simple menu won't win any prizes for originality—a simple Capricciosa pizza, perhaps, with pepperoni and artichokes, or pasta with prawns, garlic, and chili—but the cooking is excellent and the atmosphere homey. Kids are well cared for, with junior-size pizzas and calzones, all for around £5. [$] *Average main: £7* ✉ *42 Castle Arcade* ☎ *029/203-41794* 🌐 *www.restaurantminuet.co.uk* ✍ *Reservations not accepted* 🕒 *No dinner. Closed Sun.*

$ ITALIAN 🍴 **Valentino's.** With its nicely understated rustic decor and friendly Italian staff, this restaurant drips with authenticity. In addition to pizzas and pastas, there is an ever-changing selection of fresh, locally sourced meat and fish dishes. [$] *Average main: £12* ✉ *5 Windsor Pl.* ☎ *029/2022-9697* 🌐 *www.valentinocardiff.co.uk* 🕒 *Closed Sun.*

WHERE TO STAY

For expanded hotel reviews, visit Fodors.com.

$ B&B/INN 🏨 **Jolyons Boutique Hotel.** This town house, a hop and a skip from the Wales Millennium Centre in Cardiff Bay, bucks the trend in a city where big, modern hotels are usually a safer bet than boutique places. **Pros:** loads of character; comfortable bar; good online discounts. **Cons:** 10-minute drive from the city center; no parking. [$] *Rooms from: £76* ✉ *Bute Crescent* ☎ *029/2048–8775* 🌐 *www.jolyons.co.uk* 🛏 *6 rooms* 🍽 *Breakfast.*

$ B&B/INN 🏨 **Lincoln House Hotel.** Perhaps the best of the many B&Bs on Cathedral Road—a handsome enclave of Victorian houses—this place close to the city center is a great find. **Pros:** good service; handy location; free parking. **Cons:** attractive road is spoiled by traffic; no restaurant. [$] *Rooms from: £90* ✉ *118 Cathedral Rd.* ☎ *029/2039–5558* 🌐 *www.lincolnhotel.co.uk* 🛏 *24 rooms* 🍽 *Breakfast.*

$$ HOTEL 🏨 **Park Plaza.** Just off Cardiff's main shopping street, this contemporary hotel is popular with business travelers for its luxurious feel and convenient downtown location. **Pros:** central location; good spa; stainless-steel pool. **Cons:** a bit sterile. [$] *Rooms from: £110* ✉ *Greyfriars Rd.* ☎ *029/2011–1111* 🌐 *www.parkplaza.com* 🛏 *129 rooms* 🍽 *Breakfast.*

$ HOTEL 🏨 **St. David's Hotel and Spa.** Natural light from a glass atrium floods this starkly modern luxury hotel overlooking Cardiff Bay. **Pros:** a bit like staying on a cruise ship; relaxing spa; good deals. **Cons:** out-of-the-way location; service can be patchy; breakfast is pricey. [$] *Rooms from: £95* ✉ *Havannah St.* ☎ *029/2045–4045* 🌐 *www.thestdavidshotel.com* 🛏 *132 rooms* 🍽 *Multiple meal plans.*

NIGHTLIFE AND THE ARTS

NIGHTLIFE

Café Jazz. With live jazz five nights a week, Café Jazz has video monitors in the bar and restaurant so you can enjoy the on-stage action. ⊠ *21 St. Mary St.* ☎ *029/2038–7026* ⊕ *www.cafejazzcardiff.com.*

Clwb Ifor Bach. This hot spot, whose name means "Little Ivor's Club," has three floors of eclectic music, from funk to folk to rock. ⊠ *11 Womanby St.* ☎ *029/2023–2199* ⊕ *www.clwb.net.*

THE ARTS

Motorpoint Arena Cardiff. This huge venue is Cardiff's premier location for big-ticket music acts and other touring shows. ⊠ *Mary Ann St.* ☎ *029/2022–4488* ⊕ *www.livenation.co.uk.*

New Theatre. This refurbished Edwardian playhouse presents big names, including the Royal Shakespeare Company, the National Theatre, and the Northern Ballet. ⊠ *Park Pl.* ☎ *029/2087–8889* ⊕ *www. newtheatrecardiff.co.uk.*

SHOPPING

Canopied Victorian and Edwardian shopping arcades lined with specialty stores weave in and out of the city's modern shopping complexes.

Cardiff Antiques Centre. In an 1856 arcade, the Cardiff Antiques Centre is a good place to buy vintage jewelry and accessories. ⊠ *Royal Arcade* ☎ *029/2039–8891* ⊕ *www.royalarcadecardiff.com.*

Cardiff Market. The traditional Cardiff Market sells tempting fresh foods beneath its Victorian glass canopy. ⊠ *St. Mary St.* ☎ *029/2087–1214* ⊕ *www.cardiff-market.co.uk.*

Melin Tregwynt. This elegant shop sells woolen clothing, bags, and cushions woven in an old Pembrokeshire mill. ⊠ *26 Royal Arcade* ☎ *029/2022–4997* ⊕ *www.melintregwynt.co.uk.*

ABERGAVENNY Y FENNI

28 miles north of Cardiff.

The market town of Abergavenny, just outside Brecon Beacons National Park, is a popular base for walkers and hikers. It has a ruined castle and is near the industrial history sites at Blaenavon.

GETTING HERE AND AROUND

Abergavenny is on the A40 road, about an hour's drive from Cardiff. Direct trains connect with Cardiff about every half hour and take about 40 minutes.

ESSENTIALS

Visitor Information Abergavenny Tourist Information Centre
⊠ *24 Monmouth Rd.* ☎ *01873/853254* ⊕ *www.visitabergavenny.co.uk.*

EXPLORING

TOP ATTRACTIONS

Abergavenny Castle. Built early in the 11th century, this castle witnessed a tragic event on Christmas Day, 1176: the Norman knight William de Braose invited the neighboring Welsh chieftains to a feast, and in a crude attempt to gain control of the area, had them all slaughtered as they sat to dine. The Welsh retaliated and virtually demolished the castle. Most of what now remains dates from the 13th and 14th centuries. The castle's 19th-century hunting lodge houses an excellent museum of regional history. The re-creation of a Victorian Welsh farmhouse kitchen includes old utensils and butter molds. ⊠ *Castle St.* ☎ *01873/854282* ⊕ *www.abergavennymuseum.co.uk* ✉ *Free* ⊗ *Mar.–Oct., Mon.–Sat. 11–1 and 2–5, Sun. 2–5; Nov.–Feb., Mon.–Sat. 11–1 and 2–4.*

FAMILY

Fodor's Choice

★

Big Pit: National Coal Museum. For hundreds of years, South Wales has been famous for its mining industry. Decades of decline—particularly during the 1980s—left only a handful of mines in business. The mines around Blaenavon, a small town 7 miles north of Abergavenny, have been designated a UNESCO World Heritage Site, and this fascinating museum is the centerpiece. Ex-miners lead you 300 feet underground into a coal mine. You spend just under an hour examining the old stables, machine rooms, and exposed coalfaces. Afterward you can look around an exhibition housed in the old Pithead Baths, including an extraordinary section on child labor in British mines. ■ TIP→ Children under 3½ feet tall are not allowed on the underground portion of the tour. ⊠ Off A4043, Blaenavon ☎ 01495/790311 ⊕ www.museumwales. ac.uk ✎ Free ⊗ Feb.–Dec., daily 9:30–4:30; Jan., weekends 9:30–4:30. Last admission 1 hr before closing.

Blaenavon Ironworks. A UNESCO World Heritage Site, the 1789 Blaenavon Ironworks traces the entire process of iron production in the late 18th century. Well-preserved blast furnaces, a water-balance lift used to transport materials to higher ground, and a terraced row of workers' cottages show how the business operated. ⊠ A4043, Blaenavon ☎ 01495/792615 ⊕ www.cadw.wales.gov.uk ✎ Free ⊗ Apr.–Oct., daily 10–5; Nov.–Mar., Fri. and Sat. 9–4, Sun. 11–4; last admission 30 mins before closing.

14

Fodor's Choice ★ **Raglan Castle.** Impressively complete from the front, majestically ruined within, Raglan was built in the 15th century and was the childhood home of Henry Tudor (1457–1509), who seized the throne of England in 1485 and became Henry VII. Raglan's heyday was relatively short-lived. The castle was attacked by Parliamentary forces during the English Civil War, and has lain in ruins ever since. The hexagonal Great Tower survives in reasonably good condition, as do a handful of rooms on the ground floor. ⊠ A40, Raglan ☎ 01291/690228 ⊕ www. cadw.wales.gov.uk ✎ £4 ⊗ Mar.–June, Sept., and Oct., daily 9:30–5; July and Aug., daily 9:30–6; Nov.–Feb., Mon–Sat. 10–4, Sun. 11–4; last admission 30 min before closing.

OFF THE BEATEN PATH

Tintern Abbey. Literally a stone's throw from the English border, Tintern is one of the region's most romantic monastic ruins. Founded in 1131 and dissolved by Henry VIII in 1536, it has inspired its fair share of poets and painters over the years—most famously J.M.W. Turner, who painted the transept covered in moss and ivy, and William Wordsworth, who idolized the setting in his poem "Lines Composed a Few Miles Above Tintern Abbey." ■ TIP→ Come early or late to avoid the crowds. The abbey, 5 miles north of Chepstow and 19 miles southeast of Abergavenny, is on the banks of the River Wye. ⊠ A466, Tintern ☎ 01291/689251 ⊕ www.cadw.wales.gov.uk ✎ £3.80 ⊗ Mar.–Jun., Sept., and Oct., daily 9:30–5; July and Aug., daily 9:30–6; Nov.–Feb., Mon.–Sat. 10–4, Sun. 11–4; last admission 30 min before closing.

WORTH NOTING

Tretower Court. A rare surviving example of a fortified medieval manor house, Tretower Court dates mostly from the 15th century. Buildings such as these were huge status symbols in their day, as they combined the security of a castle with the luxury of a manor house. On the grounds are the ruins of an earlier Norman castle. Tretower Court, restored in the 1930s, is outside the idyllic village of Crickhowell, 5 miles northwest of Abergavenny. ⊠ A479, Crickhowell ☎ 01874/730279 ⊕ www.cadw. wales.gov.uk ✎ £4.50 ⊗ Apr.–Oct., daily 10–5; Nov.–Mar., Fri. and Sat. 10–4, Sun. 11–4.; last admission 30 min before closing.

WHERE TO EAT AND STAY

For expanded hotel reviews, visit Fodors.com.

$ ✕ **Clytha Arms.** On the banks of the River Usk between Abergavenny
MODERN BRITISH and Raglan, this restaurant serves imaginative modern Welsh dishes in
a relaxed setting. The menu makes great use of local Welsh ingredients
in the cider-roasted ham with parsley sauce and the wild boar and duck
cassoulet. There's a cheaper menu at the bar. $ *Average main: £14* ⌧ *Off
B4598* ☎ *01873/840206* ⊕ *www.clytha-arms.com* ☾ *Closed Mon.*

$ **Bear Hotel.** In the middle of town, this coaching inn is full of char-
HOTEL acter. **Pros:** friendly bar; good food. **Cons:** some rooms overlook the
road; rooms vary in size; can get busy on weekends. $ *Rooms from:
£95* ⌧ *High St., Crickhowell* ☎ *01873/810408* ⊕ *www.bearhotel.co.uk*
↘ *35 rooms* ⊖ *Breakfast.*

$ **The Lamb and Flag Inn.** This inn on the outskirts of Abergavenny
HOTEL embodies what the British like to call "cheap and cheerful," meaning
good-quality accommodations that cover all the basics. **Pros:** excellent value; good restaurant; free parking. **Cons:** a little way from
the town center; few amenities. $ *Rooms from: £60* ⌧ *Brecon Rd.*
☎ *01873/857611* ⊕ *www.lambflag.co.uk* ↘ *5 rooms* ⊖ *Breakfast.*

$$ **Llansantffraed Court Hotel.** Dating from 1400, this grand country
HOTEL house 4 miles southeast of Abergavenny is set on 20 acres of well-
Fodor'sChoice tended grounds with lovely views of the Brecon Beacons. **Pros:** excellent
★ food; peaceful setting; great for anglers. **Cons:** tired decor; out-of-
the-way location. $ *Rooms from: £115* ⌧ *Old Raglan Rd., Clytha*
☎ *01873/840678* ⊕ *www.llch.co.uk* ↘ *21 rooms* ⊖ *Breakfast.*

NIGHTLIFE AND THE ARTS

Abergavenny Food Festival. Held over a weekend in September, the Aber-
gavenny Food Festival is a celebration for foodies and a symbol of the
growing interest in Welsh cuisine. There are demonstrations, lectures,
special events, and, of course, a food market. Be sure to sample the local
cheese called Y Fenni, flavored with a piquant combination of mustard
seeds and ale. ☎ *01873/851643* ⊕ *www.abergavennyfoodfestival.com.*

BRECON ABERHONDDU

19 miles northwest of Abergavenny, 41 miles north of Cardiff.

The historic market town of Brecon is known for its Georgian buildings,
narrow passageways, and pleasant riverside walks. It's also the gateway
to Brecon Beacons National Park. The town is particularly appealing
on Tuesday and Friday, which are market days. You may want to pur-
chase a hand-carved wooden "love spoon" similar to those on display
in the Brecknock Museum.

GETTING HERE AND AROUND

Brecon's nearest railway stations are at Merthyr Tydfil and Abergavenny
(both about 19 miles away). Beacons Bus service runs to many parts of
Brecon Beacons National Park. Brecon is a handsome town to explore
on foot—especially the riverside walk along the Promenade.

ESSENTIALS

Visitor Information Brecon Beacons Tourism ⌧ *Market Car Park, Church La.*
☎ *01874/622485* ⊕ *www.breconbeaconstourism.co.uk.*

One of three national parks in Wales, Brecon Beacons offers some panoramic mountain views, whether you're on foot or in a car.

EXPLORING

TOP ATTRACTIONS

Fodor's Choice ★ **Brecon Beacons National Park.** About 5 miles southwest of Brecon you encounter mountains and wild, windswept uplands that are tipped by shafts of golden light when the weather's fine, or fingers of ghostly mist when it's not. This 519-square-mile park is one of Wales's most breathtaking areas, perfect for a hike or scenic drive. Start at the visitor center on Mynydd Illtyd, a grassy stretch of upland west of the A470. It's an excellent source of information about the park, including maps and advice on the best routes (guided or self-guided). There's also an excellent Tea Room where you can fuel up for the journey or reward yourself with an indulgent slice of cake afterwards. If you want to see it all from your car, any road that crosses the Beacons will reward you with beautiful views, but the most spectacular is the high and undulating A4069, between Brynamman and Llangadog in the park's western end. ▥ TIP→ To explore the moorlands on foot, come prepared. Mist and rain descend quickly, and the summits are exposed to high winds. ✉ *Off A470, Libanus* ☎ *01874/623366* ⊕ *www.breconbeacons.org* ✆ *Free, parking £1 for 2 hrs, £2.50 all day* ☉ *Visitor Center: Mar.–Jun., Sept. and Oct., daily 9:30–5; July–Aug., daily 9:30–5:30; Nov.–Feb., daily 9:30–4:30.*

Fodor's Choice ★ **Carreg Cennen Castle.** On the edge of Brecon Beacons National Park, about 30 miles west of Brecon, this decaying cliff-top fortress was built in the 12th century, and remains of earlier defenses have been found dating back to the Iron Age. The castle, though a ruin, has a partially intact barbican (fortified outer section) and some inner chambers hewn dramatically from the bedrock. The climb up is somewhat punishing—you have to trudge up a steep, grassy hill—but the views of the valley, with its patchwork of green fields framed by the peaks of the Black Mountains, are enough to take away whatever breath you have left. ✉ *Off Derwydd Rd., Trapp* ☎ *01443/336000* 🌐 *www.cadw.wales.gov.uk* 🎟 *£4* 🕒 *Apr.–Oct., daily 9:30–6:30; Nov.–Mar., daily 9:30–4; last admission 45 min before closing.*

LOVE SPOONS

The rural Welsh custom of giving the object of your affection a "love spoon" dates from the mid-17th century. Made from wood, the spoons are elaborately hand-carved with tokens of love, including hearts, flowers, doves, intertwined vines, and chain links. These days you don't have to make the effort yourself—you can barely turn around in a Welsh souvenir shop without seeing one.

WORTH NOTING

Brecon Cathedral. Modest on the outside but surprisingly cavernous on the inside, this cathedral stands on the hill above the middle of town. Its heritage center does a good job of telling the building's history, and there's also a handy café. Local choirs perform concerts here regularly. ✉ *Cathedral Close* ☎ *01874/623857* 🌐 *www.breconcathedral.org.uk* 🎟 *Free* 🕒 *Daily 8–6.*

FAMILY **National Show Caves of Wales.** This underground cave system was discovered by two local men in 1912—make that rediscovered, as one of the caves contained 42 human skeletons that had lain undisturbed for up to 7,000 years. The main cave system, Dan Yr Ogof (Welsh for "beneath the cave"), is an impressive natural wonder, particularly the Cathedral Cave with natural stone archways and a dramatic waterfall. The whole thing is pitched at kids, with "dramatic" piped music to "enhance" the atmosphere, and a park featuring life-size models of prehistoric creatures. There's also a petting zoo and playground. The caves are 17 miles southwest of Brecon. ✉ *Off A48 or B4310, Abercrave* ☎ *01639/730284* 🌐 *www.showcaves.co.uk* 🎟 *£14* 🕒 *Apr.–early Nov., daily 10–3.*

WHERE TO EAT AND STAY

For expanded hotel reviews, visit Fodors.com.

$$ BRITISH 🍴 **Felin Fach Griffin.** Old and new blend perfectly in this modern country-style inn with old wood floors, comfy leather sofas, and stone walls hung with bright prints. The excellent menu makes use of fresh local produce, much of it coming from the Griffin's own organic garden, in dishes such as monkfish with pancetta and parsley butter, or shin of beef with cep risotto, asparagus, and wet garlic. The inn is in Felin Fach, 5 miles northeast of Brecon. [$] *Average main: £18* ✉ *A470, Felin Fach* ☎ *01874/620111* 🌐 *www.eatdrinksleep.ltd.uk.*

$ HOTEL 🏨 **Coach House.** This former coach house in the center of Brecon has been converted into a luxurious place to stay. **Pros:** lovely staff; central location; private parking. **Cons:** on a main road. [$] *Rooms from: £81* ✉ *Orchard St.* ☎ *01874/620043* 🌐 *www.coachhousebrecon.com* 🛏 *7 rooms* 🍽 *Breakfast.*

HIKING AND BIKING IN WALES

Opened to much fanfare in 2012, the Wales Coast Path is an 870-mile walking path that snakes along the entire coastline. Linking existing routes like the Pembrokeshire Coast Path in southeast Wales with new sections, it passes as close to the coastline as possible. Managed by the Welsh government, the route can be pretty wild in places and there isn't always a guardrail, so keep a close eye on small children. Work is currently underway to link it up with other popular routes, which should create an unbroken system of walking trails extending for more than 1,000 miles within a couple of years.

Other long-distance paths include north–south Offa's Dyke Path, based on the border between England and Wales established by King Offa in the 8th century, and the Glyndr Way, a 128-mile-long highland route that traverses Mid-Wales from the border town of Knighton via Machynlleth to Welshpool. Signposted footpaths in Wales's forested areas are short and easy to follow.

Dedicated enthusiasts might prefer the wide-open spaces of Brecon Beacons National Park or the mountains of Snowdonia.

Wales's reputation as both an on-road and off-road cycling mecca is well established. There's an amazing choice of scenic routes and terrain from challenging off-road tracks (⊕ www.mbwales.com is for the serious cyclist) to long-distance road rides and gentle family trails; VisitWales has information to get you started.

CONTACTS AND RESOURCES
Cycling Wales
⊕ www.cycling.visitwales.com.

Offa's Dyke Centre
☎ 01547/528753
⊕ www.offasdyke.demon.co.uk.

Pembrokeshire Coast Path
⊕ www.nationaltrail.co.uk.

Ramblers' Association in Wales
☎ 029/2064–4308
⊕ www.ramblers.org.uk/wales.

Wales Coast Path
⊕ www.walescoastpath.gov.uk.

$
B&B/INN
  Felin Glais. In the 17th century Felin Glais was a barn; enlarged but without losing its ancient character, it provides spacious and comfortable accommodations. **Pros:** beautiful building; spacious rooms; good food. **Cons:** dog-friendly environment won't please everyone; no credit cards; 48-hours notice required for dinner. $ *Rooms from: £85* ✉ *Abersycir* ☎ *01874/623107* ⊕ *www.felinglais.co.uk* ⤳ *4 rooms* ▭ *No credit cards* ⦿ *Breakfast.*

NIGHTLIFE AND THE ARTS

Brecon Jazz. For a weekend every August, Brecon Jazz, an international music festival, takes over the town. It attracts an increasingly high-profile list of performers and includes a parade through the town on the Sunday morning. ☎ *01874/611622 box office* ⊕ *www.breconjazz.com.*

Theatr Brycheiniog. On the canal, Theatr Brycheiniog is the town's main venue for music, plays, and comedy. It also has a waterfront bistro. ✉ *Canal Wharf* ☎ *01874/611622* ⊕ *www.brycheiniog.co.uk.*

SPORTS AND THE OUTDOORS

Biped Cycles. The Brecon Beacons contain some of the best cycling routes in Britain. Biped Cycles will rent you the right bike and equipment. ⊠ *10 Ship St.* ☎ *01874/622296* ⊕ *www.bipedcycles.co.uk.*

Crickhowell Adventure Gear. This shop sells outdoor gear and climbing equipment. ⊠ *21 Ship St.* ☎ *01874/611586* ⊕ *www.crickhowelladventure.co.uk.*

MERTHYR MAWR

45 miles south of Brecon, 22 miles west of Cardiff.

As you cross over an ancient stone bridge into Merthyr Mawr, you feel as if you've entered another world. From stone cottages with beehive-shape thatched roofs to the Victorian-era Church of St. Teilo, with the pieces of its long-gone 5th-century predecessor lined up in its church-yard, it's an idyllic place to wander around. The picturesque ruin of Ogmore Castle is just off the B4524, but the most memorable way to reach it is via the walking path that starts in the car park at the very southern tip of the village. The mile-long route goes through a farm and a Shetland pony stables.

GETTING HERE AND AROUND

Merthyr Mawr is signposted from the A48 and B4524, 7 miles south-west of junction 35 on the M4. The nearest train station is in Bridgend. There's no bus service to the village.

EXPLORING

Nash Point. Just a few miles south of Merthyr Mawr is this stunning promontory overlooking the Bristol Channel. Twin lighthouses stand guard against the elements; one is still operational, but the other is open for tours. This is also a popular picnic spot, and a small snack kiosk is open during summer months. Nothing beats this place at sunset, when the evening sky ignites in a riot of color. It's one of the most romantic spots in South Wales. ■ TIP→ There's no guardrail on the cliff, so keep a close eye on children. ⊠ *Marcross* ☎ *01225/245011* 🖅 *Free; lighthouse £3.50* ☉ *Mid-Mar.–Oct., weekends 2–5.*

Ogmore Castle. Just south of the village are these atmospheric ruins, nestled by a river that can only be crossed via stepping-stones. A number of legends are associated with the castle, one concerning a ghost that supposedly forces passersby to embrace a large rock known as the "Goblin Stone." When you try to draw back, so the story goes, you find that your hands and feet have become part of the rock. ⊠ *Ogmore Rd.* 🖅 *Free.*

QUICK BITES

The Pelican in Her Piety. Up a small hill next to Ogmore Castle, The Pelican in Her Piety stands like a mirage. This friendly and fabulously named little pub is a welcome spot for a snack or restorative pint after the long walk from Merthyr Mawr. ⊠ *Ogmore Rd* ☎ *01656/880049* ⊕ *www.pelicanpub.co.uk.*

WHERE TO EAT

$ BRITISH 🍴 **The Plough and Harrow.** A short drive from Nash Point is this friendly local pub, on the edge of the tiny cliff-top village of Monknash. The food is delicious and unfussy, mostly pub classics like steaks and grilled fish. Everything is served in a cozy dining room with a fireplace. There's a small but decent wine list, and an even better selection of real ales. This place is popular locally, so call ahead or be prepared to wait. [$] *Average main: £13* ✉ *Off Hoel Las, Monknash* ☎ *01656/890209* 🌐 *www.ploughandharrow.org.*

14

SWANSEA ABERTAWE

22 miles northwest of Merthyr Mawr, 40 miles west of Cardiff.

The birthplace of poet Dylan Thomas (1914–53), Swansea adores its native son. It honors him throughout the year, especially at the Dylan Thomas Festival in October and November. But Swansea no longer seems like a place that would inspire poetry. Heavily bombed in World War II, it was clumsily rebuilt. Today it merits a stop primarily for a couple of good museums. However, the surrounding countryside tells a different story. The National Botanic Gardens and Neath Abbey make for interesting diversions, and the stunning Gower Peninsula contains some of the region's best beaches.

GETTING HERE AND AROUND

There's a half-hourly rail service from London's Paddington Station. The city has direct National Express bus connections to other parts of Wales, as well as to London and other cities.

ESSENTIALS

Visitor Information Swansea Tourist Information Centre ✉ *Plymouth St.* ☎ *01792/468321* 🌐 *www.visitswanseabay.com.*

EXPLORING

TOP ATTRACTIONS

Dylan Thomas Centre. Situated on the banks of the Tawe close to the Maritime Quarter, the Dylan Thomas Centre serves as the National Literature Centre for Wales. The center houses a permanent Dylan Thomas exhibition, art gallery, restaurant, and café-bookshop, and hosts the annual Dylan Thomas Festival. **TIP→ The poet's fans can buy a booklet that outlines the Dylan Thomas Trail around South Wales. It includes the Boathouse (now a museum), in Laugharne, where the poet lived and wrote the last four years of his life.** ✉ *Somerset Pl.* ☎ *01792/463980* 🌐 *www.dylanthomas.com* 🎟 *Free* 🕓 *Daily 10–4:30.*

FAMILY Fodor's Choice ★ **Gower Peninsula.** This peninsula, which stretches westward from Swansea, was the first part of Britain to be designated an Area of Outstanding Natural Beauty. Its shores are a succession of sheltered sandy bays and awesome headlands. The seaside resort of Mumbles, on the outskirts of Swansea, is the most famous town along the route. It's an elegantly faded place to wander on a sunny afternoon, with an amusement pier and seaside promenade. Farther along the peninsula, the secluded Pwlldu Bay can only be reached on foot from nearby villages like Southgate. A few miles westward is the more accessible (and

Stretching west of Swansea, the Gower Peninsula has some stunning beaches, including Rhossili.

very popular) Three Cliffs Bay, with its sweeping views and wide, sandy beach. At the far western tip of the peninsula, Rhossili has perhaps the best beach of all. Its unusual, snaking causeway—known locally as the Worm's Head—is inaccessible at high tide. ⊕ *www. enjoygower.com.*

Fodor's Choice ★ **National Botanic Garden of Wales.** This 568-acre, 18th-century estate is dotted with lakes, fountains, and a Japanese garden. The centerpiece is the Norman Foster–designed Great Glass House, the largest single-span greenhouse in the world, which blends into the curving landforms of the Tywi Valley. The greenhouse's interior landscape includes a 40-foot-deep ravine and thousands of plants from all over the world. The garden, 20 miles northwest of Swansea, is signposted off the main road between Swansea and Carmarthen. ⊠ *Off A48 or B4310, Llanarthne* ☎ *01558/668–7688* ⊕ *www.gardenofwales.org.uk* ✉ *£8.50* ⊙ *Apr.– Sept., daily 10–6; Oct.–Mar., daily 10–4:30.*

FAMILY **National Waterfront Museum.** Housed in a construction of steel, slate, and glass grafted onto a historic redbrick building, the National Waterfront Museum's galleries have 15 theme areas. State-of-the-art interactive technology and a host of artifacts bring Welsh maritime and industrial history to a 21st-century audience. ⊠ *Oystermouth Rd., Maritime Quarter* ☎ *029/2057–3600* ⊕ *www.museumwales.ac.uk* ✉ *Free* ⊙ *Daily 10–5.*

WORTH NOTING

5 Cwmdonkin Drive. Dylan Thomas was born in this suburban Edwardian house, which remains a place of pilgrimage for the poet's devotees. Tours (which must be booked in advance) are tailored according to how much time you want to spend here; devoted fans can hang around for hours. The house can be rented as self-catering accommodation for around £130 per night or £530 per week. ✉ *5 Cwmdonkin Dr.* ☎ *01792/405331* 🌐 *www.5cwmdonkindrive.com* 🎟 *£5* 🕒 *Call ahead for tours.*

Maritime Quarter. Swansea was extensively bombed during World War II, and its old dockland has reemerged as the splendid Maritime Quarter, a modern marina with attractive housing and shops and a seafront that commands views across the sweep of Swansea Bay.

Neath Abbey. Built in the 12th century, this abbey was, in its day, one of the largest and most important in the British Isles. Though just a shell, the main church gives an impressive sense of scale, with its tall buttresses and soaring, glassless windows. Here and there small sections of the original building have survived unscathed, including an undercroft with a vaulted stone ceiling. Neath Abbey is 9 miles northeast of Swansea. ✉ *Monastery Rd., Neath Abbey* 🌐 *www.cadw.wales.gov.uk* 🎟 *Free* 🕒 *Daily 10–4.*

14

Richard Burton Trail. Two new walking trails celebrate the early life of the revered Welsh actor, who was born in the village of Pontrhydyfen, 13 miles northeast of Swansea. The tours cover significant places from his childhood, in addition to some beautiful Welsh countryside. Illustrated maps detailing the tours can be downloaded on the Visit Neath Port Talbot website. ✉ *B4286, Pontrhydyfen* 🌐 *www.visitnpt.co.uk.*

Swansea Museum. Founded in 1841, this museum contains a quirky and eclectic collection that includes an Egyptian mummy, local archaeological exhibits, and the intriguing Cabinet of Curiosity, which holds artifacts from Swansea's past. The museum is close to the Maritime Quarter. ✉ *Victoria Rd.* ☎ *01792/653763* 🌐 *www.swanseaheritage.net* 🎟 *Free* 🕒 *Tues.–Sun. 10–5.*

WHERE TO EAT AND STAY

For expanded hotel reviews, visit Fodors.com.

$$ SPANISH

🍴 **La Braseria.** Lively and welcoming, this spot resembles a Spanish *bodega* (wine cellar), with its flamenco music, oak barrels, and whitewashed walls. Among the house specialties are sea bass in rock salt, roast suckling pig, and pheasant (in season, of course). There's a good choice of 140 Spanish and French wines. [$] *Average main: £15* ✉ *28 Wind St.* ☎ *01792/469683* 🌐 *www.labraseria.com* 🕒 *Closed Sun.*

$$$$ MODERN BRITISH

🍴 **Slice.** One of Swansea's few truly high-end restaurants, Slice is where the locals go for a properly grown-up meal. The small but ever-changing fixed-price menu makes excellent use of local Welsh meats, fish and cheese, with impeccably presentation. You may start with a pheasant boudin before moving on to venison steaks served with a miniature venison pie, or perhaps a simple, fresh lemon sole. There's also separate vegetarian menu. Note that the restaurant is accessed up a flight of stairs. [$] *Average main: £35* ✉ *74 Eversley Rd., Sketty* ☎ *01792/290929* 🌐 *www.sliceswansea.co.uk* 🕒 *No lunch.*

$$$ HOTEL Fodor's Choice ★ **Fairyhill.** Luxuriously furnished public rooms, spacious bedrooms, and delicious cooking make this 18th-century country house a restful retreat. **Pros:** peaceful surroundings; good restaurant. **Cons:** you must buy dinner on Friday and Saturday night stays; restaurant always busy. [$] *Rooms from: £180* ✉ *Off B4295, 11 miles southwest of Swansea, Reynoldston* ☎ *01792/390139* 🌐 *www.fairyhill.net* 🛏 *8 rooms* 🍴 *Some meals.*

$ HOTEL **Morgans.** Now a hotel, the Victorian-era Port Authority building in the Maritime Quarter has lost none of its period features: moldings, pillars, stained glass, and wood floors. **Pros:** near the marina; short walk to shops; maritime flair. **Cons:** No room service in Townhouse. [$] *Rooms from: £65* ✉ *Somerset Pl.* ☎ *01792/484848* 🌐 *www.morganshotel.co.uk* 🛏 *41 rooms* 🍴 *No meals.*

TENBY DINBYCH-Y-PYSGOD

53 miles west of Swansea.

Fodor's Choice ★ Pastel-color Georgian houses cluster around a harbor in this seaside town, which became a fashionable resort in the 19th century and is still popular. Two golden sandy beaches stretch below the hotel-lined cliff top. Medieval Tenby's ancient town walls still stand, enclosing narrow streets and passageways full of shops, inns, and places to eat. From the harbor you can take a short boat trip to Caldey Island, with its active Cistercian community.

GETTING HERE AND AROUND

Tenby is on the southwest Wales rail route from London's Paddington Station. You have to change trains at Swansea or Newport. The center of Tenby, a maze of narrow medieval streets, has parking restrictions. In summer, downtown is closed to traffic, so park in one of the lots and take the shuttle buses.

ESSENTIALS

Visitor Information **Tenby Information Centre** ✉ *Unit 2, Upper Park Rd.* ☎ *01834/842402* 🌐 *www.pembrokeshire.gov.uk.*

EXPLORING

Fodor's Choice ★ **Caldey Island.** This beautiful little island off the coast at Tenby has whitewashed stone buildings that lend it a Mediterranean feel. The island is best known for its Cistercian order, whose black-and-white-robed monks make a famous perfume from the local plants. You can visit tiny St. Illtud's Church to see the Caldey Stone, an early Christian artifact from circa AD 600, engraved in Latin and ancient Celtic. St. David's Church, on a hill above the village, is a simple Norman chapel noted for its art-deco stained glass. The monastery itself isn't open to the public, but its church has a public viewing gallery if you want to observe a service. Boats to Caldey Island leave from Tenby's harbor every 20 minutes or so between Easter and September. ✉ *Caldey Island* ☎ *01834/844453* 🌐 *www.caldey-island.co.uk* 🎟 *Free, boats £11 round-trip* 🕒 *Boats Easter–Oct., weekdays (also Sat. May–Sept) 10–3. Last return usually 5.*

Pembroke Castle. About 10 miles east of Tenby is this remarkably complete Norman fortress dating from 1190. Its walls remain stout, its gatehouse mighty, and the enormous cylindrical keep proved so impregnable to cannon fire in the Civil War that Cromwell's men had to starve out its Royalist defenders. Climb the towers and walk the walls for fine views. A well-stocked gift shop sells faux-medieval knickknacks. ⊠ *Westgate Hill, Pembroke* ☎ *01646/681510* ⊕ *www.pembroke-castle. co.uk* ⊑ *£5.50* ☉ *Apr.–Aug., daily 9:30–6; Sept.–Oct. and Mar., daily 10–5; Nov.–Feb., daily 10–4; last entry 45 mins before closing.*

Pembrokeshire Coast National Park. By far the smallest of the country's three national parks, Pembrokeshire Coast is no less strikingly beautiful than the other two. The park has 13 blue flag beaches and a host of spectacular clifftop drives and walks, including some of the most popular stretches of the Wales Coast Path. The park has a smattering of historic sites, including the impossibly picturesque St. David's Cathedral, built in a Viking-proof nook by the Irish Sea. The information center in Tenby is a good place to start. ⊠ *Tenby National Park Centre, South Parade* ☎ *01834/845040* ⊕ *www.pembrokeshirecoast.org.uk* ⊑ *Free* ☉ *Apr.–Sept., daily 9:30–5; Oct.–Mar., Mon.–Sat. 10:30–3:30.*

FAMILY   **Tenby Museum and Art Gallery.** Close to the castle, this small but informative museum recalls the town's maritime history and its growth as a fashionable resort. Kids will appreciate the section on Tenby's role in the golden age of piracy. Two art galleries feature works by local artists. ⊠ *Castle Hill* ☎ *01834/842809* ⊕ *www.tenbymuseum.org.uk* ⊑ *£4* ☉ *Oct.–Mar., Tues.–Sat. 10–5; Apr.–Sept., daily 10–5; last admission 30 min before closing.*

FAMILY   **Tudor Merchant's House.** This late-15th-century home shows how a prosperous trader would have lived in Tudor times. Kids can try on Tudor-style costumes. ⊠ *Quay Hill* ☎ *01834/842279* ⊕ *www.nationaltrust. org.uk* ⊑ *£3.20* ☉ *Mid-Feb.–Mar., Nov. and Dec. weekends 11–3; Apr.–mid-Jun., Sept. and Oct. Wed.–Mon. 11–5; mid-July–Aug., daily 11–5; last admission 30 min before closing.*

WHERE TO EAT AND STAY

For expanded hotel reviews, visit Fodors.com.

$$ ✕ **Plantagenet House.** Flickering candles, open fireplaces, exposed stone
BRITISH   walls, and top-notch locally sourced food are hallmarks of this popular restaurant and bar. The menu contains a selection of Welsh-reared steaks and other meat dishes, but seafood is the specialty. The romantic setting is as much of a draw as the food. Check out the huge stone "Flemish chimney," a distinctive style popularized by immigrants during the 16th century. $ *Average main: £18* ⊠ *Quay Hill* ☎ *01834/842350* ⊕ *www.plantagenettenby.co.uk* ☉ *Closed Jan.–mid-Feb.*

$ ⌂ **Ivy Bank Guest House.** This comfortable and immaculate Victorian
B&B/INN   house sits across from the train station, a five-minute stroll from the sea. **Pros:** cozy and simple; close to beach; seniors discounts. **Cons:** you have to park at the train station; color scheme not for everyone. $ *Rooms from: £36* ⊠ *Harding St.* ☎ *01834/842311* ⊕ *www.ivybanktenby.co.uk* ⇆ *5 rooms* ⑪ *Breakfast.*

$$ 🛏 **Penally Abbey.** Built on the site
HOTEL of a 6th-century abbey in 5 acres
of lush forest overlooking Cam-
arthen Bay, this dignified 18th-
century house is awash with period
details. **Pros:** informal luxury;
great views; friendly hosts. **Cons:**
small pool. $ *Rooms from: £148*
✉ *Off A4139, 2 miles west of
Tenby, Penally* ☎ *01834/843033*
⊕ *www.penally-abbey.com* ⤳ *17
rooms* ⊺◉⊺ *Breakfast.*

$$ 🛏 **St. Brides Spa Hotel.** Between Amroth and Tenby, this luxury hotel is
HOTEL perched on a breathtaking location above Carmarthen Bay; most of
the superbly appointed rooms have stunning sea views. **Pros:** amazing views; wonderful spa; fantastic restaurant. **Cons:** steep walk from
the beach; minimum stay on weekends. $ *Rooms from: £150* ✉ *St.
Brides Hill, Saundersfoot* ☎ *01834/812304* ⊕ *www.stbridesspahotel.
com* ⤳ *35 rooms* ⊺◉⊺ *Breakfast.*

SPORTS AND THE OUTDOORS

The town's beaches are hugely popular in summertime. North Beach
is the busiest, with shops and a little café along the promenade. The
adjoining Harbour Beach is prettier and more secluded. Castle Beach
is in a little cove where you can walk out to a small island at low tide.
Past that is South Beach, which stretches for more than a mile.

ST. DAVID'S TYDDEWI

35 miles northwest of Tenby.

Despite its miniscule size, this community of fewer than 1,800 people
isn't a village or a hamlet—it's actually Britain's smallest city. Historically, little St. David's has punched above its weight due to the presence
of St. David's Cathedral, the resting place of the patron saint of Wales
and once a major destination for pilgrims. These days, visitors with
time on their hands might want to consider approaching the city via
the Wales Coast Path, around the St. David's headland from St. Justin-
ian to Caerfai Bay. In May and June the town's hedgerows and coastal
paths are ablaze with wildflowers. The town's visitor center also has
a small collection of art and artifacts drawn from the collection of the
National Museum of Wales.

GETTING HERE AND AROUND

St. David's is on the A487. The nearest train station is 14 miles southeast in Haverfordwest. Bus 411 travels from Haverfordwest to St.
David's every hour or so.

ESSENTIALS

Visitor Information Oriel y Parc Gallery and Visitor Centre ✉ *1 High St.*
☎ *01437/720392* ⊕ *www.pembrokeshirecoast.org.uk.*

EXPLORING

OFF THE BEATEN PATH

Last Invasion Tapestry. The 100-foot-long Last Invasion Tapestry, on display in the Town Hall in Fishguard, is modeled on the famous Bayeux Tapestry depicting the Norman invasion of 1066. This modern version marks a lesser known, and certainly less successful assault on the country. In 1797 a unit of French soldiers, led by an Irish-American general, landed in Fishguard Harbour. They were defeated by a hastily assembled local militia, which included many women. The impressive tapestry, commissioned to mark the event's 200th anniversary, took 70 local women more than 40,000 hours to complete. Fishguard is 16 miles northeast of St. David's off the A487. ✉ *Market Sq., Fishguard* ☎ *01437/776638* 🎫 *Free* ⏲ *Apr.–Sept., Mon.–Wed., Fri. and Sat. 9:30–5; Thurs. 9:30–6:30; Oct.–Mar., Mon.–Wed. and Fri., 9:30–5; Thurs. 9:30–6:30; Sat. 9:30–1.*

Fodor's Choice ★

St. David's Cathedral. The idyllic valley location of this cathedral helped protect the church from Viking raiders by hiding it from the view of invaders who came by sea. Originally founded by St. David himself in around AD 600, the current building dates from the 12th century, although it has been added to at various times since. You must climb down 39 steps (known locally as the Thirty-Nine Articles) to enter the grounds; then start at the Gatehouse, with its exhibition on the history of the building. In the cathedral itself, the 15th-century choir stalls still have their original floor tiles, while the Holy Trinity Chapel contains an intricate fan-vaulted ceiling and a casket said to contain the patron saint's bones. **TIP→ Don't miss the Treasury and its illuminated gospels, silver chalices, and 700-year-old golden bishop's crosier.** In August, guided tours costing £4 begin Monday at 11:30 and Friday at 2:30, and on other days by arrangement. The cathedral has a good café. ✉ *The Close* ☎ *01437/720202* 🌐 *www.stdavidscathedral.org.uk* 🎫 *Free* ⏲ *Daily 8:40–5.*

Bishop's Palace. At the rear of the grounds of St. David's Cathedral are the ruins of the 13th-century Bishop's Palace, particularly beautiful at dusk. ✉ *The Close* ☎ *01437/720517* 🌐 *www.cadw.wales.gov.uk* 🎫 *£3.50* ⏲ *Mar.–June, Sept., and Oct., daily 9:30–5; July and Aug., daily 9:30– 6; Nov.–Feb., Mon.–Sat. 10–4, Sun. 11–4; last admission 30 min before closing.*

WHERE TO STAY

For expanded hotel reviews, visit Fodors.com.

$$ HOTEL

🏨 **Warpool Court Hotel.** Overlooking a stunning stretch of coastline, this hotel sits on a bluff above St. Non's Bay.**Pros:** beautiful sea views; peaceful gardens; good food. **Cons:** unattractive entrance; few restaurants nearby. [$] *Rooms from: £140* ✉ *Off Goat St.* ☎ *01437/720300* 🌐 *www.warpoolcourthotel.com* 🛏 *25 rooms* 🍴 *Breakfast.*

MID-WALES

Traditional market towns and country villages, small seaside resorts, quiet roads, and rolling landscapes filled with sheep farms, forests, and lakes make up Mid-Wales, the country's green and rural heart. There are no cities here—the area's largest town is barely more than a big village. Outside of one or two towns, such as Aberystwyth and Llandrindod Wells, accommodations are mainly country inns, small hotels, and rural farmhouses. This area also has some splendid country-house hotels.

There are no motorways through Mid-Wales, and the steam railways that once linked this area with Cardiff are long gone. Getting around requires a bit of advance planning, but it's worth the trouble. The bibliophilic charms of Hay-on-Wye have made the town world-famous, while the countryside around Abertystwyth is peppered with peaceful sandy beaches and dramatic beauty spots.

HAY-ON-WYE Y GELLI GANDRYLL

57 miles north of Cardiff, 25 miles north of Abergavenny.

Fodor's Choice
★

With its crumbling old castle and low-slung buildings framed by lolloping green hills, Hay-on-Wye is a beautiful little place. In 1961 Richard Booth established a small secondhand bookshop here. Other booksellers soon got in on the act, and now there are dozens of shops. It's now the largest secondhand bookselling center in the world, and priceless 14th-century manuscripts rub spines with "job lots" selling for a few pounds.

For 10 days every May and June, Hay-on-Wye is taken over by its Literary Festival, a celebration of literature that attracts famous writers from all over the world. (Bill Clinton, himself an attendee, once called it "the Woodstock of the mind.") Plan ahead if you want to attend, as hotels get booked several months in advance.

GETTING HERE AND AROUND

You'll need a car to get to Hay. Use one of the public lots of the outskirts of town and walk—the whole town is accessible on foot. The nearest train stations are Builth Wells in Wales (19 miles) and Hereford in England (22 miles).

ESSENTIALS

Visitor Information Hay-on-Wye Tourist Information Bureau ⊠ *Oxford Rd.* ☎ *01497/820144* ⊕ *www.hay-on-wye.co.uk/tourism.*

EXPLORING

Hay Castle. On a hilltop are the handsome remains of a 12th-century castle keep, jutting out from behind a 16th-century manor house. ⊠ *Castle St.* ⊡ *Free* ⊙ *Late Mar.–Oct., daily 9:30–6; Nov.–late Mar., daily 9:30–5:30.*

> QUICK
> BITES

Shepherd's. The delicious ice cream at Shepherd's is legendary in these parts. Produced at a local farm, its distinct, creamy flavor comes from the fact that it's made from sheep's milk. ⊠ *9 High Town* ☎ *01497/821898* ⊕ *www.shepherdsicecream.co.uk.*

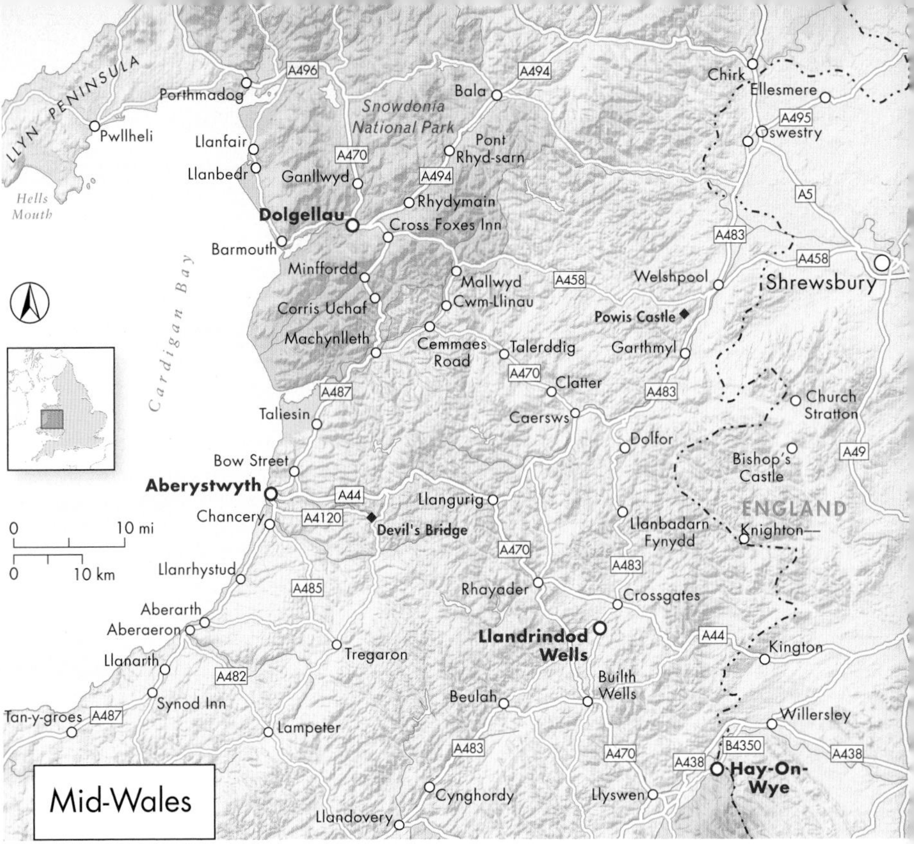

WHERE TO EAT AND STAY

For expanded hotel reviews, visit Fodors.com.

$$ BRITISH 🍴 **Old Black Lion.** A 17th-century coaching inn close to Hay's center is ideal for a lunch break while you're ransacking the bookshops. The oak-beamed bar serves food, and the breakfasts are especially good. The restaurant's sophisticated cooking has an international flavor and emphasizes local meats and produce. You can even opt for an overnight stay in one of the country-style rooms (from about £90 per night). [$] *Average main: £15* ✉ *Lion St.* ☎ *01497/820841* 🌐 *www.oldblacklion.co.uk.*

$$$ HOTEL 🏨 **Llangoed Hall.** This magnificent Jacobean mansion on the banks of the River Wye, about 7 miles west of Hay-on-Wye, has beautiful fabrics and furnishings, open fireplaces, a sweeping carved staircase, and a paneled library dating back to 1632. **Pros:** secluded setting by River Wye; wonderful art collection. **Cons:** often filled with wedding parties; minimum stay sometimes required; no attractions within walking distance. [$] *Rooms from: £160* ✉ *A470, Llyswen* ☎ *01874/754525* 🌐 *www.llangoedhall.co.uk* 🛏 *23 rooms* 🍽 *Breakfast.*

$$ HOTEL 🏨 **The Swan.** Once a coaching inn, this sophisticated lodging on the edge of town retains its sense of history. **Pros:** atmospheric building; friendly staff; good food. **Cons:** wedding parties dominate in summer;

beds a bit creaky. [$] *Rooms from: £100* ✉ *Church St.* ☎ *01497/821188* 🌐 *www.swanathay.co.uk* 🛏 *17 rooms* 🍴 *Breakfast.*

SHOPPING

The Thursday Market takes over much of the town center every Thursday morning. Traders sell everything from antiques to home-baked cakes.

Boz Books. The kind of dusty old bookshop you see in movies, Boz Books has an impressive range of 19th-century first editions, including many by Dickens. ✉ *13A Castle St.* ☎ *01497/821277* 🌐 *www.bozbooks.demon.co.uk.*

Murder and Mayhem. True to its name, this shop specializes in crime and horror. Head upstairs for a cheaper and more eclectic selection, including old pulp novellas. ✉ *5 Lion St.* ☎ *01497/821613.*

Richard Booth Books. Shopkeeper Richard Booth once tried to declare Hay an independent kindgom—with himself as king. His bookstore has a huge collection from all over the world, piled haphazardly across two labyrinthine floors. ✉ *44 Lion St.* ☎ *01497/820322* 🌐 *www.boothbooks.co.uk.*

Rose's Books. Easy to spot for its fuchsia-pink front, Rose's Books is devoted entirely to children's books, including rare first editions. ✉ *14 Broad St.* ☎ *01497/820013* 🌐 *www.rosesbooks.com.*

LLANDRINDOD WELLS LLANDRINDOD

27 miles north of Hay-on-Wye, 67 miles north of Cardiff.

Also known as Llandod, the old spa town of Llandrindod Wells preserves its Victorian look with turrets, cupolas, loggias, and balustrades everywhere. Cross over to South Crescent, passing the Glen Usk Hotel with its wrought-iron balustrade and the Victorian bandstand in the gardens opposite, and you reach Middleton Street, a Victorian thoroughfare. From there, head to Rock Park and the path that leads to the Pump Room. This historic building is now an alternative health center, but visitors can freely "take the waters."

GETTING HERE AND AROUND

There are about half a dozen trains daily from Cardiff's Craven Arms Station, and the journey takes around three hours. Direct trains from Swansea and Shrewsbury also stop here, but they're less frequent.

ESSENTIALS

Visitor Information **Llandrindod Wells Tourist information Centre** ✉ *Temple St.* ☎ *01597/822600* 🌐 *www.llandrindod.co.uk.*

EXPLORING

OFF THE BEATEN PATH

Powis Castle. Continuously occupied since the 13th century, Powis Castle rises above the town of Welshpool. One of the most elegant residential castles in Britain, Powis is equally renowned for its magnificent terraced gardens. The interior contains an outstanding art collection, from Greek vases to paintings by Thomas Gainsborough and Joshua Reynolds. The **Clive of India Museum** contains perhaps the most extensive private collection of antique Indian art in Britain. Powis Castle is north of Llandrindod Wells on the A483. ✉ *A483, Welshpool* ☎ *01938/551944* 🌐 *www.nationaltrust.org.uk* 🎟 *£12; castle only £6; garden only £9*

Hay-on-Wye's claims to fame are its many secondhand bookstores and the annual Literary Festival.

⊙ *Castle Mar.–Oct., daily 12:30–5; Nov.–Feb., weekends 12:30–3:30. Museum Mar.–Oct., daily 12:30–5. Gardens Mar.–Sept., daily 11–5:30; Oct. daily 11–4:30; Nov. daily 11–3:30.*

Radnorshire Museum. In Memorial Gardens, this museum tells the story of the town's development from prehistory onwards, and includes a small collection of Roman and medieval artifacts. The largest and most interesting section is devoted to the town's Victorian heyday, with some of the "cures" at the spa explained in gruesome detail. ⊠ *Temple St.* ☎ *01597/824513* 💷 *£1* ⊙ *Apr.–Sept., Tues.–Sat. 10–4; Oct.–Mar., Tues.–Fri. 10–4, Sat. 10–1.*

Royal Welsh Show. The town of Llanelwedd, 7 miles south of Llandrindod, comes to life in late July for the Royal Welsh Show. The old-school livestock judging, sheepdog competitions, and craft demonstrations are spiced up with events such as vintage air displays and motorbike stunt shows. ⊠ *Llanelwedd* ☎ *01982/553683* ⊕ *www.rwas.co.uk.*

Victorian Festival. The Victorian Festival takes over Llandrindod Wells for a week in late August. Everyone from shopkeepers to hotel clerks dresses up in period costume for events from tea dances to street parades. ☎ *01597/823441* ⊕ *www.victorianfestival.co.uk.*

WHERE TO EAT AND STAY
For expanded hotel reviews, visit Fodors.com.

$ × **Jules.** Cheerful and family-run, this bar and bistro in the middle of
BISTRO town offers a small but well-edited menu of bistro cooking, such as fried tilapia with coconut curry, or slow-baked chicken with chorizo, couscous, and olives. Traditional Sunday roast lunches are delicious

and popular. $ *Average main: £11* ⊠ *Temple St.* ☎ *01597/824642* ⊕ *julesrestaurant.blogspot.com.*

$
B&B/INN
▦ **Brynhir Farm.** A friendly welcome awaits at this cozy farmhouse 2 miles outside Llandrindod. **Pros:** lovely house; peaceful location; charming hosts. **Cons:** lacks modern extras; remote location is not walking distance to town. $ *Rooms from: £70* ⊠ *Chapel Rd., Howey* ☎ *01597/822425* ⊕ *www.brynhirfarm.co.uk* ⇆ *3 rooms* ⦿ *Breakfast.*

$$
HOTEL
▦ **Metropole.** This grand looking hotel from 1896 is surprisingly contemporary on the inside, with modern furnishings that complement the original architectural flourishes. **Pros:** very central; good service; inexpensive spa. **Cons:** lacks character; can be taken over by conferences. $ *Rooms from: £126* ⊠ *Temple St.* ☎ *01597/823700* ⊕ *www.metropole.co.uk* ⇆ *120 rooms* ⦿ *Breakfast.*

ABERYSTWYTH

41 miles northwest of Llandrindod Wells via A44, 118 miles northwest of Cardiff.

A pleasingly eccentric combination of faded Victorian seaside resort and artsy college town, Aberystwyth is the largest community in Mid-Wales, with a population of barely 16,000. When the weather's fine, the beaches along the bay fill up with sunbathers; when it's not, waves crash so ferociously against the sea wall that even the hotels across the street get soaked. To the east of the town are the Cambrian Mountains and the Veil of Rheidol, which can be visited by steam train.

GETTING HERE AND AROUND
All journeys from South Wales are routed through Shrewsbury and take four to five hours. From London, the trip here takes five to six hours. Long-distance buses are infrequent and painfully slow, though the local bus system is good. There are two roads to Aberystwyth, both of them among the most scenic in Wales: the coastal A487 and the mountainous A44.

ESSENTIALS
Visitor Information Aberystwyth Tourist Information Centre ⊠ *Lisburn House, Terrace Rd.* ☎ *01970/612125.*

EXPLORING
TOP ATTRACTIONS
FAMILY **Constitution Hill.** At the northern end of the beach promenade, Constitution Hill dominates the skyline. From the top you can see much of the Welsh coastline (and, on *exceptionally* clear days, Ireland). There's a small café at the top and plenty of space for a picnic. If you're feeling hale and hearty, there's a long footpath that zigzags up to the 430-foot summit. From there a 5-mile-long coastal path stretches to the village of Borth, a smaller, sleepier resort north of Aberystwyth where the remains of a 3,000-year-old petrified forest may be seen on the beach at low tide.

Aberystwyth Cliff Railway. The Victorian-era Aberystwyth Cliff Railway deposits you at the top of Constitution Hill. Opened in 1896, it's the longest electric cliff railway in Britain. ⊠ *Cliff Terr.* ☎ *01970/617642*

⊕ *www.aberystwythcliffrailway.co.uk* ⬛ *£4 round-trip* ☉ *Apr.–Oct., daily 10–5; Nov.–Mar. Wed.–Sun. 10–5. Times vary in winter.*

Great Aberystwyth Camera Obscura. A modern version of a Victorian amusement, Great Aberystwyth Camera Obscura is a massive 14-inch lens that gives you a bird's-eye view of Cardigan Bay and 26 Welsh mountain peaks. It's reached via the Aberystwyth Cliff Railway. ⊠ *Cliff Terr.* ☎ *01970/617642* ⬛ *Free* ☉ *Mar.–Oct., daily 10–5*

National Library of Wales. This massive neoclassical building next to the University of Wales houses notable Welsh and other Celtic literary works among its more than 4.5 million volumes. The cache of public records makes it an invaluable tool if you're tracing your family tree. Also here is the **National Screen and Sound Archive of Wales**, which hosts lunchtime and evening film screenings. ⊠ *Off Penglais Rd.* ☎ *01970/632800* ⊕ *www.llgc.org.uk* ⬛ *Free* ☉ *Weekdays 9:30–6, Sat. 9:30–5.*

FAMILY **Vale of Rheidol Railway.** At Aberystwyth Station you can hop on the steam-powered Vale of Rheidol Railway for an hour-long ride to the **Devil's Bridge** (*Pont y Gwr Drwg*, or, literally, "the Bridge of the Evil One") where the rivers Rheidol and Mynach meet in a series of spectacular falls. Clamped between two rocky cliffs where a torrent of water pours unceasingly, there are actually three bridges, one built on top of the other. The oldest bridge is about 800 years old. ⊠ *Park Ave.* ☎ *01970/625819* ⊕ *www.rheidolrailway.co.uk* ⬛ *£16 round-trip* ☉ *Easter–Oct.; call for schedule.*

WORTH NOTING

Aberystwyth Castle. At the southern end of the bay, a little way down from the pier, are the crumbling remains of this castle. Built in 1277, it was one of the key strongholds captured in the early 15th century by Owain Glyndwr, a Welsh prince who led the country's last serious bid for independence from England. Today it's a romantic, windswept ruin. ⊠ *New Promenade* ⬛ *Free.*

Ceredigion Museum. Housed in a flamboyant 1905 Edwardian theater, the Ceredigion Museum has collections related to folk history and the building's own music hall past. Highlights include a reconstructed mudwalled cottage from 1850 and items illustrating the region's seafaring, lead-mining, and farming history. ⊠ *Terrace Rd.* ☎ *01970/633088* ⊕ *museum.ceredigion.gov.uk* ⬛ *Free* ☉ *Apr.–Sept., Mon.–Sat. 10–5; Oct.–Mar., Mon.–Sat. noon–4:30.*

FAMILY **Llynwenog Silver-Lead Mine.** Outside the village of Ponterwyd, 10 miles east of Aberystwyth, this 200-year-old mine is now a museum where you can tour reproductions of mining buildings and some original machinery, including working waterwheels. Kids over the age of 8 can also enjoy a few harmless scares on the Black Chasm ghost tour, though very young ones will be better off sticking to the Woo Hoo Woods adventure playground. ■TIP➜ It's cold in the mine, even on hot days, so bring a jacket or sweater. ⊠ *Off A44, Ponterwyd* ☎ *01970/890620* ⊕ *www.silvermountainexperience.co.uk* ⬛ *£12* ☉ *Apr.–June, Sept., and Oct., daily 10:30–5; July and Aug., daily 10–6; last tour 1 hr before closing.*

14

FAMILY   **Ynyslas Beach.** About 9 miles up the coast from Aberystwyth is Ynyslas Beach (pronounced "*Inn*-iss-lass"), a popular local beauty spot. Where the River Dyfi flows into the sea at Cardigan Bay, enormous dunes undulate from the sandy beach in a network of hillocks crisscrossed by wooden bridges. Ynyslas Beach is part of a nature reserve that is home to several species of butterfly and—unusual for the British Isles—lizards. Ynyslas is 8 miles north of Aberystwyth on the B4572.

WHERE TO EAT

$ ✕ **Gannets.** A simple but friendly bistro, Gannets specializes in hearty
BRITISH   roasts and traditional Welsh-style dishes that use local meat and fish. Organically grown vegetables and a good wine list are further draws for a university crowd. This place is popular with locals, and you're likely to hear Welsh being spoken at the next table. $ *Average main: £11* ✉ *7 St. James's Sq.* ☎ *01970/617164* ◷ *No lunch. Closed Sun.–Tues.*

$ ✕ **Ultracomida.** This lively, modern Spanish eatery brings a splash of
SPANISH   Mediterranean color to the Mid-Wales coastline. The lunch menu is served tapas style: hake with lentils and Serrano ham, squid fried in garlic with salsa verde, or maybe just some fresh hummus and toast. Or you could just put together an upscale picnic hamper from the in-house deli. Light meals are available in the evening. $ *Average main: £5* ✉ *31 Pier St.* ☎ *01970/630686* ⊕ *www.ultracomida.co.uk* ◷ *No dinner Sun. and Mon.*

WHERE TO STAY

For expanded hotel reviews, visit Fodors.com.

$ 🏠 **Gwesty Cymru.** This seafront Edwardian house has been converted
HOTEL   into one of Aberystwyth's more stylish lodgings. **Pros:** contemporary
Fodor'sChoice   design; beautiful location. **Cons:** seafront can be noisy at night; lim-
★   ited parking. $ *Rooms from: £87* ✉ *19 Marine Terr.* ☎ *01970/612252* ⊕ *www.gwestycymru.com* ⤴ *8 rooms* ⦿| *Breakfast.*

$$ 🏠 **Harbourmaster Hotel.** A drive south on the coast road from Aberys-
HOTEL   twyth brings you to this early-19th-century Georgian-style building, right on the harbor among colorfully painted structures. **Pros:** good food; stunning harbor location; friendly hosts. **Cons:** difficult parking; often booked up; minimum stay on weekends. $ *Rooms from: £110* ✉ *Pen Cei, 15 miles south of Aberystwyth, Aberaeron* ☎ *01545/570755* ⊕ *www.harbour-master.com* ⤴ *13 rooms* ⦿| *Breakfast.*

$$$ 🏠 **Ynyshir Hall.** This luxurious Georgian mansion is *the* place to stay in
HOTEL   this part of Wales if money is no object—as the photos of its world-
Fodor'sChoice   famous guests on the lobby walls will attest. **Pros:** artsy ambience;
★   unabashed luxury; great food. **Cons:** isolated location; impossible to reach without a car. $ *Rooms from: £205* ✉ *Off A487, southwest of Machynlleth, Eglwysfach* ☎ *01654/781209* ⊕ *www.ynyshir-hall.co.uk* ⤴ *9 rooms* ⦿| *Breakfast.*

NIGHTLIFE AND THE ARTS

Aberystwyth Arts Centre. In addition to a cinema, the Aberystwyth Arts Centre has a theater, gallery, shops, and a good café and bar. The list of movies is varied, including an international horror movie festival every fall. ⊠ *Bridge St.* ☎ *01970/623232* ⊕ *www.aberystwythartscentre.co.uk.*

OUTDOORS

Glyndwr's Way. To the east of Aberystwyth, the 128-mile Glyndwr's Way walking route passes through the Cambrian Mountains before turning north through the town of Machynlleth. From there it veers east to climb above the River Dovey, with wonderful views north to Cadair Idris. ⊕ *www.nationaltrail.co.uk/glyndwrsway.*

DOLGELLAU

34 miles northeast of Aberystwyth.

A solidly Welsh town with dark stone buildings and old coaching inns made of the local gray dolerite and slate, Dolgellau (pronounced dol-*geth*-lee) thrived with the wool trade until the mid-19th century. Prosperity left striking architecture, with buildings of different eras side by side on crooked streets that are a legacy from Norman times.

Dolgellau has long been a popular base for people eager to walk the surrounding countryside, which forms the southern tip of Snowdonia National Park. To the south of Dolgellau rises the menacing bulk of 2,927-foot Cadair Idris. The name means "the Chair of Idris," a reference to a giant from ancient Celtic mythology.

GETTING HERE AND AROUND

Dolgellau's nearest railway station is at the town of Barmouth, about 10 miles away. The town is small and full of interesting nooks and crannies easily explored on foot. To discover the surrounding area you'll need a car.

ESSENTIALS

Visitor Information Dolgellau Tourist Information Centre ⊠ *Ty Meirion, Eldon Sq.* ☎ *01341/422888* ⊕ *www.visitmidwales.co.uk.*

EXPLORING

Quaker Heritage Centre. In the town square, this museum commemorates the area's strong links with the Quaker movement and the Quakers' emigration to the American colonies. ⊠ *Eldon Sq.* ☎ *01341/424680* 🎟 *Free* ☯ *Easter–Oct., daily 10–6; Nov.–Easter, Thurs.–Mon. 10–5.*

FAMILY **Ty Siamas.** The National Centre for Welsh Folk Music is in the converted Victorian Market Hall and Assembly Rooms. It has a fascinating interactive folk music exhibition, performance auditorium, and café and bar. ⊠ *Neuadd Idris, Eldon Sq.* ☎ *01341/421800* ⊕ *www.tysiamas.com* 🎟 *Free* ☯ *Easter–Sept., Wed.–Fri. 10–4, Sat. 10–1. Call for off-season hrs.*

NORTH WALES

Wales masses its most dramatic splendor and fierce beauty in the north. Dominating the area is Snowdon, at 3,560 feet the highest peak in England and Wales. The peak gives its name to the 840-square-mile Snowdonia National Park, which extends southward all the way to Machynlleth in Mid-Wales. As in other British national parks, much of the land is privately owned, so inside the park are towns, villages, and farms, in addition to some spectacular mountain scenery.

The mock-Italianate village of Portmeirion is an extraordinary architectural flight of fancy, and the seaside resort of Llandudno is as popular today as it was during its Victorian heyday. And scattered across the countryside are a ring of mighty medieval castles, built by King Edward I (1239–1307) at the end of a bloody war to bring the population under English rule.

Although North Wales is more popular with travelers than Mid-Wales, the road network is even more tortuous. In fact, you haven't really experienced North Wales until you've spent a maddening hour snaking along a narrow mountain road, all the while with your destination in plain view.

LLANGOLLEN

23 miles southwest of Chester, 60 miles southwest of Manchester.

Llangollen's setting in a deep valley carved by the River Dee gives it a typically Welsh appearance. The bridge over the Dee, a 14th-century stone structure, is named in a traditional Welsh folk song as one of the "Seven Wonders of Wales." In July the very popular International Musical Eisteddfod brings crowds to town.

For a particularly scenic drive in this area, head for the Horseshoe Pass. For other views, follow the marked footpath from the north end of the canal bridge up a steep hill to see Castell Dinas Bran, the ruins of a 13th-century castle built by a native Welsh ruler. The views of the town and the Vale of Llangollen are worth the 45-minute (one-way) walk.

GETTING HERE AND AROUND

You'll need a car to get here, but once you arrive you can take a trip on the Llangollen Railway. Along the Llangollen Canal longboat tours head both west and east. The town itself is easy to explore on foot.

ESSENTIALS

Visitor Information Llangollen Tourist Information Centre ⊠ *Y Capel, Castle St.* ☎ *01978/860828* ⊕ *www.llangollen.org.uk.*

EXPLORING

Chirk Castle. This impressive medieval fortress has evolved from its 14th-century origins into a grand home complete with an 18th-century servants hall and interiors furnished in 16th- to 19th-century styles. However, it still looks satisfyingly medieval from the outside—and also below ground, where you tour the original dungeons. Surrounding the castle are beautiful formal gardens and parkland. Chirk Castle is 5

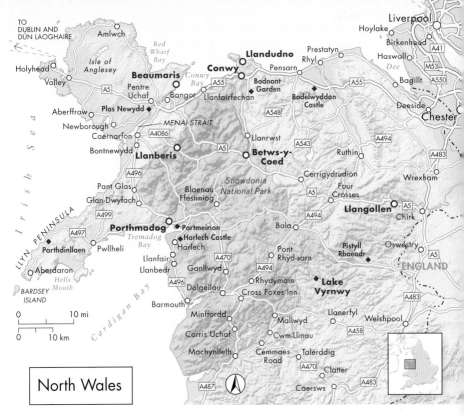

North Wales

miles southeast of Llangollen. ⊠ *Off B4500, Chirk* ☎ *01691/777701*
⊕ *www.nationaltrust.org.uk* ⬚ *£9.50* ⊙ *Castle Apr.–Sept., daily 10–4;*
Mar. and Oct., daily 10–4; Nov.–mid-Dec. and Feb., weekends 10–4.
Gardens Apr.–Sept., daily 10–5; Oct.–Mar., daily 10–4.

FAMILY **Llangollen Railway.** This restored standard-gauge steam line runs for
7 miles along the scenic Dee Valley. The terminus is near the town's
bridge. ⊠ *Abbey Rd.* ☎ *01978/860979* ⊕ *www.llangollen-railway.*
co.uk ⬚ *£12 round-trip* ⊙ *Apr.–Oct., daily 10:30–5; Nov.–Mar.,*
some weekends.

Plas Newydd. From 1778 to 1828 Plas Newydd (not to be confused
with the similarly named Isle of Anglesey estate) was the home of Lady
Eleanor Butler and Sarah Ponsonby, the eccentric Ladies of Llangollen,
who set up a then-scandalous single-sex household, collected curios and
magnificent carvings, and made it into a tourist attraction even during
their lifetimes. You can take tea there, as did Wordsworth and the Duke
of Wellington, and stroll in the attractively terraced gardens. ⊠ *Hill St.*
☎ *01978/862834* ⊕ *www.denbighshire.gov.uk* ⬚ *£5.50* ⊙ *Apr.–Sept.,*
Wed.–Sun., 10:30–5; last admission 45 min before closing.

Pontcysyllte. From the Llangollen Canal Wharf you can take a horse-
drawn boat or a narrow boat (a slender barge) along the canal to the
world's longest and highest navigable cast-iron aqueduct: Pontcysyllte

WELSH: A SHORT PRIMER

The native language of Wales, Welsh (or *Cymraeg*, as it's properly called) is spoken fluently by around a quarter of the population. (The vast majority, however, speaks a little.) Not legally recognized in Britain until the 1960s, it was suppressed beginning in the time of Henry VIII and blamed for poor literacy during the reign of Queen Victoria. Today Welsh children under 17 are required to take classes to learn the language.

Welsh may look daunting to pronounce, but it's a phonetic language, so pronunciation is fairly easy once the alphabet is learned. Remember that "dd" is sounded like "th" in they, "f" sounds like "v" in save, and "ff" is the equivalent of the English "f" in forest. The "ll" sound has no English equivalent; the closest match is the "cl" sound in "close."

Terms that crop up frequently in Welsh are *bach* or *fach* (small; also a common term of endearment similar to "dear"), *craig* or *graig* (rock), *cwm* (valley; pronounced coom), *dyffryn* (valley), *eglwys* (church), *glyn* (glen), *llyn* (lake), *mawr* or *fawr* (great, big), *pentre* (village, homestead), *plas* (hall, mansion), and *pont* or *bont* (bridge).

(Welsh for "the bridge that connects"), a UNESCO World Heritage Site. The aqueduct is more than 1,000 feet long. The aqueduct is 3 miles east of Llangollen. ✉ *Llangollen Canal Wharf, Wharf Hill,* ☎ *01978/860702 Llangollen Wharf* 🌐 *www.horsedrawnboats.co.uk* 🎟 *£12.50.*

Vale of Ceiriog. Near Llangollen is this verdant valley, known locally as "Little Switzerland." The B4500, running between Chirk and the village of Glyn Ceiriog, at the foothills of the Berwyn Mountains, is one of the region's great drives. It's just remote enough that you can often have the road to yourself.

WHERE TO EAT AND STAY

For expanded hotel reviews, visit Fodors.com.

$ BRITISH 🍴 **The Corn Mill.** In a converted mill on the River Dee, this pub and restaurant has an old water wheel that turns behind the bar. Dine on the open-air deck or in the cozy dining room, sampling stylishly updated pub fare, from smoked salmon and haddock fishcakes to chicken with grilled truffle polenta. There are light bites, too, and dessert classics such as pecan and toffee cheesecake. Several of the ales are from Welsh microbreweries. Service can be slow when things get busy, but this is a good place to unwind. [$] *Average main: £12* ✉ *Dee La.* ☎ *01978/869555* 🌐 *www.cornmill-llangollen.co.uk.*

$ B&B/INN 🏨 **Cornerstones Guesthouse.** Made up of three 16th-century cottages with views over the River Dee, this little B&B mixes period charm with modern comfort. **Pros:** spacious bedrooms; free passes for town parking lots. **Cons:** directly on the street; two-night minimum stay. [$] *Rooms from: £80* ✉ *15 Bridge St.* ☎ *01978/861569* 🌐 *www.cornerstones-guesthouse.co.uk* 🛏 *3 rooms, 2 suites* 🍽 *Breakfast.*

NIGHTLIFE AND THE ARTS

International Musical Eisteddfod. The six-day International Musical Eisteddfod, held in early July, brings together amateur choirs and dancers—more than 12,000 participants in all—from all corners of the globe for a colorful folk festival. The tradition of the *eisteddfod*, held throughout Wales, goes back to the 12th century. Originally gatherings of bards, the *eisteddfodau* of today are more like national festivals. ☎ 01978/862001 ⊕ *www.international-eisteddfod.co.uk*.

EN ROUTE
Pistyll Rhaeadr. The peat-brown water of Pistyll Rhaeadr, the highest waterfall in Wales, thunders down a 290-foot double cascade. When you're driving on the B4500 between Llangollen and Llanwddyn, take the road leading northwest from the town of Llanrhaeadr ym Mochnant, in the peaceful Tanat Valley. It was near here that, in 1588, the Bible was translated into Welsh—one of the key moments that helped to ensure the survival of the language. The waterfall is 4 miles up the road.

14

LAKE VYRNWY LLYN EFYRNWY

18 miles southwest of Llangollen.

This beautiful lake has a sense of tranquillity that doesn't entirely befit its history. Lake Vyrnwy was created in the 1880s to provide water for the people of Liverpool, 80 miles north. Unfortunately, this meant forcibly evicting the residents of a small town—an act that's still controversial in Wales. Today it's a peaceful spot surrounded by a thriving nature reserve. The closest settlement is tiny Llanwddyn, and a bit farther away is Bala, a pretty town with an almost-as-lovely natural lake of its own.

GETTING HERE AND AROUND

Rural bus service is infrequent, so you need a car to explore the area. The B4393 circles Lake Vyrnwy itself; from here, Bala is a 14-mile drive over hair-raising Bwlch y Groes pass or a circuitous drive along the B4391. Llangollen is 28 miles northeast of Lake Vyrnwy on the B4396.

EXPLORING

FAMILY **Bala Lake Railway.** The steam-powered train runs along the southern shores of Bala Lake (Llyn Tegid, or "Lake of Beauty"), a large natural reservoir just northeast of Lake Vyrnwy. Bala Lake is also popular for kayaking and other water sports. ⊠ *Off B4403, Llanuwchllyn* ☎ 01678/540666 ⊕ *www.bala-lake-railway.co.uk* ⌑ *£9.50 round-trip* ☉ *Late Apr., weekends; May, late June, and Sept., Sat.–Thurs; early June, July, and Aug., daily; call for departure times.*

Bwlch y Groes. One of the great drives of North Wales, the sweeping, vertiginous panoramas of Bwlch y Groes (Pass of the Cross) form the highest mountain pass accessible by road in the country. From Lake Vyrnwy, drive for a mile on B4393 before heading west on the mountain road.

FAMILY
Fodor's Choice
★
Lake Vyrnwy Nature Reserve. Bordered by lush forest and emerald green hills, Lake Vyrnwy is a haven for wildlife. It's rich in rare bird species, from falcons to siskins and curlews. Stretching out along the shores

Llangollen's yearly International Musical Eisteddfod, a gathering of international choirs and dancers, shows that Wales is truly a land of song.

of the lake near the visitor center, the Lake Vyrnwy Sculpture Park is a collection of pieces by the talented local artist Andy Hancock. Arranged along a paved walking trail, many of the wooden sculptures resemble oversize versions of the lake's wildlife, including a 15-foot-long dragonfly. It's an extremely popular cycling route, and there's a bike shop and coffee shop near the visitor center. ✉ *Off B4393, Llanwddyn* ☎ *01691/870278* 🌐 *www.lake-vyrnwy.com* 🎟 *Free* 🕒 *Visitor Center Apr.–Oct., daily 10:30–5:30; Nov.–Mar., weekdays 10:30–4; weekends 10:30–4:30. Park daily year-round.*

WHERE TO STAY

For expanded hotel reviews, visit Fodors.com.

$$ B&B/INN 🏨 **Cyfie Farm.** This ivy-clad 17th-century farmhouse sits in a tranquil area 5 miles from Lake Vyrnwy. **Pros:** in-room fireplaces; outdoor hot tub; hosts are trained chefs; discounts for longer stays. **Cons:** remote location; need a car to get around. [$] *Rooms from: £125* ✉ *Off B4393, Llanfihangel-yng-Ngwynfa* ☎ *01691/648451* 🌐 *www.cyfiefarm.co.uk* 🛏 *4 suites* 🍴 *Breakfast.*

$$ B&B/INN 🏨 **Lake Vyrnwy Hotel.** Awesome views of mountain-ringed Lake Vyrnwy are just one asset of this country mansion on a 24,000-acre estate. **Pros:** perfect for outdoor pursuits; luxurious spa; excellent package deals. **Cons:** too remote for some; minimum stay on some summer weekends. [$] *Rooms from: £135* ✉ *Off B4393, Llanwddyn* ☎ *01691/870692* 🌐 *www.lakevyrnwy.com* 🛏 *52 rooms* 🍴 *Breakfast.*

PORTHMADOG

35 miles southeast of Lake Vyrnwy, 16 miles southeast of Caernarfon.

The little seaside town of Porthmadog, built as a harbor to export slate from nearby Blaenau Ffestiniog, stands at the gateway to the Llŷn Peninsula (pronounced like "lean," with your tongue touching your palate), with its virtually unspoiled coastline and undulating, wildflower-covered hills. It's also near the town of Harlech, which contains one of the great castles of Wales, and the weird and wonderful Portmeirion.

GETTING HERE AND AROUND

The picturesque Cambrian Coast Railway runs from Machynlleth, near Aberystwyth, up the coast to Porthmadog. When you arrive you can take a scenic trip on the town's "little railways." Porthmadog is a stop on the excellent Snowdon Sherpa bus service. The town itself is totally walkable and has good access to coastal trails.

ESSENTIALS

Visitor Information Porthmadog Tourist Information Centre ⊠ *High St.* ☎ *01766/512981* ⊕ *www.visitsnowdonia.info.*

EXPLORING

TOP ATTRACTIONS

FAMILY **Ffestiniog Railway.** Founded in the early 19th century to carry slate, the Ffestiniog Railway starts at the quayside and climbs up 700 feet through a wooded vale, past a waterfall, and across the mountains. The northern terminus is in Blaenau Ffestiniog, where you can visit an old slate mine. The Ffestiniog Railway is perhaps the best of several small steam lines in this part of the country. ■TIP➡ **Porthmadog gets very crowded in summer, and parking is limited, so you might want to make this journey from Blaenau Ffestiniog to Porthmadog instead.** ⊠ *Harbour Station, High St.* ☎ *01766/516000* ⊕ *www.festrail.co.uk* 🎟 *£20.20 round-trip* ⊙ *Mid-Mar.–Oct., daily; call for times.*

Harlech Castle. A wealth of legend, poetry, and song is conjured up by the 13th-century Harlech Castle, built by Edward I to help subdue the Welsh. Its mighty ruins, visible for miles, are as dramatic as its history (though you have to imagine the sea, which used to crash against the rocks below but receded in the 19th century). Harlech was occupied by the Welsh Prince Owain Glyndwr from 1404 to 1408 during his revolt against the English. The music of the traditional folk song "Men of Harlech" refers to the heroic defense of this castle in 1468 by Dafydd ap Eynion, who, summoned to surrender, is alleged to have replied: "I held a castle in France until every old woman in Wales heard of it, and I will hold a castle in Wales until every old woman in France hears of it." On a clear day you can climb the battlements for a spectacular view of the surrounding countryside. The castle dominates the coastal town of Harlech, 12 miles south of Porthmadog. ⊠ *Off B4573, Harlech* ☎ *01443/336000* ⊕ *www.cadw.wales.gov.uk* 🎟 *£4.50* ⊙ *Mar.– Jun., daily 9:30–5; July and Aug., daily 9:30–6; Nov.–Feb., Mon.–Sat. 10–4; Sun. 11–4. Last admission 30 min before closing.*

Fodor'sChoice **Portmeirion.** One of the true highlights of North Wales is Portmeirion, ★ a tiny fantasy-Italianate village on a private peninsula surrounded by hills, which is said to be loosely modeled after Portofino. Designed in the 1920s by architect Clough Williams-Ellis (1883–1978), the village has a hotel and restaurant among its multicolored buildings, and gift shops sell a distinctive local pottery. On the edge of town is a peaceful woodland trail punctuated here and there by such flourishes as a red iron bridge and a miniature pagoda. William-Ellis called it his "light-opera approach to architecture," and the result is magical, though distinctly un-Welsh. Portmeirion is about 2 miles east of Porthmadog. ✉ *Off A487, Portmeirion* ☎ *01766/772311* 🌐 *www.portmeirion-village.com* 🎫 *£10* 🕑 *Daily 9:30–7:30.*

Fodor's Choice ★ **Tre'r Ceiri.** Remote, atmospheric, and astoundingly little known, Tre'r Ceiri is one of the most impressive ancient monuments in Wales. Today parts of the 4th-century fort's outer walls are still intact (rising more than 18 feet in places), and within are the ruins of 150 stone huts. They were inhabited by a Celtic tribe known as the Ordovices, and may have survived as a settlement for up to 700 years. From Porthmadog, take the A497 west, then turn left onto the A499 just before Pwllheli. At the village of Llanaelhaearn, turn left onto the B4417. Less than a mile down this road is an unmarked footpath on the right leading straight up a hill to Tre'r Ceiri. ✉ *B4417, Llanaelhaearn* 🎫 *Free.*

WORTH NOTING

FAMILY **Llechwedd Slate Caverns.** At these caverns you can take two trips: a tram ride through floodlighted tunnels where Victorian working conditions have been re-created, and a ride on Britain's deepest underground railway to a mine where you can walk by an eerie underground lake. Either tour gives a good idea of the difficult working conditions the miners endured. Above are a re-created Victorian village and slate-splitting demonstrations. ⚠ **Wear sturdy footwear—during busy times you may have to climb 70 steps as part of the tour.** ✉ *Off A470, Blaenau Ffestiniog* ☎ *01766/830306* 🌐 *www.llechwedd-slate-caverns.co.uk* 🎫 *Tram ride or deep mine tour £10.50; both tours £17* 🕑 *Mid-Mar.–Sept., daily 9:30–5:30; Oct.–mid-Mar., daily 10–5; last admission 45 mins before closing.*

Porthdinllaen. On the very tip of a thumb-shape peninsula jutting out into the Irish Sea, this miniscule but gorgeous little harbor community is 20 miles from Porthmadog. There's a wide, sheltered beach where the sand is so fine that it squeaks underfoot, and whitewashed cottages line the curving seafront. Park at the nearby visitor center. ✉ *Porthdinllaen.*

WHERE TO EAT AND STAY

For expanded hotel reviews, visit Fodors.com.

$$$$ BRITISH 🍴 **Castle Cottage.** Close to Harlech's mighty castle, this friendly "restaurant with rooms" is a wonderful find. The emphasis is on the exceptional cuisine of chef-proprietor Glyn Roberts, who uses locally sourced ingredients from lobster to lamb to create imaginative, beautifully presented contemporary dishes. There's a fixed-price dinner menu (£39.50). There are three spacious, modern rooms (from £135) in the main house and four more in the annex, a 16th-century coaching inn. [$] *Average main: £39* ✉ *Near B4573, Harlech* ☎ *01766/780479* 🌐 *www.castlecottageharlech.co.uk* 🕑 *No lunch.*

For a touch of whimsy, visit the mock-Italianate village of Portmeirion, set on the coast.

$ **✕ Ty Coch Inn.** In a seafront building in picture-postcard Porthdinllaen, this pub has what is undoubtedly one of the best locations in Wales. The lunches are honest and unpretentious: pies, sandwiches, bangers and mash, or perhaps a plate of local mussels in garlic butter. Everything is delicious and reasonably priced. The atmosphere is friendly and slightly bohemian; this is the kind of place where they're pleasantly surprised you've managed to find it. $ *Average main: £9* ⊠ *Off B4417, Porthdinllaen* ☎ *01758/720498* ⊕ *www.tycoch.co.uk* ⊗ *No dinner.*

BRITISH

$ **🛏 Hotel Maes-y-Neuadd.** Eight acres of gardens and parkland create a glorious setting for this luxurious manor house dating from the 14th century. **Pros:** magnificent location above Tremadog Bay; great restaurant. **Cons:** low ceilings in some rooms. $ *Rooms from: £90* ⊠ *Off B4573, Talsarnau* ☎ *01766/780200* ⊕ *www.neuadd.com* ⤳ *15 rooms* ⭘ *Breakfast.*

B&B/INN

$$ **🛏 Hotel Portmeirion.** One of the most elegant and unusual places to stay in Wales, this waterfront mansion is located at the heart of Portmeirion. **Pros:** unique location; beautiful building; woodland walks. **Cons:** gets crowded with day-trippers; minimum stay on weekends. $ *Rooms from: £139* ⊠ *A487, Portmeirion* ☎ *01766/770000* ⊕ *www.portmeirion-village.com* ⤳ *42 rooms, 11 suites* ⭘ *Multiple meal plans.*

HOTEL

BETWS-Y-COED

25 miles northeast of Porthmadog, 19 miles south of Llandudno.

The rivers Llugwy and Conwy meet at Betws-y-Coed, a popular village surrounded by woodland with excellent views of Snowdonia. It can be used as a base to explore the national park, although its diminutive size means that it can get overcrowded in summer. The most famous landmark in the village is the ornate iron Waterloo Bridge over the River Conwy, designed in 1815 by Thomas Telford.

GETTING HERE AND AROUND

The town is easy to reach on the Conwy Valley Railway that runs from Llandudno to Blaenau Ffestiniog. Betws-y-Coed is also a hub for the excellent Snowdon Sherpa bus service that covers most of Snowdonia's beauty spots, so it's feasible to explore this part of Wales without a car.

ESSENTIALS

Visitor Information **Betws-y-Coed Tourist Information Centre** ✉ *Royal Oak Stables, Station Rd.* ☎ *01690/710426* 🌐 *www.betws-y-coed.co.uk.*

EXPLORING

FAMILY Fodor's Choice ★ **Snowdonia National Park.** Stretching from the Welsh midlands almost to its northern coast, Snowdonia National Park covers a vast swath of North Wales. The park consists of 840 square miles of rocky mountains, valleys clothed in oak woods, moorlands, lakes, and rivers, all guaranteeing natural beauty and, to a varying extent, solitude. Its most famous attraction, by far, is the towering peak of Mt. Snowdon. The view from the top is jaw-dropping: to the northwest you can see the Menai Strait and Anglesey; to the south, Harlech Castle and the Cadair Idris mountain range. To the southwest, on an exceedingly clear day, you can make out the distant peaks of Ireland's Wicklow Mountains. There are six different walking paths to the top, but a far less punishing way is via the Snowdon Mountain Railway, in nearby Llanberis.

Perched at the top of Snowdon is Hafod Eryri, an eco-friendly replacement for the previous visitor center (once described by Prince Charles as "the highest slum in Wales"). The granite-roof building, which blends beautifully into the rocky landscape, has a café and exhibitions about the mountain, its ecology, and its history. If you're planning to make the ascent, the visitor center in Betws-y-Coed is the best place to stop for information. ✉ *Royal Oak Stables, Station Rd.* ☎ *01690/710426* 🌐 *www.eryri-npa.gov.uk/home.*

Swallow Falls. Betws-y-Coed is bordered by Gwydyr Forest, which has several well-marked walking trails. The forest also contains a half dozen or so mines, the last of which was abandoned in the 1940s. On the western approach to the village you'll find Swallow Falls, where the River Llugwy tumbles down through a wooded chasm. **TIP→ Be careful on the footpath: there's no guardrail.** ✉ *Off A5.*

WHERE TO EAT AND STAY

For expanded hotel reviews, visit Fodors.com.

$$ BRITISH 🍴 **Ty Gwyn.** This coaching inn, built in 1636, is one of the best places to eat in Snowdonia. The food is traditional Welsh fare, beautifully prepared with local ingredients. Standouts include steak with cream of Stilton cheese and coriander, or lobster with a prawn and crayfish thermidor. Vegetarians are well cared for with such dishes as Thai-style vegetable curry with fresh lime and chili. The inn also has simple, cozy bedrooms starting at £30 per night. [$] *Average main: £16* ✉ *A5* ☎ *01690/710383* 🌐 *www.tygwynhotel.co.uk.*

EATING WELL IN WALES

Talented chefs making use of the country's bountiful resources have put Wales firmly on the culinary map. Welsh Black beef and succulent Welsh lamb are world renowned, and the supply of fish and seafood (including mussels and oysters) from coasts and rivers is excellent. Organic products are available to restaurants and the public from specialty companies, farm shops, and farmers' markets.

Ty Nant Welsh spring water graces restaurant tables worldwide, and there are a few small vineyards in the south. There's even a Welsh whisky that's won awards at international tastings.

You can try traditionally named cheeses such as Llanboidy and Caws Cenarth or an extra-mature cheddar called Black Bomber.

Contemporary cuisine is more fashionable, but traditional dishes are worth seeking out. Cawl, for example, is a nourishing broth of lamb and vegetables, and laverbread is a distinctive puréed seaweed that's usually fried with eggs and bacon.

14

$ **Aberconwy House.** This luxurious Victorian house has panoramic
B&B/INN views over Betws-y-Coed. **Pros:** beautiful countryside views; great breakfasts. **Cons:** no bar or evening meal. [$] *Rooms from: £70* ⊠ *Lôn Muriau, off A470* ☎ *01690/710202* ⊕ *www.aberconwy-house.co.uk* ↝ *8 rooms* ⏐⊙⏐ *Breakfast.*

$ **Pengwern Country House.** Hosts Ian and Gwawr Mowatt are charmingly
B&B/INN adept at making their guests feel at home in this former Victorian art-
Fodor's Choice ists' colony. **Pros:** woodland location; wealth of Victorian details; lovely
★ hosts. **Cons:** close to main road; car is essential. [$] *Rooms from: £72* ⊠ *A5, Allt Dinas* ☎ *01690/710480* ⊕ *www.snowdoniaaccommodation. co.uk* ↝ *3 rooms* ⏐⊙⏐ *Breakfast.*

$$ **Tan-y-Foel Country House.** Hidden away on a wooded hillside outside
B&B/INN Betws-y-Coed, this quiet, contemporary hideaway has views over the Conwy Valley. **Pros:** striking decor; inventive cuisine. **Cons:** meals must be arranged in advance; too far to walk into town. [$] *Rooms from: £125* ⊠ *Off A5, Capel Garmon* ☎ *01690/710507* ⊕ *www.tyfhotel.co.uk* ↝ *6 rooms* ⏐⊙⏐ *Breakfast.*

LLANBERIS

17 miles west of Betws-y-Coed.

Like Betws-y-Coed, Llanberis is a focal point for people visiting Snowdonia National Park.

GETTING HERE AND AROUND

Llanberis is accessible by bus. The most convenient service, targeted at visitors, is the Snowdon Sherpa bus route.

ESSENTIALS

Visitor Information Llanberis Tourist Information Centre
⊠ *Electric Mountain, Off A4086* ☎ *01286/870765.*

EXPLORING

Fodor's Choice ★ **Caernarfon Castle.** The grim, majestic mass of Caernarfon Castle, a UNESCO World Heritage Site, looms over the waters of the River Seiont. Numerous bloody encounters were witnessed by these sullen walls, erected by Edward I in 1283 as a symbol of his determination to subdue the Welsh. The castle's towers, unlike those of Edward I's other castles, are polygonal and patterned with bands of different-color stone. In 1284 the monarch thought of a scheme to steal the Welsh throne. Knowing that the Welsh chieftains would accept no foreign prince, Edward promised to designate a ruler who could speak no word of English. Edward presented his infant son to the assembled chieftains as their prince "who spoke no English, had been born on Welsh soil, and whose first words would be spoken in Welsh." The ruse worked, and on that day was created the first prince of Wales of English lineage. In the Queen's Tower, a museum charts the history of the local regiment, the Royal Welsh Fusiliers. The castle is in the town of Caernarfon, 7 miles west of Llanberis. ⊠ *Castle Hill, Caernarfon* ☎ *01286/677617* ⊕ *cadw.wales.gov.uk* 🎫 *£5.50* ☉ *Mar.–June, Sept., and Oct., daily 9:30–5; July and Aug., daily 9:30–6; Nov.–Feb., Mon.–Sat. 10–4, Sun. 11–4; last admission 30 min before closing.*

National Slate Museum. In Padarn Country Park, this museum in the old Dinorwig Slate Quarry is dedicated to what was once an important industry for the area. The museum has quarry workshops and slate-splitting demonstrations, as well as restored worker housing, all of which convey the development of the industry and the challenges faced by those who worked in it. The narrow-gauge Llanberis Lake Railway departs from here. ⊠ *Padarn Country Park, A4086* ☎ *029/2057–3700* ⊕ *www.museumwales.ac.uk* 🎫 *Free* ☉ *Easter–Oct., daily 10–5; Nov.–Easter, Sun.–Fri. 10–4.*

FAMILY **Fodor's Choice** ★ **Snowdon Mountain Railway.** One of the region's most famous attractions is the rack-and-pinion Snowdon Mountain Railway, with some of its track at a thrillingly steep grade; the train terminates within 70 feet of the 3,560-foot-high summit. Snowdon—*Yr Wyddfa* in Welsh—is the highest peak south of Scotland and lies within the 840-square-mile national park. Weather permitting, trains go all the way to the summit; on a clear day you can see as far as the Wicklow Mountains in Ireland, about 90 miles away. You can take two types of train: a modern diesel-driven version, or the brand-new "heritage" version, complete with restored carriages and working steam engine. ⊠ *A4086* ☎ *0844/493–8120* ⊕ *www. snowdonrailway.co.uk* 🎫 *Diesel service: £27 round-trip; Heritage service: £35 round-trip* ☉ *Mid-Mar.–Oct., daily; call for schedule.*

WHERE TO STAY

For expanded hotel reviews, visit Fodors.com.

$ **HOTEL** 🖫 **Meifod Country House.** Former home of the high sheriff of Caernarfon, this opulent Victorian house has polished tile floors, wood-burning fireplaces, and bedrooms with features such as Victorian claw-foot baths and chandeliers. **Pros:** authentic atmosphere; good restaurant. **Cons:** often booked with wedding parties; not walking distance to town. 💲 *Rooms from: £90* ⊠ *Off A487, Bontnewydd* ☎ *01286/673351* ⊕ *www.meifodcountryhouse.com* 🛏 *5 rooms* 🍽 *Breakfast.*

The Llanberis Path is one route to the top of Snowdon, the highest peak in Wales, in Snowdonia National Park.

BEAUMARIS BIWMARES **AND ANGLESEY** YNYS MÔN

14 miles north of Llanberis.

Elegant Beaumaris is on the Isle of Anglesey, the largest island directly off the shore of Wales. It's linked to the mainland by the Britannia road and rail bridge and by Thomas Telford's remarkable chain suspension bridge, built in 1826 over the Menai Strait. Though its name means "beautiful marsh," Beaumaris has become a town of pretty cottages, Georgian houses, and bright shops; it also has Plas Newydd, one of the grandest stately homes in Wales.

Around 70% of Anglesey's 60,000 or so inhabitants speak Welsh, so you'll probably hear it more than English.

GETTING HERE AND AROUND

Anglesey is linked to the mainland by the A55 and A5. The roads on the island are in good condition, and there's a relatively extensive bus network. Ferries and catamarans to Ireland leave from Holyhead, on the island's western side.

EXPLORING

Beaumaris Castle. The town of Beaumaris dates from 1295, when Edward I commenced work on this impressive castle, the last and largest link in an "iron ring" of fortifications around North Wales built to contain the Welsh. Guarding the western approach to the Menai Strait, the unfinished castle (a World Heritage Site) is solid and symmetrical, with concentric lines of fortification, arrow slits, and a moat: a superb example of medieval defensive planning. ⊠ *Castle St.* ☎ *01248/810361* ⊕ *www.cadw.wales.gov.uk* ⊠ *£4* ☉ *Mar.–Jun., Sept.*

and Oct., daily 9–5; July and Aug., daily 9:30–6; Nov.–Feb., Mon.–Sat. 10–4, Sun. 11–4; last admission 30 min before closing.

Fodor's Choice ★ **Bryn Celli Ddu.** Dating from around 3000 BC, this megalithic passage tomb is the most complete site of its kind in Wales. You enter via a narrow opening built into a burial mound. The passage extends for around 25 feet before opening out into a wider burial chamber. The far wall, made of quartz, is illuminated at dawn on the summer solstice. **TIP→ Bring a flashlight, as the tomb has no artificial lighting.** Next to the entrance is a replica of a stone pillar carved with Celtic spirals, found here in 1928. The original is in the National Museum in Cardiff. The site is 7 miles southwest of Beaumaris. ✉ *Off A4080, Llanddaniel Fab* 🎟 *Free* 🕒 *Daily, dawn–dusk.*

Plas Newydd. Some historians consider Plas Newydd to be the finest mansion in Wales. Remodeled in the 18th century by James Wyatt (1747–1813) for the marquesses of Anglesey (whose descendants still live here), it stands on the Menai Strait about 7 miles southwest of Beaumaris. The interior has some fine 18th-century Gothic Revival decorations. Between 1936 and 1940 the society artist Rex Whistler (1905–44) painted the mural in the dining room. A museum commemorates the Battle of Waterloo, where the first marquess led the cavalry. The woodland walk and rhododendron gardens are worth exploring, and it's sometimes possible to take boat trips on the strait. ✉ *Off A4080, southwest of Britannia Bridge, Llanfairpwll* ☎ *01248/714795* 🌐 *www.nationaltrust.org.uk* 🎟 *House and garden £9; garden only £7* 🕒 *House mid-Mar.–early Nov., Sat.–Wed. noon–4:30. Garden mid-Mar.–early Nov., Sat.–Wed. 10–5:30.*

WHERE TO STAY

For expanded hotel reviews, visit Fodors.com.

$ B&B/INN 🏨 **Cleifiog.** This cozy manor house, mostly Georgian in style, is on the banks of the Menai Strait a short stroll from Beaumaris Castle. **Pros:** seafront location; close to town; interesting history. **Cons:** minimum stay on weekends. [$] *Rooms from: £90* ✉ *A454* ☎ *01248/811507* 🌐 *www.cleifiogbandb.co.uk* 🛏 *3 rooms* 🍴 *Breakfast.*

$$ B&B/INN 🏨 **Ye Olde Bull's Head and Townhouse.** These twin hotels, a stone's throw away from each other, could hardly be more different: one is a restored 15th- century coaching inn, the other a contemporary lodging. **Pros:** lovely blend of historic and contemporary; good food. **Cons:** Bull's Head has low ceilings. [$] *Rooms from: £100* ✉ *Castle St.* ☎ *01248/810329* 🌐 *www.bullsheadinn.co.uk* 🛏 *13 rooms* 🍴 *Breakfast.*

SPORTS AND THE OUTDOORS

Anglesey is a great place to get outdoors.

Isle of Anglesey Coastal Path. Extending 125 miles around the island, this path leads past cliffs, sandy coves, and plenty of scenic variety. Pick up information at tourist offices and choose a section; the west coast has the most dramatic scenery. 🌐 *www.angleseycoastalpath.co.uk.*

CONWY

23 miles east of Beaumaris, 48 miles northwest of Chester.

The still-authentic medieval town of Conwy grew up around its castle on the west bank of the River Conwy. A ring of ancient but well-preserved walls, built in the 13th century to protect the English merchants who lived here, enclose the old town and add to the pervading sense of history. Sections of the walls, with their 21 towers, can still be walked. The impressive views from the top take in the castle and the estuary, with mountains in the distance.

GETTING HERE AND AROUND

The A55 expressway links Conwy into the central U.K. motorway system via the M56. The town is also on the North Wales coast rail route, which ends at Holyhead on Anglesey. The town itself—surrounded by its wonderfully preserved walls—is perfect for pedestrians.

ESSENTIALS

Visitor Information Conwy Town Tourism Association ⊠ *Muriau Buildings, Rosehill St.* ☎ *01492/577566* ⊕ *www.visitconwytown.co.uk.*

EXPLORING

Aberconwy House. In what is thought to be the oldest complete medieval house in Wales, Aberconwy House's rooms have been restored to reflect three distinct periods in its history: medieval, Jacobean, and Victorian. It's a diverting and atmsoheric little place, which also holds the distinction of (supposedly) being one of the most haunted buildings in North Wales. ⊠ *Castle St.* ☎ *01492/592246* ⊕ *www.nationaltrust. org.uk* ☎ *£3.50* ☉ *Mid-Mar.–June, Sept., and Oct., Wed.–Mon. 11–5; July and Aug, daily 11–5.*

Bodnant Garden. Undoubtedly one of the best gardens in Wales, Bodnant Garden is something of a pilgrimage spot for horticulturists from around the world. Laid out in 1875, the 87 acres are particularly famed for rhododendrons, camellias, and magnolias. ■TIP➔ Visit in May to see the laburnum arch that forms a huge tunnel of golden blooms. The mountains of Snowdonia form a magnificent backdrop to the Italianate terraces, rock and rose gardens, and pinetum. The gardens, which are closed mid-November to late December, are about 5 miles south of Conwy. ⊠ *Off A470, Tal-y-Cafn* ☎ *01492/650460* ⊕ *www. nationaltrust.org.uk* ☎ *Mar–Oct., £8.50; Nov.–Feb., £4.60* ☉ *Mar.– mid-Oct., daily 10–5; mid-Oct.–mid-Nov. and late Dec.–Feb., daily 11–3; winter times may vary.*

Fodor's Choice
★

Conwy Castle. Of all Edward I's Welsh strongholds, it is perhaps Conwy Castle that best preserves a sheer sense of power and dominance. The eight large round towers and tall curtain wall, set on a rocky promontory, provide sweeping views of the area and the town walls. Although the castle is roofless (and floorless in places), the signage does a pretty good job of helping you visualize how rooms such as the Great Hall must once have looked. Conwy Castle can be approached on foot by a dramatic suspension bridge completed in 1828; engineer Thomas Telford designed the bridge with turrets to blend in with the fortress's presence. ⊠ *Rose Hill St.* ☎ *01492/592358* ⊕ *www.cadw.wales.gov.*

14

With plants and trees from around the world, Bodnant Garden, south of Conwy, is colorful in fall.

uk ✉ *£5* ⏰ *Mar.–Jun., Sept. and Oct., daily 9:30–5; July and Aug., daily 9:30–6; Nov.–Feb., Mon.–Sat. 10–4, Sun. 11–4; last admission 30 min before closing.*

Plas Mawr. Dating from 1576, Plas Mawr is one of the best-preserved Elizabethan town houses in Britain. Richly decorated with ornamental plasterwork, it gives a unique insight into the lives of the Tudor gentry and their servants. ✉ *High St.* ☎ *01492/580167* ⊕ *www.cadw. wales.gov.uk* ✉ *£5.85* ⏰ *Mar.–Sept., Tues.–Sun. 9–5; Oct., Tues –Sun., 9:30–4; last admission 45 min before closing.*

Smallest House in Britain. What is said to be Britain's smallest house is furnished in mid-Victorian Welsh style. The house, which is 6 feet wide and 10 feet high, was reputedly last occupied in 1900 by a fisherman who was more than 6 feet tall. ✉ *Lower Gate St.* ☎ *01492/593484* ✉ *£1* ⏰ *Apr.–Oct., Mon.–Sat. 10–5:30; Sun. 11–4.*

WHERE TO EAT AND STAY

For expanded hotel reviews, visit Fodors.com.

$

MODERN BRITISH

✕ **The Mulberry.** This family-run restaurant overlooking the boats bobbing in Conwy Marina is popular with families for its jovial, laid-back atmosphere. The menu consists of classic dishes like rack of lamb, burgers, curries, and pizzas. Sunday lunch is served buffet style. $ *Average main: £11* ✉ *Morfa Dr.* ☎ *01492/583350* ⊕ *www.mulberryconwy.com.*

$$

BRITISH

✕ **Watson's Bistro.** This popular bistro in central Conwy combines traditional Welsh flavors with accents of the Mediterranean. You may start with *Y fenni* mustard cheese and Parmesan beignets served with chorizo and mozzarella, before moving on to poached prawns in a sparkling wine sauce with lime fritters, or shoulder of lamb with minted garlic and honey. ■TIP→ The £10 two-course lunch menu is an exceptional value. $ *Average main: £16* ⊠ *Chapel St.* ☎*01492/596326* ⊕*www. watsonsbistroconwy.co.uk* ☷ *Closed Mon.*

$$
HOTEL **Castle Hotel.** Nestled within Conwy's medieval walls, this former coaching inn has wood beams, stone fireplaces, and plenty of antiques. **Pros:** oozes history; in the heart of Conwy; good food. **Cons:** small rooms; noisy seagulls. $ *Rooms from: £140* ⊠ *High St.* ☎*01492/582800* ⊕ *www.castlewales.co.uk* ➴*28 rooms* ⦿*Breakfast.*

$$
HOTEL **Sychnant Pass House.** On a peaceful wooded hillside 2 miles west of Conwy, this country-house hotel has a laid-back atmosphere. **Pros:** great indoor pool and hot tub; beautiful grounds; unforced hospitality. **Cons:** far outside Conwy. $ *Rooms from: £135* ⊠ *Sychnant Pass Rd.* ☎*01492/596868* ⊕ *www.sychnant-pass-house.co.uk* ➴*12 rooms* ⦿*Breakfast.*

14

LLANDUDNO

3 miles north of Conwy, 50 miles northwest of Chester.

This engagingly old-fashioned North Wales seaside resort has a wealth of well-preserved Victorian architecture and an ornate amusement pier with entertainments, shops, and places to eat. Grand-looking small hotels line the wide promenade with a view of the deep-blue waters of the bay. The shopping district beyond retains its original canopied walkways.

GETTING HERE AND AROUND

Llandudno is on the North Wales railway line, with fast access from London and other major cities. By road, it's connected to the motorway system via the A55 expressway. The scenic Conwy Valley rail line runs to Blaenau Ffestiniog, and the town is also on the network covered by the Snowdon Sherpa bus service.

ESSENTIALS

Visitor Information **Llandudno Tourist Information Centre** ⊠ *Library Building, Mostyn St.* ☎ *01492/577577* ⊕ *www.visitllandudno.org.uk.*

EXPLORING

EN ROUTE **Bodelwyddan Castle.** Between Abergele and St. Asaph, this castle is the Welsh home of London's National Portrait Gallery. Paintings on display include works by John Singer Sargent, Dante Gabriel Rossetti, and Edwin Landseer. The castle grounds contain a fascinating, if somber historical footnote: a network of overgrown World War I trenches, used by the army to train new recruits. A series of interactive displays help bring the history to life. Also on the grounds are a maze, an aviary, and pretty woodland walks. The castle is 16 miles east of Llandudno. ⊠ *Off A55, Bodelwyddan* ☎*01745/584060* ⊕*www.bodelwyddan-castle. co.uk* ➴*£6.50; park only £4* ☷ *Jan.–late Mar. and Nov.–mid-Dec., weekends 10:30–4; late Mar.–Oct., Wed.–Sun. 10:30–5; last admission 30 mins before closing.*

Great Orme. Named for the Norse word meaning "sea monster," the 679-foot headland called Great Orme towers over Llandudno, affording extraordinary views over the bay.

Grand Orme Aerial Cable Car. This cable car zips you one mile to the top of Grand Orme. At the summit there's an artificial ski slope and a toboggan run, both usable all year. ⊠ *Happy Valley Rd.* 🕾 *01492/879306* 🖃 *£7 round-trip* 🕙 *Mid-Mar.–Oct., daily 10–4:30*

Great Orme Tramway. The most picturesque way to reach the summit of Grande Orme is the Great Orme Tramway. Trips depart about every 20 minutes. The summit is a sylvan spot, with open grassland, fields of wildflowers, and rare butterflies. ⊠ *Victoria Station, Church Walks* 🕾 *01492/577877* ⊕ *www.greatormetramway.co.uk* 🖃 *£6 round-trip* 🕙 *Late Mar. and Oct., daily 10–5; Apr.–Sept. daily 10–6.*

FAMILY   **Great Orme Mines.** Discovered in 1987, these mines date back 4,000 years to when copper was first mined in the area. You can take a tour and learn about the technology that ancient people used to dig the tunnels, which are thought to be the largest surviving prehistoric mines in the world. ⊠ *Pyllau Rd.* 🕾 *01492/870447* ⊕ *www.greatormemines.info* 🖃 *£6.75* 🕙 *Mid-Mar.–Oct., daily 10–5; last admission 1 hr before closing.*

WHERE TO STAY
For expanded hotel reviews, visit Fodors.com.

$$$ 🏨 **Bodysgallen Hall.** Tasteful antiques, polished wood, and comfortable
HOTEL   chairs by cheery fires distinguish one of Wales's most luxurious country-
Fodor'sChoice   house hotels. **Pros:** superb spa and pool; rare 17th-century knot gar-
★   den; elegant dining. **Cons:** too formal for some; hard to get to without a car. 💲 *Rooms from: £189* ⊠ *Off A470* 🕾 *01492/584466* ⊕ *www. bodysgallen.com* ⤴ *15 rooms, 16 cottage suites* ⍾⊙⍾ *Breakfast.*

$ 🏨 **Bryn Derwen Hotel.** This immaculate, impeccably run Victorian hotel
HOTEL   is traditional in style, but has a contemporary edge. **Pros:** historic build-
ing; gracious touches; close to the beach. **Cons:** no sea views. 💲 *Rooms from: £84* ⊠ *34 Abbey Rd.* 🕾 *01492/876804* ⊕ *www.bryn-derwen. co.uk* ⤴ *9 rooms* ⍾⊙⍾ *Breakfast.*

$$ 🏨 **St. Tudno Hotel.** Perfectly situated on the seafront promenade over-
HOTEL   looking the beach and pier, this hotel has been run by the same family for nearly 40 years. **Pros:** ocean views; swimming pool; good food. **Cons:** some rooms are snug; overly fussy decor. 💲 *Rooms from: £104* ⊠ *Promenade* 🕾 *01492/874411* ⊕ *www.st-tudno.co.uk* ⤴ *18 rooms* ⍾⊙⍾ *Breakfast.*

TRAVEL SMART
ENGLAND

GETTING HERE AND AROUND

▌AIR TRAVEL

The least expensive airfares to England are often priced for round-trip travel and must usually be purchased in advance. Airlines generally allow you to change your return date for a fee; most low-fare tickets, however, are nonrefundable.

Flying time to London is about 6½ hours from New York, 7½ hours from Chicago, 9 hours from Dallas, 10 hours from Los Angeles, and 21½ hours from Sydney. From London, flights take an hour to Paris or Amsterdam, 1½ hours to cities in Switzerland or Luxembourg, and 2 hours to Rome.

If you're flying from England, plan to arrive at the airport 90 minutes in advance for flights to Europe, 2 hours for the United States. Security at Gatwick and Heathrow airports is always fairly intense. Most people can expect to be patted down after they pass through metal detectors. Travelers are randomly searched again at the gate before transatlantic flights.

Airline Security Issues Transportation Security Administration ☏ *866/289–9673 in U.S.* ⊕ *www.tsa.gov.*

AIRPORTS

Most international flights to London arrive at either Heathrow Airport (LHR), 15 miles west of London, or at Gatwick Airport (LGW), 27 miles south of the capital. Most flights from the United States go to Heathrow, with Terminals 3, 4, and 5 handling transatlantic flights (British Airways uses Terminal 5). Gatwick is London's second gateway, serving many U.S. destinations. A third, much smaller airport, Stansted (STN), is 40 miles northeast of the city. It handles mainly European and domestic traffic.

London City Airport (LCY), a small airport inside the city near Canary Wharf, has twice-daily business-class flights to New York on British Airways, as well as flights to European destinations. Luton Airport (LLA), 32 miles north of the city, is also quite small, and serves British and European destinations. Luton is the hub for low-cost easyJet. Manchester (MAN) in northwest England handles some flights from the United States, as does Birmingham (BHX).

Heathrow and Gatwick are enormous and can seem like shopping malls. Both airports have bars and pubs and dining options. Several hotels are connected to each airport, and both Gatwick and Heathrow are near dozens of hotels that run free shuttles to the airports. Heathrow has a Hotel Hoppa service that runs shuttles between the airport and around 20 nearby hotels for £4 each way. A free, subsidized local bus service operates between the Central Bus Station serving Terminals 1, 2, and 3 and nearby hotels. You can find out more at the Central Bus Station or at the Transport for London (TfL) Information Centre in the Underground station serving Terminals 1, 2, and 3. Yotel has budget pod hotels in both Heathrow and Gatwick with cabin-size rooms to be booked in advance in four-hour blocks or overnight. Prices begin at about £50, depending on how long you stay and the time of day.

In comparison, other British airports have much more limited shopping, hotel, and dining options; a delay of a few hours can seem like years.

Airport Information Birmingham Airport ☏ *0871/222–0072* ⊕ *www.birminghamairport. co.uk.* **Gatwick Airport** ☏ *0844/892–0322* ⊕ *www.gatwickairport.com.* **Heathrow Airport** ☏ *0844/335–1801* ⊕ *www.heathrowairport. com.* **London City Airport** ☏ *0207/646–0088* ⊕ *www.londoncityairport.com.* **Luton Airport** ☏ *01582/405100* ⊕ *www.london-luton.co.uk.* **Manchester Airport** ☏ *0871/271–0711* ⊕ *www.manchesterairport.co.uk.* **Stansted Airport** ☏ *0844/355–1803* ⊕ *www.stanstedairport.com.*

GROUND TRANSPORTATION

London has excellent bus and train connections between its airports and downtown. Train service can be the fastest, but the downside is that you must get yourself and your luggage to the terminal, often via a series of escalators and connecting trams. Airport buses (generally run by National Express) may be located nearer to the terminals and drop you closer to central hotels, but they're subject to London traffic, which can be horrendous. Taxis can be more convenient than buses, but prices can go through the roof.

The Transport for London website has helpful information, as does Airport Travel Line. The official sites for Gatwick, Heathrow, and Stansted are useful resources for transportation options.

FROM HEATHROW TO CENTRAL LONDON		
Travel Mode	Time	Cost
Taxi	40–80 minutes	£50–£80
Heathrow Express Train	15 minutes	£20 one-way
Underground	50 minutes	£5.30 one-way
National Express Bus	45–80 minutes	£6 one-way

Heathrow by Bus: National Express buses take around 90 minutes (longer at peak time) to reach the city center (Victoria Coach Station) and cost £6 to £8.50 one-way and £13.20 round-trip. Buses leave every 30 to 75 minutes from 4:20 am to 10 pm. The National Express Hotel Hoppa service runs from all terminals to around 20 hotels near the airport (£4). Alternatively, nearly every hotel in London is served by the Hotel By Bus service. Fares to Central London begin at £22.50. SkyShuttle also offers a minibus service between Heathrow and any London hotel. The N9 night bus runs every 20 minutes from 11:45 pm to 5 am to Kensington, Trafalgar Square, and Aldwych; it takes about 75 minutes and costs £2.20.

Heathrow by Train: The cheap, direct route into London is via the Piccadilly line of the Underground (London's extensive subway system, or "Tube"). Trains normally run every three to seven minutes from all terminals from around 5 am until just before midnight. The 50-minute trip into central London costs £5 and connects with other central Tube lines. The Heathrow Express train is comfortable and very convenient, if costly, speeding into London's Paddington Station in 15 minutes. Standard one-way tickets cost £20, or £28 for first class. Book online for the lowest fares. If you arrive without tickets you should purchase them at a kiosk before you board, as they're more expensive on the train. There's daily service from 5:12 am (5:08 am on Sunday) to 11:45 pm (11:53 pm on Sunday), with departures every 15 minutes. A less expensive option is the Heathrow Connect train, which stops at local stations between the airport and Paddington. Daily service is every half hour from 5:23 am (6:07 am on Sunday) to 12:01 am. The journey takes about 30 minutes and costs £9.50 one-way.

Gatwick by Bus: Hourly bus service runs from Gatwick's north and south terminals to Victoria Coach Station with stops at Hooley, Coulsdon, Mitcham, Streatham, Stockwell, and Pimlico. The journey takes two hours and costs between £6.50 and £8 one-way. Make sure you get on a direct bus not requiring a change; otherwise the journey could take much longer. The easyBus service runs a service to Earls Court in west London from as little as £2; the later the ticket is booked online, the higher the price (up to £10 on board).

Gatwick by Train: The fast, nonstop Gatwick Express leaves for Victoria Station every 15 minutes 4:35 am–1:35 am. The 30-minute trip costs £19.90 one-way. Book in advance, as tickets cost more on board. The First Capital Connect rail company's nonexpress services are cheaper. Trains runs regularly throughout the day until midnight to St. Pancras International, London Bridge, and Blackfriars stations; daytime departures are every 10–25 minutes (hourly between 1:30 am and 5 am), and the journey takes 30 to 45 minutes. Tickets are from £10 one way to St. Pancras. You can also reach Gatwick by First Capital Connect coming from Brighton in the opposite direction. First Capital Connect service is on commuter trains, and during rush hour trains can be crowded, with little room for baggage and seats at a premium.

Stansted by Bus: Hourly service on National Express Airport bus A6 (24 hours a day) to Victoria Coach Station costs from £10 one-way, and takes 85–108 minutes. Stops include Golders Green, Finchley Road, St. John's Wood, Baker Street, Marble Arch, and Hyde Park Corner. The easyBus service to Victoria via Baker Street costs from £2. The Terravision bus goes to Liverpool Street station and costs £8. Travel is extended to Victoria Coach Station between 8 pm and 6 am, and the fare is £9. Travel time is 60 minutes.

Stansted by Train: The Stansted Express to Liverpool Street Station (with a stop at Tottenham Hale) runs every 15 minutes 5:30 am–12:30 am daily (until 1:30 am Friday and Saturday). The 45-minute trip costs £23.40 each way if booked online. Tickets cost more on board.

Luton by Bus and Train: A free airport shuttle runs from Luton Airport to the nearby Luton Airport Parkway Station, where you can take a train or bus into London. From there, the First Capital Connect train service runs to St. Pancras, Farringdon, Blackfriars, and London Bridge. The journey takes about 40 minutes. Trains leave every 10 minutes or so from 5 am until midnight, hourly at other times. One-way tickets begin at £13.50. The Terravision Shuttle bus runs from Luton to Victoria Coach Station, with departures every 20 to 30 minutes during peak hours. The journey takes around an hour, with

fares from £10 each way. The Green Line 757 bus service from Luton to Victoria Station runs every 15 to 30 minutes between 7 am and midnight, takes 60 to 90 minutes, and costs from £10, while an easyBus shuttle has tickets starting from £2. National Express runs coaches from Victoria Coach Station to Luton for £15.

Heathrow, Gatwick, Stansted, and Luton by Taxi: This is an expensive and time-consuming option. If your destination is within the city's congestion zone, £10 will be added to the bill during charging hours. If you get stuck in traffic, a taxi from the stand will be even more expensive; a cab booked ahead is a set price. A taxi trip from Heathrow to Victoria, for example, can take more than an hour and cost more than £58. Private hire cars may be the same price or even less—at this writing, the fee to Victoria Station is about £50 from Heathrow and £100 from Gatwick and Stansted, not including the congestion charge. Another option, if you have friends in the London area, is to have them book a reputable minicab firm to pick you up. The cost of a minicab from Heathrow to central London is approximately £47. Your hotel may also be able to recommend a car service.

TRANSFERS BETWEEN AIRPORTS

Allow at least two to three hours for transferring between airports. The National Express Airport bus is the most direct option between Gatwick and Heathrow. Buses depart from Gatwick every 5–35 minutes between 5:35 am to 11:35 am (every hour from 1:50 am to 5:35 am) and from Heathrow every 5–35 minutes from 2:35 am to 12:35 am. The trip takes 45 to 95 minutes, and the fare is £27.50 each way. Book tickets in advance. National Express buses between Stansted and Gatwick depart every 30 to 75 minutes and take between 3 and 4½ hours. The one-way fare is from £18 to £31.50. Some airlines may offer shuttle services as well—check with your airline before your journey.

The cheapest option—but most complicated—is public transportation: from Gatwick to Stansted, for instance, catch the Gatwick Express train from Gatwick to Victoria Station, take the Tube to Liverpool Street Station, then hop on the train to Stansted. Alternatively, take the Thameslink train to Farringdon and transfer to the Tube bound for Liverpool Street. From Heathrow to Gatwick, take the Tube to King's Cross/St. Pancras, then take the Thameslink train to Gatwick, or else transfer from the Piccadilly Line to the District/Circle Line at Hammersmith, head to Victoria Station, and take the Gatwick Express.

All this should get much easier when the new Crossrail service debuts in 2014. It will travel directly from Heathrow to Liverpool Street Station for Stansted connections and directly to Farringdon for the Thameslink to Gatwick.

Contacts Crossrail ☎ *0345/602-3813* ⊕ *www.crossrail.co.uk.* **easyBus** ⊕ *www.easybus.co.uk.* **First Capital Connect** ☎ *0845/748-4950* ⊕ *www.firstcapitalconnect. co.uk.* **Gatwick Express** ☎ *0845/850-1530* ⊕ *www.gatwickexpress.com.* **Green Line** ☎ *0844/800-4411* ⊕ *www.greenline.co.uk.* **Heathrow Connect** ☎ *0845/678-6975* ⊕ *www.heathrowconnect.com.* **Heathrow Express** ☎ *0845/600-1515* ⊕ *www.heathrowexpress.com.* **Hotel By Bus** ☎ *0845/850-1900* ⊕ *www.hotelbybus. com.* **National Express** ☎ *0871/781-8178* ⊕ *www.nationalexpress.com.* **SkyShuttle** ☎ *0845/481-0960* ⊕ *www.skyshuttle. co.uk.* **Stansted Express** ☎ *0845/600-7245* ⊕ *www.stanstedexpress.com.* **Terravision** ☎ *01279/662-931* ⊕ *www.terravision. eu/london.html.* **Transport for London** ☎ *0843/222-1234* ⊕ *www.tfl.gov.uk.* **Traveline** ☎ *0871/200-2233* ⊕ *www.traveline.info.*

FLIGHTS

British Airways offers mostly nonstop flights from 28 U.S. cities to Heathrow, along with flights to Manchester and Birmingham and a vast program of discount airfare–hotel packages. Britain-based Virgin Atlantic is a strong competitor in terms of packages. London is a very popular destination, so many U.S. carriers have flights and packages, too.

Because England is such a small country, internal air travel is much less important than it is in the United States. For trips of less than 200 miles, trains are often quicker because rail stations are more centrally located. Flying tends to cost more, but for longer trips air travel has a considerable time advantage (you need to factor in time to get to and from the airport, though).

British Airways operates shuttle services between Heathrow or Gatwick and Manchester, while Virgin's Little Red takes you from London to Manchester, Edinburgh, and Aberdeen. Low-cost airlines such as easyJet and Ryanair offer flights within the United Kingdom as well as to cities in Ireland and continental Europe. Prices are low, but these airlines usually fly out of smaller British airports such as Stansted and Luton, both near London. Check ⊕ *www.cheapflights.com* for price comparisons.

Major Airline Contacts American Airlines ☎ *800/433-7300, 0844/499-7300 in U.K.* ⊕ *www.aa.com.* **British Airways** ☎ *800/247-9297, 0844/493-0787 in U.K.* ⊕ *www.britishairways.com.* **Delta Airlines** ☎ *800/241-4141 international reservations, 0871/221-1222 in U.K.* ⊕ *www.delta. com.* **United Airlines** ☎ *800/864-8331 in U.S., 0845/607-6760 in U.K.* ⊕ *www.united. com.* **US Airways** ☎ *800/428-4322 for U.S. and Canada reservations, 0845/600-3300 in U.K.* ⊕ *www.usairways.com.* **Virgin Atlantic** ☎ *800/862-8621, 0800/874-7747 in U.K.* ⊕ *www.virgin-atlantic.com.*

Within England and to Europe easyJet ☎ *0871/244-2377* ⊕ *www.easyjet.com.* **Ryanair** ☎ *0871/246-0000* ⊕ *www.ryanair.com.*

▌ BOAT TRAVEL

Ferries and other boats travel regular routes to France, Spain, Ireland, and Scandinavia. P&O runs ferries to Belgium, Spain, Ireland, and the Netherlands. DFDS Seaways serves France and the Netherlands, and Stena Line serves Ireland, Northern Ireland, and the Netherlands.

Low-cost airlines and Eurotunnel (which lets you take a car to France on the train) have cut into ferry travel, but companies have responded by cutting fares and upgrading equipment.

Prices vary; booking early ensures cheaper fares, but also ask about special deals. Seaview is a comprehensive online ferry- and cruise-booking portal for Britain and continental Europe. Ferry Cheap is a discount website.

Information DFDS Seaways ☎ *0871/574–7235* ⊕ *www.dfdsseaways.co.uk.* **Ferry Cheap** ☎ *01304/501100* ⊕ *www.ferrycheap.com.* **P&O** ☎ *0871/664–2121* ⊕ *www.poferries.com.* **Seaview** ☎ *01442/843–050* ⊕ *www.seaview. co.uk.* **Stena Line** ☎ *0137/040–100* ⊕ *www.stenaline.co.uk.*

TRANSATLANTIC AND OTHER CRUISES

Most cruise ships leave from southern England—particularly Southampton and Portsmouth. Some ships leave from Liverpool and Dover as well, or from Harwich, near Cambridge.

Cruise Lines Cunard Line ☎ *800/728–6273 in U.S., 0843/374–0033 in U.K* ⊕ *www.cunard. co.uk.* **Holland America Line** ☎ *0843/374–2300* ⊕ *www.hollandamerica.com.* **Norwegian Cruise Line** ☎ *0845/201–8900 in U.K, 866/234–7350 in U.S.* ⊕ *www.ncl.co.uk.* **Princess Cruises** ☎ *800/774–6237 in U.S., 0843/374–4444 in U.K.* ⊕ *www.princess.com.* **Royal Caribbean International** ☎ *866/562–7625 in U.S., 0844/493–4005 in U.K.* ⊕ *www.royalcaribbean.com.*

▌ BUS TRAVEL

Britain has a comprehensive bus (short-haul public transportation) and coach (faster, plusher long-distance buses) network that offers an inexpensive way of seeing England. National Express is the major coach operator, and Victoria Coach Station, near Victoria Station in central London, is its hub in the region. The company serves more than 1,000 destinations within Britain (and, via Eurolines, 500 more in continental Europe). There are 2,000 ticket agents nationwide, including offices at London's Heathrow and Gatwick airport coach stations.

Green Line is the second-largest national service, serving airports and major tourist towns. A budget option for long-distance travel, Megabus has double-decker buses that serve cities across Britain, with seats that turn into bunk beds on routes to Scotland. Greyhound has low-cost, long-distance bus service to five destinations in Wales. In London, the latter two companies depart from Victoria Coach Station as well as other stops, while Green Line buses also stop at Baker Street and Hyde Park Corner.

Bus tickets can be much less than the price of a train ticket (even lower if you take advantage of special deals). For example, an Oxford Tube bus ticket from London to Oxford is £14, whereas a train ticket may be £22. Buses are also just as comfortable as trains. However, buses often take twice as long to reach their destinations. Greyhound and Oxford Tube have onboard Wi-Fi. All bus services forbid smoking.

Double-decker buses, run by private companies, offer local bus service in cities and regions. Check with the local bus station or tourist information center for routes and schedules. Most companies offer daylong or weeklong unlimited-travel tickets, and those in popular tourist areas operate special scenic tours in summer. The top deck of a double-decker bus is a great place from which to view the countryside.

DISCOUNTS AND DEALS

National Express's Young Persons' Coach-Card for students age 16 to 26 costs £10 annually and gets 20% to 30% discounts off many fares. Most companies also offer a discount for children under 15. A Senior CoachCard for the over-sixties cuts many fares by a third. Apex tickets (advance-purchase tickets) save money on standard fares, and traveling midweek is cheaper than over weekends and holidays.

FARES AND SCHEDULES

You can find schedules online, pick them up from tourist information offices, or get them by phone from the bus companies. Fares vary based on how close to the time of travel you book—Megabus tickets, for example, are cheaper if ordered in advance online.

PAYING

Tickets for National Express can be bought from the Victoria, Heathrow, or Gatwick coach stations, by phone, online, or from most British travel agencies. Reservations are advised. Tickets for Megabus must be purchased online or by phone (avoid calling, as there's a surcharge).

Most companies accept credit cards for advance purchases, but some companies require cash for onboard transactions.

RESERVATIONS

Book in advance, as buses on busy routes fill up quickly. With most bus companies (National Express, Megabus, Green Line), advance payment means you receive an email receipt and your name is placed on a list given to the bus driver.

Bus Contacts Green Line ☎ 0844/800–4411 ⊕ www.greenline.co.uk. **Greyhound** ☎ 0900/096–0000 ⊕ www.greyhounduk.com. **Megabus** ☎ 0900/160–0900 ⊕ uk.megabus. com. **National Express** ☎ 0871/781–8178 ⊕ www.nationalexpress.com. **Traveline** ☎ 0871/200–2233 ⊕ traveline.info. **Victoria Coach Station** ✉ 164 Buckingham Palace Rd., London ☎ 0207/027–2520 ⊕ www.tfl.gov.uk.

∎ CAR TRAVEL

Britain can be a challenging place for most foreigners to drive, considering that people drive on the left side of the often disconcertingly narrow roads, many rental cars have standard transmissions, and the gearshift is on the wrong side entirely.

There's no reason to rent a car for a stay in London, because the city and its suburbs are well served by public transportation, and traffic is desperately congested. Here and in other major cities it's best to rely on public transportation.

Outside the cities, a car can be very handy. Many sights aren't easily reached without one—castles, for example, are rarely connected to any public transportation system. Small villages might have only one or two buses a day pass through them. If you're comfortable on the road, the experience of driving between the tall hedgerows or on country roads is a truly English experience.

In England and Wales your own driver's license is acceptable. However, you may choose to get an International Driving Permit (IDP), which can be used only in conjunction with a valid driver's license and which translates your license into 10 languages. Check the Automobile Association of America website for more info as well as for IDPs ($15) themselves. These permits are universally recognized, and having one in your wallet may save you a problem with the local authorities.

GASOLINE

Gasoline is called petrol in England and is sold by the liter. The price you see posted at a petrol station is the price of a liter, and there are about 4 liters in a U.S. gallon. Petrol is expensive; it was around £1.35 per liter, or $2.10 per liter, at the time of this writing. Supermarket pumps just outside city centers frequently offer the best prices. Premium and superpremium are the two varieties, and most cars run on premium. Diesel is widely used; be sure not to use it by mistake. Along busy motorways, most large stations are open 24 hours a day, 7 days a week. In rural areas, hours can vary. Most service stations accept major credit cards, and most are self-service.

PARKING

Parking regulations are strictly enforced, and fines are high. If there are no signs on a street, you can park there. Many streets have centralized "pay and display" machines, in which you deposit the required money and get a ticket allowing you to park for a set period of time. In London's City of Westminster (⊕ *www. westminster.gov.uk*) and some other boroughs, parking machines have been replaced by a pay-by-phone plan, enabling you to pay by cell phone if you've preregistered. In town centers your best bet is to park in a public lot marked with a square blue sign with a white "P" in the center.

If you park on the street, follow these basic rules: Do not park within 15 yards of an intersection. Never park in bus lanes or on double yellow lines, and do not park on single yellow lines when parking meters are in effect. On busy roads with red lines painted on the street you cannot park or stop to let a passenger out of the car.

RENTALS

Rental rates are generally reasonable, and insurance costs are lower than in the United States. If you want the car only for country trips, consider renting outside London. Rates are cheaper, and you avoid traversing London's notoriously complex road system. Rental rates vary widely, beginning at £27 a day and £110 a week for a midsize car, usually with manual transmission. As in the United States, prices rise in summer and during holidays. Car seats for children cost £10–£30, and GPS is usually around £14.

Major car-rental agencies are much the same in Britain as in the United States: Alamo, Avis, Budget, Enterprise, Hertz, and National all have offices in Britain. Europcar is another large company. Companies may not rent cars to people who are under 23. Some have an upper age limit of 75.

ROAD CONDITIONS

There's a good network of major highways (motorways) and divided highways (dual carriageways) throughout most of England and Wales. Motorways (with the prefix "M"), shown in blue on most maps, are mainly two or three lanes in each direction. Other major roads (with the prefix "A") are shown on maps in green and red. Sections of fast dual carriageways (with black-edged, thick outlines on maps) have both traffic lights and traffic circles. Turnoffs are often marked by highway numbers, rather than place names. An exit is called a junction in Britain.

The vast network of lesser roads, for the most part old coach and turnpike roads, might make your trip twice as long but show you twice as much. Minor roads are drawn in yellow or white on maps, the former prefixed by "B," the latter unlettered and unnumbered. Should you take one of these, be prepared to back up into a passing place if you meet an oncoming car.

ROADSIDE EMERGENCIES

On major highways emergency roadside telephone booths are positioned at regular intervals. Contact your car-rental company or call the police. You can also call the British Automobile Association (AA) toll-free. You can join and receive assistance from the AA or the RAC on the spot, but the charge is higher than a simple membership fee. If you're a member of the American Automobile Association, check before you travel; reciprocal agreements may give you free roadside aid.

Emergency Services Ambulance, fire, police ☎ *999 emergency, 101 police non-emergency.* **Automobile Association** ☎ *0800/887–766 emergency service, 0800/085–2721 general calls* ⊕ *www.theaa. com.* **RAC** ☎ *0333/200–0999 emergency service, 0844/891–3111 general inquiries* ⊕ *www.rac.co.uk.*

RULES OF THE ROAD

Driving on the left side of the road might be easier than you expected, as the steering and mirrors on British cars are designed for driving on the left. If you have a standard transmission car, you have to shift gears with your left hand. Give yourself time to adjust before leaving the rental-car lot. Seat belts are obligatory in the front and back seats. It's illegal to talk on a handheld cell phone while driving.

Pick up a copy of the official Highway Code (£2.50) at a service station, newsstand, or bookstore, or check it out online by going to ⊕ *www.gov.uk* and putting "Highway Code" in the search bar. Besides driving rules and illustrations of signs and road markings, this booklet contains information for motorcyclists, cyclists, and pedestrians.

Speed limits are complicated, and there are speed cameras everywhere. The speed limit (shown on circular red signs) is generally 20 or 30 mph in towns and cities, 40 to 60 mph on two-lane highways, and 70 mph on motorways. At traffic circles (called roundabouts), you turn clockwise. As cars enter the circle, they must yield to those already in the circle. If you're taking an exit all the way around the circle, signal right as you enter, stay to the center, and then signal and move left just before your own exit.

Pedestrians have the right-of-way on "zebra" crossings (black-and-white-stripe crosswalks between two orange-flashing globe lights). At other crossings, pedestrians must yield to traffic, but they do have the right-of-way over traffic turning left.

Drunk-driving laws are strictly enforced. The legal limit is 80 milligrams of alcohol per 100 milliliters of blood, which means two units of alcohol—two glasses of wine, one pint of beer, or four shots of whisky—but amounts vary, depending on your weight or what you've eaten that day.

▌TRAIN TRAVEL

Operated by several different private companies, the train system in Britain is extensive and useful, though less than perfect. Some regional trains are old, and virtually all lines suffer from occasional delays, schedule changes, and periodic repair work that runs over schedule. All major cities and many small towns are served by trains, and despite the difficulties, rail travel is the most pleasant way to cover long distances.

On long-distance runs some rail lines have buffet cars; on others you can purchase snacks from a mobile snack cart. Most train companies now have "quiet cars" where mobile-phone use is forbidden.

CLASSES

Most rail lines have first-class and second-class cars. In virtually all cases, second class is perfectly comfortable. First class is quieter and less crowded, has better furnishings, and marginally larger seats. It also usually costs two to three times the price of second class, but not always, so it's worth comparing prices. Most train operators offer a Weekend First ticket. Available on weekends and holidays, these tickets allow you to upgrade for as little as £5.

FARES AND SCHEDULES

National Rail Enquiries is a helpful, comprehensive, and free service that covers all the country's rail lines. National Rail will help you choose the best train, and then connect you with the right ticket office. You can also book tickets online. A similar service is offered by the Trainline, which provides online train information and ticket booking for all rail services. The Man in Seat 61, a website, offers objective information along with booking facilities.

Ticket prices are more expensive during rush hour, so plan accordingly. For long-distance travel, tickets cost more the longer you wait. Book in advance and tickets can be half of what you'd pay on the day of departure. A journey from London to Cardiff costs £16 if you buy a ticket two weeks in advance, but the fare rises to £40.50 if you wait until the day of your trip.

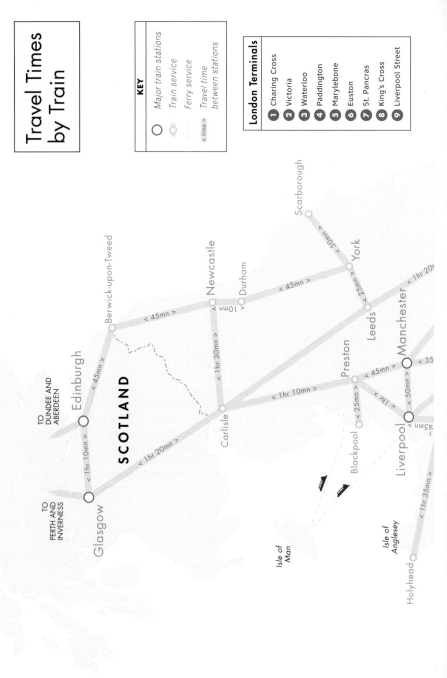

Travel Times by Train

KEY

○ Major train stations
○ Train service
⋯⋯ Ferry service
< time > Travel time between stations

London Terminals

1. Charing Cross
2. Victoria
3. Waterloo
4. Paddington
5. Marylebone
6. Euston
7. St. Pancras
8. King's Cross
9. Liverpool Street

SCOTLAND

TO PERTH AND INVERNESS

TO DUNDEE AND ABERDEEN

Glasgow
Edinburgh
< 1hr 10mn >

Berwick-upon-Tweed
< 45mn >
< 45mn >

Newcastle
10mn
Durham

< 45mn >

Scarborough
< 50mn >
York
< 25mn >
Leeds

< 1hr 30mn >

< 1hr 20mn >

Carlisle
< 1hr 10mn >

Preston
< 25mn >
Blackpool
< 45mn >
< 1hr >
< 50mn >
Manchester
< 35

Liverpool
45mn

< 1hr 20

Isle of Man

Isle of Anglesey

Holyhead
< 1hr 35mn >

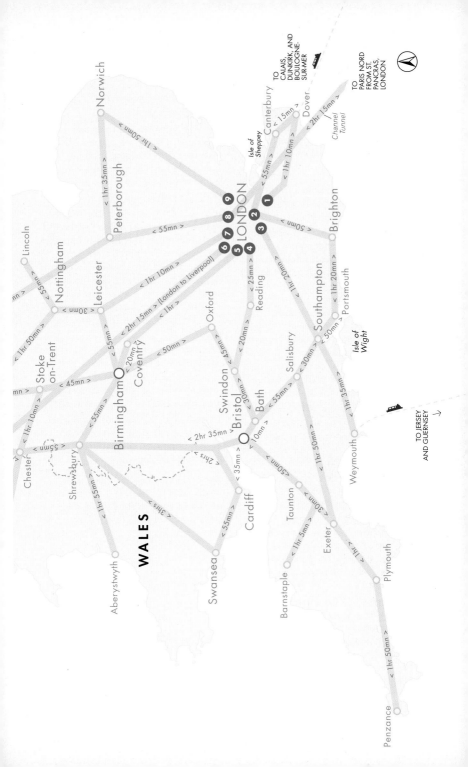

▓ TIP→ Ask the local tourist board about hotel and local transportation packages that include tickets to major events.

Information **National Rail Enquiries** ☎ *0845/748–4950, 020/7278–5240 outside U.K.* ⊕ *www.nationalrail.co.uk.* **The Man in Seat 61** ⊕ *www.seat61.com.* **Trainline** ☎ *0871/244–1545* ⊕ *www.thetrainline.com.*

PASSES

National Rail Enquiries has information about rail passes such as Rovers, which save you money on individual trips.

If you plan to travel a lot by train in England and Wales, consider purchasing a BritRail Pass, which gives unlimited travel over the entire British rail network and can save you money. If you don't plan to cover many miles, you may come out ahead by buying individual tickets. Buy your BritRail Pass before you leave home, as they are not sold in Britain. The passes are available from most U.S. travel agents or from ACP Rail International, Flight Centre, or VisitBritain. Note that Eurail Passes aren't honored in Britain.

BritRail passes come in two basic varieties: the Consecutive Pass and the FlexiPass. You can get a Consecutive Pass good for 3, 4, 8, 15, 22, or 31 consecutive days starting at $215 standard and $319 first-class for 3 days. The FlexiPass for 3, 4, 8, or 15 days of travel in two months costs $269 standard and $395 first class for 3 days.

Don't assume that a rail pass guarantees you a seat on a particular train. You need to book seats even if you're using a rail pass, especially on trains that may be crowded, particularly in summer on popular routes.

Discount Passes **ACP Rail International** ☎ *866/938–7245 in U.S., 0207/953-4062 in U.K.* ⊕ *www.acprail.com.* **BritRail** ☎ *866/938–7245 in U.S.* ⊕ *www.britrail.com.* **Flight Centre** ☎ *0870/499–0040 in U.K., 866/938–7245 in U.S.* ⊕ *www.flightcentre.com.* **VisitBritain** ☎ *877/992–4732 in U.S.* ⊕ *www.visitbritainshop.com.*

PAYING

Cash and credit cards are accepted by all train ticket offices; credit cards are accepted over the phone and online.

RESERVATIONS

Reserving your ticket in advance is recommended. Even a reservation 24 hours in advance can provide a substantial discount. Look into cheap day returns if you plan to travel a round-trip in one day.

CHANNEL TUNNEL

Short of flying, taking the Eurostar through the Channel Tunnel is the fastest way to cross the English Channel. Travel time is 2¼ hours from London's St. Pancras Station to Paris's Gare du Nord. Trains also travel to Lyon (5½ hours) and Aix-en-Provence (6¼ hours) on Saturday in May and June, and to Avignon (6 hours), on Saturday from July to September.

Early risers can easily take a day trip to Paris if time is short. Book ahead, as Eurostar ticket prices increase as the departure date approaches. If purchased in advance, round-trip tickets to Paris start at £98.

Channel Tunnel Car Transport **Eurotunnel** ☎ *0844/335–3535* ⊕ *www.eurotunnel.com.* **French Motorail/Rail Europe** ☎ *0844/848–4064* ⊕ *www.raileurope.co.uk.*

Channel Tunnel Passenger Service **Eurostar** ☎ *0843/218–6186* ⊕ *www.eurostar. com.* **Rail Europe** ☎ *800/622–8600 in U.S., 0844/848–4064 in U.K.* ⊕ *www.raileurope.com.*

ESSENTIALS

▌ ACCOMMODATIONS

Hotels, bed-and-breakfasts, rural inns, or luxurious country houses—there's a style and price to suit most travelers. Wherever you stay, make reservations well in advance. *(For additional descriptions of kinds of lodgings, see the England Lodging Primer in chapter 1.)*

Our local writers vet every hotel to recommend the best overnights in each price category, from budget to expensive. Unless otherwise specified, you can expect private bath, phone, and TV in your room. *For expanded reviews, facilities, and current deals, visit Fodors.com.*

Lodgings are indicated in the text by ⊞. Throughout Britain, lodging prices often include breakfast of some kind, but this is generally not the case in London. *Prices in the reviews are the lowest cost of a standard double room in high season, including 20% V.A.T.*

APARTMENT AND HOUSE RENTALS

If you deal directly with local agents, get a recommendation from someone who's used the company. Unlike with hotels, there's no accredited system for apartment-rental standards. *Also see Chapter 2 for London rental resources.*

BED-AND-BREAKFASTS

B&Bs can be a good budget option, and will also help you meet the locals. Cottages, unlike B&Bs, usually do not provide breakfast.

Reservation Services
Bed & Breakfast.com ☎ 512/322-2710 ⊕ www.bedandbreakfast.com. **The Bed and Breakfast Club** ☎ 01243/370692 ⊕ www.thebedandbreakfastclub.co.uk. **Wolsey Lodges** ☎ 01473/822058 ⊕ www.wolseylodges.com.

COTTAGES
Contacts Classic Cottages ☎ 01326/555555 ⊕ www.classic.co.uk. **National Trust** ☎ 0844/800-2070 ⊕ www.nationaltrustcottages.co.uk. **Rural Retreats** ☎ 01386/701177 ⊕ www.ruralretreats.co.uk. **VisitBritain** ☎ 0207/578-1000 ⊕ www.visitbritain.com.

FARMHOUSES
Contacts Farm & Cottage Holidays UK ☎ 01237/459-888 ⊕ www.holidaycottages.co.uk. **Farm Stay UK** ☎ 024/7669-6909 ⊕ www.farmstayuk.co.uk.

HISTORIC BUILDINGS
Contacts Celtic Castles ☎ 01422/323200 ⊕ www.celticcastles.com. **English Heritage** ☎ 0870/333-1181 ⊕ www.english-heritage.org.uk. **Landmark Trust** ☎ 01628/825925 ⊕ www.landmarktrust.org.uk. **National Trust** ☎ 0844/800-2070 ⊕ www.nationaltrustcottages.co.uk. **Portmeirion Cottages** ☎ 01766/770000 ⊕ www.portmeirion-village.com. **Rural Retreats** ☎ 01386/701177 ⊕ www.ruralretreats.co.uk. **Stately Holiday Cottages** ☎ 01638/674756 ⊕ www.statelyholidaycottages.co.uk. **Unique Home Stays** ☎ 01637/881183 ⊕ ww.uniquehomestays.com. **Vivat Trust** ☎ 0845/090-0194 ⊕ www.vivat-trust.org.

HOME EXCHANGES

With a direct home exchange you stay in someone else's home while they stay in yours. Some outfits handle vacation homes, so you're staying in someone's vacant weekend place. Home Exchange.com offers a one-year membership for $101; HomeLink International costs $119 for an annual online membership, which includes a directory listing; and Intervac U.S. offers international membership for $100.

Exchange Clubs Home Exchange.com ☎ 800/877-8723 ⊕ www.homeexchange.com. **HomeLink International** ☎ 800/638-3841 ⊕ www.homelink.org. **Intervac.** ☎ 800/756-4663 ⊕ www.intervac-homeexchange.com.

Online Booking Resources

CONTACTS

The Apartment Service	0208/944–1444	www.apartmentservice.com
At Home Abroad	212/421–9165	www.athomeabroadinc.com
Barclay International Group	516/364–0064 or 800/845–6636	www.barclayweb.com
English Country Cottages	0845/268–0785	www.english-country-cottages.co.uk
In the English Manner	01559/371600 or 800/422–0799	www.english-manner.com
Interhome	800/882–6864	www.interhome.us
Living Architecture	07734/323464	www.living-architecture.co.uk
National Trust	0844/800–2070	www.nationaltrustcottages.co.uk
Suzanne B. Cohen & Associates	207/622–0743	www.villaeurope.com
Vacation Rentals By Owner	877/228–3145	www.vrbo.com
Villanet	877/250–4366 or 206/417–3444	www.rentavilla.com
Villas International	415/499–9490 or 800/221–2260	www.villasintl.com

HOTELS

Most hotels have rooms with "ensuite" bathrooms—as private bathrooms are called—although some older ones may have only washbasins; in this case, showers and toilets are usually down the hall. Especially in London, rooms and bathrooms may be smaller than those you find in the United States.

Besides familiar international chains, England has some local chains that are worth a look; they provide rooms from the less expensive (Travelodge, basic but bargain, and Premier Inn are the most widespread; Jurys Inns offer good value in city centers) to the trendy (ABode, Hotel du Vin, Malmaison).

Local Chains ABode ⊕ *www.abodehotels. co.uk.* **Hotel du Vin** ☎ *0871/943–0345* ⊕ *www.hotelduvin.com.* **Jurys Inn** ☎ *0870/410–0800* ⊕ *www.jurysinn.com.* **Malmaison** ☎ *0871/943–0350* ⊕ *www. malmaison.com.* **Premier Inn** ☎ *0871/527– 9222* ⊕ *www.premierinn.com.* **Travelodge** ☎ *0800/835–2424 in U.K., 800/525–4055 in U.S.* ⊕ *www.travelodge.com.*

HOTEL GRADING SYSTEM

Hotels, guesthouses, inns, and B&Bs in the United Kingdom are all graded from one to five stars by the tourism board, VisitBritain. Basically, the more stars a property has, the more amenities it has, and the facilities will be of a higher standard. It's a fairly good reflection of lodging from small B&Bs up to palatial hotels. The most luxurious hotels will have five stars; a simple, clean, acceptable hostelry will have one star.

DISCOUNTS AND DEALS

Hotel rates in major cities tend to be cheapest on weekends, whereas rural hotels are cheapest on weeknights. The lowest occupancy is between November and April, so hotels lower their prices substantially during these months.

Lastminute.com offers deals on hotel rooms all over the United Kingdom. VisitLondon.com, London's official website, has some good deals.

Local Resources Lastminute.com ☎ *0800/083–4000* ⊕ *www.lastminute.com.*

LOCAL DOS AND TABOOS

CUSTOMS OF THE COUNTRY

In general, British and American rules of etiquette are much the same. Differences are subtle. British people find Americans' bluntness somewhat startling from time to time, but are charmed by their friendliness.

Many of the English still tend to take politeness extremely seriously, but younger people and urbanites have a more casual approach. Self-deprecating humor, however, always goes down well. The famous British reserve is still in place, but on social occasions it's best to observe what the others do, and go with the flow. If you're visiting a family home, a gift of flowers is welcome, as is a bottle of wine.

GREETINGS

Older British people will shake hands on greeting old friends or acquaintances; female friends may greet each other with a kiss on the cheek. In Britain, you can never say "please," "thank you," or "sorry" too often; to thank your host, a phone call or thank-you card does nicely. Email and other electronic messages are fine for younger hosts.

SIGHTSEEING

As in the United States, in public places it's considered polite to give up your seat to an elderly person, to a pregnant woman, or to a parent struggling with children and bags. Jaywalking isn't illegal in England and everybody does it. However, since driving is on the left in England, the traffic flow may be confusing; use caution.

British people used to take waiting in line (called queuing) incredibly seriously, but, especially in London bus queues, line discipline is breaking down. Nevertheless, many still highly value patience, and will turn on "queue jumpers" who try to cut in line. Complaining while waiting in line is considered wimpy. Enduring the wait with good humor is considered a sign of strong moral character.

The single thing you can do that will most mark you as a tourist—and an impolite one—is fail to observe the written and spoken rule that, on virtually all escalators but especially those in Tube stations, you stand on the right side of the escalator and leave room for people to walk past you on the left.

OUT ON THE TOWN

Etiquette in restaurants is much the same as in any major U.S. city. In restaurants you hail a waiter by saying, "Excuse me..." as one passes by, or by politely signaling with subtle hand signals (but no snapping fingers). It's common to have drinks before dinner, and wine with dinner. Friends and co-workers frequently gather in pubs, but you don't have to drink alcohol—some people in the pub drink juice or sodas. Nonetheless, drunkenness can be common in major cities after 10 pm.

"Smart casual" is fine for the theater, and those going to nightclubs will dress just the same here as they would in New York or Chicago—the flashier the better. Pubs are very casual places, however.

Smoking is forbidden in all public places, including bars and restaurants.

DOING BUSINESS

Punctuality is of prime importance; if you anticipate a late arrival, call ahead. For business dinners, if you proffered the invitation, it's usually assumed that you'll pick up the tab. If you're the visitor, however, it's good form for the host to pay the bill. Alternatively, play it safe and offer to split the check.

▌ COMMUNICATIONS

INTERNET

If you're traveling with a laptop, carry a spare battery and adapter. If your hotel has dial-up (a rarity these days), get a telephone cord that's compatible with a British phone jack; these are available in Britain at airports and electronics stores. Wi-Fi is increasingly available in hotels, and broadband coverage is widespread in cities. Many London Underground stations now have Wi-Fi (for a fee). Outside big cities, wireless access is relatively rare in cafés and coffee shops, but its popularity there is growing.

Contacts Cybercafes ⊕ www.cybercafes.com. **Wi-Fi Freespot** ⊕ www.wififreespot.com.

PHONES

All calls (including local calls) made within the United Kingdom are charged according to the time of day. The standard landline rate applies weekdays 7 am to 7 pm; a cheaper rate is in effect weekdays 7 pm to 7 am and all day on weekends, when it's even cheaper.

A word of warning: 0870 numbers are *not* toll-free numbers in Britain; in fact, numbers beginning with this or the 0871, 0844, or 0845 prefixes cost extra to call. The amount varies and is usually relatively small—except for numbers with the premium-rate 090 prefix, which cost an eye-watering £1 per minute when dialed from within the country—but can be excessive when dialed from outside Britain.

CALLING ENGLAND

The country code for Great Britain (and thus England) is 44. When dialing an English number from abroad, drop the initial 0 from before the local area code. For example, let's say you're calling Buckingham Palace—0207/7930–4832—from the United States. First, dial 011 (the international access code), then 44 (Great Britain's country code), then 207 (London's center-city code—without its initial 0), then the remainder of the number.

CALLING WITHIN ENGLAND

For all calls within England (and Britain), dial the area code (which usually begins with 01, except in London), followed by the telephone number.

There are two types of pay phones: those that make calls to landlines or mobiles and those that also let you send texts or email. Most coin-operated phones take 10p, 20p, 50p, and £1 coins. SIM cards for your own cell phone and inexpensive pay-as-you-go cell phones are widely available from mobile network retailers such as 3, O2, T-Mobile, Vodaphone, and Virgin, as well as the Carphone Warehouse chain.

For pay and other phones, if you hear a repeated single tone after dialing, the line is busy; a continuous tone means the number didn't work.

There are several different directory-assistance providers. For information anywhere in Britain, try dialing 118–888 or 118–118; you'll need to know the town and the street (or at least the neighborhood) of the person you're trying to reach. For the operator, dial 100. For genuine emergencies, dial 999. For nonurgent police matters, dial 101.

CALLING OUTSIDE ENGLAND

For direct overseas dialing from England (and Britain), dial 00, then the country code, area code, and number. For the international operator, credit card, or collect calls, dial 155; for international directory assistance, dial 118505. The country code for the United States is 1.

Access Codes **AT&T Direct** ☎ *0800/890–0011.* **MCI WorldPhone** ☎ *0800/279–5088.* **Sprint International Access** ☎ *817/698–4199.*

CALLING CARDS

Public card phones operate with special cards that you can buy from post offices, some newsstands, or on the Internet. Ideal for longer calls, the cards are composed of units of 10p, and come in values of £3, £5, £10, and more. To use a card phone, lift the receiver, insert your card, and dial the number. An indicator panel shows the number of units used. At the end of your call the card will be returned. Where credit cards are taken, slide the card in as indicated.

MOBILE PHONES

Any cell phone can be used in Europe if it's tri-band, quad-band, or GSM. Travelers should ask their cell-phone company if their phone fits in this category and make sure it's activated for international calling before leaving their home country. Roaming fees can be steep, however: $1 a minute is considered reasonable. And overseas you normally pay the toll charges for incoming calls. It's almost always cheaper to send a text message than to make a call, since text messages have a low set fee (often less than 25¢).

If you just want to make local calls, consider buying a new SIM card (your provider may have to unlock your phone for you) and a prepaid local service plan. You'll then have a local number and can make local calls at local rates. You can also rent a cell phone from most major car-rental agencies in England. Some upscale hotels now provide loaner cell phones to their guests. Beware, however, of the per-minute rates charged. Alternatively, you may want to buy a basic pay-as-you-go phone for around £15.

Contacts Carphone Warehouse ☎ *0870/087–0870* ⊕ *www.carphonewarehouse.com.* **Cellular Abroad** ☎ *800/287–5072* ⊕ *www.cellularabroad.com.* **Mobal** ☎ *888/888–9162* ⊕ *www.mobal.com.*

▌CUSTOMS AND DUTIES

You're always allowed to bring goods of a certain value back home without having to pay any duty or import tax. But there's a limit on the amount of tobacco and liquor you can bring back duty-free, and some countries have separate limits for perfumes; for exact figures, check with your customs department. The values of so-called duty-free goods are included in these amounts. When you shop abroad, save all your receipts, as customs inspectors may ask to see them as well as the items you purchased. If the total value of your goods is more than the duty-free limit, you'll have to pay a tax (most often a flat percentage) on the value of everything beyond that limit.

Fresh meats, plants and vegetables, controlled drugs, and firearms (including replicas) and ammunition may not be brought into the United Kingdom, nor can dairy products from non-EU countries. Pets from the United States with the proper documentation may be brought into the country without quarantine under the U.K. Pet Travel Scheme (PETS). The process takes about four months to complete and involves detailed steps.

You'll face no customs formalities if you enter Scotland or Wales from any other part of the United Kingdom.

Information in England HM Revenue and Customs ☎ *0845/010–9000* ⊕ *www.hmrc.gov. uk.* **Pet Travel Scheme** ☎ *0845/933–5577 in U.K., 207/238–6951 in U.S.* ⊕ *www.gov.uk.*

U.S. Information U.S. Customs and Border Protection ☎ *877/228–5511 in U.S.* ⊕ *www.cbp.gov.*

▌EATING OUT

The stereotypical notion of English meals as parades of roast beef, overcooked vegetables, and stodgy puddings has largely been replaced—particularly in London, other major cities, and some country hot spots—with an evolving picture of the country as foodie territory. From trendy gastro-pubs to interesting ethnic-fusion restaurants to see-and-be-seen dining shrines, English food is becoming known for having an international approach.

In general, restaurant prices are high. If you're watching your budget, seek out pubs and ethnic restaurants.

Prices in the reviews are the average cost of a main course at dinner or, if dinner isn't served, at lunch.

DISCOUNTS AND DEALS

Eating out in England's big cities in particular can be expensive, but you can do it cheaply. Try local cafés, more popularly known as "caffs," where heaping plates of English comfort food (bacon sandwiches and stuffed baked potatoes, for example) are served. England has plenty of the big names in fast food, as well as smaller places selling sandwiches, fish-and-chips, burgers, falafels, kebabs, and the like. For a local touch, check out Indian restaurants, which are found almost everywhere. Marks & Spencer, Sainsbury's, Morrison's, Tesco, and Waitrose are chain supermarkets with outlets throughout the country. They're good choices for groceries, premade sandwiches, or picnic fixings.

MEALS AND MEALTIMES

Cafés serving the traditional English breakfast (called a "fry-up") of eggs, bacon, sausage, beans, mushrooms, half a grilled tomato, toast, and strong tea are often the cheapest—and most authentic—places for breakfast. For lighter morning fare (or for real brewed coffee), try the Continental-style sandwich bars and coffee shops—the Pret-a-Manger chain being one of the largest—offering croissants and other pastries.

At lunch you can grab a sandwich between sights, pop into the local pub, or sit down in a restaurant. Dinner, too, has no set rules, but a three-course meal is standard in most midrange or high-end restaurants. Pre- or posttheater menus, offering two or three courses for a set price, are usually a good value.

Note that most traditional pubs don't have any waitstaff and you're expected to go to the bar to order a beverage and your meal. Also, in cities many pubs don't serve food after 3 pm, so they're usually a better lunch option than dinner. In rural areas it's not uncommon for pubs to stop serving dinner after 9 pm.

Breakfast is generally served between 7:30 and 9, lunch between noon and 2, dinner or supper between 7:30 and 9:30, sometimes earlier, seldom later except in large cities. These days high tea is rarely a proper meal anymore (it was once served between 4:30 and 6), and tearooms are often open all day in touristy areas (they're not found at all in nontouristy places). So you can have a cup and pastry or sandwich whenever you feel you need it. Sunday roasts at pubs last from 11 am or noon to 3 pm.

Smoking is banned in pubs, clubs, and restaurants throughout Britain.

PAYING

Credit cards are widely accepted in restaurants and pubs, though some require a minimum charge of around £10. Be sure that you don't double-pay a service charge. Many restaurants exclude service charges from the printed menu (which the law obliges them to display outside), and then add 10% to 15% to the check. Others will stamp "Service not included" along the bottom of the bill, in which case you should add 10% to 15%. Cash is always appreciated, as it's more likely to go to the specific waiter.

PUBS

A common misconception among visitors to England is that pubs are simply bars. Pubs are also community gathering places and even restaurants. In many pubs the social interaction is as important as the alcohol. Pubs are, generally speaking, where people go to meet their friends and catch up on one another's lives. In small towns pubs act almost as town halls. Traditionally pub hours are 11–11, with last orders called about 20 minutes before closing time, but pubs can choose to stay open until midnight or 1 am, or later.

Though to travelers it may appear that there's a pub on almost every corner, in fact pubs are something of an endangered species, closing at a rate of 14 a week (as of 2013), with independent, nonchain pubs at particular risk.

Most pubs tend to be child-friendly, but others have restricted hours for children. If a pub serves food, it'll generally allow children in during the day with adults. Some pubs are stricter than others, though, and won't admit anyone younger than 18. Some will allow children in during the day, but only until 6 pm. Family-friendly pubs tend to be packed with kids, parents, and all of their accoutrements.

RESERVATIONS AND DRESS

Regardless of where you are, it's a good idea to make a reservation if you can. We mention them specifically only when reservations are essential or when they're not accepted. For popular restaurants, book as far ahead as you can (often 30 days), and reconfirm as soon as you arrive. (Large parties should always call ahead to check the reservations policy.) We mention dress only when men are required to wear a jacket or a jacket and tie.

Online reservation services aren't as popular in England as in the United States, but Toptable and Square Meal have a fair number of listings in England.

Contacts Square Meal ☎ *0207/582–0222* ⊕ *www.squaremeal.co.uk.* **Toptable** ☎ *0207/299–2949* ⊕ *www.toptable.co.uk.*

WINES, BEER, AND SPIRITS

Although hundreds of varieties of beer are brewed around the country, the traditional brew is known as bitter and isn't carbonated; it's usually served at room temperature. Fizzy American-style beer is called lager. There are also plenty of other potations: stouts like Guinness and Murphy's are thick, pitch-black brews you'll either love or hate; ciders, made from apples, are alcoholic in Britain (Bulmer's and Strongbow are the big names, but look out for local micro-brews); shandies are a low-alcohol mix of lager and lemon soda. Real ales, which have a natural second fermentation in the cask, have a shorter shelf life (so many are brewed locally) but special flavor; these are worth seeking out. Generally the selection and quality of cocktails is higher in a wine bar or café than in a pub. The legal drinking age is 18.

▌ ECOTOURISM

Ecotourism is an emerging trend in the United Kingdom. The Shetland Environmental Agency Ltd. runs the Green Tourism Business Scheme, a program that evaluates lodgings in England, Scotland, and Wales and gives them gold, silver, or bronze ratings. You can find a list of green hotels, B&Bs, and apartments on the GTBS website. Also check out the VisitBritain website, which has information and tips about green travel in Britain.

Contacts Green Tourism Business Scheme ☎ *01738/632162* ⊕ *www.green-business.co.uk.*

▌ ELECTRICITY

The electrical current in Great Britain is 220–240 volts (in line with the rest of Europe), 50 cycles alternating current (AC); wall outlets take three-pin plugs, and shaver sockets take two round, oversize prongs. British bathrooms aren't permitted to have 220–240 volt outlets in them. Consider making a small investment in a universal adapter, which has several types of plugs in one lightweight, compact unit. Most laptops and mobile phone chargers are dual voltage (i.e., they operate equally well on 110 and 220 volts), so require only an adapter. These days the same is true of small appliances such as hair dryers. Always check labels and manufacturer instructions. Don't use 110-volt outlets marked "For shavers only" for high-wattage appliances such as hair dryers.

Contacts Walkabout Travel Gear
☏ 800/852–7085
⊕ www.walkabouttravelgear.com.

▌ EMERGENCIES

If you need to report an emergency, dial 999 for police, fire, or ambulance. Be prepared to give the telephone number you're calling from. 101 is the number for nonurgent police calls, such as reporting a stolen car. You can get 24-hour treatment in Accident and Emergency at British hospitals, although you may have to wait hours for treatment. Prescriptions are valid only if made out by doctors registered in the United Kingdom.

Although England has a subsidized National Health Service, free at the point of service for British residents, foreign visitors are expected to pay for any treatment they receive. Expect to receive a bill after you return home. Check with your health-insurance company to make sure you're covered. Some British hospitals now require a credit card or other payment before they'll offer treatment.

U.S. Embassies American Embassy
✉ 24 Grosvenor Sq., London ☏ 0207/499–9000 ⊕ london.usembassy.gov. **U.S. Passport Unit** ✉ 55/56 Upper Brook St., London ☏ 0207/499–9000.

▌ HEALTH

SPECIFIC ISSUES IN ENGLAND
If you take prescription drugs, keep a supply in your carry-on luggage and make a list of all your prescriptions to keep on file at home while you're abroad. You won't be able to renew a U.S. prescription at a pharmacy in Britain. Prescriptions are accepted only if issued by a U.K.-registered physician.

OVER-THE-COUNTER REMEDIES
Over-the-counter medications in England are similar to those in the United States, with a few significant differences. Medications are sold in boxes rather than bottles, and are sold in small amounts—usually no more than 24 pills. There may also be fewer brands. All headache medicine is usually filed under "painkillers." You can buy generic ibuprofen or a popular European brand of ibuprofen, Nurofen. Tylenol isn't sold in the United Kingdom, although its main ingredient, acetaminophen, is found in brands like Panadol.

Among sinus and allergy medicines, Clarityn is the main option here; it's spelled slightly differently but is the same brand sold in the United States. Some medicines are pretty much the same as brands sold in the United States—instead of Nyquil cold medicine, there's Sudafed or Lemsip. The most popular over-the-counter cough medicine is Benylin.

Drugstores are generally called pharmacies, but sometimes referred to as chemists' shops. The biggest drugstore chain in the country is Boots, which has outlets everywhere, except for the smallest towns. If you're in a rural area, look for shops marked with a sign of a green cross.

If you can't find what you want, ask at the counter; many over-the-counter medicines are kept behind the register.

SHOTS AND MEDICATIONS
No special shots are required or suggested for England.

Health Warnings National Centers for Disease Control & Prevention (CDC).
☏ 800/232–4636 travelers' health line ⊕ wwwnc.cdc.gov/travel. **World Health Organization** (WHO). ⊕ www.who.int.

▌ HOURS OF OPERATION

Most banks are open weekdays from 9:30 until 3:30 or 4:30. Some have Thursday evening hours, and a few are open Saturday morning. Normal office hours for most businesses are weekdays 9 to 5.

The major national museums and galleries are open daily 9–6, including lunchtime, but have shorter hours on Sunday. Regional museums are usually closed Monday and have shorter hours in winter. In London many museums are open late one evening a week.

Independently owned pharmacies are generally open Monday through Saturday 9:30–5:30, although in larger cities some stay open until 10 pm; local newspapers list which pharmacies are open late.

Usual retail business hours are Monday through Saturday 9–5:30 or 10–6:30, Sunday noon–4. In some small villages shops may close at 1 pm once a week, often Wednesday or Thursday. They may also close for lunch and not open on Sunday at all. In large cities—especially London—department stores stay open late (usually until 7:30 or 8) one night a week, usually Thursday. On national holidays most stores are closed, and over the Christmas holidays most restaurants are closed as well.

HOLIDAYS

Holidays are January 1, New Year's Day; Good Friday and Easter Monday; May Day (first Monday in May); spring and summer bank holidays (last Monday in May and August, respectively); December 25, Christmas Day; and December 26, Boxing Day (day after Christmas). If these holidays fall on a weekend, the holiday is observed on the following Monday. During the Christmas holidays many restaurants, as well as museums and other attractions, may close for at least a week—call to verify hours. Book hotels for Christmas travel well in advance, and check whether the hotel restaurant will be open.

▌ MAIL

Stamps can be bought from post offices (hours vary according to branch, but usual opening hours are weekdays 9–5:30, Saturday 9–noon), from stamp machines outside post offices, and from newsagents. Some post offices are located within supermarkets or general stores. Specialized shipping shops like Mail Boxes Etc. also sell stamps. Mailboxes, known as post or letter boxes, are painted bright red. Allow 7 days for a letter to reach the United States and about 10 days to two weeks to Australia or New Zealand. The useful Royal Mail website has information on everything from buying stamps to finding a post office.

Airmail letters up to 10 grams (0.35 ounce) to North America cost 88p. Letters within Britain weighing up to 100 grams (3.5 ounces) are 60p for first class, 50p for second class. Rates for envelopes larger than 353 mm (13.9 inches) long, 250 mm (9.84 inches) wide, and 25 mm (1 inch) deep are higher.

Contact Royal Mail ☎ *0845/577–4040* ⊕ *www.royalmail.com.*

SHIPPING PACKAGES

Most department stores and retail outlets can ship your goods home. You should check your insurance for coverage of possible damage. Private delivery companies such as Federal Express and DHL offer two-day delivery service to the United States, but you'll pay a considerable amount for the privilege.

Express Services DHL ☎ *0800/316–0498* ⊕ *www.dhl.co.uk.* **Federal Express** ☎ *0845/607–0809* ⊕ *www.fedex.com.* **Mail Boxes Etc.** ☎ *0800/623123* ⊕ *www.mbe.co.uk.* **Parcelforce** ☎ *0844/800–4466* ⊕ *www.parcelforce.com.* **UPS** ☎ *0845/787–7877* ⊕ *www.ups.com.*

▌ MONEY

Prices in England can seem high because of the exchange rate. London remains one of the most expensive cities in the world. But for every yin there's a yang, and travelers can get breaks: staying in bed-and-breakfasts, or renting a city apartment brings down lodging costs, and national museums are free. *The chart below gives some ideas of the prices you can expect to pay for day-to-day life.*

ITEM	AVERAGE COST
Cup of Coffee	£1.50–£3
Glass of Wine	£3.50 in a pub or wine bar, £5.50 or more in a restaurant
Glass of Beer	£2.70 or more
Sandwich	£3.50
One-Mile Taxi Ride in London	£5.50–£8.60
Museum Admission	National museums free; others £5–£10

Prices throughout this guide are given for adults. Substantially reduced fees—generally referred to as "concessions" throughout Great Britain—are almost always available for children, students, and senior citizens.

▌TIP→ Banks have limited amounts of foreign currencies on hand, and it may take as long as a week to order. If you're planning to exchange funds before leaving home, don't wait until the last minute.

ATMS AND BANKS

Make sure before leaving home that your credit and debit cards have been programmed for ATM use abroad—ATMs in England and Wales accept PINs of four or fewer digits only. If you know your PIN as a word, learn the numerical equivalent, since most keypads in England show numbers only, not letters. Most ATMs are on both the Cirrus and Plus networks. ATMs are available at most main-street banks, large supermarkets such as Sainsbury's and Tesco,

some Tube stops in London, and many rail stations. Major banks include Barclays, HSBC, and NatWest.

Your own bank will probably charge a fee for using ATMs abroad (unless you use your bank's British partner); the foreign bank you use may also charge a fee. Nevertheless, you'll usually get a better rate of exchange at an ATM than you will at a currency-exchange office or even when changing money in a bank. And extracting funds as you need them is a safer option than carrying around a large amount of cash.

CREDIT CARDS

The Discover card isn't accepted throughout Britain. Other major credit cards, except Diners Club and American Express, are accepted virtually everywhere in Britain; however, you're expected to know and use your pin number for all transactions—even for credit cards, so it's a good idea to do some quick memorization for whichever card you intend to use in England.

Keep in mind that most European credit cards store information in microchips, rather than magnetic strips. Although some banks in the United States, such as Chase and Wells Fargo, are starting to adapt this system, you may find some places in England that can't process your credit card. It's a good idea to carry enough cash to cover small purchases.

Inform your credit-card company before you travel, especially if you're going abroad and don't travel internationally very often. Otherwise, the credit-card company might put a hold on your card owing to unusual activity. Record all your credit-card numbers in a safe place. Both MasterCard and Visa have general numbers you can call (collect if you're abroad) if your card is lost, but you're better off calling the number of your issuing bank, since MasterCard and Visa usually just transfer you to your bank; your bank's number is usually printed on your card.

If you plan to use your credit card for cash advances, you'll need to apply for a PIN at least two weeks before your trip.

Although it's usually cheaper (and safer) to use a credit card abroad for large purchases (so you can cancel payments or be reimbursed if there's a problem), note that some credit-card companies *and* the banks that issue them add substantial percentages to all foreign transactions, whether they're in a foreign currency or not. Check on these fees before traveling.

Reporting Lost Cards American Express
☏ *336/393–1111 collect from abroad*
⊕ *www.americanexpress.com.* **Diners Club**
☏ *514/881–3735 collect from abroad* ⊕ *www.dinersclubus.com.* **MasterCard** ☏ *636/722–7111 collect from abroad* ⊕ *www.mastercard.com.* **Visa** ☏ *800/847–2911 collect from abroad* ⊕ *usa.visa.com.*

CURRENCY AND EXCHANGE

The unit of currency in Great Britain is the pound sterling (£), divided into 100 pence (p). The bills (called notes in Britain) are 50, 20, 10, and 5 pounds. Coins are £2, £1, 50p, 20p, 10p, 5p, 2p, and 1p. If you're traveling beyond England and Wales, note that Scotland and the Channel Islands have their own bills, and the Channel Islands their own coins, too. Scottish bills are accepted (often reluctantly) in the rest of Britain, but you can't use Channel Islands currency outside the islands.

At the time of this writing, the exchange rate was about U.S. $1.52 to £1.

British post offices exchange currency with no fee, and at decent rates.

▮▮▮TIP➜ Even if a currency-exchange booth has a sign promising no commission, rest assured that there's some kind of huge, hidden fee. And as for rates, you're almost always better off getting foreign currency at an ATM or exchanging money at a bank.

Currency Conversion
Google ⊕ *www.google.com.* **Oanda.com** ⊕ *www.oanda.com.* **XE.com** ⊕ *www.xe.com.*

▮ PACKING

England can be cool, damp, and overcast, even in summer. You'll want a heavy coat for winter and a lightweight coat or warm jacket for summer. There's no time of year when a raincoat or umbrella won't come in handy. For the cities, pack as you would for an American city: coats and ties for expensive restaurants and nightspots, casual clothes elsewhere. If you plan to stay in budget hotels, take your own soap. It's also a good idea to take a washcloth. Pack insect repellent if you plan to hike.

▮ PASSPORTS

U.S. citizens need only a valid passport to enter Great Britain for stays of up to six months. Travelers should be prepared to show sufficient funds to support and accommodate themselves while in Britain (credit cards will usually suffice for this) and to show a return or onward ticket. If you're within six months of your passport's expiration date, renew it before you leave—nearly expired passports aren't strictly banned, but they make immigration officials anxious, and may cause you problems. Health certificates aren't required.

▮ RESTROOMS

Public restrooms are sparse in England, although most big cities maintain public facilities that are clean and modern. Train stations and department stores have public restrooms that occasionally charge a small fee, usually 30p. Most pubs, restaurants, and even fast-food chains reserve their bathrooms for customers. Hotels and museums are usually a good place to find clean, free facilities. On the road, gas-station facilities are usually clean and free.

Find a Loo The Bathroom Diaries
⊕ *www.thebathroomdiaries.com.*

■ SAFETY

England has a low incidence of violent crime. However, petty crime, mostly in urban areas, is on the rise, and tourists can be the targets. Use common sense: when in a city center, if you're paying at a shop or a restaurant, never put your wallet down or let your bag out of your hand. When sitting on a chair in a public place, keep your purse on your lap or between your feet. Don't wear expensive jewelry or watches, and don't flash fancy smart phones outside Tube stations, where there have been some thefts. Store your passport in the hotel safe, and keep a copy with you. Don't leave anything in your car.

Although scams do occur in Britain, they aren't pervasive. If you're getting money out of an ATM, beware of someone bumping into you to distract you. You may want to use ATMs inside banks rather than those outside them. In London scams are most common at ATMs on Oxford Street and around Piccadilly Circus. Watch out for pickpockets, particularly in London. They often work in pairs, one distracting you in some way.

Always take a licensed black taxi or call a car service (sometimes called minicabs) recommended by your hotel. Avoid drivers who approach you on the street, as in most cases they'll overcharge you. Always buy theater tickets from a reputable dealer. If you're driving in from a British port, beware of thieves posing as customs officials who try to "confiscate illegal goods."

While traveling, don't leave any bags unattended, as they may be viewed as a security risk and destroyed by the authorities. If you see an unattended bag on the train, bus, or Tube, find a worker and report it. Never hesitate to get off a Tube, train, or bus if you feel unsafe.

■ TIP➜ Distribute your cash, credit cards, IDs, and other valuables between a deep front pocket, an inside jacket or vest pocket, and a hidden money pouch. Don't reach for the money pouch once you're in public.

General Information and Warnings
Transportation Security Administration (*TSA*). ☎ 866/289-9673 ⊕ *www.tsa. gov.* **U.K. Foreign & Commonwealth Office** ☎ 0207/008-1500 ⊕ *www.gov.uk/foreign-travel-advice.* **U.S. Department of State** ⊕ *www.travel.state.gov.*

■ SIGHTSEEING PASSES

DISCOUNT PASSES

If you plan to visit castles, gardens, and historic houses during your stay in England and Wales, look into discount passes or memberships that offer significant savings. Just be sure to match what the pass or membership offers against your itinerary to see if it's worthwhile.

The National Trust, English Heritage, and the Historic Houses Association each encompass hundreds of properties. English Heritage's Overseas Visitors Pass costs £24 for a 9-day pass and £28 for a 16-day pass for one adult. You can order it in advance by phone or online, or purchase it at a participating property in England. The National Trust Touring Pass, for overseas visitors, must be purchased in advance, either by phone or online. A 7-day pass is £24; a 14-day pass is £29.

The London Pass gets you into more than 60 attractions and tours in the capital, and can help you bypass some queues. Packages range from one day (£47) to six days (£102). Annual membership in the National Trust (through the Royal Oak Foundation, the U.S. affiliate) is $65 a year. English Heritage membership is £48, and the Historic Houses Association is £43.50. Memberships entitle you to free entry to properties.

For passes specifically for Wales, see Chapter 14.

Information **English Heritage** ☎ *0870/333–1181* ⊕ *www.english-heritage.org.uk.* **Historic Houses Association** ☎ *0207/259–5688* ⊕ *www.hha.org.uk.* **London Pass** ☎ *0870/242–9988 in U.K., 01664/485020 from U.S.* ⊕ *www.londonpass.com.* **National Trust** ☎ *0844/800–1895* ⊕ *www.nationaltrust.org.uk.* **Royal Oak Foundation** ☎ *212/480–2889, 800/913–6565* ⊕ *www.royal-oak.org.*

❚ SPORTS AND THE OUTDOORS

VisitBritain and local Tourist Information Centres can recommend places to enjoy your favorite sport.

BIKING

The national body promoting cycle touring is the Cyclists' Touring Club (£39 a year). Members get free advice and route information and a magazine. Transport for London publishes maps of recommended routes across the capital and British Cycling has online route maps of the United Kingdom. The CTC organizes cycling vacations.

Contacts **British Cycling** ☎ *0161/274–2000* ⊕ *www.britishcycling.org.uk.* **Cyclists' Touring Club** ☎ *0844/736–8450* ⊕ *www.ctc.org.uk.*

BOATING

Boating—whether on bucolic rivers or industrial canals—can be a leisurely way to explore the English landscape. For boat-rental operators along Britain's several hundred miles of historic canals and waterways, from the Norfolk Broads to the Lake District, contact the Association of Pleasure Craft Operators or Waterway Holidays. The Canal and River Trust has maps and other information. Waterway Holidays arranges boat accommodations from traditional narrow boats to wide-beam canal boats, motorboats, and sailboats.

Contacts **Association of Pleasure Craft Operators** ☎ *01784/223603* ⊕ *www.apco.org.uk.* **Canal and River Trust** ☎ *0303/040–4040* ⊕ *www.canalrivertrust.org.uk.* **Waterways Holidays** ☎ *0845/127–1020 in U.K.* ⊕ *www.waterwaysholidays.com.*

GOLF

Invented in Scotland, golf is a beloved pastime all over England. Some courses take advantage of spectacular natural settings, from the ocean to mountain backdrops. Most courses are reserved for club members and adhere to strict rules of protocol and dress. However, many famous courses can be used by visiting golfers reserving well in advance. In addition, numerous public courses are open to anyone, though advance reservations are advised. Package tours with companies such as Golf International and Owenoak International Golf Travel allow you into exclusive clubs. For further information on courses, fees, and locations, try the website English Golf Courses.

Contacts **English Golf Courses** ☎ *0141/353–2222* ⊕ *www.englishgolf-courses.co.uk.* **Golf International** ☎ *212/986–9176, 800/833–1389* ⊕ *www.golfinternational.com.* **Owenoak International Golf Travel** ☎ *203/854–9000, 800/426–4498* ⊕ *www.owenoak.com.*

WALKING

Walking and hiking, from the slowest ramble to a challenging mountainside climb, are enormously popular in England. National Trails, funded by Natural England and the Countryside Counsel for Wales, has great resources online. The Ramblers, a well-known charitable organization promoting walking and care of footpaths, has helpful information, including a list of B&Bs close to selected long-distance footpaths. Some of the best maps for walking are the Explorer Maps, published by the Ordnance Survey; check out ⊕ *www.ordnancesurvey.co.uk.*

Contacts **National Trails** ⊕ *www.nationaltrail.co.uk.* **The Ramblers** ☎ *0207/339–8500* ⊕ *www.ramblers.org.uk.*

▌ TAXES

Air Passenger Duty (APD) is a tax included in the price of your ticket. The U.K.'s APD fees, currently the highest in the world, are divided into four bands: short-haul destinations under 2,000 miles, £13 per person in economy, £26 and £52 in all first and business class; medium-haul destinations under 4,000 miles (including the United States), £67 economy, £134 and £268 first and business class; long-haul destinations under 6,000 miles, £83 economy, £166 and £332 first and business class; ultra-long-haul destinations over 6,000 miles, £94 economy, £188 and £376 first and business class.

The British sales tax (Value Added Tax, or V.A.T.) is 20%. The tax is almost always included in quoted prices in shops, hotels, and restaurants. The most common exception is at high-end hotels, where prices often exclude V.A.T. Outside of hotels and rental-car agencies, which have specific additional taxes, there's no other sales tax in England.

Refunds apply for V.A.T. only on goods being taken out of Britain. Many large stores provide a V.A.T.–refund service, but only if you request it. You must ask the store to complete Form V.A.T. 407, to be given to customs at departure along with a V.A.T. Tax Free Shopping scheme invoice. Fill in the form at the shop, have the salesperson sign it, have it stamped by customs when you leave the country, then mail the stamped form to the shop or to a commercial refund company. Alternatively, you may be able to take the form to an airport refund-service counter after you're through passport control for an on-the-spot refund. There is an extra fee for this service, and lines tend to be long.

Global Blue is a Europe-wide service with 270,000 affiliated stores. It has refund counters in the U.K. at Heathrow and Gatwick, as well as on Oxford Street and in the Westfield Shopping Centre. Its

refund form, called a Tax Free Check, is the most common across the European continent. The service issues refunds in the form of cash, check, or credit-card adjustment. The latter is useful for small purchases as the cost of cashing a foreign-currency check may exceed the amount of the refund.

V.A.T. Refunds Global Blue ☎ 866/706–6069 ⊕ www.globalblue.com. **HM Revenue and Customs** ☎ 0845/010–9000 ⊕ www.hmrc.gov. uk/customs.

▌ TIME

England sets its clocks by Greenwich Mean Time, five hours ahead of the U.S. East Coast. British summer time (GMT plus one hour) generally coincides with American daylight saving time adjustments.

Time Zones Timeanddate.com ⊕ www.timeanddate.com.

▌ TIPPING

Tipping is done in Britain just as in the United States, but at a lower level than you would back home, generally 12.5% to 15%. Tipping more can look like you're showing off. Don't tip bar staff in pubs—although you can always offer to buy them a drink. There's no need to tip at clubs (it's acceptable at posher establishments, though) unless you're being served at your table. Rounding up to the nearest pound or 50p is appreciated.

TIPPING GUIDELINES FOR ENGLAND

Bartender	£1–£2 per round of drinks, depending on the number of drinks, except in pubs, where tipping isn't the custom
Bellhop	£1 per bag, depending on the level of the hotel
Hotel Concierge	£5 or more, if he or she performs a service for you
Hotel Doorman	£1 if he helps you get a cab
Hotel Maid/ Housekeeping	£1 or £2 per day
Hotel Room-Service Waiter	Same as a waiter, unless a service charge has been added to the bill
Porter at Airport or Train Station	£1 per bag
Skycap at Airport	£1 per bag checked
Taxi Driver	10p per pound of the fare, then round up to nearest pound
Tour Guide	Tipping optional: £1 or £2 is generous
Waiter	12.5%–15%, with 15% being the norm at high-end London restaurants; nothing additional if a service charge is added to the bill, unless you want to reward particularly good service. Tips in cash preferred
Other	Restroom attendants in more expensive restaurants expect some small change or £1. Tip coat-check personnel £1 unless there's a fee, then nothing. Hairdressers and barbers get 10%–15%

▌TOURS

Visiting London on a fully escorted tour is unnecessary because of its extensive public transport and wide network of taxicabs. Many tour companies offer day tours to the main sights, and getting around is fairly easy.

If you're traveling beyond London, packaged tours can be very useful, particularly if you don't want to rent a car. Because many sights are off the beaten track and not accessible by public transportation—particularly castles, great houses, and small villages—tour groups make the country accessible to all. There are a few downsides to escorted tours: rooms in castles and medieval houses tend to be small and can feel overrun when tour groups roll in. And as on a cruise, your traveling companions are inescapable.

Dozens of companies offer fully guided tours in Britain. Most of these are full packages including lodging, food, and transportation costs in one flat fee. Do a bit of research before booking. You'll want to know about the hotels you'll be staying in, how big your group is likely to be, how your days will be structured, and who the other people are likely to be.

SPECIAL-INTEREST TOURS

CULINARY

Britain's foodie culture is increasingly rich and thriving. Gourmet on Tour, a U.S.–based tour company, offers vacations dominated by cooking, eating, and fine wine.

Contact Gourmet on Tour ☎ *646/461–6088 in U.S., 0207/558–8796 in U.K.* ⊕ *www.gourmetontour.com.*

GARDENS

England is a land of garden lovers, and its gardens are varied and impressive. Adderley and Flora are British companies; the American tour companies Coopersmiths and Lynott Tours also offer tours of gardens around Britain. The website ⊕ *www.gardenvisit.com* is a useful reference site.

Contacts Adderley Travel Ltd. ☎ *01953/606706* ⊕ *www.adderleytravel.com.* **Coopersmiths** ☎ *415/669–1914 in U.S.* ⊕ *www.coopersmiths.com.* **Flora Garden Tours** ☎ *01366/328946* ⊕ *www.flora-garden-tours.co.uk.* **Lynott Tours** ☎ *800/221–2474* ⊕ *www.lynotttours.com.*

HIKING AND WALKING

For those who prefer to spend their vacations on the move, Adventure Sports Holidays will have you surfing, kayaking, paragliding, or just walking. Country Walkers and England Lakeland Ramblers, based in the United States, or the U.K.'s Adventureline, have guided walks in Britain. The Wayfarers offer specialized walking tours, such as treks through Brontë Country.

Contacts **Adventureline** 🖀 *01209/820847* ⊕ *www.adventureline.co.uk*. **Adventure Sports Holidays** 🖀 *01273/358092* ⊕ *www. adventuresportsholidays.com*. **Country Walkers** 🖀 *800/464–9255 in U.S.* ⊕ *www.cwadventures.com*. **English Lakeland Ramblers** 🖀 *800/724–8802 in U.S.* ⊕ *www.ramblers.com*. **The Wayfarers** 🖀 *01242/620871* ⊕ *www.thewayfarers.com*.

HISTORY

England is rich in history and culture, to the point where it's developed what's known as the "heritage industry." Inscape offers tours of four days or less, oriented toward fine art and architecture led by knowledgeable academics. Classic England specializes in private tours to castles, cathedrals, and areas of historic interest.

Contacts **Classic England** 🖀 *01277/841651 in U.K.,* *866/464–7389 in U.S.* ⊕ *www.classic-england.com*. **Inscape Fine Art Study Tours** 🖀 *0208/566-7539* ⊕ *inscapestudytours. wordpress.com*.

▌ VISITOR INFORMATION

ONLINE TRAVEL TOOLS

ALL ABOUT ENGLAND

VisitEngland (⊕ *www.visitengland.com*) is a useful resource. All of England's regions, along with most major towns and cities, have their own dedicated tourism websites providing information. VisitBritain (⊕ *www.visitbritain.com*), the official visitor website, focuses on information most helpful to England-bound U.S. travelers, from practical information to money-saving deals; you can even find out about movie locations. The London visitor website (⊕ *www. visitlondon.com*) can help you book your accommodations.

GARDENS

The National Gardens Scheme opens exceptional gardens attached to private houses and private garden squares to the public on selected weekends.

Contact **National Gardens Scheme** 🖀 *01483/211535* ⊕ *www.ngs.org.uk*.

HISTORIC SITES

The British monarchy has an official website with information about visiting royal homes and more. English Heritage, the National Trust, and VisitBritain all offer discount passes.

Contacts **British Monarchy** 🖀 *0207/930–4832* ⊕ *www.royal.gov.uk*. **English Heritage** 🖀 *0870/333–1181* ⊕ *www.english-heritage. org.uk*. **National Trust** 🖀 *0844/800–1895* ⊕ *www.nationaltrust.org.uk*.

MUSEUMS AND THE ARTS

The London Theatre Guide, created by the Society of London Theatre, presents what's on and sells tickets. Their half-price ticket booths, tkts, located in London's Leicester Square and Brent Cross Shopping Centre, offer same-day bargains. Culture 24 is a nonprofit site with information about publicly funded museums, art galleries, and historic sights. Tokenline sells gift vouchers for theater tickets.

Contacts **Culture 24** 🖀 *01273/623266* ⊕ *www.culture24.org.uk*. **London Theatre Guide** 🖀 *0207/527–6700* ⊕ *www. officiallondontheatre.co.uk*. **tkts** 🖀 *0207/527–6700* ⊕ *www.tkts.co.uk*. **Tokenline** 🖀 *0844/887-7878* ⊕ *www.theatretokens.com*.

VISITOR INFORMATION OFFICES

In some towns there are local and regional tourist information centers; many have websites. Offices offer services from discounts for local attractions to visitor guides, maps, parking information, and accommodation advice.

In the U.S. **VisitBritain** ⊕ *www.visitbritain.com*.

INDEX

PHOTO CREDITS

Front cover: Brian Lawrence/Photographer's Choice/Getty Images [Description: Kings College, Cambridge]. 1, Adam Woolfi tt / age fotostock. 2, Joe Cornish/Britain on View/photolibrary.com 5, Stowe Park, Buckinghamshire by Martin Pettitt http://www.flickr.com/photos/mdpettitt/4663854507/ Attribution License. Chapter 1: Experience England: 10-11, Heeb Christian/age fotostock. 12, David Peta/Shutterstock. 13 (left), London 2012. 13 (right), Morland Abingdon by Jim Champion http://www.flickr.com/photos/treehouse1977/4524995971/ Attribution-ShareAlike License. 14, Monkey Business Images/Shutterstock. 15 (left), ChrisAngove/Wikimedia Commons. 15 (right), redlentil/Wikimedia Commons. 16, Gail Johnson/Shutterstock. 17 (left), Gail Johnson/Shutterstock. 17 (right), Stewart Smith Photography/Shutterstock. 20 (left), StraH/Shutterstock. 20 (top center), (c) Davidmartyn | Dreamstime.com. 20 (bottom center), Matthew Jacques/Shutterstock. 20 (bottom right), Pecold/Shutterstock. 20 (top right), (c) Khrizmo | Dreamstime.com. 21 (left), Bill Gats/Wikimedia Commons. 21 (top center), Adrian Zenz/Shutterstock. 21 (bottom center), Ian Woolcock/Shutterstock. 21 (top right), David Hughes/Shutterstock. 21 (bottom right), Kevin Eaves/Shutterstock. 22, [champions] Chelsea x Juventus : 3 by Crystian Cruz http://www.flickr.com/photos/crystiancruz/3310826822/ Attribution-ShareAlike License. 23, Nikki Bidgood/Hemera/Thinkstock. 24, David Hughes/Shutterstock. 25 (left), Dahlia Flower by William Warby http://www.flickr.com/photos/wwarby/4085740597/ Attribution License. 25 (right), Albert Dock by thinboyfatter http://www.flickr.com/photos/1234abcd/227827242/ Attribution License. 26, Firmdale Hotels. 27 (left), Ashdown Park by Caitlin http://www.flickr.com/photos/lizard_queen/110491647/ Attribution License. 27 (right), Kevin Eaves/Shutterstock. 28, IMG_4286 by Leon Brocard http://www.flickr.com/photos/acme/3111148216/ Attribution License. 29 (left), O'Shea Fillet by Simon Doggett http://www.flickr.com/photos/simondee/4886407274/ Attribution License. 29 (right), Elzbieta Sekowska/Shutterstock. 30, Hampton Court Palace by Roberto Arias http://www.flickr.com/photos/roberto8080/4844875392/Attribution License. 32, David Woods/Shutterstock. 33 (left), JCElv/Shutterstock. 33 (right), Debu55y/ Shutterstock. 34, Herbert Ortner/Wikimedia Commons. 36, Peekaboopink/Wikimedia Commons. Chapter 2: London: 37, Doug Pearson/age fotostock. 38 (top), Angelina Dimitrova/Shutterstock. 38 (bottom), jan kranendonk/Shutterstock. 39, Christopher Steer/iStockphoto. 40, Tan, Kim Pin/Shutterstock. 47, ktylerconk/Flickr. 54, Britain on View/photolibrary.com. 58, Jon Arnold/age fotostock. 61, Jarno Gonzalez Zarraonandia/Shutterstock. 67, iStockphoto. 69 (left), Walter Bibikow/viestiphoto.com. 69 (right), Tom Hanley / Alamy. 70, News Team International Ltd. 71, Peter Phipp/age fotostock. 72 (left), Mary Evans Picture Library /Alamy. 72 (center), Refl ex Picture Library / Alamy. 72 (right), Classic Image / Alamy. 73, Jan Kranendonk/iStockphoto. 85, Londonstills.com / Alamy. 92, Danilo Donadoni/Marka/age fotostock. 104, jason lowe ltd. 116, Harwood Arms. 129, (top left), Barbara Kraft. 129 (top right), Damian Russell. 129 (bottom left), The Dorchester. 129, (botom right), Simon Brown. 132 (top) Claridge's Hotel. 132 (bottom) The Stafford. 134 (top left), Mandarin Oriental. 134 (top right), Church Street Hotel. 134 (center left), The Hoxton. 134 (center right), Firmdale Hotels. 134 (bottom left), VIEW Pictures Ltd / Alamy. 134 (bottom right), RayMain.co.uk. 145, Gianni Muratore / Alamy. 152, Bettina Strenske/age fotostock. 160, Britain on View/photolibrary.com. 167, Jess Moss. Chapter 3: The Southeast: 173, Britain on View/photolibrary.com. 174, Dover White Cliffs_2010 08 14_0077 by Harvey Barrison http://www.flickr.com/photos/hbarrison/4930390553/ Attribution-ShareAlike License. 175 (top), Jake Keup/Wikimedia Commons. 175 (bottom), Sissinghurst Castle, Kent by Allan Harris http://www.flickr.com/photos/50638285@N00/3777894502/ Attribution-ShareAlike License. 176, High Tea by Adam Burt http://www.flickr.com/photos/aburt/3013235854/ Attribution-ShareAlike License. 177 (top), shtukicrew/Shutterstock. 177 (bottom), England 2010 - 014.jpg by David Ooms http://www.flickr.com/photos/davidooms/4507226751/Attribution License. 178, Alan Smithers/iStockphoto. 185, Hans Musil/Wikimedia Commons. 190, David Sellman/Britain on View/photolibrary.com. 202, Dave Porter/Britain on View/photolibrary.com. 206, Britain on View/photolibrary.com. 218, Dave Porter/Britain on View/photolibrary.com. 226, SuzanneKn/Wikimedia Commons. 227 (top), C Zaduck/Wikimedia Commons. 227 (bottom), Charlesdrakew/Wikimedia Commons. 228, 6mat1/Wikimedia Commons. 229, Hever Castle - 23/08/09 by Chris Parfi tt http://www.flickr.com/photos/chr1sp/3862791040/ Attribution License. 231, David Strydom/iStockphoto/Thinkstock. Chapter 4: The South: 235, Guy Edwardes/Britain on View/photolibrary.com. 236, Joe Gough/Shutterstock. 237 (top), Portsmouth City Council. 237 (bottom), Sweet/Shutterstock. 238, jurassic by Kevin Walsh http://www.flickr.com/photos/86624586@N00/10186815/ Attribution License. 239 (top), csp/Shutterstock. 239 (bottom), David Hughes/Shutterstock. 240, Britain on View/photolibrary.com. 246, Britain on View/photolibrary.com. 251, Derek Croucher/Britain on View/photolibrary.com. 256, Rod Edwards/Britain on View/photolibrary.com. 266, Graham Taylor/Shutterstock. 268, H & D Zielske / age fotostock. 271, Salisbury International Arts Festival. 274, David Nunuk / age fotostock. 275, DEA PUBBLI AER FOTO / age fotostock. 277 (left),

Stonehenge Heel Stone by Auz http://www.flickr.com/photos/auz/1399022598/ Attribution-ShareAlike License. 277 (right), Triple trilithon by tpholland http://www.flickr.com/photos/tphol-land/5127066452/ Attribution License. 278, Martin Beddall / Alamy. 279, Blueskyimages Ltd/Britain On View/photolibrary.com. 280, Martin Brent/Britain On View/photolibrary.com. 284-85, Piers Cavendish/ age fotostock. 293, Guy Edwardes/Britain on View/photolibrary.com. 300, Adam Burton/Britain on View/photolibrary.com. Chapter 5: The West Country: 303, Lee Pengelly/Silverscene Photography/Britain on View/photolibrary.com. 304 (top), St. Michael's Mount by Kay-Uwe G.tz http://www.flickr.com/photos/kayugee/3932779091/ Attribution-ShareAlike License. 304 (bottom), Portsmouth City Council. 305 (top), Tim Lewy/Wikimedia Commons. 305 (bottom), Lanhydrock by Caro11ne. http://www.flickr.com/photos/caro11ne/2647977554/ Attribution-ShareAlike License. 306, Ant Clausen/Shutterstock. 307 (top), Logan's Rock by Steve Parker http://www.flickr.com/photos/sparker/3661505821/ Attribution License. 307 (bottom), St Ives by Mark A Coleman http://www.flickr.com/photos/48509939@N07/5789336129/ Attribution-ShareAlike License. 308, Kevin O'Hara / age fotostock. 309 (top), Hicki/Shutterstock. 309 (bottom), Rachelle Burnside/Shutterstock. 310, Ben Foster. 318, Cornish Cream Tea by a.froese http://www.flickr.com/photos/anfroese/4948281599/ Attribution-ShareAlike License. 321, Guy Edwardes/Britain on View/photolibrary.com. 324, Craig Joiner / age fotostock. 326, Toby Adamson / age fotostock. 330, DAVID JEROME BALL / age fotostock. 334, Hicki/Shutterstock. 336, Martin Brent/Britain on View/photolibrary.com. 343, Markus Keller / age fotostock. 353, WJournalist/Wikimedia Commons. 357, Britain on View/photolibrary.com. 361, National Trust Photo Library/Britain on View/photolibrary.com. Chapter 6: The Thames Valley: 375, Adam Woolfi tt 7/ age fotostock. 376, Blenheim Palace - Water gardens by Andrew Rivett http://www.flickr.com/photos/veggiefrog/2125370180/Attribution License. 377 (top), Windsor Castle by Cody http://www.flickr.com/photos/codyr/660169937/Attribution License. 377 (bottom), Radcliffe Camera by Skoll World Forum http://www.flickr.com/photos/44608864@N08/5577902316/ Attribution License. 378, Jevgenija Pigozne / age fotostock. 379 (top), Suspension Bridge by Carlton Browne. http://www.flickr.com/photos/carltonbrowne/2581827928/ Attribution License. 379 (bottom), Boats, Henley-on-Thames by Dan Taylor http://www.flickr.com/photos/dantaylor/101689906/ Attribution License. 380, White Horse of Uffi ngton by Jun http://www.flickr.com/photos/biker_jun/4589269528/ Attribution ShareAlike License. 388, Travel Pix Collection / age fotostock. 391, Neil Tingle / age fotostock. 395, Howard Sayer/Britain on View/photolibrary.com. 407 (top), Michael Kemp / Alamy. 407 (bottom), Fuller, Smith & Turner. 408 (left), Britain On View/photolibrary.com. 409 , Lamb and Flag pub, Covent Garden by Phil Whitehouse http://www.flickr.com/photos/philliecasablanca/2033195503/ Attribution License. 410 (top left), adnams broadside, the landseer by Simon Frost http://www.flickr.com/photos/spli/24884750/ Attribution-ShareAlike License. 410 (bottom left), Fuller, Smith & Turner. 410 (top right), Ice Cold Magners Cider by Wapster http://www.flickr.com/photos/wapster/3830930511/Attribution License. 410 (center), Fuller, Smith & Turner. 410 (bottom right), Newcastle 1 by Zach Heller. http://www.flickr.com/photos/zachheller/5276422526/ Attribution License. 411 (left), Kelly Cline/iStockphoto. 411 (right), Elzbieta Sekowska/Shutterstock. 415, FOTOSEARCH RM / age fotostock. Chapter 7: Bath and the Cotswolds: 423, Atlantide SNC / age fotostock. 424, Patricia Hofmeester/Shutterstock. 425 (top), Thermae Bath Spa, Bath, England, UK - 4 by http://www.flickr.com/photos/profernity/4482595883/ Attribution License. 425 (bottom left), gary718/shutterstock. 425 (bottom right), VashiDonsk/Wikimedia Commons. 426, David Hughes / age fotostock. 427 (top), Jo Ann Snover/Shutterstock. 427 (bottom), Ballista/Wikimedia Commons. 428, Britain on View/photolibrary.com. 434, Andr. Viegas/Shutterstock. 445, Adam Burton / age fotostock. 449, Britain on View/photolibrary.com. 452, Rob Lacey / vividstock.net / Alamy. 456, H & D Zielske /age fotostock. 458-59, Britain on View/photolibrary.com. 460 (top left), Stowe Park, Buckinghamshire by Martin Pettitt http://www.flickr.com/photos/mdpettitt/4663854507/ Attribution License. 460 (top right), Britain On View/photolibrary.com. 460 (center)," LOOK Die Bildagentur der Fotografen GmbH / Alamy. 460 (bottom), Andreas Tille/Wikimedia Commons. 461, John Glover / age fotostock. 462, National Trust Photo Library/Britain On View/photolibrary.com. 463 (top), North Light Images /age fotostock. 463 (bottom), David Sellman/Britain On View/photolibrary.com. 464, Paul Felix/Britain On View/photolibrary.com. 465 (left), Targeman/Wikimedia Commons. 465 (right), 20100506Stourhead_Cutler_P1010967 by Wendy Cutler http://www.flickr.com/photos/wlcutler/4586726477/ Attribution License. 466, Peter Packer/Britain On View/photolibrary.com. 474, Jon Bower / age fotostock. 477, Andy Williams / age fotostock. 484, Simon Tranter / age fotostock. Chapter 8: Stratford-Upon-Avon and the Heart of En gland: 487, John Martin / Alamy. 489 (top), David Benton/Shutterstock. 489 (bottom), Stratford on Avon by Allan Harris. http://www.flickr.com/photos/allan_harris/3941380761/ Attribution-ShareAlike License. 490, Simon Reddy / Alamy. 491 (top), Monkey Business Images/Shutterstock. 491 (bottom), Foodpics/Shutterstock. 492, Ironbridge Gorge Museum Trust. 496, Cotswolds Photo Library/Britain on View/photo-

NOTES

ABOUT OUR WRITERS

Longtime contributor Robert Andrews loves warm beer and soggy moors, but hates shopping malls and the sort of weather when you're not sure if it's raining—all of which he found in abundance while updating the West Country chapter. He writes and revises other guidebooks and has penned his own guide to Devon and Cornwall.

Julius Honnor lives in London, but his Fodor's beat included rural spots in the Lake District, where he has observed chic new hotels and restaurants popping up alongside more traditional places. Julius also updated the Arts and Entertainment and Pubs and Nightlife chapters of the London chapter, as well as Soho. His work for other guidebooks has taken him around the globe.

Writer and editor Kate Hughes acquired a liking for the big city when she studied classical literature in Liverpool. Having since indulged her penchant for the country and landed gentry by getting a master's in garden history, she feels qualified to pass judgment on matters both urban and rural. She is responsible for the Experience England, Thames Valley, and Bath and the Cotswolds chapters, as well as the sections on Stratford-upon-Avon and Shakespeare Country.

A Londoner since public transportation was cheap, Jack Jewers has directed films for the BBC and reviewed pubs for *Time Out;* he also makes independent films. He updated the Southeast, Lancashire and the Peaks, East Anglia, Northeast, and Wales chapters, as well as the non-Stratford portions of the Stratford-upon-Avon and the Heart of England chapter. Jack is also responsible for the Where to Stay section of London and several London neighborhoods.

James O'Neill loves London and—as his work updating various London neighborhoods for this edition proves—loves rediscovering it, too. Over the past 15 years, he has written extensively for television and radio (mainly for the BBC and Channel 4), the stage, and the page.

Ellin Stein has written for publications on both sides of the Atlantic, including the *New York Times*, the *Times of London*, and *InStyle*. She has lived in London for two decades and is married to a native. For this edition, Ellin updated the South and Yorkshire chapters as well as Travel Smart England. Her territory also included London shopping and several London neighborhoods.

London restaurant maven Alex Wijeratna is always amazed by the capital's rocket-fueled restaurant scene. He has written for publications including *The Times, Guardian,* and *Independent*. Alex updated the Where to Eat section of London.